Source: World Bank, *The World Bank Atlas, World Tables*, 1991, pp. 6-9.

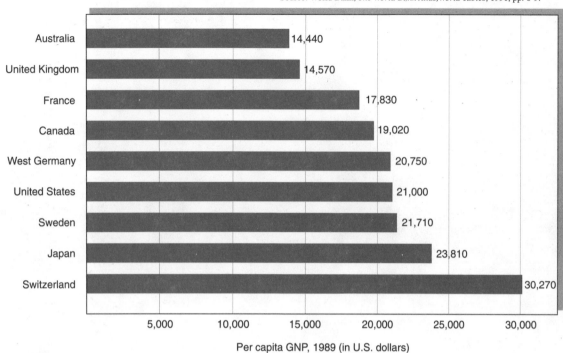

Per capita GNP, 1989 (in U.S. dollars)

EXHIBIT C The Gross National Product per Person of Nine Western Industrial Nations, 1989

Source: *Economic Report of the President, 1986*, p. 41 and *Statistical Abstract of the United States, 1991*. Table 1426

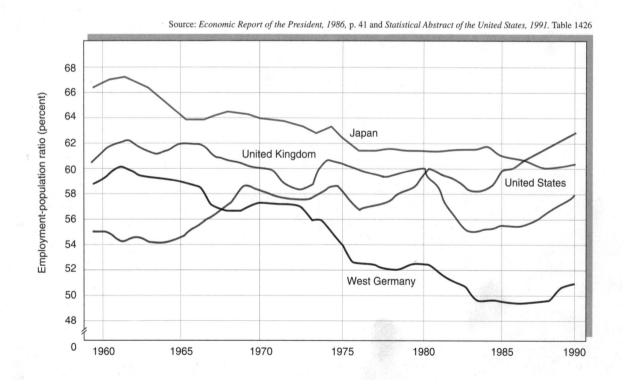

EXHIBIT D Percent of the Population Employed—An International Comparison, 1960–1989   The employment ratio in the United States and Japan is higher than that in the United Kingdom and West Germany.

ECONOMICS
Private and Public Choice
Sixth Edition

ECONOMICS
Private and Public Choice
Sixth Edition

James D. Gwartney
Florida State University

Richard L. Stroup
Montana State University

with the assistance of
A. H. Studenmund
Occidental College

The Dryden Press
Harcourt Brace College Publishers
Fort Worth   Philadelphia   San Diego
New York   Orlando   Austin   San Antonio
Toronto   Montreal   London   Sydney   Tokyo

Acquisitions Editor: Rick Hammonds
Manuscript Editor: Margie Rogers
Production Editor: Michael Kleist
Designer: Cheryl Staples
Art Editor: Avery Hallowell
Production Managers: David Hough, Lesley Lenox

ISBN: 0-15-518921-2

Library of Congress Catalog Number: 91-65874

Printed in the United States of America

Preface

We live in a world of dynamic change. During the last few years, the Berlin wall has fallen; democratic governments have emerged in Eastern Europe and Latin America; and global competition has increased in intensity. Economics helps us better understand both the underlying forces and future implications of these changes. Perhaps more than any other science, economics is about people. It enhances our understanding of today's crucial issues. Why do some people prosper, while others live on the edge of starvation? Will the adoption of democratic political institutions improve economic conditions? Is there a danger that we are about to run out of key economic resources? Is economic activity destroying the environment of planet Earth and, if so, what can be done about it? As we proceed, we will use the tools of economics to address these and many other important issues that affect our lives.

SIXTH EDITION

As in previous editions, our approach emphasizes the importance of the economic way of thinking. We want to stimulate students, challenge their reasoning ability, and teach them to *think* like economists. Examples are used freely to illustrate the power and relevance of economic analysis. Real-world data are employed to test the implications of economic theory. We think this approach will enliven the study of economics for both the student and the teacher.

While the organization of this text is basically the same as for the previous edition, almost every chapter has been thoroughly revised. Several new features have been incorporated. This edition reflects the global relevance of economic analysis. We now live in a shrinking world that is characterized by dynamic change. Pushed along by changes in technology, communications, and transportation, more and more of our economic goods are produced in one country and sold in another. The economies of countries in Latin America, Eastern Europe, and even the Soviet Union are in the midst of enormous change. Europe is moving toward political and economic unification. North America appears to be moving toward a common market. Basic economic analysis enhances our understanding of these forces and helps clarify their impact on our lives.

CHANGES IN THE CORE MACROECONOMICS

In recent years, macroeconomics has undergone enormous change. Modern macroeconomics stresses the importance of (a) expectations and decision-making in an uncertain world, (b) microeconomic elements (for example, search theory and the incentive effects of relative price changes) that influence outcomes in aggregated markets, (c) whether a change is anticipated or unanticipated, (d) interrelations among aggregate markets, (e) whether a change is expected to be temporary or permanent, and (f) differences between the long-run and short-run effects of a macroeconomic change. Our approach reflects this modern view. We now live in a world of international markets. From the outset, the basic macroeconomic model of this text is an ''open economy'' model. Constant attention is given to how changes in international markets influence output, employment, and prices across countries.

While the organization of the core macroeconomics is basically the same as for the previous edition, several new features have been incorporated into this edition. The following list highlights some of the specific changes.

■ From the outset, the basic aggregate demand/aggregate supply model is developed within an open economy framework and an international credit (loanable funds) market. Constant attention is given to how changes in international markets influence output, employment, and prices across countries.

■ Macroeconomic policy indicators and measures of performance for Japan, Canada, and Western Europe are often compared and contrasted with the U.S. data. The expanded presentation of cross country data illustrates both the broad relevance of economics and the interrelations among the economies of the world.

■ The coverage of factors contributing to the savings and loan crisis and to the increasing number of bank failures during the 1980s is expanded and integrated into our analysis of monetary policy.

■ The change in the nature of money during the 1980s is explained. Since the M1 money supply of the 1980s is not really comparable with earlier data, the broader M2 money supply data are generally used to track changes in the direction of monetary policy in this edition.

■ The economics underlying the Great Tax Debate of the 1980s is discussed in greater detail. The structural changes in the income tax which evolved from the debate are described and their impact is analyzed (Chapter 5).

■ The impact of changes in nominal interest rates on the velocity of money and the potency of monetary policy is more fully integrated into our analysis in this edition (Chapters 13 and 15).

■ The influence of international trade and finance on fiscal and monetary policy is discussed more fully. In turn, the impact of macroeconomic policy on the current account deficit (or surplus) is also analyzed in greater detail in this edition (Chapter 32).

CHANGES IN THE CORE MICROECONOMICS

Our coverage of core microeconomics stresses the ability of a limited number of basic principles (for example, opportunity costs, gains from specialization and trade, competition and adjustments to relative price changes) to enhance our understanding of real world events. Theoretical analysis is always supplemented with applications which illustrate the relevance of the theory. The following brief list indicates the major areas of substantial change.

- The discussion of rivalrous behavior and business strategy is expanded and the models of monopolistic competition and oligopoly are more fully used to explain these aspects of business competition (Chapter 21).

- The coverage of price discrimination is expanded, and its use as a competitive weapon is more fully explored in this edition (Chapter 20).

- The changing role of labor unions and the impact of product market competition and mobility of firms on the economic power of organized labor are analyzed in more detail in this edition (Chapter 26).

- Recent changes in income inequality and the economic factors contributing to these changes are analyzed in more detail.

- The coverage of environmental economics is expanded and integrated more fully into our analysis of resource economics (Chapter 28).

- A new feature on educational vouchers is integrated into our analysis of public sector economics (Chapter 30).

- The coverage of the ''new development economics'' which stresses the importance of gains from trade, monetary (price) stability, security of property rights, and an efficient capital market is expanded.

- The chapter on comparative economic systems outlines the latest economic developments in the Soviet Union, considers their importance, and analyzes the future of the Soviet economy.

DISTINGUISHING FEATURES OF OUR APPROACH

As we stated in the first edition of this text, our primary goal is to challenge students to think like economists. The following points are of specific interest in this regard:

1. *Economic Principles Are Presented in a Highly Readable Fashion.* Difficult language and terminology can often hinder successful learning, particularly of economic concepts. Without sacrificing accuracy, we have sought to employ simple language. Simplicity, however, has not been substituted for depth. Rather, our aim is to highlight the power and accessibility of economic concepts. Where complex ideas are essential to our analysis, they are developed fully. We believe that the economics required for the 1990s can be comprehensible to the student as well as challenging and applicable to the real world.

2. *Economic Reasoning and Its Applications Are Emphasized.* Although models, theories, and exercises are important, they are only tools with which to develop the economic way of thinking. We have avoided abstractions and mechanical exercises that obscure basic concepts. On the other hand, we have integrated applications and real world data in an effort to make the basic concepts come alive to the reader.

3. *Microeconomic Reasoning Is a Fundamental Component of Macroeconomic Analysis.* The central principle of economics is that incentives matter. The microstructure of an economy does have macroeconomic ramifications. Microincentives influence such macrofactors as the rate of unemployment, the level of current spending, saving, and aggregate output. In this book, the

importance of the microincentive structure that is the foundation of our macroeconomic markets is highlighted.

4. *Economic Tools Are Applied to Both the Market and the Political Process.* Most textbooks tell students how an *ideal* market economy would operate, how real-world markets differ from the hypothetical ideal, and how ideal public policy can correct the shortcomings of the market. In addition to discussing these three basic issues, we analyze what real-world public policy is *likely to do*. Building on recent developments in the area of public choice, we apply the tools of economics to the political process as well as to market allocation. We think this approach emphasizes both the power and relevance of economics.

5. *The Role of the Individual Decision-Maker Is Stressed.* Students often feel that economists exclude human beings from the economic process. In most economics textbooks, business decision-makers are depicted as having perfect knowledge of demand and cost. Like computers, they always arrive at the maximum-profit solution. Likewise, government planners are often depicted as omniscient mechanics who always do the right thing. Decision-making is treated as a mechanical exercise, removed from the real world. We reject this approach. Throughout this book, we stress the importance of information, uncertainty, trial-and-error decision-making, expectations, and other factors that influence real-world choices. Economics is more than a set of guidelines. If students are to be convinced of its applicability, these dynamic factors that influence and motivate human beings must be integrated into the analysis.

ORGANIZATIONAL FEATURES

We have employed several organizational features designed to make the presentation more understandable and interesting.

1. *Myths of Economics*   In a series of boxed articles, commonly held fallacies of economic reasoning are dispelled. Each myth is followed by a concise explanation of why it is incorrect and each one is presented within a chapter containing closely related material.

2. *Applications in Economics*   These boxed features apply economic theory to real-world issues and controversies. They add breadth on topics of special interest and illustrate the relevance of basic principles to the world in which we live.

3. *Measures of Economic Activity*   Measurement is an important element of economics. These features explain how important economic indicators such as the Consumer Price Index, unemployment rate, and index of leading indicators are assembled.

4. *Outstanding Economists*   These brief profiles stress the contributions of several economists, both current and historical, whose work has been important in the development of the field. This series is designed both to enhance the student's appreciation of economic history and to provide depth on the contributions of several present-day economists.

5. *Chapter Focus Questions and Closing Summaries*   Each chapter begins with several questions that summarize the focus of the chapter. A summary, which

provides the student with a concise statement of the material (chapter learning objectives), appears at the end of each chapter. Reviewing the focus questions and chapter summaries will help the student better understand the material and integrate it into the broader economic picture.

6. *Key Terms*   The terminology of economics is often confusing to introductory students. Key terms are introduced in the text in color type; simultaneously, each term is defined in the margin opposite the first reference to the term. A glossary containing the key terms also appears at the end of the book.

7. *Critical Analysis Questions.*   Each chapter concludes with a set of discussion questions designed to test the student's ability to analyze an economic problem and to apply economic theory to real-world events. Appendix C at the end of the text contains suggested answers for approximately half of the critical analysis questions. We think these answers, illustrating the power of economics, will interest students and will help them develop the economic way of thinking.

SUPPLEMENTARY MATERIALS

A complete set of support materials accompanies this textbook and includes:

Coursebook.   We call the student handbook accompanying the textbook a *Coursebook.* since it is more than a study guide. Of course, it contains numerous multiple choice, true-false, and discussion questions permitting students to self-test their knowledge of each chapter. Answers and short explanations for most questions are provided in the back of the *Coursebook.* Each chapter also contains problem and project exercises designed to improve the student's knowledge of the mechanics. A set of short readings chosen to supplement the classroom teaching of important topics is also included in the *Coursebook.* Several of the readings are arranged in a debate format and cover areas of controversy in economics. Discussion questions follow each article, challenging students to demonstrate their understanding of the material and their ability to distinguish a sound argument from economic nonsense. Like the textbook, the *Coursebook* is designed to help students develop the economic way of thinking.

Testbanks.   Two testbanks accompany the Sixth Edition. Testbank A contains approximately 3,500 multiple-choice questions, most of which have been extensively tested in the classroom. Within each chapter, the questions correspond to the major subheadings of the text. Testbank B, prepared by J. J. Bethune of Bellarmine College, provides approximately 2,000 additional multiple-choice questions. Both testbanks are available on computer diskette. The ExaMaster system accompanying the computerized textbanks makes it easy to create tests, print scrambled versions of the same test, modify questions, and reproduce the graphic questions. The new edition of the testbank contains a large number of graphic questions.

Instructor's Manual.   The *Instructor's Manual* is divided into two parts. The first part, which is also available on computer diskette, is a detailed outline of each chapter in lecture-note form. It is designed to help instructors organize and structure their current lecture notes according to the format of the Sixth Edition of *Economics: Private and Public Choice.* Instructors can easily prepare a detailed, personalized set of notes by revising the computerized form of the notes. The second part of the *Instructor's Manual* contains teaching tips, sources of supplementary materials, and other helpful information. Part 3 provides instructors with several games designed to illustrate and enliven important economic concepts. Suggested answers to most of the critical analysis questions that were not answered in Appendix C of the text are also provided in the *Instructor's Manual*.

Color Transparencies.   Color transparencies of the major exhibits of the Sixth Edition have been especially prepared for overhead projectors. They are available to adopters upon request.

Computer Simulation Package.   *ECO Talk,* a computer simulation package, is available free to adopters (and to their students for a nominal fee). *ECO Talk* consists of ten microeconomic and ten macroeconomic models designed to help users master important concepts through simulations, practice with graphics, and quizzes on the models. *ECO Talk* was developed by Michael Claudon of Middlebury College and Kipley Olson of Apple Computer. While it is not tied to a specific textbook, it contains the primary models presented in this textbook.

Video Package.   Milton Friedman's *Free to Choose* is available in ten half-hour videotapes.

ACKNOWLEDGMENTS

A project of this type is a team effort. Several people contributed substantially to the development of this edition. Once again, Woody Studenmund provided valuable direction and insightful comments. In addition, he provided us with a draft of several suggested changes in the chapters on macroeconomics and international trade and finance. Several of his associates at Occidental College, including Robby Moore, Jim Whitney, and Jim Halstead also provided us with helpful suggestions.

Gary Galles of Pepperdine University provided a detailed review of every chapter. In addition, he is the author of the *Instructor's Manual* for this edition. Given his creativity, communication skills, and talent for the teaching of economics, the overall Sixth Edition package is vastly improved as the result of his contributions.

We owe a special debt to David Klingaman of Ohio University and Don May of Loyola University of Chicago. Each provided a detailed review and suggested revisions for the core macro chapters. The organization and clarity of this material is significantly improved as the result of their efforts.

Several other people wrote detailed reviews and offered helpful suggestions in specific areas. Robert Crandall of the Brookings Institution and Ron Johnson of Montana State University contributed substantially to the revision of the chapter on business structure and regulation. Barry Hirsch of Florida State University provided us with several suggestions that we integrated into the chapters on labor markets and unionization. Ron Brandolini of Valencia College made several helpful suggestions for both the organization of the book and applications for the enrichment of the analysis. We also benefitted from discussions with J. J. Bethune of Bellarmine College, who is the author of *Testbook B* which accompanies the text. We would also like to thank Mark Nichols and Russell Sobel for their research assistance.

We have often revised material in light of suggestions made by reviewers, users, friends, and even a few competitors. In this regard, we would like to express our appreciation to the following: Paul Azrak, Queensborough Community College; Jacqueline Kasun, Humboldt State University; Norlin Masih, St. Cloud State University; Richard Torz, SUNY-Queens College; Lucinda Coulter-Burbach, Seminole Community College; Sue Hayes, Sonoma State; Fred Goddard, University of Florida; Larry Lichtenstein, Canisius College; Jeffrey Herbener, Washington and Jefferson College; Lawrence Martin, Michigan State University; J. P. Egan, University of Wisconsin, Eau Claire; Michael White, St. Cloud State University; Dona A. Derr, Rutgers College; Don Millman, Itasca Community College; Nathan Eric Hampton, St. Cloud State University; D. E. Morris, University of New Hampshire; James T. Bennett, George Mason University; Jeffrey Young, St. Lawrence University; Robert Puth, University of New Hampshire; Sam Osemene, Prairie View A & M University; Harold Katz, U.S. Merchant Marine Academy; James Wible, University of New Hampshire; Frank Scott, University of Kentucky; John Neal, Lake Sumter Community College; Wilson Mixon, Berry College; James Long, Auburn University; Denise Rogers, Arizona Western College; Patrick McMurry, Missouri Western State College; William Jahn, American Institute of Business; David Emery, St. Olaf College; Joseph M. Lammert, Raymond Walters College; Abdalla Gergis, Framingham State College; Darrell Irvin, Spokane Community College; Ken Somppi, Auburn University; Seren Burg, Eastern Michigan University; James A. Dunlevy, Miami University; Michael Loewy, George Washington University; John C. McCarthy, Armstrong State College; Eric N. Baklanoff, University of Alabama; William Steiden, Bellarmine College; Julia Lee, University of Louisville; Marshall Edwards, Armstrong State College; John Leevries, Brainerd Community College; Pati Crabb, Bellarmine College; Terry R. Ridgway, University of Nevada, Las Vegas; Dale Bails, Memphis State; Luther D. Lawson, University of North Carolina–Wilmington; Jack Morgan, University of North Carolina–Wilmington; William Sher, Duquesne University; Donald L. Alexander, Pennsylvania State University; Kevin C. Sontheimer, University of Pittsburgh; Kurt Rethwisch, Duquesne University; Marsha Goldfarb, University of Maryland–Baltimore County; Arthur Janssa, Emporia State University; Chas C. Milliken, Siena Heights College; Thomas Wyrick, Southwest Missouri State University; Jim Scheib, Red Rocks Community College; Alan Sleeman, Western Washington University; Robert E. Williams, The School of the Ozarks; Anthony Yezer, George Washington University; L. Aubrey Drewery, Birmingham Southern College; Ernest M. Buchholz, Santa Monica College; Shirley Svorny, California State University–Northridge; Henry Demmert, Santa Clara University; C. Fred DeKay, Seattle University; David O. Whitten, Auburn University–Main Campus; Randall G. Holcombe, Florida State University; Ralph Bristol, University of New Hampshire–Durham.

We are also indebted to the excellent team of professionals at Harcourt Brace Jovanovich. Rick Hammonds (acquisitions editor), Margie Rogers (manuscript editor), and Michael Kleist (production editor) provided us with guidance, editorial assistance, and encouragement. We would also like to thank Avery Hallowell (art editor), David Hough and Lesley Lenox (production managers) and Cheryl Staples (designer) for their contributions.

Finally, we would like to acknowledge the assistance of Amy Gwartney and Jane Shaw Stroup, both of whom contributed in numerous ways to the success of this project. Without their assistance and encouragement, we would have been unable to meet the demands and deadlines of this project.

A Note to Students

This text contains several features that we think will help you maximize (a good economics term) the returns derived from your study effort. Our past experience indicates that awareness of the following points will help you to use the book more effectively.

- Each chapter begins with a series of focus questions which communicate the central issues of the chapter. Before you read the chapter, briefly think about the focus questions, why they are important, and how they relate to the material of prior chapters.
- The textbook is organized in the form of an outline. The headings within the text are the major points of the outline. Minor headings (contained in the margins) are subpoints under the major headings. In addition, important subpoints within sections are often set off and numbered. Sometimes thumbnail sketches are used to help the reader better organize important points. Careful use of the headings and thumbnail sketches will help you better visualize the organization of the material.
- A summary appears at the end of each chapter. Use the summary as a checklist to determine whether or not you understand the major points of the chapter.
- Review of the exhibits will also provide you with a summary of each chapter. The accompanying legend briefly describes the content and analysis of each exhibit. After studying the chapter, briefly review the exhibits to ensure that you have mastered the central points.
- The key terms introduced in each chapter are defined in the margins. As you study the chapter, go over the marginal definition of each key term as it is introduced. Later, you may also find it useful to review the marginal definitions. If you have forgotten the meaning of a term introduced earlier, consult the glossary at the end of the book.
- The boxed features provide additional depth on various topics without disrupting the flow of the text. In general, the topics of the boxed features have been chosen because of their relevance as an application of the theory or because of past student interest in the topic. Reading the boxed features will supplement the text and enhance your understanding of important economic concepts.
- The Critical Analysis Questions at the end of each chapter are intended to test your understanding of the economic way of thinking. They provide you with another opportunity to review each chapter. Answers to approximately 40 percent of these questions are provided in Appendix C.

■ If you are having trouble, be sure to obtain a *Coursebook* and work the questions and problems for each chapter. The *Coursebook* also contains the answers to the multiple-choice questions and a brief explanation of why an answer is correct (and other choices incorrect). In most cases, if you master the concepts of the test items in the *Coursebook,* you will do well on the quizzes and examinations of your instructor.

Contents in Brief

Applications in Economics

Measures of Economic Activity

Myths of Economics

Contents

4 Supply and Demand for the Public Sector   81

5 Government Spending and Taxation   101

PART TWO
Macroeconomics   129

6 Taking the Nation's Economic Pulse   130

7 Economic Fluctuations, Unemployment, and Inflation   156

8 An Introduction to Basic Macroeconomic Markets   181

9 Working with Our Basic Aggregate Demand / Aggregate Supply Model   204

10 Keynesian Foundations of Modern Macroeconomics   227

11 Modern Macroeconomics: Fiscal Policy   253

12 Money and the Banking System   276

PART THREE
Microeconomics *411*

17 *Demand and Consumer Choice* *412*

18 *Costs and the Supply of Goods* *445*

19 *The Firm under Pure Competition* *474*

PART FOUR
Factor Markets and Income Distribution   581

23 The Supply of and Demand for Productive Resources   582

24 Earnings, Productivity, and the Job Market   605

25 Capital, Interest, and Profit   631

PART FIVE
Public Choice 727

29 Problem Areas for the Market 728

30 Public Choice: Understanding Government and Government Failure 752

PART SIX
International Economics
and Comparative Systems 777

31 Gaining from International Trade 778

PART ONE

The Economic Way of Thinking— An Introduction

1 *The Economic Approach*

[Economics] is not a body of concrete truth, but an engine for the discovery of concrete truth.[1]

Alfred Marshall

CHAPTER FOCUS

- Why is scarcity a key economic concept, even in an affluent economy?
- How does scarcity differ from poverty?
- What are the basics underlying the economic way of thinking? What is different about the way economists look at choices and human decision-making?
- What is the difference between positive and normative economics?

*T*his is an exciting time to study economics. The world is changing rapidly and economic conditions are the driving force behind much of the change. During the last 20 years, the United States has experienced double-digit inflation rates, widespread unemployment during two severe recessions, and the longest peacetime recovery in the history of the United States. Our tax structure has changed substantially. For the first time in our history, large government budget deficits during peacetime have become the norm.

Economic change around the world has been even more dramatic. The Berlin Wall has crumbled and the countries of Eastern Europe are experimenting with markets and moving away from central planning. The Soviet Union is in the midst of massive change—republics are seeking independence, central planning is not working well, and some Soviet leaders are calling for a market economy. Simultaneously, the market economies of Western Europe are rapidly developing into a single integrated economy with a common currency and legal structure.

In economic terms, the world is shrinking. National economies are increasingly interconnected components of one gigantic global economy. Many of the goods at your favorite shopping mall were produced, at least in part, by people who speak a different language and live in a country halfway around the world. Similarly, many Americans work for companies that market their products in Europe, Japan, Latin America, and/or Africa. Ownership shares of American companies are traded, not only in New York, but also on stock exchanges in London, Tokyo, and throughout the world.

How will our current economic policies and rapidly changing world affect the economic status of Americans? What impact will the globalization of our economy have on our living standards, lifestyles, and future opportunities? This book will help you better understand the world in which you live. This is not to imply that economics provides easy answers for problems. As Alfred Marshall stated more than a century ago, economics is a discovery process—a way of thinking—rather than ''a body of concrete truth'' (see chapter opening quote). In fact, economics is more likely to provide an appreciation of the limitations of ''grand design'' proposals than it is to offer utopian solutions. Nonetheless, ''economic thinking'' is a powerful tool capable of illuminating a broad range of real-world events. Our goals are to communicate the basics of economics and to illustrate their relevance to our changing world.

WHAT IS ECONOMICS ABOUT?

[Economics is] the science which studies human behavior as a relationship between ends and scarce means which have alternative uses.[2]
                                                                    Lionel Robbins, 1932

Economics is about people and the choices they make. The unit of analysis in economics is the individual. Of course, individuals group together to form collective organizations such as corporations, labor unions, and governments.

---

[1]Alfred Marshall, *The Present Position of Economics*, 1885, p. 25.
[2]Lionel Robbins, *An Essay on the Nature and Significance of Economic Science*, 1932.

Individual choices, however, still underlie and direct these organizations. Thus, even when we study collective organizations, we will focus on the ways in which their operation is affected by the choices of individuals.

SCARCITY AND CHOICE

Economic theory evolves from fundamental postulates about how individual human beings behave, struggle with the problem of scarcity, and respond to change. The reality of life on our planet is that productive resources—resources used to produce goods—are limited. Therefore, goods and services are also limited. In contrast, the desires of human beings are virtually unlimited. These facts confront us with the two basic ingredients of an economic topic—scarcity and choice. **Scarcity** is the term used by economists to indicate that people's desire for a ''thing'' exceeds the amount of it that is freely available from Nature. Nature has always dealt grudgingly with us; the Garden of Eden has continually eluded our grasp.

A good that is scarce is an **economic good.** The first column of Exhibit 1 contains a partial listing of scarce or economic goods. The list includes food, clothing, and many of the items that all of us commonly recognize as material goods. It also includes some items, however, that may surprise you. Is leisure a good? Would you like to have more leisure time than is currently available to you? Most of us would. Therefore, leisure time is a scarce good. What about clean air? A few years ago many economics texts classified clean air as a free good, made available by Nature in such abundant supply that everyone could have all of it they wanted. This is no longer the case. Our utilization of air to dispose of wastes has created a scarcity of clean air. Many of the residents of Los Angeles, New York, and other large cities would like to have more clean air.

Few of us usually think of environmental conditions as economic goods. However, if you would like to have more open spaces, green areas, or dogwood

Scarcity: Fundamental concept of economics which indicates that less of a good is freely available than consumers would like.

Economic Good: A good that is scarce. The desire for economic goods exceeds the amount that is freely available from Nature.

EXHIBIT 1 ■ A General Listing of Desired Economic Goods and Limited Resources	
Economic Goods	Limited Resources
Food (bread, milk, meat, eggs, vegetables, coffee, etc.)	Land (various degrees of fertility)
Clothing (shirts, pants, blouses, shoes, socks, coats, sweaters, etc.)	Natural resources (rivers, trees, minerals, oceans, etc.)
Household goods (tables, chairs, rugs, beds, dressers, television sets, etc.)	Machines and other man-made physical resources
Space exploration	Nonhuman animal resources
Education	Technology (physical and scientific ''recipes'' of history)
National defense	Human resources (the knowledge, skill, and talent of individual human beings)
Recreation	
Leisure time	
Entertainment	
Clean air	
Pleasant environment (trees, lakes, rivers, open spaces, etc.)	
Pleasant working conditions	
More productive resources	

Our history is a record of our struggle to transform available, but limited, resources into things that we would like to have—economic goods.

trees, you will recognize that these things are scarce. They, too, are economic goods.

Since scarcity of productive resources, time, and income limit the alternatives available to us, we must make choices. **Choice** is the act of selecting among restricted alternatives. A major focus of economics concerns how people choose when the alternatives open to them are restricted. The choices of the family shopper are restricted by the household budget, market prices, and the shopper's own imagination about ways to satisfy wants. The choices of business decision-makers are restricted by competition from other firms, the cost of productive resources, technology, and their own entrepreneurial ability to open new markets or use new techniques to satisfy customers' wants. The spending choices of political decision-makers are restricted by the taxable income of the citizenry and voter opposition to taxes. The selection of one alternative generally necessitates doing without others. If you choose to spend $10 going to a football game, you will have $10 less to spend on other things. Similarly, if you choose to spend an evening watching a movie, you must forgo spending the evening playing Ping-Pong (or participating in some other activity). You cannot have your cake and eat it, too.

Each day, we all make hundreds of economic choices, even though we are not normally aware of doing so. Choosing when to get up in the morning, what to eat for breakfast, how to travel to work, what television program to watch—all of these are economic decisions. They are economic decisions because they involve the utilization of scarce resources (for example, time and income). We all are constantly involved in making choices that relate to economics.

Choice: The act of selecting among alternatives.

OUR CONSTANT STRUGGLE WITH SCARCITY

Scarcity restricts us. How can we overcome it? **Resources,** including our own skills, can be used to produce economic goods. Human effort and ingenuity can be combined with machines, land, natural resources, and other productive factors (see the second column of Exhibit 1) to increase the availability of economic goods. These are "tools" in our struggle with scarcity. It is important to note that most economic goods are not like manna from heaven. Human energy is nearly always an ingredient in the production of economic goods.

The lessons of history confirm that our desire for economic goods far outstrips our resources to produce them. Are we destined to lead hopeless lives of misery and drudgery because we are involved in a losing battle with scarcity? Some might answer "Yes," pointing out that a substantial proportion of the world's population goes to bed hungry each night. The World Bank estimated that in 1990 more than one billion people were struggling to survive on less than $370 per year.

At the same time, the grip of scarcity has been loosened in most of North America, Western Europe, and Japan. Most Americans, Japanese, and Europeans have an adequate caloric intake and sufficient housing and clothing. Many own luxuries such as dishwashers, video cassette recorders, microwave ovens, and swimming pools. Over the last century, the average number of hours worked per week has fallen from 60 to about 40 in most Western nations. From a material viewpoint, life is certainly more pleasant for these people than it was for their ancestors 250 years ago. Despite this progress, though, scarcity is still a fact of life, even in relatively affluent countries. Most of us have substantially fewer goods and resources and less time than we would like to have.

It is important to note that scarcity and poverty are not the same thing. Poverty implies some basic level of need, either in absolute or relative terms. Absence of poverty means that the basic level has been attained. In contrast, the absence of

Resource: An input used to produce economic goods. Land, labor, skills, natural resources, and capital are examples.

scarcity means that we have not merely attained some basic level, but have acquired as much of all goods as we desire. Poverty is at least partially subjective, but there is an objective test for scarcity. If people are willing to pay—give up something—for a good, that good is scarce. Even though the battle against poverty may ultimately be won, the outcome of the battle against scarcity is already painfully obvious. Our productive capabilities and material desires are such that goods and services will always be scarce.

THE ECONOMIC WAY OF THINKING

It [economics] is a method rather than a doctrine, an apparatus of the mind, a technique of thinking which helps its possessor to draw correct conclusions.

J. M. Keynes, 1923[3]

Reflecting on a television appearance with economist Paul Samuelson and other social scientists (noneconomists), Milton Friedman stated that he was amazed to find that economists, although differing in their ideological viewpoints, usually find themselves to be allies in discussions with other social scientists.[4] One does not have to spend much time around economists to recognize that there is an "economic way of thinking." Admittedly, economists, like others, differ widely in their ideological views. A news commentator once remarked that "any half-dozen economists will normally come up with about six different policy prescriptions." Yet, in spite of their philosophical differences, there is a common ground to the approach of economists.

> **Economic Theory:** A set of definitions, postulates, and principles assembled in a manner that makes clear the "cause-and-effect" relationships of economic data.

That common ground is **economic theory,** developed from basic postulates of human behavior. Theory has a reputation for being abstract and difficult, but this need not be the case. Economic theory, like a road map or a guidebook, establishes reference points indicating what to look for, and how economic issues are interrelated. It helps us understand the relationships among complex and often seemingly unrelated events in the real world. A better understanding of cause-and-effect relationships will enhance our ability to accurately predict the likely consequences of alternative policy choices. Economics has sometimes been called the "science of common sense." This is as it should be. After all, common sense is nothing more than a set of beliefs based on sound theories that have been tested over a long period of time and found to be accurate.

This is not to say, however, that the person who has not studied economics will come to the same conclusions on an economic question as the serious student would. Each component of the theory may be common sense, but putting the components together can lead us to conclusions very different from those of the person thinking about the same problem without the apparatus of economics.

---

[3]John Maynard Keynes (1883–1946) was an English economist whose writings during the 1920s and 1930s exerted an enormous impact on both economic theory and policy. Keynes established the terminology and the economic framework that are still widely used today when economists study problems of unemployment and inflation.

[4]The philosophical views of Professor Friedman and Professor Samuelson differ considerably. They are often on opposite sides of economic policy issues.

EIGHT GUIDEPOSTS TO ECONOMIC THINKING

The economic way of thinking involves the incorporation of certain guidelines—some would say the building blocks of basic economic theory—into one's thought process. Once these guidelines are incorporated, we believe that economics can be a relatively easy subject to master.

Students who have difficulty with economics almost always do so because they fail to develop the economic way of thinking. Their thought processes are not consistently directed by a few simple economic concepts or guideposts. Students who do well in economics learn to use these basic concepts and allow their thought processes to reflect them. We will outline and discuss eight principles that characterize economic thinking and that are essential to the understanding of the economic approach.

1. Scarce Goods Have a Cost—There Are No Free Lunches.

The benefits of scarce goods can be obtained only if someone is willing to exert personal effort or give up something. The use of scarce goods to meet one ''need'' means less resources (time, energy, tools, and so on) to meet ''needs'' in other areas. When it comes to the use of scarce resources to produce valued products, there is not such a thing as a free lunch.

The cost of many scarce goods is obvious. The purchaser of a new car must give up $10,000 or $15,000 of purchasing power over other goods to own the car. Similarly, the cost to the purchaser of a delightful meal, new clothes, or a Las Vegas weekend is obvious. But, what about a good such as public elementary education? The ''scarce goods have a cost'' concept is just as true for goods provided through government as for goods provided by private producers. Even though the education is usually free to students, it is not free to the community. Buildings, books, and teachers' salaries must be paid for from tax revenues, which the taxpayer could have used for other goods and services. The scarce resources used to produce elementary schools and education could have been used instead to produce more recreation, entertainment, housing, and other goods. Providing for public education means that some of these other scarce goods must be forgone.

Similarly, provision of free medical service, recreation areas, tennis courts, and parking lots involves the use of scarce resources. Again, something must be given up if we are to produce these goods. Taxpayers usually bear the cost of ''free'' medical services and tennis courts. Consumers often bear the cost of ''free'' parking lots in the form of higher prices in areas where this service is provided.

By now the central point should be obvious. Economic thinking recognizes that the provision of a scarce good, any scarce good, involves a cost. We must give up other things if we are to have more of a scarce good. Economic goods are not free.

2. Decision-Makers Choose Purposefully. Therefore, They Will Economize.

Since resources are scarce, it is all the more important that decisions be made in a purposeful manner. Decision-makers do not deliberately make choices in a manner that wastes their valuable resources. Recognizing the restrictions imposed by the limited resources available to them (income, time, talent, and so on), they seek to choose wisely; they try to select the options that best advance their own personal objectives. In turn, the objectives or preferences of individuals are revealed by the choices they make. **Economizing behavior** results directly from purposeful decision-making. Economizing individuals will seek to accomplish an objective at the least possible cost to themselves. When choosing among things that yield equal

Economizing Behavior: Choosing the objective of gaining a specific benefit at the least possible cost. A corollary of economizing behavior implies that when choosing among items of equal cost, individuals will choose the option that yields the greatest benefit.

benefit, an economizer will select the cheapest option. For example, if a hamburger, a fish dinner, and a New York sirloin steak are expected to yield identical benefits, economizing behavior implies that the cheapest of the three alternatives, probably the hamburger, will be chosen. Correspondingly, when choosing among alternatives of equal cost, economizing decision-makers will select the option that yields the greatest benefit. Purposeful decision-makers will not deliberately pay more for something than is necessary.

Utility: The benefit or satisfaction expected from a choice or course of action.

Purposeful choosing implies that decision-makers have some basis for their evaluation of alternatives. Economists refer to this evaluation as utility. **Utility** is the benefit or satisfaction that an individual expects from the choice of a specific alternative. The utility of an alternative is highly subjective, often differing widely from person to person. (The Myths of Economics box in this chapter also discusses personal choice.)

3. Incentives Matter—Human Choice Is Influenced in a Predictable Way by Changes in Economic Incentives.

This guidepost to clear economic thinking might be called the basic postulate of all economics. As the personal benefits from choosing an option increase, other things constant, a person will be more likely to choose that option. In contrast, as the costs associated with the choice of an item increase, the person will be less likely to choose that option. For a group, this basic economic postulate suggests that making an option more attractive will influence more people to choose it. In contrast, as the cost of a selection to the members of a group increases, fewer of them will make this selection.

This basic postulate of economics is a powerful tool because its application is so widespread. Incentives affect behavior in virtually all aspects of our lives, ranging from household decision-making to political choices.

According to this basic postulate, what would happen to the birthrate if the U.S. government (a) removed the income tax deduction for dependents, (b) imposed a $1,500 "birth tax" on parents, and (c) made birth-control pills available, free of charge, to all? The birthrate would fall—that's what. In fact, several governments around the world recognize this, and provide economic inducements to increase or decrease birthrates. Canada, for example, provides payments to couples with larger families to encourage population growth, while China penalizes couples who have more than one child.

What would happen if the government imposed a $5,000 tax on smokestacks, required automobile owners to pay a larger license fee for cars with higher exhaust levels, and gave a 10-percent tax reduction to all corporations that did not use the air for waste disposal purposes? Answer: there would be a decline in air pollution levels. Economics suggests that any policy shift that increases the cost and/or reduces the benefits of a specific activity will reduce the frequency of that activity.

The incentives matter postulate is just as applicable to human behavior under socialism as under capitalism. For example, at one time in the Soviet Union, the managers of glass plants were rewarded according to the tons of sheet glass produced. Not surprisingly, most plants produced sheet glass so thick that one could hardly see through it. The rules were changed so that the managers were rewarded according to the square meters of glass produced. The managers reacted in a predictable way. Under the new rules, Soviet firms stretched their resources, producing only very thin glass that was easily broken. Incentives matter in both capitalist and socialist countries.

MYTHS OF ECONOMICS

"Economic analysis assumes people act only out of selfish motives. It rejects the humanitarian side of humankind."

Probably because economics focuses on the efforts of individuals to satisfy material desires, many casual observers of the subject argue that its relevance hinges on the selfish nature of humankind. Some have even charged that economists, and the study of economics, encourage people to be materialistic rather than humanitarian.

This point of view stems from a fundamental misunderstanding of personal decision-making. Obviously, people act for a variety of reasons, some selfish and some humanitarian. The economist merely assumes that actions will be influenced by costs and benefits, as viewed by the decision-maker. As an activity becomes more costly, it is less likely that a decision-

maker will choose it. As the activity becomes more attractive, it is more likely that it will be chosen.

The choices of both the humanitarian and the egocentric individual will be influenced by changes in personal costs and benefits. For example, both will be more likely to try to save the life of a small child in a three-foot swimming pool than in the rapid currents approaching Niagara Falls. Both will be more likely to give a needy person their hand-me-downs rather than their best clothes. Similarly, both will be more likely to support a policy that generates benefits for others (for example: farmers, the poor, or the elderly) when the personal cost of doing so is low. Incentives matter for both the humanitarian and the egocentric.

Observation would suggest that the right to control one's destiny is an "economic" good for most

persons. Most of us would prefer to make our own choices rather than have someone else decide for us. But, is this always greedy and selfish? If so, why do people often make choices in a way that is charitable toward others? After all, many people freely choose to give a portion of their wealth to the sick, the needy, the less fortunate, religious organizations, and charitable institutions. Economics does not imply that these choices are irrational. It does imply that if you make it more (less) costly to act charitably, fewer (more) persons will do so.

Economics deals with people as they are—not as we would like to remake them. Should people act more charitably? Perhaps so. But this is not the subject matter of economics.

Marginal: Term used to describe the effects of a change, given the current situation. For example, the marginal cost is the cost of producing an additional unit of a product, given the producer's current facility and production rate.

Like monetary incentives, nonmonetary incentives also influence human behavior. The policies of instructors can alter incentives and thereby influence the incidence of cheating on their exams. There will be little cheating on a closely monitored, individualized, essay examination. Why? Because it is difficult (that is, costly) to cheat on such an exam. Suppose, however, that an instructor gives an objective "take-home" exam, basing students' course grades entirely on the results. More students will be likely to cheat because the benefits of doing so will be great and the risk (cost) minimal.

Economic reasoning recognizes that many factors help determine how people make decisions. Morality, for example, might be a strong factor in the situations discussed above. Incentives, though, will also be important. The economic way of thinking never loses sight of the fact that changes in incentives exert a powerful and predictable influence on human decisions. (The boxed feature "Do Incentives Matter?" gives yet another application of this principle.)

4. Economic Thinking Is Marginal Thinking.
Fundamental to economic reasoning and economizing behavior are the effects of decisions made to change the status quo. Economists refer to such decisions as **marginal**. Marginal choices always involve the effects of net additions to or subtractions *from the current conditions*.

APPLICATIONS IN ECONOMICS

Do Incentives Matter?

How generally can we apply the "incentives matter" principle? Does it apply, for example, to drinking and driving? Will changing the incentives with regard to drinking and driving change behavior? Consider the case of Norway, the country that has the toughest drunk-driving laws in the Western world.[5] Drinking a single can of beer before driving can put a first offender in jail for a minimum sentence of three weeks. These drivers generally lose their licenses for up to two years and often get stiff fines as well. Repeat offenders are treated even more harshly. These laws are far more Draconian than those of the United States. And the results?

1. One out of three Norwegians arrives at parties in a taxi, while nearly all Americans drive their own cars.
2. One out of ten Norwegian partygoers spends the night at the host's home; Americans seldom do.
3. In Norway, 78 percent of drivers totally avoid drinking at parties, compared to only 17 percent of American drivers.

Norwegians do like to drink, though they consume only half as much alcohol as Americans. The strong incentives built into Norwegian law, however, clearly make a difference in the incidence of drunken driving in that country. Once again, incentives do matter, and matter in a big way.

_____

[5]The information in this feature is taken from L. Erik Calonius, "Just a Bottle of Beer Can Land a Motorist in Prison in Norway," *Wall Street Journal,* August 16, 1985, p. 1.

In fact, the word "additional" is often used as a substitute for marginal. For example, we might ask, "What is the marginal (or additional) cost of producing one more automobile?" Or, "What is the marginal (or additional) benefit derived from one more glass of water?"

Marginal decisions need not always involve small changes. The "one more unit" can be large or small. For example, the decision to build a new plant is a marginal decision. It is marginal because it involves additional costs and additional benefits. *Given the current situation,* what marginal benefits (additional sales revenues, for example) can be expected from the plant, and what will be the marginal cost of constructing the facility? The answers to these questions will determine whether or not building the new plant is a good decision.

It is important to distinguish between "average" and "marginal." Even though a manufacturer's current average cost (total cost divided by total number of cars produced) of producing automobiles may be $10,000, for example, the marginal cost of producing an additional automobile (or an additional 1,000 automobiles) might be much lower; say, $5,000 per car. Costs associated with research, testing, design, molds, heavy equipment, and similar factors of production must be incurred whether the manufacturer is going to produce 1,000 units, 10,000 units, or 100,000 units. Such costs will clearly contribute to the average cost of an automobile. However, since these activities have already been undertaken to produce the manufacturer's current output level, they may *add little* to the cost of producing *additional* units. Thus, the manufacturer's marginal cost may be substantially less than the average cost. When determining whether to expand or reduce the production of a good, the choice should be based on marginal costs, not the current average cost.

We often confront decisions involving a possible change from the current situation. The marginal benefits and marginal costs associated with the choice will determine the wisdom of our decisions. What happens at the margin is therefore an important part of economic analysis.

5. Information, like Other Resources, Is Scarce. Therefore, Knowledge About the Future Is Scarce.

It is difficult, if not impossible, to anticipate the results of many decisions. Would a different car be better than the one you now use? Would a vacation in the mountains be better than one at the seashore? Are political candidate A's positions better than those of candidate B? It is difficult to recognize what all of the options are, and to know how important each of the differences among them will be. Rational decision-makers recognize that it is costly to obtain information and make complex calculations. Although additional information and techniques that improve one's decision-making capabilities are valuable, often the potential benefit is less than its expected cost. Sensible decision-makers will conserve on these limited resources, therefore, just as they conserve on other scarce resources.

6. Remember the Secondary Effects—Economic Actions Often Generate Secondary Effects in Addition to Their Immediate Effects.

Secondary Effects: Economic consequences of an initial economic change, even though they are not immediately identifiable. Secondary effects will be felt only with the passage of time.

Frédéric Bastiat, a nineteenth-century French economist, stated that the difference between a good and a bad economist is that the bad economist considers only the immediate, visible effects, whereas the good economist is also aware of the **secondary effects,** effects that are indirectly related to the initial policy and whose influence might only be seen or felt with the passage of time.

Secondary effects are important in areas outside of economics. The immediate effect of an aspirin is a bitter taste in one's mouth. The indirect effect, which is not immediately observable, is relief from a headache. The immediate effect of drinking six glasses of beer might be a warm, jolly feeling. The indirect effect, for many, would be a pounding headache the next morning. In economics, too, the secondary effects of an action may be quite different from the initial impact. According to the economic way of thinking, the significant questions are: In addition to the initial result of this policy, what other factors will be affected? How will future actions be influenced by the changes in economic incentives that have resulted from policy A?

An economic system is much like an ecological system. An ecological action sometimes generates indirect and perhaps unintended secondary effects. For example, the heavy use of a pesticide on a field to kill a specific population of insects may have an undesirable effect on other creatures. Economic actions can generate similar results. For example, price controls on natural gas have the desired effect of reducing heating expenditures for some consumers, but they also reduce both conservation of gas by those consumers and the incentive of producers to bring more natural gas to the market. Other consumers will therefore be forced to rely more heavily on other, more expensive energy sources, pushing the prices of these energy sources upward. Thus, the controls also generate an unintended result: an increase in the energy costs for some consumers. Good economic thinking demands that we recognize the secondary effects, which will often be observed only with the passage of time.

7. The Value of a Good or a Service Is Subjective.

Preferences differ, sometimes dramatically, between individuals. How much is a ticket to see tonight's performance of the Bolshoi Ballet worth? *Different people will have very different answers!* Some would be willing to pay a high price indeed, while others might even be willing to pay to avoid the ballet if attendance were mandatory. Even for a given individual, circumstances can change from day to day. Alice, who usually would value the ballet ticket at $20, is invited to a party, and suddenly becomes uninterested in the ballet tonight. Now what is the ticket worth? If she knows a friend who would give her $5 for the ticket, it is worth at least that much. If she advertises on a bulletin board and gets $10 for it, a higher value is created. *One thing is certain: the value of the ticket depends on many things, among them who uses it and when.*

Seldom will one individual know how others value an item. Consider how difficult it often is to know what would make a good gift, even for a close friend or family member! So, arranging trades or otherwise moving items to higher-valued users and uses can be very valuable, but is not a simple task. In fact, how society promotes such coordination in the behavior of individuals is a key subject in many of the chapters that follow.

Scientific Thinking:
Development of theory from basic postulates and the testing of the implications of that theory as to their consistency with events in the real world. Good theories are consistent with and help explain real-world events. Theories that are inconsistent with the real world are invalid and must be rejected.

8. The Test of a Theory Is Its Ability to Predict. Economic Thinking Is Scientific Thinking.

The proof of the pudding is in the eating. The usefulness of an economic theory is revealed by its ability to predict the future consequences of economic action. Economists develop economic theory from an analysis of how incentives will affect decision-makers. The theory is then tested against events in the real world. Through testing, we either confirm the theory or recognize the need for amending or rejecting it. If the events in the real world are consistent with a theory, we say that the theory has predictive value. In contrast, theories that are inconsistent with real-world data must be rejected.

If it is impossible to test the theoretical relationships of a discipline, the discipline does not qualify as a science. Since economics deals with human beings, who can think and respond in a variety of ways, can economic theories really be tested? The answer to this question is yes, if, *on average,* human beings respond in predictable and consistent ways to changes in economic conditions. The economist believes that this is the case. Note that this does not necessarily imply that *all* individuals will respond in a specified manner. Economics usually does not seek to predict the behavior of a specific individual; instead, it focuses on the general behavior of a large number of individuals.

How can we test economic theory when controlled experiments with all the interactions of real life are not feasible? This is a problem, but economics is no different from astronomy in this respect. Astronomers must also deal with the world as it is. They cannot change the course of the stars or planets to see what impact the change would have on the gravitational pull of the earth.

So it is with economists. Limited experiments are sometimes possible. For example, experiments comparing the reaction of competing individuals to different forms of an auction might be conducted with actual money payoffs at stake. But economists cannot perform economy-wide tests under real-world conditions. They cannot arbitrarily change the price of cars or unskilled labor services just to observe the effect on quantity purchased or level of employment.

Still, economic theory can be tested in real-world situations. Economic conditions (for example, prices, production costs, technology, transportation cost, and so on), like the location of the planets, do change from time to time. As actual conditions change, economic theory can be tested by comparing its predictions with real-world outcomes. Just as the universe is the laboratory of the astronomer, the real world is the laboratory of the economist.

In some cases, observations of the real world may be consistent with two (or more) economic theories. Given the current state of our knowledge, we will sometimes be unable to distinguish between competitive theories. Much of the work of economists remains to be done, but in many areas substantial empirical work has been completed. Throughout this book, we will refer to this evidence in an effort to provide information with which we can judge the validity of various economic theories. We must not lose sight of the scientific method of thinking because it is a requisite for sound economic thinking.

POSITIVE AND NORMATIVE ECONOMICS

A positive science may be defined as a body of systematized knowledge concerning what is; a normative or regulative science a body of systematized knowledge relating to criteria of what ought to be, and concerned therefore with the ideal as distinguished from the actual.[6]

John Neville Keynes

Positive Economics: The scientific study of "what is" among economic relationships.

Economics as a social science is concerned with predicting or determining the impact of changes in economic variables on the actions of human beings. Scientific economics, commonly referred to as **positive economics,** attempts to determine "what is." Positive economic statements postulate a relationship that is potentially verifiable or refutable. For example: "If the price of butter were higher, people would buy less." Or, "As the money supply increases, the price level will go up." We can statistically investigate (and estimate) the relationship between butter prices and sales, or between the supply of money and the general price level. We can analyze the facts to determine the correctness of a statement about positive economics.

Normative Economics: Judgments about "what ought to be" in economic matters. Normative economic views cannot be proved false, because they are based on value judgments.

Normative economics involves the advocacy of specific policy alternatives, because it uses ethical judgments as well as knowledge of positive economics. Normative economic statements concern "what ought to be," given the philosophical views of the advocate. Value judgments may be the source of disagreement about normative economic matters. Two persons may differ on a policy matter because one is a socialist and the other a libertarian, one a liberal and the other a conservative, or one a traditionalist and the other a radical. They may agree as to the expected outcome of altering an economic variable (that is, the positive economics of an issue), but disagree as to whether that outcome is "good" or "bad."

In contrast with positive economic statements, normative economic statements cannot be tested and proved false (or confirmed to be correct). "The government *should* increase defense expenditures." "Business firms *should not* maximize profits." "Unions *should not* increase wages more rapidly than the cost of living." These normative statements cannot be scientifically tested, since their validity rests on value judgments.

---

[6]John Neville Keynes, *The Scope and Method of Political Economy,* 4th ed., 1917, pp. 34–35.

Positive economics does not tell us which policy is best. The purpose of positive economics is to increase our knowledge of all policy alternatives, thereby eliminating one source of disagreement about policy matters. The knowledge that we gain from positive economics also serves to reduce a potential source of disappointment with policy. Those who do not understand how the economy operates may advocate policies that are actually inconsistent with their philosophical views. Sometimes what one thinks will happen if a policy is instituted may be a very unlikely result in the real world.

Our normative economic views can sometimes influence our attitude toward positive economic analysis. When we agree with the objectives of a policy, it is easy to overlook its potential liabilities. Desired objectives, though, are not the same as workable solutions. The actual effects of policy alternatives often differ dramatically from the objectives of their proponents. A new law forcing employers to pay all employees at least $15 per hour might be intended to help workers, but the resulting decline in the number of workers employed (and increase in the number unemployed) would be disastrous despite the good intentions. Proponents of such a law, of course, would not want to believe the economic analysis that predicted the unfortunate outcome.

Sound positive economics will help us evaluate more accurately whether or not a policy alternative will, in fact, accomplish a desired objective. The task of the professional economist is to expand our knowledge of how the real world operates. If we do not fully understand the implications, including the secondary effects, of alternative policies, we will not be able to choose intelligently among the alternatives. It is not always easy to isolate the impact of a change in an economic variable or policy. Let us consider some of the potential pitfalls that retard the growth of economic knowledge.

PITFALLS TO AVOID IN ECONOMIC THINKING

VIOLATION OF THE CETERIS PARIBUS CONDITION

Economists often preface their statements with the words *ceteris paribus,* meaning "other things constant." "Other things constant, an increase in the price of housing will cause buyers to reduce their purchases." Unfortunately for the economic researcher, we live in a dynamic world. Other things seldom remain constant. For example, as the price of housing rises, the income of consumers may simultaneously be increasing. Both of these factors, higher housing prices and an expansion in consumer income, will have an impact on housing purchases. In fact, we would generally expect them to exert opposite effects—higher prices retarding housing purchases but the rise in consumer income stimulating the demand for housing. The task of sorting out the specific effects of interrelated variables thus becomes more complex when several changes take place simultaneously.

Economic theory acts as a guide, suggesting the probable linkages among economic variables. However, the relationships suggested by economic theory must be tested for consistency with events in the real world. Statistical procedures are often used by economists to correctly identify and more accurately measure relationships among economic variables. In fact, the major portion of the day-to-day work of many professional economists consists of statistical research.

ASSOCIATION IS NOT CAUSATION

In economics, causation is very important. The incorrect identification of causation is a potential source of error. Statistical association alone, though, does not establish causation. Perhaps an extreme example will illustrate the point. Suppose that each November a witch doctor performs a voodoo dance designed to arouse the cold-weather gods of winter and that soon after the dance is performed, the weather in fact begins to turn cold. The witch doctor's dance is *associated with* the arrival of winter, but does it cause the arrival of winter? Most of us would answer in the negative, even though the two are linked statistically.

Unfortunately, cause-and-effect relationships in economics are not always self-evident. For example, it is sometimes difficult to know whether a rise in income has caused people to buy more or, conversely, whether an increase in people's willingness to buy more has created more business and caused incomes to rise. Similarly, economists sometimes argue whether rising money wages are a cause or an effect of inflation. Economic theory, if rooted to the basic postulates, can often help to determine the source of causation, even though competitive theories may sometimes suggest differing directions of causation.

THE FALLACY OF COMPOSITION

What is true for the individual (or subcomponent) may not be true for the group (or the whole). If you stand up for an exciting play during a football game, you will be better able to see. But, what happens if everyone stands up at the same time? What benefits the individual does not benefit the group as a whole. When everyone stands up, the view for individual spectators fails to improve; in fact, it probably becomes even worse.

Fallacy of Composition: Erroneous view that what is true for the individual (or the part) will also be true for the group (or the whole).

People who argue that what is true for the part is also true for the whole may err because of the **fallacy of composition.** Consider an example from economics. If you have an extra $10,000 in your bank account, you will be better off. But, what if everyone suddenly has an additional $10,000? This increase in the money supply will result in higher prices, as people with more money bid against each other for the existing supply of goods. Without an increase in the availability (or production) of scarce economic goods, the additional money will not make everyone better off. What is true for the individual is misleading and often fallacious when applied to the entire economy.

Microeconomics: The branch of economics that focuses on how human behavior affects the conduct of affairs within narrowly defined units, such as individual households or business firms.

Potential error associated with the fallacy of composition highlights the importance of considering both a micro- and a macroview in the study of economics. Since individual human decision-makers are the moving force behind all economic action, the foundations of economics are clearly rooted in a microview. Analysis that focuses on a single consumer, producer, product, or productive resource is referred to as **microeconomics.** As Professor Abba Lerner put it, "Microeconomics consists of looking at the economy through a microscope, as it were, to see how the millions of cells in the body economic—the individuals or households as consumers, and the individuals or firms as producers—play their part in the working of the whole organisms."[7]

Macroeconomics: The branch of economics that focuses on how human behavior affects outcomes in highly aggregated markets, such as the markets for labor or consumer products.

As we have seen, however, what is true for a small unit may not be true in the aggregate. **Macroeconomics** focuses on how the aggregation of individual micro-units affects our analysis. Macroeconomics, like microeconomics, is concerned

---

[7]Abba P. Lerner, "Microeconomy Theory," in *Perspectives in Economics,* ed. A. A. Brown, E. Neuberger, and M. Palmatier (New York: McGraw-Hill, 1968), p. 29.

with incentives, prices, and output. In macroeconomics, however, the markets are highly aggregated. In our study of macroeconomics, the 90 million households in this country will be lumped together when we consider such topics as the importance of consumption spending, saving, and employment. Similarly, the nation's 18 million firms will be lumped together into something we call "the business sector."

What factors determine the level of aggregate output, the rate of inflation, the amount of unemployment, and interest rates? These are macroeconomic questions. In short, macroeconomics examines the forest rather than the individual trees. As we move from the microcomponents to a macroview of the whole, it is important that we bear in mind the potential pitfalls of the fallacy of composition.

WHAT DO ECONOMISTS DO?

The primary functions of economists are to teach, conduct research, and formulate policies. Approximately one half of all professional economists are affiliated with academic institutions. Many of these academicians are involved both in teaching and in scientific research.

OUTSTANDING ECONOMIST

Adam Smith (1723–1790) and the Historical Roots of Economics

The foundation of economics as a systematic area of study was laid in 1776, when Adam Smith published his monumental work, *An Inquiry Into the Nature and Causes of the Wealth of Nations*. Perhaps the most influential book since the Bible, *The Wealth of Nations* was nothing less than a revolutionary attack on the existing orthodoxy. Smith declared that the wealth of a nation did not lie in gold and silver, but rather was determined by the goods and services—whether produced at home or abroad—available to the people.

To increase the nation's hoard of gold and silver, the political and intellectual leaders of Smith's time placed numerous constraints on economic freedoms. Political institutions encouraged citizens to sell their produce abroad in exchange for gold and silver, and discouraged or restrained the purchase of foreign-made goods. Monopolies and guild associations were protected from competition. People thought then that economic activities motivated by private gain were antisocial.

In contrast, Smith argued that a free exchange market economy would harness self-interest as a creative force. Since one gets ahead in a market economy by helping others in exchange for income, people seeking their own gain will provide valuable goods and services to others. As Smith put it:

Man has almost constant occasion for the help of his brethren, and it is in vain for him to expect it from his benevolence *only* [emphasis added] . . . Whoever offers

The job of the research economist is to increase our understanding of economic matters. The tools of statistics and mathematics help the researcher carry out this task. Government agencies and private business firms generate a vast array of economic statistics on such matters as income, employment, prices, and expenditure patterns. A two-way street exists between statistical data and economic theory. Statistics can be used to test the consistency of economic theory and measure the responsiveness of economic variables to changes in policy. At the same time, economic theory helps to explain *which* economic variables are likely to be related and *why* they are linked. Statistics do not tell their own story. We must utilize economic theory to properly interpret and better understand the actual statistical relationships among economic variables.

Economics is a social science. The fields of political science, sociology, psychology, and economics often overlap. Because of the abundance of economic data and the ample opportunity for scientific research in the real world, economics has sometimes been called the "queen of the social sciences." Reflecting the scientific nature of economics, the Swedish Academy of Science in 1969 instituted the Nobel Prize in Economic Science. The men and women of genius in economics now take their place alongside those in physics, chemistry, physiology and medicine, peace, and literature.

A knowledge of economics is essential for wise policy-making. Policy-makers who do not understand the consequences of their actions will not likely reach their

another bargain of any kind proposes to do this: Give me that which I want, and you shall have this which you want; it is in this manner that we obtain from one another the far greater part of those good offices which we stand in need of. It is not from the benevolence of the butcher, the brewer, or the baker, that we expect our dinner, but from their regard to their own interest.

Furthermore, Smith argued that if kings and politicians would remove legal restrictions that retard productive activity and exchange, the "invisible hand" of market prices would direct individuals and resources into those areas of their greatest productivity. Coordination, order, and efficiency would result, despite the absence of a central authority that planned and directed the economy. Smith believed that this process provided the key to production and the wealth of nations.

Ideas have consequences. Even though Smith's thinking conflicted with the social environment of his time, his idea that self-interest, economic freedom, and national wealth were all in harmony eventually changed the world. English historian Henry Thomas Buckle declared that *The Wealth of Nations* represented "the most valuable contribution ever made by a single man towards establishing the principles on which government should be based."

Smith's ideas greatly influenced those who mapped out the structure of the U.S. government. By the end of the eighteenth century, institutional reform had lifted the hand of government from many areas of economic activity in England and throughout Europe.

The nineteenth century, the "era of economic freedom," was one of industrialization and growing prosperity in the Western world. Adam Smith, more than anyone else, established the intellectual climate in which this could happen.

By the time of Smith's death in 1790, five editions of *The Wealth of Nations* had been published, and it had been translated into several foreign languages. The study of the relationship between production, exchange, and wealth began to occupy the time of an increasing number of intellectuals. Political economy—later divided into economics and political science—became a new and widely accepted field of study in major universities throughout the world.

goals. Recognizing the link between economic analysis and policy, Congress in 1946 established the Council of Economic Advisers. The purpose of the council is to provide the president with analyses of how the activities of the federal government influence the economy. The chairmanship of the Council of Economic Advisers is a cabinet-level position.

FINAL WORD

The primary purpose of this book is to encourage you to develop the economic way of thinking so that you can differentiate sound reasoning from economic nonsense. Once you have developed the economic way of thinking, economics will be relatively easy. Using the economic way of thinking can also be fun. Moreover, it will help you become a better citizen. It will give you a different and fascinating perspective on what motivates people, why they act the way they do, and why their actions are sometimes in conflict with the best interest of the community or nation. It will also give you some valuable insight into how people's actions can be rechanneled for the benefit of the community at large.

Economics is a relatively young science. Current-day economists owe an enormous debt to their predecessors. The Outstanding Economist feature analyzes the contribution of Adam Smith, the father of economics.

CHAPTER SUMMARY

1. Scarcity and choice are the two essential ingredients of an economic topic. Goods are scarce because desire for them far outstrips their availability from Nature. Since scarcity prevents us from having as much of everything as we would like, we must choose among the alternatives available to us. Any choice involving the use of scarce resources requires an economic decision.

2. Scarcity and poverty are not the same thing. Absence of poverty implies that some basic level of need has been met. Absence of scarcity would mean that all of our desires for goods have been met. We may someday be able to eliminate poverty, but scarcity will always be with us.

3. Economics is a method of approach, a way of thinking. The economic way of thinking emphasizes the following:
   a. Among economic goods, there are no free lunches. Someone must give up something if we are to have more scarce goods.
   b. Individuals make decisions purposefully, always seeking to choose the option they expect to be most consistent with their personal goals. Purposeful decision-making leads to economizing behavior.
   c. Incentives matter. People will be more likely to choose an option as the benefits expected from that option increase. In contrast, higher costs will make an alternative less attractive, reducing the likelihood that it will be chosen.
   d. Marginal costs and marginal benefits (utility) are fundamental to economizing behavior. Economic reasoning focuses on the impact of marginal changes.
   e. Since information is scarce, uncertainty will be present when decisions are made.
   f. In addition to their initial impact, economic events often alter personal incentives in a manner that leads to important secondary effects that may be felt only with the passage of time.
   g. The value of a good or service is subjective and will differ among individuals.
   h. The test of an economic theory is its ability to predict and to explain events in the real world.

4. Economic science is positive. It attempts to explain the actual consequences of economic actions and alternative policies. Positive economics alone does not state that one policy is superior to another. Normative economics is advocative; using value judgments, it makes suggestions about "what ought to be."

5. Testing economic theory is not an easy task. When several economic variables change simultaneously, it is often difficult to determine the relative importance of each. The direction of economic causation is sometimes difficult to ascertain. Economists consult economic theory as a guide and use statistical techniques as tools to improve our knowledge of positive economics.

6. Microeconomics focuses on narrowly defined units, such as individual consumers or business firms. Macroeconomics is concerned with highly aggregated units, such as the markets for labor or goods and services. When shifting focus from micro- to macrounits, one must be careful not to commit the fallacy of composition. Both micro- and macroeconomics use the same postulates and tools. The level of aggregation is the distinction between the two.

7. The origin of economics as a systematic method of analysis dates back to the publication of *The Wealth of Nations* by Adam Smith in 1776. Even though legal restraints on economic activity abounded at the time, Smith argued that production and wealth would increase if individuals were left free to work, produce, and exchange goods and services. Smith believed that individuals pursuing their own interests would be led by the ''invisible hand'' of market incentives (prices) to employ their productive talents in a manner ''most advantageous to the society.'' Smith's central message is that when markets are free—when there are no legal restraints limiting the entry of producer-sellers—individual self-interest and the public interest are brought into harmony.

CRITICAL ANALYSIS QUESTIONS

1. Indicate how each of the following changes would influence the incentive of a decision-maker to undertake the action described.
   a. A reduction in the temperature from 80° to 50° on one's decision to go swimming.
   b. A change in the meeting time of the introductory economics course from 11:00 A.M. to 7:30 A.M. on one's decision to attend the lectures.
   c. A reduction in the number of exam questions that relate to the text on the student's decision to read the text.
   d. An increase in the price of beef on one's decision to have steak every night this week.
   e. An increase in the rental price of apartments on one's decision to build additional housing units.

*2. ''The government should provide goods such as health care, education, and highways because it can provide them free.'' (True or false; explain)

3. ''Reasonable rental housing could be brought within the economic means of all if the government would prevent landlords from charging more than $200 per month rent for a quality three-bedroom house.'' Use the economic way of thinking to evaluate this view.

*4. Legislation has been introduced which would require airlines to provide and parents to purchase a special safety seat for small children. Proponents of this legislation argue that it would save lives. Do you agree? Can you think of any ''secondary effects'' that might actually increase injuries and fatalities?

5. SENATOR DOGOODER: I favor an increase in the minimum wage because it would help the unskilled worker.
   SENATOR DONOTHING: I oppose an increase in the minimum wage because it would cause the unemployment rate among the young and unskilled to rise.
   Is the disagreement between Senator Dogooder and Senator Donothing positive or normative? Explain.

*6. The United States recently raised the personal exemption from $1,080 to $2,000 and thereby increased the tax-saving provided to parents of children. According to the

---

*Asterisk denotes questions for which answers are given in Appendix C, Selected Answers.

basic postulate of economics, how will this change affect the birth rate?

*7. The economic way of thinking stresses that good intentions lead to sound policy. (True or false; explain)

8. Economic theory postulates that self-interest is a powerful motivation for action. Does this imply that people are selfish and greedy? Do self-interest and selfishness mean the same thing?

*9. Congress and government agencies often make laws to help protect the safety of product consumers. New cars, for example, are required to have many safety features before they can be sold in the United States. These rules do indeed provide added safety for buyers, although they also add to the cost and price of the new vehicles. But can you think of secondary effects of the laws which tend to undercut or reduce the intended effect of increasing auto safety?

*10. "Individuals who economize are missing the point of life. Money is not so important that it should rule the way we live." Evaluate.

11. "Positive economics cannot tell us which agricultural policy is better, so it is useless to policymakers." Evaluate.

12. "I examined the statistics for our basketball team's wins last year and found that when the third team played more, the winning margin increased. If the coach played the third team more, we would win by a bigger margin." Evaluate.

ADDENDUM: UNDERSTANDING GRAPHS

Economists often use graphs to illustrate economic relations. Graphs are like pictures. They are visual aids that can communicate valuable information in a small amount of space. It has been said that a good picture is worth a thousand words. But, one must understand the picture (and the graph) if it is to be enlightening.

This addendum is designed to illustrate the use of simple graphs as an instrument of communication. Many students, particularly those with an elementary mathematics background, are already familiar with this material, and they may safely ignore it. This addendum is for those who need to be assured that they have the ability to understand graphic economic illustrations.

THE SIMPLE BAR GRAPH

A simple bar graph can often help one better visualize comparative relationships. It can be used to illustrate how an economic indicator varies among countries, time periods, or under alternative economic conditions. A bar graph is nothing more than a visual aid. Nevertheless, it is sometimes a valuable illustrative tool.

Exhibit A-1 shows how a bar graph can be used to illustrate economic data. Exhibit A-1a presents tabular data on the income per person in 1988 for several countries. Exhibit A-1b (next page) uses a bar graph to illustrate the same data. The horizontal scale of the graph indicates the total income per person in 1988. A bar is constructed indicating the income level of each country. The length of each bar is in proportion to the per person income of the country. Thus, the length of the bars makes it easy to see how the per capita income varies across the countries. For example, the extremely short bar for India makes it easy to visualize that income per person in India is only a small fraction of the comparable figure for Switzerland, Japan, the United States, and several other countries.

EXHIBIT A-1

International Comparison
of Income per Person

(a) Chart Presentation

Country	Total Income Per Person, 1988
Switzerland	27,500
Japan	21,020
United States	19,840
Sweden	19,300
Canada	16,960
France	16,090
United Kingdom	12,810
Hong Kong	9,220
Mexico	1,760
Egypt	660
India	340

Source: *World Development Report, 1990.*

(b) Bar Graph Presentation

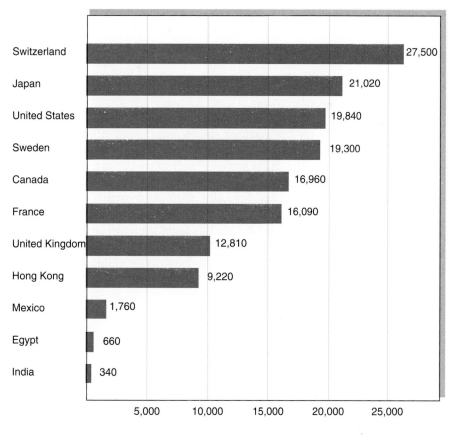

Total income per person, 1988

EXHIBIT A-2

Changes in the Level of Prices in the United States, 1960–1990

The tabular data (a) of the inflation rate is presented in graphic form in (b).

(a) Chart Presentation

Year	Percent Change in Consumer Prices	Year	Percent Change in Consumer Prices
1960	1.5	1975	7.0
1961	0.7	1976	4.8
1962	1.2	1977	6.8
1963	1.6	1978	9.0
1964	1.2	1979	13.3
1965	1.9	1980	12.4
1966	3.4	1981	8.9
1967	3.0	1982	3.9
1968	4.7	1983	3.8
1969	6.1	1984	4.0
1970	5.5	1985	3.8
1971	3.4	1986	1.1
1972	3.4	1987	4.4
1973	8.8	1988	4.4
1974	12.2	1989	4.6
		1990	6.1

Source: *Economic Report of the President, 1991*, Table B-61.

LINEAR GRAPHIC PRESENTATION

Economists are often interested in illustrating variations in economic variables with the passage of time. A linear graph with time on the horizontal axis and an economic variable on the vertical axis is a useful tool to indicate variations over time. Exhibit A-2 illustrates a simple linear graph of changes in consumer prices (the inflation rate) in the United States between 1960 and 1990. The table of the exhibit presents data on the percent change in consumer prices for each year. Beginning with 1960, the horizontal axis indicates the time period (year). The inflation rate for a country is plotted vertically above each year. Of course, the height of the plot (line) indicates the inflation rate during that year. For example, in 1975, the inflation rate was 7.0 percent. This point is plotted at the 7.0 percent vertical distance directly above the year 1975. In 1976, the inflation rate fell to 4.8 percent. Thus, the vertical plot of the 1976 inflation rate is lower than for 1975. The inflation rate for each year (frame a) is plotted at the corresponding height directly above the year. The linear graph is simply a line connecting the points plotted for each of the years 1960 through 1990.

The linear graph makes it easy to visualize what happens to the inflation rate during the period. As the graph shows, the inflation rate rose sharply between 1965 and 1969, in 1973–1974 and again in 1977–1979. It was substantially higher during the 1970s than it was in the early 1960s or the mid-1980s. While the linear graph does not communicate any information not in the table, it does make it easier to see the pattern of the data. Thus, economists often use simple graphics rather than tables to communicate information.

(b) Running Linear Graph

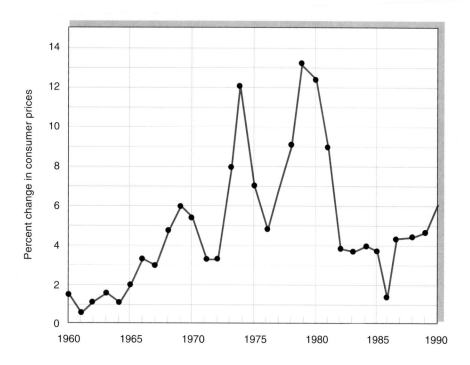

DIRECT AND INVERSE RELATIONSHIPS

Economic logic often suggests that two variables are linked in a specific way. Suppose an investigation reveals that, other things constant, farmers supply more wheat as the price of wheat increases. Exhibit A-3a presents hypothetical data indicating the relationship between the price of wheat and the quantity supplied by farmers.

The information contained in Exhibit A-3a can also be illustrated with a simple two-dimensional graph. Suppose we measure the quantity of wheat supplied by farmers on the x-axis (the horizontal axis) and the price of wheat on the y-axis (the vertical axis). Points indicating the value of x (quantity supplied) at alternative values of y (price of wheat) can then be plotted. The line (or curve) linking the points together illustrates the relationship between the price of wheat and amount supplied by farmers.

In the case of price and quantity supplied of wheat, the two variables are *directly related*. When the y-variable increases, so does the x-variable. When two variables are directly related, the graph illustrating the linkage between the two will slope upward to the right (as in the case of *SS* of Exhibit A-3b).

Sometimes the x-variable and the y-variable are *inversely related*. A decline in the y-variable is associated with an increase in the x-variable. Therefore, a curve picturing the inverse relationship between x and y slopes downward to the right.

Exhibit A-4 illustrates this case. As the data of the table indicate, consumers purchase *less* as the price of wheat increases. Measuring the price of wheat on the y-axis (by convention, economists always place price on the y-axis) and the quantity of wheat purchased on the x-axis, the relationship between these two variables can

EXHIBIT A-3

A Direct Relationship Between Variables (hypothetical data)

As the table (a) indicates, farmers are willing to supply more wheat at a higher price. Thus, there is a direct relation between the price of wheat and the quantity supplied. When the x- and y-variables are directly related, a curve mapping the relationship between the two will slope upward to the right like SS.

Price	Amount of Wheat Supplied by Farmers per Year (millions of bushels)
$1	45
2	75
3	100
4	120
5	140

(a)

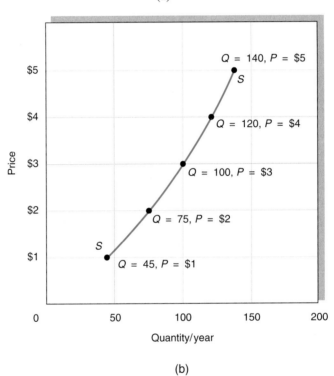

(b)

also be illustrated graphically. If the price of wheat was $5 per bushel, only 60 million bushels would be purchased by consumers. As the price declines to $4 per bushel, annual consumption increases to 75 million bushels. At still lower prices, the quantity purchased by consumers will expand to larger and larger amounts. As Exhibit A-4b illustrates, the inverse relationship between price and quantity of wheat purchased generates a curve that slopes downward to the right.

COMPLEX RELATIONSHIPS

Sometimes the initial relationship between the x- and y-variables will change. Exhibit A-5 illustrates more complex relations of this type. Frame A-5a shows the typical relationship between annual earnings and age. As a young person acquires work experience and develops skills, earnings usually expand. Thus, *initially,* age

EXHIBIT A-4

An Inverse Relationship Between Variables (hypothetical data)

As the table (a) shows, consumers will demand (purchase) more wheat as the price declines. Thus, there is an inverse relationship between the price of wheat and the quantity demanded. When the x- and y-variables are inversely related, a curve showing the relationship between the two will slope downward to the right like *DD*.

Price	Amount of Wheat Demanded by Consumers per Year (millions of bushels)
$1	170
2	130
3	100
4	75
5	60

(a)

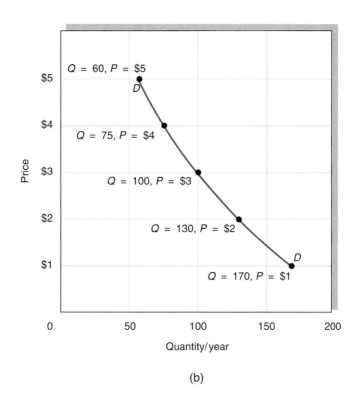

(b)

and annual earnings are directly related; annual earnings increase with age. However, beyond a certain age (approximately age 55), annual earnings generally decline as workers approach retirement. As a result, the initial direct relationship between age and earnings changes to an inverse relation. When this is the case, annual income expands to a maximum (at age 55) and then begins to decline with years of age.

Exhibit A-5b illustrates an initial inverse relation that later changes to a direct relationship. Consider the impact of travel speed on gasoline consumption per mile. At low speeds, the automobile engine will not be used efficiently. As speed increases from 5 mph to 10 mph and on to a speed of 40 mph, gasoline consumption *per mile* declines. In this range, there is an inverse relationship between speed of

EXHIBIT A-5
Complex Relationships

At first, an increase in age (and work experience) leads to a higher income, but later earnings decline as the worker approaches retirement (a). Thus, age and annual income are initially directly related but at approximately age 55 an inverse relation emerges. Frame (b) illustrates the relationship between travel speed and gasoline consumption per mile. Initially, gasoline consumption per mile declines as speed increases (an inverse relation), but as speed increases above 40 miles per hour, gasoline consumption per mile increases with the speed of travel (direct relation).

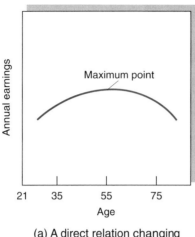

(a) A direct relation changing to inverse

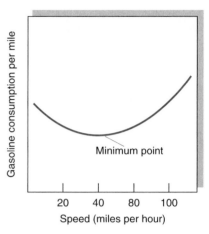

(b) An inverse relation changing to direct

travel (x) and gasoline consumption per mile (y). However, as speed increases beyond 40 mph, more gasoline per mile is required to achieve the additional acceleration. At very high speeds, gasoline consumption per mile increases substantially with speed of travel. Thus, gasoline consumption per mile reaches a minimum and a direct relationship between the x- and y-variables emerges beyond the minimum point (40 mph).

SLOPE OF A STRAIGHT LINE

In economics, we are often interested in how much the y-variable changes in response to a change in the x-variable. The slope of the line or curve reveals this information. Mathematically, the slope of a line or curve is equal to the change in the y-variable divided by the change in the x-variable.

Exhibit A-6 illustrates the calculation of the slope for a straight line. The exhibit shows how the daily earnings (y-variable) of a worker change with hours worked (the x-variable). The wage rate of the worker is $5 per hour. Thus, when 1 hour is worked earnings are equal to $5; for 2 hours of work, earnings jump to $10, and so on. A one-hour change in hours worked leads to a $5 change in earnings. Thus, the slope of the line ($\Delta Y/\Delta X$) is equal to 5. (The symbol Δ means ''change in.'') In the case of a straight line, the change in y per unit change in x is equal for all points on the line. Thus, the slope of a straight line is constant for all points along the line.

Exhibit A-6 illustrates a case in which there is a direct relation between the x- and y-variable. For an inverse relation, the y-variable decreases as the x-variable increases. So, when x and y are inversely related, the slope of the line will be negative.

SLOPE OF A CURVE

In contrast with a straight line, the slope of a curve is different at each point along the curve. The slope of a curve at a specific point is equal to the slope of a line tangent to the curve at the point. (A tangent is a line that just touches the curve.) Exhibit A-7 illustrates how the slope of a curve at a specific point is determined. First, let us consider the slope of the curve at point A. A line tangent to the curve at point A indicates that y changes by 1 unit when x changes by 2 units at point A. Thus, the slope ($\Delta Y/\Delta X$) of the curve at A is equal to 1/2.

EXHIBIT A-6

The Slope of a Straight Line

The slope of a line is equal to change in y divided by the change in x. The line above illustrates the case in which daily earnings increase by $5 per hour worked. Thus, the slope of the earnings function is 5 ($5 ÷ 1 hr). For a straight line, the slope is constant at each point on the line.

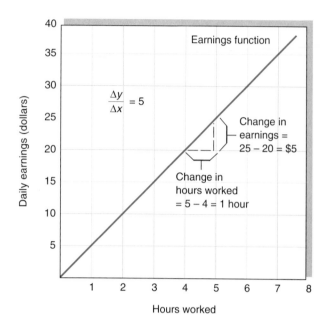

EXHIBIT A-7

The Slope of a Nonlinear Curve

The slope of a curve at any point is equal to the slope of the straight line tangent to the curve at the point. As the lines tangent to the above curve at point A and B illustrate, the slope of a curve will change from point to point along the curve.

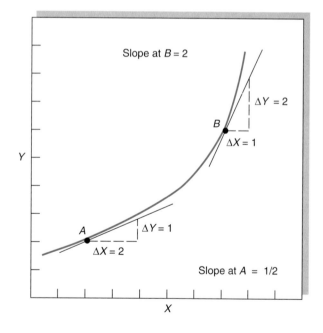

Now, consider the slope of the curve at point *B*. The line tangent to the curve at *B* indicates that *y* changes by 2 units for each one unit change in *x* at point *B*. Thus, at *B* the slope ($\Delta Y/\Delta X$) is equal to 2. At point *B,* a change in the *x*-variable leads to a much larger change in *y* than was true at point *A*. The greater slope of the curve at *B* reflects this greater change in *y* per unit change in *x* at *B* relative to *A*.

GRAPHS ARE NOT A SUBSTITUTE FOR ECONOMIC THINKING

By now you should have a fairly good understanding of how to read a graph. If you still feel uncomfortable with graphs, try drawing (graphing) the relationship between several things with which you are familiar. If you work, try graphing the relationship between *your* hours worked (*x*-axis) and *your* weekly earnings (*y*-axis). If need be, refer to Exhibit A-6 to help guide you with this exercise. Can you graph the relationship between the price of gasoline and your expenditures on gasoline? Graphing these simple relationships will give you greater confidence in your ability to grasp more complex economic relationships presented in graphs.

This text uses only simple graphs. Thus, there is no reason for you to be intimidated. Graphs look much more complex than they really are. In fact, they are nothing more than a simple device to communicate information quickly and concisely. One cannot communicate anything with a graph that cannot be communicated verbally.

Most important, graphs are not a substitute for economic thinking. While a graph may illustrate that two variables are related, it tells us nothing about the cause-and-effect relationship between the variables. To determine probable cause and effect, we must rely on economic theory. Thus, the economic way of thinking, not graphs, is the power station of economic analysis.

2 Some Tools of the Economist

The goods people sell usually are made by processes using a high proportion of the skills they are gifted in, whereas the goods people buy usually are made by processes they are comparatively ungifted in.[1]

Robert A. Mundell

CHAPTER FOCUS

- What is ''opportunity cost''? Why do economists place so much emphasis on opportunity cost?
- What does a production possibilities frontier demonstrate?
- How do specialization and exchange create value?
- What three economizing decisions are faced by every economy?
- What are the two major methods of economic organization? How do they differ?

*I*n the last chapter, you were introduced to the economic approach. In this chapter, we discuss a few important tools that will help you develop the economic way of thinking.

WHAT SHALL WE GIVE UP?

Scarcity calls the tune in economics. We cannot have as much of everything as we would like. Most of us would like to have more time for leisure, recreation, vacations, hobbies, education, and skill development. We would also like to have more wealth, a larger savings account, and more consumable goods. However, all of these things either are scarce or require the use of scarce resources. They are in conflict with one another. We can have more leisure time if we sacrifice some wealth. We can increase our current consumption if we reduce our rate of saving. Choosing one requires us to give up something of the other.

OPPORTUNITY COST IS THE HIGHEST VALUED OPPORTUNITY LOST

An unpleasant fact of economics is that the choice to do one thing is, at the same time, a choice not to do something else. Your choice to spend time reading this book is a choice not to play tennis, go out on a date, listen to a math lecture, or attend a party. These things must be given up because of your decision to read. The highest valued alternative that must be sacrificed because one chooses an option is the **opportunity cost** of the choice.[2]

Opportunity Cost: The highest valued benefit that must be sacrificed (forgone) as the result of choosing an alternative.

Costs are subjective. (So are benefits. After all, a cost is a sacrificed benefit!) A cost exists in the mind of the decision-maker. It is based on expectation—the expected value of the forgone alternative. Cost can never be directly measured by someone other than the decision-maker because only the decision-maker can place a value on what is given up.[3] In fact, this is one reason that voluntary trade is so critical in the creation of value, as we discussed in the last chapter. Only individuals are in a position to evaluate options for themselves, and to decide whether a possible trade is personally a good thing.

Cost, however, often has a monetary component that enables us to approximate its value. For example, the cost of attending a ballet is the highest valued opportunity lost due to: (a) the time necessary to attend and (b) the purchasing power (that is, money) necessary to obtain a ticket. The monetary component is, of course, objective and can be measured. When nonmonetary considerations are relatively unimportant, the monetary component will approximate the total cost of an option.

OPPORTUNITY COST AND THE REAL WORLD

Is real-world decision-making influenced by opportunity cost? Remember, the basic economic postulate states that an option is more likely to be chosen when its cost to the decision-maker is less. So, economic theory does imply that differences (or changes) in opportunity cost will influence how decisions are made.

[1]Robert A. Mundell, *Man and Economics: The Science of Choice* (New York: McGraw-Hill, 1968), p. 19.
[2]For an excellent in-depth discussion of this subject, see A. A. Alchian, ''Cost,'' in *International Encyclopedia of the Social Sciences* (New York: Macmillan, 1969), 3:404–415.
[3]See James M. Buchanan, *Cost and Choice* (Chicago: Markham, 1969), for an analysis of the relationship between cost and choice.

Some examples will demonstrate the real-world application of the opportunity cost concept. Poor people are more likely to travel long distances by bus, whereas the wealthy are more likely to travel by airplane. Why? A simple answer would be that the bus is cheaper; therefore, the poor will be more likely to purchase the cheaper good. But, is the bus cheaper for a relatively well-off individual whose opportunity cost of travel time is high? Suppose that a round-trip airline ticket from Kansas City to Denver costs $150, whereas a bus ticket costs only $110. The bus requires ten hours of travel time, however, and the airplane only two hours. Which would be cheaper? It depends on one's opportunity cost of time. The money cost of air travel is $40 more, but the time cost is 8 hours less. If one's opportunity cost is evaluated at less than $5 per hour, the bus is cheaper, but if one's time is valued at more than $5 per hour, the airplane is clearly the cheaper option. Since the opportunity cost of the travel time will usually be greater for the wealthy than for the poor, the airplane is likely to be much cheaper for those with high incomes.

The concept of opportunity cost also helps us understand labor allocation and wage differences. Setting aside the nonmonetary aspects of a job for the moment, workers whose skills make them valuable to other employers will have to be paid enough to compensate them for what they could be making elsewhere—their highest valued employment alternatives. Thus, a filling station owner is unlikely to hire a physician to pump gas because the physician would have to be paid at least his or her opportunity cost—perhaps $100 per hour or more for delivering babies or performing surgery. Similarly, since the job opportunities forgone on other jobs will be greater for a skilled carpenter than for an unskilled worker, an employer must pay the skilled carpenter a higher wage. Skills and abilities, if they create more valuable alternatives, increase one's earning capability.

Elderly retirees watch considerably more television than high-income lawyers, accountants, and other professionals. Why? Is it because the elderly can better afford the money cost of a TV? Clearly, this is not the case. The time cost, though, is another matter. Consider the difference in the opportunity cost of time between the retirees and the professionals. In terms of lost earnings, watching television costs the professional a lot more than it costs the elderly. The professional watches less TV because it is an expensive good in terms of time.

Why do students watch less television and spend less time at the movies or on the beach during final exam week? Recreation is more costly then, that's why. Using valuable study time to go to the beach might well mean lower grades in several classes, although a student's grade in economics might be unaffected if he or she kept up during the semester and developed the economic way of thinking!

By now you should have the idea. Choosing one thing means giving up others that might have been chosen. Opportunity cost is the highest valued option sacrificed as the result of choosing an alternative.

Failure to consider opportunity cost often leads to unwise decision-making. Suppose that your community builds a beautiful new civic center. The mayor, speaking at the dedication ceremony, tells the world that the center will improve the quality of life in your community. Persons who understand the concept of opportunity cost may question this view. If the center had not been built, the resources could have been used to build a new hospital, improve the educational system, or perhaps provide better housing for low-income families. Will the civic center contribute more to the well-being of the people in your community than these other facilities? If so, it was a wise investment. If not, however, your community will be worse off than it might have been if a higher valued project (that must now be forgone) had been built instead.

TRADE CREATES VALUE

We learned in the last chapter that preferences are subjective, are known only to the individual, and differ among individuals. This means that merely trading—rearranging goods and services among people—can create value. In our Chapter 1 example, the value to Alice of a ticket to attend the Bolshoi ballet performance was zero once she received the party invitation, but the value to other individuals was greater. Suppose the value of the ticket to Jim, who bought it at the advertised price of $10, was $11. An unforeseen change in Alice's schedule had destroyed the value of the performance that evening for her, but trading (selling) the ticket to Jim created $10 in value for her, and it netted $1 in value for Jim — the $11 value he placed on the performance minus the $10 he gave to Alice. The performance remained the same, and the seats available remained the same, but value had been created just as surely as if an additional seat had been made available. *It is wrong to assume that a particular good or service has value just because it exists, independently of the circumstances and who uses it.*[4] As the example of the ballet ticket illustrates, the value of goods and services depends on who uses them, when they are used, and where they are used, as well as on their own physical characteristics.

TRANSACTION COSTS— A BARRIER TO TRADE

Unfortunately, Alice did not know about Andrew, another ballet fan, who would have been willing to pay $15 for the ticket. Andrew lives off campus and failed to see the bulletin board ad, so the potential for another $4 increase in value failed to materialize. A trade to achieve the additional value by putting the ticket into Andrew's hands was overlooked. Still, if Jim and Andrew happen to meet and talk about the ballet before the show, the additional $4 in value for the ticket could be created by another transaction: Jim trading the ticket to Andrew. Such a transaction is unlikely, though, because it would be costly to arrange by other than pure chance. Andrew would have to learn that Jim has the ticket, which seat and what performance the ticket is for, and finally, a price would have to be agreed on. Given the cost of acquiring the necessary information and conducting the trade, the potential exchange between Andrew and Jim will probably not take place.

While exchange creates value, it is also costly. The costs of the time, effort, and other resources necessary to search out, negotiate, and conclude an exchange are called **transaction costs.** Transaction costs reduce our ability to gain from mutually advantageous potential trades.

Since exchange is costly, we should not expect all potentially valuable trades to take place, any more than we expect all useful knowledge to be learned, all safety measures to be taken, or all potential ''A'' grades to be earned. Frequent fliers know that if they never miss a flight, they are probably spending too much time waiting in airports. Similarly, the seller of a car, a house, or a ballet ticket knows that to find

Transaction Costs: The time, effort, and other resources needed to search out, negotiate, and consummate an exchange.

---

[4]An illuminating discussion of this, the ''physical fallacy,'' is found in Thomas Sowell, *Knowledge and Decisions* (New York: Basic Books, 1980), pp. 67–72.

OUTSTANDING ECONOMIST

**Thomas Sowell
(1930–)**

Adam Smith and his colleagues called themselves political economists because they recognized that "the wealth of nations," the prosperity of any economy, depends upon what happens in both the political and economic realms. But over the years, economics came to be separated from the study of political institutions. It also became concerned more with abstract logic, mathematics, and mechanical laws of behavior, and less with the principles underlying human interactions.

Thomas Sowell is one of the foremost economists who has revived the tradition of "political economy." Like Smith before him, he recognizes the critical importance of the institutions—the "rules of the game"—which shape human interactions. His book, *Knowledge and Decisions,* stresses the difficulty of obtaining knowledge, and the way different institutional arrangements provide different kinds and amounts of scarce information.

Knowledge and Decisions also introduces the concept of "physical fallacy"—the error that many people make when they assume that two physically identical objects must have the same value. People value things differently. An opera ticket may be worth $25 to one person, and nothing to another. Two physically identical items may differ in value for other reasons, too. The items may be in different locations in time or space. The Cuisinart on the department store shelf is worth more than one in a warehouse on the boat dock. By getting it to a place where the customer can easily see it and buy it, the distributor has added value to the product, even though the physical object itself is not changed.

Sowell points out that failure to understand the physical fallacy has been the cause of much misery. It has led people to be hostile toward "middlemen"—people who add value by bringing goods (and knowledge) from the producer to the customer—largely because their contribution to the goods' value is not physical, and thus not easily seen.

Sowell's willingness to apply economic thinking to a wide array of human activities beyond standard "textbook" markets reflects the tradition at the University of Chicago, where he earned his Ph.D. in economics after receiving earlier degrees from Columbia and Harvard Universities. In 1980 he became a Senior Fellow at the Hoover Institution. In addition to a number of books on economics, he has published extensive studies of the effects of ethnic and racial discrimination in both the United States and other countries.

that single person in the world who would be willing to pay the most money is not worth the enormous effort required to locate that buyer. The cost of perfection in exchange, as in other endeavors, is just too high.

THE MIDDLEMAN AS A COST REDUCER

Middleman: A person who buys and sells, or who arranges trades. A middleman reduces transaction costs, usually for a fee or a markup in price.

Since there are gains from exchange, some people specialize in providing information and arranging trades. Such a specialist is commonly called a **middleman.** Often, people believe that middlemen are unnecessary; that they simply add to the buyer's expense without benefitting the seller. Now that we recognize transactions costs, however, we can see the fallacy of this view. The auto dealer, for example, can help both the makers and the buyers of cars. By keeping an inventory of autos, and by hiring knowledgeable sales people, the dealer helps the car shopper learn about the many cars offered, and how each car looks, performs, and "feels." (Don't forget that preferences are subjective; they are not objectively known to others.) Car buyers also like to know that the local dealer will honor the warranty, and provide parts and service for the car when they are needed. The car maker, by using the dealer as a middleman, is able to concentrate on designing and making cars, leaving to middlemen—dealers—the task of marketing and servicing them in each community.

Grocers are another provider of middleman services. Each of us could deal with food producers directly, buying in large quantities, perhaps shopping through catalogues to choose what we want. If we did, though, we wouldn't be able to squeeze the tomatoes! Besides, we would each need giant refrigerators, freezers, and storerooms at home to hold huge quantities of food. Or, perhaps we could form consumer cooperatives, banding together to eliminate the middleman, using our own warehouses and our own volunteer labor to order, receive, display, redistribute, and collect payment for the food. In fact, some cooperatives like this do exist, but most people prefer instead to hire the space and do the planning, record keeping, and labor through the grocer, paying the usual markup for middleman services.

Stockbrokers, publishers of the yellow pages, and merchants of all sorts are middlemen—specialists in selling, guaranteeing, and servicing the items traded. For a fee, they reduce transaction costs both for the shopper and for the seller.

Transaction costs reduce our ability to realize gains from trade; middlemen reduce transaction costs. Simply by making exchange cheaper and more convenient, middlemen cause more efficient trades to happen. In so doing, they themselves create value.

WHAT IS TRADED—PROPERTY RIGHTS

Property Rights: The right to use, control, and obtain the benefits from a good or service.

The buyer of an automobile or an apple may take the item home. The buyer of a steamship or an office building, though, might never touch it. When exchange occurs, it is really the rights—the **property rights**—to the item that change hands. It is ownership and control that count, rather than physical possession.

Private property rights exist when property rights are (a) exclusively controlled by one owner and (b) transferable to others. Private ownership of property rights gives owners a chance to act selfishly. However, since they link responsibility to authority, they also make owners accountable for their actions.

Pr. ate Property Rights: Property rights that are exclusively held by an owner, and that can be transferred to others at the owner's discretion.

1. *Private owners can gain by employing their resources in ways that are beneficial to others. On the other hand, owners bear the opportunity cost of ignoring the wishes of others.* If someone values an asset more than its current owner, the current owner can gain by paying heed to the wishes of others. For example, suppose Ed owns a car that others would also like to have. What incentive is there for Ed to pay attention to the desires of the others? If someone else values the car at $2,000, while Ed values it at only $1,500, then Ed can gain by selling the car at any price higher than $1,500. Turning down the offer of $2,000 costs Ed $500. In fact, if transaction costs are low (if search is cheap and easy), Ed might gain by searching for people (potential buyers) who want the car more than he does. If he fails to yield to the desires of others, Ed ''pays'' the opportunity cost for continued ownership of the car by not receiving the $2,000. Failing to consider the wishes of others may penalize the potential buyer, but it would also hurt Ed. When

potential buyers and sellers know that cars are privately owned and thus easily transferable, each has every incentive to search out mutually advantageous trades. After all, if they find such a trade, only the buyer and seller have to approve the deal, and both will gain.

As a second example, suppose Ed owns a house and will be out of town all summer. Will the house stay vacant, or will Ed let someone else use it during those months? We don't know, but we do know that Ed can rent the house to someone else if he chooses, and that if he does not, he will pay the opportunity cost—the rental payments he could get, minus any damages, added upkeep, and transaction costs. Ownership of the private property rights has again faced Ed with the opportunity costs of his actions, and provided him with a strong incentive to consider the wishes of others regarding the use of his property.

2. *The private owner has a strong incentive to properly care for the item he or she owns.* Will Ed change the oil in his car? Will he take care to see that the seats do not get torn? Probably so, since being careless about these things would reduce the car's value, both to him and to any future owner. The car and its value—the sale price if he sells it—belong just to Ed, so he would bear the burden of a decline in the car's value if the oil ran low and ruined the engine, or if the seats were torn. As the owner, Ed has both the authority and the incentive to protect the car against harm or neglect. Private property rights give the owner a strong incentive for good stewardship.

3. *The private owner has an incentive to conserve for the future if the item is expected to be worth more then.* Suppose our man Ed owns a case of very good red wine, which is only two years old. Age will improve it substantially if he puts it in his cellar for another five years. Will he do so? Well, if he does not, he will personally bear the consequences. He (and presumably his friends) will drink wine sooner, but they will sacrifice quality. Also, Ed will forgo the chance to sell the wine later for much more than its current worth. The opportunity cost of drinking the wine now is its unavailability later. Ed bears that cost. Private property rights assure that Ed has the authority to preserve the wine, and that he gains the benefits if he does so. If the greater quality is expected to be worth the wait, then Ed can capture the benefits of not serving the wine "before its time."

In a similar way, if Ed owns land, or a house, or a factory, he has a strong incentive to bear costs now, if necessary, to preserve the asset's value. His wealth is tied up in its value, which reflects nothing more than the net benefits which will be available to the owner in the future. So Ed's wealth depends on his ability to look ahead, maintain, and conserve those things that will be highly valued in the future.

4. *With private property rights, the property owner is accountable for damage to others through misuse of the property.* Ed, the car owner, has a right to drive his car, but he has no right to drive in a drunken or reckless way that injures Alice. A chemical company has control over its products, but exactly for that reason, it is legally liable for damages if it mishandles the chemicals. Courts of law recognize and enforce the authority granted by ownership, but they also enforce the responsibility that goes with that authority. Once again, property rights hold accountable the person (owner) with authority over property.

These characteristics of property rights are very useful. When private property rights are not present or are not enforced, other methods must be found to provide the incentives for good stewardship of property, and for proper concern for others by the users of property. For example, when the owner of an automobile or a factory pollutes the air and is not made to pay for damage done to the property of others,

"Their house looks so nice. They must be getting ready to sell it."

Pepper . . . and Salt © *The Wall Street Journal*

EXHIBIT 1

The Production Possibilities Curve for Grades in English and Economics

The production possibilities for Susan, in terms of grades, are illustrated for two alternative quantities of total study time. If Susan studied six hours per week, she could attain (a) an F in English and an A in economics, (b) a D in English and a B in economics, (c) a C in both, (d) a B in English and a D in economics, or (e) an F in economics and an A in English.

Could she make higher grades in both? Yes, if she were willing to apply more resources, thereby giving up some leisure. The colored line indicates her production possibilities curve if she studied eight hours per week.

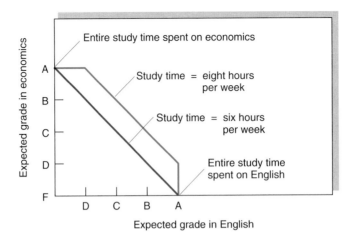

Production Possibilities Curve: A curve that outlines all possible combinations of total output that could be produced, assuming (a) the utilization of a fixed amount of productive resources, (b) full and efficient use of those resources, and (c) a specific state of technical knowledge. The slope of the curve indicates the rate at which one product can be traded off to produce more of the other.

property rights are not being enforced. Without effective property rights, other measures may be necessary to control polluting behavior. We will return to this problem in Chapter 4.

THE PRODUCTION POSSIBILITIES CURVE: SEPARATING THE POSSIBLE FROM THE IMPOSSIBLE

The resources of every individual are limited. Purposeful decision-making and economizing behavior imply that individuals seek to get the most from their limited resources. They do not deliberately waste resources.

The nature of the economizing problem can be made more clear by the use of a conceptual tool, the production possibilities diagram. A **production possibilities curve** reveals the maximum amount of any two products that can be produced from a fixed set of resources, and the possible tradeoffs in production between them.

Exhibit 1 illustrates the production possibilities curve for Susan, an intelligent economics major. This curve indicates the combinations of grades possible for two alternative amounts of study time—six hours and eight hours. If Susan uses her six hours of study time efficiently, she can choose any grade combination along the six-hour production possibilities curve. When her study time is limited to six hours per week, though, Susan is able to raise her grade in one of the subjects only by accepting a lower grade in the other. If she wants to improve her overall performance (raise at least one grade without lowering the other), she will have to spend more time on academic endeavors. For example, she might increase her weekly study time from six to eight hours. Of course, this would require her to give up something else—leisure.

Can the production possibilities concept be applied to the entire economy? The answer is yes. Having more guns means having less butter, as the old saying goes. Beefing up the military requires the use of resources that otherwise could be used to produce nonmilitary goods. If scarce resources are being used efficiently, more of one thing means the sacrifice of others.

EXHIBIT 2

The Concept of the Production Possibilities Curve for an Economy

When an economy is using its limited resources efficiently, production of more clothing requires the economy to give up some other goods—food in this simple example. *With time,* a technological discovery or expansion of the economy's resource base could make it possible to produce more of both, shifting the production possibilities curve outward. Or, the citizens of the economy might decide to give up some leisure for more of both goods. These factors aside, limited resources will constrain the production possibilities of an economy.

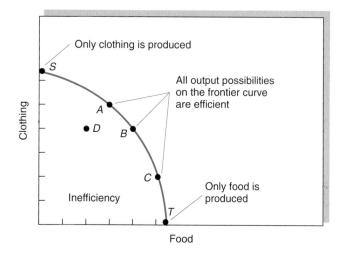

Exhibit 2 shows a production possibilities curve for an economy producing only two goods: food and clothing. The curve is concave or bowed out from the origin. Why? Resources are not equally well suited to produce food and clothing. Consider an economy that was using all of its resources to produce clothing. At that point *(S),* food production can be expanded by transferring those resources which are best suited for production of food (and least suitable for clothing production) from clothing to food production. Since the resources transferred are highly productive in food and not very productive in clothing, *in this range* the opportunity cost (clothing forgone) of additional food is low. However, as successively larger amounts of food are produced (moves from *S* to *A* to *B* and so on), the opportunity cost of food will rise. This results because as more and more food is produced, additional food output can be achieved only by using resources that are less and less suitable for the production of food. Thus, as food output is expanded, successively larger amounts of clothing must be forgone per unit of additional food.

What restricts the ability of an economy, once resources are fully utilized, from producing more of everything? The same thing that kept Susan from making a higher grade in both English and economics—lack of resources. There will be various maximum combinations of goods that an economy will be able to produce when:

1. it uses some fixed quantity of resources;
2. the resources are not unemployed or used inefficiently; and
3. the level of technology is constant.

When these three conditions are met, the economy will be at the perimeter of its production possibilities frontier (points such as *A, B,* and *C,* Exhibit 2). Producing more of one good, such as clothing, will necessitate less production of other goods (for example, food).

When the resources of an economy are unemployed or used inefficiently, the economy is operating at a point inside the production possibilities curve—point *D,* for example. Why might this happen? It happens because the economy is not properly solving the economizing problem. A major function of economics is to help us get the most out of available resources, to move us out to the production possibilities frontier. We will return to this problem again and again.

Could an economy ever have more of all goods? Could the production possibilities curve be shifted outward? The answer is yes, under certain circumstances. There are three major methods.

1. An Increase in the Economy's Resource Base Would Expand Our Ability to Produce Goods and Services.

If we had more and better resources, we could produce a greater amount of all goods. Many resources are human-made. If we were willing to give up some current consumption, we could invest more of today's resources into the production of long-lasting physical structures, machines, education, and the development of human skills. This **capital formation** would provide us with better tools and skills in the future and thereby increase our ability to produce goods and services. Exhibit 3 illustrates the link between capital formation and the future production possibilities of an economy. The two economies illustrated start with the same production possibilities curve *(RS)*. However, since Economy A (Exhibit 3a) allocates more of its resources to investment than does Economy B, A's production possibilities curve shifts outward with the passage of time by a greater amount. The growth rate of A—the expansion rate of the economy's ability to produce goods—is enhanced because the economy allocates a larger share of its output to investment. Of course, more investment in machines and human skills will necessitate less current consumption.

2. Advancements in Technology Can Expand the Economy's Production Possibilities.

Technology determines the maximum physical output obtainable from any particular set of resource inputs. New technology can make it possible to get more from our given base of resources.[5] An important form of technological change is **invention,** the use of science and engineering to discover new products or processes. Sending information instantly and cheaply by satellite, getting more oil from a well, and growing more corn from newly developed hybrid seed are all examples of technological advances resulting from inventions. Each one has pushed our production possibilities curve outward.

An economy can also benefit from technological change through **innovation,** the practical and effective adoption of new techniques. Such innovation is commonly carried out by an **entrepreneur**—one who seeks profit by introducing new products or improved techniques to satisfy consumers at a lower cost.[6] To prosper, an entrepreneur must convert and rearrange resources in a manner that will increase their value, thus expanding our production possibilities. Some examples will help us explain.

---

[5]Without modern technical knowledge, it would be impossible to produce the vast array of goods and services responsible for our standard of living. Thomas Sowell makes this point clear when he notes:

> *The cavemen had the same natural resources at their disposal as we have today, and the difference between their standard of living and ours is a difference between the knowledge they could bring to bear on those resources and the knowledge used today.*

See Thomas Sowell, *Knowledge and Decisions* (New York: Basic Books, 1980), p. 47.

[6]This French-origin word literally means "one who undertakes." The entrepreneur is the person who is ultimately responsible. Of course, this responsibility may be shared with others (partners or stockholders, for example) or it may be partially delegated to technical experts. Nevertheless, the success or failure of the entrepreneur is dependent on the outcome of the choices he or she makes.

SHIFTING THE PRODUCTION POSSIBILITIES CURVE OUTWARD

Capital Formation: The production of buildings, machinery, tools, and other equipment that will enhance the ability of future economic participants to produce. The term can also be applied to efforts to upgrade the knowledge and skill of workers and thereby increase their ability to produce in the future.

Technology: The body of skills and technological knowledge available at any given time. The level of technology establishes the relationship between inputs and the maximum output they can generate.

Invention: The discovery of a new product or process, often facilitated by the knowledge of engineering and scientific relationships.

Innovation: The successful introduction and adoption of a new product or process; the economic application of inventions and marketing techniques.

Entrepreneur: A profit-seeking decision-maker who decides which projects to undertake and how they should be undertaken. A successful entrepreneur's actions will increase the value of resources.

EXHIBIT 3

Investment and Production Possibilities in the Future

Here we illustrate two economies that initially confront identical production possibilities curves *(RS)*. The economy illustrated on the left allocates a larger share of its output to investment (I_a, compared to I_b for the economy on the right). As a result, the production possibilities of the high-investment economy will shift outward by a larger amount than will be true for the low-investment economy.

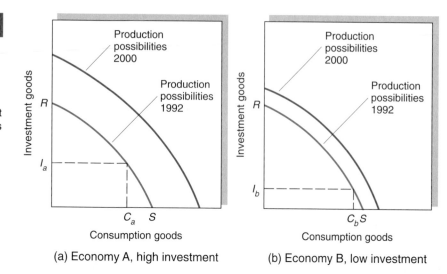

(a) Economy A, high investment　　(b) Economy B, low investment

One entrepreneur, Henry Ford, changed car-making technology by pioneering the assembly line for making cars. With the same amount of labor and materials, Ford made more cars, more cheaply. Another entrepreneur, the late Ray Kroc, founded the McDonald's hamburger chain. In addition to a popular restaurant menu, he provided information to potential customers. By carefully designing a limited menu that could be prepared according to strict formulas, setting up a training school (Hamburger University, outside of Chicago) for managers, and providing for a regular inspection program, he could guarantee uniformity (known products and quality level) to each customer. Once the McDonald's reputation spread, hungry people knew what to expect at the "golden arches" without even having to enter the restaurant. Trying McDonald's in one location provides information on thousands of others. Nationwide franchises and quality control make it easy for McDonald's fans to find these quick, cheap meals. The same information makes it easy for those who dislike the formula to avoid it. In both cases, we benefit from Mr. Kroc's entrepreneurship—an innovative way to guarantee quality and to transmit instant information cheaply.

Another type of entrepreneur takes inventions produced by others and applies them more effectively. Steven Jobs, co-founder of the Apple Computer Corporation, is an example. He and his firm used the new computer technology to create personal- and small-business computers, and arranged for the "user friendly" software needed by most of us to use such machines. Selling the combination helped make computers useful to millions of people, both at home and on the job, and brought the new technology within their financial reach. Once again, entrepreneurship expanded our production possibilities.

3. By Working Harder and Giving Up Current Leisure, We Could Increase Our Production of Goods and Services.　Strictly speaking, this is not an expansion in the production frontier because leisure is also a good. We are giving up some of that good to have more of other things.

The work effort of individuals depends not only on their personal preferences but also on public policy. For example, high tax rates may induce individuals to reduce their work time. The basic economic postulate implies that as high tax rates reduce the personal payoff from working (and earning taxable income), individuals will shift more of their time to other, untaxed activities, including the consumption of leisure, moving the production possibilities curve for market goods inward. Any reduction in market work time not only reduces output directly, but it is likely also to reduce the gains from the division of labor. We turn now to look at why this is important.

DIVISION OF LABOR AND PRODUCTION POSSIBILITIES

Division of Labor: A method that breaks down the production of a commodity into a series of specific tasks, each performed by a different worker.

In a modern economy, individuals do not produce most of the items we consume. Instead, we sell our labor services (usually agreeing to do specified productive work) and use the income we get in exchange to buy what we want. We do this because the **division of labor,** together with exchange, allow us to produce far more goods and services through cooperative effort than we could if each household produced its own food, clothing, shelter, transportation, and other desired goods.

Observing the operation of a pin manufacturer more than 200 years ago, Adam Smith noted that specialization and division of labor permitted far more output. When each worker specialized in a productive function, ten workers were able to produce 48,000 pins per day, or 4,800 pins per worker. Without specialization and division of labor, Smith doubted an individual worker would have been able to produce as many as 20 pins per day.[7]

The division of labor separates production tasks into a series of related operations. Each worker performs a single task, only one of perhaps hundreds of tasks necessary to produce a commodity. There are several reasons why the division of labor often leads to enormous gains in output per worker. First, specialization permits individuals to take advantage of their existing abilities and skills. (Put another way, specialization permits an economy to take advantage of the fact that individuals have different skills.) Productive assignments can be undertaken by those individuals who are able to accomplish them most efficiently. Second, a worker who specializes in just one task (or one narrow area) becomes more experienced and more skilled in that task with the passage of time. Most importantly, the division of labor lets us adopt complex, large-scale production techniques unthinkable for an individual household. As our knowledge of technology and the potential of machinery expand, capital-intensive production procedures and the division of labor permit us to attain living standards undreamed of just a few decades ago.

TRADE, COMPARATIVE ADVANTAGE, AND REALIZING OUR PRODUCTION POSSIBILITIES

Economizing means getting the most out of our available resources. How can this be accomplished? How can we reach our production possibilities frontier and get more value from our productive activities? To answer these questions, we must understand several important principles.

---

[7]See Adam Smith, *An Inquiry into the Nature and Causes of the Wealth of Nations* (1776; Cannan's ed., Chicago: University of Chicago Press, 1976), pp. 7–16, for additional detail on the importance of the division of labor.

First, let us consider the economizing problem of Woodward and Mason, individuals in the construction business. Exhibit 4 presents certain facts about the abilities of Woodward and Mason. Woodward is highly skilled, fast, and reliable. During one month, Woodward can build either four frame houses or two brick houses. Mason is less skilled, and is slower than Woodward at building both kinds of houses. It takes Mason an entire month to build either a frame or a brick house.

Last year, Woodward spent 8 months producing 16 brick houses and the other 4 months producing 16 frame houses. Mason was able to produce only 6 frame and 6 brick houses during the year. Their joint output was 22 frame and 22 brick houses.

Since Woodward has an absolute advantage (Woodward can build both frame and brick houses more rapidly than Mason) in the production of houses, few observers would believe that Woodward and Mason could gain from specialization and trade of products. Potential gain, though, is clearly present. Suppose Mason specialized in the production of brick houses, while Woodward spent 6 months producing both types of house. Woodward could produce 24 frame houses (4 per month) in those 6 months, and 12 brick houses (2 per month) in another 6 months. After they became more specialized, Mason and Woodward could produce 24 frame houses (all by Woodward) and 24 brick houses (12 each) in the same 12-month

---

EXHIBIT 4 ■ Comparative Advantage and Increasing Output

The monthly possibilities of Woodward and Mason are:

Frame Houses per Month		Brick Houses per Month	
Woodward	Mason	Woodward	Mason
4	1	2	1

Initially each produced an equal quantity of both frame and brick houses. Annually, Woodward could produce 16 of each, and Mason only 6 of each. Thus, their total output could reach 22 frame and 22 brick units.

After each specialized in his area of greatest comparative advantage, Mason produced only brick houses, building 12 of them (one each month). Woodward spent 6 months building frame houses, and 6 months building brick houses, producing 24 frame (4 per month) and 12 brick units (2 per month). As the chart shows, after specialization, their total output of both frame houses and brick houses increased from 22 to 24.

If Mason trades 5 brick houses to Woodward for 7 frame houses, Woodward would end up with 17 brick and 17 frame houses, one more of each than he could achieve without specialization and trade. Similarly, Mason would be left with 7 brick and 7 frame (received in the trade with Woodward) houses. Specialization and exchange permit both parties to gain.

	Annual Output Before Specialization		Annual Output After Specialization	
	Frame Houses	Brick Houses	Frame Houses	Brick Houses
Woodward	16	16	24	12
Mason	6	6	0	12
Total	22	22	24	24

period. Together, the builders would be better off. If 5 of Mason's 12 brick houses were traded to Woodward for 7 frame houses, then Mason would have 7 frame and 7 brick houses to show for his efforts, compared to last year's individual output rate of 6 frame and 6 brick. Similarly, upon receipt of the 5 brick houses from Mason in exchange for 7 frame ones, Woodward would also be left with 17 frame and 17 brick houses, definitely an improvement over last year's output of 16 frame and 16 brick. Thus, specialization and exchange could allow both Woodward and Mason to surpass last year's production rate.

Despite the fact that Woodward was better than Mason at producing both frame and brick houses, the two were able to gain from trade and specialization.[8] Was it magic? What is happening here? Our old friend, opportunity cost, will help us unravel this seemingly paradoxical result. In what sense is Woodward better at producing brick houses than Mason? True, in one month, Woodward can produce twice as many brick houses as Mason, but what is Woodward's opportunity cost of producing a brick house? Two frame ones, right? In the same time required to produce a single brick house, Woodward can produce two frame houses.

Consider Mason's opportunity cost of producing a brick house. It is only one frame house. So, who is the cheaper producer of brick houses? Mason is, because Mason's opportunity cost of producing a brick house is one frame house, compared to Woodward's opportunity cost of two frame houses.

The reason that Woodward and Mason could both gain is that their exchange allowed each of them to specialize in the production of the product that, comparatively speaking, they could produce most cheaply. Mason was the cheaper producer of brick houses. Woodward was the cheaper producer of the frame ones. They were able to economize—get more out of their resources—by trading and specializing in the thing that each did better, comparatively speaking.

This simple example demonstrates a basic truth known as the law of comparative advantage, which lies at the heart of economizing behavior for any economy. Initially developed in the early 1800s by the great English economist David Ricardo, the **law of comparative advantage** states that the total output of a group of individuals, an entire economy, or a group of nations will be greatest when the output of each good is produced by the person (or firm) with the lowest opportunity cost.

If a product, any product made, could be produced by someone else with a lower opportunity cost, the economy is giving up more than necessary. It is not economizing. Economizing, or economic efficiency, requires that output always be generated by the producer who has the lowest opportunity cost.

Perhaps one additional example will help to drive home the implications of the law of comparative advantage. Consider the situation of an attorney who can type 120 words per minute. The attorney is trying to decide whether to hire a secretary, who types only 60 words per minute, to complete some legal documents. If the lawyer does the typing job, it will take four hours; if a secretary is hired, the typing job will take eight hours. Thus, the lawyer has an absolute advantage in typing compared to the prospective employee. The attorney's time, though, is worth $50 per hour when working as a lawyer, whereas the typist's time is worth $5 per hour

Law of Comparative Advantage: A principle that states that individuals, firms, regions, or nations can gain by specializing in the production of goods that they produce cheaply (that is, at a low opportunity cost) and exchanging those goods for other desired goods for which they are high opportunity cost producers.

---

[8]Throughout this section we will assume that individuals are equally content to produce either product. Dropping this assumption would add to the complexity of the analysis, but it would not change the basic principle.

as a typist. Although a fast typist, the attorney is also a high opportunity cost producer of typing service. If the lawyer types the documents, the job will cost $200, which is the opportunity cost of four hours of lost time as a lawyer. Alternatively, if the typist is hired, the cost of having the documents typed is only $40 (eight hours of typing service at $5 per hour). The lawyer's comparative advantage thus lies in practicing law. The attorney will gain by hiring the typist and spending the additional time specializing in the practice of law.

DIVISION OF LABOR, SPECIALIZATION, AND EXCHANGE IN ACCORDANCE WITH THE LAW OF COMPARATIVE ADVANTAGE

It is difficult to exaggerate the gains derived from specialization, division of labor, and exchange in accordance with the law of comparative advantage. These factors are the primary source of our modern standard of living. Can you imagine the difficulty involved in producing one's own housing, clothing, and food, to say nothing of radios, television sets, dishwashers, automobiles, and telephone services? Yet, most families in North America, Western Europe, Japan, and Australia enjoy these conveniences. They are able to do so largely because their economies are organized in such a way that individuals can cooperate, specialize, and trade, thereby reaping the benefits of the enormous increases in output—both in quantity and diversity—thus produced. An economy not realizing the gains from specialization and division of labor is ignoring the law of comparative advantage. It is operating inside of its production possibilities curve, at a point such as *D* of Exhibit 2. This is the case for most of the less-developed economies. For various reasons, production in these economies is centered primarily in the individual household. Therefore, the output level per worker of these economies falls well below the attainable level.

When one stops to think about it, the law of comparative advantage is almost common sense. Stated in layman's terms, it simply means that if we want to accomplish a task with the least effort, each of us should specialize in that component of the task that we do best, comparatively speaking.

The principle of comparative advantage is universal. It is just as valid in socialist countries as it is in capitalist countries. Socialist planners, to get the most out of available resources, must also apply the principle of comparative advantage.

DEPENDENCE, SPECIALIZATION, AND EXCHANGE

Specialization and mutual dependence are directly related. If the United States specializes in the production of agricultural products and Middle East countries specialize in the production of oil, the two countries become interdependent. Similarly, if Texas specializes in the production of cotton and Kansas specializes in the production of wheat, interdependence results. In some cases, this dependence can have serious consequences for one or both of the parties. The potential costs of mutual dependence (for example, vulnerability to economic pressure applied by a trading partner who supplies an important economic good) and its potential benefits (for example, economic interaction that may well increase international understanding and reduce the likelihood of war) should be weighed along with the mutual consumption gains when one is evaluating the merits of specialization.

SPECIALIZATION AND WORKER ALIENATION

Specialization clearly makes it possible to produce more goods, but it may also result in many workers performing simple, boring, and monotonous functions. Our friend Woodward may get tired of building frame houses, and Mason's life may lose a certain zest because he produces only brick ones. On a more practical level, specialization often results in assembly-line production techniques. Workers may become quite skilled because they perform identical tasks over and over again, but they may also become bored if the work is personally unrewarding. Thus, strictly speaking, some of the gains associated with the expansion of physical output may result in worker dissatisfaction.

You may be thinking that economists consider only material goods and ignore the importance of human beings. It may seem that they do not care if a worker hates a job because it is repetitive, unchallenging, and boring. Our initial approach to the topic of specialization is vulnerable to this charge. We stressed only physical production because it makes the principle simpler to communicate. However, specialization could be considered strictly from the viewpoint of utility, in which both output *and* job satisfaction are economic goods.

An individual's opportunity cost of producing a good (or performing a service) includes the sacrifice of both physical production of other goods and any change in the desirability of working conditions. The consideration of working conditions and job preferences does not invalidate the basic concept. It is still true that maximum economic efficiency, in the utility sense, requires that each productive activity be performed by those persons with the lowest opportunity cost, including satisfaction given up by turning down other jobs. Individuals could still gain by producing and selling those things for which they have a comparatively low opportunity cost, including the job satisfaction component, while buying other things for which their opportunity cost is high. They would tend to specialize in the provision of those things they both do well and enjoy most. People with a strong aversion to monotonous work would be less likely to choose such work even though they might be skilled at it. Those with a smaller comparative advantage, measured strictly in terms of physical goods, might have a lower opportunity cost because they find the work more rewarding.

PERSONAL MOTIVATION AND THE GAINS FROM SPECIALIZATION AND EXCHANGE

What motivates people to act? How does the purposeful decision-maker choose? Economic thinking implies that people will choose an option only if they expect the benefits (utility) of the choice to exceed its opportunity cost. Purposeful decision-makers will be motivated by the pursuit of personal gain. They will never knowingly choose an alternative when they expect the opportunity cost to exceed the benefits. To do so would be to make a choice with the full awareness that it meant the sacrifice of another, preferred course of action. That simply would not make sense. To say that people are motivated by personal gain does not, of course, mean that they are inconsiderate of others. Other people's feelings will often affect the personal benefit received by a decision-maker.

When an individual's interest, aptitudes, abilities, and skills make it possible to gain by exchanging low opportunity cost goods for those things that he or she could only produce at a high opportunity cost, pursuit of the potential gain will motivate the individual to trade precisely in this manner. If free exchange is allowed, it will not be necessary for people to be assigned the "right" job or to be told that, comparatively speaking, they should trade A for B because they are good at producing A but not so good at producing B. In a market setting, individuals will

MYTHS OF ECONOMICS

"In exchange, when someone gains, someone else must lose."

People tend to think of making, building, and creating things as productive activities. Agriculture and manufacturing are like this. They create something genuinely new, something that was not there before. Trade, however, is only the exchange of one thing for another. Nothing is created. Therefore, it must be a zero-sum game in which one person's gain is necessarily a loss to another. So goes a popular myth.

A closer look at the motivation for trade helps one see through this myth. Mutual gain is the foundation for voluntary exchange. If the parties to the exchange do not anticipate that the trade will improve their well-being, they will not agree to it. Trade is productive because it increases the well-being of each trading partner.

There are three major reasons why trade is productive—why it is a positive-sum activity. First, it

channels goods and services to those who value them most. People have fallen into the habit of thinking of material things as wealth, but material things are not wealth until they are in the hands of someone who values them. A highly technical mathematics book is not wealth to a longshoreman with a sixth-grade education. It becomes wealth only after it is in the hands of a mathematician. A master painting may be wealth to the collector of art, but it is of little value to the average cowboy. Wealth is created by the act of channeling goods to persons who value them highly.

Second, exchange can be advantageous to trading partners because it permits each to specialize in areas in which they have a comparative advantage. For example, exchange permits a skilled carpenter to concentrate on building house frames, while contracting for electrical and plumbing services from others who have comparative advantages in

those areas. Similarly, trade permits a country such as Canada to specialize in the production of wheat, while Brazil specializes in coffee. Such specialization enlarges joint output and permits both countries to gain from the exchange of Canadian wheat for Brazilian coffee.

Third, voluntary exchange makes it possible for individuals to produce more goods through cooperative effort. In the absence of exchange, productive activity would be limited to the individual household. Self-provision and small-scale production would be the rule. Voluntary exchange permits us to realize gains derived from the division of labor and the adoption of large-scale production methods. Production can be broken down into a series of specific operations. This procedure often leads to a more efficient application of both labor and machinery. Without voluntary exchanges, these gains would be lost.

voluntarily specialize because they will gain by doing so. People following their own interests will produce and sell items for which they have a comparative advantage—items they can produce cheaply—and will buy those things that others can produce more cheaply. (See Myths of Economics box.)

THREE ECONOMIZING DECISIONS FACING ALL NATIONS: WHAT, HOW, AND FOR WHOM?

We have outlined several basic concepts that are important if one is to understand the economizing problem. In this section, we outline three general economizing questions that every economy, regardless of its institutions, must answer.

1. What Will Be Produced?   We cannot produce as many goods as we desire. What goods should we produce and in what quantities? Should we produce more food and less clothing, more consumer durables and less clean air, more national defense and less leisure? Or, should we use up some of our productive resources, producing more consumer goods today even though it will mean fewer goods in the future? If our economy is operating efficiently (that is, on its production possibilities curve), the choice to produce more of one commodity will reduce our ability to produce others. Sometimes the impact may be more indirect. Production of some goods will not only require productive resources but may, as a by-product, reduce the actual availability of other goods. For example, production of warmer houses and more automobile travel may, as a by-product, increase air pollution, and thus reduce the availability of clean air (another desired good). Use of natural resources (water, minerals, trees, and so on) to produce some goods may simultaneously reduce the quality of our environment. Every economy must answer these and similar questions concerning what should be produced.

2. How Will Goods Be Produced?   Usually, different combinations of productive resources can be used to produce a good. Education could be produced with less labor by the use of more television lectures, recording devices, and books. Wheat could be raised with less land and more fertilizer. Chairs could be constructed with more labor and fewer machines. What combinations of the alternative productive resources will be used to produce the goods of an economy?

The decision to produce does not accomplish the task. Resources must be organized and people must be motivated. How can the resources of an economy be transformed into the final output of goods and services? Economies may differ as to the combination of economic incentives, threats of force, and types of competitive behavior that are permissible, but all still face the problem of how their limited resources can be used to produce goods.

3. For Whom Will Goods Be Produced?   Who will actually consume the available products? This economic question is often referred to as the distribution problem. Property rights for resources, including labor skills, might be established and resource owners might be permitted to sell their services to the highest bidder. Income from the sale of resource services would be used to bid for goods. Prices and resource ownership would be the determining factors of distribution. Alternatively, goods might be split on a strict per capita basis, with each person getting an equal share of the pie. Or, they might be divided according to the relative political influence of citizens, with larger shares going to those who are more persuasive and skillful than others at organizing and obtaining political power. They could be distributed according to need, with a dictator or an all-powerful, democratically elected legislature deciding the various "needs" of the citizens.

THE THREE DECISIONS ARE INTERRELATED

One thing is clear—these three questions are highly interrelated. How goods are distributed will exert considerable influence on the "voluntary" availability of productive resources, including human resources. The choice of what to produce will influence how resources are used. In reality, these three basic economic questions must be resolved simultaneously and all economies, whatever their other differences, must somehow answer them. There are many ways to set up the institutions—the "rules of the game"—by which an economy makes these decisions. Each will result in a different set of answers to the universal questions.

TWO METHODS OF MAKING DECISIONS—THE MARKET AND GOVERNMENT PLANNING

Market Mechanism: A method of organization that allows unregulated prices and the decentralized decisions of private property owners to resolve the basic economic problems of consumption, production, and distribution.

Collective Decision-making: The method of organization that relies on public-sector decision-making (voting, political bargaining, lobbying, and so on). It can be used to resolve the basic economic problems of an economy.

Capitalism: An economic system based on private ownership of productive resources and allocation of goods according to the signals provided by free markets.

Socialism: A system of economic organization in which (a) the ownership and control of the basic means of production rest with the state and (b) resource allocation is determined by centralized planning rather than by market forces.

Two prominent ways to organize economic activity are through the **market mechanism** and **collective decision-making.** Let us briefly consider each of these methods.

Private ownership, voluntary contracts (often these contracts are verbal), and reliance upon market prices are the distinguishing characteristics of markets, or capitalist economies as they are often called. Under market **capitalism,** people have private ownership rights to consumption goods, their labor, and productive assets.[9] Private parties are permitted to buy and sell ownership rights at mutually agreeable prices in unregulated markets. The role of government is limited to that of a referee—a neutral party enforcing the rules of the game. The government defines and protects private ownership rights, enforces contracts, and protects people from fraud. But the government is not an active player; the political process will not be used to modify market outcomes or favor some at the expense of others. The government will not prevent a seller from using price reductions and quality improvements to compete with other sellers. Nor will the government prevent a buyer from using a higher price to bid a product or productive resource away from another potential buyer. Legal restraints (for example, government licensing) will not be used to limit potential buyers or sellers from producing, selling, or buying in the marketplace. Under market organization, planning by a central authority is absent. The three basic economic questions are answered through the market coordination of the decentralized choices of buyers and sellers.

The major alternative to market organization is the *collective decision-making process,* the use of political organization and government planning to allocate resources. In some cases, the government may own the income-producing assets (machines, buildings, and land) and directly determine what goods they will be used to produce. This form of economic organization is referred to as **socialism.** Alternatively, the government may maintain private ownership in name, but use taxes, subsidies, and regulations to answer the basic economic questions. In both instances, political powers rather than market forces are used to direct the economy. In both cases, the decision to expand or contract the output of education, medical services, automobiles, electricity, steel, consumer durables, and thousands of other commodities is made by government officials and planning boards. This is not to say that the preferences of individuals are of no importance. If the government officials and central planners are influenced by the democratic process, they have to consider how their actions will influence their election prospects. If they do not, like the firm that produces a product consumers do not want, their tenure of service is likely to be a short one.

In most economies, including that of the United States, a large number of decisions are made both through the decentralized pricing system and through public-sector decision-making. Both exert considerable influence on how we solve fundamental economic problems. Although the two arrangements are different, in

---

[9]Capitalism is a term coined by Karl Marx.

each case the choices of individuals acting as decision-makers are important. Economics is about how people make decisions; the tools of economics can be applied to both market- and public-sector action. Constraints on the individual and incentives to pursue various types of activities will differ according to whether decisions are made in the public sector or in the marketplace. Still, people are people; changes in personal costs and benefits will influence their choices. In turn, the acts of political participants—voters, lobbyists, and politicians—will influence public policy and its economic consequences.

LOOKING AHEAD

The next chapter presents an overview of the market sector. Chapter 4 focuses on how the public sector, the democratic collective decision-making process, functions. It is not enough merely to study how the pricing system works. To understand the forces influencing the allocation of economic resources in a country such as the United States, we must apply the tools of economics to both market- and public-sector choices.

We think this approach is important, fruitful, and exciting. How does the market sector really work? What does economics say about which activities should be handled by government? What types of economic policies are politically attractive to democratically elected officials? Is sound economic policy sometimes in conflict with good politics? We will tackle all these questions.

CHAPTER SUMMARY

1. Because of scarcity, when an individual chooses to do, to make, or to buy something, that individual must simultaneously give up something else that might otherwise have been chosen. The highest valued activity sacrificed is the opportunity cost of the choice.
2. Trade is productive. Voluntary exchange creates value by channeling goods into the hands of people who value them most. Recognition of this fact exposes the physical fallacy, which incorrectly assumes that a good or a service has a given value, regardless of who uses it and how it is used. Trade is a positive-sum game that improves the economic well-being of each voluntary participant.
3. The production possibilities curve reveals the maximum combination of any two products that can be produced with a fixed quantity of resources, assuming that the level of technology is constant. When an individual or an economy is operating at maximum efficiency, the combination of output chosen will be on the production possibilities curve. In such cases, greater production of one good will necessitate a reduction in the output of other goods.
4. The production possibilities curve of an economy can be shifted outward by (a) current investment that expands the future resource base of the economy, (b) technological advancement, and (c) the forgoing of leisure and an increase in work effort. The last factor indicates that the production possibilities constraint is not strictly fixed, even during the current time period. It is partly a matter of preference.
5. Production can often be expanded through division of labor and cooperative effort among individuals. With division of labor, production of a commodity can be broken down into a series of specific tasks. Specialization and division of labor often lead to an expansion in output per worker because they (a) permit productive tasks to be undertaken by the individuals who can accomplish those tasks most efficiently, (b) lead to improvement in worker efficiency as specific tasks are performed numerous times, and (c) facilitate the efficient applications of machinery and advanced technology to the production process.
6. Joint output of individuals, regions, or nations will be maximized when goods are exchanged between parties in accordance with the law of comparative advantage.

This law states that total output is maximized when parties specialize in the production of goods for which they are low opportunity cost producers and exchange these for goods for which they are high opportunity cost producers. Pursuit of personal gain will motivate people to specialize in those things they do best (that is, for which they are low opportunity cost producers) and sell their products or services for goods for which they are high opportunity cost producers.

7. Every economy must answer three basic questions: (a) What will be produced? (b) How will goods be produced? (c) How will the goods be distributed? These three questions are highly interrelated.

8. There are two basic methods of making economic decisions: The market mechanism and public-sector decision-making. The decisions of individuals will influence the result in both cases. The tools of economics are general. They are applicable to choices that influence both market- and public-sector decisions.

CRITICAL ANALYSIS QUESTIONS

1. If Jones trades $2,000 to Smith for a used car, the items exchanged must be of equal value. (True, false, or uncertain.)

*2. Economists often argue that wage rates reflect productivity. Yet, the wages of housepainters have increased nearly as rapidly as the national average, even though these workers use approximately the same methods that were applied 50 years ago. Can you explain why the wages of painters have risen substantially even though their productivity has changed so little?

3. It takes one hour to travel from New York City to Washington, D.C., by air, but it takes five hours by bus. If the air fare is $55 and the bus fare $35, which would be ·cheaper for someone whose opportunity cost of travel time is $3 per hour? for someone whose opportunity cost is $5 per hour? $7 per hour?

4. Explain why the percentage of college-educated women employed outside the home exceeds the percentage of women with eight years of schooling who are engaged in outside employment.

5. Explain why parking lots in downtown areas of large cities often have several decks, whereas many of equal size in suburban areas cover only the ground level.

*6. "People in business get ahead by exploiting the needs of their consumers. The gains of business are at the expense of suffering imposed on their customers." (Statement from the producer of a prime-time television program.) Evaluate this statement.

7. a. Do you think that your work effort is influenced by whether there is a close link between personal output and personal compensation (reward)? Explain.

   b. Suppose the grades in your class were going to be determined by a random draw at the end of the course. How would this influence your study habits?

   c. How would your study habits be influenced if everyone in the class were going to be given an A grade? if grades were based entirely on examinations composed of the multiple-choice questions in the *Coursebook* for this textbook?

   d. Do you think the total output of goods in the United States is affected by the close link between productive contribution and individual reward? Why or why not?

8. In many states, the resale of tickets to sporting events at prices above the original purchase price ("ticket scalping") is prohibited. Who is helped and who is hurt by such prohibitions? Can you think of ways ticket owners who want to sell might get around the prohibition? Do you think it would be a good idea to extend the resale prohibition to other things—automobiles, books, works of art, or stock shares, for example? Why or why not?

*9. Does a 60-year-old tree farmer have an incentive to plant and care for Douglas fir trees which will not reach optimal cutting size for another 50 years?

*Asterisk denotes questions for which answers are given in Appendix C, Selected Answers.

*10. What forms of competition does a private property, market-directed economy authorize? What forms does it prohibit?

11. With regard to the use of resources, what is the objective of the entrepreneur? What is the major function of the middleman? Is the middleman an entrepreneur?

*12. Do private property rights permit owners to use their property selfishly to the detriment of others? Do private property rights protect owners against the selfishness of others? Explain.

13. "The rancher, who owns his grazing land, may over-graze it (let the cattle eat so much of the grass that erosion ruins the land) if he is desperate to make money now. Private ownership of land is dangerous." Evaluate.

*14. "Really good agricultural land should not be developed for housing. Food is far more important." Evaluate.

15. The United States imposes tariffs (taxes) on textiles, automobiles, computer chips, and many other import products. Other trade restraints prohibit the importation of sugar and cheese products. How do these trade restraints affect the economic well-being of Americans?

*16. "When you're dealing with questions related to human life, economic costs are irrelevant." Evaluate this statement made by a congressman.

3 Supply, Demand, and the Market Process

I am convinced that if it [the market system] were the result of deliberate human design, and if the people guided by the price changes understood that their decisions have significance far beyond their immediate aim, this mechanism would have been acclaimed as one of the greatest triumphs of the human mind.[1]

Nobel Laureate
Friedrich Hayek

CHAPTER FOCUS

- What do economists mean when they talk about the laws of supply and demand?
- How do market prices respond to changes in supply and demand?
- As buyers and sellers respond to changes in supply and demand, what role does time play in the adjustment process?
- Why are waiting lines, ''sold out'' signs, and huge inventories seldom observed in market economies? What is the invisible hand?
- What happens when prices are fixed above or below the market level?
- Are rent controls an effective means of increasing the availability of rental housing?

*R*ecent events in the Soviet Union and Eastern Europe make Professor Hayek's observation, published in 1946, appear to be more and more important. The difficulty of coordinating the components of a national economy is enormous. Central planning in the Soviet Union and Eastern European economies, sophisticated though it was, could not do the job in an acceptable fashion. Yet in the larger United States economy, where economic activity is directed primarily by the market mechanism, productivity and output have continued to grow.

To appreciate these results, consider the awesome task of coordinating the economic activity of the United States, with 250,000,000 people, 65,000,000 families, and 125,000,000 workers, each having various skills and job preferences. In the market sector, roughly 18,000,000 firms produce a vast array of products ranging from toothpicks to supercomputers.

How can the actions of these economic participants be coordinated in a sensible manner? How do producers know how much of each good to produce? What keeps them from producing too many ballpoint pens and too few bicycles with reflector lights? Who directs each labor force participant to the job that best fits his or her skills and preferences? How can we be sure that business firms will choose the correct production methods? In this chapter, we analyze how a market-directed pricing system answers these questions.

In the ideal market economy, no individual or planning board tells the participants what to do. Markets are free, some would say competitive, in the sense that there are no legal restrictions limiting the entry of either buyers or sellers. The economic role of government is limited to defining property rights, enforcing contracts, protecting people from fraud, and similar activities that establish the rules of the game. Although centralized planning is absent, the participants are not without direction. As we shall see, the decentralized decision-making of market participants provides direction and leads to economic order.

In the real world, even economies that are strongly market-oriented, such as the United States economy, use a combination of market- and public-sector answers to the basic economic questions. In all economies, the institutions provide a mixture of market-sector and government allocation. Nevertheless, it is still quite useful to understand how a free-market pricing system functions, how it motivates people, and how it allocates goods and resources.

SCARCITY NECESSITATES RATIONING

Rationing: An allocation of a limited supply of a good or resource to users who would like to have more of it. Various criteria, including charging a price, can be utilized to allocate the limited supply. When price performs the rationing function, the good or resource is allocated to those willing to give up the most "other things" in order to obtain ownership rights.

When a good (or resource) is scarce, some criterion must be set up for deciding who will receive the good (or resource) and who will do without it. Scarcity makes **rationing** a necessity.

There are several possible criteria that could be used in rationing a limited amount of a good among citizens who would like to have more of it. If the criterion were first-come, first-served, goods would be allocated to those who were fastest at getting in line or to those who were most willing to wait in line. If beauty were used, goods would be allocated to those who were thought to be most beautiful. The political process might be used, and goods would be allocated on the basis of political status and ability to manipulate the political process to personal advantage.

---

[1]Friedrich Hayek, "The Use of Knowledge in Society," *American Economic Review* 35, (September, 1945), pp. 519–30.

One thing is certain: Scarcity means that methods must be established to decide who gets the limited amount of available goods and resources.

COMPETITION IS THE RESULT OF SCARCITY

Competition is not unique to a market system. Rather, it is a natural outgrowth of scarcity and the desire of human beings to improve their conditions. Competition exists both in capitalist and in socialist societies. It exists both when goods are allocated by price and when they are allocated by other means—collective decision-making, for example.

Certainly the rationing criterion will influence which competitive techniques will be used. When the rationing criterion is price, individuals will engage in income-generating activities that enhance their ability to pay the price. The market system encourages individuals to provide services to others in exchange for income. In turn, the income will permit them to procure more of the scarce goods.

A different rationing criterion will encourage other types of behavior. When the appearance of sincerity, broad knowledge, fairness, good judgment, and a positive TV image are important, as they are in the rationing of elected political positions, people will use resources to project these qualities. They will hire makeup artists, public relations experts, and advertising agencies to help them compete. We can change the form of competition, but no society has been able to eliminate it, because no society has been able to eliminate scarcity and the resulting necessity of rationing. When people who want more scarce goods seek to meet the criteria established to ration those goods, competition occurs.

The market is one method of producing and rationing scarce goods and resources. Let us investigate how it works.

CONSUMER CHOICE AND THE LAW OF DEMAND

Since our desire for goods is generally far greater than the purchasing power of our income, we have to make choices. How do consumers decide which things to buy and which things to forgo? Economizing behavior suggests that to get the most satisfaction from spending their money, rational consumers will buy the things from which they expect the most satisfaction per dollar spent. Given personal tastes, they will choose the best alternatives that their limited incomes will permit. Prices influence consumer decisions. An increase in the price of a good will increase a consumer's opportunity cost of consuming it. More of other things must be given up if the consumer chooses the higher-priced commodity.

According to a basic postulate of economics, an increase in the cost of an alternative will reduce the likelihood that it will be chosen. This basic postulate implies that higher prices will discourage consumption. Lower prices will reduce the cost of choosing a good, stimulating consumption of it. This inverse relationship between the price of a good and the amount of it that consumers choose to buy is called the **law of demand.**

Law of Demand: A principle that states that there is an inverse relationship between the price of a good and the amount of it buyers are willing to purchase.

The availability of substitutes—goods that perform similar functions— explains why consumers buy less of a product as its price increases. No single good is absolutely essential. To some extent, each good can be replaced by other goods. Margarine can be substituted for butter. Wood, aluminum, bricks, and glass can take the place of steel. Car pools, slower driving, bicycling, and smaller cars are substitutes for gasoline, allowing households to reduce their gas consumption. When the price (and therefore the consumer's opportunity cost) of a good increases,

EXHIBIT 1

The Law of Demand

As the price of VCRs fell during 1979–1987, consumers purchased more of them. The consumption level of VCRs (and other products) is inversely related to their price.

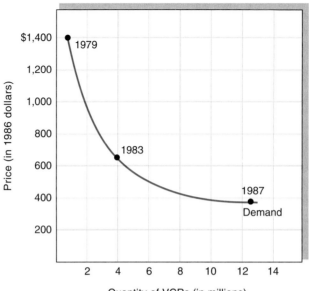

people turn to substitute products that serve almost as well and economize on their use of the more expensive good. Prices really do matter.

Exhibit 1 is a graphic presentation of the law of demand. Looking at what happened, we will assume that the price changes that occurred resulted from decreasing costs facing suppliers, and that consumer desires for video cassette recorders (VCRs), along with several other factors, did not change during this period. This allows us to estimate the influence of price on quantity demanded by constructing a demand curve. To do so, economists measure price on the vertical or y-axis, and the amount demanded on the horizontal or x-axis. The demand curve will slope downward to the right, indicating in this case that the number of VCRs demanded will increase as price declines. During 1979–1987, the price of VCRs fell sharply. Consumers happily responded by purchasing more of them. In 1979, when the average price of a VCR was $1,413 (in 1987 dollars), manufacturers sold less than half a million (478,000) of them. But costs dropped, and the price fell steadily. By 1983 the average VCR sold for only $652. In fact this reduction in average price understates the price drop, since quality and features also were improving at the same time. Sales climbed and by 1983 reached 4,020,000 units. The downward fall of price continued, and at the 1987 price of $389, people were watching a lot of movies at home! VCR sales in 1987 were 12,304,000. People are willing to use far more VCRs when the cost of doing so declines.

Some commodities are much more responsive to change in price than others. Consider a good for which there are several viable substitutes—a Florida vacation. If the price of a Florida vacation increases, perhaps because of higher air fares, consumers will substitute more movies, local camping trips, baseball games, TV programs, and other recreational activities for the Florida vacation. Exhibit 2 illustrates that, since good substitutes are available, an increase in the price of Florida vacations will cause a sharp reduction in quantity demanded. The quantity of Florida vacations demanded is quite responsive to a change in price.[2]

---

[2]The technical term for price responsiveness is elasticity. For those in a microeconomics course, this concept will be explored in the chapter on demand and consumer choice.

EXHIBIT 2

Responsiveness of Demand to a Price Change

A 15 percent increase in the price of Florida vacations (D_1) caused the quantity demanded to decline from Q_0 to Q_1, a 50 percent reduction. In contrast, a 15 percent increase in the price of physician services (D_2) resulted in only a 5 percent reduction in quantity demanded (from Q_0 to O_2).

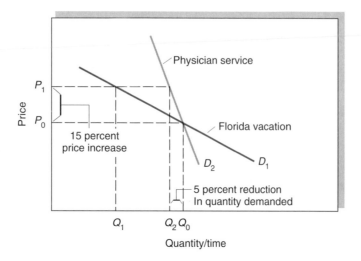

Other goods may be much less responsive to a change in price. Suppose the price of physician services were to rise 15 percent, as indicated by Exhibit 2. What impact would this price increase have on the quantity demanded? The higher prices would cause some people to prescribe their own medications for colds, flu, and minor illnesses. Others might turn to painkillers, magic potions, and faith healers for even major medical problems. Most consumers, though, would consider these to be poor substitutes for the services of a physician. Thus, higher medical prices would cause a relatively small reduction in the quantity demanded. The amount of physician services demanded is relatively unresponsive to a change in price.

However, despite differences in the degree of responsiveness, the fundamental law of demand holds for all goods. A price increase will induce consumers to turn to substitutes, leading to a reduction in the amount purchased. In contrast, a price reduction will make a commodity relatively cheaper, inducing consumers to purchase more of it as they substitute it for other goods.

The demand schedule is not something that can be observed directly by decision-makers of a business firm or planning agency. Nevertheless, when prices are used to ration goods, consumer reactions to each price communicate information about the preferences of consumers—how they value alternative commodities. The height of the unseen demand curve indicates the maximum price that consumers are willing to pay for an *additional unit* of the product. If consumers value *additional units* of a product highly, they will be willing to pay a large amount (a high price) for it. On the other hand, if their valuation of *additional units* of the good is low, they will be willing to pay only a small amount for it.

NEEDS AND WANTS VERSUS DEMAND

When discussing purchasing decisions, noneconomists often speak of what they ''need'' or ''want.'' For example, people say: ''I need a new pair of shoes'' or ''I want to see the movie.'' Two points should be recognized with regard to the relationship between (a) needs and wants and (b) demand. First, there are no critical needs, minimum requirements, or absolute necessities in the sense that one must have some fixed amount of a good or service, regardless of its price. We live in a world of substitutes. There are alternative ways of satisfying needs. Therefore, the amount needed, or more precisely, the amount demanded, is very much dependent upon price. The vertical demand curve (indicating that a fixed amount will be purchased regardless of price) is a myth. Second, just because one needs or wants a good, it does not follow that he or she should purchase (demand) it. Needs and wants are unlimited. There are literally millions of goods or services that each of us would like to have more of. The authors want (''need'') backyard tennis courts, vacations in the Far East, and summer homes in the mountains, but we have not purchased any of them. Why? Because, given the restrictions imposed by our finite incomes and limited time, our desire for other goods is even greater.

We live in a world of scarcity that restricts our consumption possibilities. Therefore, we must choose to forgo many needs and wants so that we will have the resources to satisfy other needs that are even more urgent. Demand is important precisely because it provides information about the preferences of people—how much they value alternative scarce goods. After all, the choice of a consumer to purchase a good reveals that he or she values (needs or wants) that good more than other needs and wants which must now remain unfulfilled as the result of the purchase.

PRODUCER CHOICE AND THE LAW OF SUPPLY

How does the market process determine the amount of each good that will be produced? We cannot answer this question unless we understand the factors that influence the choices of those who supply goods. Producers of goods and services, often using the business firm:

1. organize productive inputs, such as labor, land, natural resources, and intermediate goods;
2. transform and combine these factors of production into goods desired by households; and
3. sell the final products to consumers for a price.

Profit: An excess of sales revenue relative to the cost of production. The cost component includes the opportunity cost of all resources, including those owned by the firm. Therefore, profit accrues only when the value of the good produced is greater than the sum of the values of the individual resources utilized.

Production involves the conversion of resources into commodities and services. Producers have to pay the owners of scarce resources a price that is at least equal to what the resources could earn elsewhere. Stated another way, each resource employed has to be bid away from all other uses; its owner will have to be paid its opportunity cost. The sum of the amounts paid by the producer for each productive resource, including the cost of production coordination and management, will equal the product's opportunity cost. That cost represents the value of those things given up by society to produce the product.

All economic participants have a strong incentive to undertake activities that generate profit. **Profit** is a residual ''income reward'' earned by decision-makers who produce a good or service that is valued more highly than the resources that were required for its production. It is what is left over after all costs have been paid. If an activity is to be profitable, the revenue derived from the sale of the product must exceed the cost of employing the resources that have been diverted from other uses to make the product. Sometimes decision-makers use resources unwisely. They divert resources to production of an output that consumers value less than the opportunity cost of the resources used. **Losses** result, since the sales revenue derived from the project is insufficient to pay the opportunity cost of the resources.

Loss: Deficit of sales revenue relative to the cost of production, once all the resources used have received their opportunity cost. Losses are a penalty imposed on those who use resources in lower, rather than higher, valued uses as judged by buyers in the market.

Losses discipline even the largest of firms. For example, in January of 1984, IBM introduced a small personal computer, the PC Jr. The company expected it to be profitable, but 15 months later, it announced that it would quit making the machines. Of IBM's $46 billion in 1984 revenue, only $150 million was accounted for by the PC Jr. Even a $40 million Christmas advertising campaign did not help. IBM could not sell enough units at a price high enough to cover its opportunity costs. So, "Big Blue," as the firm is called, threw in the towel, announcing in March of 1985 that the line had been discontinued.

Also in 1985, the Coca-Cola Company announced its carefully planned multimillion-dollar strategy to replace its main product, Coca-Cola, with "New Coke," which had a slightly different taste. There was a lukewarm reception to the new product and an insistent demand by fans of the "old Coke" to reverse the action. Within the year, the company had reversed itself and reintroduced the older product, calling it "Coke Classic" to be sold alongside New Coke (later renamed "Coke II.") The market had once again disciplined a giant company, despite its huge advertising campaign to sell what it had thought would be a more popular product. The company had made a mistake, but was smart enough to correct it quickly in the face of strong consumer demand.

As we learned in the last chapter, entrepreneurs undertake production organization, deciding what to produce and how to produce it. The business of the entrepreneur is to figure out which projects will, in fact, be profitable. Since the profitability of a project will be affected by the price consumers are willing to pay for a product, the price of resources required to produce it, and the cost of alternative production processes, successful entrepreneurs must either be knowledgeable in each of these areas or obtain the advice of others who have such knowledge.

To prosper, entrepreneurs must convert and rearrange resources in a manner that will increase their value. An individual who purchases 100 acres of raw land, puts in a street and a sewage disposal system, divides the plot into one-acre lots, and sells them for 50 percent more than the opportunity cost of all resources used is clearly an entrepreneur. This entrepreneur "profits" because the value of the resources has been increased. Sometimes entrepreneurial activity is less complex. For example, a 15-year-old who purchases a power mower and sells lawn service to the neighbors is also an entrepreneur seeking to profit by increasing the value of resources. In a market economy, profit is the reward to the entrepreneur who discovers and acts upon an opportunity to produce a good or service that is valued more highly than the resources required for its production. It also provides an incentive for rival entrepreneurs to enter the market.

How will producer-entrepreneurs respond to a change in product price? Other things constant, a higher price will increase the producer's incentive to supply the good. New entrepreneurs, seeking personal gain, will enter the market and begin supplying the product. Established producers will expand the scale of their operations, leading to an additional expansion in output. Higher prices will induce producers to supply a greater amount. The direct relationship between the price of a product and the amount of it that will be supplied is termed the **law of supply.**

Law of Supply: A principle that states that there will be a direct relationship between the price of a good and the amount of it offered for sale.

Exhibit 3 presents a graphic picture of this law. The supply curve summarizes information about production conditions. Unless the profit-seeking producer receives a price that is at least equal to the opportunity cost of the resources employed, the producer will not continue to supply the good. The height of the supply curve indicates both (a) the minimum price necessary to induce producers to supply a specific quantity and (b) the valuation of the resources used in the production of the marginal unit of the good. This minimum supply price will be high (low) if the opportunity cost of supplying the marginal unit is high (low).

EXHIBIT 3

The Supply Curve

As the price of a product increases, *other things constant,* producers will increase the amount of the product supplied.

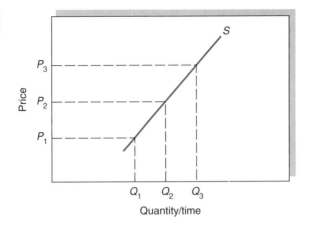

MARKETS COORDINATE SUPPLY AND DEMAND ACTIVITIES

Market: An abstract concept that encompasses the trading arrangements of buyers and sellers that underlie the forces of supply and demand.

Consumer-buyers and producer-sellers make decisions independent of each other, but markets coordinate their choices and influence their actions. To the economist, a market is not a physical location. A **market** is an abstract concept that encompasses the forces generated by the buying and selling decisions of economic participants. A market may be quite narrow (for example, the market for razor blades). Alternatively, it is sometimes useful to aggregate diverse goods into a single market, such as the market for ''consumer goods.'' There is also a broad range of sophistication among markets. The New York Stock Exchange is a highly computerized market in which each weekday buyers and sellers, who never formally meet, exchange shares of corporate ownership worth billions of dollars. In contrast, the neighborhood market for lawn-mowing services may be highly informal, since it brings together buyers and sellers primarily by word of mouth.

Equilibrium: A state of balance between conflicting forces, such as supply and demand.

Equilibrium is a state in which conflicting forces are in perfect balance. When there is a balance—an equilibrium—the tendency for change is absent. Before a market equilibrium can be attained, the decisions of consumers and producers must be coordinated. Their buying and selling activities must be brought into harmony with one another.

SHORT-RUN MARKET EQUILIBRIUM

The great English economist Alfred Marshall pioneered the development of supply and demand analysis. From the beginning, Marshall recognized that time plays a role in the market process. Marshall introduced the concept of the **short run,** a time period of such short duration that decision-makers do not have time to adjust fully to a change in market conditions. During the short run, producers are able to alter the amount of a good supplied only by using more (or less) labor and raw materials with their existing plant and heavy equipment. In the short run, there is insufficient time to build a new plant or to obtain new ''made-to-order'' heavy equipment for the producer's current facility. (For more information on Alfred Marshall, see the Outstanding Economist box.)

As Exhibit 1 illustrates, the amount of a good demanded by consumers will be inversely related to its price. On the other hand, a higher price will induce producers

EXHIBIT 4

Supply and Demand

The table below indicates the supply and demand conditions for oversize playing cards. These conditions are also illustrated by the graph on the right. When the price exceeds $10, an excess supply is present, which places downward pressure on price. In contrast, when the price is less than $10, an excess demand results, which causes the price to rise. Thus, the market price will tend toward $10, at which point supply and demand will be in balance.

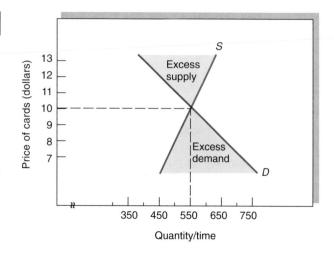

Price of Cards (dollars)	Quantity Supplied (per month)	Quantity Demanded (per month)	Condition in the Market	Direction of Pressure on Price
13	625	400	Excess supply	Downward
12	600	450	Excess supply	Downward
11	575	500	Excess supply	Downward
10	550	550	Balance	Equilibrium
9	525	600	Excess demand	Upward
8	500	650	Excess demand	Upward
7	475	700	Excess demand	Upward

Short Run: A time period of insufficient length to permit decision-makers to adjust fully to a change in market conditions. For example, in the short run, producers will have time to increase output by using more labor and raw materials, but they will not have time to expand the size of their plants or to install additional heavy equipment.

to use their existing facilities more intensively in the short run. As Exhibit 3 depicts, the amount of a good supplied will be directly related to its market price.

The market price of a commodity will tend to change in a direction that will bring the rate at which consumers want to buy into balance with the rate at which producers want to sell. If the price is too high, the quantity supplied will exceed the quantity demanded. Producers will be unable to sell as much as they would like unless they reduce their price. Alternatively, if price is too low, the quantity demanded will exceed the quantity supplied. Some consumers will be unable to get as much as they would like, unless they are willing to pay a higher price. Thus, there will be a tendency for price to move toward equilibrium—toward the single price that will bring the quantity demanded by consumers into balance with the quantity supplied by producers.

Exhibit 4 illustrates short-run supply and demand curves in the market for oversize playing cards. At a high price, $12 for example, card producers will plan to supply 600 decks of the cards per month, whereas consumers will choose to purchase only 450. An excess supply of 150 decks will result. Production exceeds sales, so inventories of producers will rise. To reduce undesired inventories, some of the oversize card producers will increase their sales by cutting their price. Other firms will have to lower their price also, or sell even fewer decks. The lower price will make production of the cards less attractive to producers. Some of the marginal producers will go out of business, and others will reduce their current output. How low will the price go? When it has declined to $10, the quantity supplied by producers and the quantity demanded by consumers will be in balance at 550 decks per month. At this price ($10), coordination of buyer and seller desires is achieved. The production plans of producers are in harmony with the purchasing plans of consumers.

What will happen if the price per deck is low—$8, for example? The amount demanded by consumers (650 units) will exceed the amount supplied by producers (500 units). An excess demand of 150 units will be present. Some consumers who are unable to purchase the cards at $8 per unit because of the inadequate supply would be willing to pay a higher price. Recognizing this fact, producers will raise their price. As the price increases to $10, producers will expand their output and consumers will cut down on their consumption. At the $10 price, short-run equilibrium will be restored.

LOCAL, NATIONAL, AND WORLD MARKETS

Consider a typical breakfast of an American consumer. It is likely to include coffee from Brazil, bananas from Honduras, jelly from Switzerland, and strawberries, apples, and milk produced by farmers hundreds, if not thousands, of miles away. This remarkable diversity is a reflection of low transportation costs, which expand the opportunity for gains for specialization and exchange. During the last 200 years, dramatic reductions in the cost of transporting goods have changed our lives and linked markets around the world.

When there are no trade barriers (legal restrictions limiting exchange), transportable goods will tend to trade for the same price in all markets, except for price differences caused by transportation costs and taxes. This **price equalization principle** reflects the fact that any inequality in the price of a good, for reasons other than taxes and transport costs, creates a profit opportunity for entrepreneurs. One could profit by buying the good in the market where its price is low and selling it in the high-price market. But the additional buying will push the good's price upward in the low-price market and the additional supply will drive its price down in the high-price market. Therefore, as entrepreneurs act on the opportunity for profit, they tend to equalize the price of each good across all markets, except for price differences reflecting transport costs and taxation among markets.

Price Equalization Principle: The tendency for markets, when trade restrictions are absent, to establish a uniform price for each good throughout the world (except for price differences due to transport costs and differential tax treatment of the good).

The price equalization principle explains why if it costs 5 cents to transport oranges from Florida to Wisconsin, oranges will not sell for 25 cents in Florida and 50 cents in Wisconsin. If those prices were present, entrepreneurs would buy the oranges at the cheap Florida price and ship them to Wisconsin, driving the price up in Florida while decreasing the Wisconsin price. This continues to be profitable until the price differential between the two locations is reduced to only the cost of transportation (assuming similar tax treatment between the two states).

The principle is just as applicable to international markets, as to a regional or national market. It explains why the price of a good, transportable at a relatively low cost, will not be cheap in one market and expensive in another if free trade is present. In fact, when the costs of transportation are low, the presence of substantial price differences between two markets is evidence that there are either substantial trade barriers or differences in the taxation of the good in the markets.

LONG-RUN MARKET EQUILIBRIUM

In the **long run,** decision-makers will have time to adjust fully to a change in market conditions. With the passage of time, producers will be able to alter their output; not only will they use their current plant more intensively, but given sufficient time, they will be able to change the size of their production facility. The long run is a time period long enough to permit producers to expand the size of their capital stock (the physical structure and heavy equipment of their plant).

Long Run: A time period of sufficient length to enable decision-makers to adjust fully to a market change. For example, in the long run, producers will have time to alter their utilization of all productive factors, including the heavy equipment and physical structure of their plants.

A balance between amount supplied and amount demanded will bring about market equilibrium in the short run. However, if the current market price is going to persist in the future, an additional condition must be present: The opportunity cost of producing the product must also be equal to the market price.

If the market price of a good is greater than the opportunity cost of producing it, suppliers will gain from an expansion in production. Profit-seeking entrepreneurs will be attracted to the industry. Investment capital will flow into the industry and output (supply) will expand until the additional supply lowers the market price sufficiently to eliminate the profits.[3] In contrast, if the market price is less than the good's opportunity cost of production, suppliers will lose money if they continue to produce the good. The losses will drive producers from the market and capital will flow away from the industry. Eventually the decline in supply and shrinkage in the capital base (durable productive assets) of the industry will push prices upward and eliminate the losses.

In a market economy, characterized by freedom of entry and exit, there will be a tendency for the *after-tax* rate of return on investment to move toward a uniform rate, the competitive or normal-profit return. Neither abnormally high nor abnormally low after-tax returns will persist for long periods of time. This tendency for returns on investment capital to move toward a uniform, normal rate is sometimes referred to as the **rate-of-return equalization principle.**

Rate-of-Return Equalization Principle: The tendency for capital investment in each market to move toward a uniform or normal rate of return. An abnormally high return in a market will attract additional investment which will drive returns down. Conversely, an abnormally low return will result in investment flight from the market which will eventually lead to the restoration of normal returns.

It is easy to see why there is a tendency for abnormal investment returns—that is, both profits and losses—to be eliminated with the passage of time in a competitive environment. Suppose the after-tax investment return on capital was abnormally high in the retail clothing industry and abnormally low in the publishing industry. The high return in retail clothing would attract additional investors (rival suppliers). Supply in the clothing industry would expand, causing both prices and returns on investment to decline. Eventually, normal returns would be restored in the clothing industry. Conversely, the abnormally low return in the publishing industry would cause investment flight and a reduction in supply. This shrinkage of the capital base and decline in supply in the publishing industry would lead to higher prices until eventually the remaining firms in the industry could once again earn normal returns.

The rate-of-return equalization principle enhances our understanding of supply changes and capital movements when the market price of a good differs from its opportunity cost of production. However, the principle also explains why it will be very difficult for public policy to alter the market returns to any activity over the long term. Suppose the government tries to enhance the returns of farmers (or small business operators, or any other group). For example, it might provide low-cost loans, tax breaks, and subsidies in other forms. Such a policy might initially increase the returns in farming, but it will fail to do so in the long run. If the subsidies increase the returns in farming, capital will flow into the industry, driving

---

[3]Bear in mind that economists use the opportunity cost concept for *all* factors of production, including those owned by the producers. Therefore, the owners are receiving a return equal to the opportunity cost of their investment capital even when profits are zero. Zero profits therefore mean that the capital owners are being paid precisely their opportunity cost, precisely what they could earn if their resources were employed in the highest valued alternative that must be forgone as the result of current use. Far from indicating that a firm is about to go out of business, zero economic profits imply that each factor of production, including the capital owned by the firm and the managerial skills of the owner-entrepreneur, is earning the market rate of return.

commodity prices down (or production costs up) until normal returns are restored. In the long run, the subsidies do not enhance the profitability of investment in farming.

Conversely, consider what will happen if the government imposes higher taxes or discriminatory regulations on an industry. Returns in the industry may temporarily fall below normal. But if they do, capital flight and reductions in supply will push prices upward and eventually restore normal returns.

SHIFTS IN DEMAND AND CHANGES IN QUANTITY DEMANDED

A demand curve isolates the impact that price has on the amount of a product purchased. Of course, factors other than price—for example, consumer income, tastes, prices of related goods, and expectations as to the future price of a product—also influence the decisions of consumers. Until now, we have assumed that these factors stay the same. If one of them changes, though, the entire demand curve will shift. Economists refer to such shifts in the demand curve as a change in *demand*.

Let us take a closer look at some of the factors that would cause the demand for a product to change. Expansion in income makes it possible for consumers to purchase more goods at current prices. They usually respond by increasing their spending on a wide cross-section of products. Changes in prices of closely related products also influence the choices of consumers. If the price of butter were to fall, many consumers would substitute it for margarine. The demand for margarine would decline (shift to the left) as a result. If coffee and cream are frequently used together, a rise in the price of coffee may decrease the demand for cream, since less coffee will be consumed at the higher price.

Our expectations about the future price of a product also influence our current decisions. For example, if you think that the price of automobiles is going to rise by 20 percent next month, this will increase your incentive to buy now, before the price rises. In contrast, if you think that the price of a product is going to decline, you will demand less now, as you attempt to extend your purchasing decision into the future, when prices are expected to be lower.

Failure to distinguish between a change in *demand* and a change in *quantity demanded* is one of the most common mistakes made by introductory economics students.[4] A change in demand is a shift in the entire demand curve. A change in quantity demanded is a movement along the same demand curve.

Exhibit 5 clearly demonstrates the difference between the two. The demand curve D_1 indicates the initial demand (the entire curve) for doorknobs. At a price of $3, consumers would purchase Q_1. If the price declined to $1, there would be an increase in quantity demanded from Q_1 to Q_3. Arrow A indicates the change in quantity demanded—a movement along demand curve D_1. Now, suppose that there were a 20 percent increase in income that caused a housing boom. The demand for doorknobs would increase from D_1 to D_2. As indicated by the B arrows, the entire

---

[4]Questions designed to test the ability of students to make this distinction are favorites of many economics instructors. A word to the wise should be sufficient.

EXHIBIT 5

The Difference Between a Change in Demand and a Change in Quantity Demanded

Arrow A indicates a change in *quantity demanded,* a movement along the demand curve D_1, in response to a change in the price of doorknobs. The B arrows illustrate a change in *demand,* a shift of the entire curve.

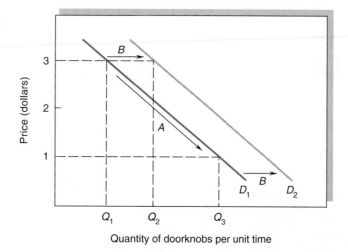

Quantity of doorknobs per unit time

demand curve would shift. At the higher income level, consumers would be willing to purchase more doorknobs at $3, at $2, at $1, and at every other price than was previously true. The increase in income leads to an increase in demand—a shift in the entire curve.

How does the market react to a change in demand? What happens to price and the amount supplied of a good if demand increases? Exhibit 6 will help to answer these questions while yielding insight into real-world events. During 1979–1981, there was a sharp rise in the price of gasoline. Many car owners attempted to economize on their use of the more expensive fuel by substituting smaller cars for their heavier, gas-guzzling models. There was an increase in demand for compact cars. The demand curve for such cars shifted to the right (from D_1 to D_2). At the original equilibrium price ($6,000, in our example), there was an excess demand for compact cars—a shortage. This caused the price of compact cars to rise. Market forces eventually brought about a new balance between supply and demand,

EXHIBIT 6

A Shift in Demand

As conditions change over time, the entire demand curve for a product may shift. Facing higher gasoline prices after the large increases of 1979 and 1980, many consumers decided to purchase compact cars. The *demand* for compact cars increased, causing both an increase in price and greater sales.

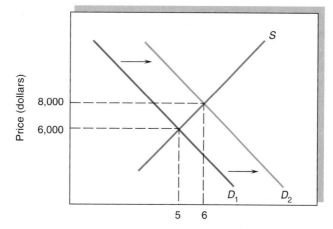

Millions of compact cars per year

OUTSTANDING ECONOMIST

**Alfred Marshall
(1842-1924)**

Early economists such as Adam Smith and David Ricardo thought that the price of a good was determined by its cost of production. Later, other economists, known as the "marginalists," emphasized the importance of demand and consumer preferences. Alfred Marshall put these two ideas together in 1890 when he introduced the concept of supply and demand.

Marshall noted that "the greater the amount to be sold, the smaller must be the price at which it is offered in order that it may find purchasers." Similarly, he argued that the supply of a commodity reflects the cost of the resources required to produce the good. In turn, the price of the commodity is determined by the balancing of these two forces—supply and demand.

In a famous analogy, Marshall likened the importance of supply and demand to the blades of a pair of scissors. When discussing which was more important, he wrote:

> We might reasonably dispute whether it is the upper or the under blade of a pair of scissors that cuts a piece of paper, as whether value is governed by utility [consumer demand] or cost of production [supply.] [5]

Although it is true that the blades of supply and demand operate jointly to determine price, Marshall recognized that the passage of time affects the relative importance of the supply and demand sides of the market in its response to change. In the short run, both supply and demand are highly significant, interacting to determine price. In contrast, in the long run, the supply side of a market is more important. As Marshall pointed out nearly a century ago, "the longer the time period, the more important will be the influence of cost of production" on price.

Alfred Marshall's father wanted him to enter the ministry, but young Marshall turned down a theological scholarship at Oxford in order to study mathematics at Cambridge.

In his *Principles of Economics* (1890), Marshall introduced many of the concepts and tools that form the core of modern microeconomics. Elasticity, the short run, the long run, equilibrium—all of these concepts were initially developed by Marshall. His influence was so great during the first 25 years of the twentieth century that this period is sometimes referred to as the "Age of Marshall."

---

[5] Alfred Marshall, *Principles of Economics*, 8th ed. (London: Macmillan, 1920), p. 348.

establishing a new equilibrium price, $8,000, at a higher sales level. The pricing system responded to the increase in demand by granting (a) producers a stronger incentive to supply more compact cars and (b) consumers an incentive to search for additional, cheaper ways to conserve gasoline other than buying compact cars.

SHIFTS IN SUPPLY

The decisions of producers lie behind the supply curve. Other things constant, the supply curve summarizes the willingness of producers to offer a product at alternative prices. As with demand it is important to note the difference between (a) a change in quantity supplied and (b) a change in supply. A change in quantity supplied is a movement along the same curve in response to a change in price. A change in supply indicates a shift in the entire supply curve.

What factors would cause a shift in the entire supply curve? How does the market for consumer goods adjust to a shift in supply? We now turn to an analysis of these two questions.

We previously indicated that a profit-seeking entrepreneur will produce a good only if the sales price of the good exceeds its opportunity cost. Factors that increase the opportunity cost of producers will discourage production and thereby decrease supply (shift the entire curve to the left). Conversely, changes that decrease the opportunity cost of producers will increase supply (shift the entire curve to the right).

Let us consider a number of important factors that will shift the supply curve.

Changes in Resource Prices.

Resource and product markets are closely linked. Firms demand labor, machines, and other resources because they contribute to the production of goods and services. In turn, individuals supply resources in order to earn income.

In resource markets, the demand curve is typically downward-sloping and the supply curve upward-sloping just as it is in product markets. An inverse relationship will exist between the amount of a resource demanded and its price because businesses will substitute away from a resource as its price rises. Less of the resource will be used at higher prices. In contrast, there will be a direct relationship between the amount of a specific resource supplied and its price. An increase in the price of a resource, for example the labor services of an automotive mechanic, will make it more attractive to supply the resource. Some people, who would choose to do other things when the wage (price) of automotive mechanics is low, will be willing to supply the resource (or more of the resource) when the payoff from doing so improves.

Just as in markets for consumer goods, prices will coordinate the choices of business firms and households in resource markets. There will be a tendency for the price of each resource to move toward an equilibrium, where the amount of the resource supplied by households is in balance with the amount demanded by businesses.

How will an increase in the price of a resource affect product markets? Higher resource prices will increase the opportunity cost of producing consumer goods that use the resource. The higher costs will reduce supply and increase price in the product market. Exhibit 7 illustrates this point. Many economists are forecasting that the wages of low-skill workers will increase substantially in the next few years, primarily because there will be fewer youthful workers (teenagers and persons in their early twenties). As Exhibit 7a illustrates, a reduction in the supply of low-skill workers will push their wage rates upward (from $4.55 to $5.45). The higher price of this resource will increase the opportunity cost of hamburgers at fast-food restaurants such as McDonald's and Wendy's. In turn, the higher opportunity cost will reduce supply (from S_1 to S_2) and increase hamburger prices at fast-food establishments (Exhibit 7b).

Of course, lower resource prices would exert the opposite effect in the product market. A reduction in resource prices will reduce costs and expand the supply (a shift to the right) of consumer goods using the lower priced resources. The increase in supply will lead to a lower price in the product market.

EXHIBIT 7

Resource Prices and
the Opportunity Cost
of Consumer Goods

Suppose a reduction in the
supply of low-skill labor pushes
the wage rates of workers hired
by fast-food restaurants
upward. In the product market,
the higher wage rates will
increase the restaurant's
opportunity cost, causing a
reduction in supply (frame b,
shift from S_1 to S_2), leading to
higher hamburger prices.

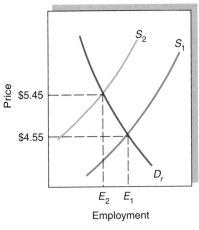

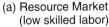

(a) Resource Market
(low skilled labor)

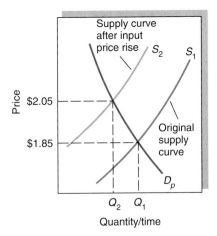

(b) Product Market
(fast food hamburgers)

Changes in Technology.   Technological improvements—the discovery of new, lower cost production techniques—will reduce the opportunity cost of production and increase supply (shift the supply curve to the right) in the product market. Previously, we indicated that consumers increased their purchases of VCRs as prices for those items declined between 1979 and 1987 (see Exhibit 1). Exhibit 8 illustrates why VCR prices fell. Technological improvements substantially reduced the opportunity cost of producing VCRs between 1979 and 1987. The reduction in cost made it more attractive for entrepreneurs to produce VCRs. Established firms expanded output. New firms began production, further contributing to the expansion of supply. The supply curve shifted to the right (from S_{79} to S_{87}). At the old $1,413 price (an average for VCRs sold in 1979, adjusted to 1987 dollars), consumers would not buy the larger supply of VCRs. A reduction in price was necessary to bring the desires of producers to expand production into line with consumers' willingness to purchase the output. By 1987, the average VCR was not only a much better machine, but its price had fallen to $389. At that price, coordination of buyer and seller decisions was achieved.

Natural Disasters and Political Disruptions.   Natural disasters and changing political conditions may also alter supply, sometimes dramatically. For example, in 1986 a drought hit Brazil, destroying a substantial portion of that year's coffee crop. War and political unrest in Iran exerted a major impact on the supply of oil in the late 1970s, as did the invasion of Kuwait by Iraq in 1990.

In the early 1980s, there was substantial overfishing in the Atlantic haddock fishery of Georges Bank, off the coasts of New England and Canada. No one owned the fishery; no one controlled access. As a result, too many fishing boats took too many fish. The breeding stock fell, and by 1986 the catch was much smaller than it had been. At the 1981 price, there would have been an excess demand for haddock. In response to the reduction in supply (shift from S_1 to S_2), price rose

EXHIBIT 8

Improved Technology and a Shift in the Supply Curve

In 1979, VCRs were selling for $1,413 (in 1987 dollars). Improved technology and manufacturing substantially reduced their production cost, shifting the supply curve to the right (from S_{79} to S_{87}). Prices declined, inducing consumers to purchase a larger quantity.

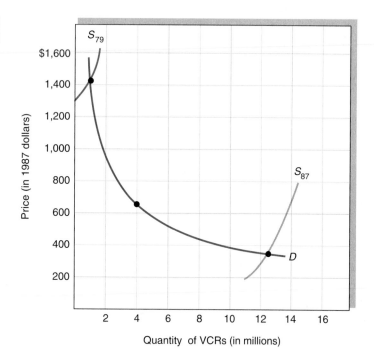

EXHIBIT 9

A Decrease in Supply

Overfishing of the Atlantic haddock fishery off Georges Bank in the early 1980s caused the number of haddock to decline dramatically. Supply was reduced—the supply curve shifted upwards, so that 1986 prices were more than double those of 1981. The smaller supply was rationed to buyers willing to pay the higher prices.

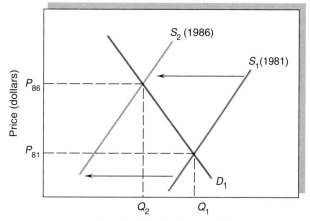

sharply (Exhibit 9). Consumers cut back on their consumption of the more expensive good. Some switched to substitutes—in this case probably other fish. By 1986, the price of haddock had risen to more than twice its 1981 level, rationing the smaller supply of haddock to those most willing to pay the higher price. Balance was maintained in the market, despite the sharp drop in the supply of haddock. The accompanying Thumbnail Sketch summarizes the major factors causing shifts in demand and supply.

THUMBNAIL SKETCH

These factors increase (decrease) the demand for a good:	These factors increase (decrease) the supply of a good:
1. A rise (fall) in consumer income 2. A rise (fall) in the price of a good used as a substitute 3. A fall(rise) in the price of a complementary good often used with the original good 4. A rise (fall) in the expected future price of the good	1. A fall (rise) in the price of a resource used in producing the good 2. A technological change allowing cheaper production of the good 3. Favorable weather (bad weather or a disruption in supply due to political factors, or war)

TIME AND THE ADJUSTMENT PROCESS

The signals that the pricing system sends to consumers and producers will change with market conditions. The market adjustment process will not be completed instantaneously, though. Sometimes various signals are sent out and understood only gradually, with the passage of time.

The response of consumers to a change in market conditions will generally be more pronounced as time passes. Consider the response of consumers when gasoline prices nearly doubled from 1978 to 1980 (corrected for inflation, gasoline prices rose more than 50 percent during the two-year period). Initially, consumers responded by cutting out some unnecessary trips and leisure driving. Some drove more slowly in order to get better gasoline mileage. As Exhibit 10 illustrates, these adjustments led to some reduction in gasoline consumption. However, while the rise in gasoline prices persisted, new car purchases began to shift toward smaller cars that used less gas. Since people usually waited for their current gas-guzzler to wear out before they bought a new, smaller car, the adjustment was still taking place years later, when gasoline prices began to drop in 1982. But, while the shift to higher-mileage automobiles was taking place, gasoline consumption declined more and more. The adjustment process for gasoline is a typical one. The demand response to a price change will usually be less in the short run than over a longer period of time.

Similarly, the adjustments of producers to changing market conditions take time. Suppose there is an increase in demand for radios. How will this change be reflected in the market? Initially, retailers will note a decline in their inventories as radios move off their shelves more rapidly. They will increase their wholesale orders, causing producer inventories to decline. At first, producers may be unsure whether the increase in demand is a random, temporary phenomenon or a lasting change. In either case, some will use a price increase to ration their limited supplies among the increased number of buyers.

A few alert entrepreneurs may have anticipated the expansion in demand and developed plans early to increase their production. With the passage of time, other

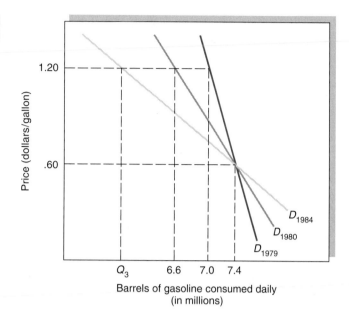

EXHIBIT 10

Time and the Buyer's Response to a Price Increase

Usually, the shorter the time period, the less responsive is consumption to a change in price. The gasoline price increases of 1979–1980 illustrate the point. Gasoline consumption declined from 7.4 million barrels per day to 7.0 million during the first year as the price of gasoline rose. The second year, consumption dropped to 6.6 million barrels. If the price had remained at the 1980 level for another four years, we would have expected a further decline, perhaps to Q_3, as consumers adjusted more fully. (The price fell after 1980.)

producers, initially oblivious to the increase in demand, will take note of the strong demand for radios. To bring more resources into radio production, some resource prices will have to be bid higher, raising costs. For this reason also, manufacturers will raise their prices. Retailers will soon pass the higher wholesale prices on to consumers.

Once the increase in demand is widely perceived by suppliers, the price of radios will rise sharply. Profits will exist in the industry. Astute entrepreneurs who anticipated the increase in demand will have expanded their production capacity. They will be rewarded with substantial profits. Other radio suppliers will hastily attempt to expand their production in order to increase their profits. A rapid increase in production, however, will be costly for producers who failed to anticipate (and plan for) the higher level of demand. Such firms will have to resort to overtime payments, air shipments of raw materials, and/or the employment of inexperienced workers to increase their output rapidly. Producers whose apt foresight gives them more time to expand their output in an orderly fashion can do so at a lower cost.

Although producers will expand their output at different rates, the profitable opportunities will induce additional supply, which will eventually moderate the price rise. All of these responses will take time, however, even though economists sometimes talk as if the process were instantaneous.

REPEALING THE LAWS OF SUPPLY AND DEMAND

Buyers often believe that prices are too high, and sellers generally perceive prices as too low. Unhappy with prices established by market forces, individuals may seek to have prices set by legislative action. Fixing prices seems like a simple, straightforward solution. Simple, straightforward solutions, though, often have unanticipated repercussions. Do not forget the secondary effects.

Price Ceiling: A legally established maximum price that sellers may charge.

Price ceilings are often popular during a period of inflation, a situation in which prices of most products are continually rising. Many people mistakenly believe that the rising prices are the cause of the inflation rather than just one of its effects. Exhibit 11a illustrates the impact of fixing a price of a product below its equilibrium level. Of course, the price ceiling does result in a lower price than market forces would produce, at least in the short-run. However, that is not the end of the story. At the below-equilibrium price, producers will be unwilling to supply as much as consumers would like to purchase. A shortage ($Q_D - Q_S$, Exhibit 11a) of the goods will result. A **shortage** is a situation in which the quantity demanded by consumers exceeds the quantity supplied by producers *at the existing price.* Normally, competing buyers would bid up the price. Fixing the price will prevent that, but will not eliminate the rationing problem. Nonprice factors will now become more important in the rationing process. Producers must discriminate on some basis other than willingness to pay as they ration their sales to eager buyers. Sellers will be partial to friends, to buyers who do them favors, and even to buyers who are willing to make illegal black-market payments.

Shortage: A condition in which the amount of a good offered by sellers is less than the amount demanded by buyers at the existing price. An increase in price would eliminate the shortage.

In addition, the below-equilibrium price reduces the incentive of sellers to expand the future supply of the good. Fewer resources will flow into the production of this good. Higher profits will be available elsewhere. With the passage of time, the shortage conditions will worsen as suppliers direct resources away from production of this commodity and into other areas.

What other secondary effects can we expect? In the real world, there are two ways that sellers can raise prices. First, they can raise their money price, holding quality constant. Or, second, they can hold the money price constant while reducing the quality of the good. Confronting a price ceiling, sellers will rely on the latter method of raising prices. Rather than do without the good, some buyers will accept the lower-quality product. It is not easy to repeal the laws of supply and demand. (See Myths of Economics box.)

EXHIBIT 11

The Impact of Price Ceilings and Price Floors

Frame a illustrates the impact of a price ceiling. When price is fixed below the equilibrium level, shortages will develop. Frame (b) illustrates the effects of a price floor. If price is fixed above its equilibrium level, then a surplus will result. When ceilings and floors prevent prices from bringing about a market equilibrium, nonprice factors will play a more important role in the rationing process.

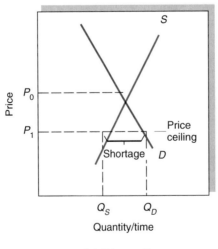

(a) Price ceiling

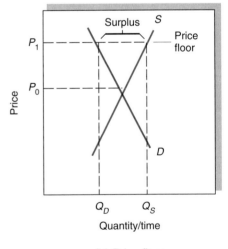

(b) Price floor

It is important to note that a shortage is not the same as scarcity. *Scarcity is inescapable*. Scarcity exists whenever people want more of a good than Nature has provided. This means, of course, that almost everything of value is scarce. *Shortages, on the other hand, are avoidable if prices are permitted to rise.* A higher, unfixed price (P_0 rather than P_1 in Exhibit 11a) would (a) stimulate additional production, (b) discourage consumption, and (c) ration the available supply to those willing to give up the most in exchange; that is, to pay the highest prices. These forces, an expansion in output and a reduction in consumption, would eliminate the shortage.

Price Floor: A legally established minimum price that buyers must pay for a good or resource.

Exhibit 11b illustrates the case of a **price floor,** which fixes the price of a good or resource above its equilibrium level. At the higher price, sellers will want to bring a larger amount to the market, while buyers will choose to buy less of the good. A **surplus** ($Q_S - Q_D$) will result. Agricultural price supports and minimum wage legislation are examples of price floors. Predictably, nonprice factors will again play a larger role in the rationing process than would be true without a price floor. Buyers can now be more selective, since sellers want to sell more than buyers, in aggregate, desire to purchase. Buyers can be expected to seek out sellers willing to offer them favors (discounts on other products, easier credit, or better service, for example). Some sellers may be unable to market their product or service.[6] Unsold merchandise and underutilized resources will result.

Surplus: A condition in which the amount of a good that sellers are willing to offer is greater than the amount that buyers will purchase at the existing price. A decline in price would eliminate the surplus.

Note that a surplus does not mean the good is no longer scarce. People still want more of the good than is freely available from Nature, even though they desire less, *at the current price,* than sellers desire to bring to the market. A decline in price would eliminate the surplus but not the scarcity of the item.

HOW THE MARKET ANSWERS THE THREE BASIC ECONOMIC QUESTIONS

How does the market's pricing mechanism resolve the three basic economic questions—what goods will be produced, how will they be produced, and for whom will they be produced?

In a market economy, what will be produced is determined by the consumer's evaluation of a good (demand) relative to its opportunity cost (supply). If consumers value a good (in terms of money) more than its opportunity cost, they will choose to purchase it. Simultaneously, profit-seeking producers will supply a good as long as consumers are willing to pay a price that is sufficient to cover the opportunity cost of producing it. The result: There is an incentive to produce those goods, and only those goods, to which consumers attach a value at least as high as the production costs of the goods.

How goods will be produced is determined by the economizing behavior of suppliers. Suppliers have a strong incentive to use production methods that minimize costs, because lower costs will mean larger profits. Thus, producers can

---

[6]Our theory indicates that minimum wage legislation (a price floor for unskilled labor) will generate an excess supply of inexperienced, low-skilled workers. The extremely high unemployment rate of teenagers—a group with little work experience—supports this view.

MYTHS OF ECONOMICS

"Rent controls are an effective method of ensuring adequate housing at a price the poor can afford."

Over 200 American cities have rent controls, intended to protect residents from high housing prices. However, economic theory suggests that when rents (a price for a good) are set below the equilibrium level, the amount of rental housing demanded by consumers will exceed the amount landlords will make available. Initially, if the mandated price is not set too much below equilibrium, the impact of rent controls may be barely noticeable. With the passage of time, however, their effects will grow. Inevitably, controls will lead to the following results.

1. *The Future Supply of Rental Houses Will Decline.* The below-equilibrium price will discourage entrepreneurs from constructing new rental housing units. Private investment will flow elsewhere, since the controls have depressed the rate of return in the rental housing market. The current owners of such housing may be forced to accept the lower price. However, potential future suppliers of rental housing have other alternatives. Many of them will opt to use their knowledge and resources in other areas. In the city of Berkeley, rental units available to students of the University of California reportedly dropped 31 percent in the first five years after the city adopted rent controls in 1978.[7]

2. *Shortages and Black Markets Will Develop.* Since the quantity of housing supplies will fail to keep pace with the quantity demanded, some persons who value rental housing highly will be unable to find it. Frustrated by the shortage, they will seek methods by which they may induce landlords to rent to them. Some will agree to prepay their rent, including a substantial damage deposit. Others will resort to tie-in agreements (for example, they might also agree to rent or buy the landlords' furniture at an exorbitant price) in their efforts to evade the controls. Still others will make under-the-table payments to secure the cheap housing.

3. *The Quality of Rental Housing Will Deteriorate.* Economic thinking suggests that there are two ways to raise prices. The nominal price can be increased, quality being held constant. Alternatively, quality can be reduced, while the same nominal price is maintained. When landlords are prohibited from adopting the former, they will use the latter. They will paint rental units less often. Normal maintenance and repair service will deteriorate. Tenant parking lots will be eliminated (or rented). Cleaning and maintenance of the general surroundings will be neglected. Eventually, the quality of the rental housing will reflect the controlled price. Cheap housing will be of cheap quality.

4. *Nonprice Methods of Rationing Will Increase in Importance.* Since price no longer plays its normal role, other forms of competition will develop. Prohibited from price rationing, landlords will rely more heavily on nonmonetary discriminating devices. They will favor friends, persons of influence, and those with life-styles similar to their own. In contrast, applicants with many children, unconventional life-styles, or perhaps dark skin will find fewer landlords who cater to their personal requirements. Since the cost to landlords of discriminating against those with characteris-

be expected to organize production efficiently—to use a division of labor, to discover and adapt new technologies, and to choose labor-capital combinations that will result in lower production costs.

What assurances are there that producers will not waste resources or exploit consumers by charging high prices? Competition provides the answer. Inefficient producers will have higher costs. They will find it difficult to meet the price competition of sellers who use resources wisely. Similarly, in a market with many sellers, competition among firms will, on the whole, keep prices from straying much above production costs. When prices are above the opportunity costs of a good, profits for the producers will result. As we have discussed, the profits will attract additional suppliers into the market, driving the price downward.

tics they do not like has been reduced, such discrimination will become more prevalent in the rationing process.

5. *Inefficient Use of Housing Space Will Result*. The tenant in a rent-controlled apartment will think twice before moving. Why? Even though the tenant might want a larger or smaller space, or even though the tenant might want to move closer to work, he or she will be less likely to move because it is much more difficult to find a vacancy if rent control ordinances are in effect. As a result, turnover will be lower, and even many who gain financially from living in rent-controlled units will find themselves in apartments not well suited to their needs.

6. *Long-term Renters Will Benefit at the Expense of Newcomers*. People who stay for lengthy time periods in the same apartment often pay rents substantially below market value (because the controls restrict rent increases), while newcomers are forced to pay exorbitant prices for units sublet from tenants, or for the limited supply of unrestricted units— typically newly constructed and thus temporarily exempted. Distortions and inequities result. A

recent book on housing and the homeless by William Tucker reports several examples, such as "actress Ann Turkel, who paid $2350 per month for a seven-room, four-and-a-half bathroom duplex on the East Side (of New York City). . .Identical apartments in the building were subletting for $6,500."[8] Turkel had been spending only 2 months each year in New York. "Former mayor Edward Koch . . . pays $441.49 a month for a large, one-bedroom apartment . . . that would probably be worth $1200 in an unregulated market. Koch kept the apartment the entire twelve years he lived in Gracie Mansion (the official mayor's residence)." Tucker reports on many other such cases, involving celebrities with other housing in addition to their rent controlled units, to illustrate the distortions brought on by the control of rental prices. Although rent controls may appear to be a simple solution, the truth of the matter is that a decline in the supply of rental housing, poor maintenance, and shortages are the inevitable results. Controls may initially lead to lower housing prices for some, but in the long-run the potential for the deteriora-

tion of urban life is almost unlimited. In the words of Swedish economist Assar Lindbeck: "In many cases rent control appears to be the most efficient technique presently known to destroy a city—except for bombing."[9] Though this may overstate the case somewhat, economic analysis suggests that the point is well-taken.

---

[7]William Tucker, *The Excluded Americans,* (Washington, D.C.: Regnery Gateway, 1990), p. 162.
[8]William Tucker, *The Excluded Americans,* (Washington, D.C.: Regnery Gateway, 1990), p. 248.
[9]Assar Lindbeck, *The Political Economy of the New Left, 1970* (New York: Harper and Row, 1972), p. 39.

To whom will the goods be distributed? Goods will be allocated to consumers willing and able to pay the market price. Of course, some consumers will be better able to pay the market price—they have larger incomes (more "dollar votes") than others. The unequal distribution of income among consumers is directly related to what is produced and how. The income of individuals will reflect the extent of their provision of resources to others. Those who supply large amounts of highly valued resources—resources for which market participants are willing to pay a high price—will have high incomes. In contrast, those who supply few resources or resources that are not valued highly by others will have low incomes.

As long as the preferences and productive abilities of individuals differ, a market solution will lead to unequal incomes. Many people are critical of the pricing system because of the income inequality that results. But, unequal incomes are not unique to a market economy. In virtually all systems, unequal income shares exist and provide at least some of the incentive for individuals to undertake productive activities. Since efforts to alter the allocation of income will also affect supply conditions, this issue is highly complex. As we proceed, we will investigate it in more detail.

THE INVISIBLE HAND PRINCIPLE

The market system is a mechanism for social cooperation. As Adam Smith (see the Outstanding Economist box in Chapter 1) noted more than 200 years ago, the remarkable thing about a market economy—an economy based on private property and freedom of exchange—is that market prices will bring the actions of self-interested individuals into harmony with the general welfare. Emphasizing his point, Smith stated:

> Every individual is continually exerting himself to find out the most advantageous employment for whatever capital he can command. It is his own advantage, indeed, and not that of the society which he has in view. But the study of his own advantage naturally, or rather necessarily, leads him to prefer that employment which is most advantageous to society. . . . He intends only his own gain, and he is in this, as in many other cases, led by an invisible hand to promote an end which was not part of his intention. By pursuing his own interest he frequently promotes that of the society more effectually than when he really intends to promote it.[10]

Invisible Hand Principle: The tendency of market prices to direct individuals pursuing their own interests into productive activities that also promote the economic well-being of the society.

Economists refer to the tendency of market prices to *communicate* information, *coordinate* the actions of self-interested individuals, and *motivate* them into engaging in activities that promote the general welfare as the **invisible hand principle.** An efficiently operating economy must communicate, coordinate, and motivate the actions of decision-makers. Let us take a closer look at how the invisible hand of market prices performs these functions.

COMMUNICATING INFORMATION TO DECISION-MAKERS

Communication of information is one of the most important functions of a market price. We cannot *directly* observe the preferences of consumers. How highly do consumers value tricycles relative to attic fans, television sets relative to trampolines, or automobiles relative to swimming pools? Product prices and quantities sold communicate up-to-date information about consumers' valuation of additional units of these and numerous other commodities. Similarly, we cannot turn to an engineering equation in order to calculate the opportunity cost of alternative commodities. But, resource prices tell the business decision-maker the relative importance others place on production factors (skill categories of labor, natural resources, and machinery, for example). With this information, in addition to knowledge of the relationship between potential input combinations and the

---

[10]Adam Smith, *An Inquiry into the Nature and Causes of the Wealth of Nations* (New York: Modern Library, 1937), p. 423.

output of a product, producers can make reliable estimates of their opportunity costs.

Without the information provided by market prices, it would be impossible for decision-makers to determine how intensively a good was desired relative to its opportunity costs—that is, relative to other things that might be produced with the resources required to produce the good. Markets collect and register bits and pieces of information reflecting the choices of consumers, producers, and resource suppliers. This vast body of information, which is almost always well beyond the comprehension of any single individual, is tabulated into a summary statistic— *the market price*. This summary statistic provides market participants with information on the relative scarcity of products.

When weather conditions, consumer preferences, technology, political revolution, or natural disasters alter the relative scarcity of a product or resource, market prices communicate this information to decision-makers. Direct knowledge of why conditions were altered is not necessary for making the appropriate adjustments. A change in the market price provides sufficient information to determine whether an item has become more or less scarce.

COORDINATING THE ACTIONS OF MARKET PARTICIPANTS

Market prices coordinate the choices of buyers and sellers, bringing their decisions into line with each other. If producers are currently supplying a larger amount than consumers are willing to purchase at the current price, then the excess supply will lead to falling prices, which discourage production and encourage consumption and thereby eliminate the excess supply. Alternatively, if consumers want to buy more than producers are willing to supply at the current price, then the excess demand will lead to price increases. The price rise will encourage consumers to economize on their uses of the good and encourage suppliers to produce more of it. Eventually, these forces will eliminate the excess demand and bring the choices of market participants into harmony.

Prices also direct entrepreneurs to undertake the production projects that are demanded most intensely (relative to their cost) by consumers. Entrepreneurial activity is guided by the signal lights of profits and losses. If consumers really want more of a good—for example, luxury apartments—the intensity of their demand will lead to a market price that exceeds the opportunity cost of constructing the apartments. A profitable opportunity will be created. Entrepreneurs will soon discover this opportunity for gain, undertake construction, and thereby expand the availability of the apartments. In contrast, if consumers want less of a good—very large cars, for example—the opportunity cost of supplying such cars will exceed the sales revenue from their production. Entrepreneurs who undertake such unprofitable production will be penalized by losses.

An understanding of the importance of the entrepreneur also sheds light on the market adjustment process. Since entrepreneurs, like the rest of us, have imperfect knowledge, they will not be able to instantaneously identify profitable opportunities and the disequilibrium conditions that accompany them. With the passage of time, however, information about a profitable opportunity will become more widely disseminated. More and more producers will move to supply a good that is intensely desired by consumers relative to its cost. Of course, as entrepreneurs expand supply, they will eventually eliminate the profit.

The move toward equilibrium will typically be a groping process. With time, successful entrepreneurial activity will be more clearly identified. Successful methods will be copied by other producers. Learning-by-doing and trial-and-error will help producers sort out attractive projects from ''losers.'' The process, though, will never quite be complete. By the time entrepreneurs discover one intensely desired product (or a new, more efficient production technique), change will have occurred elsewhere, creating other unrealized profitable opportunities. The wheels of dynamic change never stop.

MOTIVATING THE ECONOMIC PLAYERS

As many leaders of centrally planned economies have discovered, people must be motivated to act before production plans can be realized. One of the major advantages of the pricing system is its ability to motivate people. Market prices establish a reward-penalty (profit-loss) structure that induces the participants to work, cooperate with others, use efficient production methods, supply goods that are intensely desired by others, and invest for the future.

No government agency needs to tell business decision-makers to use resources wisely and thereby minimize the cost of producing their product. The pursuit of profit will encourage them to economize, and if they do not they will be unable to compete successfully with more cost effective rivals. No control authority has to force the farmer to raise wheat, the construction firm to build houses, or the furniture manufacturer to produce chairs. When the market prices of these and literally millions of other products indicate that consumers value them as much or more than their production costs, producers seeking personal gain will supply them.

Similarly, no one has to tell resource suppliers to invest and develop productive resources. Why are many young people willing to undertake the necessary work, stress, late hours of study, and financial cost to acquire a medical or law degree, a doctoral degree in economics or physics, or a master's degree in business administration? Why do others seek to master a skill requiring an apprentice program? Why do individuals save to buy businesses, machines, and other capital assets? Although many factors undoubtedly influence one's decision to acquire skills and capital assets, the expectation of financial reward is an important stimulus. Without this stimulus, the motivation to work, create, develop skills, and supply capital assets to those productive activities most desired by others would be weakened.

PRICES AND MARKET ORDER

How is it that grocery stores in thousands of different locations have approximately the right amount of milk, bread, vegetables, and other goods—an amount sufficiently large that the goods are nearly always available but not so large that spoilage and waste are a problem? How is it that refrigerators, automobiles, and VCRs, produced at diverse places around the world, are supplied in the U.S. market in approximately the same amount that they are demanded by consumers? Why are long waiting lines and ''sold out until next week'' signs that are commonplace in centrally planned economies almost completely absent in market economies? In each case, the answer is that the invisible hand of market prices directs self-interested individuals into cooperative action and brings their choices into harmony.

The market process works so automatically that most people fail to grasp the concept—they fail to understand the source of the social coordination. Perhaps an illustration will help the reader grasp the concept. Visualize a busy limited-access highway with four lanes of traffic moving in each direction. There is not a central planning agency that assigns lanes and directs traffic. No one tells drivers when to shift to the right, middle, or left lane. Drivers are left to choose for themselves. Nonetheless, they do not all try to drive in the same lane. Drivers are alert for adjustment opportunities that offer personal gain. When traffic in a lane slows due to congestion, some drivers will shift to other lanes and thereby smooth out the flow of traffic among the lanes. Even though central planning is absent, this process of mutual adjustments by the individual drivers results in order and social cooperation. In fact, the degree of social cooperation is generally well beyond what could be achieved if central coordination was attempted; if for example, each vehicle were assigned a lane.

Market participation is a lot like driving on the freeway. It is often necessary to alter one's actions in light of the choices made by others. Success is dependent upon one's ability to act upon opportunities. Like the degree of traffic in a lane, profits and losses provide market participants with information concerning the advantages and disadvantages of alternative economic activities. Losses indicate that an economic activity is congested, and as a result, producers are unable to cover their costs. Successful market participants will shift away from such activities. The most mobile resources will be moved to other, more valuable uses. Conversely, profits are indicative of an open lane, the opportunity to experience gain if one shifts into an activity where price is currently high relative to costs. As producers and resource suppliers shift away from activities characterized by congestion and into those characterized by the opportunity for gain (profit), they smooth out economic activity and enhance its flow. Order is the result, even though central authority is absent. This order in the absence of central planning is precisely what Adam Smith was referring to more than 200 years ago when he spoke of the "invisible hand" of market coordination.

QUALIFICATIONS

In this chapter, we have focused on the operation of a market economy. The efficiency of market organization is dependent on (a) competitive markets and (b) well-defined private property rights. Competition, the great regulator, can protect both buyer and seller. The presence (or possible entry) of independent alternative suppliers protects the consumer against a seller who seeks to charge prices substantially above the cost of production. The existence of alternative resource suppliers protects the producer against a supplier who might otherwise be tempted to withhold a vital resource unless granted exorbitant compensation. The existence of alternative employment opportunities protects the employee from the power of any single employer. Competition can equalize the bargaining power between buyers and sellers.

Understanding the information, coordination, and motivation results of the market mechanism helps us see all the more clearly the importance of property rights, the things actually traded in markets. Although property rights are often thought to increase selfish behavior, they are actually an arrangement to (a) force resource users—including those who own them—to bear fully the opportunity cost of their actions and (b) prohibit persons from engaging in destructive forms of competition. When property rights are well-defined, secure, and tradeable, suppliers of goods and services will be required to pay resource owners the opportunity cost of each resource employed. They will not be permitted to seize and use scarce resources without compensating the owner; that is, without bidding the resources away from alternative users.

Similarly, secure property rights eliminate the use of violence as a competitive weapon. A producer you do not buy from (or work for) will not be permitted to burn down your house. Nor will a competitive resource supplier whose prices you undercut be permitted to slash your automobile tires or threaten you with bodily injury.

Lack of competition and poorly defined property rights will alter the operation of a market economy. As we proceed, we will investigate each of these problems in detail.

CHAPTER SUMMARY

1. Because people want more of scarce goods than Nature has made freely available, a rationing mechanism is necessary. Competition is the natural outgrowth of the necessity for rationing scarce goods. A change in the rationing mechanism used will alter the form of competition, but it will not eliminate competitive tactics.

2. The law of demand holds that there is an inverse relationship between price and the amount of a good purchased. A rise in price will cause consumers to purchase less because they now have a greater incentive to use substitutes. On the other hand, a reduction in price will induce consumers to buy more, since they will substitute the cheaper good for other commodities.

3. The law of supply states that there is a direct relationship between the price of a product and the amount supplied. Other things constant, an increase in the price of a product will induce established firms to expand their output and new firms to enter the market. The quantity supplied will expand.

4. Market prices will bring the conflicting forces of supply and demand into balance. If the quantity supplied to the market by producers exceeds the quantity demanded by consumers, price will decline until the excess supply is eliminated. On the other hand, if the quantity demanded by consumers exceeds the quantity supplied by producers, price will rise until the excess demand is eliminated.

5. If there are no restrictions on the movement of a good, the good will tend to sell for the same price in all markets, except for price differences resulting from differences in transport costs and taxes among markets. This price equalization principle applies to regional, national, and global markets.

6. When a market is in long-run equilibrium, supply and demand will be in balance and the producer's opportunity cost will equal the market price. If the opportunity cost of supplying the good is less than the market price, profits will accrue. However, competition will tend to erode profit (abnormally high returns). The profits will attract additional suppliers, cause lower prices, and push the market toward an equilibrium. On the other hand, if the opportunity cost of producing a good exceeds the market price, suppliers will experience losses. The losses will induce producers to leave the market, causing price to rise until equilibrium is restored.

7. Changes in consumer income, prices of closely related goods, preferences, and expectations as to future prices will cause the entire demand curve to shift. An increase (decrease) in demand will cause prices to rise (fall) and quantity supplied to increase (decline).

8. Changes in input prices, technology, and other factors that influence the producer's cost of production will cause the entire supply curve to shift. An increase (decrease) in supply will cause prices to fall (rise) and quantity demanded to expand (decline).

9. The constraint of time temporarily limits the ability of consumers to adjust to changes in prices. With the passage of time, a price increase will usually elicit a larger reduction in quantity demanded. Similarly, the market supply curve shows more responsiveness to a change in price in the long run than during the short-term time period.

10. When a price is fixed below the market equilibrium, buyers will want to purchase more than sellers are willing to supply. A shortage will result. Nonprice factors such as waiting lines, quality deterioration, and illegal transactions will play a more

important role in the rationing process. When a price is fixed above the market equilibrium level, sellers will want to supply a larger amount than buyers are willing to purchase at the current price. A surplus will result.

11. The pricing system answers the three basic allocation questions in the following manner.
    a. What goods will be produced? Additional units of goods will be produced only if consumers value them more highly than the opportunity cost of the resources necessary to produce them.
    b. How will goods be produced? The methods that result in the lowest opportunity cost will be chosen. Since lower costs mean larger profits, markets reward producers who discover and utilize efficient (low-cost) production methods.
    c. To whom will the goods be distributed? Goods will be distributed to individuals according to the quantity and price of the productive resources they supplied in the marketplace. A large quantity of goods will be allocated to persons who are able to sell a large quantity of highly valued productive resources; few goods will be allocated to persons who supply only a small quantity of low-valued resources.

12. Market prices communicate information, coordinate the actions of buyers and sellers, and provide the incentive structure that motivates decision-makers to act. The information provided by prices instructs entrepreneurs as to (a) how to use scarce resources and (b) which products are intensely desired (relative to their opportunity cost) by consumers. Market prices establish a reward-penalty system, which induces individuals to cooperate with each other and motivates them to work efficiently, invest for the future, supply intensely desired goods, economize on the use of scarce resources, and use efficient production methods. Even though decentralized individual planning is a characteristic of the market system, there is a harmony between personal self-interest and the general welfare, as Adam Smith noted long ago. The efficiency of the system is dependent on (a) competitive market conditions and (b) securely defined private-property rights.

CRITICAL ANALYSIS QUESTIONS

*1. Which of the following do you think would lead to an increase in the current demand for beef: (a) higher pork prices, (b) higher incomes, (c) higher feed grain prices, (d) a banner-year corn crop, (e) an increase in the price of beef?

2. How many of the following "goods" do you think conform to the general law of supply: (a) gasoline, (b) cheating on exams, (c) political favors from legislators, (d) the services of heart specialists, (e) children, (f) legal divorces, (g) the services of a minister? Explain your answer in each case.

3. **What's Wrong with this Way of Thinking?**
   "Economists argue that lower prices will necessarily result in less supply. However, there are exceptions to this rule. For example, in 1970, 10-digit electronic calculators sold for $100. By 1985, the price of the same type of calculator had declined to less than $15. Yet business firms produced and sold five times as many calculators in 1985 as in 1970. Lower prices did *not* result in less production and a decline in the number of calculators supplied."

*4. A drought during the summer of 1988 sharply reduced the 1988 output of wheat, corn, soybeans, and hay. Indicate the expected impact of the drought on the following:
   a. prices of feed grains and hay during the summer of 1988
   b. price of cattle during the summer and fall of 1988
   c. price of cattle during the summer and fall of 1989

5. The County Commission recently voted $15 million for the construction of a new civic center. The chairperson of the Commission stated, "We are undertaking this

---

*Asterisk denotes questions for which answers are given in Appendix C, Selected Answers.

project because the community needs a civic center and the 500 new jobs the project will create.'' (News item)

  a. Does a "need" for a project mean it should be undertaken?

  b. What is the opportunity cost of the project?

  c. Will the project expand employment by 500 workers?

* 6. If a price ceiling is "meaningful," the ceiling must be below the market price. Conversely, a meaningful price floor must be above the market price. What impact will a meaningful price ceiling have on the quantity exchanged? What impact will a meaningful price floor have on the quantity exchanged? Explain.

  7. Which of the following statements are true? Explain your answer.

  a. The high excise tax on cigarettes reduces the profitability of cigarette manufacturers.

  b. Government-subsidized, low-interest loans to farmers increase the profitability of farming.

  c. A tariff (tax) that restricts the supply of textile products to the domestic market pushes up domestic prices and increases the profitability of domestic textile manufacturers.

* 8. "The future of our industrial strength cannot be left to chance. Somebody has to develop notions about which industries are winners and which are losers." (Newspaper columnist) Is this statement true? Who is the "somebody"?

  9. What is the "invisible hand principle"? Does the invisible hand principle indicate that "good intentions" are necessary if one's actions are going to be beneficial to others?

* 10. "Production should be for people and not for profit."

  a. If production is profitable, are people helped or hurt? Explain.

  b. Are people helped more if production results in a loss than if it leads to profit?

  c. Is there a conflict between production for people and production for profit?

  11. Suppose a disease destroys half of the cattle herds in Kansas and Missouri. Should we expect shortages and sky-high beef prices in these states as the result of the disease?

* 12. Suppose a drought destroyed half of the wheat crop in France. What is the expected impact on the market price of wheat in France?

  13. If there is a surplus of a good, does this mean that the good is not scarce? Indicate what the supply and demand curves would look like for a good that was not scarce.

* 14. When the price of a commodity (for example, rental housing or campus parking) is below equilibrium, then waiting in line rather than monetary payments will play a greater role in the allocation of the good. What is a major disadvantage of rationing by waiting in line rather than price. (Hint: How do the alternative methods affect future supply?)

  15. "Economists claim that when the price of something goes up, producers bring more of it to the market. But the last year in which the price was really high for oranges, there were not nearly as many oranges as usual. The economists are wrong!" How would an economist respond?

*16. A popular California winery, and the restaurant on its grounds, can be reached only by a tram with gondola cars, similar to those used at ski resorts. Suppose the owners are charging $3 to winery visitors and restaurant diners alike, but are thinking about providing "free rides" to diners. How would this change affect:

  a. the demand for dining at the restaurant?

  b. the price and quantity of meals served at the restaurant?

  17. If everyone had an income above the current poverty level, would substandard, shoddy housing disappear?

4 *Supply and Demand for the Public Sector*

[Public choice] analyzes the motives and activities of politicians, civil servants and government officials as people with personal interests that may or may not coincide with the interest of the general public they are supposed to serve. It is an analysis of how people behave in the world as it is.[1]

Arthur Seldon

CHAPTER FOCUS

- What does the economic way of thinking have to say about economic efficiency?
- When do markets fall short of the ideal of economic efficiency?
- Can government action improve on the efficiency of the market? When is it most likely to do so?
- What is public choice analysis? What does it reveal about how the political process works?
- Is there sometimes a conflict between good economics and good politics? Why?

*T*he economic role of government is pivotal. The government sets the rules of the game. It establishes and defines property rights, which are necessary for the smooth operation of markets. As we shall soon see, public policy is also an important determinant of economic stability. The government sometimes uses subsidies to encourage the production of some goods while it applies special taxes to reduce the availability of others. In a few cases—education, the mail service, and local electric power, for example—the government becomes directly involved in the production process.

Because of government's broad economic role, it is vital that we understand how it works and the circumstances under which it contributes to the efficient allocation of resources. In this chapter, we examine the shortcomings of the market and the potential of government policy as an alternate means for resolving economic problems. Issues involving market- and public-sector organization will be discussed repeatedly throughout this book. Political economy—how the public sector works, and how its workings compare with those of the market—is an integral and exciting aspect of economic analysis.

IDEAL ECONOMIC EFFICIENCY

Economic Efficiency:
Economizing behavior. When applied to a community, it implies that (a) an activity should be undertaken if the sum of the benefits to the individuals exceeds the sum of their costs and (b) no activity should be undertaken if the costs borne by the individuals exceed the benefits.

We need a criterion by which to judge alternative institutional arrangements— market- and public-sector policies. Economists often use the standard of **economic efficiency.** The central idea is straightforward. It simply means that for any given level of effort (cost), we want to obtain the largest possible benefit. A corollary to this is that we want to obtain any specific level of benefits with the least possible effort. Economic efficiency simply means getting the most out of the available resources—making the largest pie from the available set of ingredients, so to speak.

Why efficiency? Economists acknowledge that each individual does not have the efficiency of the economy as a primary goal. Instead, each person wants the largest possible ''piece of the pie.'' All might agree that a bigger pie is preferred, however, particularly if they and those they care most about will get a larger slice as a result. Not only will most people agree that efficiency is good in the abstract, but an alternative that is more efficient can potentially make more people better off than an inefficient alternative.

What does efficiency mean when applied to the entire economy? Individuals are the final decision-makers of an economy. Individuals will bear the costs and reap the benefits of economic activity. When applied to the entire economy, two conditions are necessary for ideal economic efficiency to exist:

Rule 1. *Undertaking an economic action will be efficient if it produces more benefits than costs for the individuals of the economy.* Such actions result in gain—improvement in the well-being of at least some individuals without creating reductions in the welfare of others. Failure to undertake such activities means that potential gain has been forgone.

Rule 2. *Undertaking an economic action will be inefficient if it produces more costs than benefits to the individuals.* When an action results in greater total costs

[1]Preface to Gordon Tullock, *The Vote Motive* (London: Institute of Economic Affairs, 1976), p. *x*.

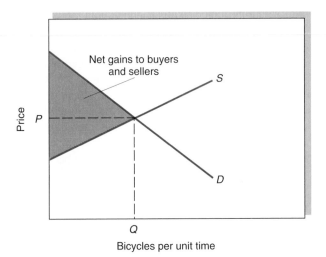

EXHIBIT 1

What Is Good About Idealized Market Exchange?

When competitive forces are present, price will tend toward the supply-demand intersection *P*. At that price, the seller's opportunity cost of producing the last unit will just equal the buyer's evaluation of that unit. All potential mutual gains from production and exchange are realized.

than benefits, somebody must be harmed. The benefits that accrue to those who gain are insufficient to compensate for the losses imposed on others. Therefore, when all persons are considered, the net impact of such an action is counterproductive.

When either rule 1 or rule 2 is violated, economic inefficiency results. The concept of economic efficiency applies to each and every possible income distribution, although a change in income distribution may alter the precise combination of goods and services that is most efficient.[2] Positive economics does not tell us how income should be distributed. Of course, we all have ideas on the subject. Most of us would like to see more income distributed our way. For each kind of income distribution, though, there will be an ideal resource allocation that will be most efficient.

A closer look at supply and demand when competitive pressures are present will help you to understand the concept of efficiency. The supply curve reflects the producer's opportunity costs. Each point along the supply curve indicates the minimum price for which the units of a good could be produced without a loss to the seller. Each point along the demand curve indicates the consumer's valuation of an extra unit of the good—the maximum amount the consumer of each unit is willing to pay for the unit. Any time the consumer's valuation exceeds the producer's opportunity cost—the producer's minimum supply price—producing and selling more of the good can generate mutual gain.

When only the buyer and seller are affected by production and exchange, competitive markets directed by the forces of supply and demand are efficient. Exhibit 1 illustrates why this is true. Suppliers of a good, bicycles in this example,

---

[2]Note to students who may pursue advanced study in economics: using the concept of efficiency to compare alternative policies typically requires that the analyst estimate costs and benefits that are difficult or impossible to measure. Costs and benefits are the values of opportunities forgone or accepted by individuals, *as evaluated by those individuals*. Then, these costs and benefits must be added up across all individuals, and compared. But does a dollar's gain for one individual really compensate for a dollar's sacrifice by another? Some economists simply reject the validity of making such comparisons. They say that neither the estimates by the economic analyst of subjectively determined costs and benefits nor the adding up of these costs and benefits across individuals is meaningful. Their case may be valid, but most economists today nevertheless use the concept of efficiency as we present it. No other way to use economic analysis to compare policy alternatives has been found.

will produce additional units as long as the market price exceeds the production cost. Similarly, consumers will gain from the purchase of additional units as long as their benefits, revealed by the height of the demand curve, exceed the market price. Market forces will result in an equilibrium output level of Q: All units for which the benefits to consumers exceed the costs to suppliers will be produced. Rule 1 is met; all potential gains from exchange (the shaded area) between consumers and producers are fully realized. Production beyond Q, however, will prove inefficient. If more than Q bicycles are produced, rule 2 is violated; consumers value the additional units less than their cost. With competitive markets, suppliers will find it unprofitable to produce units beyond Q because the cost of the additional units will exceed revenues.

Consumers and producers alike will thus be guided by the pricing system to output level Q, just the right amount. The market works beautifully. Individuals, pursuing their own interests, are guided as if by an invisible hand to promote the general welfare. This was the message of Adam Smith, more than 200 years ago.

WHY MIGHT THE INVISIBLE HAND FAIL?

Is the invisible hand still working today? Why might it fail? There are four important factors that can limit the ability of the invisible hand to perform its magic.

LACK OF COMPETITION

Competition is vital to the proper operation of the pricing mechanism. It is competition that drives the prices for consumer goods down to the level of their cost. Similarly, competition in markets for productive resources prevents (a) sellers from charging exorbitant prices to producers and (b) buyers from taking advantage of the owners of productive resources. The existence of competitors reduces the power of buyers and sellers alike to rig the market in their own favor.

Modern mass production techniques, marketing, and distributing networks often make it possible for a large-scale producer to gain a cost advantage over smaller competitors. In several industries—automobiles, aircraft, and aluminum, for example—a few large firms produce the entire output. Because an enormous amount of capital investment is required to enter these industries, existing large-scale producers may be partially insulated from the competitive pressure of new rivals.

Since competition is the enemy of high prices, sellers have a strong incentive to escape from its pressures by colluding rather than competing. Competition is something that is good when the other guy faces it. Individually, each of us would prefer to be loosened from its grip. Students do not like stiff competitors at exam time, when seeking entry to graduate school, or in their social or romantic lives. Similarly, sellers prefer few real competitors.

Exhibit 2 illustrates how sellers can gain from collusive action. If a group of sellers could eliminate the competition from new entrants to the market, they would be able to raise their prices. The total revenue of sellers is simply the market price multiplied by the quantity sold. The sellers' revenues may well be greater, and their total costs would surely be lower, if the smaller, restricted output Q_2 were sold rather than the competitive output Q_1. The artificially high price P_2 reflects not only resource scarcity, but also the reduction in output brought on by collusion among sellers.

EXHIBIT 2

Rigging the Market

If a group of sellers can restrict the entry of competitors and connive to reduce their own output, they can sometimes obtain more total revenue by selling fewer units. Note that the total sales revenue P_2Q_2 for the restricted supply exceeds the sales revenue P_1Q_1 for the competitive supply, in this case.

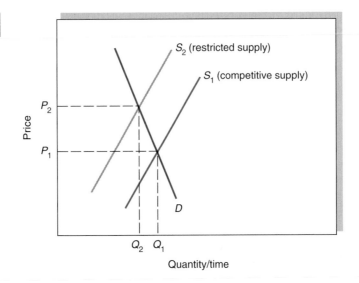

It is in the interest of consumers and the community that output be expanded to Q_1, the output consistent with economic efficiency. It is in the interest of sellers, though, to make the good artificially scarce and raise its price. If sellers can use collusion, government action, or other means of restricting supply, they can gain. However, the restricted output level would violate rule 2. Inefficiency would result. There is a conflict between the interests of sellers and what is best for the entire community.

When there are only a few firms in the industry and competition from new entrants can be restrained, sellers may be able to rig the market in their favor. Through collusion, either tacit or overt, suppliers may be able to escape competitive pressures. What can the government do to preserve competition? Congress has enacted a series of antitrust laws, most notably the Sherman Antitrust Act and the Clayton Act, making it illegal for firms to collude or attempt to monopolize a product market. Congress also established the Federal Trade Commission, which prohibits "unfair methods of competition in commerce," such as false advertising, improper grading of materials, and deceptive business practices.

For the most part, economists favor the principle of government action to ensure and promote competitive markets. There is considerable debate, however, about the effectiveness of past public policy in this area. Many economists believe that, by and large, antitrust policy has been ineffective. Others stress that governmental regulatory policies have often restricted entry, protected existing producers, and limited price competition. These critics charge that the government has often reduced the competitiveness of markets.

EXTERNALITIES—WHAT HAVE YOU BEEN DOING TO YOUR NEIGHBOR?

Production and consumption of some goods will result in spillover effects that the market will fail to register. These spillover effects, called **externalities,** are present when the actions of one individual or group affect the welfare of others without their consent.

Examples of externalities abound. If you live in an apartment house and the noisy stereo of your next-door neighbors keeps you from studying economics, your neighbors are creating an externality. Their actions are imposing an unwanted cost

Externalities: The side effects of an action that influence the well-being of nonconsenting parties. The nonconsenting parties may be either helped (by external benefits) or harmed (by external costs).

on you. Driving your car during rush hour increases the level of congestion, thereby imposing a cost on other motorists.

The existence of externality implies the lack of property rights, or of enforcement of those rights. The apartment dweller who is bothered by a neighbor's noise either does not have a right to quiet, or is unable to enforce the right. In either case, the maker of noise need not take into account the resulting discomfort of neighbors. Similarly, each motorist adding his or her car to heavy traffic will not be forced to consider the effects on others, unless there is a highway access fee reflecting the costs of congestion. When enforceable property rights are not present, externality is a normal result.

Not all externalities result in the imposition of a cost. Sometimes human actions generate benefits for nonparticipating parties. The home-owner who keeps a house in good condition and maintains a neat lawn improves the beauty of the entire community, thereby benefitting community members. A flood-control project built by upstream residents for their benefit may also generate gains for those who live downstream. Scientific theories benefit their authors, but the knowledge gained also contributes to the welfare of others who do not help to pay for the benefits. Again, a lack of enforceable property rights causes the problem. The producers of the goods or services providing the positively valued externalities do not have property rights in them. Thus, they are often unable to reap fully the benefits of their services.

Why do externalities create problems for the market mechanism? Exhibit 3 can help answer this question. With competitive markets in equilibrium, the cost of a good (including the opportunity cost borne by the producer) will be paid by consumers. Unless consumer benefits exceed the opportunity cost of production, the goods will not be produced. What happens, though, when externalities are present?

Suppose that a business firm discharges unwanted smoke into the air or sewage into a river. Valuable resources, clean air and pure water, are used essentially for garbage disposal. Neither the firm nor the consumers of its products, however, will pay for these costs. As Exhibit 3a shows, the supply curve will understate the opportunity cost of production when these external costs are present. Since the producer only has to consider the cost to the firm, and can ignore the cost imposed

EXHIBIT 3

Externalities and Problems for the Market

When external costs are present (a), the output level of a product will exceed the desired amount. In contrast, market output of goods that generate external benefits (b) will be less than the ideal level.

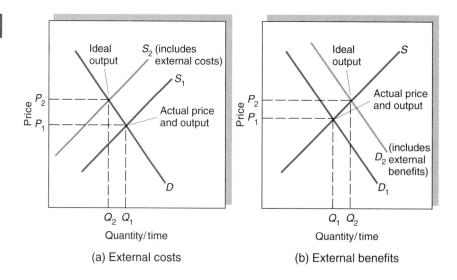

(a) External costs   (b) External benefits

on secondary parties, supply curve S_1 will result. If the producer had to pay all costs, supply would be S_2. The actual supply curve S_1 will not reflect the full opportunity cost of producing the good. For the producer, the opportunity cost paid is low enough to merit an increase in supply. Output will be expanded beyond Q_2 (to Q_1), even though the buyer's valuation of the additional units is less than their full opportunity cost. The second efficiency condition, rule 2, is violated. Inefficiency in the form of excessive air and water pollution results. In the total picture, the harm caused by the added pollution outweighs the added benefits to the buyers and sellers involved.

As Exhibit 3b shows, external benefits often result in opportunities forgone. When they are present, the market demand curve D_1 will not fully reflect the total benefits, which include those going to parties who receive the benefits without payment. They may be unwilling to pay, since they already receive benefits without payment. Output Q_1 will result. Could the community gain from a greater output of the product? Yes. The demand curve D_2 reflects both the direct benefits to paying consumers and the benefits bestowed on secondary, nonpaying parties. Expansion of output beyond Q_1 to Q_2 would result in net gain to the community. But, since neither producers nor paying consumers can capture the secondary benefits, consumption level Q_1 will result. The potential net gain from the greater output level Q_2 will be lost. Rule 1 of our ideal efficiency criterion is violated.

Competitive markets will fail to give consumers and producers the correct signals when property rights are not fully defined and enforced, so that externalities are present. The market will tend to underallocate resources to the production of goods with external benefits and overallocate resources to the production of goods that impose external costs on nonconsenting parties.

PUBLIC GOODS—MORE PROBLEMS FOR THE MARKET

Public Goods: Jointly consumed goods. When consumed by one person, they are also made available to others. National defense, poetry, and scientific theories are all public goods.

Some goods are difficult to provide commercially through the marketplace because there is no way to exclude nonpaying customers. Goods that must be consumed jointly by all are called **public goods.** National defense, the judicial and legal systems, and the monetary system are examples of public goods. The national defense that protects you also protects others. Unlike candy bars, national defense cannot be provided to some citizens but not to others. Similarly, the actions of a central monetary authority are a public good. The monetary system that influences the prices of things you buy and sell also influences the prices and incomes of others.

Why are public goods troublesome for the market? Typically, in the marketplace, there is a direct link between consumption and payment. If you do not pay, you do not consume. Similarly, the payments of consumers provide the incentive to supply products. Public goods, however, are consumed jointly. If a public good is made available to one person, it is simultaneously made available to others. Since people cannot be excluded, their incentive to pay or even to reveal their true valuation of the good is destroyed. Why would you voluntarily pay your ''fair share'' for national defense, the courts, or police protection if these goods were provided in the market? If others contribute a large amount, the public good will be provided pretty much regardless of what you do. If others do not pay, your actions will not make much difference anyway. Each person thus has an incentive to opt out, to refuse to help pay voluntarily for the public good.

When everybody opts out, what happens? Not very much of the public good is produced. This is precisely why the market cannot handle public goods very well. Resources will be underallocated to the production of public goods because self-interested consumers, recognizing that there is little relationship between their specific contribution and the quantity of a public good supplied, will fail to contribute to its costs. But when many people follow this course, too little of the public good is produced. Thus, the nature of public goods causes a conflict between self-interest and the public interest of economic efficiency.

ECONOMIC INSTABILITY

If markets are to function well, a stable monetary exchange system must be provided. Many market exchanges involve a time dimension. Houses, cars, consumer durables, land, buildings, equipment, and many other items are paid for over a period of months or even years. If the purchasing power of the monetary unit, the dollar in the United States, gyrated wildly, few would want to make transactions involving long-term commitments because of the uncertainty. The smooth functioning of the market would be retarded. Many economists believe that without the help of government, the economy would be less stable than it is.

The government's spending and monetary policies exert a powerful influence on economic stability. If properly conducted, these policies contribute to economic stability, full and efficient utilization of resources, and stable prices. Improper stabilization policies, though, can cause massive unemployment, rapidly rising prices, or both.

Economists are not in complete agreement on the extent to which public policy can stabilize the economy and promote full employment. They often debate the impact of various policy tools. All agree, however, that a stable economic environment is vital to a market economy. Those pursuing a course in macroeconomics will find both the potential and the limitations of government action as a stabilizing force in the economy discussed further in Part Two.

THE ECONOMICS OF COLLECTIVE ACTION

The pricing system will fail to meet our ideal efficiency standards if (a) markets are not competitive, (b) externalities are present, (c) public goods necessitate joint consumption, or (d) the aggregate economy is characterized by instability and the resultant uncertainty. If public-sector action can correct these deficiencies, net gains for the community are possible. Public policy does not have to be a zero-sum game.

Just because it is possible to visualize that public-sector action will promote economic welfare, it does not follow that real-world governments, including those organized democratically, will necessarily institute sound policies. Government is *not* a supraindividual that will always make decisions in the "public interest," however that nebulous term might be defined. Neither is it a corrective device available for use when market organization fails to achieve a desired outcome. It is instead an alternative method of social organization—an institutional process through which individuals collectively make choices and carry out activities.

Public Choice Analysis: The study of decision-making as it affects the formation and operation of collective organizations, such as governments. The discipline bridges the gap between economics and political science. In general, the principles and methodology of economics are applied to political science topics.

If we are going to make meaningful comparisons between market allocation and collective action, we need to develop a sound theory that will help us understand both forms of economic organization. **Public choice analysis** has significantly advanced our understanding of the collective decision-making process in recent years. Something of a cross between economics and political science, public choice theory applies the principles and methodology of economics to collective choices.

In a democratic setting, individual preferences will influence the outcome of collective decisions, just as they influence outcomes in the market. Public choice theory postulates that individual behavior in the political arena will be motivated by considerations similar to those that influence market behavior. If self-interest is a powerful motivator in the marketplace, there is every reason to believe it will also be a motivating factor when choices are made collectively. If market choices are influenced by changes in projected personal costs relative to benefits, we can expect that such changes will also influence political choices. Public choice theory, in other words, suggests that the number of saints and sinners in the two sectors will be comparable.

In analyzing the behavior of people in the marketplace, economists develop a logically consistent theory of behavior that can be tested against reality. Through theory and empirical testing, we seek to explain various economic actions of decision-makers and, in general, how the market operates.

In the public sphere, our purpose should be the same: to explain how the collective decision-making process really operates. This means developing a

APPLICATIONS IN ECONOMICS

Perspectives on the Cost of Political Competition

We all have our own ideas concerning how government should be run. Since government is such an extremely important force in our economy and in our lives, individuals and groups try to influence election outcomes by voting, by contributing to political campaigns, and by ringing doorbells, among other activities. In addition, legislative and executive branch decisions can be influenced directly, by lobbying.

Competition for elective office is fierce, and campaigns are expensive. In preparation for the 1990 elections, for example, candidates for House and Senate positions spent about $500 million. Unlike bidders in a market auction, winners and losers alike pay the full costs of the election bid. It is common for lobbying groups to donate to opposing candidates in a close race.

During and after the election,

lobbying groups compete for the attention—the ear—of elected officials. In fact, the greatest portion of campaign funds raised by incumbents is not raised at election time; rather, it accrues over their entire term in office. A large campaign contribution may not be able to "buy" a vote, but it certainly enhances the lobbyist's chance to sit down with the elected official to explain the power and the beauty of a client's position. In the competitive world of politics, the politician who does not at least listen to helpful "friends of the campaign" is less likely to survive.

Campaign contributions are only the tip of the lobbying iceberg. In Washington, D.C. alone, thousands of offices and tens of thousands of individuals, many of them extremely talented, hard-working, and well-paid, are dedicated to lobbying Congress and the executive branch of the federal

government. Trade associations, for example, have more than 3,000 offices and 80,000 employees in Washington.[3] Another indicator of the enormous amount of time and effort allocated to influencing government is that 65 percent of Fortune 200 Chief Executive Officers travel to Washington at least every two weeks, on average. Billions of dollars in budgets, in taxes, and in expenditures required by regulation are at stake, in addition to such emotional issues as gun control and abortion. The natural result is huge expenditures designed to influence governmental policy.

---

[3]More details on campaign finance can be found in Michael Barone and Grant Ujifusa, *The Almanac of American Politics: 1990* (Washington, D.C.: National Journal, 1990). See also David Boaz, "Spend Money to Make Money," *The Wall Street Journal,* November 13, 1983.

logically consistent theory linking individual behavior to collective action, analyzing the implications of that theory, and testing these implications against events in the real world.

Since the theory of collective decision-making is not as well developed as our theory of market behavior, our conclusions will, of course, be less definitive. In the last 25 years, however, social scientists have made great strides in our understanding of resource allocation by the public sector.[4] Currently, this subject is often dealt with at a more advanced academic level. Even on an introductory level, though, economic tools can be used to shed light on how the public sector handles economic activities.

DIFFERENCES AND SIMILARITIES BETWEEN MARKET AND COLLECTIVE ACTION

There are some basic characteristics that influence outcomes in both the market and the public sectors.[5] As we have noted, there is reason to believe that the motivational factors present in both sectors are similar. There are, however, basic structural differences. Voluntary exchange coordinated by prices is the dominant characteristic of a market economy (although, of course, when externalities are present, involuntary exchange may also result). In a democratic setting, the dominant characteristic of collective action is majority rule, effective either directly or through legislative procedures. Let us take a look at both the differences and similarities between the two sectors.

1. Competitive Behavior Is Present in Both the Market and Public Sectors.
Although the market sector is sometimes referred to as "the competitive sector," it is clear that competitive behavior is present in both sectors. Politicians compete with each other for elective office. Bureau chiefs and agency heads compete for additional taxpayer dollars. Public-sector employees, like their counterparts in the private sector, compete for promotions, higher incomes, and additional power. Lobbyists compete to secure funds, to receive favorable rulings, and to secure legislation for the interest groups they represent—including both private and governmental clients. (See Applications in Economics box on p. 89.) The nature of the competition and the criteria for success do differ between the two sectors. Nonetheless, competitive behavior is present in both sectors.

2. Public-Sector Organization Can Break the Individual Consumption-Payment Link.
In the market, a consumer who wants to obtain a commodity must be willing to pay the price. For each person, there is a one-to-one correspondence between consuming the commodity and paying the purchase price. In this respect, there is a fundamental difference between market and collective action. The government usually does not establish a one-to-one relationship between the individual's payment and receipt of a good.

Your tax bill will be the same whether you like or dislike the national defense, agriculture, or antipoverty policies of the government. You will be taxed for subsidies to higher education, sugarbeet growers, airlines, cultural centers, and many other **political goods**[6] regardless of whether or not you consume or use them.

Political Good: Any good (or policy) supplied through the political process.

---

[4]The contributions of Kenneth Arrow, James Buchanan, Duncan Black, Anthony Downs, Mancur Olson, Robert Tollison, and Gordon Tullock have been particularly important.

[5]The "Public Choice" section of this book analyzes the topics of alternative forms of economic organization—market versus collective action—in more detail.

[6]"Political good" is a broad term used to designate any action supplied through the public sector. Note that political goods may be either private goods or public goods.

In some cases, you may receive very large benefits (either monetary or subjective) from a governmental action without any significant impact on your tax bill. The direct link between individual consumption of the good and individual payment for the good is not required in the public sector.

3. Scarcity Imposes the Aggregate Consumption-Payment Link in Both Sectors.
Although the government can break the link between an individual's payment for a good and the right to consume the good, the reality of the *aggregate consumption-aggregate payment* link will remain. Provision of scarce goods requires sacrificing alternatives. Someone must cover the cost of providing scarce goods, regardless of the sector used to produce (or distribute) them. There are no free lunches in either the private or the public sector. Free goods provided in the public sector are "free" only to individuals. They are most certainly not free from the viewpoint of society.

An increase in the amount of goods provided by the public sector will mean an increase in the total costs of government. Given the fact of scarcity, the link between aggregate consumption and aggregate costs of production cannot be broken by public-sector action.

4. The Element of Compulsion Is Present in the Public Sector.
As we have already discussed, voluntary exchange is the dominant characteristic of market organization. Except when externalities are present, involuntary exchange is absent. In the marketplace, a minority need not yield to the majority. For example, the views of the majority, even an overwhelming majority, do not prevent minority consumers from purchasing desired goods.

Governments possess an exclusive right to the use of coercion. Large corporations like Exxon and General Motors are economically powerful, but they cannot require you to buy their products. In contrast, in the political arena, if a legislative majority decides on a particular policy, the minority must accept the policy and help pay for its cost, even if that minority strongly disagrees. If representative legislative policy allocates $10 billion for the development of a superweapon system, the dissenting minority is required to pay taxes that will help finance the project. Other dissenting minorities will be compelled to pay taxes for the support of welfare programs, farm subsidies, foreign aid, or hundreds of other projects on which reasonable people will surely differ. When issues are decided in the public sector, dissidents must, at least temporarily, yield to the current dominant view.

5. When Collective Decisions Are Made Legislatively, Voters Must Choose Among Candidates Who Represent a Bundle of Positions on Issues.
On election day, the voter cannot choose the views of Representative Free Lunch on poverty and business welfare and simultaneously choose the views of challenger Ms. Austerity on national defense and tariffs. Inability to separate a candidate's views on one issue from his or her views on another greatly reduces the voter's power to register preferences on specific issues. Since the average representative is asked to vote on roughly 2,000 different issues during a two-year term, the enormity of the problem is obvious.

To the average individual, choosing a representative is a bit like choosing an agent who will control a substantial portion of one's income and also regulate one's activities. Even if this individual voter could personally elect the agent, it would be impossible for the voter to select one agent's views on issue X and another agent's views on issue Y. Looked at another way, deciding to vote for (or against) a candidate on the basis of one issue essentially means being disenfranchised on all others. As a result of the ''bundle-purchase'' nature of the political process, the ability of each voter to express his or her preference at the ballot box, on each issue, is severely limited.

6. Income and Power Are Distributed Differently in the Two Sectors.   Individuals who supply more highly valued resources in the marketplace have larger incomes. The number of dollar votes available to an individual reflect her or his abilities, ambitions, skills, perceptiveness, past savings, inheritance, and good fortune, among other things. An unequal distribution of consumer power is the result.

In the public sector, ballots call the tune when decisions are made democratically. One citizen, one vote is the rule. This does not mean, however, that political goods and services—those resources that make up political power or political income—are allocated equally to all citizens by the collective decision-making process. Some individuals are much more astute than others at using the political process to obtain personal advantage. The political process rewards those who are most capable of delivering votes—not only their own individual votes but those of others as well. Persuasive skills (that is, lobbying, public speaking, public relations), organizational abilities, financial contributions, and knowledge are vital to success in politics. Persons who have more of these resources—and are willing to spend them in the political arena—can expect to benefit more handsomely, in terms of both money and power, from the political process than individuals who lack them.

THE SUPPLY OF AND DEMAND FOR PUBLIC-SECTOR ACTION

Consumers use their dollar votes to demand goods in the marketplace. Producers supply goods. The actions of both are influenced by self-interest. In a democratic political system, voters and legislators are counterparts to consumers and producers. Voters demand political goods using their political resources—votes, lobbying, contributions, and organizational abilities. Vote-conscious legislators are suppliers of political goods.

How does a voter decide which political supplier to support? Since there is no evidence that entrance into a voting booth or participation in the political process causes a personality transformation, there is sound reason to believe that the motivation of participants in the market and political processes is similar. The voter who selects among political alternatives is the same person who selects among market alternatives. If Jones is influenced by expected personal benefits and costs when he makes choices in the department store, it makes sense that he will be similarly influenced by personal benefits and costs when he makes choices in the voting booth.

Other things constant, voters will support those candidates whom they expect to provide them with the most benefits, net of cost. The greater the expected gains from a candidate's election, the more voters will do to ensure the candidate's success. A voter, like the consumer in the marketplace, will ask the supplier, ''What can you do for me and how much will I pay?''

The goal of the political supplier is to put together a majority coalition—to win the election. Vote-seeking politicians, like profit-seeking business decision-makers, will have a strong incentive to cater to the views of politically active constituents.

The easiest way to win votes, both politically and financially, is to give the constituents, or at least appear to give them, what they want. A politician who pays no heed to the views of his or her constituents is as rare as a business-person selling bikinis in the Arctic.

There are two major reasons that voters are likely to turn to public-sector economic organization: (a) to reduce waste and inefficiency stemming from noncompetitive markets, externalities, public goods, and economic instability and (b) to redistribute income. Public-sector action that corrects, or appears to correct, the shortcomings of the market will be attractive. If properly conducted, it will generate more benefits than costs to the community. Much real-world public policy is motivated by a desire to correct the shortcomings of the market. Antitrust action is designed to promote competition. Government provision of national defense, crime prevention, a legal system, and flood-control projects is related to the public-good nature of these activities. Similarly, externalities help justify public-sector action in such areas as pollution control, education, pure research, and disease control. Clearly, the tax, spending, and monetary policies of the government are used to influence the level of economic activity in most Western nations.

Demand for public-sector action may also stem from a desire to change the income distribution. There is no reason to presume that the unhampered market will lead to the most desirable distribution of income. In fact, the ideal distribution of income is largely a matter of personal preference. There is nothing in positive economics that tells us that one distribution of income is better than another. Some people may desire to see more income allocated to low-income citizens. The most common scientific argument for redistribution to the poor is based on the "public-good" nature of adequate income for all. Alleviation of poverty may help not only the poor but also those who are well-off. Middle- and upper-income recipients, for example, may benefit if the less fortunate members of the community enjoy better food, clothing, housing, and health care. If the rich would gain, why will they not voluntarily give to the poor? For the same reason that individuals will do little to provide national defense voluntarily. The antipoverty efforts of any single individual will exert little impact on the total amount of poverty in the community. Because individual action is so insignificant, each person has an incentive to opt out. When everyone opts out, the market provides less than the desired amount of antipoverty action.

Others may desire public-sector redistribution for less altruistic reasons—they may seek to enhance their own personal incomes. This poses a problem: How can government engage in income redistribution based on the "public-good" nature of antipoverty transfers and at the same time restrain income transfers based on the political clout of various interest groups? This is an important question because there is reason to believe that economic waste is a side effect of substantial government involvement in the determination of income shares. There are three major reasons why large-scale redistribution is likely to reduce the size of the economic pie.

First, such redistribution weakens the link between productive activity and reward. When taxes take a larger share of one's income, tax revenues are spread among all beneficiaries, so the benefits derived from hard work and productive service are reduced. The basic economic postulate suggests that when benefits allocated to producers are reduced (and benefits of nonproducers are raised), less productive effort will be supplied.

Rent Seeking: Actions by individuals and interest groups designed to restructure public policy in a manner that will either directly or indirectly redistribute more income to themselves.

Second, as public policy redistributes a larger share of income, individuals will allocate more resources to **rent seeking.**[7] Rent seeking is a term used by economists to classify actions designed to change public policy—tax structure, composition of spending, or regulation—in a manner that will redistribute income to oneself. Resources used for lobbying and other means of rent seeking (perhaps ''favor seeking'' would be more descriptive) will not be available to increase the size of the economic pie.

Third, higher taxes to finance income redistribution and an expansion in rent-seeking activities will induce taxpayers to engage in protective action. Taxpayers will be encouraged to take steps to protect their income. More accountants, lawyers, and tax-shelter experts will be retained as people seek to limit the amount of their income that is redistributed to others. Like the resources allocated to rent seeking, resources allocated to protecting one's wealth from public policy will also be wasted. They will not be available for productive activity. Therefore, given the incentive structure generated by large-scale redistribution policies, there is good reason to expect that such policies will reduce the size of the economic pie.

CONFLICTS BETWEEN GOOD ECONOMICS AND GOOD POLITICS

What reason is there to believe that political action will result in economic inefficiency? Current economic and political research is continually yielding knowledge that will help us answer this question more definitively. We deal with it in more detail in a later chapter, but three important characteristics of the political process are introduced here.

THE RATIONALLY IGNORANT VOTER

Rational Ignorance Effect: Voter ignorance that is present because people perceive their individual votes as unlikely to be decisive. Voters rationally have little incentive to inform themselves so as to cast an informed vote.

Less than one half of the American electorate can correctly identify the names of their congressmen and women, much less state where their representatives stand on various issues. Why are so many people ignorant of the simplest facts regarding the political process? The explanation does not lie with a lack of intelligence on the part of the average American. The phenomenon is explained by the incentives confronting the voter. Most citizens recognize that their vote is unlikely to determine the outcome of an election. Since their vote is highly unlikely to resolve the issue at hand, citizens have little incentive to spend much effort to seek the information needed to cast an informed ballot. Economists refer to this lack of incentive as the **rational ignorance effect.**

The rationally ignorant voter is exercising good judgment as to how his or her time and effort will yield the most personal benefits. There is a parallel between the voter's failure to acquire political knowledge and the farmer's inattention to the factors that determine the weather. Weather is probably the most important factor determining the income of an individual farmer, yet it makes no sense for the farmer

[7]See Charles K. Rowley, Robert D. Tollison, and Gordon Tullock, *The Political Economy of Rent-Seeking* (Boston: Kluewer Academic Publishers, 1988) for additional details on rent seeking.

to invest time and resources attempting to understand atmospheric science. An improved knowledge of how weather systems work will seldom enable the farmer to avoid their adverse effects. So it is with the average voter. The voter stands to gain little from acquiring more information about a wide range of issues that are decided in the political arena. Since the resolution of these issues, like the weather, is out of the individual voter's hands, he or she has little incentive to become more informed.

Because of this fact, most voters simply rely on information that is supplied to them freely by candidates and the mass media. Conversations with friends and information acquired at work, from newspapers, from TV news, and from political advertising are especially important because the voter has so little incentive to spend personal time and effort gathering information. It is not surprising, then, that few

OUTSTANDING ECONOMIST

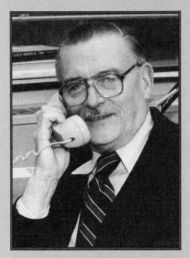

James Buchanan
(1919—)

Thirty years ago, most economists were content to concentrate on the workings of the marketplace, its shortcomings, and what government action might do to correct these deficiencies. Political scientists and economists alike envisioned the public sector as a type of supraindividual, a creature making decisions in the public interest. James Buchanan was determined to change all this. He, perhaps more than anyone else, is responsible for what some have called the "public choice revolution." For this and related contributions, he was awarded the 1986 Nobel Prize in Economics.

Buchanan refers to himself as a "constitutional political economist," which he differentiates from a "public policy economist." Buchanan argues that it is constitutional restraints and political rules, rather than the people elected to office or the experts advising them, that determine the pattern of political outcomes. Public choice theory maintains that politicians and bureaucrats are guided by essentially the same motives as consumers and business decision-makers. Therefore, unless we design rules that bring the self-

interest of the political players into harmony with the wise use of resources, the process will go awry. Waste and stagnation will result.

Much of Buchanan's research has focused on how alternative political decision rules (simple majority, supra-majority, legislative procedures, and so on) work. Buchanan's most famous work on this topic is *The Calculus of Consent* (1962), coauthored with Gordon Tullock.[8] Indeed, *The Calculus* has become a modern-day classic.

Buchanan and Tullock founded the Center for Study of Public Choice in 1969. Located on the campus of George Mason University, the Center is a focal point of public choice scholarship. Currently a Distinguished Professor of Economics at George Mason and General Director of the Center, Buchanan helped launch a new journal there, *Constitutional Political Economy*. He continues his work as a prolific writer and innovative scholar.

---

[8]J. M. Buchanan and G. Tullock, *The Calculus of Consent* (Ann Arbor: University of Michigan Press, 1962).

voters are able to accurately describe the consequences of raising tariffs on automobiles or of abolishing the farm price support program. In using their time and efforts in ways other than studying these policy issues, voters are merely responding to economic incentives.

THE PROBLEM OF SPECIAL INTEREST

Special Interest Issue: An issue that generates substantial individual benefits to a small minority while imposing a small individual cost on many other voters. In total, the net cost to the majority might either exceed or fall short of the net benefits to the special interest group.

A **special interest issue** is one that generates substantial personal benefits for a small number of constituents while imposing a small individual cost on a large number of other votes. A few gain a great deal individually, whereas a large number lose a little as individuals.

Special interest issues are very attractive to vote-conscious politicians (that is, to those most eager and most likely to win elections). Voters who have a small cost imposed on them by a policy favoring a special interest will not care enough about the issue to examine it, particularly if it is complex enough that the imposition of the cost is difficult to identify. Because information is costly, most of those harmed will not even be aware of the legislator's views on such an issue. Most voters will simply ignore special interest issues. Those representing the special interest, though, will be vitally concerned. They will let the candidate (or legislator) know when an issue is important to them. Because they are a small group, they may be able to organize and to give financial and other help to politicians receptive to their ideas, while opposing those who are not.

What would you do if you wanted to win an election? Support the special interest groups. Milk them for financial resources. Use those resources to "educate" the uninformed majority of voters to the fact that you support policies of interest to them. You would have an incentive to follow this path even if the total community benefits from the support of the special interest were less than the cost. The policy might cause economic inefficiency, but it could still be a political winner.

Why stand up for a large majority? Even though the total cost may be very large, each person bears only a small cost. Most voters are uninformed on the issue. They do not care much about it. They would do little to help you get elected even if you supported their best interests on this issue. Astute politicians will support the special interest group if they plan to be around for very long.

The political process tends to work in favor of special interest groups, even when their programs are inefficient. This means that there is sometimes a conflict between good politics (winning elections) and ideal public policy. Throughout, as we consider public policy alternatives, we will remind you to consider how public policy is likely to operate when special interest influence is strong.

POLITICAL GAINS FROM SHORTSIGHTED POLICIES

The complexity of many issues makes it difficult for voters to identify the future benefits and costs. Can a change in tax rates lead to a greater rate of economic growth? Will a change in environmental policy now lead to a healthier environment for our grandchildren, or to slower economic growth? What impact will a rise in the national debt have on future prosperity? These questions are complex. Few voters will analyze the short-run and long-run implications of policy in these areas. Instead, voters will have a tendency to rely on current conditions. To the voter, the best indicator of the success of a policy is, "How are things now?"

Politicians seeking reelection have a strong incentive to support policies that generate current benefits in exchange for future costs, particularly if the future costs will be difficult to identify on election day and will be felt after the incumbent leaves office. Public-sector action will therefore be biased in favor of legislation that offers immediate (and easily identifiable) current benefits in exchange for future costs that are complicated and difficult to identify. Simultaneously, there is a bias against legislation that involves immediate and easily identifiable costs (for example, higher taxes) while yielding future benefits that are complex and difficult to identify. Economists refer to this bias inherent in the collective decision-making process as the **shortsightedness effect.**

Shortsightedness Effect: Misallocation of resources that results because public-sector action is biased (a) in favor of proposals yielding clearly defined current benefits in exchange for difficult-to-identify future costs and (b) against proposals with clearly identifiable current costs yielding less concrete and less obvious future benefits.

The nature of democratic institutions restricts the planning horizon of elected officials. Positive results must be observable by the next election, or the incumbent is likely to be replaced by someone who promises more rapid results. Policies that will eventually pay off in the future (after the next election) will have little attractiveness to vote-seeking politicians if those policies do not exert a beneficial impact by election day. As we shall subsequently see, the shortsighted nature of the political process reduces the likelihood that it will be able to promote economic stability and a noninflationary environment.

What if shortsighted policies lead to serious problems after an election? This can be sticky for politicians, but is it not better to be an officeholder explaining why things are in a mess than a defeated candidate trying to convince people who will not listen why you were right all the time? The political entrepreneur has a strong incentive to win the next election and worry about the problems, as they arise, later.

IMPLICATIONS OF PUBLIC CHOICE

It is important to distinguish between ordinary politics and constitutional rules. Constitutions establish the procedures that will be utilized to make decisions. They also may limit the boundary of ordinary politics—place certain matters (for example, the taking of private property without compensation, restrictions on freedom of speech or worship, and various restrictions on voting) beyond the reach of majority rule or normal legislative procedures.

Both bad news and good news flow from public choice analysis. The bad news is that for certain classes of economic activity, unconstrained democratic government will predictably be a source of economic waste and inefficiency. Not only does the invisible hand of the market sometimes fail to meet our ideal efficiency criteria, so too, does political decision-making. But there is also some good news arising from public choice theory: properly structured constitutional rules can improve the expected result from government.

Whether political organization leads to desirable or undesirable economic outcomes is critically dependent upon the structure of the political (constitutional) rules. When the structure of the political rules brings the self-interest of individual voters, politicians, and bureaucrats into harmony with the general welfare, government will promote economic prosperity. On the other hand, if the rules fail to bring about this harmony, politically determined outcomes will often conflict with economic efficiency. The challenge before us is to develop political economy institutions that are more consistent with economic prosperity. As we proceed, we will discuss several modifications of the political rules that public choice theory indicates would improve the economic effectiveness of the political process.

Needless to say, this general topic—modifications in the structure of government that will make it more consistent with economic efficiency and general prosperity—is one of the most exciting and potentially fruitful areas of study in economics.

LOOKING AHEAD

In the next chapter, we will examine the government's actual spending and tax policies. In subsequent chapters, the significance of economic organization and issues of political economy will be highlighted. The tools of economics are used with a dual objective. We will point out what government ideally might do, but we will also focus on what government can be expected to do. Not surprisingly, these two are not always identical. Political economy—the use of economic tools to explain how both the market and the public sectors actually work—is a fascinating subject. It helps us to understand the "why" behind many of today's current events. Who said economics is the dismal science?

CHAPTER SUMMARY

1. Economic efficiency—creating as much value as possible from a given set of resources—is a goal by which alternative institutions and policies can be judged. Two conditions must be met to achieve economic efficiency: (a) all activities that produce more benefits than costs for the individuals within an economy must be undertaken and (b) activities that generate more costs than benefits to the individuals must not be undertaken. If only the buyer and the seller are affected, production and exchange in competitive markets are consistent with the ideal efficiency criteria.

2. Lack of competition may make it possible for a group of sellers to gain by restricting output and raising prices. There is a conflict between (a) the self-interest of sellers that leads them to collude, restrict output, and raise product prices above their production costs and (b) economic efficiency. Public-sector action—promoting competition or regulating private firms—may be able to improve economic efficiency in industries in which competitive pressures are lacking.

3. The market will tend to underallocate resources to the production of goods with external benefits and overallocate resources to those products that generate external costs.

4. Public goods are troublesome for the market to handle because nonpaying customers cannot easily be excluded. Since the amount of a public good that each individual receives is largely unaffected by whether he or she helps pay for it, many individuals will contribute little. The market will thus tend to undersupply public goods.

5. The public sector can improve the operation of markets by providing a stable economic environment.

6. The public sector is an alternative means of organizing economic activity. Public-sector decision-making will reflect the choices of individuals acting as voters, politicians, financial contributors, lobbyists, and bureaucrats. Public choice analysis applies the principles and methodology of economics to group decision-making to help us understand collective organizations.

7. Successful political candidates will seek to offer programs that appeal to voters. Voters, in turn, will be attracted to candidates who reflect the voters' own views and interests. In a democratic setting, there are two major reasons why voters will turn to collective organization: (a) to reduce waste and inefficiency stemming from noncompetitive markets, externalities, public goods, and economic instability and (b) to alter the income distribution.

8. Public-sector action may sometimes improve the market's efficiency and lead to an increase in the community's welfare, all individuals considered. However, the political process is likely to conflict with ideal economic efficiency criteria when (a)

voters have little knowledge of an issue, (b) special interests are strong, and/or (c) political figures can gain from following shortsighted policies.

CRITICAL ANALYSIS QUESTIONS

1. Explain in your own words what is meant by external costs and external benefits. Why may market allocations be less than ideal when externalities are present?

*2. If producers are to be provided with an incentive to produce a good, why is it important for them to be able to prevent nonpaying customers from receiving the good?

3. Do you think real-world politicians adopt political positions to help their election prospects? Can you name a current political figure who consistently puts "principles above politics"? If so, check with three of your classmates and see if they agree.

4. Do you think special interest groups exert much influence on local government? Why or why not? As a test, check the composition of the local zoning board in your community. How many real-estate agents, contractors, developers, and landlords are on the board? Are there any citizens without real-estate interests on the board?

*5. "Economics is a positive science. Government by its very nature is influenced by philosophical considerations. Therefore, the tools of economics cannot tell us much about how the public sector works." Do you agree or disagree? Why?

*6. Which of the following are public goods: (a) an antimissile system surrounding Washington, D.C.; (b) a fire department; (c) tennis courts; (d) Yellowstone National Park; (e) elementary schools? Explain, using the definition of a public good.

7. "A democratic government is a corrective device used to remedy inefficiencies that arise when market allocation is not working well." (True or false; explain)

8. Incentives are important in both the market and political sectors. Discuss the similarities and differences in the incentives of the following pairs of people to use resources efficiently and provide value to others.
   a. The President of General Motors and the President of a large state university
   b. A member of the Board of Directors of IBM and a congressional representative
   c. The general manager of Walt Disney World and the superintendent of Yellowstone National Park
   d. The President of a textbook publishing company and the superintendent of public schools in your state

* 9. How can you determine if a market action is efficient? How can you determine if a government action is efficient? If the majority of the citizens favor a project, does this indicate it is productive?

10. English philosopher John Locke argued that the protection of each individual's person and property was the primary function of government. Why is the secure protection of each individual's person and property acquired without the use of violence, theft, or fraud important to the efficient operation of an economy?

*11. Does the democratic political process incorporate the invisible hand principle? Is the presence or absence of the invisible hand principle important? Why or why not?

*12. "The average person is more likely to make an informed choice when he or she purchases a personal computer than when he or she votes for a congressional candidate." Evaluate this view.

13. Suppose that Abel builds a factory next to Baker's farm, and air pollution from the factory harms Baker's crops. Is Baker's property right to the land being violated? Is an externality present? What if the pollution invades Baker's home and harms her health. Are her property rights violated? Is an externality present? Explain.

---

* Asterisk denotes questions for which answers are given in Appendix C, Selected Answers.

*14. Jack, a stockholder in General Motors Corporation, lives in an apartment in Los Angeles. In two years he expects to sell the stock and retire in Florida. General Motors announces that profits will not be paid out to stockholders this year, but will be used to finance a new auto design that is expected to return more than enough money in ten years to compensate stockholders for this year's lack of dividend payments. On the same day, the Los Angeles mayor announces that a city sales tax will be imposed to finance better streets. Over the next ten years, by coincidence, the benefits to Jack would be exactly the same as the General Motors benefits (just as the costs paid this year would be the same), *if he holds the stock and stays in Los Angeles*. Explain why Jack is not bothered by the GM announcement, but is very unhappy about the mayor's announcement. (*Hint:* he will sell the stock, but can't sell his right to future benefits in Los Angeles.)

5 Government Spending and Taxation

Our Constitution is in actual operation; everything appears to promise that it will last; but in this world nothing is certain but death and taxes.

Benjamin Franklin (1789)

CHAPTER FOCUS

■ How big is government? What goods and services do we provide through government? How are they financed?

■ Why has the size of government grown more rapidly than our economy during the last several decades? Does government now provide more goods and services than it did in the past? Does it redistribute more income?

■ How do taxes influence the choices of taxpayers? If a tax rate is increased by 10 percent, will revenue from the tax increase by 10 percent?

■ How did legislation passed during the 1980s modify the structure of the income tax? How did it affect the taxes paid by the rich?

■ How does the size of government in the United States compare with the size of government in other countries?

*T*he activities of government exert an enormous impact on our lives. Governments levy taxes and organize the production of many goods and services. Sometimes governments take tax revenue from some and transfer it to others. Governments also set the rules of the game. Public policy defines property rights, enforces contracts, regulates business activities, and establishes a monetary framework. These legal and regulatory activities influence how markets work and the degree of cooperation and conflict among economic participants. In fact, the role of government as the rule-maker and referee probably exerts more influence on the economic prosperity of a nation than does its function as a producer of goods and services. Nevertheless, taxation and government expenditures are the most direct means by which the government influences the economy. Analysis of the government's spending policies and methods of finance will reveal a great deal about the size and economic character of government.

THE GROWTH OF GOVERNMENT

Prior to the 1930s, government expenditures generally amounted to less then 10 percent of our gross national product (GNP).[1] Except during times of war, federal government expenditures were quite small in the early part of this century. As Exhibit 1 illustrates, the expenditures of the federal government were only 2.6 percent of GNP in 1929, compared with 7.3 percent for state and local expenditures.

During the 1930–1970 period, both the size and composition of government changed dramatically. By 1970, total government expenditures comprised 31.3

---

[1]The gross national product (GNP) is discussed in Chapter 6. For now, it can be thought of as a measure of total output produced during a period.

EXHIBIT 1

The Growth of Government Expenditures, 1929–1989

In 1929, total government spending summed to less than 10 percent of total output. During the 1930–1970 period, the size of government as a share of the U.S. economy rose substantially, reaching 31.3 percent of GNP in 1970. In 1989, total government spending was 34.1 percent of GNP, only slightly higher than the 1970 figure.

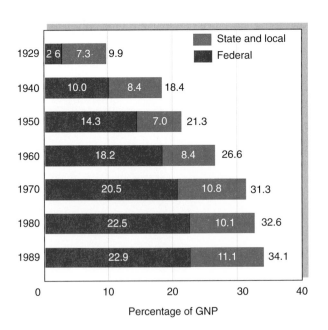

Source: *Economic Report of the President, 1990,* (Tables C-1 and C-79). Grants to state and local governments are included in federal expenditures.

percent of our economy, more than triple the level of 1929. Most of this growth of government took place at the federal level. As a share of our economy, federal expenditures quadrupled during the 1930s, while state and local expenditures increased by only a small amount. Between 1940 and 1970, federal expenditures doubled in size (from 10 percent to 20.5 percent) as a share of our economy. State and local spending grew more slowly, advancing from 8.4 percent to 10.8 percent of GNP. In contrast with 1929 when government expenditures were small and mostly at the local level, by 1970 government spending summed to nearly one-third of our total output and most of this spending was undertaken by the federal government.

Since 1970 the growth of government as a proportion of our economy has slowed substantially. In 1989, total government expenditures comprised 34.1 percent of GNP, up only slightly from 1970. Similarly, the trend toward the centralization of government expenditures has slowed during the last two decades.

FEDERALISM AND GOVERNMENT EXPENDITURES

The economic functions of government in the United States vary among the different levels. The United States has a federalist system of government. While many economic activities are conducted at the federal level, the primary responsibility for other functions remains with state and local governments. A breakdown of expenditures and revenues highlights the functional differences among the levels of government.

Exhibit 2 shows the broad categories of federal expenditures for fiscal year 1990. The federal government is solely responsible for national defense. A little less

EXHIBIT 2

How the Federal Government Spends Your Tax Dollar

The breakdown of the 1990 fiscal year federal budget is presented here. Defense accounted for 29.6 percent of federal spending. More than 50 percent of the federal tax dollar was spent on cash income maintenance, helping people buy essentials, and manpower development.

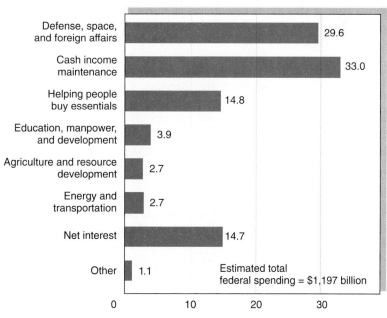

Percentage of total federal expenditures, 1990

Source: *Economic Report of the President, 1990*, Table C-77.

than 30 percent of federal expenditures went for defense and related areas (space, veterans' benefits, and foreign affairs) in 1990. The largest item in the federal budget was cash income maintenance—social security, unemployment payments, and public assistance to the poor and the disabled. These income transfers accounted for 33.0 percent of the total federal budget. Programs to help people buy essentials (medical care, housing, food, and so on) made up 14.8 percent of all federal spending in 1990. This category differs from cash income maintenance in that people must purchase specific goods in order to qualify for the assistance. Expenditures on education, manpower development, agriculture, energy, and transportation also constitute major items in the federal budget from year to year. Interest payments on the national debt for 1990 constituted 14.7 percent of total federal outlays.

Exhibit 3 is a graphic presentation of state and local government expenditures. In the United States, public education has traditionally been the responsibility of state and local governments. Thirty-four percent of state and local governmental expenditures were allocated to education during the fiscal year 1988. State governments supplement federal allocations in the areas of social welfare, public welfare, and health. These social welfare expenditures comprised 22 percent of the total spending of state governments during 1988. Highways, utilities, insurance trusts, law enforcement, and fire protection are other major areas of expenditure for state and local governments.

GOVERNMENT PURCHASES AND TRANSFER PAYMENTS

It is important to distinguish between (a) government purchases of goods and services and (b) transfer payments. **Government purchases** are expenditures incurred when goods and services are supplied through the public sector. Government purchases include items such as jet planes, missiles, highway construction and maintenance, police and fire protection, and computer equipment. Governments also purchase the labor services of teachers, clerks, lawyers, accountants, and public relation experts to produce goods ranging from public education to administrative services. Since they consume resources with alternative uses, government purchases directly reduce the supply of resources available to produce private goods and services.

Transfer payments are transfers of income from taxpayers to recipients who do not provide current goods and services in exchange for these payments. Simply put, transfer payments take income from some to provide additional income to others. Social security benefits, pensions of retired government employees, and Aid to Families with Dependent Children (AFDC) are examples of transfer payments.

Unlike government purchases, transfer payments do not *directly* reduce the resources available to the private sector. They do, however, alter the incentive structure of the economy and almost certainly exert an indirect impact on the size of the economic pie. The taxes necessary to finance transfer payments reduce the personal payoff from saving, investing, and working. If receipt of transfer payments is inversely related to income level, they will also reduce the recipient's incentive to earn taxable income. As we proceed, we will investigate the link between aggregate output and the incentive structure in more detail.

Government Purchases:
Current expenditures on goods and services provided by federal, state, and local governments; they exclude transfer payments.

Transfer Payments:
Payments to individuals or institutions that are not linked to the current supply of a good or service by the recipient.

What State and Local Governments Buy

Education, public welfare, and general administrative expenditures comprise the major budget items of state and local governments.

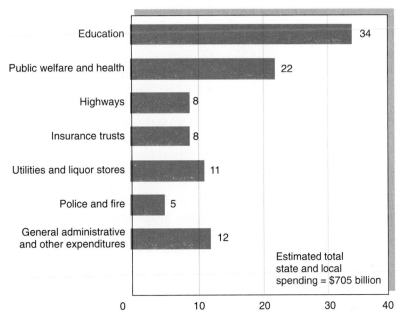

Source: U.S. Department of Commerce.

ALTERNATIVE MEASURES OF GOVERNMENT'S SIZE

Exhibit 4 presents four alternative measures of governmental size. In 1989, the purchases of federal, state, and local governments amounted to 1,025.6 billion, or 19.7 percent of total U.S. output. Government purchases thus consumed a little more than one-fifth of our resources. Government employment offers a second gauge by which we can measure the size of government. In 1989, approximately one out of every six workers (16.4 percent) was employed by a governmental unit.

EXHIBIT 4 ▪ Four Measures of the Size of Government (Federal, State, and Local), 1989		
1. Government purchases of goods and services	a) Billions of dollars b) Percentage of GNP	1,025.6 19.7
2. Government employment	a) Millions of employees b) Percentage of total employment	17.9 16.4
3. Total government expenditures including transfer payments	a) Billions of dollars b) Percentage of GNP	1,772.4 34.1
4. Total taxes and other revenues	a) Billions of dollars b) Percentage of GNP	1,684.6 32.4

Source: *The Economic Report of the President, 1991* (Washington, D.C.: U.S. Government Printing Office, 1991), and *Monthly Labor Review*, February 1991. Intergovernmental transfer payments (i.e., federal grants to state and local governments) are not counted twice.

As we have already pointed out, government purchases fail to tell the whole story. Governments not only employ people and provide goods and services, they also tax the income of some and transfer it to others. Once transfer payments are included (the third measure of size), total government expenditures in 1989 amounted to $1,772.4 billion, or 34.1 percent of the gross national product (GNP).[2] The total tax bill (the fourth measure of size) was slightly less, amounting to 32.4 percent of GNP. Therefore, during 1989, approximately one-third of the national output was channeled through the public sector.

On a per capita basis, government expenditures were equal to $7,125 in 1989. If government expenditures in 1989 had been divided equally among the 92 million households in the United States, each household would have received $19,265.

THE CHANGING COMPOSITION OF GOVERNMENT

The federal government has traditionally been responsible for national defense in the United States. Since defense is a classic example of a public good, it is not surprising that this good is supplied through the public rather than through the private sector. Police and fire protection, road maintenance, and education have traditionally been financed and distributed by state and local governments. Each of these goods either generates external "spillover effects" or exhibits public-good characteristics. The police and fire departments available to help protect my life and property are also available for your protection. At least until congestion becomes a problem, my use of the roadways does not diminish their availability to you. Education contributes to the feasibility of a modern democratic society, thereby generating a benefit to persons other than those educated.

For many years, government has been involved in the provision of national defense, police and fire protection, roads, education, and other jointly consumed goods and services. Given the characteristics of such goods, government involvement in these areas is not surprising. Interestingly, these traditional public-sector functions are not responsible for the growth of government in recent years. As Exhibit 5a illustrates, government purchases of goods and services have fluctuated within a narrow band, around 20 percent of GNP, for more than three decades. Surprising perhaps to some, *federal* purchases of goods and services consume a smaller percent of GNP today than they did in the mid-1950s. As Exhibit 5a shows, federal purchases of goods and services as a share of GNP were 7.7 percent in 1989, down from 11.1 percent in 1955.

The expansion in the relative size of the public sector during the last three decades is almost exclusively the result of increased governmental involvement in income transfer activities. The government has emerged as a major redistributor of income from one group to another—from the working population to retirees, from the employed to the unemployed, from the taxpayer to disadvantaged groups (such as low-income households with dependent children). In 1955, income transfers were 4.5 percent of the GNP. Since the mid-1970s, the government has been redistributing almost 15 percent of total output away from current producers to income-transfer recipients.

Most of the expansion in the size of the transfer sector has taken place at the federal level. As a result, there has been a major change in the composition of activities undertaken by the federal government. Exhibit 5b illustrates this point. In

---

[2]The public administration costs associated with income transfer programs do involve the direct use of resources and they therefore are counted as government purchases. Only the redistribution portion is counted as a transfer payment.

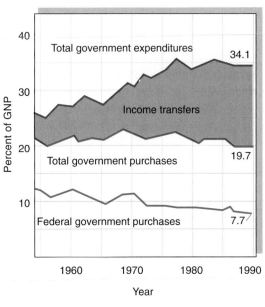

(a) Total government spending and income transfers as a share of GNP

(b) Government purchases and transfers as a share of the federal budget

---

Government Purchases, Transfer Payments, and the Changing Function of Government

State, local, and federal purchases of goods and services have accounted for approximately 20 percent of total output throughout the last three decades (frame a). The growth of transfer payments has accounted for the growth in the relative size of the public sector during this period. Frame (b) shows how government purchases and transfer payments have changed as a share of federal spending during the last three decades. Clearly, the federal government now plays a larger role as a redistributor of income and a smaller role as a purchaser of goods and services.

1989, only one-third of all federal expenditures was for the purchase of goods and services, down from two-thirds in 1955. On the other hand, income transfers consumed 37.5 percent of the federal budget in 1989, compared to less than 20 percent in 1955. It is clear that the federal government is now more heavily involved in income-redistribution activities than it is in the provision of public-sector goods and services.

FINANCING GOVERNMENT EXPENDITURES

If the government is going to supply goods, services, or income transfers, then these activities must be financed. Governments use three major sources of funds to pay for their expenditures: (1) taxes (2) user charges, and (3) borrowing.[3] In the United States, taxes are by far the largest source of governmental revenue. The power to tax sets governments apart from private businesses. Of course, a private business

---

[3]In addition to borrowing from private sources, the federal government also may borrow from its central bank. As we will see later, borrowing from a central bank is equivalent to the finance of government via the creation of money.

can put whatever price tag it wishes on its products; but no private business can force you to buy. With its power to tax, a government can force citizens to pay, regardless of whether they receive a ''good'' of equal or greater value in return.

Let's take a closer look at the taxes levied by governments and at the other sources of revenue available for the finance of government activities.

PERSONAL INCOME TAXES

Progressive Tax: A tax that requires those with higher taxable incomes to pay a larger percentage of their incomes to the government than those with lower taxable incomes.

Average Tax Rate: One's tax liability divided by one's taxable income.

The largest single source of revenue for governments is the personal income tax. The income tax is particularly important at the federal level, where it accounts for 40 percent of federal budget receipts (Exhibit 6). Since the Second World War, the income tax has also become an important source of revenue at the state level, where it now accounts for 10 percent of the tax receipts collected by the states. Only six states (Florida, Nevada, South Dakota, Texas, Washington, and Wyoming) now fail to levy a state income tax.

The structure of the federal income tax is progressive, although less so than in the past. A **progressive tax** takes a larger percentage from high-income recipients. For example, using the rate structure applicable to income in 1990, the tax liability of a single person with $20,000 of taxable income is $3,079. The **average tax rate** (ATR) can be expressed as follows:

$$ATR = \frac{\text{tax liability}}{\text{taxable income}}$$

EXHIBIT 6

Sources of Government Revenue, 1988

Personal income and payroll taxes are the major sources of revenue for the federal government. User charges, sales taxes, property taxes, and grants from the federal government provide the major revenue sources for state and local governments.

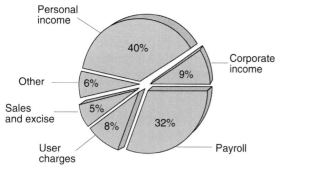

(a) Federal government

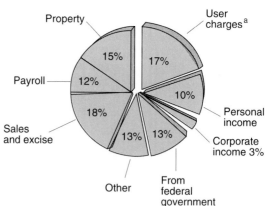

(b) State and local governments

Source: U.S. Department of Commerce, *Government Finances in 1987–1988*, (Washington, D.C.: U.S. Printing Office, 1990).

[a]Revenues from government operated utilities and liquor stores are included in this category.

The single person's average tax rate on $20,000 of income is 15.4 percent ($3,079/$20,000). Since the federal income tax structure is progressive, the average tax rate will increase with taxable income. For example, the tax liability (1990) of a single person with a taxable income of $40,000 is $8,679, resulting in an average tax rate of 21.7 percent, higher than the ATR for $20,000 of taxable income.

The economic way of thinking stresses that what happens at the margin is of crucial importance in personal decision-making. The **marginal tax rate** (MTR) can be expressed as follows:

$$MTR = \frac{change\ in\ tax\ liability}{change\ in\ income}$$

The marginal tax rate reveals both how much of one's additional income can be retained and how much must be turned over to the tax collector. For example, when the marginal tax rate is 25 percent, $25 of every $100 of additional earnings must be paid to the taxing authority. The individual is permitted to keep $75 of his or her additional income.

Marginal Tax Rate: Additional tax liability divided by additional income. Thus, if $100 of additional earnings increases one's tax liability by $30, the marginal tax rate would be 30 percent.

PAYROLL TAXES

Although income from all sources is covered by the income tax, only earnings derived from labor are subject to the payroll tax. Interest, dividends, rents, and other income derived from capital are not subject to payroll taxes. Payroll taxes on the earnings of employees and self-employed workers are used to finance social security (including Medicare) and unemployment compensation benefits. Payroll taxes constitute the second largest and most rapidly expanding source of tax revenue. In 1988, payroll taxes comprised 32 percent of all federal revenues, compared to only 16 percent in 1960.

Payroll taxes are often criticized because of their regressive structure. Actually, the payroll tax encompasses both proportional and regressive features. A **proportional tax** is one that takes the same percentage of income from all taxpayers, regardless of income level. Until the maximum taxable income ceiling is reached, the payroll tax is proportional. For example, in 1991, each employee pays a tax rate of 7.65 percent on earnings up to $53,400. Beyond that taxable income ceiling, no additional payroll tax is levied. So, a worker earning $10,000 incurs a payroll tax of $765, whereas one earning $20,000 is taxed twice that amount, or $1,530. Until the taxable income ceiling is met, all workers pay exactly the same tax rate.

A **regressive tax** takes a smaller *percentage* of income from those in high-earnings brackets than it does from low-income recipients. Since the social security payroll tax does not apply beyond the maximum income ceiling, it is regressive for incomes beyond that point. For example, a person with an income twice the taxable ceiling will pay exactly the same amount of payroll taxes (and only one-half the average tax rate) as another individual whose earnings are equal to the taxable ceiling. All people with earnings above the taxable ceiling will pay a lower average tax rate than people with earnings below the ceiling. Thus, since the payroll tax does not apply to earnings above the ceiling, its basic structure can be considered regressive.

Proportional Tax: A tax for which individuals pay the same percentage of their income (or other tax base) in taxes, regardless of income level.

Regressive Tax: A tax that takes a smaller percentage of one's income as one's income level increases. Thus, the proportion of income allocated to the tax would be greater for the poor than for the rich.

SALES AND EXCISE TAXES

Taxes levied on the consumption expenditures for a wide range of goods and services are called sales taxes. A tax levied on specific commodities, such as gasoline, cigarettes, or alcoholic beverages, is called an excise tax. There is little difference between the two, except that one is a general tax and the other is quite specific.

Sales and excise taxes provided 18 percent of the revenue for state and local governments in 1988. They are particularly important at the state level where they account for almost a third of the revenue raised by state governments.

PROPERTY TAXES

Despite their unpopularity, property taxes still constitute the bulk of local tax revenues. In 1988, 74 percent of the tax revenue raised by local governments was generated from this source. Property taxes are often criticized because they are cumbersome. The assessor must set a value on taxable property. This generally involves a certain amount of judgment and arbitrariness. During a period of rising prices, property that has recently been exchanged is likely to command a higher valuation than similar property without an easily identifiable indicator of current value. High administration costs and problems associated with providing equal treatment for similarly situated taxpayers reduce the attractiveness of property taxes.

CORPORATE INCOME TAX

The corporate income tax is levied on the accounting profits of the business firm. Its structure is relatively simple. In 1990, the first $50,000 of corporate profit was taxed at a rate of 15 percent. Corporate earnings in the range from $50,000 to $75,000 were taxed at a rate of 25 percent. All corporate earnings above $75,000 were taxed at a flat rate of 34 percent. Corporate incomes in the United States have been taxed since 1909. The tax currently generates approximately 9 percent of all federal tax receipts and 3 percent of the revenue of state and local governments (see Exhibit 6).

Inadvertently, the corporate income tax encourages debt financing rather than equity ownership. This results because no adjustment is made for factors of production owned by the firm and the equity capital invested by the owners. A corporation that uses debt financing will incur an interest cost, which will reduce its accounting profits and tax liability. In contrast, if the same firm uses equity financing (that is, raises financial capital by issuing additional stock), the interest cost will not appear on the firm's accounting statement. Therefore, even though there is an opportunity cost of capital, regardless of whether it is raised by equity financing or by debt, only the latter will reduce the firm's tax liability.

USER CHARGES

Not all government revenue comes from taxes. For some services, governments charge consumers a price, just as private businesses do. User charges differ from taxes in that one's payment is directly linked to the consumption of a good or service. Citizens who do not consume the government-provided good or service do not have to pay for it. User charges are particularly important at the state and local level where they account for 17 percent of government revenue. Local governments often provide utility services, garbage pick-up, hospital care, and bus transportation. These government-operated businesses—many of which are in competition with private firms—are often partially or entirely financed by prices charged to the users of these services. In general, when the nature of the good permits, economists favor the use of charges rather than taxes, since the former provide better information on whether consumers value the good or service produced more than its cost of production.

Sometimes taxes can be used to approximate the effects of a user charge. For example, an excise tax on gasoline used to finance roads imposes the cost of the roads on individuals roughly in proportion to their consumption (use). Similarly, if a civic auditorium is operated by the government, a ticket tax used to finance the arena's cost approximates a user charge.

BORROWING

In addition to taxes and user charges, government has one other method of financing expenditures: borrowing. When the total spending exceeds revenue from taxes and user charges, the government will have to borrow to cover its budget deficit. Governments generally borrow by issuing interest-bearing bonds. In effect, the bonds commit the government to higher future taxes in order to meet the interest obligations on the bonds.

In recent years, the federal government has borrowed funds to cover a major proportion—approximately 20 percent during the 1980s—of its expenditures. Constitutional provisions often limit the borrowing powers of state governments. Thus, state and local governments borrow much less than the federal government. In fact, state and local governments in aggregate have run substantial budget surpluses in recent years.

THE ISSUES OF EFFICIENCY AND EQUITY

There are two major factors to consider when choosing among taxation alternatives. First, taxes should be consistent with the concept of economic efficiency. Taxes should not encourage people to use scarce resources wastefully. A tax system is inconsistent with economic efficiency if it encourages individuals (a) to buy goods costing more than their value to consumers and/or (b) to channel time into tax-avoidance activities.

Second, a tax system should be equitable; that is, it should be consistent with widely accepted principles of fairness. Economists often speak of "horizontal" and "vertical" equity. Horizontal equity means equal treatment of equals. If two parties earn equal incomes, for example, horizontal equity implies that the two should be taxed equally. The corollary concept of vertical equity requires that persons who are situated differently should be taxed differently. It encompasses what economists

Ability-to-Pay Principle: The equity concept that people with larger incomes (or more consumption or more wealth) should be taxed at a higher rate because their ability to pay is presumably greater. The concept is subjective and fails to reveal how much higher the rate of taxation should be as income increases.

refer to as the **ability-to-pay principle,** the seemingly straight-forward idea that taxes should be levied according to the ability of the taxpayer to pay. Deciding exactly what this means, however, is at least partially subjective. Most people find it reasonable that the rich should pay more taxes than the poor. This would be the case under a proportional tax system since high-income taxpayers would pay the flat (constant) rate on a larger tax base. Many find it reasonable that the rich should pay a *higher proportion* of their income (or wealth or consumption) in taxes than the poor. Of course, progressive taxation incorporates this concept. But, how much higher should the rate be for those with higher incomes? At this point, the consensus breaks down. There is little agreement among either laymen or professional economists about the proper degree of tax progressivity.

A tax system must take equity into account if it is to succeed. The cost of enforcing a system widely presumed to be unreasonable or unfair is certain to be extremely high. Equity, though, must be balanced with efficiency. A tax system that ignores economic efficiency will also be extremely costly to an economy.

TAXES AND ECONOMIC EFFICIENCY

An ideal tax system would not alter the incentive of individuals to allocate their time and income into those areas that yield them the most satisfaction. A tax of this kind is called a **neutral tax.** A neutral tax would not encourage individuals to spend more of their income on business travel, housing, medical service, or professional association publications and less of their income on food and clothing because the former are tax-deductible and the latter are not. Similarly, a neutral tax would not encourage an individual to allocate more time and money to investments that reduce the tax burden (depreciable assets, municipal bonds, tax-free retirement plans, and so on), and less time and money to savings and work activities that generate taxable income.

There is a problem, though, with the concept of a neutral tax. Probably the only tax that would meet the hypothetical ideal of neutrality is a **head tax,** a tax imposing an equal lump-sum tax on all individuals. A head tax would impose the same dollar tax liability on the poor as it would on the rich (or the same liability on those who consume few goods as on those who consume many goods). Since a head tax conflicts with the concept of vertical equity—the view that persons who are situated differently should be taxed differently—it fails to pass our test of fairness.

Thus, we generally tax things such as income, consumption, and property. However, taxes on these items distort pricing signals and thereby cause individuals to forgo productive activities. Economists refer to this inefficiency and the accompanying reduction in private-sector output over and above the tax revenue collected as the **excess burden of taxation.** It is easy to think of cases that illustrate the excess burden of taxation. For example, if two individuals decide to forgo a mutually advantageous exchange because a tax makes the transaction unprofitable, they incur a burden from the taxation even though they do not pay a tax, because the transaction did not take place. Similarly, if a taxpayer decides to allocate more time to leisure or to household production and less time to market work—because the tax system limits the individual's ability to retain income generated by market work—a burden over and above tax revenues collected from the individual is imposed. Income from market work is lost to the individual, and whatever benefits for others that might have resulted from the work are sacrificed. Excess burdens reflect economic inefficiency, relative to our hypothetical ideal. They impose a **deadweight loss** on an economy, because they reflect a cost imposed on some individuals without any offsetting benefit to others.

Exhibit 7 illustrates the distinction between the tax burden associated with the transfer of purchasing power and the excess burden of taxation. Here we show the impact of a 40-cent tax imposed on each pack of cigarettes. Prior to the imposition of the tax, 35 billion packs of cigarettes were produced and sold to consumers at a market price of 80 cents per pack. The cigarette tax increases the cost of supplying and marketing cigarettes by 40 cents per pack. Thus, the supply curve of cigarettes shifts vertically by the amount of the tax. Consumers, however, would not continue to purchase as many cigarettes if the full burden of the tax were passed on to them in the form of a 40-cent increase in the per-pack price. So, when the supply curve shifts vertically, the market price of cigarettes rises by less than the amount of the tax. Since the number of cigarettes demanded is thus responsive to the higher price, some of the tax burden will fall on cigarette producers. In our hypothetical example, the new equilibrium price for cigarettes will become $1 per pack, with an annual output rate of 30 billion packs of cigarettes. The tax will raise $12 billion (40 cents

Neutral Tax: A tax that does not (a) distort consumer buying patterns or producer production methods or (b) induce individuals to engage in tax avoidance activities. There will be no excess burden if a tax is neutral.

Head Tax: A lump-sum tax levied on all individuals, regardless of their income, consumption, wealth, or other indicators of economic well-being.

Excess Burden of Taxation: A burden of taxation over and above the burden associated with the transfer of revenues to the government. An excess burden usually reflects losses that occur when beneficial activities are forgone because they are taxed.

Deadweight Loss: A net loss associated with the forgoing of an economic action. The loss does not lead to an offsetting gain for other participants. It thus reflects economic inefficiency.

EXHIBIT 7

The Impact of a Tax on Economic Activity

Here we illustrate the impact of a 40-cent tax (per pack) on cigarettes. Since the tax increases the cost of supplying cigarettes for consumption, the supply curve is shifted vertically by the amount of the tax. At the higher price, however, consumers reduce their consumption. The equilibrium price increases from 80 cents to $1 per pack. Consumers pay 20 cents more per pack and sellers receive 20 cents less as the result of the 40-cent tax. In addition, consumers and producers lose the mutual gains from exchange (triangle ABC) that would be realized if the tax did not reduce the volume of trade between cigarette producers and consumers.

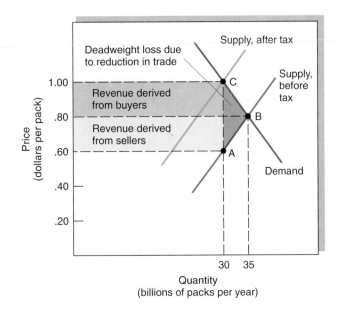

Tax Incidence: The manner in which the burden of the tax is distributed among economic units (consumers, employees, employers, and so on). The tax burden does not always fall on those who pay the tax.

times 30 billion packs) of revenue. Buyers will pay 20 cents more per pack for the 30 billion packs of cigarettes purchased after the tax is imposed. Simultaneously, sellers will receive 20 cents less per pack. The tax thus transfers $12 billion of revenue from cigarette buyers and sellers to the government. Note, though, that the quantity of cigarettes produced and consumed has fallen by 5 billion packs. The mutually advantageous gains that would have accrued to producers and consumers from these unrealized trades (the triangle ABC) are lost. (Remember that trade is a positive-sum game, so a reduction in the volume of trade will result in economic loss.) This loss of welfare (triangle ABC) associated with the unrealized exchanges imposes an excess burden on buyers and sellers over and above the burden accompanying the transfer of revenue to the government. Clearly, the triangle ABC is a deadweight loss, since it is not accompanied by an offsetting gain in the form of additional tax revenue for the government.

In our example, the burden of the tax was divided equally between sellers and buyers. This will not always be the case. If the demand curve were steeper (and the supply curve flatter), the price of the taxed good would rise by a larger amount, imposing more of the burden on buyers. In contrast, if the demand curve were flatter (and the supply curve steeper), the market price would rise by a smaller amount, and a larger share of the tax burden would fall on sellers.

The burden of taxes is not always borne by the person who writes a check to the Internal Revenue Service. Economists use the term **tax incidence** when discussing the question of how the burden of a tax is distributed among parties. Since the distribution of the tax burden is dependent on the slope of the supply and demand curves for the activity being taxed, it is not easy to determine how it is distributed among parties.

TAX RATES, WORK EFFORT, AND TAX AVOIDANCE

The 1980s were a decade of substantial debate concerning the impact of taxes, particularly high marginal tax rates, on the incentive of individuals to earn taxable income and to engage in tax avoidance activities. Prior to 1980, most economists believed that the tax rate on income exerted little adverse influence on the incentive

The Controversy Concerning the Incentive Effects of the Income Tax

Here we illustrate two alternative outcomes associated with the imposition of a 20 percent tax on income. According to the traditional view (a), when the aggregate labor supply curve is vertical, or nearly vertical, the tax will result in only a small reduction in work effort (from 40 to 39 hours per week). In contrast, according to a more recent view (b), if the labor supply curve is flatter, the tax will lead to a larger reduction (from 40 to 36 hours per week) in time spent generating taxable income.

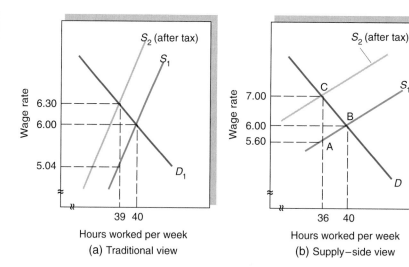

(a) Traditional view

(b) Supply–side view

Supply-Side Economists: Modern economists who believe that changes in marginal tax rates exert important effects on output and the efficiency of resource use.

Underground Economy: Unreported barter and cash transactions that take place outside recorded market channels. Some are otherwise legal activities undertaken to evade taxes. Others involve illegal activities such as trafficking in drugs, prostitution, extortion, and similar crimes.

of individuals to engage in productive activity. According to this traditional view, workers lack viable alternatives to the earning of taxable income. Because of this, they will be unable, or virtually unable, to shift from current work to other income-generating activities in order to partially avoid the tax burden.

The traditional view was seriously challenged by **supply-side economists** during the 1980s. The challengers stressed the linkage between marginal tax rates and the incentive to earn taxable income. As marginal tax rates increase, there is less incentive to earn and more incentive to engage in tax avoidance and even illegal tax evasion. Therefore, when confronting high marginal tax rates, some taxpayers will take longer vacations and reduce their hours of work. Similarly, spouses in high-income families will choose to drop out of the labor force or work only part-time. Still other workers confronting high tax rates will take jobs with lower pay but higher nonmonetary benefits. Simultaneously, tax avoidance will increase. Some will engage in business ventures designed to show an accounting loss which will shelter income from the tax collector. Others will spend more money on pleasurable, tax-deductible expenditures, such as plush offices, Hawaiian business conferences, and various fringe benefits (for example, a company luxury automobile, business entertainment, and a company retirement plan). All of these activities are perfectly legal methods of reducing one's tax liability. However, some individuals will also use illegal means to evade the payment of taxes. Participation in the **underground economy** is one device that many believe is widely used to avoid and reduce taxes (see "The Underground Economy" box). If this supply-side view is correct—if there are fairly good, feasible alternatives to the payment of the higher tax rates—both taxable income and the amount of labor supplied to taxable work activities will decrease significantly as marginal tax rates rise.

Exhibit 8 uses supply and demand analysis to illustrate the economics of this debate as it relates to the issue of work effort. Here we consider a labor market in which workers earn an equilibrium wage of $6 per hour in the absence of income taxation. Forty hours of work per week are supplied by each worker in this market at the $6 hourly wage. Now, consider the impact of a flat 20 percent tax rate on income (or payroll). Just as the cigarette tax made it more costly to supply that product, so, too, will the income tax make it more costly to supply labor. The supply curve of labor will then decline (shift vertically) by the amount of the tax. According to the traditional view, illustrated by Exhibit 8a, the income tax will exert relatively little impact on hours worked, since the aggregate supply curve of labor is vertical (or almost vertical). The equilibrium wage, including the tax, will only be slightly higher ($6.30 per hour), and the after-tax wage rate of workers will decline substantially (to $5.04). Since the labor supply curve is almost vertical, the burden of the income tax will fall primarily on workers. Furthermore, this will be true regardless of whether the tax is paid directly by the individuals (as in the case of the personal income tax) or whether the check to the IRS is made out by their employer (as in the case of the payroll tax).

The supply-side challengers to the traditional view argue that when marginal tax rates are extremely high, say 40 percent or more, the supply curve for labor will

MEASURES OF ECONOMIC ACTIVITY

The Underground Economy

High marginal tax rates increase the incentive of individuals to participate in the underground economy to escape taxation. The underground economy encompasses unreported production and exchange, often conducted in cash to avoid possible detection.

There are two major components of the underground economy: (a) production and distribution of illegal goods and services and (b) the nonreporting of transactions involving legal goods and services. Drug trafficking, smuggling, prostitution, and other criminal activities are examples of the first component. Income from such activities is generally unreported to avoid detection by law enforcement authorities.

Of course, even when the work activity is legal, it is illegal to earn income and not report it to the taxing authorities. However, the likelihood of detection by authorities is very small for certain types of activities. Since cash transactions are difficult to trace, they provide the life-blood of the underground economy. The

participants in the legal-if-reported portion of the underground economy are diverse. Taxicab drivers and waitresses may pocket fees and tips. Small-business proprietors may fail to ring up cash sales. Craft and professional workers may fail to report cash income. All of these individuals are participating in the underground economy.

In addition, it is estimated that millions of employees, ranging from farm laborers to bartenders, are paid in cash. Company books fail to record their employment. Neither income taxes nor social security deductions are withheld. The employer evades the payroll taxes, while employees pocket "tax-free" cash wage payments without endangering their eligibility for welfare or unemployment benefits.

For obvious reasons, it is difficult to accurately measure the size of the underground economy. Based on data from its special audits, the IRS estimates that underground activities constitute approximately 10 percent of the U.S. economy. Peter

Gutmann of Baruch College believes the U.S. underground economy is even larger, closer to 15 percent.[4]

The underground economy is not a problem unique to the United States. In fact, available evidence indicates it is even more widespread in Western Europe (where tax rates are higher) and in South America (where regulation makes it costly to operate legally). The Organization for Economic Cooperation and Development estimates that between 3 and 5 percent of the total labor force in Western Europe is working "off the books" and thereby evading taxes. In Italy, Great Britain, and Sweden, the estimated size of the underground economy ranges from 10 to 30 percent of the national income. Apparently, the underground economy has become a sizable sector of Western economies.

[4]Peter M. Gutmann, "The Subterranean Economy," *Taxing and Spending,* April, 1979.

be flatter, as illustrated by Exhibit 8b. If this is the case, the vertical shift in the labor supply curve will cause a larger decline in the work time allocated to activities that generate taxable income. For example, hours might decline from 40 per week to 36 per week (rather than to only 39 hours per week in the traditional view). Simultaneously, the higher tax rates will lead to an increase in tax-avoidance activities. Waste and sizable deadweight losses will be incurred.

The triangle ABC (Exhibit 8b), which indicates only the inefficiency stemming from lost hours of work, is one measure of allocative inefficiency. However, it actually understates society's excess burden. In addition to the decline in hours worked, the high marginal tax rates channel resources into tax avoidance, rent seeking, and low-return investment projects (that are undertaken because of their tax advantages), activities that are counterproductive from society's viewpoint.

TAX RATES, TAX REVENUES, AND THE LAFFER CURVE

Tax Rate: The per-unit or percentage rate at which an economic activity is taxed.

Tax Base: The level of the activity that is taxed. For example, if an excise tax is levied on each gallon of gasoline, the tax base is the number of gallons of gasoline sold. Since higher tax rates generally make the taxed activity less attractive, the size of the tax base is inversely related to the rate at which the activity is taxed.

Laffer Curve: A curve illustrating the relationship between tax rates and tax revenues. The curve reflects the fact that tax revenues are low for both very high and very low tax rates.

It is important to distinguish between a change in **tax rates** and a change in tax revenues. The quantity or level of an activity that is taxed—the **tax base**—is inversely related to the rate at which the activity is taxed. An increase in a tax rate will lead to a less-than-proportional increase in tax revenues. Higher tax rates will make it more costly to engage in the activity, thereby inducing individuals to shift to substitutes. If there are attractive substitutes, the decline in the activity due to the tax may be substantial. Perhaps a real-world example will help clarify this point. In 1981, the District of Columbia increased the tax rate on gasoline from 10 cents to 13 cents per gallon, a 30 percent increase. Tax revenues, however, did not increase by 30 percent—they expanded by only 12 percent. Why? The higher tax rate discouraged motorists from purchasing gasoline in the District of Columbia. There was a pretty good alternative to the purchase of the more highly taxed (and therefore higher-priced) gasoline—the purchase of gasoline in Virginia and Maryland, where the tax rates (and therefore prices) were slightly lower. Because of this, the quantity of gasoline sold in Washington, D.C., declined. The revenue gains associated with the higher tax rates were partially eroded by a decline in the tax base.

Economist Arthur Laffer has popularized the idea that higher tax rates can sometimes shrink the tax base so much that tax revenues will decline despite the higher tax rates. As the result of Laffer's efforts, the curve illustrating the relationship between tax rates and tax revenues is now called the **Laffer curve.** Exhibit 9 illustrates the concept of the Laffer curve for the taxation of income-generating activity. Obviously, tax revenues would be zero if the tax rate were zero. What is not so obvious is that tax revenues would also be zero (or at least very close to zero) if the tax rate were 100 percent. Confronting a 100 percent tax rate, most individuals would go fishing or find something else to do rather than engage in taxable productive activity, since the 100 percent tax rate would completely remove the material reward derived from earning taxable income. Production in the taxed sector would come to a halt, and without production, tax revenues would plummet to zero.

As tax rates are reduced from 100 percent, the incentive to work and earn taxable income increases, income expands, and tax revenues rise. Similarly, as tax rates increase from zero, tax revenues expand. Clearly, at some rate greater than zero but less than 100 percent, tax revenues will be maximized (point B, Exhibit 9). This is not to imply that the tax rate that maximizes revenue is ideal. In fact, as the maximum revenue point (B) is approached, relatively large tax rate increases will be necessary to expand tax revenues. In this range, the excess burden of taxation will be substantial.

EXHIBIT 9

The Laffer Curve

Since taxation affects the amount of the activity being taxed, a change in tax rates will not lead to a proportional change in tax revenues. As the Laffer curve indicates, beyond some point (*B*), an increase in tax rates may actually cause tax revenues to fall. Since large tax rate increases will lead to only a small expansion in tax revenue as *B* is approached, there is no presumption that point *B* is an ideal rate of taxation.

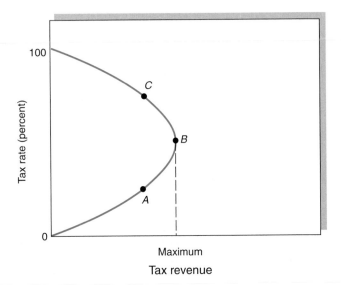

CHANGES IN TAX POLICY DURING THE 1980s

The 1980s were a period of substantial changes in tax policy in the United States. Under a nonindexed progressive income tax structure, inflation pushes more and more taxpayers into high marginal tax brackets. This was precisely what happened during the 1970s. As more and more taxpayers confronted marginal tax rates of 45 percent and up, tax avoidance activities grew. Increasingly, investment decisions were based on tax considerations rather than on profitability. The belief that lower tax rates would reduce wasteful tax avoidance and economic distortions, and thereby promote economic growth provided the foundation for the modifications in the U.S. personal income tax structure during the 1980s.

Four major structural changes in the personal income tax were instituted during the 1980s. First, the highest marginal tax rates were sharply reduced during the decade. In 1980 there were 14 different marginal tax brackets, ranging from a beginning rate of 14 percent to a top rate of 70 percent. Legislation passed in 1981 cut tax rates in all brackets by approximately 25 percent over a three-year period. The top marginal rate was sliced to 50 percent, while the beginning rate was reduced to 11 percent. Later, legislation passed in 1986 reduced the number of brackets to only three (with marginal rates of 15, 28, and 33 percent). Therefore, in less than a decade the top marginal tax rate in the United States was sliced from 70 percent to 33 percent.

Second, in order to offset revenue losses from the lower marginal tax rates, the 1986 legislation eliminated various deductions and exclusions from the taxable income base. The deductibility of state and local sales taxes, nonmortgage consumer interest expenses, and contributions to Individual Retirement Accounts was eliminated. Long-term capital gains income on the sale of assets was fully included (previously only 40 percent of capital gains income was included) in the tax base. Limitations were imposed on net losses from passive investments and from active real-estate investments in the case of high-income taxpayers. The permissible allowances for the depreciation of assets were decelerated, reversing the effects of the 1981 Act. This combination of factors—lower marginal tax rates and the more stringent limitations on the deductibility of investment losses—substantially reduces the attractiveness of investments driven by tax considerations rather than income-generating potential.

Third, the 1986 legislation also increased the personal exemption allowance for each taxpayer, spouse, and dependent from $1,080 to $2,000. The standard deduction (the income allowance to taxpayers who do not itemize their deductions) was increased substantially. As the result of these changes, a family of four can now earn approximately $12,000 without confronting any federal income tax liability. Increases in the personal exemption allowance and standard deduction reduce the average tax liability of low-income recipients more than those with higher income. Thus, these modifications contribute to the progressivity of the overall structure, partially offsetting the decline in progressivity implied by the sharp reduction in the highest marginal tax rates.

Finally, the 1981 legislation also provided for indexing of the personal income tax structure. **Indexing** adjusts money income figures for the effects of inflation and thereby prevents rising prices from pushing people into higher tax brackets. With indexing, tax brackets are widened each year to compensate for the inflation-induced component of a rising money income (see box, ''How Does Indexing Work?'').

Indexing: The automatic increasing of money values as the general level of prices increases. Economic variables that are often indexed include wage rates and tax brackets.

Critics of the 1980s' tax policies argue that the policies were a bonanza for the rich. As the result of the decline in the progressivity of the rate structure, taxes now take a smaller share of the income of high earners than was previously the case. As we begin the 1990s, numerous politicians are calling for increases in the top marginal tax rates.

In analyzing the position of the critics, once again it is important to distinguish between changes in *tax rates* and changes in *tax revenues*. As the Laffer curve analysis indicates, reduction in high marginal tax rates can sometimes increase the

MEASURES OF ECONOMIC ACTIVITY

How Does Indexing Work?

Since 1985, the personal-income-tax-structure in the United States has been indexed. Indexing expands the tax brackets (and personal-exemption allowance) in proportion to the increase in prices.

An example will help clarify how indexing works. Suppose a marginal tax rate of 10 percent is applied to the initial income bracket of $0 to $5,000, and also suppose that higher marginal tax rates are applicable at higher levels of income. In the absence of indexing, taxpayers whose

incomes merely keep pace with inflation are pushed into higher tax brackets. For example, if a 10 percent inflation rate expands the taxable income of a worker from $5,000 to $5,500, it pushes that taxpayer into a higher tax bracket. Both the taxpayer's average and marginal tax rates are increased, even though the expansion in income merely reflects the general rise in prices. Indexing widens the tax brackets for the effects of inflation and thereby keeps inflation from pushing taxpayers with incomes of constant

purchasing power into higher tax brackets. With indexing, the $0–$5,000 income bracket would be expanded to $0–$5,500, when prices increase by 10 percent. So, when inflation increases the income of a taxpayer by 10 percent, the taxpayer's average and marginal tax rates remain constant. Indexing thus protects individuals from unlegislated tax increases that, under a progressive tax system, would otherwise be automatically imposed by inflation.

EXHIBIT 10 ■ The Change in Federal Income Tax Revenue Derived from Various Income Groups, 1981–1988			
	Tax Revenue Collected from Group **(in billions of 1982–1984 dollars)**		
Income Group	*1981*	*1988*	*Percent Change* *1981–1988*
Top 10 percent of Earners	150.6	199.8	+32.7
Top 1 percent	55.9	96.2	+72.1
Top 5 percent	110.5	159.2	+44.1
All Other	161.8	149.1	−7.8
Total	312.4	348.9	+11.7

Source: U.S. Department of Treasury, Internal Revenue Service

tax revenue collected from high-income taxpayers. When high marginal rates—for example tax rates of 45 percent or more—are reduced, high-income taxpayers are encouraged to work more hours and make fewer tax-shelter investments. As a result, economic efficiency will improve since investments based on tax considerations often waste resources. Of course, the observed income of the rich will increase rapidly (as less of their income is sheltered by tax avoidance activities), but the taxes paid by the rich will increase, also. Supply-side economists believe that this is precisely what happened in 1964 when the Kennedy-Johnson administration cut tax rates (see Applications in Economics box ''The Incentive Effects of the 1964 Tax Cut'') and they believe that the same forces were at work during the 1980s.

Exhibit 10 presents data on the tax revenue collected from various income categories both before and after the structural changes of the 1980s. Adjusted for inflation, the income tax revenue collected from the top 10 percent of earners rose from $150.6 billion in 1981 to $199.8 billion in 1988, an increase of 32.7 percent. The percent increases in the real tax revenue collected from the top 1 and top 5 percent of taxpayers were even larger. In contrast, the tax liability of other taxpayers declined from $161.8 billion to $149.1 billion, a reduction of 7.8 percent. Therefore, even though their *rates* were reduced sharply, the income tax revenue collected from high-income taxpayers rose substantially during the 1980s.

It is interesting to view Exhibit 10 (and Exhibit 11 in Applications in Economics box) within the framework of the Laffer curve. The evidence indicates that most taxpayers were on the upward-sloping portion (the AB range of Exhibit 9) of the Laffer curve. For these taxpayers, changes in tax rates and tax revenues were directly related. However, a few taxpayers, perhaps 10 percent in 1980, confronted marginal tax rates at or above the revenue maximum level. For this small group, the incentive effects of rate changes were very important.[5] Therefore, the rates of these taxpayers could be reduced without substantial loss of revenue. In the case of extremely high rates, for example marginal rates of 45 percent of more, the lower rates may actually have increased tax revenues.

---

[5]A study for the National Bureau of Economic Research by Harvard professor Lawrence Lindsey estimates that, in the United States, marginal personal income rates above 43 percent reduce tax revenues. See Lawrence Lindsey, *Estimating the Revenue Maximizing Top Personal Tax Rate* (New York: National Bureau of Economic Research—Working Paper 1761, 1985) and *The Growth Experiment: How The New Tax Policy Is Transforming The U.S. Economy* (New York: Basic Books, 1989). Also see James E. Long and James D. Gwartney, ''Income Tax Avoidance: Evidence from Individual Tax Returns'' *National Tax Journal,* December 1987, for additional evidence on this topic.

APPLICATIONS IN ECONOMICS

The Incentive Effects of the 1964 Tax Cut

The incentive effects of reductions in tax rates are generally far more important in the highest tax brackets.

Consider the impact of a reduction in a marginal tax rate from 70 percent to 50 percent on the incentive of a high-income professional or business executive to earn *taxable* income. When confronting a 70 percent marginal tax rate, the taxpayer gets to keep only 30 cents of each additional dollar earned by cutting costs, producing more, or investing more wisely. However, after the tax cut, take-home pay from each dollar of taxable income jumps to 50 cents—a whopping 67 percent increase in the incentive to earn. Predictably, high-income taxpayers will then spend more time finding ways to cut business costs and increase earnings and less time on tax avoidance activities.

In contrast, consider the incentive effects of an *identical* percentage rate reduction in lower tax brackets. Suppose the 14 percent marginal rate were cut to 10 percent. Take-home pay, per dollar of additional earnings, would expand from 86 cents to 90 cents, only a 5 percent increase. Compared with the incentive effects in the upper brackets, the same percentage tax cut in the lower tax brackets would lead to a much smaller increase in take-home pay and thus a much smaller increase in the incentive to earn more taxable income.

Since the incentive effects of a proportional rate reduction (one that cuts all rates by the same percent) will be greater in the upper tax brackets, taxable income will increase most in these brackets. The growth in the taxable income base will offset, at least partially, revenue losses emanating from the lower rates. As the Laffer curve analysis indicates, if the incentive effects are strong, it is even possible for lower rates to lead to an increase in tax revenue.

Clearly, this is most likely to be the case for high income taxpayers confronting high tax rates.

The Kennedy-Johnson tax cut was consistent with this view. This 1964 tax cut sliced the top marginal bracket from 91 percent to 70 percent, leading to a 233 percent increase (from 9 cents to 30 cents per additional dollar of earnings) in take-home pay from marginal income in this bracket. The bottom rate was cut from 20 percent to 14 percent—about the same proportional tax reduction. But, after-tax income, per dollar of additional earnings, in the bottom bracket, rose from 80 cents to 86 cents, an increase of only 7.5 percent.

Just as one would expect, given the incentive effects accompanying the rate reductions, *taxable incomes* grew rapidly in the upper tax brackets after the tax cut. This growth in the tax base partially offset revenue losses due to the rate reductions, particularly

Perhaps influenced by the U.S. experience, countries around the world are beginning to question the wisdom of high marginal tax rates. Of 86 countries with an income tax, 55 reduced their top marginal tax rate during the 1985–1990 period, while only two (Luxembourg and Lebanon) increased their top rate. As Exhibit 12 illustrates, Australia, Brazil, Italy, Japan, New Zealand, Sweden, and the United Kingdom substantially reduced their top marginal tax rates during the latter half of the 1980s.

WHO PAYS THE TAX BILL?

How is the overall burden of taxation distributed among income groupings? This is not an easy question to answer. As we have discussed, several different types of taxes are levied. It is difficult to identify who actually bears the burden of many taxes. In some cases, taxes are designed to act as a proxy for a user charge for public services. Motor fuel taxes to finance roads provide an example. Taxes of this type are intended to allocate costs to users, independent of income.

in the highest tax brackets. Exhibit 11 presents data on tax revenue before and after the 1964 tax cut, according to percentile income groupings. Adjusted for inflation, the tax liability of the bottom 95 percentile of returns fell. For these taxpayers, lower tax rates meant less tax revenue. The negative impact of the rate reduction on tax revenues was dominant over the positive impact of income growth on tax revenues.

However, the picture for the top 5 percent of taxpayers was quite different. Despite the roughly 20 percent lower tax rates, measured in constant dollars, the revenues collected from the top 5 percent of earners rose from $17.17 billion in 1963 to $18.49 billion in 1965, a healthy increase of 7.7 percent. Tax revenue collected from these high-income taxpayers grew because the rapid expansion in their taxable income more than offset the loss of tax revenue associated with the rate reductions.

The experience of the 1964 tax cut convinced many economists that the incentive effects of rate reductions in the top tax brackets were important. Thus, they forecast that the 1980 rate cuts would stimulate income and tax collections in the top tax brackets. As Exhibit 10 shows, the evidence from the 1980s is supportive of this view.

EXHIBIT 11 ■ **The Change in Federal Income Tax Revenue Derived from Various Income Groupings, 1963–1965**

The tax revenues are ranked according to adjusted gross income prior to and subsequent to the 1964 reduction in tax rates.

Percentile of All Returns (ranked from lowest to highest income	Tax Revenues Collected from Group (in billions of 1963 dollars)[a]		
	1963	*1965*	*Percent Changes*
Bottom 50 percent	$ 5.01	$ 4.55	−9.2
50th and 75th percentile	10.02	9.61	−4.1
75th to 95th percentile	16.00	15.41	−3.7
Top 5 percent	17.17	18.49	+7.7
Total	$48.20	$48.06	−0.3

[a]These estimates were derived by interpolation.
Source: Internal Revenue Service, *Statistics of Income: Individual Income Tax Returns* (1963 and 1965).

The late Joseph Pechman of the Brookings Institution conducted a detailed study of the incidence of taxes in the United States.[6] Pechman's findings indicate that overall the U. S. tax structure is within the proportional-to-mildly progressive range. Even Pechman's assumptions that yielded his most progressive estimates project that high-income recipients pay only slightly higher average tax rates—27.3 percent compared with 20.6 percent—than households with much lower incomes.

Edgar Browning of Texas A&M and William Johnson of the University of Virginia dispute the findings of the Pechman study.[7] According to Browning and Johnson, the U. S. tax structure is highly progressive. The Browning-Johnson study indicates that the overall average tax rate of high-income groups is approximately three times the average rate of low-income groups.

A recent study of the federal tax structure by the Congressional Budget Office (CBO) indicates that the federal taxes are quite progressive, though somewhat less

---

[6]Joseph Pechman, *Who Paid the Taxes, 1966–85?* (Washington, D.C.: The Brookings Institution, 1985).
[7]Edgar K. Browning and William R. Johnson, *The Distribution of the Tax Burden* (Washington, D.C.: American Enterprise Institute, 1979).

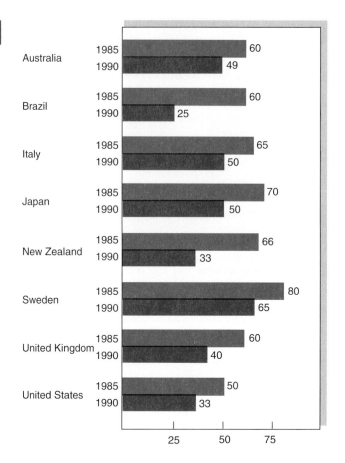

EXHIBIT 12

Cuts in Top Marginal Tax Rates

As the accompanying chart illustrates, several nations reduced their top marginal tax rates during the latter half of the 1980s.

Highest marginal tax rate

so than during the 1970s.[8] The CBO study estimated the incidence of the federal personal income, corporate income, payroll, and excise taxes. These four taxes account for 93 percent of the federal tax revenue. According to CBO projections, federal taxes consumed between 25 percent and 26.6 percent of the income of the top 20 percent of wage earners in 1988, compared with slightly less than 10 percent for the bottom decile of earners. Taxpayers in middle-income groupings paid average rates ranging from 13 percent (the third decile) to 24 percent (the ninth decile). The CBO study indicates that the progressivity of federal taxes declined during the 1980s. For example, in 1977 the CBO estimates that federal taxes took between 26.7 percent and 29.5 percent of the income of the top decile of earners, compared to approximately 8 percent for the bottom decile.

With regard to the burden of taxation, two additional points should be noted. First, middle- and upper-middle-income taxpayers earn the bulk of income and pay the bulk of the tax bill. In 1988, 55 percent of households in the United States had

---

[8]Congressional Budget Office, *The Changing Distribution of Federal Taxes: 1975–1990* (Washington, D.C.: U.S. Government Printing Office), October 1987.

"THIS NEW TAX PLAN SOUNDS PRETTY GOOD... WE GET A 9% CUT AND BUSINESS PICKS UP THE BURDEN...."

By John Trever, Albuquerque Journal © by and permission of News America Syndicate.

incomes between $30,000 and $75,000. These households earned approximately 70 percent of the total income and they shouldered slightly more than 70 percent of the tax burden. The findings of both Pechman and Browning-Johnson are consistent with this view.

Second, people pay all taxes. Politicians sometimes speak of imposing taxes on businesses, as if part of the tax burden could be transferred from individuals to nonpersons (business firms). The assumptions of this viewpoint are incorrect. Like all other taxes, business taxes are paid by individuals. A corporation or business firm may write the tax check to the government, but it does not pay the taxes. The business firm merely collects the money from someone else—its customers, employees, or stockholders—and transfers it to the government. It makes good political rhetoric to talk about ''businesses'' paying taxes, but the hard facts are that individuals provide all tax revenues.

THE COST OF GOVERNMENT

Do taxes measure the cost of government? Interestingly, the answer to this question is, ''Not entirely.'' Our old friend—the opportunity cost concept—will help us understand why. There are three types of costs incurred when governments provide goods and services.

First, there is the opportunity cost of the resources used to produce goods supplied through the public sector. When governments purchase missiles, education, highways, health care, and other goods, resources to provide these goods must be bid away from private-sector activities. If these resources were not tied-up producing goods supplied through the public sector, they would be available to produce private-sector goods. Note that this cost is incurred regardless of whether the provision of the public-sector goods is financed by current taxes, an increase in government debt, or money creation. This cost can only be diminished by reducing the size of governmental purchases.

Second, there is the cost of resources expended in the collection of the tax. Tax laws must be enforced. Tax returns must be prepared and monitored. Resources used to prepare, monitor, and enforce tax legislation are unavailable for the production of either private- or public-sector goods. In the United States, studies indicate that these compliance costs amount to between 5 percent and 7 percent of the tax revenue raised.

Finally, there is the excess burden cost due to price distortions emanating from the levying of taxes (and the provision of transfers). Less output will result because

EXHIBIT 13

The Size of Government—An International Comparison, 1988

The size of government varies substantially across countries. Government expenditures comprise nearly 60 percent of GNP in Denmark, Sweden, and the Netherlands. In contrast, government spending amounts to only about one-third of GNP in Australia, the United States, Japan, and Switzerland. In South Korea and Hong Kong, two rapidly growing Asian countries, the size of government is still smaller.

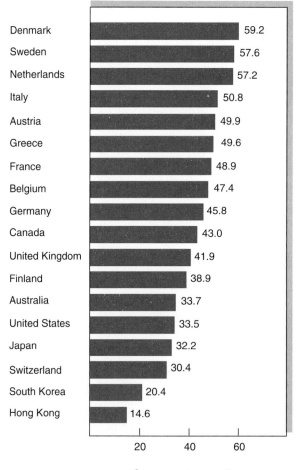

Government expenditures as
a percentage of GNP, 1988

Source: *OECD Economic Outlook,* June 1990; Government Information Services; Hong Kong, *Hong Kong 1989;* and International Monetary Fund; *Government Finance Statistics Yearbook, 1989.*

the tax-transfer structure will cause individuals to forgo productive activities and engage in counterproductive action (for example, tax-avoidance activities).

In essence, the cost of government activities is the sum of (a) the opportunity cost of resources used to produce government supplied goods and services, (b) the cost of tax compliance, and (c) the excess burden cost of taxation. Thus, government purchases of goods and services generally cost the economy a good bit more than either the size of the tax bill or the level of budget expenditures imply.

THE SIZE OF GOVERNMENT IN OTHER COUNTRIES

How does the size of the public sector in the United States compare with the size of the public sector in other countries? Exhibit 13 helps to answer that question. There is substantial variation in the size of government across countries. Government spending sums to nearly three-fifths of the total output in Denmark, Sweden, and the Netherlands. Approximately one-half of the total income of Italy, Austria, Greece, France, Belgium, and Germany is channelled through the public sector. The high level of government spending in these countries primarily reflects greater public-sector involvement in the provision of housing, health care, retirement insurance, and aid to the poor and unemployed. In Canada, public-sector spending summed to 43 percent of total output in 1988. The size of the public sectors in Australia, Japan, and Switzerland are approximately the same as in the United States. Interestingly, the size of government in South Korea and Hong Kong, two Asian nations where income has grown very rapidly in recent decades, is substantially smaller than for the United States.

LOOKING AHEAD

Government expenditures and tax rates are important determinants of an economy's output and employment. They also influence the price and output of consumer goods and income of resource suppliers. As we proceed, we will investigate these topics in greater detail.

CHAPTER SUMMARY

1. Governmental expenditures have grown more rapidly than the U.S. economy during this century. In 1929, government spending accounted for only 10 percent of GNP. Since 1929, the relative size of government expenditures has expanded every decade. In the late 1980s, more than one-third of the total output of the United States was channeled through the public sector.
2. Government purchases of goods and services constitute approximately 20 percent of the national output. Approximately one out of every six Americans works for the local, state, or federal government. Taking into account transfer payments, total government expenditures amounted to 34.1 percent of the gross national product in 1989.
3. During the last three decades, government spending in traditional areas such as national defense, highways, police and fire protection, and the provision of other goods and services has changed very little relative to the size of the economy. The growth of government in recent decades is almost exclusively the result of increased governmental involvement in the redistribution of income.
4. Personal income taxes, payroll taxes, and corporate income taxes are the major sources of federal tax revenues. Sales taxes provide the major tax base for state government, whereas local governments still rely primarily on property taxes for their revenue.

5. Payroll taxes constitute the most rapidly expanding source of tax revenues. In 1988, payroll taxes comprised 32 percent of the total tax revenue at the federal level. The social security payroll tax is a regressive tax because it is not levied on income beyond a designated maximum.

6. As the marginal tax rates increase, the proportion of income individuals are permitted to keep for private use declines. Since it determines the share of earnings available for private expenditures, the marginal tax rate exerts a major impact on the incentive of individuals to earn taxable income.

7. Both efficiency and equity should be considered when choosing among taxation alternatives. A tax system that induces inefficient behavior will be costly to a society. Similarly, it will be costly to induce compliance with a tax system that is perceived as unreasonable or unfair.

8. Ideally, we would all prefer a neutral tax system—one that does not distort prices or induce individuals to channel scarce resources into tax-avoidance activities. However, a tax on productive activity will always alter some prices. Our goal should be to adopt an equitable system that will minimize the inefficiency effects.

9. It is important to distinguish between a change in tax rates and a change in tax revenues. The size of the tax base will generally be inversely related to the rate of taxation. Therefore, an increase in tax rates will lead to a less-than-proportional increase in tax revenues, particularly if there are viable substitutes for those things that are taxed.

10. At very high rates of taxation, it is possible that an increase in tax rates will cause a reduction in tax revenues, because such a large number of people will shift away from the activity that is being taxed. The Laffer curve illustrates this possibility.

11. Tax legislation passed during the 1980s fundamentally altered the federal income tax structure. The personal income tax base was broadened and the marginal tax rates were reduced substantially. The tax policy of the 1980s was based on the belief that the lower tax rates will reduce tax avoidance and economic distortions and thereby promote economic growth. In addition to the United States, several other countries substantially reduced their top marginal tax rates during the latter half of the 1980s.

12. The cost of government activities encompasses the following components: (a) the opportunity cost of resources used to produce public-sector goods and services, (b) the compliance costs of taxation, and (c) the excess burden costs associated with price distortions and inefficiencies emanating from taxation. Generally, these costs will exceed both the size of the government budget and the dollar amount of the tax revenue collected.

13. The size of government as a share of the economy in the United States is approximately the same as for Japan, Australia, and Switzerland, but significantly smaller than for Canada and most Western European nations.

CRITICAL ANALYSIS QUESTIONS

1. Major categories of governmental spending include (a) national defense, (b) education, and (c) income transfers and antipoverty expenditures. Why do you think the public sector has become involved in these activities? Why not leave them to the market?

*2. People can avoid local taxes and, to a lesser degree, state taxes by moving. In comparison with the federal government, how does this characteristic influence people's ability to achieve value for their tax dollar at these levels of government?

*3. "User charges are simply another name for taxes. It makes no difference whether a government activity is financed by taxes or user charges." Evaluate.

4. "Transfer payments exert no influence on our economy because they merely transfer income from one group of individuals to another." Evaluate.

*Asterisk denotes questions for which answers are given in Appendix C, Selected Answers.

5. Do you think the indexing of the U.S. tax structure was a good idea? Why or why not? Will indexing make it easier or more difficult for Congress to increase tax revenues without voting for a tax increase? Explain. Do you think Congress may want to repeal indexing in the future? Why or why not?

*6. "A government project financed by taxation should be undertaken only if the expected value of the project is somewhat greater than the outlay necessary for its finance." Evaluate.

*7. How would a reduction in marginal tax rates influence the incentive of a taxpayer to incur a tax deductible expenditure?

8. As of 1990, capital gains (income from assets that were sold for more than they were purchased during an earlier time period) were taxed at the same rate as other income. From an equity viewpoint, is this policy sound?

9. Do you think your college should cover the cost of providing campus parking through user charges, higher tuition for all students, or taxation? Should waiting in line (that is, time spent hunting for a parking space) play a substantial role in the allocation of parking spaces? Discuss.

*10. A popular sticker on trucks reads: "This truck pays $6,775 (or some other figure) in annual road-use taxes." Is this statement true?

11. How would each of the following affect the ability of the invisible hand to bring self-interest and helping others into harmony?
    a. A tax transfer system that equalized incomes.
    b. High tax rates and a large public sector that allocated most goods and services.

PART TWO

Macroeconomics

6 *Taking the Nation's Economic Pulse*

It has been said that figures rule the world; maybe. I am quite sure that it is figures which show us whether it is being ruled well or badly.

Johann Wolfgang Goethe, 1830

The Gross National Product is one of the great inventions of the twentieth century, probably almost as significant as the automobile and not quite so significant as TV. The effect of physical inventions is obvious, but social inventions like the GNP change the world almost as much.[1]

Professor Kenneth Boulding

CHAPTER FOCUS

- What is GNP? What does it measure? How is it calculated?

- What is the difference between real and nominal GNP? Why is it important to adjust income and output data for changes in prices?

- How much have prices increased in recent years? How do economists and statisticians measure changes in the general level of prices?

- Is GNP a good measure of output?

- What is the relationship between real output and real income? Can a nation increase its real income without increasing its real output?

*O*ur society likes to keep score. The sports pages supply us with the won–lost records that reveal how well the various teams are doing. We also keep score on the performance of our economy. The score board for economic performance is the national income accounting system. Simon Kuznet of Harvard University and the National Bureau of Economic Research developed the concepts and outlined the measurement procedures for national income accounting in the 1920s and 1930s. In 1971, Kuznets was awarded the Nobel Prize in Economics for his work in this area.

The accounting statement of a firm provides information on the flow of revenues and expenditures necessary to assess the firm's performance. National income accounts supply similar information for the entire economy. They provide a comprehensive overview of how the economy is doing. Without a measuring rod for national output, it would be difficult to determine the health of the economy. In this chapter, we will explain how the flow of an economy's output is measured. We will also explain how changes in national income that reflect changes in production are separated from those that merely reflect inflation (changes in prices). Finally, we will analyze the strengths and weaknesses of the measurement tools used to assess the performance of our national economy.

THE CONCEPT OF THE GNP

The Gross National Product (GNP) is the most widely used measure of economic performance. GNP estimates are prepared quarterly and released a few weeks subsequent to the end of each quarter. The numbers are widely reported and closely watched, particularly in the business and financial communities. What does GNP measure and why is it important?

Gross National Product: The total market value of all "final product" goods and services produced during a specific period, usually a year.

The **gross national product** is a measure of the market value of goods and services produced during a specific time period. GNP is a "flow" concept. It is typically measured in terms of an annual rate. By analogy, a water gauge is a device designed to measure the amount of water that flows through a pipe each hour. Similarly, GNP is a device designed to measure the market value of production that "flows" through the economy's factories and shops each year.

WHAT COUNTS TOWARD GNP?

Since GNP seeks to measure only current production, it cannot be arrived at merely by summing the totals on all of the nation's cash registers. Many transactions have to be excluded. What does GNP include and what does it exclude?

1. GNP Counts Only Goods and Services Purchased by Final Users. If output is going to be measured accurately, all goods and services produced during the year must be counted once, but only once. Most goods go through several stages of production before they end up in the hands of their ultimate user. Since we do not want to double count, care must be taken to differentiate between "final goods" and goods in intermediate stages of production.

---

[1]Kenneth Boulding, "Fun and Games with the Gross National Product—The Role of Misleading Indicators in Social Policy," in *The Environmental Crisis,* (ed.) Harold W. Helfrich, Jr. (New Haven, Connecticut: Yale University Press, 1970), p. 157.

Final Goods and Services:
Goods and services purchased
by their ultimate users.

Intermediate Goods: Goods
purchased for resale or for use
in producing another good or
service.

Final goods and services are those purchased for final use rather than for resale or further processing. Goods utilized as intermediate inputs in the production of final user goods and services are called **intermediate goods.** Sales at intermediate stages of production are not counted by GNP. Why? Because the value of an intermediate good is embodied within the final user good. If we counted both the intermediate good and the final user good, double counting would result and GNP would be exaggerated. For example, when a wholesale distributor sells steak to a restaurant, the final purchase price paid by the patron of the restaurant for a steak dinner will reflect the cost of the meat. Double counting would result if we included both the sale price of the intermediate good (the steak sold by the wholesaler to the restaurant) and the final purchase price of the steak dinner. Since the price paid by the final user of a good will reflect the value of the intermediate inputs, GNP includes only the market value of goods and services being purchased for final use.

Exhibit 1 will help clarify the accounting methods for GNP. Before the final good, bread, is in the hands of the consumer, it will go through several intermediate stages of production. The farmer produces a pound of wheat and sells it to the miller for 30 cents. The miller grinds the wheat into flour and sells it to the baker for 65 cents. The miller's actions have added 35 cents to the value of the wheat. The baker combines the flour with other ingredients, makes a loaf of bread, and sells it to the grocer for 90 cents. The baker has added 25 cents to the value of the bread. The grocer stocks the bread on the grocery shelves and provides a convenient location for consumers to shop. The grocer sells the loaf of bread for $1, adding 10 cents to the value of the final product. Only the market value of the final product—the $1 for the loaf of bread—is counted by GNP.

EXHIBIT 1

GNP and Stages of Production

Most goods go through several stages of production. This chart illustrates both the market value of a loaf of bread as it passes through the various stages of production (column 1) and the amount added to the bread by each intermediate producer (column 2). GNP counts only the market value of the final product. Of course, the amount added by each intermediate producer (column 2) sums to the market value of the final product.

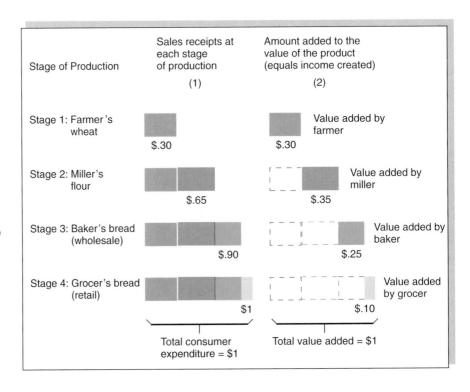

As Exhibit 1 illustrates, the price of the final product reflects the *value added* at each stage of production. Thus, the 30 cents added by the farmer, the 35 cents by the miller, the 25 cents by the baker, and the 10 cents by the grocer sum to the $1 purchase price.

If GNP counted the sales price at each intermediate stage of production, it would overstate the value of the final product. Since GNP includes only the purchase price of final goods and services, double counting is avoided. Of course, as Exhibit 1 illustrates, the price of final goods is also equal to the *value added*—that is, the amount of income created at each stage of production.

2. GNP Counts Only Goods Produced During the Period.

Keep in mind that GNP is a measurement of current production. Therefore, transactions that merely involve the exchange of goods or assets produced during an earlier period or the transfer of ownership rights are excluded since they do not contribute to current production. *Secondhand sales are excluded.* The purchase of a used car produced last year will not enhance current GNP, nor will the sale of a ''used'' home, constructed five years ago. Production of these goods was counted at the time they were produced. Current sales and purchases of such items merely involve the exchange of existing goods. They do not involve current production of additional goods. Therefore, they are not counted. (Note: If a sales commission is involved in the exchange of a used car or home, the commission would add to current GNP since it involves a service during the current period.)

Since GNP counts long-lasting goods such as automobiles and houses when they are produced, it is not always an accurate gauge of what is currently being consumed. During an economic slowdown, few new durable assets will be produced. However, the consumption of durable goods that were produced and counted during an earlier period will continue. During good times, there will be a rapid expansion in the production of durable assets, but their consumption will be extended over a longer time period. Because of this cycle, GNP tends to understate consumption during a recession and overstate it during an economic boom.

3. Financial Transactions and Income Transfers Are Excluded.

GNP does not count purely financial transactions, since they do not involve current production. Purchases or sales of stocks, bonds, and U.S. securities do not count. They represent exchange of current assets, not production of additional goods. Similarly, both private- and public-sector income transfers are excluded since they do not enhance current production. If your aunt sends you $100 to help pay for your college expenses, your aunt has less wealth and you have more, but the transaction adds nothing to current production. Thus, it is not included in GNP. Neither are government income transfer payments like social security, welfare, and veterans' payments. The recipients of these transfers are not producing goods in return for the transfers. Therefore, it would be inappropriate to add them to GNP.

DOLLARS AS THE COMMON DENOMINATOR OF GNP

In elementary school, each of us was instructed about the difficulties of adding apples and oranges. Yet, this is precisely the nature of the aggregate measurement problem. Literally millions of different commodities and services are produced each year. How can the production of houses, movies, legal services, education, automobiles, dresses, heart transplants, astrological services, and many other items be added together?

These vastly different commodities and services have only one thing in common: someone pays for each of them in terms of dollars. Dollars act as a common denominator; units of each different good are weighted according to their dollar selling price. Production of an automobile adds 100 times as much to GNP as does the production of a briefcase, because the new automobile sells for $10,000 compared to $100 for the new briefcase. A $20,000 heart transplant adds 50 times as much to GNP as does a $400 appendectomy. A fifth of whiskey adds more to GNP than does a week's supply of household water because the purchaser pays more for the whiskey than for the water. The total spending on all final goods produced during the year is then summed, in dollar terms, to obtain the annual GNP.

TWO WAYS OF MEASURING GNP

There are two ways of looking at and measuring GNP. The GNP of an economy can be reached either by totaling the spending on goods and services purchased, or by totaling the costs of producing and supplying those goods and services. That is, GNP can be calculated by adding the total expenditures on final goods and services supplied to purchasers. Or, alternatively, GNP can be determined by adding the total cost of supplying the goods and services, including the residual income of the

EXHIBIT 2

The Circular Flow of Income

Here we illustrate two alternative ways of looking at the GNP for a simple economy consisting only of households and businesses. Households supply factor inputs in exchange for income (wages, rents, interest, and profits). These exchanges flow through the resource market (bottom loop). In turn, businesses supply final goods and services in exchange for business receipts (household spending on goods and services). These exchanges flow through the goods and services market. Both the flow of household purchases of goods and services (top loop) and the flow of factor compensation payments (bottom loop) will sum to GNP.

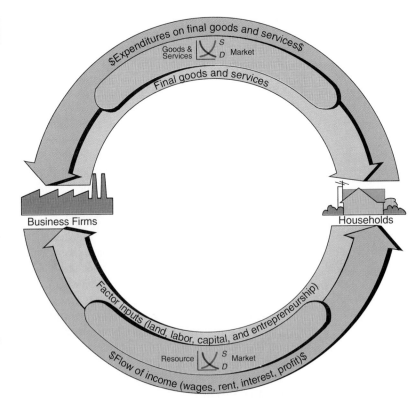

producer-entrepreneurs. Either sum will equal GNP. This is true because, in simple terms, the money spent by purchasers on final goods and services can be seen as providing the wherewithal to produce and supply those goods and services.

Exhibit 2 uses a circular flow diagram for a simple two-sector economy to illustrate the two alternative methods of measuring GNP. The dollar flow of **consumption** expenditures and receipts is indicated by the outer ring of the circular flow diagram. The flow of real products and resources is indicated by the inner ring. Goods and services produced in the business sector are sold to consumers in the household sector. Households supply the factors of production and receive income payments in exchange for their services. In turn, all the income of households is expended on the purchase of goods and services.

The bottom loop of Exhibit 2 illustrates the dollar flow of factor-cost payments (wages, rents, interest, and profits) from the business sector to the household sector in exchange for productive resources (labor, land, capital equipment, and entrepreneurship). These factor payments constitute the income of households. The price of the productive resources is determined by the forces of supply and demand operating in resource markets. Businesses use the services of the productive resources to produce goods and services.

The top loop of Exhibit 2 illustrates the dollar flow of consumer expenditures from households to businesses in exchange for goods and services. Business firms derive their revenues from the sale of products (food, clothing, medical services, and so on) they supply to households. These prices are determined in goods and services markets.

Modern economies, of course, are much more complicated than our simple two-sector circular flow model. In addition to the personal consumption expenditures of the household sector, there are governmental purchases of goods and services (for example, highways, education, warplanes, and police protection). Rather than purchase all productive inputs from households, businesses may undertake investment expenditures (business spending on machinery, production facilities, and other capital assets) out of their retained earnings, thus enhancing their future productive capabilities. In addition, foreigners may both purchase domestic goods and services and sell foreign-made products to the domestic market.

Nevertheless, the general principle still holds. Gross national product can be determined either by (a) summing the total expenditures on the "final product" goods and services produced during a period or by (b) summing the total cost incurred as a result of producing the goods and services supplied during the period. Exhibit 3 summarizes the components of GNP for both the expenditure approach and the resource cost-income approach.

It is important to note that the residual income of the producer-entrepreneur is included in the total cost of supplying goods and services, the second form of GNP measurement. Since business revenues derived from sales of goods and services will either be paid to resource suppliers or will accrue to capitalist entrepreneurs in the form of profits (or losses), the two methods of calculating GNP will yield identical outcomes. Note that profits, like contractual payments to factors of production, are considered a cost of production.[2] Since profits are residual return, some might

Consumption: Household spending on consumer goods and services during the current period. Consumption is a flow concept.

---

[2]In the national income accounts, the terms "profit" and "corporate profit" are used in the accounting sense. Thus, they reflect *both* the rate of return on assets owned by a business firm (which is sometimes referred to as normal profit) *and* the firm's economic profit and loss which was discussed in Chapter 3.

EXHIBIT 3   ■   The Two Ways of Measuring GNP

Even though modern economies are far more complicated than the two-sector circular flow model of Exhibit 2, there are still two methods of calculating GNP. It can be calculated either by summing the expenditures on the "final product" goods and services of each sector (left, below) or by summing the costs associated with the production of these goods and services (right, below).

Expenditure Approach		Resource Cost-Income Approach

Household sector (personal consumption expenditures)
+
Business sector (gross private investment expenditures)
+
Government sector (government purchases of goods and services)
+
International sector (net exports of goods and services)
	= GNP =	*Income payments to resources* (at factor cost)
		    Wages
		    Self-employment income
		    Rents
		    Profits
		    Interest
		        +
		Nonincome cost items
		    Indirect business taxes
		    Depreciation

object to this classification. This view is incorrect. Just as wage payments induce workers to supply labor, the expectation of profit induces business decision-makers to supply capital equipment, organize production, and shoulder the risk of a residual income claimant. The latter is just as much a cost of production as the former.

From an accounting viewpoint, total payments to the factors of production, including the producer's profit or loss, must be equal to the sales price generated by the good. This is true for each good or service produced, and it is also true for the aggregate economy, as must be obvious from the previous discussion. This is a fundamental accounting identity.

$$\text{Dollar flow of expenditures} = \text{GNP} = \text{dollar flow of the producers' cost}$$
$$\text{on final goods} \qquad\qquad\qquad \text{on final goods}$$

Thus, GNP obtained by adding the dollar value of final goods and services purchased will equal GNP obtained by adding the total of all "cost" items, including the producer's profits, associated with the production of final goods.

THE EXPENDITURE APPROACH

As Exhibit 3 indicates, when the expenditure approach is used to calculate GNP, four basic components of final products purchased must be considered. The left side of Exhibit 4 presents the value of these four components of GNP for 1990.

1. Consumption Purchases. Personal consumption purchases are the largest component of GNP; in 1990, they amounted to $3,658 billion. Most consumption expenditures are for nondurable goods or services. Food, clothing, recreation, medical and legal services, education, and fuel are included in this category. These items are used up or consumed in a relatively short time. Durable goods, such as appliances and automobiles, comprise approximately one-seventh of all consumer purchases. These products are enjoyed over a longer period of time even though they are fully counted at the time they are purchased.

EXHIBIT 4 ■ Two Ways of Measuring GNP—1990 data (billions of dollars)[a]				
Expenditure Approach			**Resource Cost-Income Approach**	
Personal consumption		$3,658	Employee compensaton	$3,244
Durable goods	$ 482		Proprietors' income	402
Nondurable goods	1,194			
Services	1,982		Rents	7
			Corporate profits	297
Gross private investment		745		
Fixed investment	747		Interest income	467
Inventories	−2			
Government purchases		1,098	Indirect business taxes (includes	470
Federal	424		transfers)	
State and local	674		Depreciation	576
			(capital consumption)	
Net exports		−38		
Gross national product		$5,463	Gross national product	$5,463

Source: U.S. Department of Commerce. These data are also available in the *Federal Reserve Bulletin*, which is published monthly.
[a]The left side shows the flow of expenditures and the right side the flow of resource costs. Both procedures yield GNP.

Investment: The flow of expenditures on durable assets (fixed investment) plus the addition to inventories (inventory investment) during a period. These expenditures enhance our ability to provide consumer benefits in the future.

2. Gross Investment Purchases. **Investment** is the construction or manufacture of capital goods that provide a "flow" of future consumption or production service. Unlike food or medical services, they are not immediately "used." A house, for example, is an investment good because it will provide a stream of services long into the future. Business plants and equipment are investment goods because they, too, will provide productive services in the future. Changes in business inventories are also classed as investment goods, since they measure goods that will provide future consumer benefits.

Gross investment includes expenditures for both (a) the replacement of machinery, equipment and buildings worn out during the year and (b) net additions to the stock of capital assets. Net investment is simply gross investment minus an allowance for depreciation and obsolescence of machinery and other physical assets during the year. Net investment is an important indicator of the economy's future productive capability. Substantial net investment indicates that the capital stock of the economy is growing, thereby enhancing the economy's future productive potential (shifting the economy's production-possibilities frontier outward). In contrast, a low rate of net investment, or, even worse, negative net investment, implies a stagnating or even contracting economy. In 1990, gross investment expenditures in the United States were $745 billion, including $576 billion for the replacement of assets worn out during the year. Thus, net investment was $169 billion.

Since GNP is designed to measure current production, allowance must be made for goods produced but not sold during the year. This means that we must make an allowance for **inventory investment**—changes during the year in the market value of unsold goods on shelves and in warehouses. If business firms have more goods on hand at the end of the year than they had at the beginning of the year, inventory investment will be positive. This inventory investment must be added to GNP. On the other hand, a decline in the market value of inventories would indicate that the purchases of goods and services exceeded current production. In this case, inventory disinvestment would be a subtraction from GNP. In 1990, the United States experienced an inventory disinvestment of $2 billion.

Inventory Investment: Changes in the stock of unsold goods and raw materials held during a period.

The inventory component of investment varies substantially. At the beginning of an unexpected recession, inventories often rise as the result of weak demand. Later in the recession, businesses reduce their inventories in response to weak sales. In contrast, businesses generally rebuild their inventories during prosperous times when strong future sales are anticipated.

Many goods possess both consumer- and investment-good characteristics. There is not always a clear distinction between the two. National accounting procedures have rather arbitrarily classified business purchases of final goods as investment and considered household purchases, except housing, as consumption.

3. Government Purchases. In 1990, federal, state, and local government purchases were $1,098 billion, approximately 20 percent of total GNP. The purchases of state and local governments exceeded those of the federal government by a wide margin. The government component includes both investment and consumption services. Thus, current public sector expenditures on missiles, highways, and dams for flood control as well as the operation of veterans' hospitals, public schools, and law enforcement agencies are all included in the government component. Since transfer payments are excluded, the size of the public sector greatly exceeds the amount counted as actually spent by the government on goods and services.

4. Net Exports.   **Exports** are domestically produced goods and services sold to foreigners. **Imports** are foreign-produced goods and services purchased domestically. We want GNP to measure only the nation's production. Therefore, when measuring GNP by the expenditure approach, we must (a) add exports (goods produced domestically that were sold to foreigners) and (b) subtract imports (goods produced abroad that were purchased by Americans). For national accounting purposes, we can combine these two factors into a single entry, net exports, where

Exports: Goods and services produced domestically but sold to foreigners.

Imports: Goods and services produced by foreigners but purchased by domestic consumers, investors, and governments.

$$\text{Net exports} = \text{total exports} - \text{total imports}$$

Net exports may be either positive or negative. When we sell more to foreigners than they buy from us, net exports are positive. In recent years, net exports have been negative, indicating we were buying more goods and services from foreigners than we were selling to them. In 1990, net exports were minus $38 billion.

THE RESOURCE COST-INCOME APPROACH

Exhibit 4 illustrates how, rather than summing the flow of expenditures on final goods and services, we could reach GNP by summing the flow of costs incurred in their production. Labor services play a very important role in the production process. It is therefore not surprising that employee compensation, $3,244 billion in 1990, is the largest cost incurred in the production of goods and services.

Self-employed proprietors undertake the risks of owning their own businesses and simultaneously provide their own labor services to the firm. Their earnings in 1990 contributed $402 billion to GNP, 7 percent of the total. Together, employees and self-employed proprietors accounted for approximately two-thirds of GNP.

Machines, buildings, land, and other physical assets also contribute to the production process. Rents, corporate profits, and interest are payments to persons who provide either physical resources or the financial resources with which to purchase physical assets. Rents are returns to resource owners who permit others to use their assets during a time period. Corporate profits are compensation earned by stockholders, who bear the risk of the business undertaking and who provide financial resources with which the firm purchases resources. Interest is a payment to parties who extend loans to producers.

Not all cost components of GNP result in an income payment to a resource supplier. There are two major indirect costs.

1. Indirect Business Taxes. These taxes are imposed on the sale of many goods, and they are passed on to the consumer. The sales tax is a clear example. When you make a $1 purchase in a state with a 5 percent sales tax, the purchase actually costs you $1.05. The $1 goes to the seller to pay wages, rent, interest, and managerial costs. The 5 cents goes to the government. Indirect business taxes boost the market price of goods when GNP is calculated by the expenditure approach. Similarly, when looked at from the factor-cost viewpoint, taxes are an indirect cost of supplying the goods to the purchasers.

2. Depreciation. Using machines to produce goods causes the machines to wear out. Depreciation of capital goods is a cost of producing current goods, but it is not a direct cost because it reflects what is lost to the producer when machines and facilities become less valuable. Depreciation does not involve a direct payment to a resource owner. It is an estimate, based on the expected life of the asset, of the decline in the asset's value during the year. In 1990, depreciation (sometimes called capital consumption allowance) amounted to $576 billion, a little more than 10 percent of GNP.

DEPRECIATION AND NET NATIONAL PRODUCT

Net National Product: Gross national product minus a depreciation allowance for the wearing out of machines and buildings during the period.

The inclusion of depreciation costs in GNP points out that it is indeed a "gross" rather than a "net" measure of economic production. Since GNP fails to allow for the wearing out of capital goods, it overstates the net output of an economy.

The **net national product** (NNP) is a concept designed to correct this deficiency. NNP is the total market value of the goods and services produced for consumers, governments, and net exports, plus any net additions to the nation's capital stock. In accounting terms, net national product is simply GNP minus depreciation.

Since NNP counts only net additions to the nation's capital stock, it is less than GNP. Net investment—the additions to capital stock—is always equal to gross investment minus depreciation. NNP counts only net investment.

THE RELATIVE SIZE OF GNP COMPONENTS

Of course, the relative importance of the components of GNP changes from time to time. Exhibit 5 shows the average proportion of GNP accounted for by each of the components during 1988–1990. When the expenditure approach is used, personal consumption is by far the largest and most stable component of GNP. Consumption accounted for 66 percent of GNP during 1988–1990, compared to only 15 percent for investment and 20 percent for government expenditures. When GNP is measured by the resource cost-income approach, compensation to employees is the dominant component (59 percent of GNP). During 1988–1990, rents, corporate profits, and interest combined to account for 14 percent of GNP.

EXHIBIT 5

Major Components of GNP
in the United States,
1988–1990

The relative sizes of the major
components of GNP usually
fluctuate within a fairly narrow
range. The average proportion
of each component during
1988–1990 is demonstrated
here for both (a) the
expenditure and (b) the
resource cost-income
approaches.

Source: *Economic Report of the
President, 1991.*

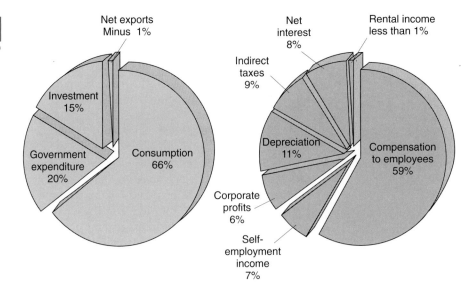

(a) Expenditure Approach   (b) Resource Cost-Income Approach

GROSS NATIONAL PRODUCT OR GROSS NATIONAL COST?

As we have indicated, the cost and the expenditure approaches both lead to the same estimate of GNP. They are simply two ways of calculating the same thing. Considering the two approaches together helps keep the GNP in perspective. From the purchaser's viewpoint, it is indeed gross national product. Good things were purchased by households, investors, governments, and foreigners. The purchasers valued the goods and services more than the purchase prices; otherwise, they would not have purchased them.

Production, though, also involves costs. The resource cost-income approach stresses the cost side of national income. The production of goods involves human toil, wear and tear on machines, sacrificing current consumption, risk, managerial responsibilities, and other of life's unpleasantries. Viewed from the producer's position, gross national cost might be a better term for GNP because resource owners had to forgo other things to produce goods and services.

As we will emphasize later, GNP is not a measure of how much "better off" we are. There are both positive and negative sides to it. Perhaps it might best be thought of as an index of current productive activity—activity that results in the goods and services that we desire, at the expense of work, waiting, risk, and depreciation, which we do not desire.

REAL AND NOMINAL GNP

It is important to distinguish between real and nominal economic values. **Nominal values** (or money values, as they are often called) are expressed in current dollars.

Nominal Values: The value of economic variables such as GNP and personal consumption expressed in current prices. A general increase in prices will cause nominal values to rise even when there is no real change in the variable (quantity produced or consumed).

Real Values: The measurement of a variable after it has been adjusted for changes in the general level of prices.

Real GNP: GNP in current dollars deflated for changes in the prices of the items included in GNP. Mathematically, real GNP_2 is equal to nominal GNP_2 multiplied by (GNP Deflator$_1$/ GNP Deflator$_2$). Thus, if prices have risen between periods 1 and 2, the ratio of the GNP deflator in period 1 to the deflator in period 2 will be less than 1. This ratio will therefore deflate the nominal GNP for the rising prices.

GNP Deflator: A price index that reveals the cost of purchasing the items included in GNP during the period relative to the cost of purchasing these same items during a base year (currently, 1982). Since the base year is assigned a value of 100, as the GNP deflator takes on values greater than 100, it indicates that prices have risen.

Nominal GNP: GNP expressed at current prices. It is often called money GNP.

Over time, nominal values reflect changes both in (a) the real size of an economic variable and in (b) the general level of prices. In contrast, **real values** eliminate the impact of changes in the price level, leaving only the real changes in the size of an economic variable. When comparing data at different points in time, economists usually are most interested in the real changes. Thus, they will focus on real wages, real income, or real GNP. The ''real'' refers to the fact that the data have been adjusted for changes in the purchasing power of the dollar.

Perhaps an example will help clarify the difference between real and nominal values. In 1990, per capita *nominal* GNP in the United States was more than $21,730, compared to only $2,800 in 1960. Does this mean we produced almost eight times as much output *per person* in 1990, as we did in 1960? Not hardly. In 1990, the general level of prices was 4.4 times the level of 1960. *Measured in terms of the price level in 1960,* **real GNP** per person in 1990 was $4,940, only about 76 percent more than GNP per person in 1960.

Nominal GNP will increase either if (a) more goods and services are produced or if (b) prices rise. Often, both (a) and (b) will contribute to an increase in GNP. Since we are usually interested in comparing only the output or actual production during two different time intervals, GNP must be adjusted for the change in prices.

How can we determine how much the prices of items included in GNP have risen during a specific period? We answer this question by constructing a price index called the **GNP deflator.** The Department of Commerce estimates how much of each item included in GNP has been produced during a year. This bundle of goods will include automobiles, houses, office buildings, medical services, bread, milk, entertainment, and all other goods included in the GNP, in the quantities actually produced during the current year. The Department then calculates the ratio of (a) the cost of purchasing this representative bundle of goods *at current prices* divided by (b) the cost of purchasing the same bundle *at the prices that were present during a designated earlier base year*. The base year chosen (currently 1982 for the GNP deflator) is assigned the value 100. The GNP deflator is equal to the calculated ratio multiplied by 100. If prices are, *on average,* higher during the current period than they were during the base year, the GNP deflator will exceed 100. The relative size of the GNP deflator is a measure of the current price level compared to the price level during the base year. (See Measures of Economic Activity for additional detail on how price indexes are constructed.)

We can use the GNP deflator to measure real GNP: GNP in dollars of constant purchasing power. If prices are rising, we simply deflate the **nominal GNP** during the latter period to account for the effects of inflation.

Exhibit 6 illustrates how real GNP is measured and why it is important to adjust for price changes. Between 1982 and 1990, nominal GNP increased 72.6 percent. However, a large portion of this increase in nominal GNP reflected higher prices rather than a larger rate of output. The GNP deflator in 1990 was 131.5, compared to 100 in 1982. Prices rose by 31.5 percent between 1982 and 1990. To determine the real GNP for 1990 in terms of 1982 dollars, we deflate the 1990 nominal GNP for the rise in prices:

$$\text{Real GNP}_{90} = \text{nominal GNP}_{90} \times \frac{\text{GNP deflator}_{82}}{\text{GNP deflator}_{90}}$$

Because prices were rising, the latter ratio is less than one. In terms of 1982 dollars, the real GNP in 1990 was $4,154 billion, only 31.2 percent more than in 1982. So,

EXHIBIT 6 ■ Changes in Prices and the Real GNP			
Between 1982 and 1990, GNP increased by 72.6 percent. But, when the 1990 GNP was deflated to account for price increases, real GNP increased by only 31.2 percent.			
	Nominal GNP (billions of dollars)	Price Index (GNP deflator, 1982 = 100)	Real GNP (1982 dollars)
1982	$3,166	100.0	$3,166
1990	5,463	131.5	4,154
Percent increase	72.6	31.5	31.2
Source: U.S. Department of Commerce.			

although money GNP expanded by 72.6 percent, real GNP increased by only 31.2 percent.

A change in money GNP tells us nothing about what is happening to the rate of real production unless we also know what is happening to prices. Money income could double while production actually declines, if prices more than double. On the other hand, money income could remain constant while real GNP increases, if prices fall during a time period. Data on money GNP and price changes are both essential for a meaningful comparison of real income between two time periods.

PROBLEMS WITH GNP AS A MEASURING ROD

GNP is not a perfect device for measuring current production and income. Some items are excluded, even though they would be properly classed as "current production." Sometimes production results in harmful "side effects," which are not fully accounted for. In this section, we will focus on some of the limitations and shortcomings of GNP as a measure of economic performance.

GNP DOES NOT COUNT NONMARKET PRODUCTION

The GNP fails to count household production because such production does not involve a market transaction. Because of this, the household services of millions of people are excluded. If you mow the yard, repair your car, paint your house, pick up relatives from school, or perform similar productive household activities, your labor services add nothing to GNP, since no market transaction is involved. Such nonmarket productive activities are sizable—10 or 15 percent of total GNP, perhaps more. Their exclusion results in some oddities in national income accounting.

For example, if a woman marries her gardener, and, if after the marriage the spouse-gardener works for love rather than for money, GNP will decline because the services of the spouse-gardener will now be excluded: there is no longer a market transaction. If a parent hires a baby-sitter in order to enter the labor force, these actions have a double-barreled impact on GNP. It will rise as a result of (a) the amount the baby-sitter is paid plus (b) the parent's on-the-job earnings.

The omission of many nonmarket productive activities makes comparisons over time and among countries at various stages of market development less meaningful. For example, more women are currently involved in market work than was true 30 years ago. There is widespread use of appliances today to perform functions previously performed by women at home. Remember that the initial purchase of the appliance contributes to GNP while the unpaid household labor is not counted. Thus, a larger share of total production was previously excluded. This implies that the current GNP, even in real dollars, is overstated relative to the earlier period.

Similarly, GNP comparisons overstate the output of developed countries when compared to underdeveloped countries. A larger share of the total production of underdeveloped countries originates in the household sector. For example, Mexican families are more likely than their U.S. counterparts to make their own clothing, raise and prepare their own food, provide their own child-rearing services, and even build their own homes. These productive labor services, originating in the household sector, are excluded from GNP. Therefore GNP understates total output in Mexico more so than in the United States.

GNP DOES NOT COUNT THE UNDERGROUND ECONOMY

In the preceding chapter, we indicated that many transactions go unreported because they involve either illegal activities or tax evasion (which is illegal, although the activities generating the income may not be). Many of these "underground" activities produce goods and services that are valued by purchasers. Nevertheless, since the activities are unreported, they do not contribute to GNP. Estimates of the size of the underground economy in the United States range from 10 to 15 percent of total output. Most observers, as we have noted, believe that since the 1960s these unrecorded transactions have grown more rapidly than measured output. If this is true, it implies that the published GNP figures are actually understating the recent growth rate of output, since an expanding proportion of total output is being excluded.

GNP FAILS TO TAKE LEISURE AND HUMAN COSTS INTO ACCOUNT

Simon Kuznets, the "inventor" of GNP, suggests that the failure to fully include leisure and human costs is one of the grave omissions of national income accounting. GNP excludes leisure, a good that is valuable to each of us. One country might attain a $20,000 per capita GNP with an average work week of 30 hours. Another might attain the same per capita GNP with a 50-hour work week. In terms of total output, the first country has the greater production because it "produces" more leisure, or sacrifices less human cost. GNP, though, does not reflect this fact.

The average number of hours worked per week in the United States has declined steadily over the years. The average nonagricultural production worker spent only 34.5 hours per week on the job in 1990, compared to more than 40 hours in 1947: a 14 percent reduction in weekly hours worked. Clearly, this reduction in the length of the work week raised the American standard of living, even though it did not enhance GNP.

GNP also fails to take into account human costs. On average, jobs today are less physically strenuous and are generally performed in a safer, more comfortable environment than was true a generation ago. To the extent that working conditions have improved through the years, GNP figures understate the growth of real income.

MEASURES OF ECONOMIC ACTIVITY

Deriving the GNP Deflator and the Consumer Price Index

When making comparisons of output and expenditures between periods, it is important to adjust for price changes. Economists measure changes in prices by constructing a price index. A price index measures the cost (or value) of a given bundle of goods at a point in time relative to the cost of the same bundle of goods during a prior base year. The base year is assigned a value of 100. If prices are higher during the current period (that is, if the cost of purchasing the given bundle of goods has risen), the value of the price index during the current period will exceed 100.

Construction of a Price Index— Simple Illustration

A simple example can be used to illustrate the concept of a price index. Imagine that students at your college purchase only four items: hamburgers, T-shirts, blue jeans, and stereo tapes. In recent years, the prices of these goods have risen. Suppose we want to determine the degree to which prices rose between 1980 (the base year) and 1990. A careful sampling of prices is used to determine the average price of each item in the student's budget for both 1980 and 1990. These data are presented in Exhibit 7. Note that price changes varied among the goods. The price of hamburgers doubled between 1980 and 1990, while the price of jeans remained unchanged. T-shirt prices rose by 80 percent (from $10 to $18), but the price of stereo tapes declined between 1980 and 1990. How can the price data for 1980 and 1990 be used to determine the difference in the

level of prices between the two years?

Method I: Using Base-Year Market Basket. A price index reveals the cost of purchasing a market basket of goods at a point in time compared to the cost of purchasing *the identical market basket* during an earlier base period. What market basket should be used? One obvious possibility would be the market basket consumed by students during the base period. Suppose a survey of the student population indicates that, on average, students purchased 60 hamburgers, four T-shirts, two pairs of blue jeans and one stereo tape monthly during the 1980 base year. This information permits us to determine the cost of the market basket purchased by the typical student in 1980 at both 1980 and 1990 prices. Exhibit 7 presents these calculations. The market basket consumed by the typical student in 1980 costs $200 at 1980

prices. At 1990 prices, the identical market basket costs $324.

We can now calculate the 1990 College Student Price Index (CSPI) based on the 1980 market basket. The CSPI is:

$$\frac{\text{Cost of base-year}}{\text{market basket at}}_{\substack{\text{current (1990) prices} \\ \hline \text{Cost of base-year} \\ \text{market basket at} \\ \text{base-year (1980) prices}}} \times 100$$

The cost of the base-year market basket in 1990 was $324, compared to a cost of $200 in 1980. Thus, the 1990 CSPI *using the base-year market basket* is equal to 162 [(324 ÷ 200) × 100].

Method II: Using Current-Year Market Basket. Rather than using the base-year market basket, we might use the current-year quantity of each good purchased to weight the 1980 and 1990 prices. Using this alternative, the formula for the CSPI would be:

EXHIBIT 7 ■ The 1990 Price Index (1980 = 100) Based on the Typical Market Basket Consumed by College Students in 1980 (hypothetical data)

Monthly Purchases, 1980	Average Price		Cost of 1980 Market Basket	
	1980	1990	1980 Prices	1990 Prices
60 Hamburgers	$ 1.60	$ 3.20	$ 96.00	$192.00
4 T-shirts	10.00	18.00	40.00	72.00
2 Jeans	24.00	24.00	48.00	48.00
1 Stereo tape	16.00	12.00	16.00	12.00
		Total	$200.00	$324.00

Price Index in 1990 (1980 = 100) $= \frac{324}{200} \times 100 = 162$

$$\frac{\text{Cost of current-year market basket at current (1990) prices}}{\text{Cost of current-year market basket at base-year (1980) prices}} \times 100$$

A 1990 survey of students indicates the quantity of each commodity purchased monthly during the year. These data can be used to calculate the cost of purchasing the 1990 typical market basket at both 1980 and 1990 prices. As Exhibit 8 shows, the typical market basket actually purchased in 1990 would have cost $196 *at 1980 prices*. The same market basket cost $280 at 1980 prices. *Based on the current-year market basket,* then, the 1990 CSPI is equal to 142.9 [(280 ÷ 196) × 100].

Why do the two alternative methods yield different values for the price index? The differences reflect the weights applied to 1980–1990 price changes. Method I uses the quantity purchased of each good during 1980 to weight the price changes; Method II uses the quantities of the current period (1990).

If the changes in purchases of goods were random, the two alternative methods would tend toward equality. However, changes in the pattern of purchases will not

Consumer Price Index: An indicator of the general level of prices. It attempts to compare the cost of purchasing the market basket bought by a typical consumer during a specific period with the cost of purchasing the same market basket during an earlier period.

be random. Consumers will systematically reduce their purchases of those items that increase the most in price. Similarly, they will tend to expand their consumption of commodities that become *relatively* cheaper. The consumption patterns of Exhibits 7 and 8 illustrate this point. As the prices of hamburgers and T-shirts rose sharply between 1980 and 1990, the quantity purchased of these items declined. In contrast, the quantity of jeans and stereo tapes purchased increased as their *relative* prices declined between 1980 and 1990.

Since Method I assumes that consumers will purchase the base-year bundle, it makes no allowance for substitution away from those goods (hamburgers and T-shirts in our hypothetical case) that increase most in price. So, it overstates the "true" increase in prices (and the inflation rate). In contrast, Method II imposes the current-year bundle on consumers during the base year.

In reality, they would substitute away from the goods that have increased most in price. The imposition of the current-year market basket overstates the level of prices *during the base year*. It thus understates the change in prices between periods.

It was therefore no coincidence that our Method I price index (using the base-year market basket) was greater than our Method II price index (based on the current-year market basket). Method I systematically overstates the increase in prices (and the inflation rate), while Method II systematically understates it.

The Consumer Price Index
The **Consumer Price Index** (CPI) is the most widely used index of price changes over time. The CPI is prepared monthly by the Bureau of Labor Statistics of the Department of Labor. The methodology underlying the CPI is *(Continued)*

EXHIBIT 8 ■ **The 1990 Price Index (1980 = 100) Based on the Typical Market Basket Consumed by College Students in 1990 (hypothetical data)**

Monthly Purchases, 1990	Average Price		Cost of 1980 Market Basket	
	1980	1990	1980 Prices	1990 Prices
50 Hamburgers	$ 1.60	$ 3.20	$ 80.00	$160.00
2 T-shirts	10.00	18.00	20.00	36.00
2 Jeans	24.00	24.00	48.00	48.00
3 Stereo tapes	16.00	12.00	48.00	36.00
		Total	196.00	$280.00

Price Index in 1990 (1980 = 100) $= \dfrac{280}{196} \times 100 = 142.9$

much like our Method I calculations of Exhibit 7, except that the market basket for the CPI is much broader. The composition (quantities) of that market basket is based on the Consumer Expenditure Survey of urban consumers conducted during 1982– 1984. This survey identified 364 items that comprised the typical bundle purchased by urban consumers during 1982–1984.[3]

Each month, some 250 survey workers call or visit approximately 21,000 stores in urban areas selected to represent all urban places in the United States. All together, the CPI *each month* uses approximately 125,000 prices for the 364 food items, consumer goods and services, housing, and property taxes included in the CPI. The average price for each of the items is then weighted according to the quantity of the item purchased during 1982–1984. Just as we illustrated for the four-item market basket of Exhibit 7, the cost of purchasing the 364-item market basket *at current prices* is then compared with the cost of purchasing the same market basket *at base-year prices*. The result is a measure of current prices compared to base-year prices.

Like Method I, the CPI measures the percent change in the cost of purchasing a *fixed* basket of goods consumed during an earlier period (1982–1984). However, consumers will tend to substitute away from the goods that increase most in price, while consuming more of goods that have become relatively cheaper. For example, if the price of beef doubles and the price of turkey falls (or increases by only a small amount), consumers will substitute turkey for the more expensive beef. Since the CPI is based on the *fixed market basket of the earlier period* and therefore fails to adjust for consumer substitution away from the goods that increase most in price, it tends to overstate the rate of inflation.

In 1990, the value of the CPI was 130.7, compared to the base of 100 during the 1982–1984 base period. This indicates the price level in 1990 was 30.7 percent higher than the price level of 1982–1984.

The GNP Deflator
The most general price index is the GNP deflator. The GNP deflator differs from the CPI in two important respects. First, the GNP

deflator is based on the typical market basket that goes into GNP—that is, all final goods and services produced. In addition to consumer goods, the GNP deflator includes prices for goods and services purchased by businesses and governments. Thus, items such as computers, airplanes, welding equipment, and office space are included in the GNP deflator. Second, the GNP deflator is calculated by Method II procedures. Prices during each period are weighted by *the current-year market basket* rather than the base-year market basket as for the CPI.

Comparison of the CPI and GNP Deflator
Exhibit 9 presents data for both the CPI and GNP deflator during the 1967–1990 period. Even though they are based on different market baskets and procedures, the two measures of the inflation rate are quite similar for most years. There were three exceptions—1974, 1979, and 1980. Since the CPI is based on the market basket of the earlier period (Method I procedure), it tends to overstate the inflation rate. The upward bias is more important when there is

THE PROBLEM OF QUALITY VARIATION AND INTRODUCTION OF NEW GOODS

In a dynamic world, changes in quality and the introduction of new goods make income comparisons over time more difficult. During the last 10 or 15 years, there have been substantial changes in the quality and availability of products. Today, new automobiles are more fuel efficient and generally safer than were new automobiles 15 years ago. Dental services are generally much less unpleasant than was true 15 years ago. Some commodities—compact disc players, video recorders, personal computers, and heart transplants, to name a few—simply were unavailable just a few years ago. Statisticians devising price indexes attempt to make some allowance for quality improvements. Many economists believe, however, that failure to fully adjust for quality improvements and the introduction of new products

substantial substitution away from items for which prices have increased sharply. Many economists believe this was the case during the 1970s, a period of sharply higher oil prices. This may well account for the differences between the CPI and GNP deflator during 1974, 1979, and 1980.

The CPI and GNP deflator were designed for different purposes. Choosing between the two depends on what we are trying to measure. If we want to determine how rising prices affect the money income of consumers, the CPI would be most appropriate since it includes only consumer goods. However, if we want an economy-wide measure of inflation with which to adjust GNP or national income data, clearly the GNP deflator is the appropriate index since it includes the price of every good and service produced.

---

[3]Actually, the Bureau of Labor Statistics now publishes two indexes of consumer prices—one for "all urban households" and the other for "urban wage earners and clerical workers." The two differ slightly because the typical bundles of goods purchased by the two groups are not identical.

EXHIBIT 9 ■ The CPI and GNP Deflator, 1967–1990				
Year	CPI (1982–84 = 100)	Inflation Rate (percent)	GNP Deflator (1982 = 100)	Inflation Rate (percent)
1967	33.4	—	35.9	—
1968	34.8	4.2	37.7	5.0
1969	36.7	5.5	39.8	5.6
1970	38.8	5.7	42.0	5.5
1971	40.5	4.4	44.4	5.7
1972	41.8	3.2	46.5	4.7
1973	44.4	6.2	49.5	6.5
1974	49.3	11.0	54.0	9.1
1975	53.8	9.1	59.3	9.8
1976	56.9	5.8	63.1	6.4
1977	60.6	6.5	67.3	6.7
1978	65.2	7.6	72.2	7.3
1979	72.6	11.3	78.6	8.9
1980	82.4	13.5	85.7	9.0
1981	90.9	10.3	94.0	9.7
1982	96.5	6.2	100.0	6.4
1983	99.6	3.2	103.9	3.9
1984	103.9	4.3	107.7	3.7
1985	107.6	3.6	111.2	3.2
1986	109.6	1.9	114.1	2.6
1987	113.6	3.6	117.5	3.0
1988	118.3	4.1	121.7	3.6
1989	124.0	4.8	126.3	3.8
1990	130.7	5.4	131.5	4.1

Source: *Economic Report of the President, 1991.*

results in an overestimation of the inflation rate by as much as 1 or 2 percent annually.

When the bundle of goods available differs substantially between years, the significance of income comparisons is reduced. As Exhibit 10 shows, per capita real GNP in 1930 was less than one-third the figure for 1990. Does this mean that, on average, Americans produced and consumed three times more goods in 1990 than in 1930? Caution should be exercised before arriving at this conclusion. In the 1930s, there were no jet planes, electric typewriters, high speed computers, television programs, automatic dishwashers, or video games. In 1930, even a millionaire could not have purchased the typical bundle consumed by Americans in

| EXHIBIT 10 ■ Per Capita Real GNP, 1930–1990 |||||

In 1990, per capita real GNP was a little more than twice the 1950 level, 2.8 times the 1940 level, and 3.3 times the 1930 value. How meaningful are these numbers?

Year	Per Capita Real GNP (in 1982 dollars)	Year	Per Capita Real GNP (in 1982 dollars)
1930	$5,085	1970	$11,785
1940	5,851	1980	13,996
1950	7,935	1990	16,530
1960	9,213		

Source: Derived from U.S. Department of Commerce data.

1990.[4] On the other hand, in 1930, there were plenty of open spaces, trees, uncongested (but rough) roads, pure-water rivers, hiking trails, and areas with low crime rates. Thus, many goods were available in 1990 that were not available in 1930, and vice versa. Under such circumstances, comparative GNP statistics lose much of their relevance.

GNP DOES NOT ACCOUNT FOR HARMFUL SIDE EFFECTS AND ECONOMIC "BADS"

GNP makes no adjustment for harmful side effects that sometimes arise from production, consumption, and the events of nature. If they do not involve market transactions, economic "bads" are ignored. In a modern industrial economy, production and consumption sometimes generate side effects that either detract from current consumption or reduce our future production possibilities. When property rights are defined imperfectly, air and water pollution are sometimes side effects of economic activity. For example, an industrial plant may pollute the air or water while producing goods. Automobiles may put harmful chemicals into the atmosphere while providing us with transportation. GNP makes no allowance for these negative side effects. In fact, expenditures on the clean-up of air and water pollution, should they be undertaken, will add to GNP.

Similarly, GNP makes no allowance for destructive acts of nature. Consider the events in the fall of 1989. Within a two-week period, San Francisco was hit by a major earthquake and the Carolina coast was devastated by hurricane Hugo. On both sides of the country, nature caused vast damage to important highways, numerous buildings, bridges, and homes. Yet nothing was subtracted from GNP since it makes no allowance for losses that operate outside of market channels. In fact, these natural disasters probably increased GNP. Several hundred million dollars were poured into the reconstruction efforts. The clean-up and replacement of items lost undoubtedly caused people to work longer and purchase more goods and

---

[4]The following quotation from Mancur Olson, Professor of economics at The University of Maryland, illustrates this point:

> The price level has risen about eight times since 1932, so a $25,000 income then would be the "equivalent" of an income of $200,000 today—one could readily afford a Rolls-Royce, the best seats in the theater, and the care of the best physicians in the country. But the 1932 Rolls-Royce, for all its many virtues, does not embody some desirable technologies available today in the humblest Ford. Nor would the imposing dollar of 1932 buy a TV set or a home videocassette recorder. And if one got an infection, the best physicians in 1932 would not be able to prescribe an antibiotic.

services, than otherwise would have been the case. Since GNP ignored the destruction, but counted the rebuilding activities, it tended to overstate the change in living standards during the period.

GNP AND MEASURING ECONOMIC WELFARE

GNP means many things to many people. Some people perceive it as a measure of economic welfare, happiness, or even social progress. This is unfortunate, because GNP was never intended to measure subjective concepts that would obviously be influenced by many factors other than economic goods.

GNP focuses on the production of goods and services without making any judgments about how useful the goods are or what makes people want them. A dollar spent for the schooling of an orphan child counts no more or no less than the alcoholic's dollar spent on another bottle of cheap wine. A dollar spent on advertising counts as much as a dollar spent on a kidney machine to preserve life. A dollar spent on a ticket to a football game counts as much as a dollar spent for admission to a concert by the Boston Symphony Orchestra. GNP makes no distinction. The only criterion is whether or not someone wants the "good" or service enough to pay for it.

Might it be possible to develop a measure, if not of social progress, then of economic welfare? Some economists think so. The task is complicated by the fact that many important items that one would like to measure do not flow through markets. Because of this, there are no market prices to tell us how much they are valued by purchasers.

The work of James Tobin, the 1981 Nobel laureate, and William Nordhaus represents the most elaborate attempt to develop a broader measure of economic well-being, a measure that encompasses both the economic "goods" and "bads" generated during a period.[5] Tobin and Nordhaus refer to their measuring rod as the **measure of economic welfare** (MEW). MEW modifies the traditional GNP data in three major ways:

Measure of Economic Welfare: A measure of economic well-being that focuses on the consumption of goods and services during a period. It differs from GNP in that (a) the estimated cost of various economic "bads" are deducted, (b) expenditures on "regrettable necessities" are excluded, and (c) the estimated benefits of leisure and various nonmarket productive activities are included.

1. The estimated cost of certain economic bads, such as pollution, litter, congestion, and noise, is subtracted from GNP.
2. Expenditures on "regrettable necessities," such as police protection and national defense, are excluded from GNP.
3. The estimated value of nonmarket goods, such as household productive activities and leisure, is added to GNP.

Tobin and Nordhaus estimate that since 1945, per capita MEW has grown less rapidly than per capita GNP. This would indicate that the growth of GNP in recent years may be an overstatement of our recent economic progress.

Of course, subjective judgments are involved when researchers seek to place a value on items that do not go through markets. Tobin and Nordhaus are aware that their estimates are both subjective and subject to error. Nevertheless, their work

---

[5]William Nordhaus and James Tobin, "Is Growth Obsolete?" in *Economic Growth,* National Bureau of Economic Research, [Proceedings on] Fiftieth Anniversary Colloquium (New York, 1972).

represents a challenge to other economists to develop alternative estimates based on different procedures and assumptions. The revision of our methods of measuring economic performance is clearly an exciting and potentially fertile field for tomorrow's economists.

THE GREAT CONTRIBUTION OF GNP

The great contribution of GNP (measured in constant dollars) is its precision, despite all of its shortcomings, as an indicator of short-term changes in productive activity. Current GNP provides a reasonably accurate indication of how we are doing relative to the recent past.

This is very important. If we could not accurately track the performance of the economy, we would be much less likely to adopt productive policies. This ability to identify short-run changes in economic performance is a valuable contribution. As Professor Boulding indicated, this contribution is sufficiently important to rank GNP, ''as one of the great inventions of the twentieth century, probably almost as significant as the automobile.''

OTHER RELATED INCOME MEASURES

Exhibit 11 illustrates the relationship among five alternative measures of aggregate income. GNP, of course, is the broadest and most frequently quoted index of economic performance. As we previously discussed, NNP is simply GNP minus depreciation. Net national product measures the total flow of consumption and government expenditures plus the *net additions* to the capital stock. It values the production of goods and services of the economy at market prices. These prices, however, include indirect business taxes, which boost market prices but which do not represent the cost of using a factor of production. When economists subtract these indirect taxes from NNP, the resulting figure is called **national income.** National income thus represents net output valued at factor cost.

National Income: The total income payments to owners of human (labor) and physical capital during a period. It is also equal to NNP minus indirect business taxes.

National income can be determined in two ways. As Exhibit 11 shows, it is NNP minus indirect business taxes, but it is also the income payments to all factors of production. So, the sum of employee compensation, interest, self-employment income, rents, and corporate profits also yields national income.

Personal Income: The total income received by individuals that is available for consumption, saving, and payment of personal taxes.

Although national income represents the earnings of all resource owners, it is not the same as personal income. **Personal income** is the total of all income received by individuals—income with which they consume goods, add to savings, and pay taxes. It differs from national income in two respects. First, some income is earned but not directly received. Stockholders do not receive all the income generated by corporations. Corporate taxes take a share. Additional profits are channeled back into the business, remaining undistributed to the stockholder. Social security taxes are deducted from the employee's paycheck, forming a component of income earned but not directly received. These factors must be subtracted when calculating personal income.

Second, some income is received even though it was not earned *during the current period*. Government transfer payments, including social security and

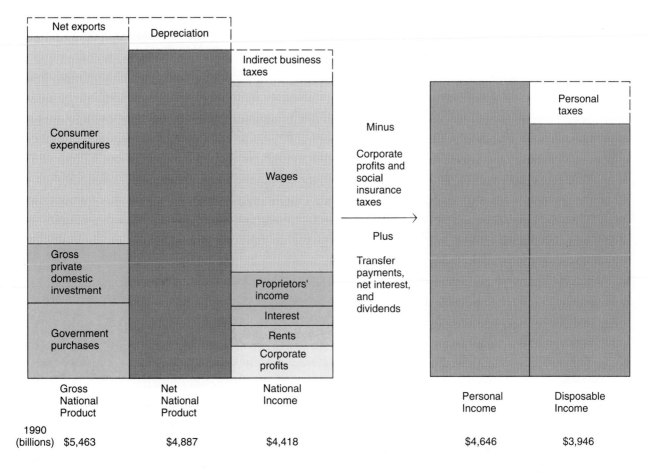

			Minus Corporate profits and social insurance taxes **Plus** Transfer payments, net interest, and dividends		
Gross National Product	Net National Product	National Income		Personal Income	Disposable Income
1990 (billions) $5,463	$4,887	$4,418		$4,646	$3,946

EXHIBIT 11

Five Alternative Measures of Income

The bars illustrate the relationship among five alternative measures of national income. The alternatives range from the gross national product, which is the broadest measure of output, to disposable income, which indicates the funds available to households for either personal consumption or saving.

Disposable Income: The income available to individuals after personal taxes. It can either be spent on consumption or saved.

interest payments, are included in this category. By the same token, dividends received add to personal income, regardless of when they were earned. These components must be added to yield personal income.

As anyone who has ever worked on a job knows, the amount shown on your paycheck does not equal your salary. Personal taxes must be deducted. **Disposable income** is the income that is yours to do with as you please. It is simply personal income minus personal taxes.

There are thus five alternative measures of national product and income:

1. Gross national product
2. Net national product
3. National income

4. Personal income
5. Disposable income

Each of the five measures something different, but they are all closely related. Movement of one of the income measures nearly always parallels movement of the other indicators. Since the five measures move together, economists often use only GNP or the terms "income," "output," or "aggregate production" when referring to the general movement of all five of the indicators of productive activity.

THE REAL INCOME–REAL OUTPUT LINK

National income accounting methods illustrate that the flow of goods and services to the household, business, government, and foreign sectors must equal the flow of income to resource suppliers (see Exhibits 2, 3, and 4). Stated another way, the total output of goods and services must equal the total income of resource suppliers. Total output (supply) and total income are merely alternative methods of viewing the same thing. Aggregate output is the value of the "final user" goods and services supplied to the household, business, government, and foreign sectors during the period. Aggregate income is the sum of payments to resource suppliers who produced those goods. They must equal one another. Since aggregate output and aggregate income must be equal, one obviously cannot change without the other changing, too.

The only way in which a nation can increase its real income is to increase its real output. Unless there is an expansion in the production of goods and services valued by customers, businesses, governments, and foreigners, there will not be an expansion in the real income of a nation. Growth of real income is entirely dependent on the growth of real output.

When evaluating policy alternatives designed to stimulate the growth of income, one must focus clearly on the link between aggregate income and aggregate output. Proponents of policies such as tax reductions, public-sector employment, higher minimum wages, and increased unionization generally argue that their proposals will lead either to a higher level of income or to more rapid economic growth. In evaluating these and other policy alternatives, the careful researchers will ask, "How will the proposal affect output?" Unless there is reason to believe that the policy alternative will stimulate the production of desired goods and services, it will clearly not increase income.

LOOKING AHEAD

GNP and the related income concepts provide us with a measure of economic performance. In the next chapter, we will take a closer look at the movements of prices and real output in the United States and in other countries. As we proceed, we will investigate the factors that underlie these movements. Models that rely heavily on the interrelationships among household consumption, business investment, and government expenditures will be central to our analysis. As we compare the implications of our analysis with the real world, measurement of GNP and related indicators of income will help us sort out sound theories from economic nonsense.

CHAPTER SUMMARY

1. Gross national product (GNP) is a measure of the market value of final goods and services produced during a specific time period.
2. Dollars act as a common denominator for GNP. Production of each final product is weighted according to its selling price. Alternatively, GNP can be calculated by adding up the dollar factor cost of producing the final goods. The two methods sum to an identical result.

3. When the expenditure approach is used, there are four major components of GNP: (a) consumption, (b) investment, (c) government, and (d) net exports.

4. The major components of GNP, as calculated by the resource cost-income approach, are (a) wages and salaries, (b) self-employment income, (c) rents, (d) interest, (e) corporate profits, and (f) non-income expenses, primarily depreciation and indirect business taxes.

5. When comparing income and output data over time, it is important to distinguish between real and nominal values. Changes in nominal values reflect changes in the general level of prices, as well as changes in the economic variable. In contrast, data measured in real terms have been adjusted to eliminate the impact of changes in the price level. Since economics focuses primarily on real changes, economists generally use real data to measure income, output, and other variables influenced by the level of prices.

6. In effect, price indexes compare the cost of purchasing a typical bundle of goods during a time period relative to the cost of the same bundle during an earlier base year. The base-year price level is assigned a value of 100. Thus, if prices have risen relative to the base year, the price index will exceed 100. The two most widely used price indexes in the United States are the GNP deflator and the consumer price index (CPI).

7. GNP may increase because of an increase in either output or prices. The GNP deflator can be used to convert nominal GNP to real GNP. Measured in period 1 dollars,

$$\text{Real GNP}_2 = \text{nominal GNP}_2 \times \frac{\text{GNP deflator}_1}{\text{GNP deflator}_2}$$

8. GNP is an imperfect measure of current production. It excludes household production and the underground (unreported) economy. It fails to account for the negative side effects of current production, such as air and water pollution, depletion of natural resources, and other factors that do not flow through markets. It adjusts imperfectly for quality changes. GNP comparisons are less meaningful when the typical bundle of available goods and services differs widely between two time periods (or between two nations).

9. Despite all its limitations, GNP is vitally important because it is an accurate tool enabling us to identify short-term fluctuations in output. Without such an indicator, our understanding of these fluctuations and their underlying causes would be substantially limited.

10. Economists frequently refer to four other income measures that are related to GNP: net national product, national income, personal income, and disposable income. All of these measures of income tend to move together.

11. The circular flow model illustrates that the aggregate supply of goods and services to households, businesses, governments, and foreigners, and the aggregate income of resource suppliers are merely alternative methods of viewing the same thing. Because of this, actual aggregate output and actual aggregate income will always be equal. The only way we can increase aggregate income is by increasing the aggregate supply of goods desired by economic participants.

CRITICAL ANALYSIS QUESTIONS

*1. Indicate how each of the following activities will affect this year's GNP:
   a. The sale of a used economics textbook to the college bookstore.
   b. Smith's $500 doctor bill for the setting of his son's broken arm.
   c. Family lawn services provided by Smith's 16-year-old child.
   d. Lawn services purchased by Smith from the neighbor's 16-year-old child who has a lawn-mowing business.

---

*Asterisk denotes questions for which answers are given in Appendix C, Selected Answers.

  e. A $5,250 purchase of 100 shares of stock at $50 per share plus the sales commission of $250.
  f. A multibillion dollar discovery of natural gas in Oklahoma.
  g. An earthquake that causes $10 billion of damage in California.
 2. Explain why the rate of growth in GNP in current dollars can sometimes be a misleading statistic.
*3. A large furniture retailer sells $100,000 of household furnishings from inventories built up last year. How does this sale influence GNP? How are the components of GNP affected?
 4. If a nation's gross investment exceeds its depreciation (capital consumption allowance) during the year, what happened to the nation's stock of capital during the year? How will this affect future output? Is it possible for the net investment of a nation to be negative? Explain. What would negative net investment during a year imply about the nation's capital stock and future production potential?
*5. Why might the GNP be a misleading index of changes in output between 1900 and 1990 in the United States? of differences in output between the United States and Mexico?
 6. "GNP counts the product of steel but not the disproduct of air pollution. It counts the product of automobiles but not the disproduct of 'blight' due to junkyards. It counts the product of cigarettes but not the disproduct of a shorter life expectancy due to cancer. Until we can come up with a more reliable index, we cannot tell whether economic welfare is progressing or regressing." Explain why you either agree or disagree with this view.
*7. In 1982, the base year for the consumer price index (1982 CPI = 100), the average earnings of private nonagricultural workers was $267.26 per week. By 1989, the average earnings of private nonagricultural workers had risen to $334.24. However, by 1989, the CPI had risen to 124. What were the real earnings of private nonagricultural workers in 1989 measured in 1982 dollars?
 8. Consider an economy with the following data:

	Nominal GNP (in trillions)	GNP Deflator
1990	$4.80	120
1991	5.25	125

  a. What was the 1991 GNP in constant 1990 dollars?
  b. What was the growth rate of real GNP between 1990 and 1991?
  c. What was the inflation rate?
*9. How much does each of the following contribute to GNP?
  a. Jones pays a repair shop $1,000 to have the engine of her automobile rebuilt.
  b. Jones spends $200 on parts and pays a mechanic $400 to rebuild the engine of her automobile.
  c. Jones spends $200 on parts and rebuilds the engine of her automobile herself.
  d. Jones sells her four-year-old automobile for $5,000 and buys Smith's two-year-old model for $10,000.
  e. Jones sells her four-year-old automobile for $5,000 and buys a new car for $10,000.
10. What is the distinction between *all* market transactions and *final good* transactions? Which is a better measure of the economy's rate of production? Why? What is the relationship between "final good" transactions and the sum of the value added of producers?

*11. Indicate whether the following statements are true or false:
   a. "For the economy as a whole, inventory investment can never be negative."
   b. "The net investment of an economy must always be positive."
   c. "An increase in GNP indicates that the standard of living of people has risen."

*12. How do the receipts and expenditures of a state-operated lottery affect GNP?

 13. Distinguish between the Consumer Price Index (CPI) and the GNP deflator. Which is the better measure of price increases?

*14. Indicate how each of the following will affect this year's GNP:
   a. You suffer $10,000 of damage when you wreck your automobile.
   b. You win $10,000 in a state lottery.
   c. You spend $5,200 in January for 100 shares of stock ($5,000 for the stock and $200 sales commission) and sell the stock in August for $8,300 ($8,000 for the stock and $300 sales commission).
   d. You pay $300 for this month's rental of your apartment.
   e. You are paid $300 for computer services provided to a client.
   f. You receive $300 from your parents.
   g. You get a raise from $4 to $5 per hour and simultaneously decide to reduce your hours worked from 20 to 16 per week.

 15. GNP does not count productive services such as child care, food preparation, cleaning, and laundry provided within the household. Why are these things excluded? Is GNP a sexist measure? Does it understate the productive contributions of women relative to men? Discuss.

 16. Suppose a group of British investors finances the construction of a plant to manufacture skateboards in St. Louis, Missouri. How will the construction of the plant affect GNP? Suppose the plant generates $100,000 in corporate profits this year. Will these profits contribute to GNP?

*17. Would you rather have a $40,000 income in 1929 or in 1989, if you could buy only the goods that were available during each of those years? Explain.

 18. Fill in the blanks a through f in the following table:

Year	Nominal GNP (in billions)	GNP Deflator (1982 = 100)	Real GNP (billions of 1982 dollars)
1940	$100.4	13.0	a._____
1955	$405.9	27.2	b._____
1965	$705.1	c._____	$2,087.6
1975	d._____	59.3	$2,695.0
1985	$4,014.9	e._____	$3,618.7
1989	$5,200.8	126.3	f._____

Economic Fluctuations, Unemployment, and Inflation

Prosperity is when the prices of the things that you sell are rising; inflation is when the prices of the things that you buy are rising. Recession is when other people are unemployed; depression is when you are unemployed.

Anonymous

CHAPTER FOCUS

- What is a business cycle? How much economic instability has the United States experienced?

- Why do we experience unemployment? Are some types of unemployment worse than others?

- What do economists mean by full employment? How is full employment related to the natural rate of unemployment?

- What are some of the side effects of inflation? Does it make any difference whether buyers and sellers anticipate inflation? Why?

- How does the economic performance of the United States stack up with other major industrial countries?

*T*hree of the most important indicators of economic performance are the growth of real GNP, level of employment, and rate of inflation. These indicators are closely watched by investors, politicians, and the media. Most governments are committed to the achievement of rapid growth in output, a high level of employment, and relatively stable prices. There is, however, substantial disagreement about what governments can do to accomplish these objectives. As we proceed, we will analyze this issue in detail.

What happens to output, employment, and prices is closely related to another central issue: economic stability. A stable environment is crucial to the efficient operation of an economy. In this chapter, we will look at the stability of real output, employment, and prices. We will analyze the historical record and discuss some of the measurement problems in these areas. The concept of full employment will be introduced and its meaning discussed. We will also analyze the side effects of inflation and consider how buyers and sellers adjust their choices when they anticipate rising prices in the future.

Our goal in this chapter is to provide the reader with basic knowledge about economic instability—why it is important and how it influences our lives. As we proceed, we will develop a model of our economy that will help us better understand the causes of economic instability. In the United States, the Employment Act of 1946 pledges that the federal government will pursue policies designed to "promote maximum employment, production, and purchasing power." In subsequent chapters, we will analyze both the potential and limitations of government as a stabilizing force.

SWINGS IN THE ECONOMIC PENDULUM

During this century, the growth rate of real GNP in the United States has averaged approximately 3.5 percent. The rate of growth, however, has not been steady. Exhibit 1 illustrates the fluctuation of real GNP, beginning with the Great Depression of the 1930s. On several occasions, the annual growth rate of real GNP has exceeded 6 percent for brief periods of time. In other instances, output as measured by real GNP actually declined. During the Great Depression, economic growth plunged. Real GNP declined by 8 percent or more each year between 1930

EXHIBIT 1

Instability in the Growth of Real GNP

Note that although fluctuations are present, the periods of positive growth outweigh the periods of declining real income. The long-run real GNP in the United States has grown approximately 3.5 percent annually.

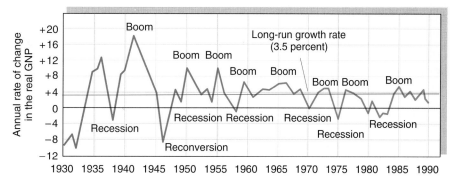

and 1932. Real GNP in 1933 was 30 percent smaller than it was in 1929. The 1929 level of real GNP was not reached again until 1939. The Second World War was characterized by a rapid expansion of GNP, which was followed by a decline after the war. Real GNP did not reach its 1944 level again until 1951, although the output of consumer goods did increase significantly in the years immediately following the war as the conversion was made to a peacetime economy.

Since 1950, growth has been more stable. Economic booms and serious declines in the rate of output, though, continue to occur. The years 1954, 1958, 1960, 1970, 1974, and 1979–1982 were characterized by downswings in economic activity. Upswings in real GNP came in 1950, 1955, most of the 1960s, 1972–1973, 1976–1977, and 1983–1988. During the last four decades, however, annual fluctuations in real GNP have fallen within the range of minus 2 percent to plus 6 percent. Compared to prior periods, this is a definite improvement.

A HYPOTHETICAL BUSINESS CYCLE

Business Cycle: Fluctuations in the general level of economic activity as measured by such variables as the rate of unemployment and changes in real GNP.

The historical data show that periods of economic expansion have traditionally been followed by economic slowdown and contraction. During the slowdown, real GNP grows at a slower rate, if at all. During the expansion phase, real GNP grows rapidly. Economists refer to these fluctuations in economic conditions as business cycles. As the term implies, a **business cycle** is a period of up-and-down motion in aggregate measures of current economic output and income. Exhibit 2 illustrates a hypothetical business cycle. When most businesses are operating at capacity level and real GNP is growing rapidly, a *business peak* or *boom* is present. A business peak is characterized by high levels of economic activity and real GNP, compared to the recent past and near future. As aggregate business conditions slow, the economy begins the contraction or recessionary phase of a business cycle. During the contraction, the sales of most businesses fall, real GNP grows at a slow rate or perhaps declines, and unemployment in the aggregate labor market increases. The bottom of the contraction phase is referred to as the *recessionary trough*. After the downturn reaches bottom and economic conditions begin to improve, the economy enters an expansionary stage. During the expansion phase, business sales rise, GNP grows rapidly, and the rate of unemployment declines. The expansion eventually

EXHIBIT 2

The Business Cycle

In the past, ups and downs have often characterized aggregate business activity. Despite these fluctuations, an upward trend in real GNP is usually observed.

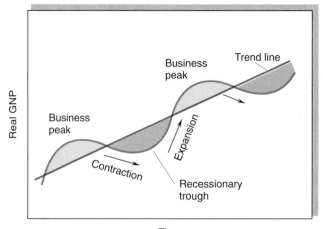

blossoms into another business peak. The peak, however, peters out and turns to a contraction, beginning the cycle anew.

Recession: A downturn in economic activity characterized by declining real GNP and rising unemployment. In an effort to be more precise, many economists define a recession as two consecutive quarters in which there is a decline in real GNP.

The term **recession** is widely used to describe conditions during the contraction and recessionary trough phases of the business cycle. Economists define a recession as a period during which real GNP declines for two or more successive quarters. When a recession is prolonged and characterized by a sharp decline in economic activity, it is called a **depression.**

Our hypothetical business cycle of Exhibit 2 indicates steady and smooth movement from business peak to recessionary trough and back again to the peak. In the real world, cycles are not nearly so regular or predictable. As Exhibit 1 shows, various phases of the cycle have sometimes been quite lengthy. As we know, 1929–1933 was a prolonged period of economic decline that clearly deserves the title of depression. In contrast, the 1960s were characterized by lengthy expansion. Nevertheless, the phases of expansion, business peak, contraction, and recessionary trough are readily observable.

Depression: A prolonged and very severe recession.

Despite these cyclical patterns, the trend in real GNP in the United States and most other industrial nations has clearly been upward. During the last 80 years, the long-run rate of growth in real GNP has been approximately 3.5 percent (see Exhibit 1). In some years, growth has been greater, and in others, less, but years of positive growth clearly outweigh the periods of falling real GNP.

EMPLOYMENT FLUCTUATIONS IN A DYNAMIC ECONOMY

Rate of Unemployment: The percent of persons in the civilian labor force who are not employed. Mathematically, it is equal to:

$$\frac{\text{Number of persons unemployed}}{\text{Number in civilian labor force}} \times 100$$

The **rate of unemployment** is one of the most widely used economic indicators. It is a key barometer of conditions in an important market, the aggregate labor market. This notwithstanding, the term is often misunderstood. At the most basic level, it is important to note that *unemployment* is different from *not working*. Persons may not be currently working in the marketplace for a variety of reasons. Some may have retired. Others may be attending school in order to acquire the knowledge and skills that will enhance their future livelihood. Still others may not be working as a result of illness or disability.

Unemployed: The term used to describe a person, not currently employed, who is either (a) actively seeking employment or (b) waiting to begin or return to a job.

Only persons not working who are either looking for work or waiting to return or begin a job are counted as **unemployed.** In turn, persons must either be employed or unemployed before they are considered in the **labor force.** The rate of unemployment is the number of persons unemployed expressed as a percentage of the labor force. (See Measures of Economic Activity box for information on how the Bureau of Labor Statistics derives the unemployment rate.)

Labor Force: The portion of the population 16 years of age and over who are either employed or unemployed.

Exhibit 3 will help explain the relationships among the important labor force classifications. We begin by grouping the noninstitutional adult population into three broad categories: (a) persons not in the labor force, (b) persons in the armed forces, and (c) persons either working or seeking work in the civilian labor force. In 1990, there were 61.6 million people aged 16 or over who were neither employed nor looking for market work. This is not to say these people were idle. Most were attending school, working in their households, vacationing, and/or recovering from illnesses. Nevertheless, their activities were outside the market labor force. They were not part of the labor force.

Rate of Labor Force Participation: The number of persons 16 years of age or over who are either employed or actively seeking employment as a percentage of the total noninstitutional population 16 years of age and over.

Labor force participants fall into two subgroups: the employed and the unemployed. The **rate of labor force participation** is the number of persons in the labor force as a percentage of the total noninstitutional population 16 years of age and over. In 1990, the rate of labor force participation was 67.2 percent, indicating that two out of every three adults were in the labor force.

Not all people who are unemployed lost their last job. A dynamic economy will be characterized by considerable labor mobility as workers move (a) from contracting to expanding industries and (b) into and out of the labor force. Spells of unemployment often accompany such changes.

MEASURES OF ECONOMIC ACTIVITY

Deriving the Unemployment Rate

Each month, the Bureau of Labor Statistics (BLS) of the U.S. Department of Labor calculates the number of people employed, unemployed, and not in the labor force. Because it would be too burdensome, the BLS does not contact each person in the United States to determine each one's employment status. Instead, the employment statistics published by the BLS are based on a random sample of 59,500 households drawn from 729 different locations in the United States. The survey is conducted during the week containing the twelfth day of each month and is designed to reflect geographic and demographic groups in proportion to their representation in the nation as a whole.

Specially trained interviewers pose identical questions in the same order to each of the 59,500 households (which include approximately 100,000 adults). People are classified as employed, unemployed, or not in the labor force on the basis of their responses to questions designed to elicit this information. People are considered "employed" if they (a) worked at all (even as little as one hour) for pay or profit during the survey week, (b) worked 15 hours or more without pay in a family-operated enterprise during the week, or (c) have a job at which they did not work during the survey week because of illness, vacation, industrial disputes, bad weather, time off, or personal reasons.

People are considered unemployed if they (a) do not have a job, (b) are available for work, and (c) have actively looked for work during the past four weeks. Looking for work may involve any of the following activities: (a) registration at a public or private employment office, (b) meeting with prospective employers, (c) checking with friends or relatives, (d) placing or answering advertisements, (e) writing letters of application, or (f) being on a union or professional register. In addition, those not working are classified as unemployed if they are either waiting to start a new job within 30 days or waiting to be recalled from a layoff. Except for temporary illness, a person must be available for work to be classified as unemployed. So, students seeking summer employment prior to their availability for employment would not be counted as unemployed.

Except for people under the age of 16 and inmates of institutions, those who are neither employed nor unemployed are classified as "not in the labor force." Major subcategories of people not in the labor force include those in school, keeping house, retired, or unable to work due to a disability.

Only people in the labor force—that is, only those classified as either employed or unemployed—enter into the calculation of the unemployment rate. The unemployment rate is the number of people unemployed divided by the number of people in the labor force. Based on its survey data, the BLS publishes the unemployment rate and other employment-related statistics monthly. Since employment and unemployment patterns vary during the year due to holidays, vacations, shifts in production schedules, and other seasonally related reasons, the unemployment data are seasonally adjusted. In addition, states use the BLS survey data and employment data from industries covered by unemployment insurance to construct state and area unemployment estimates based on BLS guidelines. The major sources of employment data are the *Monthly Labor Review* and *Employment and Earnings,* monthly publications of the U.S. Department of Labor.

As Exhibit 4 shows, the Department of Labor indicates five reasons why workers may experience unemployment. Exhibit 4 indicates the share of unemployed workers in each of these categories in 1990. Interestingly, 9.5 percent of the unemployed workers were first-time entrants into the work force. Another 27.4 percent were reentering after exiting for additional schooling, household work, or other reasons. Thus, nearly two out of five unemployed workers were experiencing unemployment as the result of entry or reentry into the labor force. Approximately 15 percent of the unemployed quit their last job. People laid off and waiting to return to their previous positions contributed 14.8 percent to the total. Workers terminated from their last job accounted for approximately a third (33.5 percent) of the unemployed workers.

One of the most interesting labor force developments of the post-Second World War era is the dramatic increase in the labor force participation rate of women.

EXHIBIT 3

Population, Employment, and Unemployment, 1990

The accompanying diagram illustrates the alternative participation status categories for the adult population.

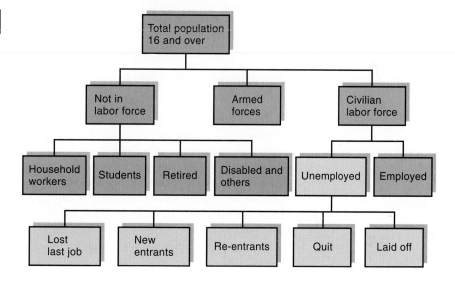

EXHIBIT 3 ■ Population, Employment, and Unemployment, 1990	
	Number of Persons, 1990[a]
Noninstitutional Population (Age 16 and over)	188.0
Not in labor force	61.6
Total labor force	126.4
Armed forces	1.6
Civilian labor force	124.8
Employed	117.9
Unemployed	6.9
Rate of labor force participation (percent)	67.2
Civilian rate of employment (as a percentage of the total noninstitutional population)	62.7
Rate of unemployment (as a percentage of the civilian labor force)	5.5

[a]Data are measured in millions, except those expressed as percentages. U.S. Department of Labor, *Monthly Labor Review,* February 1991.

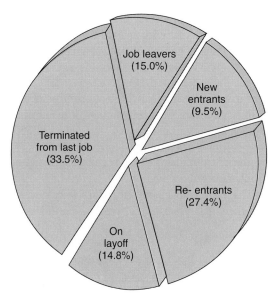

EXHIBIT 4

Composition of the Unemployed by Reason

This chart indicates the various reasons why persons were unemployed in 1990. Only one-third (33.5%) of the persons unemployed were terminated from their last job.

Approximately 37 percent of the unemployed workers were new entrants and reentrants to the labor force.

Source: *Monthly Labor Review,* February 1991

Exhibit 5 visually illustrates this point. In 1948, the labor force participation rate of women was 32.7 percent, compared to 87 percent for men. Since then, the market work participation rate of women has steadily increased while the rate for men has fallen. By 1990, 57.7 percent of adult women worked outside the home. Married women accounted for most of this increase. More than half of all married women now are in the labor force, compared to only 20 percent immediately following the Second World War. In contrast, the labor force participation rate for men fell to 76.4 percent in 1990, down from 84 percent in 1960. Clearly, the composition of work force participation within the family has changed substantially during the last four decades.

We live in a dynamic world. New products are constantly introduced and new technologies developed. Some firms are expanding, while others are contracting, and still others are going out of business. This process results in the creation of new jobs and the disappearance of old ones. Similarly, at any point in time potential workers are switching from school (or nonwork) into the labor force, while others are retiring or taking a leave from the labor force. As long as workers are mobile—as long as they can voluntarily quit and search for better opportunities in a changing world; switch positions from one job to another; and reallocate work responsibilities within the family—some unemployment will be present.

There is a positive side to job search and unemployment—it generally permits individuals to better match their skills and preferences with the requirements of a job. Such job moves enhance both employee productivity and earnings.

Young workers often switch jobs and move between schooling and the labor force as they search for a career path that best fits their abilities and preferences. As the result of this job switching, the unemployment rate of younger workers is substantially higher than for more established workers. As Exhibit 6 shows, in 1990 the unemployment rate of young men was more than double the rate for men age 25 years and over. Similarly, the unemployment rate of young women was well above the rate for older women.

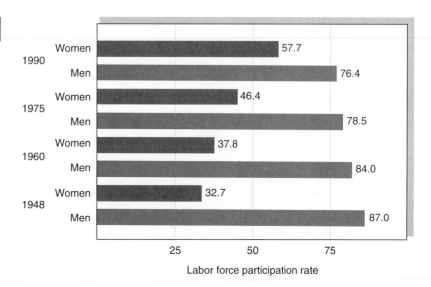

EXHIBIT 5

The Labor Force Participation of Men and Women

As the chart illustrates, the labor force participation rate for women has been steadily increasing for several decades, while the rate for men has been declining.

EXHIBIT 6 ■ Unemployment Rate by Age and Sex, 1990	
Group	Rate of Unemployment, 1990 (Percent)
Total, all workers	5.5
Men, Total	5.6
Age, 16–19	16.3
Age, 20–24	9.1
25 and over	4.4
Women, Total	5.4
Age, 16–19	14.7
Age, 20–24	8.5
25 and over	4.3

Source: *Monthly Labor Review*, February 1991.

Frictional Unemployment: Unemployment due to constant changes in the economy that prevent *qualified* unemployed workers from being immediately matched up with existing job openings. It results from lack of complete information on the part of both job seekers and employers and from the amount of unemployed time spent by job seekers in job searches (pursuit of costly information).

JOB SEARCH AND FRICTIONAL UNEMPLOYMENT

While some unemployment is perfectly consistent with economic efficiency, this is not always the case. Abnormally high rates of unemployment generally reflect weak demand conditions for labor, counter-productive policies, and/or the inability or lack of incentive on the part of potential workers and potential employers to arrive at mutually advantageous agreements. To clarify matters, economists divide unemployment into three categories: frictional, structural, and cyclical. Let us take a closer look at each of these three classifications.

Unemployment that is caused by constant changes in the labor market is called **frictional unemployment.** Frictional unemployment occurs because (a) employers are not fully aware of all available workers and their job qualifications and (b) available workers are not fully aware of the jobs being offered by employers.

The basic cause of frictional unemployment is imperfect information. The number of job vacancies may match up with the number of persons seeking

EXHIBIT 7

Benefits and Costs
of Job Search

The marginal gain from job search generally declines with time spent searching for a job, because it becomes less likely that additional search will lead to a better position. Conversely, the marginal cost of additional search rises with search time, primarily because still more search means forgoing wages on more attractive jobs discovered by prior search. When the job seeker perceives that the marginal gain from additional search no longer exceeds the marginal cost, the best option discovered by the search process will be accepted.

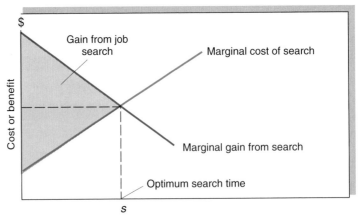

employment. The qualifications of the job seekers may even meet those required by firms seeking employees. Frictional unemployment will still occur, however, because persons seeking jobs and firms hiring employees with the qualifications of the job seekers do not know about each other. In the real world, information is scarce. Both employers and employees will search for information that will help them make better choices.

Employers looking for a new worker seldom hire the first applicant who walks into their employment office. They want to find the "best available" worker to fill their opening. It is costly to hire workers who perform poorly. It is sometimes even costly to terminate their employment. So, employers search—they expend time and resources screening applicants and choose only those who have the desired qualifications.

Similarly, unemployed workers seeking a job usually do not accept the first one offered. They, too, search among potential alternatives, seeking their best option. They make telephone calls, respond to newspaper ads, submit to job interviews, use employment services, and so on. Pursuit of personal gain—the landing of a job that is more attractive than the current options of which they are aware—motivates job seekers to engage in job search activities. Additional search leads to the discovery of higher paying, more preferable alternatives. However, as a job searcher finds out about more potential job opportunities, it becomes less likely that additional search will uncover a more preferable option. Therefore, as Exhibit 7 illustrates, the marginal gain from job search declines with time spent searching. The primary cost of job search is generally the opportunity cost of wages forgone as the result of failure to accept one's best current alternative. This cost will increase as additional search leads to the discovery of better alternatives not accepted. Thus, the marginal cost of job search will rise with time spent searching.

The rational job seeker will search for employment as long as the expected marginal gain from the search exceeds the expected marginal cost of the search. Eventually, as the marginal gains decline and marginal costs rise, the job seekers will conclude that additional search is not worth the cost. The best alternative resulting from the search process will be accepted. However, this process takes time and during this time the job seeker is contributing to the frictional unemployment of the economy.

MYTHS OF ECONOMICS

"Unemployed resources would not exist if the economy were operating efficiently."

Nobody likes unemployment. Certainly, extended unemployment can be a very painful experience. Not all unemployment, however, reflects waste and inefficiency. If the resources of an economy are going to be used effectively, the skills of workers must be matched with the jobs of employers. People must end up working on jobs that fit their knowledge, skills, and preferences. Similarly, firms must employ workers that are well suited for their jobs. Waste will result if, for example, a person with few engineering skills works as an engineer or a person who is unable to work with others occupies a foreman position.

Prospective employees searching for the right job need information on job requirements and availability, wage rates, work environment, and so on. This information is scarce and is generally acquired by "shopping"—searching for employment. Often, this shopping is easier (cheaper) if the job seeker is unemployed. Thus, job seekers usually do not take just any available job. They search, all the while acquiring valuable

information, because they believe searching will lead to a preferred job opportunity.

Similarly, employers shop when they are seeking labor services. They, too, acquire information about available workers that will help them select employees whose skills and preferences match with the demands of the job. The shopping of job seekers and employers results in some unemployment, but it also communicates information that leads to a better match between the characteristics of job seekers (including their preferences) and job requirements. Improvement in the match between employees and jobs will lead to an expansion in real output and higher wage rates. Thus, job search can yield a return (in excess of its cost) to both the individual and the society. Such job search, even though it often involves unemployment, is a natural part of an efficiently operating labor market.

Perhaps thinking about the housing market will help the reader better understand why search time can be both beneficial and productive. As with the employment market, the housing market is characterized by dynamic change. New housing structures are brought into the market; older structures

depreciate and wear out. Families move from one community to another. Within the same community, renters move among housing accommodations as they seek the housing quality, price, and location that best fit their preferences. As in the employment market, information is imperfect. So, renters shop among the available accommodations, seeking the most for their housing expenditures. Similarly, landlords search among renters, seeking to rent their accommodations to those who value them most highly. "Frictional unemployment" of houses is inevitable, but does it indicate inefficiency? No. It results from people's attempts to acquire information that will eventually promote an efficient match between housing units and renters.

Some unemployment, particularly cyclical unemployment, is indicative of inefficiency. However, the unemployment due to the shopping of job seekers and employers makes available more information, a scarce resource, and will eventually result in a more efficient match of applicants with job openings (and, thus, greater economic efficiency) than would be possible otherwise.

It is important to note that even though frictional unemployment is a side effect, the job search process typically leads to improved economic efficiency and a higher real income for employees (see Myths of Economics). If a job seeker were to search less than the optimal amount (*s* of Exhibit 7), potential gains (from the achievement of a better job) in excess of the marginal search costs would be forgone. Similarly, job search beyond the optimal level is simply not worth the cost.

Policies that influence the costs and benefits of searching will influence the level of unemployment. If the job seeker's search costs are reduced, he or she will spend more time searching. For example, higher unemployment benefits make it less costly to continue looking for a preferred job. This decline in the marginal cost of job search (a shift of the marginal cost curve to the right in Exhibit 7) will induce job seekers to expand their search time beyond the optimal level. A higher level of unemployment will result.

STRUCTURAL UNEMPLOYMENT

Structural Unemployment: Unemployment due to structural changes in the economy that eliminate some jobs while generating job openings for which the unemployed workers are *not* well qualified.

Structural unemployment occurs because of changes in the basic characteristics of the economy that prevent the ''matching up'' of available jobs with available workers. It is not always easy to distinguish between frictional and structural unemployment. In each case, job openings and potential workers searching for jobs are present. The crucial difference between the two is that with frictional unemployment, workers possess the requisite skills to fill the job openings; with structural unemployment, they do not. Essentially, the skills of a structurally unemployed worker have been rendered obsolete by changing market conditions and technology. Realistically, the structurally unemployed worker faces the prospect of either a career change or prolonged unemployment. For older workers in particular, these are bleak alternatives.

There are many causes of structural unemployment. Dynamic change is of course at the top of the list. The introduction of new products or productive methods can substantially alter the employment and earnings opportunities of even highly skilled workers, particularly if the skills are not easily transferable to other industries. Many automobile workers experienced this reality in the early 1980s, as increased competition from foreign producers and changing technology reduced employment in the U.S. automobile industry. Shifts in public-sector priorities can also cause structural unemployment. For example, increased spending on space programs coupled with a decline in spending on highway construction may lead to a shortage of aeronautical scientists and unemployment among construction workers. Institutional factors that reduce the ability of employees to obtain skills necessary to fill existing job openings also increase structural unemployment. For example, minimum wage legislation may reduce the incentive of business firms to offer on-the-job training to low-skill workers, thereby contributing to structural unemployment.

CYCLICAL UNEMPLOYMENT

Cyclical Unemployment: Unemployment due to recessionary business conditions and inadequate aggregate demand for labor.

Cyclical unemployment arises when there is a general downturn in business activity. Since fewer goods are being produced, fewer workers will be required to produce them. Employers lay off workers and cut back employment.

Unexpected reductions in the general level of demand for goods and services are the major cause of cyclical unemployment. In a world of imperfect information, adjustments to *unexpected* declines in demand will be painful. When the demand for labor declines generally, workers will at first not know whether they are being laid off because of a *specific shift* in demand away from their previous employer or because of a *general decline* in aggregate demand. Similarly, they will not be sure whether their current bleak employment prospects are *temporary* or *long-term*. Workers will search for employment, hoping to find a job at or near their old wage rate. If their situation was merely the result of *shifts* among employers in demand, or, if the downturn is brief, terminated workers will soon find new employment similar to their old jobs. When there is a general decline in demand, however, most workers' search efforts will be fruitless. Their duration of unemployment will be abnormally long.

With time, the unemployed workers will lower their expectations and be willing to take some cut in wages. However, when the reduction in aggregate demand is

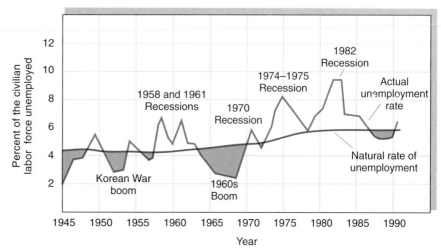

EXHIBIT 8

The Unemployment Rate, 1945–1990

The unemployment rate increases during recessions (such as those experienced in 1974–1975 and 1982) and declines during economic expansions (for example, the 1960s boom and 1983–1989 expansion). The estimated natural rate of unemployment is also indicated. Note that the actual unemployment rate is substantially greater than the natural rate during recessions.

Source: *Economic Report of the President:* 1991 and Robert J. Gordon. *Macroeconomics* (Boston: Little, Brown, 1990).

substantial, the adjustment process may be lengthy and a substantial increase in the unemployment rate is the expected result. As we proceed, we will investigate potential sources of cyclical unemployment and consider policy alternatives to reduce it.

EMPLOYMENT FLUCTUATIONS—THE HISTORICAL RECORD

Employment and output are closely linked over the business cycle. If we are going to produce more goods and services, we must either increase the number of workers or increase the *output per worker*. While output, or productivity per worker, is an important source of long-term economic growth, it changes slowly from year to year.

Thus, rapid increases in output, such as those that occur during a strong business expansion, generally require an increase in employment. As a result, output and employment tend to be positively related. Conversely, output and unemployment are inversely related—the unemployment rate generally increases when the economy dips into a recession.

The empirical evidence of Exhibit 8 illustrates the inverse relationship between output and rate of unemployment. When output declines during a recession, the unemployment rate generally rises. During the recessions of 1958 and 1960–1961, unemployment rose to approximately 7 percent. In contrast, the unemployment rate declined throughout the economic boom of the 1960s only to rise again during the recession of 1970. During the recession of 1974–1975, the unemployment rate jumped to more than 9 percent. Similarly, the unemployment rate soared to nearly 11 percent during the severe, but relatively brief recession of 1982. Conversely, the rate declined substantially during the 1976–1978 and post-1982 expansions.

THE CONCEPT OF FULL EMPLOYMENT

Full employment is a term widely used by economists and public officials alike. What does full employment mean? Clearly, full employment does not mean zero unemployment. In a world of imperfect information, employers and employees will "shop" before they buy and sell. Much of this shopping is efficient, since it leads to a better match between the skills of employees and the skills necessary to carry out productive tasks. Some unemployment is thus entirely consistent with the efficient operation of a dynamic labor market.

How much unemployment would one expect when the labor market is working well? There is not a clear answer to this question. Economists define **full employment** as the level of employment that results when the rate of unemployment is normal, considering both frictional and structural factors. Currently, most economists believe that full employment exists when between 94 and 95 percent of the labor force is employed.

Full employment incorporates the idea that at a given time there is some **natural rate of unemployment** in a dynamic exchange economy. This natural rate of unemployment arises from employees and employers shopping in a world characterized by both (a) dynamic change and (b) imperfect (scarce) information concerning job opportunities and the availability of potential workers. The natural rate of unemployment reflects both frictional and structural factors. The natural rate of unemployment is not a temporary high or low. It is sustainable into the future. Economists sometimes refer to it as the unemployment rate accompanying the economy's "maximum sustainable rate of output."

The natural rate of unemployment, though, is not immutably fixed. It is influenced both by the structure of the labor force and by changes in public policy. For example, since youthful workers experience more unemployment because they change jobs and move in and out of the labor force often (see Exhibit 6), the natural rate of unemployment increases when youthful workers comprise a larger proportion of the work force. This is precisely what happened during the 1960s and 1970s. In 1958, youthful workers (ages 16 to 24) constituted only 15.6 percent of the labor force. As the postwar "baby boom" generation entered the labor market, youthful workers as a share of the labor force rose dramatically. By 1980, one out of every four workers was in the youthful-worker grouping. In contrast, prime-age workers (over age 25) declined from 84.4 percent of the U.S. work force in 1958 to only 75.3 percent in 1980. Studies indicate that this increased representation of youthful workers pushed the natural rate of unemployment up by approximately 1.5 percent during the 1958–1980 period. (See estimated natural rate of unemployment in Exhibit 8.)

Public policies also affect the natural rate of unemployment. Policies that (a) encourage workers to reject job offers and continue to search for employment, (b) prohibit employers from offering wage rates that would induce them to employ (and train) low-skill workers, and (c) reduce the employer's opportunity cost of using layoffs to adjust rates of production will increase the natural rate of unemployment. With regard to these points, most economists believe that increases in the legislated minimum wage and higher unemployment benefits push the natural rate of unemployment upward.

Exhibit 8 illustrates the relationship between the *actual* unemployment rate and the *natural* unemployment rate during the last four decades. The actual unemployment rate fluctuates around the natural rate, in response to cyclical economic conditions. The actual rate generally rises above the natural rate during a recession and falls below the natural rate when the economy is in the midst of an economic boom. For example, the actual rate of unemployment was substantially above the natural rate during the recessions of 1974–75 and 1982, while the reverse was the

Full Employment: The level of employment that results from the efficient use of the civilian labor force after allowance is made for the normal (natural) rate of unemployment due to information cost, dynamic changes, and the structural conditions of the economy. For the United States, full employment is thought to exist when between 94 and 95 percent of the labor force is employed.

Natural Rate of Unemployment: The long-run average unemployment rate due to frictional and structural conditions of labor markets. This rate is affected both by dynamic change and by public policy. It is sustainable in the future.

case during the economic boom of the 1960s. As we proceed, we will often compare the actual and natural rates of unemployment. In a very real sense, macroeconomics studies why the actual and natural rates differ and the factors that cause the natural rate to change with the passage of time.

Without detracting from the importance of full employment (maximum sustainable employment), we must not overlook another vital point. Employment is a means to an end. We use employment to produce desired goods and services. Full employment is an empty concept if it means employment at unproductive jobs. The meaningful goal of full employment is productive employment—employment that will generate goods and services desired by consumers at the lowest possible cost.

THE RATE OF UNEMPLOYMENT OR THE RATE OF EMPLOYMENT—SOME MEASUREMENT PROBLEMS

The definition of "unemployed" is not without ambiguity. Remember that persons are counted as unemployed only if they are (a) available for and seeking work or (b) awaiting recall from a layoff. These criteria can lead to some paradoxical outcomes. For example, a person who quit looking for work because his or her job-seeking efforts have been discouraging is not counted as unemployed. On the other hand, a welder vacationing in Florida, receiving unemployment compensation while awaiting recall to a $50,000-per-year job in the automobile industry, is considered to be among the ranks of the unemployed.

One can argue that the statistical definition of "unemployment" results both in (a) people being excluded even though they would prefer to be working (or working more) and in (b) people being included who are not seriously seeking employment. **Discouraged workers** are those whose employment prospects are so bleak that they no longer consider it worthwhile to search for employment. Since they are not *actively* seeking employment, they are not counted as unemployed. Nevertheless, many discouraged workers would be willing to accept employment, were it available. When the economy turns down, the number of workers in the discouraged category rises substantially. For example, during the severe recession of 1982, the Department of Labor estimated that there were nearly 2 million discouraged workers (approximately 2 percent of the labor force) in the United States.

The method of classifying part-time workers may also result in an understatement of the number of unemployed workers. Part-time workers who desire full-time employment are classified as employed rather than unemployed if they work as much as a single hour per week. People in the latter category are certainly underemployed, if not unemployed.

On the other hand, some people who only claim to be searching for work may also be classified as unemployed. For example, an individual who rejects available employment because it is less attractive than the current combination of household work, continued job search, unemployment benefits, food stamps, and other governmental welfare programs is numbered among the unemployed. Required work registration in order to maintain eligibility for food stamps and assistance from Aid to Families with Dependent Children (AFDC) also adds to the ambiguity of the unemployment statistics. Some may register for employment (and therefore be numbered among the unemployed) with the primary objective of maintaining their

Discouraged Workers:
Persons who have given up searching for employment because they believe additional job search would be fruitless. Since they are not currently searching for work, they are not counted among the unemployed.

food stamp and/or AFDC benefits.[1] People engaged in criminal activities (for example, drug pushers, gamblers, and prostitutes) or working "off the books" in the underground economy may be counted among the unemployed if they are not otherwise gainfully employed. Although estimates are difficult to project, some researchers believe that as many as a million people classified as unemployed participate in the underground economy.

Rate of Employment: The number of persons 16 years of age and over who are employed as a percentage of the total noninstitutional population 16 years of age and over. One can calculate either (a) a civilian rate of employment, in which only civilian employees are included in the numerator, or (b) a total rate of employment, in which both civilian and military employees are included in the numerator.

As a result of these ambiguities, some economists argue that the **rate of employment** is a more objective and meaningful indicator of job availability than is the rate of unemployment. The civilian rate of employment is the number of persons employed (over the age of 16) in the civilian labor force as a percentage of the number of persons (over the age of 16) in the noninstitutional population. Both of these variables (the civilian level of employment and the noninstitutional adult population) can be readily measured. In addition, they are relatively clear. Their measurement does not require a subjective judgment as to whether a person is actually "available for work" or "actively seeking employment."

The rate of employment is relatively free of several defects that may distort the unemployment figures. For example, when a large number of discouraged job seekers stop looking for work, the rate of unemployment drops. In contrast, the rate of employment does not follow such a misleading course.

Which of the two figures should the wise observer follow? The answer is both. Our economy has been undergoing several structural changes that affect both the rate of unemployment and the rate of employment. The increased incidence of working wives, the influx of a higher percentage of youthful workers into the work force, and changes in eligibility requirements for various income transfer programs—all of these factors contribute to the diversity of the unemployed population. Clearly, "the unemployed" is not a homogeneous category.

ACTUAL AND POTENTIAL GNP

If an economy is going to realize its potential, full employment is essential. When the actual rate of unemployment exceeds the natural rate, the actual output of the economy will fall below its potential. Some resources that could be productively employed will be underutilized.

Potential Output: The level of output that can be achieved and sustained into the future, given the size of the labor force, expected productivity of labor, and natural rate of unemployment consistent with the efficient operation of the labor market. For periods of time, the actual output may differ from the economy's potential.

The Council of Economic Advisers defines the **potential output** as: ". . . the amount of output that could be expected at full employment. . . . It does not represent the absolute maximum level of production that could be generated by wartime or other abnormal levels of aggregate demand, but rather that which would be expected from high utilization rates obtainable under more normal circumstances."

The concept of potential output encompasses two important ideas: (a) full utilization of resources, including labor, and (b) an output constraint. Potential

---

[1]See Kenneth W. Clarkson and Roger E. Meiners, "Government Statistics as a Guide to Economic Policy: Food Stamps and the Spurious Increase in the Unemployment Rates," *Policy Review* (Summer 1977), pp. 25–51, for a clear statement of this view.

output might properly be thought of as the maximum sustainable output level consistent with the economy's resource base, given its institutional arrangements.

Estimates of the potential output level involve three major elements—the size of the labor force, the quality (productivity) of labor, and the natural rate of unemployment. Since these factors cannot be estimated with certainty, there is some variation in the estimated values of the potential rate of output for the U.S. economy. Relying on the projections of potential output developed by the Council of Economic Advisers, Exhibit 9 illustrates the record of the U.S. economy since 1965. During the latter half of the 1960s, output expanded and even temporarily exceeded the sustainable potential output rate of the economy. However, during the recessions of 1969–1970, 1974–1975, and 1982, output fell well below the economy's potential. Note the similarity in the pattern of the actual real GNP data of Exhibit 9 and the hypothetical data of an idealized business cycle of Exhibit 2. While the actual data of Exhibit 9 are irregular compared to the hypothetical data, nonetheless periods of expansion and economic boom followed by contraction and recession are clearly observable. During the boom phase, actual output expands rapidly and may temporarily exceed the economy's long-run potential. In contrast, recessions are characterized by an actual real GNP that is less than potential. As we proceed, we will focus on how we can achieve the maximum potential output while minimizing economic instability.

EXHIBIT 9

Actual and Potential GNP

The graph indicates the gap between the actual and potential GNP for the period from 1965 to 1990. Note the gap between the actual and potential GNP during the recessions of 1969–1970, 1974–1975, and 1982.

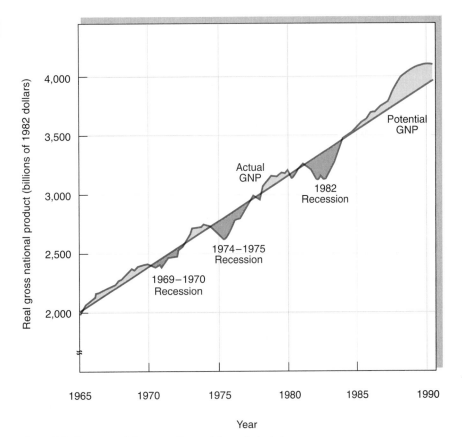

Source: U.S. Department of Commerce, Bureau of Economic Analysis.

INFLATION AND THE MODERN ECONOMY

Inflation: A continuing rise in the general level of prices of goods and services. The purchasing power of the monetary unit, such as the dollar, declines when inflation is present.

Inflation is a continuing rise in the level of prices, such that it costs more to purchase the typical bundle of goods and services chosen by consumers. Of course, even when the general level of prices is stable, some prices will be rising and others will be falling. During a period of inflation, however, the impact of the rising prices will outweigh that of falling prices. Because of the higher prices (on average), a dollar will purchase less than it did previously. Inflation, therefore, might also be defined as a decline in the value (the purchasing power) of the monetary unit.

How do we determine whether prices, in general, are rising or falling? Essentially, we answered that question in the last chapter when we indicated how a price index is constructed. When prices are rising, on average, the price index will also rise. The annual inflation rate is simply the percent change in the price index (PI) from one year to the next. Mathematically, the inflation rate (i) can be written as:

$$i = \frac{\text{This year's PI} - \text{last year's PI}}{\text{last year's PI}} \times 100$$

So, if the price index this year was 220, compared to 200 last year, the inflation rate would equal 10 percent ([220 − 200 ÷ 200] × 100). The consumer price index and

EXHIBIT 10

The Inflation Rate, 1930–1990

Prices fell as the economy plunged into the Great Depression during the 1930s. The Second World War was characterized by high rates of inflation. During the 1952–1966 period, prices increased at an annual rate of only 1.5 percent. In contrast, the inflation rate averaged 7 percent during the 1967–1981 era, reaching double-digit rates during several years. During 1982–1990 the rate of inflation averaged 4.0 percent annually.

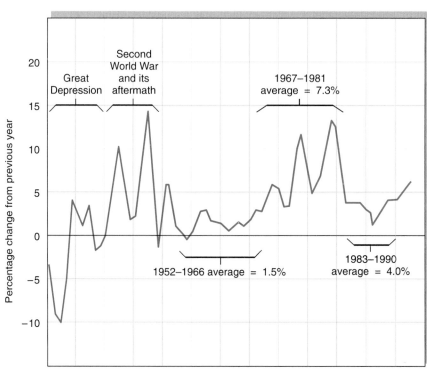

the GNP deflator are the price indexes most widely used to measure the inflation rate in the United States. Since the CPI and the GNP deflator are calculated monthly and quarterly, respectively, we often compare their value during a specific month (or quarter) with their value during the same month (or quarter) one year earlier to calculate the inflation rate during the most recent 12 months.

How rapidly have prices risen in the United States? Exhibit 10 illustrates the record since 1930. Prices declined sharply during the early years of the Great Depression. In contrast, the Second World War was characterized by a double-digit inflation rate. During the 1950s and into the mid-1960s, the annual inflation rate was usually less than 2 percent. In fact, the average inflation rate during the 1952–1966 period was 1.5 percent. Beginning in the latter half of the 1960s, inflation began to accelerate upward, jumping to 12 percent or more during 1974, 1979, and 1980. During the 1967–1981 period, the inflation rate averaged 7.3 percent. Price increases moderated again in the mid-1980s, as the inflation rate averaged 4 percent during 1982–1990.

Sometimes the focus on annual rates diverts our attention from the impact of continuous high rates of inflation. Given the lower inflation rates of the period, the price level was only 50 percent higher in 1967 than it was in 1947. In contrast, the price level tripled between 1967 and 1983.

The rate of inflation varies widely among countries. Inflation has been a way of life for many South American countries, including Argentina, Brazil, Bolivia, Uruguay, and Peru. Annual inflation rates of 50 percent or more have been a common occurrence in these countries. At the other end of the spectrum, the inflation rate in recent years has seldom climbed above 5 percent in Switzerland, Singapore, West Germany, and Japan. As we proceed, we will analyze why the price level has risen rapidly in some countries but not in others.

Unanticipated Inflation: An increase in the general level of prices that was not expected by most decision-makers. Thus, it catches them by surprise.

ANTICIPATED AND UNANTICIPATED INFLATION

Before examining the effects of inflation, it is important that we distinguish between unanticipated and anticipated inflation. **Unanticipated inflation** is an increase in the price level that comes as a surprise, at least to most individuals. The unanticipated inflation rate may either exceed or fall short of the inflation rate expected by most people. For example, suppose that based on the recent past, most people anticipate an inflation rate of 4 percent. If the actual inflation rate turns out to be 10 percent, it will catch people off guard. In this instance, the actual inflation rate exceeds the expected rate. Conversely, if the actual inflation rate had been zero when 4 percent inflation was widely anticipated, the stable price level would also have caught people by surprise. In this instance, an over-estimate of inflation would result.

Anticipated Inflation: An increase in the general level of prices that is expected by economic decision-makers. Past experience and current conditions are the major determinants of an individual's expectations with regard to future price changes.

Anticipated inflation is a change in the price level that is widely anticipated by decision-makers. For example, if individuals expect prices to rise 5 percent annually, the occurrence of 5 percent inflation merely fulfills their expectations. In contrast with unanticipated inflation, decision-makers are neither surprised nor caught off guard by inflation rates they anticipate.

THE EFFECTS OF INFLATION

Inflation reduces the purchasing power of money income received in the future (for example, payments from pensions, life insurance policies, and receipts from outstanding loans). When the inflation is unanticipated (or underestimated), debtors will gain at the expense of creditors. Unanticipated inflation victimizes those who have loaned money to others. Why is this true? Inflation erodes the purchasing power of the principal and interest repayment. Thus, in terms of command over goods and services, debtors give up less (and lenders receive less) than each anticipated at the time they agreed to the loan.

Consider a simple case. Suppose you want to borrow $10,000 to start a business. Since prices have been relatively stable in the recent past, both you and the person loaning you money anticipate stable prices in the future. As a result, you both agree to a 5 percent interest rate for a 5-year loan of $10,000. At the end of five years, you will owe the lender $12,800 (the $10,000 principal plus $2,800 in compound interest over the 5-year period). Now, consider what happens if, soon after you take out the loan, the inflation rate jumps unexpectedly to 10 percent. The 10 percent inflation rate erodes the value of the principal and interest you repay when the loan comes due. In fact, your $12,800 repayment will permit the lender to buy approximately the same market basket as could have been purchased with $7,950 at the time of the loan agreement. Far from gaining by loaning you money, the creditor ends up with even less purchasing power than his or her original principal. The unanticipated inflation redistributes income from the lender to you. Of course, the opposite would have occurred if the inflation rate had been less than was anticipated.

When the actual inflation rate is greater than was anticipated, debtors gain at the expense of lenders. Conversely, when the inflation rate is less than was anticipated, lenders gain at the expense of debtors.

Does this mean that unanticipated inflation helps poor people? Not necessarily. We must remember that people need reasonably good credit before they can borrow money. This limits the ability of persons in the lowest income brackets to acquire debt. Since they have little outstanding debt, inflation does little to improve the economic status of the poor.

A more important redistributional effect of unanticipated inflation is the transfer of wealth among age groupings. Persons under 45 years of age are more likely to be debtors. Inflation helps them repay their housing mortgages, car loans, and other outstanding debts. In contrast, those over 50 years of age are more likely to have savings, paid-up life insurance policies, bonds, and other forms of fixed future income. Inflation erodes the purchasing power of these savings. It thus tends to redistribute income from the old to the young.

Interestingly, the biggest beneficiary of an inflation rate greater than people anticipate is the federal government. Households are net lenders, and the government is the largest debtor. Unanticipated inflation therefore tends to transfer wealth from households to the government.

It is important to recognize that past experience will influence the actions of debtors and lenders. Predictably, higher inflation rates will result in an increase in the anticipated rate of inflation. When a high rate of inflation is anticipated, lenders will demand and borrowers will grant higher interest rates on loans because both parties expect the value of the dollar to depreciate. A borrower and a lender might agree to a 5 percent interest rate if they anticipate stable prices during the course of the loan. However, if both expected prices to rise 10 percent annually, they would instead agree to a 15 percent interest rate. The higher interest rate would compensate the lender for the expected decline in the purchasing power of the dollar during the course of the loan.

When borrowers and lenders accurately anticipate an inflation rate, even high rates of inflation fail to systematically redistribute income from debtors to lenders.

Debtors gain at the expense of lenders only if the actual rate of inflation exceeds the rate expected at the time the terms of the transaction are established.

When inflation is commonplace, people will adopt a variety of economic arrangements designed to protect their wealth and income against erosion by inflation. For example, collective-bargaining agreements will incorporate **escalator clauses** or contain a premium for the expected rate of inflation. Variable-rate home mortgages will be more widely used. Life and home insurance policies will be updated more often. Many long-term contracts will provide for indexing. All of these arrangements reflect the adjustments of decision-makers to an inflationary environment.

Contrary to the satirical statement at the beginning of the chapter, inflation will affect the prices of things we sell as well as the prices of goods we buy. Before we become too upset about inflation ''robbing us of the purchasing power of our paychecks,'' we should recognize that inflation influences the size of those paychecks. The weekly earnings of employees would not have risen at an annual rate of 7 percent during the 1970s if the rate of inflation had not increased rapidly during that period. Wages are a price, also. Inflation raises both wages and prices.

Escalator Clause: A contractual agreement that periodically and automatically adjusts the wage rates of a collective-bargaining agreement upward by an amount determined by the rate of inflation.

THE DANGERS OF INFLATION

Simply because money income initially tends to rise with prices, it does not follow that there is no need to be concerned about inflation, particularly high rates of inflation. Two negative aspects of inflation are particularly important.

1. Inflation Can Frustrate the Intent of a Long-Term Contract. Since the rate of inflation varies, it cannot be predicted with certainty. Most market exchanges, including long-term contracts, are made in money terms. If unanticipated inflation takes place, it can change the result of long-term contracts, such as mortgages, life insurance policies, pensions, bonds, and other arrangements that involve a debtor-lender relationship.

Studies indicate that higher rates of inflation are associated with greater variability in the inflation rate. This variability adds to the risks of time dimension contracts. If price changes are unpredictable (for example, if prices rise 10 percent one year, 5 percent the next year, and then increase again by 10 or 15 percent the following year), no one knows what to expect. Long-term money exchanges must take into account the uncertainty created by inflation. Given this additional uncertainty, many decision-makers will forgo exchanges involving long-term contracts. Because of this, mutually advantageous gains will be lost. The efficiency of markets is thus reduced.[2]

2. Real Resources Are Used Up as Decision-Makers Seek to Protect Themselves From Inflation. Since the failure to accurately anticipate the rate of inflation can have a substantial effect on one's wealth, individuals will divert scarce resources from the production of desired goods and services to the acquisition of information on the future rate of inflation. The ability of business decision-makers to forecast changes in prices becomes more valuable relative to their ability as managers and

[2]See Robert Higgs, ''Inflation and the Destruction of the Free Market Economy,'' *The Intercollegiate Review* (Spring 1979) for an excellent discussion of this point.

organizers of production. Speculative practices are encouraged as persons try to outwit each other with regard to the future direction of prices. Funds flow into speculative investments such as gold, silver, and art objects rather than into productive investments (buildings, machines, and technological research) that expand one's ability to produce goods and services. Such practices are socially counter-productive. They reduce our production possibilities.

STAGFLATION

Stagflation: A period during which an economy is experiencing both substantial inflation and a slow growth in output.

For a time, inflation may lead to temporary prosperity and economic growth. But as high rates of inflation persist, real output inevitably stagnates. The two inflationary recessions of the United States during the 1970s illustrate this point. Economists have coined the term **stagflation** to describe the phenomenon of rapid inflation and sluggish economic growth. One of the challenges of modern economic policy is to develop a solution to the problem of stagflation—to develop economic policies that will lead to stable prices, efficient utilization of resources, and expansion in the future production possibilities available to economic participants. Again and again, we will return to this issue as we probe more deeply into macroeconomics.

What causes inflation? We must acquire some additional tools before we can analyze this question in detail, but we can outline a couple of theories. First, economists emphasize the link between aggregate demand and supply. If aggregate demand rises more rapidly than supply, prices will rise. Second, nearly all economists believe that a rapid expansion in a nation's stock of money causes inflation. The old saying is that prices will rise because "there is too much money chasing too few goods." The hyperinflation experienced by South American countries has mainly been the result of monetary expansion. Once we develop additional knowledge about the operation of our economy, we will consider this issue in more detail.

ECONOMIC PERFORMANCE IN OTHER COUNTRIES

How does the economic performance of the United States compare with other major industrial countries? Exhibit 11 presents data on the economic record of the United States, Canada, Europe, and Japan during 1970–1982 and 1983–1989. The top frame provides data on the unemployment rate, the middle frame the inflation rate, and the lower frame the growth rate of real GNP.

The unemployment rate in Japan has been persistently lower than for other major industrial countries in recent years. During 1983–1989 the rate of unemployment in Japan averaged 2.7 percent, less than half the comparable rate for the United States and less than a third of the rate for Canada and Europe. Compared to other countries, Japanese employers are far more reluctant to lay off workers and bid employees away from other employers. In addition, during times of economic difficulty, Japanese employees are more likely to accept wage cuts from their current employer than workers in other countries. Thus, there is less job switching and more long-term employment relationships in Japan. No doubt, these factors contribute to Japan's low unemployment.

After experiencing high rates of inflation in the 1970s, the inflation rate in the major industrial countries declined substantially during 1983–1989. During the more recent period the inflation rate has been lowest in Japan, followed in order by the United States, Canada, and Europe.

Unemployment, Inflation, and Growth of Real GNP—An International Comparison

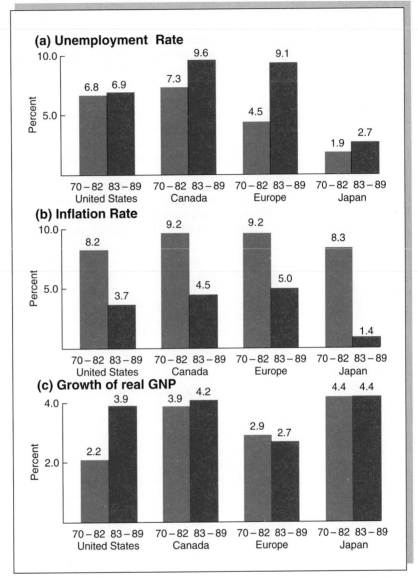

Source: *The Economic Report of the President: 1990* and *The Monthly Labor Review* (various issues).

During the 1950s and 1960s, the growth of real GNP in Japan averaged approximately 10 percent annually, well above the rates of other industrial nations. In recent years, the growth rate of Japan has slowed. Nonetheless, it continues to be impressive. Since 1970 the growth of real GNP in Japan has been slightly higher than for Canada and the United States.

Compared with other countries, clearly the economic performance of Japan has been outstanding. The recent Japanese record is one of low unemployment, relatively stable prices, and rapid economic growth. In contrast, the European economy has been characterized by a high rate of unemployment and sluggish growth. As we proceed, we will analyze important economic factors that contribute to the variation in economic performance of countries.

LOOKING AHEAD

In this chapter, we have examined the historical record for real income, employment, and prices. Measurement problems and the side effects of economic instability were discussed. In the next chapter, we will begin to develop a macroeconomic model that will help us better understand both the sources of and potential remedies for economic instability.

CHAPTER SUMMARY

1. Historically, real GNP in the United States has grown unevenly. Periods of rapid real growth have been followed by economic slowdowns. Nevertheless, the long-term trend has been upward. During the last 80 years, real GNP in the United States has grown at an average annual rate of approximately 3.5 percent.

2. Business peak, contraction, recessionary trough, and expansion are terms used by economists to describe the four phases of the business cycle. During an expansion, output increases rapidly and unemployment declines. The highest output rate of an expansion is referred to as a business peak or economic boom. Contraction is characterized by increasing unemployment, declining business conditions, and a low rate of growth. The bottom of the contraction is referred to as the recessionary trough.

3. Officially, the Commerce Department defines a recession as two successive quarters of declining real GNP. If a recession is quite severe, it is called a depression.

4. Even an efficient exchange economy will experience some unemployment. Frictional unemployment results because of imperfect information about available job openings and qualified applicants. Structural unemployment stems from the presence of factors that prevent the "matching up" of available applicants with available jobs. Currently, frictional and structural unemployment in the United States are thought to involve between 5 and 6 percent of the labor force.

5. Cyclical unemployment results because aggregate demand for labor is insufficient to maintain full employment. A primary concern of macroeconomics is how cyclical unemployment can be minimized.

6. Full employment is the employment level consistent with the economy's natural rate of unemployment. The natural rate of unemployment reflects both frictional and structural factors. It is neither a temporary high nor low, but rather the rate of unemployment associated with the economy's maximum sustainable rate of output. The natural rate of unemployment is not immutable. Public policies and changes in the composition of the labor force affect the natural rate.

7. Employment is a means to an end. The meaningful goal of full employment is full, productive employment—employment that produces desired goods and services.

8. The statistical definition of "unemployed" is imperfect. Some persons are not counted as unemployed because they are currently too discouraged to "actively seek employment." Others are counted even though they may be "employed" in the underground economy or only casually seeking employment (perhaps because of the incentive structure that they confront). Because of these ambiguities, some observers believe that the rate of employment (the percentage of the noninstitutional population, age 16 and over, who are employed) may be a more objective and accurate indicator of current employment opportunities. A prudent observer will consider both measures.

9. The concept of potential output encompasses two important ideas: (a) full utilization of resources and (b) a supply constraint that limits our ability to produce desired goods and services. When the resources of the economy are not fully and efficiently used, output will fall below its potential rate.

10. Inflation is a general rise in the level of prices. Alternatively, we might say that it is a decline in the purchasing power of the monetary unit—the dollar in the case of the United States. The inflation rate accelerated upward in the United States during the 1970s. Since 1982, the inflation rate has been more moderate.

11. It is important to distinguish between anticipated and unanticipated inflation. When the actual inflation rate is greater than the anticipated rate, debtors gain at the expense

of lenders. If the actual rate is less than the expected rate, lenders gain relative to debtors. In contrast, when inflation is accurately anticipated, the terms of loan agreements (particularly the interest rate) will be adjusted in a manner that eliminates the redistributive effects of inflation.

12. Inflation will have a harmful effect on an economy because it (a) increases the uncertainty of exchanges involving time, and (b) consumes valuable resources as individuals use their skills and talents to protect themselves from inflation.

13. During the last two decades Japan has achieved a more rapid growth rate of real output, less inflation, and a lower rate of unemployment than the United States and Western Europe. Compared to Japan and the United States, Europe has experienced both a high rate of unemployment and slow economic growth during the 1983–1989 period.

CRITICAL ANALYSIS QUESTIONS

*1. Explain why even an efficiently functioning economic system will have some unemployed resources.

2. What is full employment? How are full employment and the natural rate of unemployment related? Indicate several factors that would cause the natural rate of unemployment to change. Is the actual rate of unemployment currently greater than or less than the natural rate of unemployment? Why?

3. How does the rate of employment differ from the rate of unemployment? Which is the better indicator of employment opportunity? Why?

*4. **What's Wrong With This Way of Thinking?** ''My money wage rose by 6 percent last year, but inflation completely erased these gains. How can I get ahead when inflation continues to wipe out my increases in earnings?''

5. Does inflation help debtors relative to lenders? Why or why not? Does it help the poor relative to the rich? Explain. What is the most harmful side effect of inflation?

*6. ''As the inflation proceeds and the real value of the currency fluctuates widely from month to month, all permanent relations between debtors and lenders, which form the ultimate foundation of capitalism, become so utterly disordered as to be almost meaningless; and the process of wealth-getting degenerates into a gamble and a lottery.'' Do you agree with this well-known economists's view? Why or why not? How high do you think the inflation rate would have to climb before these effects would become pronounced? Do you see any evidence in support of this view in the United States?

*7. How are the following related to each other?
   a. Actual rate of unemployment
   b. Natural rate of unemployment
   c. Cyclical unemployment
   d. Potential GNP

*8. Use the following data to calculate the (a) labor force participation rate, (b) rate of unemployment, and (c) rate of employment: Population = 10,000; labor force = 6,000; not currently working = 4,500; employed full-time = 4,000; employed part-time = 1,500; and unemployed = 500.

*9. Persons are classified as unemployed if they are not currently working at a job and they made an effort to find a job during the past 4 weeks. Does this mean that there were no jobs available? Does it mean that there were no jobs available that unemployed workers were qualified to perform? What does it mean?

10. Classify each of the following as employed, unemployed, or not in the labor force:
   a. Brown, who is not working but is available for work, applied for a job at XYZ Company and is awaiting the result of her application.
   b. Smith is vacationing in Florida during a layoff at a General Motors plant due to a model changeover but he expects to be recalled in a couple of weeks.

---

*Asterisk denotes questions for which answers are given in Appendix C, Selected Answers.

c. Green was laid off as a carpenter when a construction project was completed. He is looking for work but has been unable to find anything except an $8 per hour job, which he turned down.

d. West works 50 to 60 hours per week as a homemaker for her family of nine.

e. Carson, a 17-year-old, works 6 hours per week as a route person for the local newspaper.

f. Johnson works 3 hours in the mornings at a clinic and for the last two weeks has spent the afternoons looking for a full-time job.

*11. Indicate how an unanticipated 5 percent jump in the inflation rate will influence the wealth of the following:

a. A person whose major asset is a house with a 30-year mortgage at a fixed interest rate.

b. A family holding most of its wealth in long-term fixed yield bonds.

c. A retiree drawing a monthly pension.

d. A heavily indebted farmer.

e. The owner of an apartment complex with substantial outstanding debt at a fixed interest rate.

f. A worker whose wages are determined by a three-year union contract ratified three months ago.

12. Is the natural rate of unemployment fixed?

*13. How does an unanticipated increase in the inflation rate influence the government's liability for the national debt?

14. If a group of employees has a relatively low opportunity cost of job search, how will this affect their unemployment rate? How do you think the opportunity cost of job search of teenagers living with their parents compares with that of a prime family earner with several dependents? How will this affect the unemployment rate of teenagers?

*15. How will each of the following affect a job seeker's decision to reject an available job offer and continue searching for a superior alternative?

a. The rumor that a major firm in the area is going to expand employment next month

b. The availability of food stamps

c. Increased optimism about the future of the economy

16. As specialization increases and an economy becomes more industrial, production in the market sector expands relative to the household sector. What does this imply about the real GNP of industrial economies relative to developing (less industrial) nations? What does it imply with regard to per capita real GNP as a measure of *growth* in real output?

17. Suppose that the Consumer Price Index at year-end 1991 were 140. By year-end 1992 the CPI had risen to 150. What was the inflation rate during 1992?

8

An Introduction to Basic Macroeconomic Markets

Macroeconomics is interesting . . . because it is challenging to reduce the complicated details of the economy to manageable essentials. Those essentials lie in the interactions among the goods, labor, and assets (loanable funds) markets of the economy.[1]

Rudiger Dornbusch and Stanley Fischer

CHAPTER FOCUS

- What are the major markets that coordinate macroeconomic activities?
- Why is the aggregate demand for goods and services inversely related to the price level?
- Why is an increase in the price level likely to expand output in the short run, but not in the long run?
- What determines the equilibrium level of GNP of an economy?
- How is the natural rate of unemployment related to the concept of long-term aggregate supply?
- What is the difference between the real interest rate and the money interest rate?

*F*rom Chapter 7, you might get the idea that unemployment and inflation are as unavoidable as death and taxes. Not so. Many economists believe that proper policies might have saved us from the horrible 25 percent unemployment rates of the Great Depression. At the other extreme, inflation in some countries is so high that prices often double in one year! What causes such rampant inflation? How can we avoid such a disaster? These and similar issues are precisely the focus of macroeconomics. Macroeconomics seeks to improve our understanding of economic instability (business cycles), inflation, unemployment, and related issues.

UNDERSTANDING MACROECONOMICS: OUR GAME PLAN

Why was the inflation rate so high during the 1970s? Do tax cuts like those instituted in the 1980s promote prosperity? And what about the large budget deficits of the 1980s and 1990s—are they leading us to economic destruction? Why do we experience economic instability? Could anything like the widespread bankruptcies and massive unemployment of the 1930s recur in our lifetime?

These are exciting questions and we want to address them. But before we can do so sensibly, we must lay a foundation. We must develop a model of the basic macroeconomic markets and analyze how these markets respond to various economic changes. In this chapter and Chapters 9 and 10 as well, we will develop several alternative versions of a basic model of our macroeconomy. The operation of this model will enhance our understanding of both how our macroeconomy works and the potential of policy alternatives that affect its operation.

Macroeconomic policy is usually divided into two components: fiscal policy and monetary policy. **Fiscal policy** entails the use of the government's taxation, spending, and debt-management policies. In the United States, fiscal policy is conducted by Congress and the president. It is thus a reflection of the collective decision-making process. **Monetary policy** encompasses actions that alter the money supply. The direction of monetary policy is determined by a nation's central bank, the Federal Reserve System in the United States. Ideally, both monetary and fiscal policy would be used to promote business stability, high employment, the growth of output, and a stable price level. It is not always easy, however, to determine which policy alternatives best serve these objectives.

Initially, as we develop our basic macroeconomic model, we will assume that monetary and fiscal policy are unchanged. Stated another way, we will proceed as if the government's tax and spending policies are unaffected by economic circumstances. Similarly, we will assume that policy-makers maintain a constant **money supply**—that they follow policies that keep the amount of cash in our billfolds and deposits in our checking accounts constant. Of course, changes in governmental expenditures, taxes, and money supply are potentially important. We will investigate their impact in detail in subsequent chapters. For now, though, things will go more smoothly if we simply assume that policy-makers are holding governmental expenditures, taxes, and the supply of money constant.

Fiscal Policy: The use of government taxation and expenditure policies for the purpose of achieving macroeconomic goals.

Monetary Policy: The deliberate control of the money supply and, in some cases, credit conditions for the purpose of achieving macroeconomic goals.

Money Supply: The supply of currency, checking account funds, and traveler's checks. These items are counted as money since they are used as the means of payment for purchases.

---

[1]Rudiger Dornbusch and Stanley Fischer, *Macroeconomics* (New York: McGraw-Hill, 1978).

THREE KEY MARKETS: RESOURCES, LOANABLE FUNDS, AND GOODS AND SERVICES

As Exhibit 1 illustrates, the basic markets of our simple macroeconomic model are: (1) goods and services, (2) resources, and (3) loanable funds. The circular flow diagram we initially introduced in Chapter 6 (Exhibit 2) will help us visualize each of the markets. In Chapter 6, we considered a strictly private economy in which households spent all of their income on consumption. We now consider an economy with government and international trade sectors in which households save as well as consume.

EXHIBIT 1

Three Key Markets and the Circular Flow of Income

A circular flow of income is coordinated by three key markets. First, the resource market (bottom loop) coordinates the actions of businesses demanding resources and households supplying them in exchange for income. Second, the loanable funds market (lower center) coordinates the saving choices of households and the borrowing decisions of businesses and governments. Finally, households, investors, governments, and foreigners (net exports) purchase products supplied by the business sector. These exchanges are coordinated in the goods and services market (top loop).

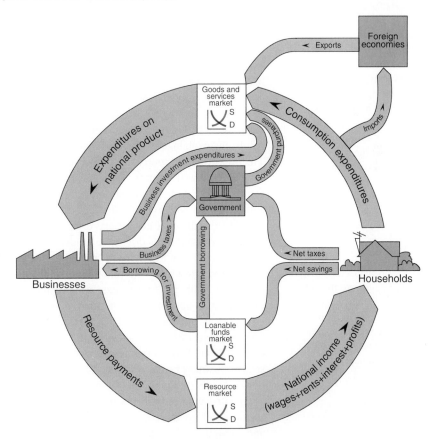

Resource Market: A highly aggregate market encompassing all resources (labor, physical capital, land, and entrepreneurship) that contribute to the production of current output. The labor market forms the largest component of this market.

Saving: Disposable income that is not spent on consumption. Saving is a "flow" concept. Thus, it is generally measured in terms of an annual rate.

Loanable Funds Market: A general term used to describe the market arrangements that coordinate the borrowing and lending decisions of business firms and households. Commercial banks, savings and loan associations, the stock and bond markets, and insurance companies are important financial institutions in this market.

Goods and Services Market: A highly aggregate market encompassing all final user goods and services during a period. The market counts all items that enter into GNP. Thus, real output in this market is equal to real GNP.

As before, the bottom loop of Exhibit 1 illustrates the flow of income from the business to the household sector in exchange for productive resources. Business firms demand resources such as labor and machines because of their contributions to the production of goods and services. The **resource market,** an aggregate market including labor and capital submarkets, coordinates the exchange of productive inputs between the household and business sectors. In turn, households supply resources in order to earn wages, interest, rents, and profits. These income payments provide households with the purchasing power necessary to buy goods now and in the future.

Much of the income of households will still be used to purchase consumption goods and housing. As Exhibit 1 illustrates, however, there are also two indirect routes by which funds can flow from the household to the business sector. First, the net savings of households can flow through the loanable funds market to (a) business firms purchasing investment goods and (b) governments purchasing public services. **Saving** is that portion of one's disposable income that is not spent on consumption. It is income not consumed. Net saving by the household sector supplies funds to the **loanable funds market.** In turn, businesses borrow loanable funds to finance investment expenditures. In addition, governments often finance their expenditures by borrowing. When the borrowed funds are spent on investment goods and government purchases, they return to the circular flow. The price of loanable funds is the interest rate. The actions of borrowers and lenders are coordinated by the interest rate in the loanable funds market.

Second, tax revenues can flow to the government to finance government expenditures. In effect, taxes are a leakage from the circular flow that is injected back into the income stream by the government when they are used to finance the purchase (or production) of goods and services provided by the government.

We live in a world where instant communications and shrinking transportation costs facilitate exchange between trading partners thousands of miles apart. As a result, the exchange partners of modern economies often live in different countries. The import-export loop of Exhibit 1 depicts this interaction with foreign economies. Households will import some of the goods and services that they purchase. Similarly, in addition to their domestic sales, business firms will export some goods and services. Net exports are the amount sold to foreigners minus the amount bought from them. If net exports are positive, they will increase the demand for the goods and services of domestic producers. Similarly, if net exports are negative, they will decrease the demand for the goods and services of domestic producers.

As the arrows flowing into the **goods and services market** (top loop) indicate, there are four major sources of expenditures in this market: (a) household expenditures on consumption (and new housing), (b) business investment, (c) government purchases, and (d) net exports. These expenditures of households, business investors, governments and foreigners (net exports) comprise the aggregate (total) demand for goods and services. Purchasing resources from the household sector, business firms supply goods and services. These exchanges are coordinated by the forces of supply and demand in the goods and services market. This highly aggregated market includes items such as stereo tapes, movie tickets, pizza, hair styling, and air travel—goods purchased primarily by consumers, both domestic and foreign. It also includes things bought by businesses such as tools, machines, and factory buildings. Finally, items such as education, fire protection, and national defense, which are usually purchased by governments, are also part of the goods and services market.

AGGREGATE DEMAND FOR GOODS AND SERVICES

What goes on in the aggregate goods and services market is vital to the health of an economy. Indeed, if we could keep our eye on just one market in an economy, we would choose the goods and services market since it exerts a vital impact on our economic opportunity and standard of living. It is important to note that the "quantity" and "price" variables in this highly aggregated market differ from their counterparts in the market for a specific good.

When we measure aggregate demand, the "quantity" variable is real GNP; it is the flow of goods and services produced and purchased in the goods and services market during a period. The "price" variable in the goods and services market represents the average price of goods and services purchased during the period. In essence, it is the economy's price level, as measured by a general price index (for example, the GNP deflator).

Just as the concepts of demand and supply enhance our understanding of markets for specific goods, they also contribute to our understanding of a highly aggregate market such as goods and services. The purchases of consumers, investors, governments, and foreigners comprise the nation's demand for goods and services. The **aggregate demand curve** indicates the various quantities of goods and services that purchasers are willing to buy at different price levels. As Exhibit 2 illustrates, the aggregate demand curve slopes downward to the right indicating an inverse relationship between the amount of goods and services demanded and the price level.

In Chapter 3, we noted that the amount of a specific commodity demanded, such as television sets, is inversely related to price. This inverse relationship reflects the fact that consumers turn to substitutes when a price increase makes a good more expensive. An increase in the price level, though, indicates that, on average, the prices of *all* goods have risen. When all prices increase, there is no incentive to substitute among goods. Thus, the aggregate demand schedule is not simply a reflection of the negative relationship between price and quantity demanded for specific goods.

Aggregate Demand Curve: A downward sloping curve indicating an inverse relationship between the price level and the quantity of goods and services that households, business firms, governments and foreigners (net exports) are willing to purchase during a period.

EXHIBIT 2

The Aggregate Demand Curve

There are three reasons why the quantity of goods and services purchased will decline as the price level increases: (a) an increase in the price level reduces the wealth of persons holding the nation's fixed money supply, causing them to reduce their purchases; (b) the higher price level pushes up the interest rate, which leads to a reduction in the purchases of interest-sensitive goods; and (c) net exports decline as foreigners buy less from us and we buy more from them at the higher price level.

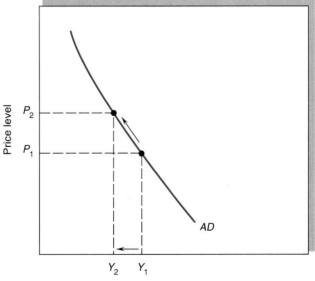

Why then, does the aggregate demand curve slope downward to the right? There are three major reasons.

1. The Real Balance Effect. Suppose you have a bank account of $2,000. Consider how a 25 percent increase in the level of prices will influence your wealth and spending. The 25 percent increase in prices reduces your real wealth because it reduces the amount of goods and services you can buy with the $2,000 in your checking account. After the increase in prices, your $2,000 will only buy as much as $1,600 would have bought before prices jumped. Of course, an increase in the price level reduces not only your wealth, but it also reduces the wealth of others holding money balances. Economists refer to this inverse relationship between the price level and the wealth of households and businesses holding a fixed supply of money as the **real balance effect.**

Real Balance Effect: The decrease in wealth emanating from a decline in the purchasing power of a constant money supply as the price level increases. This wealth effect leads to a negative relationship between price (level) and quantity demanded in the goods and services market.

The real balance effect helps to explain the downward slope of the aggregate demand curve. When the price level increases, the purchasing power of the fixed quantity of money balances declines. As the result of this reduction in the wealth of households and businesses, people will cut back their purchases of goods and services at the higher price level.

In contrast, a decline in the price level will increase the purchasing power of money and the real wealth of people holding money balances. As their wealth increases, people will increase their purchases. Therefore, a negative relationship between the price level and the quantity of goods and services purchased emerges from the real balance effect.

2. The Interest Rate Effect. Remember, when we construct an aggregate demand curve, the supply of money is fixed all along the curve. An increase in the price level reduces the real money supply—the nominal money supply deflated for the higher price level. When there is an increase in the average price of all goods and services, larger money balances will be necessary for the conduct of business. Households will try to expand their checking account funds to pay the higher prices for food, clothing, and other items regularly purchased. Similarly, businesses will want to increase their money balances to pay larger wage bills and supplier costs accompanying the higher price level. Since the actual supply of money is constant, it will not be possible for everybody to increase their money balances simultaneously. The additional demand for money will create a shortage. Many households and firms will try to borrow funds to increase their money balances. As they attempt to do so, they increase the demand for loanable funds and drive up the interest rate.[2]

What impact will a higher interest rate have on the demand for goods and services? The higher interest rate makes it more costly to purchase goods and services during the current period, particularly those that are financed. Households will cut back on their purchases of interest-sensitive consumption goods such as automobiles and consumer durables. Similarly, firms will reduce their current investment expenditures on business expansion and new construction. Thus, a rise in the price level leads to a higher interest rate that discourages both consumption and investment spending. This interest rate effect also contributes to the downward slope of the aggregate demand curve.

3. The International Substitution Effect. Other things the same, an increase in the U.S. price level will make American goods more expensive relative to foreign

---

[2]We will provide additional detail on this topic when we analyze the demand for money in Chapter 13.

goods. Foreigners will cut back on their purchases of U.S.-produced goods as they increase in price. Simultaneously, U.S. consumers will purchase more Japanese automobiles, Korean textiles, and Italian shoes, substituting these and other foreign-produced goods and services for the more expensive domestically produced goods.

Therefore, as the price level increases, foreigners will switch away from U.S.-produced goods, while domestic consumers will purchase more goods and services abroad (and fewer from domestic producers). Net exports will decline (or net imports rise). Of course, the decline in net exports as the U.S. price level increases will directly reduce the quantity demanded of U.S.-produced goods. Thus, the international substitution effect provides a third reason for the downward sloping aggregate demand curve.

SUMMARY

The accompanying Thumbnail Sketch indicates why the price level is inversely related to the amount demanded in the aggregate goods and services market. Higher prices (a) reduce the purchasing power of the fixed money supply, (b) cause higher interest rates which make current goods more expensive, and (c) encourage the substitution of foreign goods for domestically-produced goods. Each of these factors reduces the amount of goods and services demanded as the price level increases. So, even though the explanation differs, the aggregate demand curve, like the demand curve for a specific product, slopes downward to the right.

THUMBNAIL SKETCH

Why the Aggregate Quantity Demanded Is Inversely Related to the Price Level

An *increase* in the price level will *lower* aggregate quantity demanded because:	A *decrease* in the price level will *raise* aggregate quantity demanded because:
1. the real wealth of persons holding money balances declines when prices rise;	1. the real wealth of persons holding money balances increases when prices fall;
2. higher real interest rates due to an increased scarcity of money discourage current investment and consumption; and	2. lower real interest rates due to a reduction in the scarcity of money encourage current investment and consumption; and
3. net exports decline (since the prices of domestic goods have increased relative to foreign goods).	3. net exports expand (since the prices of domestic goods have fallen relative to foreign goods).

AGGREGATE SUPPLY

After reading the previous section, it should come as no great surprise that aggregate supply is a bit more interesting and complex than is the supply of a specific good. In particular, we cannot explain the upward slope of the aggregate supply curve with the same logic that explains the upward slope of the supply curve for a specific good. One reason for this difference is that in the goods and services market, the price variable measures the price *level*, an index of the prices of all goods not just the price of one good. An increase in the price of a specific good offers producers profit as an incentive to increase output. But in the case of an increase in the aggregate price level, the impact on profitability is different in the short run than in the long run.

Therefore, when considering aggregate supply, it is particularly important to distinguish between the short run and the long run. In this context, the short run is the time period during which some prices, particularly those in labor markets, are set by prior contracts and agreements. Therefore, in the short run, households and businesses are unable to adjust these prices in light of *unexpected* recent changes, including unexpected changes in the price level. In contrast, the long run is a time period of sufficient duration that people have the opportunity to learn more fully about recent price changes and to modify their prior choices in response to them. We now consider both the short-run and long-run aggregate supply curves.

AGGREGATE SUPPLY IN THE SHORT RUN

Aggregate Supply Curve: A curve indicating the relationship between the nation's price level and quantity of goods supplied by its producers. In the short run, it is probably an upward sloping curve, but in the long run most economists believe the aggregate supply curve is vertical (or nearly so).

The short-run **aggregate supply** (SRAS) **curve** indicates the various quantities of goods and services that firms will supply at different price levels during the period immediately following a change in the price level. As Exhibit 3 illustrates, the short-run aggregate supply (SRAS) curve in the goods and services market slopes upward to the right. The upward slope reflects the fact that in the short run an unexpected increase in the price level will improve the profitability of firms. They will respond with an expansion in output.

The short-run aggregate supply curve is based on a specific expected price level, P_{100} in the case of Exhibit 3. When that price level is achieved, firms will earn normal profits and supply output Y_0. Why will an increase in the price level (to P_{105}, for example) enhance profitability, at least in the short run? Profit per unit equals price minus the producer's per unit costs. Important components of producers' costs will be determined by long-term contracts. Interest rates on loans, collective bargaining agreements with employees, lease agreements on buildings and machines, and other contracts with resource suppliers will influence production costs during the current period. The prices incorporated into these long-term contracts at the time of the agreement are based on the expectation of price level (P_{100}) for the current period. These resource costs tend to be temporarily fixed. If an increase in demand causes the price level to rise unexpectedly during the current period, prices of goods and services will increase relative to the temporarily fixed components of costs. Profit margins will improve and business firms will happily respond with an expansion in output (to Y_1).

In addition, widespread price increases may cause many producers to mistakenly believe that the price (and demand) for their product has increased *relative to other products*. When prices are increasing, specific firms are likely to be most aware of price changes for their products. They may act on this observation. For example, many floral shop operators may think that higher prices for floral goods indicate that people want to buy more of their products relative to other goods. Other firms may arrive at a similar conclusion. Fooled by the unexpected general price increase, they expand output in anticipation of strong future sales and attractive profit margins. However, when all, or almost all, firms try to expand, they will bid up resource prices. Rising costs and shrinking profit margins (relative to what was expected) will result. Disappointed by the unexpected increase in costs,

EXHIBIT 3

The Short-Run Aggregate Supply Curve

The short-run aggregate supply curve shows the relationship between the price level and the production of goods and services by domestic suppliers during the period immediately following the change in aggregate demand leading to the change in the price level. In the short run, firms will generally expand output as the price level increases because the higher prices (a) improve profit margins since many components of costs are temporarily fixed and (b) lead many producers to believe the relative price of their product has increased.

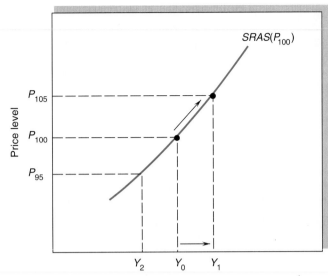

Goods and services (real GNP)

producers will eventually scale back output in response to the smaller-than-expected profit margins. Until then, misled by the general increase in prices, many businesses will temporarily expand output and thereby contribute to the short-run increase in production (aggregate supply).

An unexpected reduction in the price level to P_{95} would exert just the opposite effects. It would decrease product prices *relative to costs* and thereby reduce profitability. In response, firms would reduce output to Y_2. Therefore, *in the short run*, there will be a direct relationship between amount supplied and the price level in the goods and services market.

AGGREGATE SUPPLY IN THE LONG RUN

The *long-run aggregate supply (LRAS)* curve indicates the relationship between the price level and quantity of output, after decision-makers have had sufficient time to adjust their prior commitments in the light of any previously unexpected changes in market prices. A higher price level in the goods and services market will fail to alter the relationship between product and resource prices in the long run. Once people have time to adjust fully their prior commitments, competitive forces will restore the usual relationship between product prices and costs. *Profit rates will return to normal,* removing the incentive of firms to supply a larger rate of output. Therefore, as Exhibit 4 illustrates, the long-run aggregate supply curve is vertical.

The forces that provided for an upward-sloping short-run aggregate supply curve are absent in the long run. Costs that are temporarily fixed due to long-term contracts will eventually rise. With time, the long-term contracts will expire and be renegotiated. The new contracts will reflect the higher level of prices. Similarly, business decision-makers will eventually correct production errors based on the mistaken view that the price of their product has risen relative to costs and other prices.

Once the contracts are renegotiated, resource prices will increase in the same proportion as product prices. A proportional increase in costs and product prices will leave the incentive to produce unchanged. Consider how a firm with a selling price of $20 and per unit costs of $20 will be affected by the doubling of both

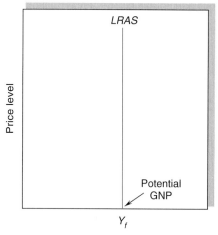

product and resource prices. After the price increase, the firm's sales price will be $40, but so too, will its per unit costs. Thus, neither the firm's profit rate nor the incentive to earn is changed. Therefore, in the long run an increase in the nominal value of the price level will fail to exert a lasting impact on aggregate output.

Reflecting on the production possibilities of an economy also sheds light on *why* the long-run aggregate supply curve is vertical. As we discussed in Chapter 2, at a point in time, our production possibilities are constrained by the supply of resources, level of technology, and institutional arrangements that influence the efficiency of resource use. A higher price level does not loosen these constraints. For example, a doubling of prices will not improve technology. Neither will it expand the availability of productive resources nor improve the efficiency of our economic institutions. Thus, there is no reason for a higher price level to increase our ability to produce goods and services. This is precisely what the vertical long-run aggregate supply curve implies. The accompanying Thumbnail Sketch on the following page summarizes the factors that underlie both the short-run and long-run aggregate supply curves.

EQUILIBRIUM IN THE GOODS AND SERVICES MARKET

Equilibrium: A balance of forces permitting the simultaneous fulfillment of plans by buyers and sellers.

We are now ready to combine our analysis of aggregate demand and aggregate supply and consider how they act to determine the price level and rate of output. When a market is in **equilibrium,** there is a balance of forces such that the actions of buyers and sellers are consistent with one another.

EQUILIBRIUM IN THE SHORT RUN

As Exhibit 5 illustrates, short-run equilibrium is present in the goods and services market at the price level (P) where the aggregate quantity demanded is equal to the aggregate quantity supplied. This occurs at the output rate (Y) where the AD and *SRAS* curves intersect.

Short-Run Equilibrium in the Goods and Services Market

Short-run equilibrium in the goods and services market occurs at the price level (*P*) where *AD* and *SRAS* intersect. If the price level were lower than *P*, general excess demand in goods and services markets would push prices upward. Conversely, if the price level were higher than *P*, excess supply would result in falling prices.

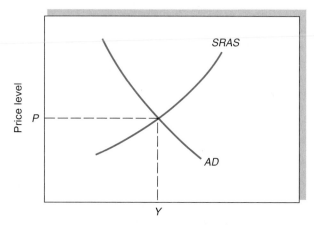

Goods and services (real GNP)

If a price level of less than *P* were present, the aggregate quantity demanded would exceed the aggregate quantity supplied. Purchasers would be seeking to buy more goods and services than producers were willing to produce. This excess demand would place upward pressure on prices, causing the price level to rise toward *P*. On the other hand, at a price level greater than *P*, the aggregate quantity supplied would exceed the aggregate quantity demanded. Producers would be unable to sell all the goods produced. This would result in downward pressure (toward *P*) on prices. Only at the price level *P* would there be a balance of forces between the amount of goods demanded by consumers, investors, governments, and foreigners, and the amount supplied by domestic firms.

THUMBNAIL SKETCH

Why the Short-Run Aggregate Quantity Supplied Is Directly Related to the Price Level

1. As the price level increases, profit margins of firms increase, because initially product prices increase relative to costs (important components of which are fixed by long-term contracts).

2. As the price level increases, some firms mistakenly believe that the demand for their product has increased relative to other goods.

Why the Long-Run Aggregate Supply Curve is Vertical

1. Once people have the time to adjust fully to a new price level, the normal relationship between product prices and resource costs is restored.

2. The sustainable potential output of a national economy is determined by its quantity of resources, technology, and the efficiency of its institutional structures, *not* by the price level.

EQUILIBRIUM IN THE LONG RUN

The price level in the economy-wide goods and services market will tend to bring quantity demanded and quantity supplied into balance. However, a second condition is required for long-run equilibrium: the buyers and sellers must be happy with their prior choices. If they are not satisfied, they will want to change their actions in the future. Thus, long-run equilibrium requires that decision-makers who agreed to long-term contracts influencing current prices and costs must have *correctly anticipated the current price level at the time they arrived at the agreements*. If this was not the case, they will modify those agreements when the long-term contracts expire. In turn, their modifications will affect costs, profit margins, and output.

Exhibit 6 illustrates a long-run equilibrium in the goods and services market. As in Exhibit 3, the subscripts attached to the *SRAS* and *AD* curves indicate the price level (an index of prices) that was anticipated by decision-makers at the time they made decisions affecting the schedules. In this case, when buyers and sellers made their purchasing and production choices, they anticipated that the price level during the current period would be P_{100}, where the 100 refers to an index of prices during an earlier base year. As the intersection of the *AD* and *SRAS* curves reveals, the P_{100} was actually attained.

When the price level expectations imbedded in the long-term contracts turn out to be correct, there is no reason for buyers and sellers in resource markets to modify resource prices when their contracts come up for renegotiation. Therefore, the resource prices, costs, and profits will continue into the future. Since the price/cost relationship is unchanged, firms have no incentive to alter either their product prices or rate of output. Thus, the equilibrium price level and output will persist into the future (until changes in other factors alter AD or SRAS). *It is a long-run equilibrium*.

LONG-RUN EQUILIBRIUM, POTENTIAL OUTPUT AND FULL EMPLOYMENT

When long-run equilibrium is present, the actual output achieved is equal to the economy's potential GNP. In other words, when a short-run equilibrium (AD intersects with SRAS) occurs along the economy's vertical aggregate supply curve (LRAS), long-run equilibrium will also be present. Exhibit 6 illustrates this case.

As we discussed in Chapter 7, potential GNP is equal to the economy's maximum *sustainable* output consistent with its resource base, current technology, and institutional structure. Potential GNP is neither a temporary high nor an abnormal low. Rather, it reflects the normal operation of markets, the situation when decision-makers (including those involved in long-term agreements) neither systematically underestimate nor overestimate the current price level.

The long-run equilibrium output rate (Y_f of Exhibit 6) also corresponds with the full-employment of resources. When full-employment output is present, the job search time of unemployed workers will be normal, given the characteristics of the labor force and the institutional structure of the economy. Only frictional and structural unemployment will be present; cyclical unemployment will be absent. When an economy is at full employment, the unemployment rate that exists is equivalent to the *natural* rate of unemployment. (See boxed feature, "How Large Is the Natural Rate of Unemployment?")

WHAT HAPPENS WHEN THE PRICE LEVEL DIFFERS FROM WHAT WAS EXPECTED?

Changes in the price level may catch buyers and sellers by surprise. When the actual price level differs from the level forecast by buyers and sellers, some decision-makers will enter into agreements that they will later regret.

Consider a case in which the price level increases more than was anticipated. Failing to foresee the price increase, lenders in the loanable funds market agreed to

EXHIBIT 6

Long-Run Equilibrium in the Goods and Services Market

When the goods and services market is in long-run equilibrium, two conditions must be present. First, the quantity demanded must equal the quantity supplied at the current price level. Second, the price level anticipated by decision-makers must equal the actual price level. The subscripts on the *SRAS* and *AD* curves indicate that buyers and sellers alike anticipated the price level P_{100}, where the 100 represents an index of prices during an earlier base year. When the anticipated price level is actually attained, current output (Y_f) will equal the economy's potential GNP when full employment is present.

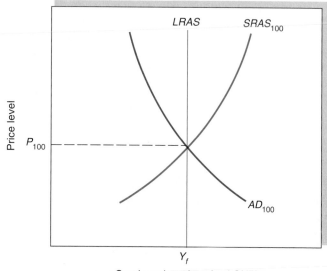

interest rates that are lower than they are willing to accept once the general increase in prices (inflation) is taken into account. Similarly, anticipating a lower current price level, union officials accept money-wage increases that end up reducing real wages during the period. In the short run, the atypically low interest rates and real wages reduce costs relative to product prices. Profit margins will be abnormally high and firms will respond with a larger output. Employment will expand. Unemployment will fall below its natural rate. But this abnormally large output and high level of employment is not sustainable. The "mistakes", based on a prior failure to estimate fully the strength of current demand, will be recognized and corrected when contracts expire. Real wages and interest rates will increase and eventually reflect the higher price level and rate of inflation. Profit margins will return to normal. When these adjustments are completed, the temporarily large output rate and high employment level will decline and return to normal.

What would happen if product prices increase less rapidly than decision-makers anticipate? Anticipating larger price increases (a higher inflation rate than actually occurs), borrowers agree to interest rates that later prove to be unacceptably high in terms of the current price level. Similarly, employers agree to wage increases that result in higher real wages than expected, since the price level rises more slowly than was anticipated. The abnormally high interest and wage rates increase costs relative to product prices. As profit margins are squeezed, producers reduce output and lay off employees. Unemployment rises above the natural rate of unemployment. Current output falls short of the economy's potential GNP.

Many economists think this is precisely what happened during 1982. After inflation rates of 13 percent in 1979 and 12 percent in 1980, price increases plummeted to 4 percent in 1982. This sharp reduction in the inflation rate caught many decision-makers by surprise. Unable to pass along to consumers the large increases in money wages agreed to in 1980 and 1981, employers cut back production and laid off workers. The unemployment rate soared to 10.8 percent in late 1982, up from 7.6 percent in 1981. Eventually, new agreements provided for smaller money wage increases or even wage reductions in 1983 and 1984.

Unemployment fell. Nevertheless, in 1982, unemployment was well above its natural rate. The necessary adjustments could not be made instantaneously.

In summary, a current output rate will be sustained into the future only when the price agreements of buyers and sellers were based on an accurate forecast of the current price level. If the decision-makers were able to accurately forecast the current price level when they arrived at their agreements, then the current resource prices and real interest rates will tend to persist into the future. Profit rates will be normal. When this is the case, the economy's sustainable potential rate of output (Y_f, Exhibit 6) will be achieved.

MEASURES OF ECONOMIC ACTIVITY

How Large Is the Natural Rate of Unemployment?

When an economy is in long-run equilibrium, unemployment will be at the natural rate. However, since the natural rate of unemployment is a theoretical concept, it cannot be directly observed. It must be estimated.

Economists use two different methods to estimate the natural rate of unemployment. First, they estimate a statistical equation relating aggregate unemployment to changes in the rate of inflation. Conceptually, the natural rate of unemployment is present when the inflation rate is neither rising nor falling. Therefore, when the inflation rate is constant, the equation linking unemployment to the change in the inflation rate provides an estimate for the natural rate of unemployment.

The second method of estimating the natural rate of unemployment uses historical data to estimate the natural rate for several different demographic groups. These estimates are then used to estimate the aggregate natural rate, based on the size of the various demographic groups at different times.

Several researchers have used one or both of these techniques to estimate the natural rate at various times. Perhaps the most widely cited estimates are those by Robert Gordon of Northwestern University. The accompanying chart presents the estimates of Gordon, along with the low and high estimates of other researchers for 1955, 1970, 1980, and 1988.

In the mid-1950s, the natural rate of unemployment was estimated at between 4 percent and 5.5 percent. Gordon's estimate for the natural rate in 1955 was 5.1 percent. Researchers agree that the natural rate increased during the 1960s and 1970s, primarily as the result of a large influx of youthful workers into the labor force. Since younger workers are more likely than their older counterparts both to switch jobs and enter (and reenter) the labor force, the natural unemployment rate increases when youthful workers grow as a proportion of the labor force. By 1980, the estimated natural rate had risen to between 5 percent and 7 percent. As the baby-boom generation matured and the growth of the labor force slowed during the 1980s, the natural rate declined. In the late 1980s, researchers placed the natural rate of unemployment between 4.5 percent and 6.5 percent.

Estimated Natural Rate of Unemployment

Year	Low Estimate	Robert Gordon	High Estimate
1955	4.0	5.1	5.5
1970	4.5	5.6	6.0
1980	5.0	5.9	7.0
1988	4.5	6.0	6.5

Sources: Robert Gordon, *Macroeconomics,* 5th ed. (Glenview, Ill.: Scott Foresman Company, 1990); Stuart E. Weiner, "The Natural Rate of Unemployment: Concepts and Issues," *Economic Review—Federal Reserve Bank of Kansas City,* January 1986, pp. 11–24; Keith M. Carlson, "How Much Lower Can the Unemployment Rate Go?" *Review—Federal Reserve Bank of St. Louis,* July/August 1988, pp. 44–57; and Lowell E. Gallaway and Richard K. Vedder, *The Natural Rate of Unemployment,* Joint Economic Committee, Congress of the United States (Washington: Government Printing Office, 1982).

It is this long-run maximum sustainable output that economists are referring to when they speak of "full employment output" or "potential GNP." When this output rate is present, the actual and natural rates of unemployment will be equal. The choices of buyers and sellers will harmonize and neither will have reason to alter their choices. Thus, long-run equilibrium is present.

RESOURCE MARKET

Until now in this chapter, we have discussed only the aggregate goods and services market, but there are two other basic macroeconomic markets that are almost as important. These two markets are the resource market and the loanable funds market. After we discuss the resource market in this section and the loanable funds market in the section that follows, we will be ready to link all three markets together and analyze general macroeconomic equilibrium.

It is not hard to guess that the resource market is a market for resources, but what does that mean? Resources are factors of production such as labor, natural resources, and machines, so the resource market is nothing more than a place where such items are bought and sold. The resource market thus coordinates the choices of business firms that demand resources and resource owners who supply them. When you hunt for a summer job, for instance, you're participating in the resource market.

Why do business firms demand resources? In a market economy, the demand for resources is merely a reflection of the contribution of the resources to the production of goods and services. Business firms employ labor and other resources because they contribute to the production of goods the firm believes it can sell at a profit. For example, a builder purchases resources such as lumber, cement, and glass windows, and hires the labor services of carpenters, bricklayers, and roofers because they are required in order to produce houses that the contractor hopes to sell for a profit. The demand for a resource such as labor reflects the law of demand, which says that the higher the price of something the less the quantity demanded. If the wages that firms must pay for workers increase, the firms will choose to hire fewer workers. In contrast, a lower wage rate will increase the quantity of labor demanded by firms. Therefore, the demand for resources, like the demand for goods and services, slopes downward to the right.

Why are labor and other resources supplied? Most people work and supply resources to earn income. Working, though, requires us to give up something else that is valuable—leisure; time to do nonmarket work and other things. So, a trade-off must be made between working for income and leisure time for nonmarket activities. Higher real wages increase the opportunity cost of leisure. Because of this, as real wages increase, individuals generally make substitutions that permit them to supply more market work time. Therefore, the quantity of labor and other resources supplied expands as resource prices increase.

Exhibit 7 illustrates equilibrium in the aggregate resource market. Price coordinates the actions of buyers and sellers. In equilibrium, the market price of resources will bring the amount demanded by business firms into balance with the amount supplied by resource owners. An above-equilibrium price will result in an excess supply of resources. The excess supply will push resource prices downward toward equilibrium. In contrast, if resource prices are below equilibrium, excess demand will place upward pressure on the price of resources. Market forces will thus tend to move resource prices toward equilibrium.

EXHIBIT 7

Equilibrium in the Resource Market

In general, as resource prices increase, the amount demanded by producers declines and the amount supplied by resource owners expands. In equilibrium, resource price brings amount demanded into equality with amount supplied in the aggregate resource market. The labor market is a major component of the resource market.

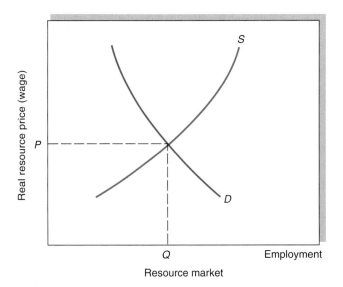

As we discussed in Chapter 3, the markets for resources and products are highly interrelated. The cost of producing goods and services is influenced directly by the price of resources. Other things remaining constant, an increase in resource prices will increase costs and squeeze profit margins in the goods and services market. Aggregate supply will decline (*SRAS* will shift to the left). Conversely, a reduction in resource prices will lower costs and improve profit margins in the goods and services markets. An increase in aggregate supply (a shift to the right in *SRAS*) will result.

The demand for resources is directly linked to the demand for goods and services. In fact, the demand for resources is a derived demand—it emanates from the demand for goods and services. An increase in aggregate demand will increase the demand for resources. Similarly, a reduction in aggregate demand will reduce the demand for resources.

Since the resource and goods and services markets are highly interrelated, obviously changes in either one of these markets will have repercussions in the other. Much of macroeconomics is about how changes in one of these markets affects conditions in the other. As we proceed, we will consider these two important markets in more depth and utilize them to enhance our understanding of macroeconomic relationships.

While we have lumped all resources together into a single aggregated market, it is important to recognize that the market for labor services is the dominant resource market. In the United States, wage costs make up approximately 70 percent of production costs. Since the labor market is both large and very important, we will often concentrate on the labor market rather than the general resource market.

LOANABLE FUNDS MARKET

The loanable funds market coordinates the actions of borrowers and lenders. This market permits households, businesses, and governments to borrow against their assets or against future expected income. As the circular flow of income implies, households are generally *net* suppliers of loanable funds (see Exhibit 1). Businesses and governments often demand loanable funds to finance capital investment projects and other expenditures. Financial institutions, such as savings and loan associations, commercial banks, insurance companies, pension funds, and the stock and bond markets, form the core of this market.

In essence, borrowers are exchanging *future* income for purchasing power *now*. The interest rate is the price they must pay to do so. Why do you have to pay an interest premium when you borrow? Most of us are impatient. We want things now rather than in the future. Interest is the cost one pays for impatience. From the lender's viewpoint, interest is a premium one receives for waiting, for delaying possible expenditures into the future.

The interest rate can be thought of as the price of credit. Lenders are supplying credit and borrowers are demanding credit. The interest rate brings the choices of borrowers and lenders into harmony.

It is helpful to think of the interest rate in two ways. First, there is the **money interest rate,** the percentage of the amount borrowed that must be paid to the lender in the future, in addition to the principal amount borrowed. It is money interest rates that are typically quoted in newspapers and business publications. When there is inflation, the money rate of interest may be a misleading indicator of real borrowing costs. During a period of inflation, rising prices shrink the purchasing power of the loan's principal. When the principal is repaid in the future, it will not purchase as much as when the funds were initially loaned. Recognizing this fact, borrowers and lenders implicitly agree on an interest premium when they expect inflation. So, the inflation leads to a higher money interest rate, which is necessary to compensate the lender for the decline in the purchasing power of money during the lifetime of the loan.

Second, there is the **real interest rate.** The real interest rate reflects the real burden to borrowers and the payoff to lenders, in terms of command over goods and services. The real interest rate is simply the money rate of interest adjusted for the expected rate of inflation.

Perhaps an example will clarify the distinction between the two. Suppose a person borrows $1,000 for one year at an 8 percent interest rate. After a year, the borrower must pay the lender $1,080—the $1,000 principal plus the 8 percent interest. Now, suppose during the year prices rose 8 percent as the result of inflation. Because of this, the $1,080 repayment after a year commands exactly the same purchasing power as the original $1,000 did when it was loaned. In effect, the borrower pays back exactly the same amount of purchasing power as was borrowed. The lender receives nothing for making the purchasing power available to the borrower. In this case, the effective real interest rate was zero.

Lenders are unlikely to continue making funds available at such bargain rates. When they anticipate the 8 percent inflation rate, lenders will demand (and borrowers will agree to) a higher money interest rate to compensate for the decline in the purchasing power of the dollar. This premium for the expected decline in purchasing power of the dollar is called the **inflation premium.** Once borrowers and lenders anticipate the inflation, they may agree to a 16 percent money interest rate, 8 percent of which reflects an inflationary premium and 8 percent a real interest return.

We can reflect the relationship between the real interest rate and the money interest rate as follows:

Money Interest Rate: The interest rate measured in dollars. It overstates the real cost of borrowing during an inflationary period. When inflation is anticipated, an inflationary premium will be incorporated into the nominal value of this rate. The money interest rate is often referred to as the nominal interest rate.

Real Interest Rate: The interest rate adjusted for expected inflation; it indicates the real cost to the borrower (and yield to the lender) in terms of goods and services.

Inflation Premium: A component of the money interest rate that reflects compensation to the lender for the expected decrease, due to inflation, in the purchasing power of the principal and interest during the course of the loan. It is determined by the expected rate of future inflation.

$$\text{Real interest rate} = \text{money interest rate} - \text{inflation premium}$$

The size of the inflation premium, of course, varies directly with the expected rate of future inflation. It is the real interest rate, not the money rate, that indicates the true burden of borrowers and the yield to lenders derived from a loan.

Thus, the real interest rate reflects the "true" cost of borrowing and the true yield from lending. An increase in the real interest rate makes borrowing more costly. Households, investors, and governments will reduce the amount of funds demanded as the real interest rate rises. On the other hand, a higher interest rate increases the payoff derived from waiting. Lenders will therefore supply more funds as the real interest rate increases. So, as Exhibit 8 illustrates, the supply curve for loanable funds slopes upward to the right, while the demand curve has the usual downward slope. Equilibrium is present in the loanable funds market at the real interest rate when the amount of funds demanded by borrowers is equal to the amount supplied by lenders.

Businesses and governments often borrow funds by issuing bonds that yield an interest rate. Issuing bonds is simply a method of demanding loanable funds. In turn, the purchasers of bonds are supplying loanable funds. It is important to note that there is an inverse relationship between bond prices and interest rates. Higher bond prices are the same thing as lower interest rates (see boxed feature, "Bonds, Interest Rates, and Bond Prices").

As was true for the resource market, the loanable funds and goods and services markets are closely interrelated. We previously indicated that a higher interest rate accompanying an increase in the price level when the supply of money is constant helps explain why the *AD* curve slopes downward to the right. In addition, the real interest rate may change for other reasons. When it does, it will affect the aggregate demand schedule. The real interest rate influences aggregate demand because people who borrow money generally do so in order to buy things. Since a higher real interest rate would discourage borrowing, it would also discourage spending. As we proceed, we will analyze in more detail the interrelationship between the loanable funds market and the goods and services market.

EXHIBIT 8

Equilibrium in the Loanable Funds Market

As illustrated, the quantity of loanable funds demanded is inversely related to the real interest rate. The quantity of funds lenders are willing to supply is directly related to the real interest rate. In equilibrium, the real interest rate (*r*) will bring the quantity demanded and quantity supplied in balance.

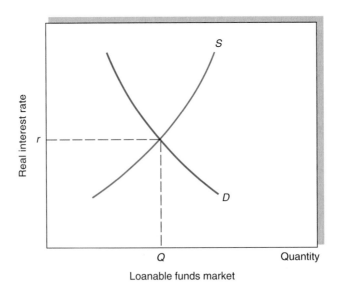

Loanable funds market

APPLICATIONS IN ECONOMICS

Bonds, Interest Rates, and Bond Prices

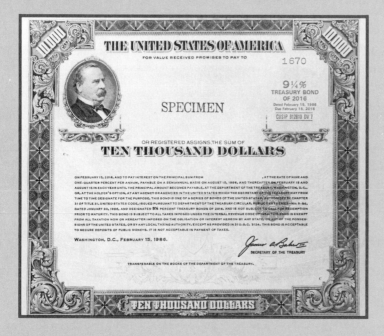

What Is a Bond?

Bonds are simply IOUs issued by firms and governments. Issuing bonds is a method of borrowing money to finance economic activity. The entity issuing the bond promises to pay the bondholder the amount borrowed (called "principal") at a designated future date plus a fixed amount of interest. Some bonds pay the interest at designated intervals (i.e., on a specific date each year). Others pay both principal and interest when the bonds mature at a specified date in the future. The bond shown here is a typical government bond. The face value of the bond is $10,000 and the bond will pay the owner 9¼ percent interest paid annually (half in August and half in February) over a 30-year period. The bond matures on February 15, 2016. At that time, the owner

of the bond will receive from the Treasury Department the $10,000 principal, plus the interest for the final six months.

Even though most bonds are issued for long periods of time, they can be sold to another party prior to their maturity. Each day, sales of previously issued bonds comprise the majority of bonds bought and sold on the bond market. Like most stocks traded on the stock market, new issues of bonds account for only a small portion of all bond sales.

How Does a Change in the Market Interest Rate Affect Bond Prices?

Suppose you have just bought a newly issued $1,000 bond that pays 8 percent per year in perpetuity (forever) on the $1,000 principal.[3] As long as you own the bond, you are entitled to a fixed

return of $80 per year. Let us also assume that, after you have held the bond for one year and have collected your $80 interest for that year, the market interest rate increases to 10 percent.[4] How will the increase in the interest rate affect the market price of your bond? Since bond purchasers can now earn 10 percent interest if they buy newly issued bonds, they will be unwilling to pay more than $800 for your bond, which pays only $80 interest per year. After all, why would anyone pay $1,000 for a bond that yields only $80 interest per year when the same $1,000 will now purchase a bond that yields $100 (10 percent) per year? Once the interest rate has risen to 10 percent, your 8 percent $1,000 bond will no longer sell for its original value. If potential buyers expect the new 10 percent rate to continue, the market value of your bond will fall to $800. You have experienced a $200 capital loss on the bond during the year. Rising market interest rates cause bond prices to decline.

On the other hand, falling interest rates will cause bond prices to rise. If the market interest rate had fallen to 6 percent, what would have happened to the market value of your bond? (Hint: $80 is 6 percent of $1,333.) Bond prices and interest rates are inversely linked to each other.

---

[3]Undated securities of this sort are available in the United Kingdom. They are called consols.

[4]The astute reader will recognize an oversimplification in this discussion. In reality, the economy supports a variety of interest rates, which usually tend to move together.

EQUILIBRIUM IN OUR THREE-MARKET MACROECONOMY

We have now discussed all three basic macroeconomic markets: the goods and services market, the resource market, and the loanable funds market. From these discussions it would be easy to get the impression that each market exists more or less independently. Nothing could be further from the truth. Instead, the three basic macroeconomic markets are as dependent on one another as the legs of a three-legged stool.

Exhibit 9 illustrates equilibrium conditions in the three basic macroeconomic markets of our circular flow model of Exhibit 1. Aggregate demand and aggregate supply are in equilibrium at the price level P_1 and output rate Y_f (frame a). Since the P_1 price level was anticipated both by buyers and by sellers, the economy is operating at its long-run (full employment) capacity. In the resource market, price

EXHIBIT 9

The Three Basic Macroeconomic Markets

Here we indicate equilibrium conditions in the three basic markets that coordinate macroeconomic activity. These markets are highly interrelated. Changes in one influence equilibrium conditions in the other two. In the next chapter, we will focus on how these markets respond to changing economic conditions.

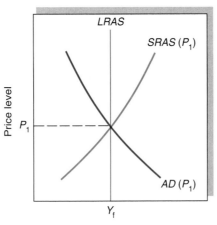

(a) Goods and services (real GNP)

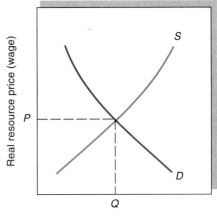

(b) Resource market

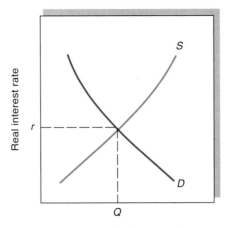

(c) Loanable funds market

also equates amount demanded and amount supplied (frame b). Since the economy is at long-run capacity, only normal unemployment is present in the labor market, an important subcomponent of the resource market. Finally, the real interest (*r*) has brought the amount demanded and amount supplied into balance in the loanable funds market (frame c).

How are these three basic macroeconomic markets interrelated? When an economy is in macroeconomic equilibrium, each of the three basic macromarkets must be in equilibrium. Changes in any one of the basic macro economic markets will influence the equilibrium price and quantity in other markets. In fact, macroeconomics largely concerns tracing the impact of a change in one market through to other markets, particularly the goods and services market.

In macroeconomic equilibrium, the interrelations among the three markets must be internally consistent. The price of resources *relative* to the price of goods and services must permit the firms to cover their cost of production, including a competitive return on their investment. If this were not the case, producers would seek to either contract or expand output. For example, if the prices of resources were so high (*relative* to producers' prices) that firms were unable to cover their costs, many producers would cut back output or perhaps even discontinue production. Aggregate output would thereby be altered. Conversely, if resource prices were so low that firms were able to earn *an above market return,* profit-seeking firms would expand output. New firms would begin production. Again, these forces would alter conditions in the goods and services market.

The incentive of producers in the goods and services market is influenced not only by resource prices relative to product prices, but also by the real interest rate. In macroeconomic equilibrium, the returns of producers must equal the real interest rate—that is, the opportunity cost of capital. Higher returns would induce producers to expand output, while lower returns would cause them to cut back on production. Therefore, when macroeconomic equilibrium is present, prices in these three markets will be such that buyers and sellers in each of the markets are willing to continue with the current arrangements.

LOOKING AHEAD

In the next chapter, we will consider how our simple aggregate demand/aggregate supply model adjusts to changing conditions. Factors that shift demand and supply in one or more of the markets will be analyzed. The interrelationships among the basic macroeconomic markets will be discussed in more detail. As we proceed, we will use our model of basic macroeconomic markets to address these questions.

CHAPTER SUMMARY

1. The circular flow of income illustrates the significance of three highly aggregated markets: (a) goods and services, (b) resources, and (c) loanable funds. The resource market coordinates the exchange of labor and other inputs between the household and business sectors. The goods and services market coordinates the demand of households, business investors, governments, and foreigners with the supply of commodities produced. The loanable funds market coordinates the actions of borrowers and lenders, and thereby channels the *net* saving of households back into the flow of income as investment or government expenditures.

2. The willingness of consumers, investors, governments, and foreigners (net exports) to purchase goods and services determines aggregate demand. The aggregate demand curve indicates the various quantities of goods and services purchasers want to buy at different price levels.

3. Assuming the money supply is constant, there are three reasons why the aggregate demand for goods and services will decline as the price level rises. First, the higher price level reduces the wealth of persons holding money balances. This reduction in wealth will induce them to cut back on their spending. Second, the higher price level will increase the demand for money relative to its fixed supply, causing households and businesses to borrow more to build up their money balances. This increased borrowing leads to higher interest rates, which discourage expenditures on interest-sensitive goods such as automobiles, homes, and investment projects. Third, a higher price level makes domestic goods more expensive and foreign goods cheaper, inducing a decline in net exports (or rise in *net* imports). Each of these factors reduces the quantity of domestic goods and services purchased as the price level rises.

4. The aggregate supply curve indicates the various quantities of goods and services suppliers will produce at different price levels. *In the short run,* the aggregate supply curve will generally slope upward to the right because a higher price level (a) improves profit margins since important cost components are temporarily fixed and (b) misleads some business decision-makers into thinking there has been an increase in *relative* demand for their product.

5. Once decision-makers adjust fully to a higher price level, the factors that justified the upward sloping short-run aggregate supply curve are no longer present. Output is constrained by factors such as technology and resource supply. A higher price level does not loosen these constraints. Thus, the *long-run* aggregate supply curve is vertical.

6. Long-run aggregate supply is closely related to the natural rate of unemployment. When unemployment is at its natural rate (the rate that can be *sustained* into the future), output will also be at its maximum sustainable rate. Thus, the economy's long-run aggregate supply curve is vertical at the output rate that corresponds to the natural rate of unemployment.

7. Two conditions are necessary for long-run equilibrium in the goods and services market: (a) quantity demanded must equal quantity supplied and (b) the actual price level must equal the price level decision-makers anticipated when they made buying and selling decisions for the current period.

8. The aggregate demand and aggregate supply model tells us where the nation's price level and real output will be moving toward. In the short run, price and output will move toward an intersection of the aggregate demand and short-run aggregate supply (SRAS) curves. In the long run, price and output will gravitate to the levels represented by the intersection of AD, SRAS, and LRAS.

9. When the current price level differs from what was expected, output will differ from the economy's long-run capacity. When the current price level is *higher* than was anticipated, real wages and interest rates will be abnormally low. Unemployment will temporarily fall below its natural rate. Current output will temporarily exceed the economy's long-run capacity. In contrast, when the current price level is lower than was anticipated, real wages and interest rates will be abnormally high. Unemployment will exceed its natural rate. Under such circumstances, current output will be lower than the economy's long-run capacity.

10. Business firms demand labor and other resources because they contribute to the production of goods and services that the firms hope to sell at a profit. Individuals supply resources in order to earn income. Price in the resource market coordinates the actions of buyers and sellers. The labor market is the largest component of the general resource market.

11. The interest rate in the loanable funds market is the price borrowers pay to obtain purchasing power now rather than in the future. From the lender's viewpoint, interest is a premium one receives for delaying expenditures into the future. It is the price of credit.

12. It is important to distinguish between the real interest and money interest rates. The real interest rate reflects the real burden to borrowers and the payoff to lenders in

terms of command over goods and services. In addition to this real burden, the money rate of interest also reflects the expected rate of inflation during the period the loan is outstanding. The real rate of interest is equal to the money rate of interest minus the inflation premium. The latter depends on the expected rate of inflation.

13. The presence of macroeconomic equilibrium requires equilibrium in the (a) goods and services, (b) resource, and (c) loanable funds markets. Changes in any one of these markets will influence price and quantity in the other markets. Macroeconomics primarily concerns the adjustment of the basic aggregate markets to various changes in economic conditions.

CRITICAL ANALYSIS QUESTIONS

1. In your own words, explain why aggregate demand is inversely related to the price level. Why isn't the aggregate demand curve simply a reflection of the downward sloping demand curve for an individual good?

2. What are the major factors influencing aggregate supply in the long run? Why doesn't the long run aggregate supply curve slope upward to the right like *SRAS?*

3. What is the natural rate of unemployment? Why is the natural rate of unemployment an important determinant of long-run aggregate supply?

*4. Suppose prices had been rising at a 3 percent annual rate in recent years. A major union signs a 3-year contract calling for increases in money wage rates of 6 percent annually. What will happen to the real wages of the union members if the price level is constant (unchanged) during the next three years? If other unions signed similar contracts, what will probably happen to the unemployment rate? Why? Answer the same questions under conditions in which the price level increases at an annual rate of 8 percent during the next three years.

5. What is the current money interest rate on 30-year government bonds? Is this also the real interest rate? Why or why not?

6. Do you think workers are more concerned about money wages or real wages? Explain. If real wages increase, what happens to the quantity of labor supplied? The quantity demanded? Why?

*7. In Chapter 3, we indicated the other things that are held constant when the supply and demand schedules *for a specific good* are constructed. What were they? What are the key "other things" held constant when the *AS, LRAS,* and *SRAS* schedules are constructed?

8. Under what conditions would the actual unemployment rate be less than the natural rate? Can this condition be sustained in the future? Why or why not?

9. What conditions are required for a short-run equilibrium in the goods and services market? for a long-run equilibrium?

*10. How are the following related to each other?
   a. The long-run equilibrium rate of output
   b. The potential real GNP of the economy
   c. The output rate resulting in the equality of the *actual* and *natural* rates of unemployment

*11. Can the real interest rate ever be negative? Can you cite any examples of a negative real interest rate? Is a negative real interest likely to persist over a long period of time? Why or why not?

*12. If a bond pays $1,000 per year in perpetuity (each year in the future), what will be the market price of the bond when the long-term interest rate is 10 percent? What would it be if the interest rate were 5 percent?

13. If the money interest rate is 10 percent and the inflation rate in recent years has been steady at 7 percent, what is the estimated real interest rate?

*14. How are bond prices related to interest rates? Why are they related?

---

*Asterisk denotes questions for which answers are given in Appendix C, Selected Answers.

9

Working with Our Basic Aggregate Demand/ Aggregate Supply Model

We might as well reasonably dispute whether it is the upper or under blade of a pair of scissors that cuts a piece of paper, as whether value is governed by[demand] or [supply].[1]

Alfred Marshall

CHAPTER FOCUS

- What factors will cause shifts in aggregate demand? What factors will shift aggregate supply?
- How will the goods and services market adjust to changes in aggregate demand?
- How does the economy adjust to unanticipated changes in aggregate supply?
- What causes fluctuations in output and employment?
- Does a market economy have a self-correcting mechanism that will lead it to full employment?

*I*n Chapter 8, we focused on the equilibrium conditions in the three basic macroeconomic markets. Equilibrium is important, but we live in a dynamic world. Markets are constantly affected by unexpected changes such as the discovery of a vastly improved computer chip, shifts in consumer confidence, drought in midwestern agricultural states, or even war in the Middle East. Changes like these will disrupt equilibrium conditions in markets. Thus, if we want to understand how the real world works, analysis of how macroeconomic markets adjust to dynamic change is of crucial importance.

We are now ready to consider how macroeconomic markets adjust to changes in aggregate demand and aggregate supply. As in the last chapter, we will continue to assume that the government's tax, spending, and monetary policies are unchanged. For now, we want to help the reader understand how macroeconomic markets work. Once this objective is achieved, we will be better able to understand both the potential and the limitations of macroeconomic policy.

SHIFTS IN AGGREGATE DEMAND

The aggregate demand curve isolates the impact of the price level on the quantity demanded of goods and services. However, the price level is not the only factor that influences the demand for goods and services. When we constructed the aggregate demand curve, we assumed that several other factors affecting the choices of buyers in the goods and services market were constant. Changes in these "other factors" will shift the entire aggregate demand schedule, altering the amount purchased at each price level. Let us take a closer look at the major factors capable of shifting the aggregate demand schedule.

CHANGES IN REAL WEALTH

In Chapter 8, we indicated that changes in the price level will alter the real value of money balances and therefore the real wealth of people. The wealth of individuals—the value of their assets—may change for reasons other than a change in the price level. For example, during the 1982–1987 period, stock prices in the United States nearly tripled. This stock market boom increased the real wealth of stockholders. In contrast, both stock prices and housing prices declined during 1990. These declines in stock and housing prices reduced the wealth of Americans.

How will changes in the wealth of households affect their demand for goods and services? As the real wealth of households increases—perhaps as the result of higher prices in stock, housing, and/or real estate markets—people will demand more goods and services. As Exhibit 1 illustrates, the increase in wealth will shift the entire aggregate demand schedule to the right (from AD_0 to AD_1). More goods and services are purchased at each price level.

Conversely, a reduction in wealth will reduce the demand for goods and services. The aggregate demand schedule will shift to the left (to AD_2, Exhibit 1) as the result of a decline in the wealth of households.

CHANGES IN THE REAL INTEREST RATE

As we discussed previously, the major macroeconomic markets are closely related. Changes in the real interest rate in the loanable funds market will influence the choices of consumers and investors in the goods and services market. A lower real interest rate makes it cheaper for consumers to buy major appliances, automobiles,

---

[1]Alfred Marshall, *Principles of Economics,* 8th ed. (London: Macmillan, 1920), p. 348.

EXHIBIT 1

Shifts in Aggregate Demand

An increase in real wealth, such as would result from a stock market boom, for example, will increase aggregate demand, shifting the entire curve to the right (from AD_0 to AD_1). In contrast, a reduction in real wealth decreases the demand for goods and services, causing AD to shift to the left (from AD_0 to AD_2). As the following Thumbnail Sketch indicates, changes in the real interest rate, business optimism, expectations concerning the future rate of inflation, incomes abroad, and exchange rates will also shift aggregate demand.

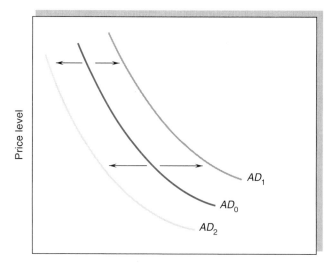

Goods and services (real GNP)

and houses now rather than in the future. Simultaneously, a lower rate will also stimulate business spending on capital goods (investment). The interest rate influences the opportunity cost of all investment projects. If the firm must borrow, the real interest rate will contribute directly to the cost of an investment project. If the firm uses its own funds, it sacrifices real interest that could have been earned by loaning the funds to someone else rather than by investing them. Therefore, a lower real interest rate reduces the opportunity cost of a project, regardless of whether it is financed with internal funds or by borrowing.

Predictably, both households and investors will increase their current expenditures on goods and services in response to a reduction in the real interest rate. A lower real interest rate will increase aggregate demand, shifting the entire schedule to the right. In contrast, a higher real interest rate makes current consumption and investment goods more expensive. A higher real interest rate will tend to reduce aggregate demand, shifting the AD curve to the left.

BUSINESS AND HOUSEHOLD EXPECTATIONS ABOUT THE ECONOMY

What people think will happen in the future will influence current purchasing decisions. Consumers are more likely to buy big ticket items such as automobiles and houses when they expect an expanding economy to provide them with both job security and rising income in the future. Similarly, optimism concerning the future direction of the economy will stimulate current investment. Business decision-makers know that an expanding economy will mean strong sales and improved profit margins. Investment today may be necessary if business firms are going to benefit fully from these opportunities. So, increased optimism encourages additional expenditures by both consumers and investors, increasing aggregate demand.

Of course, pessimism about the future state of the economy exerts just the opposite impact. When consumers and investors expect an economic downturn (a recession), they will cut back on their current spending for fear of becoming overextended. This pessimism leads to a decline in aggregate demand, shifting the AD schedule to the left. Changes in the confidence level of households and businesses concerning the expected future direction of the economy can be a powerful force affecting aggregate demand.

THE EXPECTED RATE OF INFLATION

When consumers and investors believe that the inflation rate is going to accelerate in the future, they have an incentive to spend more during the current period. "Buy now before prices go higher" becomes the order of the day. Thus, the expectation of an acceleration in the inflation rate will stimulate current aggregate demand, shifting *AD* to the right.

In contrast, the expectation of a deceleration in the inflation rate will tend to discourage current spending. When prices are expected to stabilize (or at least increase less rapidly), the gain obtained by moving expenditures forward in time is reduced. The expectation of a deceleration in the inflation rate will thus reduce current aggregate demand (shift the *AD* curve to the left).

CHANGES IN INCOME ABROAD

Changes in the income of a nation's trading partners will influence the demand for the nation's exports. If the income of a nation's trading partners is increasing rapidly, the demand for exports will expand. In turn, the strong demand for exports will stimulate aggregate demand. For example, rapid growth of income in Europe and Japan increases the demand of European and Japanese consumers for U.S. produced goods. As U.S. exports expand, aggregate demand increases (the AD schedule shifts to the right).

Conversely, when a nation's trading partners are experiencing recessionary conditions, they reduce their purchases, including their purchases abroad. Thus, a decline in the income of a nation's trading partners tends to reduce both exports and aggregate demand.

Currently, nearly 10 percent of the goods and services produced in the United States are sold to purchasers abroad. The export sector is still larger for Canada, Japan, and most Western European countries. The larger the size of the trade sector, the greater the potential importance of fluctuations in income abroad as a source of instability in aggregate demand. If the demand of foreign buyers does not rise and fall at the same time as domestic demand however, the diversity of markets will reduce the impact of fluctuations in domestic demand.

CHANGES IN EXCHANGE RATES

As we previously explained, a change in a nation's price level relative to that of its trading partners will influence both net exports and the quantity of goods and services demanded at home. A change in the exchange rate will also affect net exports, and hence aggregate demand. The exchange rate is the value of a nation's currency in terms of the currency of another country. Changes in the value of the dollar on the foreign exchange rate market will alter the prices of imports to U.S. consumers and the prices of U.S. exports to foreign consumers. Consider the impact of an increase in the exchange rate value of the U.S. dollar relative to the British pound. The increase in the exchange rate value of the dollar will make the dollar price of British goods cheaper to U.S. consumers because each dollar will now buy more pounds. In turn, this reduction in the dollar price of British goods will stimulate U.S. imports. Simultaneously, the increase in the exchange rate value of the dollar will make the price tag on U.S. goods (in terms of pounds) more expensive to British consumers, since it will take more pounds to purchase a dollar than was previously the case. Predictably, British consumers will reduce their purchases of American-made goods. Thus, the increase in the exchange rate value of the dollar will stimulate imports and retard exports to the United States. Net exports will decline which will retard aggregate demand (that is, shift the AD schedule to the left.)

A decline in the exchange rate value of the dollar will have just the opposite effect. When there is a decline in the value of the dollar on the exchange rate market, foreign-produced goods become more expensive for U.S. consumers, while U.S.-produced goods become cheaper for foreigners. As a result, net exports will increase and thereby stimulate aggregate demand (shifting AD to the right).[2]

SUMMARY

The accompanying Thumbnail Sketch summarizes the major factors causing shifts in aggregate demand. Shortly, we will analyze how the goods and services market adjusts to changes in demand. The government's spending, taxing, and monetary policies also influence aggregate demand. Knowledge of how the goods and services market works will help us better understand how fiscal and monetary policies work.

THUMBNAIL SKETCH

The major factors causing shifts in the aggregate demand schedule are listed below. The list excludes one important factor—macroeconomic policy. The impact of macroeconomic policy will be considered later.

These factors will increase (decrease) aggregate demand:

1. An increase (decrease) in real wealth.
2. A decrease (increase) in the real rate of interest.
3. An increase in the optimism (pessimism) of businesses and consumers about future economic conditions.
4. An increase (decrease) in the expected rate of inflation.
5. Higher (lower) real incomes abroad.
6. A reduction (increase) in the exchange rate value of the nation's currency.

SHIFTS IN AGGREGATE SUPPLY

What happens if aggregate demand stays the same but aggregate supply changes? The answer to this question depends on whether the aggregate supply change is long run or short run.

By a long-run change in aggregate supply, we mean a change in the economy's long-run production possibilities (sustainable potential output). For example, the invention of a more efficient source of energy would cause a long-run change in aggregate supply. In such a situation, both long-run (LRAS) and short-run (SRAS) aggregate supply would change.

By a short-run change in aggregate supply, we mean a temporary alteration in current output. A drought in California would be an example of such a short-run

---

[2]Later, when we consider the topic of international finance, we will analyze in more detail the determinants of the exchange rate and consider more fully the impact of changes in the exchange rate value of a nation's currency.

change. The drought will hurt in the short run, but it will eventually end, and output will return to the long-run normal rate. Changes that are temporary in nature will shift only SRAS. Let us now consider the major factors capable of shifting the long-run and short-run aggregate supply schedules.

CHANGES IN LONG-RUN AGGREGATE SUPPLY

When constructing the *long-run* aggregate supply curve, the quantity of resources, level of technology, and institutional arrangements that influence the productivity and efficiency of resource use are held constant. Since these factors are generally insensitive to changes in the price level, the long-run aggregate supply curve is vertical. In other words, changes in the price level have no long-run impact on real GNP.

As Exhibit 2 illustrates, changes that increase the economy's productive capacity—its maximum sustainable output at full employment—will shift the long-run aggregate supply to the right. With the passage of time, the economy's resource base can expand and thereby increase *LRAS*. Net investment can increase the future availability of productive equipment and other physical capital. Search and discovery can increase the supply of natural resources. With the passage of time, changes in population and labor force participation may affect the supply of labor. The size of the labor force in the United States doubled between 1950 and 1989, primarily as the result of population growth and the increased participation of females in the labor force. Similarly, education, training, and skill-enhancing experience can improve the quality of the labor force, and thereby expand the supply of human resources.

Increases in the quantity and quality of capital, natural resources, and labor will permit an economy to produce and sustain a larger rate of output. Both LRAS and short-run aggregate supply will increase (shift to the right). On the other hand, a

EXHIBIT 2

Shifts in Aggregate Supply

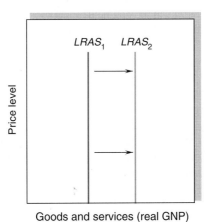

(a) Increase in *LRAS*

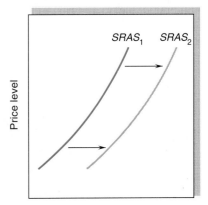

(b) Increase in *SRAS*

Frame (a) illustrates an increase in *LRAS* supply, such as might accompany an increase in the stock of capital or an improvement in technology. These and other factors which expand the economy's potential output will shift the *LRAS* to the right. Frame (b) illustrates a shift in *SRAS*, such as might result from a reduction in resource prices, favorable weather, or a temporary decrease in the world price of an important imported resource. Of course, changes that resulted in a decrease in either *LRAS* or *SRAS* would shift the respective schedules to the left. The following Thumbnail Sketch summarizes the major factors that shift *LRAS* and *SRAS*.

Productivity: The average output produced per worker during a specific time period. It is usually measured in terms of output per hour worked.

lasting reduction in the quantity (or quality) of resources will reduce both the current and long-term production capacity of the economy, shifting both LRAS and SRAS to the left.

Improvements in technology and increases in productivity can also alter long-run aggregate supply. These two factors are closely related. Technological improvements—the discovery of economical new products or less costly ways of producing goods and services—permit us to squeeze a larger output from a specific resource supply. **Productivity** describes the amount of goods and services produced per worker, per hour. As we previously discussed, entrepreneurs have a strong incentive to figure out better ways of doing things and discover new products that are highly valued relative to their costs. Within the framework of a market economy, entrepreneurship is a driving force underlying technological advancements and increases in productivity. For the most part, the enormous improvement in our living standards during the last 250 years is a reflection of the discovery process, technological advancements, and accompanying improvements in productivity. The discovery of the steam engine, and later the internal combustion engine and the jet engine, vastly altered our energy sources. The development of the railroad, the automobile, and the airplane dramatically changed both the cost and speed of transportation. More recently, the discovery of a new, low-cost method of converting sand into silicon chips with a computing power a thousand times greater than the human brain is rapidly changing the way we work and play. Improvements in technology and productivity enhance the economy's long-term productive capacity and thereby shift *LRAS* to the right.

Finally, institutional changes may also influence the efficiency of resource use and thereby alter the long-run aggregate supply schedule. Institutional changes may either increase or decrease aggregate supply. Public policy increases aggregate supply when it enhances economic efficiency by providing, for example, public goods at a low cost, or efficient remedies in instances where externalities would otherwise be a source of waste. In contrast, institutional arrangements sometimes promote waste and increase production costs. For example, studies indicate that minimum-wage legislation reduces employment and restricts the opportunity for training, particularly in the case of youthful workers. Output restrictions accompanying agricultural price supports generally result in inefficient production methods and reductions in output. Such arrangements reduce aggregate supply.

The long-run growth trend of real GNP in the United States has been approximately 3 percent per year. This indicates that increases in the supply of resources and improvements in productivity have gradually expanded potential real output. Hence, the LRAS and SRAS have gradually drifted to the right at about a 3 percent annual rate, sometimes a little faster and sometimes a little slower.

CHANGES IN SHORT-RUN AGGREGATE SUPPLY

Changes can sometimes influence current output without altering the economy's long-run capacity. When this is the case, the *SRAS* curve will shift, even though *LRAS* is unchanged.

What types of changes would influence output in the short run but not in the long run? When we derived the short-run aggregate supply schedule in Chapter 8, we noted explicitly that resource prices and the expected price level (and therefore the inflation rate in the immediate future) were being held constant. Changes in either of these factors will alter *SRAS* but not necessarily *LRAS*.

A reduction in resource prices will lower costs and therefore shift the *SRAS* curve to the right, as illustrated by Exhibit 2b. However, unless the lower prices of resources reflect a *long-term* increase in the supply of resources, they will not alter *LRAS*. Conversely, an increase in the price of resources will increase costs, shifting the *SRAS* curve to the left. But unless the higher prices are the result of a long-term reduction in the size of the economy's resource base, they will not reduce *LRAS*.[3]

Supply Shock: An unexpected event that temporarily either increases or decreases aggregate supply.

In addition, various supply shocks may also alter current output without directly affecting the productive capacity of the economy. **Supply shocks** are surprise occurrences that temporarily increase or decrease current output. For example, adverse weather conditions, a natural disaster, or a temporary increase in the price of imported resources (for example, oil in the case of the United States) will reduce current supply, even though they do not alter the economy's long-term production capacity. They will thus decrease short-run aggregate supply (shift *SRAS* to the left) without directly affecting *LRAS*. On the other hand, favorable weather conditions or temporary reductions in the world price of imported resources will increase current output, even though the economy's long-run capacity remains unchanged.

The accompanying Thumbnail Sketch summarizes the major factors influencing both long-run and short-run aggregate supply. Of course, macroeconomic policy may also influence aggregate supply. As in the case of aggregate demand, we will consider the impact of macroeconomic policy on supply in subsequent chapters.

THUMBNAIL SKETCH

The major factors causing shifts in the long-run and short-run aggregate supply schedules are indicated below. As in the case of aggregate demand, we will analyze the impact of macroeconomic policy on aggregate supply later.

These factors will increase (decrease) long-run aggregate supply *(LRAS):*

1. An increase (decrease) in the supply of resources.
2. An improvement (deterioration) in technology and productivity.
3. Institutional changes that increase (reduce) the efficiency of resource use.

These factors will increase (decrease) short-run aggregate supply *(SRAS):*

1. A decrease (increase) in resource prices, that is, production costs.
2. Favorable (unfavorable) supply shocks such as good (bad) weather.
3. A decrease (increase) in the world price of imported resources.

---

[3]The definition of long-run aggregate supply helps clarify why a change in resource prices will affect short-run aggregate supply, but not long-run aggregate supply. When an economy is operating on its long-run aggregate supply curve, the relationship between resource prices (costs) and product prices will reflect normal competitive market conditions. Since both profit and unemployment rates are at their normal levels, there is no tendency for resource prices to change *relative* to product prices when current output is equal to the economy's long-run potential. Therefore, *when an economy is operating on its long-run aggregate supply schedule,* any change in resource prices will be matched by a proportional change in product prices, leaving the incentive to supply resources (and output) unchanged.

ANTICIPATED AND UNANTICIPATED CHANGES

Anticipated Change: A change that is foreseen by decision-makers, in time for them to adjust.

It is important to distinguish between anticipated and unanticipated changes in markets. **Anticipated changes** are foreseen by economic participants. Decision-makers have time to adjust to anticipated changes *even before they occur*. For example, suppose that under normal weather conditions, a drought-resistant hybrid seed can be expected to expand the production of feed grain in the Midwest by 10 percent next year. As a result, buyers and sellers will plan for a larger supply and probable lower prices in the future. They will adjust their decision-making and behavior accordingly.

Unanticipated Change: A change that decision-makers could not reasonably foresee. Thus, choices made prior to the event did not take the event into account.

In contrast, **unanticipated changes** catch people by surprise. Our world is characterized by dynamic change. Unexpected new products, crop failures, expanding markets, cheaper imports—markets are constantly changing in light of unexpected events. Economics largely concerns how markets adjust to unanticipated changes. To see the importance of this distinction, let's investigate the impact of anticipated versus unanticipated changes on aggregate supply and demand.

ECONOMIC GROWTH AND ANTICIPATED CHANGES IN SUPPLY AND DEMAND

How does the market for goods and services adjust to anticipated changes in aggregate demand and supply? Interestingly, the major source of anticipated changes in aggregate supply and demand is economic growth. Why are the changes due to economic growth usually anticipated? Economic growth is the slow but steady increase in the productive capacity of the economy due to net investment, technological advancement, and growth in the labor force. Significant changes of this type usually take place gradually, over a matter of years. Month to month changes in the resource base and level of technology are almost always quite modest.

Exhibit 3 illustrates the impact of economic growth on the goods and services market. Initially, the economy is in long-run equilibrium at price level P_1 and output Y_{f_1}. The growth expands the economy's potential output, shifting both the long- and short-run aggregate supply curves to the right (to $LRAS_2$ and $SRAS_2$). Since these changes are gradual, decision-makers have time to anticipate the changing market conditions and adjust their behavior accordingly.

Of course, the economic growth has expanded the economy's production possibilities. It will now be possible to *produce* and *sustain* a higher rate of real output (Y_{f_2}). *The larger output rate can be achieved even while unemployment remains at its natural rate. Since the money supply is constant, the increase in aggregate supply will lead to a lower price level (P_2).* Of course, changes in technology and relative resource prices will lead to movement of resources among industries. In addition, other changes will almost certainly disturb the economy's long-run equilibrium as it grows over time. However, as markets adjust to these factors, the result will be a new long-run equilibrium at a higher *sustainable* output.

During the last 50 years, real output has expanded significantly in the United States and other countries. However, contrary to the presentation of Exhibit 3, the price level has generally not declined. This is because the monetary authorities have

EXHIBIT 3

The Growth of Aggregate Supply

Here we illustrate impact of economic growth due to capital formation or a technological advancement, for example. The full employment output of the economy expands from Y_{f_1} to Y_{f_2}. Thus, both long- and short-run aggregate supply increase (to $LRAS_2$ and $SRAS_2$). A *sustainable,* higher level of real output and real income is the result. If the money supply is held constant, a new long-run equilibrium will emerge at a larger output rate (Y_{f_2}) and lower price level (P_2).

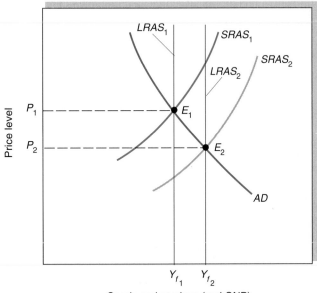

Goods and services (real GNP)

expanded the supply of money. As we will see later, an increase in the money supply stimulates aggregate demand (shifts *AD* to the right) and thereby pushes the price level upward.[4]

UNANTICIPATED CHANGES IN AGGREGATE DEMAND

Markets do not adjust instantaneously to unanticipated changes in market conditions. For a time, it may be unclear whether a change in sales, for example, reflects a random occurrence or a lasting change. It takes time to differentiate between temporary and permanent changes. Even after decision-makers are convinced that market conditions have changed, it will take time to carry out new decisions. In some cases, complete adjustment will also be delayed by the presence of long-term contracts.

Since it takes time for markets to adjust, unanticipated changes in aggregate demand and supply will not immediately lead to a new long-run equilibrium. Nonetheless, unpredictable events occur. We now turn to an analysis of how markets react to unexpected changes.

UNANTICIPATED INCREASES IN AGGREGATE DEMAND

Exhibit 4a illustrates an economy that is initially in long-run equilibrium (E_1) at output Y_f and price level P_{100}. Aggregate demand and aggregate supply are in balance. Decision-makers have correctly anticipated the current price level. Thus, AD_1 and $SRAS_1$ intersect at the economy's full employment capacity (Y_f).

What would happen if this long-run equilibrium (E_1) were disrupted by an unanticipated increase in aggregate demand? For example, suppose consumers and

---

[4]In subsequent chapters, we will explain how stable prices can be achieved as real output increases.

Short- and Long-Run Effects of an Unanticipated Increase in Aggregate Demand

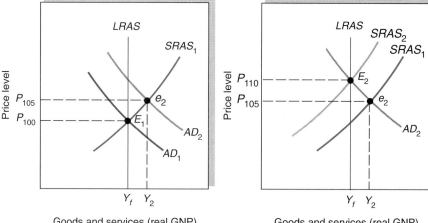

(a) Short-run effects of increase in *AD*

(b) Long-run effects of increase in *AD*

In response to an unanticipated increase in aggregate demand for goods and services (shift from AD_1 to AD_2), in the short-run prices will rise (to P_{105}) and output will temporarily exceed full employment capacity (frame a). However, with the passage of time, prices in resource markets, including the labor market, will rise as the result of the strong demand. As frame (b) illustrates, the higher resource prices will mean higher costs which will reduce aggregate supply (to $SRAS_2$, frame b). In the long run, a new equilibrium at a higher price level (P_{110}) and an output consistent with the economy's sustainable potential will result. Thus, the increase in demand will expand output only temporarily.

Inflationary Gap: The situation present when the short-run equilibrium output exceeds full employment potential GNP. The strong demand places upward pressure on prices.

investors suddenly become more optimistic about future business conditions, causing an unanticipated increase in aggregate demand (shift from AD_1 to AD_2).

At the initial price level, (P_{100}), excess demand would be present. Given the excess demand, businesses will increase their prices, improve their profit margins (since product prices increase relative to the cost of resources), and expand their output along SRAS. The economy will move to a short-run equilibrium (e_2), at a larger output (Y_2) and higher price level (P_{105}). (Note: a short-run equilibrium is indicated with a small *e*, while a capital *E* is used to designate a long-run equilibrium.) For a time, many wage rates, interest payments, rents, and other resource prices will still reflect the initial price level (P_{100}) and the previously weaker demand. Since markets do not adjust instantaneously, these resource prices and therefore *costs will lag behind prices* in the goods and services market. Thus, the higher price level temporarily improves profit margins, which, in turn, provides the incentive for business firms to expand both output and employment in the short run. As a result, the unemployment rate will drop below its natural rate, and output will temporarily exceed the economy's long-run potential output level.[5]

This is not the end of the story, however. An **inflationary gap** is present at the short-run equilibrium depicted by Exhibit 4a. Inflationary gap is a term used to describe the upward pressure on resource prices and costs when an economy is operating at an output (Y_2) beyond its full employment potential (Y_f). The strong demand accompanying this high level of output will place upward pressure on prices

[5]Thoughtful students may wonder how output (and by implication, the quantity of resources) can be increased, even temporarily, when *real* wages and resource prices more generally are declining. There are two reasons why this may be the case. First, in an inflationary environment workers (and other resource suppliers) may be fooled, at least temporarily, by an increase in *money* wages (and resource prices) that is *less rapid than the inflation rate*. Responding to the higher money wages, workers may supply more labor even though their real wages have fallen. While we have presented the analysis within the framework of a noninflationary environment, the basic linkage between real wages (costs) and SRAS still holds. A reduction in the real wage rate, even when it takes the form of a nominal wage increase that is less than the inflation rate, will reduce real costs, and thereby increase SRAS. Second, the resource base may also temporarily expand in response to strong demand conditions because the *cost of entering* the labor force will decline during this boom phase of the business cycle. Potential new labor force entrants will be able to find jobs quickly at this time. Thus, the size of the labor force will tend to grow rapidly during an economic expansion. Conversely, the labor force will tend to shrink (or grow less rapidly) during a business contraction, when the *cost of entering* the labor force will be high.

An Unanticipated Reduction in Aggregate Demand

As frame (a) illustrates, the short-run impact of an unanticipated reduction in aggregate demand (shift from AD_1 to AD_2) will be a decline in output (to Y_2) and a lower price level (P_{95}). Temporarily, unemployment will rise above its natural rate. In the long run, weak demand and excess supply in the resource market will lead to lower wage rates and resource prices. This will reduce costs, leading to an expansion in short-run aggregate supply (shift to $SRAS_2$, frame b). However, this method of restoring equilibrium (E_2) may be both highly painful and quite lengthy.

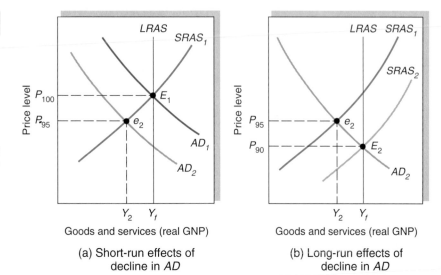

(a) Short-run effects of decline in *AD*

(b) Long-run effects of decline in *AD*

in resource and loanable funds markets. With time, the strong demand conditions will push wages, other resource prices, and real interest rates upward. As Exhibit 4b illustrates, the rising resource prices and costs will shift the short-run aggregate supply to the left (to $SRAS_2$). Eventually, a new *long-run* equilibrium (E_2) will be established at a higher price level (P_{110}) that is correctly anticipated by decision-makers.

Thus, the increase in real GNP above the economy's long-run potential is only temporary. It will last only until there is an opportunity to alter the temporarily fixed resource prices (and interest rates) upward in light of the new stronger demand conditions. As this happens, profit margins return to their normal level, output recedes to the economy's long-run potential, and unemployment returns to its natural rate.

Since an increase in aggregate demand does not alter the economy's productive capacity, it cannot permanently expand output (beyond Y_f). The expansion in demand temporarily expands output, but over the long-term its major effect will be higher prices (inflation).

UNANTICIPATED REDUCTIONS IN AGGREGATE DEMAND

Deflationary Gap: The situation present when the short-run equilibrium output is less than full employment potential. Weak demand conditions place downward pressure on prices.

How would the goods and services market adjust to an unanticipated reduction in aggregate demand? For example, suppose decision-makers become more pessimistic about the future or that an unexpected decline in income abroad reduced the demand for exports. Exhibit 5 will help us analyze this issue. Once again, we consider an economy that is in long-run equilibrium (E_1) at output Y_1 and price level P_{100} (frame a). Long-run equilibrium is disturbed by the reduction in aggregate demand: the shift from AD_1 to AD_2. As the result of the decline in demand, businesses will be unable to sell Y_f units of output at the initial price level (P_{100}). In the short run, business firms will both reduce output (to Y_2) and cut prices (to P_{95}) in response to the weak demand conditions. Since many costs of business firms are temporarily fixed, profit margins will decline. Workers will be laid off, causing unemployment to increase to an abnormally high rate.

The short-run equilibrium (e_2) depicts a **deflationary gap.** A deflationary gap is present when output is less than the economy's potential. When a deflationary gap exists, unemployment will exceed the natural rate of unemployment. Weak demand

and excess supply will be widespread in resource markets. These forces will place downward pressure on resource prices.

If resource prices quickly adjusted downward in response to the weak demand and rising unemployment, then the decline in output to Y_2 would be brief. Lower resource prices would reduce costs and thereby increase aggregate supply (shift to $SRAS_2$). As frame b illustrates, the result would be a new equilibrium (E_2) at the economy's full employment output rate (Y_f) and a lower price level (P_{90}).

Resource prices, though, may not adjust quickly. Long-term contracts and uncertainty as to whether the weak demand conditions are merely temporary will slow the adjustment process. In addition, individual workers and union officials may be highly reluctant to be the first to accept lower nominal wages.

If resource prices are inflexible in a downward direction, as many economists believe, the adjustment to a reduction in aggregate demand will be both lengthy and painful. Prolonged periods of economic recession—below capacity output rates and abnormally high unemployment—may occur before long-run equilibrium is restored.

UNANTICIPATED CHANGES IN AGGREGATE SUPPLY

As we previously discussed, factors that alter aggregate supply in the *long run* generally operate slowly. For example, it takes time to expand the supply of capital or adopt a new, improved technology. In contrast, changes in factors influencing the *short-run* aggregate supply curve are more likely to be unanticipated. By their nature, supply shocks are unpredictable. We now turn to an analysis of unexpected changes in aggregate supply.

UNANTICIPATED INCREASES IN SRAS

What would happen if highly favorable weather conditions or a temporary decline in the world market price of a critical imported resource increased the current output and income of a nation? Exhibit 6 addresses this issue. Since the temporarily favorable supply conditions cannot be counted on in the future, they will not directly alter the economy's long-term production capacity. Given that the favorable supply conditions are temporary, short-run aggregate supply will increase (to $SRAS_2$), while LRAS will remain constant. Output (and income) will temporarily expand beyond the economy's full employment constraints. The increase in current supply will place downward pressure on the price level.

How will households respond to their temporarily higher incomes? The **permanent income hypothesis,** developed by Nobel Prize-winning economist Milton Friedman, will help us answer this question. According to the permanent income hypothesis, the consumption of households is determined largely by their long-range expected or permanent income. Since temporary changes in income generally do not exert much impact on long-term expected income, transitory increases or decreases in income do not exert a large impact on current consumption. Thus, a large proportion of a temporary income gain usually flows into saving and debt reduction.

Permanent Income Hypothesis: The hypothesis that consumption depends on some measure of long-run expected (permanent) income rather than on current income.

Perhaps a personal application will help explain why it is important to distinguish between temporary and long-term changes in income. Think for a moment how you would adjust your *current* spending on goods and services if an aunt left you $10,000 next month. No doubt you would spend some of the money almost immediately. Perhaps you would buy a new stereo or take a nice vacation.

An Unanticipated, Temporary Increase in Aggregate Supply

Here we illustrate the impact of an unanticipated, but temporary increase in aggregate supply such as might result from a bumper crop due to highly favorable weather conditions. The increase in aggregate supply (shift to $SRAS_2$) would lead to a lower price level (P_{95}) and an increase in current GNP (to Y_2). Since the favorable supply conditions cannot be counted on in the future, the economy's long-run aggregate supply will not increase. Predictably, decision-makers will save a large proportion of their temporarily higher real income, spreading the benefits into the future. Thus, the supply of loanable funds will increase. The real interest rate will fall (to r_2), encouraging expenditures on interest-sensitive capital goods and consumer durables.

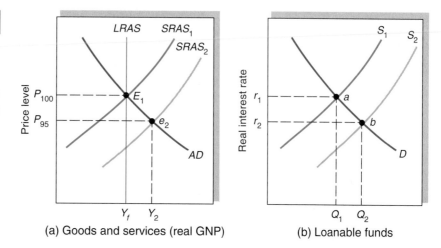

(a) Goods and services (real GNP)   (b) Loanable funds

However, you would probably also use a significant portion of this temporary (one-time only) increase in income to pay bills or save for future education. Now, consider how you would alter your *current* spending if your aunt indicated you were to receive $10,000 *per year* for the next 20 years. In this case, you are likely to spend most of this year's $10,000 almost immediately. You might even borrow money to buy an automobile or make some major expenditures, and thereby expand your spending on goods and services *this year* by more than $10,000.

The permanent income hypothesis indicates that a substantial share of a temporarily high income resulting from unexpectedly favorable supply conditions will flow into saving as individuals seek to spread the benefits over a longer time period. The increased saving will expand the supply of loanable funds (shift to S_2, frame b), causing the real interest rate to decline. The lower real interest rate will stimulate investment and encourage the purchase of consumer durables such as automobiles and appliances.

An increase in aggregate supply that is expected to be temporary will place downward pressure on prices and reduce the real rate of interest. The lower interest rate will encourage capital formation that will expand the resource base, permitting individuals to spread some of the benefits of the current high level of income into the future.

What would happen if the favorable conditions increasing supply reflected long-term factors? For example, suppose that worldwide production conditions changed, such that a decline in the price of a major imported resource such as oil was expected to be permanent rather than temporary. If this were the case, both the *LRAS* and the *SRAS* would increase (shift to the right). This case would parallel the analysis of Exhibit 3. A new long-run equilibrium at a higher output would result.

UNANTICIPATED DECREASES IN SRAS

In recent decades, the U.S. economy has been jolted by several unfavorable supply-side factors. In 1973 and again in 1979, the United States and other oil-importing countries were hit with sharply higher oil prices as the result of unstable conditions in the Middle East. During the summer of 1988, the most severe drought conditions in 50 years resulted in an extremely poor harvest in the U.S. agricultural belt. In August of 1990, Iraq suddenly invaded Kuwait and threatened the oil fields of Saudi Arabia. Once again the world price of oil shot up, sharply increasing the cost of energy in the United States and other oil importing countries.

EXHIBIT 7

The Effects of an Adverse Supply Shock

Suppose there is an unanticipated reduction in the supply of resources, perhaps as the result of a crop failure or sharp increase in the world price of a major imported resource such as oil. Resource prices would rise (from P_r to P'_r, frame a). The higher resource prices would shift the *SRAS* curve to the left. In the short run, the price level would rise (to P_{110}, frame b) and output would decline (to Y_2). What happens in the long run depends on whether the reduction in the supply of resources is temporary or permanent. If it is temporary, resource prices will fall in the future, permitting the economy to return to its initial equilibrium (E_1). Conversely, if the reduced supply of resources is permanent, the productive potential of the economy will shrink (*LRAS* will shift to the left) and e_2 will become a long-run equilibrium.

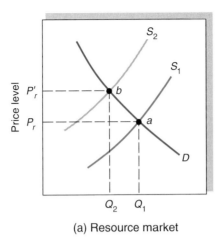

(a) Resource market

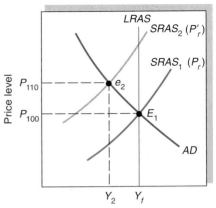

(b) Goods and services (real GNP)

How do such supply-side shocks influence macroeconomic markets? Exhibit 7 illustrates the answer. Both an unfavorable harvest due to adverse weather conditions and a higher world price of oil will reduce the supply of resources (from S_1 to S_2, frame a) in the domestic market. Resource prices will rise (to P'_r). In turn, the higher resource prices will reduce short-run aggregate supply (the shift from $SRAS_1$ to $SRAS_2$, frame b) in the goods and services market. Since supply shocks of this type are generally unanticipated, initially they will reduce output and place upward pressure on prices (the rate of inflation) in the goods and services market.

If an unfavorable supply shock is expected to be temporary, as will generally be the case for a bad harvest, long-run aggregate supply will be unaffected. After all, unfavorable growing conditions for a year or two do not represent a permanent change in climate. Therefore, as normal weather patterns return with the passage of time, both supply and price conditions in the resource market will return to normal, permitting the economy to return to long-run equilibrium at output Y_f. As in the case of the temporary increase in output depicted by Exhibit 6, people will use the loanable funds market to smooth consumption in response to a temporary reduction in income. Believing that their lower incomes are temporary, households will reduce their current saving level (and dip into past savings) to maintain a current consumption level more consistent with their longer-term perceived opportunities. But, when everyone reduces their saving level, the supply of loanable funds decreases causing an increase in the real interest rate. The higher real interest rate rations funds to those willing to pay the most to maintain their current spending during the economic hard times. Of course, a higher real interest rate will also retard capital investment. A reduction in net investment and an accompanying decline in near-term economic growth are predictable side effects of a temporary reduction in aggregate supply.

When an adverse supply-side factor is more permanent, as in the case of a *long-term* increase in the price of oil imports, the long-run supply curve would also shift to the left. Under these circumstances, the economy would have to adjust to a lower level of real output.

Regardless of whether the decline in aggregate supply is temporary or permanent, other things constant, the price level will rise. Similarly, output will decline, at least temporarily. Theory thus indicates that the adverse supply shocks of recent years contributed to the sluggish growth and inflation of the era.

DOES A MARKET ECONOMY HAVE A SELF-CORRECTING MECHANISM?

Does a market economy contain built-in forces that will prevent (a) economic downturns from plunging the economy to the depths of depression and (b) economic booms from soaring into runaway inflation? Will market forces help to stabilize the economy and cushion the effects of economic shocks? There are three important reasons to believe that they will.

1. *Consumption demand is relatively stable over the business cycle.* By far, consumption is the largest component of aggregate demand. The permanent income hypothesis indicates that the consumption component of aggregate demand will be substantially more stable than income. When income falls during a recession, households will reduce their current saving in order to maintain a high level of current consumption. Thus, consumer demand will decline by a smaller amount than income during a recession.

Similarly, during an economic expansion, a substantial amount of the above-normal gains in income enjoyed by most households will be allocated to saving. So, consumption demand will increase less rapidly than income during a business expansion. The relative stability of consumption will help keep aggregate demand from plunging downward during a recession and soaring upward during an economic boom.

2. *Changes in real interest rates will help to stabilize aggregate demand and redirect economic fluctuations.* Previously, we noted that sudden changes in the confidence of consumers and investors were a potential source of instability. However, interest rate adjustments will, at least partially, offset disturbances arising from this source. Suppose consumers and investors, motivated by a burst of optimism, suddenly decide to spend more of their current income on goods and services. In order to do so, they will either have to reduce their saving or increase their borrowing. But these actions will reduce the supply of loanable funds relative to the demand. Predictably, the real rate of interest will rise. But the higher real interest rate will make current consumption and investment spending more expensive. Thus, the rising real interest rate will limit the increases in spending of consumers and investors, and thereby help to stabilize aggregate demand.

Interest rate changes will also help to offset reductions in aggregate demand stemming from business pessimism. If consumers and investors suddenly reduce their spending of current income, other things being constant, an increase in saving is implied. The supply of loanable funds will increase relative to the demand. Real interest rates will fall, which will stimulate additional current spending. When changes in aggregate demand arise from business pessimism, adjustments in the loanable funds market will exert a stabilizing effect.

Perhaps even more important, changes in the real interest rate tend to redirect both recessions and booms. During an economic downturn, business demand for new investment projects and therefore loanable funds is generally quite weak. The weak demand, however, leads to a lower real interest rate. In turn, the lower interest rate both encourages current consumption and reduces the opportunity cost of investment projects, dampening the decline in aggregate demand. On the other hand, the real interest rate increases as many businesses borrow in order to undertake investment projects during an economic expansion. The higher real interest rate discourages both consumption and investment and thereby minimizes

EXHIBIT 8

Employment of Resources and the Dynamics of Resource Prices

When aggregate output is less than the economy's full employment potential (Y_f), the weak demand and slack employment in resource markets place downward pressure on wages and other resource prices (P_r). Conversely, when output exceeds Y_f, strong demand and tight market conditions result in rising real prices in resource markets.

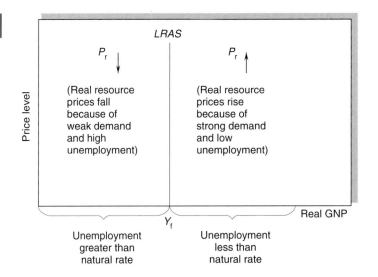

the increase in aggregate demand during a business expansion. Thus, the interest rate acts as a shock absorber helping both to stabilize aggregate demand and redirect economic fluctuations.

3. *Changes in real resource prices will redirect economic fluctuations*. Price adjustments in the resource market will also help to keep the economy on an even keel. Exhibits 8 and 9 illustrate this point. Exhibit 8 depicts the response of resource prices to business cycle conditions. When the current output of an economy is less than its full employment potential (Y_f), weak demand and slack employment in resource markets will place downward pressure on *real* resource prices. Under these conditions, real wages and other resource prices will decline (or increase at a very slow rate). In contrast, when an economy is operating beyond its full employment capacity (Y_f)—when unemployment is less than the natural unemployment rate—strong demand will push the real price of resources up rapidly.

Exhibit 9 indicates the significance of this pattern of dynamic change in resource prices in response to business conditions. Exhibit 9a illustrates the supply and demand conditions in the goods and services market such as might result from an unanticipated increase in aggregate demand. Current output exceeds the economy's full employment capacity. An inflationary gap is present. A high level of employment will be required to achieve the output (Y_1, frame a) beyond the economy's potential sustainable rate. Initially, unemployment is less than the natural rate of unemployment. When these conditions are present, however, real resource prices will increase rapidly, pushing costs upward. The higher resource prices will reduce short-run aggregate supply (shift to $SRAS_2$, frame a). As resource prices and costs rise, profit margins will decline to normal competitive rates and output will recede to its long-run potential. Thus, market forces will help direct the overemployment economy back to long-run equilibrium.

Exhibit 9b illustrates an economy initially operating at less than full employment capacity. A deflationary gap is present. When current output is less than an economy's long-run potential, resource prices will decline *relative to product prices*. An abnormally high unemployment rate (in excess of the natural rate) in resource markets will eventually induce suppliers to accept lower wage rates and prices for other resources. The declining real cost of labor and other resources

Resource Prices and Directing the Economy to Long-Run Equilibrium

In the short run, output may either exceed or fall short of the economy's full employment capacity (Y_f). If output is temporarily greater than the economy's potential (frame a), resource prices and production costs will rise. The higher production costs will decrease aggregate supply (to $SRAS_2$, frame a), restoring equilibrium at full employment capacity and a higher price level (P_{105}).

When an economy is temporarily operating at less than capacity (frame b), abnormally high unemployment and an excess supply in the resource market may lead to lower resource prices and production costs. The lower cost would increase aggregate supply (to $SRAS_2$, frame b). Thus, the output of a market economy would tend to move toward full employment capacity. However, this self-correction process may require considerable time. As we proceed, we will consider alternative methods of attaining full employment equilibrium more rapidly.

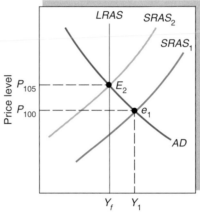

(a) Inflationary gap — output greater than long-run potential

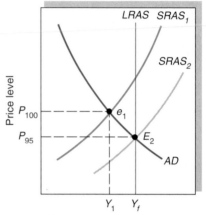

(b) Deflationary gap — output less than long-run potential

will shift *SRAS* to the right. With time, the lower resource prices will restore long-run equilibrium (E_2) at the full employment rate of output.

THE BUSINESS CYCLE REVISITED

Our aggregate demand/aggregate supply (*AD/AS*) model enhances our understanding of economic instability. In a dynamic world of changing demand conditions and supply-side shocks, the model indicates that economic ups and downs will be present. Macroeconomic markets do not adjust instantaneously and decision-makers do not always accurately anticipate changes in the price level. Therefore, *in the short run,* output sometimes exceeds and sometimes falls short of its long-run potential. This is precisely what periods of economic boom and recession imply.

Exhibit 10 presents a picture of the economic fluctuations during the last 25 years. It is interesting to reflect on these cycles within the framework of our model. Periods of economic boom, such as were present in the late 1960s, 1973, 1978, and 1986 – 1988, imply that the *AD* and *SRAS* curves look something like the initial conditions (associated with e_1) of Exhibit 9a. The intersection of the *AD* and *SRAS* curves would be at an output rate beyond the economy's full employment potential. Conversely, when an economy is in a recession, such as was experienced in the United States during 1970, 1974– 1975, and 1979– 1982, conditions similar to the initial situation (associated with e_1) depicted by Exhibit 9b are implied. During a recession, the intersection of the *AD* and *SRAS* curves will be at an output rate that is less than full employment. Therefore, as Exhibit 10b illustrates, the unemployment rate will fall below the natural rate during a period of economic boom and rise above the natural rate during recessions. (Note: Since the natural rate of unemployment is not directly observable, a range of estimates is provided in Exhibit 10b).

However, our *AD/AS* model also indicates that market forces will redirect both an expansionary boom and a recessionary contraction. A boom will not continue to spiral upward. Neither will a contraction continue to plunge downward.

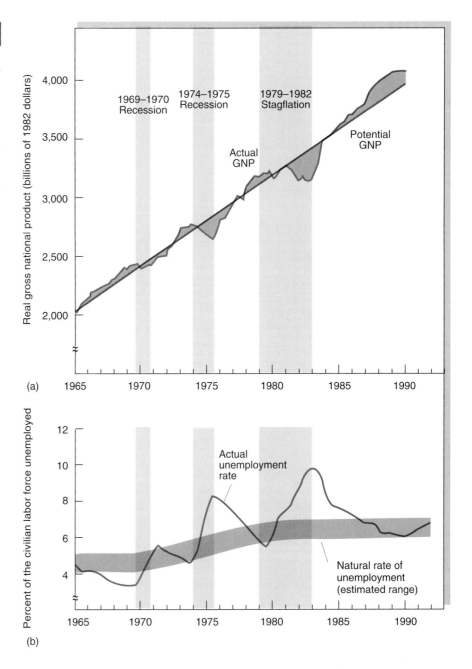

EXHIBIT 10

Output and Employment—The 1965–1990 Record

Recent periods of economic expansion and contraction are illustrated above. Our analysis indicates that real interest rates and wages will *rise* during expansions and *fall* during recessions, and thereby help to stabilize the economy. Exhibit 11 presents data on this topic.

During periods of weak resource demand, high unemployment, and output less than the economy's potential GNP, our analysis indicates that real interest rates and real wages will eventually decline (or increase at a sluggish rate.) Conversely, they will rise during periods of economic boom. Exhibit 11 presents data on the estimated real interest rate and annual rate of change in the real hourly compensation of nonfarm employees for the 1966–1987 period. Real interest rates did tend to increase during economic expansions and recede during recessionary periods. The estimated real interest rate declined to less than 1 percent during the recession of

EXHIBIT 11 ■ Business Cycle Conditions and Real Wages, 1966–1987		
Expansions and Recessions	Estimated Real Interest Rate (at peak for expansion and at trough for recession)	Annual Percent Rate of Change in Real Compensation per Hour (non-farm business sector)
1966–68 Expansion	1.5	2.9
1969–70 Recession	0.5	1.0
1971–73 Expansion	1.0	2.2
1974–75 Recession	−2.0	−0.4
1976–78 Expansion	3.5	1.5
1979–82 Recessions	0.0	−1.0
1983–87 Expansion	5.0	0.5

Source: The real interest rate data are from the Board of Governors of the Federal Reserve System and the University of Michigan Household Survey. The real compensation data are from the Department of Labor, Bureau of Labor Statistics.

1970 and, for a time, it was actually negative during the severe 1974–1975 recession. It also declined sharply (from 3.5 percent to zero) during the 1979–1982 period.[6] Similarly, real wages increased less rapidly during each of the three recessions than during the preceding and subsequent periods of economic expansion. In fact, real compensation actually declined during the 1974–1975 and 1979–1982 recessions. Clearly, this pattern of change in real interest rates and real wages is consistent with our analysis of macroeconomic markets.

THE GREAT DEBATE: HOW RAPIDLY DOES THE SELF-CORRECTION PROCESS WORK?

Following the Great Depression, many economists thought that market economies were inherently unstable. They argued that unless monetary and fiscal policy were used to stimulate and guide the macroeconomy, prolonged recessions would result. Influenced by both a reevaluation of the 1930s and the experience of the last 50 years, most modern economists reject this stagnation view of market economies.[7] Today, there is a widespread consensus that market economies possess stabilizing forces.

What divides economists is disagreement about how rapidly the self-correcting forces work. This is a key issue. If the self-corrective process works quite slowly, then market economies will still experience prolonged periods of abnormally high

---

[6]Officially, there were two recessions during the 1979–1982 stagnation: one of approximately 6 months duration in 1980 and a second lasting approximately 18 months during 1981–1982. In the 1980 recession, the short-term real interest rate fell from 3.5 percent to zero. During the sharp deceleration of the inflation rate and more severe recession of 1981–1982, the real interest rate tumbled from nearly 10 percent to approximately 3 percent.

[7]A detailed analysis of the forces causing and prolonging the Great Depression is presented in Chapter 13.

unemployment and below-capacity output. Many economists believe this is the case. As a result, they have a good deal of confidence that discretionary monetary and fiscal policy will promote stability and prosperity.

Conversely, other economists believe that the self-corrective mechanism of a market economy works reasonably well when monetary and fiscal policy follow a stable course. This latter group argues that macroeconomic policy mistakes are the major source of economic instability. Because of this, they call for the use of policy rules, such as a constant growth rate in the supply of money and balanced budgets, rather than discretionary use of macroeconomic policy. We will return to this debate when we consider the impact of monetary and fiscal policy.

LOOKING AHEAD

Modern macroeconomics reflects an evolutionary process. The Great Depression and the accompanying prolonged unemployment exerted an enormous impact on macroeconomics. John Maynard Keynes, the brilliant English economist, developed a theory that sheds light on the operation of an economy experiencing high rates of unemployment. The next chapter focuses on the Keynesian theory.

CHAPTER SUMMARY

1. An increase in aggregate demand involves a shift of the entire *AD* schedule to the right. Other than policy, major factors causing an increase in aggregate demand are: (a) an increase in real wealth, (b) a lower real interest rate, (c) increased optimism on the part of businesses and consumers, (d) an increase in the expected rate of inflation, (e) higher real income abroad and (f) a reduction in a nation's exchange rate. Conversely, if these factors change in the opposite direction, a decrease in aggregate demand will result.

2. Changes that alter the economy's maximum sustainable output will shift the *LRAS* curve. The following factors will increase *LRAS:* (a) increases in the supply of labor and capital resources, (b) improvements in technology and productivity and (c) institutional changes improving the efficiency of resource use.

3. In the short run, output may change as the result of temporary factors that do not directly alter the economy's long-run capacity. The major factors leading to an increase in *SRAS* (a shift of the schedule to the right) are: (a) a reduction in resource prices, (b) favorable weather conditions, and (c) a decline in the world price of imported resources. Conversely, if these factors changed in the opposite direction, *SRAS* would decline (shift to the left).

4. An increase in output due to economic growth (an increase in the economy's production capacity) will increase both short-run and long-run aggregate supply. The economy will now be able to produce and sustain a larger output level. If the supply of money is constant, a lower price level will result.

5. When the long-run equilibrium of an economy is disrupted by an unanticipated increase in aggregate demand, output will temporarily increase beyond the economy's long-run capacity and unemployment will fall below its natural rate. However, as decision-makers adjust to the increase in demand, resource prices will rise and output will recede to long-run capacity. In the long run, the major impact of the increase in aggregate demand will be a higher price level (inflation).

6. An unanticipated reduction in aggregate demand will temporarily reduce output below capacity and push unemployment above its natural rate. Eventually, unemployment and excess supply in resource markets will reduce wage rates and resource prices. Costs will decline and output will return to its long-run potential. However, if wages and prices are inflexible downward, less-than-capacity output and abnormally high unemployment may persist for a substantial period of time.

7. When an economy in long-run equilibrium experiences an unanticipated favorable supply shock, output (and income) will temporarily rise above capacity and prices will decline. A lower real interest rate is also a predicted result, since a large amount of a temporary increase in income will flow into saving. The lower real interest rate will stimulate capital formation and, other things constant, will lead to more rapid short-run economic growth.

8. An adverse supply shock (decrease in *SRAS*) will reduce output and increase the price level. If the reduction in income is expected to be temporary, people will increase their borrowing (and reduce their saving) to maintain a consumption level more consistent with their longer-term income. As a result, the real interest rate will rise. Many economists think adverse supply shocks, particularly the sharp increase in the price of imported oil, contributed to the slow rate of growth and rapid increase in the price level during the 1970s.

9. When output and employment exceed the rates associated with an economy's long-run equilibrium, real interest rates and resource prices (including real wages) will rise, increasing costs and thereby shifting the *SRAS* to the left until long-run equilibrium is restored at full employment output and a higher price level. Similarly, when current output is less than the economy's potential GNP, lower real interest rates and falling real resource prices (and wages) will reduce costs and thereby shift *SRAS* to the right until long-run equilibrium is restored. These forces provide the economy with a self-corrective mechanism directing it toward the full employment rate of output.

10. Many economists believe the economy's self-corrective mechanism works quite slowly and that discretionary monetary and fiscal policy changes are necessary to minimize economic instability. Others believe that the self-corrective mechanism works reasonably well and that discretionary policy is likely to do more harm than good.

CRITICAL ANALYSIS QUESTIONS

*1. Explain how and why each of the following factors would influence current aggregate demand in the United States:
   a. an increase in recession fears;
   b. increased fear of inflation;
   c. rapid growth in real income in Japan and Western Europe;
   d. a reduction in the real interest rate;
   e. a higher price level (be careful).

*2. Indicate how each of the following would influence U.S. aggregate supply in the short run:
   a. an increase in real wage rates;
   b. a severe freeze that destroys half of the orange trees in Florida;
   c. a drought in the midwest agricultural states;
   d. an increase in the world price of oil, a major import;
   e. abundant rainfall during the growing season of agricultural states.

3. It is often argued that if everyone simultaneously tried to save more, the result might well be a decline in real GNP. Use our basic three-market macroeconomic model to analyze the impact of an increase in thriftiness on prices, output, employment, and interest rates.

*4. When an economy is at a short-run equilibrium below the full-employment output rate, explain how the self-correcting mechanism will direct the economy back to its long-run potential rate of output. Can you think of any reason why this mechanism might not work? Discuss.

---

*Asterisk denotes questions for which answers are given in Appendix C, Selected Answers.

5. What is the difference between an anticipated and an unanticipated increase in aggregate demand? Provide an example of each. Which is most likely to result in a temporary spurt in the growth of real output?

*6. Both union and management representatives agreed to wage increases reflecting the expectation that prices will rise 10 percent during the next year. Explain why the unemployment rate will probably increase if the actual rate of inflation next year is only 3 percent.

7. During 1980–1985, the exchange rate value of the dollar increased sharply. How did this change influence aggregate demand, output, and the inflation rate during the 1980–1985 period? During 1986–1988, the exchange value of the dollar fell. What impact did this decline in the exchange rate value of the U.S. dollar have on *AD*, output, and inflation?

*8. When the actual output exceeds the long-run potential of the economy, how will the self-correcting mechanism direct the economy to long-run equilibrium? Why can't the above-normal output be maintained?

*9. Are the real wages of workers likely to increase more rapidly when the unemployment rate is high or when it is low? Why?

10. Suppose that the key macroeconomic markets are initially in long-run equilibrium. How will an unanticipated reduction in aggregate demand affect real output, employment, and the price level in the short run? In the long run?

11. "Unemployment benefits should replace 100% of an employee's earnings from his or her previous job when the employee is terminated or laid off through no fault of his or her own." Do you think this is a good idea? How will it affect the search time of the unemployed workers? What impact will it have on the unemployment rate?

*12. An unexpectedly rapid growth in real income abroad leads to a sharp increase in demand for U.S. exports. What impact will this change have on the price level, output, and employment in the short run? What is the likely impact in the long run?

13. Many collective bargaining agreements now contain "indexing provisions" which adjust wage rates periodically to changes in the price level. How do these provisions influence the response of firms and employees to an unexpected change in the price level?

14. If the real interest rate increases, how will this affect the incentive of consumers and investors to purchase goods and services? How will this affect the *AD* curve? How will a higher real interest rate affect the cost of producing goods? How will this influence the *SRAS* curve?

15. Construct the *AD, SRAS* and *LRAS* curves for an economy experiencing a recession. Do the same for economies experiencing (a) full employment and (b) an economic boom.

Keynesian Foundations of Modern Macroeconomics

I believe myself to be writing a book on economic theory which will largely revolutionize—not, I suppose, at once but in the course of the next ten years—the way the world thinks about economic problems.[1]

John Maynard Keynes

CHAPTER FOCUS

■ What was Keynes's explanation for the high rates of unemployment that persisted during the Great Depression?

■ What are the major components of the Keynesian model? What is the major factor that causes the level of output and employment to change?

■ What determines the equilibrium level of output in the Keynesian model?

■ What is the multiplier principle? Why is it important?

■ Why do Keynesians believe market economies experience business instability?

*R*eal world events provide the laboratory for the testing of economic theories. Sometimes real world events are inconsistent with a theory. When this is the case, the theory is discarded or modified. New theories with greater predictive power arise. This is the way sciences develop.

Modern macroeconomics is the product of this evolutionary process. Prior to the Great Depression of the 1930s, most economists thought market adjustments would automatically guide an economy to full employment within a relatively brief time. A decade of double-digit unemployment rates during the 1930s undermined the credibility of this view. The experience of the Great Depression also provided the background for the development of a new theory, one capable of explaining the prolonged unemployment of the period.

The new theory, developed by the English economist John Maynard Keynes (pronounced "canes") has exerted enormous influence on modern macroeconomics.[2] For three decades following the Second World War, Keynesian economics represented the core of macroeconomics. Several basic concepts and much of the terminology we use today can be traced to Keynes. Modern macroeconomics is built on the foundation of Keynesian analysis. This chapter presents the Keynesian view and illuminates its influence on modern macroeconomic theory.

KEYNESIAN EXPLANATION OF THE GREAT DEPRESSION

Classical Economists:
Economists from Adam Smith to the time of Keynes who focused their analyses on economic efficiency and production. With regard to business instability, they thought market prices would adjust quickly in a manner that would guide an economy out of a recession back to full employment.

Mainstream economists prior to the time of Keynes (often called **classical economists**) emphasized the importance of supply. In contrast, they paid little heed to aggregate demand. The lack of interest in demand issues by classical economists stemmed from their adherence to Say's Law. Named for the nineteenth-century French economist J. B. Say, **Say's Law** maintains that a general overproduction of goods relative to total demand is impossible since supply (production) creates its own demand. Say's Law is based on the view that people do not work just for the sake of working. Rather, they work to obtain the income required to purchase desired goods and services. The purchasing power necessary to buy (demand) desired products is generated by production. A farmer's supply of wheat generates income to meet the farmer's demand for shoes, clothes, automobiles, and other desired goods. Similarly, the supply of shoes generates the purchasing power with which shoemakers (and their employees) demand the farmer's wheat and other desired goods.

---

[1]Letter from John Maynard Keynes to George Bernard Shaw, New Year's Day, 1935.

[2]See the classic book John Maynard Keynes, *The General Theory of Employment, Interest, and Money* (London: Macmillan, 1936) for the presentation of this theory.

Say's Law: The view that production creates its own demand. Thus, there cannot be a general over-supply because the total value of goods and services produced (income) will always be available for purchasing them.

Classical economists understood that it was possible to produce too much of some goods and not enough of others. At such times, they reasoned, the prices of goods in excess supply would fall, and the prices of products in excess demand would rise. The pricing system would correct such imbalances as might temporarily exist. They did not believe, though, that a general overproduction of goods was possible. In aggregate, they thought demand would always be sufficient to purchase the goods produced.

Prior to the Great Depression, the classical view seemed reasonable. But the depth and the prolonged duration of the decline during the 1930s undermined the classical view and provided the foundation for what we now refer to as Keynesian economics. The extent of the economic decline during the 1930s is difficult to comprehend, particularly for those who are only familiar with the relative stability of the last four decades. In 1933, 25 percent of the U.S. labor force was unemployed. Numerous plants closed down or operated at 50 percent of capacity. International trade came to a virtual standstill. Real GNP in the United States declined by 9.5 percent in 1930, 8.4 percent in 1931, 13.8 percent in 1932, and by another 2.2 percent in 1933. By way of comparison, real GNP fell by only 2.5 percent in 1982, the most severe of the post-Second World War recessions. After a rebound during 1934–37, the U.S. economy experienced still another 4.6 percent decline in output in 1938. In 1939, a decade after the plunge began, the unemployment rate stood at 17 percent of the work force. Per capita income in 1939 was nearly 10 percent less than 1929, and the depressed conditions were worldwide; other industrial countries experienced similar conditions.

KEYNESIAN VIEW OF SPENDING AND OUTPUT

Against this background of the 1930s, Keynes developed a theory that provided an explanation for the prolonged depressed conditions of the era. Keynes rejected the classical view and offered a completely new concept of output determination. He believed that spending induced business firms to supply goods and services. From this, he argued that if total spending fell (as it might, for example, if consumers and investors became pessimistic about the future or tried to save more of their current income), then business firms would respond by cutting back production. Less spending would thus lead to less output.

Of course, classical economists were aware of this possibility, but they believed the labor surplus would drive down wages, reducing costs and lowering prices until the surplus was eliminated and the economy was directed to full employment within a reasonable time. Keynes and his followers disagreed. They argued that wages and prices are highly inflexible, particularly in a downward direction, in modern economies characterized by large business firms and powerful trade unions. Because of this, they did not believe that flexible wages and prices would direct the economy to equilibrium at full employment.

Keynes also introduced a different concept of equilibrium and a different mechanism for its achievement. In the Keynesian view, equilibrium takes place when the level of total spending is equal to current output. When this is the case, producers will have no reason to either expand or contract output. Moreover, according to Keynes, this equilibrium rate of output need not be associated with the full employment of resources. In the Keynesian view, *changes in output* rather than *changes in prices* direct the economy to equilibrium. If total spending is less than full employment output, output will be cut back to the level of spending and, most significantly, it will remain there until the level of spending changes. Therefore, if total spending is deficient, high rates of unemployment and other recessionary conditions will continue. This is precisely what Keynes believed was happening during the 1930s.

Within the Keynesian framework, equilibrium takes place at the output rate consistent with the level of total spending at current prices. This output rate need not be associated with the full employment of resources.

The message of Keynes could be summarized as follows: Spending (demand) leads to current production. Businesses will produce only the quantity of goods and services they believe consumers, investors, governments, and foreigners will plan to buy. If these planned aggregate expenditures are less than the economy's full employment output, output will fall short of its potential. When aggregate expenditures are deficient, there are no automatic forces capable of assuring full employment. Less than capacity output will result. Prolonged unemployment will persist. Against the background of the Great Depression, this was a compelling argument.

OUTSTANDING ECONOMIST

**John Maynard Keynes
(1883–1946)**

The General Theory of Employment, Interest, and Money was published in 1936. It would not be an exaggeration to rank this book alongside Adam Smith's *Wealth of Nations* and Karl Marx's *Das Kapital* as one of the most influential economic treatises ever written. In the midst of the Great Depression, Keynes provided both a plausible explanation for the massive unemployment and a strategy for ending it. He believed additional demand was needed to put people back to work. Furthermore, his analysis indicated that increases in government spending financed by budget deficits would provide the required demand stimulus and thereby restore full employment. A generation searching for answers in the midst of the Great Depression provided a receptive audience for Keynesian analysis. Keynes married an idea with a moment in history.

Keynes correctly anticipated that his ideas would, with the passage of time, exert a powerful influence (see chapter opening quote). By the 1950s, the Keynesian analysis was dominant in academic circles throughout the Western world. By the 1960s, the Keynesian view formed the foundation for the macroeconomic policy of the United States and most other Western nations. Keynes died rather suddenly in 1946, so he did not live to observe the enormous impact of his ideas on public policy.

The economic events of the 1970s tempered the confidence of macroeconomists in the basic analysis of Keynes. Nevertheless, his imprint is sure to endure. He revolutionized our way of thinking about macroeconomic issues.

THE BASIC KEYNESIAN AGGREGATE EXPENDITURE MODEL

As we will show, the Keynesian analysis could be presented within the framework of our *AD/AS* model. However, an alternative framework, an aggregate expenditure model, is generally used to present the Keynesian view. Equality between aggregate expenditures and output is central to the Keynesian analysis. The Keynesian aggregate expenditure model helps us visualize this point. The model will also help us better understand why Keynesians believe that changes in aggregate spending exert a powerful influence on equilibrium output and employment. The aggregate expenditure model has occupied a central position in macroeconomics for several decades. It is an integral part of the evolutionary process that led to modern macroeconomic theory.

As we develop the Keynesian aggregate expenditure model, we will make several assumptions to simplify the analysis. First, as with our *AD/AS* model, we will assume there is a specific full employment level of output. Only the natural rate of unemployment is present when full employment capacity is attained. Second, following in the Keynesian tradition, we will assume that wages and prices are completely inflexible until full employment is reached. Once full employment is achieved, though, additional demand will lead only to higher prices. Strictly speaking, these polar assumptions will not hold in the real world. They may, however, approximate conditions in the short run. Finally, we will continue to assume that the government's taxing, spending, and monetary policies are constant.

The concept of planned aggregate expenditures is central to the Keynesian analysis. As with aggregate demand, the four components of aggregate expenditures are consumption, investment, government purchases, and net exports. The Keynesian model postulates a specific relationship between total income and each component of planned expenditures. We turn now to these issues.

PLANNED CONSUMPTION EXPENDITURES

Keynes believed that current income is the primary determinant of consumption expenditures. As he stated:

> Men are disposed, as a rule and on the average, to increase their consumption as their income increases, but not by as much as the increase in their income.[3]

According to Keynes, disposable income is by far the major determinant of current consumption. If disposable income increases, consumers will increase their planned expenditures.

This positive relationship between consumption spending and disposable income is called the **consumption function.** Exhibit 1 illustrates this relationship for an economy. At low levels of aggregate income (less than $2 trillion), the consumption expenditures of households will exceed their disposable income. When income is low, households dissave. They either borrow or draw from their past savings to purchase consumption goods. Since consumption does not increase as rapidly as income, the slope of the consumption function will be less than one.

Consumption Function:
A fundamental relationship between disposable income and consumption. As disposable income increases, current consumption expenditures will rise, but by a smaller amount than the increase in income.

---

[3]John Maynard Keynes, *The General Theory of Employment, Interest, and Money* (London: Macmillan, 1936), p. 96.

EXHIBIT 1

The Aggregate Consumption Function

The Keynesian model assumes that there is a positive relationship between consumption and income. However, as income increases, consumption expands by a smaller amount. Thus, the slope of the consumption function (line *C*) is less than one (less than the slope of the 45-degree line).

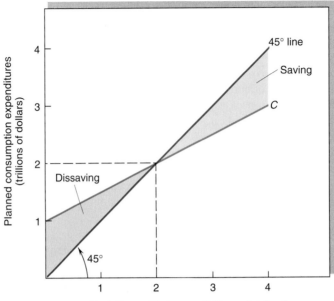

So, the consumption schedule is flatter than the 45-degree line of Exhibit 1. As income increases, household aggregate income eventually equals and exceeds current consumption. For aggregate incomes above $2 trillion, saving increases as income rises.

PLANNED INVESTMENT EXPENDITURES

Autonomous Expenditures: Expenditures that do not vary with the level of income. They are determined by factors (such as business expectations and economic policy) that are outside the basic income-expenditure model.

Investment encompasses (a) expenditures on fixed assets such as buildings and machines and (b) changes in the inventories of raw materials and final products not yet sold. Keynes argued that in the short run, investment was best viewed as an **autonomous expenditure,** independent of income.

Exhibit 2 illustrates an autonomous investment schedule. The flat investment schedule indicates that businesses plan to spend $700 billion on investment, regardless of current income. Planned investment is thus independent of income. In the Keynesian model, investment is primarily a function of current sales relative to plant capacity, expected future sales, and the interest rate. Changes in these latter factors would alter investment—they would cause the entire schedule to shift either upward or downward. But, when focusing on the forces pushing an economy toward an equilibrium level of output, the basic Keynesian model postulates a constant level of planned investment expenditures.

PLANNED GOVERNMENT EXPENDITURES

As with investment, planned government expenditures in the basic Keynesian model are assumed to be independent of income. Exhibit 2 illustrates an autonomous government expenditure function of $1,000 billion. The combined investment and government expenditures sum to $1,700 billion.

The forces underlying government expenditures differ from those influencing private consumption and investment. Government expenditures need not be constrained by income (tax revenues) or the pursuit of profit. Governments can, and often do, spend more than they receive in taxes. Planned government expenditures

Autonomous Investment and Government Expenditures

Within the basic Keynesian model, planned investment (line *I*) is autonomous of income. Investment may shift either up or down in response to changes in factors such as business optimism or the real interest rate, but it is independent of the income level. Similarly, government expenditures (line *G*) are a policy variable, independent of income. Thus, as income changes, planned investment and government expenditures (*I* + *G*) remain constant.

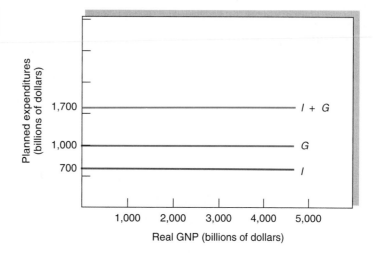

are best viewed as a policy variable, subject to alteration by the political process. Perceiving them as autonomous of income allows us to focus more clearly on the stability characteristics of a private economy. Later, we will analyze how changes in government expenditures influence output and employment within the framework of the Keynesian aggregate expenditure model.

PLANNED NET EXPORTS

Exports are dependent on spending choices and income levels abroad. These decisions are, by and large, unaffected by changes in a nation's domestic income level. Therefore, as Exhibit 3 illustrates, exports remain constant when income changes. In contrast, increases in domestic income will induce consumers to purchase more foreign as well as domestic goods. So, the level of imports increases as income rises.

Since exports remain constant and imports increase as aggregate income expands, net exports will decline as income expands (see Exhibit 3). From this, the Keynesian model postulates a negative relationship between income and net exports.

EXHIBIT 3 ■ Income and Net Exports			
Since exports are determined by income abroad, they are constant at $350 billion. Imports increase as domestic income expands. Thus, planned net exports fall as domestic income increases.			
Total Output (Real GNP in billions)	Planned Exports (billions)	Planned Imports (billions)	Planned Net Exports (billions)
$4,600	$350	$150	$200
4,900	350	200	150
5,200	350	250	100
5,500	350	300	50
5,800	350	350	0

**PLANNED VERSUS
ACTUAL EXPENDITURES**

It is important to distinguish between planned and actual expenditures. Planned expenditures reflect the choices of consumers, investors, governments and foreigners, *given their expectations as to the choices of other decision-makers.* Planned expenditures, though, need not equal actual expenditures. Remember, inventories are a component of investment in our national income accounts. *Actual* investment is equal to *planned* investment *plus* any unplanned changes in inventories. If purchasers spend a different amount on goods and services than business firms anticipate, the firms will experience unplanned changes in inventories. When this is the case, actual investment will differ from planned investment.

Consider what would happen if the planned expenditures of consumers, investors, governments, and foreigners on goods and services were less than what business firms thought they would be. If this were the case, business firms would be unable to sell as much of their current output as they had anticipated. Their *actual* inventories would increase as they unintentionally made larger inventory investments than they planned. On the other hand, consider what would happen if purchasers bought more goods and services than business expected. The unexpected brisk sales would draw down inventories and result in less inventory investment than business firms planned. In this case, *actual* inventory investment would be less than they *planned*.

Actual and planned expenditures are equal only when purchasers buy the quantity of goods and services business decision-makers anticipate. Only then will the plans of buyers and sellers in the goods and services market harmonize.

KEYNESIAN EQUILIBRIUM

In our basic Keynesian model, planned expenditures on consumption, investment, government, and net exports sum to planned aggregate expenditures *(AE)*. In turn, business firms will plan to produce only the quantity of goods they believe consumers, investors, governments, and foreigners (net exports) will purchase *at existing prices.*

Equilibrium is present in the Keynesian model when planned aggregate expenditures equal the value of current output. When this is the case, businesses are able to sell the total amount of goods and services that they produce. There are no unexpected changes in inventories. Thus, producers have no incentive to either expand or contract their output during the next period. In equation form, Keynesian macroequilibrium is attained when:

$$\underbrace{\text{total output}}_{\text{Real GNP}} = \underbrace{\text{planned } C + I + G + X}_{\substack{\text{planned aggregate} \\ \text{expenditures}}}$$

**KEYNESIAN
EQUILIBRIUM—TABULAR
PRESENTATION**

To grasp the Keynesian concept of equilibrium, it is helpful to view the major components in tabular form. Exhibit 4 presents data for planned consumption, investment, government purchases, and net exports. Reflecting the assumptions of the Keynesian model, investment is assumed to be determined by such factors as

EXHIBIT 4 ■ Equilibrium Level of Income, Output, and Employment							
Possible Levels of Employment (millions of persons) (1)	Total Output (Real GNP) (billions of dollars) (2)	Planned Consumption (billions of dollars) (3)	Planned Injections (I + G) (billions of dollars) (4)	Planned Net Exports (billions of dollars) (5)	Planned Aggregate Expenditures (billions of dollars)[a] (6)	Unplanned Inventory Change[b] (billions of dollars) (7)	Tendency of Employment, Output, and Income (8)
90	4,600	3,000	1,700	200	4,900	−300	Increase
100	4,900	3,200	1,700	150	5,050	−150	Increase
110	5,200	3,400	1,700	100	5,200	0	Equilibrium
120[c]	5,500	3,600	1,700	50	5,350	+150	Decrease
130	5,800	3,800	1,700	0	5,500	+300	Decrease

[a]Planned $C + I + G + X$ as indicated by columns 3, 4, and 5.
[b]Total output (column 2) less planned aggregate expenditures (column 6).
[c]Full employment.

business expectations and technological change. It is thus not dependent on level of income. Similarly, government expenditures are subject to economic policy. They, too, are assumed to be independent of income. So, for all levels of income, the injections of investment and government purchases into the income streams are assumed to be constant (at $1,700 billion). Within the Keynesian model, planned consumption increases with income, but it increases by a smaller amount than does income (because some of the additional income is allocated to saving and taxes). As income increases by $300 billion (from $4,600 billion to $4,900 billion, for example), consumption increases by $200 billion. While planned net exports decline with income, they fail to offset the increase in consumption since they are relatively small. Thus, aggregate expenditures (Exhibit 4, column 6) increase as income expands.

For the economy illustrated by Exhibit 4, Keynesian equilibrium takes place at a GNP of $5.2 trillion, the income level at which planned aggregate expenditures are just equal to total output (aggregate supply). An employment level of 110 million is associated with the $5.2 trillion output. When GNP is equal to $5.2 trillion, the planned expenditures of consumers, investors, governments, and foreigners (net exports) are precisely equal to the value of the output produced by business firms. Because of this, the spending plans of purchasers mesh precisely with the production plans of business decision-makers. Given this balance, there is no reason for producers to change their plans for the next period.

At other output levels, the plans of producers and purchasers will conflict. Consider what will happen if the output of the economy temporarily expands to $5.5 trillion. Employment will increase from 110 to 120 million. At the higher income level, households will increase their spending to $3.6 trillion. When added to the $1.7 trillion of spending by investors and governments, and the $50 billion in net exports, total spending is equal to $5.35 trillion, $150 billion less than output. The total spending of consumers, investors, and governments will thus be insufficient to purchase the $5.5 billion of output. Unwanted and unplanned business inventories of $150 billion will arise. Of course, business firms will not continue to produce goods they cannot sell, so they will reduce production during the subsequent period.

As production is cut back, output and employment will fall. The unemployment rate will rise. Given the spending plans of decision-makers, the $5.5 trillion income level cannot be maintained in the future.

What will happen if income falls temporarily below the Keynesian equilibrium? Suppose the income level of the economy pictured in Exhibit 4 were $4.9 trillion. At that income level, purchasers of goods and services would spend $5.05 billion (column 6) on current output. Business firms would be selling more than they are currently producing. Their inventories would decline below normal levels. Business firms would respond to this happy state of affairs by expanding output. Production would increase, providing jobs for previously unemployed workers. Income would rise toward the Keynesian equilibrium level of $5.2 trillion.

LESS THAN FULL EMPLOYMENT EQUILIBRIUM

Since Keynesian equilibrium is dependent on equality between planned aggregate expenditures and output, it need not take place at full employment. If an economy is in Keynesian equilibrium, there will be no tendency for output to change even if output is well below full employment capacity.

Exhibit 4 illustrates this point. Suppose full employment for the economy is present at an employment level of 120 million. This notwithstanding, given the current planned spending, the economy will always move toward the $5.2 trillion equilibrium income level. In equilibrium, employment will be 110 million, 10 million less than for full employment. Reflecting the view that wages and prices are inflexible downward, in the Keynesian model neither wages nor other resource prices decline in the face of abnormally high unemployment and excess capacity. Therefore, output remains at less than the full employment rate as long as the planned aggregate expenditures are $5.2 trillion. Insufficient spending prevents the economy from reaching its full potential.

This is precisely what Keynes thought was happening during the Great Depression. He believed that Western economies were in equilibrium at an employment rate substantially below capacity. Unless aggregate expenditures

EXHIBIT 5

Keynesian Equilibrium

Aggregate expenditure will be equal to total output for all points along a 45-degree line from the origin. The 45-degree line thus maps out potential equilibrium levels of output for the Keynesian model.

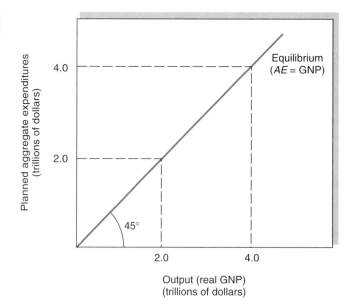

increased, the prolonged unemployment would continue. Keynesian economics provided a theory to explain the persistently high level of unemployment during the 1930s.

KEYNESIAN EQUILIBRIUM—GRAPHIC PRESENTATION

The Keynesian analysis can also be presented graphically. Exhibit 5 presents a graph for which the planned aggregate consumption, investment, government, and net export expenditures are measured on the *Y*-axis and total output is measured on the *X*-axis. The 45-degree line extends from the origin and maps out all points that are equidistant from the *X*- and *Y*-axes. So, along the 45-degree line, aggregate expenditures *(AE)* are equal to total output (GNP).

Since aggregate expenditures equal total output for all points along the 45-degree line, the line maps out all possible equilibrium income levels. As long as the economy is operating at less than its full employment capacity, producers will produce any output along the 45-degree line they believe purchasers will buy. Producers, though, will supply a level of output only if they believe planned expenditures will be large enough to purchase it. Depending on the level of aggregate expenditures, each point along the 45-degree line is a potential equilibrium. Within the Keynesian model, then, there are many possible equilibrium levels of output and employment, not just one.

Using the data of Exhibit 4, Exhibit 6 graphically depicts the Keynesian equilibrium. The $C + I + G + X$ line indicates the total planned expenditures of

EXHIBIT 6

Aggregate Expenditures and Keynesian Equilibrium

Here the data of Exhibit 4 are presented within the Keynesian graphic framework. The equilibrium level of output is $5.2 trillion since planned expenditures ($C + I + G + X$) are just equal to output at that level of income. At a lower level of income, $4.9 trillion for example, unplanned inventory reduction would cause business firms to expand output (right-hand arrow). Conversely, at a higher income level, such as $5.5 trillion, accumulation of inventories would lead to a reduction in future output (left-hand arrow). Given current aggregate expenditures, only the $5.2 trillion output could be sustained. Note the $5.2 trillion equilibrium income level is less than the economy's potential of $5.5 trillion.

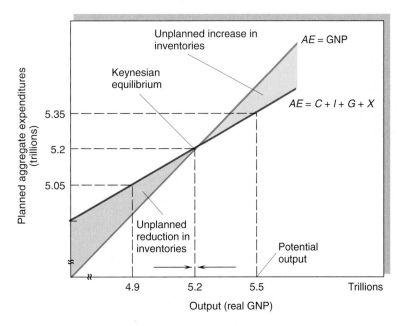

consumers, investors, governments, and foreigners (net exports) at each income level. Reflecting the consumption function, the aggregate expenditure *(AE)* line is flatter than the 45-degree line. Remember, as income rises, consumption also increases, but by less than the increase in income. Therefore, as income expands, total expenditures increase by less than the expansion in income.

The equilibrium level of output will be $5.2 trillion, the point at which the total expenditures (measured vertically) are just equal to total output (measured horizontally). Of course, the aggregate expenditure function $C + I + G + X$ will cross the 45-degree line at the $5.2 trillion equilibrium level of output.

As long as the aggregate expenditures function remains unchanged, no other level of output can be sustained. When total output exceeds $5.2 trillion (for example, $5.5 trillion), the aggregate expenditure line lies below the 45-degree line. Remember that the $C + I + G + X$ line indicates how much people want to spend at each income level. When the height of the $C + I + G + X$ line is less than the 45-degree line, total spending is less than total output. Unwanted inventories will then accumulate, leading businesses to reduce their future production. Employment will decline. Output will fall back from $5.5 trillion to the equilibrium level of $5.2 trillion. Note that it is changes in output and employment, not price changes, that restore equilibrium in the Keynesian model.

In contrast, if total output is temporarily below equilibrium, there is a tendency for income to rise. Suppose output is temporarily at $4.9 trillion. At that output level, the $C + I + G + X$ function lies above the 45-degree line. Aggregate expenditures exceed aggregate output. Businesses are selling more than they currently produce. Their inventories are falling. Excess demand is present. They will react to this state of affairs by hiring more workers and expanding production. Income will rise to the $5.2 trillion equilibrium level. Only at the equilibrium level, the point at which the $C + I + G + X$ function crosses the 45-degree line, will the spending plans of consumers, investors, and governments sustain the existing output level into the future.

As Exhibit 6 illustrates, the economy's full employment potential income level is $5.2 trillion. At this income level, though, aggregate expenditures are insufficient to purchase the output produced. Given the aggregate expenditure function, output will remain below its potential. Unemployment will persist. Within the Keynesian model, equilibrium need not coincide with full employment.

SHIFTS IN AGGREGATE EXPENDITURES AND CHANGES IN OUTPUT AND EMPLOYMENT

How could the economy reach its full employment capacity? According to the Keynesian model, it will not do so unless there is a change in the aggregate expenditure schedule. Since the Keynesian model assumes that prices are fixed until potential capacity is reached, wage and price reductions are ruled out as a feasible mechanism for directing the economy to full employment.

If consumers, investors, governments, and foreigners could be induced to expand their expenditures, output would expand to full employment capacity. Exhibit 7 illustrates this point. If additional spending shifted the aggregate expenditure schedule *(AE)* upward to AE_2, equilibrium output would expand to its potential capacity. At the higher level of expenditures, AE_2, total spending would equal output at $5.5 trillion.

What would happen if aggregate expenditures exceeded the economy's production capacity? For example, suppose aggregate expenditures rose to AE_3. Within the basic Keynesian model, aggregate expenditures in excess of output lead

Shifts in Aggregate Expenditures and Changes in Equilibrium Output

When equilibrium output is less than the economy's capacity, only an increase in expenditures (a shift in *AE*) will lead to full employment. If consumers, investors, governments, or foreigners would spend more and thereby shift the aggregate expenditure schedule to AE_2, output would reach its full employment potential ($5.5 trillion). Once full employment is reached, further increases in aggregate expenditures, such as indicated by the shift to AE_3, would lead only to higher prices. Nominal output will expand (the dotted segment of the $AE = GNP$ schedule), but real output will not.

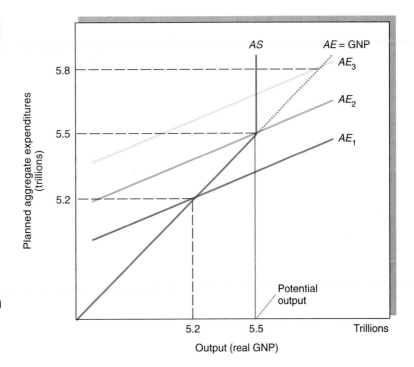

to a higher price level, once the economy reaches full employment. Nominal output will increase, but it merely reflects higher prices, rather than additional real output. Total spending in excess of full employment capacity is inflationary within the Keynesian model.

Aggregate expenditures are the catalyst of the Keynesian model. Changes in expenditures make things happen. Until full employment is attained, supply is always accommodative. An increase in aggregate expenditures will thus lead to an increase in real output and employment. Once full employment is reached, however, additional aggregate expenditures lead merely to higher prices.

The Keynesian model implies that regulation of aggregate expenditures is the crux of sound macroeconomic policy. If we could assure aggregate expenditures large enough to achieve capacity output, but not so large as to result in inflation, the Keynesian view implies that maximum output, full employment, and price stability could be attained.

THE KEYNESIAN MODEL WITHIN THE AD/AS FRAMEWORK

The Keynesian model can also be presented within the now familiar aggregate demand/aggregate supply framework. Given the polar assumptions of the model, the Keynesian supply conditions could be described as follows: Until the economy reaches its capacity, individual firms hold their price constant at the level that would be most profitable if they were operating at capacity. When demand is weak, firms simply reduce output, while maintaining the same price. Conversely, if demand

EXHIBIT 8

The Keynesian Aggregate
Supply Curves

The Keynesian model implies a
90-degree angle-shaped
aggregate supply curve. Since
the model postulates downward
wage and price inflexibility, the
SRAS curve is flat for outputs
less than potential GNP (Y_f). In
this range, often referred to as
the Keynesian range, output is
entirely dependent on the level
of aggregate demand. The
Keynesian model implies that
real output rates beyond full
employment are unattainable.
Thus, both *SRAS* and *LRAS*
are vertical at the economy's
full employment potential
output.

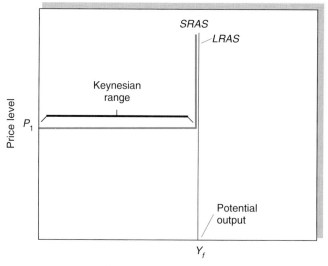

Goods and services (real GNP)

increases, they will expand output while maintaining the same price until normal
operating capacity is achieved. This means that the firms have a horizontal supply
curve when operating below normal capacity. As a result, the short-run aggregate
supply curve for the economy as a whole is perfectly horizontal until full
employment capacity is attained. Once capacity is reached, firms raise their prices
to ration the capacity output to those willing to pay the highest prices. Thus, the
economy's *SRAS* is vertical at full employment capacity.

Exhibit 8 illustrates the shape of a Keynesian *SRAS* curve. *SRAS* is completely
flat at the existing price level until potential capacity is reached. In this range, output
is entirely dependent on aggregate demand. Any change in aggregate demand will
lead to a corresponding change in output. Economists refer to this horizontal
segment as the Keynesian range of the aggregate supply curve. Once potential
capacity is attained, output can no longer be expanded. So, both *SRAS* and *LRAS* are
vertical at the capacity rate of output (Y_f) .

Exhibit 9a illustrates the impact of a change in aggregate demand within the
polar assumptions of the Keynesian model. When aggregate demand is less than
AD_2 (for example, AD_1), the economy will languish below potential capacity. Since
prices and wages are inflexible downward, below-capacity output rates (Y_1, for
example) and abnormally high unemployment will persist unless there is an increase
in aggregate demand. When output is below its potential, any increase in aggregate
demand (for example, the shift from AD_1 to AD_2) brings previously idle resources
into the productive process at an unchanged price level. In this range, the Keynesian
analysis essentially turns Say's Law (supply creates an equivalent amount of
demand) on its head. In the Keynesian range, an increase in demand creates its own
supply.

Of course, once the economy's potential output constraint (Y_f) is reached,
additional demand would merely lead to higher prices rather than to more output.
Since both the *SRAS* and *LRAS* curves are vertical at capacity output, an increase in
aggregate demand to AD_3 fails to expand real output.

EXHIBIT 9

AD/AS Presentation of Keynesian Model

Frame (a) illustrates the polar implications of the Keynesian model. When output is less than capacity (for example, Y_1), an increase in aggregate demand such as illustrated by the shift from AD_1 to AD_2 will expand output without increasing prices. But, increases in demand beyond AD_2, such as a shift to AD_3, lead only to a higher price level (P_2, frame a).

Frame (b) relaxes the assumption of complete price inflexibility and short-run output inflexibility beyond Y_f. The *SRAS* therefore turns from horizontal to vertical more gradually. This would imply that unanticipated increases in aggregate demand would lead (a) primarily to increases in output when output is below capacity (for example, Y_1, frame b) and (b) primarily to increases in the price level when output is greater than capacity (for example, Y_3, frame b).

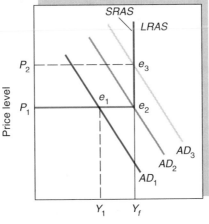

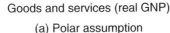

Goods and services (real GNP)

(a) Polar assumption

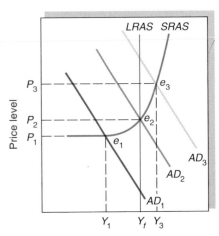

Goods and services (real GNP)

(b) Central implication

When constructing models, we often make polar assumptions to illustrate various points. The Keynesian model is no exception. In the real world, prices will not be completely inflexible. Similarly, in the short run, unanticipated increases in demand will not lead solely to higher prices. Nevertheless, the Keynesian model implies an important point that is illustrated more realistically by Exhibit 9b. The horizontal segment of the *SRAS* curve is an oversimplification intended to reinforce the idea that changes in aggregate demand exert little impact on prices and substantial impact on output when an economy is operating well below capacity. Therefore, under conditions like those of the 1930s—when idle factories and widespread unemployment are present—an increase in aggregate demand will exert its primary impact on output.

On the other hand, the vertical segment of the aggregate supply curve is a simplifying assumption meant to illustrate the concept that there is an attainable output rate beyond which increases in demand will lead almost exclusively to price increases (and only small increases in real output). So, when aggregate demand is already quite strong (for example, AD_3), increases in aggregate demand will predictably exert their primary impact on prices rather than output.

THE MULTIPLIER PRINCIPLE

Multiplier: The ratio of the change in equilibrium output to the independent change in investment, consumption, or government spending that brings about the change. Numerically, the multiplier is equal to 1/(1-MPC) when the price level is constant.

The multiplier principle occupies a central position in the Keynesian model. A change in autonomous expenditures, investment for example, generally leads to an even larger change in aggregate income. The **multiplier** is defined as the change in total income (equilibrium output) divided by the autonomous expenditure change that brought about the enlarged income.

The multiplier principle builds on the point that one individual's expenditure becomes the income of another. As we previously discussed, consumption expenditures are directly related to income—an increase in income (or wealth) will lead to an increase in consumption. Predictably, income recipients will spend a portion of their additional earnings on consumption. In turn, their consumption expenditures will generate additional income for others who will also spend a portion of it.

Perhaps an example will illuminate the concept. Suppose that there were idle unemployed resources and that an entrepreneur decided to undertake a $1 million investment project. Since investment is a component of aggregate demand, the project will increase demand directly by $1 million. This is not the entire story, however. The investment project will require plumbers, carpenters, masons, lumber, cement, and many other resources. The incomes of the suppliers of these resources will increase by $1 million. What will they do with this additional income? Given the link between one's income and consumption, the resource suppliers will predictably spend a fraction of the additional income. They will buy more food, clothing, recreation, medical care, and thousands of other items. How will this spending influence the incomes of those who supply these additional consumption products and services? Their incomes will increase, also. After setting aside (saving) a portion of this additional income, these persons will also spend some of their additional income on current consumption. Their consumption spending will result in still more additional income for other product and service suppliers.

Within the Keynesian framework, an initial increase in investment (or any other autonomous shift in expenditures) expands income, which in turn leads to additional consumption spending that generates still more income. As the process moves through successive rounds, the initial spending exerts an amplified impact on income (and output). The initial investment triggers a chain reaction that causes the total increase in income to be a multiple of the initial investment. Economists refer to this process as the **multiplier principle.**

The term multiplier is also used to indicate the number by which the initial investment would be multiplied to obtain the total summation of the increases in income. If the $1 million investment resulted in $4 million of additional income, the multiplier would be 4. The total increase in income would be four times the amount of the initial increase in spending. Similarly, if total income increased by $3 million, the multiplier would be 3.

Multiplier Principle: The concept that an induced increase in consumption, investment, or government expenditures leads to additional income and consumption spending by secondary parties and therefore expands total spending by a larger amount than the initial increase in expenditures.

WHAT DETERMINES THE SIZE OF THE MULTIPLIER?

The size of the multiplier is dependent on the proportion of the additional income that households choose to spend on consumption.[4] Keynes referred to this fraction as the **marginal propensity to consume** (MPC). Mathematically:

$$MPC = \frac{\text{additional consumption}}{\text{additional income}}$$

For example, if your income increases by $100 and you therefore increase your current consumption expenditures by $75, your marginal propensity to consume is ¾ or .75.

Marginal Propensity to Consume: Additional current consumption divided by additional current disposable income.

[4]For the purposes of simplicity when calculating the size of the multiplier, we will assume that all additions to income are either (a) spent on domestically produced goods or (b) saved. This assumption means that we are ignoring the impact of taxes and spending on imports as income expands via the multiplier process. At the conclusion of our analysis, we will indicate the significance of this assumption.

EXHIBIT 10 ■ The Multiplier Principle			
Expenditure Stage	Additional Income (dollars)	Additional Consumption (dollars)	Marginal Propensity to Consume
Round 1	1,000,000	750,000	3/4
Round 2	750,000	562,500	3/4
Round 3	562,500	421,875	3/4
Round 4	421,875	316,406	3/4
Round 5	316,406	237,305	3/4
Round 6	237,305	177,979	3/4
Round 7	177,979	133,484	3/4
Round 8	133,484	100,113	3/4
Round 9	100,113	75,085	3/4
Round 10	75,085	56,314	3/4
All Others	225,253	168,939	3/4
Total	4,000,000	3,000,000	

Exhibit 10 illustrates why the size of the multiplier is dependent on MPC. Suppose the MPC was equal to ¾ , indicating that consumers spend 75 cents of each additional dollar earned. Continuing with our previous example, we know that a $1 million investment would initially result in $1 million of additional income in round 1. Since the MPC is ¾, consumption would increase by $750,000 (the other $250,000 would flow into saving), contributing that amount to income in round 2. The recipients of the round-2 income of $750,000 would spend three-fourths of it on current consumption. Hence, their spending would increase income by $562,500 in round 3. Exhibit 10 illustrates the additions to income through other rounds. In total, income would increase by $4 million, given an MPC of ¾. The multiplier is 4.

If the MPC had been greater, income recipients would have spent a larger share of their additional income on current consumption during each round. Thus, the additional income generated in each round would have been greater, increasing the size of the multiplier. There is a precise relationship between the expenditure multiplier and the MPC. The *expenditure multiplier M* is:

$$M = \frac{1}{1 - \text{MPC}}$$

Exhibit 11 indicates the size of the multiplier for several different values of MPC.

Exhibit 12 illustrates the multiplier within the framework of the Keynesian aggregate expenditure model. Suppose that aggregate demand is initially equal to total output at $4.9 trillion. What will happen if business decision-makers suddenly become very optimistic about the future? Perhaps a technological breakthrough or some other event has triggered favorable business expectations. Because of this

EXHIBIT 11 ■
A Higher MPC Means a Larger Multiplier

MPC	Size of Multiplier
9/10	10
4/5	5
3/4	4
2/3	3
1/2	2
1/3	1.5

THE MULTIPLIER PRINCIPLE AND THE KEYNESIAN AGGREGATE EXPENDITURE MODEL

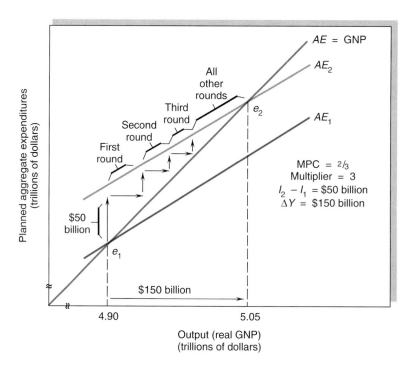

EXHIBIT 12

The Multiplier in the Keynesian Aggregate Expenditure Model

Here we illustrate the impact of the multiplier for an economy operating below its potential capacity. An increase in planned investment triggers successive rounds of additional consumption spending, causing income to rise by a multiple of the initial increase in aggregate expenditures (shift from AE_1 to AE_2). When the MPC is 2/3, a $50 billion increase in planned investment will cause equilibrium output to expand from $4.90 trillion to $5.05 trillion, an increase of $150 billion. Hence, the multiplier is 3. Since excess capacity is present, the increase in expenditures does not lead to higher prices.

optimism, business decision-makers plan to spend an additional $50 billion on investment. This additional investment will cause the aggregate expenditure function to shift upward $50 billion. At every income level, $50 billion of additional investment is planned, as indicated by the new *AE* schedule. A new equilibrium will result in which aggregate expenditures are equal to output.

How much will equilibrium output increase? This will depend on the size of MPC. The example of Exhibit 12 illustrates the multiplier when MPC is 2/3 . The $50 billion of additional investment will directly increase income by that amount (first round). Persons receiving the $50 billion will increase their spending by $33.3 billion ($50 billion multiplied by 2/3—the MPC) during the second round, causing an additional expansion in income. Of course, this additional consumption spending in round 2 will generate additional income for others. During round 3, the round-2 income recipients will increase their spending, triggering an additional expansion in income. After the process has continued through successive rounds, income will have increased by $150 billion. The $50 billion increase in initial investment eventually will thus result in a $150 billion increase in income. The multiplier is 3, since income will rise by three times the initial expansion in investment.

Although we have used an increase in investment spending to demonstrate the multiplier concept, the general principle applies to all components of aggregate expenditures. In the Keynesian model, any autonomous shift in consumption, government expenditures, or net exports will have the same amplified impact on income as we illustrated for investment.

THE REAL WORLD SIGNIFICANCE OF THE MULTIPLIER

Within the framework of the Keynesian model, the multiplier is important because it explains why even small changes in investment, government, or consumption spending can trigger much larger changes in output. The multiplier magnifies the fluctuations in output and employment that emanate from autonomous changes in spending.

There are both positive and negative sides to the amplified effects. On the negative side, the multiplier principle indicates that a small reduction in expenditures on investment and consumption durables, perhaps due to a decline in business and consumer optimism about the future, can be an important source of economic instability. As a result, most Keynesian economists believe that the stability of a market economy is quite fragile and constantly susceptible to even modest disruptions. On the positive side, the multiplier principle illustrates the potential of macroeconomic policy to stimulate output even if it is able to exert only a small impact on autonomous expenditures.

In evaluating the significance of the multiplier, it is important to keep three points in mind. First, in addition to saving, leakages in the form of taxes and spending on imports will also reduce the size of the multiplier. In order to keep things simple, we assumed that all income was either saved or spent on domestically produced goods throughout our analysis. As we have noted, as a larger portion of each round of income is saved, the size of the multiplier declines. In a broader context, some portion of the additional income will also flow into taxes and another portion will be used to purchase goods imported from abroad. Like saving, taxes and imports will siphon some of the additional income away from spending on *domestic* goods and services. These leakages from the flow of spending will dampen the effects of the multiplier. Therefore, the actual multiplier will be somewhat smaller than the simple expenditure multiplier of our analysis.

Second, it takes time for the multiplier to work. In the real world, several weeks or perhaps even months will be required for each successive round of spending. Only a fraction of the multiplier effect will be observed quickly. Most researchers believe that only about one-half of the total multiplier effect will be felt during the first six months following a change in expenditures.

Third, the multiplier implies that the additional spending brings idle resources into production, leading to additional real output rather than to increased prices. When unemployment is widespread, this is a realistic assumption. However, when there is an absence of abundant idle resources, the multiplier effect will be dampened by an increase in the price level. Exhibit 13 uses the *AD/AS* framework to illustrate this point. Reflecting a total increase in expenditures accompanying a $50 billion increase in autonomous investment when MPC is equal to $\frac{2}{3}$ (see Exhibit 12), Exhibit 13 illustrates the impact of a $150 billion increase in aggregate demand (shift from AD_1 to AD_2). If the price level remained constant at P_{100}, real output would expand by $150 billion, implying a multiplier of 3. This will not be the case, though, when resource scarcity leads to an upward sloping *SRAS*. When the *SRAS* curve is upward sloping, part of the expansionary impact of the increase in demand is dissipated by a rise in the price level (to P_{101}). Rather than increasing by $150 billion (from $4.90 to $5.05 trillion) real output only expands by $100 billion (to $5.0 trillion). When there is an absence of abundant idle resources, the *SRAS* curve will slope upward and the multiplier will be smaller than the simple multiplier derived for a specific price level.

MAJOR INSIGHTS OF KEYNESIAN ECONOMICS

Keynesian economics dominated the thinking of macroeconomists for three decades following the Second World War. What are its major insights? Three points stand out.

EXHIBIT 13

The Multiplier When *SRAS* Is Positively Sloped

When *SRAS* is positively sloped, equilibrium output will expand by less than the full multiplier effect. Continuing with the example of Exhibit 12, we illustrate the impact of a $50 billion increase in demand that would have expanded output by $150 billion (MPC = 2/3) *if the price level was constant.* However, some of the additional demand merely leads to higher prices. Thus, real GNP only expands from $4.9 trillion to $5.0 trillion, a $100 billion increase. The increase in the price level reduces the multiplier effect. (Note, e_2 is a short-run equilibrium. If the economy's output potential is less than $5.0 trillion, even this output rate cannot be sustained in the long run.)

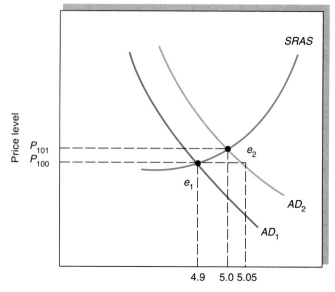

Goods and services (real GNP)
(trillions of dollars)

1. *Changes in output, as well as changes in prices, play a role in the macroeconomic adjustment process, particularly in the short run.* The classical model emphasized the role of prices in directing an economy to macroeconomic equilibrium. Keynesian analysis highlights the importance of changes in output. Modern analysis incorporates both. Market prices do not adjust instantaneously to economic change. In the short run, changes in output and employment often signal economic change to decision-makers and provide the impetus for price adjustments. Hence, modern economists believe that both price and output conditions play a role in the adjustment process.

2. *The responsiveness of aggregate supply to changes in demand will be directly related to the availability of unemployed resources.* Keynesian analysis emphasizes that when idle resources are present, output will be highly responsive to changes in aggregate demand. Conversely, when an economy is operating at or near its capacity, output will be much less sensitive to changes in demand. So, the *SRAS* curve is relatively flat when an economy is well below capacity and relatively steep when the economy is operating near and beyond capacity (see Exhibit 9).

3. *Fluctuations in aggregate demand are an important potential source of business instability.* Abrupt changes in demand are a potential source of both recession and inflation. Policies that effectively stabilize aggregated demand—that minimize abrupt changes in demand—will substantially reduce economic instability.

For more on the Keynesian viewpoint, see the Applications in Economics box.

THE EVOLUTION OF MODERN MACROECONOMICS

As we previously discussed, the prolonged unemployment of the Great Depression undermined the classical view that markets will quickly restore full employment. Keynesian analysis provides an explanation for what happened during the 1930s.

However, other explanations are also possible. As we will discuss in Chapter 13, many economists believe that misguided economic policies, particularly monetary policy, contributed to the depth and duration of the Great Depression. According to this view, markets were unable to restore full employment within a reasonable length of time during the 1930s because policies were inadvertently adopted that not only hampered recovery, but actually depressed economic conditions.

The presence of an alternative explanation for the events of the 1930s, plus the experience of the post-Second World War era, has led to a reevaluation of the stability characteristics of market economies. Greatly influenced by the Great Depression, Keynesian economists in the 1950s and 1960s feared that market economies were both depression-prone and inherently unstable. During the last two decades, there has been a reconsideration of this view. Most economists now believe that real wage and interest rate adjustments cushion economic shocks and redirect economic downturns. Thus, while markets do not direct the economy to full employment as easily and quickly as classical analysis implied, neither is a market economy as fragile and depression-prone as early Keynesians perceived.

What emerges as the modern view is a hybrid, reflecting elements of both classical and Keynesian analysis, as well as some unique insights drawn from other areas of economics. As we discussed in the previous chapter, various shocks (unanticipated changes in *AD* or *AS*) can disrupt full employment equilibrium and lead either to recessionary unemployment or to an inflationary boom in the short run. Furthermore, since macroeconomic markets do not adjust immediately, the short-run disequilibrium conditions may persist for a significant time period, perhaps a year or two. On this point, modern analysis is highly consistent with the Keynesian view.

However, the long-run implications of modern analysis are more consistent with the classical view. In the long run, modern analysis indicates that changes in real wages and interest rates will act as a stabilizing force. When an economy is operating below its potential during a recession, falling real wages and interest rates will help restore full employment. Similarly, rising real wages and interest rates will tend to retard an economic boom.

Economic conditions during the last several decades are consistent with the modern view. We continue to experience economic ups and downs, short-run disequilibrium conditions resulting from various shocks. But economic downturns do not spiral downward and result in prolonged periods of stagnation. Rather, market forces respond and redirect the economy. For example, during the 1982 recession, real wages even in several highly unionized industries declined. Similarly, real interest rates fell. Both of these forces helped to reverse the recessionary forces and direct the economy to a strong recovery.

Market adjustments also helped keep the economy on track following the 1987 stock market crash. Some commentators predicted dire consequences ahead, after the crash of 1987 eroded approximately one-third of the market value of stocks around the world. But markets handled the shock quite well. Real interest rates fell and thereby encouraged current spending on interest-sensitive goods and investment projects. In contrast with 1929, the disruptions in the financial sector did not spill over and disrupt economic activity in the production and employment sectors of the economy. In spite of the shock, the expansion of the 1980s continued.

While modern macroeconomics contains elements of both classical and Keynesian analysis, it also indicates that the impact of economic change is more complex than either view indicated. When analyzing the impact of a change, it

APPLICATIONS IN ECONOMICS

The Keynesian View of the Business Cycle

Keynesian economists believe that a market economy, if left to its own devices, will fluctuate between economic recession and inflationary boom.

The Keynesian view emphasizes the destabilizing potential of changes in expenditures powered by changes in optimism and the multiplier. Suppose there is an increase in income triggered by what appears to be a relatively minor disruption—a new innovation, an increase in consumer optimism, or a reduction in taxes, for example. The process of increased expansion will have a tendency to feed on itself. Higher incomes will lead to additional consumption and strong business sales. Inventories will decline and business will expand output (to rebuild inventories) and move investment projects forward as they become more optimistic about the future. The additional investment, magnified by the multiplier, will

lead to an expansion in employment and a rapid growth of income and consumption. Unemployment will decline to a low level. Stock prices will rise as the future begins to look rosy.

Can this expansionary phase continue indefinitely? The answer is no. Eventually, full employment of both manpower and machines will result. The economy will reach its sustainable capacity. Constrained by the short supply of resources, the growth rate of the economy will have to slow. As the growth rate decelerates, business investors will become less optimistic about the future and will cut back fixed investment. The combination of a reduction in investment and increased pessimism about the future will cause consumers to spend less, further reducing aggregate expenditures. The decline in aggregate expenditures, again magnified by the multiplier, will

reduce the equilibrium level of income. As the economy plunges into a recession, inventories will rise as businesses are unable to sell their goods because of the low level of demand. Workers will be laid off. The ranks of unemployed workers will grow. Bankruptcies will become more common.

This is what Keynes perceived was happening in the 1930s. Consumers were not spending because their incomes had fallen and they were extremely pessimistic about the future. Similarly, businesses were not producing because there was little demand for their products. Investment had come to a complete standstill because underutilized resources and capacity were abundantly available. Lack of aggregate demand, the moving force of the Keynesian model, paralyzed Western economies during the 1930s. Keynes believed that his underemployment

makes a difference whether the change is anticipated or unanticipated. It is also important whether people expect the change to be temporary or permanent. In addition, the impact may differ depending on whether long-run equilibrium, underemployment, or overemployment is initially present. As we proceed, we will stress the importance of these factors continually as we use modern macroeconomic theory to enhance our understanding of the real-world economy.

AD/AS *OR* AE—*WHICH MODEL SHOULD WE USE?*

Our three-market basic macroeconomic models featuring *AD* and *AS* and the aggregate expenditure model developed in this chapter offer alternative tools with which to analyze macroeconomic change. Which model should we use? Until recent years, the aggregate expenditure model has been a central focus of macroeconomics. We have shown that it continues to provide valuable insight in various areas.

equilibrium model explained why.

Could an economy caught in the web of a depression ever turn upward? The answer is yes. Eventually, machines will wear out, and capital stock will decline to a level consistent with current income and consumption. At that point, some investment will be necessary for replacement purposes. With time, inventories will be depleted, and businesses will begin placing new orders, which will stimulate production. The gradual upturn in investment and production will generate additional income, which will stimulate consumption and start the cycle anew.

Investment Instability and the Business Cycle

Private investment is the villain in the Keynesian theory of the business cycle. An economic expansion accelerates into a boom because investment, amplified by the multiplier, stimulates other sectors of the economy. At the first sign of a slowdown, though, investment plans are sharply curtailed. The Keynesian theory implies that the investment component, responsive to even small shifts in other economic sectors, acts as the moving force behind the business cycle.

The inventory component of investment is particularly likely to fluctuate throughout the business cycle. During the expansionary phase, inventories will be reduced, since producers will be unable to keep up with the rapid expansion in demand. In contrast, during a downturn, inventories will rise sharply, reflecting the unexpectedly slow growth of aggregate demand.

Is the empirical evidence consistent with the Keynesian view? Clearly, investment is more volatile than aggregate income. Similarly, inventories tend to rise during the early phase of an economic downturn and decline to a low level during the early phase of a business expansion, just as Keynesian theory predicts. Association, however, is not the same thing as causation. The fact that investment fluctuates substantially over the business cycle does not prove that changes in investment cause business instability. Many economists believe that economic fluctuations originate from other sources, particularly fluctuation in the supply of money. We will analyze alternative theories of the business cycle in Chapters 13 and 14.

Nevertheless, we believe that reliance upon the multimarket macroeconomic model offers several advantages.

First, the simultaneous occurrence of high unemployment and inflation is easier to visualize within the *AD/AS* framework. The aggregate expenditure model makes it easy to see why an economy might experience unemployment (demand is deficient). It also offers a straightforward explanation for inflation (excess demand). But, the *AE* model does not readily explain the simultaneous occurrence of the two. Given the reliance on the *AE* model in the 1960s and 1970s, it is no coincidence that the simultaneous occurrence of inflation and unemployment during the 1970s took many macroeconomists by surprise.

Second, recent developments in macroeconomics place much more emphasis on price changes in aggregate markets, expectations, and interrelationships among macroeconomic markets. These factors are more easily visualized within the framework of the multimarket *AD/AS* model, which emphasizes *both* price and quantity (output) changes. Similarly, the *AD/AS* model enables us to see why it makes a difference whether an event is anticipated or unanticipated. These factors are the heart of modern macroeconomics.

Finally, the *AD/AS* model makes it easier to understand and make a distinction between long-run and short-run conditions. In essence, the aggregate expenditure model is a short-run excess-capacity model. Since the *AE* model assumes that prices are inflexible downward, price adjustments fail to direct the economy toward full employment. For short periods of time, the Keynesian assumption of price inflexibility may be a reasonable approximation of real world macroeconomic markets. In the long run, however, this will not be the case. With the passage of time, weak demand will result in downward real price adjustments. The *AE* model conceals the significance of factors that are important in the long run. In contrast, the *AD/AS* model emphasizes the importance of both ''sticky prices'' in the short run and price adjustments in the long run. Thus, it sheds light on the likely impact of macroeconomic changes during both the immediate time period and the longer time period as markets adjust.

We believe the *AD/AS* model is more flexible and will help us better understand a broader range of economic issues. Thus, it will be our primary tool as we seek to develop more depth in our understanding of macroeconomic issues.

LOOKING AHEAD

Although Keynes emphasized that a market economy might fail to automatically reach its potential capacity, he argued that governments could use their tax and expenditure policies to stabilize aggregate demand and assure full employment. Keynes and his followers forced a reluctant economics profession to think seriously about macroeconomic policy. We turn next to this issue. We will begin by considering the potential of fiscal policy as a tool with which to promote full employment, stable prices, and the growth of real output.

CHAPTER SUMMARY

1. Classical economists emphasized the importance of supply because they believed that production created an equivalent amount of current demand (Say's Law) and that flexible wages and prices would assure full employment. The Great Depression undermined the credibility of the classical view.

2. The concept of planned aggregate expenditures is central to the Keynesian analysis. Aggregate expenditures are the sum of spending on consumption, investment, government purchases, and net exports.

3. In the Keynesian model, planned consumption expenditures are positively related to income. As income expands, though, consumption increases by a lesser amount. Both planned investment and government expenditures are independent of income in the Keynesian model. Planned *net* exports decline as income increases. The Keynesian model postulates that business firms will produce the amount of goods and services they believe consumers, investors, governments, and foreigners (net exports) plan to buy.

4. In the Keynesian model, equilibrium is present when planned total expenditures are equal to output. The equilibrium output level may take place at less than full employment. When it does, the high rate of unemployment will persist into the future. Since the Keynesian model assumes that wages and prices are inflexible downward, reductions in real wages are ruled out as a mechanism to restore full employment. Unless aggregate spending (demand) increases, there is no mechanism for the restoration of full employment.

5. Planned expenditures need not equal actual expenditures. If purchasers spend less than business firms anticipate, unplanned additions to inventories will result. Rather than continuing to accumulate undesired inventories, businesses will cut back output. Income will recede to the equilibrium level.

6. If planned total expenditures temporarily exceed output, businesses will sell more of their products than they anticipate. An unplanned decline in inventories will result. In an effort to restore their abnormally low inventories, businesses will expand future output, and income will rise toward the equilibrium level.

7. Aggregate expenditures are the catalyst of the Keynesian model. Until full employment is attained, supply (real GNP) is always accommodative. Increases in aggregate expenditures thus lead to an expansion in both output and employment as long as the economy is operating below potential capacity. Once capacity is reached, further expansions in expenditures lead only to higher prices, without expanding real output. The Keynesian model implies that maintaining aggregate expenditures at the level consistent with full employment and stable prices is the primary function of sound macroeconomic policy.

8. According to the multiplier principle, independent changes in planned investment, government expenditures, and consumption have a magnified impact on income. Income will increase by some multiple of the initial increase in spending. The multiplier is the number by which the initial change in spending is multiplied to obtain the total amplified increase in income. The size of the multiplier increases with the marginal propensity to consume.

9. The multiplier principle indicates that small changes in spending can exert a major impact on output. In evaluating the importance of the multiplier, it is important to remember that (a) taxes and spending on imports will dampen the size of the multiplier; (b) it takes time for the multiplier to work; and (c) the amplified effect on real output will only be valid when the additional spending brings idle resources into production without price changes.

10. The Keynesian view of the business cycle emphasizes that market forces, once begun, tend to move together, reinforcing either expansion or contraction. Upswings and downswings feed on themselves. During a downturn, business pessimism, declining investment, and the multiplier principle combine to plunge the economy further toward recession. During an economic upswing, business and consumer optimism and expanding investment interact with the multiplier principle to propel the economy further upward. Keynesian theory suggests that a market-directed economy, left to its own devices, will be inherently unstable and fluctuate between economic recession and inflationary boom.

11. Modern macroeconomic analysis incorporates elements of both Keynesian and classical economics. In the short run, market adjustments will not quickly restore full employment. Thus, a less-than-capacity output rate may exist for a period of time, much as the Keynesian model implies. However, in the long run modern analysis indicates that the changes in real wages and interest rates cushion economic shocks and direct the economy toward full employment, much as the classical model implies.

CRITICAL ANALYSIS QUESTIONS

1. You have just been appointed to the president's Council of Economic Advisers. Write a short essay explaining to the president the Keynesian view concerning why a market economy may be unable to generate the full employment level of income. Be sure to explain why equilibrium may result at less than full employment.

*2. How will each of the following factors influence the consumption schedule?
   a. The expectation that consumer prices will rise more rapidly in the future.
   b. Pessimism about future employment conditions.
   c. A reduction in income taxes.
   d. An increase in the interest rate.
   e. A decline in stock prices.

*Asterisk denotes questions for which answers are given in Appendix C, Selected Answers.

f. A redistribution of income from older workers (age 45 and over) to younger workers (under 35).

g. A redistribution of income from the wealthy to the poor.

3. Why does output change in the Keynesian model? Can the Keynesian model explain prolonged unemployment such as was present during the 1930s? How?

*4. What is the multiplier principle? What determines the size of the multiplier? Does the multiplier principle make it more or less difficult to stabilize the economy? Explain.

5. "How can the Keynesian model be correct? According to Keynes, falling income, unemployment, and bad times result because people have so much income that they fail to spend enough to buy all of the goods produced. Paradoxically, rising income and good times result because people are reducing their savings, and spending more than they are making. This doesn't make sense." Explain why you either agree or disagree with this view.

6. Widespread acceptance of the Keynesian aggregate expenditure model took place during and immediately following the Great Depression. Can you explain why? The aggregate expenditure model declined in popularity when many economies experienced *both* high rates of unemployment and inflation during the 1970s. Was this surprising? Explain.

*7. In the Keynesian aggregate expenditure model, if people suddenly decide they want to spend more of their current income on consumption, where do they get the funds for the additional spending? What does the model assume with regard to this source of funds?

8. Suppose that individuals suddenly decided to spend less and save more of their current income. Compare and contrast this change within the framework of the Keynesian aggregate expenditure and the *AS/AD* models.

*9. "Historically, interest rates have generally been higher during periods of economic boom than during recessions. This indicates that higher interest rates stimulate additional investment." Evaluate this view.

10. How would an increase in income *abroad* influence the equilibrium level of output *at home* within the framework of the Keynesian aggregate expenditure model? Would the results differ within the framework of the *AD/AS* model?

*11. When is a change in expenditures most likely to cause a corresponding change in production and employment *in a specific industry?*

12. Economists often state that the Keynesian aggregate expenditure model has its greatest relevance in the short run, while the classical model is most relevant to the long run. In what sense is this true?

*13. What role do declining real wages and resource prices play in the restoration of full employment in the Keynesian model? If output is currently below the full employment rate, what will direct the economy to full employment in the Keynesian model?

14. In the Keynesian aggregate expenditure model, why does an increase in aggregate spending lead to an equal increase in real GNP as long as output is at less than full employment capacity? What does this imply about the shape of the aggregate supply curve?

*15. Within the framework of the Keynesian model, what is the expected impact of a stock market crash such as the one experienced in October 1987? What adjustments would take place within the framework of the *AD/AS* model?

16. In recent years, approximately 25 percent of the income of Canadians has been spent on imports. In the United States, imports constitute about 10 percent of income. Would you expect the size of the multiplier to be larger or smaller in Canada than in the United States? Explain.

11 Modern Macroeconomics: Fiscal Policy

Fiscal policy has come almost full cycle in the past 50 years. From a position of no status in the classical model that dominated economic thinking until 1935, contracyclical fiscal policy reached its pinnacle in the 1960s— the heyday of Keynesian macroeconomics. It may now be on the wane as the "new macroeconomics" . . . replaces the Keynesian model.[1]

Professor J. Ernest Tanner (1982)
Tulane University

CHAPTER FOCUS

- How does fiscal policy affect aggregate demand? How does it affect aggregate supply?

- What is the Keynesian view of fiscal policy? How do the crowding-out and new classical models modify the basic Keynesian analysis?

- Are there supply-side effects of fiscal policy?

- How difficult is it to time fiscal policy properly? Why is proper timing important?

- Do budget deficits cause inflation? Do they cause high interest rates?

- What are the components of the modern synthesis view of fiscal policy?

*A*s we indicated in Chapter 8, fiscal policy involves the use of the government's spending and taxing authority. We are now ready to use our basic macroeconomic model to investigate the impact of fiscal policy on output, prices, and employment.

Previously, we assumed that the government's taxing and spending policies remained unchanged. We will now relax that assumption. However, we want to isolate the impact of changes in fiscal policy from changes in monetary policy. Because of this, we will continue to assume that the monetary authorities maintain a constant supply of money. The impact of monetary policy will be considered beginning in Chapter 12.

BUDGET DEFICITS AND SURPLUSES

Balanced Budget: A situation in which current government revenue from taxes, fees, and other sources is just equal to current expenditures.

Budget Deficit: A situation in which total government spending exceeds total government revenue during a specific time period, usually one year.

Budget Surplus: A situation in which total government spending is less than total government revenue during a time period, usually a year.

Active Budget Deficits: Deficits that reflect planned increases in government spending or reductions in taxes designed purposely to generate a budget deficit.

Passive Budget Deficits: Deficits that merely reflect reduced tax revenues due to a decline in economic activity during a recession.

Since fiscal policy encompasses both government spending and revenues, the government's budget provides information about fiscal policy. When government revenues from all sources are equal to government expenditures (including both purchases of goods and services and transfer payments), the government has a **balanced budget.** The budget need not be in balance, however. A **budget deficit** is present when total government spending exceeds total revenue from taxes and user charges. When the government runs a budget deficit, where does it get the money to finance the excess of its spending relative to revenue? It borrows by issuing interest-bearing bonds that we refer to as the national debt. A **budget surplus** is present when the government's revenues from taxes and user charges exceed the government's spending.

The federal budget is much more than merely a revenue and expenditure statement of a large organization. Of course, its sheer size means that it exerts a substantial influence on the economy. Its importance, though, emanates from its position as a policy variable. The federal budget is the primary tool of fiscal policy. In contrast with private organizations that are directed by the pursuit of income and profit, the federal government can alter its budget with an eye toward influencing the future direction of the economy.

The size of the federal deficit or surplus is often used to gauge whether fiscal policy is adding demand stimulus or imposing demand restraint. When using it as such a gauge, however, it is important to note that changes in the size of the deficit may arise from two different sources. First, the deficit may reflect discretionary changes in fiscal policy. That is, policy-makers may institute deliberate changes in government spending or in tax policies and thereby influence the budget deficit. Economists often refer to deficits emanating from this source as **active budget deficits.** Second, changes in the size of the deficit may merely reflect the state of the economy. During a recession, tax revenues, reflecting the decline in income, generally fall. Therefore, even if government expenditures are not increased or tax rates cut, an economic recession will tend to increase the size of the budget deficit. Deficits arising from recessionary conditions are often termed **passive budget deficits.** When we speak of "changes in fiscal policy," we are referring to active budget deficits—deliberate changes in government expenditures and/or tax policy.

---

[1]J. Ernest Tanner, "Fiscal Policy: An Ineffective Stabilizer?" *Economic Review: Federal Reserve Bank of Atlanta,* August 1982.

KEYNESIAN VIEW OF FISCAL POLICY

Prior to the 1960s, the desirability of a balanced federal budget was widely accepted among business and political leaders. Keynesian economists, though, were highly critical of this view. They argued that the federal budget should be used to promote a level of aggregate demand consistent with full employment output.

How does the federal budget influence aggregate demand? First, government purchases contribute directly to aggregate demand. The demand for goods and services expands as the government spends more on highways, education, national defense, and medical services, for example. Second, changes in tax policy also influence demand. A reduction in personal taxes increases the disposable income of households. As their after-tax income rises, individuals spend more on consumption. Similarly, a reduction in business taxes increases after-tax profitability and thereby encourages business investment spending.

According to the Keynesian view, fluctuations in aggregate demand are the major source of economic disturbances. If demand could therefore be stabilized and maintained at a level consistent with the economy's full employment productive capacity, the major source of economic instability would be eliminated.

OUTSTANDING ECONOMIST

Paul Samuelson (1915–)

Two generations of economists have been brought up on Paul Samuelson. His best-selling introductory text has gone through twelve editions, and literally millions of students have used it. However, as Professor Samuelson noted, "They don't give Nobel Prizes for writing textbooks." The first American to win the Nobel Prize in economics, he was so honored for "raising the level of analysis in economic science." His book, *Foundations of Economic Analysis*,[2] gave precise mathematical meaning to much of economic reasoning.

Professor Samuelson's interests are wide-ranging, and his contributions to economics reflect this fact. International trade theory, welfare economics, theory of the firm, theory of public goods, and monetary and fiscal theory have all "felt the brush" of this master artist. His *Collected Scientific Papers* encompass five lengthy volumes.[3]

A professor of economics at Massachusetts Institute of Technology for four decades, Samuelson often criticizes those who perceive economics to be a precise science that yields definitive answers. He argues that economic problems are extremely complex and that generalized conclusions can seldom be drawn. Professor Samuelson is one of the few economists who is well known and respected by both professional economists and the general public. He has bridged the gap between academia and the real world.

[2]Paul Samuelson, *Foundations of Economic Analysis* (Cambridge: Harvard University Press, 1947).

[3]Paul Samuelson, *Collected Scientific Papers of Paul Samuelson* (Cambridge: MIT Press, 1966).

EXHIBIT 1

Expansionary Fiscal Policy to Promote Full Employment

Here we illustrate an economy operating in the short run at Y_1, below its potential capacity Y_f. There are two routes to a long-run full employment equilibrium. First, policy-makers could wait for lower wages and resource prices to reduce costs, increase supply to $SRAS_3$, and restore equilibrium at E_3. Keynesians believe this market adjustment method will be slow and uncertain. Alternatively, expansionary fiscal policy could stimulate aggregate demand (shift to AD_2) and guide the economy to E_2.

Expansionary Fiscal Policy: An increase in government expenditures and/or a reduction in tax rates such that the expected size of the budget deficit expands.

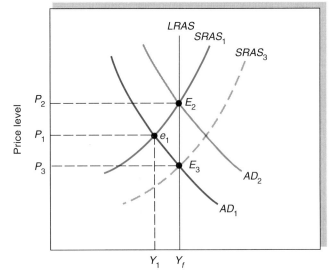

Goods and services (real GNP)

Keynesian theory highlights the potential of fiscal policy as a tool capable of reducing fluctuations in demand. When an economy is operating below its potential output, the Keynesian model suggests that government should institute **expansionary fiscal policy.** In other words, the government should either increase its purchases of goods and services and/or cut taxes. The enlargement of the government's budget deficit stemming from this policy should be financed by borrowing. The budget deficit can be covered by borrowing from private sources: individuals, business firms, and other sources of loanable funds.[4]

Exhibit 1 illustrates the case for expansionary fiscal policy when an economy is experiencing abnormally high unemployment due to deficient aggregate demand. Initially, the economy is operating at e_1. Output is below potential capacity, Y_f, and unemployment is above its natural rate. As we have previously discussed, if there is no change in policy, abnormally high unemployment and excess supply in the resource market would eventually reduce real wages and other resource prices. The accompanying lower costs would increase supply (shift to dotted $SRAS_3$) and guide the economy to a full employment equilibrium (E_3) at a lower price level (P_3). In addition, lower real interest rates resulting from weak business demand for investment funds may help stimulate aggregate demand and restore full employment.

However, most Keynesian economists believe that it would take quite a long time for adjustments in market prices and interest rates to restore full employment equilibrium. Therefore, they believe that policymakers often will be able to shift to a more expansionary fiscal policy and thereby restore full employment more rapidly. An increase in government purchases and/or a reduction in taxes would trigger the multiplier process. Thus, the total increase in aggregate demand would be substantially greater than the increase in government purchases and/or the cut in

---

[4]Alternatively, the government could borrow from its central bank, the Federal Reserve Bank in the United States. However, as we will see in the following chapter, this method of financing a budget deficit would expand the money supply. Since we want to differentiate between fiscal and monetary effects, we must hold the supply of money constant. So, for now, we assume that the government deficit must be financed by borrowing from private sources.

EXHIBIT 2

Restrictive Fiscal Policy to Combat Inflation

Strong demand such as AD_1 will temporarily lead to an output rate beyond the economy's long-run potential (Y_f). If maintained, the high level of demand will lead to long-run equilibrium (E_3) at a higher price level. However, restrictive fiscal policy could restrain demand to AD_2 (or better still, prevent demand from expanding to AD_1 in the first place) and thereby guide the economy to a noninflationary equilibrium (E_2).

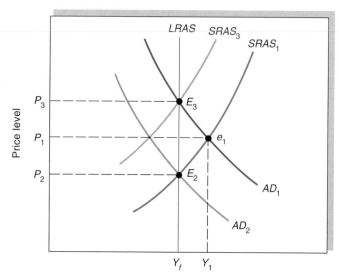

Goods and services (real GNP)

Restrictive Fiscal Policy:
A reduction in government expenditures and/or an increase in tax rates such that the expected size of the budget deficit declines (or the budget surplus increases).

Countercyclical Policy:
A policy that tends to move the economy in an opposite direction from the forces of the business cycle. Such a policy would stimulate demand during the contraction phase of the business cycle and restrain demand during the expansionary phase.

taxes. An appropriate dosage of expansionary fiscal policy, if timed properly, would stimulate aggregate demand (shift to AD_2) and guide the economy to full employment equilibrium at E_2. So, when an economy is operating below its potential capacity, the Keynesian prescription calls for an active budget deficit.

What would happen if a business expansion led to a level of demand that exceeds the economy's potential output? As Exhibit 2 illustrates, in the absence of a change in policy, the strong demand (AD_1) would push up wages and other resource prices. In time, the higher resource prices would increase costs, reduce aggregate supply (from $SRAS_1$ to $SRAS_3$), and lead to a higher price level (P_3). The basic Keynesian model, however, indicates that **restrictive fiscal policy** could be used to reduce aggregate demand (shift to AD_2) and guide the economy to a noninflationary equilibrium (E_2). A reduced level of government purchases would diminish aggregate demand directly. Alternatively, taxes could be increased. An increase in personal taxation would reduce disposable income, causing consumption to decline. An increase in business taxes would dampen investment. Of course, the combination of reduced government expenditures and higher taxes would lead to a budget surplus (or smaller budget deficit). The Keynesian analysis indicates that this is precisely the proper policy prescription with which to combat inflation generated by excessive aggregate demand.

In the Keynesian view, general economic conditions replaced the concept of the annually balanced budget as the proper criterion for evaluating the appropriateness of budget policy. **Countercyclical policy** suggests the government should seek an active budget deficit when the economy is threatened by recession and an active budget surplus (or smaller deficit) in response to the threat of inflation. Fiscal policy is a tool with which to ensure that the level of demand is sufficient to provide for full employment but not so large as to trigger an inflationary price increase.

As we stressed in the very first chapter, economic changes often exert secondary effects. Building on the basic Keynesian analysis, modern macroeconomics recognizes that budget deficits and surpluses may exert important secondary effects in other markets, particularly the loanable funds market. We turn now to an analysis of potentially important secondary effects.

FISCAL POLICY AND THE CROWDING-OUT EFFECT

Holding the supply of money constant, when the government runs a deficit, it must borrow from private lenders. Typically, the government will finance its deficit by issuing bonds. As we previously discussed, issuing bonds is simply a means of demanding loanable funds. The total demand for loanable funds will increase as government borrowing competes with private borrowing for the available supply of funds. If the supply of loanable funds does not increase, government borrowing to finance a larger deficit will drive up the real rate of interest.

What impact will a higher real interest rate have on private spending? Consumers will reduce their purchases of interest-sensitive goods such as automobiles and consumer durables in response to a higher real interest rate. More importantly, a higher interest rate will increase the opportunity cost of investment projects. Businesses will postpone spending on plant expansions, heavy equipment, and capital improvements. Residential housing construction and sales will also be hurt. Thus, the higher real interest rates emanating from the larger deficit will retard private spending. Economists refer to this squeezing out of private spending by a deficit-induced increase in the real interest rate as the **crowding-out effect.**

Crowding-Out Effect:
A reduction in private spending as a result of higher interest rates generated by budget deficits that are financed by borrowing in the private loanable funds market.

The crowding-out effect suggests that budget deficits will exert less impact on aggregate demand than the basic Keynesian model implies. Since financing the deficit pushes up interest rates, a *reduction in private spending,* particularly spending on investment, will at least partially offset additional spending emanating from the deficit. In the long run, the decline in private investment may also adversely affect aggregate supply. A lower rate of private investment will reduce the stock of capital (for example, heavy equipment, other machines, and buildings) available in the future. If this is the case, the productivity and income of future workers will be lower than it would have been if private investment had not been crowded-out by the budget deficits and higher interest rates.[5]

While most modern economists accept the logic of the crowding-out effect, many would argue that it is unlikely to be very important during a recession. If expansionary fiscal policy is applied when an economy is operating at less than capacity, then the accompanying demand stimulus will lead to an increase in both real output and income. At the higher income level, households will save more, which will permit the government to finance its enlarged deficit without much upward pressure on interest rates. In addition, when applied during a recession, the demand stimulus may improve business profit expectations and thereby stimulate additional private investment. Thus, an active budget deficit during a recession may not crowd-out much private investment.

Finally, it should be noted that the impact of a shift to restrictive fiscal policy is symmetrical. Restrictive fiscal policy will crowd-in private spending. If the government increases taxes and/or cuts back on expenditures and thereby reduces its demand for loanable funds, the real interest rate will decline. The lower real interest rate will stimulate additional private investment and consumption. So, the fiscal policy restraint will be at least partially offset by an expansion in private spending. As the result of this crowding-in, restrictive fiscal policy will be less potent as a weapon against inflation than the basic Keynesian model implies.

---

[5]The impact of budget deficits on the welfare of future generations is dealt with in detail in Chapter 16.

**THE INTERNATIONAL
LOANABLE FUNDS
MARKET**

In Chapter 3, we explained that when legal restraints on trade are absent, there will be a tendency for goods to exchange for the same price in all markets, except for price differences due to taxes and transportation costs. This *price equalization principle* reflects the incentive of producers to expand supply in markets when prices are high relative to costs (and reduce supply in markets when prices are low relative to costs).

The price equalization principle also applies to the loanable funds market. People with funds available for loan (or the purchase of bonds) can supply them to markets in London, New York, Toronto, Tokyo, Hong Kong, Sydney and elsewhere around the world. Adjusted for taxes and transaction costs (including those of a political nature), the real interest rate in one location will be approximately the same as the real interest rate in other locations (and countries). Suppose the United States cuts taxes and therefore runs a larger budget deficit. The financing of the deficit increases the demand for loanable funds and pushes up the real interest rate as the crowding-out effect implies. How will foreigners respond to this situation? The higher after-tax real interest yield will attract funds from abroad. In turn, this in-flow of loanable funds will moderate the rise in the real interest rates in the United States.

How does the in-flow of foreign credit influence the crowding-out effect? At first glance, it appears to moderate the reduction in private demand implied by the crowding-out effect. Closer inspection, though, indicates this will not be the case. Foreigners must acquire dollars before they can make financial investments in the United States. Therefore, the higher real interest rates in the United States will not only attract foreign investors, they also will result in an increase in the demand for the U.S. dollar in the foreign exchange market—the market that coordinates exchanges of the various national currencies. The increased demand of foreigners for the dollar will bid up its price. The dollar will appreciate in terms of other currencies.

How will the increased value of the dollar relative to other currencies influence the U.S. flow of exports and imports? The appreciation of the dollar will make imports cheaper for Americans. Simultaneously, it will make U.S. exports more expensive for foreigners. Predictably, the United States will import more and export less. Net exports will decline (or net imports increase), causing a reduction in aggregate demand. Therefore, some of the crowding out of domestic demand will come in the form of a decline in net exports. The in-flow of loanable funds from abroad will moderate the rise in the real rate of interest. However, the capital in-flow merely changes the form of the crowding-out effect. Rather than high, real interest rates crowding-out investment and interest-sensitive consumer goods, the appreciation in the foreign exchange value of the dollar crowds-out net exports (and stimulates imports). In either case, the crowding-out acts as an offset to demand stimulus emanating from budget deficits.

FISCAL POLICY—THE NEW CLASSICAL ECONOMICS MODEL

Some economists stress still another possible secondary effect of budget deficits—the impact of the deficits on saving. Until now, we have implicitly assumed that the current saving decisions of taxpayers are unaffected by the higher future taxes implied by budget deficits. Some economists argue that this is an unrealistic view. During the 1970s, Robert Lucas (University of Chicago), Thomas Sargent (University of Minnesota), and Robert Barro (Harvard University) were leaders among a group of economists who argued that taxpayers would reduce their current consumption and increase saving in anticipation of higher future taxes implied by debt financing. Since this position has its foundation in classical economics, these economists and their followers are referred to as **new classical economists.**

New Classical Economists: Modern economists who believe there are strong forces pushing a market economy toward full employment equilibrium and that macroeconomic policy is an ineffective tool with which to reduce economic instability.

In the basic Keynesian model, a reduction in current taxes financed by borrowing increases the current disposable income of households. Given their additional disposable income, households increase their current consumption. New classical economists argue that this analysis is incorrect because it ignores the impact of the higher future taxes implied by the budget deficit. The borrowing—the additions to the government's outstanding debt—implies a higher future tax liability. The public will have to pay higher future taxes to finance the interest payments on the additional bonds. Thus, debt financing affects the *timing* of taxes, rather than their magnitude. It merely substitutes *higher future* taxes for *lower current* taxes.

Since budget deficits merely affect the timing of the tax liability, new classical economists argue that additional government debt (and the higher taxes that it implies) will reduce the current consumption of households just as surely as an equivalent amount of current taxes. Therefore, according to the new classical view, the current consumption of households will not increase when current taxes are cut and government debt is increased by an equivalent amount. In essence, households will simply save the reduction in their current taxes so they will have the income with which to pay the higher future taxes implied by the additional government debt. Since current consumption declines as the result of the additional debt—just as it would have declined if the equivalent amount of taxes had been levied—new classical economists do not believe that the substitution of debt for taxes will stimulate either private consumption or aggregate demand. According to this view, taxes and debt financing are essentially equivalent.

Perhaps an illustration will help explain the underlying logic of the new classical view. Consider the following alternative methods of paying a $10,000 liability: (a) a one-time payment of $10,000, or (b) payments of $1,000 *each year* in the future. When the interest rate is 10 percent, a $1,000 liability each year imposes a current cost of $10,000. Therefore, just as option (a) reduces current wealth by $10,000, so, too, does option (b). Now, let us consider the impact of the two options on future income. If you dip into your savings to make a one-time $10,000 payment, your future interest income will be reduced by $1,000 each year in the future (assuming a 10 percent interest rate). Just as option (b) reduces your future net income by $1,000 each year, so, too, does option (a). In both cases, current wealth is reduced by $10,000. Similarly, in both cases the flow of future net income is reduced by $1,000 each year. Because of this, the new classical economists believe the two options are essentially the same.

Exhibit 3 illustrates the implications of the new classical view as to the potency of fiscal policy. Suppose the fiscal authorities issue $50 billion of additional debt in order to cut taxes by an equal amount. The government borrowing increases the demand for loanable funds (shift from D_1 to D_2, frame b) by $50 billion. If the taxpayers did not recognize the higher future taxes implied by the debt, they would expand consumption in response to the lower taxes and the increase in disposable

EXHIBIT 3

New Classical View— Higher Expected Future Taxes Crowd-Out Private Spending

New classical economists emphasize that budget deficits merely substitute future taxes for current taxes. If households did not anticipate the higher future taxes, aggregate demand would increase to AD_2 (frame a). However, demand remains unchanged at AD_1 when households fully anticipate the future increase in taxes. Simultaneously, the additional saving to meet the higher future taxes will increase the supply of loanable funds to S_2 (frame b) and permit the government to borrow the funds to finance its deficit without pushing up the real interest rate. In this model, fiscal policy exerts no effect. The real interest rate, real GNP, and level of employment all remain unchanged.

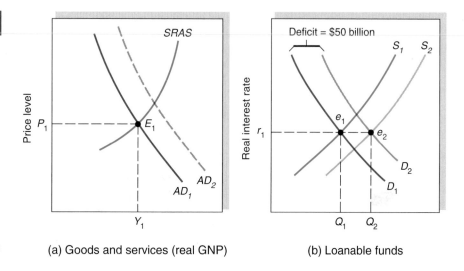

(a) Goods and services (real GNP)   (b) Loanable funds

income. Under such circumstances, aggregate demand in the goods and services market would expand to AD_2. In the new classical model, though, this will not be the case. Recognizing the higher future taxes, taxpayers will cut back their spending and increase their savings by $50 billion—the amount of saving necessary to generate the income required to pay the higher future taxes implied by the additional debt. This additional saving will allow the government to finance its deficit without an increase in the real interest rate. Since debt financing, like tax financing, causes taxpayers to reduce their expenditures, aggregate demand in the goods and services market is unchanged (at AD_1). In this polar case, fiscal policy exerts no demand stimulus. Output, employment, and the price level are all unchanged.

The new classical view might be summarized as follows: Higher current taxes and an equivalent increase in government debt reduce the wealth (and permanent income) of taxpayers by identical amounts. Substituting government debt for current taxation does not change anything. Taxpayers will recognize the higher future taxes implied by the debt and reduce their current expenditures just as if the equivalent taxes had been levied now. Thus, budget deficits do not stimulate aggregate demand. Similarly, the real interest rate is unaffected by deficits since people will save more in order to pay the higher future taxes. According to the new classical view, fiscal policy is completely impotent.

The new classical theory of fiscal policy is controversial.[6] The critics argue that it is unrealistic to expect that taxpayers will anticipate all or even most of the increase in future taxes implied by additional government debt. In addition, even if people did anticipate the higher future taxes, in our world of limited life spans, many would recognize that they will not be around to pay, at least not in full, the future tax liability implied by debt financing. Thus, many economists reject the new

---

[6]See Robert J. Barro, ''Are Government Bonds Net Wealth?'', *Journal of Political Economy,* November/December 1974, pp. 1095–1117; James M. Buchanan, ''Barro on the Ricardian Equivalence Theorem,'' *Journal of Political Economy,* April 1976, pp. 337–42; Gerald P. O'Driscoll, Jr., ''The Ricardian Nonequivalence Theorem, *Journal of Political Economy,* February 1977, pp. 207–10; and R. G. Holcombe, John D. Jackson, and A. Zardkoohi, ''The National Debt Controversy,'' *Kyklos,* vol. 34, 1981, pp. 186–202.

classical view of fiscal policy, at least in its pure form. Nonetheless, the significance of the new classical theory and its implications with regard to fiscal policy continue to provide one of the lively topics of debate in modern macroeconomics.

SUPPLY-SIDE EFFECTS OF FISCAL POLICY

Supply-Side Economists:
Modern economists who believe that changes in marginal tax rates exert important effects on aggregate supply.

Thus far, we have focused on the potential demand-side effects of fiscal policy. However, when fiscal changes alter *tax rates,* they may also influence aggregate supply. In the past, macroeconomists have often ignored the impact of changes in tax rates, thinking they were of little importance. In recent years, **supply-side economists** have challenged this view.[7] The supply-side argument provided the foundation for the Reagan tax policy, which led to significant reductions in marginal tax rates in the United States during the 1980s.

From a supply-side viewpoint, the *marginal tax rate* is of crucial importance. As we discussed in Chapter 5, the marginal tax rate determines the breakdown of one's additional income between tax payments on the one hand and personal income on the other. A reduction in marginal tax rates increases the reward derived from added work, investment, saving, and other activities that become less heavily taxed. People shift into these activities away from leisure (and leisure-intensive activities), tax shelters, consumption of tax-deductible goods, and other forms of tax avoidance. These substitutions both enlarge the effective resource base and improve the efficiency with which the resources are applied (see Applications in Economics box).

The source of the supply-side effects accompanying a change in tax rates is fundamentally different than the source of the demand-side effects. A change in tax rates affects aggregate demand through its impact on disposable income and the flow of expenditures. In contrast, it affects aggregate supply through changes in marginal tax rates, which influence the relative attractiveness of productive activity in comparison to leisure and tax avoidance.

Other things constant, lower marginal tax rates will increase the attractiveness of productive activity relative to tax avoidance. As resources shift from the latter to the former, aggregate supply increases. Conversely, higher marginal tax rates reduce the payoff from productive activity, encourage tax avoidance, and thereby retard aggregate supply.

Exhibit 4 graphically depicts the impact of a supply-side tax cut, one that reduces marginal tax rates. The lower marginal tax rates increase aggregate supply as the new incentive structure encourages taxpayers to earn additional income and use resources more efficiently. If the tax change is perceived as long-term, both *LRAS* and *SRAS* will increase. Real output and income expand. Of course, the increase in real income will also increase demand (shift to AD_2). If the lower

[7]See Dwight Lee (ed.), *Taxation and the Deficit Economy* (San Francisco: Pacific Institute, 1986) and Lawrence Lindsey, *The Growth Experiment: How the New Tax Policy Is Transforming the U.S. Economy* (New York: Basic Books, 1989) for additional information on supply-side economics. Also see Michael J. Boskin, "Tax Policy and Economic Growth: Lessons from the 1980s," *Journal of Economic Perspectives,* Fall 1988, pp. 71–97 for an evaluation of U.S. tax policy during the 1980s.

EXHIBIT 4

Tax Rate Effects and Supply-Side Economics

Here we illustrate the supply-side effects of a reduction in marginal tax rates. The lower marginal tax rates increase the incentive to earn and use resources efficiently. Since these effects are long-run, as well as short-run, both *LRAS* and *SRAS* increase (shift to the right). Real output expands. If the lower tax rates are financed by a budget deficit, aggregate demand may expand by a larger amount than aggregate supply, leading to an increase in the price level.

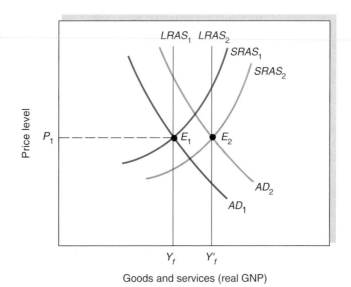

Goods and services (real GNP)

marginal rates are financed by a budget deficit, depending on the strength of the crowding-out effect and the anticipation of higher future taxes (new classical theory), aggregate demand may increase by more than aggregate supply. If this is the case, the price level will rise.

How important are the supply-side effects accompanying lower marginal tax rates? In the early 1980s, some supply-side economists suggested that lower rates might expand output so much that tax revenues would actually increase. For taxpayers confronting exceedingly high tax rates, say marginal rates of 50 percent or more, this view may well have some validity. As we discussed in Chapter 5, the real tax revenue derived from the top 10 percent of taxpayers increased sharply during the 1981–1988 period, even though their tax rates were reduced substantially (see Exhibit 10, page 119). However, this clearly was not the case for other taxpayers. The empirical evidence indicates that for taxpayers confronting top marginal tax rates of 30 percent or less, lower tax rates will invariably lead to a reduction in tax revenue.

When considering potential supply-side effects, it is important to keep two points in mind. First, the key relationship is between tax rates and output, not tax rates and tax revenues. If a 10 percent reduction in tax rates led to a 2 percent increase in annual output, tax revenues would decline (because the revenue loss due to the lower rates would exceed the revenue gain due to the increase in output). Nevertheless, the lower tax rates would significantly enlarge the size of the economic pie. Second, in the short run, the demand-side effects of a tax change will generally dominate. Supply-side economics should not be viewed as a short-run countercyclical tool. It will take time for changing market incentives to move resources out of tax-motivated investments and into higher-yield activities. The full positive effects of lower marginal tax rates will not be observed until labor and capital markets have time to fully adjust to the new incentive structure. Clearly, supply-side economics is a long-run growth-oriented strategy, not a countercyclical fiscal policy tool.

APPLICATIONS IN ECONOMICS

Marginal Tax Rates and Aggregate Supply

Changes in marginal tax rates influence the incentive of decision-makers to supply and effectively use productive resources. There are three major reasons why an increase (decrease) in marginal tax rates reduces (expands) aggregate supply.

First, higher marginal rates discourage work effort and reduce the productive efficiency of labor. Some individuals will substitute leisure for work. Economists refer to this as the **work-leisure substitution effect.** The higher marginal tax rates will induce some individuals to opt out of the labor force. Others will simply work less. Still others will decide to

Work-Leisure Substitution Effect: The substitution of leisure time for work time when higher tax rates reduce after-tax personal earnings. In effect, the reduction in the take-home (after-tax) portion of earnings reduces the opportunity cost of leisure, and thereby induces individuals to work less (and less intensively). Of course, lower tax rates would exert the opposite effect.

take more lengthy vacations, forgo overtime opportunities, retire earlier, be more particular about accepting jobs when unemployed, or forget about pursuing that promising but risky business venture. These substitutions of "leisure" for taxable work effort will reduce the available labor supply, causing aggregate supply to fall.

High marginal tax rates will also result in inefficient utilization of labor. Some individuals will substitute less-productive activities that are not taxed (for example, do-it-yourself projects) or that provide the opportunity for tax avoidance (for example, pleasurable business activities) for work opportunities yielding taxable income. Waste and economic inefficiency result.

Second, higher marginal tax rates also encourage investors to turn to projects that shelter current income from taxation and to turn away from projects with a higher rate of return but fewer tax-avoidance benefits. Investments in depreciable assets can often provide substantial tax advantages. Projects that supply investors with rapid depreciation write-offs and paper losses can be used to push

one's tax liability into the future and into tax periods (for example, retirement) when one expects to be in a lower tax bracket. Investment projects that are unprofitable when pretax earnings are compared with pretax costs are undertaken because they provide tax shelter benefits. Such tax shelter investments are wasteful because they channel resources away from their most productive uses.

Third, high marginal tax rates encourage individuals to substitute less-desired tax deductible goods for more-desired, nondeductible goods. Here the inefficiency stems from the fact that individuals do not bear the full cost of tax deductible purchases. High marginal tax rates make tax deductible expenditures cheap for persons in high tax brackets. Since the personal cost, *but not the cost to society,* is cheap, high income taxpayers consume large amounts of deductible items (for example, business-related lunches, vacations, luxury automobiles, plush offices, medical and other fringe benefits). Waste and inefficiency are byproducts of this incentive structure.

TIMING FISCAL STIMULUS AND RESTRAINT

Discretionary Fiscal Policy: A change in laws or appropriation levels that alters government revenues and/or expenditures.

If fiscal policy is going to reduce economic instability, stimulus and restraint must be properly timed. This is not an easy task. **Discretionary fiscal policy** requires changes in tax laws and government expenditure programs. It takes time to institute such changes. Congress must act. Congressional committees must meet, hear testimony, and draft legislation. Decisions by Congress to change tax rates often require such a long time that their timing as a countercyclical weapon is impaired. The same is true for congressional decisions authorizing changes in spending. Proposals to establish new spending programs or to expand (or cut back) old

EXHIBIT 5

Why Proper Timing of
Fiscal Policy Is Difficult

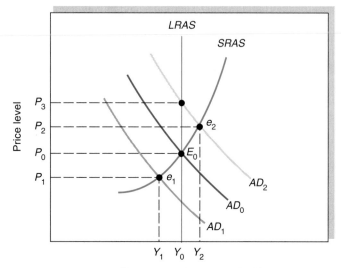

Goods and services (real GNP)

Here we consider an economy that experiences shifts in *AD* that are not easy to forecast. Initially, the economy is in long-run equilibrium (E_0) at price level P_0 and output Y_0. At this output, only the natural rate of unemployment is present. However, an investment slump and business pessimism result in an unanticipated decline in aggregate demand (to AD_1). Output falls and unemployment increases. After a time, policy-makers institute expansionary fiscal policy seeking to shift aggregate demand back to AD_0. By the time fiscal policy begins to exert its primary effect, though, private investment has recovered and decision-makers have become increasingly optimistic about the future. So AD_1 is already, on its own accord, shifting back to AD_0. Thus, the expansionary fiscal policy over-shifts aggregate demand to AD_2, rather than AD_0. Prices rise as the economy is now overheated. Unless the expansionary fiscal policy is reversed, wages and other resource prices will eventually increase, shifting *SRAS* to the left, thus pushing the price level still higher (to P_3).

Alternatively, suppose an investment boom disrupts the initial equilibrium. The increases in investment shift aggregate demand to AD_2, placing upward pressure on prices. Policy-makers respond by increasing taxes and cutting government expenditures. By the time the restrictive fiscal policy exerts its primary impact, though, investment returns to its normal rate. As a result, the restrictive fiscal policy over-shifts aggregate demand to AD_1 and throws the economy into a recession. Since fiscal policy does not work instantaneously and since dynamic factors are constantly influencing private demand, proper timing of fiscal policy is not an easy task.

programs require time-consuming deliberations. Even after a policy is adopted, it may be 6 to 12 months before its major impact is felt. Given our limited ability to forecast economic conditions 6 to 18 months in the future, mistakes are not only possible, they are probable.

To a large extent, macroeconomic policy-making is like shooting at a moving target you cannot see very well. Exhibit 5 illustrates this point. The use of expansionary fiscal policy to stimulate aggregate demand during an economic downturn may lead to excess demand if the economy recovers on its own by the time the fiscal stimulus exerts its major impact. Similarly, restrictive fiscal policy to cool an overheated economy may cause a recession if aggregate demand declines prior to the fiscal restraint. Since we live in a dynamic world characterized by unpredictable events, policy-makers can never be sure what macroeconomic conditions will be like 6, 12, or 18 months down the road. But, information on the state of the economy in the future is precisely what is needed if policy-makers are going to institute the proper dosage of countercyclical fiscal policy. All of this makes it exceedingly difficult to properly time discretionary changes in fiscal policy.

AUTOMATIC STABILIZERS

Automatic Stabilizers:
Built-in features that tend automatically to promote a budget deficit during a recession and a budget surplus during an inflationary boom, even without a change in policy.

Fortunately, there are a few fiscal programs that tend automatically to apply demand stimulus during a recession and demand restraint during an economic boom. Programs of this type are called **automatic stabilizers.** They are automatic in that, *without any new legislative action,* they tend to increase the budget deficit (or reduce the surplus) during a recession *and* increase the surplus (or reduce the deficit) during an economic boom.

The major advantage of automatic stabilizers is that they institute countercyclical fiscal policy without the delays that inevitably accompany legislation. Thus, they minimize the problem of proper timing. When unemployment is rising and business conditions are slow, these stabilizers automatically reduce taxes and increase government expenditures, giving the economy a shot in the arm. On the other hand, automatic stabilizers help to apply the brakes to an economic boom, increasing tax revenues and decreasing government spending. Three of these built-in-stabilizers deserve specific mention.

1. *Unemployment Compensation.* When unemployment is high, the receipts from the unemployment compensation tax will decline because of the reduction in employment. Payments will increase because more laid-off workers are now eligible to receive unemployment compensation benefits. The program will automatically run a deficit during a business slow-down. In contrast, when the unemployment rate is low, tax receipts from the program will increase because more people are now working. The amount paid in benefits will decline because fewer people are unemployed. The program will automatically tend to run a surplus during good times. So, without any change in policy, the program has the desired countercyclical effect on aggregate demand.[8]

2. *Corporate Profit Tax.* Tax studies show that the corporate profit tax is the most countercyclical of all the automatic stabilizers. This results because corporate profits are highly sensitive to cyclical conditions. Under recessionary conditions, corporate profits will decline sharply and so will corporate tax payments. This sharp decline in tax revenues will tend to enlarge the size of the government deficit. During economic expansion, corporate profits typically increase much more rapidly than wages, income, or consumption. This increase in corporate profits will result in a rapid increase in the ''tax take'' from the business sector during expansion. Thus, corporate tax payments will go up during an expansion and fall rapidly during a contraction if there is no change in tax policy.

3. *Progressive Income Tax.* When income grows rapidly, the average, personal-income-tax liability of individuals and families increases. With rising incomes, more people will find their income above the ''no tax due'' cutoff. Others will be pushed into a higher tax bracket. Therefore, during an economic expansion, revenue from the personal income tax increases more rapidly than income. Other things constant, the budget moves toward a surplus (or smaller deficit), even though the economy's tax rate structure is unchanged. On the other hand, when income

---

[8]Although unemployment compensation has the desired countercyclical effects on demand, it also reduces the incentive to accept available employment opportunities. As a result, researchers have found that the existing unemployment compensation system actually increases the long-run normal unemployment rate. This issue is discussed in more detail in Chapter 14.

declines, many individuals will be taxed at a lower rate or not at all. Income tax revenues will fall more rapidly than income, automatically enlarging the size of the budget deficit during a recession.

THE FISCAL POLICY RECORD

Prior to the Keynesian Revolution, it was widely believed that a responsible government would constrain spending within the bounds of its revenues. Of course, during a time of war this principle was often set aside. For example, the United States government ran very large deficits during the First and Second World Wars. But during periods of peace following wars, surpluses were often present, and they were used to pay off debt accumulated primarily during periods of war.

The Keynesian Revolution eventually altered our view of budgetary policy. The balanced budget ethic was shoved into the background. By the early 1960s, policy-makers and citizens, as well as most economists, believed that the size of the budget deficit or surplus should reflect the state of the economy.

When judging whether fiscal policy is expansionary or restrictive, economists generally focus on *changes* in the size of the deficit, rather than on the absolute amount of a deficit or surplus. An increase in the size of the deficit relative to the size of GNP indicates that fiscal policy is shifting toward expansion. Conversely, a reduction in the size of the deficit relative to GNP would imply a more restrictive fiscal policy.

Exhibit 6 illustrates the fiscal policy record of the United States during the last three decades. In general, the data indicate that the budget deficits as a percentage

EXHIBIT 6

Federal Expenditures and Revenues as Percent of GNP, 1960–1991

Since 1960 the federal budget deficit as a percent of GNP has generally increased during recessions and declined during periods of economic expansion. (The blue areas indicate periods of recession.)

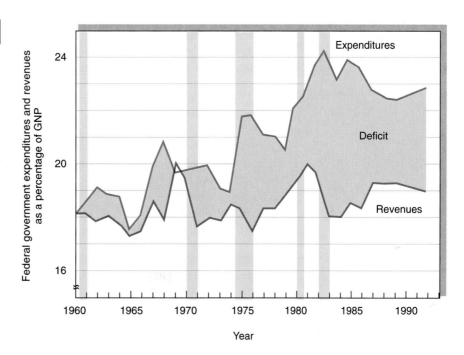

Source: *Economic Report of the President.*

of GNP expanded during recessions (shaded in blue in Exhibit 6) and contracted during business expansions. For example, revenues declined sharply, leading to a substantial increase in the size of the deficit, during the recession of 1970. In contrast, even though a budget surplus was not achieved, the budget deficit declined as a share of GNP during the 1971–1973 expansion. The deficit also increased sharply during the recessions of 1974–1975 and 1980–1982. Correspondingly, it shrank during the periods of growth following each of these recessions. This pattern of deficits and surpluses indicates that fiscal policy was countercyclical—that it added stimulus during recessions and moved toward restraints during periods of expansion.

However, closer inspection of the 1960–1988 period indicates that the generally countercyclical pattern of fiscal policy was primarily the result of automatic stabilizers, rather than active discretionary changes in fiscal policy. Perhaps the most effective discretionary fiscal change of recent decades was the 1964 tax cut. Persuaded by his economic advisors, President John F. Kennedy recommended legislation cutting personal income tax rates by almost 20 percent over a two-year period. After President Kennedy's assassination in 1963, the legislation was passed by Congress and signed into law by President Lyndon B. Johnson in early 1964. The 1964 tax cut worked marvelously. Output increased, and unemployment, which had been hovering near 6 percent, fell below 4 percent in 1966. Fiscal policy had worked just as the President's economic advisors had predicted. It was a golden era for economists, particularly Keynesian economists.

Unfortunately, it did not last very long. As Exhibit 6 shows, federal expenditures expanded rapidly during 1966–1968. Even though the economy was operating at a high level of employment, fiscal policy was nonetheless highly expansionary. What is the predicted result of fiscal stimulus when an economy is already operating at capacity? Answer: an increase in the price level—inflation. Pushed along by the demand stimulus of both the Vietnam War and Great Society programs, the inflation rate began to accelerate in 1966. In early 1966, many economists—including close advisors of President Johnson—called for a tax increase to reduce the fiscal stimulus and retard the rising inflationary pressure. Both President Johnson and Congress failed to heed these early warnings. Finally, after months of delay, President Johnson recommended and Congress passed a temporary (one-year only) 10 percent "surcharge" on personal income tax payments. The tax increase was a case of too little, too late. Since the surtax was for only one year, households did not reduce their spending very much. In fact, personal saving declined as individuals borrowed to pay their temporarily higher tax bill. Since the tax increase was not instituted until the deficit was expanding and the inflation rate accelerating, the modest policy shift was unable to turn the tide against the rising prices of the late 1960s.

In 1975 the United States had a similar experience with discretionary fiscal policy—this time in the case of a tax cut. With the economy already in the midst of serious recession, President Gerald Ford and Congress agreed to a tax rebate package. The legislation granted taxpayers a partial rebate of their 1974 tax payments and reduced rates for the balance of 1975. The change did little to minimize the effects of the 1974–1975 recession. It came too late—the economy was already beginning to recover when it was instituted. Since the tax cut was temporary and partially in the form of an unanticipated rebate, consumers saved a large portion of the tax cut. This reduced its demand-stimulus effects. In addition, since it failed to reduce *marginal* tax rates, supply-side effects were absent.

While the discretionary fiscal policy changes of 1964, 1968, and 1975 were motivated by cyclical conditions, the tax changes of the 1980s were overtly tied to the supply-side view that high tax rates retarded long-term economic growth. Nonetheless, the 1982–1984 rate reductions did coincide with the sharp decelera-tion in the inflation rate and severe recession of 1982. Thus, fiscal policy during the 1982 recession was expansionary (see Exhibit 6) and the lower tax rates enhanced aggregate supply. Later, the Tax Reform Act of 1986 further reduced marginal tax rates, while broadening the tax base. Whereas the top marginal tax rate in 1981 was 70 percent, by 1988 the effective rate had been sliced to 33 percent. Economists who stress the supply-side effects of lower marginal tax rates believe that the rate reductions in the 1980s provided the foundation for the longest peacetime expansion in the history of the United States.

DO DEFICITS CAUSE HIGH INTEREST RATES?

The major models of fiscal policy provide different answers to this question. The crowding-out model indicates that deficits will increase the demand for loanable funds and thereby place upward pressure on the real rate of interest. On the other hand, the new classical model implies that the higher expected future taxes will stimulate additional saving and thereby permit the government to expand its borrowing at an unchanged interest rate.

There have been a number of empirical studies of this issue. Thus far, the results are mixed. The Congressional Budget Office surveyed 24 studies on this topic.[9] The results of the survey indicated that while some empirical studies find a significant positive link between budget deficits and real interest rates, most of the studies indicate no statistically significant relationship. Seemingly, these findings would buttress the new classical view that deficits exert little impact on interest rates. They must, however, be interpreted with caution. Most of the studies cover the post-Second World War period. During most of that period, budget deficits were relatively small as a percent of GNP. Except for a couple of recessionary years, the budget was generally balanced during the 1950s. Budget deficits averaged less than 1 percent of GNP during the 1960s. Persistent budget deficits running 4 or 5 percent of GNP during prosperous peacetime periods are a recent occurrence. The impact of relatively small, generally temporary deficits, such as those experienced by the United States throughout most of the post-war period, may be a misleading indicator of the interest rate impact of large, long-term deficits.

Exhibit 7 presents data on both the size of the deficit as a share of GNP and the real interest rate during the last three decades. While the year-to-year linkage between the size of the deficit and the real interest rate is weak, there is some

---

[9]Congressional Budget Office, "Deficits and Interest Rates: Empirical Findings and Selected Biography," Appendix A in *The Economic Outlook,* February, 1984, pp. 99–102. Also see Charles Plosser, "The Effects of Government Financing Decisions on Asset Returns," *Journal of Monetary Economics,* May, 1982, and Paul Evans, "Do Large Deficits Produce High Interest Rates?" *American Economic Review,* March, 1985.

EXHIBIT 7

Deficits and the Real Rate of Interest, 1960–1990

While the real interest rate is not closely associated with year-to-year changes in the budget deficit, the persistent large deficits of the 1980s have been associated with high real interest rates.

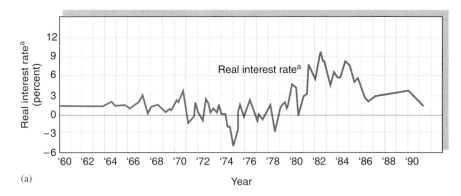

(a)

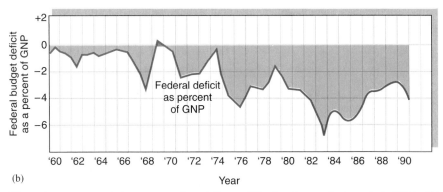

(b)

[a]We use the average quarterly interest rate on 3-month Treasury bills minus the quarterly change in the GNP implicit price deflator to approximate the real interest rate.

Source: Board of Governors, Federal Reserve System and the Office of Management and Budget.

evidence that the persistent large deficits of the 1980s have pushed the real interest rate upward.[10] Prior to the late 1970s, the real interest rate was generally less than 2 percent. In fact, the real interest rate hovered in the 2 percent range for three decades following the Second World War. In contrast, during 1981–1986, the real interest rate fluctuated between 4 and 9 percent. Even as the historically large deficits declined as a share of GNP during 1986–1988, the real rate of interest remained around 3 percent, a high rate in comparison with the rates during the three decades following the Second World War. Thus, the behavior of the real interest rate in the face of the persistently large deficits of the 1980s provides support for the crowding-out model.

Did the higher real interest rates in the United States during the 1980s attract loanable funds from abroad, as our analysis implies? Between 1980 and 1986, real foreign investment in the United States more than doubled. The U.S. trade deficit, exports minus imports, rose from $25 billion in 1980 to $144 billion in 1986. In turn, this trade deficit provided foreigners with the dollars necessary to fund their expanded financial investments in the United States. These figures are precisely the predicted side effects of large deficits and high real interest rates within the framework of the crowding-out model and an open economy.

[10]Of course, the real interest rate is the money interest rate minus the expected rate of inflation. Since the expected rate of inflation cannot be directly observed, it must be approximated. Exhibit 7 uses the actual change in the GNP deflator as a proxy for the expected rate of inflation.

DO BUDGET DEFICITS CAUSE INFLATION?

Despite the continued popularity of the "budget-deficits-cause-inflation" view, macroeconomic analysis provides little support for the theory. The crowding-out model indicates that, when the supply of money is constant, budget deficits will merely lead to a higher real interest rate, which will crowd-out private spending and thereby dampen the stimulus effect of the deficit. In the new classical model, the expectation of higher future taxes crowds-out private spending and thereby retards the inflationary effects of deficits.

The Keynesian model does indicate that an increase in the size of the deficit will shift the aggregate demand schedule to the right and lead to a higher price level. This adjustment to a higher price level will take place over time, and during the transition period, the inflation rate will accelerate. However, *once the adjustment to the higher price level occurs,* the impact of the deficit on the inflation rate will cease. Thus, while a larger deficit may permanently increase the *level* of prices, it will not exert a lasting impact on the inflation rate. Thus, none of the major macroeconomic models indicates that budget deficits financed by borrowing from the general public will cause sustained inflation.[11]

The major statistical analysis in this area is supportive of this view. *Independent of monetary expansion,* the major empirical studies have failed to find a significant relationship between budget deficits and the rate of inflation.[12] Recent economic events in the United States also illustrate the uncertainty of the frequently alleged relationship between deficits and inflation. Since 1960, the federal government has run a budget *surplus* during only one year, 1969. This surplus was associated with an acceleration in the inflation rate from 4.7 percent in 1968 to 6.1 percent in 1969. Perhaps the 1980s offer the strongest evidence conflicting with the deficits-cause-inflation view. As Exhibit 7b illustrates, budget deficits were quite large during the 1980s. Did the large deficits cause inflation? Hardly. The inflation rate decelerated from 9.2 percent in 1979–1981 to 3.5 percent during the 1983–1985 period. The inflation rate remained in the 3 to 4 percent range during 1986–1989 even though the deficit remained quite large. Of course, other factors, including a deceleration in the growth rate of the money supply, contributed to the decline in the inflation rate during the early 1980s. Nevertheless, the point is that even highly expansionary fiscal policy failed to offset the other factors placing downward pressure on the inflation rate. This is precisely what modern macroeconomic theory would predict.

FISCAL POLICY—A MODERN SYNTHESIS

During the last three decades, the impact of fiscal policy has been one of the most hotly debated topics in economics. The accompanying Thumbnail Sketch summarizes the alternative perspectives with regard to the impact of *expansionary* fiscal

---

[11]Some economists argue that large budget deficits will induce the monetary authorities to expand the supply of money more rapidly and thereby promote inflation. According to this theory, budget deficits are an indirect cause of inflation.

[12]For evidence on this point, see Gerald P. Dwyer, Jr., "Inflation and Government Deficits," *Economy Inquiry,* July, 1982, and Scott E. Hein, "Deficits and Inflation," *Review-Federal Reserve Bank of St. Louis,* March, 1981.

THUMBNAIL SKETCH

The Impact of Expansionary Fiscal Policy—a Summary

1. **Basic Keynesian Model:** An increase in government spending and/or reduction in taxes will be magnified by the multiplier process and lead to a substantial increase in aggregate demand. When an economy is operating below capacity, real output and employment will also increase subtantially.

2. **Crowding-Out Model:** The potency of expansionary fiscal policy will be dampened because borrowing to finance the budget deficit will push up interest rates and crowd out private spending, particularly investment.

3. **New Classical Model:** The potency of expansionary fiscal policy will be dampened because households will anticipate the higher future taxes implied by the debt and reduce their spending (and increase their saving) in order to pay them. Like current taxes, debt (future taxes) will crowd out private spending.

4. **Supply-Side Model:** A reduction in *marginal* tax rates will increase the incentive to earn (produce) and improve the efficiency of resource use, leading to an increase in aggregate supply (real output) *in the long run.*

policy. During the 1960s, the basic Keynesian view was widely accepted. Most economists believed that expansionary fiscal policy magnified by the multiplier process was highly potent. The crowding-out and new classical models modify this view. These models indicate that higher interest rates (crowding-out model) and higher expected future taxes (new classical model) will reduce private spending and thereby dampen the impact of expansionary fiscal policy. In addition, the supply-side view stresses the potential, long-run impact of changes in marginal tax rates on aggregate supply.

Given the alternative models of fiscal policy, one might think that there is little harmony of opinion among economists concerning fiscal policy. This impression is false. While disagreements remain in certain areas, a synthesis position reflecting contributions from all of the major models has emerged from the modern fiscal policy debate. Most macroeconomists accept the following synthesis position.

1. *During a depression or severe recession, expansionary fiscal policy can stimulate real output and thereby help to minimize economic instability.* During serious recessions, budget deficits stimulate aggregate demand and therefore output and employment, much as the basic Keynesian model implies. Fiscal policy is capable of preventing a recurrence of anything like the experiences of the 1930s. This is a major accomplishment that those who grew up during the *relatively* stable post-Second World War era often fail to appreciate.

2. *During more normal times, the ability of fiscal policy to influence real output is far more limited than the basic Keynesian model implies, and much more*

limited than most economists perceived during the 1960s. The major debate among macroeconomists about the impact of fiscal policy during normal times is not *whether* crowding-out takes place, but rather, *how* it takes place. The interest rate crowding-out and new classical models highlight this point. Both models indicate there are side effects of the deficits that substantially, if not entirely, offset increases in aggregate demand emanating from the deficits. In the one, higher real interest rates crowd-out private demand while higher anticipated future taxes accomplish the task in the other. In both cases, however, business and household decision-makers adjust in a manner that largely offsets the potency of fiscal policy—particularly its ability to promote more rapid growth of real output.

3. *Proper timing of discretionary fiscal policy is both highly difficult to achieve and of crucial importance. Given the potential of ill-timed policy changes to add to economic instability, active discretionary fiscal policy should respond only to major economic disturbances.* During the 1950s and 1960s, many macroeconomists thought that fiscal policy changes could smooth even minor economic fluctuations. Few now adhere to that position. It is widely recognized now that in a world of dynamic change and imperfect information concerning the future, active changes in fiscal policy in response to minor economic ups and downs can themselves become a source of economic instability.

LOOKING AHEAD

As we proceed, we will use our knowledge of fiscal policy to investigate several other issues. Later, in Chapter 16, we will consider a related topic—the impact of the national debt on the future health of the economy. We are now ready, though, to integrate the monetary system into our analysis. Chapter 12 will focus on the operation of the banking system and the factors that determine the supply of money. In Chapter 13, we will analyze the impact of monetary policy on real output, interest rates, and the price level. Once we understand how both fiscal and monetary policy work, we will be better able to comprehend the potential of policy as a tool for the promotion of high employment, stable prices, and the growth of income.

CHAPTER SUMMARY

1. The federal budget is the primary tool of fiscal policy. Discretionary fiscal policy encompasses deliberate changes in the government's spending and tax policies designed to alter the size of the budget deficit and thereby influence the overall level of economic activity.

2. According to the Keynesian view, fluctuations in aggregate demand are the major source of economic instability. Policies that help to maintain aggregate demand at a level consistent with the economy's full employment capacity will reduce economic instability.

3. When an economy's resources are underutilized, the Keynesian model indicates that expansionary fiscal policy—that is, an increase in government spending and/or reduction in taxes—will stimulate aggregate demand and help direct the economy to its full employment capacity. Conversely, restrictive fiscal policy—higher taxes and/or a reduction in government expenditures—can be used to combat inflationary pressures due to excess aggregate demand.

4. Modern macroeconomists stress the potential importance of secondary effects that modify the basic Keynesian analysis. The crowding-out model stresses one of these effects. The crowding-out model indicates that budget deficits increase the demand for loanable funds and thereby increase the real interest rate. In turn, the higher real interest rate will crowd out private spending, particularly investment, and thereby dampen the stimulus effects of expansionary fiscal policy. Similarly, restrictive fiscal policy will reduce the demand for loanable funds and lower the real interest rate. The

decline in the interest rate will stimulate private spending and thereby retard the effectiveness of restrictive policy as an anti-inflation weapon.

5. The new classical model introduces another secondary effect—the impact of debt on future taxes. New classical economists argue that substitution of debt for tax financing merely changes the timing, not the level, of taxes. According to this view, taxpayers will anticipate the higher future taxes implied by additional government debt, save more to pay the high future taxes, and as a result, reduce their current consumption just as if the equivalent taxes had been levied during the current period. The expansion in saving will permit the government to finance its deficit without an increase in the real interest rate. According to the new classical view, substitution of debt for tax financing will leave real interest rates, aggregate demand, output, and employment unchanged.

6. When fiscal policy changes marginal tax rates, it influences aggregate supply by altering the relative attractiveness of productive activity compared to leisure and tax avoidance. Other things constant, lower marginal tax rates will increase aggregate supply. Most economists believe that the demand-side effects of changes in taxes will dominate the supply-side effects in the short run. Supply-side economics should be viewed as a long-run strategy, not a countercyclical tool.

7. Since dynamic change alters market conditions and our ability to forecast future macroeconomic changes is highly imperfect, it is difficult to time discretionary changes in fiscal policy so as to reduce economic instability. The problem of proper timing is reduced in the case of automatic stabilizers, programs that apply stimulus during a recession and restraint during a boom, even though no legislative action has been taken. Unemployment compensation, corporate profit taxes, and the progressive income tax are examples of automatic stabilizers.

8. During the last several decades, the budget deficit has generally expanded as a percentage of GNP during recessions and declined during periods of expansion. This countercyclical pattern of fiscal policy primarily reflects automatic stabilizers rather than discretionary changes in fiscal policy.

9. The weak year-to-year relationship between budget deficits and real interest rates is supportive of the new classical view. However, the high real interest rates accompanying the large, long-term deficits of the 1980s provide support for the crowding-out theory.

10. Independent of monetary expansion, neither economic theory nor the empirical evidence indicates that budget deficits are a major cause of inflation.

11. The modern synthesis of fiscal policy emphasizes three major points: (a) During a depression or severe recession, expansionary fiscal policy can stimulate real output as the Keynesian model implies; (b) during normal times, higher real interest rates and/ or higher expected future taxes substantially dampen the stimulative effects of expansionary fiscal policy; and (c) since discretionary changes in fiscal policy are difficult to time properly, fiscal policy should be altered only in response to major disturbances.

CRITICAL ANALYSIS QUESTIONS

1. Suppose that you are a member of the Council of Economic Advisers. The president has asked you to prepare a statement on "What is the proper fiscal policy for the next 12 months?" Prepare such a statement, indicating (a) the current state of the economy (that is, unemployment rate, growth in real income, and rate of inflation) and (b) your fiscal policy suggestions. Should the budget be in balance? Present the reasoning behind your suggestions.

*2. What is the crowding-out effect? How does the crowding-out effect modify the implications of the basic Keynesian model with regard to fiscal policy? How does the new classical theory of fiscal policy differ from the crowding-out model?

---

*Asterisk denotes questions for which answers are given in Appendix C, Selected Answers.

3. Why is it difficult to properly time discretionary changes in fiscal policy? Do you think political factors, as well as economic factors, limit the use of fiscal policy as a stabilization tool? Why or why not?

*4. What are automatic stabilizers? Explain the major advantage of automatic stabilizers.

5. Which of the following changes in the personal income tax would a supply-side economist be most likely to favor? Explain.
   a. an increase in the personal exemption allowance.
   b. a flat-rate tax.
   c. lower tax rates financed by elimination of various tax deductible items (interest expense, medical expenditures, and state and local taxes, for example).

6. **What's Wrong with This Way of Thinking?**
   ''Keynesians argue that a budget deficit will stimulate the economy. The historical evidence is highly inconsistent with this view. A $12 billion budget deficit in 1958 was associated with a serious recession, not expansion. We experienced recessions in both 1961 and 1974–1975, despite budget deficits. The federal budget ran a deficit every year from 1931 through 1939. Yet the economy continued to wallow in the Depression. Budget deficits do not stimulate GNP and employment.''

7. ''The economic stimulus of deficit spending is based on money illusion. When the government issues bonds to finance its deficit, it is promising to levy future taxes so that bondholders can be paid back with interest. Bond financing is merely a substitution of future taxation for current taxation. The stimulus results because taxpayers, failing to recognize fully their greater future tax liability, are deceived into thinking that their wealth has increased. Thus, they increase their current spending.'' Is this view correct? Why or why not?

*8. ''If we set aside our reluctance to use fiscal policy as a stabilization force, it is quite easy to achieve full employment and price stability. When output is at less than full employment, we run a budget deficit. If inflation is a problem, we run a budget surplus. Quick implementation of proper fiscal policy will stabilize the economy.'' Evaluate this view.

9. In 1968, President Johnson recommended and Congress passed a 10 percent increase in taxes *for one year only* in order to combat the strong demand and inflationary pressure accompanying the Vietnam War. Would you have expected this temporary increase in taxes to have been very potent as an anti-inflation weapon? Explain.

*10. Some people argue that the growth of output and employment in the 1980s was the result of the large budget deficits. As one politician put it, ''Anyone could create prosperity, if they wrote $200 billion of hot checks every year.'' Evaluate this view.

11. Suppose the federal government decided to systematically reduce the budget deficit by $25 billion each year and eventually run a budget surplus which would be used to reduce its outstanding debt. What would be the consequences of this policy?

12. If deficits tend to be larger during a recession, how will this affect the relationship between budget deficits and real interest rates?

*13. ''If the MPC is .75, a $10 billion increase in government expenditures will stimulate $40 billion of additional expenditures ($10 billion times the multiplier of 4), while a $10 billion tax increase will reduce spending by only $30 billion ($7.5 billion times the multiplier of 4). Thus, a $10 billion increase in both government expenditures and taxes will stimulate aggregate output by $10 billion.'' Evaluate this statement.

*14. If the impact on tax revenues is the same, does it make any difference whether the government cuts taxes by (a) reducing marginal tax rates or (b) increasing the personal exemption allowance?

15. The Thumbnail Sketch on page 272 summarizes the Keynesian, crowding-out, new classical, and supply-side models concerning the impact of *expansionary* fiscal policy. As an exercise, summarize the implications of the four models with regard to the impact of *restrictive* fiscal policy.

12 Money and the Banking System

*Money is the only commodity that is good for nothing but to be gotten rid of.
It will not feed you, clothe you, shelter you, or amuse you unless you spend
it or invest it. It imparts value only in parting.[1]*

CHAPTER FOCUS

■ What is money? How is the money supply defined?

■ How have recent regulatory changes affected the banking and
financial industries?

■ What is a fractional reserve banking system? How does it influence the ability
of banks to create money?

■ What are the major functions of the Federal Reserve System?

■ What are the major tools with which the Federal Reserve controls the supply
of money? How do changes in Fed policy influence the supply of money?

■ Why has the United States experienced so many bank failures in the 1980s?
What caused the savings and loan crisis? Have other industrial countries been
plagued with recent bank failures?

■ How can the U.S. banking system be strengthened?

*T*he purposes of this chapter are to explain the operation of our banking/finance system and to analyze the determinants of the money supply. In recent years, both financial innovations and policy changes have affected the nature of money. We have also experienced several changes that have altered the operation and stability of our banking system. All of these issues will be analyzed in this chapter.

Economists are interested in money and monetary policy because they affect the way the economy works. For many economists, money plays a role similar to the quarterback in football—it is the central moving force that makes things happen. While the majority of economists would assign a somewhat lesser role to money, almost all recognize that money matters a great deal. As we proceed, we will consider the influence of money on prices, employment, output, and other important economic variables. But before we are able to deal with that topic, we need to know something about the nature of money, how it is measured, and the factors that influence its availability.

WHAT IS MONEY?

Money makes the world go around. Intrinsically, most modern money is worthless Nonetheless, most of us would like to have more of it. What is money? Money is an asset that performs three basic functions.

THE THREE BASIC FUNCTIONS OF MONEY

Medium of Exchange: An asset that is used to buy and sell goods or services.

1. Money Serves as a Medium of Exchange. Money is one of the most important inventions in human history because of its role as a **medium of exchange.** This function separates money from other assets. Without money, exchange would be complicated, time-consuming, and enormously costly. Think what it would be like to live in a barter economy—one without money, where goods were traded for goods. If you wanted to buy a pair of jeans, for example, you would have to first find someone willing to sell you the jeans who also wanted to purchase something you were willing to supply. Such an economy would be highly inefficient.

Since money trades in all markets, it simplifies exchanges and oils the wheels of trade. The reduction in transaction cost accompanying the use of money permits us to realize the enormous gains from specialization, division of labor, and mass production techniques that underlie our modern standard of living. Money makes it possible for each of us to specialize in the supply of those things that we do best and to purchase (and consume) a broad cross-section of goods and services consistent with our individual preferences. People simply sell their productive services or assets for money and, in turn, use the money to buy precisely the goods and services they want. For example, if a farmer wants to exchange a cow for electricity and medical services, the cow is sold for money, which is then used to buy the electricity and the medical services. Money permits a society to escape the cumbersome procedures of a barter economy.

2. Money Serves as an Accounting Unit. Since money is widely used in exchange, it also serves as a yardstick that can be used to compare the value of goods and

---

[1]Federal Reserve Bank of Philadelphia, "Creeping Inflation," *Business Review,* August 1957, p. 3.

services. If consumers are going to spend their income wisely, they must be able to compare the value of a vast array of goods and services. Similarly, sound business decision-making will require comparisons among vastly different productive services. Money serves as a unit of account, a common denominator into which the current value of all goods and services can be expressed.

3. Money Is Used as a Store of Value.   Money is a financial asset, a form of savings. There are some disadvantages to using money as a vehicle for storing value (wealth), though. Many methods of holding money do not yield an interest return. During a time of inflation, the purchasing power of money will decline, imposing a cost on those who are holding wealth in the form of money. Money, though, has the advantage of being a perfectly **liquid asset**. It can be easily and quickly transformed into other goods at a low transaction cost and without an appreciable loss in its nominal value. Because of this, most people hold some of their wealth in the form of money because it provides readily available purchasing power for dealing with an uncertain future.

Liquid Asset: An asset that can be easily and quickly converted to purchasing power without loss of value.

WHY IS MONEY VALUABLE?

Fiat Money: Money that has neither intrinsic value nor the backing of a commodity with intrinsic value; paper currency is an example.

Transaction Accounts: Accounts including demand deposits, NOW accounts, and other checkable deposits against which the account holder is permitted to transfer funds for the purpose of making payment to a third party.

Demand Deposits: Non-interest-earning deposits in a bank that either can be withdrawn or made payable on demand to a third party via check. In essence, they are "checkbook money" because they permit transactions to be paid for by check rather than by currency.

Other Checkable Deposits: Interest-earning deposits that are also available for checking.

At various times in the past, societies have used gold, silver, beads, sea shells, cigarettes, precious stones, and other commodities as money. When commodities are used as money, people use valuable resources to expand the supply of the commodity money. Because of this, the opportunity cost of commodity-based money is high.

If a society uses something as money that costs little or nothing to produce, more scarce resources are available for the production of desired goods and services. Thus, most modern nations use **fiat money**, money that has little or no intrinsic value. A dollar bill is just a piece of paper. Checkable deposits are nothing more than accounting numbers. Coins have some intrinsic value as metal, but in most cases it is considerably less than their value as money.

Why is fiat money valuable? The confidence of people is important. People are willing to accept fiat money because they know it can be used to purchase real goods and services. This is partly a matter of law. The government has designated that currency is "legal tender"—acceptable for payment of debts.

Money's main source of value, however, is the same as for other commodities; it is determined by demand relative to supply. People demand money because it reduces the cost of exchange. When the supply of money is limited relative to the demand, money will be valuable.

The value of a unit of money, a dollar for example, is measured in terms of what it will buy. Its value, therefore, is inversely related to the level of prices. An increase in the level of prices and a decline in the purchasing power of a unit of money are the same thing. If the purchasing power of money is to remain stable over time, the supply of money must be controlled. Assuming a constant rate of use, if the supply of money grows more rapidly than the real output of goods and services, prices will rise. In layman's terms, there is "too much money chasing too few goods."

When governmental authorities rapidly expand the supply of money, the purchasing power of money deteriorates. Money is less valuable in exchange and is virtually useless as a store of value. The rapid growth in the supply of money in Germany following the First World War provides a dramatic illustration of this point. During 1922–1923, the supply of German marks increased by 250 percent

Money Supply (M1): The sum of (a) currency in circulation (including coins), (b) demand deposits, (c) other checkable deposits of depository institutions, and (d) traveler's checks.

per month for a time. The German government was printing money almost as fast as the printing presses would run. Since money became substantially more plentiful in relation to goods and services, it quickly lost its value. As a result, an egg cost 80 billion marks and a loaf of bread 200 billion. Workers picked up their wages in suitcases. Shops closed at lunch hour to change price tags. The value of money had eroded.

HOW IS THE SUPPLY OF MONEY DEFINED?

There is not a completely unambiguous answer to this question. In fact, economists and policymakers have developed several alternative measures.

THE M1 MONEY SUPPLY

Commercial Banks: Financial institutions that offer a wide range of services (for example, checking accounts, savings accounts, and extension of loans) to their customers. Commercial banks are owned by stockholders and seek to operate at a profit.

Savings and Loan Associations: Financial institutions that accept deposits in exchange for shares that pay dividends. Historically, these funds have been channeled into residential mortgage loans. Under recent banking legislation, S&Ls are now permitted to offer checkable deposits (NOW accounts) and extend a broad range of services similar to those of commercial banks.

Above all else, money is a medium of exchange. The narrowest definition of the money supply, M1, focuses on this function. Based on its role as a medium of exchange, it is clear that currency (including both coins and paper bills) and checkable deposits should be included in the supply of money. Deposits that can be drawn from by writing a check are called **transaction accounts.** There are two general categories of transaction accounts. First, there are **demand deposits,** non-interest-earning deposits with banking institutions that are available for withdrawal (''on demand'') at any time without restrictions. Demand deposits are usually withdrawn by writing a check. Second, there are **other checkable deposits** that earn interest but that carry some restrictions on their transferability. Interest-earning checkable deposits generally either limit the number of checks written each month or require the depositor to maintain a substantial minimum balance ($1,000, for example). NOW (negotiable order of withdrawal) accounts and ATS (automatic transfer savings) accounts are the most common types of interest-earning checking accounts. Like currency and demand deposits, interest-earning checkable deposits are available for use as a medium of exchange. Traveler's checks are also a means of payment. They can be freely converted to cash at parity (equal value).

The **money supply (M1)** reflects the function of money as a medium of exchange. The M1 money supply is composed of (a) currency in circulation, (b) demand deposits, (c) other (interest-earning) checkable deposits and (d) traveler's checks. M1 is the narrowest and most commonly used definition of the money supply.

As Exhibit 1 shows, the total money supply (M1) in the United States was $826 billion in December 1990. Demand and other checkable deposits accounted for almost 70 percent of the M1 money supply. This reflects that most of the nation's business—more than 75 percent—is conducted by check.

BROADER DEFINITIONS OF MONEY

Prior to the late 1970s, there was a clear distinction between (a) checking accounts, which were used to conduct transactions, and (b) savings accounts, which were not. There was also a fairly clear distinction between **commercial banks** and other financial institutions. If one wanted a checking account, a personal or business loan, or a credit card, one would go to a commercial bank. For maximum interest on a savings account, or to obtain funds to buy a home, one would patronize a **savings and loan association. Credit unions** specialized in small personal loans, frequently offering the advantage of automatic deductions from one's paychecks.

EXHIBIT 1

Composition of the Money Supply in the United States (December 1990)

The size (as of 1990) of three alternative measures of the money supply are shown. M1 is the narrowest and most commonly used definition of the money supply. M2, which contains M1 plus the various savings components indicated, is approximately four times the size of M1. The broadest measure, M3, contains less liquid forms of savings. M3 is nearly five times the size of M1.

Source: *Federal Reserve Bulletin,* April 1991.

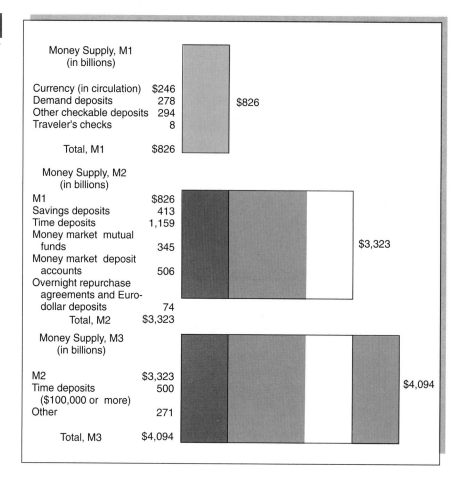

Credit Unions: Financial cooperative organizations of individuals with a common affiliation (such as an employer or labor union). They accept deposits, including checkable deposits, pay interest (or dividends) on them out of earnings, and channel funds primarily into loans to members.

Money Supply (M2): Equal to M1, plus (a) savings and time deposits (accounts of less than $100,000) of all depository institutions, (b) money market mutual fund shares, (c) money market deposit accounts, (d) overnight loans from customers to commercial banks, and (e) overnight Eurodollar deposits held by U.S. residents.

Recent developments since the late 1970s have blurred these distinctions. Banks are now permitted to both pay interest on checking accounts and provide checking privileges to savings depositors. Under legislation passed in 1980, savings and loan associations, credit unions, and commercial banks *all* now offer both checking and savings accounts and extend a wide variety of loans to customers. Similar regulations apply to each of these depository institutions. Therefore, when we speak of the banking industry, we are referring to not only commercial banks, but savings and loan associations and credit unions as well.

In addition to these changes, both banks and other financial institutions (for example, investment and brokerage firms) now offer their customers money market mutual funds. Since these funds are used to purchase short-term securities (for example U.S. Treasury bills), they are highly liquid. Therefore, shareholders not only earn interest, they are also permitted to sell their shares simply by writing a check, provided the size of the check exceeds a minimum amount (usually $500).

In modern economies, financial assets are used for both the conduct of transactions and for saving. Thus, the line between money and ''near monies'' is a fine one. Therefore, some economists—particularly those who stress the store of value function of money—argue that the supply of money is broader than the items included in M1. Clearly, a broader concept of the money supply would include various highly liquid forms of savings. The most common broad definition of the

EXHIBIT 2

The Changing Nature of
the Money Supply, M1

As the result of deregulation
during the 1980s, interest-
earning checkable deposits
now constitute more than a
third of the money supply.
Since the opportunity cost of
holding these other checkable
deposits is less than for other
forms of money, strictly
speaking, the money supply
today is not exactly comparable
to the money supply prior to
1980.

Source: *Federal Reserve Bulletin,*
April 1991

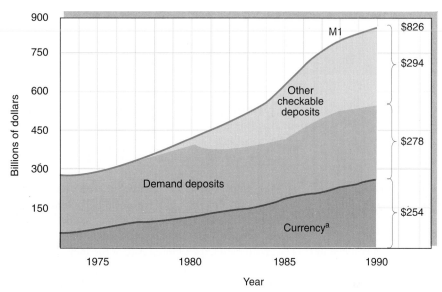

^aTravelers checks are included in this category.

money supply is M2. The **money supply (M2)** includes M1, plus (a) savings and
small-denomination time deposits at all depository institutions, (b) money market
mutual fund shares, (c) money market deposit accounts, (d) overnight loans of
customers to commercial banks (called repurchase agreements) and (e) overnight
Eurodollar deposits of U.S. residents. In each case, these financial assets can be
easily converted to checking account funds. Their owners may perceive them as
funds available for use as payment. In some cases, the assets may even be directly
used as a means of exchange. So, regardless of whether they are counted as part of
the money supply, the additional assets incorporated into M2 are close substitutes
for money.

There is a third method of measuring the money supply, M3. Under this
definition, the **money supply (M3)** is composed of M2, plus (a) large-denomination
(more than $100,000) time deposits at all depository institutions and (b) longer-term
(more than overnight) loans from customers to commercial banks and savings and
loan associations. The additional assets included in M3 are not quite as liquid as the
items that comprise M2. As Exhibit 1 notes, M2 and M3 are, respectively, about
four and five times larger than M1.

Eurodollar Deposits:
Deposits denominated in U.S.
dollars at banks and other
financial institutions outside
the United States. Although
this name originated because
of the large amounts of such
deposits held at banks in
Western Europe, similar
deposits in other parts of the
world are also called
Eurodollars.

*CHANGES IN THE
NATURE OF M1 AND
MEASUREMENT
PROBLEMS*

Money Supply (M3): Equal
to M2, plus (a) time deposits
(accounts of more than
$100,000) at all depository
institutions and (b) longer-
term (more than overnight)
loans of customers to
commercial banks and savings
and loan associations.

Recent developments in financial markets have, to some extent, changed the nature of the money supply, M1. As Exhibit 2 illustrates, during the 1970s M1
was almost entirely composed of currency and demand deposits, neither of which
earned interest. The situation changed substantially during the 1980s. Responding to the availability of interest-earning checking accounts, many depositors held
some of their savings in these accounts. By 1990, these other checking accounts
exceeded demand deposits, and they comprised more than one-third of the M1
money supply.

Since other checking accounts earn interest, they are less costly to hold than
currency and demand deposits. In essence, these other checking accounts are ''part
transactions money'' and ''part savings.'' The rapid growth of other checking
accounts during the mid-1980s accelerated the growth rate of the M1 money supply.
But they also reduced its comparability with earlier data. Today, the M1 money

supply has a larger "savings" component and a smaller "transactions" component than was true during the 1970s.

The changes in the nature of M1 during the 1980s have caused economists and monetary planners to pay more attention to M2. Since both savings and interest-earning checking accounts are components of M2, the financial innovations of the 1980s exerted less impact on M2 than on M1. Most analysts now rely more extensively on M2 (rather than M1) when making comparisons of the money supply (and its growth rate) across time periods that include the 1980s. Reflecting these views, when we use money supply data over the last several decades to assess the impact of monetary policy, we will generally use the M2 definition of money.

WHY CREDIT CARDS ARE NOT MONEY

Credit: Funds acquired by borrowing.

It is important to distinguish between money and credit. Money is a financial *asset* that provides the holder with future purchasing power. **Credit** is *liability* acquired when one borrows funds. This distinction sheds light on a question students frequently ask, "Since credit cards are often used to make purchases, why aren't credit card expenditures part of the money supply?" In contrast with money, credit cards are not purchasing power. They are merely a convenient means of arranging a loan. When you use your Visa or MasterCard to buy a disc player, for example, you are not using money to pay for the player. Instead, you are merely taking out a loan from the institution issuing your card. Payment is not made until later when you write a check to settle your credit card bill and thereby reduce your money balances. Thus, credit card purchases are not money; they are a *liability* in the form of an easy and convenient personal loan, not an *asset* representing future purchasing power.

THE BUSINESS OF BANKING

Federal Reserve System: The central bank of the United States; it carries out banking regulatory policies and is responsible for the conduct of monetary policy.

We must understand a few things about the business of banking before we can explain the factors that influence the supply of money. The banking industry in the United States operates under the jurisdiction of the **Federal Reserve System,** the nation's central bank. Not all banks belong to the Federal Reserve, but under legislation enacted in 1980 only a nominal difference exists between member and nonmember banks.

Banks are in business to make a profit. They provide checking and savings account services to their customers. Interest-earning investments, though, are the major source of income for most banks. Banks use a sizable share of both their demand and time deposits for interest-earning purposes—primarily the extension of loans and the undertaking of financial investments.

The consolidated balance sheet of commercial banking institutions (Exhibit 3) illustrates the major banking functions. It shows that the major liabilities of banks are transactions, savings, and time deposits. *From the viewpoint of a bank,* these are liabilities because they represent an obligation of the bank to its depositors. Outstanding interest-earning loans comprise the major class of banking assets. In addition, most banks own sizable amounts of interest-earning securities, both government and private.

Banking differs from most businesses in that a large portion of its liabilities are payable on demand. However, even though it would be possible for all depositors to demand the money in their checking accounts on the same day, the probability of this occurring is quite remote. Typically, while some individuals are making

EXHIBIT 3 ■ The Functions of Commercial Banking Institutions			

Banks provide services and pay interest to attract transaction, savings, and time deposits (liabilities). A portion of their assets is held as reserves (either cash or deposits with the Fed) to meet their daily obligations toward their depositors. Most of the rest is invested and loaned out, providing interest income for the bank.

Consolidated Balance Sheet of Commercial Banking Institutions,
Year-end 1990 (billions of dollars)

Assets		Liabilities	
Vault cash	$ 33	Transaction deposits	$ 599
Reserves at the Fed	33	Savings and time deposits	1,717
Loans outstanding	2,293	Borrowings	566
U.S. government securities	436	Other liabilities	257
Other securities	165	Net worth	220
Other assets	399		
Total	$3,359	Total	$3,359

Source: *Federal Reserve Bulletin*, February 1991.

withdrawals, others are making deposits. These transactions tend to balance out, eliminating sudden changes in demand deposits.

Thus, banks maintain only a fraction of their assets in reserves to meet the requirements of depositors. As Exhibit 3 illustrates, **bank reserves**—vault cash plus reserve deposits with the Federal Reserve were only $66 billion at year-end 1990, compared to transaction (checking) deposits of $599 billion. Thus, on average, banks were maintaining only slightly more than 10 percent of their assets in reserve against the checking deposits of their customers.

Bank Reserves: Vault cash plus deposits of the bank with Federal Reserve Banks.

FRACTIONAL RESERVE GOLDSMITHING

Economists often like to draw an analogy between the goldsmith of the past and our current banking system. In the past, gold was used as the means of making payments. It was money. People would store their money with a goldsmith for safekeeping, just as many of us open a checking account for safety reasons. Gold owners received a certificate granting them the right to withdraw their gold anytime they wished. If they wanted to buy something, they would go to the goldsmith, withdraw gold, and use it as a means of making a payment. Thus, the money supply was equal to the amount of gold in circulation plus the gold deposited with goldsmiths.

The day-to-day deposits of and requests for gold were always only a fraction of the total amount of gold deposited. A major portion of the gold simply "lay idle in the goldsmiths' vaults." Taking notice of this fact, goldsmiths soon began loaning gold to local merchants. After a time, the merchants would pay back the gold, plus pay interest for its use. What happened to the money supply when a goldsmith extended loans to local merchants? The deposits of persons who initially brought their gold to the goldsmith were not reduced. Depositors could still withdraw their gold anytime they wished (as long as they did not all try to do so at once). The merchants were now able to use the gold they borrowed from the goldsmith as a means of payment. As goldsmiths lent gold, they increased the amount of gold in circulation, thereby increasing the money supply.

It was inconvenient to make a trip to the goldsmith every time one wanted to buy something. Since people knew that the certificates were redeemable in gold, certificates began circulating as a means of payment. The depositors were pleased with this arrangement because it eliminated the need for a trip to the goldsmith every time something was exchanged for gold. As long as they had confidence in the goldsmith, sellers were glad to accept the certificates as payment.

Since depositors were now able to use the gold certificates as money, the daily withdrawals and deposits with goldsmiths declined even more. Local goldsmiths would keep about 20 percent of the total gold deposited with them so they could meet the current requests to redeem gold certificates in circulation. The remaining 80 percent of their gold deposits would be loaned out to business merchants, traders, and other citizens. Therefore, 100 percent of the gold certificates was circulating as money; and that portion of gold that had been loaned out, 80 percent of the total deposits, was also circulating as money. The total money supply, gold certificates plus gold, was now 1.8 times the amount of gold that had been originally deposited with the goldsmith. Since the goldsmiths issued loans and kept only a fraction of the total gold deposited with them, they were able to increase the money supply.

As long as the goldsmiths held enough reserves to meet the current requests of the depositors, everything went along smoothly. Most gold depositors probably did not even realize that the goldsmiths did not have their actual gold and that of other depositors, precisely designated as such, sitting in the "vaults."

Goldsmiths derived income from loaning gold. The more gold they loaned, the greater their total income. Some goldsmiths, trying to increase their income by extending more and more interest-earning loans, depleted the gold in their vaults to imprudently low levels. If an unexpectedly large number of depositors wanted their gold, these greedy goldsmiths would have been unable to meet their requests. They would lose the confidence of their depositors, and the system of fractional reserve goldsmithing would tend to break down.

Fractional Reserve Banking: A system that enables banks to keep less than 100 percent reserves against their deposits. Required reserves are a fraction of deposits.

FRACTIONAL RESERVE BANKING

In principle, our modern banking system is very similar to goldsmithing. The United States has a **fractional reserve banking** system. Banks are required to maintain only a fraction of their deposits in the form of cash and other reserves. Just as the early goldsmiths did not have enough gold to pay all their depositors simultaneously, neither do our banks have enough reserves (vault cash and deposits with Federal Reserve banks) to pay all their depositors simultaneously (see Exhibit 3). The early goldsmiths expanded the money supply by issuing loans. So do present-day bankers. The amount of gold held in reserve to meet the requirements of depositors limited the ability of the goldsmiths to expand the money supply. The amount of cash and other **required reserves** limits the ability of present-day banks to expand the money supply.

Required Reserves: The minimum amount of reserves that a bank is required by law to keep on hand to back up its deposits. Thus, if reserve requirements were 15 percent, banks would be required to keep $150,000 in reserves against each $1 million of deposits.

However, there are also important differences between modern banking and early goldsmithing. Today, the actions of individual banks are regulated by a central bank. The central bank is supposed to follow policies designed to promote a healthy economy. It also acts as a lender of last resort. If all depositors in a specific bank suddenly attempted to withdraw their funds simultaneously, the central bank would intervene and supply the bank with enough funds to meet the demand.

THE FEDERAL DEPOSIT INSURANCE CORPORATION

There is another reason for having greater confidence in today's banks than the early "goldsmith banks": the Federal Deposit Insurance Corporation (FDIC). Television ads often boast that a given bank is "a member of the FDIC." Why should a depositor care? The FDIC guarantees the deposits of almost all banks—both state and national—up to a $100,000 limit per account. Even if the bank should fail, the depositors will be able to get their money (up to the $100,000 limit). Individual member banks pay a small insurance premium to the FDIC for each dollar on deposit, and the FDIC uses these premiums to reimburse depositors with funds in a bank that fails. Thus, deposit insurance gives people confidence that their deposits are safe.

The confidence emanating from deposit insurance, however, does more than just give depositors peace of mind. It also reduces the level of risk for those making deposits, thus helping to avoid "runs" on banks. Before the FDIC was created in 1933, a rumor (true or false) that a bank was running short on funds often caused a panic withdrawal of funds by many depositors fearing that the bank would fail. Remember, under a fractional reserve system, banks do not have a sufficient amount of reserves to redeem the funds of all (or even most) depositors seeking to withdraw their funds at the same time. Prior to the establishment of the FDIC in 1933, more than 10,000 banks (one-third of the total) failed between 1922 and 1933. Most of these failures were the result of "bank runs," panic withdrawals as people lost confidence in the banking system. Since the advent of the FDIC, bank failures stemming from such runs are virtually nonexistent.[2]

HOW BANKS CREATE MONEY

Under a fractional reserve system, an increase in reserves will permit banks to extend additional loans and thereby create additional transaction (checking) deposits. Since transaction deposits are money, the extension of the additional loans expands the supply of money.

To enhance our understanding of this process, let us consider a banking system without a central bank, one in which only currency acts as a reserve against deposits. Initially, we will assume that all banks are required by law to maintain vault currency equal to at least 20 percent of the checking accounts of their depositors. Suppose you found $1,000 that your long-deceased uncle had apparently hidden in the basement of his house. How much would this newly found $1,000 of currency expand the money supply? You take the bills to the First National Bank, open a checking account of $1,000, and deposit the cash with the banker. First National is now required to keep an additional $200 in vault cash, 20 percent of your deposit. However, they received $1,000 of additional cash, so after placing $200 in the bank vault, First National has $800 of **excess reserves,** reserves over and above the amount they are required by law to maintain. Given their current excess reserves, First National can now extend an $800 loan. Suppose they loan $800 to a local citizen to buy a car. At the time the loan is extended, the money supply will increase by $800 as the bank adds the funds to the checking account of the borrower. No one else has less money. You still have your $1,000 checking account and the borrower has $800 for a new car.

When the borrower buys a new car, the seller accepts a check and deposits the $800 in a bank, Citizen's State Bank. What happens when the check clears? The temporary excess reserves of the First National Bank will be eliminated when it pays $800 to the Citizen's State Bank. But, when Citizen's State Bank receives $800 in currency (or as a deposit in its account with a Federal Reserve bank), it will now

Excess Reserves: Actual reserves that exceed the legal requirement.

---

[2]There has been a substantial increase in bank failures during the 1980s. However these failures are fundamentally different than the bank failures of the 1920s and 1930s. The underlying causes of the recent bank failures are analyzed later in this chapter.

EXHIBIT 4 ■ Creating Money from New Reserves			
When banks are required to maintain 20 percent reserves against demand deposits, the creation of $1,000 of new reserves will potentially increase the supply of money by $5,000.			
Bank	New Cash Deposits (Actual Reserves) (Dollars)	New Required Reserves (Dollars)	Potential Demand Deposits Created by Extending New Loans (Dollars)
Initial deposit (Bank A)	1,000.00	200.00	800.00
Second stage (Bank B)	800.00	160.00	640.00
Third stage (Bank C)	640.00	128.00	512.00
Fourth stage (Bank D)	512.00	102.40	409.60
Fifth stage (Bank E)	409.60	81.92	327.68
Sixth stage (Bank F)	327.68	65.54	262.14
Seventh stage (Bank G)	262.14	52.43	209.71
All others (other banks)	1,048.58	209.71	838.87
Total	5,000.00	1,000.00	4,000.00

have excess reserves. It must keep 20 percent, an additional $160, in the reserve against the $800 checking account deposit of the automobile seller. The remaining $640 could be loaned out. Since Citizen's State, like other banks, is in business to make money, it will be quite happy to "extend a helping hand" to a borrower. When the second bank loans out its excess reserves, the deposits of the persons borrowing the money will increase by $640. Another $640 has now been added to the money supply. You still have your $1,000, the automobile seller has an additional $800, and the new borrower has just received an additional $640. Because you found the $1,000 that had been stashed away by your uncle, the money supply has increased by $2,440.

Of course, the process can continue. Exhibit 4 follows the potential creation of money resulting from the initial $1,000 through several additional stages. In total, the money supply can increase by a maximum of $5,000, the $1,000 initial deposit plus an additional $4,000 in demand deposits that can be created by extending new loans.

The multiple by which new reserves increase the stock of money is referred to as the **deposit expansion multiplier.** The amount by which additional reserves can increase the supply of money is determined by the ratio of required reserves to demand deposits. In fact, the deposit expansion multiplier is merely the reciprocal of the required reserve ratio. In our example, the required reserves are 20 percent, or 1/5 of the total deposits. So, the potential deposit expansion multiplier is 5. If only 10 percent reserves were required, the deposit expansion multiplier would be 10, the reciprocal of 1/10.

Deposit Expansion Multiplier: The multiple by which an increase (decrease) in reserves will increase (decrease) the money supply. It is inversely related to the required reserve ratio.

The lower the percentage of the reserve requirement, the greater the potential expansion in the money supply resulting from the creation of new reserves. The fractional reserve requirement places a ceiling on potential money creation from new reserves.

THE ACTUAL DEPOSIT MULTIPLIER

Will the introduction of the new currency reserves necessarily have a full deposit expansion multiplier effect? The answer is no. The actual deposit multiplier may be less than the potential for two reasons.

EXHIBIT 5

Banking and Excess Reserves

Profit-maximizing banks use their excess reserves to extend loans and other forms of credit. Thus, excess reserves are very small, between 1 and 2 percent of the total reserves in recent years.

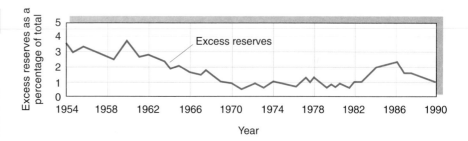

First, the deposit expansion multiplier will be reduced if some persons decide to hold the currency rather than deposit it in a bank. For example, suppose the person who borrowed the $800 in the preceding example spends only $700 and stashes the remaining $100 away for a possible emergency. Only $700 can then end up as a deposit in the second stage and contribute to the excess reserves necessary for expansion. The potential of new loans in the second stage and in all subsequent stages will be reduced proportionally. When currency remains in circulation, outside of banks, it will reduce the size of the deposit expansion multiplier.

Second, the deposit multiplier will be less than its maximum when banks fail to use all the new excess reserves to extend loans. Banks, though, have a strong incentive to loan out most of their new excess reserves. Idle excess reserves do not draw interest. Banks want to use most of these excess reserves so they can generate interest income. Exhibit 5 shows that this is indeed the case. In recent years, excess reserves have accounted for only 1 or 2 percent of the total reserves of banks.

Currency leakages and idle excess bank reserves will result in a deposit expansion multiplier that is less than its potential maximum. However, since people generally maintain most of their money in bank deposits rather than as currency, and since banks typically eliminate most of their excess reserves by extending loans, strong forces are present that will lead to multiple expansion.

THE FEDERAL RESERVE SYSTEM

As we previously indicated, the Federal Reserve System is the central monetary authority or "central bank" for the United States. Every major country has a central banking authority. The Bank of England and the Bank of France, for example, perform central banking functions for their respective countries.

Central banks are charged with the responsibility of carrying out monetary policy. The major purpose of the Federal Reserve System (and other central banks) is to regulate the money supply and provide a monetary climate that is in the best interest of the entire economy.

The Fed, a term often used to refer to the Federal Reserve System, was created in 1913. Exhibit 6 illustrates the structure of the Federal Reserve System. While there are 12 Federal Reserve District banks, the Board of Governors is the decision-making center of the Fed. This powerful board consists of seven members, each appointed to a staggered 14-year term by the president with the advice and consent of the Senate. The president designates one of the seven members as chair for a four-year term. However, since a new member of the governing board is

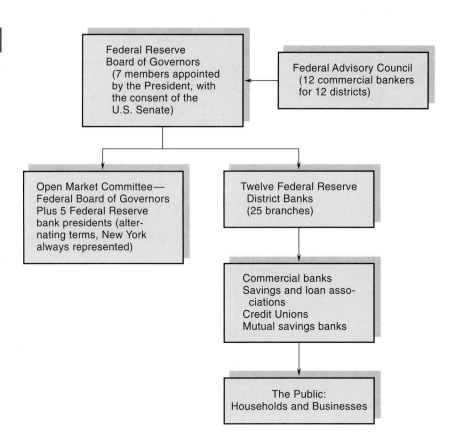

EXHIBIT 6

The Structure of the Federal Reserve System

The Board of Governors of the Federal Reserve System is at the center of the banking system in the United States. The board sets the rules and regulations for all depository institutions. The seven members of the Board of Governors also serve on the Federal Open Market Committee, a 12-member board that establishes Fed policy with regard to the buying and selling of government securities, the primary mechanism used to control the money supply in the United States.

appointed only every other year, each president has only limited power over the Fed. This enhances the independence of the Fed and makes monetary policy less subject to political manipulation. Because the Fed operates with considerable independence of both Congress and the executive branch, it often becomes the "whipping boy" for legislative leaders and presidents during difficult times.

The Board of Governors and the Fed in general have the responsibility of monitoring the health of the banking industry, supervising its procedures, and enforcing Fed regulations. Thus, the country looks to the Fed to act to keep the bankruptcy of a few banks or savings and loan institutions from having a "domino effect" and from threatening the integrity and safety of the system as a whole. The Board of Governors establishes rules and regulations applicable to all depository institutions. It sets the reserve requirements and regulates the composition of the asset holdings of depository institutions. The board is the rule-maker, and often the umpire, of the banking industry.

The Federal Advisory Council provides the Board of Governors with input from the banking industry. The Federal Advisory Council is composed of 12 commercial bankers, one from each of the 12 Federal Reserve districts. As the name implies, this council is purely advisory.

In addition to the Board of Governors, the Federal Open Market Committee (FOMC) exerts an important influence on monetary policy. This powerful policy-making arm of the Fed is made up of (a) the seven members of the Board of Governors, (b) the president of the New York District Bank, and (c) four (of the remaining eleven) additional presidents of the Fed's District Banks, who rotate on the committee. While they do not always have a vote, all 12 presidents of the Federal Reserve regional banks attend the FOMC meetings, held every five to eight weeks. The FOMC determines the Fed's policy with respect to the purchase and sale of government bonds. As we shall soon see, this is the Fed's most frequently used method of controlling the money supply in the United States.

The 12 Federal Reserve District Banks operate under the control of the Board of Governors.[3] These district banks handle approximately 85 percent of all check-clearing services of the banking system. Federal Reserve District Banks differ from commercial banks in several important respects.

1. Federal Reserve Banks Are Not Profit-Making Institutions. Instead, they are an arm of the government. All of their earnings, above minimum expenses, belong to the Treasury.

2. Unlike Other Banks, Federal Reserve Banks Can Actually Issue Money. Approximately 90 percent of the currency in circulation was issued by the Fed. Look at the dollar bill in your pocket. Chances are that is has "Federal Reserve Note" engraved on it, indicating that it was issued by the Federal Reserve System. The Fed is the only bank that can issue money.

3. Federal Reserve Banks Act as Bankers' Banks. Private citizens and corporations do not bank with Federal Reserve Banks. Commercial depository institutions and the federal government are the only banking customers of the Fed. Most depository institutions, regardless of their membership status with the Fed, usually maintain some deposits with the Federal Reserve System. Of course, deposits with the Fed count as reserves. The Fed audits the books of depository institutions regularly to assure regulatory compliance and the protection of depositors against fraud. The Fed also plays an important role in the clearing of checks through the banking system. Since most banks maintain deposits with the Fed, the clearing of checks becomes merely an accounting transaction.

Initially, the Fed was made independent of the executive branch so that the Treasury would not use it for political purposes. The policies of the Treasury and the Fed, though, are usually closely coordinated. For example, the chair of the Board of Governors of the Federal Reserve, the Secretary of the Treasury, and the chair of the President's Council of Economic Advisers meet weekly to discuss and plan macroeconomic policy. In reality, it would be more accurate to think of the Fed and the executive branch as equal partners in the determination of policies designed to promote full employment and stable prices.

HOW THE FED CONTROLS OUR MONEY SUPPLY

The Fed has three major means of controlling the money stock: (a) establishing reserve requirements for depository institutions, (b) buying and selling U.S. government securities in the open market, and (c) setting the interest rate at which it will loan funds to commercial banks and other depository institutions. We will analyze in detail how each of these tools can be used to regulate the amount of money in circulation.

---

[3]Federal Reserve District Banks are located in Boston, New York, Philadelphia, Cleveland, Richmond, Atlanta, Chicago, St. Louis, Minneapolis, Kansas City, Dallas, and San Francisco. There are also 25 district "branch banks."

EXHIBIT 7 ■ The Required Reserve Ratio of Banking Institutions		
Banking institutions are required to maintain 3 percent reserves against transaction-account deposits of less than $41.1 million and 12 percent reserves for transaction deposits over $41.1 million (in effect December 1990).		
	Transaction Accounts	
	$0–$41.1 million	Over $41.1 million
Required reserves as a percent of deposits	3	12
Source: *Federal Reserve Bulletin*, February 1991		

Reserve Requirements.   The Federal Reserve System requires banking institutions (including credit unions and savings and loan associations) to maintain reserves against the demand deposits of its customers. The reserves of banking institutions are composed of (a) currency held by the bank (vault cash) and (b) deposits of the bank with the Federal Reserve System. A bank can always obtain additional currency by drawing on its deposits with the Federal Reserve. So, both cash-on-hand and the bank's deposits with the Fed can be used to meet the demands of depositors. Both therefore count as reserves.

Required Reserve Ratio:
A percentage of a specified liability category (for example, transaction accounts) that banking institutions are required to hold as reserves against that type of liability.

Exhibit 7 indicates the **required reserve ratio**—the percentage of each deposit category that banks are required to keep in reserve (that is, their cash plus deposits with the Fed). As of December 1990, the reserve requirement for transactions accounts was set at 3 percent for amounts under $41.1 million and 12 percent for amounts in excess of $41.1 million.[4] Currently, banks are not required to keep additional reserves against their savings and time deposits.

Why are commercial banks required to maintain assets in the form of reserves? One reason is to prevent imprudent bankers from overextending loans and thereby placing themselves in a poor position to deal with any sudden increase in withdrawals by depositors. The quantity of reserves needed to meet such emergencies is not left totally to the judgment of individual bankers. The Fed sets the rules.

The Fed's control over reserve requirements, however, is important for another reason. By altering reserve requirements, the Fed can alter the money supply. The law does not prevent commercial banks from holding reserves over and above those required by the Fed, but, as we have noted, profit-seeking banking institutions prefer to hold interest-bearing assets such as loans rather than large amounts of excess reserves. Since reserves draw no interest, banks seek to minimize their excess reserves.

Exhibit 8 shows the actual reserve position of commercial banks (see also Exhibit 5). Not surprisingly, the actual reserves of these banks are very close to the required level. Since the excess reserves of banks are very small, they respond in a manner that changes the money supply when the Fed changes the required reserve ratio.

---

[4]The $41.1 million dividing point is adjusted each year by 80 percent of the change in total transaction account deposits in all banking institutions.

EXHIBIT 8 ■ The Reserves of Banking Institutions

The actual and required reserves of banking institutions (November 1990) are indicated below. The required reserves average approximately 10 percent against transaction deposits and 4 percent against total time deposits. Note that excess reserves of banking institutions are exceedingly small.

	Total—Banking Institutions (November 1990) (billions of dollars)
Total transaction deposits	599.1
Total time deposits	1,717.1
Actual reserves	62.1
Required reserves	61.1
Excess reserves	1.0

Source: *Federal Reserve Bulletin*, February 1991.

If the Fed reduced the required reserve ratio, it would free additional reserves that banks could loan out. Profit-seeking banks would not allow these excess reserves to lie idle—they would extend additional loans. The extension of new loans would then expand the money supply.

What would happen if the Fed increased the reserve requirements? Since banks typically have very small excess reserves, they would have to extend fewer loans in the future. This reduction in loans outstanding would then cause a decline in the money supply.

Reserve requirements are an important determinant of the money supply because they influence both the availability of excess reserves and the size of the deposit expansion multiplier. Higher reserve requirements reduce the size of the deposit expansion multiplier and force banks to extend fewer loans. An increase in the required reserve ratio therefore reduces the money supply. On the other hand, a decline in the required reserve ratio increases the potential deposit expansion multiplier and the availability of excess reserves. Banks then tend to extend additional loans, thereby expanding the money supply.

In recent years, the Fed has seldom used its regulatory power over reserve requirements to alter the supply of money. Because of the deposit expansion multiplier, small changes in reserve requirements can cause large changes in the money supply. In addition, the precise magnitude and timing of a change in the money stock resulting from a change in reserve requirements are difficult to predict. For these reasons, the Fed has usually preferred to use other monetary tools.

Open Market Operations. Unlike individuals, businesses, and even other government agencies, the Fed can write a check without having funds in its account. When the Fed buys things, it creates money. The primary thing that the Fed buys is the national debt, bonds that were originally issued by the U.S. Treasury and sold to private parties in order to finance budget deficits. The Fed's purchase and sale of these U.S. securities determines the size of the monetary base. The **monetary base** is equal to the reserves of commercial banks (vault cash and reserve deposits with the Fed) plus the currency in circulation.

Monetary Base: The sum of currency in circulation plus bank reserves (vault cash and reserves with the Fed). It reflects the stock of U.S. securities held by the Fed.

Open Market Operations:
The buying and selling of U.S. government securities (national debt) by the Federal Reserve.

As we indicated earlier, the Federal Open Market Committee (FOMC), a special committee of the Fed, decides when and how open market operations will be used. The members meet every five or six weeks to map out the Fed's policy concerning the purchase and sale of U.S. securities.

Since the Fed's buying and selling of U.S. securities takes place in the open market, such activity is often referred to as **open market operations.** By far, open market operations are the most important tool that the Fed uses to control the money supply. When the Fed purchases U.S. securities, it injects "new money"—new potential reserves—into the economy and thereby expands the monetary base. This new money shows up as an increase in either bank reserves or currency in circulation. The sellers of the securities receive checks drawn on a Federal Reserve Bank. If a seller cashes the check, the amount of currency in circulation expands. If, as is more likely to be the case, the seller deposits the check with a commercial bank, the supply of checking-account money increases directly and new bank reserves are created. When the check is deposited in a bank, the receiving bank acquires a deposit or credit with the Federal Reserve as the check clears. This increases the reserves of the bank, placing it in a position to extend additional loans. As the new loans are extended, the money supply expands by a still larger amount. Eventually, the money supply will increase by the amount of the securities purchased by the Fed times the actual deposit multiplier.

Let us consider a hypothetical case. Suppose the Fed purchases $10,000 of U.S. securities from Mary Jones. The Fed receives the securities and Jones receives a check for $10,000, which she deposits in her checking account at City Bank. Her deposit increases the money supply by $10,000, only a fraction of which must be held as required reserves against the new deposits of Jones. Assuming a 10 percent required reserve ratio, City Bank can now extend new loans of up to $9,000 while maintaining its initial reserve position. As the new loans are extended, they too will contribute to a further expansion in the money supply. Part of the new loans will eventually be deposited in other banks, and they also will be able to extend additional loans. As the process continues, the money supply expands by a multiple of the securities purchased by the Fed.

Open market operations can also be used to reduce the money stock, or reduce its rate of increase. If the Fed wants to reduce the money stock, it sells some of its current holdings of government securities. When the Fed sells securities, the buyer pays for them with a check drawn on a commercial bank. As the check clears, the reserves of that bank with the Fed will decline. The reserves available to commercial banks are reduced, and the money stock falls.

Every dollar of securities that the Fed buys increases the money supply by several dollars. Conversely, every dollar of securities that the Fed sells reduces the money supply by several dollars. This happens because open market operations affect not only the money supply directly, but they also expand the potential reserves—the monetary base—available to the banking system.

How much does the money supply increase per dollar of new reserves (monetary base) injected into the banking system through open market operations? The reserve requirements present in the late 1980s (see Exhibit 7) suggest that, potentially, an increase in the monetary base could expand the money supply (M1) by a multiple of 9 or 10. However, as new reserves are injected into the banking system, there is some leakage either because of potential currency reserves circulating as cash or because some banks may be accumulating excess reserves.

EXHIBIT 9 ■ How Big Is the Actual Money Deposit Multiplier?

In recent years, the actual deposit expansion multiplier has been between 2.67 and 3.02. Of course, if the reserve requirements were lowered (raised), the deposit expansion multiplier would rise (fall).

Year (December)	Money Supply (M1) (billions of dollars)	Monetary Base (billions of dollars)	Actual Money Deposit Expansion Multiplier
1970	214.5	71.0	3.02
1972	249.3	82.5	3.02
1974	274.4	96.4	2.85
1976	306.4	110.2	2.78
1978	358.5	130.0	2.76
1980	408.9	152.5	2.68
1982	474.5	172.9	2.74
1984	552.1	201.7	2.74
1985	620.1	219.4	2.83
1986	724.7	241.4	3.00
1987	750.4	258.1	2.91
1988	787.5	275.2	2.86
1989	794.8	284.9	2.79
1990	825.5	309.5	2.67

Source: Board of Governors of the Federal Reserve System and *Economic Report of the President, 1991*.

Exhibit 9 shows that since 1970, the money supply (M1) has been between 2.67 and 3.02 times greater than the monetary base, suggesting that the actual deposit expansion multiplier is generally slightly less than 3. Therefore, when the Fed purchases U.S. securities, injecting additional reserves into the system, the money supply, on average, tends to increase by approximately $3 for each dollar of securities purchased.

The Discount Rate—The Cost of Borrowing from the Fed. When banking institutions borrow from the Federal Reserve, they must pay interest on the loan. The interest rate that banks pay on loans from the Federal Reserve is called the **discount rate.** Borrowing from the Fed is a privilege, not a right. The Fed does not have to loan funds to banking institutions. Banks borrow from the Fed primarily to meet temporary shortages of reserves. They are most likely to borrow from the Fed for a brief period of time while they are making other adjustments in their loan and investment portfolios that will permit them to meet their reserve requirement.

An increase in the discount rate makes it more expensive for banking institutions to borrow from the Fed. Borrowing is discouraged, and banks are more likely to build up their reserves to ensure that they will not have to borrow from the Fed. An increase in the discount rate is thus restrictive. It tends to discourage banks from shaving their excess reserves to a low level.

In contrast, a reduction in the discount rate is expansionary. At the lower interest rate, it costs banks less if they have to turn to the Fed to meet a temporary emergency. Therefore, as the cost of borrowing from the Fed declines, banks are more likely to reduce their excess reserves to a minimum, extending more loans and increasing the money supply.

Discount Rate: The interest rate the Federal Reserve charges banking institutions for borrowing funds.

EXHIBIT 10

The Monetary Base and the Money Supply

The monetary base (currency plus bank reserves) provides the foundation for the money supply. The currency in circulation contributes directly to the money supply, while the bank reserves provide the underpinnings for checking deposits. Fed actions that alter the monetary base will affect the money supply.

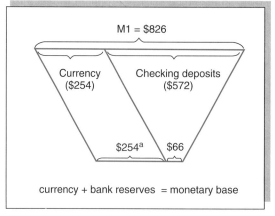

[a]Travelers checks are included in this category.

The general public has a tendency to overestimate the importance of a change in the discount rate. Many people think an increase in the discount rate means their local banker will (or must) charge them a higher interest rate for a loan.[5] This is not necessarily so. Reserves acquired through transaction and time deposits are the major source of loanable funds for commercial banks. Borrowing from the Fed amounts to less than one-tenth of 1 percent of the available loanable funds of commercial banks. Since borrowing from the Fed is such a negligible source of funds, a 0.5 percent change in the discount rate has something less than a profound impact on the availability of credit and the supply of money. Certainly, it does not necessarily mean that your local bank will raise the rate at which it will lend to you.

If a bank has to borrow to meet its reserve requirements, it need not turn to the Fed. Instead, it can go to the **federal funds market.** In this market, banks with excess reserves extend short-term (sometimes for as little as a day) loans to other banks seeking additional reserves. If the federal funds rate (the interest rate in the federal funds market) is less than the discount rate, banks seeking additional reserves will tap this source rather than borrow from the Fed. In recent years, the Fed has kept its loans to banking institutions at a low level by altering the discount rate to match the federal funds rate more closely. As a result, the federal funds rate and the discount rate tend to move together. If the federal funds rate is significantly higher than the discount rate, banks will attempt to borrow heavily from the Fed. Typically, when this happens, the Fed will raise its discount rate, removing the incentive of banks to borrow from the Fed rather than from the federal funds market.

Federal Funds Market:
A loanable funds market in which banks seeking additional reserves borrow short-term (generally for seven days or less) funds from banks with excess reserves. The interest rate in this market is called the federal funds rate.

CONTROLLING THE MONEY STOCK—A SUMMARY

As Exhibit 10 illustrates, the foundation of the M1 money supply is the monetary base, primarily composed of the Fed's holdings of U.S. securities. The monetary base can be decomposed into (a) currency in circulation and (b) bank reserves. Of course, the currency in circulation ($254 billion in December 1990) contributes directly to the money supply. In turn, the bank reserves ($66 billion in December 1990) underpin the checking deposits ($572 billion).

The Fed can determine the size of the monetary base through its buying and selling of securities and its discount rate policy. It can also use adjustments in the

---

[5]The discount rate is also sometimes confused with the prime interest rate, the rate at which banks loan money to low-risk customers. The two rates are different. A change in the discount rate will not necessarily affect the prime interest rate.

EXHIBIT 11 ■ Summary of the Monetary Tools of the Federal Reserve		
Federal Reserve Policy	Expansionary Monetary Policy	Restrictive Monetary Policy
1. Reserve requirements	*Reduce reserve requirements,* because this will free additional excess reserves and induce banks to extend additional loans, which will expand the money supply	*Raise reserve requirements,* because this will reduce the excess reserves of banks, causing them to make fewer loans; as the outstanding loans of banks decline, the money stock will be reduced
2. Open market operations	*Purchase additional U.S. securities,* which will expand the money stock directly, and increase the reserves of banks, inducing bankers in turn to extend more loans; this will expand the money stock indirectly	*Sell previously purchased U.S. securities,* which will reduce both the money stock and excess reserves; the decline in excess reserves will indirectly lead to an additional reduction in the money supply
3. Discount rate	*Lower the discount rate,* which will encourage more borrowing from the Fed; banks will tend to reduce their reserves and extend more loans because of the lower cost of borrowing from the Fed if they temporarily run short on reserves	*Raise the discount rate,* thereby discouraging borrowing from the Fed; banks will tend to extend fewer loans and build up their reserves so they will not have to borrow from the Fed

reserve requirements to influence the size of checking deposits relative to bank reserves. If the Fed wants to follow an expansionary policy, it can decrease reserve requirements, purchase additional U.S. securities, and/or lower the discount rate. If the Fed wants to reduce the money stock, it can increase the reserve requirements, sell U.S. securities, and/or raise the discount rate. Since the Fed typically seeks only small changes in the money supply (or its rate of increase), it typically uses only one or two of these tools at a time to accomplish a desired objective. Exhibit 11 summarizes the monetary tools of the Federal Reserve.

CHANGES IN THE MONEY SUPPLY

As the economy grows, the money supply is generally expanded, also. In a dynamic setting, therefore, the direction of monetary policy is best gauged by the rate of change in the money supply. When economists say that monetary policy is expansionary, they mean that the rate of growth of the money stock is rapid. Similarly, restrictive monetary policy implies a slow rate of growth or a decline in the money stock.

Since open market operations have been the Fed's primary tool of monetary control in recent years, the monetary base and money stock have followed similar paths. When the Fed purchases U.S. securities and thereby expands the monetary base at a rapid rate, the money stock grows rapidly. Conversely, when the Fed expands its holdings of securities (and therefore the monetary base), the money supply grows less rapidly.

EXHIBIT 12

Open Market Operations,
the Monetary Base, and
Changes in the Money
Supply

Here we show that changes in
the *growth rates* of the
monetary base and money
supply are associated. This is
what we would expect when
open market operations are the
primary tool of monetary policy.
The numbers in parentheses
indicate the quarter of the year.

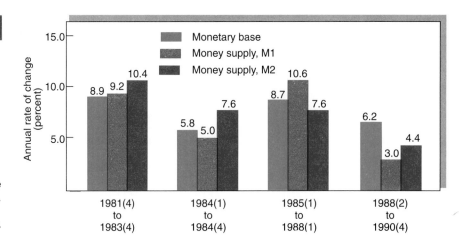

Exhibit 12 illustrates the relationship between the monetary base and the money supply during the 1980s. From 1981 (4th quarter) through 1983 (4th quarter), the monetary base grew at an 8.9 percent annual rate, while M1 and M2 grew at slightly higher rates. During 1984, the Fed shifted to a more restrictive monetary policy. Between 1984(1) and 1984(4), the monetary base grew at an annual rate of 5.8 percent. Correspondingly, the growth rates of both M1 and M2 also decelerated during 1984. During the 1985(1) to 1988(1) period, the growth rate of the monetary base accelerated again, and the M1 money supply followed suit. From 1988(2) through 1990(4), as the growth of the monetary base decelerated to 6.2 percent, once again the growth rate of the money supply measures slowed. There is a strong tendency for the monetary base and money supply measures to move together. This is precisely what we would expect when open market operations are the primary tool used by the Fed to control the money supply.

THE FED AND THE TREASURY

Many students have a tendency to confuse the Federal Reserve and the U.S. Treasury, probably because both sound like monetary agencies. The Treasury is a budgetary agency. If there is a budgetary deficit, the Treasury will issue U.S. securities as a method of financing the deficit. Newly issued U.S. securities are almost always sold to private investors (or invested in government trust funds). Bonds issued by the Treasury to finance a budget deficit are seldom purchased directly by the Fed. In any case, the Treasury is primarily interested in obtaining funds so it can pay Uncle Sam's bills. Except for nominal amounts, mostly coins, the Treasury does not issue money. Borrowing—the public sale of new U.S. securities—is the primary method used by the Treasury to cover any excess of expenditures in relation to revenues from taxes and other sources.

Whereas the Treasury is concerned with the revenues and expenditures of the government, the Fed is concerned primarily with the availability of money and credit for the entire economy. The Fed does not issue U.S. securities. It merely purchases and sells government securities issued by the Treasury as a means of controlling the economy's money supply. Unlike the Treasury, the Fed can purchase government bonds by writing a check on itself without having deposits, gold, or anything else to back it up. In doing so, the Fed creates money out of thin air. The Treasury does not have this power. The Fed does not have an obligation to meet the financial responsibilities of the U.S. government. That is the domain of the Treasury. The Fed's responsibility is to provide a stable monetary framework for the entire economy. So, although the two agencies cooperate with each other, they are distinctly different institutions established for different purposes (see accompanying Thumbnail Sketch).

It is important to recognize that the buying and selling of bonds by the Treasury and by the Fed exert different effects on the supply of money. The key to seeing this point lies in the recognition that the Treasury and the Fed handle revenues collected from the selling of bonds in a different manner. When the Treasury issues and sells bonds, it does so to pay for Federal government expenditures. After all, the Treasury issues the bonds in order to generate the required revenue for its spending. The people who sell the bonds to the Treasury have less money, but when the Treasury spends, the recipients of its spending will have more money. Thus, there is no change in the supply of money. In contrast, when the Fed sells bonds, in effect, it takes the revenues and holds them, keeping them out of circulation. Because this money is out of circulation and can no longer be used for the purchase of goods and services, the money supply shrinks. If the Fed later wishes to increase the money supply, it can buy bonds with this ''stored'' money and re-inject it into circulation. However, as long as the Fed simply holds the revenues from its bond sales, the money supply will decline.

THUMBNAIL SKETCH

The differences between the U.S. Treasury and the Federal Reserve Bank.

U.S. Treasury	**Federal Reserve**
1. Concerned with the finance of the federal government.	1. Concerned with the monetary climate for the economy.
2. Issues bonds to the general public to finance the budget deficits of federal government.	2. Does *not* issue bonds.
3. Does *not* determine the money supply.	3. Determines the money supply—primarily through its buying and selling of Treasury bonds.

RECENT DEVELOPMENTS AND CURRENT PROBLEMS IN THE BANKING INDUSTRY

During the 1940–1975 period, banking was a quiet industry. Checking accounts were available only at commercial banks. Regulations prevented banks from paying their customers interest on checking deposits. The interest-free checking deposits, along with savings accounts, provided commercial banks with a low-cost source of funds, which were invested and loaned to customers at market interest rates. The interest rate differential provided banks with a steady source of income.

APPLICATIONS IN ECONOMICS

The Savings and Loan Crisis

Savings and loan associations (S&Ls) are institutions similar to commercial banks that have traditionally concentrated on the financing of home mortgages. In 1980, there were approximately 4,600 S&Ls in the United States. During the last decade almost half of these S&Ls either failed or merged with other banking institutions. Just as deposits in commercial banks are insured by the FDIC, the Federal Savings and Loan Insurance Corporation (FSLIC) insures the accounts of depositors in S&Ls. During the 1980s, however, S&L failures were so numerous that the funds of the FSLIC were depleted. Congress intervened by appropriating more than $150 billion (as of 1991) to make the insured accounts of depositors good and to assist with the phasing out of troubled S&Ls. During the last several years, these developments—broadly referred to as ''the S&L crisis''—often occupied the front pages of our newspapers. What caused this crisis? Why have the S&L failures been far more numerous than commercial bank failures?

The Origin of the S&L Crisis

In a few isolated cases that sometimes dominated the news, managers of S&Ls defrauded customers and used institutional funds for private purposes. In some of these cases, political contributions were used in an effort to get bank regulators to look the other way. The basic cause of the S&L crisis, however, was more fundamental, though perhaps less intriguing. Having specialized in the fixed-rate home mortgage market, the value of the primary asset of S&Ls was highly vulnerable to the inflation, high interest rates, and competitive financial markets of the late 1970s and early 1980s.

In the 1970s, S&Ls were financing home mortgages (typically long-term, fixed-rate assets) with deposits that were generally short-term in nature. This financing of long-term fixed-rate loans with short-term deposits is extremely risky. To see why, consider a typical S&L with assets of 30-year mortgages paying 8 percent (for instance) and with liabilities of short-term (say one year) deposits whose interest rates can rise or fall. If nominal interest rates rise, the S&L cannot change the interest rates on its outstanding mortgages, but it still has to pay a higher interest rate on the short-term deposits. If it does not, savers will take their funds elsewhere. As interest rates rose during the inflationary 1970s, many S&Ls found themselves, for example, paying 10 percent on deposits while they were earning only 8 percent on their mortgage loans. It was situations like this that resulted in industry-wide losses and the bankruptcy of many S&Ls during the 1980s.

The single-premium deposit insurance system added to the problem. The banking deregulation of the 1980s allowed S&Ls to

---

Simultaneously, savings and loan associations were the primary source of mortgage funds for the housing industry; regulations protected S&Ls from competition from commercial banks in the home mortgage market. Generally, S&Ls attracted funds by paying savers a little higher interest rate than commercial banks, marking-up the funds a few percentage points, and then loaning the funds to home buyers. In essence, both banks and S&Ls operated in protected markets; they were largely insulated from the rigors of competition.

INCREASED COMPETITION FOR FUNDS

This quiet life began to change in the mid-1970s. Merrill Lynch and other investment firms introduced the money market mutual fund. These funds were invested in a diverse portfolio of highly liquid assets, particularly Treasury bills and highly rated bonds. Shareholders could sell shares in their fund simply by writing a check. Thus, these funds were able to provide shareholders with checking privileges and a safe investment with a high interest yield.

acquire assets that were riskier but that paid higher interest rates than fixed-rate mortgages. Unfortunately, the insurance premiums that the S&Ls paid were not adjusted for the additional risk the S&Ls undertook; all S&Ls paid the same premium rate regardless of whether they purchased risky or conservative assets. This is similar to charging a race car driver (while racing) the same automobile insurance premium you would charge a Sunday-only driver!

Not surprisingly, the single-premium element of the deposit insurance system encouraged a type of "reverse bank run"— the movement of funds *from* low-risk *to* high-risk depository institutions—which plagued the S&L industry during the 1980s.[6] Why did this occur? Since their deposit insurance premium was not linked to the soundness of their investment practices, many troubled S&Ls turned to risky investments as they sought to

escape the losses caused by the rising interest rates of the inflationary 1970s. In order to attract funds, these troubled S&Ls offered depositors higher interest rates than could be earned elsewhere. Recognizing that federal deposit insurance protected their funds, savers were encouraged to shift funds from more prudent to the riskier institutions paying higher interest rates. This shift of funds to shaky S&Ls, many of which eventually failed, substantially increased the federal government's deposit insurance liability (and eventually the size of the congressional bailout).

Currently, policymakers are seeking ways to keep the S&L crisis from spreading throughout the banking system. The large, fixed-rate mortgage portfolio of S&Ls in the 1970s made them far more vulnerable than commercial banks. However, the perverse incentive that accompanies a single-premium deposit insurance system is present for both

commercial banks and S&Ls. In essence, this single-rate system provides an implicit subsidy to banks that make risky (or imprudent) investments at the expense of healthy institutions. Removal of this implicit subsidy is one of the most urgent problems confronting policymakers. A deposit insurance system that charges individual banks insurance premiums that reflect the riskiness of their asset portfolios is essential to the long-term health of our banking system.

---

[6]For an additional analysis of the problems accompanying the current deposit insurance system, see Edward Kane, *The Gathering Crisis in Federal Deposit Insurance* (Cambridge,: MIT Press, 1985), R. Dan Brumbaugh, Jr., Andrew S. Carron, and Robert E. Litan, "Cleaning Up the Depository Institutions Mess," *Brookings Papers on Economic Activity,* 1989, no. 1, and David O. Beim, "Beyond the Savings-and-Loan Crisis," *The Public Interest,* Spring 1989, pp. 88–99.

In the 1970s, a government-imposed interest rate ceiling limited the amount banks and S&Ls could pay on saving deposits. This interest rate ceiling reduced the competition for deposits *within* the banking industry and helped provide banks with a low-cost source of funds. The newly introduced money market mutual funds undermined this anti-competitive practice.

When many depositors shifted funds from banking institutions to money market mutual funds, banks were forced to borrow from other sources at higher interest rates. Since most of the loans of commercial banks were short-term, they were well-positioned to pass the higher cost of funds onto their customers. However, the increase in the cost of funds was a much more serious problem for savings and loan associations. In the late 1970s, the primary asset of S&Ls was long-term, fixed-interest-rate mortgages. Income from these assets failed to keep up with rising interest costs. Thus, the increased competitiveness, higher inflation rates, and the accompanying rise in the cost of funds really put the squeeze on S&Ls (see the Applications in Economics box, "The Savings and Loan Crisis").

MONETARY CONTROL ACT OF 1980

Responding to the pressures on the banking industry, Congress passed the Monetary Control Act of 1980. In effect, this act restructured the banking industry, eroding the prior distinctions between commercial banks, savings and loan associations, and credit unions. The legislation lifted most of the restrictions on the types of loans and investments that savings and loan associations and credit unions could make. Interest rate ceilings on time and savings deposits were phased out. S&Ls and credit unions were permitted to offer checking account deposits. All banking institutions were allowed to pay interest on checking accounts. Finally, all depository institutions were placed under the jurisdiction of the Federal Reserve System, which was instructed to apply uniform reserve requirements and to offer similar services (for example, check clearing and access to borrowing from the Fed) to all banking institutions. In essence, the 1980 legislation transformed S&Ls and credit unions into banks and placed them under the control of the Fed.

BANK FAILURES DURING THE 1980S

In a market economy, the investment loans of the banking industry play an important role in the allocation of resources. The financing of projects provides a reality check on the hopes and dreams of business entrepreneurs. If a business cannot find funding for a project, this is strong evidence that the viability (and profitability) of the project is highly questionable. Bankers and other financial investors such as stock and bond holders have a strong incentive to finance winners (profitable projects) and shun losers (business failures). Borrowers may be unable to repay their loans if the funds are channeled into unprofitable investments. In turn, lenders who finance business failures may lose all or part of their funds. Efficient allocation of investment funds is an important source of economic growth. Profitable business projects increase the value of resources and promote economic growth; unprofitable projects have the opposite effect. An efficient operating capital market, of which the banking system is an integral part, will be good at picking winners—providing funds for profitable rather than unprofitable projects.

There are two major reasons for bank failures. First, there are bank runs. If a large number of depositors lose confidence in a bank and, for whatever reason, seek to withdraw their funds at the same time, they will be unable to do so under a fractional reserve banking system. The numerous banking failures of the 1920s and 1930s emanated from this source. As we mentioned earlier, the Federal Deposit Insurance Corporation stemmed the tide against bank failures of this type. As Exhibit 13 illustrates, the annual number of bank failures declined to a trickle, usually fewer than 15 per year, during the 1940–1980 period.

The second reason for bank failures is loan defaults. When banks finance investments that turn sour, borrowers are often unable to repay their loans. The bank loses funds when borrowers default. Banks that extend a high percentage of such bad loans will eventually fail.

As Exhibit 13 shows, commercial bank failures increased sharply during the 1980s, soaring to more than 200 per year during 1986–1988. In contrast with the earlier wave of bank failures during the 1920s and 1930s, the bank failures of the 1980s were generally the result of loan defaults (rather than bank runs).

Why were there so many commercial bank failures and loan defaults during the 1980s?

1. Banks operated in a more competitive environment during the 1980s. In recent years, both financial innovations and deregulation increased the intensity of

EXHIBIT 13

Commercial Bank Failures, 1935–1990

Following the establishment of the FDIC in 1933, bank failures in the United States numbered only 10 or 15 per year during the 1940–1980 period. In contrast, the number of bank failures jumped sharply during the 1980s, soaring to over 200 in 1986, 1987, and 1988.

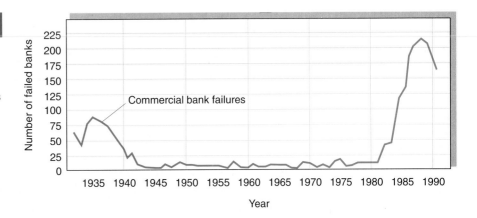

competition in financial markets. Increasingly, banks faced stiff competition from other financial institutions for both deposits and customers. Some banks, perhaps accustomed to the quiet world of a protected market, were ill-prepared to deal with the competitive environment of the 1980s.

2. Instability in regional markets and industries increased the number of bad loans. After rising rapidly during the 1970s, oil prices collapsed during 1981–1985. Many loans extended to oil industry interests in the late 1970s went into default in the 1980s. Banks in states such as Oklahoma, Texas, and Louisiana were particularly hard hit by these defaults. Similarly, agricultural land values in the Midwest, after rising sharply during the 1970s, declined in the early 1980s. Later, housing prices declined substantially throughout much of the Northeast. Many borrowers financing agricultural land and houses in these regions were unable to repay their loans. Since the assets declined in value, even foreclosure would not allow the banks extending the ''bad loans'' to fully recoup their funds. During the mid-1980s, most of the bank failures were in states hard hit by recessionary conditions in important regional industries.

3. The U.S. has many small banks holding poorly diversified asset portfolios. In contrast with the United States, bank failures have not been a serious problem in other industrial countries. Why? In other countries there are fewer banks and the existing banks tend to operate over a larger market area. There are more than 12,000 commercial banks in the United States. By comparison, there are approximately 150 banks in Japan, 65 in Canada, 550 in the United Kingdom, and 900 in Germany. Given their size and national scope, banks in these countries finance a more diverse portfolio of loans than U.S. banks. Thus, they are not as vulnerable to changing conditions in geographic regions and local markets.

4. Deposit insurance premiums are not based on the financial strength of the bank. Unlike the premiums for other forms of insurance, banks pay a single premium on deposits, regardless of the risk accompanying the loan portfolio of the bank. When insuring deposits, the FDIC does not consider the financial health of the bank. When banking institutions got into financial trouble during the 1980s, they often attracted funds by offering depositors higher interest rates and sought to restore their financial health by investing these funds in high-yield, risky areas (for example, junk bonds and businesses with low credit ratings). With time, these actions increased both the number of bank failures and the liability of the FDIC. (These forces were also present in the savings and loan industry.) If banks were charged premiums that reflected the riskiness of their portfolio, the incentive to pursue this strategy would be eliminated.

REDUCING FUTURE BANK FAILURES

Motivated by the cost of the S&L bailout, Congress is currently considering legislative alternatives to avoid a similar crisis among commercial banks. What can be done to strengthen the banking system and reduce the likelihood of future bank failures? Given the nature of the problem, action on two fronts is quite important. First, restrictions on interstate banking should be repealed. As conditions in other countries indicate, large banks operating in a national market are less likely to get into trouble than small banks dependent on local market conditions. While several banks do operate across state lines, they have to use a bank holding company and obtain separate corporate charters in each state. These restrictions increase costs and reduce profitability. Second, deposit insurance premiums should reflect risk—banks holding a more risky asset portfolio should pay higher deposit insurance premiums. Reform in this area would encourage banks to evaluate loan applications more carefully and to extend fewer risky loans.

LOOKING AHEAD

In this chapter, we focused on the banking industry and the mechanics of monetary policy. We are now ready to analyze the impact of monetary policy on output, growth, and prices. What factors does the Fed consider when deciding whether to expand or contract the money supply? Have Fed policies exerted a stabilizing influence on the economy? These topics will be considered in subsequent chapters.

CHAPTER SUMMARY

1. Money is a financial asset that is widely accepted as a medium of exchange. It also provides a means of storing current purchasing power for the future and acts as a unit of account. Without money, exchange would be both costly and tedious.

2. There is some debate among economists as to precisely how the money supply should be defined. The narrowest definition of the money supply (M1) includes only (a) currency in the hands of the public, (b) demand deposits, (c) other (interest-earning) checkable deposits in depository institutions, and (d) traveler's checks. None of these categories of money has significant intrinsic value. Money derives its value from its scarcity relative to its usefulness.

3. The M2 money supply includes M1 plus (a) savings and small-denomination time deposits, (b) money market mutual funds shares, (c) money market deposit accounts, (d) overnight loans of customers to commercial banks, and (e) Eurodollar deposits. The introduction of interest-earning checkable deposits has changed the nature of M1 and reduced the comparability of M1 data over time. As a result, most analysts now rely more extensively on M2 data when making comparisons of money supply growth rates across time periods that include the 1980s.

4. Banking is a business. Banks provide their depositors with safekeeping of money, check-clearing services on demand deposits, and interest payments on time deposits.

Banks derive most of their income from the extension of loans and investments in interest-earning securities.

5. Recent legislation and regulatory changes have altered the structure of the banking industry. Currently, savings and loan associations and credit unions offer services, including checking accounts, similar to those of commercial banks. The Federal Reserve System now regulates all of these depository institutions and is legally required to apply uniform reserve requirements to each. In essence, these changes have integrated these institutions into the banking industry.

6. Under a fractional reserve banking system, banks are required to maintain only a fraction of their deposits in the form of reserves (vault cash or deposits with the Fed). Excess reserves may be invested or loaned to customers. When banks extend additional loans, they create additional deposits and thereby expand the money supply.

7. The Federal Reserve System is a central banking authority designed to provide a stable monetary framework for the entire economy. It establishes regulations that determine the supply of money. It issues most of the currency in the United States. It is a banker's bank.

8. The Fed has three major tools with which to control the money supply.
   a. *Establishment of the Required Reserve Ratio.* Under a fractional reserve banking system, reserve requirements limit the ability of banking institutions to expand the money supply by extending more loans. When the Fed lowers the required reserve ratio, it creates excess reserves and allows banks to extend new loans, expanding the money supply. Raising the reserve requirements has the opposite effect.
   b. *Open Market Operations.* The open market operations of the Fed can directly influence both the money supply and available reserves. When the Fed buys U.S. securities, the money supply will expand because bond buyers will acquire money and the reserves of banks will increase as checks drawn on Federal Reserve Banks are cleared. When the Fed sells securities, the money supply will contract because bond buyers are giving up money in exchange for securities. The reserves available to banks will decline, causing banks to issue fewer loans and thereby reduce the money supply.
   c. *The Discount Rate.* An increase in the discount rate is restrictive because it discourages banks from borrowing from the Fed to extend new loans. A reduction in the discount rate is expansionary because it makes borrowing from the Fed less costly.

9. For a dynamic, growing economy, monetary policy can best be judged by the *rate of change* in the money supply and the monetary base—its primary determinant. When open market operations are the primary tool of monetary policy, the monetary base and money supply measures will tend to follow similar paths. Rapid growth of the monetary base and the money supply is indicative of expansionary monetary policy. Conversely, slow growth (or a decline) in the size of the monetary base and the money supply is indicative of restrictive money policy.

10. The Federal Reserve and the U.S. Treasury are distinct agencies. The Fed is concerned primarily with the money supply and the establishment of a stable monetary climate. The Treasury focuses on budgetary matters—tax revenues, government expenditures, and the financing of government debt.

11. During the 1980s, there was a sharp increase in the number of bank failures in the United States. The primary reasons for these bank failures were (a) an increase in the competitiveness of the financial industry; (b) bad loans resulting from instability in land values, regional housing markets, and the oil industry; (c) a large number of small, poorly diversified banks; and (d) deposit insurance premiums that failed to reflect the financial health of individual banks.

**CRITICAL ANALYSIS
QUESTIONS**

*1. What is meant by the statement, "This asset is illiquid"? List some things that you own, ranking them from most liquid to most illiquid.

2. What determines whether or not a financial asset is included in the money supply, M1? Why are interest-earning checkable deposits included in M1, while interest-earning savings accounts and Treasury bills are not?

*3. What makes money valuable? Does money perform an economic service? Explain. Could money perform its function better if there were twice as much of it? Why or why not?

4. "People are poor because they don't have very much money. Yet, central bankers keep money scarce. If poor people had more money, poverty could be eliminated." Explain the confused thinking this statement reflects and why it is misleading.

5. Why can banks continue to hold reserves that are only a fraction of the demand deposits of their customers? Is your money safe in a bank? Why or why not?

*6. Suppose you withdraw $100 from your checking account. How does this transaction affect (a) the supply of money, (b) the reserves of your bank, and (c) the excess reserves of your bank?

7. Explain how the creation of new reserves would cause the money supply to increase by some multiple of the newly created reserves.

*8. How will the following actions affect the money supply?
a. A reduction in the discount rate.
b. An increase in the reserve requirements.
c. Purchase by the Fed of $10 million of U.S. securities from a commercial bank.
d. Sale by the U.S. Treasury of $10 million of newly issued bonds to a commercial bank.
e. An increase in the discount rate.
f. Sale by the Fed of $20 million of U.S. securities to a private investor.

9. **What's Wrong with this Way of Thinking?**
"When the government runs a budget deficit, it simply pays its bills by printing more money. As the newly printed money works its way through the economy, it waters down the value of paper money already in circulation. Thus, it takes more money to buy things. The major source of inflation is newly created paper money resulting from budget deficits."

*10. If the Federal Reserve does not take any offsetting action, what would happen to the supply of money if the general public decided to increase its holdings of currency and decrease its checking deposits by an equal amount?

11. If market interest rates on short-term loans (including the federal funds rate) are declining, does a reduction in the discount rate indicate that the Fed is trying to increase the money supply?

*12. If the Fed wants to expand the money supply, why is it more likely to do so by purchasing bonds rather than by lowering reserve requirements?

*13. Are the following true or false?
a. "You can never have too much money."
b. "When you deposit currency in a commercial bank, cash goes out of circulation and the money supply declines."
c. "If the Fed would create more money, Americans would achieve a higher standard of living."

14. "The bank failures of the 1980s are a replay of the 1920s and 1930s." Evaluate.

15. How has the nature of the money supply, M1, changed in recent years? How have these changes influenced the usefulness of M1 as an indicator of monetary policy?

*Asterisk denotes questions for which answers are given in Appendix C, Selected Answers.

Why do many analysts prefer to use M2 rather than M1 when comparing the monetary policy of the 1980s with earlier periods?

16. During the 1980s, the failure rate of savings and loan associations was considerably higher than the rate for commercial banks. Why was the failure rate of S&Ls so high during the 1980s?

13 Modern Macroeconomics: Monetary Policy

In the early editions of the book, fiscal policy was top banana. In later editions that emphasis changed to equality. In this edition we've taken a stand that monetary policy is most important.

Paul Samuelson[1]
(1985 comment on the 12th edition of his classic text)

CHAPTER FOCUS

■ Why do individuals and businesses hold part of their wealth in the form of money?

■ How does monetary policy affect interest rates, output, and employment?

■ Can monetary policy stimulate real GNP in the short run? Can it do so in the long run?

■ Does it make any difference whether people quickly anticipate the effects of a change in monetary policy? Why?

■ Does an increase in the stock of money cause inflation?

■ Did macroeconomic policy cause the Great Depression?

*N*ow that we have an understanding of the banking system and the determinants of the money supply, we can relax our prior assumption that the monetary authorities hold the supply of money constant. In this chapter, we will integrate the market for money balances into our basic macroeconomic model. As in the case of fiscal policy, modern views on the impact of monetary policy reflect an evolutionary process. We will consider briefly the historical roots of modern monetary theory. The primary focus of this chapter is an analysis of how monetary policy works—how shifts in monetary policy affect interest rates, output, and prices.

THE DEMAND FOR MONEY

Demand for Money: At any given interest rate, the amount of wealth that people desire to hold in the form of money balances; that is, cash and checking account deposits. The quantity demanded is inversely related to the interest rate.

The amount of wealth that households and businesses desire to hold in the form of money balances is called the **demand for money.** Why do individuals and businesses want to hold cash and checking account money rather than stocks, automobiles, buildings, and consumer durables? When considering this question, it's important not to confuse (a) the demand for money balances with (b) the desire for more wealth (or income). Of course, all of us would like to have more wealth, but we may be perfectly satisfied with our holdings of money in relation to our holdings of other goods, given our current level of wealth. When we say people want to hold more (or less) money, we mean that they want to restructure their wealth toward larger (smaller) money balances.

REASONS FOR HOLDING MONEY

Economists emphasize three major reasons why people hold money.

1. Transactions Demand. Money provides us with instant purchasing power. At the most basic level, we hold money so we can conduct transactions for almost any commodity quickly and easily with numerous people. Households demand money so they can pay for the weekly groceries, the monthly house payment, gasoline for the car, lunch for the kids, and other items purchased regularly. Businesses demand money so they can meet the weekly payroll, pay the utility bill, purchase supplies, and conduct other transactions. Money balances are necessary for transaction purposes because we do not always receive our income at the time we want to buy things. So, we keep a little cash or money in the bank to bridge the gap between everyday expenses and payday.

How much money will people desire in order to conduct their transactions? Other things constant, money balances for transaction purposes will increase with the nominal value of transactions. If prices remain constant, while the quantity of goods bought and sold increases, larger money balances will be required to conduct the larger volume of business. Similarly, if wages and prices increase, more money will be required by households to purchase the costlier weekly market basket and more money will be required by businesses to pay the larger wage bill. In essence, as money GNP increases as the result of either the growth of real output or higher

---

[1]Prior to the 1970s, most economists thought that fiscal policy was far more important than monetary policy. As the statement of Nobel laureate Paul Samuelson implies, this is no longer true. Since Professor Samuelson is a long-time Keynesian economist, the change in his views concerning the importance of monetary policy is particularly revealing.

prices, the demand for money balances will also increase. This transactions demand is the principal motive for holding money balances.

2. Precautionary Demand.   Households and firms confront an uncertain future. Uncertainty produces two side effects that influence decisions: (a) risk and (b) opportunity for profit. Risk-averse households and firms, those that are uncertain about the amount and timing of the receipt of their income, will hold additional cash, checking account balances, and other highly liquid assets as a precaution against unforeseen circumstances. Economists refer to the demand for money due to risk-averse behavior associated with uncertainty over future income and expenditure patterns as the *precautionary demand for money*. While the transactions demand relates to the use of money for planned expenditures, precautionary demand stems from the recognition that unplanned expenditures may be necessary as the result of unforeseen events—a medical emergency, an unexpected decline in income, an auto accident, or such. Generally, the amount of money people wish to hold as insurance against unforeseen circumstances rises with nominal income. The precautionary demand for money balances, like transactions demand, increases with nominal GNP.

3. Speculative Demand.   Unforeseen changes may also present decision-makers with an unexpected opportunity to purchase commodities or assets at bargain prices. Individuals and businesses may want to maintain part of their wealth in the form of money so they will be in a position to take ready advantage of opportunities to purchase desired items at very low prices. Of course, money is the most liquid form of wealth. Unlike land or houses, money places an individual (or business) in a position to respond quickly to a profit-making opportunity. Money balances maintained for this purpose are termed the *speculative demand for money*.

THE OPPORTUNITY COST OF HOLDING MONEY

The motives for holding money indicate that the demand for money is linked to money income (nominal GNP). As nominal income expands, larger money balances are required to conduct transactions and respond effectively to unforeseen events. Money balances are like other goods, though, in that price influences the amount demanded. The price, or perhaps more accurately, the opportunity cost of holding money, is directly related to the nominal interest rate. Rather than maintaining $1,000 in cash or in a checking account that does not pay interest, you could earn interest by purchasing a $1,000 bond. Even if you are maintaining money balances in an interest-earning checking account, you could earn a higher rate of interest if you were willing to tie up the funds in a bond or some other less liquid form of savings.

As the nominal interest rate rises, the cost of continuing to hold money balances increases. Therefore, at the higher interest rate, individuals and businesses will try to manage their affairs with smaller money balances. As Exhibit 1a illustrates, there is an inverse relationship between the quantity of money demanded and the interest rate.

With the passage of time, changes in institutional factors will influence the demand schedule for money. Both evidence and logic indicate that changes in institutional arrangements have reduced the demand for money in recent years. The widespread use of general-purpose credit cards helps households reconcile their bills with their receipt of income. Readily available short-term loans have reduced the need to maintain a substantial cash balance for emergencies. The movement away

The Demand and Supply of Money

The demand for money is inversely related to the money interest rate (a). The supply of money is determined by the monetary authorities (the Fed) through their open market operations, discount rate policy, and reserve requirements (b).

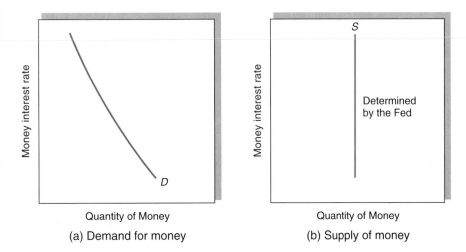

(a) Demand for money

(b) Supply of money

from agriculture means that more families have a steady income every two weeks or so, rather than an unpredictable income two or three times per year. This steady income makes planning easier. These factors have reduced the need for households to maintain large cash balances (shifting the demand for money schedule to the left).

THE SUPPLY OF MONEY

Exhibit 1b illustrates the supply schedule for money. Since the money supply is determined by the monetary authorities (the Fed in the United States), the supply curve is vertical. This implies that the supply of money is insensitive to the interest rate. It is whatever the Fed decides it should be, largely independent of the interest rate. In equilibrium, the quantity of money demanded must equal the quantity supplied at the economy's money interest rate.

What impact do changes in the money supply have on price and output? Like the modern view of fiscal policy, the modern view of monetary policy is the product of an evolutionary process. Let us consider prior views that have contributed to our modern outlook on the importance of money.

THE QUANTITY THEORY OF MONEY

Quantity Theory of Money: A theory that hypothesizes that a change in the money supply will cause a proportional change in the price level because velocity and real output are unaffected by the quantity of money.

For centuries, both laymen and economists recognized that increases in the money supply were a major determinant of changes in price level. Even prior to Adam Smith, early social philosophers such as David Hume argued that rapid growth in the supply of money caused inflation. Nearly a hundred years ago, the great classical economists, Englishman Alfred Marshall and American Irving Fisher, formalized a theory in support of this view. Economists refer to the theory as the **quantity theory of money**. According to the quantity theory, an increase in the supply of money will lead to a proportional increase in the price level.

The quantity theory of money can be easily understood once we recognize that there are two ways of viewing GNP. As we previously discussed, nominal GNP is the sum of the price, P, times the output, Y, of each "final product" good purchased during the period. In aggregate, P represents the economy's price level, while Y indicates real income or real GNP. There is also a second way of visualizing GNP.

When the existing money stock, M, is multiplied by the number of times, V, that money is used to buy final products, this, too, yields the economy's nominal GNP. Therefore,

$$PY = \text{GNP} = MV$$

Velocity of Money:
The average number of times a dollar is used to purchase final goods and services during a year. It is equal to GNP divided by the stock of money.

The **velocity of money** (V) is simply the average number of times a dollar is used to purchase a final product or service during a year. Velocity is equal to nominal GNP divided by the size of the money stock. For example, in 1990 GNP was equal to $5,463 billion while the M1 money supply was $826 billion. On average, each dollar in the M1 money supply was used 6.6 times to purchase final product goods and services included in GNP. The velocity of the M1 money stock therefore was 6.6. The velocity of the M2 money stock can be derived in a similar manner. In 1990, the M2 money stock was $3,323 billion. Thus, the velocity of M2 was 1.64 ($5,463 billion ÷ $3,323 billion).

The concept of velocity is closely related to the demand for money. When decision-makers conduct a specific amount of business with a smaller amount of money, their demand for money balances is reduced. Each dollar, though, is now being used more often. Therefore, the velocity of money is increasing. Thus, for a given income level, when the demand for money declines, the velocity of money increases.

When considering the behavior of prices, output, money, and velocity over time, we can write the quantity theory equation in terms of growth rates:

Growth of Real Output + Rate of Inflation= Growth Rate of the Money Supply
+ Growth Rate of Velocity

Equation of Exchange:
$MV = PY$, where M is the money supply, V is the velocity of money, P is the price level, and Y is the output of goods and services produced.

The $MV = PY$ relationship is simply an identity, or a tautology. Economists refer to it as the **equation of exchange,** since it reflects both the monetary and real sides of each final product exchange. The quantity theory of money, though, postulates that Y and V are determined by factors other than the amount of money in circulation. Classical economists believed that real output Y was determined by such factors as technology, the size of the economy's resource base, and the skill of the labor force. These factors were thought to be insensitive to changes in the money supply.

Similarly, classical economists thought the velocity of money was determined primarily by institutional factors such as the organization of banking and credit, the frequency of income payments, the rapidity of transportation, and the communication system. These factors would change quite slowly. Thus, classical economists thought that for all practical purposes, the velocity or "turn over" rate of money in the short run was constant.

If both Y and V are constant, the $MV = PY$ relationship indicates that an increase in the money supply will lead to a proportional increase in the price level. For classical economists, the link between the money supply and the price level was quite mechanical. An increase in the quantity of money led to a proportional increase in the price level. Of course, they recognized that the link might not always be exact. For the purposes of theory, though, it was a reasonably close approximation to reality according to the classical theory.

EARLY KEYNESIAN VIEWS ON MONEY

The Keynesian revolution emphasized the importance of aggregate demand. This notwithstanding, early Keynesians had little confidence in the ability of changes in the money supply to stimulate additional demand, particularly during an economic recession. During the 1950s, it was popular to draw an analogy between monetary policy and the workings of a string. Like a string, monetary policy could be used to pull (hold back) the economy and thereby control inflation. However, just as one cannot push with a string, monetary policy could not be used to push (stimulate) aggregate demand.

In his book, *General Theory,* John Maynard Keynes offered a plausible explanation for why monetary policy might be an ineffective method of stimulating demand. What if the direction of changes in velocity were opposite to the direction of changes in the money stock? If a 5 percent increase in the supply of money led to a 5 percent reduction in velocity, monetary policy would directly influence neither real income nor the price level. Keynes himself recognized this was a highly atypical situation. He was *not* an advocate of the extreme position that held that changes in the money supply were of no consequence.[2] In the shadow of the Great Depression, though, many of his early followers took the unusual to be typical.

THE VIEWS OF THE MONETARISTS

Monetarists: A group of economists who believe that (a) monetary instability is the major cause of fluctuations in real GNP and (b) rapid growth of the money supply is the major cause of inflation.

Beginning in the late 1950s, economists hotly debated the potency of changes in the supply of money. Led by Milton Friedman, later a Nobel laureate, a group of economists, subsequently called **monetarists,** challenged the existing Keynesian view. In contrast with the early Keynesians, the monetarists argued that changes in the stock of money exerted a powerful influence on both nominal and real GNP, as well as on the level of prices.

The monetarists charged that erratic monetary policy was the primary source of both business instability and inflation. As Milton Friedman stated in his 1967 presidential address to the American Economic Association:

> Every major contraction in this country has been either produced by monetary disorder or greatly exacerbated by monetary disorder. Every major inflation has been produced by monetary expansion.[3]

Discretionary Monetary Policy: Changes in monetary policy instituted at the discretion of policy-makers. The policy is not predetermined by rules or formulas.

While monetarists believe that monetary policy exerts a powerful influence on the economy, they reject active use of **discretionary monetary policy** as an effective stabilization tool. According to the monetarist view, there are lengthy and unpredictable time lags between the implementation of a policy change and the observation of its primary effects. When policy-makers change the direction of monetary policy, it may be between 6 and 18 months before the change exerts much effect on output. Correspondingly, the effects on the price level may not be felt for 12 to 36 months. During such lengthy time periods, market conditions may change dramatically. A policy that is appropriate now may be highly inappropriate when it exerts its primary impact 12, 18, or 24 months in the future. Given the length and

---

[2]Keynes thought that money did matter, even during a recession. He stated: "So long as there is unemployment, employment will change in the same proportion as the quantity of money, and when there is full employment, prices will change in the same proportion as the quantity of money."[*The General Theory of Employment, Interest, and Money* (New York: Harcourt, 1936), p. 296.

[3]Milton Friedman, "The Role of Monetary Policy," *American Economic Review* (March 1968), p. 12.

variability of these lags, monetarists argue that it is a mistake for decision-makers to alter monetary policy in light of current economic conditions. Monetarists believe that economic stability would be enhanced if the money supply were simply expanded at a rate equal to the economy's long-run rate of economic growth (approximately 3 percent).

THE MODERN VIEW OF MONETARY POLICY

After nearly three decades of debate between Keynesians and monetarists concerning various aspects of monetary policy, a consensus view has emerged in some areas, while differences remain in others. Both modern Keynesians and monetarists, however, agree that monetary policy exerts an important impact on our economy.

THE TRANSMISSION OF MONETARY POLICY

The modern consensus view of monetary policy transmission has both Keynesian and monetarist roots. The modern view indicates that there are two channels through which changes in monetary policy are transmitted to the goods and services market. One of the channels was previously stressed by Keynesians and the other primarily by monetarists. Exhibits 2 and 3 illustrate both of the channels.

First, let us consider the interest rate transmission of monetary policy, the mechanism generally stressed by economists of Keynesian persuasion. Consider an economy initially experiencing equilibrium in the money, loanable funds, and goods and services markets. As Exhibit 2 illustrates, the public is just willing to hold the existing money stock (S_1) provided by the Fed at the money interest rate (i). Initially, the money interest is equal to the real interest rate (r_1), indicating that the expected rate of inflation is zero.

Expansionary Monetary Policy: An acceleration in the growth rate of the money supply.

What will happen if the Fed shifts to **expansionary monetary policy**— if it unexpectedly increases the supply of money from S_1 to S_2? The increase in the money supply leaves decision-makers with larger money balances than they desire to hold. The public will take steps to reduce their **excess supply of money.** Exhibit 2 shows how the public's response to an excess supply of money is transmitted through the interest rate to the goods and services market. To reduce their excess holdings of money balances, people will transfer funds from their checking accounts into savings accounts, bonds, stocks, and other financial assets. As they do, the supply of loanable funds will increase to S_2 (Exhibit 2, frame b). In the short run, the real interest rate will fall to r_2.

Excess Supply of Money: Situation in which the actual money balances of individuals and business firms are in excess of their desired level. Thus, decision-makers will increase their spending on other assets and goods until they reduce their actual balances to the desired level.

The Fed generally pumps additional money into the economy via open market operations—the purchase of bonds in the open market. This method of increasing the money supply highlights the impact of expansionary monetary policy on the real rate of interest. When the Fed purchases bonds, it bids up bond prices and creates excess reserves for the banking system. The higher bond prices directly reduce interest rates. The additional reserves will increase the incentive of banks to cut interest rates in order to extend more loans. Expansionary monetary policy thus places downward pressure on the real interest rate, *in the short run*.

How will the lower interest rate influence the demand for goods and services? The lower real interest rate makes *current* investment and consumption cheaper relative to future spending. At the lower interest rate, entrepreneurs will undertake some investment projects they otherwise would have forgone. Spending by firms on plant and equipment will increase. Similarly, consumers will decide to expand their purchases of automobiles and consumer durables, which can now be enjoyed with smaller monthly payments. As Exhibit 2c illustrates, aggregate demand increases to AD_2.

Many economists, particularly monetarists, believe that monetary policy also can be transmitted via a more direct path. Exhibit 3 illustrates this point. Once again, an unanticipated increase in the money supply (shift from S_1 to S_2) leaves the public with an excess supply of money balances. Instead of increasing their spending exclusively or even primarily on bonds (and other saving instruments), suppose decision-makers reduce their unexpected build-up of money balances by spending more on a broad cross-section of goods and services. Households increase their spending on clothes, appliances, personal computers, automobiles and recreational activities. Businesses purchase additional machinery or add to their fixed investments. To the extent this route is chosen, there will be a direct increase in the aggregate demand for goods and services. Again, AD_1 shifts rightward to AD_2.

EXHIBIT 2

The Transmission of Monetary Policy— Interest Rate Path

Here we illustrate the transmission of monetary policy via changes in interest rates. The monetary expansion creates an excess supply of money balances, which induces individuals to purchase more bonds and thereby expand the supply of loanable funds (to S_2). The real interest rate falls (to r_2), which increases aggregate demand (to AD_2). Since the effects of the monetary expansion were unanticipated, the expansion in AD leads to both an increase in current output (to Y_2) and higher prices (inflation) in the short run.

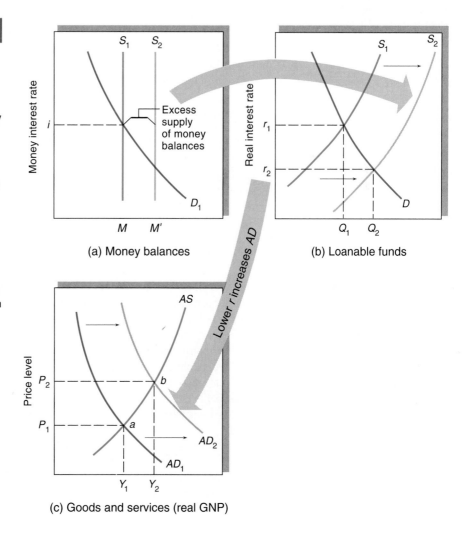

(a) Money balances

(b) Loanable funds

(c) Goods and services (real GNP)

EXHIBIT 3

The Short-Run Effects of Monetary Policy—Direct Path

Here we illustrate the direct transmission of monetary policy to the goods and services market. An unanticipated increase in the supply of money (shift to S_2, frame a) generates an excess supply of money, which causes individuals to spend more, not just on bonds, but also on goods and services directly. Aggregate demand increases. As in the case of transmission via the real interest rate, the predicted results are higher prices (inflation) and an increase in real GNP *in the short run*.

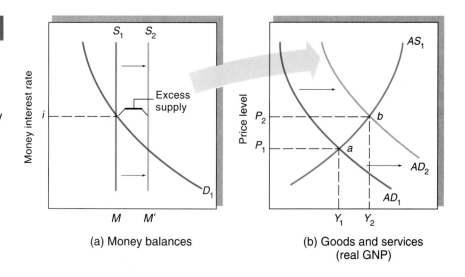

(a) Money balances

(b) Goods and services (real GNP)

UNANTICIPATED EXPANSIONARY MONETARY POLICY

Aggregate demand (nominal spending on GNP) is closely linked to the money supply (M) and the velocity of money (V). As the equation of exchange highlights, in a sense, MV is the same thing as aggregate demand (AD). An increase in either M or V will increase spending and thereby shift the AD schedule to the right. In contrast, a decrease in either M or V will shift the AD schedule to the left.

As we have previously discussed, modern macroeconomic analysis stresses the importance of whether a change is anticipated or unanticipated. If people do not anticipate the increase in aggregate demand accompanying an expansionary monetary policy, costs will rise less than prices in the short run. Profit margins will improve. Businesses will respond with an expansion in the output of goods and services (as illustrated by the increase in real output from Y_1 to Y_2 in both Exhibits 2 and 3).

Modern analysis indicates that an unexpected increase in the supply of money will lower the real interest rate and/or directly expand the demand for goods and services. As a result, aggregate demand will increase, leading to a short-run expansion in real output and employment.

Exhibit 4a illustrates the potential of expansionary monetary policy to direct a recessionary economy to full employment capacity. Consider an economy initially at output Y_1, below full employment capacity (Y_f). Expansionary monetary policy will increase aggregate demand (to AD_2). Real output will expand (to Y_f). In essence, the expansionary monetary policy provides an alternative to the economy's self-corrective mechanism. In the absence of demand stimulus, declining resource prices and real interest rates would eventually restore full employment. But many economists believe that this mechanism works too slowly. If this is the case, expansionary monetary policy will restore long-run, full employment equilibrium more rapidly.

How would a shift to expansionary monetary policy influence output and the price level if the economy were already at full employment? While this is generally not a desirable strategy, nonetheless, it is interesting to analyze the outcome. As Exhibit 4b illustrates, in the short run, an unanticipated increase in aggregate

Initial Economic Conditions and the Effects of Expansionary Monetary Policy

If the impact of an increase in aggregate demand accompanying expansionary monetary policy is felt when the economy is operating below capacity, the policy will help direct the economy to a long-run full employment equilibrium (frame a). In this case, the increase in output from Y_1 to Y_f will be long term. In contrast, if the demand stimulus effects are imposed on an economy already at full employment (frame b), they will lead to an inflationary gap. Output will temporarily increase (to Y_2, frame b). However, in the long run, the strong demand will push up resource prices shifting short-run aggregate supply to $SRAS_2$. The price level will rise to P_3 and output will recede (to Y_f) from its temporary high.

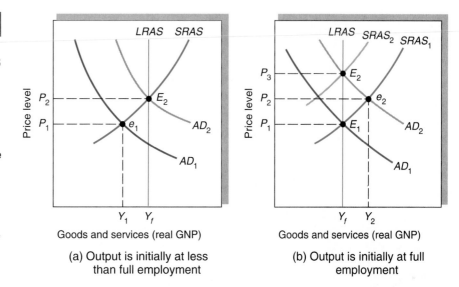

(a) Output is initially at less than full employment

(b) Output is initially at full employment

demand resulting from a shift to a more expansionary monetary policy will temporarily push real output (to Y_2) beyond the economy's long-run capacity (Y_f). Since important components of costs (for example, union wage contracts, fixed-interest loans, and lease agreements) are fixed in the short run, the strong demand for goods and services will temporarily increase product prices relative to costs. Profit margins will improve, providing the incentive for business firms to produce the larger output. Unemployment will fall below the natural rate of unemployment.

However, the high rate of output (Y_2, Exhibit 4b) and employment will not be sustainable. Eventually, long-term contracts based on the previously weaker demand (AD_1) will expire. New agreements will reflect the stronger demand. Resource prices will rise, shifting *SRAS* upward to the left. Eventually, long-run equilibrium (E_2, Exhibit 4b) will result at a higher price level (P_3). Output will recede to Y_f. Therefore, when an economy is already at full employment, an unexpected increase in the money supply will temporarily increase output, but in the long run it merely leads to higher prices. Hence, the wisdom of a shift to a more expansionary monetary policy is highly questionable when an economy is already operating at (or beyond) its full-employment capacity.

Restrictive Monetary Policy: A deceleration in the growth rate of the money supply.

UNANTICIPATED RESTRICTIVE MONETARY POLICY

Suppose the Fed moves toward a more **restrictive monetary policy** and reduces the money supply (or in dynamic terms, reduces its rate of growth). How would a reduction in the money supply influence the economy? To stimulate your thoughts on this topic, consider what would happen if someone, perhaps a foreign agent, destroyed half of the U.S. money stock. We simply awake one morning and find that half of the cash in our billfolds and half of the checkable deposits in our banks are gone. Ignore, for the sake of analysis, the liability of bankers and the fact that the federal government would take corrective action. Just ask yourself, ''What has changed because of the drastic reduction in the money supply?'' The work force is the same. Our buildings, machines, land, and other productive resources are untouched. There are no consumer durables missing. Only the money, half of yesterday's money supply, is gone.

OUTSTANDING ECONOMIST

Milton Friedman (1912–   )

Always provocative and energetic, Friedman is perhaps the most influential spokesman for a free society in the twentieth century. Through his numerous articles and lectures, best-selling books (several co-authored with his wife, Rose, who is also an economist), and widely viewed television series *Free to Choose,* he has exerted an enormous impact on both economists and the general public.

Friedman was the 1976 recipient of the Nobel Prize in economics. His scholarly activity has focused on macroeconomics. He developed the permanent income hypothesis of consumption. But, his most influential work may very well be an 850-page treatise (coauthored with Anna Schwartz), entitled *A Monetary History of the United States*. The book, already a classic, is a gold mine of monetary and aggregate economic data. Based on this analysis and related work, Friedman argues that business fluctuations are the result of short-run changes in the supply of money. According to Friedman, the key to a healthy, stable economy is a constant rate of growth in the money supply.

Friedman retired from his professorship at the University of Chicago in 1977. He continues his scholarly work at Stanford's Hoover Institution, while continuing to challenge a new generation of economists with writings and lectures.

Exhibit 5 sheds some light on the situation. To make things simple, let us assume that before the calamity, the money balances of individuals and businesses were at the desired level, given current incomes and interest rates. Hence, the reduction in the supply of money (shift from S_1 to S_2) leaves people with less than the desired amount of money. People want to hold larger money balances, but the reduction in the money stock prevents them from doing so. Attempting to remedy the situation, people will try to restore at least part of their shrunken money balances.

How do people increase their money balances? Answer: they draw on their past savings, sell bonds and other liquid assets, and cut back on their current spending. As people reduce their savings and purchase fewer bonds, the supply of loanable funds will fall (relative to demand), causing the real rate of interest to increase. In turn, the higher real interest rate will induce both investors and consumers to cut back on their purchases of current goods and services. Simultaneously, others will seek to rebuild their money balances directly by spending less during the current period. Both the higher real interest rate and the direct reduction in current purchases will reduce aggregate demand (shift from AD_1 to AD_2, Exhibit 5b).

In turn, the unexpected decline in the demand for goods and services will place downward pressure on prices, squeeze profit margins, and reduce output. As Exhibit 5b illustrates, the price level tends to move toward P_2 and output tends to move toward Y_2 as the result of the restrictive monetary policy.

The appropriateness of a restrictive policy is dependent upon the initial state of the economy. Exhibit 6 illustrates this point. When an economy is experiencing

The Short-Run Effects of a Reduction in the Money Supply When the Effects Are Unanticipated

A reduction in the money supply creates an excess demand for money balances. Economic agents will seek to restore their money balances by drawing on their savings, purchasing fewer bonds, and/or spending less on goods and services. As a result, aggregate demand will decline (shift to AD_2). When the reduction in aggregate demand is unanticipated, real output will decline (to Y_2) and downward pressure on prices will result.

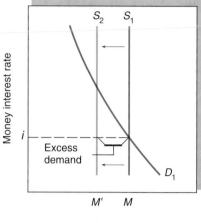

(a) Money balances

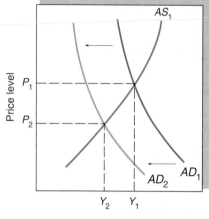

(b) Goods and services (real GNP)

upward pressure on prices as the result of strong demand, restrictive policy is an effective weapon against inflation. Suppose that, as illustrated by Exhibit 6a, an economy is temporarily operating at e_1 and Y_1, beyond its full-employment real GNP of Y_f. Strong aggregate demand is placing upward pressure on prices. The problem is inflation, not recession. Under these circumstances, restrictive policy makes good sense. It would help control the inflation. If the proper dosage is timed correctly, restrictive policy would retard aggregate demand (to AD_2) and direct the economy to a noninflationary, long-run equilibrium at P_2 and Y_f (E_2).

As Exhibit 6b illustrates, however, an unanticipated shift to restrictive policy would be damaging if applied to an economy in full-employment equilibrium. If the output of an economy is at full employment (or worse still, at less than full employment), a shift to restrictive policy would reduce aggregate demand (shift to AD_2) and throw the economy into a recession. Real GNP would decline from Y_f to Y_2. Output would fall below the economy's full-employment capacity and unemployment would rise above the natural rate of unemployment.

PROPER TIMING

As with fiscal policy, monetary policy must be properly timed if it is to help stabilize an economy. Exhibits 4 and 6 emphasize this point. When an economy is operating below its long-run capacity, expansionary monetary policy can stimulate demand and push the output of the economy to its sustainable potential (Exhibit 4a). Similarly, if properly timed, restrictive monetary policy can help control (or prevent) inflation (Exhibit 6a). But if improperly timed, monetary policy can be destabilizing. Expansionary monetary policy is a source of inflation if the effects of the policy are felt when the economy is already at or beyond its capacity (Exhibit 4b). Similarly, if the effects of a restrictive policy come when an economy is operating at its potential GNP, recession is the likely outcome (Exhibit 6b). Worse still, the impact of restrictive policy may be disastrous if imposed on an economy already in the midst of a recession (see the Applications in Economics box ''What Caused the Great Depression?'').

Proper timing of monetary policy is not an easy task. In contrast with fiscal policy changes requiring time-consuming congressional action, the Federal Reserve can institute a change in monetary policy quite rapidly. However, as an economy drifts toward a recession or an inflationary boom, policy-makers may not

EXHIBIT 6

Initial Economic Conditions and the Effects of Restrictive Monetary Policy

The stabilization effects of restrictive monetary policy are dependent upon the state of the economy when the policy exerts its primary impact. Restrictive monetary policy will reduce aggregate demand. If the demand restraint comes during a period of strong demand and an overheated economy, then it will limit or even prevent the occurrence of an inflationary boom (frame a). In contrast, if the reduction in aggregate demand takes place when the economy is at full employment, then it will disrupt long-run equilibrium, reduce output, and result in a recession (frame b).

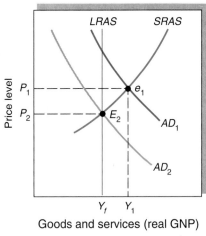

(a) Restrictive policy to control inflation

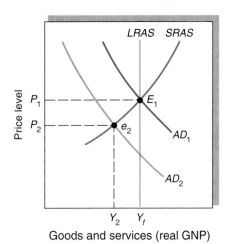

(b) Restrictive policy which causes a recession

immediately recognize the need for a change. Therefore, there may be a time lag of several months between the change in economic conditions and when policy-makers at the Fed recognize that change. More importantly, there will be an additional time lag between the institution of a policy and when it exerts an impact on aggregate demand. Economists who have studied this issue estimate that this *effectiveness lag* will be 5 or 6 months at a minimum. Some economists, particularly monetarists, estimate that the primary impact of a change in monetary policy on the price level is sometimes as much as 18 to 36 months after the change is instituted. Given our limited ability to forecast the future, such time lags make it extremely difficult to institute monetary policy in a countercyclical manner. Therefore, most economists now believe that monetary policy-makers should respond only to major economic disturbances, rather than attempting to smooth out every turn in the economic road.

MONETARY POLICY IN THE LONG RUN

Thus far, we have focused on the impact of monetary policy in a static framework. Of course, in a static framework, an increase in the price level implies inflation. However, inflation is a dynamic concept—a *rate of increase* in prices, not a once-and-for-all movement to a higher price level. It is also important to distinguish between the static and dynamic with regard to the money supply. Static analysis focuses on the change in the supply of money. In a dynamic setting, though, a change in the *growth rate* of the money supply is more indicative of the direction of monetary policy.

In this section, we want to recast our analysis slightly so we can better illustrate both dynamic factors and the long-run adjustment process. We will begin with a simple dynamic case. Suppose that the output of an economy is growing at a 3 percent annual rate and that the monetary authorities are expanding the money supply by 3 percent each year. In addition, let's assume that the velocity of money is constant. This would imply that the 3 percent increase in output would lead to a

3 percent increase in the demand for money. Under these circumstances, the 3 percent monetary growth would be consistent with stable prices (zero inflation). Initially, we will assume that the economy's real interest rate is 4 percent. Since the inflation rate is zero, the nominal rate of interest is also equal to 4 percent. Exhibits 7 and 8 illustrate an economy initially (period 1) characterized by these conditions.

What will happen if the monetary authorities permanently increase the growth rate of the money supply from 3 percent to 8 percent annually (Exhibit 7a, beginning in period 2)? In the short run, the expansionary monetary policy will reduce the real interest rate and stimulate aggregate demand (shift to AD_2), just as we previously explained (Exhibits 2 and 3). For a time, real output may exceed the economy's potential. However, as they confront strong demand conditions, many resource suppliers (who previously committed to long-term agreements) will wish they had anticipated the strength of demand and driven harder bargains. With the passage of time, more and more resource suppliers (including labor represented by union officials) will have the opportunity to raise prices and wages in order to rectify past mistakes. As they do so, costs will rise and profit margins will be squeezed. The higher costs will reduce aggregate supply (shift to AS_2). As the rapid monetary growth continues in subsequent periods (3, 4, 5, and so on), both AD and AS will shift upward. The price level will rise to P_{105}, P_{110}, and on to still higher levels as the money supply continues to grow more rapidly than the monetary growth rate consistent with stable prices. The rapid monetary growth leads to a continual rise in the price level—that is, a sustained inflation.

EXHIBIT 7

The Long-run Effects of More Rapid Expansion in the Money Supply— Goods and Services Market

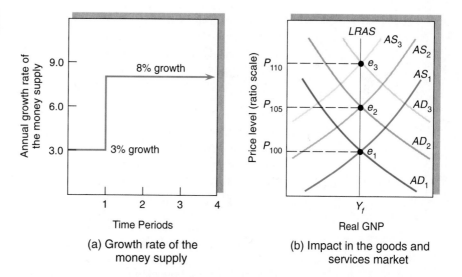

(a) Growth rate of the money supply

(b) Impact in the goods and services market

Here we illustrate the long-term impact of an increase in the annual growth rate of the money supply from 3 to 8 percent. Initially, prices are stable (P_{100}) when the money supply is expanding 3 percent annually. The acceleration in the growth rate of the money supply increases aggregate demand (shift to AD_2). At first, real output may expand beyond the economy's potential (Y_f). However, abnormally low unemployment and strong demand conditions will create upward pressure on wages and other resource prices, shifting aggregate supply to AS_2. Output will return to its long-run potential and the price level will increase to $P_{105}(e_2)$. If the more rapid monetary growth continues in subsequent periods, AD and AS will continue to shift upward, leading to still higher prices (e_3 and points beyond). The net result of this process is sustained inflation.

EXHIBIT 8

The Long-Run Effects of More Rapid Expansion in the Money Supply— Loanable Funds Market

When prices are stable, supply and demand in the loanable funds market are in balance at a real and nominal interest rate of 4 percent. If more rapid monetary expansion leads to a long-term 5 percent inflation rate (see Exhibit 7), borrowers and lenders will build the higher inflation rate into their decision-making. As a result, the nominal interest rate (i) will rise to 9 percent—the 4 percent real rate plus a 5 percent inflationary premium.

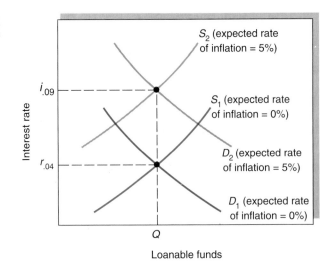

Suppose an inflation rate of 5 percent eventually emerges from the more rapid growth rate (8 percent rather than 3 percent) of the money supply. With the passage of time, more and more people will adjust their decision-making in light of the persistent 5 percent inflation. In the resource market, both buyers and sellers will eventually incorporate the expectation of the 5 percent inflation rate into long-term contracts such as collective bargaining agreements. Once that happens, resource prices and costs will rise as rapidly as prices in the goods and services market. *When the inflation rate is anticipated fully, it will fail to either reduce real wages or improve profit margins.* Unemployment will return to its natural rate.

Exhibit 8 illustrates the adjustments in the loanable funds market once borrowers and lenders expect the 5 percent inflation rate. When lenders anticipate a 5 percent annual increase in the price level, a 9 percent interest rate will be necessary to provide them with as much incentive to supply loanable funds as 4 percent interest provided when stable prices were expected. Thus, the supply of loanable funds will shift vertically by the 5 percent expected rate of inflation. Simultaneously, borrowers who were willing to pay 4 percent interest on loans when they expected stable prices will be willing to pay 9 percent when they expect prices to increase 5 percent annually. The demand for loanable funds will therefore also increase (shift vertically) by the expected rate of inflation. Once borrowers and lenders anticipate the higher (5 percent) inflation rate, the equilibrium money interest rate will rise to 9 percent. Of course, the real interest rate is equal to the money interest rate (9 percent) minus the expected rate of inflation (5 percent). In the long run, a 4 percent real interest rate will emerge with inflation, just as it did with stable prices.[4] Inflation will fail to reduce the real interest rate in the long run.

Modern analysis indicates that the long-run effects of rapid monetary growth differ from the short-run effects of an *un*anticipated move to expansionary monetary

---

[4]Higher rates of inflation are generally associated with an increase in the *variability* of the inflation rate. Thus, greater risk (the possibility of either a substantial gain or loss associated with a sharp change in the inflation rate) accompanies exchange in the loanable funds market when inflation rates are high. This additional risk may result in *higher* real interest rates than would prevail at lower rates of inflation. The text discussion does not introduce this consideration.

policy. In the long run, the major consequences of rapid monetary growth are inflation and higher nominal interest rates. Rapid monetary growth will neither reduce unemployment nor stimulate real output in the long run.

MONETARY POLICY WHEN THE EFFECTS ARE ANTICIPATED

Thus far, we have assumed that decision-makers come to anticipate the effects of monetary policy only *after they begin to occur*. For example, we assumed that borrowers and lenders began to anticipate a higher inflation rate only after prices began to rise more rapidly. Similarly, resource suppliers anticipated the inflation only after it had begun.

What if enough decision-makers in the market catch on to the link between expansionary monetary policy and an acceleration in the inflation rate? What if, in effect, they learn the model that you have learned? Suppose borrowers and lenders start paying attention to the money supply figures. Observing substantial increases in the money supply, they revise upward their expectation of the inflation rate. Lenders become more reluctant to supply loanable funds. Simultaneously, borrowers increase their demand for loanable funds at existing rates of interest because they also anticipate a higher rate of future inflation and they want to buy now before prices rise. Under these circumstances, a reduction in supply and an increase in demand for loanable funds will quickly push up the money interest rate. If borrowers and lenders *quickly and accurately* forecast the future rate of inflation accompanying the monetary expansion, the real interest rate will decline only for a short period of time, if at all.

If buyers and sellers in the goods and services market also watch the money supply figures, they too may anticipate its inflationary consequences. As buyers anticipate the future price increases, many will buy now rather than later. Current aggregate demand will rise. Similarly, expecting an acceleration in the inflation rate, sellers will be reluctant to sell except at premium prices. Current aggregate supply will fall. This combination of factors will quickly push prices of goods and services upward.

Simultaneously, if buyers and sellers in the resource market believe that more rapid monetary growth will lead to a higher rate of inflation, they too will build this view into long-run contracts. Union officials will demand and employers will pay an inflationary premium for future money wages, based on their expectation of inflation. Alternatively, they may write an **escalator clause** into their collective bargaining agreements that will automatically raise money wages when the inflation transpires. If decision-makers in the resource market correctly anticipate the inflation, *real* resource prices will not decline once prices accelerate upward.

As Exhibit 9 illustrates, when individuals correctly anticipate the effects of expansionary monetary policy *prior to their occurrence*, the short-run impact of monetary policy is much like its impact in the long run. The price level will increase, pushing up money income (P_2Y_1), but real income (Y_1) will be unchanged. Nominal interest rates will rise, but real interest rates will be unchanged. Thus, when the effects of expansionary monetary policy are fully anticipated, it exerts little impact on real economic activity.

Escalator Clause:
A contractual agreement that periodically and automatically adjusts money wage rates upward as the price level rises. They are sometimes referred to as cost-of-living adjustments or COLAs.

The Short-Run Effects of
Monetary Expansion
When the Effects Are
Anticipated

When decision-makers fully
anticipate the effects of
monetary expansion, monetary
policy does not alter real output
even in the short run.
Suppliers, including resource
suppliers, build the expected
price rise into their decisions.
The anticipated inflation leads
to a rise in nominal costs
(including wages), causing
aggregate supply to decline
(shift to AS_2). While nominal
wages, prices, and interest
rates rise, their real
counterparts are unchanged.
The result: inflation without any
change in real output (Y_1).

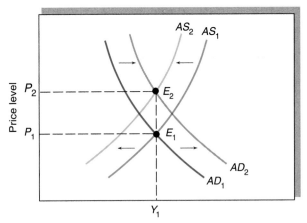

Goods and services (real GNP)

Are people likely to anticipate the effects of monetary policy? This is a topic of hot debate among economists. We will consider the topic in more detail in the next chapter. Since the effects of monetary policy differ substantially depending on whether they are anticipated, this is clearly a very important topic.

NOMINAL INTEREST RATES, THE VELOCITY OF MONEY, AND MONETARY POLICY

How will an increase in nominal interest rates affect the velocity of money? Higher interest rates will increase the opportunity cost of holding money. As the result of this increase in cost, people will reduce their money balances. They will seek to conduct a given volume of business with a smaller average money balance. This is simply another way of saying that the velocity of money will increase as interest rates rise. Hence, there will be a direct relationship between the nominal interest rate and the velocity of money.

This linkage between nominal interest rates and the velocity of money helps explain why the *immediate* effects of shifts in monetary policy on output and prices (nominal GNP) may be dampened. Remember, when the Fed shifts toward monetary expansion, it generally does so by purchasing more bonds in the open market. These bond purchases will tend to increase bond prices and push interest rates downward. Initially, *nominal* interest rates, as well as real rates, may decline. If nominal interest rates fall, the velocity of money will also decline. In turn, the decline in velocity will dampen the *initial* expansionary effects of the monetary policy. As the monetary expansion persists, however, the lower *real* interest rates will stimulate aggregate demand and output (see Exhibit 2). Eventually, strong demand and upward pressure on prices will lead to an increase in the expected rate of inflation, which will cause nominal interest rates to rise and the velocity of money to increase. However, several quarters may pass before nominal interest rates and the velocity of money reverse and begin to rise. Once this reversal takes place, the expansionary effects of the initial monetary expansion will be amplified by the high nominal interest rates. So long as the high nominal interest rates continue, the velocity of money will remain at a high level. This will make it more difficult for policy-makers to control inflation. Therefore, to the extent that expansionary monetary policy *temporarily* reduces nominal interest rates and the velocity of money, the *initial* demand stimulus effects will be dampened and the *primary* expansionary effects pushed (perhaps 12 to 30 months) into the future.

The same forces are also present in the case of a shift to a more restrictive monetary policy. When shifting toward restriction, the Fed generally sells bonds, which tends to push bond prices down and interest rates up. For a time, both nominal and real interest rates may rise as the result of the tight money policy. If nominal interest rates rise, the velocity of money will tend to increase, which will promote additional spending and, *for a time,* dampen the restrictive effects of this policy. Of course, the restrictive policy, if continued, will eventually begin to retard inflation and lower nominal interest rates, which will reduce the velocity of money. Once this happens, and many months may pass before it does, the restrictive policy will be highly potent.

Is there any evidence that the initial effects of monetary policy shifts are dampened as the result of changes in nominal interest rates and the velocity of money? Exhibit 10 presents data on this topic. During the last three decades, there

EXHIBIT 10 ■ Shifts in Monetary Policy, Interest Rates, and the Velocity of Money				
Monetary Policy	Changes in the Money Supply		Nominal Interest Rate[a]	Velocity M2
	M1	M2		
Shifts to Expansion[b]				
1966	2.5	4.5	4.88	1.61
1967	6.5	9.2	4.32	1.56
1970	5.1	6.5	6.46	1.62
1971	6.5	13.5	4.35	1.55
1975	4.8	12.6	5.84	1.56
1976	6.5	13.7	4.99	1.53
1982	8.7	8.9	10.69	1.62
1983	9.8	12.0	8.63	1.56
1985	12.3	8.4	7.48	1.56
1986	16.3	9.5	5.98	1.50
Shifts to Restriction[b]				
1965	4.7	8.1	3.95	1.53
1966	2.5	4.5	4.88	1.61
1968	7.7	8.0	5.34	1.58
1969	3.3	4.1	6.68	1.73
1972	9.2	13.0	4.07	1.51
1973	5.5	6.9	7.04	1.58
1983	9.8	12.0	8.63	1.56
1984	5.9	8.5	9.58	1.59
1986	16.9	9.5	5.98	1.50
1987	3.5	3.5	5.82	1.55

[a]The 3-month Treasury bill rate.
[b] As measured by changes in the growth rate of both M1 and M2.
Source: *Economic Report of the President, 1991.*

have been five major year-to-year shifts toward expansionary monetary policy (as measured by the acceleration in the growth rates of *both* M1 and M2). In each case, the monetary acceleration was associated with a decline in both nominal interest rates and the velocity of money (M2). Therefore, while lower real interest rates were stimulating additional spending, the short-run decline in nominal interest rates and velocity was retarding it. Thus, the full expansionary effects of these monetary accelerations were pushed into the future.

Exhibit 10 also presents data for the last five major shifts toward restrictive monetary policy. Again, the data indicate that initially the shifts to the more restrictive policy were associated with both higher nominal interest rates and an increase in the velocity of money. As the result of these increases in the velocity of money, the changes in nominal income (output and prices) were initially less pronounced than the deceleration in monetary growth.

EFFECTS OF MONETARY POLICY—A SUMMARY

The accompanying Thumbnail Sketch summarizes the theoretical implications of our analysis. The impact of monetary policy on major economic variables is indicated for three alternatives: (1) the short run when the effects are unanticipated, (2) the short run when the effects are anticipated, and (3) the long run. Note that the impact of monetary policy in the latter two cases is the same. When decision-makers quickly anticipate the effects of monetary policy, the adjustment process speeds up, and therefore the short-run effects are identical to the long-run effects. Under these circumstances, only nominal variables (money interest rates and the inflation rate) are affected. Real variables (real GNP, employment, and the real interest rate) are unaffected.

Five major predictions flow from our analysis.

1. An unanticipated shift to a more expansionary (restrictive) monetary policy will temporarily stimulate (retard) output and employment. As Exhibits 2 and 3 illustrate, an increase in aggregate demand emanating from an unanticipated increase in the money supply will lead to a short-run expansion in real output and employment. Conversely, as Exhibit 5 shows, an unanticipated move toward more restrictive monetary policy reduces aggregate demand and retards real output.

2. The stabilizing effects of a change in monetary policy are dependent upon the state of the economy when the effects of the policy change are observed. If the effects of an expansionary policy come when the economy is operating at less than capacity, then the demand stimulus will push the economy toward full employment. However, if the demand stimulus comes when the economy is operating at or beyond capacity, it will contribute to an acceleration in the inflation rate. Correspondingly, restrictive policy will help to control inflation if the demand-restraining effects are felt when output is beyond the economy's long-run capacity. On the other hand, restrictive policy will result in recession if the reduction in demand comes when the economy is at or below long-run capacity.

3. Persistent growth of the money supply at a rapid rate will cause inflation. While the short-run effects of expansionary monetary policy may be primarily on output,

THUMBNAIL SKETCH

Impact of Monetary Policy—A Summary

	The Short-Run Effects When the Policy Is Unanticipated (1)	The Short-Run Effects When the Policy Is Anticipated[a] (2)	and The Long-Run Effects (3)
Impact of expansionary monetary policy on:			
Inflation rate	Only a small increase, particularly if excess capacity is present	Increases	
Real output and employment	Long-term increase if excess capacity is present; otherwise they increase temporarily	No change	
Money interest rate	Small increase (perhaps following an initial decrease)	Increases	
Real interest rate	Decreases	No change	
Impact of restrictive monetary policy on:			
Inflation rate	Only a small decrease	Decreases	
Real output and employment	Decrease, particularly if economy at less than capacity	No change	
Money interest rate	Small decrease (perhaps following an initial increase)	Decreases	
Real interest rate	Increases	No change	

[a]Beginning from long-run equilibrium.

particularly if excess capacity is present, a persistent expansion in the money supply at a rate greater than the growth of real output will cause inflation. The more rapid the sustained growth rate of the money supply (relative to real output), the higher the accompanying rate of inflation.

4. Money interest rates and the inflation rate will be directly related. As the inflation rate rises, money interest rates will increase because both borrowers and lenders will begin to expect the higher rate of inflation and build it into their decision-making. Conversely, as the inflation rate declines, a reduction in the expected rate of inflation will lead to lower money interest rates. Therefore, when monetary expansion leads to an acceleration in the inflation rate, it will also result in an increase in nominal interest rates.

5. There will be only a loose year-to-year relationship between (a) shifts in monetary policy and (b) changes in output and prices.   It takes time for markets to adjust to changing demand conditions. Some prices in both product and resource markets are set by long-term contracts. Obviously price responses in these markets will take time. In some cases, people may anticipate the effects of a policy change and adjust quickly; in other instances, the reaction to a policy change may take more time. Differences in this area will also weaken the year-to-year relationship between monetary indicators and important economic variables. In addition, movements in nominal interest rates and the velocity of money may dampen the short-term effects and amplify the long-term effects of shifts in monetary policy. This, too, will tend to weaken the year-to-year link between changes in monetary policy and changes in output and prices. Therefore, even though our analysis indicates that monetary policy does influence output and prices, the year-to-year relationships are likely to be weak.

THE MONETARY POLICY RECORD

How well does our theory predict? The next four Exhibits will help us answer this question.

A major implication of our analysis is that rapid growth rates in the money supply over long periods of time will be associated with high rates of inflation. Exhibit 11 presents data on this issue for 50 countries throughout the world. Data on the annual growth rate of the money supply (adjusted for the growth rate of the nation's output) and the rate of inflation during the 1980–1988 period are presented for each country. The results clearly illustrate the linkage between monetary policy and inflation. Just as our analysis implies, countries with low rates of monetary growth tend to experience low rates of inflation. The growth rate of the money supply was less than 5 percent in five countries (Germany, Netherlands, Canada, Japan, and Cote d'Ivoire) during 1980–1988; the accompanying inflation rate for each of these countries was also less than 5 percent. Of 17 countries that expanded the supply of money at a single-digit annual rate between 1980 and 1988, all but one (Spain, which had an inflation rate of 10.1 percent) also experienced a single-digit average rate of inflation. In contrast, of the 29 countries that expanded the supply of money at an annual rate in excess of 12 percent, all but one (Indonesia) experienced a double-digit average inflation rate during 1980–1988. Five countries (Peru, Israel, Brazil, Argentina, and Bolivia) expanded the money supply at annual rates of 99 percent or more; each of the five experienced a triple-digit average inflation rate. Similarly, countries with monetary growth rates in the 20 percent to 50 percent range tended to experience similar rates of inflation. These data indicate that in the long run there is a close relationship between monetary expansion and the rate of inflation.

EXHIBIT 11 ■ Money and Inflation—An International Comparison

Country (ranked according to low rate of money growth)	Average Annual Growth Rate of the Money Supply 1980–1988[a]	Average Annual Inflation Rate 1980–1988	Country (ranked according to low rate of money growth)	Average Annual Growth Rate of the Money Supply 1980–1988[a]	Average Annual Inflation Rate 1980–1988
Germany	3.9	2.8	Zimbabwe	15.4	12.1
Netherlands	4.2	2.0	Madagascar	15.7	17.3
Canada	4.5	4.6	Phillipines	16.0	15.6
Japan	4.9	1.3	Chile	16.3[b]	20.8
Cote d'Ivoire	4.9	3.8	Egpyt	16.5	10.6
Belgium	5.4	4.8	Venezuela	16.6	13.0
Cameroon	5.4	7.0	Indonesia	18.7	8.5
Austria	5.6	4.0	Syria	19.3	12.9
United States	6.0	4.0	Tanzania	19.5	25.7
Switzerland	6.1	3.8	Bangladesh	20.1	11.1
Spain	7.2	10.1	Portugal	20.6	20.1
Pakistan	7.9	6.5	Greece	22.7	18.9
France	8.1	7.1	Colombia	25.3	24.1
Malaysia	8.4	1.3	Sudan	25.6	33.5
Sweden	9.0	7.5	Zambia	28.2	33.5
Australia	9.4	7.8	Ghana	42.9	46.1
Korea	9.6	5.0	Turkey	45.0	39.3
Italy	10.0	11.0	Zaire	57.5	56.1
United Kingdom	10.4	5.7	Mexico	62.1	73.8
Kenya	10.7	9.6	Uganda	76.4	100.7
India	11.7	7.4	Peru	99.7	119.1
Nigeria	13.0	11.6	Israel	134.7	136.6
New Zealand	14.2	11.4	Brazil	141.7[b]	188.7
South Africa	14.5	13.9	Argentina	284.2	290.5
Guatemala	14.9	13.3	Bolivia	590.8	482.8

[a]The money supply data are for the actual growth rate of the money supply minus the growth rate of real GNP. Thus, it is the actual supply of money adjusted to reflect the country's growth rate.
[b]Data are for 1980–1985.
Source: World Book, *World Development Report: 1990*. Only countries with a population of more than 6 million in 1988 were included.

Exhibit 12 shows the relationship between changes in the growth rate of the money supply and real output since the mid-1950s for the United States. Since the introduction of interest-earning checking accounts changed the nature of M1 (and affected its growth rate) during the 1980s, the M2 money supply measure is used here. As expected, the relationship between changes in the money supply and the growth of real output is far from perfect. However, close inspection of the data does indicate that periods of sharp acceleration in the growth rate of the money supply were often associated with an acceleration in the growth rate of real GNP. For example, an acceleration in the growth rate of the money supply during 1961–1964, 1971–1972, 1976, and 1983 was associated with an increase in the growth rate of real GNP during each of the periods. The converse was also true: periods of sharp deceleration in the growth rate of the money supply were generally associated with (or followed by) economic recession. A decline in the growth rate

EXHIBIT 12

Monetary Policy and Real Output

Periods of sharp acceleration in the growth rate of the money supply, such as 1961–1964, 1971–1972, and 1976 have generally been followed by a rapid growth of GNP. In contrast, sharp declines in the growth rate of the money supply such as those experienced in 1968–1969, 1973–1974, 1977–1979, and 1987–1989 have often been associated with (or closely followed by) reductions in real GNP and economic recession. The shaded years represent periods of recession.

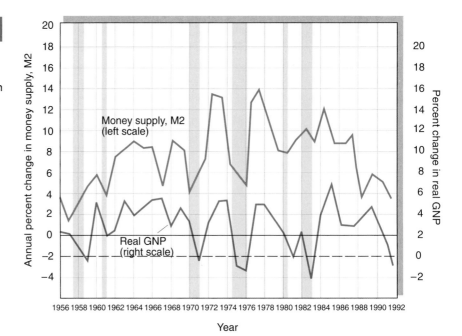

of the money supply preceded the recessions of 1958, 1960, 1970, and 1974–1975. Similarly, a sharp decline in the growth rate of the money stock from 13.7 percent in 1976 to 8 percent in 1978–1979 preceded the recession and sluggish growth of 1979–1982. Most recently, the recession of late 1990 was preceded by a substantial deceleration in the growth rate of the money supply. Hence, just as our theory predicts, there does appear to be a relationship between shifts in monetary policy and changes in real GNP. (See Applications in Economics box ''What Caused the Great Depression'' for evidence on the impact of a decline in the money supply on real output and employment.)

Exhibit 13 presents a graphic picture of the relationship between monetary policy and the inflation rate for the United States. While our theory indicates that persistent, long-term growth of the money supply will be closely associated with inflation (as illustrated by Exhibit 11), it also indicates that it will take time for a monetary expansion (or contraction) to alter demand relationships and impact prices. Most economists believe that the time lag between shifts in monetary policy and observable changes in the level of prices is often two or three years. Reflecting these views, Exhibit 13 compares the current money supply (M2) data with the inflation rate three years in the future. Once again, while the linkage is far from perfect, a definite positive relationship is observable. Most noticeably, the rapid monetary acceleration during 1971–1973 was followed by a similar acceleration in the inflation rate during 1973–1975. Similarly, the sharp monetary contraction of 1974–1975 was accompanied by, not only the recession of 1974–1975, but also a sharp deceleration in the inflation rate during 1976–1977. However, as monetary policy again shifted toward expansion in 1976–1977, the double digit inflation rates of 1979–1980 were soon to follow. During the 1980s, the linkage between monetary growth and the inflation rate a few years later appeared to weaken. To some degree this may reflect the financial innovations and changing nature of money during the 1980s. However, during the 1987–1990 period, there was a clear

EXHIBIT 13

Changes in the Money Supply and Inflation

Here we illustrate the relationship between the rate of growth in the money supply (M2) and the annual inflation rate *three years later*. While the two are not perfectly correlated, the data do indicate that periods of monetary acceleration (for example: 1971–1973, and 1976–1977) tend to be associated with an increase in the inflation rate about three years later.

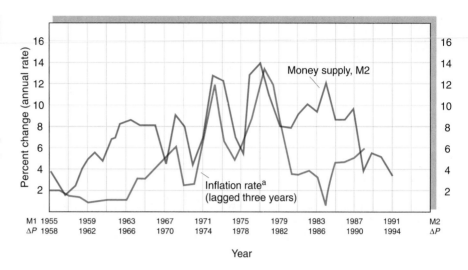

deceleration in the growth rate of the money supply (both M1 and M2). It will be interesting to see whether the inflation rate in the early 1990s follows a similar path.

Exhibit 14 shows the relationship between the inflation rate (change in CPI) and the money rate of interest. As our theory implies, the two are closely linked. As the inflation rate rose gradually throughout the 1960s, so too, did the nominal rate of interest. During the 1970s, both sharp increases and reductions in the inflation rate were accompanied by similar changes in the nominal interest rate. Similarly, the money interest rate fell sharply during the 1980s as the inflation rate decelerated from the double-digit levels of the late 1970s. Later, as the inflation rate rose again during 1987–1989, so too, did the nominal interest rate. These data provide strong evidence that, just as our theory postulates, the choices of borrowers and lenders are strongly influenced by the inflation rate.

EXHIBIT 14

Inflation Rate and the Money Interest Rate

The expectation of inflation (a) reduces the supply and (b) increases the demand of loanable funds, causing money interest rates to rise (see Exhibit 8). Note how the money rate of interest has tended to increase when the inflation rate accelerates (and decline as the inflation rate falls).

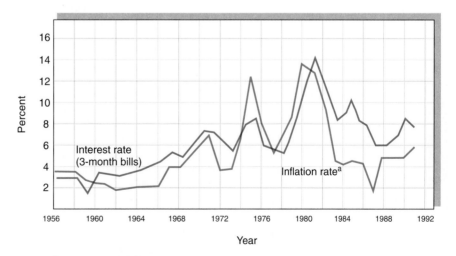

[a]As indicated by CPI.

APPLICATIONS IN ECONOMICS

What Caused the Great Depression?

As we previously discussed, the Great Depression exerted an enormous impact both on economic thought and on economic institutions. Prior to and since the Great Depression, business recessions in the United States, as well as in other countries, have reversed themselves after a year or two. The Great Depression, though, was different. Exhibit 15 presents the economic record during the period. For four successive years (1930–1933), real output fell. Unemployment soared to nearly one-quarter of the work force in 1932 and 1933. Although recovery did take place during 1934–1937, the economy again fell into the depth of depression in 1938. Ten years after the catastrophe began, real GNP was virtually the same as it had been in 1929.

Why did the economic system break down? Analysis of the period yields some surprising answers. Armed with knowledge of how monetary and fiscal policy work, we are now in a position to understand what actually took place during the 1930s. Let us consider four important factors that contributed to the economic collapse of the 1930s.

1. *A sharp reduction in the supply of money during 1930–1933 reduced aggregate demand and real output*. The supply of money expanded slowly but steadily throughout the 1920s.[5] Beginning in 1930, monetary policy suddenly shifted. The supply of money *declined* by 6.9 percent during 1930, by 10.9 percent in 1931, and by 4.7 percent in 1932. Banks failed, and the Fed also failed to act as a lender of last resort to head off the huge decline in the supply of money. From 1929 to 1933, the quantity of money in circulation declined by 27 percent!

What is the predicted impact of a sharp unexpected reduction in the money supply? Our analysis indicates it will lead to reductions both in prices and in real output (see Exhibit 5). This is precisely what happened. By 1933, prices were 27 percent below the level of 1929. Real output also plunged. By 1933, real GNP was 30 percent lower than the 1929 level. Changes in the purchasing power of money altered the terms of long-term contracts. During the 1930s, farmers, business people, and others who had signed long-term contracts (for example, mortgages) in the 1920s were unable to meet their fixed money commitments in an economy dominated by falling prices and wages. Bankruptcies resulted. Those trends bred fear and uncertainty, causing still more people to avoid investments involving long-term money commitments. Production and exchange dropped substantially. Gains previously derived from comparative advantage, specialization, and exchange were lost.[6]

2. *A large tax increase in the midst of a severe recession made a bad situation worse*. Prior to the Keynesian revolution, the dominant view was that the federal budget should be balanced. Reflecting the ongoing economic downturn, the federal budget ran a deficit in 1931 and an even larger deficit was shaping up for 1932. Assisted by the newly elected Democratic majority in the House of Representatives, the Republican Hoover administration passed the largest peacetime tax-rate increase in the history of the United States. At the bottom of the income scale, marginal tax rates were raised from 1.5 percent to 4 percent in 1932. At the top of the scale, tax rates were raised from 25 percent to 63 percent.

Our prior analysis of fiscal policy indicates the counterproductiveness of higher tax rates during a recession. Predictably, the tax increase reduced disposable income and placed still more downward pressure on aggregate demand, which had already fallen sharply in response to the monetary contraction. Simultaneously, the higher marginal tax rates reduced the incentive to earn taxable income. The restrictive fiscal policy further added to the severity of the economic decline. Exhibit 15 shows the degree to which this happened. As tax rates were increased in 1932, real GNP fell by 14.8 percent. Unemployment rose from 15.9 percent in 1931 to 23.6 percent in 1932.

3. *Tariff policy: tariff increases retarded international exchange*. Concern about low agricultural

---

[5]From 1921 through 1929, the money stock expanded at an annual rate of 2.7 percent, slightly less rapidly than the growth in the output of goods and services. Thus, the 1920s were a decade of price stability, even of slight deflation.

[6]For a detailed analysis of the role of monetary policy during the 1930s, see Milton Friedman and Anna J. Schwartz, *A Monetary History of the United States, 1867–1960* (Princeton: Princeton University Press, 1963), particularly the chapter entitled "The Great Contraction."

EXHIBIT 15 ■ The Economic Record of the Great Depression				
Year	Real GNP in 1972 Dollars (billions)	Implicit GNP Deflator (1929 = 100)	Unemployment Rate	Changes in the Money Supply (M1)
1929	315.7	100.0	3.2	+ 1.0
1930	285.6	96.8	8.7	− 6.9
1931	263.5	87.9	15.9	−10.9
1932	227.1	78.2	23.6	− 4.7
1933	222.1	76.4	24.9	− 2.9
1934	239.1	83.0	21.7	+10.0
1935	260.0	84.6	20.1	+18.2
1936	295.5	85.0	16.9	+13.9
1937	310.2	89.1	14.3	+ 4.7
1938	296.7	87.0	19.0	− 1.3
1939	319.8	86.4	17.2	+12.1

Source: Bureau of the Census, *The Statistical History of the United States from Colonial Times to Present* (New York: Basic Books, 1976).

prices, an influx of imports, rising unemployment, and declining tax revenues generated public sentiment for trade restraints. Responding to this pressure, the Hoover administration pushed for a substantial increase in tariffs on a wide range of products in early 1930. The tariff legislation took effect in June of 1930. Other countries promptly responded by increasing their tariffs, further slowing the flow of goods between nations. A tariff is, of course, nothing more than a tax on exchanges between parties residing in different countries. Since the increase in tariff rates made such transactions more costly and reduced their volume, additional gains from specialization and exchange were lost.

The high tariff policy of the Hoover administration not only retarded our ability to generate output, it was also ineffective as a revenue measure. The tariff legislation increased the duty (tax) rate on imports into the United States by approximately 50 percent.[7] However, the value of the goods and services imported declined even more sharply. By 1932, the volume of imports to the United States had fallen to $2.1 billion, down from $5.9 billion in 1929. Exports declined by a similar amount. Tariff revenues fell from $602 million in 1929 to $328 million in 1932.[8] Like the monetary and fiscal policies of the era, tariff policy retarded exchange and contributed to the uncertainty of the period.

4. *The stock market crash and the business pessimism that followed reduced both consumption and investment demand.* Economists generally think of the stock market as an economic thermometer. Although it may register the temperature, it is not the major cause of the fever. While historians may exaggerate the importance of the stock market crash of 1929, there is reason to believe that it was of significance. As the stock market rose

substantially during the 1920s, business optimism soared. In contrast, as stock prices plummeted, beginning in October of 1929, aggregate demand fell. The falling stock prices reduced the wealth in the hands of consumers. This decline in wealth contributed to the sharp reduction in consumption expenditures in the early 1930s. In addition, the stock market crash changed the expectations of consumers and investors. Both reduced their *(continued)*

---

[7]The ratio of duty revenue to the value of imports on which duties were levied rose from 40.1 percent in 1929 to 59.1 percent in 1932. See U.S. Census Bureau, *The Statistical History of the United States from Colonial Times to the Present* (New York: Basic Books, 1979), p. 888.

[8]See Jude Wanniski, *The Way the World Works: How Economies Fail and Succeed* (New York: Basic Books, 1978), pp. 125–48, for additional information on the tariff policy of the period and its impact upon the economy.

expenditures as they became more pessimistic about the future. As spending continued to decline, unemployment rose and the situation worsened. Given the impact of both the business pessimism and the perverse policies previously discussed, a minor recession was turned into an economic debacle.

Could It Happen Again?

This question was on the minds of many people following the stock market crash of October 1987. Numerous parallels were drawn between the crash of 1929 and the crash of 1987. In both cases, the stock market lost a third of its value in just a few days. But that is where the parallel ends. The Great Depression was the result of disastrous macroeconomic policy, not an inevitable consequence of a stock market crash. The experience following the October 1987 crash illustrates this point. In contrast with the crash of 1929, in 1987 the Fed moved quickly to supply reserves to the banking system. The money supply did not fall. Tax rates were not increased. And even though there was a lot of political rhetoric about "the need to protect American businesses," trade barriers were not raised. In short, sensible policies were followed subsequent to the crash of 1987. Continued growth and stability were the result. Inadvertently, perverse macroeconomic policies were followed subsequent to the crash of 1929. Economic disaster was the result.

In addition to advances in our understanding of macroeconomic policy and its effects on the economy, institutional changes also reduce the likelihood of a recurrence of the Great Depression. Foremost among these is the Federal Deposit Insurance Corporation (FDIC). As we discussed in the last chapter, the FDIC removes the underlying motivation for "bank runs," and thereby eliminates a major source of monetary contraction and economic instability.

Today, as in the 1930s, our living standard is critically dependent on the gains from specialization and exchange. If something caused our exchange system to break down, our standard of living would plummet just as it did during the 1930s. There is no law able to guarantee that we will not pursue perverse policies again. However, given our current knowledge of macroeconomics, most economists believe that the likelihood of another Great Depression is remote.

LOOKING AHEAD

The stability of the velocity of money is an important issue related to stabilization policy. For several decades, monetarists have argued that there are long and unpredictable lags between the implementation of a change in monetary policy and the impact of the change. Hence, monetarists have little confidence in the ability of monetary authorities to time policy changes properly. They believe that the economy would be more stable if policy-makers followed a monetary rule—if they simply increased the money supply, month after month, at a rate approximately equal to the economy's long-term rate of economic growth. On the other hand, if the velocity of money is unstable, as many Keynesians believe, the case for a steady-growth monetary rule is significantly weakened. If the velocity of money fluctuates substantially, steady monetary growth would not only fail to reduce the economic instability, it would prevent policy-makers from taking discretionary action to offset economic disturbances emanating from changes in the velocity of money. We will take up this issue when we analyze stabilization policy in Chapter 15.

As we discussed in this chapter, theory indicates that the impact of monetary policy will be influenced by whether economic agents anticipate its effects. Thus far, we have said little concerning how decision-makers form expectations about the future. The next chapter will consider this important issue.

CHAPTER SUMMARY

1. There are three major reasons why households and businesses demand (hold) money balances. People demand money (a) in order to conduct planned transactions, (b) as a precaution against an uncertain future that may require unplanned expenditures, and (c) for speculative purposes so they can quickly respond to profit-making opportunities.

2. The quantity of money demanded is inversely related to the nominal interest rate and directly related to nominal income (GNP). The quantity of money supplied is determined by the central monetary authority (the Fed in the United States).

3. Classical economists developed the quantity theory of money that postulated that the velocity of money was constant (or approximately so) and that real output was independent of monetary factors. According to the quantity theory, therefore, an increase in the stock of money resulted in a proportional increase in prices, while output remained unchanged.

4. Modern economists stress that there are two channels through which monetary policy may influence the demand for goods and services: (a) an indirect path via the real interest rate and (b) a direct path through changes in spending on a broad cross-section of goods resulting from an excess supply of (or demand for) money balances.

5. When monetary policy is transmitted by the interest rate, an unanticipated increase in the money supply will reduce the real interest rate and thereby cause investors and consumers to purchase more goods and services in the current period. In the short run, the unanticipated increase in aggregate demand will expand real output, although with the passage of time more and more of the demand stimulus will be transformed into price increases when output is pushed beyond long-run capacity. The analysis is symmetrical for an unanticipated reduction in the money supply. Restrictive policy will temporarily raise the real interest rate, reduce aggregate demand, and thereby cause a reduction in real output in the short run.

6. Expansionary monetary policy creates an excess supply of money. In addition to buying bonds (and thereby reducing the interest rate), people may reduce their money balances by increasing their spending in several markets, including the market for goods and services. This increased spending will directly increase aggregate demand. By parallel reasoning, a reduction in the supply of money will lead to a fall in aggregate demand.

7. Monetary policy is a potential tool of economic stabilization. If the effects of expansionary monetary policy are felt when aggregate output is at less than capacity, then the policy will stimulate demand, and push the economy toward full employment. Correspondingly, if restrictive monetary policy is properly timed, then it can help to control inflation.

8. In the long run, the primary impact of monetary policy will be on prices rather than on real output. When expansionary monetary policy leads to rising prices, decision-makers eventually anticipate the higher inflation rate and build it into their choices. As this happens, *money* interest rates, wages, and incomes will reflect the expectation of inflation and *real* interest rates, wages, and output will return to their long-run normal levels.

9. When the effects of expansionary monetary policy are anticipated *prior to their occurrence,* the short-run impact of an increase in the money supply is like its impact in the long run. Nominal prices and interest rates rise, but real output remains

unchanged. Thus, theory indicates the short-run impact of monetary policy is dependent on whether the effects of the policy are anticipated.

10. Both international comparisons and the U.S. experience strongly indicate that prolonged, rapid growth in the money supply is closely linked with inflation. The international data show that countries with low (high) rates of growth in the money supply tend to experience low (high) rates of inflation. Similarly, the U. S. data illustrate that shifts to rapid monetary growth for an extended period of time are generally followed by an acceleration in the inflation rate.

11. The empirical evidence also indicates that changes in monetary policy influence real GNP in the short run. *Shifts* toward monetary acceleration tend to be associated with a temporary increase in the growth rate of real GNP. Conversely, *shifts* toward monetary contraction have generally been associated with a slowdown in real output.

12. Analysis of the Great Depression suggests that the depth of the economic plunge, if not its onset, was the result of perverse monetary and fiscal policies. The 27 percent reduction in the money supply between 1929 and 1933 is without parallel in United States history. It reduced aggregate demand, changed the intended real terms of the time dimension exchanges, and created enormous uncertainty. The substantial increase in tariffs (taxes on imports) in 1930 and the huge increases in tax rates in 1932 further reduced aggregate demand and the incentive to earn taxable income. Lacking understanding of monetary and fiscal tools, policy-makers followed precisely the wrong course during this period.

CRITICAL ANALYSIS QUESTIONS

*1. How would each of the following influence the quantity of money that you would like to hold?
   a. An increase in the interest rate on checking deposits.
   b. An increase in the expected rate of inflation.
   c. An increase in income.
   d. An increase in the differential interest rate between savings deposits and checking deposits.

*2. a. What is the opportunity cost of *obtaining* a $100,000 house? What is the opportunity cost of *holding* the house?
   b. What is the cost of *obtaining* a dollar? What is the cost of *holding* the dollar?

3. What impact will an unanticipated increase in the money supply have on the real interest rate, real output, and employment in the short run? How will expansionary monetary policy affect the economy when the effects are widely anticipated? Why does it make a difference whether the effects of monetary policy are anticipated?

4. How rapidly has the money supply (M1) grown during the last 12 months? How rapidly has M2 grown? Do you think the monetary authorities should increase or decrease the growth rate of the money supply during the next year? Why? (The data necessary to answer this question for the United States are available in the *Federal Reserve Bulletin*.)

5. Will a budget deficit be more expansionary if it is financed by borrowing from the Federal Reserve or from the general public? Explain.

6. "Inappropriate monetary and fiscal policy was the major cause of economic instability during the 1930s, and it was the major cause of inflation in the 1970s." Evaluate this view, presenting empirical evidence to defend your position.

7. Shifts toward more expansionary monetary policy have often been associated with *lower* interest rates. Nonetheless, the *highest* interest rates in the world are found in countries that expand the supply of money rapidly. Can you explain these seemingly contradictory facts?

*Asterisk denotes questions for which answers are given in Appendix C, Selected Answers.

*8. Generally, monetarists argue that there is a "long and variable time lag" between when a change in monetary policy is instituted and when the change exerts its primary impact on output, employment, and prices. How does this long and variable time lag affect the case for discretionary monetary policy compared to the case for a monetary rule?

*9. Generally, Keynesians argue that the velocity of money is "variable and unpredictable." If velocity fluctuates substantially, how does this influence the case for discretionary monetary policy compared to the case for a monetary rule?

10. What do economists mean when they say "the demand for money has increased?" How will an increase in the demand for money affect the velocity of money?

*11. "Historically, when interest rates are high, the inflation rate is high. High interest rates are a major cause of inflation." Evaluate this statement.

*12. If the supply of money is constant, how will an increase in the demand for money influence aggregate demand?

13. Historically, shifts toward more expansionary monetary policy have often been associated with increases in real output. Why? Would a more expansionary policy increase the long-term growth rate of real GNP? Why or why not?

*14. Suppose that innovations in financial management during the 1990s permit individuals and business firms to conduct a given volume of transactions with an increasingly smaller average money balance. As a result, the velocity of money increases at a 3 percent annual rate during the decade. If the monetary authorities want to maintain stable prices, what growth rate of the money supply should they choose?

15. It is commonly held that the stock market crash caused the Great Depression. Do you think this is true? Why or why not? Why has this belief been so widely accepted?

14 Expectations, Inflation, and Unemployment

Inflation does give a stimulus . . . when it starts from a condition that is noninflationary. If the inflation continues, people get adjusted to it. But when people get adjusted to it, when they expect rising prices, the mere occurrence of what has been expected is no longer stimulating.[1]

Sir John R. Hicks

CHAPTER FOCUS

■ Why does it make a difference whether a change in macroeconomic policy is anticipated or unanticipated?

■ How do individuals form expectations about what will happen in the future?

■ Can a nation reduce its unemployment rate if it is willing to pay the price of a higher inflation rate?

■ How can one explain the simultaneous occurrence of inflation and a high rate of unemployment? Is this occurrence inconsistent with economic theory?

■ Can economic policy reduce the natural rate of unemployment? If so, how?

■ How has the natural rate of unemployment changed in recent years? How is it likely to change during the 1990s?

People make decisions on the basis of perceptions: the perceived costs and benefits associated with choices. What individuals think is going to happen in the future is important because it affects the choices they make in the present. Sometimes the choices of people will turn out differently than they anticipated. When this is true, people will often modify their future choices. In this chapter, we will explicitly incorporate the idea that expectations about the future influence the choices of individuals who think and learn from previous experience. We will consider alternative theories concerning how expectations are formed and investigate their implications.

What impact will a shift to a more expansionary macroeconomic policy have on output and employment? Can expansionary policies reduce the unemployment rate? If so, how long can the lower unemployment rate be maintained and at what cost? Expectations provide the key to the understanding of these questions. Hence, we must more fully integrate expectations into our economic way of thinking about output, employment, and prices.

UNANTICIPATED AND ANTICIPATED DEMAND STIMULUS

Throughout this text, we have carefully differentiated between unanticipated and anticipated changes. Exhibit 1 illustrates why this distinction is crucial. Beginning from a position of long-run equilibrium, the impact of expansionary macropolicy is indicated under two alternative assumptions. Exhibit 1a assumes that decision-makers fail to anticipate the effects of the expansionary policies and therefore they do not expect the resulting cost and price increases. As we have previously discussed, unanticipated increases in aggregate demand will temporarily increase both output and employment. For a time, output will expand to a rate (Y_2) beyond the economy's long-run potential. Correspondingly, employment will expand and unemployment will recede below the economy's natural rate. When the effects of expansionary policy are unanticipated, both output and employment increase *in the short run*.

Exhibit 1b illustrates the impact of expansionary macroeconomic policy under the assumption that decision-makers anticipate its effects prior to their occurrence. Recognizing that expansionary policies will strengthen demand and lead to inflation, market participants alter their choices accordingly. Agreements specifying future wage rates and resource prices immediately make allowance for an expected increase in the price level. These agreements may even include escalator clauses providing for automatic cost-of-living increases in nominal wages tied to the general price level. When buyers and sellers in the resource market fully anticipate and quickly adjust to the effects of the demand stimulus policies, wage rates and resource prices will rise as rapidly as product prices. Profit margins will fail to improve. The rising nominal costs will decrease aggregate supply, offsetting the impact of the demand stimulus on output. The result: a higher price level, while real output is unchanged (move from E_1 to E_2 in Exhibit 1b).

Thus, the impact of expansionary macroeconomic policy is dependent on whether decision-makers anticipate the eventual effects. If decision-makers fail to

---

[1]J. R. Hicks, "Monetary Theory and Keynesian Economics," in R. W. Clower (ed.), *Monetary Theory* (Harmondsworth: Penguin, 1969), p. 260.

EXHIBIT 1

The Short-Run Effects of Unanticipated Versus Anticipated Demand Stimulus Policies

When expansionary policies catch decision-makers by surprise, the increase in aggregate demand will lead to an increase in real GNP (from Y_f to Y_2, frame a) *in the short run*. In contrast, when suppliers correctly anticipate the inflationary impact of demand stimulus policies, nominal costs will rise, causing a decline in aggregate supply (shift to $SRAS_2$, frame b). When the effects are anticipated, demand stimulus policies merely increase prices without altering the rate of output.

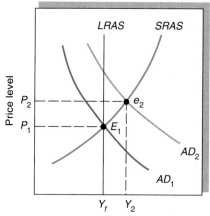

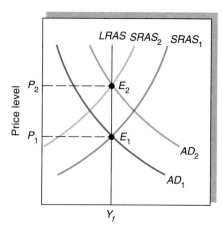

(a) Expansionary policy that leads to an unanticipated increase in aggregate demand

(b) Expansionary policy that leads to an anticipated increase in aggregate demand

anticipate the strong demand and the increase in the price level that will eventually accompany the expansionary policy, the demand stimulus will temporarily increase output and reduce unemployment. In contrast, when the inflationary side effects of expansionary policies are anticipated quickly, the primary impact of the demand stimulus will be an increase in the price level (see chapter opening quote by Nobel laureate Sir John R. Hicks).

HOW ARE EXPECTATIONS FORMED?

As Exhibit 1 illustrates, expectations concerning the future exert an important impact on the effectiveness of macroeconomic policy. Thus, it is vitally important that we understand how expectations are formed. There are two general theories in this area. Let us outline the essentials of each.

ADAPTIVE EXPECTATIONS

The simplest theory concerning the formulation of expectations is that people rely on the past to predict future trends. According to this theory, which economists call the **adaptive expectations hypothesis,** decision-makers believe that the best indicator of the future is what has happened in the recent past.

For example, under adaptive expectations, people would expect the price level to be stable next year if stable prices had been present during the last two or three years. Similarly, if prices had risen at an annual rate of 4 or 5 percent during the last several years, adaptive expectations implies that similar increases will be expected next year. Exhibit 2 presents a graphic illustration of the adaptive expectations hypothesis. In period 1, prices were actually stable (frame a). Therefore, on the basis of the experience of period 1, decision-makers assume that prices will be stable in period 2 (frame b). However, the actual rate of inflation in period 2 jumps to 4 percent. Continuation of the 4 percent inflation rate throughout period 2 (the periods may range from six months to several years in length) causes decision-makers to change their expectations. Relying on the experience of period 2,

EXHIBIT 2

The Adaptive Expectations Hypothesis

According to the adaptive expectations hypothesis, the actual occurrence during the most recent period (or set of periods) determines people's future expectations. Thus, the expected future rate of inflation (b) lags behind the actual rate of inflation (a) by one period as expectations are altered over time.

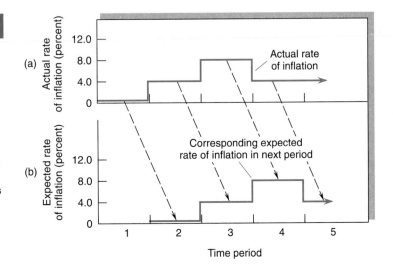

Adaptive Expectations Hypothesis: The hypothesis that economic decision-makers base their future expectations on actual outcomes observed during recent periods. For example, according to this view, the rate of inflation actually experienced during the last two or three years would be the major determinant of the rate of inflation expected for next year.

decision-makers anticipate 4 percent inflation in period 3. When their expectations turn out to be incorrect (the actual rate of inflation during period 3 is 8 percent), they again alter their expectations accordingly. During period 4, the actual rate of inflation declines to 4 percent, less than the expected rate. Again, decision-makers adjust their expectations as to the expected rate of inflation in period 5.

In the real world, of course, one would not expect the precise mechanical link between past occurrences and future expectations outlined in Exhibit 2. Rather than simply using the inflation rate of the immediate past period, people may use a weighted average of recent inflation rates when forming their expectations about the future. Nevertheless, the general point illustrated by Exhibit 2 remains valid.

With adaptive expectations, past experience determines the future expectations of decision-makers. If the inflation rate has been low (high) in the recent past, individuals will anticipate a continuation of the low (high) rate in the future.

Under adaptive expectations, forecasts of the future rate of inflation will exhibit systematic error. A systematic error is a mistake that is made over and over again in a regular methodical way. When the inflation rate is accelerating, decision-makers will systematically tend to *under*estimate the future inflation rate. In contrast, when the rate of inflation is decelerating, individuals will tend systematically to *over*estimate its future rate. We will investigate the implication of this occurrence as we proceed.

RATIONAL EXPECTATIONS

The idea that people form their expectations concerning what will happen in the future on the basis of all available information, including their understanding of how the economy works, is called the **rational expectations hypothesis.** Rather than merely assuming the future will be pretty much like the immediate past, people also consider the expected effects of changes in policy. Based on their understanding of economic policy, people alter their expectations with regard to the future when the government, for example, runs a larger deficit, expands the supply of money more rapidly, or cuts the size of its expenditures.

An important feature of the rational expectations view is its consistency with economizing behavior. When individuals economize, they will not ignore potentially valuable information—for example, the recent growth rate of the money

Rational Expectations Hypothesis: This viewpoint expects individuals to weigh all available evidence, including information concerning the probable effects of current and future economic policy, when they formulate their expectations about future economic events (such as the probable future inflation rate).

supply—that would help them more accurately forecast the future inflation rate. According to the proponents of the rational expectations view, this is precisely the problem with adaptive expectations. The adaptive expectations theory, at least in its pure form, fails to consider the impact of current economic policy on the future direction of inflation.

Perhaps an example will help clarify the rational expectations hypothesis. Suppose prices had increased at an annual rate of 6 percent during each of the last three years. In addition, let us assume that decision-makers believe there is a relationship between the growth rate of the money supply and rising prices. Individuals note that the money stock has expanded at a 12 percent annual rate during the last nine months, up from the 7 percent rate of the past several years. According to the rational expectations hypothesis, decision-makers will integrate the recent monetary acceleration into their forecast of the future inflation rate. With rational expectations, decision-makers will project an acceleration in the inflation rate, perhaps in the 10 to 12 percent range, since they believe the future inflation rate will respond to the more rapid growth of the money supply. In contrast, the adaptive expectations hypothesis implies that people will continue to predict that the inflation rate for the next period will be like it was for the last period (or the last several periods).

Under rational expectations, people do consider the expected effects of macroeconomic policy when they make choices. Just as a football team alters its strategy in light of moves by an opponent, rational decision-makers alter their expectations and strategies in light of policy developments. Contrary to the views of some, the rational expectations hypothesis does not assume that people do not make forecasting errors. Under rational expectations, however, errors will tend to be random. For example, sometimes decision-makers may overestimate the increase in the inflation rate caused by monetary expansion, and at other times they may underestimate it. But, since they learn from prior experience, people will not continue to make the same kinds of systematic errors year after year.

THE PHILLIPS CURVE—THE DREAM AND THE REALITY

Phillips Curve: A curve that illustrates the relationship between the rate of change in prices (or money wages) and the rate of unemployment.

The integration of expectations into our analysis places us in a position to better understand the effects of inflation on unemployment. A curve indicating the relationship between the unemployment rate and the inflation rate is termed the **Phillips curve** after its originator, the British economist A. W. Phillips. When tracing the link between the rate of change in wages and the unemployment rate over nearly a century for the United Kingdom, Phillips discovered an inverse relationship. When wage rates were rising rapidly, unemployment was low. Correspondingly, wage rates rose more slowly when the unemployment rate was high.[2]

Phillips did not draw any policy conclusions from his study, but others did. Noting that a similar inverse relationship was present between inflation and unemployment during the post-Second World War period in the United States, many economists and policy-makers concluded that demand stimulus (inflationary)

---

[2]A. W. Phillips, "The Relationship between Unemployment and the Rate of Change of Money Wages in the United Kingdom, 1861–1957," *Economica,* 25 (1958), pp. 238–99.

OUTSTANDING ECONOMIST

Proponents of Rational Expectations—
Robert Barro, Robert Lucas, and Thomas Sargent

While Keynesian economists were struggling to develop policy prescriptions to reduce unemployment in the late 1960s, another group of economists was busy developing theoretical models implying that the Keynesian efforts would come to naught. The latter effort led to the theory of rational expectations, a breakthrough that vastly alters, even "revolutionizes" the way we think about macroeconomics. Foremost among the leaders of the new way of thinking about macroeconomics were Robert Barro (University of Chicago), Robert Lucas (University of Chicago), and Thomas Sargent (University of Minnesota).

While Lucas is generally given credit for the introduction of rational expectations into macroeconomics, John Muth first developed the concept in 1961. Muth, though, applied it only to commodities markets. Lucas went much further. He used the idea to analyze the operation of labor and capital markets, monetary policy, and business cycles. As the simultaneous occurrence of inflation and high unemployment led to

a breakdown of the Keynesian consensus during the 1970s, Lucas's work attracted followers, particularly among youthful, mathematical economists.

Sargent and Barro have also exerted a lasting imprint on the development of rational expectations theory. Sargent, while completing his doctoral degree at Harvard (1968), first developed a discomfort with Keynesian models that assumed individuals responded passively to changes in macropolicy. Independent of Lucas, Sargent integrated the notion of rational expectations into a macroeconomic model as early as 1971. Both his theoretical and empirical work contributed to the development of the rational expectations analysis during the 1970s and 1980s.

Barro also completed his doctoral degree at Harvard, just one year after Sargent. His work in the early 1970s dealt primarily with the operation of economies under conditions of extreme inflation. He is the author of a widely acclaimed intermediate text that provides a comprehensive

view of new classical macroeconomics.

Most of the leaders of the rational expectations school are not very interested in economic policy. This is perhaps not surprising, considering that according to the rational expectations theory, policy-makers cannot fine-tune the economy by systematically injecting stimulus during a recession and restraint during an economic boom. Rather, the proponents of rational expectations favor preannounced stable policies that remain unchanged over the business cycle. In this manner, the government can at least keep its policies from becoming a source of instability.

To date, the rational expectations view has exerted little impact on economic policy. This, however, should not be taken as evidence that the theory is unimportant. After all, nearly two decades passed after the publication of Keynes's *General Theory* before the budgetary policies of Western nations began to reflect its implications.

policies could permanently reduce the unemployment rate. As early as 1959, Paul Samuelson and Robert Solow (each of whom would later win a Nobel Prize in economics) argued that we could trade a little more inflation for less unemployment. Samuelson and Solow told the American Economic Association:

> In order to achieve the nonperfectionist's goal of high enough output to give us no more than 3 percent unemployment, the price index might have to rise by as much as 4 to 5 percent per year. That much price rise [inflation] would seem to be the necessary cost of high employment and production in the years immediately ahead.[3]

Many leading economists of the 1960s concluded that a nation could reduce its unemployment rate if it were willing to pay the price of a higher rate of inflation. As Exhibit 3 indicates, even the prestigious annual *Economic Report of the President* argued that moderate inflation would reduce the unemployment rate. At the time, most economists thought the inflation-unemployment relationship was stable. In other words, they thought that the *short-run* equilibrium presented in Exhibit 1a was, in fact, a long-lasting relationship (a long-run equilibrium).

THE LABOR MARKET AND THE PHILLIPS CURVE UNDER ADAPTIVE EXPECTATIONS

For a while, it did seem that demand stimulus policies could reduce the unemployment rate. Both monetary and fiscal policy were more expansionary during the latter half of the 1960s. As Exhibit 3 illustrates, the unemployment rate declined while the inflation rate increased, just as the proponents of the inflation-unemployment trade-off theory anticipated.

The adaptive expectations hypothesis explains why the unemployment rate will decline when the inflation rate is accelerating due to expansionary macropolicy. Since adaptive expectations are based on past history, the theory implies the people will always *under*estimate the future inflation during a period of accelerating inflation.

When labor market participants underestimate the inflation rate, there are two reasons why inflation will stimulate employment. First, unanticipated inflation will reduce the real wages of workers employed under long-term contracts and thereby stimulate employment. Union wage contracts and other wage agreements, both explicit and implicit, often determine money wage rates over periods ranging from one to three years. Unanticipated inflation means that the impact of wage and price inflation has not been fully factored into long-term money wage agreements. Once an employer-employee agreement establishes money rates, an unexpected increase in the inflation rate will reduce the employee's real wage rate and the employer's real wage costs.

Suppose that employees and employers anticipate an 8 percent inflation rate during the next year. From this, they concur on a collective bargaining agreement calling for money wages of $10 during the current year and $10.80 for the year beginning 12 months from now. If the *actual* inflation rate this year equals the 8 percent expected rate, the $10.80 money wage rate 12 months from now translates to a $10 real wage rate at today's price level. What happens to the real wage rate if the inflation rate exceeds the expected rate of 8 percent? If actual inflation during the next 12 months is 12 percent, for example, the *real wage rate* one year from now will fall to $9.64 at current prices. The higher the actual inflation rate, the lower the real wages of the employees. Unanticipated inflation tends to reduce the

[3]Paul A. Samuelson and Robert Solow, "Our Menu of Policy Changes," *American Economic Review,* May 1960.

EXHIBIT 3

The Phillips Curve—Before the Inflation of the 1970s

This exhibit is from the *1969 Economic Report of the President,* prepared by the President's Council of Economic Advisers. Each dot on the diagram indicates, as a coordinate point on the graph, the inflation rate and unemployment rate for the year. The report stated that the chart "reveals a fairly close association of more rapid price increases with lower rates of unemployment." Economists refer to this link as the Phillips curve. In the 1960s, it was widely believed that policy-makers could pursue expansionary macroeconomic policies and thereby permanently reduce the unemployment rate. More recent experience has caused most economists to reject this view.

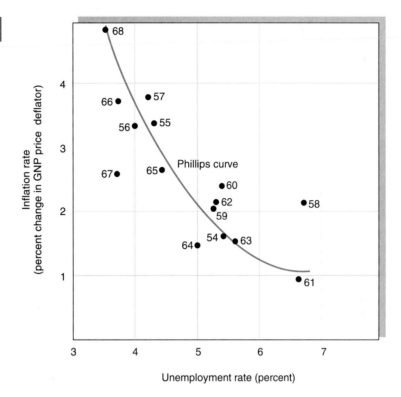

Source: *Economic Report of the President, 1969,* p. 95. The Phillips curve is fitted to the points to illustrate the relationship.

real wage rates of employees whose money wages are fixed by long-term contracts. At the lower real wage rate, firms will hire more workers and employment will expand.

There is a second reason why underestimation of the inflation rate will tend to expand employment. Misled by inflation, some job seekers will quickly accept job offers on the basis of a mistaken belief that the offers are particularly goods ones *in relation to the market for their labor services.* As we discussed in Chapter 7, in a world characterized by imperfect information, unemployed workers will search for job opportunities that fit their skills and preferences. They expect that their additional search will pay off in the form of a better job. Job search is costly, however. It involves both personal costs and loss of potential earnings. Economizing behavior indicates that workers will continue searching for employment only so long as their perceived benefits (finding a better job) exceed the cost of their search.

When people underestimate the extent that inflation has increased both prices and money wages, many job seekers will fail to recognize how much nominal wages have increased in their skill category. Unaware of just how much their money wage opportunities have improved, job seekers will tend to accept offers that are not as attractive as workers think (relative to jobs that could be found). Unemployed workers thus shorten their search time, which lowers the unemployment rate.

Thus, unanticipated (or underestimated) inflation reduces the real wage rate of workers whose money wages are determined by long-term contracts and reduces the search time of job seekers. Both of these factors will expand employment and reduce the unemployment rate below its natural rate.

With adaptive expectations, though, decision-makers will eventually anticipate a higher inflation rate after it has been present for a period of time. Individuals will build the higher expected inflation rate into their decision-making. Eventually, workers and their union representatives will demand and employers will agree to money wage increases that fully reflect the higher current and expected future inflation rate. Similarly, job seekers will become fully aware of the extent that inflation has increased (and continues to increase) their *money* wage alternatives. As they do so, their search time will return to normal. Once decision-makers fully anticipate the higher rate of inflation and reflect it in their choices, the inflation rate will neither depress real wage rates nor reduce the search time of job seekers.[4] As this happens, employment and real output will return to their natural (long-run) rates.

Exhibit 4 uses our *AD/AS* model to illustrate the implications of adaptive expectations with regard to the Phillips curve analysis. Beginning from a position of stable prices and long-run equilibrium (point *A*), Exhibit 4a illustrates the impact of an unanticipated increase in aggregate demand. As we previously discussed, *initially* the demand stimulus will increase output (to Y_2) and employment. The unemployment rate will recede below the economy's natural rate. The strong demand and tight resource markets will place upward pressure on resource prices. For a time, the economy will experience both rising prices and an output beyond its full-employment potential (point *B*). Under adaptive expectations, however, this high level of output will not be long-lasting. After a period of time, people will begin to anticipate the rising prices. When this happens, resource prices (and costs) will rise *relative to product prices,* causing the SRAS curve to shift to the left. As the previous relationship between resource prices and product prices is restored, output will recede to the economy's full-employment equilibrium level (point *C*).

Exhibit 4b illustrates the same case within the Phillips curve framework. Since initially stable prices are present and the economy is in long-run equilibrium, unemployment is equal to the natural rate of unemployment (point *A*). We assume that the economy's natural rate of unemployment is 5 percent. The condition of long-run equilibrium implies that the stable prices are both anticipated and observed. *Under adaptive expectations,* an unanticipated shift to a more expansionary policy will temporarily increase output and reduce unemployment. It will also place upward pressure on prices. Suppose that demand stimulus policies lead to 4 percent inflation and a reduction in the unemployment rate from 5 percent to 3 percent (move from *A* to *B* along the short-run Phillips Curve PC_1). While point *B* is *attainable,* it will not be *sustainable*. After an extended period of 4 percent inflation, decision-makers will begin to anticipate the higher rate of inflation. Workers and their union representatives will take the higher expected rate of inflation into account in their job search and collective-bargaining decision-making. Once the 4 percent rate of inflation is fully anticipated, the economy will confront a new, higher short-run Phillips curve (PC_2). The rate of unemployment will return to the long-run natural rate of 5 percent, even though prices will continue to rise at an annual rate of 4 percent (point *C*).

The moves from *A* to *B* in Exhibits 4a and 4b are simply alternative ways of representing the same phenomenon—a temporary increase in output and reduction in unemployment as the result of an unanticipated increase in aggregate demand.

---

[4]For an analysis of how rapidly these adjustments take place, see Robert J. Gordon, ''Price Inertia and Policy Ineffectiveness in the United States, 1890–1980,'' *Journal of Political Economy*, 90, December 1982, pp. 1087–1117.

EXHIBIT 4

The *AD/AS* Model,
Adaptive Expectations
and the Phillips Curve

When stable prices are observed *and* anticipated, both full-employment output and the natural rate of unemployment will be present (*A* in both panels). *With adaptive expectations,* a shift to a more expansionary policy will increase prices, expand output beyond its full employment potential, and reduce the unemployment rate below its natural level (move from *A* to *B* in both panels). Decision-makers, though, will eventually anticipate the rising prices and incorporate them into their decision-making. When this happens, the *SRAS* curve shifts to the left, output recedes to the economy's full-employment potential, and unemployment returns to the natural rate (move from *B* to *C* in both panels). Inflation fails to reduce the unemployment rate when it is anticipated by decision-makers. Thus, the *long-run* Phillips curve is vertical at the natural rate of unemployment.

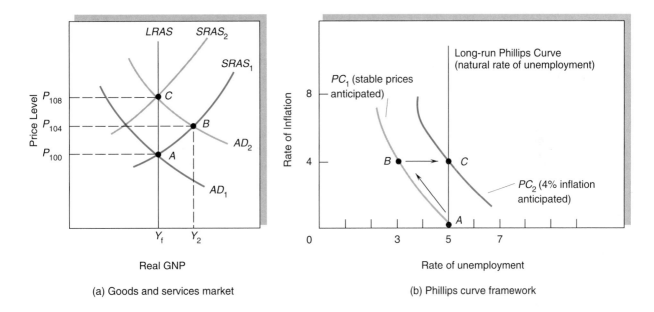

(a) Goods and services market

(b) Phillips curve framework

Similarly, the moves from *B* to *C* in the two panels also represent the same thing: the return of output to its long-run potential and unemployment to its natural rate, once decision-makers fully anticipate the observed rate of inflation.

What would happen if the macroplanners attempted to keep the unemployment rate low (below its natural rate) by shifting to a still more expansionary policy? As Exhibit 5 illustrates, this course of action will accelerate the inflation rate to still higher levels. Under adaptive expectations, once the 4 percent inflation rate is anticipated, the rate of unemployment can, for a time, be reduced to 3 percent only if the macroplanners are willing to tolerate 8 percent inflation (movement from *C* to *D*). Of course, once the 8 percent rate has persisted for a while, it, too, will be fully anticipated. The short-run Phillips curve will again shift to the right (to PC_3), unemployment will return to its long-run natural rate, and inflation will continue at a rate of 8 percent (point *E*).

Once decision-makers anticipate a higher rate of inflation (for example, the 8 percent rate), what will happen if macroplanners shift to a more restrictive policy designed to reduce the rate of inflation? When the inflation rate is declining, decision-makers will systematically *over*estimate the future inflation rate under the adaptive expectations hypothesis. Suppose that wage rates are based on agreements that anticipated a continuation of the 8 percent inflation rate (point *E* of Exhibit 5). If the actual inflation rate falls to 4 percent when 8 percent inflation was expected, the real wages of workers will exceed the real wage present when the actual and

EXHIBIT 5

Adaptive Expectations and Shifts in the Short-Run Phillips Curve

Continuing with the example of Exhibit 4b, point *C* illustrates an economy experiencing 4 percent inflation which was anticipated by decision-makers. Since the inflation was anticipated, the natural rate of unemployment is present. With adaptive expectations, demand stimulus policies that result in a still higher rate of inflation (8 percent, for example) would once again temporarily reduce the unemployment rate below its long-run, normal level (move from *C* to *D* along PC_2). After a time, however, decision-makers, would come to anticipate the higher inflation rate and the short-run Phillips curve would shift still further to the right to PC_3 (move from *D* to *E*). Once the higher rate is anticipated, if macroplanners try to decelerate the rate of inflation, unemployment will temporarily rise above its long-run natural rate (for example, move from *E* to *F*).

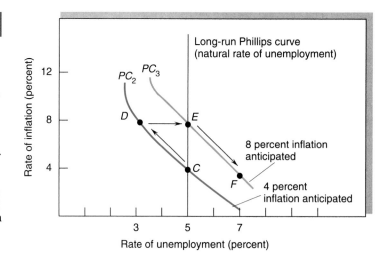

expected rates of inflation were equal at 8 percent. The more the actual inflation rate falls short of the expected rate, the higher the real wages of workers. Similarly, the search time of job seekers will be longer when they overestimate the impact of inflation on money wage rates. Unaware that the attractive money wage offers they seek are unavailable, job hunters will lengthen their job search. In the short run, rising unemployment will be a side effect of the higher real wages and more lengthy job searches.

As Exhibit 5 illustrates, with adaptive expectations, once a high (8 percent) inflation rate is anticipated by decision-makers, a shift to a more restrictive policy designed to decelerate the inflation rate will cause abnormally high unemployment (the move from *E* to *F* along PC_3) and economic recession. The abnormally high unemployment rate will continue until a lower rate of inflation convinces decision-makers to alter their inflationary expectations downward and revise long-term contracts accordingly.

We can now summarize the implications of adaptive expectations for the Phillips curve. Under adaptive expectations, decision-makers will underestimate the future inflation rate when the rate is rising and overestimate it when the inflation rate is falling. As the result of this systematic pattern, a shift to a more expansionary policy will temporarily reduce the unemployment rate, while a move to a more restrictive policy will temporarily increase the unemployment rate. As an inflation rate persists over time, decision-makers will eventually anticipate it and unemployment will return to its natural rate. There is no long-run (permanent) trade-off between inflation and unemployment under adaptive expectations. Like the *LRAS* curve, the long-run Phillips curve is vertical at the natural rate of unemployment.

THE LABOR MARKET AND THE PHILLIPS CURVE UNDER RATIONAL EXPECTATIONS

What difference does it make if we assume that expectations are formed rationally, rather than adaptively? In a world of rational expectations, individuals anticipate the effects of policy changes and adjust their actions accordingly. For example, if people see a surge in the money supply or a tax cut coming, they will adjust their expectations in light of the shift toward expansionary policy. Anticipating the strong future demand, workers and union representatives will immediately press for higher wages and/or inclusion of cost-of-living provisions to prevent the erosion of their real wages by inflation. Business firms, also anticipating the increase in demand,

EXHIBIT 6

Expansionary Policy with Rational Expectations

Initially, the actual and expected rates of inflation are equal at 4 percent and unemployment is equal to the economy's natural rate (point *A*). Policy-makers try to reduce unemployment by shifting to a more expansionary macropolicy consistent with an 8 percent inflationary rate. Proponents of rational explanations argue that the outcome is unpredictable. If people accurately anticipate the inflationary impact of the more expansionary course, the inflation rate will rise while unemployment remains unchanged (shift from *A* to *B*). On the other hand, if people underestimate the future inflation, unemployment will temporarily fall (as illustrated by shift from *A* to *C*). In contrast, if individuals overestimate the actual increase in the inflation rate, unemployment will rise temporarily above its long-run natural rate (shift from *A* to *D*).

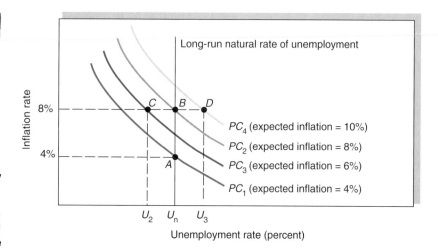

will consent to the demands of labor, but they will also raise prices. By the time the demand stimulus arrives, it will have *already been counteracted* by higher money wages, costs, and product prices.[5] Rather than increasing real output and employment as intended, the demand stimulus merely leads to higher prices since it was fully anticipated by decision-makers.

With the regard to demand stimulus policies, Exhibit 1b illustrates the implications of rational expectations within the framework of our *AD/AS* model. Exhibit 6 provides parallel analysis for the Phillips curve framework. Suppose an economy is initially at point *A,* where a 4 percent inflation rate is both observed and expected. Since the actual and expected inflation rates are equal, the long-run natural rate of unemployment (U_n) is initially observed. Now, suppose policy-makers shift to a more expansionary policy: a demand stimulus policy consistent with an 8 percent rate of inflation. With rational expectations, the Phillips curve will *immediately* shift upward as decision-makers anticipate an acceleration in the inflation rate due to the more expansionary macropolicy. If decision-makers correctly forecast the rise in the inflation rate (to 8 percent), short-run Phillips curve PC_2 will result. Even though the inflation rate increases to 8 percent, unemployment remains at its long-run natural rate (shift from *A* to *B*).

Of course, rational expectations do not imply that decision-makers are *always right*. People may either underestimate or overestimate the inflationary effects of the demand stimulus. When they *under*estimate the inflationary effects, the actual inflation rate will temporarily exceed the expected rate. Suppose that even though the actual inflation rate rises to 8 percent, decision-makers only anticipate an increase to 6 percent. When this is the case, the short-run Phillips curve (PC_3, Exhibit 6) will shift out by a lesser amount than if the increase in inflation had been accurately forecast. Since individuals do not *fully* build the higher (8 percent) inflation rate into their decision-making, the current unemployment rate declines to U_2 in the short run (move from *A* to *C*).

In contrast, when individuals *over*estimate the increase in inflation, the current unemployment rate will temporarily increase. For example, if decision-makers

---

[5]As we discussed in the last chapter, expansionary monetary policy will also increase the expected rate of inflation and lead to a higher money interest rate in the loanable funds markets. The rational expectations hypothesis also implies that money interest rates will rise quickly in response to expansionary monetary policy.

expect the inflation rate to rise to 10 percent while the expansionary policies only generate an increase to 8 percent, the short-run Phillips curve will shift by a larger amount (PC_4, Exhibit 6) than if the increase in inflation had been correctly forecast. In the short run, unemployment will rise above its long-run normal rate (move from A to D).

How can policy-makers know whether rational decision-makers will over- or underestimate the effects of a policy change? According to the proponents of rational expectations, they cannot. If the errors of decision-makers are random, as the rational expectation theory implies, people will be as likely to overestimate as underestimate the inflationary impact of demand stimulus policies. Under rational expectations, then, the impact of expansionary policy on real output and employment is *unpredictable,* even in the short run. If decision-makers accurately anticipate the inflationary impact of expansionary policy, the unemployment rate will remain unchanged even though the inflation rate accelerates. However, if they underestimate the future inflation impact, the unemployment rate will temporarily decline. Conversely, the unemployment rate will temporarily rise if they overestimate the inflationary impact of the policy.

The rational expectations hypothesis indicates that it will be extremely difficult for policy-makers to use demand stimulus policies to reduce the unemployment rate. Such a strategy is effective, even temporarily, only when it catches people by surprise. However, if policy-makers follow a systematic strategy, such as persistent demand stimulus or even countercyclical demand stimulus, rational human beings will catch on to the pattern. Most importantly, once the systematic policy moves are widely anticipated, they will fail to exert the intended effect.

RATIONAL EXPECTATIONS AND MACROECONOMIC POLICY

The policy implications of rational expectations are clear. The best policies are pre-announced, stable policies (for example, steady growth of the money supply and a balanced federal budget). Macroeconomic policy should be directed toward long-term objectives and changes should be weighed very carefully. Policy should not attempt to fine-tune the economy. Efforts to do so will only contribute to economic uncertainty.

On the positive side, the rational expectations hypothesis indicates that a move from inflation to stable prices can be achieved more easily than adaptive expectations imply. If policy-makers shift to a more restrictive course *and* convince the public they are going to stick to it until stable prices are achieved, the rational expectations hypothesis implies that the expected rate of inflation will decline quickly (shifting the short-run Phillips curve down and toward the origin). As the expectation of inflation declines, money wage rates will be correspondingly scaled back. Money interest rates will fall. If a restrictive policy is really credible, the rational expectations hypothesis implies that the inflation rate can be reduced without the economy going through a prolonged period of recession and high unemployment—a situation that is implied by the adaptive expectations hypothesis. Credibility that policy-makers will ''stay the course'' until inflation is brought under control, though, is absolutely essential.[6] If market participants lack confidence in the long-term anti-inflationary commitment of policy-makers, they will reduce their

---

[6]For evidence that even hyperinflations can be brought under control quickly (with little loss of output) when credibility is present, see Thomas Sargent, ''The Ends of Four Big Inflations,'' in Robert E. Hall (ed.), *Inflation: Causes and Effects* (Chicago: University of Chicago Press for the National Bureau of Economic Research, 1982), pp. 41–98.

expectations for the future rate of inflation slowly even if current policy is restrictive. When policy-makers have a past history of policy reversals and saying one thing while doing another, it will be difficult for them to establish credibility. Proponents of rational expectations are thus not surprised that restrictive policies have often led to recession and abnormally high unemployment.

EXPECTATIONS AND THE MODERN VIEW OF THE PHILLIPS CURVE

Expectations substantially alter the naive Phillips curve view of the 1960s. With regard to the Phillips curve, three major points follow from modern analysis.

1. Demand stimulus will lead to inflation without permanently reducing the unemployment rate. Once people fully anticipate the inflationary side effects of expansionary policies, the short-run Phillips curve shifts upward to the right and unemployment returns to its natural rate. In the long run, inflation will not reduce the unemployment rate. Under adaptive expectations, higher inflation rates are anticipated only after they are observed for a period of time. With adaptive expectations, then, accelerating rates of inflation will temporarily reduce unemployment. With rational expectations, decision-makers respond to expansionary policies by immediately adjusting their inflationary expectations upward. So, expansionary policies fail to even temporarily reduce the unemployment rate when expectations are rational. In the long run, though, the implications of adaptive and rational expectations are identical—persistent expansionary policy will lead to inflation without permanently reducing the unemployment rate. Neither the adaptive nor the rational expectations hypotheses indicate that expansionary policies can sustain unemployment below its natural rate. If the natural rate of unemployment in the United States, for example, happens to be 5 percent, macroplanners will be unable to maintain a 3 percent rate of unemployment.

2. When inflation is greater than was anticipated, unemployment falls below the natural rate. When inflation is less than was anticipated, unemployment will rise above the natural rate. It is the *differences* between the actual and expected rates of inflation that influence unemployment, not the magnitude of inflation, as some economists previously thought. Exhibit 7 illustrates this point by recasting the Phillips curve within the expectations framework. When people underestimate the actual rate of inflation, abnormally low unemployment will occur. Conversely, when decision-makers expect a higher rate of inflation than what actually occurs—when they overestimate the inflation rate—unemployment will rise above its natural rate. Equal changes in the actual and expected inflation rates, though, will fail to reduce the unemployment rate. If actual inflation rates of 5 percent, 10 percent, 20 percent, or even higher are *accurately anticipated,* they will fail to reduce unemployment below its natural rate.[7]

---

[7]Empirically, higher rates of inflation are generally associated with greater *variability* in the inflation rate. Erratic variability increases economic uncertainty. It is likely to inhibit business activity, reduce the volume of mutually advantageous exchange, and cause the level of employment to fall. Thus, higher, more variable inflation rates may actually increase the natural rate of unemployment.

EXHIBIT 7

The Modern Expectational Phillips Curve

It is the *differences* between the actual and expected rates of inflation that influence the unemployment rate, not merely the size of the inflation rate as the naive Phillips curve analysis implied. When inflation is greater than anticipated (people underestimate it), unemployment will fall below the natural rate. In contrast, when inflation is less than people anticipate, unemployment will rise above the natural rate. If the inflation rate is correctly anticipated by decision-makers, the natural rate of unemployment will result.

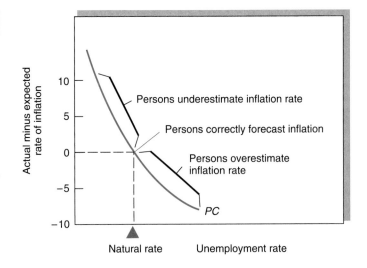

INFLATION, UNEMPLOYMENT, AND THE PHILLIPS CURVE, 1961–1990

3. *When the inflation rate is steady—when it is neither rising nor falling—the actual rate of unemployment will equal the economy's natural rate of unemployment.* If the inflation rate of an economy is constant (or approximately so), decision-makers will come to anticipate the rate. This rate will be reflected in both long-term contracts and the job search of workers. Once this happens, unemployment will return to its natural rate. In fact, the natural rate of unemployment is sometimes defined as the unemployment rate present when the inflation rate is neither rising nor falling.

Modern Phillips curve analysis enhances our understanding of the U.S. inflation-unemployment experience during the last three decades. After nearly 20 years of low inflation (and moderate monetary and fiscal policy) following the Second World War, decision-makers were accustomed to relative price stability. Against this background, the *expected* rate of inflation was low. As a result, the shift toward expansionary policies in the mid-1960s caught people by surprise.[8] Therefore, as Exhibit 3 shows, these policies initially reduced the unemployment rate.

Contrary to the popular view of the 1960s, though, the abnormally low unemployment did not last. Exhibit 8 makes this point clear. Exhibit 8 is an updated version of Exhibit 3. Just as our theory predicts, the inflation-unemployment conditions worsened substantially as the expansionary policy persisted. The Phillips curve (PC_2) consistent with the 1970–1973 data was well to the right of PC_1. During the 1974–1982 period, still higher rates of inflation were observed. As inflation rates in the 6 to 10 percent range became commonplace in the latter half of the 1970s, the Phillips curve once again shifted upward to PC_3. As monetary policy tightened in 1981–1982 and the Reagan administration promised to bring inflation under control, the inflation rate decelerated sharply in the mid-1980s.

---

[8]The following data are indicative of the shift toward more expansionary macroeconomic policies beginning in the mid-1960s. Between 1965 and 1980, the M1 money supply grew at an annual rate of 6.3 percent, compared to only 2.5 percent during the previous 15 years. Similarly, perpetual federal deficits replaced balanced budgets. During the 1950–65 period, there were 8 budget deficits and 7 surpluses. On average, the federal budget was approximately in balance during the 15-year period. During the 1965–80 period, however, there was only one year of budget surplus, and annual deficits averaged 1.5 percent of GNP.

EXHIBIT 8

Inflation and Real-World Shifts in the Phillips Curve

The 1982 Report of the Council of Economic Advisers (CEA) contained this unemployment-inflation rate chart. While the 1961–1969 data mapped Phillips curve PC_1, as demand stimulus policies led to higher inflation rates, the Phillips curve shifted out to PC_2 (for the 1970–1973 period) and PC_3 (for the 1974–1982 period). In contrast with the 1969 CEA Report (see Exhibit 3), the 1982 Report stated:

> Nothing in Phillips' works or in subsequent studies showed that higher inflation was associated with sustainable lower unemployment, and nothing in economic theory gave reason to believe that the relationship uncovered by Phillips was a dependable basis for policies designed to accept more inflation or less unemployment.

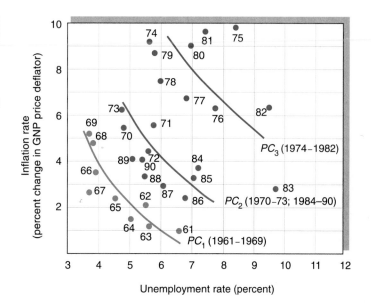

Source: *Economic Report of the President, 1982,* p. 51. The Phillips curves have been fitted and the 1982–1990 data added to the chart.

Initially, the unemployment rate soared (see 1982 and 1983 data). However, as the restraint continued, people scaled their expectations for the inflation rate downward and the Phillips curve shifted inward. As Exhibit 8 indicates, the 1984–1990 data are approximately consistent with PC_2, well below the Phillips curve for the 1974–1982 period.

Exhibit 9 presents the 1961–1990 inflation-unemployment data in a form that provides a still better test of our theory. Our analysis indicates that when the actual inflation rate is higher than people anticipate, unemployment will fall short of the natural rate. On the other hand, if the inflation rate is less than was anticipated, unemployment will exceed its natural rate. Of course, we cannot directly observe the expected inflation rate. However, we would expect that it will be influenced by recent experiences. In Exhibit 9, for each year shown, the average inflation rate during the previous three years is used as a proxy for the expected rate of inflation. The exhibit illustrates that when the inflation rate was *higher* than anticipated (higher than the average of the last 3 years), the unemployment was generally less than the natural rate. For example, as the inflation rate rose in the late 1960s, the actual inflation rate was approximately 2 percent higher than anticipated during 1966, 1968, and 1969. Just as our theory implies, unemployment was well below the natural rate during each of these years. Conversely, when the inflation rate was less than anticipated, unemployment rose above the natural rate. Look at the dots for the years 1976, 1977, 1982, 1983, and 1984. During each of these years, the actual inflation rate was significantly less than the anticipated rate. And during each of these years, unemployment well above the natural rate was observed.

While the data of Exhibit 9 show an obvious negative relationship between *un*anticipated inflation and unemployment, the observations for five years (1974–1975 and 1979–1981) do not fit as well as the others. Interestingly, these five years encompass periods of soaring oil prices. Oil prices quadrupled (from $1.50 to $10 per barrel) between 1973 and 1975, and more than tripled (from $12 to $40 per

EXHIBIT 9

Unanticipated Inflation and Deviations from the Natural Rate of Unemployment, 1961–1990

Here we show the relationship between unanticipated inflation and actual unemployment compared to the natural rate. When the inflation rate is *greater* than anticipated, unemployment tends to fall below the natural rate. Conversely, when the inflation rate is *less* than anticipated, the unemployment rate is generally above the natural rate.

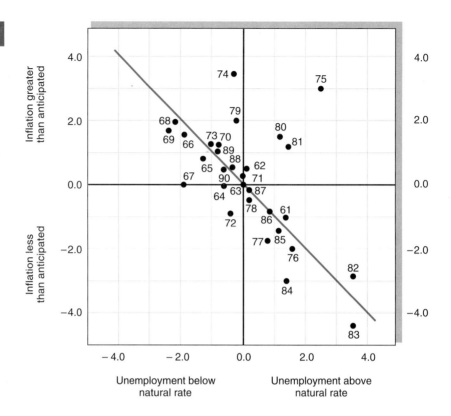

Source: *Economic Report of the President, 1990* and Robert J. Gordon, *Macroeconomics* (Boston: Little Brown, 1990). The natural rate of unemployment data are from Gordon. The average inflation rate for the previous three years was used as a proxy for the anticipated inflation rate for each year.

barrel) between 1978 and 1981. As we previously discussed (see Chapter 9, Exhibit 7), supply shocks of this type tend to push the price level up. Predictably, they lead to dislocations and adjustments that weaken the normal relationship between inflation and unemployment.

THE ADAPTIVE VERSUS RATIONAL EXPECTATIONS DEBATE

Are expectations determined adaptively or rationally? There is a continuing debate among economists concerning this question. The rational expectations proponents charge that the adaptive expectation hypothesis is naive. They find it difficult to accept the notion that individuals look only at past price changes while ignoring information on variables (for example, changes in the money supply, interest rates, and exchange rates) that play an important role in the actual generation of inflation.

The advocates of adaptive expectations reply that the rational expectations theory implies that individuals possess an inordinate amount of information about highly complex issues. They note that the average person neither keeps up with the latest moves of the Fed nor forecasts changes in the Federal budget. The proponents of adaptive expectations charge that it is unrealistic to assume that most people will

MEASURES IN ECONOMICS

The Natural Rate of Unemployment in Europe, Canada, Japan, and the United States

Our analysis indicates that when the inflation rate of a country is steady (when it is neither rising nor falling) for an extended period of time, people will anticipate the rate and unemployment will move to the economy's natural rate of unemployment. Interestingly, the inflation rates in the United States, Canada, Europe, and Japan were quite steady during 1986–1990. The inflation rate averaged approximately 4 percent during 1986–1990 in the United States, Europe, and Canada. More importantly, in each of these areas the inflation rate fluctuated within a narrow band (between 3 percent and 5 percent) during the five-year period. In Japan, the inflation rate was lower and it was virtually constant at approximately 1.5 percent during 1986–1990.

Given these steady rates of inflation, the actual unemployment rates during the latter part of the period should approximate the natural rate of unemployment for each of these economies. The unemployment rates in 1989 and 1990 were:

	1989	1990
United States	5.3	5.5
Europe		
(11 EEC Countries)	7.3	7.0
Canada	7.5	8.1
Japan	2.3	2.1

Thus, after an extended period of inflation at a steady rate, the unemployment rate during 1989–1990 was approximately 5.5 percent in the United States, approximately 7 percent in Europe, 8 percent in Canada, and 2 percent in Japan. These numbers imply

that, compared to the United States, the natural rate of unemployment in the late 1980s was higher in Europe and Canada, but lower in Japan.

Why might the natural rate of unemployment be high in Europe and Canada but low in Japan? There are two major reasons why this may be the case. First, wages tend to be more flexible in Japan, but less flexible in Europe and Canada, than in the United States. Unions in Japan are almost exclusively of the "company union" variety. They seldom set wages for an entire industry, and they are much more likely than their U.S. counterparts to accept wage cuts during a period of declining demand for the products that they produced. Compared to the United States, a decline in demand in an industry in Japan is more likely to result in wage reductions and less likely to result in termination and worker layoffs. In contrast, wages tend to be less flexible in Europe and Canada than in the United States. Unionism is more prevalent in Europe and Canada than in the United States. For example, between 40 percent and 50 percent of the nonagricultural labor force is unionized in the United Kingdom, Italy, and Germany.[9] In Canada, 37 percent of the nonfarm workers belong to a union. By way of comparison, only 16 percent of the U.S. nonagricultural labor force is unionized. To the extent that strong unions in Europe and Japan push wages above the market level and reduce wage flexibility, they tend to increase the natural rate of unemployment. In addition, many

of the governments in Europe set wages—often at or above equilibrium rates—in various occupations and industries. This, too, contributes to wage rigidity and tends to push the natural rate of unemployment up.

Second, the unemployment compensation system is generally more lucrative (and less restrictive with regard to eligibility) in Europe and Canada than in the United States.[10] This encourages more lengthy periods of job search and thereby pushes up the natural rate of unemployment in Europe. In contrast, unemployment compensation and other income transfer programs are less lucrative in Japan than in the United States. This, too, contributes to the low natural rate of unemployment in Japan.

Restrictions limiting the mobility of workers and businesses across national boundaries may also contribute to the high unemployment rate in Europe. Many of these barriers will be falling with the unification of Europe in 1992. Thus, it will be interesting to follow the natural rate of unemployment in Europe during the 1990s.

---

[9]Richard B. Freeman, "Contraction and Expansion: The Divergence of Private and Public Sector Unionism in the United States," *Journal of Economic Perspectives,* Spring 1988, pp. 63–88.
[10]See Vivek Moorthy, "Unemployment in Canada and the United States: The Role of Unemployment Insurance Benefits," *Federal Reserve Bank of New York: Quarterly Review,* Winter 1990, pp. 48–61.

(a) develop reliable theories about the operation of a highly complex economy, (b) monitor the necessary policy variables, and (c) consistently make the implied adjustments to changes in macropolicy. They believe most people will find a simple rule of thumb such as "inflation next year will be about the same as the recent past" to be both sensible and "rational."

The proponents of rational expectations are unmoved by this argument. They believe that it overlooks several facts. After all, business firms and labor unions hire specialists to make forecasts about the future. Predictions made by prominent economists are often widely disseminated via television news and daily newspapers. Because of this, even relatively uninformed citizens, whether they realize it or not, develop a view on the expected rate of inflation.

The proponents of adaptive expectations also emphasize that long-term contracts constrain the responses of decision-makers. For example, if long-term contracts specify nominal wages and prices over a longer time period than it takes the monetary authorities to alter the direction of monetary policy, the authorities are in a position to reduce real wages and thereby stimulate employment. Suppose that the wages of a group of workers are set by a three-year collective bargaining agreement that calls for raises of 5 percent during each of the years. If the inflation rate accelerates upward to say 8 percent, the workers will still get only 5 percent annual pay increases during the period of their contract. Hence, even if decision-makers anticipate the consequences of a shift toward monetary expansion, long-term contracts will limit their ability to respond quickly. To the extent that this is true, shifts in monetary policy will exert an impact on real wages, employment, and real GNP in the short run.

Advocates of rational expectations respond by pointing out that the nature of contracts is influenced by macroeconomic policy. If the monetary authorities seek to exploit long-term contracts, individuals will predictably respond by including cost-of-living provisions, choosing contracts of shorter duration, and permitting renegotiation at various time intervals. According to the proponents of rational expectations, then, if expansionary policies seek to reduce *real* wages and costs, they will only induce decision-makers to alter the nature of long-term contracts. The growth of collective bargaining agreements containing escalator clauses (provisions for automatic money wage increases as the price level rises) during the 1970s is consistent with this view. As inflation accelerated upward, the number of collective bargaining agreements providing for cost-of-living wage adjustments rose from 20 percent in 1965 to nearly 70 percent in the late 1970s.

The proponents of adaptive expectations argue that the past performance of the economy is supportive of their view. For example, more rapid growth of the money supply has generally been associated with an expansion in real GNP, followed a year or two later by increases in the inflation rate. Similarly, deceleration in monetary growth has consistently led to a recession, prior to any significant reduction in the inflation rate (see Exhibits 12 and 13, Chapter 13). These findings indicate that people alter their expectations slowly as the adaptive expectations theory implies, not rapidly as suggested by the rational expectations theory.

The proponents of rational expectations remain unconvinced. They point out that a rapid change in the public's expectations in response to a policy change is dependent on confidence that the change is both real and long-term. In contrast, even rational expectations theory implies that people will respond cautiously to an *apparent change* when policy-makers have a past history of policy reversals. When the credibility of policy-makers is low, a gradual change in expectations in response to an apparent change in direction is the expected behavior. Thus, advocates of rational expectations do not believe that past evidence indicating expectations have often changed slowly is damaging to their theory.

Of course, the adaptive versus rational expectations controversy is important because the two theories have different implications for the short-run Phillips curve. We must not forget, however, that the implications of the two theories for the *long-run* Phillips curve are essentially the same. Both theories imply that expansionary macropolicy that increases aggregate demand relative to aggregate supply will lead to inflation without *permanently* reducing unemployment below its normal, long-run rate.

MICROECONOMICS AND REDUCING THE NATURAL RATE OF UNEMPLOYMENT

The integration of expectations into our analysis highlights the difficulties involved in the use of monetary and fiscal policy to promote high levels of employment. Can other methods be used to reduce the unemployment rate? In recent years, economists have turned to microeconomics as a means of addressing the traditional macroeconomic problem of high unemployment. The microeconomics approach to employment focuses on how the economy's *natural* rate of unemployment might be reduced and LRAS increased. Remember, the natural rate of unemployment is not immutable. Among other things, it reflects the incentive structure emanating from the economy's institutional arrangements. If changes in that incentive structure could improve the efficiency of job search and remove barriers to employment, the economy's natural rate of unemployment would decline. In terms of the Phillips curve, the long-run (vertical) Phillips curve would shift to the left.

What kinds of institutional changes would be most likely to reduce the natural rate of unemployment? We will consider three changes that have been widely discussed.

REVISING THE UNEMPLOYMENT COMPENSATION SYSTEM

The unemployment compensation system was designed to reduce the hardships of unemployment. As desirable as this program is from a humanitarian standpoint, it diminishes the opportunity cost of job search, leisure, nonproductive activities, and continued unemployment. The conflict between high benefit levels and low rates of unemployment should therefore not be surprising.

There are two major reasons why the current unemployment compensation system increases the natural rate of unemployment. First, it reduces, and in some cases virtually eliminates, the personal cost of unemployment. The benefits in most states provide covered unemployed workers with payments of 50 to 60 percent of their *previous gross earnings*. Unemployment benefits are not subject to payroll taxes (and in some cases, income taxes). In addition, unemployed workers may also qualify for other transfer benefits such as food stamps and Medicaid. It is not unusual, then, for the benefit package of a covered unemployed worker to replace 75 percent or more of previous net earnings. Clearly, benefit levels in this range substantially reduce the incentive of individuals to search quickly and diligently for jobs and to accept employment at marginally lower wages prior to the exhaustion of their benefits.

Second, unemployment compensation acts as a subsidy to employers who offer unstable or seasonal employment opportunities. Employees would be more reluctant to work for such employers (for example, northern contractors who generally lay off workers in the winter) were it not for the fact that these employees can supplement their earnings with unemployment compensation benefits during their layoffs. The system makes seasonal, temporary, and casual employment opportunities more attractive than would otherwise be the case. In essence, it encourages employers to adopt production methods and work rules that rely extensively on temporary employees and supplementary layoff benefits.

There is little doubt that the current unemployment compensation system increases the natural rate of unemployment. Most researchers in the area believe that the long-run rate of unemployment is between 0.5 and 1.0 percent higher than it would be if the negative employment effects of the system could be eliminated.[11] In effect, unemployment benefits subsidize job search. There is one positive element accompanying this subsidy—the additional job search emanating from this subsidy may improve the match between the skills of unemployed workers and the requirements of potential jobs. To the extent this is true, the average productivity of workers is higher.

How can the unemployment compensation system be reformed without undercutting the original humanitarian objectives of the program? Several policy alternatives exist. Firms that regularly terminate and lay off a high percentage of their work force might be charged a payroll tax that more accurately reflects the cost of employment instability. (The current system performs this function imperfectly.) In addition, after a specified period of time, three months, for example, unemployment compensation recipients might be required to accept available jobs (including public-sector employment) that provide wage rates equal to their unemployment compensation benefits. Alternatively, recipients' benefits might be gradually reduced as they engaged in more lengthy periods of job search and unemployment. This would reduce the incentive of individuals to wait until their benefits run out (generally 26 weeks) before accepting employment. Each of these proposals would increase the incentive of employers to offer stable employment and job searchers to seek out and accept employment more quickly.

REFORMING THE MINIMUM WAGE

Despite the good intentions, minimum wage laws reduce the employment prospects of low-skilled, inexperienced workers. Many youthful workers fall into this category. As in the case of other price floors, minimum wages lead to an excess supply. By mandating artificially high wage rates for jobs requiring few skills, the minimum wage reduces the employment opportunities available to low-skill workers.[12]

---

[11]See Ray Thorne, *The Unemployment Compensation System: Paying People Not to Work* (Dallas: National Center for Policy Analysis, 1988) and Bruce Meyer, *Unemployment Insurance and Unemployment Spells* (Cambridge: National Bureau of Economic Research, 1988) for additional detail on this topic.

[12]For additional information on this topic, see Charles Brown, Curtis Gilroy, and Andrew Cohen, ''The Effect of Minimum Wage on Employment and Unemployment,'' *Journal of Economic Literature*, 20, June 1982, pp. 487–528.

The adverse impact of the minimum wage on the on-the-job training opportunities available to low-skill workers is also important. The legislation often makes it unfeasible for an employer to (a) provide training to inexperienced workers and (b) pay the legal minimum wage at the same time. Thus, there are few (temporarily) low-paying jobs offering a combination of informal (or formal) training and skill-building experience. This makes it difficult for low-skill workers to acquire the training and experience necessary to move up to better, higher-paying jobs.

Several proposals have been suggested to minimize these negative effects. Some economists favor abolition of the minimum wage. Others would exempt teenagers from the legislation's coverage. Still others would exempt long-term unemployed workers from the legislation. In each case, the advocates argue that the wages of low-skill workers would settle at a market equilibrium, and the long-run employment and training opportunities available to such workers would improve.

PROVIDING TRAINING OPPORTUNITIES

Youth Work Scholarship:
A proposed scholarship providing subsidies to younger workers who maintain jobs. Some scholarships would limit the subsidies to employment that offered on-the-job training.

Unemployment may result from mismatches between the requirements of available jobs and the skills of potential workers. Many economists believe that programs designed to improve the basic skills of workers and facilitate the development of new skills could reduce the natural rate of unemployment. Of course, improvement in our elementary and secondary educational system would be a step in that direction. Others believe that a vocational training loan program, similar in design to present college loan programs, would assist low- and middle-income youths in developing technical skills. Martin Feldstein, chairman of the Council of Economic Advisers under President Reagan, has suggested that we provide youthful workers, those under 25 years of age, for example, with a **youth work scholarship.** This plan would offer subsidies for technical training to young people who did not go on to college. Feldstein's plan would reward youthful workers for continuous employment and the acquisition of craft, clerical, operative, and perhaps even managerial skills.

The long-run goal of training programs is to improve the quality and flexibility of the labor force. Accomplishment of this objective would lead to a lower natural rate of unemployment because it would reduce the frequency and duration of unemployment.

DEMOGRAPHICS AND THE NATURAL RATE OF UNEMPLOYMENT

Compared to their elders, youthful workers are more likely to switch back and forth between the labor force and school. Even after they permanently enter the labor force, youthful workers are more likely to switch jobs as they search for a career path. Because of this, younger workers historically experience higher unemployment rates. In fact, the unemployment rate of persons under age 25 has typically run three times or more the rate for workers age 35 and over. For people age 25–34, the unemployment rate has generally been at least one and one-half times the rate for their older counterparts (see Exhibit 10b for 1980 and 1990 data).

Since the employment pattern of youthful workers is less stable, the natural rate of unemployment rises as these workers make up a larger share of the labor force.

EXHIBIT 10

Demographics and
the Natural Rate of
Unemployment,
1958–2000

Since younger workers have
less stable employment
patterns, the natural rate of
unemployment rises when they
comprise a larger share of the
labor force. This was the case
during the 1958–1980 period.
During the next decade,
however, youthful workers will
become a smaller proportion of
the labor force. This will reduce
the natural rate of
unemployment during the
1990s.

(a) Percent of labor force by age

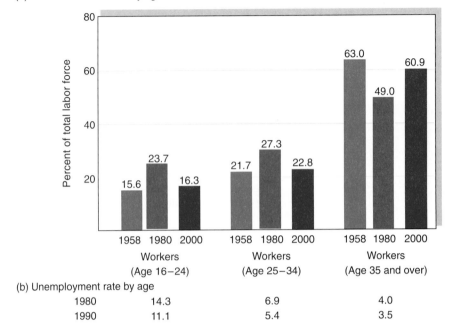

(b) Unemployment rate by age

	Workers (Age 16–24)	Workers (Age 25–34)	Workers (Age 35 and over)
1980	14.3	6.9	4.0
1990	11.1	5.4	3.5

As Exhibit 10a shows, this is precisely what happened during the 1958–1980 period. As those born during the "baby boom" following the Second World War entered the work force during the 1960s and 1970s, the labor force grew rapidly and became progressively younger. In 1958, workers age 16 to 24 constituted only 15.6 percent of the labor force. By 1980, nearly one out of every four (23.7 percent) labor force participants was in this age group. Similarly, young adults age 25 to 34 also increased as a proportion of the work force between 1958 and 1980. In contrast, workers over age 35 were a shrinking proportion of the labor force during the 1958–1980 period. As the youthful segments of the labor force grew rapidly, the natural rate of unemployment rose. Research in this area indicates that the natural rate of unemployment was between 0.5 percent and 1.5 percent higher in 1980 than in 1958 as a result of this factor. Obviously, it has contributed to the high unemployment rates of the 1970s and 1980s.

However, this adverse demographic factor has now reversed itself. By 2000, people age 16–24 are projected to comprise 16.3 percent of the work force, substantially lower than the 1980 figure. Conversely, projections indicate that workers age 35 and over will comprise 60.9 percent of the labor force in 2000, up from 49 percent in 1980 (Exhibit 10a). Economic theory indicates that this maturing of the U.S. work force during the next decade will reduce the natural rate of unemployment.

LOOKING AHEAD

Now that we have integrated expectations into our analysis, we are prepared to take a closer look at the potential of macroeconomic policy as a stabilization tool. The next chapter focuses on stabilization policy and related issues.

CHAPTER SUMMARY

1. The impact of demand stimulus policies is dependent on whether the effects are anticipated. When the effects are unanticipated, an increase in aggregate demand will

temporarily expand real GNP beyond the economy's long-run output potential. In contrast, when decision-makers correctly anticipate the effects of expansionary policy, real output will remain unchanged even though the price level increases.

2. There are two major theories as to how expectations are formed: (a) the adaptive expectations hypothesis and (b) the rational expectations hypothesis.

3. According to the adaptive expectations hypothesis, individuals base their expectations for the future on observations of the recent past. Expectations for the future will lag behind observed changes.

4. The rational expectations hypothesis assumes that people use all pertinent information, including data on the conduct of current policy, when formulating their expectations about the future. While decision-makers make forecasting errors under rational expectations, the errors are not systematic. That is, they are equally likely to either overestimate or underestimate the future change in an economic variable.

5. The Phillips curve indicates the relationship between the unemployment rate and inflation rate. Prior to the 1970s, there was a widespread belief that higher inflation would lower the rate of unemployment.

6. Integrating expectations into macroeconomics makes it clear that any trade-off between unemployment and inflation is unstable. With adaptive expectations, expansionary policies will lead to a *short-run* trade-off of lower unemployment for an acceleration in the inflation rate. Individuals, though, will eventually come to expect the higher inflation rate and alter their decisions accordingly. This will cause unemployment to return to the natural rate.

7. With rational expectations, there is no consistent unemployment-inflation trade-off even in the short run. The impact of expansionary macropolicy is unpredictable. If decision-makers accurately forecast the inflationary effects, expansionary policies will cause inflation while leaving the unemployment rate unchanged. However, if expansionary policy leads to an increase in inflation that exceeds (is less than) the expected increase, unemployment will temporarily fall below (rise above) its long-run normal level.

8. Contrary to the expectations of the 1960s, expansionary policy during the post-1965 period did not consistently reduce the unemployment rate. There is no evidence that in the long run inflationary policies can reduce the unemployment rate—that inflation can be "traded off" for unemployment. Both adaptive and rational expectations theories imply that the long-run Phillips curve is vertical at the natural rate of unemployment.

9. The modern view of the Phillips curve integrates expectations. When the inflation rate is greater than was previously anticipated, unemployment will tend to fall below the natural rate. Conversely, when the inflation rate is less than was previously anticipated, unemployment will rise above its natural rate. Even high rates of inflation will fail to reduce unemployment once they are anticipated by decision-makers.

10. The validity of the adaptive versus rational expectations hypotheses is a topic of current debate among economists. The proponents of adaptive expectations believe that the expectations used in real-world decision-making are typically based on a simple rule of thumb (the future rate of inflation will be similar to the recent past). They charge that the rational expectations hypothesis implies that people possess an unrealistic amount of knowledge about how the economy works. The proponents of rational expectations counter that it is naive to believe that decision-makers ignore information concerning how inflation is actually generated. They argue that relatively uninformed people will consult specialists and alter the nature of long-term contracts and thereby reduce the impact of inflation on real economic variables.

11. In recent years, economists have given increased attention to the importance of incentives in the determination of the natural rate of unemployment. Many economists believe that the unemployment compensation system, minimum wage legislation, and inadequate educational and training programs contribute to the high

current rate of unemployment. Reform in these areas could lower the natural rate of unemployment.

12. During the 1960s and 1970s, rapid growth in the number of youthful labor force participants increased the natural rate of unemployment. This demographic factor has now been reversed. As a share of the labor force, youthful workers will decline during the next decade. This will tend to reduce the natural rate of unemployment in the 1990s.

CRITICAL ANALYSIS QUESTIONS

1. Suppose the monetary authorities accelerate the annual growth rate of the money supply from a long-term trend of 5 percent to 10 percent. If decision-makers do not anticipate the effects of this policy change, how will it influence output, employment, and prices in the short run? If the effects are anticipated, how will the expansionary policy influence output, employment, and prices in the short run?

2. State in your own words the adaptive expectations hypothesis. Explain why adaptive expectations imply that macroacceleration will only temporarily reduce the rate of unemployment.

3. Compare and contrast the rational expectations hypothesis with the adaptive expectations hypothesis. If expectations are formed ''rationally'' rather than ''adaptively,'' will it be easier or more difficult to decelerate the inflation rate without causing an economic recession? Explain.

*4. How does the microeconomic approach to the problems of unemployment and economic growth differ from the traditional monetary and fiscal policy approach to these problems? Is the microeconomic approach a substitute for traditional monetary and fiscal policy? Explain.

5. After a period of persistent inflation, such as was experienced in the United States during the 1974–1981 period, most economists believe that a shift to restrictive monetary policy to reduce the inflation rate will cause a recession. Why? How could the monetary authorities minimize the danger of a severe, lengthy recession?

*6. Prior to the mid-1970s, many economists thought a higher rate of unemployment would reduce the inflation rate. Why? How does the modern view of the Phillips curve differ from the earlier view?

7. Why do most economists think the natural rate of unemployment rose during the 1960s and 1970s? Why do these same economists think the natural rate will fall during the next decade?

8. Throughout the 1960s, many economists believed that expansionary macroeconomic policy would result in both more inflation and less unemployment. How would acceptance of this theory influence policy-makers? Did the theory exert any impact on policy? Cite supportive evidence.

*9. Modern analysis rejects the view that inflationary policies reduce the long-term unemployment rate. How does this theory influence macroeconomic policy? Explain.

10. Suppose that a country were currently experiencing 10 percent inflation. Policy-makers want to achieve stable prices with a minimum reduction in output. What advice would you give them?

11. Evaluate each of the following:
    a. ''The primary cause of inflation is excessive government spending.''
    b. ''The primary cause of inflation is large budget deficits.''
    c. ''The primary cause of inflation is the greed of business and labor leaders.''

*12. Suppose that after 10 weeks of drawing unemployment compensation, the benefits were reduced weekly until they were phased out after 26 weeks. How would this policy influence the natural rate of unemployment? Discuss the pros and cons of such a policy.

---

*Asterisk denotes questions for which answers are given in Appendix C, Selected Answers.

13. How would you expect the actual unemployment rate to compare with the natural unemployment rate in the following cases?
    a. Prices are stable and have been stable for the last four years.
    b. The current inflation rate is 3 percent and this rate was widely anticipated more than a year ago.
    c. Expansionary policies lead to an unexpected increase in the inflation rate from 3 percent to 7 percent.
    d. There is an unexpected reduction in the inflation rate from 7 percent to 2 percent.

*14. Explain what happens to real wages, the job search time of workers, and the unemployment rate when there is unanticipated inflation. What happens when the inflation is anticipated?

15. The proponents of rational expectations argue that the cost of decelerating the inflation rate and moving to price stability will be reduced if people believe that the monetary authorities are really going to achieve and maintain stable prices. Why is this credibility important? How might the monetary authorities enhance the credibility of their policies?

*16. a. What would cause the short-run Phillips curve to shift?
     b. What would cause the long-run Phillips curve to shift?

*17. Several European countries provide weekly unemployment benefits to persons *for as long as they remain unemployed*. Can you think of problems that are likely to accompany a program of this type? What impact will it have on the rate of unemployment?

15 Stabilization Policy, Output, and Employment

Unfortunately, policymakers cannot act as if the economy is an automobile that can quickly be steered back and forth. Rather, the procedure of changing aggregate demand is much closer to that of a captain navigating a giant super-tanker. Even if he gives a signal for a hard turn, it takes a mile before he can see a change, and ten miles before the ship makes the turn.[1]

Robert J. Gordon

CHAPTER FOCUS

- Historically, how much has real output fluctuated? Are economic fluctuations becoming more or less severe?

- Can macroeconomic policy moderate the business cycle?

- Why is proper timing of changes in macroeconomic policy crucial to the effectiveness of stabilization policy? Why is proper timing difficult to achieve?

- Would we have more or less instability if policy-makers simply expanded the money supply at a low, constant rate each year while balancing the federal budget?

- Should policy-makers try to smooth minor ups and downs in the growth path of real GNP?

*D*uring the 1960s, economists were highly confident that macroeconomic policy could neutralize the economic ups and downs of the business cycle. Some even thought that the business cycle, like polio, would soon be banished to the pages of history. In the 1973 edition of his all-time best-selling text, Nobel laureate Paul Samuelson reflected this general optimism when he forecast that we may have to redefine "the cycle so that stagnant growth below the trend potential of growth is to be called recession even though absolute growth has not vanished."[2]

Subsequent events have tempered this optimism. We now know that proper timing of macroeconomic policy is far more difficult than was perceived during the 1960s and 1970s. Although we have already discussed the effects of monetary and fiscal policy, we have generally glossed over the problem of proper timing. However, proper timing is crucial if macroeconomic policy is going to smooth the ups and downs of the business cycle. In this chapter, we will focus on the tools that enhance and the factors that limit our ability to time macropolicy properly. We will begin by taking a look at the historical record.

ECONOMIC FLUCTUATIONS—THE HISTORICAL RECORD

Wide fluctuations in the general level of business activity—in income, employment, and the price level—make personal economic planning extremely difficult. Such changes can cause even well-devised investment plans to go awry. The tragic stories of unemployed workers begging for food and newly impoverished investors jumping out of windows during the Great Depression vividly portray the enormous personal and social costs of economic instability and the uncertainty that it generates.

Historically, substantial fluctuations in real output have occurred. Exhibit 1 illustrates the growth record of real GNP in the United States during the last 75 years. Prior to the Second World War, double-digit swings in real GNP during a single year were not uncommon. Real GNP rose by more than 10 percent annually during the First World War, during an economic boom in 1922, during a mid-1930s recovery, and again during the Second World War. In contrast, output fell at an annual rate of 5 percent or more during the 1920–21 recession, in the Depression years 1930, 1931, 1932, and 1938, and again following the Second World War. During the last four decades, economic ups and downs have been more moderate. Nevertheless, substantial fluctuations are still observable.

ACTIVISM VERSUS NONACTIVISM—AN OVERVIEW

There is widespread agreement concerning the goals of macroeconomic policy. Economists of most all persuasions believe that the performance of a market economy would be improved if economic fluctuations were minimal, prices were

---

[1]Robert J. Gordon, *Macroeconomics* (Boston: Little, Brown, and Co., 1978), p. 334.
[2]Paul Samuelson, *Economics,* 9th edition (New York: McGraw-Hill, 1973), p. 266.

EXHIBIT 1

The Post-Second World War Decline in Economic Instability

Prior to the conclusion of the Second World War, the United States experienced double-digit increases in real GNP (in 1918, 1922, 1935–36, 1941–43) and double-digit declines in real GNP (in 1930–32 and 1946). In contrast, fluctuations in real GNP have moderated during the last four decades. Most economists believe that more appropriate macropolicy —particularly monetary policy—deserves much of the credit (see Exhibit 3).

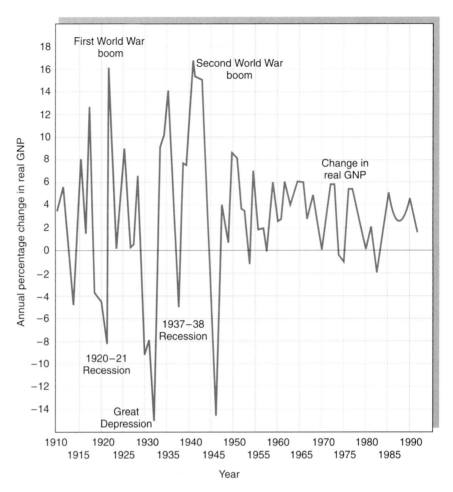

Sources: *Historical Statistics of the United States*, p. 224; *Economic Report of the President, 1991.*

---

stable, and employment were at a high level (unemployment at the natural rate). How to achieve these goals is, however, a hot topic of debate among macroeconomists. In some respects, the current debate is an extension of earlier disagreements between Keynesians and monetarists. While consensus positions emerged from the Keynesian-monetarist debate in several areas—the potency of money and the transmission of monetary policy, for example—this was not true with regard to the conduct of stabilization policy.

Most macroeconomists, particularly those of Keynesian persuasion, favor an **activist strategy.** According to the activist's view, it is reasonable to expect that discretionary macroeconomic policy will reduce economic instability. Not all activists are Keynesians. However activism generally reflects the Keynesian tradition. Activists have little confidence in the ability of a market economy to self-correct in response to inevitable economic shocks such as poor harvests, drastic changes in oil prices, or a strike in a major industry. Some activists charge that market economies are inherently unstable—that both economic expansions and contractions tend to feed on themselves. According to this view, business expansion

Activist Strategy: The view that deliberate changes in monetary and fiscal policy can be used to inject demand stimulus during a recession and apply restraint during an inflationary boom and thereby minimize economic instability.

will induce additional investment and consumption that exert a multiplier effect and lead to an inflationary boom. Resources, though, constrain the economy. Rapid expansion in real output cannot proceed indefinitely. Growth of output will eventually slow. When this happens, optimism often turns to pessimism, which triggers a downturn. The multiplier effect also amplifies the downswing, causing unused industrial capacity and widespread unemployment. The proponents of the inherent instability view generally point to the volatile behavior of expenditures on consumer durables and private investment as evidence for their position.

Other activists argue that the self-corrective mechanism of a market economy works slowly. They emphasize that restoration of full employment via lower real wage rates and interest rates is likely to be a lengthy process. They thus believe that prudent use of monetary and fiscal policy can speed the adjustment process and minimize the cost of economic instability.

Exhibit 2 illustrates the basic idea of the activists' strategy. Ideally, macroeconomic policy would apply demand restraint during an economic boom and apply demand stimulus during a recession. During an economic boom, then, proper macroeconomic policy would couple a deceleration in the growth rate of the money supply with movement toward a budget surplus (or smaller deficit). This would help restrain aggregate demand and thereby minimize the potential inflationary side effects of the boom. In contrast, when the economy dips into a recession, activist stabilization policy would shift toward stimulus. The money supply would be expanded more rapidly than normal, while budgetary policy would plan a budget deficit.

EXHIBIT 2

Activists' Countercyclical Policy—Hypothetical Ideal

Activists believe that macropolicy based on economic conditions can help stabilize the economy. Here we illustrate the hypothetical ideal in which both monetary and fiscal policy restrain demand during an inflationary boom and add stimulus during a recession.

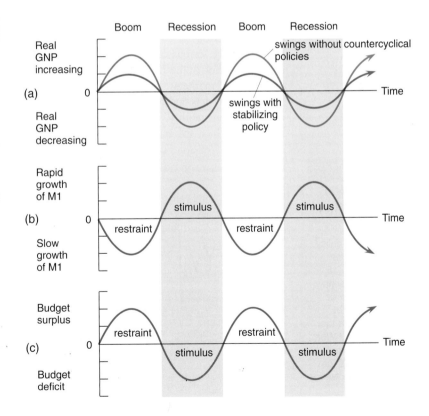

Activists believe it is feasible to apply macropolicy so that restraint will retard inflation during an economic boom and stimulus will minimize the decline in output during a recession. When macroeconomic policy is applied in this manner, it will reduce the swings in real GNP (as illustrated by the red line of Exhibit 2a) and employment.

Nonactivist Strategy: The maintenance of the same monetary and fiscal policy—that is, no change in money growth, tax rates, or expenditures—during all phases of the business cycle.

In contrast with activists, the **nonactivist strategy** is based on the foundation that we can best moderate the business cycle by adopting rules and guidelines (for example, a constant growth rate in the money supply and a balanced budget over the business cycle) that provide for stable monetary and fiscal policy, *independent of current economic conditions*. Furthermore, nonactivists argue that *discretionary* use of monetary and fiscal policy in response to changing economic conditions is likely to do more damage than good. They charge that erratic policy, particularly the instability of monetary policy, is a major source of economic fluctuations.

Clearly, the nonactivist view is reflective of the monetarists' tradition and the more recent developments in new classical economics. Nonactivists reject the view that minor disturbances, magnified by a multiplier effect, inevitably lead to either a recession or inflationary boom. They emphasize that consumption, the major component of spending, is relatively stable over the business cycle. Counter to the "instability feeds on itself" view, individuals cushion the effects of a downturn by dipping into their savings and maintaining a high level of consumer demand during a recession. Simultaneously, lower real wages will stimulate employment and lower real interest rates will encourage the purchase of both investment goods and consumer durables during a recession.

According to the nonactivist view, the self-corrective mechanism of a market economy works quite well. If not stifled by perverse macroeconomic policy, nonactivists believe that the economy's self-correcting mechanism will prevent prolonged periods of economic decline and high unemployment. Nonactivists note that the really serious cases of economic instability, such as the Great Depression and the inflation of the 1970s, were primarily the result of policy errors, not inherent instability of markets.

Both activists and nonactivists agree that in the past, policy errors contributed to economic instability. Prior to the Keynesian revolution, governments often *raised* taxes to balance the budget as revenue declined during a recession. Of course,

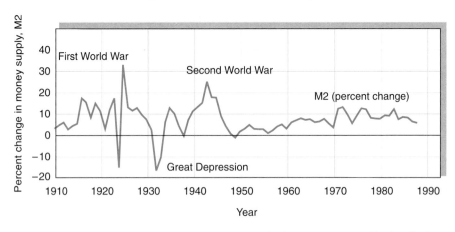

EXHIBIT 3:

The Post-Second World War Decline in Monetary Instability

Prior to 1950, monetary policy was characterized by wide swings. Huge increases (15 percent or more) in the supply of money (M2) for a year or two were often followed by sharp contractions. Since the end of the Second World War, the fluctuations in the supply of money have declined, as the monetary authorities followed a more stable course.

Source: *The Economic Report of the President, 1991* and Robert J. Gordon, *Macroeconomics* (Glenview, Ill.: Scott, Foresman and Company, 1990).

modern analysis implies that such a policy would add to the severity of the recession. Correspondingly, as Exhibit 3 illustrates, extreme gyrations in the money supply characterized monetary policy prior to the Second World War. Prior to 1947, sharp contractions in the money supply often accompanied major recessions. For example, the M2 money supply *declined* at an annual rate of 6 percent during the 1920–1921 recession, and by 15 percent annually as the United States entered into the Great Depression; it dipped again during the 1937–1938 relapse of the depression. In contrast, double-digit growth rates in the money supply were observed during the inflationary periods of the First and Second World Wars. One need not be a monetarist (or nonactivist) to recognize that the erratic changes in the money supply contributed to instability prior to the Second World War.[3]

While monetary fluctuations have continued since the post-Second World War period, they have been much less erratic. As Exhibit 3 illustrates, during the last four decades, the annual growth rate of the M2 money supply has generally been within the 3 percent to 9 percent range. Correspondingly, modern governments seldom raise taxes during a business recession. As Exhibit 1 shows, more moderate swings in real output have accompanied the increased stability of monetary and fiscal policy during the post-war era. Activists and nonactivists agree that the link between the more stable macroeconomic policy and moderation of the business cycle is no coincidence.

INSTITUTING ACTIVIST STABILIZATION POLICY

Macroeconomic policy reduces instability only if it injects stimulus and applies restraint at the proper phase of the business cycle. Proper timing is the key to effective stabilization policy. How can policy-makers know whether they should be stimulating aggregate demand or applying the economic brake?

Industrial Capacity Utilization Rate: An index designed to measure the extent to which the economy's existing plant and equipment capacity is being used.

Of course, economic indicators such as the unemployment rate, growth of real GNP, and the **industrial capacity utilization rate** will provide policy-makers with information concerning the *current* state of the economy (see Measures of Economic Activity box, "The Capacity Utilization Rate"). It takes time, though, for macroeconomic policy to work. Because of this, policy-makers really need to know about the future—where the economy is going to be 6 to 12 months from now. They need to know whether a business recession or an inflationary boom is around the corner. If they do not know where the economy is going, a policy change may fail to exert its primary impact quickly enough to offset a downturn or restrain future inflation.

How can policy-makers find out when the economy is about to take a turn in the macroeconomic road? The two most widely used sources of information on the future direction of the economy are the index of leading economic indicators and economic forecasting models.

---

[3]Macropolicy during the heyday of classical economic theory once again illustrates that ideas have consequences "both when they are right and when they are wrong" (to quote Keynes). Since classical economists thought the budget should be balanced annually, taxes were often *raised* during recessions prior to the Keynesian revolution. Similarly, classical economists, thinking price adjustments were both quick and painless, did not think that changes in the supply of money exerted much influence on real output. Thus, they paid little heed to monetary instability. For a detailed analysis of monetary instability, see Milton Friedman and Anna Schwartz, *A Monetary History of the United States, 1867–1960* (Princeton: Princeton University Press, 1963).

MEASURES OF ECONOMIC ACTIVITY

The Capacity Utilization Rate

The capacity utilization rate is a ratio of actual output to capacity output. It is expressed as a percent. The utilization rate is intended to measure the extent to which industrial facilities are used to attain their potential output.

The Bureau of Economic Analysis (BEA) conducts a quarterly survey that asks a random sample of industrial firms to report their capacity utilization as a percent of practical capacity. Practical capacity is defined as the greatest level of output that the firm's *existing plant and equipment* could achieve assuming (a) the availability of labor and other variable inputs and (b) normal expected down-time for maintenance. The company

utilization rates are weighted by asset size and then used to derive utilization rates for total industry and various subsectors (for example, manufacturing, mining, and utilities).

Just as one would not expect 100 percent employment in a world of uncertainty and imperfect information, neither would one expect 100 percent utilization of plant capacity. Since the measure of capacity is based on the subjective views of firms' managers rather than actual experience, we cannot even be sure that it would be possible for a firm to achieve 100 percent capacity. It is not surprising, then, that broad capacity utilization rates are generally well below 100 percent.

During the last three decades, the industrial capacity utilization rate has averaged approximately 83 percent. Utilization rates as high as 90 percent have been achieved only during wartime. Most economists interpret the significance of current capacity utilization rates by comparing them with past peaks and lows. A low utilization rate compared to the rates of recent years indicates the presence of underutilized industrial capacity, while relatively high utilization rates imply intensive use of industrial facilities. Capacity utilization rates are reported monthly in the *Federal Reserve Bulletin*.

THE INDEX OF LEADING INDICATORS

Index of Leading Indicators: An index of economic variables that historically has tended to turn down prior to the beginning of a recession and turn up prior to the beginning of a business expansion.

The **index of leading indicators** is a composite statistic based on 11 key variables that generally turn down prior to a recession and turn up before the beginning of a business expansion (see Measures of Economic Activity box, "The Index of Leading Indicators"). Exhibit 4 illustrates the path of the index during the 1950–1991 period. Clearly, the index does provide information on the future direction of the economy. It has forecasted each of the seven recessions since 1950. Generally, the index turned down 8 to 11 months prior to a recession. This would provide policy-makers with sufficient lead time to modify policy, particularly monetary policy. There has been significant variability, however, in the lead time of the index. The downturn in the index was only three months prior to the 1982 recession and four months prior to the recession of 1954. In contrast, the index turned down 23 months prior to the recession of 1957–1958.

Unfortunately, the index is not always an accurate indicator of the future. On three occasions (1950–1951, 1962, and 1966), a downturn in the index of leading indicators forecast a future recession that did not materialize. This has given rise to the quip that the index has accurately forecast ten of the last seven recessions.

FORECASTING MODELS

Economists have developed highly complex econometric (statistical) models to improve the accuracy of macroeconomic forecasts. In essence, these models use past data on economic interrelationships to project how currently observed changes will influence the future path of key economic variables such as real GNP,

MEASURES OF ECONOMIC ACTIVITY

The Index of Leading Indicators

History indicates that no single indicator is able to accurately forecast the future direction of the economy. However, several economic variables do tend to reach a high or low prior to the peak of a business expansion or the trough of an economic recession. Such variables are called leading economic indictors.

To provide more reliable information on the future direction of the economy, economists have devised an index of 11 leading economic indicators. The indicators included in the index are: (a) length of the average work week in hours; (b) initial weekly claims for unemployment compensation; (c) new orders placed with manufacturers; (d) percent of companies receiving slower deliveries from suppliers; (e) contracts and orders for plant and equipment; (f) permits for new housing starts; (g) change in

unfilled orders for durable goods; (h) change in sensitive materials prices; (i) change in stock prices; (j) change in money supply (M2); and (k) index of consumer expectations. Each component in the series is standardized and weighted. The weight attached to each variable is based on its past performance as an indicator of macroeconomic turns.

In some cases, it is easy to see why a change in an economic indicator precedes a change in general economic activity. Consider the indicator "new orders placed with manufacturers" (measured in constant dollars). Manufacturers are usually quite willing to expand output in response to new orders. Thus, an expansion in the volume of orders is generally followed by an expansion in manufacturing output. Similarly, manufacturers will tend to scale back their future

production when a decline in new orders signals the probability of weak future demand for their products.

The components of the index of leading indicators sometimes provide conflicting information. One component may be signalling continued expansion while another indicates that a recession is just around the corner. It often takes several months of continuous expansion or contraction in the index before all (or most all) of the components provide a consistent signal. Thus, an up or down turn in the index for just a few months should be interpreted with caution.

The index of leading indicators is calculated and published monthly by the Bureau of Economic Analysis of the Department of Commerce. It is reported monthly in the *Business Conditions Digest*.

EXHIBIT 4

The Index of Leading Indicators and the Future Direction of the Economy

The shaded periods represent business recessions. The index of leading indicators forecasted each recession during the 1955–1991 period. As the arrows show, however, the time lag between when the index turned down and when the economy fell into a recession varied. In addition, on three occasions (1950, 1962, and 1966), the index forecasted a recession that did not occur.

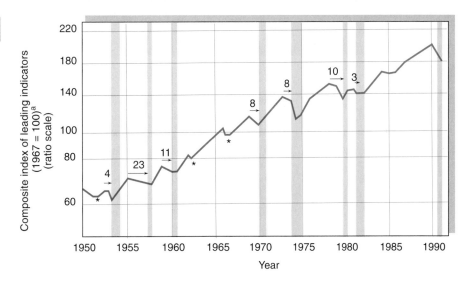

[a]The arrows indicate the number of months that the downturn in the index preceded a recession. An asterisk (*) indicates a false signal of a recession.

APPLICATIONS IN ECONOMICS

Can Economists Forecast the Future?

Economic forecasting is the occupation that makes astrology respectable.[4]   *David Dremas*

Businesses and governmental units often pay thousands of dollars for the projections of highly complex computer forecasting models of the economy. Critical business and financial decisions are often based on the forecasts. In the past, persons marketing these forecasts have sometimes oversold the ability of economic theory as a tool with which to forecast the future. There are two major reasons why the ability of economists to forecast the future is extremely limited.

1. *Future changes in market conditions will primarily reflect events that cannot be foreseen at this time.* Current market prices already reflect current conditions *and* future changes that are widely anticipated. For example, today's grain prices will already reflect current and normal future weather conditions in the grain belt. Future grain prices will differ from the present primarily as the result of unanticipated future developments, such as abnormal future rainfall. The same logic also applies to macroeconomic markets. Future market conditions will differ from the present, primarily as the result of economic changes that we cannot now foresee—for example, an unexpected policy change, discovery of a new resource or technology, abnormal weather, or political upheaval in an important oil exporting nation. There is no reason to believe that economists or anyone else will be able to predict such changes with any degree of accuracy. Thus, while economic theory helps to predict the *implications* of unforeseen events, it cannot foretell what market-changing events will occur in the future.

2. *Decision-makers will often make different choices in the future because of what they learned from the past. The past is thus an imperfect indicator of the future.* Almost all forecasters, including those who rely on complex computer models, use past relationships to project the future. In a world where people learn from experience, though, forecasts based on past relationships will never fully capture the future. The experience of the 1970s illustrates this point. Prior to 1970, the unemployment rate generally declined when prices rose more rapidly. Most forecasting models in the 1970s thus assumed that a higher inflation rate would reduce unemployment. Things did not turn out that way. The 1970s were different because people adjusted their decision-making in light of past experience with inflation.

While macroeconomic forecasts are often quite accurate during normal times (when the growth of real GNP and the inflation rate are relatively steady), they often miss

---

[4]David Dremas, "The Madness of Crowds," *Forbes,* September 27, 1982, p. 201.

---

employment, and the price level. The most elaborate of these models use hundreds of variables and equations to simulate the various sectors and macroeconomic markets. Powerful, high-speed computers are employed to analyze the effects of various policy alternatives and to predict the future.

To date, the record of computer forecasting models is mixed. When economic conditions are relatively stable, the models have generally provided highly accurate forecasts for both aggregate economic variables and important subcomponents of the economy. Unfortunately, the models have been much less effective at accurately forecasting turns in the business cycle and the impact of major economic shocks. Of course, the models are only as accurate as the programmed relationships developed by their builders. Model builders are constantly restructuring their models, based on more accurate data and recent experience. Clearly, perfection must await the future. In fact, accuracy in forecasting may be beyond the reach of economics. Many

major turns in the economic road. Unfortunately, it is precisely these turns that are most important from the viewpoint of economic policy-makers. Exhibit 5 provides data on the forecasts of five leading forecasting models released one year prior to the 1982 recession. None of the five models forecasted the 1982 recession. In fact, the five models projected an average 1982 growth rate of 3.5 percent (with a range of 2.1 to 4.9 percent). The actual change in real GNP in 1982 was *minus* 2.1 percent. Similarly, none of the major forecasting models anticipated the sharp reduction in the inflation rate during 1981–1984. Most of the models forecasted inflation rates approximately twice the actual rate for 1982–1984.

With regard to forecasting major trend *changes* of real GNP and the inflation rate, these results are highly typical. They should not be surprising. After all, economic theory indicates that forecasting is a hazardous profession.

EXHIBIT 5 ■ The Record of Five Major Forecasting Models During the Early 1980s				
	1980 Year-End Forecast For:			
	1981	1982	1983	1984
Change in Real GNP				
Chase Econometrics	1.3	3.6	3.9	3.1
Data Resources	2.7	2.4	3.2	3.8
Wharton Model	2.2	2.1	3.4	3.4
Evans Econometrics	2.5	4.7	4.6	4.2
Merrill Lynch	0.6	4.9	6.0	4.3
Average of the Five Forecasts	**1.9**	**3.5**	**4.2**	**3.8**
Actual	**2.5**	**−2.1**	**3.7**	**6.8**
Inflation Rate				
Chase Econometrics	10.2	9.1	7.7	7.7
Data Resources	10.4	9.6	9.0	8.1
Wharton Model	10.3	9.6	8.3	8.0
Evans Econometrics	10.0	8.8	8.4	8.4
Merrill Lynch	9.5	7.1	6.0	6.2
Average of the Five Forecasts	**10.1**	**8.8**	**7.9**	**7.7**
Actual	**8.9**	**3.9**	**3.8**	**4.0**

Source: "Where The Big Econometric Models Go Wrong." *Business Week,* March 30, 1981.

economists, particularly those of rational expectations persuasion, argue that this is indeed the case. (See the Applications in Economics box).

CAN INFORMATION SUPPLIED BY MARKETS IMPROVE DISCRETIONARY MONETARY POLICY?

Some economists, including several members of the Board of Governors of the Federal Reserve, believe that information supplied by key market relationships can help Fed decision-makers determine more quickly and more accurately when changes in policy are in order. There are three market indicators that policy-makers who adhere to this approach generally monitor quite closely: (1) commodity prices, (2) the *slope* of the yield curve, and (3) exchange rates.

Since they fluctuate daily and are determined in auction markets, changes in commodity prices provide readily available information that is often an early indicator of future movement in the price level. Thus, an increase in a broad index of commodity prices often indicates that money is plentiful. This provides the Fed with an early signal to shift toward a more restrictive policy. In contrast, falling commodity prices may indicate that deflation is a potential future danger. In this case, Fed decision-makers might want to shift toward a more expansionary policy.

The yield curve maps the relationship between short-term and long-term interest rates. The longer the duration of a loan, the greater the possibility of change that will adversely affect the borrower's ability to repay. Thus, longer-term loans are more risky and therefore they generally command a higher interest rate. As a result, the normal yield curve will slope upward as one moves from short-term to long-term interest rates. The further away the maturity date of the bond, the higher the interest rate. For example, a 30-year government security might have an interest rate of 9 percent, while a one-year security might have an interest rate of only 6 percent. However, when the demand for money is strong relative to the supply, short-term rates will rise *relative* to the long-term rates because short-term instruments, such as three-month Treasury bills and 90-day Certificates of Deposit, are a close substitute for money. Higher short-term interest rates relative to long-term rates imply that money is scarcer. This is a signal for the Fed to move toward a more expansionary policy. Alternatively, if long-term interest rates were abnormally high relative to short-term rates, this would imply that markets fear future inflation and think the current policy is too expansionary. This would be a signal to the Fed to shift to a more restrictive policy.

Finally, the exchange-rate data provides additional information about what markets think of current monetary policy. A decline in the exchange-rate value of the dollar (the value of the dollar relative to other currencies) often implies a fear of higher inflation and a reluctance to hold dollars. This would signal the need to shift to a more restrictive policy. Conversely, an increase in the exchange-rate value of the dollar is a strong vote of confidence in the future purchasing power of the dollar. This provides the Fed with some leeway to move toward a more expansionary policy.

If all three of these market indicators point in the same direction, then this would provide the Fed with a strong signal. For example, if commodity prices were falling, if short-term interest rates were abnormally high *relative* to long-term rates, and if the dollar were appreciating on the foreign-exchange market, then these would provide strong evidence that current policy was restrictive. A shift toward a more expansionary policy would be in order. However, the world is generally not this simple. The signals often provide inconclusive or conflicting signals. In any case, most proponents of these signals currently believe that they should be used as a supplement to, rather than as a substitute for, other indicators monitored in the formulation of activist policy.

THE ACTIVIST VIEW OF DISCRETIONARY POLICY

Activists recognize that it is difficult to institute countercyclical macroeconomic policy. Nevertheless, they believe that discretionary action by policy-makers can help smooth business ups and downs.

The activist view stresses that the index of leading indicators, forecasting models, sensitive market variables, and other economic indicators provide policy-makers with an early warning system, alerting them to the need for a change in a macroeconomic policy. This will provide policy-makers with sufficient time to institute moderate changes in macroeconomic policy quickly and more substantial changes with the passage of time if additional information indicates such changes are needed.

The following scenario outlines the essentials of the activists' view. Suppose the economy was about to dip into a recession. *Prior to the recession,* the index of leading indicators would almost surely alert policy-makers to the possibility of a downturn. This would permit them to shift toward macroeconomic stimulus, expanding the money supply more rapidly. Initially, the shift toward macroeconomic stimulus could be applied in moderate doses. It could then be easily offset with future action. On the other hand, if the signs of a downturn became more pronounced and *current* business conditions actually weakened, additional stimulus could be injected. Perhaps a tax reduction or a speed-up in government expenditures might be used to supplement the more expansionary monetary policy. Policy-makers can constantly monitor the situation as they inject additional stimulus. As economic indicators provide additional information with the passage of time, policy-makers can adjust their actions accordingly. If the weakness persists, the expansionary policy can be continued. Conversely, when the signs point to a strong recovery, policy-makers can move toward restraint and thereby head off potential inflationary pressure. According to the activist's view, the economy is more likely to stay on track when policy-makers are free to apply stimulus or restraint based on current information and economic conditions.

Activists point to the reduction in instability during the post-Second World War period as proof that discretionary policies enhance stability (see Exhibit 1). The United States has experienced five decades of economic growth without either a Great Depression or hyperinflation. Activists ask, ''Who knows what disasters stabilization policies have prevented?'' Even though minor mistakes have been made, activist policies have kept the economy on track. And activists believe that the future record will be even better. We continue to develop better models to explain the causes of business fluctuations. Data providing early warnings of economic change are improving. Experience with activist policies will lead to better timing. Activists argue that now is not the time to discard a system that is working, in favor of an unproven alternative.

THE NONACTIVIST CASE

Nonactivists argue that economic and political factors undermine the potential effectiveness of discretionary macroeconomic policy. There are three major reasons why they believe discretionary policy will be ineffective as a stabilization tool.

TIME LAGS AND THE DIFFICULTIES OF TIMING THE EFFECTS PROPERLY

Recognition Lag: The time period between when a policy change is needed from a stabilization standpoint and when the need is recognized by policy-makers.

It takes time for monetary policy to be instituted and for it to take effect. Nonactivists believe that three time lags seriously undermine the potential of discretionary policy. First, there is the **recognition lag,** the time period between when economic conditions have changed and when policy-makers are cognizant of the change. Our ability to forecast the future is highly limited. It will even take a few months to gather and tabulate reliable information on the performance of the economy in the recent past. Predictably, it will take policy-makers a few months to recognize that the economy has dipped into a recession or that the inflation rate has accelerated.

Second, even after the need for a policy change is recognized, there is generally an additional time period before the policy change is instituted. Economists refer to

Administrative Lag: The time period between when the need for a policy change is recognized and when the policy is actually implemented.

Impact Lag: The time period between when a policy change is implemented and when the change begins to exert its primary effects.

this delay as **administrative lag.** In the case of monetary policy, the administrative lag is generally quite short. The Federal Open Market Committee meets monthly, and is at least potentially capable of instituting a change in monetary policy quickly. This is a major advantage of monetary policy. For discretionary fiscal policy, the administrative lag is likely to be much longer. Congressional committees must meet. Legislation must be proposed and debated. Congress must act and the president must consent. Each of these steps take time.

Finally, there is the **impact lag,** the time period between the implementation of a macropolicy change and when the change exerts its primary impact on the economy. While the impact of a change in tax rates is generally felt quickly, the expansionary effects of an increase in government expenditures are usually much less rapid. It will take time for the submission of competitive bids and the letting of new contracts. Several months may pass before work on a new project actually begins.

Economists who have studied this topic, including Milton Friedman and Robert Gordon, conclude that the combined duration of these time lags is generally 12 to 18 months in the case of monetary policy, and even longer in the case of fiscal policy. This means that if a policy is going to exert the desired effect at the proper time, policy-makers cannot wait until a problem develops before they act. Rather, they must act *before* an economic downturn or upturn in the inflation rate is observable. It will be necessary for them to correctly forecast *turns* in the economy if they are going to properly time changes in policy. Nonactivists argue this is highly unrealistic. Rhetoric aside, economic forecasters cannot accurately predict such turns, nor can we expect them to do so in the foreseeable future (see the Applications in Economics box).

Nonactivists argue that since the future direction of our economy is influenced by complex dynamic changes and unforeseen shocks, policy-makers are unable to determine accurately where the economy is going. And, even if they could forecast accurately, the time lags accompanying changes in monetary and fiscal policies are so *long and variable,* it is highly unlikely that the primary effects of a policy change will come at the proper time. Therefore, nonactivists believe that discretionary policy is likely to be destabilizing rather than stabilizing.

Exhibit 6 illustrates the views of activists and nonactivists. When the economy begins to dip into a recession, activists argue that policy-makers can reasonably be expected to recognize that danger and shift to a more expansionary policy at *B.* Given the expected length of the impact lag, the expansionary policy will exert its primary *effects* at *C,* just in time to help minimize the business downturn. In contrast, nonactivists believe the lags are likely to be more lengthy and less predictable. They fear the shift to more expansionary policy will not come until *C* and that its *effects* will not be significant until *D.* If this is the case, the expansionary policy will contribute to the severity of the inflationary boom (dotted line beyond *D*). Similarly, a subsequent shift to an anti-inflationary policy may begin to exert its major impact at *F,* just in time to make an oncoming recession worse (dotted line beyond *F*).

POLITICS AND THE TIMING OF POLICY CHANGES

Public choice analysis has led to an increased awareness of an additional pitfall of discretionary policy-making—macropolicy might be used to pursue political objectives rather than stabilization. In a democracy, macropolicy will be designed by elected representatives, an elected president, and officials (such as the Board of

EXHIBIT 6

Time Lags and the Effects
of Discretionary Policy

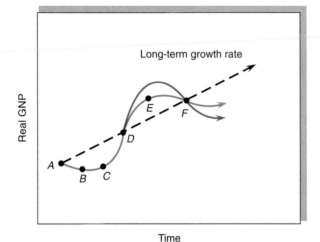

Beginning with *A*, we illustrate the path of a hypothetical business cycle. If a forthcoming recession can be recognized quickly and a more expansionary policy instituted at point *B*, the policy may add stimulus at point *C* and help to minimize the magnitude of the downturn. Activists believe that discretionary policy is likely to achieve this outcome.

However, if delays result in the adoption of the expansionary policy at *C* and if it does not exert its major impact until *D*, the demand stimulus will exacerbate the inflationary boom. In turn, an anti-inflationary strategy instituted at *E* may exert its primary effects at *F*, just in time to increase the severity of a recession beyond *F*. Nonactivists fear that improper timing of discretionary macropolicy will exert such destabilizing effects.

Governors of the Federal Reserve) who are appointed by the elected president. Like other policy choices, macropolicy provides political entrepreneurs with a potential tool with which to further their political objectives. Predictably, discretionary macropolicy choices will be influenced by political considerations. It is naive to expect otherwise.

The nature of the political process, particularly the shortsightedness effect, provides politicians with little incentive to look beyond the next election. If the adaptive expectations view is correct, expansionary policies 12 to 18 months prior to an election would stimulate output and employment, getting the economy in great shape by election day. Since demand stimulus policies generally affect output before they begin to exert a major impact on the price level, the inflationary effects of such a policy would be most observable *after the election*.

Studies indicate that incumbents are far more successful at retaining their offices when real income grows rapidly, and the inflation rate is moderate.[5] Exhibit 7 presents the findings of a recent study by David Wyss and Jeanne Blondia of Data Resources, Inc., that dramatically illustrate this point. Using an estimated premium if a candidate is an incumbent and just two economic variables, the growth rate of real GNP in the year just prior to the election and the inflation rate during the same

---

[5]See David Wyss and Jeanne Blondia, "The Economy and Presidential Elections," *Data Resources U.S. Review,* April 1988; Kevin B. Grier, "Presidential Elections and Federal Reserve Policy" (*Southern Economic Journal,* October 1987, 475–86); and Ray C. Fair, "The Effect of Economic Conditions on Votes for the President," *Review of Economics and Statistics,* May 1978, 159–73 for additional evidence on this point.

EXHIBIT 7 ■ Growth of Real GNP, Inflation, and Winning Presidential Elections				
			The Projected Percent of Two-party Vote Based on Growth of Real GNP and Inflation during Year before Election	
Year	Democratic Candidate[a]	Republican Candidate[a]	Projected Vote of Incumbent Party[b]	Actual Vote of Incumbent Party[b]
1948	*Truman* *	Dewey	52.4	50.7
1952	*Stevenson*	Eisenhower*	44.6	46.7
1956	Stevenson	*Eisenhower* *	57.7	59.5
1960	Kennedy*	*Nixon*	49.9	48.0
1964	*Johnson* *	Goldwater	61.3	61.9
1968	*Humphrey*	Nixon*	49.6	49.4
1972	McGovern	*Nixon* *	61.8	59.5
1976	Carter*	*Ford*	48.9	48.8
1980	*Carter*	Reagan*	44.7	43.6
1984	Mondale	*Reagan* *	59.2	60.8
1988	Dukakis	*Bush* *	55.0	54.0

[a]The asterisks indicate the winners; italics indicate the incumbent party candidates.
[b]Percentages shown are the share of the two-party vote won by the candidate of the incumbent party in each election.
Source: David Wyss and Jeanne Blondia, "The Economy and Presidential Elections," *Data Resources U.S. Review*, April 1988.

time period, the Wyss-Blondia model has accurately forecast the last 10 presidential elections. In fact, while the pollsters were showing fluctuating results through the summer of 1988, more than 6 months prior to the 1988 election Wyss and Blondia used the data on real GNP and inflation to forecast that George Bush would get 55 percent of the vote. When the final returns were in, Bush received 54 percent of the vote.

Given the political importance of economic conditions, political entrepreneurs have a strong incentive to stimulate the economy prior to a major election. However, to the extent that politicians use macroeconomic policy for political purposes, they reduce its effectiveness as a stabilization weapon.

There is some evidence that politicians have sought to use macropolicy for political gain. During the 18 months prior to the 1968 election, the unemployment rate was less than 4 percent. Nevertheless, monetary policy was quite expansionary and the Johnson Administration ran a large deficit during 1967–1968 rather than increase taxes to finance expenditures for domestic programs and the Vietnam War. Similarly, the Nixon Administration followed an expansionary monetary and fiscal course prior to the 1972 election even though real growth was strong during the 1971–1972 period. Many economists believe that the expansionary policies preceding both the 1968 and 1972 elections laid the foundation for the inflation of the 1970s.

Political scientist Edward Tufte has conducted extensive research on this issue. While reviewing evidence from 90 elections in 27 different countries, Tufte found that real disposable income accelerated in 77 percent of the election years compared to only 46 percent of the years without an election.[6] This suggests that there is at least a moderate tendency to follow more expansionary policies prior to major elections.

RATIONAL EXPECTATIONS AND POLICY INEFFECTIVENESS

The theory of rational expectations indicates that predictable changes in macropolicy will fail to promote economic stability. Unlike a machine, the moving parts of our economy are living, breathing human beings, capable of modifying their choices when the situation changes. As they learn from prior experience, their future response to a policy change may differ from their past responses.

As we have already discussed, the impact of macropolicy varies depending on whether it is anticipated by decision-makers (see Chapter 14, Exhibit 1). The proponents of rational expectations believe that, sooner or later, the public will figure out any systematic policy, including countercyclical stabilization policy. However, once a policy is widely anticipated and individuals adjust their decision-making in light of the expected effects (for example, rising prices or higher interest rates), the policy no longer exerts the predicted impact on real output and employment. Economists refer to this phenomenon as the **policy ineffectiveness theorem.**

Policy Ineffectiveness Theorem: The proposition that any systematic policy will be rendered ineffective once decision-makers figure out the policy pattern and adjust their decision-making in light of its expected effects. The theorem is a corollary of the theory of rational expectations.

Perhaps an example will illustrate why rational expectations economists have little confidence that even properly timed macropolicy will be effective. Suppose it is widely anticipated that the government will employ expansionary macropolicy in response to a recession. As the signs of an economic slowdown appear, the public anticipates that policy-makers will increase the growth of the money supply and cut taxes (perhaps by allowing a more attractive depreciation allowance or an investment tax credit) to spur business investment. It makes sense, once this strategy is anticipated, for investors to delay investment projects and wait for the expected lower interest rates and investment tax incentives. This delay, though, only increases the severity of the current downturn and leads to pent-up investment demand. Once the anticipated expansionary policy is instituted, investment expenditures will tend to grow more rapidly than past experience indicated would be the case (and more rapidly than is desirable from a stabilization viewpoint). In essence, once decision-makers adjust their choices in light of the anticipated countercyclical policy, the policy fails to exert the desired stabilizing effects.

The logic of the analysis applies symmetrically to an economic boom. If the public anticipates that slower money growth, higher interest rates, and higher taxes will be used to restrain an economic boom, they will spend and invest *more* prior to the expected restrictive policy. In turn, the increase in spending will contribute to the development of an economic boom.

The message of rational expectations theory to stabilization policy-makers is clear. Human decision-makers will foil your good intentions. Countercyclical macropolicy will fail because, once people expect your systematic response to recessions and booms, it will be in their personal interest to respond in a manner that will undermine the policy.

In the *long run,* of course, rational expectations theory also suggests that the intentions of political entrepreneurs seeking to "hype" the economy prior to election time will be undermined. If the public expects expansionary policy during

---

[6]Edward R. Tufte, *Political Control of the Economy* (Princeton: Princeton University Press, 1978).

a pre-election period, the primary impact of the policy will be on prices (inflation) and nominal interest rates, not real output and employment.

NONACTIVIST STABILIZATION POLICY

While the underlying logic of the monetarists, public choice economists, and proponents of rational expectations differs, the three groups arrive at the same conclusion. They agree on the following two points: (a) discretionary policy is an important source of instability, and (b) greater stability would result if stable, predictable policies based on predetermined rules were followed.

Exhibit 8 illustrates empirical data that nonactivists cite in their criticism of discretionary policy. Since 1960, the U.S. economy has experienced six recessions (indicated by an *R* in Exhibit 8), periods of at least two consecutive quarters of declining real GNP. If the effects of monetary policy are going to speed recovery, monetary policy must be expansionary prior to and during the recession. Nonactivists stress that discretionary policy has failed to achieve this outcome. In fact, the growth rate of the money supply has *declined* prior to and/or during each of the six recessions. Far from offsetting recessionary forces, monetary policy has actually contributed to the downturns and slowed the recovery process, according to the nonactivists.

Given the obstacles to the proper timing of policy changes, how can errors be minimized? Nonactivists recommend that policy-makers choose a long-run policy path (for example, 3 percent monetary growth and no change in tax rates or real government expenditures) and inform the public of this choice. This course should then be pursued regardless of cyclical ups and downs. As policy-makers stay on course, they will gain credibility. The public will develop confidence in the future stability of the policy. Uncertainty will be reduced, thereby increasing the efficiency of private decision-making. Nonactivists are confident this strategy would result both in less instability and in more rapid growth than Western economies have experienced in the past.

NONACTIVIST MONETARY POLICY

Suppose we were going to adopt a nonactivist strategy. What rules or guidelines would we choose? In the area of monetary policy, nonactivists argue that monetary policy should utilize one of the following: (a) a monetary growth rule, (b) a nominal income growth rate rule, or (c) a price level rule.

Monetary Rule. The most widely advocated nonactivist monetary policy is the constant money growth rate long-championed by Milton Friedman. Under this plan, the money supply would be expanded continuously at an annual rate (3 percent, for example) that approximates the long-run growth of the U.S. economy. When real output was growing rapidly (for example, 5 percent annually), the supply of money would decline *relative* to real GNP. Thus, monetary policy would automatically exert a restraining influence during a period of rapid growth. In contrast, during a recession, the constant money growth rate would exceed the growth of real output, offsetting any tendency toward a downward spiral.

EXHIBIT 8

The Monetary Policy Record and the Nonactivists' Case for a Monetary Rule

While monetary instability has declined in recent decades (see Exhibit 3), instability and poor timing persist. Here we show the annual growth rate of the M2 money supply for each year, 1960–1990. The graph also indicates the years of recession (labeled with an *R*). The money supply was decelerating during or immediately prior to each of the recessions. If the effects of monetary policy are going to be stabilizing, this is the *opposite* of the desired pattern. According to nonactivists, a steady growth of the money supply or some other key aggregate variable (for example, nominal income) would result in more stability than discretionary monetary policy.

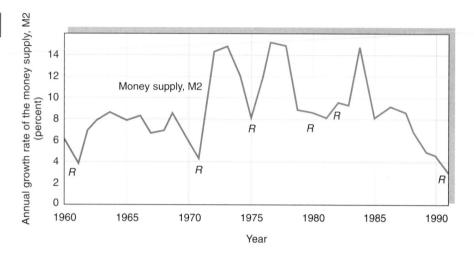

Source: *Economic Report of the President, 1991* and Robert J. Gordon, *Macroeconomics* (Glenview, Ill.: Scott, Foresman and Company, 1990).

Nonactivists, particularly those with monetarist leanings, argue that *steady growth* of the money supply would eliminate instability arising from stop–go policies on the part of the Fed. The nonactivist critics of the Fed point out that it has often expanded the money supply more rapidly than the economy's long-term growth rate, and thereby caused inflation. Responding to the inflation, the Fed then steps on the monetary brake, which pushes the economy into a recession (see Exhibit 8). Nonactivists believe that the fluctuations in the money supply accompanying discretionary monetary policies are, in fact, a major source of economic instability. Rather than responding to forecasts and current economic indicators, nonactivists believe that the Fed would be more of a stabilizing force if it simply increased the supply of money, month after month, at a low (noninflationary) constant annual rate.

If steady growth in the money supply is going to exert a stabilizing influence on aggregate demand, the velocity of money must be relatively stable. As we indicated when discussing the quantity theory of money in Chapter 13, one could think of aggregate demand (PY) as MV, the money supply (M) times velocity of circulation (V). However, the Fed controls only M. Therefore, unless V is relatively stable (or unless it changes at a steady rate), steady monetary growth will not stabilize aggregate demand. Thus, the case for a monetary rule is critically dependent upon the relative stability of the velocity of money.[7]

How stable is velocity? Exhibit 9 illustrates the velocity of both M1 and M2 for the 1955–1990 period. During 1955–1980, the velocity of the M1 money supply increased at a fairly steady rate, approximately 3 percent annually. However, between 1982 and 1987, the velocity of M1 declined sharply. Most nonactivists believe that the decline in the velocity of M1 during the 1980s was a one-time

---

[7]As we discussed in Chapter 13, *initially,* shifts to monetary acceleration tend to reduce short-term, nominal interest rates. Similarly, shifts to more restrictive monetary policy tend to increase short-term rates. Since the interest rate fluctuations affect the opportunity cost of holding money, they also influence velocity. Monetarists believe that more stable monetary growth would also result in greater stability for both interest rates and the velocity of money than what we have observed under the stop–go policies of the Fed.

EXHIBIT 9

The Velocity of M1 and M2, 1955–1990

If steady growth in the money supply at a low rate is going to stabilize the economy, the velocity of money must be relatively stable (or grow at a stable rate). Between 1955 and 1980, the velocity of the M1 money supply grew at a relatively stable annual rate of approximately 3 percent. However, the velocity of M1 declined sharply with the introduction of interest-earning checking accounts during the 1980s. During the 1955–1990 period, the velocity of M2 has been relatively stable and at a value of approximately 1.65. As the result of this stability, most advocates of the monetary rule believe that the steady growth rule should be applied to the M2 money supply.

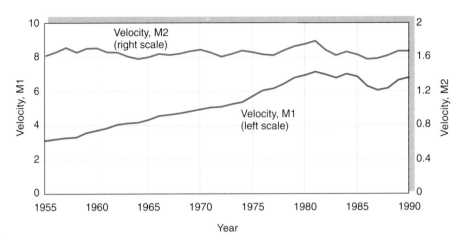

[a]Nominal GNP *(PY)* divided by the M2 money supply during the year.
[b]Nominal GNP *(PY)* divided by the M1 money supply during the year.
Source: *Economic Report of the President, 1991* and Robert J. Gordon, *Macroeconomics* (Glenview, Ill.: Scott, Foresman and Company, 1990).

occurrence, reflecting banking deregulation, the sharp deceleration in the inflation rate, and most importantly, the introduction of interest-earning checking accounts. Since the opportunity to earn interest on checking deposits reduces the opportunity cost of holding M1 money, the decline in M1 velocity during the 1982–1987 period is not really surprising. Nonetheless, the experience of the 1980s did take some of the luster off of the case for a monetary rule.

Once the transitional period is completed, most monetarists expect the stable growth of velocity for the M1 money supply to reemerge. Indeed, some argue this has already happened during 1987–1990. However, the experience of the 1980s has also directed attention toward the M2 money supply. The banking changes of the 1980s exerted much less impact on the M2 money supply. As Exhibit 9 illustrates, the velocity of M2 has been fairly constant at approximately 1.65 during the last several decades. As the result of this long-term stability in velocity, most nonactivists now prefer that the monetary rule be applied to the M2 money supply.

In 1975, Congress passed legislation requiring the Federal Reserve to adopt and announce target growth rates for the money supply during the next year. At the beginning of each year, the Fed announces its target range for the growth rates of various monetary aggregates. How does the steady growth rule differ from the monetary targets actually employed by the Fed? According to the nonactivists, the problem with the monetary targets is that the Fed does not take them very seriously. The Fed did not choose to adopt the targets. Rather, Congress imposed them. The Fed responded to the 1975 legislation by adopting target ranges that are wide enough to allow for substantial monetary variability. Finally, if the Fed wants to change policy course, it simply changes the targets. Nonactivists believe the targets are more cosmetic than real. Thus, they fail to exert the stabilizing effects of a constant money growth rate rule.

Nominal Income Rule. Nonactivists argue that even if the velocity of money sometimes changes unexpectedly, problems emanating from this source would be resolved if monetary authorities used monetary policy to provide for the steady growth of *nominal* income at a rate equal to the economy's long-run *real* growth of output (approximately 3 percent in the U.S. case). This rule would also provide long-run price stability because a stable price level is implied when nominal and real income expand at the same rate. In essence, this rule is a modified monetary rule long advocated by Allan Meltzer of Carnegie Mellon University. Rather than expanding the supply of money by a constant amount, under this rule the supply of money would be increased by the economy's long-run growth rate (approximately 3 percent) *minus* the change in the velocity of money. If the velocity of money declined, as was the case for M1 during the 1980s, the money supply would grow more rapidly than real income. Alternatively, if velocity rose, the money supply would be slowed accordingly. In effect, the policy would adjust the monetary growth rate to offset fluctuations in velocity (the demand for money).

Price Level Rule.   Some nonactivists argue that it would be better if the monetary authorities directly targeted a broad price index such as the GNP deflator. The advocates of this approach argue that, in the long run, monetary policy cannot determine real output, employment, interest rates, or other real variables. What it can and does determine is the level of prices. Therefore, why not target the price level directly? Under this plan, if the general price index were rising, monetary growth would be slowed. Conversely, if the price index were falling, the money supply would be expanded more rapidly. The proponents of this rule argue that it would reduce both instability arising from monetary sources and the uncertainty of time-dimension transactions (for example, loan agreements and other long-term contracts).

From the viewpoint of nonactivists, the important point is not the precise rule, but rather the removal of monetary policy from the hands of activist policy-makers. If left to their own discretion, policy-makers will inevitably make destabilizing errors, according to nonactivists.

NONACTIVIST FISCAL POLICY

In the area of fiscal policy, the simplest rule would require that the budget be balanced annually. Since revenues and expenditures fluctuate over the business cycle, however, a balanced budget rule would require tax increases and/or expenditure reductions during a recession. The opposite changes would be required during a period of rapid growth. Such changes are inconsistent with the nonactivist pursuit of stable (unchanged) policies.

In theory, the proper nonactivist fiscal strategy is a balanced budget over the business cycle. Under this plan, the same tax rates and expenditure policies would remain in effect during both booms and recessions. Surpluses would result during periods of prosperity, while deficits would accrue during recessions. The problem with this strategy is that it fails to provide a precise indicator revealing how well the policy-makers are adhering to the steady course. Thus, nonactivists, particularly those with a public choice background, recognize that a "balance the budget over the business cycle" rule is unlikely to impose a steady course on policy-makers.

Some nonactivists believe that a constitutional amendment limiting both government spending and budget deficits is a necessary ingredient for stable fiscal policy. These nonactivists believe pressure from special interest groups and the short-time horizon of political officials elected for limited terms bias the political process toward expansionary fiscal policy (expanding debt and spending increases). Because of this, they favor a constitutional amendment that would require supramajority (for example, 60 percent) Congressional approval for either (a) deficit-financed government spending or (b) rapid increases (more rapid than the growth of national income) in federal spending.

It is one thing to favor a general strategy and another to develop a practical, workable policy to implement the strategy. Clearly, the nonactivists have not yet arrived at a detailed fiscal policy program that would command wide acceptance among even the proponents of nonactivism.

IS THERE AN EMERGING CONSENSUS?

The accompanying Thumbnail Sketch summarizes the differences between activists and nonactivists. From a policy viewpoint, the central focus of disagreement between the two groups centers on the merits of policy-making flexibility. Activists fear that if strictly followed, inflexible rules would prevent an appropriate response to uncertain future economic changes. In their view, failure to respond to a major shock, perhaps stemming from war, another oil price run, or a collapse of investment, might well result in a major economic disaster.

On the other hand, the nonactivists fear that discretion will consistently be abused. If left with discretion, nonactivists fear that politicians will use policy to pursue either unattainable objectives or political goals. According to the nonactiv-

THUMBNAIL SKETCH

A Summary of the Major Differences Between Activists and Nonactivists

Area of Difference	Activists	Nonactivists
1. Source of Instability	Economy is inherently unstable.	Perverse policies are the primary source of instability.
2. Speed of Self-Correcting Mechanism	Self-correcting mechanism works slowly and ineffectually.	Self-correcting mechanism works with reasonable speed if it is not stifled by perverse macroeconomic policy.
3. Proper Timing of Discretionary Policy	Even though timing is difficult, discretionary policy can and has promoted stability.	Given time lags, forecasting deficiencies, and the political incentive structure, discretionary policy is an ineffective stabilization tool.
4. Impact of Monetary and Fiscal Rules	Inflexible rules would prevent policy-makers from responding to unanticipated shocks; thus, they would increase instability.	Rules providing for stable monetary and fiscal policy would reduce instability.

ists, unless you tie the hands of policy-makers, they will inevitably pursue an activist's strategy that will magnify instability and result in inflation.

While stressing the fundamental differences, however, we must not fail to recognize emerging points of agreement. Similarly, we must not forget that most economists are hybrids. They are influenced by the analysis of alternative schools of thought.

Activists and nonactivists actually share a great deal of common ground. Activists, as well as nonactivists, are aware of the difficulties involved in the proper timing of macropolicy. Fine-tuning, the idea that policy-makers can successfully promote stability by responding to each short-term bump in the economic road, has lost its luster. Recognizing that fine-tuning is beyond our current knowledge and capability, most activists now favor a policy response only in the case of major cyclical disturbances.

Both activists and nonactivists also recognize that policy instability is a potential source of economic instability. Both are sensitive to the potential destructiveness of erratic policy swings like those present prior to 1945.

Given the common ground between the two views, perhaps some combination of inflexible rules that would apply during relatively normal times and policy-maker discretion to override the rules in response to a major economic swing will emerge as a point of consensus between activism and nonactivism.

CONCLUDING THOUGHT

Economists who pronounced the death of business instability during the 1960s clearly underestimated the difficulties involved in steering a stable economic course. Unfortunately, economic bumps in the road are likely to continue in the foreseeable future. Recent economic instability must be placed in perspective, though. We must not allow failure to achieve perfection to conceal progress that has already been made.

As Exhibit 1 clearly shows, economic fluctuations have been much less pronounced since the Second World War. Sensible macroeconomic policy deserves most of the credit for this increased stability (see Exhibit 3). The Keynesian revolution convinced economists and policy-makers alike that macroeconomic policy mattered—that it was too important to be left to fate. Beginning with the Keynesian revolution, fiscal and monetary policy has been instituted in a manner that prevented economic disturbances from becoming catastrophic depressions. This is an important achievement to which macroeconomists can point with a sense of pride.

CHAPTER SUMMARY

1. Historically, the United States has experienced substantial swings in real output. Prior to the Second World War, year-to-year changes in real GNP of 5 to 10 percent were experienced on several occasions. Since the Second World War, the fluctuations in real output have been more moderate.

2. Macropolicy activists believe that a market economy is inherently unstable or that the market's self-corrective process works slowly. They are confident that discretionary monetary and fiscal policy will promote economic stability.

3. Nonactivists believe that a market economy has self-correcting tendencies that work quite well in a stable policy environment. They argue that policy-makers would make fewer errors if they merely instituted stable monetary and fiscal policies, rather than altering policy in response to current economic conditions.

4. The index of leading indicators and other forecasting devices warn policy-makers when a turn in the economic road is just ahead. While recognizing that forecasting devices sometimes give false signals, activists argue that policy-makers can initially respond cautiously to signals indicating the need for a policy change and then act more aggressively if the situation requires it. Activists thus believe that discretionary macroeconomic policy can effectively restrain the economy during an inflationary boom and stimulate output during a business recession.

5. Nonactivists stress that inability to accurately forecast the future and quickly modify macroeconomic policy, along with uncertainty as to when a policy change will exert its primary impact, substantially reduce the effectiveness of discretionary policy as a stabilization tool.

6. Public choice theory indicates that politicians have a strong incentive to follow an expansionary course prior to major elections. Political use of macropolicy reduces its effectiveness as a stabilization tool.

7. The theory of rational expectations argues that even properly timed countercyclical policy will fail to reduce instability once decision-makers figure out the systematic pattern and adjust their choices in light of the expected effects. According to rational expectations theory, any systematic policy that is widely anticipated will fail to exert a predictable impact on real output and employment once the public adjusts to the policy.

8. Rather than attempting countercyclical policies, nonactivists argue that stability would be enhanced if policy-makers simply pursued stable, predictable policies. In the area of monetary policy, nonactivists recommend that decision-makers target one of the following: (a) slow, steady growth of the money supply, (b) growth of nominal GNP at a rate equal to the economy's long-run *real* growth rate, or (c) a constant price level. With regard to fiscal policy, nonactivists favor the maintenance of a stable tax and expenditure policy based on long-run considerations rather than current cyclical conditions.

9. The major disagreement between activists and nonactivists involves the merits of a policy response to changing circumstances. Activists fear that strict adherence to a policy such as the constant (fixed) money growth rule will prevent policy-makers from responding correctly to major recessions and inflations. Correspondingly, nonactivists fear that policy-maker discretion will result in destabilizing policies.

10. Despite their differences, activists and nonactivists agree on several important points. Both agree that (a) it is more difficult to properly time stabilization policy than was generally perceived during the 1960s, (b) past errors have contributed to economic instability, and (c) it is a mistake for policy-makers to respond to minor changes in economic indicators.

11. While stabilization policy has not eliminated economic ups and downs, it has virtually eliminated the likelihood that an economic disturbance will become a catastrophic depression. This is an important achievement that is often overlooked today.

CRITICAL ANALYSIS QUESTIONS

1. Compare the views of activists and nonactivists with regard to the following points: (a) the self-stabilizing characteristics of a market economy; (b) the ability of policy-makers to forecast the future; (c) the validity of the rational expectations hypothesis; and (d) the use of rules versus discretion in the institution of monetary and fiscal policy.

2. What is the index of leading indicators? Evaluate its potential usefulness to policy-makers.

3. Do you think more detailed computer models of the economy will enhance the ability of economists to forecast future economic changes more accurately? Why or why not?

*4. How does economic instability during the last four decades compare with instability prior to the Second World War? Is there any evidence that stabilization policy has either increased or decreased economic stability during the post-Second World War period?

*5. Why do most nonactivists favor a monetary rule such as expansion of the money supply at a constant annual rate? What are some of the potential problems with a monetary rule? How does the stability of the velocity of money affect the case for a monetary rule? Do you think a monetary rule could be devised that would reduce economic instability? Why or why not?

6. The Chair of the Council of Economic Advisers has requested that you write a short paper indicating how economic policy can be used to stabilize the economy and achieve a high level of economic growth during the next five years. Be sure to make specific proposals. Indicate why your recommendations will work. You may submit your paper to your instructor.

7. Evaluate the effectiveness of monetary and fiscal policy during the last three years. Has it helped to promote stable prices, rapid growth, and high employment? Do you think policy-makers have made mistakes during this period? If so, indicate why.

8. "The Great Depression indicates that the self-correcting mechanism of a market economy is weak and unreliable." Evaluate.

*9. Both activists and nonactivists point to the increased stability of the last four decades as evidence supportive of their view. Explain each of their positions.

10. What are some of the problems that would arise if the monetary authorities sought to maintain a constant price level?

*11. Suppose that the Fed tried to peg the real interest rate below the market level. How would it do so and what would be the result of this policy?

12. In recent years, there has been less reliance on the use of discretionary fiscal policy changes as a stabilization tool. Why?

13. Suppose that presidents were limited to a single six-year term. Would this reform influence economic stability? Why or why not?

*14. What does the accuracy of the growth of real GNP and the inflation rate as a predictor of votes in presidential elections imply about the importance candidate personalities, campaign strategies, choice of vice-presidential candidates, expenditures for television commercials, performance in television debates, and similar factors that most people believe determine the outcome in presidential elections?

15. According to David Wyss and Jeanne Blondia, the following equation will predict V_i, which is the percent of the two-party vote won by the candidate of the incumbent party in a presidential election:

$$V_i = 52.56 + 6.67 X_1 - 0.84 X_2 + 1.69 X_3$$

where X_1 = one if the incumbent president is running for
reelection, otherwise zero;

X_2 = percent change in consumer prices during the last 12
months, and

X_3 = percent change in real GNP during the last 12 months.

Use current data on changes in consumer prices and changes in real GNP to predict the percent of the two-party vote the incumbent party would receive if a presidential election were held today.

---

*Asterisk denotes questions for which answers are given in Appendix C, Selected Answers.

16 Budget Deficits and the National Debt

*The attractiveness of financing spending by debt issue to the elected
politicians should be obvious. Borrowing allows spending to be made that
will yield immediate political payoffs without the incurring of any immediate
political cost.[1]*

James Buchanan

CHAPTER FOCUS

■ How large is the national debt? Will the debt have to be paid off?

■ Are we mortgaging the future of our children and grandchildren? How do
budget deficits affect future generations?

■ Have the budget deficits of recent years pushed the debt to a dangerous level?

■ How does the budget deficit of the United States compare with deficits of
other countries?

■ Are the large budget deficits of recent years an aberration or do they reflect a
fundamental problem with the budget process?

*D*eficit spending and the national debt are enduring topics. They were hot topics during the 1940s and 1950s, as Keynesian economists challenged the reigning orthodoxy—the view that the federal budget should be balanced annually. By the 1960s, the Keynesians had clearly won the debate in both the academic and political arenas. Thus, no one paid much attention as the federal government incurred a string of budget deficits during the 1960s and 1970s. These deficits were assumed to be temporary and the result of scientifically determined demand-management policies.

All of this changed in the 1980s. Large and persistent deficits during a time of peace and prosperity brought the debt issue back to center stage. News commentators, business leaders, and others often told us that the "monstrous" deficits were the most critical problem facing America. Is this really true? If so, what is the nature of the problem? Why is it a crisis now? What can be done to deal with it? This chapter focuses on these topics and related issues.

EXPENDITURES, REVENUES, BUDGET DEFICITS, AND THE NATIONAL DEBT

Exhibit 1 illustrates the path of federal expenditures and revenues during the last 35 years. During the last half of the 1950s, federal revenues averaged approximately 18 percent of GNP. Of course, revenues have fluctuated with economic conditions. Their trend, however, has clearly been upward. During the last half of the 1980s, federal revenues averaged approximately 20 percent of GNP, well above the figure for the 1950s. While revenues have increased, federal expenditures have risen even

---

[1]James Buchanan, *The Deficit and American Democracy* (Memphis: P. K. Steidman Foundation, 1984).

EXHIBIT 1

Federal Expenditures and Revenues as a Percent of GNP, 1955–1990

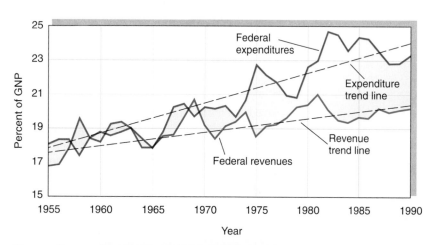

Here we illustrate the path of both federal revenues and expenditures *as a percent of GNP.* Federal revenues increased from approximately 18 percent of GNP during the 1955–1960 period to 20 percent in the late 1980s. Federal expenditures, however, have increased even more rapidly, rising from approximately 18 percent of GNP in the late 1950s to approximately 24 percent of GNP during the 1980s.

more rapidly. During the 1980s, federal expenditures averaged approximately 24 percent of GNP, up from 18 percent during the late 1950s. In recent years, there has been a persistent, sizeable gap between federal expenditures and revenues. Thus, the government has had to borrow heavily in order to cover its expenditures.

When the federal government uses debt rather than taxes and user charges to pay for its expenditures, the U.S. Treasury issues interest-bearing bonds that are sold to private investors, government agencies, and the Federal Reserve Bank. These interest-bearing bonds comprise the **national debt.** In effect, the national debt consists of outstanding loans from financial investors to the general fund of the U.S. Treasury.

National Debt: The sum of the indebtedness of the federal government in the form of outstanding interest-earning bonds. It reflects the cumulative impact of budget deficits and surpluses.

The federal budget deficit and the national debt are directly related. The deficit is a "flow" concept (like water running into a bathtub), while the national debt is a "stock" figure (like the amount of water in the tub at a point in time). In essence, the national debt represents the cumulative effect of all the prior budget deficits and surpluses. A budget deficit increases the size of the national debt by the amount of the deficit. Conversely, a budget surplus allows the federal government to pay off bondholders and thereby reduce the size of the national debt.

The credit worthiness of an organization is dependent upon the size of its debt *relative to its income base*. Therefore, when analyzing the significance of budget deficits and the national debt, it is important to consider their size relative to the entire economy. Exhibit 2 presents data during the last four decades for both the federal budget deficit and the national debt *as a percent of GNP*. Since the defense effort during the Second World War was financed substantially with debt rather than with taxes, the national debt was quite large at the end of war. Following the war, the combination of economic growth and small budget deficits reduced the size of the national debt as a percent of GNP. During the 1950–1974 period, budget deficits averaged less than 1 percent of GNP. Historically, real output in the United States has grown at an annual rate of approximately 3 percent. As long as the budget deficit *as a percent of GNP* is less than the growth of real output, the federal debt will get smaller relative to the size of the economy. This is precisely what happened during the 1950–1974 period. Budget deficits were present, and they pushed up the nominal national debt (from $256.7 billion at year-end 1950 to $492.7 billion at the end of 1974). But GNP grew even more rapidly. By 1974, the national debt had fallen to 34 percent of GNP, down from 89 percent in 1950 (and 127 percent in 1946).

This situation reversed in the mid-1970s. Since 1974, federal budget deficits have been much larger, averaging nearly 4 percent of GNP (Exhibit 2a). When the budget deficit as a percent of GNP exceeds the growth of real GNP, the national debt will increase relative to the size of the economy. As Exhibit 2 illustrates, this was the case during the 1975–1990 period. Pushed along by the large budget deficits of the 1980s, the national debt expanded to 62 percent of GNP in 1990, up from 34 percent in 1974.

A CLOSER LOOK AT THE NATIONAL DEBT

Who owns the national debt? As Exhibit 3 illustrates, the biggest share of the national debt (55.7 percent) is held internally by U.S. citizens and private institutions, such as insurance companies and commercial banks. Foreigners hold

EXHIBIT 2

Budget Deficits and the
National Debt as a
Percent of GNP

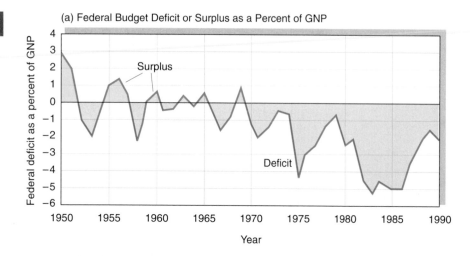

(a) Federal Budget Deficit or Surplus as a Percent of GNP

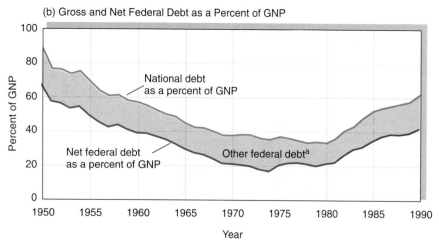

(b) Gross and Net Federal Debt as a Percent of GNP

[a]Federal debt held by U.S. Government agencies and Federal Reserve banks.

Throughout most of the 1950s and 1960s, federal budget deficits were small as a percent of GNP, and occasionally the government ran a budget surplus (panel a). During this period, the national debt declined as a proportion of GNP (panel b). Since 1974, however, the budget deficits have been quite large, larger (as a percent of GNP) than the growth of real GNP. As a result, the national debt has increased as a percent of GNP in recent years.

External Debt: That portion of the national debt owed to foreign investors.

approximately one-eighth of the total. The portion owned by foreigners is sometimes referred to as **external debt.** Almost 25 percent of the debt is held by agencies of the federal government. For example, social security trust funds are often used to purchase U.S. bonds. When the debt is owned by a government agency, it is little more than an accounting transaction indicating that one government agency (for example, the Social Security Administration) is making a loan to another (the U.S. Treasury). Even the interest payments, in this case, represent little more than an internal government transfer.

Approximately 7 percent of the public debt is held by the Federal Reserve System. As we have previously discussed, when the Fed purchases U.S. securities, it creates money. The bonds held by the Fed, therefore, are indicative of prior government expenditures that have been paid for with ''printing press'' money—

EXHIBIT 3 ■ Ownership of the National Debt (1990:Q3)		
Ownership of U.S. Securities	Dollar Value (Billion)	Percent of National Debt
Total National Debt	3,235.6	100.0
U.S. Government agencies	795.8	24.6
Federal Reserve Banks	232.5	7.2
Net Federal Debt	2207.3	68.2
Domestic investors	1802.6	55.7
Foreign investors	404.7	12.5

Source: *Federal Reserve Bulletin*, March 1991.

money created by the central bank. As in the case of the securities held by government agencies, the interest on the bonds held by the Fed is returned to the Treasury after the Fed has covered its costs of operation.

Since the government both pays and receives the interest on the bonds held by government agencies and the Federal Reserve (minus Fed expenses), these bonds do not represent a net interest obligation. Only the bonds held by domestic and foreign investors will require additional taxes to meet future net interest payments. Thus, the portion of the debt owed to domestic and foreign investors is sometimes referred to as the **net federal debt** (or net public debt). As Exhibit 3 illustrates, the net public debt accounted for 68.2 percent of the national debt in 1990.

Exhibit 2b presents data on the size of the net federal debt as a percent of GNP for the 1950–1990 period. Like the overall national debt, the net federal debt as a share of GNP declined sharply during the 1950s and moderately during the 1960–1974 period. However, since 1974, it too, has been rising as a percent of GNP.

Net Federal Debt: The portion of the national debt owed to domestic and foreign investors. It does *not* include bonds held by agencies of the federal government or the Federal Reserve.

CONCERNS ABOUT THE DEBT

Are large, persistent budget deficits harmful to the health of the U.S. economy? Persons who answer this question in the affirmative generally argue that the deficits (1) are harmful to the welfare of future generations, (2) result in a dangerous dependency on foreign capital, and (3) generate a large interest liability that threatens the financial stability of the federal government. Let us consider each of these concerns in some detail.

HOW DOES DEBT-FINANCING AFFECT FUTURE GENERATIONS?

Laymen, politicians, and economists have debated about the burden of national debt for many years.[2] One side has argued that we are mortgaging the future of our children and grandchildren—that debt-financing permits us to consume today, then send the bill to future generations. The other side, noting that most of the national

[2]See Richard H. Fink and Jack High, eds., *A Nation in Debt: Economists Debate the Federal Budget Deficit* (Frederick: University Publications of America, 1987) for an excellent set of readings summarizing this debate.

debt is held by domestic citizens (see Exhibit 3), has retorted, "we owe it to ourselves."

When considering our ability to shift the cost of government onto future generations, two points must be kept in mind. First, when government debt is financed internally, future generations of Americans will inherit both a higher tax liability and additional interest income. Other things constant, debt-financing does imply higher future taxes. But it also implies the receipt of additional interest income. Thus, in the case of domestically held debt, our children and grandchildren will both pay the taxes to service the debt and receive the interest payments. Admittedly, the people paying the taxes and receiving the interest payments will not always be the same. Some people will gain and others will lose. But both those who gain and those who lose will be members of the future generation.

Second, debt-financing of a government activity cannot push the opportunity cost of the resources used by government onto future generations. If current GNP is $5 trillion and the federal government is spending $1.2 trillion, then $3.8 trillion will remain for private individuals, businesses, and state and local governments to spend or invest. This will be true regardless of whether the federal government finances its expenditures with taxes or debt. Debt financing cannot push the opportunity cost of resources used by the government into the future. When the government builds a highway, constructs an anti-missile defense system, or provides police protection, it draws resources with alternative uses away from the private sector. *Current* output of goods for private consumption and investment will decline as the result of the government's employment of resources that otherwise would be available for use in the private sector. This cost is incurred in the present; it cannot be avoided through debt-finance.

What debt *can* push into the future is the deadweight losses and disincentive effects of taxes. In some cases, these costs may be substantial. In most instances, however, they will be considerably smaller than the opportunity cost of the resources used by the government in the provision of goods and services.

If the opportunity cost of resources occurs during the current period, does this mean that there is little reason to be concerned about an adverse impact of deficits on future generations? Not necessarily. Debt-financing influences future generations primarily through its potential impact on saving and capital formation. If the current generation bequeaths lots of factories, machines, houses, knowledge, and other productive assets to their children, then the productive potential of the next generation will be high. Alternatively, if fewer productive assets are passed along to the next generation, then their productive capability will decline accordingly. Thus, the true measure of how government debt influences future generations involves knowledge of its impact on capital formation.

When excess capacity is present, a deficit can stimulate aggregate demand and bring otherwise idle resources into the production of houses and factories, as well as consumption goods. Under such circumstances, budget deficits enlarge the stock of capital available to future generations and thereby enhance their well-being.

The impact of budget deficits *during normal times* on capital formation and the welfare of future generations is a complex issue. Consider an economy that is operating at productive capacity. *Holding government expenditures constant,* how would the substitution of debt-finance for current taxation influence capital formation? As our fiscal policy models imply, economists sometimes differ in their responses to this question. There are two alternative theories and they imply different answers. We will consider both of the theories.

***The Traditional View of Budget Deficits—They Reduce the Capital Stock of Future
Generations.*** Most economists embrace the traditional view that implies that
budget deficits will retard private investment and thereby reduce the welfare of
future generations. The traditional view stresses that people will tend to treat their
additional holdings of government bonds (used to finance the debt) as wealth. After
all, the bonds represent future income to their holders. On the other hand, the
proponents of the traditional view argue that it is absurd to believe that taxpayers
think through the implications of the budget deficit for their future taxes. If
bondholders recognize the asset value of the government bonds while taxpayers fail
to recognize fully the accompanying tax liability, then the general populace will
have an exaggerated view of its true wealth position. Wealth is an important
determinant of consumption. With an exaggerated view of their wealth, people will
consume more and save less than they would otherwise. Given the high
consumption and low saving rates, the strong government demand for loanable
funds to finance its deficit will push real interest rates upward.[3] In turn, the higher
interest rates will crowd out private investment, and with the passage of time,
reduce the capital stock available to future generations.

In addition, the higher interest rates will attract foreign investors. But
investments in the United States will require dollars. As foreigners increase their
investments in the United States, they will demand dollars in the international
currency market. This strong demand will cause the dollar to appreciate. In turn, the
appreciation in the exchange rate value of the dollar will make foreign goods
cheaper to Americans and American goods more expensive to foreigners. Thus,
U.S. imports will rise relative to exports. A balance of trade deficit (an excess of
imports over exports) follows directly from the inflow of foreign capital.

While the inflow of capital from abroad will dampen both the increase in
interest rates and the reduction in domestic investment, it also implies that
foreigners will receive larger future incomes from their asset holdings in the United
States. Therefore, compared with the financing of government by current taxation,
future generations of Americans will inherit both a smaller stock of physical capital
and less income from that capital (since the share owned by foreigners has
increased). Succeeding generations will be less well-off as a result.

In summary, the traditional view argues that the substitution of debt-financing
for current taxation will *indirectly* alter the composition of private domestic
spending toward consumption and away from investment. Since households view
government securities as wealth, they consume more and save (and invest) less than
would be the case if government expenditures were financed by taxation. As a
result, interest rates will increase and crowd out private investment. In turn, the
growth rate of the capital stock will slow. Since future generations will be working
with less capital (fewer productivity-enhancing tools and machines), their productivity and wages will be lower than would have been the case had the budget deficits
not crowded out private investment. Thus, according to the traditional view, budget
deficits will retard the growth rate of income and thereby reduce the living standard
of future generations of Americans.

---

[3]The substitution of debt for taxes will increase the disposable income of households, causing both
consumption and saving to expand. But saving will increase by much less than the additional
government demand for loanable funds to finance the deficit. Thus, real interest rates rise.

New Classical View of Budget Deficits—the Substitution of Debt for Taxes Exerts Little Impact on Either the Economy or the Welfare of Future Generations. Not all economists accept the traditional view of budget deficits. An alternative view, most closely associated with Robert Barro of Harvard University, encompasses the new classical perspective of fiscal policy.[4] The new classical view stresses that additional debt implies an equivalent amount of future taxes. If, as the new classical model assumes, individuals fully anticipate the added future tax liability accompanying the debt, current consumption will be unaffected when the taxes are levied. According to this view, if future taxes (debt) are substituted for current taxes, then people will save the reduction in current taxes so that they will have the required income to pay the higher future taxes implied by the additional debt. As a result, the increase in the demand for loanable funds emanating from the budget deficit is offset by an equivalent increase in private saving. Therefore, neither real interest rates nor private investment is altered. Since real interest yields are unaffected, neither is there an influx of foreign capital. Since neither capital formation nor wealth is altered, the substitution of debt for taxes does not affect the welfare of future generations in the new classical model.

Empirical Evidence on the Impact of the Deficit. What does the empirical evidence indicate with regard to the validity of the two theories? Studies focusing on the period prior to the 1980s have found only a weak relationship, if any, between budget deficits and real interest rates. New classical economists argue that these findings are supportive of their theory.

However, the experience with the big budget deficits of the 1980s would appear to be highly supportive of the traditional theory of deficit finance. Exhibit 4 compares consumption, investment, and net exports *as a share of GNP* during the five years following the recession of 1982 with the five years subsequent to the recession of 1974–75. Since the budget deficits averaged 5.1 percent of GNP

---

[4]See Robert Barro, "Are Government Bonds Net Wealth?" *Journal of Political Economy* 82 (November/December 1974), pp. 1,095–1,117, and "The Ricardian Approach to Budget Deficits," *Journal of Economic Perspectives* 2 (Spring 1989).

EXHIBIT 4 ■ Recent Changes in Personal Consumption, Investment, and Net Exports as a Share of GNP					
	Component as a Percent of GNP				
Time Period	Federal Deficit	Personal Consumption	Gross Private Investment	Gross Investment Less Net Foreign Investment	Net Exports
1976–1980	2.8	62.9	17.1	17.1	+0.7
1983–1987	5.1	65.6	16.0	13.4	−1.9
Differential (Later period minus earlier period)	+2.3	+ 2.7	− 1.1	− 3.7	−2.6

Source: *Economic Report of the President, 1988.*

during 1983–1987, compared with 2.8 percent during the 1976–1980 period, a comparison of the two periods sheds light on how larger budget deficits affect the economy. During the 1983–1987 period of larger budget deficits, personal consumption rose to 65.6 percent of GNP, compared with 62.9 percent during the earlier period. Gross investment as a percent of GNP declined from 17.1 percent in 1976–1980 to 16.0 percent during 1983–1987, as an inflow of foreign capital moderated the reduction. But look what happened to the investment spending of Americans. The investment expenditures of Americans (gross investment less net foreign investment) fell from 17.1 percent of GNP in 1976–1980 to 13.4 percent in 1983–1987. Net exports decreased. Thus, during the period of larger sustained deficits, Americans cut their *domestically financed* capital formation, increased their imports (negative net exports), and expanded their current consumption. This pattern is precisely what the traditional theory predicts will happen when debt-financing is substituted for current taxation.

Nominal data were used to derive the gross investment/GNP ratio presented in Exhibit 4. If the prices of investment goods and other components of GNP rose at approximately the same rate, it would not make any difference whether nominal or real numbers were used to calculate the ratio. However, this was not the case. While prices in general *rose* more than 30 percent during 1982–1990, the price index for durable equipment, a large component of private investment, *declined* during the same period. These price declines for investment equipment reflected the rapid technological change and cost reductions accompanying the computer revolution of the 1980s.

As Barro and other leading new classical economists have stressed, a different picture emerges when the investment/GNP ratio is calculated in real terms. As Exhibit 5 illustrates, while *nominal* gross investment fell (from 17.1 percent to 16.0 percent) as a share of *nominal* GNP between 1976–1980 and 1983–1987, *real* investment as a percent of *real* GNP rose from 17.2 percent to 17.5 percent.[5] Moreover, like investment, purchases of long-lasting consumer durables (such as

---

[5]Why was the gross investment/GNP ratio substantially different when calculated in real rather than nominal terms during the 1980s? The following table provides the answer:

	Implicit Price Deflator	
	GNP (1982 = 100)	Producer's Durable Equipment (1982 = 100)
1976	63.1	64.4
1980	85.7	86.0
1983	103.9	99.5
1987	117.5	95.5
Percent change:		
1976–1980	+35.8	+33.5
1983–1987	+13.1	−4.0

Broad components of a price index usually follow a pattern similar to that of the aggregate index. However, this was not true for producer's durable equipment during the 1980s. Between 1983 and 1987, durable equipment prices *fell* by 4 percent while the price index for GNP as a whole *rose* 13.1 percent. The lower durable equipment prices permitted producers to increase their real investment expenditures as a share of GNP even though their nominal expenditures *as a share of GNP* were falling. Declining prices for computers and computer-related equipment were the primary factor pushing the price index of durable equipment down in the mid-1980s.

EXHIBIT 5 ■ Have the Deficits Really Reduced Private Investment?				
	Component as a Share of GNP			
	Gross Investment		Gross Investment plus Purchases of Durable Goods	
Period	Nominal	Real	Nominal	Real
1976–1980	17.1	17.2	25.9	25.5
1983–1987	16.0	17.5	25.1	27.1
1988–1990	15.0	17.2	24.1	27.6
1965–1969	15.9	17.0	24.8	23.6

Source: *Economic Report of the President, 1991* (Tables 1, 2, and 3).

appliances, furniture, and personally owned automobiles) also enhance our future welfare. Surprisingly, *real* spending on consumer durables and gross investment summed to 27.1 percent of real GNP during the 1983–1987 period, compared with only 25.5 percent during the earlier period of smaller deficits.

Exhibit 5 also presents data for 1988–1990 and for 1965–1969, a period of sustained prosperity. During each of these periods, real gross investment averaged approximately 17 percent of real GNP. Thus, when measured in real terms, gross investment as a share of GNP during the 1980s is not out of line with the parallel figures during the 1960s and 1970s. Interestingly, expenditures on real gross investment *and* consumer durables were quite high during the 1980s. In fact, when measured in real terms, the spending on gross investment and consumer durables as a percent of GNP was at a post-Second World War high during the large deficit years of the 1980s. In contrast with the more widely cited nominal data, the real investment figures do not indicate that the budget deficits of the 1980s stimulated consumption and crowded out capital investment.

DOES DEPENDENCE ON FOREIGN INVESTORS POSE A DANGER?

While the real data indicate that gross investment was approximately constant as a share of GNP during the mid-1980s, a significant portion of the investment was financed by foreigners. Foreign investors now supply approximately one-seventh of the investment capital in the United States.

How does foreign investment affect the U.S. economy? When considering a possible burden emanating from foreign investment, it is important to keep an eye on both sides of the transaction. The inflow of foreign capital leads to lower interest rates and a higher level of investment than would take place in its absence. An increase in machines, structures, and other forms of capital formation from foreign investment will increase the productivity and income of American workers. Of course, the inflow of investment funds also enlarges the future profit and interest claims of foreigners. However, if the funds are invested wisely, the projects will generate returns (future income) that provide an offset against the future income claims of foreigners. On the other hand, if the funds are squandered on low-return projects, the wealth of investors will be reduced. But this would be equally true for projects financed solely with domestic funds.

Does the inflow of capital from abroad subject the U.S. economy to possible manipulation by foreign interests? Fear of foreign dependency has been intensified as the result of the recent financial difficulties of governments in Mexico, Argentina, and Brazil. However, the forces underlying the financial difficulties of these countries are vastly different than the current situation of the United States. The governments of Mexico, Argentina, and Brazil borrowed money from Western banks and international lending institutions at adjustable interest rates. Most importantly, the loans were not payable in the domestic currencies of the debtor countries. Therefore, the ability of the debtor nations to repay was subject to change depending upon what happened to both international exchange rates and interest rates in other countries. Needless to say, the sharp appreciation in the exchange rate value of the dollar and the high real interest rates in the United States during the 1980–1985 period dramatically affected the real liability of the loans and the ability of the debtor countries to meet their contractual commitments.

In contrast, it is really a misnomer to call much of the recent inflow of capital into the United States "borrowing." Substantial portions of these funds are in the form of risk capital—investments in stocks, land, physical structures, and business ventures. Such investments do not involve a contractual repayment commitment. Others are invested in bonds, both corporate and government. These investments are almost entirely *fixed* interest rate obligations. And their repayment is in dollars, not some foreign currency.

What would happen if foreigners suddenly decided to take their "money" home and quit financing investments in the United States? It is not obvious why literally tens of thousands of foreign investors would be any more likely to suddenly "sell out" than tens of thousands of domestic investors. But, even if they did, market adjustments would exert a stabilizing effect. Remember, the "money" of foreigners is in the form of stocks, bonds, and physical assets. If foreigners suddenly tried to sell these assets, falling prices would create some real bargains for domestic investors. Domestic investors would gain and foreign investors would lose. Similarly, if foreigners cut back their financial investments in the United States, real interest rates would rise. But the higher real interest rates would make U.S. investments more attractive and thereby help deter any outflow of funds.

Finally, the vulnerability accompanying foreign investment almost certainly lies with the foreign investor rather than with the recipient country. It is much easier for a government to expropriate the property of a foreigner than it is for an investor to exercise much control over the policies of a foreign government. History illustrates the vulnerability of the foreign investor. The United States expropriated the property of Germans and Japanese during the Second World War. Several Middle Eastern countries expropriated the property of foreign investors when they nationalized their domestic oil industries in the 1950s and 1960s. Under Fidel Castro, the Cuban government expropriated the assets of foreigners. Foreign investment is a hostage to the domestic policies of the recipient country. A major reason why foreign investment is attracted to the United States is the confidence of foreigners that the U.S. government will not abuse its superior position.

THE FINANCIAL CONSEQUENCES OF A GROWING INTEREST COST

Borrowing is an everyday method of doing business. Many of the nation's largest and most profitable corporations continually have debt outstanding. As long as the net income of a business firm is large relative to this interest liability, the outstanding debt poses little problem.

So it is with the federal government. As long as people have confidence that it can raise the tax revenue necessary to meet its debt obligations, the federal government will have no trouble financing and refinancing its outstanding debt. And it can do so in perpetuity. There is no date in the future at which the federal debt must be paid off.

The key to credit-worthiness is expected future income relative to the interest liability. This is true for individuals, private businesses, and governments. What is happening to the government's interest liability relative to its source of income? Exhibit 6 addresses this issue. Since the early 1970s, the funding necessary to pay the interest on the national debt has increased substantially. For 25 years following the Second World War, the net interest cost of the federal government was approximately 1.5 percent of GNP. In recent years, however, interest costs have increased sharply. *As a share of GNP,* the net interest costs of the federal government rose from 1.5 percent in 1972 to 3.4 percent in 1990. Thus, the federal government's current interest burden is approximately twice the level of the 1950s and 1960s.

The 1972–1990 trend cannot continue, at least not without serious consequences. What would happen if increasingly larger deficits continued to push up the federal government's interest obligations *as a share of GNP?* As interest costs increased as a proportion of the total budget, it would become increasingly difficult to cut spending and thereby reduce the size of the deficit. As the government borrowed more and more money to both refinance debt and meet interest payments, fear that it might resort to printing-press money in an effort to escape its loan obligations would arise. In turn, both strong demand and increased inflationary fears would push interest rates higher and complicate the government's difficulties. If sufficiently intense, the fear of inflation alone could seriously disrupt the long-term capital market for not only the federal government, but other borrowers as well. And, if the government did resort to "printing press" money in order to pay off its debt, hyperinflation and a breakdown in the positive-sum exchange system would result. The economy would be severely crippled.

Most economists are confident that in the United States constructive action would be taken well before such a crisis develops. However, it has happened elsewhere. Several countries, including Bolivia, Argentina, Chile, Brazil, and

EXHIBIT 6

Interest Payments as a Percentage of Gross National Product

During the period from 1954 to 1972, the interest payments on the portion of the national debt held by the public comprised approximately 1.5 percent of GNP. In recent years, the percentage has risen. The interest on the national debt rose to 3.4 percent of GNP in 1990.

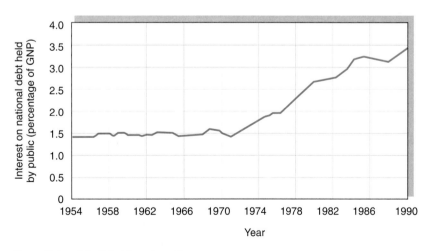

Source: Budget of the United States (annual).

Israel, have experienced the results of excessive debt, money creation, and runaway inflation in recent years. If the interest liability of the federal government consistently grew more rapidly than income, clearly the United States would not be immune to such an occurrence.

IS THE SIZE OF THE DEFICIT EXAGGERATED?

Some economists believe that the magnitude of the "deficit problem" has been exaggerated due to (a) lack of recognition that state and local governments have been running large surpluses; (b) the failure of the federal accounting procedures to make the appropriate allowance for capital expenditures; and (c) the impact of inflation on the nominal budget deficit.

STATE AND LOCAL SURPLUSES PARTIALLY OFFSET RECENT FEDERAL DEFICITS

While the federal government was running larger deficits throughout the 1980s, state and local governments were experiencing sizeable budget surpluses. Therefore, the aggregate deficit of all governmental units was not as large as the federal data indicate.

Exhibit 7 presents the data on the deficit, including state and local governments. During the 1970s, the combined budgets of state and local governments were roughly in balance. However, in recent years, the budget surpluses of state and local governments have generally exceeded 1 percent of GNP. As a percent of GNP, the aggregate deficit of all governments in the 1980s was almost one-third smaller than the federal deficit alone. For example, while the federal deficit was 4.9 percent of GNP ($206.9 billion) in 1986, the deficit for total government was only 3.4 percent of GNP ($144.1 billion). By 1989 the aggregate government deficit had fallen to 1.7 percent of GNP, a rate well below the long-term growth of income.

Inclusion of state and local government finance does not negate the point that the size of government deficits has grown as a proportion of GNP during the last 15 years. But it does indicate that reliance upon the federal data alone tends to exaggerate the growth of deficit finance.

ADJUSTMENT FOR CAPITAL EXPENDITURES

In private affairs, we recognize that it makes a difference whether borrowing is for long-lasting assets or current consumption. Borrowing to purchase a new home expected to last 30 years is one thing, borrowing to finance a weekend caper in Las Vegas is quite another. Businesses establish capital and current expense budgets in order to distinguish between expenditures for long-lasting assets and resources used during the current period. When undertaking a major capital expenditure, borrowing is a perfectly acceptable method of doing business.

In contrast, the federal government makes no distinction between expenditures for a new highway or aircraft and expenditures for current services or transfer payments. To the extent the budget deficit is used to finance long-lasting assets, future taxpayers will receive a stream of services as an offset to the tax liability. For example, suppose the federal government spends $100 million to provide office space that is currently rented for $12 million. If the expenditure is debt-financed at an annual interest rate of 12 percent, then $100 million is added to the national debt. But there is no change in government's current expenditures; rent expense goes down by $12 million, and interest expense increases by $12 million.

EXHIBIT 7 ■ The Impact of State and Local Finance on the Total Government Deficit					
	Government Deficit (−) or Surplus (+)			Deficit as a Percent of GNP	
Year	Federal (billions)	State and Local (billions)	Total (billions)	Federal	Total Government
1970	−$ 12.4	+$ 1.8	−$ 10.6	−1.2	−1.0
1975	− 69.4	+ 4.5	− 64.9	−4.3	−4.1
1980	− 61.3	+ 26.8	− 34.5	−2.2	−1.3
1985	− 196.9	+ 65.1	− 131.8	−4.9	−3.3
1986	− 206.9	+ 62.8	− 144.1	−4.9	−3.4
1987	− 158.2	+ 51.0	− 107.1	−3.5	−2.4
1988	− 141.7	+ 46.5	− 95.3	−2.9	−1.9
1989	− 134.3	+ 46.4	− 87.8	−2.6	−1.7
1990	− 161.3	+ 35.4	− 126.0	−3.0	−2.3

Source: *Economic Report of the President, 1991*.

Many economists believe that the government's inclusion of capital investment as a current expenditure exaggerates the magnitude of the deficit problem. While it is difficult to determine the precise magnitude of the federal government's net capital expenditures, it is clear that they are substantial. Recent research of the topic indicates that they were more than $20 billion in the mid-1980s.[6]

INFLATION DISTORTS THE BUDGET DEFICIT

By now you should be well aware that inflation affects nominal interest rates. Once people come to expect a given rate of inflation, it gets built into the nominal rate of interest.

Inflation can also distort data on the deficit and interest costs. Exhibit 8 will help us illustrate this point. Here we consider two economies with the same real GNP ($5,000 billion last year) and real growth rate (3 percent). Economy A is experiencing stable prices, while the annual inflation rate of B is 5 percent. In both instances, we assume that the real interest rate is 2 percent and the initial outstanding debt is equal to $2,000 billion, approximately the *net* federal debt of the United States. Furthermore, we assume that both A and B pay the *real* interest on the debt and therefore the real value of the outstanding debt remains constant during the year. When stable prices are maintained and expected, the real and nominal interest rates will be equal. Under these circumstances, the nominal interest of the outstanding debt will equal $40 billion (2 percent of $2,000 billion). The revenues of Economy A's government are sufficient to pay all other expenditures plus the $40 billion in real interest. Economy A is experiencing a balanced budget.

Now consider the situation for Economy B, which is experiencing a sustained inflation rate of 5 percent. Since the 5 percent inflation rate is anticipated, it is reflected in the 7 percent nominal interest rate. Under these circumstances, the nominal interest payments of the government will be $140 billion (7 percent of $2,000 billion). Once again we suppose that the revenues are sufficient to pay all

---

[6]Robert Eisner, "Which Budget Deficit? Some Issues of Measurement and Their Implications," *American Economic Review*, vol. 74 (May 1988), pp. 138–43.

	Growth, Budget, and Debt Related Data (dollar amounts in billions)	
Item	Inflation Rate of Economy A = 0	Inflation Rate of Economy B = 5%
Economic Growth		
GNP last year	$5,000	$5,000
GNP this year		
nominal	$5,150	$5,408
real	$5,150	$5,150
Real Growth Rate	3 %	3 %
Debt Related Variables		
a. real interest rate	2 %	2 %
b. nominal interest rate	2 %	7 %
c. net debt (beginning of year)	$2,000	$2,000
d. nominal interest on the debt	$ 40	$ 140
e. real interest paid	$ 40	$ 40
f. nominal net debt at the end of the year	$2,000	$2,100
g. loss in value of outstanding bonds due to inflation	0	$ 100
h. real debt at the end of the year	$2,000	$2,000
i. nominal deficit (−)	0	−$ 100
j. real deficit (change in real outstanding debt)	0	0
k. nominal deficit/nominal GNP	0	− 1.8%
l. nominal interest cost/GNP	0.8%	2.6%

EXHIBIT 8 ■ Inflation, Nominal Deficits, and Real Deficits (Hypothetical Data)

expenses plus the $40 billion in *real* interest. A nominal budget deficit of $100 billion results. At the end of the year, the government's nominal outstanding debt is $2,100 billion. However, the price level has increased by 5 percent. Thus, the *real* debt outstanding (in terms of the purchasing power of the dollar at the beginning of the year) remains constant at $2,000 billion ($2,100 billion deflated for the 5 percent price increase). Even though the nominal deficit is $100 billion, there is no change in real debt outstanding. Just as in the case when prices were stable, the real outstanding debt is constant and the *real* budget deficit is zero. But look at the deficit/GNP ratio and the interest cost/GNP ratio. Both of these ratios increased for the economy (B) experiencing inflation. These ratios make it appear that the burden of the deficit and accompanying interest costs are rising even though the real outstanding debt of Economy B is constant.

It is no mystery why the nominal budget deficit of Economy B rose by $100 billion even though the real outstanding debt was constant. The 5 percent inflation rate pushed up nominal interest rates (from 2 percent to 7 percent) and increased the government's interest cost. This results in $100 billion of *additional* nominal interest which shows up as an expense item in the budget. However, the 5 percent inflation also erodes the real burden of the $2,000 billion of outstanding debt by $100 billion. This is a real capital gain (a decline in the liability of the government), *but it does not appear in the budget*. Therefore, even though the $100 billion of additional interest and $100 billion reduction in the government's real liability on outstanding debt are offsetting items resulting from the 5 percent inflation rate, only the additional nominal interest cost affects the budget.

What are the implications of this analysis for the U.S. budget deficit? First, it indicates that an increase in the budget deficit/GNP ratio (see Exhibit 2) and the interest cost/GNP ratio (see Exhibit 6) are expected results of the higher inflation rates during the last 20 years. Second, if we want to find out what is happening to the real debt outstanding, the nominal deficit figure needs to be reduced by the change in the real value of the outstanding bonds. In 1990, the inflation rate was 4 percent and the net public debt was approximately $2,000 billion at the beginning of the year. This would imply that inflation reduced the real value of this outstanding debt by approximately $80 billion during 1990. If this figure were included as an offset to the higher nominal interest payments emanating from inflation, then the 1990 aggregate government deficit would have been about $46 billion (0.8 percent of GNP). This figure is still larger than the comparable deficits during the relatively stable price era of the 1960s. However, it does not indicate that an impending catastrophe is right around the corner, as persons focusing on the nominal deficit figures have sometimes charged.

IS THE SOCIAL SECURITY SURPLUS CONCEALING THE SIZE OF THE DEBT?

As conventionally measured, the budget deficit includes the revenues and expenditures of government trust funds, including the social security trust fund. Until recently, the *net* revenue (or expenditure) flowing into these funds was small relative to the size of the budget. Therefore, it really did not make much difference whether these funds were included in or excluded from budget deficit calculations.

All of this began to change in the late 1980s. Under legislation passed in 1983, the social security trust fund is scheduled to run huge budget surpluses throughout the 1990s and into the next century. As Exhibit 9 illustrates, the size of budget deficits is drastically affected by whether the social security trust funds are included in the deficit calculations. If the social security trust fund surplus had been excluded from the 1990 deficit calculations, the federal deficit would have been $286 billion, rather than $220 billion. The Bush Administration is forecasting a 1992 budget deficit of $281 billion. If the social security surplus were omitted, however, the 1992 forecast deficit would soar to $367 billion. During the 1990s, inclusion of the social security trust fund surpluses will reduce the size of the perceived annual budget deficits by approximately $100 billion.

EXHIBIT 9

The Social Security Surplus and the Budget Deficit

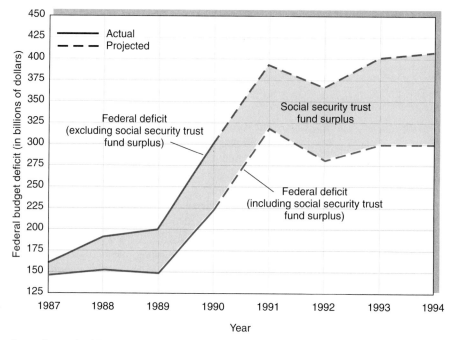

Source: Congressional Budget Office.CHAPTER 1

The budget deficits during the 1990s would be between $75 billion and $120 billion larger if the surpluses of the social security trust fund were excluded from the deficit calculations. Thus, the budget deficit is currently a substantial understatement of the "current operations" deficit.

More is at stake here than just a definitional issue. There was a reason for the planned social security surpluses. During the 15 years following the Second World War, there was a huge group of people born in the United States. When this "baby boom generation" is in the retirement phase of their life during 2020 to 2050, enormous strain will be placed on the social security system. Unless funds are set aside to finance the retirement benefits of the baby-boomers, the solvency of the social security system will be endangered. This is precisely the strategy underlying the planned social security surpluses. The surpluses are intended to increase the national saving rate and stimulate additional investment, which will help finance the retirement benefits of the baby-boom generation. Using the trust funds to finance current government expenditures completely undermines this strategy.

Given the future demands of the social security system, many economists argue that it will not be enough for the federal government to just balance its budget in the 1990s. They argue that the government should be running a budget *surplus* equal to the surplus in the social security trust fund.

DEBT FINANCING IN OTHER COUNTRIES

In recent years, the size of budget deficits has been a source of friction between the United States and its allies. However, international data indicate that the United

EXHIBIT 10	■ The Budget Deficits of Seven Industrial Countries, 1985–1989		
	Average Budget Deficit as a Percent of GNP, 1985–1989		Net Public Debt as a Percent of GNP, 1989
Country	All Government Units	Central Government Only	
Canada	−4.7	−4.3	39.6
United States	−2.6	−3.8	30.3
Japan	+0.4	−2.4	19.4
France	−2.0	−2.0	25.3
Germany	−1.3	−1.4	22.8
Italy	−10.9	−12.2	94.6
United Kingdom	−0.8	−0.6	33.5

Source: International Monetary Fund, *World Economic Outlook,* October 1988 and June 1989, Tables 6, 7, and 34.

States has not been alone in its reliance on deficit finance. In fact, deficits have become a way of life for most all industrial countries. Exhibit 10 illustrates this point. When considering all levels of government, budget deficits during 1985–1989 averaged between 0.8 percent and 2.0 percent of GNP in France, Germany, and the United Kingdom. As a share of GNP, the budget deficits of Canada and Italy were even larger. Among the major industrial countries, only Japan failed to run a budget deficit during the relatively prosperous 1985–1989 period. The widespread use of budget deficits among democratic industrial nations indicates that modern politicians have a preference for spending and debt, rather than taxes and user charges.

Exhibit 10 also provides data on the net public debt relative to the GNP for each country. As of 1989, the net public debt/GNP ratio was lowest in Japan, Germany, and France, and highest for Italy, Canada, and the United Kingdom. The United States was the median observation for the seven countries.

UNCONSTRAINED POLITICS AND BUDGET DEFICITS

Why has the federal government run a string of deficits during the last three decades, deficits that have become progressively larger? Many public choice economists, including the 1986 Nobel laureate James Buchanan, argue that their analysis provides the answer. Buchanan and others charge that politicians like to spend money in order to buy the favor of various interest groups and voting blocs, but they dislike taxes that impose visible costs on voting constituents. However, government expenditures must be financed in some manner. Borrowing provides an alternative to current taxation. Since they push the taxes into the future, deficits are less visible to people than current taxation. In essence, the substitution of debt for taxes permits politicians to conceal the full cost of government from voters. People imagine that government services cost less than is really the case. Thus, borrowing allows politicians to supply voters with *immediate* benefits without having to impose a parallel visible cost in the form of higher taxes or user charges. Therefore, if unconstrained by constitutional rules or powerful social forces, predictably politicians will use deficits to conceal partially the cost of their programs from voters. According to the public choice view, deficit spending is a natural outgrowth of unconstrained democratic politics.

For 150 years, various constitutional restrictions substantially reduced both the spending and borrowing proclivity of politicians. Even after the Constitution was amended, authorizing the income tax in 1913, and subsequent court decisions loosened the spending inclinations at the federal level, it was widely believed that prudent policy required the balancing of the federal budget, at least during times of peace. In essence, until approximately 1960, the United States had an *implicit* constitutional rule that the federal budget be balanced. During peace time, most politicians in both political parties were strongly supportive of the balanced budget concept.

However, the Keynesian revolution changed all of this, first among economists in the 1940s and 1950s, and later among the politicians. The problem was not with Keynesian theory, but rather with the *political implications* of the theory. Properly understood, Keynesian theory does not provide support for continued large budget deficits. In recent years, many Keynesian economists have been at the forefront of those criticizing such deficits. What Keynesian theory did, however, was erode the discipline that emanated from the implicit balanced budget concept. Released from this discipline, politicians of all persuasions found it politically attractive to support spending in excess of taxes.[7]

In fact, the current budget decision-making process encourages this course of action.[8] Under current procedures, Congress makes spending decisions in a series of separate appropriations made prior to and independent of the funding issue. Since a budget constraint is absent when spending decisions are made, the opportunity cost of programs is concealed from voters and even from politicians.

Rather than program-by-program comparison of benefits and costs, the budget process is driven by claims of "need." Of course, in a world of scarce resources, we always need more of most everything. The process plays into the hands of politically powerful interest groups and also encourages "pork barrel" spending— each representative has a strong incentive to fight hard for expenditures beneficial to his or her constituents and favored interest groups. The legislator will get full credit for these benefits. In contrast, a legislator does not have much incentive to oppose spending by others. A legislator who is a spending "watch dog" will incur the wrath of colleagues favoring special programs for their districts. More importantly, the benefits (for example, tax reductions and lower interest rates) of spending cuts and deficit reductions will be spread thinly among the voters in all districts. Thus, the legislator's constituents will reap only a small part of these benefits.

---

[7]See James M. Buchanan and Richard Wagner, *Democracy in Deficit: The Political Legacy of Lord Keynes* (New York: Academic Press, 1977) for a detailed account of the changes wrought by the Keynesian revolution.

[8]This section borrows freely from James Gwartney and Richard Wagner, *The Federal Budget Process: Why It Is Broken and How It Can Be Fixed* (Tallahassee: James Madison Institute, 1988).

It is as if 535 families go out to dinner knowing that after the meal each will receive a bill for 1/535th of the cost. No family representative has much incentive to conserve on the amount ordered by his or her family because less spending by one family will exert little impact on the total bill. Why not order shrimp for an appetizer, entrees of steak and lobster, and a large piece of cheesecake for dessert? After all, the extra spending will add only a few pennies to each family's share of the total bill. However, when everybody follows this course of action, the result is that many items are purchased whose value is less than their cost.[9]

So it is with congressional decision-making. Representatives have a strong incentive to push for "desserts" helpful to their own districts, particularly when each recognizes that other legislators are doing so. Then, after the spending decisions are made, Congress sums up the total and tries to figure out how to pay for it. Given the procedures, the presence of budget deficits should not come as a surprise. They are a natural outgrowth of the process.

STRUCTURAL CHANGE AND DOING SOMETHING ABOUT THE DEFICIT

Public choice analysis indicates that budget deficits are an expected result of ordinary politics in the post-Keynesian era. Paradoxically, there is little reason to believe that a tax increase would do much to reduce the deficit—at least not for long. Given the spending inclinations built into the ordinary political process, additional revenue would merely lead to additional spending (rather than a reduction in the deficit). According to this view, the budget deficits reflect the current rules of the game. If we want a different outcome, rule changes will be necessary.

GRAMM-RUDMAN-HOLLINGS ACT

The chronic tendency toward over-spending relative to taxation has not gone unnoticed in Congress. On several occasions, Congress has passed legislation mandating spending cuts and deficit reductions. In 1985, Congress passed the Gramm-Rudman-Hollings Act mandating across-the-board spending reductions in most government programs if the deficit was not lowered to specific target levels by various years in the future. This act illustrates the strength of the congressional tendency toward budget deficits. Each time the deficit reduction targets really started to constrain spending, Congress pushed the target dates for the lower deficits further into the future. Like other legislative efforts to restrain budget deficits, Gramm-Rudman-Hollings suffers from a major defect: anything that simple

---

[9]As E. C. Pasour, Jr., of North Carolina State University, has pointed out to the authors, the federal "dinner check" analogy can be carried one step further. Suppose the check is to be divided evenly among the large group, but the ordering will be done by committee so there will be separate committees for drinks, appetizers, entrees, salads, and desserts. Since each person can serve on the committees of his (or her) choice, lushes end up on the drinks committee, vegetarians on the salad committee, sweettooths on the dessert committee, and so on. This arrangement further exacerbates the tendency toward overordering and overspending. The arrangement just described closely resembles the committee structure of the U.S. Congress.

majorities of Congress pass, simple majorities may also repeal, modify, or set aside. Thus, legislative action has been unable to control the tendency of Congress to spend more than it taxes.

CONSTITUTIONAL ALTERNATIVES

Most public choice economists believe that effective restraint on deficit spending will require constitutional action. The simplest approach would be a constitutional amendment mandating that the federal government balance its budget. Proposed amendments of this type would allow only a supra-majority (for example, two-thirds or three-fourths) of Congress to override the restriction. In essence, this approach calls for an explicit constitutional restraint that its backers hope would apply the discipline present prior to the Keynesian revolution.

Is the balanced budget requirement a good idea? Two criticisms are generally levied against the idea. First, some charge that it would reduce the effectiveness of fiscal policy as a stabilization tool. According to this view, Congress might feel compelled to raise taxes in the midst of a recession. Of course, the supramajority override provision would reduce the likelihood of this occurrence. Given the usual reluctance of Congress to raise taxes, particularly during difficult times, the danger arising from this source would surely be quite remote. More directly to the point, the large budget deficits of recent years have already eroded the usefulness of fiscal policy as a stabilization tool. Whether we like it or not, we are primarily dependent upon monetary policy to keep the economy on track in the foreseeable future. A second group of critics argues that a balanced budget requirement would be easily evaded and largely ineffective. According to this view, Congress would use things like off-budget expenditures, mandated spending, and unrealistic budget projections in order to escape the proposed discipline.

In the 1970s and 1980s, 32 of the required 34 states passed resolutions calling for a constitutional convention mandating a balanced federal budget. However, the movement seems to have lost its momentum in recent years.

There are other ways that fundamental rule changes might retard the deficit spending tendencies of Congress. Many believe that providing the president with a line-item reduction veto (the authority to reduce or eliminate spending on specific line items without having to veto an entire appropriations bill) would reduce pork barrel spending and retard the power of special interests. William Niskanen, a member of the President's Council of Economic Advisers in the 1980s, has proposed that the Constitution be amended to require the approval of two-thirds of the members of both houses for an increase in either debt or taxes. Without eliminating the use of deficit financing, this proposal would stiffen the federal budget constraint. Others have proposed that Congress be required to adopt an aggregate spending constraint six months, for example, prior to the beginning of each fiscal year. Once the constraint was adopted, approval of any budget expenditure beyond the constraint would require a three-fourths majority.

Finally, Dwight Lee and Richard McKenzie have proposed that congressional salaries be inversely linked to the size of the deficit.[10] For example, congressional salaries might be reduced by ten percent for each one percent increase in the

---

[10]Dwight R. Lee and Richard B. McKenzie, *Regulating Government: A Preface to Constitutional Economics* (Lexington: Lexington Books, 1987), pp. 149–63.

deficit/GNP ratio. Therefore, if the budget deficit were five percent of GNP, as was the case in the mid-1980s, congressional salaries would be cut by fifty percent! The same pay scale could also be applied to the president and all cabinet officials. This proposal would not only let Congress and the president know that they were expected to balance the budget, it would provide them with an incentive to do so.

CONCLUDING THOUGHTS

The topic of the budget deficit is both interesting and complex. It encompasses both economic and political dimensions. It is a topic about which the popular media is constantly disseminating false information and half-truths, usually because they do not understand the issue.

Our analysis indicates that the recent growth of the federal debt is troublesome, but not catastrophic. It is troublesome because debt-finance *may* be misleading Americans with regard to their true wealth position and thereby causing them to save and invest less than would otherwise be the case. It is also troublesome because the deficit may be partially hiding the true cost of government and thereby contributing to the inefficient use of resources. But these effects imply a gradual slowdown in economic growth, not a future "day of reckoning."

If action is taken now to reduce the *growth* of the debt relative to GNP, there is no reason why a combination of expenditure cuts, revenue increases, and economic growth cannot return the ratio of debt to GNP to the downward path of the three decades following the Second World War. However, there is reason to doubt that this will happen in the current political environment. The budget discipline previously applied by explicit constitutional restraints, and the balanced budget orthodoxy is no longer present. Legislators favoring budget cuts are reluctant to support higher taxes, because, without meaningful restraints on spending, there is no assurance that the additional revenues will be used for deficit reductions rather than spending increases. Correspondingly, legislators favoring a high level of spending are reluctant to support spending reductions because such cuts reduce the pressure for a tax increase. Thus, the deficits and the political gridlock continue. The Gramm-Rudman-Hollings Act was an attempt, apparently unsuccessful, to break the gridlock. If the situation persists or perhaps worsens, no doubt there will be other attempts, including more serious efforts to bring about structural changes. Given the political pressures, a quick resolution is unlikely. The "deficit issue" will almost surely be with us in the foreseeable future.

CHAPTER SUMMARY

1. The national debt is the sum of the outstanding bonds of the U.S. Treasury. Budget deficits increase the national debt. In fact, the national debt reflects the cumulative effect of all prior budget deficits and surpluses.

2. Nearly one-third of the national debt is owned by U.S. government agencies and Federal Reserve banks. For this portion of the debt, the government both pays and receives (except for the expenses of the Fed) the interest. Therefore, only the net federal debt—the portion of the national debt owned by domestic and foreign investors—generates a net interest liability for the government. Most of the net federal debt is owed to domestic investors.

3. When considering the impact of the national debt on future generations, it is important to keep two points in mind. First, the future generations that inherit the tax liability of the debt will also receive the interest income implied by the debt. Second, the opportunity cost of using scarce resources to produce goods and services through the public sector is the decline in current private sector output. This opportunity cost is incurred during the current period regardless of how the government activity is financed.

4. Budget deficits affect future generations through their impact on capital formation. When an economy is operating below capacity, a budget deficit may stimulate output and expand the stock of future capital assets available to future generations.

5. According to the traditional view, the substitution of debt-financing for taxes during normal times will indirectly alter the composition of private spending toward consumption and away from investment. From the standpoint of the entire nation, government securities do not represent wealth since they imply a tax liability precisely equal to the future income the bond represents. However, since households are unlikely to recognize fully the implied future taxes, they will tend to view the securities as wealth, and therefore have an exaggerated view of their true wealth position. As a result, they will consume more and invest less than if government were fully financed by current taxation.

6. The traditional view of debt-financing also stresses that the strong demand for loanable funds will push real interest rates up and lead to an inflow of foreign capital. A persistent trade deficit will be required for the finance of the capital inflow.

7. In contrast with the traditional view, the new classical theory argues that households will anticipate fully the added future tax liability implied by debt financing and increase their savings in order to meet the higher future taxes. This increase in saving offsets the increase in demand for loanable funds emanating from the debt. In the new classical model, the substitution of debt for taxes leaves interest rates, consumption, and investment unaffected.

8. The high real interest rates, inflow of foreign capital, persistent trade deficits, and apparent reduction in domestically financed investment accompanying the large budget deficits of the 1980s were all highly consistent with the traditional view. However, the proponents of the new classical theory argue that *real* investment as a share of *real* GNP during the 1980s was similar to the real investment/GNP ratio of earlier decades. This suggests that the large deficits of the 1980s exerted little impact on capital formation, a finding consistent with the new classical view.

9. As long as the interest liability accompanying the debt grows less rapidly than national income, the burden imposed on the economy by the debt is declining. The increase in net interest cost relative to GNP during the last 15 years is a worrisome trend.

10. While the federal government was running large deficits during the 1980s, state and local governments were running surpluses equal to approximately 1 percent of GNP. Therefore, the general government deficit was smaller than the federal deficit.

11. Persistent inflation both increases the nominal interest payments on the debt and erodes the real value of the debt. Even though these two factors offset each other, only the higher nominal interest payments affect the budget. Some economists believe that during a period of inflation this method of accounting makes the deficit appear more serious than is justified.

12. Many public choice economists believe that the current budget process is structurally unsound. They argue that it encourages deficit financing and fails to confront Congress with a firm budget constraint. These economists believe that constitutional changes are necessary to deal with the ''budget problem.''

CRITICAL ANALYSIS QUESTIONS

*1. Does the national debt have to be paid off at sometime in the future? What will happen if it is not?

2. Do we owe the national debt to ourselves? Does this mean the size of the national debt is of little concern? Why or why not?

3. "The national debt is a mortgage against the future of our children and grandchildren. We are forcing them to pay for our current consumption of goods and services." Evaluate.

*4. When government bonds are held by foreigners, the interest income from the bonds goes to foreigners rather than to Americans. Would Americans be better off if we prohibited the sale of bonds to foreigners?

*5. If citizen-taxpayers fail to anticipate the future tax liability accompanying debt finance, what does this imply about their perception of the cost of government? How do you think this affects the political popularity of debt-financing relative to taxes?

*6. Even if it were unable or unwilling to raise taxes in order to meet the interest payments on outstanding debt, the federal government would be unlikely to default on its outstanding bonds. Why? What would happen in the event of such a crisis?

7. Is the federal government more or less likely than state and local governments to default on outstanding bonds? Why?

*8. When there is a budget deficit, what happens to the *nominal* national debt? Could the *real* outstanding government debt decline even though a budget deficit is present?

*9. Use the accompanying hypothetical data to calculate the (a) 1991 budget deficit, (b) the nominal outstanding debt at the end of the year, and (c) the real outstanding debt at the end of the year. What happened to the real indebtedness of the government during the year?

> 1991 Revenues = $800 billion
> 1991 Expenditures = $900 billion
> Net outstanding debt (beginning of 1991) = $2,525 billion
> 1991 Inflation rate = 5%

*10. Does an increase in the national debt increase the supply of money (MI)? Can the money supply increase when the U.S. Treasury is running a budget surplus?

11. "If the government is spending $20 billion to maintain and improve highways, these costs are incurred during the current period regardless of whether they are financed with taxes or debt." Evaluate this statement.

12. Will the $3.3 trillion debt of the United States impose a cost on future generations? When government expenditures are paid for with debt rather than with taxes, what is the likely impact on the growth of the U.S. economy? Explain.

13. Are the large deficits of the federal government a threat to our economy? Why or why not? Would our economy be healthier if taxes were raised sufficiently to generate a substantial budget surplus? Why or why not?

*14. Suppose that the Federal Reserve were a government agency under the direct control of Congress. Thus, the discount rate, open market policy, and growth rate of the money supply would be determined by Congress. How do you think this would affect the inflation rate and economic stability of the nation?

*15. Would you predict that government expenditures would be higher or lower if taxes (and user charges) were required for the finance of all expenditures? Why? Do you

---

*Asterisk denotes questions for which answers are given in Appendix C, Selected Answers.

think the government would spend funds more or less efficiently if it could not issue debt? Why?

16. What are the implications of the shortsightedness effect with regard to the comparative attractiveness of tax and debt financing?

17. (a) Does it make any difference whether government debt is owed to foreign investors, rather than to domestic investors? Why? (b) Does it make any difference whether government debt is owed to private investors or held by a government agency or by the Fed? Why?

18. "We must start paying for what we get from government. A government worth having is worth paying for!" Evaluate this statement. Can we get things from government without paying for them?

PART THREE

Microeconomics

17 Demand and Consumer Choice

A thing is worth whatever a buyer will pay for it.[1]

Publilius Syrus
First Century B.C.

CHAPTER FOCUS

- How do economists analyze consumer choice? What assumptions do they make?

- What role does time play in the consumption of goods?

- What factors will cause a demand curve to shift?

- What determines the demand for a specific item? Is advertising effective? Is it useful, or just misleading?

- What is demand elasticity, and what factors determine its size? How is the elasticity concept used?

*M*acroeconomics focuses on aggregate markets—the big picture. Aggregate outcomes, though, are the result of many individual decisions. We cannot understand or successfully influence the big picture without a solid knowledge of how microeconomic decisions are made. In this section, we will examine microeconomic markets for specific products.

Microeconomics focuses on how changes in *relative* prices influence consumer decisions. As we stressed in Chapter 3, the price system guides individuals in their production and consumption decisions.[2] Prices coordinate the vast array of individual economic activities by signaling relative wants and needs, and by motivating market participants to bring their own activities into harmony with those of others. Changes in one market affect conditions in others. In this chapter, we take a closer look at (a) the inter-relationships among markets and (b) the factors underlying the demand for specific products.

The quotation on the previous page, from Publilius Syrus twenty centuries ago, points out the importance of individual demand in determining the valuation of a product. Given the amount of an item supplied into a market, it is the valuation of individual buyers which determines the price of the item. Demand is a critical determinant of price, which in turn signals information about relative scarcity and value to all potential buyers and sellers of the item. The other critical element of price—the cost of supplying the item into the market—will be examined in the next chapter.

CHOICE AND INDIVIDUAL DEMAND

Exhibit 1 shows how consumers allocated their spending among alternative goods in 1950 and 1989. Why did consumers spend less on transportation than on medical care, or more on alcoholic beverages than on personal care? Why have consumer expenditures on food declined (as a percentage of the total), while spending on housing has expanded? Economists generally assume that the following factors influence the behavior of consumers.

1. *Limited Income Necessitates Choice.* Most of us are all too aware that our desire for goods far exceeds our limited incomes. People do not have enough resources to produce everything they would like. A limited income forces each of us to make choices. When one good or service is purchased, many others must be sacrificed. That is precisely the meaning of cost.

2. *Consumers Make Decisions Purposefully.* Consumption decisions are made with the desire to upgrade one's personal welfare in mind. A foolish purchase means giving up something more worthwhile. The purpose or goal behind a consumer decision can usually be met in many different ways, so that careful consideration of alternatives is useful. Consumers generally choose the alternative that is expected to enhance their personal welfare the most, relative to cost. They do not *intentionally* choose a lesser-valued alternative when they know that another of equal cost but greater projected benefit is available.

3. *One Good Can Be Substituted for Another.* Consumers have many goals, each with alternative means of satisfaction. No single good is so precious that some

---

[1]Quoted in Michael Jackman, ed., *Macmillan Book of Business and Economic Quotations* (New York: Macmillan, 1984), p. 150.

[2]You may want to review Chapter 3 before proceeding with this chapter.

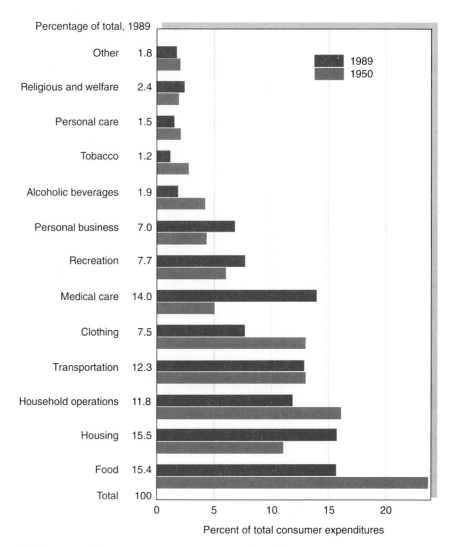

EXHIBIT 1

How Consumers Spent Their Income, 1950 and 1989

Percentage of total, 1989

Category	%
Other	1.8
Religious and welfare	2.4
Personal care	1.5
Tobacco	1.2
Alcoholic beverages	1.9
Personal business	7.0
Recreation	7.7
Medical care	14.0
Clothing	7.5
Transportation	12.3
Household operations	11.8
Housing	15.5
Food	15.4
Total	100

1989 / 1950

Percent of total consumer expenditures

U.S. Department of Commerce. *Survey of Current Business,* July 1990.

of it will not be given up in exchange for a large enough quantity of other goods. For example, consumers will give up some fried chicken to have more pizza, hamburgers, fish, ham sandwiches, or apple pie. Similarly, reading, watching movies and television, or playing cards can be substituted for playing football. Then, too, a recreational activity may partially substitute for food, as when a hamburger and a movie replace a more elaborate four-course dinner. The buyer wants utility from the substitute goods, not necessarily the same services. There are many alternative ways to satisfy the individual's wants and needs.

How about our "need" for basic commodities such as water or energy? The "need" of a person for an item is closely related to its cost—what must be given up to obtain the item. Southern California residents "need" water from the north, but the individual resident, when faced with a high water cost, finds that cactus gardens can be substituted for lawns, a plumber's bill for a faucet drip, and flow constrictors for full-force showers. The need for water depends on its cost. People living in Montana, where household electricity costs about twice as much as in nearby Washington, use half as much electricity per household. Montanans reduce their ''need'' for electricity by substituting gas, fuel oil, insulation, and wool sweaters, which cost about the same as in Washington.

4. *Consumers Must Make Decisions without Perfect Information, but Knowledge and Past Experience Will Help.* No human being has perfect foresight. Napoleon did not anticipate Waterloo; Julius Caesar did not anticipate the actions of Brutus. Consumers will not always correctly anticipate the consequences of their choices.

Consumer choices, however, are not made in a vacuum. You have a pretty good idea of what to expect when you buy a cup of coffee, five gallons of gasoline, or lunch at your favorite café. Why? Because you have learned from experience— your own and that of others. When you buy a product, your expectations may not be fulfilled precisely (for example, the coffee may be stronger than expected or the gasoline may make your car knock), but even these experiences will give you valuable information that can be used in making future decisions.

5. *The Law of Diminishing Marginal Utility Applies: As the Rate of Consumption Increases, the Utility Derived from Consuming Additional Units of a Good Will Decline.* Utility is a term economists use to describe the subjective personal benefits that result from an action. The **law of diminishing marginal utility** states that the **marginal** (or additional) **utility** derived from consuming successive units of a product will *eventually* decline as the rate of utilization increases. For example, the law implies that even though you might like ice cream, your marginal satisfaction from *additional* ice cream will eventually decline. Ice cream at lunchtime might be great. An additional helping for dinner might be even better. However, after you have had it for evening dessert and a midnight snack, ice cream for breakfast will begin to lose some of its attraction. The law of diminishing marginal utility will have set in, and thus the marginal utility derived from the consumption of additional units of ice cream will decline.

Law of Diminishing Marginal Utility: A basic economic principle which states that as the consumption of a commodity increases, the marginal utility derived from consuming more of the commodity (per unit of time) will eventually decline. Marginal utility may decline even though total utility continues to increase, albeit at a reduced rate.

Marginal Utility: The additional utility received by a person from the consumption of an additional unit of a good within a given time period.

MARGINAL UTILITY AND CONSUMER CHOICE

Consumer choices, like other decisions, are influenced by changes in benefits and costs. If a consumer wants to get the most out of his or her expenditures, how much of each good should be purchased? As more of a good is consumed per unit of time, the law of diminishing marginal utility states that the consumer's marginal benefit per unit of time will decline. A consumer will gain by purchasing more of a product as long as the benefit, or marginal utility (MU), derived from the consumption of an additional unit exceeds the cost of the unit (the expected marginal utility from other consumption alternatives that must now be given up).

Given a fixed income and specified prices for the commodities to be purchased, consumers will maximize their satisfaction (or total utility) by ensuring that the last dollar spent on each commodity purchased yields an equal degree of marginal utility. If consumers are to get the most for their money, the last dollar spent on product A must yield the same utility as the last dollar spent on product B (or any other product).[3] After all, if tickets for football games, for example, yielded less marginal utility *per dollar* than did opera tickets, the obvious thing for a consumer to do would be to cut back spending on football games and allocate more funds for opera tickets. If people really attempt to spend their money in a way that yields the greatest amount of satisfaction, the applicability of the consumer decision-making theory outlined above is difficult to question.

PRICE CHANGES AND CONSUMPTION DECISIONS

Substitution Effect: That part of an increase (decrease) in amount consumed that is the result of a good being cheaper (more expensive) in relation to other goods because of a reduction (increase) in price.

Demand is the schedule of the amount of a product that consumers would be willing to purchase at alternative prices during a specific time period. The first law of demand states that the amount of a product purchased is inversely related to its price. Why? First, as the price of a product declines, the lower opportunity cost will induce consumers to buy more of it. Economists refer to this tendency to substitute a product that has become relatively cheaper for goods that are now more expensive as the **substitution effect.** What will happen to the marginal utility derived from the product, though, as they increase their rate of consumption? It will fall. Each additional unit consumed adds less to total utility. Thus, as more of the product is consumed, a point is reached where the benefits (marginal utility) derived from the consumption of still more units will again be less than the cost. Purposeful decision-makers will not choose such units. A price reduction will thus induce consumers to purchase more of a product, but the response will be limited because of the law of diminishing marginal utility.

Second, since the money income of consumers is constant, a reduction in the price of a product will increase their real income—the amount of goods and services they are able to purchase. Typically, consumers will respond by purchasing more of the cheaper product (as well as other products) because they can now better afford to do so. This factor is referred to as the **income effect.** (Both the income and substitution effects are derived graphically in the addendum to this chapter, entitled "Consumer Choice and Indifference Curves.")

Income Effect: That part of an increase (decrease) in amount consumed that is the result of the consumer's real income (the consumption possibilities available to the consumer) being expanded (contracted) by a reduction (rise) in the price of a good.

Of course, the substitution and income effects will generally induce consumers to purchase less of a good if its price rises. Why will consumers curtail their consumption of a product that has risen in price? The rising opportunity cost of consuming the product makes it a less attractive buy. However, as consumption is reduced, remaining units have a higher marginal utility. If the price increase is not so great as to price the consumer out of the market completely, consumption of the item will fall until the product's marginal utility is high enough to again equal its new, higher opportunity cost. With moderate increases in price, the consumer's reduction in consumption will be limited. We must also bear in mind that if the consumer's money income is constant, and other prices have not fallen, the price increase reduces the individual's real income. A reduction in real income will tend to result in a reduction in the consumption of many goods, generally including the good that has increased in price.

Exhibit 2 illustrates the adjustment of consumers to a change in price. During 1985–1986, gasoline prices fell rapidly in the United States. As demand theory would predict, consumers increased their rate of consumption. As gasoline prices fell from $1.20 to $.80, Jones's average weekly consumption rose from 16 gallons to 20 gallons. The availability of less expensive fuel resulted in his postponement

---

[3]Mathematically, this implies that the consumer's total utility is at a maximum when limited income is spent on products such that

$$\frac{MU_a}{P_a} = \frac{MU_b}{P_b} = \cdot \cdot \cdot = \frac{MU_n}{P_n}$$

where MU represents the marginal utility derived from the last unit of a product, and P represents the price of the good. The subscripts a, b, . . ., n indicate the different products available to the consumer. In the continuous case, the above expression implies that the consumer will get the most for his or her money when the consumption of each product is increased only to the point at which the marginal utility from one more unit of the good is equal to the marginal utility obtainable from the best alternative purchase that must now be forgone. For more advanced students, this proposition is developed in an alternative, more formal manner in the Addendum on indifference curves.

EXHIBIT 2

Gas Prices, Consumption, and Marginal Utility

An individual, Jones in this case, will increase his rate of consumption of a product as long as MU exceeds its opportunity cost (principally the price of the good). Lower prices will induce him to consume more, but the increase in consumption will be limited because the MU of the product will fall as consumption is expanded.

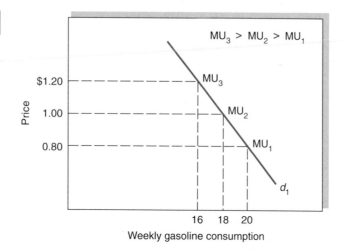

of a costly tuneup on his car, which would have saved some fuel. He went to the grocery store a little more often, rather than waiting as usual to combine shopping trips with other business near the shopping center. He and his family took a vacation by car, which would have been much more expensive at the 1985 gasoline price level. At the higher rate of use, the marginal utility of gasoline fell, bringing it into line with the lower price. Further price declines would have brought on even greater increases in consumption, but the price stabilized near its 1986 level for about four years. In late 1990 the price of gasoline jumped back up nearly to the 1985 level as the result of both higher gasoline taxes and Iraq's invasion of Kuwait. Responding to the higher price, consumers such as Jones once again began economizing more carefully on their use of the more expensive gasoline.

TIME COST AND CONSUMER CHOICE

The monetary price of a good is not always a complete measure of its cost to the consumer. Consumption of most goods requires time as well as money. Time, like money, is scarce to the consumer. A lower time cost, like a lower money price, will make a product more attractive to consumers.[4]

Some commodities are demanded primarily because of their ability to reduce the consumer's time cost. Consumers are often willing to pay higher money prices for such goods. The popularity of automatic dishwashers, prepared foods, air travel, and taxi service is based partly on their low time cost in comparison with substitutes.

What is the cost of a college education? Tuition payments and the price of books comprise only a small component. The major cost of a college education is the time cost—approximately 4,000 working hours. Even if a student's time is valued at only $5 per hour, the time cost of a college education is $20,000!

Time costs, unlike money prices, differ among individuals. They are higher for persons with greater earning power. Other things being equal, high-wage consumers choose fewer time-intensive (and more time-saving) commodities than persons with

[4]For a technical treatment of the importance of time as a component of cost from the vantage point of the consumer, see Gary Becker, "A Theory of the Allocation of Time," *Economic Journal* (September 1965), pp. 493–517.

a lower time cost. High-wage consumers are overrepresented among air and taxicab passengers but underrepresented among television watchers, chess players, and long-distance automobile travelers. Can you explain why? You can, if you understand how both money and time cost influence the choices of consumers.

CONSUMER CHOICE AND MARKET DEMAND

The market demand schedule is the amount demanded by all the individuals in the market area at various prices. Since individual consumers purchase less at higher prices, the amount demanded in a market area is also inversely related to price.

Exhibit 3 illustrates the relationship between individual demand and market demand for a hypothetical two-person market. The individual demand curves for both Jones and Smith are shown. Jones and Smith each consume 20 gallons of gasoline weekly at 80 cents per gallon. The amount demanded in the two-person market is 40 gallons. If the price rises to $1.20 per gallon, the amount demanded in the market will fall to 28 gallons, 16 demanded by Jones and 12 by Smith. The market demand is simply the horizontal sum of the individual demand curves.

Market demand reflects individual demand. Individuals buy less as price increases. Therefore, the total amount demanded in the market declines as price increases.

CONSUMER SURPLUS

Consumer Surplus: The difference between the maximum amount a consumer would be willing to pay for a unit of a good and the payment that is actually made.

The demand curve reveals how many units consumers will purchase at various prices. In so doing, it reveals consumers' evaluation of units of a good. The height of the demand curve indicates how much consumers value an added unit. The difference between the amount that consumers would be willing to pay and the amount they actually pay for a good is called **consumer surplus.** As Exhibit 4 illustrates, it is measured by the area under the demand curve but above the market price.

Previously, we indicated that voluntary exchange is advantageous to buyer and seller alike. Consumer surplus is a measure of the net gain to the buyer/consumer. Consumer surplus also reflects the law of diminishing marginal utility. Consumers will continue purchasing additional units of a good, each yielding less marginal

EXHIBIT 3

Individual and Market Demand Curves

The market demand curve is merely the horizontal sum of the individual demand curves. The market demand curve will slope downward to the right just as the individual demand curves do.

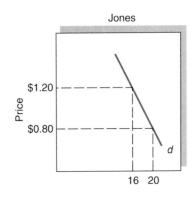 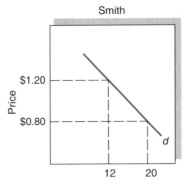 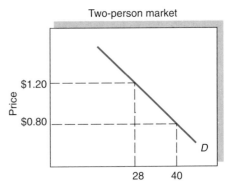

Weekly gasoline consumption (gallons)

EXHIBIT 4

Consumer Surplus

As the shaded area indicates, the difference between the largest amount consumers would be willing to pay for each unit and the price they actually pay for the unit is called consumer surplus.

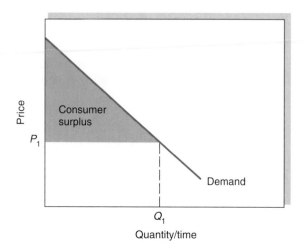

utility than the previous unit, until the marginal utility is just enough to justify paying the market price. Up to that point, however, consumption of each unit generates a surplus for the consumer, since the value of the unit generally exceeds the market price. In aggregate, the total value (utility) to consumers of a good may be far greater than the total cost to them.

The size of the consumer surplus is affected by the market price. A reduction in the market price will lead to an expansion in quantity purchased and a larger consumer surplus. Conversely, a higher market price will reduce the amount purchased and shrink the surplus (net gain) of consumers.

CONSUMER SURPLUS AND TOTAL VALUE

Nothing is more useful than water, yet it will purchase scarce anything. . . . A diamond, on the contrary, has scarce any value in use, but a very great quantity of other goods may frequently be had in exchange for it.[5]

Adam Smith

The classical economists, including Adam Smith, were puzzled that water, which is necessary for life, sells so cheaply, while diamonds have a far greater price. A century after Smith's time, economists discovered the importance of the marginal analysis we used in our discussions in the preceeding sections. The willingness to pay for additional units depends on one's valuation of the marginal unit, not the value of all units taken together. When additional units are available at a low cost, they will be consumed until their marginal value is also low. Price is determined by the cost and value of marginal units, not average units. Thus, marginal value may be quite low, even though the total value is exceedingly high. This is the case for water and other commodities when they are plentiful. The total value (and average value) of a good includes consumer surplus; thus, the *total* value and the *average* value of goods like water can be quite large even though their price is low. If we fail to recognize these facts, then we too might wonder, just as Adam Smith did, why market price has so little to do with the *total* contribution that a good makes to the welfare of users.

---

[5]Adam Smith, *Wealth of Nations*, E. Cannan, ed., 1937 (New York: Modern Library), p. 28.

WHAT CAUSES THE DEMAND CURVE TO SHIFT?

The demand schedule isolates the impact of price on the amount purchased, assuming other factors are held constant. What are these "other factors"? How do they influence demand? Since a market demand is the sum of individual demands, there are two kinds of factors, other than the price of the good, which can shift its demand.[6] First, the number of individuals in the market—the market's "demographics"—can change. All other factors shift market demands by influencing the demands of individuals.

Changes in Market Demographics Influence the Demand for Products.   The demand for products in a market is directly related to the number of consumers in that market. Changes in population and its composition can have a large influence in markets. For example, young people age 15 to 24 are a major part of the U.S. market for jeans. As the population in that group fell by more than 5 million during the 1980s, fewer jeans were demanded. Sales had topped 500 million pairs in 1980, but fell to less than 400 million pairs in 1989.[7] An increase in the number of elderly people in the same time period increased the demand for medical care, retirement housing, and vacation travel.

Changes in Consumer Income Influence the Demand for a Product.   The demand for most products is positively related to income. As their income expands, individuals typically spend more on consumption. Thus, the demand curve for most products shifts outward as the income of consumers increases. Conversely, a reduction in income generally causes the demand for a product to contract.

Changes in the Distribution of Income Influence the Demand for Specific Products.
If more income were allocated to alcoholics and less to vegetarians, the demand for liquor would increase, whereas the demand for vegetables would fall. Consider another example. Suppose a law were passed that taxed all inheritances over $500,000 at a 90 percent rate. If the law effectively reduced the income of sons and daughters of the wealthy, it would also reduce their demand for yachts, around-the-world cruises, diamonds, and expensive sports cars. If the revenues from the tax were redistributed to persons with incomes below $10,000, the demand for hamburgers, used cars, moderately priced housing, and other commodities that low-income families purchase would increase relative to yachts, cruises, diamonds, and sports cars. Thus, even if aggregate income does not change, a *redistribution* of income among individuals will often shift the demand curves for various products, increasing the demand for some products while reducing the demand for others.

Substitutes: Products that are related such that an increase in the price of one will cause an increase in demand for the other (for example, butter and margarine, Chevrolets and Fords).

The Prices of Closely Related Goods Influence the Demand for a Product.   Related goods may be either substitutes or complements. When two products perform similar functions or fulfill similar needs, they are **substitutes.** There is a direct

---

[6]Do not forget that a change in *quantity demanded* is a movement along a demand curve in response to a change in price, but a change in *demand* is a shift in the entire demand curve. Review Chapter 3 if you find this point confusing.

[7]These figures are from Suzanne Tregarthen, "Market for Jeans Shrinks," *The Margin*, Vol. 6, No. 3 (January/February 1991), p. 28.

relationship between the cost of a product and the demand for its close substitutes. For example, margarine is a substitute for butter. A supply problem that raises butter prices, or causes a butter shortage, will increase the demand for margarine. Consumers substitute margarine for the more expensive butter. Similarly, higher coffee prices will increase the demand for such substitutes as cocoa and tea. On the other hand, if technology, good weather, or some other factor reduces the price of a good, then the demand for its substitutes will decline. A substitute relationship exists between beef and pork, pencils and pens, apples and oranges, and so forth.

Other closely related products are consumed jointly. Goods that "go together," so to speak, are called **complements**. Ham and eggs are complementary items, as are tents and other camping equipment. With complements, there is an inverse relationship between the price of one and the demand for the other. For example, as the experiences of the 1970s illustrate quite well, higher gasoline prices cause the demand for *large* automobiles to decline. Gasoline and large automobiles are complementary. Similarly, lower prices for video cassette players during the 1980s increased the demand for video cassettes, and declining prices for compact discs raised the demand for compact disc players.

> **Complements:** Products that are usually consumed jointly (for example, lamps and light bulbs). An increase in the price of one will cause the demand for the other to fall.

Changes in Consumer Preferences Influence Demand.

Why do preferences change? Preferences change because people change. New information, for example, might change their valuation of a good. How did consumers respond in the 1980s to new medical information linking certain fats and oils to heart disease? They purchased less of products such as whole milk and butter (which were thought to be dangerous) and increased their demand for such goods as olive oil and canola oil, thought to be much more "heart-healthy." Sales of olive oil doubled between 1984 and 1989, while canola oil sales doubled between 1988 and 1990. Consumption of butterfat fell at the same time. In 1987, for the first time, Americans bought more low-fat and skimmed milk than whole milk. As more consumers became aware of the health implications of their diet, their demand for various foods shifted.

Expectations Influence Demand.

When consumers expect the future price of a product to rise (fall), their current demand for it will expand (decline). "Buy now, before the price goes even higher" becomes the order of the day. When the price of coffee rose sharply in 1986, how did shoppers respond? Initially, current sales increased; consumers hoarded the product because they expected its price to continue rising. Conversely, if consumers thought the price of automobiles, for example, would be 10 percent lower next year, would their actions be influenced? Yes. Many consumers would defer their automobile purchases until next year, waiting for bargain prices. Demand today would be lower as a result.

An economist constructing a demand schedule for a product assumes that factors other than the price of the product are held constant. As Exhibit 5 shows, a change in any of these other factors that influence consumer decisions will cause the entire demand curve to shift. The accompanying Thumbnail Sketch (a) points out that *quantity demanded* (but not demand) will change in response to a change in the price of a product and (b) summarizes the major factors that cause a change in *demand* (a shift of the entire curve).

EXHIBIT 5

Price Is Not All That Matters

Other things constant, the demand schedule will slope downward to the right. However, changes in income and its distribution, the prices of closely related products, preferences, population (market demographics), and expectations about future prices will also influence consumer decisions. Changes in these factors will cause the entire demand curve to shift (for example, increase from D_1 to D_2).

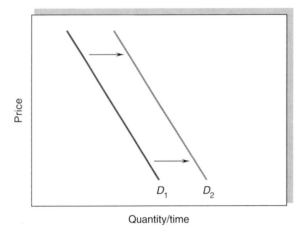

THUMBNAIL SKETCH

Change in Quantity Demanded and Change in Demand

A change in this factor will cause the quantity demanded (but not demand) to change:

1. The current price of the product

Changes in these factors will cause the entire demand curve to shift:

1. Market demographics (population) in the market
2. Consumer income
3. The distribution of consumer income
4. Price of related products (substitutes and complements)
5. Consumer preferences
6. Expectations about the future price of the product

DETERMINANTS OF SPECIFIC PREFERENCES— WHY DO CONSUMERS BUY THAT?

Did you ever wonder why a friend spent hard-earned money on something that you would not have even if it were free? Tastes differ, and as we have already shown, they influence demand. What determines preferences? Why do people like one thing but not another? Economists have not been able to explain very much about how preferences are determined. The best strategy has generally been to take preferences as given, using price and other demand-related factors to explain and predict human behavior. Still, there are some observations about consumer preferences worth noting.

First, the preferences behind any one choice are frequently complex. The person looking for a house wants far more than just a shelter: an attractive setting, a convenient location, quality of public services, and a great many other factors will enter the housing decision. Each person may evaluate the same attribute differently. For example, living near a school may be a high priority for a family with children but a nuisance to a retired couple.

Second, the individual consumer's choice is not always independent of other consumers. Not wanting to be left out, a person might buy an item to "get on the bandwagon"—just because others are buying the same item. Or, a good may have "snob appeal," setting owners apart from the crowd or elevating them into an exclusive group. Even relatively inexpensive items, such as torn jeans or faded sweat shirts, sometimes have snob appeal.[8]

A third factor influencing consumer choice is advertising. Advertisers would not spend tens of billions of dollars each year if they did not get results. How does advertising affect consumers? Does it simply provide valuable information about product quality, price, and availability? Or, does it use repetition and misleading information to manipulate consumers? Economists are not of one opinion. Let us take a closer look at this important issue.

ADVERTISING—HOW USEFUL IS IT?

What does advertising do for Americans? What were the results of the $124 billion spent on advertising in 1989? Advertising is often used as a sponsoring medium; it reduces the purchase price of newspapers, magazines, and, most obviously, television viewing. It is the consumer of the advertised products who indirectly pays for these benefits, though. Advertising thus cannot be defended solely on the basis of its sponsorship role.

Advertising does convey information about product price, quality, and availability. New firms or those with new products, new hours, new locations, or new services use advertising to keep consumers informed. Such advertising facilitates trade and increases efficiency. But, what about those repetitious television commercials that offer little or no new information? Critics charge that such advertising is wasteful, misleading, and manipulative. Let us look at each of these charges.

Is Advertising Wasteful? A great deal of media advertising simply seems to say "We are better" without providing supportive evidence. An advertiser may wish to take customers from a competitor or establish a brand name for a product. A multimillion-dollar media campaign by a soap, cigarette, or automobile manufacturer may largely be offset by a similar campaign waged by a competitor. The consumers of these products end up paying the costs of these battles for their attention and their dollars. We must remember, however, that consumers are under no obligation to purchase advertised products. If advertising results in higher prices with no compensating benefits, consumers can turn to cheaper, nonadvertised products.

A brand name in which people have confidence, even if it has been established by advertising, has another function. It is an asset at risk for the seller. People value buying from sellers in whom they have confidence, and will pay a premium to do

---

[8]See Harvey Leibenstein, "Bandwagon, Snob, and Veblen Effects in the Theory of Consumer Demand," *Quarterly Journal of Economics* (May 1950), pp. 183–207; and R. Joseph Monsen and Anthony Downs, "Public Goods and Private Status," *Public Interest* (Spring 1971), pp. 64–76, for a more complete discussion of bandwagon and snob effects.

so. If something happens to damage a brand name, the willingness of consumers to pay falls, and the value of the brand name falls, too. When brand names are not allowed, as in the case of alcoholic beverages during the Prohibition era, consumers often suffer. Without brand names to protect, anonymous moonshiners sometimes were careless and allowed dangerous impurities into the moonshine. Some consumers of moonshine were blinded, and others died. Today the situation is different. Those who buy Jack Daniels or Jim Beam whiskey know that besides skill and integrity, the distillers have an enormous sum of money tied up in their brands. A brand-name distiller would spend a large amount of money to avoid even one death from an impure batch. Is a brand name, promoted by costly advertising, worthwhile to the customer? Each customer must decide.

Is Advertising Misleading?   Unfair and deceptive advertising—including false promises, whether spoken by a seller or packaged by an advertising agency—is illegal under the Federal Trade Commission Act. The fact that a publicly advertised false claim is easier to establish and prosecute than the same words spoken in private is an argument for freedom in advertising. But, what about general, unsupported claims that a product is superior to the alternative or that it will help one enjoy life more? Some believe that such noninformational advertising should be prohibited. They would establish a government agency to evaluate the ''informativeness'' of advertising. But if consumers are misled by slick advertisers to part with their money without good reason, might they not also be misled by a slick media campaign to support politicians and regulatory policies that are not in their interest? Why should we expect consumers to make poor decisions when they make market choices, but wise decisions when they act in the political (and regulatory) arena? Clearly, additional regulation is not a cure-all. Like freedom in advertising, it has some defects.

Does Advertising Manipulate the Preferences of Consumers?   The demand for some products would surely be much lower without advertising. Some people's preferences may, in fact, be shaped by advertising. However, in evaluating the manipulative effect of advertising, we must keep two things in mind. First, business decision-makers are likely to choose the simplest route to economic gain. Generally, it is easier for business firms to cater to the actual desires of consumers than attempt to reshape their preferences or persuade them to purchase an undesired product. Second, even if advertising does influence preferences, does it follow that this is bad? College classes in music and art appreciation, for example, may also change preferences for various forms of art and music. Does this make them bad? Economic theory is neutral. It neither condemns nor defends advertising or the college classes as they try to change the tastes of target audiences.

THE ELASTICITY OF DEMAND

If the tuition charges at your school go up 50 percent next year, how many of your classmates will be back? If the price of salt doubles, how much less will you purchase? These are questions about price elasticity of demand.

Price Elasticity of Demand:
The percent change in the quantity of a product demanded divided by the percent change in the price causing the change in quantity. Price elasticity of demand indicates the degree of consumer response to variation in price.

Price elasticity of demand[9] is defined as:

$$\frac{\text{Percent change in quantity demanded}}{\text{Percent change in price}}$$

This ratio is called the elasticity coefficient. Elasticity of demand refers to the flexibility of consumers' desires for a product—the degree to which they can easily and cheaply find substitutes in response to a rise in the product's price, or can take advantage of the product's price if it falls. If a small rise in price causes consumers to choose a much smaller amount of a product, the demand for the product is elastic. In contrast, if a substantial increase in price results only in a small reduction in quantity demanded, the demand is inelastic. On an elastic demand curve, the quantity demanded is highly sensitive to a change in price. In contrast, an inelastic demand curve indicates inflexibility or little consumer response to variation in price.

The precise distinction between elastic and inelastic can be determined by the elasticity coefficient. When the elasticity coefficient is greater than 1 (ignoring the sign), demand is elastic. An elasticity coefficient of less than 1 means that demand is inelastic. "Unitary elasticity" is the term used to denote a price elasticity of 1. Although the sign of the coefficient of price elasticity is often ignored, it is always negative, since a change in price causes the quantity demanded to change in the opposite direction.

GRAPHIC REPRESENTATION OF DEMAND ELASTICITY

Exhibit 6 presents demand curves of varying elasticity. A demand curve that is completely vertical is termed "perfectly inelastic." The addict's demand for heroin or the diabetic's demand for insulin might *approximate* perfect inelasticity over a range of prices, although no demand curve will be perfectly inelastic at all prices (Exhibit 6a).

The more inelastic the demand, the steeper the demand curve *over any specific price range*. Inspection of the demand for cigarettes (Exhibit 6b), which is highly inelastic, and the demand for portable television sets (Exhibit 6d), which is relatively elastic, indicates that the inelastic curve tends to be steeper. When demand elasticity is unitary, as Exhibit 6c illustrates, a demand curve that is convex to the origin will result. When a demand curve is completely horizontal, an economist would say that it is perfectly elastic. Demand for the wheat of a single wheat farmer, for example, would approximate perfect elasticity (Exhibit 6e).

Since elasticity is a relative concept, the elasticity of a straight-line demand curve will differ at each point along the line. As Exhibit 7 illustrates, the elasticity

---

[9]You might want to distinguish between (a) the elasticity at a point on the demand curve and (b) the *arc* elasticity *between* two points on the demand curve. The formula for point elasticity is:

$$\frac{\text{Change in quantity demanded}}{\text{Initial Quantity demanded}} \div \frac{\text{Change in Price}}{\text{Initial Price}}$$

The formula for arc elasticity is:

$$[(q_0 - q_1)/(q_0 + q_1)] \div [(P_0 - P_1)/(P_0 + P_1)]$$

where the subscripts 0 and 1 refer to the respective prices and amounts demanded at two alternative points on a specific demand curve. The arc elasticity is really the point elasticity at the midpoint of a line between the two points on the curve. See William Sher and Rudy Pinola, *Modern Microeconomics* (Amsterdam, North-Holland, 1986), pp. 167–69.

EXHIBIT 6
Demand Elasticity

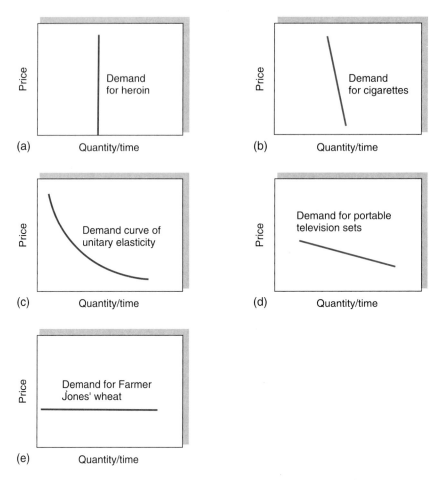

(a) *Perfectly inelastic*—Despite an increase in price, consumers still purchase the same amount. The price elasticity of an addict's demand for heroin or a diabetic's demand for insulin in some price ranges might be approximated by this curve.

(b) *Relatively inelastic*—A percent increase in price results in a smaller percent reduction in sales. The demand for cigarettes has been estimated to be highly inelastic.

(c) *Unitary elasticity*—The percent change in quantity demanded is equal to the percent change in price. A curve of decreasing slope results. Sales revenue (price times quantity sold) is constant.

(d) *Relatively elastic*—A percent increase in price leads to a larger percent reduction in purchases. Consumers substitute other products for the more expensive good.

(e) *Perfectly elastic* —Consumers will buy all of farmer Jones's wheat at the market price, but none will be sold above the market price.

of a straight-line demand curve (one with a constant slope) will range from highly elastic to highly inelastic. For Exhibit 7, when the price rises from $10 to $11, sales decline from 20 to 10. According to the arc elasticity formula, the price elasticity of demand is −7.0. Demand is very elastic in this region. In contrast, demand is quite inelastic in the $1 to $2 price range. As the price increases from $1 to $2, the amount demanded declines from 110 to 100. The arc elasticity of demand in this range is only −0.14; demand is highly inelastic.

EXHIBIT 7

The Slope of a Demand Curve Is Not the Same as the Price Elasticity

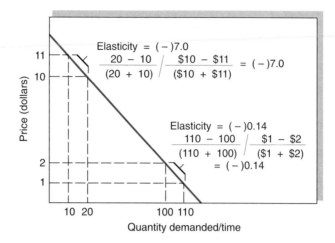

With this straight-line (constant-slope) demand curve, demand is more elastic in the high-price range. The formula for arc elasticity (see footnote 7) shows that when price rises from $1 to $2 and quantity falls from 110 to 100, demand is inelastic. A price rise of the same magnitude (but of a smaller percentage), from $10 to $11, leads to a decline in quantity of the same size (but of a larger percentage), so that elasticity is much greater. (Price elasticities are negative, but we typically ignore the sign and look only at the absolute value.)

Why do we bother with elasticity? Why not talk only about the slope of a demand curve? We use elasticities because they are independent of the units of measure. Whether we talk about dollars per gallon or cents per quart, the elasticities, given in percentages, remain the same. This is appropriate because people do not care what units of measurement are used; their response depends on the actual terms of exchange.

DETERMINANTS OF ELASTICITY OF DEMAND

Economists have estimated the price elasticity of demand for many products. Exhibit 8 presents some of these estimates, which vary a great deal. The demand for several products—salt, toothpicks, matches, light bulbs, or newspapers, for example—is highly inelastic. On the other hand, the demand for fresh tomatoes, Chevrolet automobiles, or fresh green peas is highly elastic. What factors explain this variation? Why is demand highly responsive to changes in price for some products but not for others?

The Availability of Substitutes. This factor is the most important determinant of demand elasticity. When good substitutes for a product are available, a price rise simply induces consumers to switch to other products. Demand is elastic. For example, if the price of fountain pens increased, many consumers would simply switch to pencils, ballpoint pens, and felt-tip pens. If the price of Chevrolets increased, consumers would substitute Fords, Volkswagens, and other cars.

When good substitutes are unavailable, the demand for a product tends to be inelastic. Medical services are an example. When we are sick, most of us find witch doctors, faith healers, palm readers, and cod-liver oil to be highly imperfect substitutes for a physician. Not surprisingly, the demand for physician services is inelastic.

The availability of substitutes increases as the product class becomes more specific, thus enhancing price elasticity. For example, as Exhibit 8 shows, the price

EXHIBIT 8 ■ The Estimated Price Elasticity of Demand for Selected Products

Inelastic		Approximate unitary elasticity	
Salt	0.1	Movies	0.9
Matches	0.1	Housing, owner occupied,	1.2
Toothpicks	0.1	long-run	
Airline travel, short-run	0.1	Shellfish, consumed at home	0.9
Gasoline, short-run	0.2	Oysters, consumed at home	1.1
Gasoline, long-run	0.7	Private education	1.1
Residential natural gas,	0.1	Tires, short-run	0.9
short-run		Tires, long-run	1.2
Residential natural gas,	0.5	Radio and television receivers	1.2
long-run		Elastic	
Coffee	0.25	Restaurant meals	2.3
Fish (cod) consumed at home	0.5	Foreign travel, long-run	4.0
Tobacco products, short-run	0.45	Airline travel, long-run	2.4
Legal services, short-run	0.4	Fresh green peas	2.8
Physician services	0.6	Automobiles, short-run	1.2-1.5
Taxi, short-run	0.6	Chevrolet automobiles	4.0
Automobiles, long-run	0.2	Fresh tomatoes	4.6

Hendrik S. Houthakker and Lester D. Taylor, *Consumer Demand in the United States, 1929–1970* (Cambridge: Harvard University Press, 1966, 1970); Douglas R. Bohi, *Analyzing Demand Behavior* (Baltimore: Johns Hopkins University Press, 1981); and Hsaing-tai Cheng and Oral Capps, Jr., "Demand for Fish," *American Journal of Agricultural Economics,* August 1988; and U.S. Department of Agriculture.

elasticity of Chevrolets, a narrow product class, exceeds that of the broad class of automobiles in general.

The Share of Total Budget Expended on the Product. If the expenditures on a product are quite small relative to the consumer's budget, demand tends to be more inelastic. Compared to one's total budget, expenditures on some commodities are almost inconsequential. Matches, toothpicks, and salt are good examples. Most consumers spend only $1 or $2 per year on each of these items. A doubling of their price would exert little influence on the family budget. Therefore, even if the price of such a product were to rise sharply, consumers would still not find it in their interest to spend much time and effort looking for substitutes.

Time and Adjustment to a Price Change. It takes time for consumers to recognize and to respond fully to a change in the price of a product. Initially, not all consumers are aware of the price change. Many are slow to change their buying and consumption habits. But over time, people learn of the price change; they learn how to conserve more effectively on newly expensive items and how to use cheaper items more effectively. New habits of consumption are formed, and the quantity demanded adjusts to the new price pattern.

Generally, the longer a price change persists, the greater the price elasticity of demand. The direct relationship between the elasticity coefficient of demand and the length of the time period allowed for consumer adjustment is often referred to as the second law of demand. According to this law, the elasticity of demand for a product is generally greater in the long run than in the short run.

Gasoline consumption patterns in the 1980s provide a vivid illustration of the second law of demand. When gasoline prices rose from 67 cents in 1978 to $1.25 in 1980, did consumers *immediately* stop driving their large, gas-guzzling cars? No.

When their larger cars wore out, though, many consumers did switch to compact cars providing better gas mileage. In the short run, consumers responded to higher gas prices by reducing speeds, forming car pools, and driving less often. Given more time, however, they also substituted compact cars for full-sized models, reducing gasoline consumption even more. As Exhibit 8 shows, then, the long-run demand for gasoline (0.7) proved more elastic than the short-run demand (0.2).

The same sort of process occurred in reverse when gasoline prices fell back from $1.20 to 80 or 90 cents in 1985–1986, then stabilized. New technologies that had been developed in the quest for fuel savings were retained, but cheaper fuel allowed consumers to pay more attention to convenience and speed and less attention to carpools and gas mileage. With time, people gradually replaced many small cars with larger cars that delivered more performance, comfort, and safety. As the lower fuel prices persisted (until August 1990 when Iraq invaded Kuwait), even many small cars were redesigned to take advantage of the lower gasoline prices. New high-performance and luxury cars appeared. Once again the response proved to be greater when consumers (and producers) had more time to react to the price change.

Even though the demand for most products will be more elastic in the long run than in the short run, there are a few exceptions, primarily among durable consumer goods. Often, such purchases can initially be delayed into the future as prices rise. Repairs to existing goods can at first be a substitute for a purchase; repairing the old washing machine one more time is an example. Thus, higher prices result in a greater reduction in quantity demanded in the short run than is possible over an extended time period.

ELASTICITY AND TOTAL EXPENDITURES

Price elasticity shows us the relationship between a change in price and the resulting change in total expenditure on the product. When demand is inelastic, the percent change in unit sales is less than the percent change in price. Since quantity demanded changes by a smaller amount than price, the change in price will exert a larger impact on total expenditures than will the change in quantity demanded. Therefore, total expenditures will change in the same direction as price when demand is inelastic. For example, a higher product price will lead to an increase in expenditures on the product. Suppose that when the price of beef rises from $2 to $2.40 (a 20 percent increase), the quantity demanded by an average consumer falls from 100 pounds to 90 pounds (a 10 percent reduction) per year. Since the percent reduction in quantity demanded is less than the percent increase in price, we know that demand is inelastic.[10] At the $2 price, the average person spends $200 annually on beef. When the price rises to $2.40, the average annual expenditures rise to $216. The higher beef prices cause total expenditures to increase because demand is inelastic.

When demand is elastic, on the other hand, quantity demanded is more responsive to a change in price. The percent decline in quantity demanded will exceed the percent increase in price. The loss of sales will exert a greater influence on total expenditures than the rise in price. Therefore, a price increase will reduce total expenditures when the demand for a product is elastic.

Exhibit 9 summarizes the relationship between changes in price and total expenditures for demand curves of varying elasticity. When demand is inelastic, a

---

[10]Calculate the elasticity coefficient as an exercise. Is it less than 1?

EXHIBIT 9 ■ Demand Elasticity, Change in Price, and Change in Total Expenditures		
Price Elasticity of Demand	Numerical Elasticity Coefficient[a]	The Impact of a Change in Price on Total Expenditures (and Sales Revenues)
Elastic	1 to ∞	Price and total expenditures change in opposite directions
Unitary	1	Total expenditures remain constant as price changes
Inelastic	0 to 1	Price and total expenditures change in the same direction

[a]The sign of the elasticity coefficient is negative.

change in price will cause total expenditures to change in the same direction. If demand is elastic, price and total expenditures will change in opposite directions. For unitary elasticity, total expenditures will remain constant as price changes.

HOW DOES INCOME INFLUENCE DEMAND?

Income Elasticity: The percent change in the quantity of a product demanded divided by the percent change in consumer income causing the change in quantity demanded. It measures the responsiveness of the demand for a good to a change in income.

As income expands, the demand for most goods will increase. **Income elasticity** indicates the responsiveness of the demand for a product to a change in income. It is defined as:

$$\frac{\text{Percent change in quantity demanded}}{\text{Percent change in income}}$$

As Exhibit 10 shows, the income elasticity coefficients for products vary; they are normally positive, however. In general, goods that people regard as "necessities" will have a low income elasticity of demand. Therefore, it is understandable that items such as fuel, electricity, bread, tobacco, economy clothing, and potatoes have a low income elasticity. A few commodities, such as navy beans, low-quality meat cuts, and bus travel have a negative income elasticity. Economists refer to goods with a negative income elasticity as **inferior goods.** As income expands, the demand for inferior goods will decline.

Goods that consumers regard as "luxuries" generally have a high (greater than 1) income elasticity. For example, private education, new automobiles, recreational

EXHIBIT 10 ■ The Estimated Income Elasticity of Demand for Selected Products			
Low income elasticity		High income elasticity	
Margarine	−0.20	Private education	2.46
Fuel	0.38	New cars	2.45
Electricity	0.20	Recreation and amusements	1.57
Fish (Haddock)	0.46	Alcohol	1.54
Food	0.51		
Tobacco	0.64		
Hospital care	0.69		

Hendrik S. Houthakker and Lester D. Taylor, *Consumer Demand in the United States, 1929–1970* (Cambridge: Harvard University Press, 1966); L. Taylor, "The Demand for Electricity: A Survey," *Bell Journal of Economics* (Spring 1975); F. W. Bell, "The Pope and the Price of Fish," *American Economic Review,* vol. 58 (December 1968).

Inferior Goods: Goods for which the income elasticity is negative. Thus, an increase in consumer income causes the demand for such a good to decline.

activities, expensive foods, swimming pools, and air travel are all income-elastic. As income increases, the demand for these products thus expands even more rapidly.

USING THE CONCEPT OF ELASTICITY—THE BURDEN OF A TAX

When a tax is placed on the sale of a good, who pays it? How much does the price rise? How much is paid by the seller, rather than being passed on to the customer in the form of a higher price? When the price of a good rises, we have seen that the effect on revenue and on sales depends on the price elasticity of demand. In determining the relative burden of a tax, price elasticity again plays a major role.

Sellers would like to pass the entire tax on to buyers, raising price by the full amount of the tax, rather than paying any part of it themselves. However, as price rises, customers respond by purchasing less. Sales decline and sellers must then lower their price, accepting part of the tax burden themselves by receiving less revenue. In Chapter 5 we learned that when taxes raise the amount paid by consumers and reduce the *net* (after-tax) price received by sellers, both buyer and seller share in the tax burden. Using the concept of elasticity, we can now say more about how the burden is divided and the size of the deadweight loss associated with the tax. (Now would be a good time for the reader to review the ''Taxes and Economic Efficiency'' section, pages 112–116.)

Exhibit 11 illustrates the results of a new tax on gasoline. Panel (a) shows the result in the short run, when the price elasticity of demand is 0.2. Panel (b) shows the result in the long run, when demand elasticity is 0.7. In order to demonstrate what happens when demand elasticity changes but supply is the same, in panel (b) we temporarily assume the same supply curve applies in the long run as in the short.

In panel (a) the equilibrium price of gasoline before the new tax is $1 per gallon. The $.20 tax shifts the supply upward by the amount of the tax. Since they must turn over $.20 to the government for each gallon sold, sellers must receive the old price plus $.20 per gallon in order to maintain their prior incentive to produce. This is precisely what happens when the pre-tax supply curve is shifted vertically by the $.20 tax.

Of course, sellers would like to raise prices to $1.20 and pass the entire amount of the tax onto motorists. However, they will be unable to do so since motorists reduce their purchases in response to higher prices. If the price of gasoline rose to $1.20, then an excess supply (ab) would result. Therefore, sellers are only able to increase the price to $1.15, where they are able to sell 194 million gallons, 6 million fewer than before the tax was imposed. *Short-run equilibrium* is present at that price ($1.15) and output (194 million). In the short run, the buyers pay $.15 more and the sellers receive $.05 less per gallon.

There are relatively few ways that buyers can substitute away from the more expensive gasoline in the short run. Since their responsiveness—the price elasticity of their demand—is relatively small in the short run, consumers shoulder most of the tax burden.

In the long run, though, consumers will find more ways to economize on the more expensive gasoline (for example, they will shift to smaller cars). As consumer purchases decline by a larger amount, sellers must further decrease the price they will accept (reducing the quantity they will supply). As Exhibit 11b illustrates, in the long run the equilibrium price will decline to $1.10, and quantity exchanged will fall to 186 million gallons per week. In this case, buyers and sellers divide the burden of the $.20 tax equally. Comparing Exhibit 11a with Exhibit 11b, where supply is the same but the elasticities of demand differ, we can see that *ceteris paribus, when demand is more elastic, buyers pay a smaller share of the tax burden*. This makes good intuitive sense. When consumers find more ways to economize—when they reduce their purchases more in response to the higher price—in the long run, they put more pressure on sellers to lower the price they will accept.

Elasticity of Supply: The percent change in quantity supplied, divided by the percent change in the price that causes that change in quantity supplied.

Exhibit 11c introduces the other factor determining the burden of a tax: the elasticity of supply. The **elasticity of supply** is the percent change in quantity supplied, divided by the percent change in the price that causes the change. Since it measures the responsiveness of sellers to a change in price, it is analogous to the price elasticity of demand. In the next two chapters we will discuss the factors that determine supply elasticity. For now, it is important simply to recognize the concept of supply elasticity and the fact that suppliers (like buyers) will be more responsive to price changes when they have more time to react to a change in price.

Earlier, in going from panel (a) to panel (b), we allowed demand to become more elastic, since panel (b) represented the long run. However, we unrealistically assumed that the elasticity of supply was the same in the long run as in the short run in order to isolate what would happen if only demand changed. Exhibit 11c shows the more realistic case in which supply, like demand, is more elastic in the long run. By comparing panels (b) and (c), we can see that when supply elasticity is greater

EXHIBIT 11(A)

A Gasoline Tax When Demand Is Highly Inelastic

When a $.20 gasoline tax is imposed, the supply curve shifts vertically by the amount of the tax. Since consumers will buy less as the price increases, sellers will not be able to pass all of the tax along to consumers. The new short-run equilibrium will be at a price of $1.15. As the result of the tax, consumers pay $.15 more and sellers receive $.05 less.

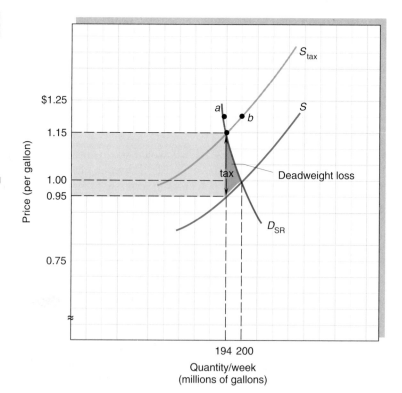

EXHIBIT 11(B)

A Gasoline Tax with More Elastic Demand

When demand is more elastic, consumers reduce their purchases by greater amounts. As a result, sellers must reduce price further[to $1.10 in this case, compared with $1.15 in panel (a)], and the tax burden falls more heavily on sellers, due to the greater demand elasticity. Here we assume that supply is unchanged.

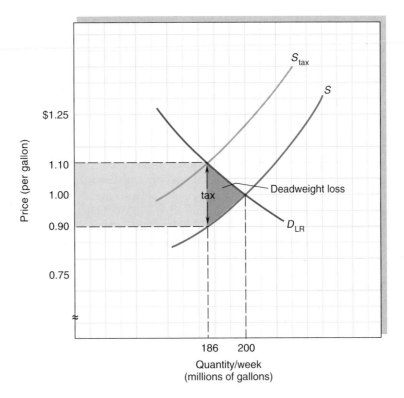

EXHIBIT 11(C)

A Gasoline Tax with More Elastic Demand and Supply

When supply is more elastic, resources have other good alternative uses, so suppliers are less willing to reduce the price they receive in response to a tax. Instead, quantity supplied is reduced by a greater amount. The price to consumers rises from $1.00 to $1.15. Compared with panel (b), where demand is the same as in (c), the greater supply elasticity in (c) causes less of the tax burden to be placed on suppliers.

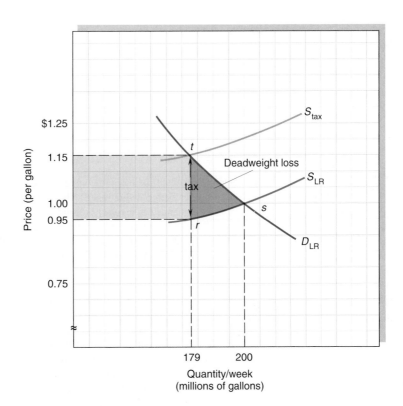

(and demand is the same), a smaller share of the tax burden is borne by suppliers. Here, supply is drawn so the gasoline price, tax included, happens to rise to $1.15, just as it did in the short-run case. That would not necessarily be the case in the real world. In general, however, *when supply is more elastic, ceteris paribus, suppliers will bear a smaller part of the tax burden.*

ELASTICITY AND THE DEADWEIGHT LOSS DUE TO A TAX

We have seen that elasticity of supply and demand plays an important part in determining how the burden of a tax is distributed between buyer and seller. Exhibit 11 also illustrates how these elasticities influence the size of the excess burden, or deadweight loss caused by the tax. As we saw in Chapter 5 (Exhibit 7), reducing trade by taxing it not only transfers revenue (amount of the tax per unit, multiplied by the number of units sold after the tax) from buyers and sellers to the government; it reduces the gains from trade for both buyers and sellers by the transferred amount, plus somewhat more. Trades which would take place without the tax are eliminated by the presence of the tax. When either demand or supply is inelastic, so that few trades are eliminated when the tax is imposed, the excess burden is smaller. Exhibit 11a illustrates this point in the case of a highly inelastic demand. Since demand is highly inelastic, the quantity of gasoline traded declines by only 6 million gallons as the result of the $.20 tax.

In contrast, when both demand and supply are elastic as in Exhibit 11c, more trades are cut off by the tax. Given the more elastic demand and supply curves of Exhibit 11c, the quantity of gasoline produced and sold declines by 21 million gallons (from 200 million to 179 million). As the triangle *rst* illustrates, the excess burden of a tax increases as it cuts off more exchanges. Therefore, the burden of excise taxes will be less if they are levied on goods and services for which either demand or supply is highly inelastic.

LOOKING AHEAD

In this chapter, we outlined the mechanism by which consumers' wants and tastes are communicated to producers. Consumer choices underlie the market demand curve. Discovering the market demand for a product tells producers how strongly consumers desire each commodity relative to others. In the following chapter, we turn to costs of production, which arise because resources have alternative uses. In fact, the cost of producing a good tells the producer how badly the resources are desired in *other* areas. An understanding of these two topics—consumer demand and cost of production—is essential if we are to understand how markets allocate goods and resources.

CHAPTER SUMMARY

1. The demand schedule indicates the amount of a good that consumers would be willing to buy at each potential price. The first law of demand states that the quantity of a product demanded is inversely related to its price. A reduction in the price of a product reduces the opportunity cost of consuming it. At the lower price, many consumers will substitute the now cheaper good for other products. In contrast, higher prices will induce consumers to buy less as they turn to substitutes that are now *relatively* cheaper.

2. The market demand curve reflects the demand of individuals. It is simply the horizontal sum of the demand curves of individuals in that particular market. The market price is a marginal valuation, not an average valuation of the item.

3. Time, like money, is scarce for consumers. Consumers consider both time and money costs when they make decisions. Other things constant, a reduction in the time cost of consuming a good will induce consumers to purchase more of the good.

4. Consumers usually gain from the purchase of a good. The difference between the amount that consumers would be willing to pay for a good and the amount they

actually pay is called consumer surplus. It is measured by the area under the demand curve but above the market price.

5. In addition to price, the demand for a product is influenced (shifted) by the (a) size and composition of the population in the market, (b) level of consumer income, (c) distribution of income among consumers, (d) cost of obtaining related products (substitutes and complements), (e) preferences of consumers, and (f) consumer expectations about the future price of the product. Changes in any of these six factors will cause the *demand* for the product to change (the entire curve to shift).

6. Both functional and subjective factors influence the demand for a product. Some goods are chosen because they have "snob appeal." Goods may also have a "bandwagon effect," fulfilling a consumer's desire to be fashionable. Observation suggests that goods are demanded for a variety of reasons.

7. The precise effect of advertising on consumer decisions is difficult to evaluate. The magnitude of advertising by profit-seeking business firms is strong evidence that it influences consumer decisions. Advertising often reduces the amount of time consumers must spend looking for a product and helps them make more informed choices. However, a sizable share of all advertising expenditures is largely for noninformational messages. Although this is a controversial area, it is clearly much easier to point out the shortcomings of advertising than to devise an alternative that would not have similar imperfections.

8. Price elasticity reveals the responsiveness of the amount purchased to a change in price. When there are good substitutes available and the item forms a sizable component of the consumer's budget, its demand will tend to be more elastic. Typically, the price elasticity of a product will increase as more time is allowed for consumers to adjust to the price change. This direct relationship between the size of the elasticity coefficient and the length of the adjustment time period is often referred to as the second law of demand.

9. The concept of elasticity is useful in explaining the effects of a policy change, such as the imposition of a sales tax. When demand is more elastic, buyers bear less of the tax burden; when supply is more elastic, sellers bear less of the burden. When either is inelastic, the excess burden of the tax is smaller.

CRITICAL ANALYSIS QUESTIONS

*1. What impact did the substantially lower gasoline prices of the mid-1980s have on (a) the demand for big cars, (b) the demand for small cars, (c) the incentive to experiment and develop electric and other non-gas-powered cars, (d) the demand for gasoline *(Be careful)*, and (e) the demand for vacations by automobile in Florida?

2. "As the price of beef rises, the demand of consumers will begin to decline. Economists estimate that a 5 percent rise in beef prices will cause demand to decline by 1 percent." Indicate the two errors in this statement.

*3. The following chart presents data on the price of fuel oil, the amount of it demanded, and the demand for insulation. (a) Calculate the price elasticity of demand for fuel oil as its price rises from 30 cents to 50 cents; from 50 cents to 70 cents. (b) Are fuel oil and insulation substitutes or complements? How can you tell from the figures alone?

	Fuel Oil	**Insulation**
Price per Gallon (cents)	*Quantity Demanded (millions of gallons)*	*Quantity demanded (millions of tons)*
30	100	30
50	90	35
70	60	40

*Asterisk denotes questions for which answers are given in appendix C, Selected Answers.

4. "Since the same price rise causes a reduction in the demand of each consumer, and since market demand is the sum of individual demands, the demand elasticity for the market must be much greater than for any individual. The same percent price change brings about a much larger quantity change in the market." Evaluate this statement.

5. "As soon as they heard about the shortage of peaches in this year's crop, suppliers of canned peaches raised the price of peaches already on the shelf! This price increase serves no economic purpose, since those on the shelf now were from last year's plentiful crop." Explain why this statement is false.

6. "Economists recommend that taxes be levied on goods with inelastic demand. This means that consumers have no place to go. Their demand is inelastic, so no good substitutes exist for such goods. Taxing such goods hurts market participants, rather than helps them." Evaluate.

7. Residential electricity in the state of Washington costs about half as much as in nearby Montana. A study showed that in Washington, the average household used about 1200 kilowatt-hours per month, whereas Montanans used about half that much per household. Do these data provide us with two points on the average household's demand curve for residential electricity in this region? Why or why not?

*8. **What's Wrong with this Way of Thinking?**
"Economics is unable to explain the value of goods in a sensible manner. A quart of water is much cheaper than a quart of oil. Yet water is essential to both animal and plant life. Without it, we could not survive. How can oil be more valuable than water? Yet economics says that it is."

*9. The wealthy are widely believed to have more leisure time than the poor. However, even though we are a good deal wealthier today than our great-grandparents were 100 years ago, we appear to live more hectic lives and have less free time. Can you explain why?

10. Recently, two researchers used variables such as hospital beds and doctors per capita, expenditures on public education, and percent of income expended on highways to construct an index of "livability." Florida ranked as one of the "least desirable" places to live. Yet, the migration rate to Florida is one of the highest in the nation. What conclusions would you draw from these facts?

11. Most systems of medical insurance substantially reduce the costs of physician services and hospitalization. Some reduce these costs to zero. How does this method of payment affect the consumption levels of medical services? Might this method of organization result in "too much" consumption of medical services? Discuss.

*12. Indicate whether the following statements are true or false. Explain.
   a. A 10 percent reduction in price that leads to a 15 percent increase in amount purchased indicates a price elasticity of more than one.
   b. A 10 percent reduction in price that leads to a 2 percent increase in total expenditures indicates a price elasticity of more than one.
   c. If the percent change in price is less than the resultant percent change in quantity demanded, demand is elastic.

*13. a. If you really like pizza, should you try to consume as much pizza as possible?
   b. If you want to succeed, should you try to make the highest possible grade in your economics class?

*14. Sue loves ice cream but cannot stand yogurt. In contrast, Carole cannot tell the difference between ice cream and yogurt. Who will have the more elastic demand for yogurt?

* 15. "If all the farmers reduced their output to one-half of the current rate, farm incomes would increase, the total utility derived from farm output would rise, and the nation would be better off." True or false? Evaluate.

16. Can you think of any circumstances under which an *increase* in price might temporarily lead to an *increase* in amount purchased?

17. Can you think of any reason why the prices of shares of stock of a specific company, gold, and other commodities for which the supply is (approximately) fixed will fluctuate more than the prices of goods that are reproduceable at a constant cost?

*18. "Market competition encourages deceitful advertising and dishonesty." True or false? Explain.

*19. What is the nature of the deadweight loss accompanying sales taxes? Why is it often referred to as an "excess burden" of the tax?

**ADDENDUM:
CONSUMER CHOICE
AND INDIFFERENCE
CURVES**

In the text of this chapter, we used marginal utility analysis to develop the demand curve of an individual. In developing the theory of consumer choice, economists usually rely on a more formal technique—indifference curve analysis. Since this technique is widely used at a more advanced level, many instructors like to include it in their introductory course. In this addendum, we use indifference curve analysis to develop the theory of demand in a more formal—some would say more elegant—manner.

WHAT ARE INDIFFERENCE CURVES?

Indifference Curve: A curve, convex from below, that separates the consumption bundles that are more preferred by an individual from those that are less preferred. The points *on* the curve represent combinations of goods that are equally preferred by the individual.

There are two elements in every choice: (a) preferences (the desirability of various goods) and (b) opportunities (the attainability of various goods). The **indifference curve** concept is useful for portraying a person's preferences. An indifference curve simply separates better (more preferred) bundles of goods from inferior (less preferred) bundles. It provides a diagrammatic picture of how an individual ranks alternative consumption bundles.

In Exhibit A-1, we assume that Robinson Crusoe is initially consuming 8 fish and 8 breadfruit per week (point *A*). This initial bundle provides him with a certain level of satisfaction (utility). He would, however, be willing to trade this initial bundle for certain other consumption alternatives if the opportunity presented itself.

EXHIBIT A-1

The Indifference Curve of Robinson Crusoe

The curve generated by connecting Crusoe's "I do not care" answers separates the combinations of fish and breadfruit that he prefers to the bundle *A* from those that he judges to be inferior to *A*. The *I* points map out an indifference curve.

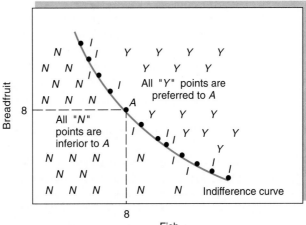

Since he likes both fish and breadfruit, he would especially like to obtain bundles to the northeast of *A,* since they represent more of both goods. However, he would also be willing to give up some breadfruit if in return he received a compensatory amount of fish. Similarly, if the terms of trade were right, he would be willing to exchange fish for breadfruit. The trade-offs he is just willing to make lie *along* the indifference curve. Of course, he is quite willing to move to any bundle on a higher indifference curve.

Starting from point *A* (8 fish and 8 breadfruit), we ask Crusoe if he is willing to trade that bundle for various other bundles. He answers "Yes" *(Y),* "No" *(N),* or "I do not care" *(I).* Exhibit A-1 illustrates the pattern of his response. Crusoe's "I do not care" answers indicate that the original bundle (point *A*) and each alternative indicated by an *I* are valued equally by Crusoe. These *I* points, when connected, form the indifference curve. This line separates the preferred bundles of fish and breadfruit from the less valued combinations. Note that such a curve may be entirely different for any two people. The preferences of different individuals vary widely.

We can establish a new indifference curve by starting from any point not on the original curve and following the same procedure. If we start with a point (a consumption bundle) to the northeast of the original indifference curve, all points on the new curve will have a higher level of satisfaction for Crusoe than any on the old curve. The new curve will probably have about the same shape as the original.

CHARACTERISTICS OF INDIFFERENCE CURVES

In developing consumer theory, economists assume that the preferences of consumers exhibit certain properties. These properties enable us to make statements about the general pattern of indifference curves. What are these properties, and what do they imply about the characteristics of indifference curves?

1. More Goods Are Preferable to Fewer Goods—Thus, Bundles on Indifference Curves Lying Farthest to the Northeast Are Always Preferred. Assuming the consumption of only two commodities, since *both* commodities are desired, the individual will always prefer to have more of at least one of the goods without loss of any of the others. This means that combinations to the northeast of a point on the diagram will always be preferred to points lying to the southwest.

2. Goods Are Substitutable—Therefore, Indifference Curves Slope Downward to the Right. As we indicated in the text of this chapter, individuals are willing to substitute one good for another. Crusoe will be willing to give up some breadfruit if he is compensated with enough fish. Stated another way, there will be some amount of additional fish such that Crusoe will stay on the same indifference curve, even though his consumption of breadfruit has declined. However, in order to remain on the same indifference curve, Crusoe must always acquire more of one good to compensate for the loss of the other. The indifference curve for goods thus will always slope downward to the right (run northwest to southeast).

3. The Valuation of a Good Declines As It Is Consumed More Intensively—Therefore, Indifference Curves Are Always Convex When Viewed from Below. The slope of the indifference curve represents the willingness of the individual to substitute one good for the other. Economists refer to the amount of one good that is just sufficient to compensate the consumer for the loss of a unit of the other good as the **marginal rate of substitution.** The marginal rate of substitution is equal to

Marginal Rate of Substitution: The change in the consumption level of one good that is just sufficient to offset a unit change in the consumption of another good without causing a shift to another indifference curve. At any point on an indifference curve, it will be equal to the slope of the curve at that point.

EXHIBIT A-2

Indifference Curves Cannot Cross

If the indifference curves of an individual crossed, it would lead to the inconsistency pictured here. Points X and Y must be equally valued. since they are both on the same indifference curve (i_1). Similarly, points X and Z must be equally valued, since they are both on indifference curve i_2. If this is true, Y and Z must also be equally preferred, since they are both equally preferred to X. However, point Y represents more of both goods than Z, so Y has to be preferred to Z. When indifference curves cross, this type of internal inconsistency always arises.

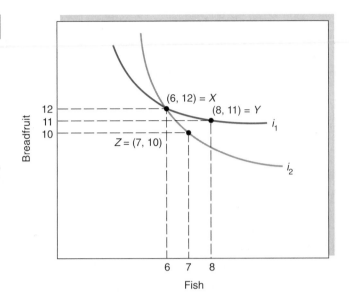

the slope of the indifference curve. Reflecting the principle of diminishing marginal utility, the marginal rate of substitution of a good will decline as the good is consumed more intensively relative to other goods. Suppose Crusoe remains on the same indifference curve while continuing to expand his consumption of fish relative to breadfruit. As his consumption of fish increases (and his consumption of breadfruit declines), his valuation of fish relative to breadfruit will decline. It will take more and more units of fish to compensate for the loss of still another unit of breadfruit. The indifference curve will become flatter and flatter, reflecting the decline in the marginal rate of substitution of fish for breadfruit as Crusoe consumes more fish relative to breadfruit.

Of course, just the opposite will happen if Crusoe's consumption of breadfruit increases relative to that of fish—if he moves northwest along the same indifference curve. In this case, as breadfruit is consumed more intensively, Crusoe's valuation of it will decline relative to that of fish, and the marginal rate of substitution of fish for breadfruit will rise (the indifference curve will become steeper and steeper). Therefore, since the valuation of each good declines as it is consumed more intensively, indifference curves must be convex when viewed from the origin.

4. Indifference Curves Are Everywhere Dense. We can draw an indifference curve through any point on the diagram. This simply means that any two bundles of goods can be compared by the individual.

5. Indifference Curves Cannot Cross—If They Did, Rational Ordering Would Be Violated. If indifference curves crossed, our postulate that more goods are better than fewer goods would be violated. Exhibit A-2 illustrates this point. The crossing of the indifference curves implies that points Y and Z are equally preferred, since they both are on the same indifference curve as X. Consumption bundle Y, though, represents more of both fish and breadfruit than bundle Z, so Y must be preferred to Z. Whenever indifference curves cross, this type of internal inconsistency (irrational ranking) will arise. So, the indifference curves of an individual must not cross.

THE CONSUMER'S PREFERRED BUNDLE

Consumption Opportunity Constraint: The constraint that separates the consumption bundles that are attainable from those that are unattainable. In a money income economy, it is usually called a budget constraint.

Together with the opportunity constraint of the individual, indifference curves can be used to indicate the most preferred consumption alternatives available to an individual. The **consumption opportunity constraint** separates consumption bundles that are attainable from those that are unattainable.

Assuming that Crusoe could produce only for himself, his consumption opportunity constraint would look like the production possibilities curves discussed in Chapter 2. What would happen if natives from another island visited Crusoe and offered to make exchanges with him? If a barter market existed that permitted Crusoe to exchange fish for breadfruit at a specified exchange rate, his options would resemble those of the market constraint illustrated by Exhibit A-3. First, let us consider the case where Crusoe inhabits a barter economy in which the current market exchange rate is 2 fish equal 1 breadfruit. Suppose as a result of his expertise as a fisherman, Crusoe specializes in this activity and is able to bring 16 fish to the market per week. What consumption alternatives will be open to him? Since 2 fish can be bartered in the market for 1 breadfruit, Crusoe will be able to consume 16 fish, or 8 breadfruit, or any combination on the market constraint indicated by the line between these two points. For example, if he trades 2 of his 16 fish for 1 breadfruit, he will be able to consume a bundle consisting of 14 fish and 1 breadfruit. Assuming that the set of indifference curves of Exhibit A-3 outlines Crusoe's preferences, he will choose to consume 8 fish and 4 breadfruit. Of course, it would be possible for Crusoe to choose many other combinations of breadfruit and fish, but none of the other attainable combinations would enable him to reach as high a level of satisfaction. Since he is able to bring only 16 fish to the market, it would be impossible for him to attain an indifference curve higher than i_2.

Crusoe's indifference curve and the market constraint curve will coincide (they will be tangent) at the point at which his attainable level of satisfaction is maximized. At that point (8 fish and 4 breadfruit), the rate at which Crusoe is *willing* to exchange fish for breadfruit (as indicated by the slope of the indifference curve) will be just equal to the rate at which the market will *permit* him to exchange the two (the slope of the market constraint).[11] If the two slopes differ at a point, Crusoe will always be able to find an attainable combination that will permit him to reach a *higher* indifference curve. He will always move down the market constraint when it is flatter than his indifference curve, and up if the market constraint is steeper.[12]

---

[11]This actually is required only if the two goods are available in completely divisible amounts, not just as whole fish or whole breadfruit. For simplicity, we assume here that fractional availability is not a problem.

[12]Mathematically, the satisfaction of the consumer is maximized when the marginal rate of substitution of fish for breadfruit is equal to the price ratio. In utility terms, the marginal rate of substitution of fish for breadfruit is equal to the MU of fish divided by the MU of breadfruit. Therefore, the following expression is a condition for maximum consumer satisfaction:

$$\frac{MU_f}{MU_b} = \frac{P_f}{P_b}$$

This can be rewritten as follows:

$$\frac{MU_f}{P_f} = \frac{MU_b}{P_b}$$

Note that this is precisely the condition of consumer maximization that we indicated earlier in this chapter (see footnote 3).

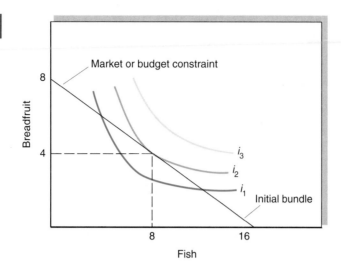

EXHIBIT A-3

Consumer Maximization—Barter Economy

Suppose that the set of indifference curves shown here outlines Crusoe's preferences. The slope of the market (or budget) constraint indicates that 2 fish trade for 1 breadfruit in this barter economy. If Crusoe produces 16 fish per week, he will trade 8 fish for 4 breadfruit in order to move to the consumption bundle (8 fish and 4 breadfruit) that maximizes his level of satisfaction.

CRUSOE IN A MONEY ECONOMY

As far as the condition for maximization of consumer satisfaction is concerned, moving from a barter economy to a money income economy changes little. Exhibit A-4 illustrates this point. Initially, the price of fish is $1, and the price of breadfruit $2. The market therefore permits an exchange of 2 fish for 1 breadfruit, just as was the case in Exhibit A-3. In Exhibit A-4, we assume Crusoe's money income is $16. At this level of income, he confronts the same market constraint (usually called a **budget constraint** in an economy with money) as for Exhibit A-3. Given the product prices and his income, Crusoe can choose to consume 16 fish, or 8 breadfruit, or any combination indicated by a line (the budget constraint) connecting these two points. Given his preferences, Crusoe will again choose the combination of 8 fish and 4 breadfruit if he wishes to maximize his level of satisfaction. As was true for the barter economy, when Crusoe maximizes his satisfaction (moves to the highest attainable indifference curve), the rate at which he is willing to exchange fish for breadfruit will just equal the rate at which the market will permit him to exchange the two goods. Stated in more technical terms, when his level of satisfaction is at a maximum, Crusoe's marginal rate of substitution of fish for breadfruit, as indicated by the slope of the indifference curve at E_1, will just equal the price ratio (P_f/P_b, which is also the slope of the budget constraint).

What will happen if the price of fish increases? Exhibit A-4 also answers this question. Since the price of breadfruit and Crusoe's money income are constant, a higher fish price will have two effects. First, it will make Crusoe poorer, even though his *money* income will be unchanged. His budget constraint will turn clockwise around point *A,* illustrating that his consumption options are now more limited—that is, his real income has declined. Second, the budget line will be steeper, indicating that a larger number of breadfruit must now be sacrificed to obtain an additional unit of fish. It will no longer be possible for Crusoe to attain indifference curve i_2. The best he can do is indifference curve i_1, which he can attain by choosing the bundle of 5 fish and 3 breadfruit.

Using the information supplied by Exhibit A-4, we can now locate two points on Crusoe's demand curve for fish. When the price of fish was $1, Crusoe chose 8

Budget Constraint: The constraint that separates the bundles of goods that the consumer can purchase from those that cannot be purchased, given a limited income and the prices of products.

EXHIBIT A-4

Consumer
Maximization—Money
Income Economy

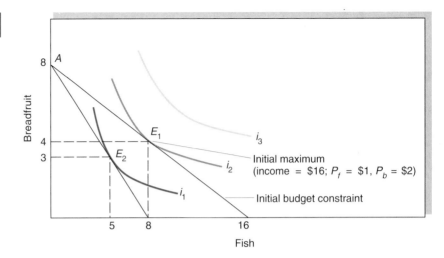

Suppose that Crusoe's income is $16 per day, the price of fish (P_f) is $1, and the price of breadfruit (P_b) is $2. Thus, Crusoe confronts exactly the same price ratio and budget constraint as in Exhibit A-3. Assuming that his preferences are unchanged, he will again maximize his satisfaction by choosing to consume 8 fish and 4 breadfruit. What will happen if the price of fish rises to $2? Crusoe's consumption opportunities will be reduced. His budget constraint will turn clockwise around point *A*, reflecting the higher price of fish. Crusoe's fish consumption will decline to 5 units. (Note: since Crusoe's real income has been reduced, his consumption of breadfruit will also decline.)

fish; when the price rose to $2, Crusoe reduced his consumption to 5 (see Exhibit A-5). Of course, other points on Crusoe's demand curve could also be located if we considered other prices for fish.

The demand curve of Exhibit A-5 is constructed on the assumption that the price of breadfruit remains $2 and that Crusoe's money income remains constant at $16. If either of these factors were to change, the entire demand curve for fish, illustrated by Exhibit A-5, would shift.

The indifference curve approach is a useful way to illustrate how a person with a fixed budget chooses between two goods. In the real world, of course, people have hundreds, or even thousands, of goods to choose from, and the doubling of only one price usually has a small impact on a person's overall consumption and satisfaction possibilities. In our simple example, the twofold increase in the price of fish makes Crusoe much worse off, since he spends a large portion of his budget on the item.

**THE INCOME AND
SUBSTITUTION EFFECTS**

In the text, we indicated that when the price of a product rises, the amount consumed will change as a result of both an "income effect" and a "substitution effect." Indifference curve analysis can be used to separate these two effects. Exhibit A-6 is similar to Exhibit A-4. Both exhibits illustrate Crusoe's response to an increase in the price of fish from $1 to $2 when money income ($16) and the price of breadfruit ($2) are held constant. Exhibit A-6 however, breaks down his total response into the substitution effect and the income effect. The reduction in the consumption of fish solely because of the substitution (price) effect, holding Crusoe's real income (level of utility) constant, can be found by constructing a line tangent to Crusoe's original indifference curve (i_2), and having a slope indicating the higher price of fish. This line (the broken line of Exhibit A-6), which is parallel

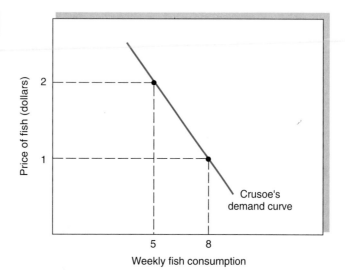

EXHIBIT A-5

Crusoe's Demand for Fish

As Exhibit A-4 illustrates, when the price of fish is $1, Crusoe chooses 8 units. When the price of fish increases to $2, he reduces his consumption to 5 units. This gives us two points on Crusoe's demand curve for fish. Other points on the demand curve could be derived by confronting Crusoe with still other prices of fish.[Note: Crusoe's money income ($16) and the price of breadfruit ($2) are unchanged in this analysis.]

to Crusoe's actual budget constraint (the line containing point E_2), reflects the higher price of fish. It is tangent to the original indifference curve i_2, so Crusoe's real income is held constant. As this line indicates, Crusoe's consumption of fish will fall from 8 to 7, due strictly to the fact that fish are now more expensive. This move from E_1 to F is a pure substitution effect.

Real income, though, has actually been reduced. As a result, Crusoe will be unable to attain point F on indifference curve i_2. The best he can attain is point E_2, which decreases his consumption of fish by another 2 units to 5. Since the broken line containing F and the budget constraint containing E_2 are parallel, the relative prices of fish and breadfruit are held constant as Crusoe moves from F to E_2. The move from F to E_2 is thus a pure income effect. The reduction in the consumption of fish (and breadfruit) is due entirely to the decline in Crusoe's real income.

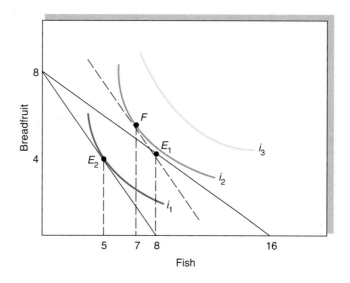

EXHIBIT A-6

The Income and Substitution Effects

Here we break down Crusoe's response to the rise in the price of fish from $1 to $2 (see Exhibit A-4) into the substitution and income effects. The move from E_1 to F illustrates the substitution effect, whereas the move from F to E_2 reflects the income effect.

Indifference curve analysis highlights the assumptions and considerations that enter into consumer decisions. The logic of the proof that there is an inverse relationship between the price and the amount demanded is both elegant and reassuring. It is elegant because of the internal consistency of the logic and the precision of the analysis. It is reassuring because it conforms with our expectations, which are based on the central postulate of economics—that incentives matter in a predictable way.

18 Costs and the Supply of Goods

Opportunity cost is the value of the best alternative that must be sacrificed in order to engage in an activity. This is the only relevant cost in economic analysis because it is based on the very nature of the science—the formulation of principles for maximum satisfaction of human wants and scarce resources. The supply curve of any commodity or service consequently reflects opportunity costs which are determined indirectly by consumers clamoring for a myriad of goods.[1]

Marshall Colberg

CHAPTER FOCUS

■ Why are business firms used by societies everywhere to organize production?

■ How are firms organized in market economies? What internal information and incentive problems must they solve?

■ What are explicit and implicit costs, and what role do they play in guiding the behavior of the firm?

■ How does economic profit differ from accounting profit? What is the role of profit for a firm, and for an industry?

■ How do short-run costs differ from long-run costs for the firm?

■ What factors can shift the firm's cost curves?

*D*emand and supply interact to determine the market price of a product. In the last chapter, we illustrated that the demand for a product reflects the preferences of consumers. In this chapter, we focus on costs of production, which are the major determinants of both the nature and the position of the supply curve for a good. If the cost of producing a good exceeds its price, producers will not continue to supply it. Most persons recognize that supply and cost of production are closely linked. For example, if it costs $400 to produce a stereo set, manufacturers will not supply the sets, at least not for very long, at a price of $200. In the long run, the sets will be supplied only if they can command a price of at least $400.

In this chapter, we lay the foundation for a detailed investigation of the link between costs and market supply. The nature and function of costs are central to economic analysis. The economist's use of the term "costs" differs sometimes from that of business decision-makers and accountants. What do economists mean by costs? Why are costs so important? What is the function of costs in a market economy? We discuss these and related questions in this chapter.

ORGANIZATION OF THE BUSINESS FIRM

The business firm is an entity designed to organize raw materials, labor, and machines with the goal of producing goods and/or services. Firms (a) purchase productive resources from households and other firms, (b) transform them into a different commodity, and (c) sell the transformed product or service to consumers.

Economies may differ in the amount of freedom they allow business decision-makers. They may also differ in the incentive structure used to stimulate and guide business activity. Nevertheless, every society relies on business firms to organize resources and transform them into products. In Western economies, most business firms choose their own price, output level, and productive techniques. In socialist countries, government policy often establishes the selling price and constrains the actions of business firms in various other ways. In any case, the central position of the business firm as the organized productive unit is universal to capitalist and socialist economies alike.

INCENTIVES, COOPERATION, AND THE NATURE OF THE FIRM[2]

Residual Claimant:
Individuals who personally receive the excess, if any, of revenues over costs. Residual claimants gain if the firm's costs are reduced and if revenues are increased.

Most firms are privately owned in capitalist countries. The owners, who may or may not act as entrepreneurs, are the individuals who risk their wealth on the success of the business. If the firm is successful and makes profits, these financial gains go to the owners. Conversely, if things go badly and the firm suffers losses, the owners must bear the consequences. Because the owners gain (or lose) what remains after the revenue of the firm is used to pay the costs, they are called **residual claimants.** Their wealth is directly influenced by the success or failure of the firm. More than anyone else in the firm, they have an incentive to see that resources are used efficiently.

---

[1]Marshall R. Colberg, Dascomb R. Forbush, and Gilbert R. Whitaker, *Business Economics* (Homewood, Illinois: Irwin, 1980), p. 12.

[2]A classic article on this topic is Ronald Coase, "The Nature of the Firm," *Economica,* (1937), pp. 386–405. See also Armen Alchian and Harold Demsetz, "Production, Information Costs, and Economic Organization," *American Economic Review,* (Dec. 1972), pp. 777–95.

Business firms rely primarily on two organizational methods when producing a good or service: team production and contracting. In team production, employees work together under the supervision of the owner, or the owner's representative. The owner must direct the efforts of the employees, maintain morale and provide an incentive system, and monitor the work of each employee to prevent shirking. Team members are **shirking** if they are reducing output by working at less than a normal rate of productivity. Taking long work breaks, paying more attention to worker convenience than to results, and wasting time when diligence is called for are examples of shirking. A worker will shirk more when the costs of doing so are shifted to other members of the team. Hired managers, even including those at the top, must be monitored and provided with incentives.

When team production is utilized, the problem of imperfect monitoring and incentives is difficult, and it is always present. It is part of a larger class of problems called **"principal-agent problems."** (See Applications in Economics box, "The Principal-Agent Problem.") The owner's gains from the firm depend directly on successful monitoring techniques, worker motivation, and incentive management, as well as on wise choices of outputs and production techniques. The form of business organization used can strongly influence the monitoring, motivation, and incentive methods available to owners and managers of a firm.

Contracting is another option, used by many firms when producing goods or services. The Boeing Company, for example, hires many employees, but when it builds a giant 747 airliner, it also contracts with hundreds of other firms to provide many of the needed parts and services. This reduces the employee monitoring problem for Boeing. The company only has to monitor the product of the contractor supplying the jet engines, rather than monitor all the engine-building workers. This adds some additional transactions costs, though, since it must search out reliable suppliers and negotiate and enforce contracts.

How do owners share the risks and liabilities of the firm? How do they carry out or participate in the decision-making? There are three major legal structures under which business firms may be organized in a market economy—proprietorships, partnerships, or corporations. The role of residual claimants (owners), and the liability faced by them, differs in each of the three structures.

A **proprietorship** is a business firm that is owned by a single individual who is fully liable for the debts of the firm. In addition to assuming the responsibilities of ownership, the proprietor often works directly for the firm, providing managerial and other labor services. Many small businesses, including neighborhood grocery stores, barbershops, and farms, are business proprietorships. As Exhibit 1 shows, proprietorships comprised 70 percent of all business firms in 1986. Because most proprietorships are small, however, they generated only 6 percent of all business receipts for that year.

A **partnership** consists of two or more persons acting as co-owners of a business firm. The partners share risks and responsibilities in some pre-arranged manner. There is no difference between a proprietorship and a partnership in terms of owner liability. In both cases, the owners are fully liable for all business debts incurred by the firm. Many law, medical, and accounting firms are organized along partnership lines. This form of business structure accounts for only 10 percent of the total number of firms and 4 percent of all business receipts.

Shirking: Working at less than a normal rate of productivity, thus reducing output. Shirking is more likely when workers are not monitored, so that the cost of lower output falls on others.

Principal-Agent Problem: The incentive problem arising when the purchaser of services (the principal) lacks full information about the circumstances faced by the seller (the agent) and thus cannot know how well the agent performs the purchased services. The agent may to some extent work toward objectives other than those sought by the principal paying for the service.

Proprietorship: A business firm owned by an individual who possesses the ownership right to the firm's profits and is personally liable for the firm's debts.

THREE TYPES OF BUSINESS FIRMS

Partnership: A business firm owned by two or more individuals who possess ownership rights to the firm's profits and are personally liable for the debts of the firm.

Corporation: A business firm owned by shareholders who possess ownership rights to the firm's profits, but whose liability is limited to the amount of their investment in the firm.

Measured in terms of business receipts, the corporate business structure is by far the most important. Even though **corporations** comprised only 20 percent of all business firms in 1986, they accounted for 90 percent of all business receipts. What are the distinctive characteristics of the corporation? What accounts for its attractiveness?

First, the stockholders of the corporation are the legal owners of the firm. Any profits of the firm belong to them. Their liability, however, is strictly limited. They are liable for corporate debts only to the extent of their explicit investment. If a corporation owes you money, you cannot directly sue the stockholders. You can, of course, sue the corporation. But, what if it goes bankrupt? You and others to whom the firm owes money will simply be out of luck.

Second, the limited liability makes it possible for corporations to attract investment funds from a large number of "owners" who do not participate in the day-to-day management of the firm. The stockholders of many large corporations simply hire managers to operate the firm. Corporations are thus often characterized by a separation of ownership and operational management.

Third, ownership can easily be transferred. The shares, or ownership rights, of an owner who dies can be sold by the heirs to another owner without disrupting the business firm. Because of this, the corporation is an ongoing concern. Similarly, any stockholders who become unhappy with the way a corporation is run can bail out merely by selling their stock.

APPLICATIONS IN ECONOMICS

The Principal-Agent Problem

In recent years, economists have focused a great deal of attention on a class of problems in which one individual is hired to act on behalf of another. A *principal-agent problem* arises when the purchaser of services (the principal) lacks full information about the circumstances faced by the seller (the agent), and thus cannot know how well the agent performs the purchased services. As a result, the agent may to some extent work toward objectives other than those sought by the principal, who is paying for the services. Because the agent exercises judgment in performing the work and cannot be completely monitored, he or she has opportunities to shirk, and, in general, to serve the agent's own ends rather than those of the principal.

We all run into the principal-agent problem when we pay a dentist, a mechanic, or a lawyer to perform services for us. The agents we hire know more than we do about their work and about the circumstances of the specific job we pay them to do. We cannot be sure that they are doing the best possible job for us. The owner of a business firm faces similar incentive problems with every employee hired. A large firm has many managers who spend a good deal of time monitoring the work of employees and providing them with the incentive to work efficiently. But they cannot monitor perfectly and, in any case, who will monitor the monitors?

Even top-level executives hired to manage a firm do not have the same objectives as owners—primarily profit maximization—unless, of course, the managers *are* the owners. So the judgments of executives, too, are influenced by what is in their personal best interests. They want perks, personal job security, and other benefits that may not be consistent with profit maximization for the firm. The problem is more serious as firms grow larger and acquire more managers and employees. Ultimately it is the job of the owners, as residual claimants, to develop an incentive structure that minimizes the principal-agent problem. For the owner, the saying "the buck stops here" always applies.

EXHIBIT 1

How Business Firms Are Organized

Nearly three out of every four firms is a proprietorship, but only 6% of all business revenue is generated by proprietorships. Corporations account for only one out of every five firms, but generate 90% of all revenues.

Source: *Statistical Abstract of the United States: 1990, Table 858 (Data are for 1986).*

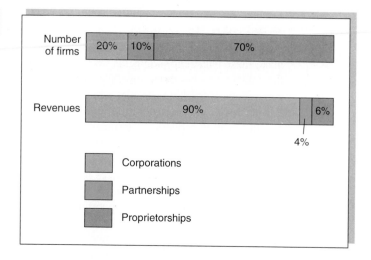

The corporate form of ownership is flexible enough to adjust easily to a different location or to many locations. Multinational corporations can do business wherever comparative advantage dictates. IBM is an American corporation, but 55 percent of its employees were in foreign countries in 1990, and that percentage was growing. IBM Japan had more than 18,000 Japanese employees and annual sales of more than $6 billion, making it one of Japan's largest exporters of computers. The Whirlpool corporation in 1990 employed 43,000 people in 45 countries. In aggregate, foreign-owned firms employed more than 8 percent of the U.S. manufacturing labor force.[3] Corporations seeking lower production costs and higher-valued outputs are quite flexible in both hiring and location decisions.

The managers of a large corporation might be thought of as trained experts hired by the stockholders to run the firm. The decisions of stockholders to buy and sell shares of stock mirror the confidence of investors in the management of the firm. If enough current and prospective stockholders alike come to believe that the managers will do a good job, the demand for the firm's stock will increase. Rising stock prices will reflect this increase in demand. Conversely, when the number of investors wanting to hold shares in the firm declines because they are dissatisfied with the current management, the stock's price will tumble. Falling stock prices will often lead to a shake-up in the management of the firm. (See Applications in Economics boxes, "Corporate Takeovers: Harmful or Productive?" and "Cost, Sensitivity to Consumers, and the Structure of the Modern Corporation.")

THE ROLE OF COSTS

Consumers would like to have more economic goods, but resources to produce them are scarce. We cannot produce as much of all goods as we would like. The use of

---

[3]These figures are from Robert Reich, "Does Corporate Nationality Matter?" *Issues in Science and Technology*, Winter 1990–1991, pp. 40–44.

resources to make one commodity takes resources from the production of other desired goods. The desire for product A must be balanced against the desire for other items which must be sacrificed to produce A. Every economic system must make these balancing judgments. When decisions are made in the political arena, the budget process performs this balancing function. Congress (or the central committee, or the king) decides which goods are most highly valued compared to others. Taxes and budgets are set accordingly.

In a market economy, consumer demand and cost of production are central to the performance of this balancing function. The desire of consumers for a specific good must be balanced against the desire for *other goods* that could be produced with the resources. Since resources have alternative uses, the use of resources to produce one good necessitates a reduction in the output of other goods. The most highly valued of these forgone opportunities when a good is produced comprise the good's costs of production. The owner of a resource employed in the production of one good must be paid at least as much as the resource would be worth in alternative uses that must be forgone. The production cost of a good reveals the value of the resources used to produce it, in terms of other opportunities forgone.

The demand for a product can be thought of as the voice of consumers instructing firms to produce a good. On the other hand, costs of production represent the voice of consumers saying that other items that could be produced with the

APPLICATIONS IN ECONOMICS

Corporate Takeovers: Harmful or Productive?

Since the early 1970s, the number of corporate mergers and takeovers has increased substantially. There is an ongoing debate on whether this trend is good for the economy. Are these takeovers actually attempts by new owners to use resources more productively, or are they primarily a financial game, where stock prices are manipulated and purely speculative gains pursued? One careful look at this question was taken in 1987 by Lichtenberg and Siegel.[4]

Examining data on more than 20,000 manufacturing plants, owned by nearly 6,000 firms and accounting for two-thirds of total U.S. manufacturing shipments, the two economists found evidence to support the hypothesis that productivity gains were intended, and indeed were achieved. In

their view, the economic performance of many operating plants deteriorates over time as conditions change. When this happens, potential new owners may be better situated than current owners to deal with the new conditions. In such cases, a sale of the plants could be productive.

When Lichtenberg and Siegel examined the productivity of plants that changed ownership, the results were striking. They found that, controlling for other factors, these plants had previously been significantly less productive, on average, than plants that did not change ownership, Also, relative productivity in the plants destined for ownership change had been deteriorating prior to the change, but starting about a year after the change, productivity figures

began to increase, rising until they nearly matched those of plants with no ownership change.

Such studies as this can never be totally conclusive, because there are always other factors which are not included, and not all cases, in all years, can be fully examined. This study was large and carefully done, however, and does provide some important evidence in support of those who say that corporate takeovers are not just financial games, but are an important way in which resources in the economy can be moved to higher-valued uses.

---

[4]Frank Lichtenberg and Donald Siegel, ''Productivity and Changes of Ownership of Manufacturing Plants,'' *Brookings Papers on Economic Activity,* Vol. 3, 1987, pp. 643–673.

Explicit Costs: Money paid by a firm to purchase the services of productive resources.

resources are also desired. The demand for a product indicates the intensity of consumers' desires for the item. The cost of producing a product indicates the desire of consumers for other goods that must now be forgone because the necessary resources have been employed in the production of the first item.

CALCULATING ECONOMIC COSTS AND PROFITS

Business firms, regardless of their size, are primarily concerned with profit. What is profit? It is the firm's total revenue, minus the sum of its costs. But to state profit correctly, it is imperative that cost be measured properly. Most people, including some who are in business, think of costs as the amount paid for raw materials, labor, machines, and similar inputs. However this concept of cost, which stems from accounting procedures, may fail to include some of the firm's real costs. When this happens and cost is miscalculated, economists recognize that profit is misstated and that uneconomic decisions may result.

Implicit Costs: The opportunity costs associated with a firm's use of resources that it owns. These costs do *not* involve a direct money payment. Examples include wage income and interest forgone by the owner of a firm who also provides labor services and equity capital to the firm.

The key to understanding the economist's concept of profit is our old friend—opportunity cost. The firm incurs a cost whenever it uses a resource, thereby requiring the resource owner to forgo the highest valued alternative. These costs may either be explicit or implicit. **Explicit costs** result when the firm makes a monetary payment to resource owners. Money wages, interest, and rental payments are a measure of what the firm gives up to employ the services of labor and capital resources. Firms may also incur **implicit costs**—costs associated with the use of resources owned by the firm. Since implicit costs do not involve a direct money or contractual payment, they are sometimes excluded from accounting statements. For example, the owners of small proprietorships often supply labor services to their businesses. There is an opportunity cost associated with the use of this resource; other opportunities have to be given up because of the time spent by the owner in the operation of the business. The highest valued alternative forgone is the opportunity cost of the labor service provided by the owner. The **total cost** of production is the sum of the explicit and implicit costs incurred by the employment of all resources involved in the production process.

Total Cost: The costs, both explicit and implicit, of all the resources used by the firm. Total cost includes an imputed normal rate of return for the firm's equity capital.

PROFIT AND THE OPPORTUNITY COST OF CAPITAL

The most important implicit cost generally omitted from accounting statements is the cost of capital. Persons who supply equity capital to a firm expect their financial investment to yield at least a normal rate of return, which could be derived from other investment opportunities. If investors do not earn this normal rate of return on their investment, they will not continue to supply financial capital to the business.

Opportunity Cost of Capital: The implicit rate of return that must be paid to investors to induce them to continuously supply the funds necessary to maintain a firm's capital assets.

This normal rate of return is the **opportunity cost of capital.** If the normal rate of return on equity capital is 10 percent, investors will not continue to supply funds to firms unable to earn a 10 percent rate of return on capital assets. As a result, earning the normal rate of return—that is, covering the opportunity cost of capital—is vital to the survival of a business firm.

ACCOUNTING PROFIT AND ECONOMIC PROFIT

Since economists seek to measure the opportunities lost due to the production of a good or service, they include both explicit and implicit costs in total cost. **Economic profit** is equal to total revenues minus total costs, including both the explicit and implicit cost components. Economic profits will be present only if the earnings of a business are in excess of the opportunity cost of using the assets owned by the firm. Economic losses result when the earnings of the firm are insufficient to cover explicit and implicit costs. When the firm's revenues are just equal to its costs, both explicit and implicit, economic profits will be zero.

Economic Profit: The difference between the firm's total revenues and total costs.

APPLICATIONS IN ECONOMICS

Costs, Sensitivity to Consumers, and the Structure of the Modern Corporation

How can we be sure that business firms will operate efficiently and respond to the interests of customers? In the case of owner-managed firms, clearly there is a strong incentive for efficient management, cost-effective production, and sensitivity to the interest of consumers. Offering consumers value at a low cost is the ticket to profitability. Since owner-managers are residual income claimants, they have a strong incentive to manage firms wisely.

However, in the case of a large corporation with millions of stockholders, the situation is more complex. While the stockholders hold the legal claim to residual income, professional managers direct the operation of the firm. There is a separation between ownership and management. The objectives of managers may conflict with those of stockholders. For example, managers may prefer high salaries, large offices, and first-class travel. They may also prefer the power and prestige of business expansion, even if it reduces profitability.

Can the stockholders control the actions of managers and direct them toward the pursuit of profitability? For large corporations, *direct* control is unlikely. Most large corporations are owned by shareholders, none of whom owns more than a tiny fraction of the firm's outstanding stock. While they elect a Board of Directors, which in turn appoints high-level managers, individual

stockholders have neither the incentive nor the information to exercise direct control. Most find it too expensive even to attend the annual shareholder's meeting. They can, of course, send a "proxy"— a designated person to vote their shares. But management generally solicits the proxies of shareholders prior to the annual meeting. If they do not throw it in the wastebasket, most stockholders turn their proxy over to the present management, and thereby provide management with the votes to reelect themselves.

Given this organizational structure, what keeps managers from using corporate resources as a personal feifdom? What prevents management from pursuing its own objectives at the expense of stockholders and consumers? There are three major factors that promote cost efficiency and limit the power of corporate managers. Let us consider each.

Competition for Investment Funds and Customers
Nobody forces stockholders to invest in corporations. Unless they are able to earn a competitive return, shareholders will invest their funds elsewhere—in bonds, real estate, or personal business activities, for example. In fact, stockholders have an incentive to monitor management in order to *anticipate* problems or constructive innovations. Investors who are the first to spot a good, new management strategy can buy stock early, before others realize the

opportunity and bid the price up. Stockholders who are the first to spot a problem can "bail out" by selling their stock before others see the problem and dump their stock, thus depressing the price. So managers get constant feedback via the stock price, which can be just as important as current profits to stockholders and boards of directors.

Similarly, consumers have an incentive to monitor the quality and price of the firm's output. No one forces them to buy the corporation's product; so if other firms supply superior products or offer a lower price, consumers can take their business to rival firms.

The corporation's need to meet the competition limits the ability of managers to pursue their personal objectives at the expense of either stockholders or customers.

Compensation and Management Incentives
The compensation of managers can be structured in a manner that will bring the interests of managers into harmony with shareholders. Market determination of managerial salaries will help achieve this objective. The market tends to reward managers who establish a track record of business profitability. In contrast, the demand for managers associated with losing enterprises and business failures is weak.

Internally, corporate firms can, and generally do, tie the

compensation of managers to the market success of the business. Salary increases and bonuses can be directly related to the firm's profitability. Senior managers can be paid in part with shares of corporate stock that will encourage them to follow policies that maximize the wealth holdings of all shareholders. Many firms have designed stock option-to-buy plans available to management that are extremely valuable if the market value of the firm's shares rise, but worthless if they fall. All of these factors tend to reduce the conflict between the interests of managers and shareholders.

The Threat of a Corporate Takeover

Managers who do not serve the interests of their shareholders are vulnerable to a *takeover,* a move by an outside person or group to gain the control of the firm. As we previously noted, shareholders who lose confidence in management can "fire" management by selling their shares. When a significant number of shareholders follows this course of action, the market value of the firm's stock will decline. This will increase the attractiveness of the firm to takeover specialists shopping for a poorly run business, the value of which could be substantially increased by a new management team.[5]

Consider a firm, currently earning $1.50 per share. Reflecting current earnings, the market value of the firm's stock is $15 per share (assuming a 10 percent interest

rate). If the earnings of the firm are reduced because the current management team is pursuing its own objectives at the expense of profitability, then a corporate takeover could lead to substantial gain. Suppose an outside person or group believes that they could restructure the firm, improve the management, and thereby increase the firm's earnings to $3 per share. Therefore, they tender a takeover bid—an offer to buy shares of the firm's stock—for $20 per share. If the takeover team is correct, and if it is able to increase the firm's earnings to $3 per share, then the stock value of the firm will rise accordingly (to $30 per share).

Of course, the current management has an incentive to resist the takeover. After all, the current operating plans are their own, and the jobs they now hold are the best available to them. The outsiders who say that the current management is wrong and should be replaced will seldom be welcomed with open arms.

If the takeover specialists are right—if the new management is able to improve the cost efficiency and profitability of the firm—they will experience a handsome profit. Of course, they may sometimes be wrong and experience losses as a consequence. However, the important point is that the potential of a takeover acts as a check against managerial strategies that conflict with profit maximization. Managers who pursue their own interest at the expense of stockholders make themselves

vulnerable to a takeover. The mere potential of the takeover reduces the likelihood that managers will stray too far from the profit maximum strategy.

Concluding Thought

How efficient is the corporate business structure? Perhaps history provides the best answer. If the corporate structure were not an efficient form of business organization, it would not continue to survive. Rival forms of business organization, including proprietorships, partnerships, consumer cooperatives, employee ownership, and mutually owned companies can and do compete in the marketplace for investment funds. In certain industries, some of these alternative forms of business organization are dominant. Nonetheless, in most industries, the corporate structure is the dominant form of business organization (see Exhibit 1). This is strong evidence that, despite its defects, it is generally a cost efficient, consumer sensitive form of organization. If it were not, it would not be so prevalent.

---

[5]For a discussion of corporate takeovers from various points of view, see Hal R. Varian, et al., "Symposium on Takeovers," *The Journal of Economic Perspectives,* Vol. 2, No. 1 (Winter 1988) pp. 3–81. See also John R. Coffee, Jr., et al., "Corporate Takeovers: Who Wins; Who Loses; Who Should Regulate?" p. 23. *Regulation,* 1988, No. 1.

Remember that zero economic profits do not imply that the firm is about to go out of business. On the contrary, they indicate that the owners are receiving exactly the market (normal) rate of return on their investment (assets owned by the firms).

Accounting Profits: The sales revenues minus the expenses of a firm over a designated time period, usually one year. Accounting profits typically make allowances for changes in the firm's inventories and depreciation of its assets. No allowance is made, however, for the opportunity cost of the equity capital of the firm's owners, or other implicit costs.

Since accounting procedures often omit implicit costs, such as those associated with owner-provided labor services or capital assets, the accounting costs of the firm generally understate the opportunity costs of production. This understatement of cost leads to an overstatement of economic profits. Therefore, the **accounting profits** of a firm are generally greater than the firm's economic profits (see Applications in Economics box, "Economic and Accounting Cost—A Hypothetical Example"). When the omission of the costs of owner-provided services is unimportant, as is the case for most large corporations, accounting profits approximate the returns to the firm's equity capital. High accounting profits (measured as a rate of return on a firm's assets), relative to the average for other firms, suggest that a firm is earning an economic profit. Correspondingly, a low rate of accounting profit implies economic losses.

APPLICATIONS IN ECONOMICS

Economic and Accounting Cost—A Hypothetical Example

The revenue-cost statement for a corner grocery store owned and operated by Terry Smith is presented below.

Terry works full-time as the manager, chief cashier, and janitor. Terry has $30,000 worth of refrigeration and other equipment invested in the store. Last year, Terry's total sales were $85,000; suppliers and employees were paid $50,000. Terry's revenues exceeded explicit costs by $35,000. Did Terry make a profit last year? The accounting statement for the store will probably show a net profit of $35,000. However, if Terry did not have a $30,000 personal investment in equipment, these funds could be collecting 10 percent interest. Thus, Terry is forgoing $3,000 of interest each

year. Similarly, if the building that Terry owns were not being used as a grocery store, it could be rented to someone else for $500 per month. Rental income thus forgone is $6,000 per year. In addition, since Terry is tied up working in the grocery store, a $28,000 managerial position with the local A&P is forgone. Considering the interest, rental, and salary income that Terry had to forgo in order to operate the grocery store last year, Terry's implicit costs were $37,000. The total costs were $87,000. The total revenue of Terry's grocery store was less than the opportunity cost of the resources utilized. Terry incurred an economic loss of $2,000, despite the accounting profit of $35,000.

Total revenue		**$85,000**
Sales (groceries)		
Total (explicit costs)		
Groceries, wholesale	$38,000	
Utilities	2,000	
Taxes	3,000	
Advertising	1,000	
Labor services (employees)	6,000	
Total (explicit) costs		$50,000
Net (accounting) profit		$35,000
Additional (implicit) costs		
Interest (personal investment)		$ 3,000
Rent (Terry's building)		6,000
Salary (Terry's labor)		28,000
Total implicit costs		$37,000
Total explicit and implicit costs		**$87,000**
Economic profit (**total revenue minus explicit and implicit costs**)		**-$2,000**

SHORT RUN AND LONG RUN

Short Run (in Production): A time period so short that a firm is unable to vary some of its factors of production. The firm's plant size typically cannot be altered in the short run.

A firm cannot instantaneously adjust its output. Time plays an important role in the production process. All of a firm's resources can be expanded (contracted) over time, but for specialized or heavy equipment, expanding (contracting) availability quickly may be very expensive or even impossible. Economists often speak of the **short run** as a time period so short that the firm is unable to alter its present plant size. In the short run, the firm is "stuck" with its existing plant and heavy equipment. They are "fixed" for a given time period. The firm can alter output, however, by applying larger or smaller amounts of variable resources, such as labor and raw materials. The firm's existing plant capacity can thus be used more or less intensively in the short run.

In sum, we can say that the short run is that period of time during which at least one factor of production, usually the size of the firm's plant, cannot be varied.

How long is the short run? The length varies from industry to industry. In some industries, substantial changes in plant size can be accomplished in a few months. In other industries, particularly those that use assembly lines and mass production techniques (for example, aircraft and automobiles), the short run might be a year or even several years.

Long Run (in Production): A time period long enough to allow the firm to vary all factors of production.

The **long run** is a time period of sufficient length to allow a firm the opportunity to alter its plant size and capacity and all other factors of production. All resources of the firm are variable in the long run. In the long run, from the viewpoint of an entire industry, new firms may be established and enter the industry; other firms may dissolve and leave the industry.

Perhaps an example will help to clarify the distinction between the short- and long-run time periods. If a battery manufacturer hired 200 additional workers and ordered more raw materials to squeeze a larger output from the existing plant, this would be a short-run adjustment. In contrast, if the manufacturer built an additional plant (or expanded the size of its current facility) and installed additional heavy equipment, this would be a long-run adjustment.

COSTS IN THE SHORT RUN

We have emphasized that in the short run some of a firm's factors of production, such as the size of the plant, will be fixed. Other productive resources will be variable. In the short run, then, we can break the firm's costs into these two categories—fixed and variable. Examining how each category of costs behaves, and seeing that behavior graphically, will help us to understand how decision-makers determine the profit-maximizing level of output for a firm.

Fixed Costs: Costs that do not vary with output. However, fixed costs will be incurred as long as a firm continues in business and the assets have alternative uses.

Fixed costs will remain unchanged even though output is altered. For example, a firm's insurance premiums, its property taxes, and, most significantly, the opportunity cost of using its fixed assets will be present whether the firm produces a large or a small rate of output. These costs will not vary with output. They are "fixed" as long as the firm remains in business. Fixed costs will be present at all levels of output, including zero. They can be avoided only if the firm goes out of business.

Average Fixed Cost: Fixed cost divided by the number of units produced. It always declines as output increases.

Variable Costs: Costs that vary with the rate of output. Examples include wages paid to workers and payments for raw materials.

Average Variable Cost: The total variable cost divided by the number of units produced.

Average Total Cost: Total cost divided by the number of units produced. It is sometimes called per unit cost.

Marginal Cost: The change in total cost required to produce an additional unit of output.

What will happen to **average fixed cost** (AFC) as output expands? Remember that the firm's fixed cost will be the same whether output is 1, 100, or 1,000. The average fixed cost is simply fixed cost divided by output. As output increases, AFC declines since the fixed cost will be spread over more and more units (see Exhibit 2a).

Variable costs are those costs that vary with output. For example, additional output can usually be produced by hiring more workers and expending additional funds on raw materials. Variable costs involve expenditures on these and other variable inputs. At any given level of output, the firm's **average variable cost** is the total variable cost divided by output.

We have noted that total cost includes explicit and implicit costs. The total cost of producing a good is also the sum of the fixed and variable costs at each output level. At zero output, total cost will equal fixed cost. As output expands from zero, variable cost and fixed cost must be added to obtain total cost. **Average total cost** (ATC), sometimes referred to as "unit cost," can be found by dividing total cost by the total number of units produced. Average total cost is also equal to the sum of the average fixed and average variable costs. ATC indicates the amount per unit of output that must be gained in revenue, if total cost is to be covered.

The economic way of thinking emphasizes the importance of what happens "at the margin." How much does it cost to produce an additional unit? **Marginal cost** is the change in total cost that results from the production of one additional unit. The profit-conscious decision-maker recognizes marginal cost as the addition to cost which must be covered by additional revenue, if producing the marginal unit is to be profitable. In the short run, as illustrated by Exhibit 2, marginal costs will generally decline if output is increased, then eventually reach a minimum, and then increase. The rising marginal costs simply reflect the fact that it becomes increasingly difficult to squeeze additional output from a plant as the facility's maximum capacity (the dotted line of Exhibit 2b) is approached. The Thumbnail Sketch summarizes the interrelationships among a firm's various costs.

As a firm alters its rate of output in the short run, how will unit cost be affected? First, let us look at this question intuitively. In the short run, the firm can vary output by using its fixed plant size more (or less) intensively. As Exhibit 2 illustrates, there are two extreme situations that will result in a high unit cost of output. First, when the output rate of a plant is small relative to its capacity, it is obviously being underutilized. Under these circumstances, average fixed cost will

THUMBNAIL SKETCH

Relationships among a Firm's Costs

1. Total cost includes both explicit and implicit costs.
2. Total cost = fixed cost + variable cost.
3. Marginal cost = change in total cost per additional unit of output.
4. Average total cost = total cost ÷ output.
5. Average fixed cost = fixed cost ÷ output.
6. Average variable cost = variable cost ÷ output.
7. Average total cost = average fixed cost + average variable cost.

be high, and therefore average total cost will also be high. It will be costly and inefficient to operate a large plant substantially below its production capacity. At the other extreme, overutilization can also result in high unit cost. An overutilized plant will mean congestion, time spent by workers waiting for machines, and similar costly delays. As output approaches the maximum capacity of a plant, overutilization will lead to high marginal costs and therefore to high average total costs.

Thus, the average total cost curve will be U-shaped, as pictured in Exhibit 2c. Average total cost will be high for both an underutilized plant (because AFC is high) and an overutilized plant (because MC is high).

DIMINISHING RETURNS AND PRODUCTION IN THE SHORT RUN

Law of Diminishing Returns: The postulate that as more and more units of a variable resource are combined with a fixed amount of other resources, employment of *additional* units of the variable resource will eventually increase output only at a decreasing rate. Once diminishing returns are reached, it will take successively larger amounts of the variable factor to expand output by one unit.

Our analysis of the link between unit cost and output rate is corroborated by a long-established economic law, the law of diminishing returns. The **law of diminishing returns** states that as more and more units of a variable factor are applied to a fixed amount of other resources, output will eventually increase by smaller and smaller amounts. Therefore, in terms of their impact on output, the returns to the variable factor will diminish.

The law of diminishing returns is as famous in economics as the law of gravity is in physics. The law is based on common sense. Have you ever noticed that as you apply a single resource more intensively, the resource eventually tends to accomplish less and less? Consider a farmer who applies fertilizer more and more intensively to an acre of land (a fixed factor). At some point, the application of additional 100-pound units of fertilizer will expand the wheat yield by successively smaller amounts.

Essentially, the law of diminishing returns is a constraint imposed by Nature. If it were not valid, it would be possible to raise all the world's foodstuffs on an acre of land, or even in a flowerpot. Suppose we did *not* experience diminishing returns when we applied more labor and fertilizer to land. Would it ever make sense to cultivate any of the less fertile land? Of course not. We would be able to increase output more rapidly simply by applying another unit of labor and fertilizer to the

EXHIBIT 2

General Characteristics of the Short-run Cost Curves

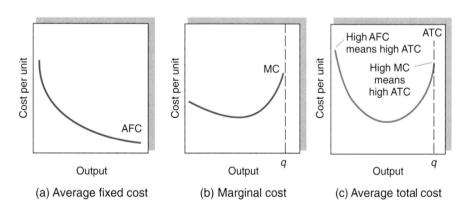

(a) Average fixed cost

(b) Marginal cost

(c) Average total cost

Average fixed costs (a) will be high for small rates of output, but they will always decline as output expands. Marginal cost (b) will rise sharply as the plant's production capacity q is approached. As graph (c) illustrates, ATC will be a U-shaped curve, since AFC will be high for small rates of output and MC will be high as the plant's production capacity is approached.

world's most fertile flowerpot! But, of course, that would be a fairy tale; the law of diminishing returns applies in the real world.

Exhibit 3 illustrates the law of diminishing returns numerically. Column 1 indicates the quantity of the variable resource, labor in this example, that is combined with a specified amount of the fixed resource. Column 2 shows the **total product** that will result as the utilization rate of labor increases. Column 3 provides data on the **marginal product,** the change in total output associated with each additional unit of labor. Without the application of labor, output would be zero. As additional units of labor are applied, total product (output) expands. As the first three units of labor are applied, total product increases by successively larger amounts (8, then 12, then 14). Beginning with the fourth unit, however, diminishing returns are confronted. When the fourth unit is added, marginal product—the change in the total product—declines to 12 (down from 14, when the third unit was applied). As additional units of labor are applied, marginal product continues to decline. It is increasingly difficult to squeeze a larger total product from the fixed resources (for example, plant size and equipment). Eventually, marginal product becomes negative (beginning with the tenth unit).

Column 4 of Exhibit 3 provides data for the **average product** of labor. The average product is simply the total product divided by the units of labor applied. Note the average product increases as long as the marginal product is greater than the average product. Whenever the marginal unit's contribution is greater than the average, it must cause the average to rise. This is true through the first four units. The marginal product of the fifth unit of labor, though, is 10, less than the average product for the first four units of labor (11.5). Therefore, beginning with the fifth unit the average product declines as additional labor is applied. When marginal productivity is below the average, it brings down the average product.

Total Product: The total output of a good that is associated with alternative utilization rates of a variable input.

Marginal Product: The increase in the total product resulting from a unit increase in the employment of a variable input. Mathematically, it is the ratio of (a) change in total product to the (b) change in the quantity of the variable input.

Average Product: The total product (output) divided by the number of units of the variable input required to produce that output level.

EXHIBIT 3	■ The Law of Diminishing Returns (hypothetical data)		
(1) Units of the Variable Resource, Labor (per Day)	(2) Total Product (Output)	(3) Marginal Product	(4) Average Product
0	0		—
		8	
1	8		8.0
		12	
2	20		10.0
		14	
3	34		11.3
		12	
4	46		11.5
		10	
5	56		11.2
		8	
6	64		10.7
		6	
7	70		10.0
		4	
8	74		9.3
		1	
9	75		8.3
		−2	
10	73		7.3

EXHIBIT 4

The Law of Diminishing Returns

As units of the variable input (labor) are added to a fixed input, total product will increase, first at an increasing rate and then at a declining rate (frame a). This will cause both the marginal and average product curves (frame b) to rise at first and then decline. Note that the marginal product curve intersects the average product curve at its maximum (when 4 units of labor are used). The smooth curves indicate that labor can be increased by amounts of less than a single unit.

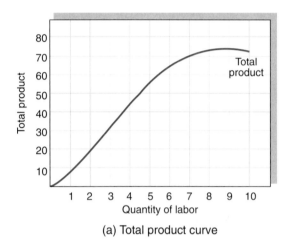

(a) Total product curve

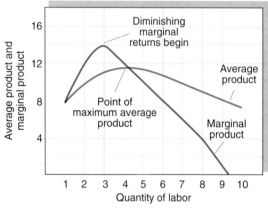

(b) Average and marginal product curve

Using the data from Exhibit 3, Exhibit 4 illustrates the law of diminishing returns graphically. Initially, the total product curve (Exhibit 4a) increases quite rapidly. As diminishing marginal returns are confronted (beginning with the fourth unit of labor), total product increases more slowly. Eventually, a maximum output (75) is reached with the application of the ninth unit of labor. The marginal product curve (Exhibit 4b) reflects the total product curve. Geometrically, marginal product is the slope—the rate of increase—of the total product curve. That slope, the marginal product, reaches its maximum with the application of three units of labor. Beyond three units, diminishing returns are present. Eventually, at ten units of labor, the marginal product becomes negative. When marginal product becomes negative, total product is necessarily declining. The average product curve rises as long as the marginal product curve is above it, since each added unit of labor is raising the average. The average product reaches its maximum at four units of labor. Beyond that, each additional unit of labor brings down the average product, and the curve declines.

DIMINISHING RETURNS AND COST CURVES

What impact will diminishing returns have on a firm's costs? Once a firm confronts diminishing returns, larger and larger additions of the variable factor are required to expand output by one unit. Marginal costs rise until, eventually, they exceed average total cost. When marginal costs are greater than ATC, ATC increases. It is easy to see why. What happens when an above-average student is added to a class? The class average goes up. What happens if a unit of above-average cost is added to output? Average total cost rises. The firm's marginal cost curve therefore crosses the ATC curve at the ATC's lowest point. For output rates beyond the minimum ATC, the rising marginal cost causes average total cost to increase. Again, the average total cost curve is U-shaped.

Exhibit 5 numerically illustrates the implications of the law of diminishing returns for a firm's short-run cost curve. Here, we assume that Royal Roller Blades, Inc., combines units of a variable input with a fixed factor to produce units of output (pairs of blades). Columns 2, 3, and 4 indicate how total cost schedules vary as output is expanded. Total fixed costs, representing the opportunity cost of the fixed factors of production, are $50 per day. For the first four units of output, total variable costs increase at a *decreasing rate*. Why? In this range, there are increasing returns to the variable input. Beginning with the fifth unit of output, however, diminishing marginal returns are present. From this point on, total variable costs and total costs increase by successively larger amounts as output is expanded.

Columns 5 through 8 of Exhibit 5 reveal the general pattern of the average and marginal cost schedules. For small output rates, the average total cost of producing roller blades is high, primarily because of the high AFC. Initially, marginal costs are less than ATC. When diminishing returns set in for output rates beginning with five units, however, marginal cost rises. Beginning with the sixth unit of output, marginal cost exceeds average variable cost, causing AVC to rise. Beginning with the eighth unit of output, MC exceeds ATC, causing it also to rise. ATC thus reaches a minimum at seven units of output. Observe the data of Exhibit 5 carefully to ensure that you fully understand the relationships among the various cost curves.

Using the numeric data of Exhibit 5, Exhibit 6 graphically illustrates both the total and the average/marginal cost curves. Note that the marginal cost curve intersects both the average variable cost and average total cost curves at the minimum points (Exhibit 6b). As marginal costs continue to rise above average total cost, unit costs rise higher and higher as output increases beyond seven units.

In sum, the firm's short-run cost curves are merely a reflection of the law of diminishing marginal returns. Assuming that the price of the variable resource is constant, marginal costs decline so long as the marginal product of the variable

EXHIBIT 5 ■ Numerical Short-Run Cost Schedules of Royal Roller Blades, Inc.

	Total Cost Data (per Day)			Average/Marginal Cost Data (per Day)			
(1)	(2)	(3)	(4)	(5)	(6)	(7)	(8)
Output per Day	Total Fixed Cost	Total Variable Cost	Total Cost, (2) + (3)	Average Fixed Cost, (2) ÷ (1)	Average Variable Cost, (3) ÷ (1)	Average Total Cost, (4) ÷ (1)	Marginal Cost, $\Delta(4) \div \Delta(1)$
0	$50	$ 0	$ 50	—	—	—	—
1	50	15	65	$50.00	$15.00	$65.00	$15
2	50	25	75	25.00	12.50	37.50	10
3	50	34	84	16.67	11.33	28.00	9
4	50	42	92	12.50	10.50	23.00	8
5	50	52	102	10.00	10.40	20.40	10
6	50	64	114	8.33	10.67	19.00	12
7	50	79	129	7.14	11.29	18.43	15
8	50	98	148	6.25	12.25	18.50	19
9	50	122	172	5.56	13.56	19.11	24
10	50	152	202	5.00	15.20	20.20	30
11	50	202	252	4.55	18.36	22.91	50

EXHIBIT 6

Costs in the Short Run

Using data of Exhibit 5, frame a illustrates the general shape of the firm's short-run total cost curves; frame b illustrates the general shape of the firm's average and marginal cost curves. Note that when output is small (for example, 2 units), average total cost will be high because the average fixed costs are so high. Similarly, when output is large (for example, 11 units) per unit cost (ATC) will be high because it is extremely costly to produce the marginal units. Thus, the short-run ATC curve will be U-shaped.

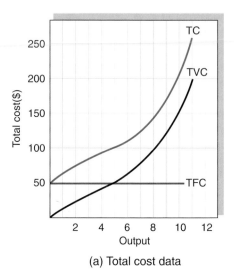

(a) Total cost data

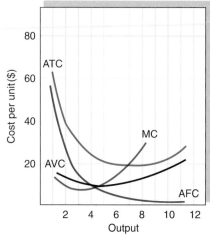

(b) Average/marginal cost data

input is rising. This results because, in this range, smaller and smaller additions of the variable input are required to produce each extra unit of output. This situation is reversed, however, when diminishing returns are confronted. Once diminishing returns set in, more and more units of the variable factor are required to generate each additional unit of output. Marginal cost will rise, because the marginal product of the variable resources is declining. Eventually, marginal costs exceed average variable and average total costs, causing these costs also to rise. A U-shaped short-run average total cost curve results.

COSTS IN THE LONG RUN

The short-run analysis relates costs to output *for a specific size of plant*. Firms, though, are not committed forever to their existing plant. In the long run, a firm can alter its plant size and all other factors of production. All resources used by the firm are variable in the long run.

How will the firm's choice of plant size affect production costs? Exhibit 7 illustrates the short-run average total cost curves for three plant sizes, ranging from small to large. If these three plant sizes were the only possible choices, which one would be best? The answer depends on the rate of output the firm expects to produce. The smallest plant would have the lowest cost if an output rate of less than q_1 were produced. The medium-sized plant would provide the least-cost method of producing output rates between q_1 and q_2. For any output level greater than q_2, the largest plant would be the most cost-efficient.

The long-run average total cost curve shows the minimum average cost of producing each output level when the firm is free to choose among all possible plant sizes. It can best be thought of as a ''planning curve,'' because it reflects the expected per unit cost of producing alternative rates of output while plants are still in the blueprint stage.

EXHIBIT 7

The Long-run Average Cost

The short-run average cost curves are shown for three alternative plant sizes. If these three were the only possible plant sizes, the long-run average curve would be *ABCD*.

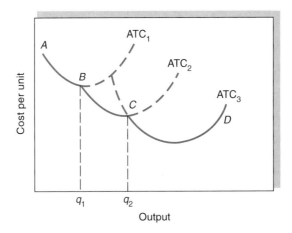

Exhibit 7 illustrates the long-run average total cost curve when only three plant sizes are possible. The planning curve *ABCD* is mapped out. Given sufficient time, of course, firms can usually choose among many plants of various sizes. Exhibit 8 presents the long-run planning curve under these circumstances. A smooth planning curve results. Each short-run average total cost curve will be tangent to the long-run planning curve.[6]

It is important to keep in mind that no single plant size could produce the alternative output rates at the costs indicated by the planning curve (LRATC). Any of the planning curve options are available before a plant size is chosen and the plant is built, but while the firm can plan for the long run, choosing among many options, it can only *operate* in the short run. The LRATC outlines the possibilities available in the planning stage, indicating the expected average costs of production for each of a large number of plants, which differ in size.

SIZE OF FIRM AND UNIT COST IN THE LONG RUN

Do larger firms have lower minimum unit costs than smaller ones? The answer to this question depends on which industries are being considered. There is a sound basis, though, for *initially* expecting some cost reductions from large-scale production methods. Why? Large firms typically produce a large total volume of output[7] . Volume of output denotes the total number of units of a product that the firm expects to produce.[8] There are three major reasons why unit costs initially decline as firms plan a larger total volume of output (and a larger size of plant).

---

[6]The tangency, though, will occur at the least-cost output level for the short run only when the long-run curve is parallel to the *x*-axis, as in q_n, Exhibit 8.

[7]Throughout this section, we assume that firms with larger plants necessarily plan a larger volume of output than do their smaller counterparts. Reality approximates these conditions. Firms choose large plants because they are planning to produce a large volume.

[8]Note the distinction between rate and volume of output. *Rate* of output is the number of units produced during a specific period (for example, the next six months). *Volume* is the total number of units produced during all time periods. For example, Boeing might produce two 767 airplanes per month (rate of output) while planning to produce a volume of two hundred 767s during the expected life of the model. Increasing the rate (reducing the time period during which a given output is produced) tends to raise costs, whereas increasing the volume (total amount produced) tends to lower costs. For additional information on production and costs, see Armen Alchian, ''Costs,'' in *International Encyclopedia of the Social Sciences* (New York: Macmillan, 1968), pp. 404–15, and Jack Hirshleifer, ''The Firm's Cost Function: A Successful Reconstruction,'' *Journal of Business* (July 1962), pp. 235–55.

EXHIBIT 8

The Planning Curve

When many alternative plant sizes are possible, the long-run average total cost curve LRATC is mapped out.

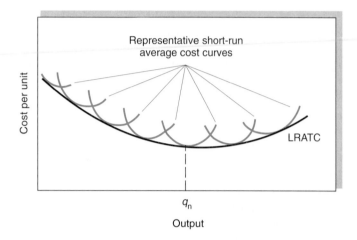

Representative short-run average cost curves

Cost per unit

LRATC

q_n

Output

1. Adoption of Mass Production Techniques.   Large firms are often able to use mass production techniques that are economical *only* when large volumes of output are planned. Mass production usually involves large development and setup costs. Once the production methods are established, though, marginal costs are low. Because of the large setup costs, mass production techniques are uneconomical for small volumes of output. For example, the use of molds, dies, and assembly line production methods reduce the per unit cost of automobiles only when the planned volume is in the millions. Machines designed to make five times as many welds on the assembly line per day (and five times as many over their lifetime) will probably not be five times as costly. High volume methods, although cheaper to use for high rates of output and high volumes, will typically be far more costly if utilized for low volumes of production.

2. Specialization.   Large-scale operation results in greater opportunity for specialized use of labor and machines. Adam Smith noted 200 years ago that the output of a pin factory is much greater when one worker draws the wire, another straightens it, a third cuts it, a fourth grinds the point, a fifth makes the head of the pin, and so on.[9] In economics, the whole can sometimes be greater than the sum of the parts. Specialization provides the opportunity for people to become exceptionally proficient at performing small but essential functions. When each of them acts as a specialist, more is produced than if each made the final product from start to finish.

3. Learning by Doing.   Workers and managers in a firm that has made more units have probably learned more from their experience. Improvements in the production

---

[9]Smith went on to state: ''I have seen a small manufactory of this kind where ten men only were employed, and where some of them consequently performed two or three distinct operations. Those ten persons, therefore, could make among them upwards of forty-eight thousand pins in a day. But if they had all wrought separately and independently, and without any of them having been educated to this peculiar business, they certainly could not each of them have made twenty, perhaps not one pin in a day,'' (Adam Smith, *An Inquiry into the Nature and Causes of the Wealth of Nations,* 1776 [Cannan's edition, Chicago: University of Chicago Press, 1976], pp. 8–9).

process result. Baseball players improve by playing, and musicians improve by performing. Similarly, workers and management improve their skills as they "practice" productive techniques. This factor has been found to be tremendously important in the aircraft and automobile industries, among others.

ECONOMIES AND DISECONOMIES OF SCALE

Economies of Scale:
Reductions in the firm's per unit costs that are associated with the use of large plants to produce a large volume of output.

Economic theory suggests that compared to smaller firms, larger firms have lower unit costs. When unit costs decline as output expands, **economies of scale** are present over the initial range of outputs. The long-run average total cost curve is falling.

Are diseconomies of scale possible—that is, are there ever situations in which the long-run average costs are greater for larger firms than they are for smaller ones? The economic justification for diseconomies of scale is less obvious (and less tenable) than that for economies of scale. However, as a firm gets bigger and bigger, bureaucratic inefficiencies *may* result. Code-book procedures tend to replace managerial genius. Motivating the work force and carrying out managerial

EXHIBIT 9

Three Different Types of Long-run Average Cost Curves

Frame (a) indicates that for output levels less than *q*, economies of scale are present. Immediately beyond *q*, diseconomies of scale dominate. Frame (b), opposite page, indicates that economies of scale are important until some minimum output level q_1 is attained. Once the minimum has been attained, there is a wide range of output levels (q_1 to q_2) that are consistent with the minimum ATC for the industry. Frame c indicates that economies of scale exist for all relevant output levels. As we will see later, this type of long-run ATC curve has important implications for the structure of the industry.

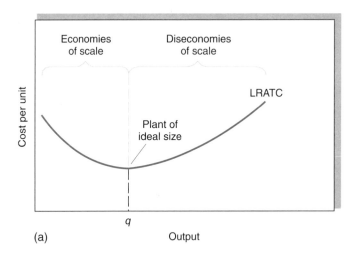

directives is also more complex when the firm is larger. Principal-agent problems grow as there are more employees and more levels of monitoring to be done. Coordinating more people and conveying information to them is more difficult. These factors combine to cause rising long-run average total costs in some, but certainly not all, industries.

Economies and diseconomies of scale stem from different sources than do increasing and diminishing returns. Economies and diseconomies of scale are long-run concepts. They relate to conditions of production when all factors are variable. In contrast, increasing and diminishing returns are short-run concepts. They are applicable only when the firm has a fixed factor of production.

Exhibit 9 outlines three different long-run average total cost (LRATC) curves that describe real-world conditions in differing situations. For Exhibit 9a, both economies and diseconomies of scale are present. Higher per unit costs will result if the firm chooses a plant size other than the one that minimizes the cost of producing output q. If each firm in an industry faces the same cost conditions, we

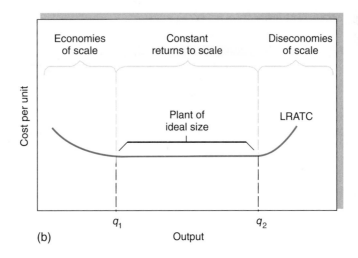

(b)

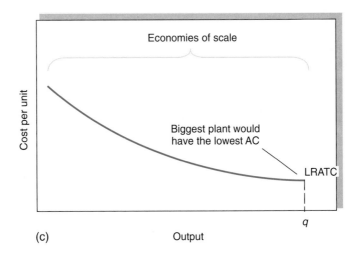

(c)

can generalize and say that any plants that are larger or smaller than this ideal size will experience higher unit costs. A very narrow range of plant sizes would be possible in industries with LRATC depicted by Exhibit 9a. Some lines of retail sales and agriculture might approximate these conditions.

Exhibit 9b demonstrates the general shape of the LRATC that economists believe is present in most industries. Initially, economies of scale exist, but once a minimum efficient scale is reached, wide variation in firm size is possible. Firms smaller than the minimum efficient size would have higher per unit costs, but firms larger than that would not gain a cost advantage. **Constant returns to scale** are present for a broad range of output rates (between q_1 and q_2). This situation is consistent with real-world conditions in many industries. For example, small firms can be as efficient as larger ones in such industries as apparel, lumber, shoes, publishing, and in many lines of retailing.

Exhibit 9c indicates that economies of scale exist for all relevant output levels. The larger the firm size, the lower the per unit cost. The LRATC in the local telephone service industry may approximate the curve of Exhibit 9c.

Constant Returns to Scale:
Unit costs are constant as the scale of the firm is altered. Neither economies nor diseconomies of scale are present.

WHAT FACTORS CAUSE THE FIRM'S COST CURVES TO SHIFT?

In outlining the general shapes of a firm's cost curves in both the long run and short run, we assumed that certain other factors remained constant, not changing with the firm's output. What are those other factors, and how will they affect production costs?

EXHIBIT 10

Higher Resource Prices and Cost

An increase in resource prices will cause the firm's cost curves to shift upward.

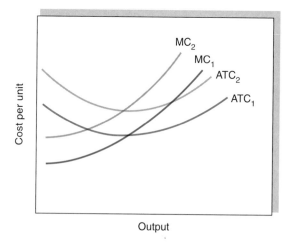

1. Prices of Resources. If the price of resources used should rise, the firm's cost curves will shift upward, as Exhibit 10 illustrates. Higher resource prices will increase the cost of producing each alternative output level. For example, what happens to the cost of producing automobiles when the price of steel rises? The cost of producing automobiles also rises. Conversely, lower resource prices will result in cost reductions. Thus, the cost curves for any specific plant size will shift downward.

2. Taxes. Taxes are a component of a firm's cost. Suppose that an excise tax of 20 cents were levied on each gallon of gasoline sold by a service station. What would happen to the seller's costs? They would increase, just as they did in Exhibit 10. The firm's average total and marginal cost curves would shift upward by the amount of the tax. If the tax were an annual business license fee instead, the average cost would rise, but variable costs would not.

3. Technology. Technological improvements often make it possible to produce a specific output with fewer resources. For example, the printing press drastically reduced the number of labor-hours required to print newspapers and books. The spinning wheel reduced the labor-hours necessary to weave cotton into cloth. More recently, computers and robots have reduced costs in many industries. As Exhibit 11 shows, a technological improvement will shift the firm's cost curves downward, reflecting the reduction in the amount of resources used to produce alternative levels of output.

EXHIBIT 11

Egg Production, Costs, and Technological Change

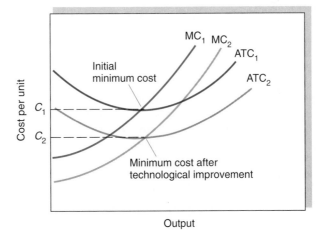

Suppose that an egg producer discovers (or develops) a "super" mineral water that makes it possible to get more eggs from the same number of chickens. Because of this technological improvement, various output levels of eggs can now be produced with less feed, space, water, and labor. Costs will be reduced. The egg producer's ATC and MC curves will shift downward.

COST AND THE ECONOMIC WAY OF THINKING

When analyzing the firm's costs, economists often present a highly mechanical—some would say unrealistic—view. The role of personal choice tends to be glossed over.

It is important to keep in mind that costs are incurred when choices are made. When business decision-makers choose to purchase raw materials, hire new employees, or renew the lease on a plant, they incur costs. All these decisions, like other choices, must be made under conditions of uncertainty. Of course, past experience acts as a useful guide, yielding valuable information. Because of this, business decision-makers will have a good idea of the costs that will be associated with alternative decisions.

Opportunity costs are usually "expected costs"—they represent the highest valued option which the decision-maker expects to give up as the result of a choice. Think for a moment of what the cost curves developed in this chapter really mean. The firm's short-run marginal cost curve represents the opportunity cost of expanding output, *given the firm's current plant size*. The firm's long-run average total cost curve represents the opportunity cost per unit of output associated with varying plant sizes and rates of output, *given that the alternative plants are still on the drawing boards*. Opportunity costs look forward, reflecting expectations—often based on the past record—as to what will be forgone as a result of current decisions. At decision time, neither the short-run marginal cost nor the long-run average total cost can be determined from accounting records. Accounting costs look backward. They yield valuable information about historical costs.

SUNK COSTS

Sunk Costs: Costs that have already been incurred as a result of past decisions. They are sometimes referred to as historical costs.

Historical costs associated with past decisions—economists call them **sunk costs**—should exert no direct influence on current choices. The outcome of past choices will provide knowledge relevant to current decisions, but the specific costs themselves are no longer relevant. Past choices cannot be reversed; money that has been spent is gone for good. Current choices should be based on the costs and benefits expected in relation to *current* market conditions. (See the Myths of Economics box.)

If they are to minimize costs, business decision-makers must recognize the irrelevance of sunk costs. Let us consider a simple example that emphasizes this point. Suppose that the firm of Exhibit 5 pays $100,000 to purchase and install a roller blade producing machine. The machine is expected to last ten years. The company's books record the cost of the machine as $10,000 each year under the heading of depreciation. The machine can be used only to make roller blades. Since dismantling and reinstallation costs are high, the machine cannot be leased or sold to another firm. It has no scrap value. In other words, there are no alternative uses for the machine. The machine's annual production of roller blades will generate $50,000 of revenues for the firm when it is employed with raw materials and other factors of production that cost $45,000.

Should the firm continue to use the machine? The annual depreciation cost of the machine suggests that the firm loses $5,000 annually on the output of the machine. The depreciation cost, however, is a sunk cost. It was incurred when the machine was installed. The current opportunity cost of the machine is precisely zero. The firm is not giving up anything by continuing to operate it. Since the machine generates $5,000 of additional net revenue, the firm should continue using it. Of course, if current market conditions are expected to continue, the firm will not purchase a similar machine or replace the machine when it wears out, but this should not influence the decision of whether to continue operating the current one. The irrelevance of sunk costs helps explain why it often makes sense to continue operating older equipment (it has a low opportunity cost), even though it might not be wise to purchase similar equipment again.

COST AND SUPPLY

Economists are interested in cost because they seek to explain the supply decisions of firms. A strictly profit-maximizing firm will compare the expected revenues derived from a decision or a course of action with the expected costs. If the expected revenues exceed costs, the course of action will be chosen because it will expand profits (or reduce losses).

MYTHS OF ECONOMICS

"A good business decision-maker will never sell a product for less than its production costs."

This statement contains a grain of truth. A profit-seeking entrepreneur would not *undertake* a project knowing that the costs could not be covered. However, this view fails to emphasize (a) the time dimension of the production process and (b) the uncertainty associated with business decisions. The production process takes time. Raw materials must be purchased, employees hired, and plants equipped. Retailers must contract with suppliers. As these decisions are made, costs result. Many of the firm's costs of production are incurred long before the product is ready for marketing.

Even a good business decision-maker is not always able to predict the future correctly. Market conditions may change in an unexpected manner. At the time the product is ready for sale, buyers may be unwilling to pay a price that will cover the seller's past costs of production. These past costs, however, are now sunk costs and no longer relevant. Current decisions must be made on the basis of current cost and revenue considerations.

Should a grocer refuse to sell oranges that are about to spoil because their wholesale cost cannot be covered? The grocer's current opportunity cost of selling the oranges may be nearly zero. The alternative may be to throw them in the garbage next week. Almost any price, even one far below past costs, would be better than letting the oranges spoil.

Consider another example. Suppose a couple who own a house plan to relocate temporarily.

Should they refuse to rent their house for $400 (if this is the best offer available) because their monthly house payment is $600? Of course not. The house payment will go on, regardless of whether they rent the house. If the homeowners can cover their opportunity costs (perhaps wear and tear plus a $60 monthly fee for a property management service), they will gain by renting rather than leaving the house vacant.

Past mistakes provide useful lessons for the future, but they cannot be reversed. Bygones are bygones, even if they resulted in business loss. Only current revenue and cost considerations are relevant to current decisions about prices and profitability. There is no need to fret over spilt milk, burnt toast, or yesterday's business losses.

In the short run, when making supply decisions, the marginal cost of producing additional units is the relevant cost consideration. A profit-maximizing decision-maker will compare the expected marginal costs with the expected additional revenue from larger sales. If the latter exceeds the former, output (the quantity supplied) will be expanded.

Whereas marginal costs are central to the choice of short-run output, the expected average total cost is vital to a firm's long-run supply decision. *Before entry into an industry,* a profit-maximizing decision-maker will compare the expected market price with the expected long-run average total cost. Profit-seeking potential entrants will supply the product if, and only if, they expect the market price to exceed their long-run average total cost. Similarly, existing firms will continue to supply a product only if they expect that the market price will enable them at least to cover their long-run average total cost.

LOOKING AHEAD

In this chapter, we outlined several basic principles that affect costs for business firms. We will use these basic principles when we analyze the price and output decisions of firms under alternative market structures in the chapters that follow.

CHAPTER SUMMARY

1. The business firm is used to organize productive resources and transform them into goods and services. There are three major business structures—proprietorships, partnerships, and corporations. Proprietorships are the most numerous, but most of the nation's business activity is conducted through corporations. To solve the principal-agent problem, which tends to reduce worker efficiency in team production, every firm must provide work incentives and monitoring. The business structure chosen can influence the cost of those provisions and ultimately, of course, the cost of the product.

2. The demand for a product indicates the intensity of consumers' desires for the item. The (opportunity) cost of producing the item indicates the desire of consumers for other goods that must now be given up because the necessary resources have been used in the production of the item. In a market economy, these two forces—demand and costs of production—balance the desire of consumers for more of a good against the reality of scarce resources, which requires that other goods be forgone as more of any one specific item is supplied.

3. Economists employ the opportunity cost concept when figuring a firm's costs. Therefore, total cost includes not only explicit (money) costs but also implicit costs associated with the use of productive resources owned by the firm.

4. Since accounting procedures generally omit the opportunity cost of the firm's equity capital and sometimes (in the case of owner-operated firms) omit the cost of owner-provided services, accounting costs understate the opportunity cost of producing a good. As a result of these omissions, the accounting profits of a firm are generally larger than the firm's economic profits.

5. Economic profit (loss) results when a firm's sales revenues exceed (are less than) its total costs, both explicit and implicit. Firms that are making the market rate of return on their assets will therefore make zero economic profit. Firms that transform resources into products of greater value than the opportunity cost of the resources used will make an economic profit. On the other hand, if the opportunity cost of the resources used exceeds the value of the product, losses will result.

6. The firm's short-run average total cost curve will tend to be U-shaped. When output is small (relative to plant size), average fixed cost (and therefore ATC) will be high. As output expands, however, AFC (and ATC) will fall. As the firm attempts to produce a larger and larger rate of output using its fixed plant size, diminishing returns will eventually set in, and marginal cost will rise quite rapidly as the plant's maximum capacity is approached. Thus, the short-run ATC will also be high for large output levels because marginal costs are high.

7. The law of diminishing returns explains why a firm's short-run marginal and average costs will eventually rise. When diminishing marginal returns are present, successively larger amounts of the variable input will be required to increase output by one more unit. Thus, marginal costs will eventually rise as output expands. Eventually, marginal costs will exceed average total costs, causing the latter to rise, also.

8. The ability to plan a larger volume of output often leads to cost reductions. These cost reductions associated with the scale of one's operation result from (a) a greater opportunity to employ mass production methods, (b) specialized use of resources, and (c) learning by doing.

9. The LRATC reflects the costs of production for plants of various sizes. When economies of scale are present (that is, when larger plants have lower per unit costs of production), LRATC will decline. When constant returns to scale are experienced, LRATC will be constant. A rising LRATC is also possible. Bureaucratic decision-making and other diseconomies of scale may in some cases cause LRATC to rise.

10. In analyzing the general shapes of a firm's cost curves, we assumed that the following factors remained constant: (a) resource prices, (b) technology, and (c) taxes. Changes in any of these factors would cause the cost curves of a firm to shift.

11. In any analysis of business decision-making, it is important to keep the opportunity cost principle in mind. Economists are interested in costs primarily because costs affect the decisions of suppliers. Short-run marginal costs represent the supplier's opportunity cost of producing additional units with the existing plant facilities of the firm. The long-run average total cost represents the opportunity cost of supplying alternative rates of output, given sufficient time to vary all factors, including plant size.

12. Sunk costs are costs that have already been incurred. They should not exert a *direct* influence on current business choices. However, they may provide a source of information that will be useful in making current decisions.

CRITICAL ANALYSIS QUESTIONS

*1. What is economic profit? How might it differ from accounting profit? Explain why firms that are making zero economic profit are likely to continue in business.

*2. Which of the following do you think reflect sound economic thinking? Explain your answer.
   a. "I paid $200 for this economics course. Therefore, I'm going to attend the lectures even if they are useless and boring."
   b. "Since we own rather than rent, housing doesn't cost us anything."
   c. "I own 100 shares of stock that I can't afford to sell until the price goes up enough for me to get back at least my original investment."
   d. "It costs to produce private education, whereas public schooling is free."

3. Suppose a firm produces bicycles. Will the firm's accounting statement reflect the opportunity cost of producing bicycles? Why or why not? What costs would an

---

*Asterisk denotes questions for which answers are given in Appendix C, Selected Answers.

accounting statement reveal? Should current decisions be based on accounting costs? Explain.

4. Suppose that Ajax, Inc., is the target of a takeover attempt by the management of Beta Corporation, which is offering to buy stock from any Ajax stockholder who wants to sell at 20 percent above its current rate. Explain how the resistance of Ajax management to the takeover attempt might illustrate the principal-agent problem. Is it possible that the Beta Corporation management's action is itself an illustration of the principal-agent problem? Explain.

5. Explain the factors that cause a firm's short-run average total costs to decline initially, but eventually to increase, as the rate of output rises.

6. Which of the following are relevant to a firm's decision to increase output: (a) short-run average total cost; (b) short-run marginal cost; (c) long-run average total cost? Justify your answer.

7. Economics students often confuse (a) diminishing returns to the variable factor and (b) diseconomies of scale. Explain the difference between the two and give one example of each.

8. **What's Wrong with This Way of Thinking?**
"The American steel industry cannot compete with Korean and Japanese steel producers. These countries built modern, efficient mills that made use of the latest technology. In contrast, American mills are older and less efficient. Our costs are higher because we are stuck with old facilities."

*9. Is profit maximization consistent with the self-interest of corporate owners? Is it consistent with the self-interest of corporate managers? Is there a conflict between the self-interest of owners and of managers?

*10. What is the opportunity cost of (a) borrowed funds and (b) equity capital? Under current tax law, firms can take the opportunity cost of borrowed funds, but not equity capital, as an expense. How does this tax feature affect the debt/equity ratio of business firms?

*11. "If a firm maximizes profit it must minimize the cost of producing the profit-maximum output." True or false? Explain.

12. Why do economists consider normal returns to capital as a cost? How does economic profit differ from normal returns (or "normal profit")?

*13. Draw a U-shaped short-run average total cost curve for a firm. Construct the accompanying marginal cost and average variable cost curves.

14. a. Prior to legislation passed in 1986, appreciation in the market value of a stock was taxed at a lower rate than dividends from the stocks. How would this affect the incentive of firms to use internal financing relative to debt?

   b. Subsequent to the 1986 legislation, capital gains (appreciation in the stock) and dividends were taxed at identical rates. The 1986 legislation was followed by a rash of takeover moves against firms with low debt/equity ratios. Did the 1986 tax change contribute to these moves? Why or why not?

15. "Diminishing marginal returns to labor reflect the fact that the best workers are hired first. That is why, as additional workers are hired, marginal productivity falls." Evaluate.

16. What are implicit costs? Do implicit costs contribute to the opportunity cost of production? Should an implicit cost be counted as cost? Give three examples of implicit costs. Does the firm's accounting statement take implicit costs into account? Why or why not?

*17. Consider a machine purchased one year ago for $12,000. The machine is being depreciated $4,000 per year over a three-year period. Its current market value is $5,000, and the expected market value of the machine one year from now is $3,000. If the interest rate is 10 percent, what is the expected cost of holding the machine during the next year?

*18. Investors seeking to take over a firm often bid a positive price for the business even though it is currently experiencing losses. Why would anyone ever bid a positive price for a firm operating at a loss?

19. "A wise business decision-maker is on the lookout for diminishing marginal returns and will not operate where diminishing returns have set in." Evaluate.

19 The Firm under Pure Competition

Competition means decentralized planning by many separate persons.[1]

Friedrich A. von Hayek

Competition is conducive to the continuous improvements of industrial efficiency. It leads some producers to eliminate wastes and cut costs so that they may undersell others. It compels others to adopt similar measures in order that they may survive. It weeds out those whose costs remain high and thus operates to concentrate production in the hands of those whose costs are low.[2]

Clair Wilcox

CHAPTER FOCUS

- What does the term ''competition'' mean in economics?
- What is the purely competitive model and why is it important?
- What determines the output of a competitive firm?
- How do competitive firms change their output when price changes, in the short run? In the long run?
- What is the role of time in determining the elasticity of supply?
- How do consumers fare under pure competition?
- How is the competitive model related to economic efficiency?

*I*n the last chapter, we outlined some basic principles that determine the general relationship between output and costs of production for any firm. Of course, a firm's output decisions will be influenced by its costs and its revenues. In this and the next two chapters, we will illustrate how the structure of an industry affects the revenues and output levels of firms. We will analyze four models of industrial structure: (a) pure competition, (b) monopoly, (c) monopolistic competition, and (d) oligopoly. These models will help us understand the role of competitive forces under various market conditions. This chapter focuses on pure competition.

THE PROCESS OF COMPETITION

Competition as a Dynamic Process: A term that denotes rivalry or competitiveness between or among parties (for example, producers or input suppliers), each of which seeks to deliver a better deal to buyers when quality, price, and product information are all considered. Competing implies a lack of collusion among sellers.

Before we introduce the model of pure competition, a few comments about the use of the term "competition" are in order. It is important not to lose sight of the function of **competition as a dynamic process** to explain the mechanics of alternative forms of industrial structure. The competitive process emphasizes the rivalry among firms—the effort on the part of a seller to outperform the alternative suppliers. Competing firms may use a variety of methods—quality of product, style, convenience of location, advertising, and price—to attract consumers. Decentralized planning in competitive markets is the key to market productivity. Independent action and rivalry are the essential ingredients of the competitive process.

Markets serve consumers well when they are open to rival sellers so that each is under intense competition to cater to consumer preferences. Open markets have both rewards and risks for producers. Profits are possible for entrepreneurs who are good at finding ways to satisfy consumer wants better or more cheaply, and who successfully implement them. But producers who offer only low quality at a high price find that their customers turn to rival sellers.

As the quotation from Professor Wilcox indicates, competition also places pressure on producers to operate efficiently and to avoid waste. Competition weeds out the inefficient—those who are incapable of providing consumers with quality goods at low prices. Competition also keeps producers on their toes in other areas. The production techniques and product offerings that lead to success today will not necessarily pass the competitive market test tomorrow. Producers who survive in a competitive environment cannot be complacent. They must be forward-looking and innovative. They must be willing to experiment and quick to adopt improved methods.

Each competitor is, of course, in business to make a profit. Rival firms struggle for the dollar votes of consumers. Competition, though, is the taskmaster that forces producers to serve the interests of consumers and to do so at the lowest possible level of profit. As Adam Smith noted more than 200 years ago, competition harnesses the profit motive and puts it to work, elevating our standard of living and directing our resources toward the production of those goods that we desire most

---

[1] F. A. Hayek, "The Use of Knowledge in Society," *American Economic Review, 35,* (Sept. 1945), pp. 519–30.

[2] Clair Wilcox, *Competition and Monopoly in American Industry,* Monograph no. 21, Temporary National Economic Committee, Investigation of Concentration of Economic Power, 76th Congress, 3rd session (Washington, D.C.: U.S. Government Printing Office, 1940).

intensely relative to their cost. Smith pointed out that aggregate output would be vastly expanded if individuals specialized in those things they did best and cooperated with others desirous of their services. He believed that self-interest directed by competitive markets would generate precisely these two ingredients—specialization and cooperation. Smith emphasized this theme in Book 1 of *The Wealth of Nations:*

> It is not from the benevolence of the butcher, the brewer, or the baker, that we expect our dinner, but from their regard to their own self-interest. We address ourselves, not to their humanity but to their self-love, and never talk to them of our own necessities, but of their advantages.[3]

In Smith's time, as today, many thinkers erred because they did not understand that productive action and voluntary exchange offer the potential for mutual gain. Both parties to an economic exchange generally gain (see Myths of Economics box, p. 45). Bridled by competition, self-interest leads to economic cooperation and provides a powerful fuel for the benefit of humankind. Paradoxical as it seems, even though benevolence may be the more admirable attitude, it cannot generate the cooperative effort that is a natural outgrowth of self-interest directed by competition. Unilateral giving does not generate the information and feedback to buyers and sellers inherent in the competitive market process. Thus, the competitive process occupies center stage in economic analysis, as one of the forces directing the economic behavior of human beings.

Before we move on to more technical material, two additional points should be addressed. First, a dual usage of the term ''competition'' has evolved through the years. The term is used to describe a rivalry or competitiveness among sellers, as we have already noted. In addition, the term ''competition,'' or more precisely, ''pure competition,'' is used to describe a hypothetical model of industrial structure characterized by independent firms and a large number of sellers. This dual usage can sometimes be confusing. It is important to recognize that firms can be competitive in the sense of rivalry even though they may not be competitive in the industrial structure sense. To avoid confusion, we will use the complete expression ''pure competition'' when we discuss the competitive model of industrial structure.

Second, we have emphasized the role of competition as the taskmaster forcing sellers to obey the desires of consumers. Nobody likes a taskmaster, and sellers often try to escape the discipline imposed by competitive forces. The models of industrial structure that we examine are useful because they provide a framework for analyzing both the likelihood of a business firm escaping the directives of competition and the economic implications of its doing so.

THE PURELY COMPETITIVE MODEL

Pure competition presupposes that the following conditions exist in a market.

*1. All Firms in the Market Are Producing a **Homogeneous Product**.*   The product of firm A is identical to the product offered by firm B and all other firms. This

Pure Competition: A model of industrial structure characterized by a large number of small firms producing a homogeneous product in an industry (market area) that permits complete freedom of entry and exit.

---

[3]Adam Smith, *An Inquiry into the Nature and Causes of the Wealth of Nations* (1776; Cannan's ed., Chicago: University of Chicago Press, 1976), p. 18.

Homogeneous Product:
A product of one firm that is identical to the product of every other firm in the industry. Consumers see no difference in units of the product offered by alternative sellers.

presupposition rules out advertising, location preferences, quality difference, and other forms of nonprice competition.

2. A Large Number of Independent Firms Produce the Product. The independence of the firms rules out joint actions designed to restrict output and raise prices.

3. Each Buyer and Seller Is Small Relative to the Total Market. Therefore, no single buyer or seller is able to exert any noticeable influence on the market supply and demand conditions. For example, a wheat farmer selling 5,000 bushels annually would not have a noticeable impact on the U.S. wheat market in which 2,500,000,000 bushels are traded annually.

Barriers to Entry: Obstacles that limit the freedom of potential rivals to enter an industry.

4. There Are No Artificial Barriers to Entry into or Exit from the Market. Under pure competition, any entrepreneur is free either to produce or fail to produce in the industry. New entrants need not obtain permission from the government or the existing firms before they are free to compete. Nor does control of an essential resource limit market entry.

The purely competitive model, like other theories, is abstract. Keep in mind that the test of a theory is not the realism of its assumptions but its ability to make *predictions* that are consistent with the real world (see Chapter 1). Assumptions are made and ideas are simplified so that we can better organize our thoughts. Models, based on simplifications and assumptions, can often help us develop the economic way of thinking.

WHY IS PURE COMPETITION IMPORTANT?

Previously, we discussed how supply and demand jointly determine market price. The model of pure competition is another way of looking at the operation of market forces. This model will help us understand the relationship between the decision-making of individual firms and market supply. If we familiarize ourselves with the way in which economic incentives influence the supply decisions of firms within the competitive model, we will be better able to understand the behavior of firms in markets that are less than purely competitive.

There are other reasons for the model's importance. Its conditions are approximated in a few important industries, most notably in many parts of agriculture. The model will help us understand these industries. In addition, as we will show later, the equilibrium conditions in the competitive model yield results that are identical with the conditions necessary for ideal static efficiency. Many economists thus use the competitive model as a standard by which to judge other industrial structures.

Price Takers: Sellers who must take the market price in order to sell their product. Because each price taker's output is small relative to the total market, price takers can sell all of their output at the market price, but are unable to sell any of their output at a price higher than the market price. Thus, they face a horizontal demand curve.

THE WORKINGS OF THE COMPETITIVE MODEL

Since a competitive firm by itself produces an output that is small relative to the total market, it cannot influence the market price. A purely competitive firm must accept the market price if it is to sell any of its product. Competitive firms are sometimes called **price takers,** because they must take the market price in order to sell.

EXHIBIT 1

The Firm's Demand Curve Under Pure Competition

The market forces of supply and demand determine price (b). Under pure competition, individual firms have no control over price. Thus, the demand for the product of the firm is perfectly elastic (a).

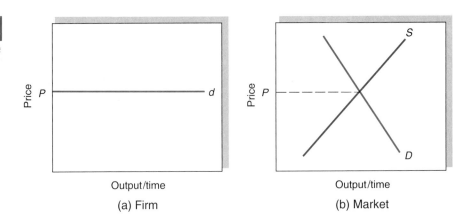

(a) Firm

(b) Market

Exhibit 1 illustrates the relationship between market forces (frame b) and the demand curve facing the purely competitive firm (frame a). If a pure competitor sets a price above the market level, consumers will simply buy from other sellers. Why pay the higher price when the identical good is available elsewhere at a lower price? For example, if the price of wheat were $3 per bushel, a farmer would be unable to find buyers for wheat at $3.50 per bushel. A firm could lower its price, but since it is small relative to the total market, it can already sell as much as it wants at the market price. A price reduction would merely reduce revenues. A purely competitive *firm* thus confronts a perfectly elastic demand for *its* product.

DECIDING HOW MUCH TO PRODUCE—THE SHORT RUN

The firm's output decision is based on comparison of benefits with costs. If a firm produces at all, it will continue expanding output as long as the benefits (additional revenues) from the production of the additional units exceed their marginal costs.

How will changes in output influence the firm's costs? In the last chapter, we discovered that the firm's short-run marginal costs will *eventually* increase as the firm expands its output by working its fixed plant facilities more intensively. The law of diminishing marginal returns assures us that this will be the case. *Eventually,* both the firm's short-run marginal and average total cost curves will turn upward.

What about the benefits or additional revenues from output expansion? **Marginal revenue** (MR) is the change in the firm's total revenue per unit of output. It is the additional revenue derived from the sale of an additional unit of output. Mathematically,

Marginal Revenue: The incremental change in total revenue derived from the sale of one additional unit of a product.

$$MR = \frac{\text{Change in total revenue}}{\text{Change in output}}$$

Since the purely competitive firm sells all units at the same price, its marginal revenue will be equal to the market price.

In the short run, the purely competitive firm will expand output until marginal revenue (its price) is just equal to marginal cost. This decision-making rule will maximize the firm's profits (or minimize its losses).

Exhibit 2 helps explain why. Since the firm can sell as many units as it would like at the market price, the sale of one additional unit will increase revenue by the price of the product. As long as price exceeds marginal cost, revenue will increase

EXHIBIT 2

Profit Maximization and
the Purely Competitive
Firm

The purely competitive firm
would maximize profits by
producing the output level *q*,
where *P* = MC.

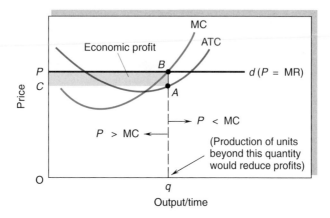

more than cost as output is expanded. Since profit is merely the difference between total revenue and total cost, production of units that add more to revenue than to cost will increase profit. This happy state of affairs comes to an end when MC has risen enough to make MC = MR = *P*. For the pure competitor then, profit will be at a maximum when *P* = MR = MC. In Exhibit 2, this occurs at output level *q*.

Why would the firm not expand output beyond *q*? The cost of producing such units is given by the height of the MC curve. The sale of these units would increase revenues only by *P*, the price of the product. Production of units beyond *q* would add more to cost than to revenue. Therefore, production beyond *q*, the *P* = MC output level, would reduce the firm's profits.

A profit-maximizing firm with the cost curves indicated by Exhibit 2 would produce exactly *q*. The total revenue of the firm would be the sales price *P* multiplied by output sold *q*. Geometrically, the firm's total revenues would be *POqB*. The firm's total cost would be found by multiplying the average total cost by the output level. Geometrically, total costs are represented by *COqA*. The firm's total revenues exceed total costs, and the firm is making short-run economic profit (the shaded area).

In the real world, of course, decisions are not made by entrepreneurs who sit around drawing curves labeled MC and *P*. Many have not even heard of these concepts. Our model also ignores the problem of uncertainty. Very often, businesspeople must make decisions without complete knowledge of what costs or product price will be. In addition, there may be problems of ''lumpiness.'' The manager may prefer to use 1.7 machines and 2.5 people to carry out a production process. Managers, however, know that machines and people alike come in discrete ''lumps,'' or whole units. They may not be able to approximate what they want even by renting, or changing the machine size they use, or hiring part-time employees.

Despite the inconvenient and uncertain facts of real life, our simple model does make fairly accurate predictions. A business decision-maker who has never heard of the *P* = MC rule for profit maximization probably has another rule that yields approximately the same outcome. For example, the rule might be: Produce those units, and only those units, that add more to revenue than to cost. This ensures maximum profit (or minimum loss). It also takes the firm to the point at which *P* = MC. Why? To stop short of that point would mean not producing some profitable units—units that would add more to revenue than to cost. Similarly, the decision-maker would not go beyond that point because production of such units would add more to costs than to revenues. This common sense rule thus leads to the same outcome as the competitive model, even when the decision-maker knows none of the technical jargon of economics. No wonder economics is sometimes thought of as "organized common sense."

Just how accurate is the purely competitive model in predicting behavior in real markets? Do other models, which assume that sellers collude to eliminate competition, make better predictions? Direct scientific evidence bearing on such questions is highly desirable. As the Applications in Economics box, "Experimental Economics—Testing the Purely Competitive Model," indicates, such evidence has been produced repeatedly in recent decades by the relatively new subdiscipline of experimental economics. The evidence supports the purely competitive model surprisingly well under a variety of circumstances.

PROFIT MAXIMIZING— A NUMERIC EXAMPLE

Exhibit 3 uses numeric data to illustrate profit-maximizing decision-making for a competitive firm. The firm's short-run total and marginal cost schedules have the general characteristics we discussed in the previous chapter. Since the firm confronts a market price of $5 per unit, its marginal revenue is $5. Total revenue thus *increases* by $5 per additional unit of output. The firm maximizes its profit when it supplies an output of 15 units.

There are two ways of viewing this profit-maximizing output rate. First, we could examine the difference between total revenue and total cost, identifying the

EXHIBIT 3 ■ Profit Maximization of a Competitive Firm—A Numeric Illustration					
(1) Output (per Day)	(2) Total Revenue	(3) Total Cost	(4) Marginal Revenue	(5) Marginal Cost	(6) Profit (TR − TC)
0	$ 0.00	$ 25.00	$0.00	$ 0.00	$−25.00
1	5.00	29.80	5.00	4.80	−24.80
2	10.00	33.75	5.00	3.95	−23.75
3	15.00	37.25	5.00	3.50	−22.25
4	20.00	40.25	5.00	3.00	−20.25
5	25.00	42.75	5.00	2.50	−17.75
6	30.00	44.75	5.00	2.00	−14.75
7	35.00	46.50	5.00	1.75	−11.50
8	40.00	48.00	5.00	1.50	− 8.00
9	45.00	49.25	5.00	1.25	− 4.25
10	50.00	50.25	5.00	1.00	− 0.25
11	55.00	51.50	5.00	1.25	3.50
12	60.00	53.25	5.00	1.75	6.75
13	65.00	55.75	5.00	2.50	9.25
14	70.00	59.25	5.00	3.50	10.75
15	75.00	64.00	5.00	4.75	11.00
16	80.00	70.00	5.00	6.00	10.00
17	85.00	77.25	5.00	7.25	7.75
18	90.00	85.50	5.00	8.25	4.50
19	95.00	95.00	5.00	9.50	0.00
20	100.00	108.00	5.00	13.00	− 8.00
21	105.00	125.00	5.00	17.00	−20.00

output rate at which this difference is greatest. Column 6, the profit data, provides this information. For small output rates (less than 11), the firm would actually experience losses. But, at 15 units of output, an $11 profit is earned ($75 total revenue minus $64 total cost). Inspection of the profit column indicates that it is impossible to earn a profit larger than $11 at any other rate of output.

Exhibit 4a presents the total revenue and total cost approach in graph form. (However, the curves are drawn smoothly, as though output could be increased in any amounts including tiny amounts, not just in whole unit increments as shown in Exhibit 3.) Profits will be maximized when the total revenue line exceeds the total cost curve by the largest vertical amount. That takes place, of course, at 15 units of output.

The marginal approach also can be used to determine the profit-maximizing rate of output for the competitive firm. Remember, as long as price (marginal revenue) exceeds marginal cost, production and sale of additional units will add to the firm's profit (or reduce its losses). Inspection of columns 4 and 5 of Exhibit 3 indicates that MR is greater than MC for the first 15 units of output. Production of these units will expand the firm's profit. In contrast, the production of each unit beyond 15 adds more to cost than to revenue. Profit will therefore decline if output is expanded beyond 15 units. Given the firm's cost and revenue schedule, the profit-maximizing manager will choose to produce 15, and only 15, units per day.

Exhibit 4b graphically illustrates the marginal approach. Note here that the output rate (15 units) at which the marginal cost and marginal revenue curves intersect coincides with the output rate in Exhibit 4a at which the total revenue curve exceeds the total cost curve by the largest amount.

LOSSES AND GOING OUT OF BUSINESS

Suppose changes take place in the market that depress the price below a firm's average total cost. How will a profit-maximizing (or loss-minimizing) firm respond to this situation? The answer to this question depends on both the firm's current

EXHIBIT 4

Profit Maximization—The Total and Marginal Approaches

Using the data of Exhibit 3, here we provide two alternative ways of viewing profit maximization. As frame (a) illustrates, the profits of the competitive firm are maximized at the output level at which total revenue exceeds total cost by the maximum amount. Frame (b) demonstrates that the maximum-profit output can also be identified by comparing marginal revenue and marginal cost.

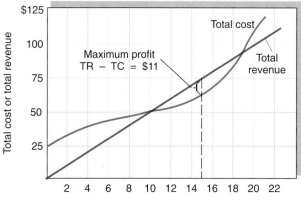

(a) Total revenue/total cost approach

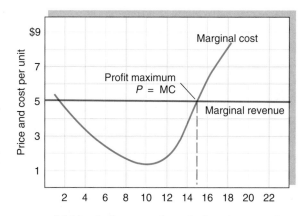

(b) Marginal revenue/marginal cost approach

APPLICATIONS IN ECONOMICS

Experimental Economics—Testing the Purely Competitive Model

Do individual decision-makers, without any economics training, behave as if they understand marginal cost? Do they act according to the competitive model, even though not all of the assumptions of that model are satisfied? Or when there are only a few sellers, do they collude successfully so as to raise price above marginal cost?

Answering such questions is important, but verifying economic principles and comparing alternative economic models by scientific testing is not an easy task. Simply observing people to see whether they behave as economic principles suggest is not completely satisfying. Since a normal economic event that we can observe is the result of more than one cause, the economist trying to isolate the impact of one causal factor must try to be sure that other

factors influencing the outcome do not vary, or else try to take them into account in the analysis. To isolate the impact of a change in the price of a product on consumer behavior for example, the economist must somehow account for the impact of all other price changes, income changes, and so on, that may have occurred. In other disciplines, scientists use experiments in the laboratory, with all factors controlled, to tackle this problem. They test the principles on which their science is built, using carefully detailed methods, so that other scientists can replicate the experiment.

Beginning about the middle of the twentieth century, economists also began to conduct laboratory experiments. A good many experiments have been conducted to investigate the predictive power of the purely competitive model.

In one of the earliest, conducted in 1956 by Vernon Smith of the University of Arizona, individual subjects were brought into a laboratory setting and arbitrarily assigned roles as buyers and sellers, in a game-like setting.

Each buyer was given a different "limit price" (that is, a maximum price he or she was allowed to pay) for a paper asset. If the buyer could purchase the paper commodity for less than the limit price, he or she received a cash payment equal to the difference between the limit price and the amount actually paid. Therefore, as in other markets, each buyer gained financially by purchasing at lower prices. The sellers were treated in a parallel fashion. Each had a "limit price" (a minimum selling price) and received in cash any extra revenue above that price.

sales revenues relative to its *variable cost* and its expectations about the future. The firm has three options—it can (a) continue to operate in the short run, (b) shut down temporarily, or (c) go out of business.

If the firm anticipates that the lower market price is temporary, it may want to continue operating in the short run as long as it is able to cover its variable cost.[5] Exhibit 5 illustrates why. The firm shown in this exhibit would minimize its loss at output level q, where $P = $ MC. At q, total revenues ($OqBP_1$) are, however, less

---

[5]In thinking about this issue, we must keep in mind the opportunity cost concept. The firm's fixed costs are *opportunity costs* that do not vary with the level of output. They can be avoided if, and only if, the firm goes out of business. Following this course releases the fixed-cost resources to their best alternative use, and thus eliminates the fixed costs. Fixed costs are *not* (as some economics texts have stated) the depreciated value of the firm's fixed assets. Such accounting measures may have little to do with the firm's opportunity cost of those fixed assets. To specify fixed costs, we need to know (a) how much the firm's fixed assets would bring if they were sold or rented to others and (b) any other costs, such as operating license fees and debts, which could be avoided if the firm declared bankruptcy and/or went out of business. Although these costs can be avoided if the firm goes out of business, the firm could not operate even in the short run if it cannot cover its fixed costs (unless it expects conditions to improve; then it would have to pay extra costs to get back into business at that future time). See Marshall Colberg and James King, "Theory of Production Abandonment," *Revista Internazionale di Scienze Economiche e Commerciali* 20 (1973), pp. 961–1072.

Buyers and sellers were free to make verbal offers to buy or sell. How did markets develop? Did the outcomes resemble a competitive market, or did sellers collude, controlling the market price for their own benefit, so that a monopoly model would better describe the outcome?

The competitive model predicts that trades among buyers and sellers will occur at a market price, which will allow every efficient trade to take place. The market price equates the quantity demanded with the quantity willingly supplied.

Prior to the work in experimental economics, many economists thought the competitive model was relevant only under highly restrictive conditions. The experimental work indicates that this is not the case. The wide applicability of the purely

competitive model surprised many observers. As Vernon Smith, a leading experimental economist, points out, "Since 1956, several hundred experiments using different supply and demand conditions, experienced as well as inexperienced subjects, buyers and sellers with multiple unit trading capacity, a great variation in the numbers of buyers and sellers, and different trading institutions have established the replicability and robustness of these results [competitive outcomes]."[4]

The experimental approach allows researchers to test theories under a wide range of conditions. By changing the number of sellers, the type of trading rules, and so on, researchers can find out whether predicted outcomes hold only in special cases or under a wide variety of circumstances. Without the control that is possible

in the laboratory, questions about the relevance of a theory might lead only to heated debate, with little light shed on the topic.

Experimental economics, like laboratory work in other sciences, cannot answer all questions about what might happen in nonlaboratory settings. But it has already provided a great deal of precision and certainty to a world of economics needing just those things. And its contributions undoubtedly will continue.

---

[4] See Vernon L. Smith, "Experimental Methods in Economics," in *The New Palgrave: A Dictionary of Economics,* ed. by John Eatwell, et al., (London: Macmillan Press Ltd., 1987), pp. 241–49 for a good overview of experimental economics. Also see Charles R. Plott, "Will Economics Become an Experimental Science" *Southern Economic Journal* (April 1991).

Shutdown: A temporary halt in the operation of a business. The firm does *not* sell its assets. Its variable cost will be eliminated, but the firm's fixed costs will continue. The shut-down firm anticipates a return to operation in the future.

than total costs ($OqAC$). The firm confronts short-run economic losses. Even if it shuts down completely, it will still incur fixed costs, *unless it goes out of business.* If the firm anticipates that the market price will increase enough that it will be able to cover its average total costs in the future, it may not want to sell out. It may choose to produce q units in the short run, even though losses are incurred. At price P_1, production of output q is clearly more advantageous than shutting down, because the firm is able to cover its variable costs and pay some of its fixed costs. If it were to shut down, *but not sell out,* the firm would lose the entire amount of its fixed cost.

What if the market price declines below the firm's average variable cost (for example, P_2)? Under these circumstances, a temporary **shutdown** is preferable to short-run operation. If the firm continues to operate in the short run, operating losses merely supplement losses resulting from the firm's fixed costs. Therefore, even if the firm expects the market price to increase, enabling it to survive and prosper in the future, it will shut down in the short run when the market price falls below its average variable cost.

Going Out of Business: The sale of a firm's assets and its permanent exit from the market. By going out of business, a firm is able to avoid fixed cost, which would continue during a shutdown.

The firm's third option is **going out of business** immediately. After all, even the losses resulting from the firm's fixed costs (remember that if they are costs of doing business, they must be avoidable by not doing business) can be avoided if the

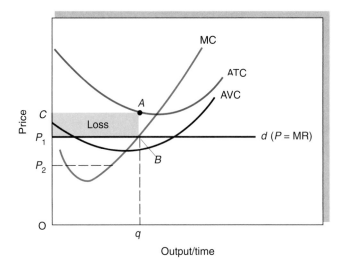

EXHIBIT 5

Operating with Short-run Losses

A firm making losses will operate in the short run if it (a) can cover its variable costs now and (b) expects price to be high enough in the future to cover all its costs.

firm sells out. If market conditions are not expected to change for the better, then going out of business is the preferred option.

THE COMPETITIVE FIRM'S SHORT-RUN SUPPLY CURVE

The competitive firm that intends to stay in business will maximize profits (or minimize losses) when it produces the output level at which $P = MC$ and variable costs are covered. Therefore, the portion of the firm's short-run marginal cost curve that lies above its average variable cost is the short-run supply curve of the firm.

Exhibit 6 illustrates that as the market price increases, the competitive firm will expand output along its MC curve. If the market price were less than P_1, the firm would shut down immediately because it would be unable to cover even its variable costs. If the market price is P_1, however, a price equal to the firm's average variable cost, the firm may supply output q_1 *in the short run*. Economic losses will result, but the firm would incur similar losses if it shut down completely. As the market price increases to P_2, the firm will happily expand output along its MC curve to q_2. At P_2, price is also equal to average total costs. The firm is making a "normal rate of return," or zero economic profits. Higher prices will result in a still larger short-run output. The firm will supply q_3 units at market price P_3. At this price, economic profits will result. At still higher prices, output will be expanded even more. As long as price exceeds average variable cost, the firm will expand supply along its MC curve, which therefore becomes the firm's short-run supply curve.

THE SHORT-RUN MARKET SUPPLY CURVE

The short-run market supply curve corresponds to the total amount supplied by all of the firms in the industry. For a purely competitive industry, the short-run market supply curve is the horizontal summation of the marginal cost curves (above the level of average variable cost) for all firms in the industry. Since individual firms will supply a larger amount at a higher price, the short-run market supply curve will slope upward to the right.

Exhibit 6 illustrates this relationship. As the price of the product rises from P_1 to P_2 to P_3, the individual firms expand their output along their marginal cost curves. Since the individual competitive firms supply a larger output as the market price increases, the total amount supplied to the market also expands.

EXHIBIT 6

The Supply Curve for the Firm and the Market

When resource prices are constant, the short-run market supply is merely the sum of the supply produced by all the firms in the market area (b).

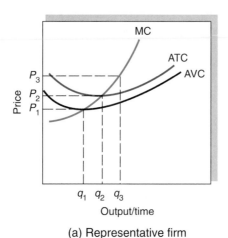

(a) Representative firm

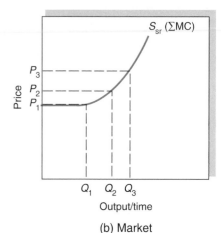

(b) Market

Our construction of the short-run market supply curve assumes that the prices of the resources used by the industry are constant. When the entire industry (rather than just a single firm) expands output, resource prices may rise. If this does happen, the short-run market supply curve (reflecting the higher prices of purchased inputs) will be slightly more inelastic (steeper) than the sum of the supply curves of the individual firms.

The short-run market supply curve, together with the demand curve for the industry's product, will determine the market price. At the short-run equilibrium market price, each of the firms will have expanded output until marginal costs have risen to the market price. They will have no desire to change output, *given their current size of plant.*

OUTPUT ADJUSTMENTS IN THE LONG RUN

In the long run, firms have the opportunity to alter their plant size and enter or exit from an industry. As long-run adjustments are made, output in the whole industry may either expand or contract.

LONG-RUN EQUILIBRIUM

In addition to the balance between quantity supplied and quantity demanded necessary for short-run equilibrium, the firms in a competitive industry must earn the normal rate of return, and only the normal rate, before long-run equilibrium can be attained. If economic profit is present, new firms will enter the industry, and the current producers will have an incentive to expand the scale of their operations. This will lead to an increase in supply, placing downward pressure on prices. In contrast, if firms in the industry are suffering economic losses, they will leave the market. Supply will decline, placing upward pressure on prices.

Therefore, as Exhibit 7 illustrates, when a competitive industry is in long-run equilibrium, (a) the quantity supplied and the quantity demanded will be equal at the market price, and (b) the firms in the industry will be earning normal (zero) economic profit (that is, their minimum ATC will just equal the market price).

EXHIBIT 7

Long-run Equilibrium in a Competitive Market

The two conditions necessary for equilibrium in a competitive market are depicted here. First, quantity supplied and quantity demanded must be equal in the market (b). Second, the firm must earn zero economic profit, that is, the "normal rate of return," at the established market price (a).

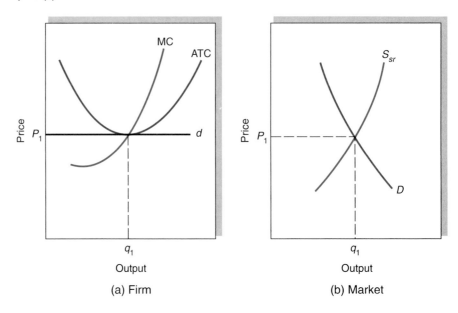

(a) Firm

(b) Market

EXHIBIT 8

How the Market Responds to an Increase in Demand

The introduction of a new candy product that sticks to one's teeth causes the demand for toothpicks to increase to D_2 (frame b). Toothpick prices rise to P_2, inducing firms to expand output. Toothpick firms make short-run profits (frame a), which draw new competitors into the industry. Thus, the toothpick supply expands (shifts from S_1 to S_2). If cost conditions are unchanged, the expansion in supply will continue until the market price of toothpicks has declined to its initial level P_1.

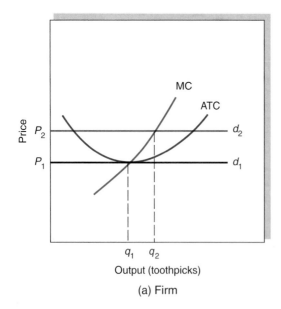

(a) Firm

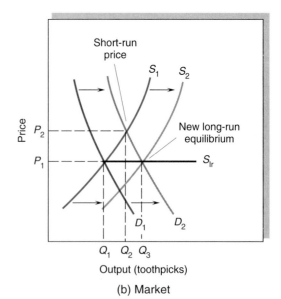

(b) Market

ADJUSTING TO AN EXPANSION IN DEMAND

Suppose a purely competitive market is in equilibrium. What will happen if there is an increase in demand? Exhibit 8 presents an example. An entrepreneur introduces a fantastic new candy product. Consumers go wild over it. However, since it sticks to one's teeth, the market demand for toothpicks increases from D_1 to D_2. The price of toothpicks rises from P_1 to P_2. What impact will the higher market price have on the output level of toothpick-producing firms? It will increase (from q_1 to q_2, Exhibit 8a) as the firms expand output along their marginal cost curves. In the short run, the toothpick producers will make economic profits. The profits will attract new toothpick producers to the industry and cause the existing firms to expand the scale of their plants.[6] Hence, the market supply will increase (shift from S_1 to S_2) and eventually eliminate the short-run profits. If cost conditions are unchanged in the industry, the market price for toothpicks will return to its initial level, even though output has expanded to Q_3.

ADJUSTING TO A DECLINE IN DEMAND

Economic profits attract new firms to an industry. In contrast, economic losses (when they are expected to continue) encourage capital and entrepreneurship to move out of the industry and into other areas where the profitability potential is more favorable. Economic losses mean that the owners of capital in the industry are earning less than the market rate of return. The opportunity cost of continuing in the industry exceeds the gain.

Exhibit 9 illustrates how market forces react to economic losses. Initially, an equilibrium price exists in the industry. The firms are able to cover their average costs of production. Now, suppose there is a reduction in consumer income, causing

---

[6]If the *long-run* average total cost curve results in only one possible minimum-cost output level (see Exhibit 9a of the previous chapter), the expansion in the long-run supply will be generated entirely by the entry of new firms. However, when the long-run average total cost is such that a wide range of minimum-cost output levels is possible (see Exhibit 9b of the previous chapter), both the entry of new firms and expansion by the established firms will contribute to the increase in supply.

EXHIBIT 9

Impact of a Decline in Demand

A reduction in market demand will cause price to fall and short-run losses to occur. The losses will cause some firms to go out of business and others to reduce their scale. In the long run, the market supply will fall, causing the market price to rise. The supply will continue to decline and price will continue to rise until the short-run losses have been eliminated (S_2).

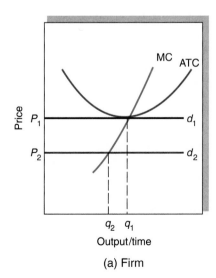

(a) Firm

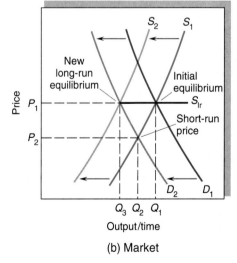

(b) Market

APPLICATIONS IN ECONOMICS

A Shift in Demand—The Impact of a Papal Decree on the Price of Fish[7]

Sometimes changes in institutions, legal restrictions, or regulatory policies influence the demand for a product. The 1966 papal decree lifting the Catholic Church's ban on the eating of meat on Fridays provides an interesting illustration of this point. Prior to the lifting of the ban, most of the nearly 600 million Roman Catholics consumed fish on Fridays. After the decree, many shifted to substitute goods such as beef, pork, and chicken. The demand for fish therefore declined. As our analysis indicates, a decline in demand will lead to a lower market price in the short run.

Economist Frederick Bell of Florida State University estimated the impact of the reduction in demand on the market price of fish in the Northeastern United States, an area where Catholics comprise a large proportion of the total population. As we discussed earlier, changes in personal income and the price of related commodities (beef, pork, and poultry in this case) will influence the demand for a good. Bell utilized statistical techniques to adjust for these factors. This permitted him to isolate the independent effect of the papal decree on the price of fish.

Bell estimated the impact of the decree on the price of seven different species of fish during the period following the decree. As Exhibit 10 shows, his analysis indicates that the price of each variety of fish fell. In the case of large haddock, the price was 21 percent lower after the papal decree than for the 10 years prior to the lifting of the ban. In other instances, the decline in price was smaller. On average, Bell estimates, the price of fish in the Northeastern United States fell by 12.5 percent as the result of the papal decree. Just as economic theory indicates, a reduction in

the market demand for the product to decrease and the market price to decline. At the new, lower price, firms in the industry will not be able to cover their costs of production. In the short run, they will reduce output along their MC curve. This reduction in output by the individual firms results in a reduction in the quantity supplied in the market. For an illustration of demand reduction from a different source, see the Applications in Economics box feature on ''A Shift in Demand— The Impact of a Papal Decree on the Price of Fish.''

In the face of short-run losses, there will be a reduction even in replacement capital into this industry. Some firms will leave the industry as their fixed costs become variable when they are no longer able to cover their variable cost at the prevailing price. Others will reduce the scale of their operations. These factors will cause the industry supply to decline, to shift from S_1 to S_2. What impact will this have on price? It will rise. In the long run, the market supply will decline until the price rises sufficiently to permit ''normal profits'' in the industry.

THE LONG-RUN SUPPLY CURVE

The long-run market supply curve indicates the minimum price at which firms will supply various market output levels, given sufficient time both to adjust plant size (or other fixed factors) and to enter or exit from the industry. The shape of the long-run market supply curve is dependent on what happens to the cost of production as the output of an industry is altered. Three possibilities emerge, although one is far more likely than the other two.

demand for a product leads to a lower price in the short run (see Exhibit 9).

[7]Frederick W. Bell, ''The Pope and The Price of Fish,'' *American Economic Review*, 58 (December 1968), pp. 1346–1350.

EXHIBIT 10 ■ The Papal Decree and the Price of Fish	
The papal decree lifting the ban against the eating of meat on Fridays reduced the demand for fish and resulted in lower prices for fish.	
Species	Percent Change in the Price of Fish after Papal Decree
Sea scallops	−17
Yellowtail flounder	−14
Large haddock	−21
Small haddock (scrod)	−2
Cod	−16
Ocean perch	−10
Whiting	−20
All species (average)	−12.5

Source: F. W. Bell, ''The Pope and the Price of Fish,'' *American Economic Review* (December 1968).

Constant Cost Industry: An industry for which factor prices and costs of production remain constant as market output is expanded. Thus, the long-run market supply curve is horizontal.

If factor prices remain unchanged, the long-run market supply curve will be perfectly elastic. In terms of economics, this describes a **constant cost industry.** Exhibits 8 and 9 both picture constant cost industries. As Exhibit 8 illustrates, an expansion in demand causes prices to increase *temporarily*. The high prices and profits stimulate additional production. The short-run market supply continues to expand (the entire schedule shifts to the right) until the market price returns to its initial level and profits return to their normal level. In the long run, the larger supply will not require a permanent price increase. The *long-run* supply curve (S_{lr}) is thus perfectly elastic. Exhibit 9 illustrates the impact of a decline in demand in a constant cost industry. Again, the long-run supply curve is perfectly elastic, reflecting the basically unchanged cost at the lower rate of industry output.

A constant cost industry is most likely to arise when the industry's demand for resource inputs is quite small relative to the total demand for these resources. For example, since demand of the matches industry for wood, chemicals, and labor is so small relative to the total demand for these resources, doubling the output of matches would exert only a negligible impact on the price of the resources used by the industry. Matches therefore approximate a constant cost industry.

Increasing Cost Industries: Industries for which costs of production rise as the industry output is expanded. Thus, the long-run quantity supplied to the market is directly related to price.

INCREASING COST INDUSTRIES

For most industries, called **increasing cost industries** by economists, an expansion in total output causes a firm's production cost to rise. As the output of an industry increases, demand for resources used by the industry expands. This usually results in higher resource prices, which cause the firm's cost curves to shift upward. For example, an increase in demand for housing places upward pressure on the prices of lumber, roofing, window frames, and construction labor, causing the cost of housing to rise. Similarly, an increase in demand (and market output) for beef may cause the prices of feed grains, hay, and grazing land to rise. Thus, the production costs of beef rise as more of it is produced.

In some industries, additional demand may lead to industrial congestion, which will reduce the efficiency of the industry and cause costs to rise, even though resource prices are constant. For example, as the demand for lobster increases, additional fishermen are attracted to the industry. However, the increase in the number of fishermen combing lobster beds typically leads to congestion, which reduces the catch per hour of individual fishermen. The production cost in the lobster industry therefore rises as output per labor-hour declines.

For an increasing cost industry, an expansion in market demand will bid up resource prices and/or lead to industrial congestion, causing the per unit cost of the firms to rise. As a result, a larger market output will be forthcoming only at a higher price. The long-run market supply curve for the product will therefore slope upward.

Exhibit 11 depicts an increasing cost industry. An expansion in demand causes higher prices and a larger market output. The presence of short-run profit attracts new competitors to the industry, expanding the market output even more. *As the industry expands,* factor prices rise and congestion costs increase. What happens to the firm's cost curves? Both the average and marginal cost curves rise (shift to ATC_2 and MC_2). This increase in production cost necessitates a higher long-run price (P_2). Hence, the long-run supply curve slopes upward to the right.

EXHIBIT 11

Increasing Costs and the Long-run Supply

Most often, higher factor prices and industrial congestion will cause costs to rise as the *market* output increases. For such increasing cost industries, the long-run supply curve (S_{lr}, frame b) will slope upward to the right.

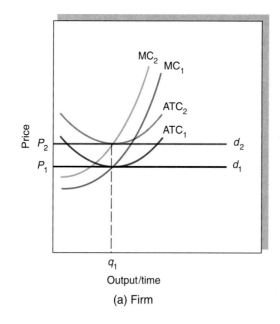

(a) Firm

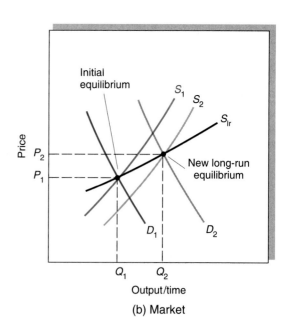

(b) Market

DECREASING COST INDUSTRIES

Decreasing Cost Industries:
Industries for which costs of production decline as the industry expands. The market supply is therefore inversely related to price. Such industries are atypical.

Conceivably, factor prices could decline if the market output of a product were expanded. Since a reduction in factor prices would lead to a lower long-run competitive market price for the product, economists refer to such industries as **decreasing cost industries.** The long-run (but not the short-run) market supply curve for a decreasing cost industry would slope downward to the right. For example, as the electronics industry expands, suppliers of components may be able to adopt large-scale techniques that will lead to lower component prices. If this occurs, the cost curves of the electronics firms may drift downward, causing the industry supply curve for electronics products to slope downward to the right (at least temporarily). However, since expansion of an industry is far more likely to cause rising rather than falling input prices, decreasing cost industries are atypical.

SUPPLY ELASTICITY AND THE ROLE OF TIME

The market supply curve is more elastic in the long run than in the short run because the firm's short-run response is limited by the "fixed" nature of some of its factors. The short- and long-run distinction offers a convenient two-stage analysis, but in the real world there are many intermediate production "runs." Some factors that could not be easily varied in a one-week time period can be varied over a two-week period. Expansion of other factors might require a month, and still others, six months. To be more precise, the cost penalty for quicker availability is greater for some production factors than for others. In any case, a faster expansion usually means that greater cost penalties are necessary to provide for an earlier availability of productive factors.

When a firm has a longer time period to plan output and adjust all of its productive inputs to the desired utilization levels, it will be able to produce any specific rate of output at a lower cost. Because it is less costly to expand output slowly in response to a demand increase, the expansion of output by firms will increase with time, as long as price exceeds cost. Therefore, the elasticity of the market supply curve will be greater when more time is allowed for firms to adjust output.

Exhibit 12 illustrates the impact of time on the response by producers to an increase in price resulting from an expansion in demand. When the price of a product increases from P_1 to P_2, the *immediate* supply response of the firms is small

EXHIBIT 12

Time and the Elasticity of Supply

The elasticity of the market supply curve usually increases as more time is allowed for adjustment to a change in price.

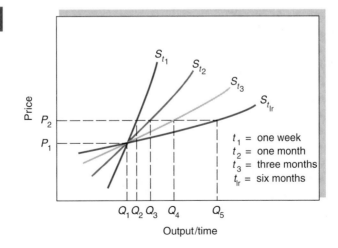

t_1 = one week
t_2 = one month
t_3 = three months
t_{lr} = six months

because it is costly to expand output hastily. After one week, firms are willing to expand output only from Q_1 to Q_2. After one month, due to cost reductions possible because of the longer production planning period, firms are willing to offer Q_3 units at the price P_2. After three months, the rate of output expands to Q_4. In the long run, when it is possible to adjust all inputs to the desired utilization levels (after a six-month time period, for example), firms are willing to supply Q_5 units of output at the market price of P_2. The supply curve for products is typically more elastic over a longer time period than for a shorter period. The length of time necessary to bring about large changes in quantity supplied can vary dramatically across industries. The Applications in Economics box, ''Increasing Milk Supplies— Slowly,'' shows that the adjustment process there takes many years.

APPLICATIONS IN ECONOMICS

Increasing Milk Supplies—Slowly

When milk prices rise and are expected to remain higher, other things equal, dairies will expand their output of milk. They will retain more older cows past their prime—cows that would have been sent to slaughter. New dairy cows will be added to the herd, and more expensive feed rations may be used to boost milk output from each cow in the herd. Research will be conducted to more effectively utilize feed rations, medicines, and other techniques to raise milk output. Genetically advanced cows, capable of producing more milk, will be sought. New firms will enter the dairy business.

Some of these changes will begin immediately. Others, though, especially research efforts and changes in the size and composition of the dairy herd, will take years to complete. Similarly, a decrease in milk production will take many years, if milk prices fall.

Just how slow is the response in the dairy industry? The supply elasticity numbers that follow,

from a study published in 1985 at the University of Wisconsin, indicate that even after 25 years, some of the long-run effects of a milk price increase are felt. A 10 percent increase in the price of milk will, after one year, lead to only a 1.2 percent increase in the quantity of milk supplied. But, after six years, the same price increase would lead to a 12 percent

quantity increase, and after 10 years, the response would be 25 percent. Given 20 years to react, dairies would provide a 50 percent increase in the quantity of milk supplied, in response to the same 10 percent price increase. After 30 years, the response would be greater still. On the dairy farm, at least, changes can take a great deal of time.

EXHIBIT 13 ■ Supply Elasticities for Milk	
Length of Run (Years)	Percent Change in the Quantity of Milk Supplied Due to a 10% Rise in the Price of Milk
1	1.2
3	2.3
6	11.7
10	24.6
15	39.0
20	50.3
25	59.5
30	67.0

Source: Richard Klemme and Jean-Paul Chavas, ''The Effects of Changing Milk Price on Milk Supply and National Dairy Herd Size,'' *Economic Issues,* University of Wisconsin, June 1985.

THE ROLE OF PROFITS IN THE COMPETITIVE MODEL

In the competitive model, profits and losses are signals sent to producers by consumers. Economic profits will be largest in those areas in which consumer wants at the margin are greatest *relative to costs of production*. Profit-seeking entrepreneurs will guide additional resources into these areas. Supply will increase, driving prices down and eliminating the profits. Free entry and the competitive process will protect the consumer from arbitrarily high prices. In the long run, competitive prices will reflect costs of production.

Economic profits result because a firm or entrepreneur increases the value of resources. The successful firm produces a product that is valued more highly (as measured by buyers' willingness to pay for it) than the resources required for its production (as measured by the cost of bidding the resources away from all other users). Losses discipline firms that waste resources producing products that cost more than they are valued by consumers. Losses and bankruptcies are the market mechanism's way of bringing wasteful activities to a halt.

Producers, like other decision-makers, of course, confront uncertainty and dynamic change. Entrepreneurs, at the time they must make investment decisions, cannot be sure of either future market prices or costs of production. They must base their decisions on expectations. Within the framework of the competitive model, however, the reward-penalty system is clear. Firms that efficiently produce and correctly anticipate the products and services for which future demand will be most urgent (relative to production cost) will make economic profits. Those that are inefficient and incorrectly allocate resources into areas of weak future demand will be penalized with losses.

A look at the market for videotape rental business shows how profits are a powerful—but temporary and potentially treacherous—lure for new entrants, when entry barriers are low.[8] In 1982, videotape rental stores were new and there were only an estimated 5,000 stores in the United States. They could charge $5 and more per 24-hour rental. The availability of rentals and the falling prices of home video players meant that profits could at times reach 80 percent of rental revenues. More importantly, *expected* profits were very high. This optimism led to the rapid entry of many new stores which increased competition and forced prices down. By 1990, there were about 25,000 stores. Prices had fallen dramatically. Even new releases were typically renting for $1.99, and most videos rented for even less. At times, video rental supply expanded faster than the demand for rentals, and some of the firms had to leave the business. Even for those who were efficient and stayed in the business, profits were slim. Consumers, however, benefitted tremendously from the highly competitive nature of the video rental business.

EFFICIENCY AND THE COMPETITIVE MODEL

Economists often seem to be enchanted by the purely competitive model. They sometimes use it as the standard by which to judge other models. What accounts for the special significance of pure competition? Most economists agree that under

---

[8]The facts in this example are taken from Tim Tregarthen, "Supply, Demand, and Videotape," *The Margin,* 6 (September/October, 1990), p. 29.

rather restrictive assumptions resource allocation within the purely competitive model is ideal from society's viewpoint. In what sense can we say that it is "ideal"?

PRODUCTION EFFICIENCY (P = ATC)

In the long run, competition forces firms to minimize their average total cost of production and to charge a price just sufficient to cover production costs. Competitive firms must use production methods that minimize costs if they are going to survive. In addition, they must choose a scale of operation that minimizes their long-run average total cost of production. Consumers of competitively produced goods will benefit, since they will receive the largest quantity at the lowest possible price, given the prevailing cost conditions. Competitive markets will eliminate waste and production inefficiency. Inefficient, high-cost producers will confront economic losses and be driven from a competitive industry.

ALLOCATIVE EFFICIENCY (P = MC)

Allocative efficiency refers to the balance achieved by the allocation of available resources to the production of goods and services most desired by consumers, given their incomes. Allocative efficiency is present when all markets are in long-run competitive equilibrium. Each good is produced as long as consumers value it more than the alternative goods that might be produced with the same resources.

OUTSTANDING ECONOMIST

Friedrich A. von Hayek (1899–   )

For six decades, Professor Hayek has been a consistent eloquent defender of classical liberalism, even when most of the world was moving toward central planning and big government. Born in Vienna, Hayek was a lecturer in Austria during the 1920s. In 1931,

he accepted a professorship of economics at the London School of Economics. After the Second World War, he joined the faculty of the University of Chicago, where he taught for many years.

Hayek has made important contributions in areas as diverse as monetary theory, markets and knowledge, capital theory, and the theory of business cycles. In 1974, he was the joint recipient (along with Gunnar Myrdal) of the Nobel Prize in economics.

Hayek believes that the competitive process is far more important than the perfect competition which so often preoccupies economists. According to Hayek, competition is a process that "creates the views people have about what is best and cheapest." In the absence of entry barriers created by government, the competitive process will drive prices down to the level of production costs. "The practical lesson of all this," Hayek states,

"is that we should worry much less about whether competition in a given case is perfect and worry much more whether there is competition at all."[9]

Hayek is much more than an economist—he is a social critic, philosopher, political theorist, and scholar. In the 1970s, he published the three volumes of *Law, Legislation, and Liberty,* in which he articulates his views on the importance of rules over discretionary authority, the interrelationship of economic and political freedom, and the illusory concept of social justice.

Nearing the age of 90 in 1988, he published *The Fatal Conceit,* his manifesto on the "errors of socialism." In the tradition of Hayek, it is both scholarly and in some respects controversial.

[9]Friedrich A. Hayek, *Individualism and Economic Order* (Chicago: University of Chicago Press, 1948), pp. 105–106.

Allocative Efficiency:
The allocation of resources to the production of goods and services most desired by consumers. The allocation is ''balanced'' in such a way that reallocation of resources could not benefit anyone without hurting someone else.

Conversely, no unit of the good is produced if a more valuable alternative must be forgone. Therefore, no reallocation of resources toward production of different goods—or different combinations of goods—could benefit any one person without simultaneously hurting someone else.

The profit-maximization rule ($P = MC$) assures allocative efficiency within the competitive model. The market demand (price) reflects consumers' valuation of an additional unit of a good. The seller's marginal cost indicates the value of the resources (in their alternative uses) necessary to produce an additional unit of the good. When the production of each good is expanded so long as price exceeds marginal cost, each good will be produced if, and only if, consumers value it more than the alternatives that might have been produced. In purely competitive markets, therefore, profit-maximizing producers will be led to produce the combination of goods most desired by consumers.

PURE COMPETITION AND THE REAL WORLD

In the purely competitive model, the ''invisible hand'' that Adam Smith spoke of does its job very well indeed. Producers who are motivated purely by the desire to make a profit act no differently than they would if they cared only about the efficient satisfaction of consumers' desires. Because of the resulting price structure, even the desire of a very selfish consumer for a consumption item is balanced against the value of the good (and the resources embodied within it) to other people. In other words, prevailing prices provide each person with the information and incentive to heed the wishes of others. An incredibly complex array of consumer desires, production possibilities, and resource availabilities can be optimally coordinated in the model. No central person or group need know or understand all the aspects of the model. A few market prices condense the needed information and convey it to each decision-maker.

However, remember that pure competition is a hypothetical model. Even though it predicts fairly well in many circumstances, it ignores some important features of real markets. First, in many industries, the production costs of large firms are less than those of small firms, due to economies of scale. Under these circumstances, it may not be economical to have the industry's output divided among a large number of small producers.

Second, the preferences of consumers differ widely with regard to product design, quality, and location of purchase. Sometimes consumers want variety rather than the homogeneous products implied by the purely competitive model.

Third, we live in a dynamic world. Frequent changes in knowledge and technology bring about a continual parade of new products that are better, or cheaper, or both. Surprises are normal. Profit seeking behavior, where firms take those actions for which they expect added revenues to exceed costs, replaces the neat and tidy profit maximization of the economic model. Although the model often accurately predicts the directions of change, adjustments take time, and the expectations of decision-makers are frequently disappointed. In the real world we often observe disequilibrium, rather than the stable equilibrium of the purely competitive model.

Fourth, competition in the sense of rivalry is multidimensional. Pure competition features only one dimension—price. But product quality, producer reliability, convenience, location of service, and other competitive factors are important in the real world.

LOOKING AHEAD

Pure competition is important because it can help us understand real-world markets characterized by low barriers to entry and a substantial number of independent sellers. At the opposite end of the spectrum lie markets characterized by high barriers to entry and a single seller. The following chapter focuses on the hypothetical model developed by economists to analyze markets of this type—pure monopoly.

CHAPTER SUMMARY

1. Competition as a process should not be confused with pure competition, a model of industrial structure. Competition as a process implies rivalry and entrepreneurial behavior. Rival firms use quality, style, location, advertising, and price to attract consumers. Pure competition, on the other hand, is a model of industrial structure that assumes the presence of a large number of small (relative to the total market) firms, each producing a homogeneous product in a market for which there is complete freedom of entry and exit.

2. The competitive process places producers under strong pressure to operate efficiently and heed the views of consumers. Those who do not offer quality goods at economical prices lose customers to rivals. As Adam Smith recognized long ago, self-interest is a powerful motivator of human beings. If it is bridled by competition, self-interest leads to economic cooperation and productive effort.

3. Under pure competition, firms are price takers—they face a perfectly elastic demand curve. Profit-maximizing (or loss-minimizing) firms will expand output as long as the additional output adds more to revenues than to costs. Therefore, the competitive firm will produce the output level at which marginal revenue (and price) equals marginal cost.

4. The firm's short-run marginal cost curve (above its average variable cost) is its supply curve. Under pure competition, the short-run *market* supply curve is the horizontal sum of the marginal cost curves (when MC is above AVC) for all firms in the industry.

5. If a firm (a) is covering its average variable cost and (b) anticipates that the price is only temporarily below average total cost, it may operate in the short run even though it is experiencing a loss. However, even if it anticipates more favorable market conditions in the future, loss minimization will require the firm to shut down if it is unable to cover its average variable cost. If the firm does not anticipate that it will be able to cover its average total cost even in the long run, loss minimization requires that it immediately go out of business (even if it is covering its average *variable* cost) so that it can at least avoid its fixed cost.

6. When price exceeds average total cost, a firm will make economic profits. Under pure competition, profits will attract new firms into the industry and stimulate the existing firms to expand. The market supply will increase, pushing price down to the level of average total cost. Competitive firms will be unable to make long-run economic profits.

7. Losses exist when the market price is less than the firm's average total cost. Losses will cause firms to leave the industry or reduce the scale of their operations. Market supply will decline until price rises sufficiently for firms to earn normal (that is, zero economic) profits.

8. As the output of an industry expands, marginal costs will increase in the short run, causing the short-run market supply curve to slope upward to the right. If the prices of resources purchased by the industry remain unchanged, as the market output is expanded, the long-run supply curve will be perfectly elastic. However, as the output of an industry expands, rising factor prices and industrial congestion will normally cause the firm's costs to increase. The long-run market supply curve for such an increasing cost industry will slope upward to the right.

9. Within the framework of the purely competitive model, firms that efficiently produce and correctly anticipate those goods for which future demand will be most urgent

(relative to costs of production) will make profits. Firms that inefficiently produce and incorrectly allocate resources to the production of goods for which future demand turns out to be weak (relative to costs of production) will be penalized with losses. In the short run, firms might make either profits or losses, but in the long run, competitive pressures will eliminate economic profits (and losses).

10. Economists often argue that pure competition leads to ideal economic efficiency because (a) average costs of production are minimized and (b) output is expanded to the level at which the consumer's evaluation of an additional unit of a good is just equal to its marginal cost.

CRITICAL ANALYSIS QUESTIONS

*1. Farmers are often heard to complain about the high cost of machinery, labor, and fertilizer, suggesting that these costs drive down their profit rate. Does it follow that if, for example, the price of fertilizer fell by 10 percent, farming (a highly competitive industry with low barriers to entry) would be more profitable? Explain.

*2. If the firms in a competitive industry are making short-run profits, what will happen to the market price in the long run? Explain.

3. What factors will cause the supply curve for a product to slope upward in the long run? Be specific.

4. A sales tax collected from the seller will shift the firm's cost curves upward. Outline the impact of a sales tax within the framework of the competitive model. Use diagrams to indicate both the short-run and long-run impact of the tax. Who will bear the burden of the sales tax?

5. "In the model of perfect competition, there is no room for the entrepreneur." How would you defend this position? Is it always true? Is it true in equilibrium?

*6. "In long-run equilibrium for a competitive industry, the firms in the industry are just able to cover their cost of production. Economic profit is zero. Therefore, if there were a reduction in demand causing prices to go down even a little bit, all of the firms in the industry would be driven out of business." Evaluate.

7. "Under pure competition, the average total cost of production determines the price of each good." True or false?

*8. Within the framework of the pure competition model, how will an unanticipated increase in demand for a product affect each of the following in a market that was initially in long-run equilibrium?
   a. the short-run market price of the product.
   b. industry output in the short run.
   c. profitability in the short run.
   d. the long-run market price in the industry.
   e. industry output in the long run.
   f. profitability in the long run.

*9. Suppose that the development of a new drought-resistant hybrid seed corn leads to a 50 percent increase in the average yield per acre without increasing the cost to the farmers who use the new technology. If the conditions in the corn production industry are approximated by the pure competition model, what will happen to the following:
   a. the price of corn.
   b. the profitability of corn farmers who quickly adopt the new technology.
   c. the profitability of corn farmers who are slow to adopt the new technology.
   d. the price of soybeans, a substitute product for corn.

10. Indicate whether the following statements are true or false:
   a. "If the demand for a product is inelastic, a technological change that reduces the production cost of the good will lead to a reduction in the expenditures on the good."

*Asterisk denotes questions for which answers are given in Appendix C, Selected Answers.

    b. "If the demand for a product is inelastic, a reduction in the good's cost of production will reduce the total utility derived from the good."

*11. Explain why the firms in a highly competitive industry are unable to earn long-term economic profit. Since long-run economic profit in a competitive industry is absent, does it follow that profits and losses are unimportant in industries that are competitive? Why or why not?

12. "In a competitive market, if a business operator produces efficiently—that is, if the cost of producing the good is minimized—the operator will be able to make at least a normal profit." True or false?

13. During the summer of 1988, drought conditions throughout much of the United States substantially reduced the size of the corn, wheat, and soybean crops, three commodities for which demand is inelastic. Use the competitive model to determine how the drought affected (a) grain prices, (b) revenue from the three crops, and (c) the profitability of farming.

*14. Suppose that the government of a large city levies a 5 percent sales tax on hotel rooms. How will the tax affect (a) prices of hotel rooms, (b) the profits of hotel owners, and (c) gross (including the tax) expenditures on hotel rooms.

15. Explain why the market supply curve is slightly less elastic than the summation of the marginal cost curves for the firms in a competitive industry.

*16. "Competition is never between the buyer and the seller. It is always between a seller and other sellers (both actual and potential) and a buyer and other buyers (both actual and potential)." True or false?

*17. The following table presents the expected cost and revenue data for the Tucker Tomato Farm. The Tuckers produce tomatoes in a greenhouse and sell them wholesale in a purely competitive market. (a) Fill in the firm's marginal cost, average variable cost, average total cost, and profit schedules. (b) If the Tuckers are profit maximizers, how many tomatoes should they produce when the market price is $500 per ton? Indicate their profits. (c) Indicate the firm's output level and maximum profit if the market price of tomatoes increases to $550 per ton. (d) How many units would the Tucker Tomato Farm produce if the price of tomatoes declined to $450? Indicate the firm's profits. Should the firm continue in business? Explain.

Cost and Revenue Schedules—Tucker Tomato Farm, Inc.

Output (Tons per Month)	Total Cost	Price per Ton	Marginal Cost	Average Variable Cost	Average Total Cost	Profits (Monthly)
0	$1000	$500	—	—	—	—
1	1200	500	_____	_____	_____	_____
2	1350	500	_____	_____	_____	_____
3	1550	500	_____	_____	_____	_____
4	1900	500	_____	_____	_____	_____
5	2300	500	_____	_____	_____	_____
6	2750	500	_____	_____	_____	_____
7	3250	500	_____	_____	_____	_____
8	3800	500	_____	_____	_____	_____
9	4400	500	_____	_____	_____	_____
10	5150	500	_____	_____	_____	_____

20 Monopoly and High Barriers to Entry

Monopoly affords the consumer little protection against exorbitant prices.[1]

Walter Adams, 1971

CHAPTER FOCUS

- What, exactly, is a monopoly? What are the barriers that allow monopoly to exist?
- What price will a monopolist set?
- Why is monopoly a problem?
- What are the reasons for trying to regulate monopolies? What problems occur when we do regulate monopolies?
- In dealing with monopoly, what are the policy alternatives, and what can we expect from each one?
- What impact does dynamic change have on the monopoly power of a business?

*I*n the last chapter, we analyzed pure competition, a hypothetical market structure characterized by numerous sellers. We now turn to the other extreme of market structure—pure monopoly. The word "monopoly," derived from two Greek words, means "single seller." When only a single seller for a product exists, the firm will exert more control over price and output. This does not mean that a monopolist is completely free from competitive pressures. Consumers are not forced to buy from any business firm, including those with monopoly power. Thus, even a monopolist must compete with other sellers of goods and services for the dollar votes of consumers.

However, the presence of substantial entry barriers and the absence of direct rivals producing close substitutes does influence both decision-making within the firm and the operation of markets. When barriers to entry are high, what price will a monopolist charge? How does the presence of monopoly influence the efficiency of a market? Can government regulation promote economic efficiency when monopoly is present? This chapter focuses on these questions and related issues.

DEFINING MONOPOLY

Monopoly: A market structure characterized by a single seller of a well-defined product for which there are no good substitutes and by high barriers to the entry of any other firms into the market for that product.

We will define **monopoly** as a market structure characterized by (a) high barriers to entry and (b) a single seller of a well-defined product for which there are no good substitutes. Even this definition is ambiguous because "high barriers" and "good substitutes" are both relative terms. Are the barriers to entry into the automobile or steel industries high? Many observers would argue that they are. After all, it would take a great deal of financial capital to compete successfully in these industries. However, there are no *legal* restraints that prevent an entrepreneur from producing automobiles or steel. If price is well above cost, so that substantial profits are being made, it should not be difficult to find the necessary investment capital. After all, even a tiny portion of the investors who make up the capital market would be enough to finance a full-scale steel plant, for example. And profit, it seems, draws investment capital the way honey draws bears. Then again, would the new factory, perhaps one making cars, require a new and extensive marketing network? Or could other sales outlets be enticed into carrying the new competitor? Barriers to entry are like expected profits: in both cases, assessing their size requires subjective judgments.

"Good substitutes" is also a subjective term. There is always some substitutability among products, even those produced by a monopolist. Is a letter a good substitute for telephone communication? For some purposes, legal correspondence for example, a letter is a very good substitute. In other cases, when the speed of communication and immediacy of response are important, telephone communication has a tremendous advantage over letter writing. Are there any good substitutes for electricity? Most of the known substitutes for electric lighting (candles, oil lamps, and battery lights, for example) are inferior to electric lights. Natural gas, fuel oil, and wood, though, are often excellent substitutes for electric heating.

---

[1]Walter Adams, *The Structure of American Industry, 4e,* (New York: Macmillan Co., 1971), p. 460.

Monopoly, then, is always a matter of degree. Pure monopoly, like pure competition, is a rare phenomenon. Nevertheless, there are two reasons why it is important to understand how markets work under pure monopoly. First, the monopoly model will help us understand markets in which there are few sellers and little active rivalry. When there are only two or three producers in a market, rather than competing with each other, they may seek to collude and thus together behave like a monopoly. Second, in a few important industries there is usually only a single producer. Local telephone and electricity services provide examples. The monopoly model will illuminate the operation of such markets.

BARRIERS TO ENTRY

What makes it difficult for potential competitors to enter a market? Four factors are of particular importance.

1. Economies of Scale. In some industries, firms experience declining average total costs over the full range of output that consumers are willing to buy. When this is the case, larger firms, relative to the total market, will have lower unit costs. Since small firms have high per unit costs, they will be unable to enter the market, build a reputation, and compete effectively with larger firms. Under these circumstances, a single firm will tend to emerge from the competitive process in the industry, and the cost advantage resulting from its size will provide the firm with protection from potential rivals.

2. Government Licensing. Legal barriers are the oldest and most effective method of protecting a business firm from potential competitors. Kings once granted exclusive business rights to favored citizens or groups. Today, governments continue to establish barriers, restricting the right to buy and sell goods. To compete in the communications industry in the United States (for example, in order to operate a radio or television station), one must obtain a government franchise. The Post Office, a corporation formed by government, is granted the exclusive right to deliver first-class mail, although this is sometimes challenged. Potential private competitors are eliminated by law. Local governments generally grant exclusive franchises to public utilities in most areas of the United States.

Licensing, a process by which one obtains permission from the government to enter a specific occupation or business, often limits entry. In many states, a person must obtain a license before operating a liquor store, barbershop, taxicab, funeral home, or drugstore. Sometimes, these licenses cost little and are designed to ensure certain minimum standards. In other cases, they are expensive and designed primarily to limit competition.

Patent: The grant of an exclusive right to use a specific process or produce a specific product for a period of time (17 years in the United States).

3. Patents. Most countries have established patent laws designed to provide inventors with a property right to their inventions. Patent laws grant the owner a legal monopoly on the commercial use of a newly invented product or process for a limited period of time, 17 years in the United States. Once a patent is granted, other persons are prevented from producing the product or using the procedure unless they obtain permission from the patent holder. Costs, as well as benefits, accompany a patent system. As we will soon illustrate, the monopoly created by the grant of a patent generally leads to higher prices for consumers. On the positive side, however, patents encourage scientific research and technological improvements since they help inventors reap the benefits of their inventions. Patent laws increase the incentive of individuals and firms to invest the time and money that is often involved in the discovery and development of improved products and machines. If other firms could merely copy new products and techniques, there would be less incentive to develop them. Without patents, the pace of technological development would be slowed.

4. Control over an Essential Resource.   If a single firm has sole control over a resource essential for entry into an industry, it can eliminate potential competitors. An example often cited is the Aluminum Company of America, which before the Second World War controlled the known supply of bauxite conveniently available to American firms. Without this critical raw material, potential competitors could not produce aluminum. With time, however, other supplies of bauxite were found, and this source of monopoly was lost to the company.

New technology, mineral exploration, and other ways to exploit profitable situations are always sought. Over time, they are usually found. Nevertheless, let us move on to see what happens when at least a temporary monopoly is gained.

THE HYPOTHETICAL MODEL OF MONOPOLY

Suppose you invent, patent, and produce a microwave device that locks the hammer of any firearm in the immediate area. This fabulous invention can be used to immobilize potential robbers or hijackers. Since you own the exclusive patent right to the device, you are not concerned about a competitive supplier in the foreseeable future. Although other products are competitive with your invention, they are poor substitutes. In short, you are a monopolist.

What price should you charge for your product? Like the purely competitive firm, you will want to expand output as long as marginal revenue exceeds marginal cost. Unlike the purely competitive firm, however, you will face a downward-sloping demand curve. Since you are the only firm in the industry, the industry demand curve will coincide with your demand curve. Consumers will buy less of your product at a higher price. At high prices, even a monopolist will have few customers.

TOTAL REVENUE, MARGINAL REVENUE, AND ELASTICITY OF DEMAND

Since the demand curve of a monopolist slopes downward, there are two conflicting influences on total revenue when the seller reduces price in order to expand output and sales. As Exhibit 1 illustrates, the resultant increase in sales (from q_1 to q_2) will, by itself, add to the revenue of the monopolist. But since the price reduction also applies to units that *would have been* sold at a higher price (P_1, rather than the lower price P_2) this factor by itself would cause a *reduction* in total revenue for the monopolist. Together, the higher quantity and the lower price produce a change in total revenue (the marginal revenue associated with the added sales) that is smaller than the price at which the added units are sold.

The marginal revenue derived from additional sales by a monopolist will be less than the sales price. Thus, as shown in Exhibit 1, the marginal revenue curve of the monopolist will lie inside (below) the demand curve of the firm.[2]

---

[2]For a straight-line demand curve, the marginal revenue curve will bisect any line parallel to the *x*-axis. For example, the MR curve will divide the line P_2F into two equal parts, P_2E and *EF*.

EXHIBIT 1

The Effect of Increases in Sales on Revenue

When a firm faces a downward-sloping demand curve, a price reduction that increases sales will exert two conflicting influences on total revenue. First, total revenue will rise because of an increase in the number of units sold (from q_1 to q_2). However, revenue losses from the lower price (P_2) on units that could have been sold at a higher price (P_1) will at least partially offset the additional revenues due to increased sales. Therefore, the marginal revenue curve will lie inside the firm's demand curve.

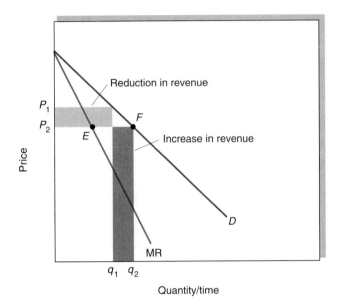

While the demand curve shows the number of units that can be sold at different prices, it also reveals how revenues vary as price and output are altered. Using a straight-line demand curve, Exhibit 2 illustrates how total and marginal revenue are related to elasticity of demand. At very high prices, the sales of the monopolist will be small and demand will tend to be elastic. As price is reduced and output is expanded on the elastic portion of the monopolist's demand curve, total revenue will rise. Marginal revenue will be positive. Suppose the monopolist charged $15 for a product and sold 25 units, yielding a total revenue of $375. If the monopolist cut the price to $10, sales would expand to 50 units. Total revenue would rise to $500. A price reduction from $15 to $10 would thus increase the total revenue of the monopolist.

Consider the output rate at which elasticity of demand is equal to unity. At that point, total revenue reaches its maximum. Marginal revenue is equal to zero. As price falls below $10 into the inelastic portion of the monopolist's demand curve, total revenue declines as output is expanded. For this range of price and output, marginal revenue will be negative. Thus, marginal revenue goes from positive to negative as the elasticity of demand changes from elastic to inelastic (at output 50 in Exhibit 2).

This analysis has clear implications. For a monopolist operating on the inelastic portion of its demand curve, a price increase would lead to more total revenue *and* less total cost (since fewer units would be produced and sold). Because of this, we would never expect a profit-maximizing monopolist to push the sales of a product into the range in which the product's demand curve becomes inelastic.

THE PROFIT-MAXIMIZING OUTPUT

Both costs and revenues must be considered when we analyze the profit-maximizing decision rule for the monopolist. The profit-maximizing monopolist will continue expanding output until marginal revenue equals marginal cost. The price at which that output level can be sold is given by the demand curve of the monopolist.

EXHIBIT 2

Price, Total Revenue, and Marginal Revenue of a Monopolist

In the elastic portion of the monopolist's demand curve (prices greater than $10), a price reduction will be associated with rising total revenue (frame b) and positive marginal revenue. At unitary elasticity (output of 50 units), total revenue will reach a maximum. When the monopolist's demand curve is inelastic (output beyond 50 units), lower prices will lead to declining total revenue and negative marginal revenue.

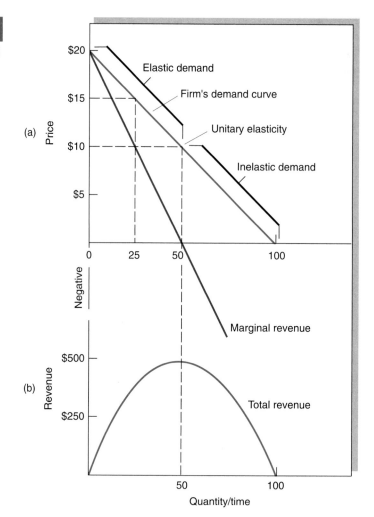

Exhibit 3 provides a graphic illustration of profit maximization. The monopolist will continue to expand output as long as marginal revenue exceeds marginal cost. Therefore, output will be expanded to *Q,* where MR = MC. The monopolist will be able to sell the profit-maximizing output *Q* for a price indicated by the height of the demand curve. At any output less than *Q,* the benefits (marginal revenue) of producing the *additional* units will exceed their costs. The monopolist will gain by expanding output. For any output greater than *Q,* the monopolist's costs of producing *additional* units will be greater than the benefits (marginal revenue). Production of such units will reduce profits.

Exhibit 3 also depicts the profits of a monopolist. At output *Q,* the monopolist would charge price *P.* Price times the number of units sold yields the firm's total revenue *(PAQO).* The firm's total cost would be *CBQO,* the average per unit cost multiplied by the number of units sold. The firm's profits are merely total revenue less total cost, the shaded area of Exhibit 3.

Even though competitive and monopolistic firms alike expand output until MR = MC, there is one important difference. For the competitive firm, price is

EXHIBIT 3

The Short-Run Price and Output of a Monopolist

The monopolist will reduce price and expand output as long as MR exceeds MC. Output Q will result. When price exceeds average cost at any output level, profit will accrue at that output level.

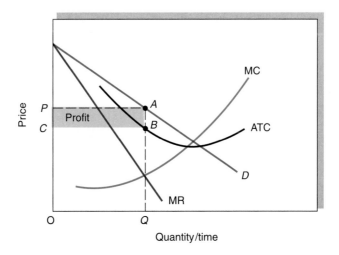

always equal to marginal revenue, so that price will also equal marginal cost when profit is maximized. For the monopolist, however, price is always greater than marginal revenue, so that when profit is maximized and MR = MC, price will exceed marginal cost. This difference has implications for efficiency in the market, which we will discuss later in this chapter.

Exhibit 4 provides a numeric illustration of profit-maximizing decision-making. At low output rates, marginal revenue exceeds marginal cost. The monopolist will continue expanding output as long as MR is greater than MC. Thus, an output rate of eight units per day will be chosen. Given the demand for the product, the monopolist can sell eight units at a price of $17.25 each. Total revenue will be $138, compared to a total cost of $108.50. The monopolist will make a profit

EXHIBIT 4 ■ Profit Maximization for a Monopolist

Rate of Output (per Day) (1)	Price (per Unit) (2)	Total Revenue (1) × (2) (3)	Total Cost (per Day) (4)	Profit (3) − (4) (5)	Marginal Cost (6)	Marginal Revenue (7)
0	—	—	$ 50.00	$−50.00	—	—
1	$25.00	$ 25.00	60.00	−35.00	$10.00	$ 25.00
2	24.00	48.00	69.00	−21.00	9.00	23.00
3	23.00	69.00	77.00	−8.00	8.00	21.00
4	22.00	88.00	84.00	4.00	7.00	19.00
5	21.00	105.00	90.50	14.50	6.50	17.00
6	19.75	118.50	96.75	21.75	6.25	13.50
7	18.50	129.50	102.75	26.75	6.00	11.00
8	17.25	138.00	108.50	29.50	5.75	8.50
9	16.00	144.00	114.75	29.25	6.25	6.00
10	14.75	147.50	121.25	26.25	6.50	3.50
11	13.50	148.50	128.00	20.50	6.75	1.00
12	12.25	147.00	135.00	12.00	7.00	−1.50
13	11.00	143.00	142.25	.75	7.25	−4.00

of $29.50. The profit rate will be smaller at all other output rates. For example, if the monopolist reduces the price to $16 in order to sell nine units per day, revenue will increase by $6. However, the marginal cost of producing the ninth unit is $6.25. Since the cost of producing the ninth unit is greater than the revenue it brings in, profits will decline.

MARKET FORCES AND THE MONOPOLIST

High barriers to entry insulate monopolists from direct competition with rival firms producing a similar product. In contrast with competitive markets, in a monopolized industry profits will not attract—at least not quickly—rivals who will expand supply, cut prices, and spoil the market. Protected by high entry barriers, a monopolist may be able to earn profit, even in the long run.

Does this mean that monopolists can charge as high a price as they want? Monopolists are often charged with price gouging. In evaluating this charge, however, it is important to recognize that, like other sellers, monopolists will seek to maximize *profit,* not *price*. Consumers will buy less as price increases. Thus, a higher price is not always best for monopolists. Exhibit 4 illustrates this point. What would happen to the profit of the monopolist if price was increased from $17.25 to $18.50? At the higher price, only seven units will be sold and total revenue will equal $129.50. The cost of producing seven units will be $102.75. Thus, when price is $18.50 and output seven, profit is only $26.75, less than could be attained at the lower price ($17.25) and larger output (eight). The highest price is not always the best price for the monopolist. Sometimes a price reduction will increase the firm's total revenue more than its total cost.

Will a monopolist always be able to make economic profit? The profitability of a monopolist is limited by the demand for the product that it produces. In some cases, even a monopolist may be unable to sell for a profit. For example, there are thousands of clever, patented items that are never produced because demand-cost conditions are not favorable. Exhibit 5 illustrates this possibility. When the average cost curve of a monopolist is always above its demand curve, economic losses will result. Even a monopolist will not want to operate under these conditions. If market conditions are expected to improve, the monopolist will produce output Q (at which $MR = MC$) and charge price P, *operating in the short run* as long as variable cost can be covered. If the loss-producing conditions persist, however, the monopolist will discontinue production.

REALITY AND THE MONOPOLY MODEL

Price Searcher: A seller with imperfect information, facing a downward sloping demand curve, who tries to find the price that maximizes profit.

Thus far, we have proceeded as if monopolists always knew exactly what their revenue and cost curves looked like. Of course, this is not true in the real world. A monopolist cannot be sure of the demand conditions for a product. Demand curves frequently shift, and choices must be made without the benefit of perfect knowledge.

The monopolist is, in fact, a **price searcher;** a seller trying to find the price at which profit will be maximized. How many sales will be lost if the price is raised? How many sales will be added if the price is lowered? Trial and error are often necessary to learn the answers. A firm that is a price searcher will price its product on the basis of what it *expects* to happen if the price is changed.

The revenue and cost data illustrated in Exhibits 3, 4, and 5 might be thought of as representing *expected* revenues and costs associated with various output levels.

EXHIBIT 5

When a Monopolist
Incurs Losses

Even a monopolist will incur
short-run losses if the average
total cost curve lies above the
demand curve.

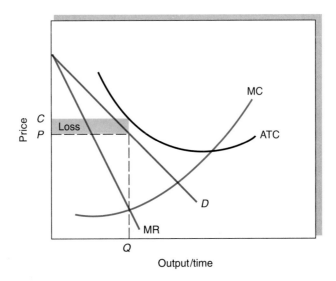

A monopolist, of course, seldom calculates what we have called demand, marginal revenue, and cost curves. Even so, the same questions are asked: Would a lower price add more to revenue than to cost? Would a higher price decrease revenue more than cost? The profit-maximizing price is usually just approximated. However, the monopolist who *is* maximizing profits acts *as if* MR and MC had been calculated, so our model of monopoly shows what a profit-maximizing monopolist is trying to do.

DEFECTS AND PROBLEMS OF MONOPOLY

Monopolists, by keeping the market constantly understocked, by never fully supplying the effectual demand, sell their commodities much above the natural price, and raise their emoluments, whether they consist of wages or profit, greatly above their natural rate.[3]

Adam Smith, 1776

What types of problems arise under monopoly? Can public policy improve resource allocation in markets characterized by monopoly?

FOUR DEFECTS OF MONOPOLY

From Adam Smith's time to the present, economists have generally considered monopoly a necessary evil at best. There are four major reasons for this view.

1. Monopoly Severely Limits the Options Available to Consumers. If you do not like the food at a local restaurant, you can go to another restaurant. If you do not like the wares of a local department store, you can buy good substitutes somewhere

[3]Adam Smith, *An Inquiry into the Nature and Causes of the Wealth of Nations* (1776; Cannan's ed., Chicago: University of Chicago Press, 1976), p. 69.

else. The competition of rivals protects the consumer from the arbitrary behavior of a single seller. What, though, are your alternatives if you do not like the *local* telephone service? You can send a letter or deliver your message in person, or you can write to your legislative representative and complain. These are not always satisfactory alternatives to the service of the monopolist, however. If the monopolist "pushes you around," you often have no feasible alternative but to accept poor service, rude treatment, or high prices.

In the absence of monopoly, the consumer can buy a product either from firm A or from a competitor. In the presence of monopoly, the option is to buy from the monopolist or do without. This reduction in the options available to the consumer greatly reduces the consumer's ability to discipline monopolists.

2. Monopoly Results in Allocative Inefficiency.   Allocative efficiency requires that an activity be undertaken when it generates additional benefits that exceed its added costs. This requires that a firm expand output as long as price exceeds marginal cost. A profit-maximizing monopolist, however, would restrict output below this level. The monopolist will expand output only to the point where marginal revenue is equal to marginal cost, an output rate less than that at which price is equal to marginal cost.

The logic of this criticism is pictured in Exhibit 6. Demand is a measure of the degree to which consumers value additional units of a product. The marginal cost curve represents the opportunity cost of the resources used to produce the additional units. Ideally, economic efficiency would require output to be expanded as long as the height of the demand curve exceeded that of the marginal cost curve. From the viewpoint of the entire community, output level Q_i would be best.

The monopolist, however, would produce only Q_m units, the profit-maximizing output rate. If output were expanded beyond Q_m to Q_i, how much would consumers

EXHIBIT 6

Under-stocking in the Market

A monopolist will produce only output Q_m, even though Q_i is best for the entire community. If output were expanded from Q_m to Q_i, the benefits *to the community* would exceed the costs by *ABC*. However, since the profit of the monopolist is maximized at Q_m, units beyond Q_m will not be produced. What is best for the monopolist (output Q_m) conflicts with what is best for the community (output Q_i).

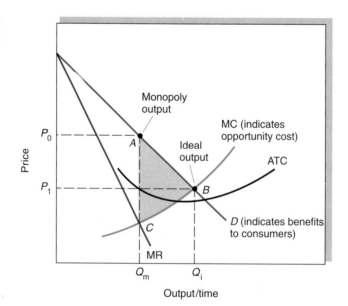

"And though in 1969, as in previous years, your company had to contend with spiralling labor costs, exorbitant interest rates, and unconscionable government interference, management was able once more, through a combination of deceptive marketing practices, false advertising, and price fixing, to show a profit which, in all modesty, can only be called excessive."

Drawing by Lorenz © 1970 The New Yorker Magazine, Inc.

gain? The area under the demand curve, ABQ_iQ_m, reveals the answer. How much would it cost the monopolist to produce these units? CBQ_iQ_m reflects the monopolist's costs. The benefits of expanding output from Q_m to Q_i exceed the costs by ABC. The monopolist, though, would not produce these additional units because they would add less to the monopoly's revenues (assuming that all consumers are charged the same price) than to its costs. Potential gains represented by ABC are lost under monopoly. As Adam Smith observed 200 years ago, the monopolist understocks the market in order to charge a higher price.

3. Under Monopoly, Profits and Losses Do Not Properly Induce Firms to Enter and to Exit from Industries.

When barriers to entry are low, profits induce firms to produce goods for which consumers are willing (because of the expected benefits) to pay prices sufficient to cover costs of production. Inefficient firms face competition and are unable to cover their costs. They are forced to either improve efficiency or leave the market. Losses also constrain firms from producing goods for which consumers are not willing to cover costs of production. Profits and losses direct resources into those activities for which consumer valuation is highest.

For the monopolist, profits play a smaller role because entry barriers are high. The discipline of close competition is missing. Even though losses will induce exit from the market, when costs are high relative to demand, the ability of profits and losses to discipline firms under monopoly is weakened. Firms that are earning profits, or that are inefficient, may nonetheless be protected from potential new competitors by barriers to entry. Their benefits are enjoyed at the consumer's expense.

4. Government Grants of Monopoly Will Encourage Rent Seeking; Resources Will Be Wasted by Firms Attempting to Secure and Maintain Grants of Monopoly Power. The inefficiency emanating from government licenses, franchises, and other grants of monopoly power will exceed the welfare losses due to allocative inefficiency. As we discussed in Chapter 4, grants of special favor by the government will lead to rent-seeking activities. Individuals, firms, and organized interest groups will compete for the government favors. When government licenses or other grants of monopoly power increase profitability and provide protection from the rigors of market competition, people will expend scarce resources in an attempt to secure and maintain these monopoly grants. From an efficiency standpoint, such rent-seeking activities are wasteful; they consume valuable resources without contributing to output. In aggregate, output is reduced as the result of these wasteful activities.[4]

By way of illustration, suppose the government issues a license providing a seller with the exclusive right to sell liquor in a specific market. If this grant of monopoly power permits the licensee to earn monopoly profit, potential suppliers will expend resources trying to convince government officials that they should be granted the license. The potential monopolists will lobby government officials, make political contributions, hire representatives to do consulting studies, and undertake other action designed to convince politicians and their appointees that they can best "serve the public interest" as a monopoly supplier. Any firm that expects its rent-seeking activities to be successful will be willing to spend up to the present value of the future expected monopoly profits, if necessary, to obtain the monopoly protection. Other suppliers, of course, may also be willing to invest in rent-seeking activities. When several suppliers believe they can win, the total expenditures of all firms on rent-seeking activities may actually consume resources worth more than the economic profit expected from the monopoly enterprise.

PRICE DISCRIMINATION

Price Discrimination: A practice whereby a seller charges different consumers different prices for the same product or service.

Thus far, we have assumed that all sellers of a product will charge each customer the same price. Sometimes, though, sellers can increase their revenues (and profits) by charging different prices to different groups of consumers. This practice is called **price discrimination.** As we will see, this practice can help sellers, but it can also increase market efficiency and lower the price available to buyers whose demands are elastic.

If price discrimination is going to be attractive to a seller, three conditions must be met. First, the firm must confront a downward-sloping demand curve for its product. A monopolist will meet this criterion; a pure competitor will not. Second, there must be at least two identifiable groups of consumers whose price elasticities of demand for the firm's product differ. The seller must be able to identify and separate these consumers at a low cost. Third, the sellers must be able to prevent the customers who are charged a low price from reselling the product to customers who are charged higher prices.

Can you think of any examples of price discrimination? Businesses such as hotels, fast-food restaurants, and drug stores often charge senior citizens less than

---

[4]See Gordon Tullock, "The Welfare Costs of Tariffs, Monopolies, and Theft," *Western Economic Journal* 5 (June 1967), pp. 224–32.

other customers. Students (and children) are often given discounts at movie theaters and athletic events. Sometimes bars and sports teams charge women lower prices than men.

GAINING FROM PRICE DISCRIMINATION

Why do sellers charge different prices to their customers? When a seller can identify specific groups of customers and distinguish among them at a relatively low cost, profits can be increased when (a) groups with the most inelastic demand are charged high prices and (b) groups with a more elastic demand are charged low prices. Pricing of airline tickets illustrates this point. The airline industry has found that the demand of business fliers is substantially more inelastic than the demand of vacationers, students, and other travelers. Thus, airlines usually charge high fares to persons who are unwilling to stay over a weekend, who spend only a day or two at their destination, and who make reservations a short time before their flight. These high fares fall primarily on business travelers who are less sensitive to price. In contrast, discount fares are offered to fliers willing to make reservations well in advance, travel during off-peak hours, and stay at their destinations over a weekend before returning home. Such travelers are likely to be vacationers and students, who are highly sensitive to price.

Exhibit 7 illustrates the logic of this policy. Panel (a) shows what would happen if a single price were charged to all customers. Given demand, the profit-maximizing firm expands output to 100, where MR equals MC. The profit-maximizing price on coast-to-coast flights is $400, which generates $40,000 of revenue per flight. Since the marginal cost per passenger is $100, this provides the airline with net operating revenue of $30,000 with which to cover other costs.

However, as Exhibit 7b shows, even though the market demand schedule is unchanged, the airline can do even better if it uses price discrimination. When it charges business travelers (those who travel on weekdays, do not stay over a weekend, and who make their reservations only a few days in advance) $600, most of these passengers continue to travel since their demand is highly inelastic. On the other hand, since their demand is more elastic, a $100 price cut generates substantial additional ticket sales from vacationers, students, and others. Therefore, with price discrimination, the airline can sell 60 tickets (primarily to business travelers) at $600 and 60 additional tickets to others at $300. Total revenue jumps to $54,000 and leaves the airline with $42,000 ($54,000 minus 120 times $100) of revenue in excess of variable cost. Compared to the single price outcome (Exhibit 7a), the price discrimination strategy expands profit by $12,000.

When sellers can segment their market (at a low cost) into groups with differing price elasticities of demand, price discrimination can increase profits. *For each group,* the seller will maximize profit by equating marginal cost and marginal revenue. This rule will lead to higher prices for groups with the most inelastic demand (and lower prices for the groups with the most elastic demand). Compared to the single-price situation, price discrimination increases profitability because a higher price increases the net revenue from groups with an inelastic demand, while a lower price increases the net revenue from price-sensitive customers. With price discrimination, the number of units sold also increases (compare Exhibit 7a with 7b) because the discounts provided to price-sensitive groups increase the quantity sold more than the higher prices charged the less price-sensitive groups reduce sales.

A seller need not be a pure monopolist to gain from price discrimination. Any firm that faces a downward-sloping demand curve for its product may employ the technique. In fact, differential prices accompanying discounts and economy fares

Price Discrimination

As panel (a) illustrates, a $400 ticket price will maximize profits on coast-to-coast flights *if an airline charges a single price.* However, the airline can do still better if it raises the price to $600 for passengers (business travelers) with a highly inelastic demand and *reduces* the price to $300 for travelers (for example, students and vacationers) with a more elastic demand. When sellers can segment their market, they can gain by (a) charging a higher price to consumers with a less elastic demand and (b) offering discounts to customers whose demand is more elastic.

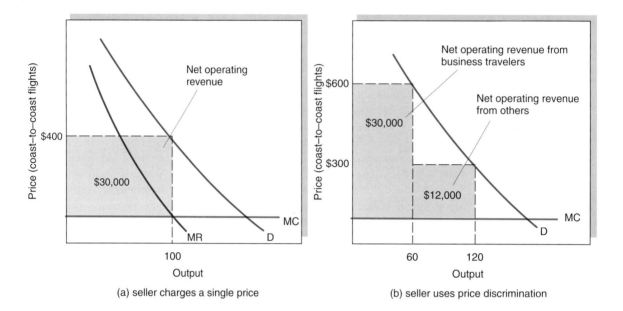

(a) seller charges a single price   (b) seller uses price discrimination

are often indicative of intense rivalry among firms. We introduce the concept while discussing monopoly merely to illustrate the general point.

Sometimes price discrimination is quite subtle. Discount coupons, for example, reflect the use of price discrimination as a competitive strategy. Many businesses recognize that shoppers who take the time and effort to cut out and save coupons are more price-sensitive (their demand is more elastic) than other consumers. As our analysis indicates, it makes sense to charge these customers a lower price. Even colleges engage in price discrimination. Many colleges charge a high standard tuition, which allows them to get additional revenue from wealthy families with a more inelastic demand. At the same time, however, they provide low-income students with scholarships based on need (tuition ''discounts''). The partial tuition scholarships given to students whose parents are less wealthy saves the college from losing students who have a more elastic demand. Poorer students thus are not priced out of their market by the high standard tuition.

WINNERS AND LOSERS FROM PRICE DISCRIMINATION

When a monopolist can price discriminate, some buyers are forced to pay more than they would if a single intermediate price were offered. They purchase fewer units, and they are worse off. In contrast, those for whom the price discrimination process lowers the price are better off. (Of course with some products, such as airline transportation, a single buyer might be better off with some purchases and worse off with others.)

On balance, however, we can expect that output will be greater with price discrimination than it would be with a single price. The market is not as understocked as it would have been in the absence of the price discrimination. Thus, from an allocative standpoint, price discrimination gets high marks; it reduces the allocative inefficiency due to monopolistic pricing. Some of the gains that would accrue to consumers with an inelastic demand are transferred to the monopolist as increased revenue, but additional gains from trade are created by the increased output of goods which would be lost if the monopolist did not (or could not) price discriminate.

In some markets, there is an additional gain emanating from price discrimination: production may occur that would be lost if price discrimination were absent. Remember, a monopolist is not guaranteed a profit. Sometimes, even a monopolist, charging *a single price* to all customers, may be unable to cover cost (see Exhibit 5). With price discrimination, however, some otherwise unprofitable firms may be able to generate enough additional revenue to operate successfully in the marketplace. For example, some small towns in Montana might not provide enough revenue at a single price to enable a local physician to cover his or her opportunity costs. However, if the physician is able to discriminate on the basis of income, charging wealthier people more and poorer people less than normal rates, the resulting revenues from practice in the small town may enable the physician to stay in the community. In this case, all residents of the town may be better off as the result of the price discrimination, since it provides them with access to a local physician. After all, even those being charged the highest prices are not disadvantaged if the price discrimination keeps the physician in town. They are just as able to seek physician services elsewhere as they would have been in the absence of the price-discriminating local doctor.

WHEN CAN A MONOPOLIZED INDUSTRY BE MADE COMPETITIVE?

The most serious problems raised by a monopoly would be avoided if the monopolist faced the threat of rivals producing the same product or even close substitutes. The presence of competitors would prevent independent firms from restricting output and raising prices.

Why not break up the monopoly into several rival units, substituting competition for monopoly? If it were not for economies of scale, this would be a very good strategy.

Exhibit 8 compares competition and monopoly, assuming that economies of scale are unimportant in the industry. The minimum-cost output conditions for purely competitive firms thus would not differ from those of monopolists. If the industry were purely competitive, price would be determined by supply and demand. As Exhibit 8a illustrates, under these conditions, competition would drive price down to P_c in the long run. An industry output of Q_c would result. The market price would just equal the *marginal* opportunity costs of production.

In contrast, if the industry were monopolized, the profit-maximizing monopolist would equate marginal revenue with marginal cost (Exhibit 8b). This would lead to an output level of Q_m. The monopolist would charge P_m, a price higher than would exist in a competitive industry. When economies of scale are unimportant, imposition of competitive conditions on a monopolized industry would result in lower prices, a larger output, and improved economic efficiency.

EXHIBIT 8

Pure Competition and
Pure Monopoly in the
Absence of Economies of
Scale

Here we assume that a product can be produced by either numerous small firms or a monopolist at the same average total and marginal costs. When there are no cost disadvantages of small-scale production, competition serves to reduce price. For a purely competitive industry (a), supply and demand would dictate price P_c. The firms would just be able to cover their cost. If all the firms merged into a monopoly and *cost conditions remained the same*, the monopolist would restrict output to Q_m (where MC would equal MR). Price would rise to P_m.

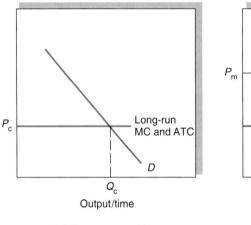

(a) Pure competition

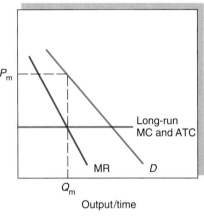

(b) Pure monopoly

ECONOMIES OF SCALE AND NATURAL MONOPOLY

Unfortunately, it is often unrealistic to expect similar cost conditions for pure competition and monopoly. Economies of scale may be the reason that certain industries tend to be monopolized. If economies of scale are important, larger firms will have lower per unit cost than smaller rivals. Sometimes economies of scale may be so important that per unit cost of production will be lowest when the entire output of the industry is produced by a single firm. In the absence of government intervention, the "natural" tendency will then be toward monopoly, because increases in firm size through merger, or "survival of the fittest," will lead to lower per unit cost.

Exhibit 9 depicts the **natural monopoly** case. The long-run average total cost in the industry declines and eventually crosses the demand curve. To take full advantage of the economies of scale, given the demand for the product, the total output of the industry would have to be produced by a single firm. If the firm were an unregulated monopolist, it would produce output Q_m and charge price P_m. The firm would realize economic profits, because average total cost would be less than price at the profit-maximizing output level. It would be very difficult for any firm to begin to compete with the natural monopolist; initially, while the new competitor was still small, it would have very high costs of production and would be unable to make profits at price P_m. The "natural" monopoly conditions of the industry would act as an entry barrier to potential competitors.

Therefore, when "natural" monopoly exists, a "competitive" market structure will be both costly and difficult to maintain. Suppose the output of an industry were divided among ten firms of size Q_c (see Exhibit 9). These small firms would have per unit average costs of P_c. Even if they charged a price equal to their average total cost, the price would be higher than the monopolistic price P_m. In addition, since firms larger than Q_c would always have lower per unit costs, there would be a strong

Natural Monopoly: A market situation in which the average costs of production continually decline with increased output. Therefore, average costs of production will be lowest when a single large firm produces the entire output demanded.

EXHIBIT 9

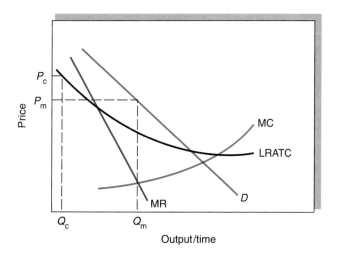

EXHIBIT 9

Monopoly and Competition with Economies of Scale

When economies of scale are important, efforts to impose a competitive market structure are self-defeating. For an industry with cost (and demand) curves like those indicated here, prices (and costs) would be lower under monopoly than if there were ten competitors of size Q_c.

tendency for firms to merge and become larger. Imposition of a competitive structure would be self-defeating in cases in which monopoly "naturally" exists because of the economies of scale.

In what situations are substantial economies of scale present? It is difficult for an observer to know, especially when technology is constantly changing. Existing and potential suppliers sometimes have different opinions as to the importance of scale economies, at a given time and place. However, it is commonly assumed that delivery of local telephone service, water, and electricity exhibit natural monopoly conditions. If there were several telephone companies operating in the same area, each with its own lines and transmission equipment, the resulting duplication would be costly. In such industries, a large number of firms might not be feasible.

POLICY ALTERNATIVES TO NATURAL MONOPOLY

When monopoly or near monopoly results from economies of scale, there are three policy alternatives. First, monopolists could be permitted to operate freely. We have already pointed out that this option limits consumer choice and results in a higher product price (and smaller output) than is consistent with ideal economic efficiency. Second, government regulation could be imposed on the monopolists. Third, the government could completely take over production in the industry. Government operation is an alternative to private monopoly. Let us take a closer look at the last two alternatives, and compare them with private monopoly.

REGULATING THE MONOPOLIST

Can government regulation improve the allocative efficiency of unregulated monopoly? In theory, the answer to this question is clearly yes. Government regulation *can* force the monopoly to reduce its price; at the lower government-imposed price ceiling, the monopolist will voluntarily produce a larger output.

Exhibit 10 illustrates why ideal government price regulation would improve resource allocation. The profit-maximizing monopolist sets price at P_0 and produces output Q_0, where MR = MC. Consumers, however, would value *additional* units more than the opportunity cost. How can the regulatory agency improve on the situation that would result from unregulated monopoly?

EXHIBIT 10

Regulation of a Monopolist

If unregulated, a profit-maximizing monopolist with the costs indicated here would produce Q_0 units and charge P_0. If a regulatory agency forced the monopolist to reduce price to P_1, the monopolist would expand output to Q_1. Ideally, we would like output to be expanded to Q_2, where $P =$ MC, but regulatory agencies usually do not attempt to keep prices as low as P_2. Can you explain why?

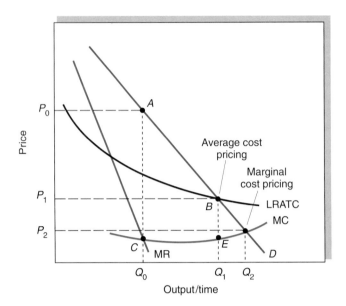

1. *Average Cost Pricing.*

If a regulatory agency forces the monopolist to reduce price to P_1, at which the firm's ATC curve intersects with the market (and firm) demand curve, the monopolist will expand output to Q_1. Since the firm cannot charge a price above P_1, it cannot increase revenues by selling a smaller output at a higher price. Once the price ceiling is instituted, the firm can increase revenues by P_1, and by only P_1, for each unit it sells. The regulated firm's MR is constant at P_1 for all units sold until output is increased to Q_1. Since the firm's MC is less than P_1 (and therefore less than MR), the profit-maximizing, regulated monopolist will expand output from Q_0 to Q_1. The benefits from the consumption of these units (ABQ_1Q_0) clearly exceed their costs (CEQ_1Q_0). Social welfare has improved as a result of the regulative action (we will ignore the impact on the distribution of income). At that output level, revenues are sufficient to cover costs. The firm is making zero economic profit (or "normal" accounting profit).

2. *Marginal Cost Pricing.*

Ideally, since even at the Q_1 output level marginal cost is still less than price, additional welfare gains are possible if output is increased to Q_2. However, if a regulatory agency forced the monopolist to reduce price to P_2 (so that price would equal marginal cost at the output level Q_2), economic losses would result. Even a monopolist, unless subsidized, would not undertake production if the regulatory agency set the price at P_2 or any price below P_1. Usually, problems associated with determining and allocating the necessary subsidy would make this option infeasible.

WHY REGULATION MAY GO ASTRAY

It is not easy to regulate an industry well. The cost-plus orientation toward which pricing methods gravitate weakens incentives for efficiency.[5]

F. M. Scherer

Even though government regulation of monopoly seems capable of improving market results, as in the average cost pricing example above, economic analysis

---

[5]F. M. Scherer, *Industrial Market Structure and Economic Performance,* 2nd ed. (Boston: Houghton Mifflin, 1980), p. 485.

suggests that regulating monopolies will usually not be an ideal solution. Why? As Professor Scherer indicates in the quote above, the lack of incentive to produce at a low cost is important. Information is another factor. Together, the lack of incentives and information form a serious principal-agent problem for regulators who would act on behalf of citizens to control monopoly. Let us look at the various factors that make this such a difficult task.

Lack of Information. In discussing ideal regulation, we assumed that we knew what the firm's ATC, MC, and demand curves looked like. In reality, of course, this would not be the case. The firms themselves have difficulty knowing their costs, and especially their demand curves, with any precision.

Because estimates of demand and marginal costs are difficult to obtain, regulatory agencies usually use profits (or rate of return) as a gauge to determine whether the regulated price is too high or too low. The regulatory agency, guarding the public interest, seeks to impose a "fair" or "normal" rate of return on the firm. If the firm is making profits (that is, an abnormally high rate of return), the price must be higher than P_1 and should be lowered. If the firm is incurring losses (less than the fair or normal rate of return), the regulated price must be less than P_1, and the firm should be allowed to increase price.

The actual existence of profits, though, is not easily identified. Accounting profit, even allowing for a normal rate of profit, is not the same as economic profit. In addition, regulated firms have a definite incentive to adopt reporting techniques and accounting methods that conceal profits. This will make it difficult for a regulatory agency to identify and impose the price consistent with allocative efficiency.

Cost Shifting. When demand is sufficient, the owners of the regulated firm can expect the long-run rate of profit to be essentially fixed regardless of whether efficient management reduces costs or inefficient management allows costs to increase. If costs decrease, the "fair return" rule imposed by the regulatory agency will force a price reduction; if costs increase, the "fair return" rule will allow a price increase. Thus, the *owners* of the regulated firm have less incentive to be concerned about costs than the owners of unregulated firms. Managers will have a freer hand to pursue personal objectives. They will be more likely to fly first-class, entertain lavishly on an expense account, give their relatives and friends good jobs, grant unwarranted wage increases, and in general make decisions that increase costs, but yield personal benefits to the managers. Since monopoly means that buyers do not have a close substitute to turn to, consumers will bear the burden of managerial inefficiency. Normally, wasteful activities would be policed by the owners, but since the firm's rate of return is set by the regulatory agency, the owners have little incentive to be concerned.

Exhibit 11 demonstrates the impact of inefficient management. If the firm's costs were effectively policed, average total cost curve ATC_1 would result. Because of production inefficiency, however, the firm's average total cost curve shifts to ATC_2. A regulatory agency, granting the firm a fair return, would then allow a price increase to P_2. Even though P_2 might be less than the unregulated profit-maximizing monopolist would charge, some of the gains of the regulatory policy would be lost to inefficiency.

Alternatively, Exhibit 11 could represent a very different situation. Suppose that the firm's costs previously were ATC_2, but now ATC_1 has been attained due to

Cost Shifting and
Monopoly Regulation

Managers of a regulated firm
have a greater incentive to
follow policies that yield
personal gain at the expense of
higher cost. With time, this may
cause the cost curves of the
regulated monopolistic firm to
rise, resulting in higher prices
even though the monetary
profits are still normal.

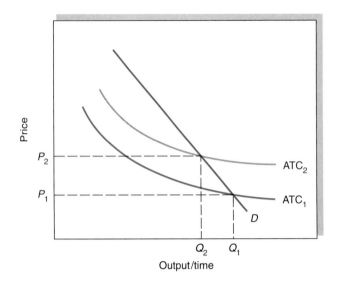

the firm's innovative and efficient operation. In this case, ironically, if the rate
adjustments by the regulatory agency come only after a delay, permitting the firm
temporarily to continue charging P_2 despite the lower costs, then there is a
beneficial incentive effect. The temporary ability to profit from increased efficiency
is a spur to generating more efficiency. In the short run, consumers may have failed
to gain immediately from the lower costs, but when innovation and increased
efficiency are rewarded, even temporarily, cost-reducing innovation is encouraged.

The Impact of Inflation.   Regulatory lag is not always beneficial. Regulation based
on normal rate of return will encounter serious difficulties during inflationary times.
If the costs of labor, energy resources, and other factors of production rise along
with other prices, the cost of producing the product or service of the regulated firm
will increase during the period of inflation. A rate structure based on *last year's cost
figures* will not permit the firm to earn a normal rate of return. Of course, as its rate
of return drops below normal, the firm's case for a rate increase *next* year will be
strengthened. If the inflation continues, however, the regulated firm's rate of return
will continue to be below normal. The firm will be unable to earn the normal rate
of return during inflationary times as long as its rate structure is based on historical
costs. As a result of low earnings, the regulated firm will have difficulty raising
funds in the capital market. If the normal rate of return on capital is 12 percent, who
will want to invest with a firm that is able to earn only 9 percent? Many regulated
utilities were caught in precisely this cost-regulated price squeeze as the price of
energy and other resources soared during the inflation of the 1970s.

Quality Regulation.   It is much easier to regulate product price than to regulate
quality. Regulated firms desiring to raise the price of their product can often do so
by taking cost-reducing steps that result in quality deterioration. Consider the
quality dimension of a seemingly uniform good such as telephone service. The
speed at which your call goes through, the likelihood that you will have to redial the
desired number, how often your phone is out of order, and how quickly you can get
it repaired are included in the quality of telephone service. Since these factors are
hard to control, it is extremely difficult for a regulatory agency to impose a price *per
constant quality unit.* During inflationary times, regulated firms caught in a

cost-regulated price squeeze may be particularly tempted to lower the quality of their product.

Special Interest Effect. The difficulties of government regulation discussed thus far are practical limitations that a regulatory agency, seeking to perform its duties efficiently, would confront. But, the special interest effect suggests that regulatory authorities cannot necessarily be expected to pursue only efficiency. Regulated firms have a strong incentive to see that "friendly," "reasonable" people serve as regulators, and they will invest political and economic resources to this end. Just as rent-seeking activities designed to gain monopoly privileges can be expected, so can activities to influence regulatory decisions.

What about consumer interests? Do you know who serves on the Interstate Commerce Commission or the public utility regulatory boards? Do you know any consumer who voted against a politician because of his or her appointments to a regulatory commission? Chances are that you do not. Consumer interests are widely dispersed and disorganized. Ordinarily, consumers cannot be expected to invest time, resources, votes, and political contributions to ensure that a particular regulatory commission represents their views. The firms that are regulated can, however, be expected to make such investments.[6] Even though the initial stimulus for a regulating agency might come from consumer interests, economic theory suggests that such agencies will eventually reflect the views of the business and labor interests they are supposed to regulate.

THE GOVERNMENT-OPERATED FIRM

Government-operated firms—socialized firms such as the Post Office, the Tennessee Valley Authority, and many local public utilities—present an alternative to both private monopoly and regulation. How do socialized firms operate in the real world? The decision-makers of firms owned by the government are influenced by political and economic factors alike. With the rise of public-sector action, economists have recently expressed renewed interest in the socialized firm.

The ideal theoretical solution is straightforward. The socialized firm should (a) operate efficiently and (b) set price equal to marginal cost. When cost conditions are like those illustrated by Exhibit 6, the government-operated monopoly firm will ideally expand output to Q_i (where $P = MC$) and charge price P_1. The firm will make profits that can be channeled into the public treasury. On the other hand, marginal cost pricing may sometimes result in economic losses, requiring a subsidy for the government-operated firm. Exhibit 10 illustrates this possibility. Output should be expanded to Q_2 if the potential marginal welfare gains are to be fully realized. Price P_2 will be charged. The consumer's valuation of the marginal unit (P_2) will equal its marginal cost. Since losses result at this price and output, it will be necessary to subsidize the public enterprise.

This analysis assumes that the socialized firm will both operate efficiently and set the proper price. How realistic are these assumptions? The same "perverse" managerial incentives—incentives to ignore efficiency and pursue personal or professional objectives at the firm's expense—that regulated firms confront also tend to plague the government-operated firm. Professor John Kenneth Galbraith and others have pointed out that there is a principal-agent problem in private corporations. Poorly informed stockholders may be unable to police management

---

[6]The special interest effect will be weaker when regulatory commissions are elected rather than appointed, allowing the voter to separate this issue from other issues of greater importance.

inefficiency. Managers may pursue their own objectives at the expense of "owners."

The socialized firm, however, is the extreme case of a principal-agent problem. The "owners" (voters) are typically uninformed about how well a socialized firm is run, or how it might be run better. This is especially true when the firm has no direct competitors. As we indicated in Chapter 4, voters tend to be rationally ignorant about matters on which, as individuals, they have no decisive vote. This is in sharp contrast with individual stockholders in a firm, any one of whom can personally "bail out" simply by selling their stock upon seeing trouble coming for the firm, or can buy more stock upon seeing promising management initiatives. Unlike investors in the private sector, no small group of voters normally is in a position to gain substantial wealth by taking over the socialized firm and improving its management. Even more than with monopoly in the private sector, customers of the socialized monopoly (voter-taxpayers) cannot easily switch their business to other sellers. Even those voter-taxpayers who do not consume the product have to pay taxes to support the socialized firm. The end result is that when the government operates a business—particularly one with monopoly power—there is typically less consumer and investor scrutiny, less reward for efficiency, and less penalty for inefficiency. Higher costs result.

In much the same way, special interests also affect incentives—usually in terms of political or group gain—and result in inefficiency. The managers, employees, and specialized users of public enterprises often comprise special interest groups, particularly if the employees are well organized (for example, unionized) for political action. Should the wages of public-sector employees be raised and their working conditions improved? Should comfortable offices, lengthy coffee breaks, and lucrative fringe benefits be provided to employees? Should attractive positions in the public enterprise be provided to the politically faithful? Should management resist pressure to lay off unneeded workers (particularly at election time), abandon unprofitable service areas, and charge users low prices (that is, less than the marginal cost) when the opportunity cost of providing the service is high? On all these issues, the interests of special interest groups involved with public-sector production and its consumption will be in conflict with the interests of the disorganized, uninformed taxpayers. Under these circumstances, economic theory suggests that the views of the special interest groups will usually dominate, even when inefficiency and higher costs result.

Public enterprises can thus be expected to use at least some of their monopoly power, not to benefit the wide cross-section of disorganized taxpayers and consumers, but as a cloak for inefficient operation and actions that advance the personal and political objectives of those who exercise control over the firm. Government ownership, like unregulated monopoly and government regulation, is a less than ideal solution. It is not especially surprising that those who denounce monopoly in, for instance, the telephone industry seldom point to a government-operated monopoly—such as the Post Office—as an example of how an industry should be run.[7]

SUMMARY

The policy implications that can legitimately be drawn from an analysis of monopoly are more limited than might initially appear. We may not like

[7]For an analysis of potential cost savings in the case of the U.S. Postal Service, see *Privatization: Toward More Effective Government,* Report of the President's Commission on Privatization, (March 1988), Chapter 7, pp. 101–128.

monopolistic power or its effects, but the alternatives are not terribly attractive. Monopoly power based on economies of scale poses a particularly troublesome problem. When average total costs decline with the size of firm, per unit costs will be minimized if a single firm produces the entire market output. However, if a monopolist is permitted to dominate the market, inefficiency will arise because a monopolist will restrict output and charge a price in excess of marginal cost. Since smaller firms have higher per unit costs, restructuring the industry to increase the number of firms is unattractive. Neither is regulation an ideal solution. Since regulators do not possess the information necessary to impose an efficient outcome and since the special interest effect indicates that regulators are susceptible to manipulation by the industrial interests, regulation is unlikely to achieve our hypothetical ideal efficiency conditions. Finally, since public-sector managers are likely to pursue political objectives at the expense of economic efficiency, public ownership is also a less than ideal solution. Thus, economic theory indicates that there are no ideal solutions when natural monopoly is present. Choices must be made among alternatives, all of which are imperfect.

DYNAMIC CHANGE, MONOPOLY POWER, AND RESOURCE ALLOCATION

We have analyzed monopoly within a static framework and emphasized the lack of competition (sellers of alternative products) *within the industry*. No firm, though, is an island unto itself. Each firm competes with every other firm for the dollar votes of consumers. Dynamic change is present in the real world and the expectation of monopoly profit may influence its speed. If a monopoly is profitable, rivals will seek to develop substitutes. Actual and potential substitutes exist for almost every product. With the passage of time, dynamic competition in the form of technological change and the development of new substitute products will threaten the position of firms with monopoly power. For example, the recent development of fax machines has reduced the monopoly power of the postal service.

In fact, high monopoly prices will encourage the development of substitutes. For example, the high price of natural rubber spurred the development of synthetic rubber. High rail-shipping rates accelerated the development of long-distance trucking. The strong exercise of monopoly power by the Organization of Petroleum Exporting Countries (OPEC) subjected oil to vastly intensified competition from coal, solar energy, and other nonpetroleum energy sources, as well as from greatly expanded exploration efforts. The result was a long tumble in the price OPEC could charge for its oil. What seemed to be a secure monopoly position for OPEC in the 1970s turned out to be something very different during the 1980s.

This dynamic competition from substitute products and suppliers, both actual and potential, is important for two reasons. First, a monopolist will sometimes choose to produce a larger output and charge a lower price—lower than the short-run profit-maximizing price—to discourage potential rivals from developing substitutes. When this happens, the allocative inefficiency associated with monopoly will be less than our static model implies. Second, the expectation of monopoly profits may spur product development. In fact, the patent system is based on this premise. (See Applications in Economics box.) When a new product or production method is patented, monopoly power is granted to the patent owner for

APPLICATIONS IN ECONOMICS

Product Obsolescence, Monopoly Power, and the Dynamics of Product Development

Many Americans believe that business firms can gain by producing shoddy merchandise that wears out quickly. It is often charged that business firms, over the objections of consumers, produce goods with a short life expectancy so they can sell replacements. Economists have sometimes been at the forefront of those deploring such planned obsolescence.

Yet, a solid majority of economists believe that price indexes overstate the measured rate of inflation because they fail to make an adequate allowance for actual observed improvements in product quality. Why has the quality of products, on the average, risen, if firms have an incentive to produce shoddy, nondurable goods?

Should a Car Last a Lifetime?

There are three important points to keep in mind. First, the production of longer-lasting, higher-quality goods will increase costs. There are no free lunches. A car that lasts 15 years will be more expensive than one with a shorter life expectancy. We should expect consumers to trade off lower prices for more durability. At some point, the greater durability will not be worth the price.

Second, "newness," product variability, and style changes are often valued by consumers. For example, operational reliability aside, many consumers would prefer three differently styled, new-model cars lasting 5 years each to a single car of equal cost that lasts 15 years. *Under these conditions,* the production of goods with less

than maximum life expectancy is perfectly consistent with consumer tastes.[8]

Third, goods engineered to last a relatively short time put their owners in a more adaptable position. For example, buyers of new American cars in 1971–1972 preferred large cars. At the time, this made good sense because gasoline prices were low and had been falling in real terms for many years. The value of large, gas-guzzling cars dropped sharply in 1974, though, as gasoline prices soared and spot shortages developed. Years later, in the mid-1980s, the reverse happened: gasoline prices fell sharply, and buyers found it economical to buy cars with more size, comfort, and safety. If those who bought large cars in 1971–1972 and small cars in the early 1980s had paid for years of extra durability, their losses (and the nation's) would have been greater. In a dynamic world, one decision every ten years is less flexible (and, if wrong, more costly to correct) than a decision every five years.

Durability of Products and Producer Choices

In a competitive environment, producers have a strong incentive to cater to the preferences of consumers. Product quality, including durability, is a competitive weapon. If customers really want longer-lasting products, competitive firms have a strong incentive to introduce them. If consumers are willing to pay the price for greater durability, firms that cater to their views can gain. Durability, however, is only one

facet of a product that is attractive to consumers. Low prices, newness, and product variation are also preferred by many people. Much of our planned obsolescence undoubtedly stems from the choice of consumers to give up some of the former (durability) to have more of the latter.

The Monopolist and the Durability of Products

Will a monopolist ever introduce a new, improved, longer-lasting product, even if the new product is expected to drive the existing profitable product off the market? Strange as it may seem, a monopolist will introduce the new product if two conditions are met.

1. The product must be a genuine improvement—it must give the consumer more service per dollar of opportunity cost (to the monopolist) than the monopolist's current product.
2. The monopolist must be able to enforce property rights over gains from the new product. A patent preventing others from copying the innovative idea serves this purpose.

If these two conditions are met, the monopolist will be able to price the new product such that it will be profitable to introduce, even though it may eventually replace the monopolist's current product line. Two examples will help to clarify this point.

Super Sharp: The Better Blade

Suppose Super Sharp Razor, Inc., has a monopoly on razor blades, which sell for 5 cents and give one week of comfortable shaves. Currently, Super Sharp makes a 3-cent profit (return above opportunity cost) on each blade. Assume the firm discovers (and quickly patents) a blade made with the same machines at the same cost but with a slightly different metal alloy.[9] It gives two weeks of comfortable shaves instead of one. Will the firm market the new blade, even though it will lose one half of its weekly sales of blades? Yes! Customers will gladly pay up to 10 cents per blade for the new blades, which last twice as long. Instead of making 3 cents net profit per customer per week, the firm now will make up to 8 cents per customer every two weeks. Profits will rise. In fact, a price of 9 cents per blade will benefit the buyer *and* Super Sharp alike.

Would Monopoly Oil Sell the Miracle Carburetor?

For years, it has been rumored that a much more efficient "miracle carburetor" for automobiles has been discovered, but that the big oil companies have plotted to keep it off the market because it would reduce their profits from the sale of gasoline.

Suppose an oil cartel, Monopoly Oil, sells all the oil and gasoline in the world. This hypothetical organization has also obtained the patent on a miracle carburetor. The real improvement is simply a little plastic gizmo that can be inserted into ordinary carburetors. The gizmo can be made in quantity for 1 cent each, and each gizmo lasts just long enough (one year, on average) to save its buyer 1,000 gallons of

gas. If Monopoly Oil makes 5 cents per gallon economic profit on each gallon of gasoline, the sales lost *per gizmo* will cost the firm $50 per year. Will Monopoly Oil sell the gizmo? Of course! If gas sells for 95 cents per gallon (but the opportunity cost of crude oil, refining, and so on is only 90 cents), the cartel will *increase* its profit by selling the gizmo (cost 1 cent), which replaces 1,000 gallons of gasoline, as long as the price of the gizmo exceeds $50.01. The consumer would certainly pay far more than $50.01 to save 1,000 gallons of gas. Indeed, any price below $950 per gizmo would help the motorist.[10]

Do Patents Help or Hurt the Consumer?

A patent right is crucial, of course, to both of the above examples. If firms could not at least partially capture the gains to be made from introducing a new product, they might prefer to keep it off the market and thereby prevent other firms from cutting into their profits by copying the new idea.

The patent system has a dual impact on the allocation of resources. First, the patent monopoly grants, as any monopoly does, the patent owner the ability (for a limited time) to keep the price of the patented item higher than costs of production warrant. Thus, *for patented inventions that have already been introduced,* consumers would be better off if competition replaced patent monopolies.

There is, however, a second effect. The fact that one can patent a new product or production

process encourages the development of improved, lower-cost goods. Public policy in the United States allows temporary patent monopolies, which are costly to consumers in the short-run, in order to provide firms (and individuals) with a strong incentive to undertake the risk and effort involved in the development of technological improvements, which may lead to lower costs and greater efficiency in the long-run.

---

[8]Both the authors and reader may disagree with such "vulgar taste." We should be aware, however, that such disagreement stems from our views about how consumers should behave and does not necessarily mean that the system that caters to that taste is defective.

[9]If the blade requires new and different machines that render the firm's current machines obsolete, the firm will still introduce the product. It will do so, however, at a slower pace, because the cost associated with new machines is higher than the zero *opportunity cost* (assuming the old machines have no alternative use) of using existing machines. Phasing in the new product so that the existing machines may be more fully used could be a cheaper alternative for Super Sharp. If so, it will also be cheaper for society.

[10]If the gizmo were invented by someone other than Monopoly Oil, the inventor would have an even stronger incentive to introduce the product. However, the introduction of the product *by someone else* would detract from the net profit of Monopoly Oil. The latter would have an incentive to suppress the product, if possible. The cartel might attempt to use political power or extralegal methods to keep the product off the market. Of course, such actions would conflict with the efficient use of resources.

a period of 17 years. Others are prohibited from copying the product or technique. If this "reward" of temporary monopoly power and profit did not exist, businesses would be less inclined to undertake research designed to reduce costs and improve product quality. Thus, even though some of these dynamic competitive forces will operate more slowly than when barriers to entry into an industry are low, the development of substitutes will nonetheless tend with the passage of time to erode the market power of a monopolist.

LOOKING AHEAD

Most markets do not fit neatly into either the pure competition or pure monopoly models. Many markets are characterized by low barriers to entry and competition on the basis of product quality, design, convenience of location, and producer reliability. Other markets involve a small number of rival firms, operating under widely varying entry conditions. In the next chapter, we will investigate market structures that lie between pure competition and monopoly.

CHAPTER SUMMARY

1. Pure monopoly is a market structure characterized by (a) high barriers to entry and (b) a single seller of a well-defined product for which there are no good substitutes. Pure monopoly is at the opposite end of the market-structure spectrum from pure competition.

2. Analysis of pure monopoly is important for two reasons. First, the monopoly model will help us understand the operation of markets dominated by a few firms. Second, in a few important industries, such as local telephone services and utilities, there is often only a single producer in a market area. The monopoly model will help us understand these markets.

3. The four major barriers to entry into a market are government licensing, economies of scale, patents, and control of an essential resource.

4. The monopolist's demand curve is the market demand curve. It slopes downward to the right. The marginal revenue curve for a monopolist will lie inside the demand curve because of revenue losses from the lower price for units that could have been sold at a higher price.

5. For the elastic portion of a monopolist's demand curve, a lower price will increase total revenue. For the inelastic portion of the monopolist's demand curve, a price reduction will cause total revenue to decline. A profit-maximizing monopolist will not operate on the inelastic portion of the demand curve because in that range it is always possible to increase total revenue by raising the price and producing fewer units.

6. A profit-maximizing monopolist will lower price and expand output as long as marginal revenue exceeds marginal cost. At the maximum-profit output, MR will equal MC. The monopolist will charge the price on its demand curve corresponding to that rate of sales.

7. If losses occur in the long run, a monopolist will go out of business. If profit results, high barriers to entry will shield a monopolist from competitive pressures. Therefore, *long-run* economic profits for a monopoly are sometimes possible.

8. Economists are critical of a monopoly because (a) it severely limits the role of demand in the market for a good and thus consumers' "control" over the producer; (b) the unregulated monopolist produces too little output and charges a price in excess of the marginal cost; (c) profits are less able to stimulate new entry, which would expand the supply of the product until price declined to the level of average production costs; and (d) legal monopoly encourages rent-seeking activity.

9. Under certain conditions, a monopolist will sell output at more than one price. Price discrimination reduces the degree to which a monopolist understocks the market. This

practice allows the seller to convert some of the market's consumer surplus into revenue, and to profit by offering some units at lower prices.

10. Natural monopoly exists when long-run average total costs continue to decline as firm size increases (economies of scale). Thus, a larger firm always has lower costs. When natural monopoly is present, costs of production will be lowest when a single firm generates the entire output of the industry.

11. In the presence of natural monopoly, there are three policy alternatives: (a) private, unregulated monopoly; (b) private, regulated monopoly; and (c) government ownership. Economic theory suggests that each of the three will fail to meet our criteria for ideal efficiency. Private monopoly will result in higher prices and less output than would be ideal. Regulation will often fail to meet our ideal efficiency criteria because (a) the regulators will not have knowledge of the firm's cost curves and market demand conditions; (b) firms have an incentive to conceal their actual cost conditions and take profits in disguised forms; and (c) the regulators often end up being influenced by the firms they are supposed to regulate. Under public ownership, managers often derive personal gain from policies that conflict with cost control and cater to the views of special interest groups (for example, well-organized employees and specialized customers) who will be able to help them further their political objectives.

12. Even a monopolist is not completely free from competitive pressures. All products have some type of substitute. Monopolists who raise the price of their products provide encouragement for other firms to develop substitutes, which may eventually erode the market power of the monopolist. Some monopolists may charge less than the short-run, profit-maximizing price to discourage *potential* competitors from developing substitute products.

13. Monopoly profits derived from patents have two conflicting effects on resource allocation. *Once a product or process has been discovered,* the monopoly rights permit the firm to restrict output and raise price above the current marginal (and average) cost of production. However, the possibility of future monopoly rights granted by a patent encourages entrepreneurs to improve products and develop lower-cost methods of production.

CRITICAL ANALYSIS QUESTIONS

*1. "Barriers to entry are crucial to the existence of long-run profits, but they cannot guarantee the existence of profits." Evaluate.

2. "Monopoly is good for producers but bad for consumers. The gains of the former offset the losses of the latter. On balance, there is no reason to think that monopoly is bad for the economy." Evaluate.

*3. Do monopolists charge the highest prices for which they can sell their products? Do they maximize their average profit per sale? Are monopolistic firms always profitable? Why or why not?

4. The retail liquor industry is potentially a competitive industry. However, the liquor retailers of a southern state organized a trade association that sets prices for all firms. For all practical purposes, the trade association transformed a competitive industry into a monopoly. Compare the price and output policy for a purely competitive industry with the policy that would be established by a profit-maximizing monopolist or trade association. Who benefits and who is hurt by the formation of the monopoly?

5. Does economic theory indicate that a monopoly forced by an ideal regulatory agency to set prices according to either marginal or average cost would be more efficient than an unregulated monopoly? Explain. Does economic theory suggest that a regulatory agency *will* follow a proper regulation policy? What are some of the factors that complicate the regulatory function?

*Asterisk denotes questions for which answers are given in Appendix C, Selected Answers.

6. Is a monopolist subject to any competitive pressures? Explain. Would an unregulated monopolist have an incentive to operate and produce efficiently? If so, why?

*7. If a university has some monopoly power, explain why it would allocate more of its financial aid to students from low-income families than those from richer families if it seeks to maximize revenue.

8. Explain why it is impossible to draw a supply curve for a monopolist.

*9. "The patent system provides a monopoly to the producer and raises consumer prices. It is inefficient." Evaluate, giving economic arguments for and against this point of view.

10. Which of the following are monopolists: (a) your local newspaper, (b) the Boston Celtics, (c) General Motors, (d) the U.S. Postal Service, (e) Johnny Carson, (f) the American Medical Association? Is the definition of an industry or market area important in the determination of a seller's monopoly position? Explain.

11. How can a firm, through rent-seeking activities, hope to "buy" monopoly profits? Is there competition for monopoly-seller positions? How does competition among rent seekers for monopoly profit influence the efficiency of resource allocation?

*12. Suppose that there is an increase in demand for a product such that a monopolist confronting a straight line demand curve is able to sell a 10-percent-larger quantity at each price. If the product is produced at a constant marginal cost, will the increase in demand cause the monopolist to raise its price? Explain.

*13. In the midst of the sharply higher oil prices of the 1970s, it was often charged that (a) the big oil companies colluded and set prices as if they were a monopolist and (b) the higher prices of petroleum products failed to reduce consumption. Is there a conflict between these two propositions?

14. Once a manuscript is supplied to the publisher, the personal services of the author are a sunk cost. Generally, authors bear none of the production cost and are paid a percentage of total revenue. Given this arrangement, would authors generally prefer a lower sales price for the book than would their publishers? Explain.

*15. Historically, the real cost of transporting both goods and people has declined substantially. What impact does a reduction in transportation cost have on the monopoly power of producers? Do you think the U.S. economy is more or less competitive today than it was 100 years ago? Explain.

16. Is price discrimination harmful to the U.S. economy? How does price discrimination affect the gains from exchange? Why do firms often charge students, the elderly, or people with coupons different prices than others? Explain.

17. Adam Smith, writing before the importance of marginal costs and marginal revenues was discovered by economists, stated that "The price of monopoly is upon every occasion the highest which can be got." Explain why, taken literally, this would seldom be correct. When would it be true, for a profit-maximizing seller?

*18. There is only one National Basketball Association team in Seattle—the Seattle Supersonics. Do the Supersonics have a monopoly in Seattle? A monopoly on what? Discuss.

19. When the Alcoa aluminum company was the only large aluminum producer in the United States for several decades prior to the Second World War, they were accused of monopolizing the industry by expanding output in anticipation of demand and by keeping prices so low that competitors had no chance to enter. If the accusation is true, how did it affect the welfare of consumers?

20. Why do the owners of theaters and sports teams often provide students, senior citizens, and the military with discount admission tickets, but they almost never provide these groups with discounts on food and drinks at the event?

21

Between Competition and Monopoly: Models of Rivalry and Strategy

*Differences in tastes, desires, incomes and locations of buyers, and
differences in the uses which they wish to make of commodities all indicate
the need for variety and the necessity of substituting for the concept of a
"competitive ideal," an ideal involving both monopoly and competition.[1]*

Edward H. Chamberlin

CHAPTER FOCUS

■ How do economists account for competitive advertising, price cutting, coupons for shoppers, and other rivalrous behavior by firms?

■ What are the characteristics of monopolistic competition? How do consumers fare under monopolistic competition?

■ How do markets work when there are only a few rival firms competing?

■ Why have economists been unable to construct a general theory of oligopoly?

■ What is the theory of contestable markets? What can we say about the outcomes in such markets?

■ What do we know about competitiveness within the U.S. economy, and how it has changed over the last several decades?

■ How large are accounting profits, and what changes have occurred in profit levels over the years? What would happen if accounting profits were eliminated?

The models of pure competition and monopoly presented in the two previous chapters are extremely useful in predicting the pricing and output behavior of firms and how they react to changes in costs and changes in demand. But there is no room in those simplified models for the rivalrous behavior that we see every day in markets around us.

Consider the huge sums spent by Ford and Chevrolet, each advertising that its pickup trucks are best. This does not fit the monopoly model: A monopolist has no direct rivals. Although the firms clearly are competing, it also does not fit the model of pure competition: a pure competitor can sell any desired amount at the market price and is unable to raise that price by advertising. Or think about the weekly grocery store fliers and newspaper ads, with their "cents-off" coupons and special sale prices to bring in more customers. Once again, the actions of these competitors do not fit into either the pure competition or pure monopoly models.

Airlines wage "price wars" and use frequent-flier programs to gain customers and earn their loyalty. Producers of breakfast cereal advertise extensively, and some even give away prizes for children in their cereal boxes. Active rivalries among sellers are all around us.

How do economists explain these activities within the context of the economic way of thinking? How are the pricing policies and the profits of rivalrous firms determined in markets with advertising, price wars, and other practices which are costly to the firms? To answer these questions we turn now to some different models of the firm—models in which the firm has rivals and in which the firm must predict how those rivals will react to alternative pricing, output, and product quality decisions it is considering. We will look at models of the firm operating in markets that are competitive, but in which each firm can charge higher prices without losing all its customers and must lower its price if it is to sell a larger quantity. These markets are between competition and monopoly, sharing some of the characteristics of each, but with the added factor of active rivalry among the firms.

THE DIFFERENT TYPES OF MARKET STRUCTURE

Market Structure: The classification of a market with regard to key characteristics including the number of sellers, entry barriers into the market, the control of firms over price, and type of products (homogeneous or differentiated) in the market.

Market structure is a way to classify markets according to the degree of competition among sellers in each market. Competitiveness in a market is influenced by the number of sellers, by whether similar products are available from alternative firms, and by the existence of barriers to entry and exit. Competitiveness is also correlated with the firm's degree of control over price.

The two preceding chapters dealt with models of two forms of market structure: pure competition and monopoly. In their pure form, these models are rarely seen in the real world. Most real-world firms are better described by one of the two additional forms of market structure used by economists to describe and analyze the behavior of firms when rivalry is present. The first is called monopolistic competition. It pertains to a market with many sellers, in which no small group of

---

[1]Edward H. Chamberlin, *The Theory of Monopolistic Competition* (Cambridge: Harvard University Press, 1948), p. 214.

EXHIBIT 1

Models of Market Structure

These four market structures form a continuum from most competitive, on the left, to least competitive, on the right. In general, the closer a market is to the competitive end, the better the consumers will be served.

More Competitive → *Less Competitive*

	Pure Competition	*Monopolistic Competition*	*Oligopoly*	*Monopoly*
Number of sellers	Many	Many	Few	One
Products in market	Identical	Differentiated	Identical or differentiated	No close substitutes
Barriers to entry	None	No legal or scale barriers	Economies of scale	Economies of scale or legal barriers
Firm's control over price	None	Some	Considerable	Considerable, if not regulated
Examples	Wheat, corn	Retail food, clothing, home construction	Automobiles, breakfast cereals	Local phone service, electric and gas utilities

firms dominates the market. The second is oligopoly, and it applies when the market is dominated by a few sellers.

The four types of market structure, ranging from pure competition to monopoly, are listed in Exhibit 1, along with their market structure characteristics. They form a continuum from left to right, from market types that are more competitive to those that are less competitive. In general, the closer a market is to the purely competitive end, the more efficiently it will operate, and the better off consumers will be. Toward that end of the competitive spectrum, more substitutes are available for consumers; firms' demand curves are more elastic; and firms are closer to selling and producing at marginal costs. In addition, profits are more likely to result in the entry of firms and/or an increase in quantity supplied by existing firms, while losses generally lead to the exit of firms and a reduction in production.

The market structure characteristics listed in Exhibit 1 suggest that monopolistically competitive and oligopolistic firms have different degrees of freedom in setting prices, altering quality, and choosing a marketing strategy than do firms in purely competitive or purely monopolistic markets. Most firms, unlike those under purely competitive conditions, will lose some *but not all* of their customers when they increase the price of their product. These firms face a downward-sloping demand curve. Like monopolists, they are price searchers: they must search for the price most consistent with their overall goal—maximum profit, for example. As we have indicated, though, just as they are not pure competitors, most price searchers are not monopolists, either. Thus, their freedom to raise prices is limited by the existence of actual and potential competitors offering similar products.

The major difference between the two models of rivalrous competition is the number of firms in the market. Under monopolistic competition, each seller confronts many rivals. In contrast, there are only a few rivals in an oligopolistic market. This variation in the number of rivals results in two important differences between monopolistic competition and oligopoly. First, monopolistic competitors generally are more limited than oligopolists in their ability to raise price. There are lots of firms producing good substitutes for the product or service of a monopolistic competitor. Thus, if the firm increases its price very much, sales will decline sharply. Put another way, the demand curve confronting a monopolistic competitor is generally quite elastic.

Second, since all have many rivals, economists assume that each monopolistic competitor reacts to general conditions in the market rather than the actions of any specific firm. In contrast, oligopolistic firms face only a few rivals, and therefore, they are expected to think strategically about how rivals will react to any change in product price, quality, or location decision it makes. There is little chance that rivals will fail to notice any significant action by an oligopolist attempting to lure customers away from the few rivals in the oligopolistic market.

Both of these models can incorporate the competitive advertising, product differentiation, and other rivalrous behavior which neither pure competition nor monopoly models can explain. We turn now to a discussion of how the models have developed and how they work.

CHARACTERISTICS OF MONOPOLISTIC COMPETITION

Monopolistic Competition: A situation in which there are a large number of independent sellers, each producing a differentiated product in a market with low barriers to entry. Construction, retail sales, and service stations are good examples of monopolistically competitive industries.

Neither pure competition nor pure monopoly are descriptive of markets such as retail sales, construction, service businesses, and small manufacturing, which are generally characterized by numerous firms offering different but closely related products or services. The need for a more accurate model for markets of this type led to the theory of **monopolistic competition.** The theory was developed independently by Joan Robinson, a British economist, and Edward Chamberlin, an American economist. The major works of Robinson and Chamberlin were both published in 1933.[2] These economists outlined three distinguishing characteristics of monopolistic competition.

PRODUCT DIFFERENTIATION

Differentiated Products: Products distinguished from similar products by such characteristics as quality, design, location, and method of promotion.

Monopolistic competitors offer **differentiated products** to consumers. Goods and services of one seller are differentiated from those of another by convenience of location, product quality, reputation of the seller, advertising, and various other product characteristics.

Since the product of each monopolistic competitor is slightly different from that of its rivals, the individual firm faces a downward-sloping demand curve. A price reduction will enable the firm to attract new customers. Alternatively, the firm will be able to increase its price by a small amount and still retain many of its customers, who prefer the location, style, dependability, or other product characteristics offered by the firm. The demand curve confronted by the monopolistic competitor is highly elastic, however. Even though each firm has some control over price, that control is extremely limited, since the firm faces competition from rivals offering very similar products. The availability of close substitutes and the ease with which consumers can turn to rival firms (including new firms that are free to enter the market) force a monopolistically competitive firm to think twice before raising its price.

[2]See Joan Robinson, *The Economics of Imperfect Competition* (1933, reprint ed., New York: St. Martin's, 1969), and Edward H. Chamberlin, *The Theory of Monopolistic Competition* (Cambridge: Harvard University Press, 1933).

OUTSTANDING ECONOMIST

**Joan Robinson
(1903–1983)**

Along with Edward Chamberlin, Joan Robinson is given credit for developing the theory of monopolistic competition. In her book *The Economics of Imperfect Competition* (1933), she redefined the market demand curve to account for interdependence among firms. Following Alfred Marshall, she used differences among products to define an industry. Essentially, she viewed each firm as a monopolist facing a downward-sloping demand curve that is affected by the behavior of other "monopolists" in the industry. Unlike Chamberlin, she did not introduce product differentiation and quality competition *within an industry* into her analysis.

Professor Robinson's contribution to economics goes far beyond her role in developing the theory of monopolistic competition. A long-time professor emerita of economics at Cambridge University, she was one of a select group of economists who worked with Keynes during the developmental stage of his *General Theory*. Her work in economics ran the gamut. Capital theory, international trade, Marxian economics, growth theory, and comparative systems are among the many areas that felt the touch of her pen.

During the latter years of her life, Professor Robinson was a vocal critic of the capitalist system. Nevertheless, her scholarly work was highly acclaimed by economists of all persuasions. The *Collected Economic Papers* of Professor Robinson fill four volumes.[3]

---

[3]Joan Robinson, *Collected Papers*, 4 vols. (New York: Humanities Press, 1960–1972).

**LOW BARRIERS
TO ENTRY**

Under monopolistic competition, firms are free to enter into or exit from the market. There are neither legal barriers nor market obstacles hindering the movement of competitors into and out of a monopolistically competitive market. Monopolistic competition resembles pure competition in this respect; firms in both these types of markets confront the constant threat of competition from new, innovative rivals.

**MANY INDEPENDENT
FIRMS**

A monopolistic competitor faces not only the potential threat posed by new rivals but competition from many current sellers as well. Each firm is small relative to the total market. No single firm or small group of firms is able to dominate the market.

Retailing is perhaps the sector of our economy that best typifies monopolistic competition. In most market areas, there are a large number of retail stores offering similar products and services. Rivalry is intense, and stores are constantly trying new combinations of price and quality of service (or merchandise) to win customers. The *free entry* that typifies most retailing makes for rapid change. Yesterday's novelty can quickly become obsolete as new rivals develop still better (or more attractive) products and marketing methods.

PRICE AND OUTPUT UNDER MONOPOLISTIC COMPETITION

How does a monopolistic competitor decide what price to charge and what level of output to produce? Like a pure monopolist, a monopolistic competitor will face a downward-sloping demand curve for its product. Additional units can be sold only at a lower price. Therefore, the marginal revenue curve of the monopolistic competitor will always lie below the firm's demand curve.

Any firm can increase profits by expanding output as long as marginal revenue exceeds marginal cost. Therefore, a monopolistic competitor will lower its prices and expand its output until marginal revenue is equal to marginal cost.

Exhibit 2 illustrates the profit-maximizing price and output under monopolistic competition. A profit-maximizing monopolistic competitor will expand output to q, where marginal revenue is equal to marginal cost and price P can be charged. Beyond q, to sell more output would require a reduction in price so large that profit would be reduced. For any output level less than q (for example, R), a price reduction and sales expansion will add more to total revenues than to total costs. At output R, marginal revenues exceed marginal costs. Thus, profits will be greater if price is reduced so output can be expanded. On the other hand, if output exceeds q (for example, S), sale of additional units beyond q will *add* more to costs (MC) than to revenues (MR). The firm will therefore gain by raising the price to P, even though the price rise will result in the loss of customers. Profits will be maximized by charging price P and producing the output level q, where MC =MR. At this stage, the analysis resembles that for a monopolist. Under monopolistic competition, however, there are no barriers to entry or exit. Therefore in contrast with monopoly, the number of firms in the market will respond to changes in profitability.

The firm pictured by Exhibit 2 is making economic profit. Total revenues $PAqO$ exceeds the firm's total costs $CBqO$ at the profit-maximizing output level. Since barriers to entry in monopolistically competitive markets are low, profits will attract

EXHIBIT 2

The Monopolistic Competitor's Price and Output

A monopolistic competitor maximizes profits by producing output q, for which MR = MC, and charging price P. The firm is making economic profits. What impact will they have, if this is a typical firm?

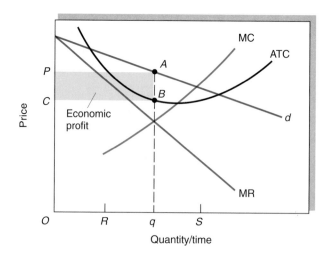

rival competitors. If this is a typical firm, other firms will attempt to duplicate the product (or service) offered by the profit-making firms.

What impact will the entry of new rivals have on the demand for the products of profit-making firms already in the market? These new rivals will draw customers away from existing firms. As long as monopolistically competitive firms can make economic profits, new competitors will be attracted to the market. This pressure will continue until the competition among rivals has shifted the demand curve for monopolistic competitors inward far enough to eliminate economic profits. In the long run, as illustrated by Exhibit 3, a monopolistically competitive firm will just be able to cover its production costs. It will produce to the MR = MC output level, but for the typical firm, the entry of new competition will force the price down to the average per unit cost.

If losses exist in a monopolistically competitive industry, some of the existing firms in the industry will go out of business over a period of time. As firms leave the industry, some of their previous customers will buy from other firms. The demand curve facing the remaining firms in the industry will shift out until the economic losses are eliminated and the long-run, zero-profit equilibrium illustrated by Exhibit 3 is again restored.

Under monopolistic competition, profits and losses play basically the same role as they do under pure competition. Economic profits will attract new competitors to the market. The increased availability of the product (and similar products) will drive the price down until the profits are eliminated. Conversely, economic losses will induce competitors to exit from the market. The decline in the availability of the product (supply) will allow the price to rise until firms are once again able to cover their average cost.

In the short run, a monopolistic competitor may make either economic profits or losses, depending on market conditions. In the long run, however, only a normal profit rate (that is, zero economic profits) will be possible because of competitive conditions and freedom of entry.

As we use the model of monopolistic competition, it is important to keep in mind that like all models, it is a simplification of the real world. The market process

EXHIBIT 3

Monopolistic Competition and Long-Run Normal Profit

Since entry and exit are free, competition will eventually drive prices down to the level of average total cost, for the representative firm.

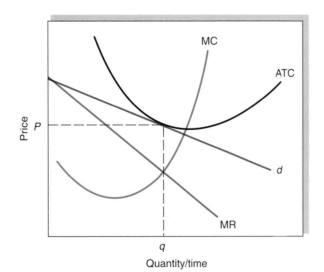

is more complex. Entrepreneurs in a monopolistically competitive situation recognize that, since each firm is producing a slightly different product that is sold into a slightly different market, losses for one firm do not necessarily mean that another, slightly different strategy might not succeed. Similarly, just because some of the firms in a market have discovered a successful combination of product, service, location, marketing, and operational efficiency, there is no guarantee that others will do so. The restaurant business in most cities illustrates this point. While some restauranteurs are operating successfully and earning economic profit, others may be closing their doors. Competition is an ongoing, dynamic process. Entrepreneurs who are good at discovering and producing things consumers value highly relative to their cost will prosper. Those who are not, will fail. Therefore, while we often focus on what is happening to the *typical* firm under monopolistic competition, it important to recognize that there is an ongoing competitive process at work. Thus, the experience of a *specific* market participant many differ from that of the typical firm in the market.

COMPARING PURE AND MONOPOLISTIC COMPETITION

As you can see, determination of price and output under monopolistic competition is in some ways very similar to that under pure competition. Also, since the long-run equilibrium conditions under pure competition are consistent with ideal economic efficiency, it is useful to compare and contrast other market structures with pure competition. There are both similarities and differences between pure and monopolistic competition.

EXHIBIT 4

Comparing Pure and Monopolistic Competition

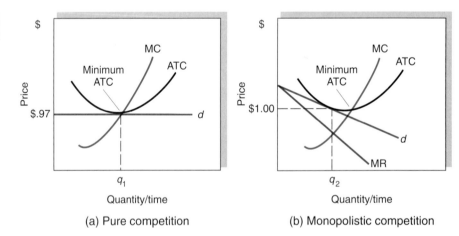

(a) Pure competition

(b) Monopolistic competition

The long-run equilibrium conditions of firms under pure and monopolistic competition are illustrated here. In both cases, price is equal to average total cost, and economic profit is absent. However, since the monopolistically competitive firm confronts a downward-sloping demand curve for its product, its equilibrium price exceeds marginal cost, and equilibrium output is not large enough to minimize average total cost. *For identical cost conditions,* the price of the monopolistic competitor will be slightly higher than that of the pure competitor. Chamberlin referred to this slightly higher price as the premium a society pays for variety and convenience (product differentiation).

SIMILARITIES BETWEEN PURE AND MONOPOLISTIC COMPETITION

Since barriers to entry are low, neither pure nor monopolistic competitors will be able to earn long-run economic profit. In the long run, competition will drive the price of pure and monopolistic competitors down to the level of average total cost.

In each case, entrepreneurs have a strong incentive to manage and operate their businesses efficiently. Inefficient operation will lead to losses and forced exit from the market. Pure and monopolistic competitors alike will be motivated to develop and adopt new cost-reducing procedures and techniques because lower costs will mean higher short-run profits (or at least smaller losses).

The response of pure and monopolistic competitors to changing demand conditions is very similar. In both cases, an increase in market demand leads to higher prices, short-run profits, and the entry of additional firms. With the entry of new producers, and the concurrent expansion of existing firms, the market supply will increase, lowering the demand facing each firm. The process will continue until the market price falls to the level of average total cost, squeezing out all economic profit. Similarly, a reduction in demand will lead to lower prices and short-run losses, causing output to fall and some firms to exit. The remaining firms can raise prices until short-run losses are eliminated. Profits and losses will direct the activities of firms under both pure and monopolistic competition.

DIFFERENCES BETWEEN PURE AND MONOPOLISTIC COMPETITION

As Exhibit 4 illustrates, the pure competitor confronts a horizontal demand curve; the demand curve faced by a monopolistic competitor is downward-sloping. This is important because it means that the marginal revenue of the monopolistic competitor will be less than, rather than equal to, price. So, when the profit-maximizing monopolistic competitor expands output until MR = MC, price will still exceed marginal cost (Exhibit 4b). In contrast, in long-run equilibrium, the price charged by the pure competitor will *equal* marginal cost (Exhibit 4a). Also, for a firm in monopolistic competition, unlike one in pure competition, the equilibrium (zero economic profit) output rate fails to minimize the firm's long-run average total cost, as Exhibit 4 illustrates. The monopolistic competitor would have a lower per unit cost (97 cents rather than $1.00) if a larger output were produced.

ALLOCATIVE EFFICIENCY UNDER MONOPOLISTIC COMPETITION

The efficiency of monopolistic competition has been the subject of debate among economists for years. At one time, the dominant view seemed to be that allocative inefficiency results because monopolistic competitors fail to operate at an output level that minimizes their long-run average total cost. Due to the proliferation in the number of monopolistic competitors, the sales of each competitor fall short of their least-cost capacity level. The potential social gain associated with the expansion of production to the $P = MC$ output rate is lost. The advocates of this view point out that if there were fewer producers, they would each be able to operate at a minimum-cost output rate. Instead, there is costly duplication—too many producers each operating below their minimum-cost output capacity. According to this traditional view, the location of two or more filling stations, restaurants, grocery stores, or similar establishments side by side is indicative of the economic waste generated by monopolistic competition.

In addition, the critics of monopolistic competition argue that it often leads to self-defeating, wasteful advertising. Firms have an incentive to use advertising to promote artificial distinctions between similar products. Each firm bombards consumers with advertisements proclaiming (or implying) that its own product is fancier, has greater sex appeal, and/or brings quicker relief than any product of rival firms. Firms that do not engage in such advertising can expect their sales to decline. Advertising, though, results in higher prices for consumers and thus is costly from society's point of view.

In recent years, this traditional view has been seriously challenged. Many economists now believe that such a view is mechanistic and fails to take into account the significance of dynamic competition. Most important, the traditional view assumes that consumers place no value on the wider variety of qualities and styles that results from monopolistic competition. Prices might very well be slightly lower if there were fewer gasoline stations, if they were located farther apart, and if they offered a more limited variety of service and credit plan options. Similarly, the prices of groceries might very well be slightly lower if there were fewer supermarkets, each a bit more congested and located less conveniently for some customers. However, since customers value product diversity as well as lower prices, they might be better off under the conditions created by monopolistic competition. Edward Chamberlin, one of the developers of the theory, argues that higher prices (and costs) are simply the premium consumers pay for variety and convenience. When consumers receive utility from product diversity, one cannot conclude that pure competition with a lower price, but less variety from which to select, would be preferable to monopolistic competition. The fact that consumers willingly pay more for a variety of products, rather than all flocking to a single, cheaper version of the product, suggests that many consumers, at least, prefer the variety.

The defenders of monopolistic competition also deny that this leads to excessive, wasteful advertising. They point out that advertising often reduces the consumer's search time and provides valuable information on prices. If advertising really raises prices, it must provide the consumer with something valuable. Otherwise, the consumer will purchase lower-priced, nonadvertised goods. When consumers really prefer lower prices and less advertising, firms offering that combination do quite well. In fact, proponents argue that monopolistic competitors actually do often use higher quality service and lower prices to compete with rivals who advertise heavily.

The debate among economists has helped clarify this topic's issues. Nevertheless, for some observers the efficiency of monopolistic competition continues to be an unresolved issue.

REAL-WORLD MONOPOLISTIC COMPETITORS

In our model, we assume that firms have perfect knowledge of their costs and demand conditions. Real-world firms do not have such information. They must rely on past experience, market surveys, experimentation, and other business skills when they make price, output, and production decisions. (See the Applications in Economics box, "The Left-Out Variable: Entrepreneurship.")

APPLICATIONS IN ECONOMICS

The Left-Out Variable: Entrepreneurship[4]

To help us understand facts and make predictions, a scientific model must simplify what it describes, and draw attention to the most important relationships. Economic models are no exception. Our model of decision-making in business firms is designed to highlight for us the decision-making elements common to all firms, and it performs this job quite well. But it leaves out some important steps in the decision-making process of real-world firms. Typically, a great many judgments are needed before the process we describe can even begin.

Would profits increase if prices were raised, or would lower prices lead to larger profits? Real-world decision-makers cannot go into the back room and look at their demand-cost diagram to answer these questions. They must search for clues, experiment with actual price changes, and interpret what they see, often using a great deal of "seat-of-the-pants" judgment. The successful entrepreneur will search and find (or at least approximate) the profit-maximizing price—the MR = MC price and output combination that our model shows so simply.

For real-world entrepreneurs, the problem of uncertainty goes well beyond setting the profit-maximizing price and output. How can an entrepreneur decide whether demand and cost conditions will make entry into a monopolistically competitive field profitable? How large should the plant be? How should production be organized? How much variety,

and what combination of qualities should be built into the firm's product or service? What location will be best? What forms of advertising will be most effective? These questions and many more require entrepreneurial judgment. Entrepreneurial judgment is necessary when there is no decision rule that can be applied using only information that is freely available. For this reason, the entrepreneurial function has not been put into economic models. There simply is no way to model such judgmental decisions. All we can do is note their importance and recognize that our models are limited by the fact that they are missing this critical element of successful business decision-making.

The Entrepreneur: A Job Description

If we cannot put entrepreneurship into our models, what can we say about its function? One way to answer this question is to consider a generalized job description for an entrepreneurial position. An investor who lacks the desire, or perhaps the skill, to be an entrepreneur, but nonetheless wants to be in business, may well seek someone to act as the business entrepreneur, while the investor provides some of the capital. A newspaper ad to find such a person (while perhaps not the usual way for the investor to search) might read as follows:

Wanted: Entrepreneur. Must have many qualities: 1) Alert to new business opportunities and to new

problems before they become obvious. 2) Willing to back judgments with investments of hard work and creative effort before others recognize correctness of judgments. 3) Able to make correct decisions and to convince others of their validity, so as to attract additional financial backing. 4) Able to recognize own inevitable mistakes and to back away from incorrect decisions without wasting additional resources. Exciting, exhausting, high risk position. Pay will be very good for success, and very poor for failure.

Entrepreneurship is not for the faint-hearted or the lazy. Entrepreneurs are at the center of the action in the real world, even if they do not have a place in most economic models.

---

[4]For a more complete overview of entrepreneurship, and references on the topic, see Mark Crosson, "Entrepreneurship," in *The New Palgrave: a Dictionary of Economics* edited by John Eatwell, et. al., (New York: Stockton Press, 1987) pp. 151–53.

Despite their high hopes, many firms go out of business every year. In recent years, among corporate establishments alone, the number of firms going out of business has generally exceeded 250,000 annually. A great many of these unsuccessful businesses are small, monopolistically competitive firms that are the victims of losses stemming from market competition.

Why do losses occur in the real world? Since business decisions must be made with imperfect information, mistakes sometimes result. A firm may mistakenly produce a good for which consumers are unwilling to pay a price that will enable the producer to cover the costs of production. Losses are the market's method of bringing such activities to a halt. Economic losses signal that the resources would be valued more highly if they were put to other uses. That is, the opportunity cost of production exceeds the value of the output. The fact that losses reduce the wealth of firms' owners also provides the incentive to correct this allocative inefficiency.

CHARACTERISTICS OF OLIGOPOLY

Oligopoly: A market situation in which a small number of sellers comprise the entire industry. It is competition among the few.

"Oligopoly" means "few sellers." When there are only a few firms in an industry, the industrial structure is called an **oligopoly.** In the United States, the great majority of output in such industries as automobiles, steel, cigarettes, and aircraft is produced by five or fewer dominant firms. In addition to a small number of producers, there are several other characteristics that oligopolistic industries have in common.

INTERDEPENDENCE AMONG FIRMS

Since the number of sellers in an oligopolistic industry is small, each firm must take the potential reactions of rivals into account when it makes business decisions. The decisions of one seller often influence the price of products and the profits of rival firms. In an oligopoly, the welfare of each seller is dependent on the policies followed by its major rivals.

SUBSTANTIAL ECONOMIES OF SCALE

In an oligopolistic industry, large-scale production (relative to the total market) is necessary to attain a low per unit cost. Economies of scale are significant. A small number of the large-scale, cost-efficient firms will meet the demand for the industry's product.

Using the automobile industry as an example, Exhibit 5 illustrates the importance of economies of scale as a source of oligopoly. It has been estimated that each firm must produce approximately one million automobiles annually before its per unit cost of production is minimized. However, when the selling price of automobiles is barely sufficient for firms to cover their costs, the total quantity demanded from these producers is only six million. To minimize costs, then, each firm must produce at least one sixth (one million of the six million) of the output demanded. In other words, the industry can support no more than five or six domestic firms of cost-efficient size.

SIGNIFICANT BARRIERS TO ENTRY

As with monopoly, barriers to entry limit the ability of new firms to compete effectively in oligopolistic industries. Economies of scale are probably the most significant entry barrier. A potential competitor may be unable to start out small and gradually grow to the optimal size, since a firm in an oligopolistic industry must gain a large share of the market before it can minimize per unit cost. The

Economies of Scale and Oligopoly

Oligopoly exists in the automobile industry because firms do not fully realize the cost reductions from large-scale output until they produce approximately one-sixth of the total market.

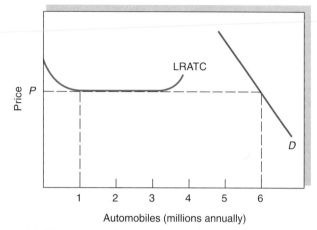

manufacture of refrigerators and diesel engines, as well as automobile production, seems to fall into this category.

Other factors, including patent rights, control over an essential resource, and government-imposed monopoly may also prevent new competitors from entering profitable oligopolistic industries. Without substantial barriers to entry, oligopolistic competition would be similar to monopolistic competition.

PRODUCTS MAY BE EITHER HOMOGENEOUS OR DIFFERENTIATED

The products of sellers in an oligopolistic industry may be either homogeneous or differentiated. When firms produce identical products, such as milk or gasoline, there is less opportunity for nonprice competition. On the other hand, rival firms producing differentiated products are more likely to use style, quality, and advertising as competitive weapons.

PRICE AND OUTPUT UNDER OLIGOPOLY

Unlike a monopolist or a pure competitor, an oligopolist cannot determine the product price that will deliver maximum profit simply by estimating market demand and cost conditions. An oligopolist must also predict how rival firms (that is, the rest of the industry) will react to price (and quality) adjustments. Since each oligopolist confronts such a complex problem, it is impossible to determine the precise price and output policy that will emerge in oligopolistic industries. Economics does, however, indicate a potential range of prices, and the factors that will determine whether prices in the industry will be high or low relative to costs of production.

Consider an oligopolistic industry in which seven or eight rival firms produce the entire market output. Substantial economies of scale are present. The firms produce identical products and have similar costs of production. Exhibit 6 depicts the market demand conditions and long-run costs of production of the individual firms for such an industry.

What price will prevail? We can answer this question for two extreme cases. First, suppose that each firm sets its price independently of the other firms. There is no collusion, and each competitive firm acts independently, seeking to maximize profits by offering consumers a better deal than its rivals. Under these conditions, the market price would be driven down to P_c. Firms would be just able to cover their per unit costs of production. What would happen if a *single firm* raised its price? Its customers would switch to rival firms, which would now expand to accommodate the new customers. The firm that raised its price would lose out. It would be self-defeating for any one firm to raise its price if the other firms did not raise theirs.

What would happen if supply conditions were such that the market price was above P_c? Since the demand curve faced by each *individual firm* is relatively elastic, rival sellers would have a strong incentive to reduce their price. Any firm that reduced its price slightly, by 1 percent, for example, would gain numerous customers. The price-cutting firm would attract some new buyers to the market, but more importantly, that firm would also lure many buyers away from rival firms charging higher prices. Total profit would expand as the price-cutter gained a larger share of the total market. But, what would happen if all firms attempted to undercut their rivals? Price would be driven down to P_c, and the economic profit of the firms would be eliminated.

When rival oligopolists compete (pricewise) with one another, they drive the market price down to the level of costs of production. They do not always compete, however. There is a strong incentive for oligopolists to collude, raise price, and restrict output.

Cartel: An organization of sellers designed to coordinate supply decisions so that the joint profits of the members will be maximized. A cartel will seek to create a monopoly in the market.

Suppose the oligopolists, recognizing their interdependence, acted cooperatively to maximize their joint profit. They might form a **cartel,** such as OPEC, to accomplish this objective. Alternatively, they might collude without the aid of a formal organization. Under federal antitrust laws, collusive action to raise price and expand the joint profit of the firms would, of course, be illegal. Nevertheless, let us see what would happen if oligopolists followed this course. Exhibit 6 shows the marginal revenue curve that would accompany the market demand D for the product. Under perfect cooperation, the oligopolists would refuse to produce units for which marginal revenue was less than marginal cost. Thus, they would restrict joint output to Q_m, where MR = MC. Market price would rise to P_m. With collusion, substantial joint profits (the shaded area of Exhibit 6) could thus be attained. The case of perfect cooperation would be identical with the outcome under monopoly.

EXHIBIT 6

The Range of Price and Output under Oligopoly

If oligopolists competed with one another, price-cutting would drive price down to P_c. In contrast, perfect cooperation among firms would lead to a higher price P_m and a smaller output (Q_m rather than Q_c). The shaded area shows profit if firms collude. Demand here is the market demand.

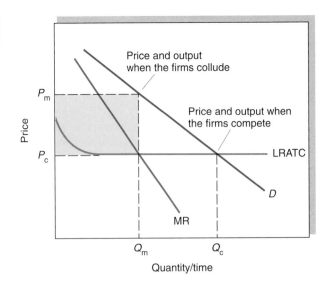

In the real world, however, the outcome is likely to fall between the extremes of price competition and perfect cooperation. Oligopolists generally recognize their interdependence and try to avoid vigorous price competition, which would drive price down to the level of per unit costs. But, there are also obstacles to collusion. Thus, prices in oligopolistic industries do not rise to the monopolistic level. Oligopolistic prices are typically above the purely competitive level but below those for pure monopoly.

OBSTACLES TO COLLUSION

Collusion: Agreement among firms to avoid various competitive practices, particularly price reductions. It may involve either formal agreements or merely tacit recognition that competitive practices will be self-defeating in the long run. Tacit collusion is difficult to detect. The Sherman Act prohibits collusion and conspiracies to restrain interstate trade.

Collusion is the opposite of competition. It involves cooperative actions by sellers to turn the terms of trade in favor of the group, and against buyers. Since oligopolists can profit by colluding to restrict output and raise price, economic theory suggests that they will have a strong incentive to do so. To accomplish this however, the firms must also agree on production quotas for each firm, or a division of the market so that production is limited to the level that will be purchased at the chosen cartel price.

Each *individual* oligopolist, though, also has an incentive to cheat on collusive agreements. Exhibit 7 will help us understand why. An undetected price cut will enable a firm to attract (a) customers who would not buy from any firm at the higher price *and* (b) those who would normally buy from other firms. The demand facing the oligopolistic *firm* will thus be considerably more elastic than the industry demand curve. As Exhibit 7 shows, the price P_i that maximizes the industry's profits will be higher than the price P_f that is best for each individual oligopolist. If a firm can find a way to undercut the price set by the collusive agreement, while other sellers maintain the higher price, expanded sales, beyond the level agreed

EXHIBIT 7

Gaining from Cheating

The industry demand (D_i) and marginal revenue curves are shown in frame b. The joint profits of oligopolists would be maximized at Q_i, where $MR_i = MC$. Price P_i would be best for the industry as a whole. However, the demand curve (d_f) facing each firm (frame a, drawn under the assumption that no other firms cheat) would be much more elastic than D_i. Given the greater elasticity of its demand curve, an individual firm would maximize its profit by cutting its price to P_f and expanding output to q_f, where $MR_f = MC$. Thus, individual oligopolists could gain by secretly shaving price and cheating on the collusive agreement.

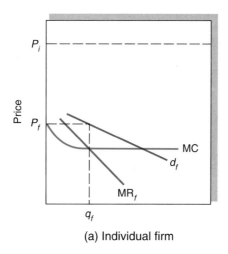

(a) Individual firm

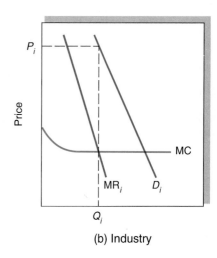

(b) Industry

upon by the cartel, will more than make up for the reduction in per unit profit margin.

In oligopolistic industries, there are two conflicting tendencies. An oligopolistic firm has a strong incentive to cooperate with its rivals so that joint profit can be maximized. However, it also has a strong incentive to cheat secretly on any collusive agreement in order to increase its share of the joint profit. Oligopolistic agreements therefore tend to be unstable. This instability exists whether the cooperative behavior is formal, as in the case of a cartel, or informal.

There are certain situations in which it is difficult for oligopolists to collude. Five major obstacles can limit collusive behavior.

When the Number of Oligopolists Is Larger, Effective Collusion Is Less Likely.

Other things constant, as the number of major firms in an industry increases, it becomes more costly for the oligopolists to communicate, negotiate, and enforce agreements among themselves. Developing and maintaining collusive agreements become more difficult. In addition, the greater the number of firms, the more likely it is that the objectives of individual firms will conflict with those of the industry. Each firm will want a bigger slice of the pie. Opinions about the best collusive price arrangement will differ because marginal costs, unused plant capacity, and estimates of market demand elasticity are likely to differ among firms. Aggressive, less mature firms may want to expand their share of total output. These conflicting interests contribute to the breakdown of collusive agreements.

When It Is Difficult to Detect and Eliminate Price Cuts, Collusion Is Less Attractive.

Unless a firm has a way of policing the pricing activities of its rivals, it may be the "sucker" in a collusive agreement. Firms that secretly cut prices may gain a larger share of the market, while others maintain their higher prices and lose customers and profits. Price-cutting can sometimes be accomplished in ways that are difficult for the other firms to identify. For example, a firm might provide better credit terms, faster delivery, and other related services "free" to improve slightly the package offered to the consumer.[5]

When firms sell a differentiated product, improvements in quality and style can be used as competitive weapons. "Price cuts" of this variety are particularly attractive to an oligopolist because they cannot be easily and quickly duplicated by rivals. Competitors can quickly match a reduction in money price, but it will take time for them to match an improvement in quality. When firms can freely use improvements in quality to gain a larger share of the market, collusive agreements on price are of limited value. When cheating (price-cutting) is profitable and difficult for rivals to police, it is a good bet that oligopolistic rivals will be induced to cheat.

Low Entry Barriers Are an Obstacle to Collusion.

Unless potential rivals can be excluded, oligopolists will be unable to make unusually large profits. Successful collusion will merely attract competitors into the industry, which will eliminate the profits. Even with collusion, long-run profits will not be possible unless entry into the industry can be blocked.

---

[5]See Marshall R. Colberg, Dascomb Forbush, and Gilbert R. Whitaker, *Business Economics,* 5th ed. (Homewood: Irwin, 1975), for an extensive discussion of the alternative methods by which business firms are able to alter price.

Local markets are sometimes dominated by a few firms. For example, many communities have only a small number of ready-mix concrete producers, bowling alleys, accounting firms, and furniture stores. In the absence of government restrictions, however, entry barriers into these markets are often low (see Applications in Economics box on Contestable Markets). The threat of potential rivals reduces the gains from collusive behavior under these conditions.

APPLICATIONS IN ECONOMICS

Contestable Markets: Low Entry Barriers May Yield Competitive Results

Markets with few sellers are sometimes more competitive than they seem. Consider the case of the airline route between Salt Lake City, Utah, and Albuquerque, New Mexico. Only two airlines serve this route directly, since it has so little traffic. Further, there would seem to be high barriers to entry, since it takes multimillion dollar airplanes to compete, as well as facilities for reservations, ticketing, baggage handling and so on. The two airlines are well aware of the rivalry (with or without competition) between them, and they both charge the same price. One might expect that price to be high, perhaps close to the monopoly level. But, there is reason to believe that the two airlines, much as they would like to collude and drive up the price, will not be able to do so, as long as other airlines are free to enter this market.

Contestable Market: A market in which the costs of entry and exit are low, so that a firm risks little by entering. Efficient production and zero economic profits should prevail in a contestable market. A market can be contestable even if capital requirements are high.

To compete on an airline route may require millions of dollars in equipment, but the barriers to entry are much lower than that fact suggests. The Salt Lake City—Albuquerque market, for example, can be entered simply by shifting aircraft, personnel, and equipment from other locations. The aircraft can even be rented or leased. By the same token, if a new entrant (or an established firm) wants to leave that market, nearly all the invested capital values can be recovered, through shifting the aircraft and other capital equipment to other routes, or leasing them to other firms. An airline route then, in the absence of legal barriers, is a classic case of a **contestable market:** the costs of entry and exit are low, so that a firm risks little by entering.[6] If entry is later judged to be a mistake, exit is relatively easy because fixed costs are not sunk costs, but are instead recoverable. Entry into a contestable market may require the use of large amounts of capital, but so long as the capital is recoverable, and not a sunk cost, the large capital requirement is not a high barrier to entry.

In a contestable market, potential competition, as well as actual entry, can discipline firms selling in the market. When entry and exit are not expensive, even a single seller in a market faces the serious prospect of

competition. Contestable markets yield two important results: (a) prices will not for long be higher than the level necessary to achieve zero economic profits, and (b) least-cost production will occur. The reason is that both inefficiency and prices above costs present a profitable opportunity to new entrants. Potential competitors who see an opportunity for economic profit can be expected to enter and move the market toward the perfectly competitive result.

These results do have a policy implication: if policy-makers want to correct an oligopoly (or monopoly) situation, they should consider what might be done to make the market in question contestable. Much of the enthusiasm of economists for deregulation can be traced to the fact that regulation often is the primary restraint to entry. Many economists believe that deregulation permitting new entry can make many markets contestable, achieving lower prices and more efficiency than can direct regulation of producers. We will have more to say about this in the next chapter.

[6]The classic article on this topic is William J. Baumol's "Contestable Markets: An Uprising in the Theory of Industry Structure," *American Econonmic Review* 72 (March 1982), pp. 1–15.

Unstable Demand Conditions Are an Obstacle to Collusion.   Demand instability tends to increase the honest differences of opinion among oligopolists about what is best for the industry. One firm may want to expand because it anticipates a sharp increase in future demand, while a more pessimistic rival may want to hold the line on existing industrial capacity. Greater differences in expectations about future demand create greater conflict among oligopolistic firms. Successful collusion is more likely when demand is relatively stable.

Vigorous Antitrust Action Increases the Cost of Collusion.   Under existing antitrust laws, collusive behavior is prohibited. Secret agreements are, of course, possible. Simple informal cooperation might be conducted without discussions or collusive agreements. However, like other illegal behavior, all such agreements are not legally enforceable by any firm. Vigorous antitrust action can discourage firms from making such illegal agreements. As the threat of getting caught increases, participants will be less likely to attempt collusive behavior.

LIMITS OF THE OLIGOPOLY MODEL

Market Power:
The ability of a firm to profit by raising its price significantly above the competitive level for a considerable period of time.

Uncertainty and imprecision characterize the theory of oligopoly. We know that firms will gain if they can successfully agree to restrict output and raise price. However, collusion also has its costs. We have outlined some of the conflicts and difficulties (costs) associated with the establishment of perfect cooperation among oligopolistic firms. In some industries, these difficulties are considerable, and the **market power** of the oligopolists is therefore relatively small. In other industries, oligopolistic cooperation, although not perfect, may raise prices significantly. Economists would say that such firms have market power, indicating that even though these firms are not pure monopolists, they do have some monopoly power. Analysis of the costs and benefits of collusive behavior, while it does not yield precise predictions on oligopoly pricing, at least allows us to determine when discipline by competitive pressures is more likely for an oligopolist.

CONCENTRATION AND REAL-WORLD OLIGOPOLISTIC POWER

Concentration Ratio:
The total sales of the four (or sometimes eight) largest firms in an industry as a percentage of the total sales of the industry. The higher the ratio, the greater is the market dominance of a small number of firms. The ratio can be seen as a measure of the potential for oligopolistic power.

Which industries are dominated by a small number of firms? How important is oligopoly? Economists have traditionally used a tool, the concentration ratio, to help answer these questions.

The **concentration ratio** is the percentage of total industry sales made by the four (or sometimes eight) largest firms of an industry. This ratio can vary from nearly zero to 100, with 100 indicating that the sales of the four largest firms comprise those of the entire industry.

The concentration ratio can be thought of as a broad indicator of competitiveness. In general, the higher (lower) the concentration ratio, the more (less) likely that the firms of the industry will be able to successfully collude against the interests of consumers. This ratio, though, is by no means a perfect measure of competitiveness. Since the sales of foreign producers are excluded, it overstates the degree of concentration in industries in which foreign firms compete. Neither does the concentration ratio reveal the elasticity of demand for products, even though concentration is not as great a problem if good substitutes for a product are available. For example, the market power of aluminum producers is partially limited by competition from steel, plastics, copper, and similar products. Similarly, the monopoly power of commercial airlines is substantially reduced by the availability of automobiles, buses, chartered private flights, and even conference telephone calls. Concentration ratios tend to conceal such competitiveness among products.

The concentration ratio can also overstate the competitiveness in instances in which the relevant market area is a city or region. For example, consider the case of newspaper publishing companies. In 1982, there were more than 7500 such companies in the United States. Sales of the four largest companies amounted to only 22 percent of the national market. Most cities, however, were served by only one or two newspapers. In most market areas, newspaper publishing is a highly concentrated industry, even though this is not true nationally. In this instance, the low concentration ratio for the nation in the newspaper publishing industry probably understates the market power of local newspapers.

What do concentration ratios reveal about the U.S. economy? Exhibit 8 presents concentration data for several manufacturing industries in 1947 and in 1982, the most recent year for which the Census Bureau concentration ratios for

EXHIBIT 8 ■	Concentration Ratios for Selected Manufacturing Industries in 1947 and 1982		
Industry	1947	1982	Change
High concentration (40 or more)			
Motor vehicles and car bodies	71	92	+21
Blast furnaces and steel mills	50	42	− 8
Tires and inner tubes	70[a]	66	− 4
Aircraft and parts	72	64	− 8
Telephone and telegraph	92	76	−16
Farm machinery	36	53	+17
Soap and other detergents	72[a]	60	−12
Photographic equipment and supplies	61	74	+13
Electronic computing equipment	66[a]	43	−23
Medium concentration (20–39)			
Petroleum	37	28	− 9
Bread, cake, and related products	16	34	+18
Periodicals	34	20	−14
Gray iron foundries	16	29	+13
Toilet preparations	24	34	+10
Pharmaceuticals	28	26	− 2
Newspapers	21	22	+ 1
Meat packing	41	29	−12
Low concentration (less than 20)			
Bottled and canned soft drinks	12[a]	14	+ 2
Commercial printing	13[a]	7	− 6
Sporting and athletic goods	24	17	− 7
Sawmills	11[a]	17	+ 6

[a]Data are for 1963.

Source: U.S. Bureau of the Census, *Census of Manufacturing, 1947* and *1982*.

industries economy-wide are available. Several industries, including the automobile, steel, aircraft, telephone and telegraph, computer equipment, and soap industries, are dominated by a few firms. They are oligopolistic. At the other end of the spectrum, the "big four" accounted for less than 20 percent of the sales of sporting goods, saw mill products, bottled and canned soft drinks, and commercial printing.

Most research suggests that there has been, if anything, an increase in business competitiveness over the last several decades. *Within specific industries,* there are cases of both increases and decreases in the degree of concentration. For example, concentration increased in the motor vehicle, farm machinery, and photographic equipment industries between 1947 and 1982. On the other hand, the degree of concentration in aircraft, computer equipment, steel, telephone and telegraph equipment, and meat packing has declined significantly in recent years.

CONCENTRATION AND MERGERS

Horizontal Merger: The combining of the assets of two or more firms engaged in the production of *similar products* into a single firm.

At some points in American history, especially during the early developmental stages of American manufacturing, mergers had an important influence on the structure of markets in our economy. The desire of oligopolistic firms to merge is not surprising. A **horizontal merger,** the combining of two or more firms' assets under the same ownership, provides the firms with an alternative to both the rigors of competition and the insecurity of collusion.

There have been two great waves of horizontal mergers. The first occurred between 1887 and 1904; the second between 1916 and 1929. Many corporations whose names are now household words—U.S. Steel, General Electric, Standard Oil, General Foods, General Mills, and American Can, for example—are products of mergers formed during these periods. Mergers led to a dominant firm in manufacturing industries such as steel, sugar refining, agricultural implements, leather, rubber, distilleries, and tin cans.

Analysis of these horizontal mergers leads to two interesting observations. First, horizontal mergers can create a highly profitable dominant firm, even if there is freedom of entry into an industry. The entry of new competitors takes time. A firm formed by merger that controls a substantial share of the market for a product can often realize oligopolistic profits for a period of time before the entry of new firms drives prices back down to the level of average cost. Of course, if entry barriers can be established to limit or retard the entry of new rivals, the incentive to merge is further strengthened.[7] Second, with the passage of time, competitive forces have generally eroded the position of the dominant firms created by horizontal mergers. Almost without exception, the market share of the dominant firms created by horizontal mergers began to decline soon after the mergers were consummated. Smaller firms gained ground relative to the dominant firm. This suggests that temporary profits stemming from market power, rather than economies of scale, were the primary motivation for the horizontal mergers. In 1950, the Celler-Kefauver Act made it substantially more difficult to use horizontal mergers as a means of developing oligopolistic power. Today, mergers involving large firms seldom involve former competitors.

---

[7]See George Stigler, "Monopoly and Oligopoly by Merger," *American Economic Review* (May 1950), pp. 23–34, for a detailed analysis of this issue.

Vertical Merger: The creation of a single firm from two firms, one of which was a supplier or customer of the other—for example, a merger of a lumber company with a furniture manufacturer.

Conglomerate Merger: The combining under one ownership of two or more firms that produce *unrelated products*.

Another type of merger, the **vertical merger,** joins a supplier and a buyer—for example, an automobile maker and a steel producer. A vertical merger might simplify the long-range planning process for both firms and reduce the need for costly legal contracting between the two. Even though vertical mergers generally do not increase concentration within industries, some economists are concerned that such mergers may reduce competition if either the buyer or the supplier grants a market advantage to the other.

A **conglomerate merger** combines two firms in unrelated industries. The stated intent is usually to introduce new and superior management into the firm being absorbed. This type of merger results in increased size but not necessarily in reduced competition. Since the 1960s, when some very large corporations were formed by conglomerate merger, some observers have expressed concern that the concentration of political power created by such mergers and the enormous financial assets available to the operating units may be potentially dangerous. Others have argued that conglomerate mergers often lead to more efficient management and increased competitiveness within specific industries.

CONCENTRATION AND PROFITS

The model of oligopoly implies that if the firms in concentrated industries cooperate with one another, they can *jointly* exercise monopoly power. Is there a relationship between industrial concentration and profitability in the real world? Researchers in this area have not been able to arrive at a definite conclusion. An early study by Joe Bain showed a distinctly positive relationship between concentration and profitability. George Stigler, in a detailed study of manufacturing industries, found that from 1947 to 1954 "the average[profit] rate in the concentrated industries was 8.00 percent, while that in the unconcentrated industries was 7.16 percent." Later, both a study by William Shepherd covering the period from 1960 to 1969 and the White House Task Force on Antitrust Policy presented evidence that the rate of profitability is higher in concentrated industries.

More recent research results indicate that greater profits for larger firms are likely to come from greater efficiency, so that prices are lower. As Sam Peltzman concluded in his 1977 study, "Briefly, more concentration raises profitability not because prices rise, but because they fall less than costs."[8] Other researchers are not fully convinced. In any case, the weight of the evidence is that the profit rate of firms in concentrated industries is only slightly higher than the profit rate of other firms. Demand conditions, efficient management, and superior entrepreneurship are the main determinants of profitability. Thus, the odds are only a little better than 50–50 that a more concentrated industry will be more profitable than a less concentrated one.

MARKET POWER AND PROFIT—THE EARLY BIRD CATCHES THE WORM

In the last chapter, we saw that under certain conditions an unregulated monopolist can earn economic profit, even in the long run. Similarly, our analysis of oligopoly suggests that if barriers to entry are high, firms might be consistently able to earn above-average profits, even in the long run. Suppose a well-established firm, such

---

[8]Sam Peltzman, "The Gains and Losses from Industrial Concentration," *Journal of Law and Economics* 20 (Oct. 1977): 257. For a detailed analysis of this issue, see Leonard W. Weiss, "The Concentration–Profits Relationship and Antitrust," in H. J. Goldschmid et al., eds. *Industrial Concentration: the New Learning.* (Boston: Little, Brown, 1974), 184–232; and John S. McGee, *Industrial Organization.* (Englewood Cliffs: Prentice Hall 1988), 332–37.

MYTHS OF ECONOMICS

Profits are about as popular with consumers as failing grades are with students at the end of a term. When food prices rise, the profits of farmers, meat processors, and food store chains are heavily publicized by the news media. If gasoline prices jump, many people believe that they are being pushed up by greedy profiteering on the part of the major oil companies. The casual observer might easily be left with the impression that large profits are the major source of the high cost of living.

This issue is clouded by the fact that both the size of profits and their function are largely misunderstood by most people. Surveys show that young people believe the after-tax profits of corporations comprise between 25 and 30 percent of sales. A national sample poll of adults conducted by Opinion Research of Princeton found that the average person thought profits comprised 29 cents of every dollar of sales in manufacturing. In reality, as Exhibit 9b shows, the after-tax accounting profits of manufacturing corporations are about 4 to 5 percent of sales. Thus, the public believes that the rate of profit as a percentage of sales is nearly six times as great as the actual figure!

Why are people so misinformed on this issue? The popular media are one source of confusion. They nearly always report the accounting profits of firms in dollar terms, instead of comparing them to sales, stockholder equity, or the value of the firms' assets. A favorite device is to report that profits, either annually or quarterly, were up by some astonishing percentage.[9] Unless we know whether profits were high, normal, or low during the previous period, this type of statement tells little or nothing about the firm's earnings rate on its capital assets. For example, suppose a corporation with $100 million of assets earned a profit of $2 million last year, a 2 percent rate of return on its capital assets. Now, suppose the firm's earnings this year are $4 million, generating only a 4 percent rate of return. It would not be unusual for the popular media to report, ''The profits of corporation X soared to $4 million, a 100 percent increase over last year.'' What this statement conceals is that the profits of the firm as a percentage of its capital assets were less than one could earn on a savings account.

Not only is the average person misinformed about the size of profits, but most people do not understand their function. Many believe that if profits were eliminated, our economy would continue to operate as if nothing had happened. This erroneous view indicates a misunderstanding of what accounting profits are. Accounting profits are primarily a monetary return to those who have invested in machines, buildings, and nonhuman productive resources. Investment in physical capital involves both risk and the forgoing of current consumption. If profits were eliminated, the incentive of persons to invest and provide the tools that make the American worker the most productive in the world would be destroyed. Who would invest in either physical or human capital (for example, education) if such investments did not lead to an increase in future income—that is, if investment did not lead to accounting profit?

---

[9]This is equally true for large wage increases. Apparently, the extreme example rather than the norm helps to sell newspapers. We should note that such reports do not imply an antibusiness bias. The *Wall Street Journal*, not noted for such bias, regularly headlines its stories in the same manner.

---

as Exxon or General Motors, is able to use its market power to earn consistent economic profits. Do its current stockholders gain because of its monopoly power? Surprisingly, the answer is no. The ownership value of a share of corporate stock for such a corporation long ago began to reflect its market power and profitability. Many of the *present* stockholders paid high prices for their stock because they expected the firm to be highly profitable. In other words, they paid for any above-normal economic profits that the firm was expected to earn because of its monopoly power.

Profits play an important role in our economy. People who increase the value of resources—who produce something that is worth more than the resources that went into it—are rewarded with economic profit (and generally an above-average accounting profit). Those who allocate resources to a venture producing outputs that consumers value less than the venture's opportunity cost will experience economic losses (below-average accounting profits). Without this reward-penalty system, individuals (and firms) would have neither the information nor the incentives to use resources wisely and produce the goods that consumers desire most, relative to the goods' opportunity costs.

EXHIBIT 9

How Great Are Profits?

After-tax corporate profits average about 12 percent of stockholder equity and 5 percent of sales in the United States.

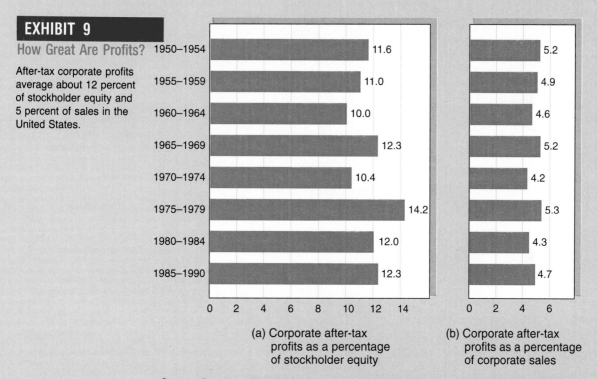

(a) Corporate after-tax profits as a percentage of stockholder equity

(b) Corporate after-tax profits as a percentage of corporate sales

Source: *Economic Report of the President, 1991.* As the result of changes in definitions and accounting procedures, the data for one period may not be perfectly comparable to the figures for other periods.

Do not expect to get rich buying the stock of monopolistic or oligopolistic firms known to be highly profitable. You are already too late. The early bird catches the worm. Those who owned the stock when these firms initially developed their market position have already captured the gain. The value of their stock increased at that time. After a firm's future prospects are widely recognized, subsequent stockholders fail to gain a higher-than-normal rate of return on their financial investment.

LOOKING AHEAD

The competitiveness of a market economy is influenced not only by the various market structures operating within it but also by public policy. Business activity is often directly regulated by the government. In the next chapter, we will investigate the business structure of markets in the U.S. economy and consider the impact of regulatory activities.

CHAPTER SUMMARY

1. Economic models of monopoly and competition, while quite useful, do not explain rivalrous business behavior, such as competitive advertising, ''cents-off'' coupons, and airline frequent-flier programs. Economists use models of monopolistic competition and oligopoly to illustrate and analyze the behavior of firms when these factors are present, and when firms attempt to collude.

2. The distinguishing characteristics of monopolistic competition are (a) firms that produce differentiated products, (b) low barriers to entry into and exit from the market, and (c) a substantial number of independent, rival firms.

3. Monopolistically competitive firms face a gently downward-sloping demand curve. They often use product quality, style, convenience of location, advertising, and price as competitive weapons. Since all rivals within a monopolistically competitive industry are free to duplicate another's products (or services), the demand for the product of any one firm is highly elastic.

4. A profit-maximizing firm will expand output as long as marginal revenue exceeds marginal cost. Thus, a firm under monopolistic competition will lower its price so that output can be expanded until MR = MC. The price charged by the profit-maximizing monopolistic competitor will be greater than its marginal cost.

5. If monopolistic competitors are making economic profits, rival firms will be induced to enter the market. They will expand the supply of the product (and similar products), enticing some customers away from established firms. The demand curve faced by an individual firm will fall (shift inward) until the profits have been eliminated.

6. Economic losses will cause monopolistic competitors to exit from the market. The demand for the products of each remaining firm will rise (shift outward) until the losses have been eliminated.

7. Since barriers to entry are low, firms in a monopolistically competitive industry will make only normal profits in the long run. In the short run, they may make either economic profits or losses, depending on market conditions.

8. Traditional economic theory has emphasized that monopolistic competition is inefficient because (a) price exceeds marginal cost at the long-run equilibrium output level; (b) long-run average cost is not minimized; and (c) excessive advertising is sometimes encouraged. However, other economists have argued more recently that this criticism is misdirected. According to the newer view, firms under monopolistic competition have an incentive to (a) produce efficiently; (b) undertake production if and only if their actions will increase the value of resources used; (c) offer a variety of products; and (d) be innovative in offering new product options.

9. Although standard economic models do not include the judgments made under uncertainty by entrepreneurs, economists generally recognize that the world is not so simple as our models indicate, and that entrepreneurial judgments are, in fact, important.

10. Oligopolistic market structure is characterized by (a) an interdependence among firms, (b) substantial economies of scale that result in only a small number of firms in the industry, and (c) significant barriers to entry. Oligopolists may produce either homogeneous or differentiated products.

11. There is no general theory of price, output, and equilibrium for oligopolistic markets. If rival oligopolists acted totally independently of their competitors, they would drive price down to the level of cost of production. Alternatively, if they used collusion to obtain perfect cooperation, price would rise to the level that a monopolist would

charge. The actual outcome lies between these two extremes.

12. Collusion is the opposite of competition. Oligopolists have a strong incentive to collude and raise their prices. However, the interests of individual firms will conflict with those of the industry as a whole. Since the demand curve faced by individual firms is far more elastic than the industry demand curve, each firm could gain by cutting its price (or raising product quality) by a small amount so that it could attract customers from rivals. If several firms tried to do this, however, the collusive agreement would break down.

13. Oligopolistic firms are less likely to collude successfully against the interests of consumers if (a) the number of rival firms is large; (b) it is costly to prohibit competitors from offering secret price cuts (or quality improvements) to customers; (c) entry barriers are low; (d) market demand conditions tend to be unstable; and/or (e) the threat of antitrust action is present.

14. Competition can come from potential, as well as actual rivals. If entry and exit are not expensive, and if there are no legal barriers to entry, the theory of contestable markets indicates that competitive results may occur even if only one or a few firms are actually in the market.

15. Analysis of concentration ratios suggests that, on balance, there has been an increase in the competitiveness of the U.S. economy in recent decades.

16. Accounting profits as a share of stockholder equity are probably slightly greater in highly concentrated industries than in those that are less concentrated. The relationship between profits and concentration, however, is not a close one. This suggests that several other factors, such as changing market conditions, quality competition, risk, and ability to exclude rivals, are the major determinants of profitability.

17. The after-tax accounting profits of business firms average about 5 cents of each dollar of sales, substantially less than most Americans believe to be the case. Accounting profits average approximately 12 percent of stockholder equity. This rate of return (accounting profit) provides investors with the incentive to sacrifice current consumption, assume the risk of undertaking a business venture, and supply the funds to purchase buildings, machines, and other assets.

CRITICAL ANALYSIS QUESTIONS

1. Street-corner vendors using pushcarts have sometimes engaged in price wars at popular locations within Washington, D.C. Each vendor would like to drive out the other sellers and have the prime location to himself. Explain why a strategy of cutting price below cost in order to drive out other vendors would not make sense, if there are no legal barriers to entry.

*2. Suppose that a group of investors wants to start a business operated out of a popular Utah ski area, and the group is considering either building a new resort or starting a new local airline serving that market. Each new business would require about the same amount of capital and personnel hiring. The group believes each to have the same profit potential. Which is the safer (less likely to result in a substantial capital loss) investment? Why? Is there an offsetting advantage to the other investment?

3. "Monopolistic competition is inefficient. Not only are prices higher than marginal cost, and average cost above the minimum in long-run equilibrium, the firms do not make long-run profits! Consumers lose, and even the firms don't gain." Evaluate.

4. "The important functions of entrepreneurs cannot be put into an economic model. The models therefore are useless." Evaluate.

*5. "My uncle just bought stock in Mammoth Insurance, Incorporated. It has long been one of the most profitable firms in the business. He'll make a bundle on that one!" Evaluate.

---

*Asterisk denotes questions for which answers are given in Appendix C, Selected Answers.

*6. Why is oligopolistic collusion more difficult when there is product variation than when the products of all firms are identical?

7. "Market conditions in the world oil market are constantly changing. This makes it difficult for the Organization of Petroleum Exporting Countries (OPEC) to collude successfully and hold price far above the marginal cost of oil." Evaluate.

8. "World markets are impossible to control, because you cannot keep out new competitors. Brazil, once a major oil importer, illustrated the problem when it reached a production level of 600,000 barrels a day. OPEC, the oil cartel, will never again be able to raise prices as they did for a time at the beginning, and again at the end, of the 1970s." Evaluate.

*9. "A high concentration ratio virtually guarantees monopoly pricing and excess profits." Evaluate.

10. We have a theory to explain the equilibrium price and output for monopoly, but not for oligopoly. Why?

11. "Successful collusion by a group of oligopolists contains the seeds of its own destruction, generating incentives that will destroy cooperation." Evaluate.

*12. What determines the *variety* of styles, designs, and sizes of different products? Why do you think there are only a few different varieties of toothpicks, but lots of different types of napkins on the market?

*13. How would the imposition of a fixed, per unit tax of $2,000 on new automobiles affect the average *quality* of automobiles, if the proceeds of the tax were used to subsidize a government operated lottery?

14. What is the primary function of the entrepreneur? Some economists have charged that the major market-structure models of economic theory assume away the function of the entrepreneur. In what sense is this true? Is the function of the entrepreneur important? Discuss.

15. Is quality and style competition as important as price competition? Would you like to live in a country where government regulation restricted the use of quality and style competition? Why or why not? Do you think you would get more or less for your consumer dollar if quality and style competition were restricted? Discuss.

16. Suppose that a monopolistic competitor is currently charging a price that maximizes the firm's total revenue. Will this price also maximize the firm's profit? Why or why not? Explain.

Business Structure, Regulation, and Deregulation

People of the same trade seldom meet together, even for merriment and diversion, but the conversation ends in a conspiracy against the public, or in some contrivance to raise prices.[1]

Adam Smith (1776)

CHAPTER FOCUS

- How is the U.S. economy structured? In particular, what role does big business play? How important is competition?
- What forms of antitrust legislation are important? What are its policy objectives? How effective has it been?
- What new directions have appeared for antitrust policy in recent years?
- What theories do economists put forth to explain and predict government regulation of business?
- What has been the history of traditional economic regulation? What changes have been occurring?
- What is "the new social regulation," and how does it differ from traditional economic regulation? What can we say about its costs and benefits?

*M*ost contemporary economists believe, just as Adam Smith did, that competition and rivalry among business firms provide benefits to consumers and workers alike. Competition forces producers to operate efficiently and to supply consumers with the goods they most intensely desire (relative to costs). Similarly, competition for resources forces each producer to treat workers and other resource suppliers fairly, offering them pay rates and work environments that are attractive relative to those available elsewhere.

But as Adam Smith was keenly aware, and as we have seen in the last two chapters, forces are present which may sometimes undermine competition. Is real-world competition strong enough to protect consumers and workers? Have the actions of government promoted or retarded the development of competitive markets? Economists often disagree on the answers to these two questions. As we have seen, competitive elements will eventually be introduced into even highly concentrated oligopolistic industries, if a profit is being earned. But at the same time, tendencies toward collusion must also be considered. Reduced competition and other market imperfections (relative to the purely competitive model) may make it possible for government policies to improve upon market results in the real world.

Some economists point out that regulatory policy, by limiting various types of noncompetitive behavior, effectively increases the discipline of the market. Others charge that past regulatory policies have often reduced market competitiveness, contributed to economic inefficiency, and in general, ignored major concerns of consumers and workers. In this chapter, we will analyze the structure of the U.S. economy and examine how regulatory policies of various kinds can influence economic behavior in the light of these controversies.

THE STRUCTURE OF THE U.S. ECONOMY

The structure of the U.S. economy is extremely diverse. About 85 percent of all firms hire fewer than 20 employees. These workers add up to approximately one quarter of the labor force. Very large firms, employing more than 5000 workers each, comprise only 1.5 percent of all companies but provide employment for about 20 percent of the labor force.

The structure of our economy has changed significantly over the years. In 1870, 50 percent of all workers were employed in agriculture, 24 percent were in service industries, and 18 percent worked in manufacturing. By 1989, agricultural employment had declined to less than 3 percent, services had risen gradually to 60 percent, and manufacturing, which had risen to a peak of 35 percent in 1948, totaled 18 percent. These changes have been pronounced since 1950, and the decline in manufacturing employment has prompted concern that manufacturing in the United States is in serious decline.

Output in manufacturing, however, has not changed in the same way as employment. Exhibit 1, which graphs the falling proportion of the U.S. work force in manufacturing since 1960, also indicates that the value of manufacturing output *as a share of GNP* has remained roughly constant throughout the period. Labor

---

[1]See Adam Smith, *An Inquiry into the Nature and Causes of the Wealth of Nations* (1776; Cannan's ed., Chicago: University of Chicago Press, 1976), p. 144.

EXHIBIT 1

Real Output and Employment Shares in Manufacturing

While manufacturing took a smaller share of the work force over the period 1960 to 1988, its share of real output stayed roughly constant. Labor productivity rose substantially, so that fewer workers were required to produce the same output. This made possible additional output (and higher real wages) in the economy as a whole.

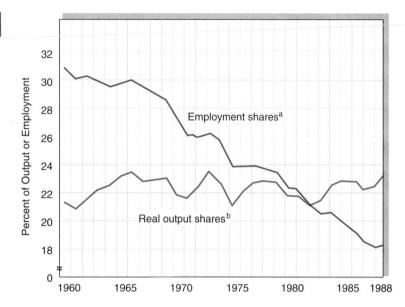

[a]Manufacturing as a percent of nonfarm payroll employment.
[b]Manufacturing as a percent of real gross domestic product less agriculture, forestry, and fisheries.
Source: *Economic Report of the President, 1988.* p. 65, and 1991, pp. 299, 334.

productivity in manufacturing has grown more rapidly than in other sectors. Why? An important part of the answer lies in the fact that labor unions have succeeded in driving up the wages of their members, particularly in manufacturing industries.[2] As wages rose in such key manufacturing industries as automobiles and steel, employers sought to minimize the cost penalty of the higher wages by substituting capital for the increasingly expensive union labor. The use of fewer workers and more capital raised the productivity *per worker* in manufacturing. Thus, manufacturing firms were able to produce a steady proportion of aggregate output even while manufacturing employment was declining as a share of the total.

Changes in the occupational composition of the labor force also shed light on how our economy has changed. Federal Reserve Bank economist Mack Ott researched changes in the labor force over more than 100 years.[3] (Some of his findings are shown in Exhibit 2.) Dividing workers' occupations into three categories, Ott found a very long and steady trend in the United States away from direct, physical production work—including such occupations as farmers and farm workers, craft workers, factory supervisors, machine operators, and nonfarm laborers—which we usually think of as "blue collar" work.

Blue collar workers declined from 73 percent of the work force in 1900 to only 34 percent in 1980. Nonetheless, there has been little growth in the number of

---

[2]We explain the ability of unions to raise wages, and the results of their doing so, more thoroughly in the upcoming chapter on "Labor Unions and Collective Bargaining."

[3]The evidence cited here is largely from Mack Ott, "The Growing Share of Services in the U.S. Economy—Degeneration or Evolution?" *Review,* Federal Reserve Bank of St. Louis, Vol. 69. No. 6, June/July 1987; *The Statistical History of the United States, from Colonial Times to the Present,* Basic Books, 1976, pp. 164, 165; *Economic Report of the President, 1988,* pp. 60–75; and Dave M. O'Neil, "We're Not Losing Our Industrial Base," *Challenge,* May-June 1986, pp. 19–25.

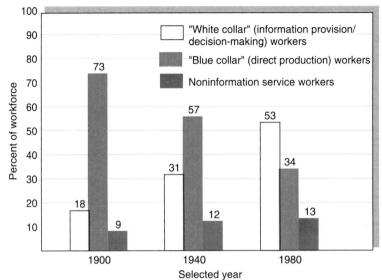

More White Collars, Fewer Blue Collars, in America's Work Force

A dramatic shift has steadily occurred over the past century and more, from direct production, or blue collar jobs, to white collar occupations that provide information or decision-making services. At the same time, annual earnings per worker rose more than 500 percent.

Source: Mack Ott, "The Growing Share of Services in the U.S. Economy—Degeneration or Evolution?" *Review,* Federal Reserve Bank of St. Louis, vol. 69, No. 6, June/July 1987. (Derived from Table 5.)

noninformational service jobs. Thus, the data do not suggest that we are becoming a nation of food service and laundry workers, as some have charged. The shift has been primarily toward "information provision/decision-making" occupations, or "white collar" jobs. This category includes professional and technical workers, managers, clerks, and sales workers. White collar workers rose from an 18 percent share of the work force in 1900 to a 53 percent share in 1980. As these large, but gradual changes took place, annual earnings per worker rose more than 500 percent! Meanwhile the noninformational service work force rose much less, from 9 percent to 13 percent during the same period.

Significant labor force shifts have accompanied the dynamic changes that have characterized the American economy. These shifts have been one key to our sustained growth of output.

HOW MUCH OF OUR ECONOMY IS COMPETITIVE?

The question, "how much of our economy is competitive," is a difficult one to answer. In a very real sense, every firm competes with every other firm for the consumer's additional dollar of spending. Competition is everywhere; the seller of compact discs, for example, competes with the book store and the local restaurant for our entertainment budgets.

As we have discussed, competition, even within an industry, is multidimensional. Dynamic innovation, entrepreneurship, and product-quality competition may be important even in highly concentrated industries. The concentration ratio of an industry, as we found in the previous chapter, provides an indication of competitiveness, but it is an imperfect measure. Available substitutes reduce the monopoly power of firms in some concentrated industries. Other firms are restrained by the threat of entry from potential rivals. Still others face stiff competition from foreign producers.

Product-quality competition may also account for strong rivalry even among a limited number of competitors. Moreover, in a firm as big as General Motors, even the rivalry among divisions (Buick versus Oldsmobile, for example) may be intense. Direct price competition within the firm is presumably controlled, but competition involving quality remains. Leaders in each division compete for recognition and advancement, and each is judged by monthly sales and profit figures. Thus, competitive forces are not entirely absent even in a concentrated industry.

One factor that affects the degree of competition in an industry is the merger of firms. Mergers may increase competition when two firms combine and become a greater challenge to larger firms. However, the merger of large firms might serve to reduce competition without cost savings or lower prices.

The relative importance of competitive and noncompetitive sectors within the economy changes with time. Moreover—and perhaps most important—it is not clear where the line should be drawn between competitive and noncompetitive industries. Most economists would probably classify unregulated industries in which the four largest firms produce less than 20 or 25 percent of the market as competitive. On the other hand, industries in which the largest firms produce more than half of the output would generally be classified as oligopolistic, suggesting the presence of noncompetitive elements. These categories, however, are arbitrary.

Economist William G. Shepherd has examined the structure of the U.S. economy in depth, and uses four categories to classify the structure of various industries. He has also looked at how much of the U.S. national income is produced by firms in each category, and how those percentages have changed over time. As Exhibit 3 shows, he finds that firms in competitive industries have produced a rising share of national income, while monopolies have produced a falling share. The intermediate categories have also declined in importance. Shepherd attributes the sharp increase in competition from 1958 to 1980 to antitrust policy, increased import competition, and deregulation. Other economists also point to reductions in transportation costs as a contributing factor to the increase in competition.

EXHIBIT 3 ■ **The Increasing Competitiveness of the U.S. Economy, 1939–1980**

This chart presents the findings of a study by William Shepherd, an industrial economist from the University of Michigan. Shepherd found that the share of national income produced by the competitive sectors of the U.S. economy has been rising for several decades, while the share produced in less competitive markets has been falling. The "single dominant firm" here is one with more than a 50 percent market share, high barriers to entry, and the ability of the dominant firm to control pricing and to influence innovation. A "tight oligopoly" means a 4-firm concentration ratio above 60 percent and stable market shares, or government-regulated firms with the ability to strongly influence the regulated prices.

Market Structure Category	*Percentage Shares of National Income Produced in Each Category*		
	1939	1958	1980
1. Pure Monopoly	6.2	3.1	2.5
2. Single Dominant Firm	5.0	5.0	2.8
3. Tight Oligopoly	36.4	35.6	18.0
4. Effectively Competitive	52.4	56.3	76.7
Total	100.0	100.0	100.0

Source: William G. Shepherd, "Causes of Increased Competition in the U.S. Economy, 1939–1980," *Review of Economics and Statistics,* November 1982, p. 618.

PUBLIC POLICY AND BIG BUSINESS IN THE U.S. ECONOMY

The stated objective of public policy has been to restrain various aspects of big business activity, especially when competition seems threatened. Many believe that antitrust action can help promote efficiency and keep political power and income more equally distributed. To what extent does the economic and political power of large corporations threaten competitiveness? Some observers argue that large firms threaten our decentralized economic institutions and our democratic political structure. Certainly, public choice theory indicates that concentrated business interests, like other special interest organizations, often exert a disproportional influence on the political process. This notwithstanding, we should keep three points in mind as we evaluate this issue and the effectiveness of the government's antitrust policies.

First, bigness and absence of competition are not necessarily the same thing. A firm can be big and yet function in a highly competitive industry. For example, Sears and K Mart are both large, but they are also part of a highly competitive industry—retail sales.

Second, large size does not ensure greater profitability. The real-world data indicate that profits as a percentage of stockholder equity are unrelated to corporate size.[4] Many of the companies formed by conglomerate mergers discovered this when their earnings took a nose dive during the 1970s.

Third, the firms that comprise the largest 100 or 200 corporations are heterogeneous and constantly changing. As successful management and the vagaries of business fortune exert their influences, some firms are pushed out of the top group and others enter. Following the fate of various firms over time is not easy, since mergers occur and names change, but historical research indicates that of the largest 100 manufacturing corporations in 1909, only 36 remained on the list in 1948. Of the 50 largest in 1947, only 25 remained on the list in 1972, and 5 failed to make even the top 200. Of the firms on the *Fortune* 500 list in 1980, only about half were able to make the list in 1990. With time even giants tumble and fall, as technology and preferences change.

ANTITRUST LEGISLATION—THE POLICY OBJECTIVES

If we can avoid the creation of undue market power, by and large we expect to achieve better market performance—better in terms of lower prices, higher quality products and innovations both in product and technology.[5]

Donald F. Turner

Antitrust legislation seeks to (a) ensure that the economy is structured such that competition exists among firms in the same industry (or market area) and to (b) prohibit business practices that tend to stifle competition. Once these objectives are accomplished, it is assumed that market forces can be relied on to allocate goods and services. (See above quote from a former chief of the antitrust division.)

---

[4]See William G. Shepherd, *The Economics of Industrial Organization* (Englewood Cliffs: Prentice-Hall, 1979), pp. 270–72, for evidence on this issue. Shepherd found that large corporate size had a mild *negative* impact on the rate of profit of firms.

[5]Donald F. Turner, "The Antitrust Chief Dissents," *Fortune* (April 1966), p. 113.

Predatory Pricing: The practice by which a dominant firm in an industry temporarily reduces price to damage or eliminate weaker rivals, so that prices can be raised above the level of costs at a later time.

Exclusive Contract: An agreement between manufacturer and retailer that prohibits the retailer from carrying the product lines of firms that are rivals of the manufacturer. Such contracts are illegal under the Clayton Act when they "lessen competition."

There are numerous tactics business entrepreneurs might use to avoid the rigors of competition. We have already stressed that collusion and price agreements are potential weapons with which to turn trade in favor of the seller. Potential competitors might also decide to divide a market geographically, agreeing not to compete in certain market areas. Large, diversified firms might use **predatory pricing,** a practice by which a firm *temporarily* reduces its price below cost in certain market areas in order to damage or eliminate weaker rivals. Once the rivals have been eliminated, the firm then uses its monopoly power to raise prices above costs. A competitor might also use exclusive contracts and reciprocal agreements to maintain an advantage over rivals. An **exclusive contract** (or dealership) is an arrangement whereby the manufacturer of a line of products prohibits retailers from selling any of the products of rival producers. An established firm offering many product lines might use this tactic to limit the entry by rivals into retail markets offering only narrow product lines.

These and other business practices can be used to increase market power, rather than to achieve superior performance. In one form or another, they are illegal under current antitrust legislation.

MAJOR ANTITRUST LEGISLATION

The United States, to a greater degree than most Western countries, has adopted antitrust legislation designed to promote competitive markets. Three major legislative acts—the Sherman Act, the Clayton Act, and the Federal Trade Commission Act—form the foundation of antitrust policy in the United States.

The Sherman Act.   The Sherman Act was passed in 1890, largely in response to the great number of cartels formed in the United States in the late 1800s. Many of these cartels were in the form of trusts. In a **trust,** the assets of several firms are placed in the custody of trustees who manage the trust for the benefit of the owners. Producers in the oil, railroad, sugar, and tobacco industries, among others, formed trusts to fix prices and control output, in an attempt to increase their profits. Many Americans were enraged and the Sherman Act was passed to limit the economic power of trusts.

Trust: In American history, an arrangement in which the assets of several firms were placed in the custody of trustees, who managed the trust for the benefit of the owners. Trusts were used to form cartels in the United States in the late 1800s.

The most important provisions of the act are:

> Section 1: Every contract, combination in the form of trust or otherwise, or conspiracy, in restraint of trade or commerce among the several states or with foreign nations, is hereby declared illegal.
> Section 2: Every person who shall monopolize, or conspire with any other person or persons to monopolize any part of the trade or commerce among the several states, or with foreign nations, shall be guilty of a misdemeanor.

The language of the Sherman Act is vague and subject to interpretation. What does it mean to attempt to "monopolize" or combine or "conspire" with another person? Initially, the courts were hesitant to apply the act to manufacturing corporations. In 1911, however, the Supreme Court ruled that Standard Oil and American Tobacco had used "unreasonable" tactics to restrain trade. At the time, the Standard Oil trust controlled 90 percent of the country's refinery capacity. American Tobacco controlled three-fourths of the tobacco manufacturing market. Both firms were broken up into several smaller rival firms.

The Supreme Court, however, did not prohibit monopoly *per se.* In fact, passage of the Sherman Act was followed by a great wave of mergers, which between 1898 and 1902 alone, involved perhaps half of the U.S. manufacturing capacity. Firms that could not conspire, could merge. It was "unfair or unethical" business practices that the courts would not condone. Since the Sherman act did not clearly define unfair or unethical business practices, additional legislation was required. In 1914, Congress passed two other antitrust laws to remedy the situation.

The Clayton Act.   The Clayton Act was passed in an effort to spell out and prohibit specific business practices. The following are prohibited by the Clayton Act when they "substantially lessen competition or tend to create a monopoly": (a) *price discrimination*—charging purchasers in different markets different prices that are unrelated to transportation or other costs; (b) *tying contracts*—a practice whereby the seller requires the buyer to purchase another item; (c) *exclusive dealings*—an agreement between a manufacturer and retail distributor that prohibits the distributor from handling the products of firms that are competitors of the manufacturer; (d) *interlocking stockholding*—one firm purchasing the stock of a competing firm; and (e) *interlocking directorates*—the same individual(s) serving on the boards of directors of competing firms.

Although somewhat more specific than the Sherman Act, the Clayton Act is still vague. At what point do the prohibited actions actually become illegal? Under what circumstances do these actions "substantially lessen competition"? The task of interpreting this ambiguous phrase still remains with the courts.

The Federal Trade Commission Act.   The Federal Trade Commission Act declared unlawful all "unfair methods of competition in commerce." The Federal Trade Commission (FTC), composed of five members appointed by the president to seven-year terms, was established to determine the exact meaning of "unfair methods." However, a 1919 Supreme Court decision held that the courts, not the FTC, had the ultimate responsibility for interpreting the law. Today, the FTC is concerned primarily with (a) enforcing consumer protection legislation, (b) prohibiting deceptive advertising, a power it acquired in 1938, and (c) preventing overt collusion.

When a complaint is filed with the FTC, usually by a third party, the commission investigates. If there is a violation, the FTC initially attempts to settle the dispute by negotiation between the parties. If the attempts to negotiate a settlement fail, a hearing is conducted before one of the commission's examiners. The decision of the hearing examiner may be appealed to the U.S. Court of Appeals. The great majority of cases brought before the FTC are now settled by mutual consent of the parties involved.

MORE RECENT ANTITRUST LEGISLATION

Additional antitrust legislation was passed in the 1930s. The Robinson-Patman Act of 1936 prohibits selling "at unreasonably low prices" when such practices reduce competition. The section of the Clayton Act dealing with price discrimination was aimed at eliminating predatory pricing. The Robinson-Patman Act went beyond this. It was intended to protect competitors not just from stronger rivals who might temporarily sell below cost but also from more efficient rivals who were actually producing at a lower cost. Chain stores and mass distributors were the initial targets of the legislation. Economists have often been critical of the Robinson-Patman Act, since it has tended to reduce price competition and thereby protect inefficient producers.

In 1938, Congress passed the Wheeler-Lea Act, which was designed to strengthen sectors of the Federal Trade Commission Act that had been weakened by restrictive court decisions. Before the passage of the act, the courts were reluctant to prohibit unfair business practices, such as false and deceptive advertising, unless there was proof of damages to either consumers or rival firms. The Wheeler-Lea Act removed this limitation and gave the FTC extended powers to prosecute and ban false or deceptive advertising.

In 1950, Congress passed the Celler-Kefauver Act (sometimes referred to as the antimerger act), which prohibits a firm from acquiring the assets of a competitor if the transaction substantially lessens competition. The Clayton Act, though it prohibits mergers through stock acquisition, proved unable to prevent business combinations from being formed by sale of assets. The Celler-Kefauver Act closed this loophole, further limiting the ability of firms to combine to escape competitive pressures.

Since the intent of the Celler-Kefauver Act is to maintain industrial competition, its applicability to mergers between large firms in the same industry is obvious. The act also prohibits vertical mergers between large firms if competition is reduced by such mergers. For example, the merger of a publishing company with a paper producer is illegal if the courts find that it lessens competition. However, few vertical merger cases have been brought under this act since the early 1970s, when antitrust policy began to focus more on consumer welfare and less directly on the structure of industries.

THUMBNAIL SKETCH

Antitrust Legislation

Antitrust laws prohibit the following:

1. Collusion—contracts and conspiracies to restrain trade (Sherman Act, Sec. 1)
2. Monopoly and attempts to monopolize any part of trade or commerce among the several states (Sherman Act, Sec. 2)
3. Persons serving on the board of directors of competing firms with more than $1 million of assets (Clayton Act, Sec. 8)
4. Unfair and deceptive advertising (Federal Trade Commission Act as amended by Wheeler-Lea Act)
5. Price discrimination if the intent is to injure a competitor (Robinson-Patman Act)

The following practices are also illegal when they substantially lessen competition or tend to create a monopoly:

1. Tying contracts (Clayton Act, Sec. 3)
2. Exclusive dealings (Clayton Act, Sec. 3)
3. Interlocking stockholdings and horizontal mergers (Clayton Act, Sec. 7, as amended by Celler-Kefauver Act)
4. Interlocking directorates (Clayton Act, Sec. 8)

CURRENT ANTITRUST POLICY

An important trend over the past two decades has been the increased weight given by antitrust policymakers to consumer welfare. If a proposed merger would increase a firm's market share, but is expected to reduce the prices paid by buyers of the industry's output, then opposition to the merger is less likely than before. This position was particularly emphasized by the Reagan administration in the 1980s. One clear signal that the shift had occurred came with the Justice Department's 1982 Merger Guidelines, which recognize the potential value of mergers for efficiency purposes and call for a challenge to a proposed merger only if it is likely to result in harm to consumers.

Herfindahl Index: A measure of industry concentration, calculated by squaring the percentage share of each firm in the industry, then summing the squares. The index can range from zero to 10,000. It is a more sophisticated measure of concentration than the traditional concentration ratio, and is used by the Justice Department in antitrust policy.

The new merger policy uses a relatively new tool, the **Herfindahl index,** to measure market concentration. The new index measures market power in a way that strongly emphasizes any existing large market share, and gives relatively little weight to any firms holding small market shares, compared with the traditional concentration ratio. (See the Measures of Economic Activity box.) For example, the older measure of concentration does not distinguish between a market in which four firms divide the market equally, and one in which one firm has a large market share, and there are three other much smaller firms. The Herfindahl index gives the latter market a much larger index number, indicating a larger possibility of the presence of significant market power.

The 1982 Merger Guidelines, as clarified and extended in 1984 by the Justice Department—and agreed upon in effect by the Federal Trade Commission—indicate that if a merger results in a Herfindahl index of less than 1,000, then the resulting market is unconcentrated, and the merger generally will not be challenged. If the index would be above 1,000 after the merger, and the merger would add at least 100 points to the index, then a challenge is likely.

Other factors also are considered under the guidelines, especially in borderline cases. A merger is less likely to be challenged if:

1. foreign firms are an important source of competition in the industry;
2. one of the firms might otherwise go out of business;
3. the firms in the industry do not produce a homogeneous product (thus, quality competition is more likely); and
4. new competitors are likely to enter the industry if the current producers increase their prices.

MEASURES OF ECONOMIC ACTIVITY

The Herfindahl Index

The Herfindahl index measures market concentration in a way that gives a great deal of weight to the share of the largest one or two firms in the market. It does so by squaring the percentage each firm has in the market, and summing the squares. If there are n firms in the market, then H, the Herfindahl index, is:

$$H = S_1^2 + S_2^2 + S_3^2 + \cdots + S_n^2$$

where S_1 in the formula is the percentage share of the largest firm in the market, S_2 is the percentage share of the second largest firm, and so on. Each S can vary from 100 (a pure monopoly, with only one firm in the market) down to almost zero. For a pure monopoly,

$$H = (100)^2 = 10,000$$

This is the largest possible value for the Herfindahl index. By contrast, if there are 100 firms in a market, each with an equal 1 percent share, then

$$H = (1)^2 + (1)^2 + (1)^2 + \cdots + (1)^2 = 100$$

The Herfindahl index is a more sophisticated tool for measuring market power than is the traditional concentration ratio, which treats a market with four firms of equal size the same as a market with four firms, one of which has 70 percent of the market and three that have 10 percent each. The Herfindahl index would assign the equal-shares market an index of 2,500 (4×25^2) and the unequal-shares market an index of 5,200 ($70^2 + 10^2 + 10^2 + 10^2$), indicating the larger potential for market power when one firm has a 70 percent share of the market. Only the shares of the larger firms are needed to approximate the index, since firms with small shares add little to the Herfindahl index.

In general, the purpose of the new guidelines is to bring a challenge against only those mergers likely to harm consumers by significantly increasing the market power of affected firms. The guidelines have resulted in far fewer challenges to mergers, especially vertical mergers. For example, challenges to proposed vertical mergers, in the form of preliminary investigations by the Antitrust Division of the Justice Department, fell from 460 in 1969 to 7 in 1984. Similar challenges to proposed horizontal mergers rose during the same period from 26 to 108. Clearly, vertical mergers had come to be seen as generally posing little threat to the interests of consumers.

WHICH ACTIONS ARE ANTICOMPETITIVE?

Unfortunately for the conduct of good antitrust policy, it is often difficult to know when observed behavior is really anticompetitive. The same actions described earlier as ways to reduce competition can also be used to produce and sell more economically, or better satisfy customers.

Consider predatory pricing. Price cutting by a more efficient firm in an industry will tend to drive less efficient firms out of business. Is the lower price a bad thing? If pricing below cost is the essence of predatory pricing, how do we know whether the price is truly below the cost of production and delivery, without knowing intimate details about how the firm's costs vary with the season, the territory, with other products produced, and so on? Investigating many cases of alleged predatory pricing over the years, economists have found that the evidence often failed to support the charges. A price cutter's competitors may be unhappy, but that may simply reflect vigorous competition, rather than the presence of anticompetitive behavior.

Exclusive contracts, or dealerships, are another tool that can have legitimate uses. If two manufacturers sell competing products, and one advertises heavily to stimulate consumer interest, the other may benefit without bearing the cost. For example, suppose that A-OK and X-tra Good are both manufacturers of lawn mowers. The A-OK company decides to spend $20 million on a massive advertising campaign. Customers, drawn by the campaign, flock to Marty's Mower Mart, where X-tra Good mowers are also sold, and they are able to make price and performance comparisons between the two brands. Obviously, without spending a penny on advertising, X-tra Good will benefit from the expensive campaign of its competitor and since its advertising costs are lower, it may be able to sell at a lower price. Similarly, if A-OK trains Marty's personnel in service methods that could be used for both products, X-tra Good also gets a free ride on the service offered. A-OK could avoid the spillover effects of its advertising campaign and its training program if it were able to require that Marty's Mower Mart carry only the A-OK brand. If A-OK is unable to do so, it may forgo these activities and consumers may therefore end up with less information and poorer service than would otherwise be the case.

Unfortunately, it is often difficult to identify and separate anticompetitive behavior from competitive actions that cut the costs of marketing and product service. Thus, formulating and administering a set of antitrust laws that consistently promote competition in the marketplace is not an easy task.

ANTITRUST POLICY— DISSENTING VIEWS

For the reasons listed above and for others as well, antitrust policy has its critics. People in business often argue that current legislation is vague, making it difficult to determine whether a proposed action is in compliance. In addition to more clarity, some analysts believe that stronger laws and more vigorous enforcement are needed. Another school of thought holds that antitrust policy does more harm than good and that such policy actually is unnecessary. Let us look briefly at each of these positions.

Antitrust Policies Should Be Stronger and More Vigorously Enforced.

The proponents of this position argue that greater effort is required to ensure the existence of competitive markets. They often point out that antitrust policy has functioned primarily as a holding action. That is, it prevents large firms from *increasing* their market share, but it is ineffective as a means for *reducing* industrial concentration. Policy can end up working against its own objectives. For example, an established firm controlling 50 or 60 percent of a market is generally left untouched, whereas two smaller firms with a combined market share of as little as 10 percent may be prohibited from merging. Current policy, therefore, often protects strong, established firms while weakening their smaller rivals. Those who view current policy as self-defeating typically favor an antitrust policy that would more thoroughly restructure concentrated industries, dividing large firms into smaller, independent units.

Antitrust Policy Is Unnecessary.

The advocates of this position argue that antitrust legislation places too much emphasis on the number of competitors without recognizing the positive role of dynamic competition. They believe an antitrust policy that limits business concentration will often promote inefficient business organization and will therefore encourage higher prices. They reject the notion that pure competition is a proper standard of economic efficiency.[6] As Joseph Schumpeter, an early proponent of this view of competition and regulation, emphasized more than two decades ago:

> It . . . is a mistake to base the theory of government regulation of industry on
> the principle that big business should be made to work as the respective industry
> would work in perfect competition.[7]

Like Schumpeter, current advocates of this position believe innovative activity is at the heart of competition. An ingenious innovator may forge ahead of competitors, but competition from other innovators will always be present. Competition is a perpetual game of leapfrog, not a process that is dependent on the number of firms in an industry. Bigness is a natural outgrowth of efficiency and successful innovation. One of the leading proponents of this position, John McGee, of the University of Washington, argues that concentration is neither inefficient nor indicative of a lack of competition:

> Take an industry of many independent producers, each of which is efficiently
> using small scale and simple methods to make the same product. . . . Suppose
> that a revolution in technology or management techniques now occurs, so that
> there is room in the market for only one firm using the new and most efficient

---

[6]See Dominick T. Armentano, *Antitrust and Monopoly: Anatomy of a Policy Failure* (New York: John Wiley, 1982), for an excellent presentation of this viewpoint.

[7]Joseph Schumpeter, *Capitalism, Socialism and Democracy* (New York: Harper Torchbooks, 1950), p. 106.

methods. Whether it occurs quickly through merger or gradually through bankruptcy, an atomistic industry is transformed into a "monopoly," albeit one selling the same product at a lower price than before. If expected long-run price should rise, resort can still be had to the old and less efficient ways, which were compatible with . . . small firms. It would be incomplete and misleading to describe that process as a "decline of competition."[8]

THE MERGER WAVE OF THE 1980s

Of the hundred largest mergers and acquisitions on record up to 1984, 65 occurred between 1981 and 1983, and only 11 occurred prior to 1979. During the 1981–1984 period, there were at least 45 transactions of over a billion dollars apiece; prior to this period there were only a dozen or so transactions of such magnitude.[9]

Hal R. Varian

As these numbers indicate, a merger wave began with a surge in the early 1980s. It continued strongly into the second half of the decade. The largest acquisition occurred in 1988 when the investment firm of Kohlberg Kravis Roberts & Co. (KKR) bought the RJR Nabisco Co. for $24.7 billion.

A new method of financing was used in the KKR takeover, and in many others that received so much attention during the period. These were "leveraged buyouts," or "LBOs," in which the acquiring firm borrowed large amounts of money in order to make the purchases. KKR borrowed $18 billion by selling bonds secured by RJR Nabisco's assets and future profits. These were called "junk bonds" because the risk of nonrepayment was considered to be high. The high risk meant that lenders (the bond buyers) demanded a high rate of return on the bonds, and so the newly formed firms had a large debt to repay, at a high interest rate. KKR did very well, as it sold off some parts of RJR Nabisco at attractive prices, and paid off much of the debt. Some of the other acquiring firms did not perform so well, however, and could not fully pay off the junk bonds.

PROS AND CONS OF THE MERGERS

On balance, were the leveraged buyouts a good thing? Economists are not in total agreement on their evaluations of the costs and benefits of the 1980s' wave of mergers and acquisitions. Their discussions shed light on the current state of economic thinking on the benefits and costs of corporate reorganization via the market for corporate control.[10]

Economists who defend the merger and acquisition wave of the 1980s point to several ways in which the additional corporate reorganizations may have enhanced economic productivity.

Larger (or Smaller) Firms May Be More Efficient. The merger of Piedmont Airlines and U.S. Air gave the combined firm the ability to provide better service by integrating their routes and schedules. With other reorganizations, such as RJR

---

[8]John S. McGee, *In Defense of Industrial Concentration* (New York: Praeger, 1971), pp. 21–22.

[9]Hal R. Varian, "Symposium on Takeovers," *Journal of Economic Perspectives,* Vol. 2, No. 1, Winter, 1988, p. 3.

[10]The remainder of this section draws heavily on the symposium on takeovers printed in *The Journal of Economic Perspectives,* Vol. 2, No. 1, Winter 1988, pp. 3–82.

Nabisco, decentralization (breaking up the parts of the firm) created more market value. As junk bonds reduced the costs of large mergers and acquisitions, the restructuring of large corporations by outsiders as well as by corporate officials became more practical.

Complementary Strengths.   If one firm is very good at making textbooks, and another is very good at marketing texts, then merging the two may make a new firm which is more productive than the two had been separately. Merging two complementary firms can make both of them more productive and more profitable.

Management Efficiencies.   Suppose that Oil Incorporated, a hypothetical firm, earns a high profit now because of wise choices made years ago, but it is using those profits to support unproductive parts of the firm. As a result of such wasteful activity, it is earning only a normal profit on average. Our imaginary firm is worth less, and its stock price is lower, than it could be if the unproductive components were shut down or sold off to more productive uses. Its managers do not want to drop the unproductive activities however, and stockholders have not been able to elect a board of directors that will force the needed change. In such a situation another, more profit-oriented firm might profit by taking over (buying) Oil, Inc., and making the productive changes. The value of the combined firms would be increased.

For these and other reasons, the mergers and takeovers in the 1980s created some benefits in the form of greater economic efficiency. However, some economists are skeptical that increased productivity was always the purpose of the many deals made during the decade of the 1980s. They point out that in addition to the productive reasons listed above, deals might be undertaken for reasons that have little to do with greater efficiency, as the following list points out.

Tax Benefits.   If Corporation X makes large accounting profits, it will pay high taxes. If Firm Y shows accounting losses, it will pay no tax. If the two firms merge, so that the profits of X are offset by the accounting losses of Y, then the combined firm pays little or no taxes. A merger might be arranged simply to reduce the total taxes paid by the participants.

Gains in Market or Political Power.   If a merger reduces competition between firms in an industry, their combined market power may be enhanced. Product price would increase, and output would fall. Even if that is not the case, the combined firms might gain political power, enabling them to influence legislation in their own interest at the expense of other market participants. Either of these changes would probably decrease total productivity even though the firms might become more profitable.

Manager Ambitions.   The personal ambitions of managers might lead them to seek mergers to add to the size and visibility of the firms they manage, independent of whether productivity is enhanced. Their personal desire to control a larger firm may cloud their judgment about the profitability of a merger.

These and other factors mean that not every merger or acquisition is likely to increase efficiency in the economy. What can be said on balance, then, about the net benefits of the merger wave of the 1980s? Studies indicate that stock market participants, at least, believed that on average, the mergers and acquisitions were productive. Buyers and sellers in the stock market clearly were more willing to buy and hold stock in firms targeted for takeover mergers, demonstrating their belief that takeovers are likely to improve the performance of firms being purchased. Takeovers usually caused the value of stock in the ''target'' firm—the one purchased—to rise. The value of stock in acquiring firms did not do as well, however, especially when other firms had made competing bids for the target firm. The price of stock in acquiring companies went down as often as it went up for the winning firms when there was more than one bid for a target firm. While market results suggest that takeovers were productive on average, they also indicate that most of the productivity gains occurred in target firms. Certainly most of the market benefits flowed to those holding stock in the target firms.

THEORIES OF REGULATION AND REGULATORY POLICY

Antitrust policy seeks to assure that the structure of industry is competitive. Modern monopoly is often the result of government policy, however, as we see in the markets for local telephone service, broadcasting, airports, and taxi service. When government itself has established the monopoly, antitrust policy is not useful to protect market participants from monopoly results. For this reason and for other purposes as well, business regulation is often used.

Dunagin's People by Ralph Dunagin © Field Enterprises, Inc. 1977. Permission of News America Syndicate.

Regulatory policies are usually direct and specific, often dictating prices or operating procedures of business firms. What can economics tell us about how regulation can be expected to work? To date, economists have been unable to develop a complete theory of regulation. Given the complex array of political and economic factors involved, this should not be surprising. In regulated markets, predicting what sellers will offer and how much consumers will be willing to buy at various prices is not enough. The regulatory process also must take account of (a) buyers who are unwilling to pay the full cost; (b) sellers who are inefficient producers; (c) politicians who are simultaneously considering thousands of pieces of legislation; and (d) voters, many of whom are ''rationally uninformed'' on regulatory issues. It is not easy to predict how such a complex system will deal with economic problems.

We can, however, facilitate our discussion of regulation by breaking it down into two major types: traditional economic regulation and the newer social regulation. We can also draw some conclusions about the decision-making of economic and political participants in the regulatory process. Economic analysis indicates that decision-makers in the regulatory process, like those in other areas, respond to incentives. There are three incentive-related characteristics of the regulatory process that should be kept in mind.

The Demand for Regulation Often Stems from Special Interest Effects and Redistribution Considerations Rather Than from the Pursuit of Economic Efficiency.

APPLICATIONS IN ECONOMICS

AT&T and Cross-Subsidies

Cross-subsidies are a perennial issue in regulation. When a regulated firm serves more than one market, regulators must allocate fixed costs to each market if they are to set prices according to the average (or total) costs of production. In economics, there is no logical way to allocate such joint costs between the two markets. An unregulated firm has no need to do so. Based on marginal costs and marginal revenues, the firm charges a price to maximize profit (or minimize loss) in each market. Any economic profit leads to more entry, until the price is driven down to average cost. When price (and entry) are regulated, however, the arbitrary division of joint costs is necessary, and consumers in one market may be required to subsidize those in the other market. So it was in the case of telephones.

Local telephone lines are a fixed cost of providing both local and long-distance services. Until the AT&T divestiture settlement in 1982, state and federal regulators had agreed to load much of the fixed cost of the local lines onto the long-distance bills, which were charged according to minutes of use by customers. Rather than recognize the fixed nature of these costs (the same wires had to be in place and maintained regardless of how many minutes they were used, and whether any long-distance calls were made) and charge each customer the true (fixed) cost, fixed charges were kept low. Long-distance rates were set high enough to make up the difference.

The result of this system was to provide large subsidies to local service at the expense of long-distance telephone customers. Those who used more than 50 minutes per month [11] of long-distance service paid more than their share of the combined system's costs, while those using less than 50 minutes (a large majority) paid less than the costs they generated. In general, businesses and a few other users paid far more than their share.

The system was politically very popular at the state and local level,

[11]This estimate, and the others in this feature, were reported by Professor John T. Wenders in ''. . . And Now Learn to Love the Chaos,'' *Wall Street Journal,* Nov. 29, 1985.

The wealth of an individual (or business firm) can be increased by an improvement in efficiency and an expansion in production. Regulation introduces another possibility. Sellers can gain if competition in their market is restricted. Buyers can gain, at least in the short run, if a legal requirement forcing producers to supply goods below cost is passed. Regulation opens up an additional avenue whereby those most capable of bending the political process to their advantage can increase their wealth.

Our earlier analysis suggested that special interest groups, such as well-organized, concentrated groups of buyers or sellers, exert a disproportionate influence on the political process. In addition, the regulators themselves often comprise a politically powerful interest group. Bureaucratic entrepreneurs are key figures in the regulatory process. Their cooperation is important to those who are regulated. In exchange for cooperation, politicians and bureaucrats are offered all manner of political support.

These factors suggest that there will be demand for economic regulation even if it contributes to economic inefficiency. The wealth of specific groups of buyers, sellers, and political participants may be enhanced, even though the total size of the economic pie is reduced. This is particularly true if the burden of economic inefficiency is widely dispersed among rationally uninformed taxpayers and groups of consumers.

Regulation Is Inflexible—It Often Fails to Adjust to Changing Market Conditions.
Dynamic change often makes regulatory procedures obsolete. The introduction of

because as telephone customers paid their bills each month, they had detailed information before them. Seldom is there a situation like this in which consumers know just who to blame in case of a rate increase. In large numbers, they complained to their state regulatory commissions whenever commissioners allowed those bills to rise. The large users were unable to counter the popular pressure on politically selected commissioners. The majority was understandably less upset when others paid the higher bills. This system was very inefficient, however. Long-distance calls costing only 7 to 9 cents a minute at the margin were charged at 30 to 40 cents, so everyone used far less than the optimal amount of

long-distance service. The net result was an estimated loss to the economy of $10 to $14 billion. AT&T did not mind the cross-subsidy of local service by long distance, since it provided both, and was assured a fixed rate of return by the regulators.

When technological advances made it possible for new suppliers to enter the industry and serve large customers at a lower rate, the system began to come apart. If the new suppliers could offer a better deal to the biggest customers, the source of the cross-subsidies would disappear. Regulators could keep newcomers out, but now the really huge size of the penalties paid by large users was becoming obvious, and the politics of continuing the system of cross-subsidies to large

customers became less attractive.

Following the divestiture agreement, AT&T continued to provide long-distance service at rates regulated by the Federal Communications Commission, but MCI, GTE Sprint, and other competitors were also allowed into the market. State regulators still would like to keep local rates low and load costs onto long-distance users, but now AT&T and the other long-distance suppliers, not owning the local firms, are hurt by such an arrangement and will fight it. Lower long-distance rates and a higher fixed charges for local service are observable effects of the competitive forces now in place.

the truck vastly changed the competitiveness of the ground transportation industry (previously dominated by railroad interests). Nevertheless, the regulation of price, entry, and routes continued for years, even though competitive forces had long since eliminated the monopoly power of firms in this industry. Similarly, city building codes that may have been appropriate when adopted have become obsolete and now retard the introduction of new, more efficient materials and procedures. In many cities, for example, regulatory procedures have prevented builders from introducing such cost-saving materials as plastic pipes, preconstructed septic tanks, and prefabricated housing units. Why does the process work this way? In contrast with the market process, regulatory procedures generally grant a controlling voice to established producers. The introduction of new, more efficient products would reduce the wealth of the existing producers of protected products. The political (regulatory) process is often responsive to these producers' charges that substitute materials (or new producers) would create unfair competition, violate safety codes, or generally be unreliable. Hearings are held. Lawsuits are often filed. Regulatory commissions meet and investigate—again and again. These procedures result in costs, delay, and inflexibility.

With the Passage of Time, Regulatory Agencies Often Adopt the Views of the Business Interests They Are Supposed to Regulate.   Although the initial demand for regulatory action sometimes originates with disorganized groups seeking protection from practices they consider unfair or indicative of monopolistic power, forces are present that will generally dilute or negate the impact of such groups in the long run. Individual consumers (and taxpayers) have little incentive to be greatly concerned with regulatory actions. Often, they are lulled into thinking that since there is a regulatory agency, the "public interest" is served. In contrast, firms (and employees) in regulated industries are vitally interested in the structure and composition of regulatory commissions. Favorable actions by the commission could lead to larger profits, higher-paying jobs, and insulation from the uncertainties of

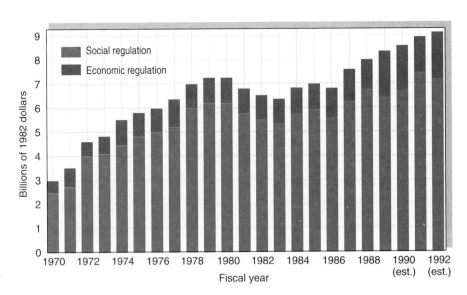

EXHIBIT 4

Federal Outlays for Regulatory Activities (in constant 1982 dollars)

One index of federal regulatory activity is the expenditures by the government on those activities. This measure of regulation rose rapidly in the 1970s, reached a peak in 1980, declined, then rose again during the latter half of the 1980s.

Source: Center for the Study of American Business. Derived from Budget of the United States and related documents.

competition. Thus, firms and employee groups, recognizing their potential gain, invest both economic and political resources to influence the actions of regulatory agencies.

How do vote-maximizing political entrepreneurs behave under these conditions? The payoffs from supporting the views of an apathetic public are small. Clearly, the special interest effect is present. When setting policy and making appointments to regulatory agencies, political entrepreneurs have a strong incentive to support the position of well-organized business and labor interests—often the very groups the regulatory practices were originally designed to police.

Regulatory activity in the United States has expanded substantially in the past two decades. As Exhibit 4 shows, federal regulatory spending levels increased rapidly in the 1970s, dropped in the early 1980s, then resumed their expansion in the late 1980s and early 1990s. Estimated 1991 federal spending for economic regulation was $2.1 billion, while the figure for social regulation expenditures was $10.2 billion. Compliance costs are much larger. For example, budgeted federal expenditures on environmental regulation for 1991 were $4.7 billion, but the Environmental Protection Agency estimates that annual expenditures by others to meet the objectives of environmental regulation brought the national spending total to $115 billion.

TRADITIONAL ECONOMIC REGULATION

Economic Regulation:
Regulation of product price or industrial structure, usually imposed on a specific industry. By and large, the production processes used by the regulated firms are unaffected by this type of regulation.

Regulation of business activity is not a new development. In 1887, Congress established the Interstate Commerce Commission (ICC), providing it with the authority to regulate the railroad industry. In 1935, the trucking industry was also brought under the ICC's regulatory jurisdiction. State regulatory commissions began to oversee local delivery of electricity, natural gas, and telephone services as early as 1907. Little was done at the federal level to expand regulation beyond the railroads until the 1930s, when commissions were formed during the Roosevelt administration to regulate interstate telephone service, broadcasting, airlines, natural gas pipelines, and other industries. These activities focus on **economic regulation** and usually control the product price or the structure of a particular industry, rather than specifying the production processes used by the regulated firm.

Regulation is normally justified as action taken to protect the general public. There are three main purposes given for the economic regulation of firms:

1. Control a Natural Monopoly. If the delivery of electricity in a local area is thought to be a natural monopoly, then encouraging competition by increasing the numbers of firms in the industry would be an inefficient way to try to keep prices from high monopoly levels; regulation is typically used instead.

2. Prevent "Cutthroat" Competition. If firms in an industry have low marginal cost, but high fixed cost—railroads might be an example—then some observers fear that as each firm competes for extra business, the industry price might be driven down to marginal cost. If this happens and fixed costs are not covered, firms will eventually be driven out of business until survivors can raise the price enough to cover full cost. Instability in the industry may result. Regulators, by fixing prices, might help to provide orderly competition.

3. Cross-Subsidize Certain Services. Some customers, such as rural families wanting electrical service from a utility, can only be served at a high cost. Regulators, however, can require that an average price be charged in order to serve high-cost customers at a low price without government subsidies. Other customers pay more to provide the low price to high-cost users.

Regulation may be established to promote orderly competition and to keep prices more equal across classes of customers, but it will have other effects as well. Rules designed to restrict entry and control competition among members of an industry are not likely to encourage efficient production. Detailed restrictions on what firms can produce, when and where they can sell it, and on other actions may be needed to prevent disputes among potentially competing firms with many incentives to get around the rules. But in a constantly changing economic environment, and without the discipline of competition from new entrants, such regulations often become costly. High costs and production inefficiencies helped to generate widespread dissatisfaction with the traditional regulation of several industries during the 1970s. Major steps toward deregulation were taken in the ground and air transportation industries. A look at how regulation developed, and at the deregulation of these two industries will help us to see more clearly how regulation works, and why it does not always work well.

Regulation and Deregulation in the Trucking Industry.   The ICC was initially established to regulate rates in the railroad industry. Actually, much of the railroad industry supported the ICC's establishment. For many years, the commission regulated rates and allocated hauls to various rail shippers. Beginning in the 1930s, however, the railroads began to confront stiff competition from the developing trucking industry. Since the trucking industry could be entered with relative ease, competitive forces were pushing rates downward. In response to the demands of railroad and large trucking interests, in 1935, the regulatory control of the ICC was extended to include the trucking industry.

The ICC influenced the structure of the ground transportation industry in several ways. First, it limited the number of shippers in interstate commerce. Rail and truck shippers were required to obtain licenses from the ICC before they were permitted to compete in interstate transportation. The ICC issued such licenses only when the proposed new service was deemed "necessary for the public convenience." Established shippers were granted the opportunity to present the ICC with counter-evidence attesting that the entry of a new shipper was unnecessary or even harmful. The ICC's policies severely limited entry into the trucking industry.

Second, the ICC regulated shipping rates and permitted the rail and truck industries to establish price-fixing rate bureaus. Competitors who wanted to *reduce* their prices below the schedule established by the rate bureau had to ask the ICC to hear the cases. Typically, it would take six to eight months to obtain a ruling from the ICC. These arrangements strongly discouraged price competition in interstate shipping.

Third, the ICC limited the products that carriers could haul, the routes they could travel, and the number of cities along the route they could serve. Carriers were prohibited from using price reductions as a means to arrange a "return haul." A carrier that was granted a license to haul from St. Louis to Denver might simultaneously have been prohibited from hauling a return shipment along the way, from Kansas City. A carrier's assigned route from New Orleans to Chicago might have required an intermediate stop in Atlanta. The result: miles of wasteful travel and trucks that were empty nearly 40 percent of the time.

The ICC's strict regulation of the trucking industry has been relaxed considerably in recent years. The Motor Carrier Act of 1980 allows freer entry. As a result, the number of ICC-authorized carriers rose from about 18,000 in 1980 to 33,548 in 1984. The act also allowed rate reductions (without the requirement of ICC approval), and existing firms were allowed to expand their service and take advantage of economies of scale. The ICC was instructed to eliminate its restrictions on service to intermediate points on a delivery route and on return-trip haulage. In addition, the antitrust immunity of the rate-setting bureaus was removed.

Studies by the Federal Trade Commission and others indicate that the relaxation of entry barriers and rate-fixing policies has exerted a significant impact on the trucking industry.[12] During the first year after passage of the trucking deregulation legislation, the ICC granted 27,960 additional routes to new and existing carriers, compared to only 2,710 during fiscal year 1976. Some 2,452 new firms entered the trucking industry. Discount rates were widespread, and in general, freight rates fell between 5 and 20 percent during 1980–1981. By 1986, revenue per ton for a truckload had fallen by 22 percent. Non-price competition also occurred, as schedule reliability increased, and truckers made more specialized equipment available. There was an influx of small, primarily nonunion carriers into the industry. Price competition led to the acceptance of a temporary wage freeze by the Teamsters union. For the industry as a whole, wages fell. New competition led to a shakeout in the trucking industry. Failure rates were much higher after deregulation than before, as profits for the least efficient firms were reduced.[13] Both efficiency and accident rates improved, however, after trucking was deregulated.

Regulation and Deregulation in the Airline Industry. The history of the airline industry has followed a similar pattern. For decades, the airline business was operated under the close supervision of the Civil Aeronautics Board (CAB).[14] In effect, the regulatory powers of the CAB imposed a monopolistic structure on the industry. The CAB blocked competitive entry and outlawed competitive pricing. Any carrier that wanted to compete in an interstate route had to convince the CAB that its services were needed. To say that the CAB limited entry on major routes would be an understatement. Despite more than 150 requests, the CAB did not grant a single trunk (long-distance) route to a new carrier between 1938 and 1978. CAB policy also stifled price competition. Carriers that wanted to lower prices were required to present an application to the CAB. A hearing would be held, at which time the firm's competitors would have ample opportunity to indicate why the impending rate reduction was unfair or potentially harmful to their operations.

At least partially in response to evidence that regulatory policies were leading to excessive fares, half-empty planes, and a uniform product offering, airline regulatory policies in the United States were substantially relaxed in the late 1970s. Under the direction of economist Alfred Kahn, the CAB moved toward

---

[12]See for example Thomas Gale Moore, "Transportation Policy," *Regulation,* No. 3, 1988, and Dennis W. Carlton and Jeffrey M. Perloff, *Modern Industrial Organization* (Glenview, Ill.: Scott, Foresman/Little, Brown, 1990), pp. 825–34, for summaries of deregulation results in the United States.

[13]See Daniel Machalaba, "More Companies Push Freight Haulers to Get Better Rate, Service" *Wall Street Journal,* December 18, 1985.

[14]Many people incorrectly associate the CAB with regulation of air safety, a function that it did perform in the past. However, since 1958, the Federal Aviation Agency has been responsible for air safety rules.

deregulation. Carriers were permitted to raise prices by as much as 10 percent and lower them by as much as 70 percent merely by giving the CAB notice 45 days in advance. In 1978, Congress passed the Airline Deregulation Act, which reduced the restrictions on price competition and entry into the industry.

What has been the result of the move toward deregulation? A 1986 Brookings Institution study by Clifford Winston and Stephen Morrison concluded that airline passengers gained about $11.5 billion annually, in 1988 dollars, from deregulation. The airline industry has expanded; employment increased approximately one third between 1977 and 1986.[15] During the same period, flights increased 28 percent and miles flown by paying passengers rose 61 percent. Despite the large increase in the number of flights, safety has improved. Contrary to the fears of some, free entry into the airline industry has not meant a reduction in the number of flights into small cities, although smaller planes are now used more often on low passenger-density routes.

Deregulation substantially increased airline efficiency. Previously, with high regulated fares, airlines competed by having more flights on the most lucrative routes. Each flight carried fewer passengers, who enjoyed the luxury of half-empty planes. After deregulation, increased entry and price competition made it necessary for airlines to lower fares and operate with a larger proportion of their seats filled. The loads hauled per airline employee rose nearly 20 percent on the major airlines.

THE NEW SOCIAL REGULATION

Social Regulation:
Legislation designed to improve the health, safety, and environmental conditions available to workers and/or consumers. The legislation usually mandates production procedures, minimum standards, and/or product characteristics to be met by producers and employers.

Along with movement toward deregulation of industrial structure and prices, there has been a sharp increase in what economists call **social regulation.** In the late 1960s and early 1970s, people had great faith in the ability of government to improve the quality of life. The economy was prospering, and people turned their attention more toward reducing health hazards, preserving the environment, and reducing the negative impacts of new technologies and the booming economy. For a wealthier nation, reducing air and water pollution and other externalities became more feasible and more desirable. Added regulation to protect individuals against risks from occupational hazards as well as risks from newly developed drugs and other consumer products was also demanded by activist groups.

The new social regulation resulted from these demands. As Exhibit 4 indicates, agencies such as the Occupational Safety and Health Administration (OSHA), Consumer Product Safety Commission (CPSC), Food and Drug Administration (FDA), and Environmental Protection Agency (EPA) grew rapidly. These new agencies as a group are now larger, in terms of number of employees and size of budgets, than the older regulatory agencies.

There are several significant differences between the two types of regulation. The older economic regulation focuses on a specific industry, whereas the new social regulation applies to the entire economy. Also, though more broadly based, social regulation is much more involved than economic regulation in the actual operation of individual firms. Economic regulation confines its attention to price and product quality—the final outcomes of production. The social regulatory agencies, on the other hand, frequently specify in detail the engineering processes to be followed by regulated firms and industries.

The major cost of social regulation is generally felt in the form of higher production costs and higher prices. Social regulation requires producers to alter

---

[15]See Thomas Gale Moore, ''Transportation Policy,'' *Regulation,* No. 3, 1988, p. 59, and the *Economic Report of the President, 1988,* pp. 199–229 for more details.

EXHIBIT 5

The Regulation "Tax"

Regulation that requires businesses to adopt more costly production techniques is similar to a tax. If the regulation increases per unit costs by *t*, the supply curve shifts upward by that amount. Higher prices and a smaller output result.

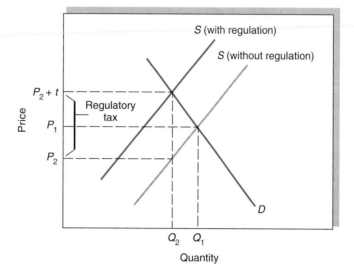

production techniques and facilities in accordance with dictated standards—to install more restrooms, to emit less pollution, or to reduce noise levels, for example—and most of the mandated changes increase costs. Of course, there are costs associated with the process of regulation itself; employment and operating costs of regulatory agencies must be met, which means higher taxes. The primary cost of social regulation, however, comes in the form of higher operating costs of firms as the result of the mandated regulations. In effect, these higher costs are like a tax. As Exhibit 5 illustrates, the higher cost shifts the supply curve for a good affected by the regulation to the left. Higher prices and a decline in the output of the good result.

Who pays the cost? As with any tax, the burden is shared by buyers and sellers according to the elasticity of supply and demand. When consumers have more options to the taxed good, so that their demand is more elastic, they will pay a smaller portion of the tax. In Exhibit 5, the new price $(P_2 + t)$ will be closer to P_1 when demand is more elastic. On the other hand, sellers will pay a smaller portion when the supply curve is more elastic, meaning that they have other options. In the short run, suppliers of goods may have few options for the use of capital already committed to the production process. Therefore, the short-run supply is likely to be inelastic. In the long run, of course, capital is quite mobile among uses, and the supply should be more elastic.

Sometimes the opportunity cost of social regulation is nearly impossible to calculate. For example, the FDA often bans the sale of a new drug until years of tests costing millions of dollars are completed, demonstrating that the drug is safe. Two important costs of this regulation, if the drug finally proves (or would have proven) to be safe, are: (a) some drugs are never developed because of the expensive tests and delays, and (b) people who could have been helped by the drug have to forgo it for several years. Deaths may even result from these delays. These opportunity costs may be very large, but they do not show up as expenditures.

Even when the costs of a regulation are measurable largely in cash, it is frequently difficult to assess the costs per unit of results. For example, there is strong disagreement about the costs and benefits of proposed new regulations for

APPLICATIONS IN ECONOMICS

Buying Fuel Conservation—Expensively

Fear of global warming—which some scientists think could be caused by rising levels of carbon dioxide in the air—has led to new calls for more fuel-efficient cars; cars that burn less fuel emit less carbon dioxide. In 1991, U.S. Senator Richard Bryan introduced a bill into Congress that would require automakers to boost their average mileage per gallon (mpg) from 27.5 mpg to 40 mpg.

Would such a mandatory fuel economy reduce fuel usage significantly? And if so, at what cost? We have some answers to these questions because Congress has been mandating fuel economy standards since 1975. Experience with these standards reveals some severe problems and the large sacrifices that would be required if standards are further tightened. The problems also illustrate the complex effects of government regulations.

Congress mandated Corporate Average Fuel Economy (CAFE) standards in 1975 after the price of oil went up dramatically. Supporters said that the standards

would conserve energy and make the U.S. less dependent on foreign oil. However, if Congress had simply allowed gasoline prices to rise, the higher prices would have encouraged people to adjust their habits in ways that suited them individually and minimized their personal cost. Some consumers would have simply driven less; others would have saved on gasoline by buying smaller cars or having more tune-ups. Some people who lived far from their workplaces might have bought larger cars and car-pooled; others might have chosen to live in places where they could walk to work.

Indeed, before the CAFE standards had an impact, people began to respond to higher gasoline prices by purchasing fuel-efficient cars. According to the *1986 Economic Report of the President,* average fuel economy in the United States increased by 43 percent between 1973 and 1979, as consumers responded to higher fuel prices. By the time the fuel efficiency standards influenced the design of cars, which probably

occurred with model year 1986, much fuel economy had already been achieved and the price of gasoline was going down.

By that time, some consumers wanted larger cars, but the CAFE standards forced automakers to offer smaller cars. Although they could make some reductions in fuel usage by such steps as redesigning transmissions or fuel-injection systems, car companies had to reduce vehicle weight to meet the standards. Robert W. Crandall of the Brookings Institution and John Graham of the Harvard School of Public Health estimate that model year 1989 cars were on average 500 pounds lighter than they would have been without the CAFE standards.[17]

A serious problem with lighter cars is that they are less safe than larger cars in crashes. Crandall and Graham estimated that 2200 to

---

[17]Robert W. Crandall and John D. Graham, "The Effect of Fuel Economy Standards on Automobile Safety," *Journal of Law and Economics*, Vol. 32, No. 1 (April 1989) pp. 97–118.

---

automobile safety. However, a study by the Brookings Institution[16] indicates that the auto safety regulations prevailing in the early 1980s probably provided enough benefits to at least offset their costs. The same study, however, concluded that regulations requiring emission controls to reduce air pollution, and requiring increases in fuel efficiency for automobiles have been very costly, while yielding few, if any, benefits. An unintended result of the increased regulatory costs of buying and operating new automobiles has been to reduce their sales, keeping older cars on the road longer. The earlier design of these older cars, and the wear they have experienced, increase the pollution they emit while decreasing the safety and fuel efficiency they provide. The study criticizes the lack of coordination among the

---

[16]See Robert W. Crandall, Howard K. Gruenspecht, Theodore E. Keeler, and Lester B. Lave, *Regulating the Automobile* (Washington, D.C.: The Brookings Institution, 1986).

3900 lives would be lost over a ten-year period as a result of the application of the CAFE standards to the cars of the 1989 model year, with similar numbers of lives likely to be lost with each succeeding model year. These findings led Jerry Ralph Curry, administrator of the National Highway Traffic Safety Administration, to oppose tighter standards in 1991. ''The bottom line is drastically smaller cars and more injuries and deaths,'' he wrote in *The Washington Post*.

The CAFE standards have had other unwanted effects. To sell enough small cars to raise the fuel economy average, domestic auto makers reduced small car prices and raised prices for large cars. Buying decisions were distorted and consumers paid more on balance for their cars.

Because Congress required the car companies to calculate average fuel economy separately for their domestic-manufactured cars and their imports, they cannot use their smaller, more fuel-efficient imports to bring down their domestic fleets'

average. This has encouraged small-car production in the U.S., even though production might be cheaper overseas, and led the Ford Motor Company to move some of its large-car production out of the country.

Another outcome of the CAFE regulations was to set in motion a big lobbying effort in Washington, D.C.—taking creative skills and energy away from productive activity. General Motors and Ford have lobbied to keep the government from tightening the standards. In contrast, Chrysler Corporation, which specializes in small cars, has a vested interest in keeping the standards tight, because the standards increase the costs of their rivals.

Were the CAFE standards effective in reducing fuel use? Not very. According to the Federal Highway Administration, even though fuel usage per vehicle has fallen since 1969, total fuel consumption has been rising since 1982. With large cars more expensive as a result of the standards, some people probably

kept their old cars longer, increasing gas consumption (and pollution). The lower prices of small cars probably increased the total number of cars purchased. More cars on the road meant greater fuel consumption because the marginal cost of driving in a small car is lower than in a large car, and because smaller car sizes lead people to share fewer rides. Robert A. Leone of Boston University estimates that a 2- or 3-cent tax on gasoline beginning in 1984 would have saved as much fuel as the CAFE standards did, at much less cost to society. In sum, the evidence suggests that the standards did not accomplish what was intended and placed costly burdens on society.

—Jane S. Shaw, Senior Associate, Political Economy Research Center, Bozeman, Montana.

many regulations on automobiles. Rules requiring greater fuel economy, for example, make cars smaller, lighter, and less safe. Emission controls often reduce fuel economy, while safety requirements increase weight and decrease performance and fuel economy. Yet, each regulation is established with little regard to these conflicting impacts on the consumers.

The new social regulation is costly, but it can have important benefits. The primary goal of social regulation is the attainment of a cleaner, safer, healthier environment. Nearly everyone agrees that this is a worthy objective. There is, however, considerable disagreement about the procedures that are most likely to accomplish this objective and the price that should be paid to make improvements. Resources are scarce. More social regulation will mean less of other things.

It should not be any more surprising that people differ with regard to the proper consumption level of environmental amenities than it is that they differ with regard to the proper consumption level of ice cream, for example. If 100 people were asked the best rate of consumption for strawberry ice cream, there would be a wide variety of answers. Similarly, the extent to which we should bear costs to make our air and water cleaner, and drugs safer, for example, is a question that each person may answer quite differently. One's preferred consumption rate for these benefits, like the preferred rate for strawberry ice cream, will depend in part on the expected cost and who pays that cost. Those who expect others to foot the bill will naturally prefer more of any valued good, whether it is ice cream or safety.

Differing preferences as to how much of other goods should be given up to attain a safer, cleaner, healthier environment comprise only part of the problem faced by regulators. An important characteristic of most socially regulated activities is a lack of information about their effects. This is not a coincidence. In most cases, the lack of information contributes directly to the demand for the regulation. For example, if consumers knew exactly what the effect of a particular drug would be, there would be little need for the FDA to regulate its availability. Many people, though, are unaware of the precise effects of drugs, air pollution, or work-place hazards, even when the information is available to experts. It is costly to communicate information, particularly highly technical information. A case can be made, therefore, that we should let the experts decide which drugs, how much air pollution, and what forms of work-place safety should be sought. While the lack of solid information generates much of the demand for social regulation, it also makes it difficult to evaluate the effectiveness of the regulatory activity.

Future Directions.   Most people concede that regulation, both economic and social, is an imperfect solution. It is quite difficult, however, to separate beneficial regulations from those that are counterproductive. Even though there is strong support for the continuation and expansion of social regulatory activities, recent experience indicates that forces favoring deregulation are also present. Improved empirical evidence on the effectiveness of specific social regulation programs will continue to emerge during the next decade.

CHAPTER SUMMARY

1. For more than a century, the relative size of the agricultural sector has declined, while the service sector has expanded. Manufacturing rose in importance, employing an increasing fraction of the labor force until 1948, but a declining fraction since then.
2. Even though manufacturing employment has declined, manufacturing output as a share of the total has been approximately constant during the last several decades. This pattern reflects the rising wages and productivity in the manufacturing sector. Over the past century, large shifts in worker occupations have accompanied the dynamic changes in the U.S. economy.
3. An increasing proportion of the U.S. economy has become competitive over the past several decades, probably due to antitrust policy, rising import competition, and deregulation.
4. Antitrust legislation seeks to (a) maintain a competitive structure in the unregulated private sector and (b) prohibit business practices that are thought to stifle competition.
5. The Sherman, Clayton, and Federal Trade Commission Acts form the foundation of antitrust policy in the United States. The Sherman Act prohibits conspiracies to restrain trade and/or monopolize an industry. The Clayton Act prohibits specific business practices, such as price discrimination, tying contracts, exclusive dealings, and mergers and acquisitions (as amended), when they "substantially lessen

competition or tend to create a monopoly.'' As it has evolved through the years, the Federal Trade Commission is concerned primarily with enforcing consumer protection legislation, prohibiting deceptive advertising, and investigating industrial structure.

6. The merger wave of the 1980s included many hostile takeovers and leveraged buyouts, financed in part by junk bonds. Research to date indicates that such mergers usually increased the efficiency of the target firms, but did not necessarily benefit the acquiring firms.

7. Antitrust policy is made more difficult by the fact that it is not always easy to determine when a business practice is being used to further competition, and when it will have an anticompetitive result. Most economists believe that antitrust policy in the U.S. has promoted competition and reduced industrial concentration, but not to a dramatic extent.

8. Regulation often involves cross-subsidies, resulting in pressures on regulators from affected classes of customers. The breakup of AT&T reduced the cross-subsidy of local telephone service by long-distance customers, raising just such disputes among classes of users.

9. To date, economists have been unable to develop a complete theory of regulation. However economic analysis does suggest that: (a) the demand for regulation often stems from special interest and redistribution considerations rather than from the pursuit of economic efficiency; (b) regulation often fails to adjust to changing market conditions; and (c) with the passage of time, regulatory agencies are likely to adopt the views of the interest groups they are supposed to regulate.

10. Traditional economic regulation has generally sought to fix prices and/or influence industrial structure. During the 1970s, changing market conditions and empirical studies generated widespread dissatisfaction with economic regulation. Significant moves toward deregulation were made in the late 1970s, particularly in the trucking and airline industries. New entrants, intense competition, and discount prices have accompanied the deregulation of these industries.

11. In recent years, economic regulation has been relaxed, and social regulatory activities have expanded rapidly. Social regulation seeks to provide a cleaner, safer, healthier environment for workers and consumers. Pursuit of this objective is costly—higher product prices and higher taxes accompany such regulation. Since the costs and particularly the benefits are often difficult to measure and evaluate, the efficiency of social regulatory programs is a controversial topic, and the subject of much current research.

CRITICAL ANALYSIS QUESTIONS

*1. ''Manufacturing is dying in the U.S. economy. We are becoming a nation of service workers—hamburger flippers and people who take in each others' laundry—and inevitably a second-rate economy.'' Evaluate.

2. ''Big business is taking over the U.S. economy. Giant firms decide what we can buy, and even what government does.'' Evaluate.

3. Does the fact that a firm is large indicate that it does not face important competition? Do large firms usually earn a high rate of profit?

*4. ''Any merger that reduces competition hurts consumers and clearly should be stopped.'' Evaluate.

5. ''Efficiency requires large-scale production. Yet big businesses mean monopoly power, high prices, and market inefficiency. We must choose between production efficiency and monopoly.'' Evaluate.

*6. Legislation mandating stronger automobile bumpers has presumably made cars both safer and more expensive, as would legislation requiring air bags for front-seat drivers and passengers. Should these laws be imposed? Why or why not?

---

*Asterisk denotes questions for which answers are given in Appendix C, Selected Answers.

7. "Without legal safety requirements, products such as lawn mowers would be unsafe." Evaluate.

*8. Will social legislation mandating work-place and product safety reduce the profitability of the regulated firms? Who bears the cost, and who gains the benefits of such legislation?

*9. If tariff and quota barriers for foreign imports are lifted, making imports easier to obtain, does this strengthen or weaken the case for strict antitrust legislation and enforcement?

10. AT&T, which sells long-distance service but no longer is in the local phone service business, now opposes the higher long-distance rates it previously supported. Why?

11. "Voters in our state should insist on state utility regulators who are tough on business. Consumers will benefit if prices are kept from rising above the per unit cost of production." Evaluate.

*12. With rate regulation and control of routes, as the Civil Aeronautics Board imposed on interstate airlines before deregulation, new entry was permitted only when it was shown to be "necessary." What definitions of "necessary" would you expect to hear from (a) existing airlines and (b) customers? Which one would you expect to prevail, and why?

13. "The leveraged buyout craze of the 1980s was an example of capitalism at its worst. Greedy corporate heads were just trying to expand their empires. Huge mountains of debt were generated simply to feed the egos of a few executives." Why might an economist disagree with this statement? Might there be some truth in it, from an economic point of view?

14. "We owe it to our coal miners to see that mines become much safer. Regulations can accomplish this and the mine owners will pay. Since users of coal have many sources of supply, they will not pay for these regulations. Workers will clearly be better off." Explain the logic here, and show what additional assumptions must be made about mine owners, and about workers, before the statement can be true.

*15. "If we force increased safety measures in the workplace by regulation, business may bear the cost in the short run, but capital will receive that market rate of return in the long run." Evaluate and explain.

16. "Regulations on the introduction of new drugs should be strengthened. Fewer people would die if more research were required prior to the introduction of new drugs. Only an economist could possibly disagree. Sure, it would cost more, but saving even one life would surely be worth more than whatever it costs." Evaluate.

*17. "People cannot be expected to make good decisions on their own regarding auto safety. Only experts know enough to make such decisions." Evaluate.

18. "Safety regulation is not an economic question. Where lives and health are at stake, economics has no place." Evaluate.

19. In large cities, taxi fares are often set above the market equilibrium rate. Sometimes the number of licenses is limited in order to maintain the above market price. In another case, licenses are automatically granted to anyone wanting to operate a taxi. When taxi fares are set above market equilibrium, compare and contrast resource allocation under the restricted license system (assume the licenses are tradable) and the free-entry system. In which case will it be easier for customers to get a taxi? In which case will the amount of capital required to enter the taxi business be greater?

PART FOUR

Factor Markets and Income Distribution

23

The Supply of and Demand for Productive Resources

It is . . . necessary to attach price tags to the various factors of production . . . in order to guide those who have the day-to-day decisions to make as to what is plentiful and what is scarce.[1]

Professor James Meade

CHAPTER FOCUS

- Why do business firms demand labor, machines, and other resources?

- Why is the demand for a productive resource inversely related to its price?

- How do business firms decide how many skilled laborers, unskilled laborers, machines, and other factors of production to employ?

- How is the quantity supplied of a resource related to its price in the short run? . . . in the long run?

- What determines the market price in resource markets?

Resource Markets: Markets in which business firms demand factors of production (for example, labor, capital, and natural resources) from household suppliers. The resources are then used to produce goods and services. These markets are sometimes called factor markets.

*I*n previous chapters we focused on the demand and supply conditions in *product* markets. In these markets, consumers purchased goods and services which were produced by business firms. We now turn to an analysis of **resource markets,** or, as they are sometimes called, *factor markets*.

When producing commodities, business firms hire productive resources, which are either directly or indirectly owned by households. The roles of households and business firms in resource markets are reversed from what they were in product markets. In resource markets, households are sellers; they supply resources in exchange for income. On the other hand, business firms are purchasers; they demand resources which are used to produce goods and services.

There is a close relationship between resource and product markets. The circular flow diagram of Exhibit 1 illustrates this point. Households get their income by selling factors of production—for example, the services of their labor and

---

[1]James E. Meade, ''Economic Efficiency and Distributional Justice,'' in *Contemporary Issues in Economics*, ed. Robert W. Crandall and Richard S. Eckaus (Boston: Little, Brown, 1972), p. 319.

EXHIBIT 1

The Market for Resources

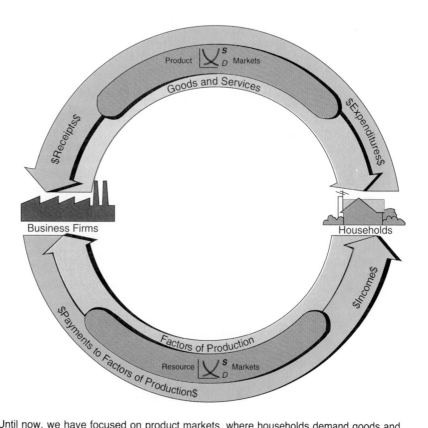

Until now, we have focused on product markets, where households demand goods and services which are supplied by firms (upper loop). We now turn to resource markets, where firms demand factors of production—human capital (for example, skills and knowledge of workers) and physical capital (for example, machines, buildings, and land) which are supplied by households in exchange for income (bottom loop). In resource markets, firms are buyers and households are sellers, just the reverse of the case for product markets.

capital—to business firms. Their offers to sell form the supply curve in resource markets (bottom loop). In turn, the income households derive from the sale of resources provides them with the buying power required to purchase goods and services in product markets. These household expenditures for products generate revenues which provide business firms with the incentive to produce goods and services (top loop). Finally, the revenues of business firms from product sales underlie their demand for resources.

Business firms demand resources because they contribute to the production of goods and services. Since resources must be bid away from competitive firms seeking to put them to alternative uses, costs are incurred whenever resources are employed. Prices in resource markets coordinate the actions of the firms demanding factors of production and the households supplying them. Resource prices provide both resource suppliers and resource-using producers with information about scarcity. Resource prices (and the accompanying income payments) provide individuals with the incentive to offer their productive services to producers. An increase in the price of a resource will encourage potential suppliers to provide more of the resource. Resource prices also provide profit-seeking firms with an incentive to economize on resource use. Firms will find that it is profitable to hire a resource, if, and only if, the resource adds more to the firm's revenue than to its cost. Thus, an increase in resource prices will encourage firms to cut back on their use of the resource.

HUMAN AND NONHUMAN RESOURCES

Nonhuman Resources: The durable, nonhuman inputs that can be used to produce both current and future output. Machines, buildings, land, and raw materials are examples. Investment can increase the supply of nonhuman resources. Economists often use the term "physical capital" when referring to nonhuman resources.

Broadly speaking, there are two different types of productive inputs—nonhuman and human resources. **Nonhuman resources** are further broken down into the categories of physical capital, land, and natural resources. Capital consists of man-made goods used to produce other goods. Tools, machines, and buildings are part of the capital stock.

Net investment can increase the supply of nonhuman resources. Increasing the available stock of nonhuman resources, though, involves the sacrifice of current consumption goods. Resources that are used to produce machines, upgrade the quality of land, or discover natural resources could be used to produce current goods and services directly. Why take the round-about path? The answer is that sometimes indirect methods of producing goods are less costly in the long run. Robinson Crusoe found he could catch more fish by taking some time off from hand-fishing to build a net. Even though his initial investment in the net reduced his current catch, once the net was completed he was able to more than make up for his earlier loss of output.

Additions to capital stock, whether they are fishing nets or complex machines, involve current sacrifices. Capital-intensive methods of production are adopted only when decision-makers expect the benefits of a larger future output to more than offset the current reduction in the production of consumption goods.

Just as the supply of machines can be increased, so too can wise land-clearing and soil conservation practices be used to upgrade both the quantity and quality of land. Similarly, the supply of natural resources can be increased (within limits) by the application of more resources to discovery and development.

OUTSTANDING ECONOMIST

**Gary Becker
(1930—   )**

This innovative economist is perhaps best known for his ingenious application of economics to several areas that many had previously considered noneconomic by nature. His pioneering book, *The Economics of Discrimination,*[3] developed a general theory that could be used to analyze (and measure) the impact of discrimination in several areas on the status of minorities and women. His work in this area laid the foundation for the burgeoning of research interest in the economics of discrimination that took place during the 1970s and 1980s.

Later, Becker applied economic analysis to such seemingly noneconomic subjects as crime prevention, family development, an individual's allocation of time, and even the selection of a marriage partner.[4] The human capital approach underlies much of Becker's research. His widely acclaimed book, *Human Capital,*[5] is already a classic. The work developed a theoretical foundation for human investment decisions in education, on-the-job training, migration, and health.

Becker is a past president of the American Economic Association and a recipient of the organization's prestigious John Bates Clark Award.

---

[3]Gary Becker, *The Economics of Discrimination* (Chicago: University of Chicago Press, 1957).
[4]Gary Becker, *The Economic Approach to Human Behavior* (Chicago: University of Chicago Press, 1976), and Gary Becker and W. M. Landes, *Essays in the Economics of Crime and Punishment* (New York: Columbia University Press, 1974).
[5]Gary Becker, *Human Capital* (New York: Columbia University Press, 1964).

Human Resources: The abilities, skills, and health of human beings that can contribute to the production of both current and future output. Investment in training and education can increase the supply of human resources.

Investment in Human Capital: Expenditures on training, education, and skill development designed to increase the productivity of an individual.

Human resources are comprised of the skills and knowledge of workers. Lay persons sometimes act as if these resources are strictly the result of inheritance or happenstance. This is not the case. Investment in such things as education, training, health, and skill-building experience can increase worker productivity and thereby the availability of human resources. Economists refer to such activities as **investment in human capital.**[2]

Decisions to invest in human capital involve all the basic ingredients of other investment decisions. Consider the decision of whether to go to college. For most people, it is partly an investment decision. As many of you will testify, an investment in a college education requires the sacrifice of current earnings as well as payment for direct expenses such as tuition and books. The investment is expected to lead to a better job, considering both monetary and nonmonetary factors, and other benefits associated with a college education. The rational investor will weigh the current costs against the expected future benefits. College will be chosen only if the latter are greater than the former.

---

[2]The contributions of T. W. Schultz and Gary Becker to the literature on human capital have been particularly significant. See Daniel S. Hamermesh and Albert Rees, *The Economics of Work and Pay* (New York: Harper & Row, 1988), Chapter 3, for additional detail on human capital theory.

Some may find it offensive to refer to human beings as though they were machines. No ethical connotations are implied by the term "human capital." Men and women are, of course, not factors of production. They are human beings. However, the effort, skill, ability, and ingenuity of individuals can be applied productively. They can be used to improve human welfare. It is these productive resources that we refer to as human resources, or human capital.

Human resources differ from nonhuman resources in two important respects. First, human capital is embodied in the individual. Choices concerning the use of human resources are vitally affected by working conditions, location, job prestige, and similar nonpecuniary factors. Although monetary factors influence human capital decisions, individuals have some leeway in trading off money income for better working conditions. Second, human resources cannot be bought and sold in nonslave societies. However, the *services* of human resources are bought and sold daily. Individuals have the right to quit, to sell their labor services to another employer, or to use them in an alternative manner in a nonslave society.

In competitive markets, the price of resources, like the price of products, is determined by supply and demand. To develop the theory of price for resource markets, we must first develop a theory for each of these determining factors. Let us begin by focusing on the demand for resources, both human and nonhuman.

THE DEMAND FOR RESOURCES

Derived Demand: Demand for an item based on the demand for products the item helps to produce. The demand for resources is a derived demand.

Producers employ laborers, machines, raw materials, and the other resources required to produce goods and services they hope to sell for a profit. The demand for a resource exists because there is a demand for goods that the resource helps to produce. The demand for each resource is thus a **derived demand;** it is derived from the demand of consumers for products.

For example, a service station hires mechanics because customers demand repair service, not because the service station owner receives benefits simply from having mechanics around. If customers did not demand repair service, mechanics would not be employed for long. Similarly, the demand for such inputs as carpenters, plumbers, lumber, and glass windows is derived from the demand of consumers for houses and other consumer products these resources help to make.

Most resources contribute to the production of numerous goods. For example, glass is used to produce windows, ornaments, dishes, light bulbs, and mirrors, among other things. The total demand for a resource is the sum of the derived demand for it in each of its uses. Consequently, when economists study the demand for factors of production, they must trace changes in resource prices to their impact in the product market.

How will firms respond to an increase in the price of a resource? In the long run, the higher price of a resource will lead to two distinct adjustments, which will ensure an inverse relationship between price and the amount of the resource demanded. First, firms will seek to reduce their use of the now more expensive input by substituting other resources for it. Second, the increase in the price of the resource will lead to both higher costs and higher product prices. Consumers will buy less of the higher-priced product and substitute other goods for it, leading to a decline in the demand for resources used to make it. Therefore, the amount demanded of a factor of production will decline as its price increases. The demand curve for a resource will slope downward.

Let us look a little more closely at both of these adjustments.

Substitution in Production.   Firms will use the input combination that minimizes their cost. When the price of a resource goes up, cost-conscious firms will turn to lower-cost substitutes and cut back on their use of the more expensive resource. For example, if the price of walnut lumber increases, furniture manufacturers will use other wood varieties, metals, and plastics more intensely. Similarly, if the price of copper tubing increases, construction firms and plumbers will substitute plastic pipe for the more expensive tubing. The methods of substitution may differ. Sometimes producers will alter the style and dimensions of a product in order to conserve on the use of a more expensive resource. In other cases, a shift in location may play a role in the substitution process. For example, if prices of office space and land increase in the downtown area of a large city, firms may move to the suburbs in order to cut back on their use of the more expensive resources. The degree to which firms will be able to reduce their use of a more expensive resource will vary. If good substitutes in production are available and, therefore, it is relatively easy to conserve on the use of a more expensive resource, then this substitution effect ensures not only that quantity demanded will be inversely related to price but also that the demand for the resource will be highly elastic.

Substitution in Consumption.   An increase in the price of a resource will lead to higher prices for products that the input helps to produce. The higher product prices will encourage consumers to purchase substitute goods, reducing the consumption of the more expensive product. When less of that product is produced, however, producer demand for resources (including the one that has risen in price) will decline. The experience of the American automobile industry in the early 1980s illustrates the point. Throughout much of the 1970s, wages in the U.S. automobile industry increased quite rapidly. The higher wages placed upward pressure on the prices of American-made automobiles. However, as auto prices rose, many consumers switched to substitute products, particularly foreign-produced automobiles. American auto sales declined, causing a reduction in quantity of labor demanded in the automobile industry and therefore widespread layoffs.

Other things constant, the more elastic the demand for the product, the more elastic the demand for the resource. This relationship stems from the derived nature of resource demand. An increase in the price of a product for which the demand is highly elastic will cause a sharp reduction in the sales of the good. There will thus also be a relatively sharp decline in the demand for the resources used to produce the good.

How important is the factor pricing mechanism? Some economies use a planning process rather than factor markets to allocate resources. When a resource becomes more scarce, planners in these economies do not have the necessary information to reallocate resources among users. Neither do the users have the incentive to voluntarily cut back on their use of the resource. As a result, resource conservation in response to increased scarcity is weaker in centrally planned economies. See Applications in Economics Box, "The Importance of Factor Markets: The Case of Energy," for evidence on this point.

APPLICATIONS IN ECONOMICS

The Importance of Factor Markets: The Case of Energy

The job of factor markets is to provide each firm with the information and incentive to economize on the resources used to produce the firm's output. The same job can be done in other ways, of course. Central planning replaces factor markets in economies where resources are not privately owned. But will planners be able to recognize all the places where a resource, such as energy, is most valuable? In such an economy, will technology evolve to reduce energy use when (and where) it is more costly? Without a factor market to formulate prices that reflect energy cost and demand information, how will planners know the least costly sources and the most highly valued uses for energy?

Economic thinking suggests that efficient use of a factor of production such as energy is more difficult without resource markets for energy. Is this view supported by what we see in the real world? Economist Mikhail Bernstam, in a book written for London's

Institute of Economic Affairs, compares the efficiency of energy use in socialist nations, which use central planning, with energy efficiency in nations where factor markets are used to allocate energy resources such as oil, electricity, and coal. The results of his research are striking. Socialist economies use nearly three times as much energy per unit of GNP as economies using factor markets. The comparison holds also for countries that are similar except for their use of markets. Centrally planned North Korea consumes three times as much energy per unit of GNP as South Korea, where factor markets distribute energy. Similarly, what until recently was centrally planned East Germany consumed 3.5 times as much energy per unit of GNP as West Germany.[6]

Energy prices rose sharply during the 1973–1980 period. Exhibit 2 illustrates the impact of the higher prices on energy use in North America, Europe, and the Soviet Union. In North America

and Europe, per capita energy consumption (which had been increasing) began to decline during the period following the price increases of the 1970s. Resource markets in these areas directed users toward substitutes and away from the more expensive energy resources during the post-1973 period. In contrast, there was no evidence of a similar response on the part of central planners in the Soviet Union. Per capita energy consumption continued to rise in the Soviet Union throughout the 1970s and 1980s.

As our theory indicates, resource markets are able to encourage conservation and direct users away from more expensive resources. In contrast, centrally planned economies often find it difficult to achieve a similar response without the information and incentives generated by prices determined in markets.

---

[6]Mikhail S. Bernstam, *The Wealth of Nations and the Environment* London: Institute of Economics Affairs, 1991).

TIME AND THE DEMAND FOR RESOURCES

It will take time for producers to adjust fully to a change in the price of a resource. Typically, a producer will be unable to alter a production process or the design of a product immediately to conserve on the use of a more expensive input or to use more efficiently an input whose price has declined. Similarly, consumers may be unable to alter their consumption patterns immediately in response to price changes. Thus, the short-run demand for resources is typically less elastic than the demand in the long run.

Using steel as an example, Exhibit 3 illustrates the relationship between time and the demand for resources. Initially, higher steel prices may lead to only a small reduction in usage. If the high price of steel persists, however, automobile manufacturers will alter their designs, moving toward lighter-weight cars that require less steel. Architectural firms will design buildings that permit more substitution of plastics, wood, aluminum, glass, and other resources for steel. Products made with steel will increase in price, which will encourage consumers to

EXHIBIT 2

Resource Prices and Energy Use—Europe and the United States Compared to the Soviet Union

Energy consumption per capita declined in North America and Europe after the rapid increase in energy prices during the 1973–1981 period. In contrast, energy consumption continued to increase in the Soviet Union. This indicates that centrally planned economies have a more difficult time adjusting energy use to changing prices than is true for market economies.

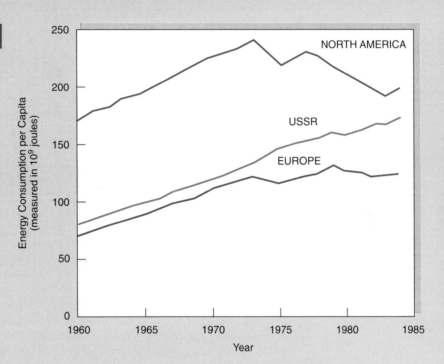

Source: UN Environment Programme, *Environmental Data Report* (London: Basil Blackwell, 1987), p. 247. Reprinted in Mikhail S. Bernstam, *The Wealth of Nations and the Environment* (London: Institute of Economic Affairs, 1991), Figure 1, p. 26.

find more and more ways to cut back on their use. These and numerous similar adjustments will help conserve on the use of the more expensive steel. It will take time, however, for decision-makers to carry out many of these adjustments. Therefore, the demand (D_{sr}) for steel, like that for most other resources, will be more inelastic in the short run than in the long run.

SHIFTS IN THE DEMAND FOR RESOURCES

The entire demand curve for a resource, like that for a product, may shift, for one of three reasons.

1. A Change in the Demand for a Product Will Cause a Similar Change in the Demand for the Resources Used to Make the Product. Anything that increases the demand for a consumer good simultaneously increases the demand for resources required to make it; a decline in product demand and price will reduce the demand for resources embodied in the product. During the 1970s, the demand for

EXHIBIT 3

Time and the Demand Elasticity of Resources

An increase in the price of steel will lead to a much larger reduction in consumption in the long run than in the short run. Typically, the demand for resources will be more inelastic in the short run.

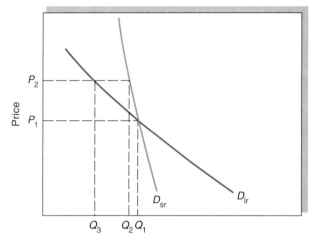

small automobiles increased sharply, primarily because of higher gasoline prices. The increase in demand for small cars led to an increase in demand for workers to produce them. Employment at plants producing small cars expanded during the 1970s, even while auto workers were being laid off at plants producing large cars. Falling gasoline prices in the mid-1980s reversed this situation. Propelled by lower gasoline prices, the demand for larger automobiles increased, while the demand for small cars declined. Reflecting the demand in product markets, employment at automobile plants making full-size cars expanded, while employment at plants producing small cars fell.

2. Changes in the Productivity of a Resource Will Alter the Demand for the Resource.   The higher the productivity of a resource, the greater the demand for it. Several factors combine to determine the productivity of a resource. First, the **marginal product** of any resource will depend on the amount of other resources with which it is working. In general, additional capital will tend to increase the productivity of labor. For example, someone with a lawn mower can mow more grass than the same person with a pair of shears. A student working with a textbook, class notes, and tutor can learn more economics than the same student without these tools. The quantity and quality of the tools with which we work significantly affects our productivity.

Marginal Product: The change in total output that results from the employment of one additional unit of a factor of production—one workday of skilled labor, for example.

Second, technological advances can improve the productivity of resources, including labor. Advances in the computer industry illustrate this point. Working with computer technology, an accountant and a data-entry person can maintain business records and create bookkeeping reports that previously would have required 10 to 15 workers. Improvements in word processing equipment have vastly increased the productivity of typists, journalists, lawyers, and writers. Similarly, computers have substantially increased the productivity of typesetters, telephone operators, quality-control technicians, and workers in many other occupations.

Third, improvements in the quality (skill level) of a resource will increase productivity and therefore the demand for the resource. As workers obtain valuable new knowledge and/or upgrade their skills, they enhance their productivity. In essence, such workers move into a different skill category, where demand is greater.

All these factors help explain why wage rates in the United States, Canada, Western Europe, and Japan are higher than in most other areas of the world. Given the skill level of workers, the technology, and the capital equipment with which they work, individuals in these countries produce more goods and services per hour of labor. The demand for labor (relative to supply) is greater because of labor's increased productivity. Essentially, the workers' greater productivity leads to higher wage rates.

3. A Change in the Price of a Related Resource Will Affect the Demand for the Original Resource.

An increase in the price of a substitute resource will lead to an increase in demand for the given resource. For example, when the wage rates of unionized workers in a given field or industry increase, demand for non-union workers who are good substitutes for the union workers will expand. Conversely, an increase in the price of a resource that is a complement to a given resource will decrease the demand for the given resource. For example, higher prices for computers would most likely cause the demand for computer programmers to fall.

MARGINAL PRODUCTIVITY AND THE FIRM'S HIRING DECISION

Marginal Revenue Product: The change in the total revenue of a firm that results from the employment of one additional unit of a factor of production. The marginal revenue product of an input is equal to its marginal product multiplied by the marginal revenue (price) of the good or service produced.

How does a producer decide whether to employ additional units of a resource? We noted previously that the marginal product of a resource is the increase in output that results when the employment of a resource is expanded by one unit. The resource's marginal product multiplied by the marginal revenue of the product being produced yields what is known as the **marginal revenue product,** or MRP. The MRP is simply the change in the firm's total revenue brought about by the employment of one extra unit of a resource. The marginal revenue product reveals how much employment of the additional unit of the resource adds to the firm's revenue.

A profit-maximizing firm will, of course, continue to expand output as long as marginal cost is less than marginal revenue. This rule can be generalized to include the firm's employment of resources. Since firms are usually price takers when they buy resources, the price of a resource is its marginal cost. Firms maximize profits by hiring units of a resource so long as the employment of each additional unit adds more to the firm's revenues than it adds to the firm's cost. Thus, additional units of a variable resource will be hired up to the employment level at which the price of the resource (the firm's marginal cost) is just equal to the marginal revenue product of the resource (the firm's additional revenue generated by the employment of the resource). This profit maximization rule applies to all firms, pure competitors and price searchers alike.

Value Marginal Product: The marginal product of a resource multiplied by the selling price of the product it helps to produce. Under pure competition, a firm's marginal revenue product will be equal to the value marginal product.

The marginal product of a resource multiplied by the selling price of the product yields the resource's **value marginal product** (VMP). When a firm sells its product in a competitive market, the selling price and the marginal revenue of the

EXHIBIT 4   ■   The Short-run Demand Schedule of a Firm

Compute-Accounting, Inc., uses computer technology and data-entry operators to provide accounting services in a competitive market. For each accounting statement processed, the firm receives a $200 fee (column 4). Given the firm's current fixed capital, column 2 shows how total output changes as additional data-entry operators are hired. The marginal revenue product schedule (column 6) indicates how hiring an additional operator affects the total revenue of the firm. Since a profit-maximizing firm will hire an additional employee if, and only if, the employee adds more to revenues than to costs, the marginal revenue product curve is the firm's short-run demand curve for the resource (see Exhibit 5).

Units of the Variable Factor (data-entry operators) (1)	Total Output (accounting statements processed per week) (2)	Marginal Product [change in (2) divided by change in (1)] (3)	Sales Price per Statement (4)	Total Revenue (2) × (4) (5)	Marginal Revenue Product (3) × (4) (6)
0	0.0	—	$200	$ 0	—
1	5.0	5.0	200	1,000	1,000
2	9.0	4.0	200	1,800	800
3	12.0	3.0	200	2,400	600
4	14.0	2.0	200	2,800	400
5	15.5	1.5	200	3,100	300
6	16.5	1.0	200	3,300	200
7	17.0	0.5	200	3,400	100

product are equal. Under pure competition, therefore, the marginal revenue product of a resource is equal to its value marginal product.

Exhibit 4 illustrates how a firm decides how much of a resource to employ. Compute-Accounting, Inc., uses computer equipment and data-entry operators to supply clients with monthly accounting statements. The firm sells its service in a competitive market for $200 per statement. Given the fixed quantity of computer equipment owned by Compute-Accounting, column 2 relates the employment of data-entry operators to the expected total output (quantity of accounting statements). One data-entry operator can process five statements per week. When two operators are employed, nine statements can be completed. Column 2 indicates how total output is expected to change as additional data-entry operators are employed. Column 3 presents the marginal product schedule for data-entry operators. Column 6, the marginal revenue product schedule, shows how the employment of each additional operator affects total revenues.

Since Compute-Accounting sells its service competitively, both the marginal revenue product and the value marginal product of labor equal MP (column 3) times the sales price per accounting statement (column 4). What if the firm is not a perfect competitor? The marginal revenue product must always equal MR multiplied by MP. When the firm confronts a downward-sloping demand curve for its product, the marginal revenue of the product will be less than its price. When this is the case, the marginal revenue product of a resource will be less than its value marginal product.

How does Compute-Accounting decide how many operators to employ? As additional operators are employed, the output of processed statements (column 2) will increase, which will expand total revenue (column 5). Employment of additional operators, though, will also add to production costs since the operators

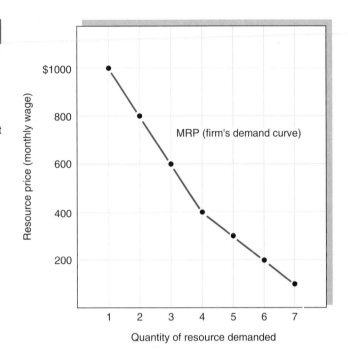

EXHIBIT 5

The Firm's Demand Curve for a Resource

The firm's demand curve for a resource will reflect the marginal revenue product of the resource. In the short run, it will slope downward because the marginal product of the resource will fall as more of it is used with a fixed amount of other resources. The location of the MRP curve will depend on (a) the price of the product and (b) the productivity of the resource, which depends on technology and the quantity of other factors working with the resource.

must be paid. Applying the profit maximization rule, Compute-Accounting will hire additional operators as long as their employment adds more to revenues than to costs. This will be the case, as long as the marginal revenue product (Exhibit 4, column 6) of the data entry operators exceeds their wage rate. Thus, as Exhibit 5 illustrates, the marginal revenue product curve of operators is also the firm's short-run demand curve for the resource.[7] At a weekly wage of $1,000, Compute-Accounting would hire only one operator. If the weekly wage dropped to $800, two operators would be hired. At still lower wage rates, additional operators would be hired.

The location of the firm's MRP curve depends on (a) the price of the product, (b) the productivity of the resource, and (c) the amount of other resources with which the resource is working. Changes in any one of these three factors will cause the MRP curve to shift. For example, if Compute-Accounting obtained additional computer equipment that made it possible for the operators to complete more statements each week, the MRP curve for labor would increase. This increase in the quantity of the other resources working with labor would increase labor's productivity.

ADDING OTHER FACTORS OF PRODUCTION

Thus far, we have analyzed the firm's hiring decision, assuming that it employed one variable resource (labor) and one fixed resource. Production, though, usually involves the use of many resources. When a firm employs multiple resources, how should the resources be combined to produce the product? We can answer this question by considering either the conditions for profit maximization or the conditions for cost minimization.

---

[7]Strictly speaking, this is true only for a variable resource that is employed with a fixed amount of another factor.

Profit Maximization When Multiple Resources Are Employed.   The same decision-making considerations apply when the firm employs several factors of production. The profit-maximizing firm will expand its employment of a resource as long as the marginal revenue product of the resource exceeds its employment cost. If we assume that resources are perfectly divisible, the profit-maximizing decision rule implies that, in equilibrium, the marginal revenue product of each resource will be equal to the price of the resource. Therefore, the following conditions will exist for the profit-maximizing firm:

MRP of skilled labor $= P_{SL}$ (wage rate of skilled labor)

MRP of unskilled labor $= P_{UL}$ (wage rate of unskilled labor)

MRP of machine $= P_M$ (explicit or implicit rental price of machine A)

and so on, for all other factors.

Cost Minimization When Multiple Resources Are Employed.   If the firm is maximizing profits, clearly it must produce the profit-maximizing output at the least possible cost. If the firm is minimizing costs, the marginal dollar expenditure for each resource will have the same impact on output as every other marginal resource expenditure. Factors of production will be employed such that the marginal product per last dollar spent on each factor is the same for all factors.

Suppose that a dollar expenditure on labor caused output to rise by ten units, whereas an additional dollar expenditure on machines generated only a five-unit expansion in output. Under these circumstances, five more units of output (at no added cost) would result if the firm spent $1 less on machines and $1 more on labor. The firm's per unit cost would be reduced if it substituted labor for machines.

If the marginal dollar spent on one resource increases output by a larger amount than a dollar expenditure on other resources, costs can always be reduced by substituting resources with a high marginal product per dollar for those with a low marginal product per dollar expenditure. This substitution continues to reduce costs (and add profit) until the marginal product per dollar expenditure is equalized—that is, until the resource combination that minimizes cost is attained. When this is true, the proportional relationship between the price of each resource and its marginal product will be equal for all resources.

Therefore, the following condition exists when per unit costs are minimized:

$$\frac{\text{MP of skilled labor}}{\text{price of skilled labor}} = \frac{\text{MP of unskilled labor}}{\text{price of unskilled labor}}$$

$$= \frac{\text{MP of machine A}}{\text{price (rental value) of machine A}}$$

and so on, for the other factors.

This relationship indicates why, with competition, there will be a tendency for wage differences across skill categories to reflect productivity differences. If skilled workers are twice as productive as unskilled workers, their wage rates will tend toward twice the wage rates of unskilled workers. For example, suppose that a construction firm hiring workers to hang doors was choosing among skilled and unskilled workers. If skilled door hangers could complete four doors per hour, while unskilled workers could hang only two doors per hour, a cost minimizing firm would hire only skilled workers if their wages were *less than twice* the wages of unskilled workers. On the other hand, only unskilled workers would be hired if the wages of skilled workers were *more than twice* the wages of unskilled workers. With competition, wages across skill categories will tend to mirror productivity differences. If skilled workers are twice as productive (at the margin) as unskilled workers, their wages will tend to be twice as high, *but only twice as high,* as the wages of unskilled workers.

In the real world, it is sometimes difficult to measure the marginal product of a factor. Businesspeople may not necessarily think in terms of equating the marginal product/price ratio for each factor of production. Nevertheless, if they are minimizing cost, the marginal product/price ratio will be equal for all factors of production. Real-world decision-makers may use experience, trial and error, and intuitive rules but the question always is: "Can we reduce costs by using more of one resource and less of another?" Thus, when profits are maximized and the cost-minimization method of production is attained, regardless of the procedures used, the outcome will be as if the employer had followed the profit-maximization and cost-minimization decision-making rules just discussed.

MARGINAL PRODUCTIVITY, DEMAND, AND ECONOMIC JUSTICE

According to the law of diminishing marginal returns, as the employment level of a resource increases, other things constant, the marginal product (and marginal revenue product) of the resource will decline. As we have just seen, a profit-maximizing employer will expand the use of a resource until its marginal revenue product is equal to the price of the resource. If the price of the resource declines, employers will increase their utilization level of that resource. Therefore, as Exhibit 6 shows, the marginal productivity approach can be used to illustrate the inverse relationship between quantity demanded and resource price.

EXHIBIT 6

Marginal Productivity and Demand

Other things constant, an increase in the employment level will cause the MRP of a resource to decline. The larger quantity of the resource can be employed only at a lower price.

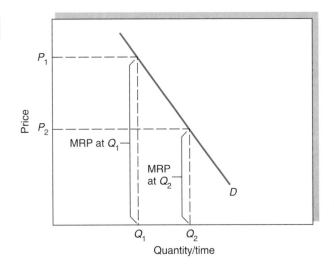

Some observers, noting that under pure competition the price of each resource is equal to the value of what it produces (that is, input price equals the marginal product of the input multiplied by the price of the product), have argued that competitive markets are ''just'' or ''equitable'' because each resource gets paid exactly what it is worth. There is a major defect in this line of reasoning, however. When a product is produced by a combination of factors, as is almost invariably the case, it is impossible to assign a specific proportion of the total output to each resource. For example, if one uses a tractor, an acre of land, and seed to produce wheat, one cannot accurately state that labor (or the seed or the land) produced one half or any other proportion of the output. Hence, those who argue that the factor payments generated by competitive markets are just, because each resource gets paid according to its productive contribution, assume that one can assign a specific proportion of the total output to each resource. This is impossible when output is produced by a combination of factors. The marginal product can be used as a measure of the change in total output associated with the use of an additional unit of a resource, but this measurement does not directly link one resource with one segment of output.

The marginal productivity theory is really a theory about the demand for resources. The central proposition of the theory is that profit-maximizing employers will never pay more for a unit of input, whether it is skilled labor, a machine, or an acre of land, than the input is worth to them. The worth of a unit of input to the firm is determined by how much additional revenue (marginal revenue product) is expected when the unit is used. That is, pursuit of profit will induce employers to hire additional units of each resource as long as the units' marginal productivity generates revenues in excess of costs. Resource prices will tend to reflect—though somewhat roughly in the real world—the marginal productivity of the resource.

However, the price of each resource is determined by conditions of supply as well as conditions of demand. Even though marginal productivity theory helps us understand the demand side of the market, it reveals nothing about the share of the total product produced by a resource or the justice of a resource price. We must analyze the supply of resources in order to complete the picture.

THE SUPPLY OF RESOURCES

In essence, our analysis of resource demand indicates that employers will hire a resource so long as they can gain by doing so. The same basic postulate also applies to resource suppliers. Resource owners will supply their services to an employer only if they perceive that the benefits of doing so exceed their costs (other things they could do with their time or resources). Thus, in order to attract factors of production, employers must offer resource owners at least as good a deal as they can get elsewhere. For example, if an employer does not offer a potential employee a package of income payments and working conditions that is as good or better than the employee can get elsewhere, the employer will be unable to attract the employee. Resource owners will supply their services to those who offer them the best job, all factors considered.

Resource owners will seek to use their factors of production in a manner that leads to their greatest net advantage. Others things constant, as the price of a specific resource (for example engineering services, craft labor, or wheat farm land) increases, the incentive of potential suppliers to provide the resource increases.

An increase in the price of a resource will attract potential resource suppliers into the market. In contrast, potential resource suppliers will shift into other activities when the price of a resource falls. Thus, the supply curve for a specific resource will slope upward to the right.

SHORT-RUN SUPPLY

As in the case of demand, the supply response in resource markets may vary between the short run and long run. The short run is a period so brief that there is insufficient time to alter the availability of a resource through investment in human and physical capital. In contrast, in the long run, resource suppliers have time to fully adjust their investment choices to a change in resource prices. Let us begin by considering the supply response in the short run.

Most resources have alternative uses; they can be used to perform a variety of functions. The elasticity of supply to a particular use will be dependent on **resource mobility.** Resources that can be easily transferred from one use to another in response to changing price incentives (in other words, those resources with a great many alternative uses or locations) are said to be highly mobile. The supply of such factors to any specific use will be elastic. Factors that have few alternative uses are said to be immobile and will have an inelastic short-run supply.

Resource Mobility: A term that refers to the ease with which factors of production are able to move among alternative uses. Resources that can easily be transferred to a different use or location are said to be highly mobile. In contrast, when a resource has few alternative uses, it is immobile. For example, the skills of a trained rodeo rider would be highly immobile, since they cannot be easily transferred to other lines of work.

What can we say about resource mobility in the real world? First, let us consider the mobility of labor. When labor skills can be transferred easily and quickly, human capital is highly mobile. Within a skill category (for example, plumber, store manager, accountant, or secretary), labor will be highly mobile within the same geographical area. Movements between geographical areas and from one skill category to another are more costly to accomplish. Labor will thus be less mobile for movements of this variety.

What about the mobility of land? Land is highly mobile among uses when location does not matter. For example, the same land can often be used to raise corn, wheat, soybeans, or oats. Thus, the supply of land allocated to production of each of these commodities will be highly responsive to changes in their relative prices. Undeveloped land on the outskirts of cities is particularly mobile among uses. In addition to its value in agriculture, such land might be quickly subdivided and used for a housing development or a shopping center. However, since land is totally immobile physically, supply is unresponsive to changes in price that reflect the desirability of a location.

Machines are typically not very mobile among uses. A machine developed to produce airplane wings is seldom of much use in the production of automobiles, appliances, or other products. Steel mills cannot easily be converted to produce aluminum. There are, of course, some exceptions. Trucks can typically be used to haul a variety of products. Building space can often be converted from one use to another. In the short run, however, immobility and inelasticity of supply characterize of much of our physical capital.

LONG-RUN SUPPLY

In the long run, the supply of resources can change substantially. Machines wear out, human skills depreciate, and even the fertility of land declines with use and erosion. These factors reduce the supply of resources. Through investment, though, the supply of productive resources can be expanded. Resources can be invested to maintain and expand the stock of machines, buildings, and durable assets. Alternatively, current resources can be used to train, educate, and develop the skills of future labor force participants. The supply of both physical and human resources in the long run is determined primarily by investment and depreciation.

Price incentives will, of course, influence the investment decisions of firms and individuals. Considering both monetary and nonmonetary factors, investors will choose those alternatives they believe to be most advantageous. Higher resource prices will induce utility-maximizing individuals to undertake investments that will permit them to supply more of the higher priced resource. In contrast, other things constant, lower resource prices will reduce the incentive of individuals to invest and expand the future supply of a resource. Thus, resource prices will influence the incentive to invest and acquire resources and thereby lead to a direct relationship between the price of a resource and quantity supplied in the long run.

The theory of long-run resource supply is general. The expected payoff from an investment alternative will influence the decisions of investors in human, as well as physical, capital. For example, the higher salaries of physical and space scientists employed in the expanding space program during the early 1960s induced an increasing number of college students to enter these fields. Similarly, attractive earning opportunities in accounting and law led to an increase in investment and quantity supplied in these areas during the period from 1965 to 1975. During the last decade, job opportunities for computer programmers, systems analysts, and computer technicians have been highly attractive as the computer revolution spread throughout our economy. As salaries in these areas rose, the number of students in computer science and technology courses expanded substantially. As in other markets, suppliers respond to changing incentives in resource markets.

Considering both monetary and nonmonetary factors, investors will not knowingly invest in areas of low return when higher returns are available elsewhere. Of course, since human capital is embodied in the individual, nonpecuniary considerations will typically be more important for human than for physical capital. Nevertheless, expected monetary payoffs will influence investment decisions in both areas.

The long run, of course, is not a specified length of time. Investment can increase the availability of some resources fairly quickly. For example, it does not take very long to train additional over-the-road truck drivers. Thus, in the absence of barriers to entry, the quantity of truck drivers supplied will expand rapidly in response to higher wages. However, the gestation period between expansion in investment and an increase in quantity supplied is substantially longer for some resources. It takes a long time to train physicians, dentists, lawyers, and pharmacists. Higher earnings in these occupations may have only a small impact on their current availability. Additional investment will go into these areas, but it will typically be several years before there is any substantial increase in the quantity supplied in response to higher earnings for these resources.

Because supply can be substantially expanded over time by investment, the supply of a resource will be much more elastic in the long run than in the short run. This is particularly true when there is a lengthy gestation period between an increase in investment and an actual increase in the availability of a resource.

Time and the Elasticity of Supply for Resources

The supply of engineering services (and other resources that require a substantial period of time between current investment and expansion in the future quantity supplied) will be far more inelastic in the short run than in the long run.

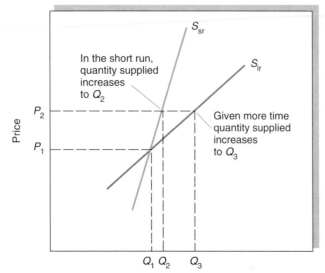

Quantity of engineering services per unit of time

Using engineering services as an example, Exhibit 7 illustrates the relationship between the short- and long-run supply of resources. An increase in the price of engineering services (the wage rate of engineers) will result in some immediate increase in quantity supplied. Persons currently employed as engineers may choose to work more hours. In addition, the higher wage may induce workers with engineering skills currently employed in mathematics, physics, or similar fields to switch to engineering. While these adjustments are important, they may fail to substantially increase the quantity supplied in the short run. With time, however, the more attractive earning opportunities in engineering will raise the level of investment in human capital in this area. More students will enter engineering programs. It takes time, though, to acquire an engineering degree. Several years may pass before the additional newly acquired engineering degrees exert a major impact on supply. Nevertheless, the expanded human capital investments will eventually exert important effects. Thus, in the long run, the quantity of engineering services may be quite elastic, even though supply is highly inelastic in the short run.

SUPPLY, DEMAND, AND RESOURCE PRICES

The theories of supply and demand for resources have been analyzed. This is all we need to develop the theory of resource pricing in competitive markets. When factor prices are free to vary, resource prices will bring the choices of buyers and sellers into line with each other. Continuing with our example of engineers, Exhibit 8 illustrates how the forces of supply and demand push the market price toward equilibrium, where quantity demanded and quantity supplied are equal. Equilibrium is achieved when the price (wage) of engineering services is P_1. Given the market conditions illustrated by Exhibit 8, excess supply is present if the price of

EXHIBIT 8

Equilibrium in a
Resource Market

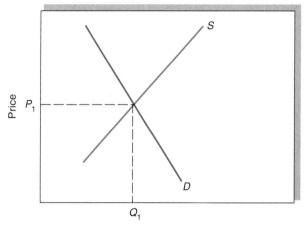

The market demand for a resource, such as engineering services, is a downward sloping curve reflecting the declining marginal revenue product of the resource. The market supply slopes upward since higher resource prices (wage rates) will induce individuals to supply more of the resource. Resource price P_1 brings the choices of buyers and sellers into harmony. At the equilibrium price (P_1), the quantity demanded will just equal the quantity supplied.

engineering services exceeds P_1. Some resource owners are unable to sell their services at the above-equilibrium price. Responding to this situation, they will cut their price (wage) and thereby push the market toward equilibrium. In contrast, if the resource price is less than P_1, excess demand is present. Employers are unable to obtain the desired amount of engineering services at a below-equilibrium resource price. Rather than doing without the resource, employers will bid the price up to P_1 and thereby eliminate the excess demand.

How will a resource market adjust to an unexpected change in market conditions? As is true for product markets, adjustment to changes do not take place instantaneously in resource markets. Our analysis of short-run and long-run responses makes the nature of the adjustment process clear. Suppose there is an unanticipated increase in demand for a resource. As Exhibit 9 illustrates, an increase in market demand (from D_1 to D_2) initially leads to a sharp rise in the price of the resource (from P_1 to P_2), particularly if the short-run supply is quite inelastic. However, at the higher price, the quantity of the resource supplied will expand with time. If it is a natural resource, individuals and firms will put forth a greater effort to discover and develop the now more valuable productive factor. If it is physical capital (for example a building or machine), current suppliers will have greater incentive to work intensively to expand production. New suppliers will be drawn into the market. Higher prices for human capital resources will also lead to an expansion in the quantity supplied. With time, more people will acquire the training, education, and experience necessary to supply the service that now commands a higher price. The expansion of the supply will eventually moderate the price rise. Because of these forces, as Exhibit 9 illustrates, the long-run price increase will be less than the short-run increase.

The market adjustment to an unexpected reduction in demand for a resource is symmetrical. A reduction in demand will cause the price of the resource to fall

EXHIBIT 9

Adjusting to
Dynamic Change

An increase in demand for a
resource will typically cause
price to rise more in the short
run than in the long run. Can
you explain why?

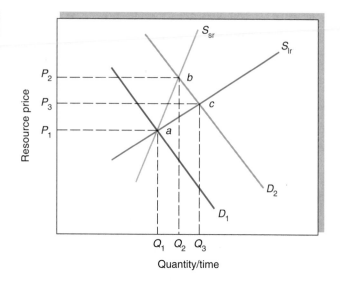

further in the short run than over a longer period of time. At the lower price, some
resource suppliers will use their talents in other areas. The incentive for potential
new suppliers to offer the resource will be reduced by the fall in price. With time,
the quantity of the resource supplied will decline, making the long-run decline in
price more moderate. Those with the poorest alternatives (that is, lowest
opportunity cost) will continue to provide the resource at the lower prices. Those
with better alternatives will move to other areas.

LOOKING AHEAD

Now that we have outlined the theoretical underpinnings of factor markets, we can apply the
analysis to a broad range of economic issues. The next chapter will focus on the labor market
and the determination of wage rates. Later, we will focus on the capital market and the
allocation of resources over time. The operation of these two markets plays an important role
in determining the distribution of income, a topic that will also be analyzed in detail in a
subsequent chapter.

CHAPTER SUMMARY

1. Factor markets, where productive resources and services are bought and sold, help to
   determine what is produced, how it is produced, and how the distribution of income
   (output) is accomplished. There are two broad classes of productive
   resources—nonhuman capital and human capital. Both are durable in the sense that
   they will last into the future, thereby enhancing future productive capabilities. Both
   yield income to their owners. Investment can expand the future supply of both.
2. The demand for resources is derived from demand for products that the resources
   help to produce. The quantity of a resource demanded is inversely related to its price.
   There are two reasons why if the price of a resource increases, less of it will be used.
   First, producers will substitute other resources for the now more expensive input
   (substitution in production). Second, the higher resource price will lead to higher
   prices for products that the resource helps to make, inducing consumers to reduce
   their purchases of those goods (substitution in consumption).
3. The short-run market demand curve will be more inelastic than the long-run curve. It
   will take time for producers to adjust their production process to use more of the
   resources that are now cheaper and less of the ones that are more expensive.

4. The demand curve for a resource, like the demand for a product, may shift. The major factors that can increase the demand for a resource are (a) an increase in demand for products that use the resource, (b) an increase in the productivity of the resource, and (c) an increase in the price of substitute resources.

5. Profit-maximizing firms will hire additional units of a resource as long as the marginal revenue product of the resource exceeds its hiring cost, usually the price of the resource. If resources are perfectly divisible, firms will expand their usage of each resource until the marginal revenue product of each resource is just equal to its price.

6. When a firm is minimizing its costs, it will employ each factor of production up to the point at which the marginal product per last dollar spent on the factor is equal for all factors. This condition implies that the marginal product of labor divided by the price of labor must equal the marginal product of capital (machines) divided by the price of capital, and that this ratio (MP_i/P_i) must be the same for all other inputs used by the firm. When real-world decision-makers minimize per unit costs, the outcome will be as if they had followed these mathematical procedures, even though they may not consciously do so.

7. Resource owners will use their factors of production in the manner that they consider most personally advantageous. Many resources will be relatively immobile in the short run. The less mobile a resource, the more inelastic its short-run supply. There will be a positive relationship, however, between amount supplied and resource price even in the short run.

8. In the long run, investment and depreciation will alter resource supply. Resource owners will shift factors of production toward areas in which resource prices have risen and away from areas in which resource prices have fallen. Thus, the long-run supply will be more elastic than the short-run supply.

9. The prices of resources will be determined by both supply and demand. The demand for a resource will reflect the demand for products that it helps to produce. The supply of resources will reflect the human and physical capital investment decisions of individuals and firms.

10. Changing resource prices will influence the decisions of users and suppliers alike. Higher resource prices give users a greater incentive to turn to substitutes and suppliers a greater incentive to provide more of the resource. Since these adjustments take time, when the demand for a resource expands, the price will usually rise more in the short run than in the long run. Similarly, when there is a fall in resource demand, price will decline more in the short run than in the long run.

CRITICAL ANALYSIS QUESTIONS

1. What is the meaning of the expression "invest in human capital"? In what sense is the decision to invest in human capital like the decision to invest in physical capital? Is human capital investment risky? Explain.

2. "The demand for resources is a derived demand." What is meant by that statement? Why is the employment of a resource inversely related to its price?

*3. Use the information of Exhibit 3 to answer the following:
   a. How many employees (operators) would Compute-Accounting hire at a weekly wage of $250 if it were attempting to maximize profits?
   b. What would the firm's maximum profit be if its fixed costs were $1,500 per week?

---

*Asterisk denotes questions for which answers are given in Appendix C, Selected Answers.

    c. Suppose there was a decline in demand for accounting services, reducing the market price per monthly statement to $150. At this demand level, how many employees would Compute-Accounting hire at $250 per week in the short run? Would Compute-Accounting stay in business at the lower market price? Explain.

*4. Are productivity gains the major source of higher wages? If so, how does one account for the rising real wages of barbers, who by and large have used the same technique for half a century? (Hint: Do not forget opportunity cost and supply.)

  5. a. "Firms will hire a resource only if they can make money by doing so."

    b. "In a market economy, each resource will tend to be paid according to its marginal product. Highly productive resources will command high prices, whereas less productive resources will command lower prices."

    Are (a) and (b) both correct? Are they inconsistent with each other? Explain.

  6. "However desirable they might be from an equity viewpoint, programs designed to reduce wage differentials will necessarily reduce the incentive of people to act efficiently and use their productive abilities in those areas where demand is greatest relative to supply." Do you agree or disagree? Why?

  7. **What's Wrong with This Way of Thinking?**

    "The downward-sloping marginal revenue product curve of labor shows that better workers are hired first. The workers hired later are less productive."

*8. A dressmaker uses labor and capital (sewing machines) to produce dresses in a competitive market. The last unit of labor hired cost $1,000 per month and increased output by 100 dresses. The last unit of capital hired (rented) cost $500 per month and increased output by 80 dresses. Is the dressmaker minimizing cost? If not, what changes need to made?

  9. Suppose that lawn service operators always use one worker with one mower to produce output. The resources are always used in the same proportion; there is no substitutability between labor and capital. Under these circumstances, would a change in wages influence employment? Explain.

*10. "The earnings of engineers, doctors, and lawyers are high because lots of education is necessary to practice in these fields." Evaluate this statement.

11. Other things constant, what impact will a highly elastic demand for a product have on the elasticity of demand for the resources used to produce the product? Explain.

*12. The following chart provides information on a firm that hires labor competitively and sells its product in a competitive market:

Units of Labor	Total Output	Marginal Product	Product Price	Total Revenue	Marginal Revenue Product
1	14	———	$5	———	———
2	26	———	$5	———	———
3	37	———	$5	———	———
4	46	———	$5	———	———
5	53	———	$5	———	———
6	58	———	$5	———	———
7	62	———	$5	———	———

  a. Fill in the missing columns.

  b. How many units of labor would be employed if the market wage rate was $40? Why?

  c. What would happen to employment if the wage rate rose to $50? Explain.

13. College professors in subjects such as accounting, engineering, computer science, and even economics generally have more attractive nonteaching employment opportunities than their colleagues in such areas as history, English, physical education, and home economics. Nonetheless, colleges sometimes pay faculty members in the same rank the same salary across all disciplines. How will this strategy influence the unemployment rate and the ability of colleges to hire (and retain) quality faculty members across disciplines? How easy will it be for a person in computer science to find an academic job relative to a similarly qualified person in history?

24 Earnings, Productivity, and the Job Market

A fair day's-wages for a fair day's-work; it is as just a demand as governed men ever made of governing. It is the everlasting right of man.

Thomas Carlyle

CHAPTER FOCUS

■ Why do some people earn more than others?

■ How does employment discrimination affect the earnings of minorities and women? Are the earnings differences according to race and sex the result of employment discrimination?

■ Who pays for fringe benefits? Do government-mandated fringe benefits increase employee compensation?

■ Why are wages higher in the United States than they are in India or China? Why are the wages of Americans higher today than they were 50 years ago?

■ Does automation destroy jobs? Does it harm workers?

■ Can we legislate higher wages?

*T*he major source of income for most people is labor earnings, income derived from current work. The earnings of U.S. workers are among the highest in the world and they have been increasing. The earnings of individuals, however, vary widely. An unskilled laborer may earn $5 per hour, or even less. Lawyers and physicians often earn $75 per hour. Dentists and even economists might receive $50 per hour. This chapter focuses on earnings—the source of high earnings, the explanation of why earnings vary, and the reasons why some groups earn more than others.

WHY DO EARNINGS DIFFER?

The earnings of paired individuals in the same occupation or with the same amount of education very often differ substantially. The earnings of persons with the same family background also vary widely. For example, one researcher found that the average earnings differential between brothers was $21,000, compared with $23,250 (figures are in 1990 dollars) for men paired randomly.[1] In addition, the earnings of persons with the same IQ, level of training, or amount of experience typically differ. How do economists explain these variations? Several factors combine to determine the earning power of an individual. Some seem to be the result of good or bad fortune. Others are clearly the result of conscious decisions made by individuals. In the previous chapter, we analyzed how the market forces of supply and demand operate to determine resource prices. The subject of earnings differentials can be usefully approached within the framework of this model.

If (a) all individuals were homogeneous, (b) all jobs were equally attractive, and (c) workers were perfectly mobile among jobs, the earnings of all employees in a competitive economy would be equal. If, given these conditions, higher wages existed in any area of the economy, the supply of workers to that area would expand until the wage differential was eliminated. Similarly, low wages in any area would cause workers to exit until wages in that area returned to parity. However, the conditions necessary for earnings equality do not exist in the real world. Thus, earnings differentials are present.

EARNINGS DIFFERENTIALS DUE TO NONHOMOGENEOUS LABOR

All workers are clearly not the same. They differ in several important respects, which influence both the supply of and demand for their services.

Worker Productivity and Specialized Skills. The demand for employees who are highly productive—those with a higher marginal revenue product—will be greater than the demand for those who are less productive. Persons who can operate a machine more skillfully, hit a baseball more consistently, or sell life insurance policies with greater regularity will have a higher marginal revenue product than their less skillful counterparts. Because they are more productive, their services will command a higher wage from employers.

Worker productivity is the result of a combination of factors, including native ability, parental training, hard work, and investment in human capital. The link between higher productivity and higher earnings provides individuals with the

---

[1]Christopher Jencks, *Inequality* (New York: Basic Books, 1972), p. 220.

incentive to invest in themselves and thereby upgrade their knowledge and skills. If additional worker productivity did not lead to higher earnings, individuals would have little incentive to incur the direct and indirect cost of productivity-enhancing educational and training programs.

Exhibit 1 illustrates the impact of worker productivity and the cost of investment in human capital on the wages of skilled and unskilled workers. Since the productivity of skilled workers exceeds the productivity of unskilled workers, the demand for skilled workers (D_s) exceeds the demand for unskilled workers (D_u). The vertical distance between the two demand curves reflects the higher marginal product of skilled workers relative to the unskilled workers (frame a). Since investments in human capital (for example, education or training) are costly, the supply of skilled workers (S_s) will be smaller than the supply of unskilled workers (S_u). The vertical distance between the two supply curves indicates the wage differential that is necessary to compensate workers for the costs incurred in the acquisition of their skills (frame b). As Exhibit 1c illustrates, wages are determined by demand *relative* to supply. Since the demand for skilled workers is large, while their supply is small, the equilibrium wage of skilled workers will be high. In contrast, since the supply of unskilled workers is large relative to the demand, the wages of unskilled workers will be substantially lower.

Of course, native ability and motivation will influence the rate at which an individual can transform educational and training experience into greater productivity. Individuals differ in the amount of valuable skills they develop from a year of education, vocational school, or on-the-job training. We should not expect, therefore, a rigid relationship to exist between years of training (or education) and skill level.

Nevertheless, detailed empirical studies indicate that investment in human capital leads to higher earnings *once the person enters the labor force full-time*. For example, in 1989, the median income of full-time workers age 25 and over with a college degree was $32,570, compared to $22,165 for high school graduates. Some

---

EXHIBIT 1

The Demand, Supply, and Wage Rates of Skilled and Unskilled Workers

The productivity (and therefore MP) of skilled workers is greater than unskilled workers. Therefore, as frame (a) illustrates, the demand for skilled workers (D_s) will exceed the demand for unskilled workers (D_u). Education and training generally enhance skills. Since upgrading skills through investments in human capital is costly, the supply of skilled workers (S_s) is smaller than the supply of unskilled workers (frame b). As frame (c) illustrates, the wages of skilled workers are high relative to unskilled workers due to the strong demand and small supply of skilled workers relative to unskilled workers.

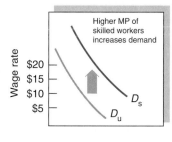

(a) Demand for Skilled and Unskilled Labor

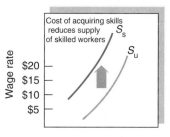

(b) Supply of Skilled and Unskilled Labor

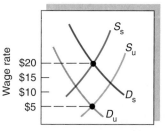

(c) Wages of Skilled and Unskilled Labor

of the additional earnings of college graduates may reflect native ability, intelligence, and motivation. Research, however, indicates that a large proportion of the additional earnings also reflects knowledge and skills acquired as the result of investment in additional education. Similarly, economic research has shown that training enhances the earnings of workers.

Investment in human capital and development of specialized skills can protect high-wage workers from the competition of others willing to offer their services at a lower price. Few persons could develop the specialized skills of a Barbara Mandrell or a Bill Cosby. Similarly, the supply of heart surgeons, trial lawyers, engineers, business entrepreneurs, and many other specialized workers is limited in occupations where specific skills, knowledge, and human capital investments contribute to job performance.

Other things constant, a skilled specialist will command a higher wage than one with less skill, but high skill will not guarantee high wages in the absence of demand. For example, expert harness makers and blacksmiths typically command low wages today, even though the supply of these workers is small—because demand is low even for the services of experts in these areas.

Worker Preferences.   This very important source of earnings differentials is sometimes overlooked. People have different objectives in life. Some want to make a great deal of money. Many are willing to work long hours, undergo agonizing training and many years of education, and sacrifice social and family life to make money. Others may be ''workaholics'' because they enjoy their jobs. Still others may be satisfied with enough money to get by on, preferring to spend more time with their family, the Boy Scouts, and television, or the local tavern keeper.

Economics does not indicate that one set of worker preferences is more desirable than another, any more than it suggests that people should eat more spinach and less pastrami. Economics does indicate, however, that these factors contribute to differences in wages and earnings. Other things constant, persons who are more highly motivated by monetary objectives will be more likely to do the things necessary to command higher wage rates.

Race and Sex.   Discrimination on the basis of race or sex contributes to earnings differences among individuals. Employment discrimination may directly limit the earnings opportunities of minorities and women. **Employment discrimination** exists when minorities or women employees are treated in a manner different from similarly productive whites or men. Of course, the earnings of minority employees, for example, may differ from whites for reasons other than employment discrimination. Nonemployment discrimination may limit the opportunity of minority groups and women to acquire human capital (for example, quality education or specialized training) that would enhance both their productivity and earnings. Thus, discrimination in employment and in other areas will contribute to earnings differences among individuals. The following section will analyze the impact of employment discrimination in some detail.

Employment Discrimination:
Unequal treatment of persons on the basis of their race, sex, or religion, which restricts their employment and earnings opportunities compared to others of similar productivity. Employment discrimination may stem from the prejudices of employers, consumers and/ or fellow employees.

EARNINGS DIFFERENTIALS DUE TO NONHOMOGENEOUS JOBS

When individuals evaluate employment alternatives, they consider working conditions as well as wage rates. Is a job dangerous? Does it offer the opportunity to acquire the experience and training that will enhance future earnings? Is the work strenuous and nerve-racking? Are the working hours, job location, and means of transportation convenient? These factors are what economists call **nonpecuniary**

Nonpecuniary Job Characteristics: Working conditions, prestige, variety, location, employee freedom and responsibilities, and other nonwage characteristics of a job that influence how employees evaluate the job.

Compensating Wage Differentials: Wage differences that compensate workers for risk, unpleasant working conditions, and other undesirable nonpecuniary aspects of a job.

job characteristics. People will accept jobs with unpleasant working conditions if the wages are high enough (compared to jobs with better working conditions for which the workers are qualified) to compensate for the undesirable nonpecuniary job characteristics. Since the higher wages, in essence, compensate workers for the unpleasant nonpecuniary attributes of a job, economists refer to wage differences stemming from this source as **compensating wage differentials.** There are numerous examples of compensating wage differences. Because of the dangers involved, aerial window washers (those who hang from windows 20 stories up) earn higher wages than other window washers. Sales jobs involving a great deal of out-of-town travel typically pay more than similar jobs without such inconvenience. Coal miners and sewer workers accept these jobs because they generally pay more than the alternatives available to low-skill workers. Compensating factors even influence the earnings of economists. When economists work for colleges or universities, they generally enjoy a more independent work environment and stimulating intellectual climate than when they are employed in the business sector. Unsurprisingly, the earnings of economists in academia are typically lower than those of economists in business.

EARNINGS DIFFERENTIALS DUE TO IMMOBILITY OF LABOR

It is costly to move to a new location or train for a new occupation in order to obtain a job. Such movements do not take place instantaneously. In the real world, labor, like other resources, does not possess perfect mobility. Some wage differentials thus result from an incomplete adjustment to change.

Since the demand for labor resources is a derived demand, it is affected by changes in product markets. An expansion in the demand for a product causes a rise in the demand for specialized labor to produce the product. Since resources are often highly immobile (that is, the supply is inelastic) in the short run, the expansion in demand may cause the wages of the specialized laborers to rise sharply. This is what happened in the oil-drilling industry in the late 1970s. An expansion in demand triggered a rapid increase in the earnings of petroleum engineers, oil rig operators, and other specialized personnel. Falling oil prices triggered the opposite effect in the mid-1980s. The demand and employment opportunities of specialized resources declined substantially as output in the oil industry fell during 1985–1986. Demand shifts in the product market favor those in expanding industries but work against those in contracting industries.

Institutional barriers may also limit the mobility of labor. Licensing requirements limit the mobility of labor into many occupations—medicine, taxicab driving, architecture, and mortuary science among them. Unions may also follow policies that limit labor mobility and alter the free-market forces of supply and demand. Minimum wage rates may retard the ability of low-skill workers to obtain employment in certain sectors of the economy. These restrictions on labor mobility will influence the size of wage differentials among workers.

SUMMARY OF WAGE DIFFERENTIALS

As the Thumbnail Sketch shows, wage differentials stem from many sources. Many of them play an important allocative role, compensating people for (a) human capital investments that increase their productivity or (b) unfavorable working conditions. Other wage differentials reflect, at least partially, locational preferences or the desires of individuals for higher money income rather than nonmonetary benefits. Still other differentials, such as those related to discrimination and occupational restrictions, are unrelated to worker preferences and are not required to promote efficient production.

THUMBNAIL SKETCH

Sources of Earnings Differentials

Differences in workers:
1. Productivity and specialized skills (reflects native ability, parental training, and investment in human capital)
2. Worker preferences (trade-off between money earnings and other things)
3. Race and sex discrimination

Differences in jobs:
1. Location of job
2. Working conditions (for example job safety, likelihood of temporary layoffs, and comfort of work environment)
3. Opportunity for training and skill-enhancement work experience.

Immobility of resources:
1. Temporary disequilibrium resulting from dynamic change
2. Institutional restrictions (for example, occupational licensing and union-imposed restraints)

THE ECONOMICS OF EMPLOYMENT DISCRIMINATION

How does employment discrimination affect the job opportunities available to women and minorities? Do employers gain from discrimination? Economics sheds light on both of these questions. There are two outlets for labor market discrimination: wage rates and employment restrictions. Exhibit 2 illustrates the impact of wage discrimination. When majority employees are preferred to minority and female workers, the demand for the latter two groups is reduced. The wages of blacks and women decline relative to those of white men.

Essentially, there is a dual labor market—one market for the favored group and another for the group toward which the discrimination is directed. The favored group, such as whites, is preferred, but the less expensive labor of minority workers is a substitute productive resource. Both white and minority employees are employed, but the whites are paid a higher wage rate.

Exclusionary practices may also be an outlet for employment discrimination. Either in response to outside pressure or because of their own views, employers may primarily hire whites and males for certain types of jobs. When minority and female workers are excluded from a large number of occupations, they are crowded into a smaller number of remaining jobs and occupations. (See Applications in Economics box.) If entry restraints prevent people from becoming supervisors, bank officers, plumbers, electricians, and truck drivers, they will be forced to accept alternatives. The supply of labor in the unrestricted occupations will increase, causing wage rates to fall. The exclusionary practices will result in higher wages for white males holding jobs from which blacks and females are excluded. The outcome will be an overrepresentation of white males in the higher paying occupations, while a disproportionate number of blacks and women will occupy the lower-paying,

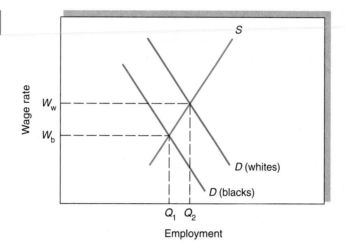

EXHIBIT 2

The Impact of Direct Wage Discrimination

If there is employment discrimination against blacks or women, the demand for their services will decline, and their wage rate will fall from W_w to W_b.

nonrestricted positions. The impact will be a reduction in the earnings of minorities and women relative to white males.

While employment discrimination undoubtedly influences earning opportunities available to minorities and women, economic theory indicates that discrimination is costly to employers when they are merely reflecting their own prejudices. If employers can hire *equally productive* minority employees (or women) at a lower wage than whites (or men), the profit motive gives them a strong incentive to do so. Hiring the higher-wage whites when similar minority employees are available will increase the costs of firms that discriminate. Employers who offer a wage and hire employees regardless of their race or sex will have lower costs and higher profits than rival firms who try to fill positions with (mostly) white males. Thus, competitive forces tend to reduce the profitability of firms that discriminate.[2]

EMPLOYMENT DISCRIMINATION AND THE EARNINGS OF MINORITIES

Earnings may differ among groups for reasons other than employment discrimination. If we want to isolate the impact of employment discrimination, we must (a) adjust for differences between groups in education, experience, and other productivity-related factors and (b) then make comparisons between similarly qualified groups of employees who differ only with regard to race (or sex). This is precisely the methodology followed by Leonard Carlson and Caroline Swartz of Emory University in their detailed study of earnings differences among minority groups.[3] In essence, Carlson and Swartz calculated what the earnings of white men would be if they had the same average education, age, language (English), marital status, native birth, annual hours worked, and regional location as minority men. The actual earnings of minority men were then compared to the "corrected" (productivity-adjusted) earnings of white men.

---

[2]For empirical evidence that competition reduces the effects of employer discrimination, see James Gwartney and Charles Haworth, "Employer Cost and Discrimination: The Case of Baseball," *Journal of Political Economy* (June 1974).

[3]Leonard A. Carlson and Caroline Swartz, "The Earnings of Women and Ethnic Minorities, 1959–1979," *Industrial and Labor Relations Review*, Vol. 41 (July 1988). Also see Barry R. Chiswick, "Differences in Education and Earnings Across Racial and Ethnic Groups: Tastes, Discrimination, and Investments in Child Quality", *Quarterly Journal of Economics* (August 1988): pp. 571–99 and June O'Neill, "The Role of Human Capital in Earnings Differences Between Black and White Men," *Journal of Economic Perspectives* (Fall 1990): pp. 25–45.

APPLICATIONS IN ECONOMICS

Employment Discrimination and the Earnings of Women

Since the Second World War, there has been a dramatic shift in the household/work force role of women, particularly married women. In 1989, 57.9 percent of women were in the labor force, compared with 33.2 percent in 1949, and 37.6 percent in 1960 (see Exhibit 3). Married women accounted for most of this dramatic increase in the labor force participation rate of women. The labor force participation rate of married women has doubled since 1960.

While more women were working, prior to 1980 their earnings changed little relative to men. In fact, the female/male, (F/M), earnings ratio for *full-time workers* was approximately 60 percent throughout the 1950–1980 period. As Exhibit 3 shows, the earnings of women have improved relative to men in the 1980s. Nevertheless, women working full-time earned only 68.9 percent as much as their male counterparts in 1989.

Employment Discrimination and Family Specialization

Why are the earnings of women so low compared to men? Most people blame employment discrimination. A Presidential Task Force in the 1970s concluded that widespread and pervasive discrimination accounted for the lower earnings of women relative to men. There is substantial evidence supportive of this view. In contrast with minorities relative to whites, the age, education, marital status, language, and regional locational characteristics of men and women are similar. Thus, correcting for these factors does little to reduce the earnings deferential between men and women. Occupational data are consistent with the view that women are crowded into a few low-paying jobs. Until recently, more than half of all women were employed in just four occupations—clerical workers, teachers, nurses, and food service workers. High-paying professional,

managerial, and craft occupations, particularly occupations where on-the-job experience leads to upward mobility, appear to be reserved primarily for men.

Despite this evidence, the case that employment discrimination is the sole or even the major source of the earnings differential between men and women is less than airtight. First, the size of even the adjusted differential should cause one to pause. If an employer could really hire women who are *willing and able to do the same work as men* for 30 percent less, the profit motive would provide the employer with a strong incentive to do so. Remember, the average business earns a profit of about 5 percent on total sales (or total cost). If an employer could really cut labor cost 30 percent merely by hiring women (primarily) rather than men, surely many less "sexist" employers, perhaps even women employers, would jump at the chance. Of course, as more and more employers substituted women

EXHIBIT 3

The Labor Force Experience of Females, 1960–1989

Between 1960 and 1989, the labor force participation of females rose from 35 to 57.9 percent. However, the F/M earning ratio fluctuated around 60 percent during the 1960–1980 period, before climbing to 68.7 percent in 1989.

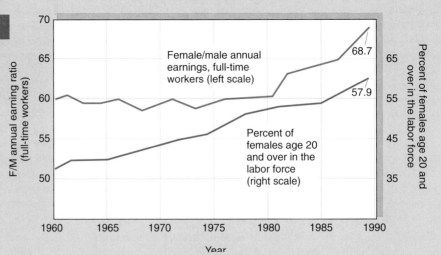

for men workers, the earnings ratio of women to men would move toward parity.[4]

Second, it is important to recognize that *married* men and women have different areas of traditional specialization within the family. Married men typically pursue paid employment aggressively because they are expected to be the family's primary breadwinner. Since men envision continuous labor force participation, they are more likely to make a geographic move to improve their earnings and choose jobs for which employment experience leads to higher earnings. Given their traditional responsibility for monetary earnings, men are also more likely to accept jobs with long hours, uncertain schedules, and out-of-town travel.

In contrast, married women have generally had the primary responsibility for operating the household and caring for children. Given these areas of specialization, many women anticipate intermittent labor force participation. Thus, women seek different sorts of jobs than men. They seek jobs with less travel time, flexible hours, and other characteristics that are complementary with household responsibilities. Similarly, many women seek jobs that will allow them to reenter the labor force with only a small reduction in earning power.[5] Viewed in this light, it is not particularly surprising that women find nursing, teaching, secretarial, and other jobs with easily transportable skills and credentials highly attractive.

Is there evidence in support of the view that differing areas of

specialization within the family are an important source of earnings differences according to sex? Since preferences cannot be directly observed, the family specialization theory is difficult to test. However, Exhibit 4 sheds some light on its importance. Here we illustrate the median annual earnings of women relative to men, *according to marital status*. Clearly, married women earn substantially less than married men. Even when working full-time, year-round, married women earn only 61 percent as much as men. However, the earnings gap between men and women is substantially less for singles, the group least influenced by actual and potential differences in specialization within the traditional family. In 1989, the female/male annual earning ratio for full-time, full-year workers was 92 percent for singles.

Even this 8 percent disparity may not be entirely attributable to employment discrimination. Among current labor force participants, women are less likely than men to have studied mathematics, engineering, medicine, law, and similar fields leading to high-paying professional jobs (see Exhibit 5). Similarly, they are probably less likely than men to find construction work, coal mining, and other physically demanding jobs very attractive. Moreover, recent increases in the number of unwed mothers imply that the earnings of a significant number of never-married women are also constrained by family responsibilities.

Therefore, while a huge earnings disparity is present between married men and married women, the differential is quite

small for singles. This pattern of earnings differences according to martial status implies that, although employment discrimination may well be a contributing factor, family specialization is also an important determinant of the overall earnings differential between men and women.

The Future

What can we say about the future direction of earnings according to sex? There is evidence that the career plans of young women have changed dramatically in recent

(continued)

---

[4]The employment and earnings data of self-employed workers are also inconsistent with the employment discrimination hypothesis. If employment discrimination is the primary cause of the low earnings of women relative to men, one would expect that many women would shift to self-employment in order to escape the effects of discrimination. As the result of employment discrimination, one would expect an over-representation of women and a higher women/men earnings ratio in self-employment occupations. In fact, the opposite results occur. See Robert L. Moore, "Employer Discrimination: Evidence from Self-Employed Workers," *Review of Economics and Statistics*, vol. LXV (August 1983).

[5]For an analysis of how family specialization influences the employment and earnings of women, see Solomon Polachek, "Discontinuous Labor Force Participation and Its Effect on Women's Market Earnings," in Cynthia B. Lloyd (ed.), *Sex Discrimination and the Division of Labor* (New York: Columbia University Press, 1975), and James Gwartney and Richard Stroup, "Measurement of Employment Discrimination According to Sex," *Southern Economic Journal* (April 1973).

EXHIBIT 4
Female/Male Earnings According to Marital Status—1989

Although the female/male earning ratio varies considerably according to marital status and time worked, the earnings of single women relative to the earnings of single men are much higher than the earnings of women in other marital status groupings. Source: U.S. Department of Commerce, *Current Population Reports,* Series P–60.

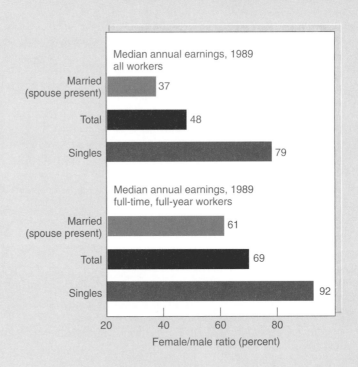

Median annual earnings, 1989 all workers

Married (spouse present) 37
Total 48
Singles 79

Median annual earnings, 1989 full-time, full-year workers

Married (spouse present) 61
Total 69
Singles 92

Female/male ratio (percent)

years. In 1968, a national sample of women 14 to 24 years of age found that only 27 percent expected to be working at age 35. In contrast, a similar sample of young women in 1979 found that 72 percent expected to be working at age 35.[6] These figures indicate that there has been a dramatic increase in the proportion of young women who are preparing for a career and planning for a lifetime of labor force participation.

The dramatic change in the career plans of women is also reflected in their educational choices. As Exhibit 5 illustrates, more and more women are preparing for the professions rather than for the office. For example, women earned 52.6 percent of the accounting degrees in 1987–1988, up from only 10.1 percent in 1970–1971. In 1987–1988, half of the persons earning a degree in veterinary medicine were women,

compared with only 7.8 percent in 1970–1971. During the last 20 years, there has also been a dramatic increase in the number of women earning degrees in

[6]See Chapter 7 of the *Economic Report of the President: 1987.* The numbers presented here are from Table 7–3 of the *Report.*

Exhibit 6 summarizes the findings of Carlson and Swartz. The actual earnings of black men were only 67 percent of the earnings of white men in 1979. However, when the work force characteristics (education, age, language, marital status, and so on) of black men were taken into account, the corrected earnings of black men rose to 83 percent of the white male earnings. Productivity-related factors accounted for almost half of the earnings differential between white and black men. Nonetheless, the 17 percent earnings difference between similarly qualified whites and blacks indicates that the earnings of blacks are substantially reduced as the result of employment discrimination.

EXHIBIT 5 ■ Women as a Proportion of Persons Earning Selected Professional Degrees, 1970–1971 and 1987–1988		
	Women as a Percentage of Persons Earning First Professional Degree in the Field	
Field of Study	1970–1971	1987–1988
Engineering	0.8	15.3
Dentistry	1.2	26.1
Optometry	2.4	34.3
Law	7.3	40.4
Veterinary Medicine	7.8	50.0
Medicine	9.2	33.0
Accounting	10.1	52.6
Economics	11.2	32.8
Architecture	12.0	38.7
Pharmacy	25.2	59.7

Source: Commission on Professionals in Science and Technology, *Professional Women and Minority* (Washington, D.C.: CPST, 1987) and U.S. Department of Education, *Digest of Educational Statistics, 1990,* (Washington, D.C.: Government Printing Office, 1991).

medicine, law, architecture, pharmacy, economics, and several other professional areas.

The dramatic changes in the labor force participation and career plans of women are now beginning to exert an impact on their earnings relative to men.[7] As we previously indicated, the F/M earning ratio was virtually constant at approximately 60 percent throughout the 1950–1980 period. Apparently, the 1964 Civil Rights law and other legislation prohibiting employment discrimination passed during the mid-1960s exerted little effect on the earnings of women relative to men. But things began to change during the 1980s. As more women were participating in the labor force on a continuous basis and as their career plans became more similar to those of men, the F/M earning ratio began to rise. This is a trend that will almost surely continue in the 1990s.

[7]James P. Smith and Michael P. Ward, *Women's Wages and Work in the Twentieth Century* (Los Angeles: Rand Foundation, 1984).

Mexican-Americans constitute the second-largest minority group in the United States. Even though the actual earnings of Mexican-American men were only 66 percent of the earnings of white men, their "corrected" earnings were almost equal (98 percent) to the white earnings. This implies that if Mexican men possessed the same worker characteristics as white men, their earnings would be very close to parity with their white counterparts.

The actual and corrected earnings for other minority groups are also presented in Exhibit 6. Interestingly, both the actual and corrected earnings of Japanese-American men were slightly greater than for their white counterparts. The two most

EXHIBIT 6 ■	The Actual and Productivity-Corrected Wages of Minority Males Compared with White Males, 1979	
	The Wage of Minority Men Relative to White Men, 1979	
	Actual	Corrected
White	100	100
Black	67	83
Mexican American	66	98
Japanese American	105	101
Chinese American	89	88
Puerto Rican American	63	95
American Indian	74	90
Cuban American	79	96
Vietnamese American	64	98

Source: Leonard A. Carlson and Caroline Swartz, "The Earnings of Women and Ethnic Minorities, 1959–1979," *Industrial and Labor Relations Review,* vol. 41 (July 1988). The estimates are based on 1980 census data.

recent arrivals among the minority groups—Cubans and Vietnamese—appear to be doing quite well, given their worker characteristics. The corrected relative wage of both groups was only a little less than the white wage. The corrected earnings of both Chinese-Americans and American Indians were approximately 10 percent less than those of similar whites. Except for Japanese- and Chinese-Americans, the corrected earnings of each minority group were significantly higher relative to whites than their actual earnings figure. This indicates that differences in worker characteristics as well as employment discrimination contribute to earnings differences between white and minority men.

THE ECONOMICS OF FRINGE AND MANDATED BENEFITS

Fringe Benefits: Benefits other than normal money wages that are supplied to employees in exchange for their labor services.

When referring to wages or compensation, we have proceeded as if employees were compensated only with money payments. Of course, this is a simplification. There are generally two components of employee compensation; (a) money wages and (b) **fringe benefits.** Fringe benefits include items such as health care insurance, layoff benefits, pension benefits, on-the-job training, on-the-premises child care services, severance benefits, use of an automobile, discounts on life and auto insurance, parental leave benefits, and paid time-off for sickness, personal business, vacation, jury duty, and holidays. In 1989, fringe benefits comprised approximately 27 percent of the total compensation of employees in the United States.

Like money wages, provision of fringe benefits will be costly to employers. When deciding whether to employ a worker, an employer will consider the *total cost* of the compensation package. Employment will be expanded as long as the employee's marginal revenue product exceeds the cost of the employee's total compensation package, including the cost of the fringe benefits. Conversely, workers will not be hired if their employment adds more to cost than to revenue.

In any specific skill category, the compensation package of employees will reflect market conditions. Employers will have to pay a compensation package equal to the market wage, or they will lose employees to rival firms. On the other hand, employees who demand a compensation package in excess of the market wage will be unable to find employment. Fringe benefits are nothing more than a component of the market-determined compensation package. Employers who offer more attractive fringe benefits will be able to attract workers with a lower money wage. Conversely, employers who offer little in the way of fringe benefits will have to pay higher money wages in order to attract workers. In essence, employees pay for fringe benefits in the form of lower money wages. Contrary to the view of some, fringe benefits are not a "gift" from the employer. Rather, they are earned by the employees as a component of their total compensation package.

Why might employers and employees find a compensation package that included fringe benefits mutually advantageous? There are two major reasons. First, it may be cheaper for the employees of a firm to purchase certain benefits as a group rather than separately as individuals. When this is the case, employees may prefer the group-purchased benefit rather than additional money wages of equal cost. Health care insurance premiums provide an example. It will often be cheaper for an insurance company to provide a single policy covering 100 employees (and their families) than it would be for workers themselves to buy 100 separate policies. Therefore, group-purchase provides the employees of a firm with a more economical insurance coverage than they could achieve if they were paid a higher wage (equal to the cost of the insurance) and bought the insurance separately. Second, compensation in the form of fringe benefits may lead to a tax savings. For example, employer-provided child care services or use of company-purchased football tickets generate "income" to the employee, but such in-kind benefits are usually not taxable. Therefore, compensation in this form may increase the employee's *after-tax* compensation more than an equivalent amount of money earnings.

The cost of providing fringe benefits will vary among employers. For example, large firms may be able to provide some fringe benefits—health care insurance and child care services, for example—much more cheaply than small firms. Simultaneously, employees will vary in their personal valuation of various fringe benefits. For example, employer-provided parental leave benefits or child care services may be a highly valued benefit to one employee, while yielding little or no utility to another.

In the absence of legislation, agreement between employers and employees (and their representatives) determines the proportion of money wages and fringe benefits in the total compensation package. Employers and employees have an incentive to structure the compensation package so that it will transfer the maximum amount of value to employees for any given cost to the employer. Compensation packages of this type will attract employees, and thereby minimize the employer's labor costs.

The extent to which any given fringe benefit will be included in a compensation package will be dependent upon both the cost of the employer's provision and the employee's personal valuation of the benefit. It will cost an employer the same to pay an employee (a) $1,000 per month or (b) $800 per month plus a fringe benefit package that costs $200 per month. In both cases, the employer's monthly cost is $1,000. When the employer's cost of providing a fringe benefit is low (relative to its cost if purchased directly by the employee) and the employee's valuation of the benefit is high, employers and employees will find it mutually advantageous to substitute the fringe benefits for higher money wages. Conversely, when there is little or no advantage derived from employer-coordinated group provision, or when employees value a fringe benefit less than its cost, employees will prefer higher money wages rather than the fringe benefit. In fact, failure to include a fringe benefit in a wage package is strong evidence that it costs more than the value it provides to employees.

THE IMPACT OF MANDATED BENEFITS

Mandated Benefits: Fringe benefits that the government forces employers to include in their total compensation package paid to employees.

In recent years, several congressional bills have been introduced mandating that employers supply their employees with various fringe benefits, including health care insurance, parental leave, and child care services. The proponents of **mandated benefits** argue that the legislation will increase the compensation of employees, particularly those working for employers who do not provide their employees with important fringe benefits. In response, the critics often charge that mandated benefits will push up labor costs and thereby reduce employment.

In analyzing the impact of legislation mandating benefits, there are three key points to keep in mind. First, a mandated benefit is only one component of the total compensation package. Increasing a single component of the package will not necessarily increase the size of the overall package. The parties will adjust. As they adjust, money wages and other fringe benefits will be reduced *below what they would have been in the absence of the mandated benefits*. Legislation mandating benefits reduces flexibility. It forces employers and employees to include a specific item in the total compensation package even when the parties would have preferred to structure the compensation package differently. In many cases, employer-provision of a benefit—particularly provision by small firms—will cost more than the benefit is valued by employees. When this is the case, mandated benefits will increase labor costs without providing a proportional increase in value to employees.

Second, employees earn and ultimately pay for all components of their compensation package—including any benefits mandated by government. Workers will not be hired if their employment adds more to costs than to revenues. The view that fringe benefits are a gift from the employer, and that the size of the benefits package can be increased by requiring employers to include various government-mandated benefits, is purely and simply wrong.

Third, fringe benefits are often an inefficient form of compensating employees. When there are neither savings from group purchase nor tax advantages, employees will prefer money wages to in-kind benefits. When in-kind compensation is efficient—when employees value a fringe benefit more than the additional money that it costs—an employer has a strong incentive to adopt (and employees have a strong incentive to bargain for) this form of compensation. When efficient, a fringe benefit will increase the total employee compensation without increasing the employer's cost. However, failure of a fringe benefit to emerge in a given employment setting is strong evidence that it is inefficient—that employees would prefer additional money wages to the fringe benefit.

How are mandated benefits likely to affect the welfare of workers? Our analysis indicates that adjustments in other dimensions of employment contracts will erode much of their impact. Even when they alter the structure of compensation, it is unlikely that mandated benefits will significantly increase the overall level of employee compensation. In cases where employees would prefer additional money wages rather than the benefits, forcing the mandated benefits into the compensation package will *reduce* the welfare of employees (even though it increases the employer's costs). However, adjustments in other components of the compensation package will often minimize the adverse effects of the mandated benefits. Thus, any positive impact of mandated benefits on the total compensation of employees will generally be substantially less than the proponents believe. Similarly, the negative impact on labor costs and employment will generally be substantially less than the critics charge.

PRODUCTIVITY AND WAGES

Productivity and real wages are closely linked. Real earnings are vastly greater in the United States than they are in India or China, because the output per hour of U.S. workers is much greater than the output of their counterparts in India and China. The U.S. workers earn more because they produce more. Similarly, average real earnings per hour in the United States in 1990 were approximately double the earnings of U.S. workers 40 years earlier. Again, productivity explains the difference in earnings. The output of goods and services per hour of U.S. workers in 1990 was twice the level of the early 1950s.

Differences in labor productivity—output produced per worker-hour—are the major source of variation in real wages between nations and between time periods. When the amount produced per worker-hour is high, real wages will be high.

In the last chapter, we showed that the productivity of a resource, including labor, is dependent on the amount of other resources with which it works. Contrary to what many believe, physical capital (for example, modern labor-saving machines) is not the enemy of high real wages (see the Myths of Economics box). In fact, just the opposite is true.

Machines make it possible for labor to produce more per worker-hour. Are jobs destroyed in the process? Specific jobs are sometimes eliminated, but this merely releases human resources so that they can be used to expand output in other areas. Output and productivity, not jobs, are the source of high real wages.

Not surprisingly, the *growth* of productivity and real earnings is also closely linked. The growth of real earnings is dependent upon the growth of real output. Without an expansion of output, we will be unable to increase our real earnings and improve our living standard.

Increasing productivity is brought about by a cooperative process. Investment, both in human and nonhuman capital, is vital to the growth of productivity. For several decades, the educational level of members of the work force in the United States has steadily increased. The median number of years of schooling of persons in the labor force in 1989 was 13, compared with 10.6 years in 1949. Simultaneously, the nonhuman capital per worker has expanded (although the

MYTHS OF ECONOMICS

"Automation is the major cause of unemployment. If we keep allowing machines to replace people, we are going to run out of jobs."

Machines are substituted for people if, and only if, the machines reduce costs of production. Why has the automatic elevator replaced the operator, the tractor replaced the horse, and the power shovel replaced the ditch digger? Because each is a cheaper method of accomplishing a task.

The fallacy that **automation** causes unemployment stems from a

Automation: A production technique that reduces the amount of labor required to produce a good or service. It is beneficial to adopt the new labor-saving technology only if it reduces the cost of production.

failure to recognize the secondary effects. Employment may decline in a specific industry as the result of automation. However, lower per unit costs in that industry will lead to either (a) additional spending and jobs in other industries or (b) additional output and employment in the specific industry as consumers buy more of the now cheaper good.

Perhaps an example will help illustrate the secondary effects of automation. Suppose someone develops a new toothpaste that actually prevents cavities and sells it for half the current price of Colgate. Think of the impact the invention will have on dentists, producers of the old toothpaste and their employees, and even the advertising agencies that give us those marvelous toothpaste commercials. What are these people to do? Haven't their jobs been destroyed?

These are the obvious effects; they are seen to be the direct result of the toothpaste invention. What most people do not see are the additional jobs that will indirectly be created by the invention; assuming an inelastic demand, consumers will now spend less on toothpaste, dental bills, and pain relievers. Their real income will be higher. They will now be able to spend more on other products they would have forgone had it not been for the new invention. Their spending on clothes, recreation, vacations, swimming pools, education, and many other items will increase. This additional spending, which would not have taken place if dental costs had not been reduced by the technological advancement, will generate additional demand and employment in other sectors.

When the demand for a product is elastic, a cost-saving invention

---

growth rate of capital investment per worker has slowed considerably in recent years). Both the development and innovative application of improved technological methods are also important determinants of the growth in productivity. Technological improvements make it possible to obtain a larger output from the same resource base. Of course, modern technological advancements are often linked to investments in both physical and human capital.

THE GREAT PRODUCTIVITY SLOWDOWN

What has happened to productivity in recent decades? Exhibit 7 sheds light on this question. For two decades following the Second World War, the output per worker in the United States increased at an annual rate of 3 percent or more. As would be expected, the real compensation per hour grew at a similar rate. However, since 1968 productivity has sagged badly. During the 1974–1990 period, the annual growth rate of output per hour of U.S. workers fell to less than one percent. Real compensation per hour barely grew at all during that period.

Productivity growth has lagged in other countries as well. Exhibit 8 presents data on the growth of per capita GNP during 1955–1973 and 1974–1990 for seven major industrial economies. In every case, the growth of GNP per capita declined substantially subsequent to 1973. For the seven countries in aggregate, per capita

can even generate an increase in employment *in the industry affected by the invention*. This was essentially what happened in the automobile industry when Henry Ford's mass production techniques reduced the cost (and price) of cars. When the price of automobiles fell 50 percent, consumers bought three times as many cars. Even though the worker-hours per car decreased by 25 percent between 1920 and 1930, employment in the industry increased from 250,000 to 380,000 during the period, an increase of approximately 50 percent.

Of course, technological advances that release labor resources may well harm specific individuals or groups. Home appliances such as automatic washers and dryers, dishwashers, and microwave ovens reduced the job opportunities of maids. Computer technology has reduced

the demand for telephone operators. In the future, videotaped lectures may even reduce the job opportunities available to college professors. Thus, the earnings opportunities of specific persons may, at least temporarily, be adversely affected by cost-reducing automated methods. It is understandable why groups directly affected fear and oppose automation.

Focusing on jobs alone, though, can lead to a fundamental misunderstanding about the importance of machines, automation, and technological improvements. The real impact of cost-reducing machines and technological improvements is an increase in production. Technological advances make it possible for us to produce as much with fewer resources, thereby releasing valuable resources so that production (and consumption) can

be expanded in other areas. Other tasks can be accomplished with the newly available resources.

Since there is a direct link between improved technology and rising output, automation exerts a positive influence on economic welfare from the viewpoint of society as a whole. In aggregate, running out of jobs is not a problem. Jobs represent obstacles, tasks that must be accomplished if we desire to loosen the bonds of scarcity. As long as our ability to produce goods and services falls short of our consumption desires, there will be jobs. A society running out of jobs would be in an enviable position: It would be nearing the impossible goal—victory over scarcity.

---

real GNP declined from *more than 4 percent* during the 1955–1973 period to *approximately 2 percent* subsequent to 1973.

What accounts for the decline in the growth rate of productivity and real earnings during the last two decades? Researchers in this area believe that at least four major factors contributed to the slowdown in productivity. First, there was a slowdown in net capital formation *per worker* during the 1970s and 1980s. Workers are generally able to produce more when they are working with more equipment and better tools. Thus, when the supply of productivity-enhancing capital assets grows more slowly, the growth of labor productivity also tends to slow. This is precisely what happened during the last two decades. During the 1950–1970 period, the net annual growth rate of the fixed capital stock increased 2.5 percent faster than the number of persons in the labor force. During the 1970s and 1980s, however, the growth of the capital stock per worker slowed to only 1.0 percent. Both a decline in the rate of net capital formation and an acceleration in the growth rate of the labor force contributed to the slowdown in the growth of the capital stock per worker.

Second, both sharply higher energy prices and an increase in government regulation of business activities also reduced the productivity of capital during the last two decades. The sharply higher oil prices of the 1973–1981 period

EXHIBIT 7

Productivity and
Employee Compensation
in the United States,
1948–1990

As illustrated in the graph,
worker productivity and
employee compensation per
hour are closely linked. During
the last two decades, the
growth rate of worker
productivity in the United
States has been sagging.

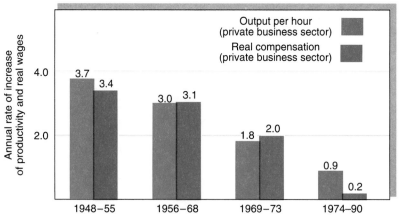

Source: *The Economic Report of the President, 1991.*

substantially reduced the efficiency of vast amounts of capital. Machines and structures designed for cost effectiveness at pre-1973 energy prices were suddenly rendered obsolete. They were too costly to operate at the higher level of energy prices. At this same time, regulations designed to improve the environment and reduce the level of pollution also reduced the effectiveness of capital. Many firms were forced either to terminate their use of various equipment or to undertake costly modifications in order to meet the more rigid regulatory standards of the 1970s and 1980s.[8] As Robert Solow, the 1987 recipient of the Nobel Prize in Economics, notes:

> Since the 1970s a substantial fraction of all investment has gone into pollution control and environmental improvement. That may be very valuable, but it doesn't contribute to the output we measure for the economy.[9]

Third, changing demographic factors in the United States also adversely affected productivity. Beginning in the latter half of the 1960s, there was a sharp influx of less experienced workers into the work force as the labor force participation of women increased and the children of the post-Second World War "baby boom" came of working age. Economics indicates that a rapid growth of the labor force—particularly the growth of inexperienced and less skilled workers—will reduce productivity.

Finally, recent evidence indicates that a decline in the average achievement level of the new labor force entrants has also retarded the growth rate of productivity.[10] The SAT scores of high school graduates and other measures of basic skills have been declining in the United States since the late 1960s. Prior to that time, these basic skill test scores had been improving for at least 50 years. Thus, compared with the 1950s and 1960s, the new labor force entrants during the

---

[8]See Edward F. Denison, *Trends in American Economic Growth, 1929–1982* (Washington, D.C.: Brookings Institution, 1985) and the articles in *The Journal of Economic Perspectives* (Fall 1988) for additional details on this topic.

[9]Robert Solow, quoted in Timothy Tregarthen, "Explaining the Great Slowdown," *The Margin* (November/December 1988).

[10]See John H. Bishop, "Is the Test Score Decline Responsible for the Productivity Decline?," *American Economic Review,* March 1989: 178–97.

EXHIBIT 8 ■ The Post-1973 Decline in the Growth Rates of Major Industrial Economies		
	Annual Growth Rate of Per Capita GNP	
	1955–1973	1974–1990
United States	2.0	1.4
Japan	8.8	3.5
Germany	4.2	2.3
United Kingdom	2.5	1.4
Italy	4.9	2.2
France	4.6	2.1
Canada	3.0	2.1

Source: Stanley Fischer, "Symposium on the Slowdown in Productivity Growth," *Journal of Economic Perspectives,* vol. 2 (Fall 1988), Table 1. Data from the *Economic Report of the President, 1991*, were used to update the figures.

last two decades have been less well-qualified than was previously the case. With the passage of time, these declining achievement levels reduce the quality of the labor force and retard the growth of productivity.

Clearly, the lagging growth rate of productivity is a serious matter. Unless it is reversed, the future growth of income will be quite slow compared with previous historical rates. For example, a 3 percent annual growth rate means that annual earnings expand by 35 percent during a decade, while a one percent growth rate increases earnings only by approximately 10 percent during the same period. Some of the unfavorable trends—for example, the oil price increases and the rapid growth of inexperienced workers—have reversed. Perhaps these positive developments will lead to productivity improvements in the near future. However, most researchers in this area are pessimistic. Few are predicting a return to the 3 percent growth rate of productivity experienced during the two decades subsequent to the Second World War.

HOW IS THE ECONOMIC PIE DIVIDED?

We have emphasized that wage rates generally reflect the availability of tools (physical capital) and the skills and abilities of individual workers (human capital). Wages tend to be high when physical capital is plentiful, technology is advanced, and the work force is highly skilled. When the equipment available to the typical worker is primitive and most workers lack education and skills, wages are low. Human capital and physical capital alike contribute to the productive process.

How is the pie divided between these two broad factors of production in the United States? Exhibit 9 provides an answer. In 1950, 81 percent of the national income was earned by employees and self-employed proprietors, the major categories reflecting the earnings of human capital. In 1989, the share of national income allocated to human capital was 81.9 percent. Income earned by nonhuman capital—rents, interests, and corporate profits—accounted for between 18 and 19 percent of the national income during both years. These earnings shares of labor and capital have been relatively constant for several decades.

EXHIBIT 9

The Shares of Income Going to Physical and Human Capital

Including self-employment income, approximately four-fifths of the national income is earned by owners of human capital.

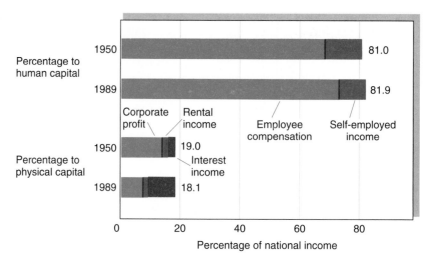

Source: *Economic Report of the President, 1991*, Table B–24.

CAN HIGHER WAGES BE LEGISLATED?

Minimum Wage Legislation:
Legislation requiring that all workers in specified industries be paid at least the stated minimum hourly rate of pay.

In 1938, Congress passed the Fair Labor Standards Act, which provided for a national **minimum wage** of 25 cents per hour. During the last 40 years, the minimum wage has been increased several times. Currently, federal legislation requires most employers to pay wage rates of at least $4.25 per hour. Minimum wage legislation is intended to help the working poor. There is good reason to question, however, whether it actually does so.

Economic theory indicates that the quantity demanded of labor, particularly a specific skill category of labor, will be inversely related to its wage rate. If a higher minimum wage increases the wage rates of unskilled workers above the level that would be established by market forces, the quantity of unskilled workers employed will fall. The minimum wage will price the services of the least productive (and therefore lowest-wage) workers out of the market.

Exhibit 10 provides a graphic illustration of the direct effect of a $4.25 minimum wage on the employment opportunities of a group of low-skill workers. Without a minimum wage, the supply of and demand for these low-skill workers would be in balance at a wage rate of $3.50. The $4.25 minimum wage makes the low-skill labor service more expensive. Employers will substitute machines and highly skilled workers (whose wages have not been raised by the minimum) for the now more expensive low-productivity employees. Jobs in which low-skill employees are unable to produce a marginal revenue product equal to or greater than the minimum will be eliminated. As the cost (and price) of goods and services produced by low-skill employees rises, consumers will rely more heavily on substitute goods produced by highly skilled labor or in foreign markets. The net effect of this substitution process will be a reduction in the quantity demanded of low-skill labor.

Of course, some low-skill workers will be able to maintain their jobs, but others will be driven into sectors not covered by the legislation or onto the unemployment and welfare rolls. Workers who retain their jobs will gain. The most adverse effects

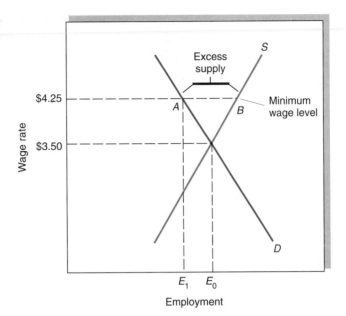

EXHIBIT 10

Employment and the Minimum Wage

If the market wage of a group of employees were $3.50 per hour, a $4.25-per-hour minimum wage would (a) increase the earnings of persons who were able to maintain employment and (b) reduce the employment of others (E_o to E_1), pushing them onto the unemployment rolls or into less-preferred jobs.

will fall on those workers who are already most disadvantaged—those whose market earnings are lowest relative to the minimum wage—because it will be so costly to bring their wages up to the minimum.

The direct results of minimum wage legislation are clearly mixed. Some workers, most likely the better qualified among those whose previous wages were near the minimum, will enjoy higher wages. Others, particularly those with the lowest prelegislation wage rates and skill levels, will be unable to find work.[11] They will be pushed into the ranks of the unemployed or out of the labor force.

INDIRECT EFFECTS OF THE MINIMUM WAGE

When analyzing the effects of the minimum wage, we must not forget that money wages are only one dimension of the exchange. Other aspects of the labor-service exchange will be affected by the imposition of the minimum wage. When a minimum rate pushes wages of low-skill workers above the market level, employers will have no trouble hiring workers. Therefore, they have little incentive to offer workers training, convenient working hours, continuous employment, fringe benefits, and other nonwage components of the total compensation package. Predictably, a higher minimum wage will lead to an erosion in the quality of the nonwage components of minimum wage jobs.[12] As we discussed previously, higher mandated benefits do not necessarily increase total compensation. Correspondingly,

---

[11]The impact of minimum wage legislation could differ from the theoretical results we have outlined if labor markets were dominated by a single buyer. Economists refer to this situation as "monopsony." We choose not to present the monopsony model here because (a) in a modern society, where labor is highly mobile, the major assumptions of the model are seldom met, and (b) the bulk of the empirical evidence in this area is consistent with the competitive model.

[12]Our treatment here is parallel to that for rent controls in Chapter 3. There we noted that in response to a *below*-market price and accompanying excess demand, the quality of rental housing deteriorates because sellers (landlords) have little incentive to maintain quality in order to attract buyers (renters). Correspondingly, in response to an *above*-equilibrium price and accompanying excess supply, the nonwage characteristics of jobs deteriorate because buyers (employers) have little incentive to maintain the quality of working conditions and fringe benefits necessary to attract sellers (workers). It is hard to repeal the laws of supply and demand.

neither does a higher mandated money wage necessarily increase total compensation—at least not by the increase in the money wage.

Of the nonwage elements adversely affected by minimum wage legislation, the decline in training opportunities is particularly important. Many inexperienced workers face a dilemma: they cannot find a job without experience (or skills), but they cannot obtain experience without a job. This is particularly true for younger workers. Employment experience obtained at an early age, even on seemingly menial tasks, can help one acquire work habits (for example, promptness and self-confidence), skills, and attitudes that will enhance one's value to employers in the future. Since minimum wage legislation prohibits the payment of even a temporarily low wage, it substantially limits the employer's ability to offer employment to inexperienced workers. In effect, the minimum wage acts as an institutional barrier limiting the on-the-job training opportunities available to low-skill workers.

MINIMUM WAGE AND TEENAGE UNEMPLOYMENT

Most empirical studies of the minimum wage in the United States have focused on teenagers, since there is a higher proportion of low-wage workers (reflecting their lack of skill-building experience) in this age group. There have been several studies of the impact of the minimum wage on the employment opportunities of youth. Most of these studies indicate that a 10 percent increase in the minimum wage reduces teenage employment by 1 to 3 percent.[13] Given the expected adverse impact of the minimum wage on other forms of compensation, this relatively small decline in employment is not surprising.

The minimum wage exerts its greatest impact on the employment opportunities of younger workers (ages 16–24), particularly blacks. When a minimum wage pushes earnings in a skill category above the market level, an excess supply of labor will result. Employers will be in a position to choose among a surplus of applicants for each position. They will generally choose those workers, within the low-productivity group, who have the most skill, experience, and education. These are generally not younger blacks. In addition, since all workers must be paid the minimum, the employer's incentive to hire less skilled and less favored groups is destroyed.

Black economists such as Walter Williams of George Mason University and Andrew Brimmer, a former member of the Federal Reserve Board, have been among the leading critics of the minimum wage. Brimmer argues:

> A growing body of statistical and other evidence accumulated by economists shows that increases in the statutory minimum wage dampen the expansion of employment and lengthen the lineup of those seeking jobs. Advances in the minimum wage have a noticeably adverse impact on young people—with the effects on black teenagers being considerably more severe.[14]

---

[13] See Jacob Mincer, "Unemployment Effects of Minimum Wages," *Journal of Political Economy*, vol. 84 (August 1976); James Ragan, "Minimum Wages and the Youth Labor Market," *Review of Economics and Statistics*, vol. 59 (May 1977); Finis Welch, *Minimum Wages: Issues and Evidence* (Washington, D.C.: American Enterprise Institute, 1978); Charles L. Betsey and Bruce H. Dunson, "Federal Minimum Wage Laws and the Employment of Minority Youth," *American Economic Review*, vol. 71 (May 1981); and Charles Brown, Curtis Gilroy, and Andrew Kohen, "The Effect of the Minimum Wage on Employment and Unemployment," *Journal of Economic Literature*, vol. 20 (June 1982).

[14] Andrew Brimmer, quoted in Louis Rukeyser, "Jobs Are Eliminated," Naught News Service (August 1978).

WOULD A HIGHER MINIMUM WAGE HELP THE POOR?

The proponents of a higher minimum wage argue that the current minimum wage will not provide the head of a family with enough income to keep the family out of poverty. This is true. When considering the relevance of this fact, however, it is important to keep two points in mind. First, the minimum wage does not assure one a job. A minimum wage high enough for a worker to support a family of three or four at an above-poverty income level will reduce the employment of low-skill workers, including some supporting families. Presumably, these people would be better off working at a low wage than they would be unemployed. Second, and perhaps more importantly, most minimum wage workers are not supporting a family. In 1988, less than 7 percent of the workers earning the minimum wage were heads of families with incomes below the poverty level. Perhaps surprising to some, more than half of all of the minimum wage workers were members of a family with an income *above* the median. Most (two thirds) of the minimum wage workers were employed only part-time. Nearly 40 percent were teenagers.

The typical minimum wage worker is a spouse or a teenage member of a household with an income well above the poverty level. Therefore, even if the adverse impact of a higher minimum wage on both employment and nonwage forms of compensation is ignored, a higher minimum wage would exert little impact on the income of the poor. This is precisely the conclusion reached in a recent study by William R. Johnson and Edgar K. Browning. Johnson and Browning estimated that a 22 percent increase in the minimum wage would add less than one-half of one percent to the income of households in the bottom 30 percent of the income distribution *even if there were no reductions in employment.*[15] The view that a higher minimum wage is an effective device with which to assist the poor is, purely and simply, incorrect.

LOOKING AHEAD

While this chapter focused on the labor market, the following chapter will analyze the capital market. The real income and output of a nation is strongly influenced by the capital equipment with which people work. The next chapter analyzes the factors that underlie the availability of capital and the investment choices of decision-makers.

CHAPTER SUMMARY

1. There are three major sources of wage differentials among individuals: differences in workers, differences in jobs, and degree of labor mobility. Individual workers differ with respect to productivity (skills, human capital, motivation, native ability, and so on), specialized skills, employment preferences, race, and sex. These factors influence either the demand for or the supply of labor. In addition, differences in nonpecuniary job characteristics, changes in product markets, and institutional restrictions that limit labor mobility contribute to variations in wages among workers.

2. Both employment discrimination and differences in employability characteristics (the quality and quantity of schooling, skill level, prior job experience, and other human capital factors) contribute to earning differentials among groups. Economic research indicates that more than half of the earnings disparity between whites and blacks is due to differences in employability (productivity) characteristics rather than employment discrimination.

3. In the late-1980s, women working full-time, year-round, earned only about 69 percent as much as men. Some of this differential may emanate from discrimination

---

[15]William R. Johnson and Edgar K. Browning, ''The Distributional and Efficiency Effects of Increasing the Minimum Wage: A Simulation,'' *American Economic Review* 73 (March 1983), 204–11.

in the labor market. However, differences between men and women in other areas that influence earnings—particularly differences in the degree of their attachment to the labor force and historical roles of specialization within the family—also have been important sources of earnings differences between men and women. There is evidence that the differences between men and women in these areas have changed substantially during the last two decades. Increasingly, women are continuously in the labor force and choosing professional careers. These developments pushed the F/M earnings ratio upward during the 1980s.

4. Fringe benefits are a component of employee compensation. When the employer's cost of providing a fringe benefit is low, and the employee's personal valuation of the benefit is high, employers and employees will find it mutually advantageous to substitute fringe benefits for money wages in the total compensation package. Conversely, when these conditions are absent, money wages are the more efficient form of compensation.

5. Other forms of compensation will be scaled back as markets adjust to legislation mandating various fringe benefits. These adjustments will largely erode both the positive effects of the mandated benefits on employee compensation and the adverse effects of the benefits on labor costs and employment.

6. Productivity is the ultimate source of high wages. Workers in the United States, Canada, Japan, and other industrial countries earn high wages because their output per hour is high as the result of (a) worker knowledge and skills (human capital) and (b) the use of modern machinery (physical capital).

7. During the last 20 years, the growth of productivity in the United States and other major industrial nations has lagged well below the growth rate achieved during the two decades following the Second World War. A slowdown in the growth of capital per worker, higher energy prices, environment regulations, an influx of inexperienced younger workers, and a decline in the basic skill levels of new labor force entrants contributed to the slowdown in productivity in the United States. If the slowdown in productivity continues, future improvements in our standard of living will come about more slowly.

8. Approximately 80 percent of national income in the United States is allocated to human capital (labor); 20 percent is allocated to owners of physical (nonhuman) capital.

9. Automated methods of production will be adopted only if they reduce costs. Although automation might reduce revenues and employment in a specific industry, the lower cost of production will increase real income, causing demand in other industries to expand. These secondary effects will cause employment to rise in other industries. Improved technology expands our ability to produce. It is expanded production, not the number of jobs, that contributes to our economic well-being.

10. Minimum wage legislation increases the earnings of some low-skill workers, but others are forced to accept inferior employment opportunities, join the ranks of the unemployed, or drop out of the labor force. The direct effects, however, will be moderated by an erosion in the quality of the nonwage components of compensation in response to the minimum rate. These adjustments will moderate both (a) the increase in total compensation and (b) the adverse employment effects emanating from the minimum wage. The minimum wage exerts its most adverse effects on the employment and training opportunities of teenagers, particularly minority teenagers.

CRITICAL ANALYSIS QUESTIONS

1. What are the major reasons for the differences in earnings among individuals? Why are wages in some occupations higher than in others? How do wage differentials influence the allocation of resources? How important is this function? Explain.

*2. Why are real wages in the United States higher than in other countries? Is the labor force itself responsible for the higher wages of American workers? Explain.

---

*Asterisk denotes questions for which answers are given in Appendix C, Selected Answers.

3. What are the major factors that would normally explain earnings differences between (a) a lawyer and a minister, (b) an accountant and an elementary school teacher, (c) a business executive and a social worker, (d) a country lawyer and a Wall Street lawyer, (e) an experienced, skilled craftsperson and a 20-year-old high school dropout, and (f) an upper-story and a ground-floor window washer?

4. Is employment discrimination the major cause of earnings differences between whites and blacks? Is it the cause of earnings differences between males and females? Carefully justify your answer.

5. **What's Wrong with This Way of Thinking?**
   "Higher wages help everybody. Workers are helped because they can now purchase more of the things they need. Business is helped because the increase in the worker's purchasing power will increase the demand for products. Taxpayers are helped because workers will now pay more taxes. Union activities and legislation mandating higher wages for workers will promote economic progress."

*6. "Jobs are the key to economic progress. Unless we create more jobs, our standard of living will fall." (True or false? Explain.)

7. If Jones has a skill that is highly valued, she will be able to achieve high market earnings. In contrast, Smith may work just as hard or even harder, and still earn only a low income.
   a. Does hard work necessarily lead to a high income?
   b. Why are the incomes of some workers high and others low?
   c. Do you think the market system of wage determination is fair? Why or why not?
   d. Can you think of a more equitable system? If so, explain why it is more equitable.

*8. People who have invested heavily in human capital (for example, lawyers, doctors, and even college professors) generally have higher wages, but they also generally work more hours than other workers. Can you explain why?

*9. Analyze the impact of an increase in the minimum wage from the current level to $7.00 per hour. How would the following be affected:
   a. employment in skill categories previously earning less than $7 per hour?
   b. the unemployment rate of teenagers?
   c. the availability of on-the-job training for low-skill workers?
   d. the demand for high-skill workers who provide good substitutes for the labor services offered by low-skill workers who are paid higher wage rates due to the increase in the minimum wage?

*10. "If individuals had identical abilities and opportunities, earnings would be equal." True or false?

11. "If it were not for employment discrimination against women, the average earnings of men and women would be equal." True or false?

*12. Other things being constant, how will the following factors influence hourly earnings?
   a. The employee must work the midnight to 8:00 A.M. shift.
   b. The job involves broken intervals (work 3 hours, off 2 hours, work 3 additional hours, and so on) of employment during the day.
   c. The employer provides low-cost child care services on the premises.
   d. The job is widely viewed as prestigious.
   e. The job requires employees to move often from city to city.
   f. The job requires substantial amounts of out-of-town travel.

*13. In addition to money wage compensation, some employers provide employees with health care benefits, paid time-off for sickness, vacation, and jury duty, on-the-premises child care services, and severance benefits in case of termination.
   a. How do these benefits affect the employer's cost of employment? Do you think employers offering the benefits would be willing to pay higher wages if the benefits were not offered?
   b. Would you be willing to work for an employer who did not offer any of these benefits if the money wage payments were high enough?

c. Are these benefits "gifts" from employers offering them? Who really pays for the benefits?

14. Does it sometimes make sense for employers to pay workers with in-kind benefits (health care insurance, child care services, termination payments, and the like) rather than higher money wages? Why? Discuss.

*15. Congress is currently considering legislation that would require businesses to provide a minimum level of health insurance to all employees working more than 17.5 hours per week.

   a. If the current money wages of part-time workers employed more than 17.5 hours per week are unchanged compared to full-time workers, how would the legislation affect the cost of employing the part-time workers? How would it affect the availability of part-time (but more than 17.5 hours per week) employment?

   b. If passed, what impact would the legislation have on the *money* wages of part-time workers employed more than 17.5 hours per week, but less than full-time?

*16. Consider two occupations (A and B) that employ persons with the same skill and ability. When employed, workers in the two occupations work the same number of hours *per day*. In occupation A, employment is stable throughout the year, while employment in B is characterized by seasonal layoffs. In which occupation will the *hourly* wage rate be highest? Why? In which occupation will the *annual* wage rate be highest? Why?

*17. Recognizing that one cannot support a large family at the current minimum wage, Congress passes legislation requiring that businesses employing workers with 3 or more children pay these employees at least $7.50 per hour. How would this legislation affect the employment level of low-skill workers with 3 or more children? Do you think some workers with large families might attempt to conceal the fact? Why?

18. Top officials of large firms already offering health care insurance, parental leaves, and child care benefits are often at the forefront of those favoring legislation mandating that *all* firms provide these benefits. They usually argue that "good corporate citizens" should provide the benefits to their employees. Can you think of a less altruistic reason why the officials may favor the mandated benefits?

*19. In 1989, the median earnings of single men working full-time, year-round were only 61 percent those of their married counterparts. Does this indicate that there was employment discrimination against single men and in favor of married men?

25 Capital, Interest, and Profit

A greater result is obtained by producing goods in round-about ways than by producing them directly. . . . That round-about methods lead to greater results than direct methods is one of the most important and fundamental propositions in the whole theory of production.[1]

Eugen von Bohm-Bawerk, 1884

CHAPTER FOCUS

■ What are roundabout methods of production? Why are roundabout production methods often used to produce consumption goods?

■ Why are investors willing to pay interest in order to acquire loanable funds? Why are consumers willing to pay interest for funds?

■ How does the interest rate bring the choices of borrowers and lenders into harmony? How does a change in the interest rate affect the price of current goods relative to future goods?

■ How does inflation influence the interest rate? What are the three components of the money interest rate?

■ Why is the interest rate so important when choices involve comparisons of revenue or cost across time periods? What is the present value of $100 of income one year from now?

■ How does an investor decide if an investment project is profitable? Why is the interest rate central to this decision?

■ What are the sources of economic profit? How does expected profitability influence investment decisions?

■ What role do interest and profit play in the allocation of resources?

When we focused in previous chapters on the employment of resources, we proceeded as if the firm would both bear the employment cost and reap the return (for example, the resource's MRP) *within a relatively short time period*. With regard to the employment of labor and raw materials, this is generally true. It is not the case, however, for long-lasting capital resources. Consider choices such as whether to construct an office building, purchase a harvesting machine, or go to law school. The returns derived from investments such as these are generally spread over several years (or even decades). In some cases, the costs of investments may also be incurred over a lengthy time period. How can decision-makers compare the benefits and costs of such investment? What factors determine whether an investment project should be undertaken?

Clearly these questions and related issues are quite important. Investments in machines, buildings, skills, and other capital assets exert a major impact on our productivity and standard of living. If investment choices are made unwisely, our future income will suffer.

THE ROLE OF TIME IN PRODUCTION AND CONSUMPTION

Thus far, we have generally ignored the role of time in both production and consumption. We have proceeded as if firms both incurred the costs and derived the revenues from the use of resources *during the current period*. Similarly, we have ignored the role of time with regard to the decision-making of consumers. We are now ready to integrate decision-making across time periods into our analysis.

PRODUCTION, CAPITAL, AND TIME

Capital is a term used to describe long-lasting resources that are utilized to produce goods and services. In contrast with consumption goods that yield direct benefits to consumers, capital resources enhance our ability to produce in the future. There are two broad categories of capital goods: (1) physical capital—for example, buildings, machines, tools, and natural resources and (2) human capital—the knowledge and skills of people.

Consumption is the ultimate objective of all production. But the use of physical and human capital can sometimes magnify our productive capabilities. Often we can produce a larger amount of a consumption good with the same quantity of resources by first using our resources to produce tools, machines, and even factories, and then later using the capital resources to produce the consumption good. Economists refer to this procedure as a **roundabout method of production.**

Roundabout Method of Production: The use of productive effort to make tools and other capital assets, which are then used to produce the desired consumer good.

Resources used to produce capital goods will be unavailable for the direct production of consumption goods. Therefore, when roundabout production methods are used, current consumption must be reduced. If the use of capital goods enhances our productivity, more consumption goods will be available in the future. Nonetheless, if we produce more capital goods *today,* we must give up current consumption.

---

[1]Eugen von Bohm-Bawerk, ''Capitalist Production,'' in *The Capitalist Reader,* ed. Lawrence S. Stepelevich (New Rochelle: Arlington House, 1977), pp. 26–27.

Perhaps a simple illustration will help identify the major elements involved in the use of capital and roundabout methods of production. Suppose that Robinson Crusoe could catch fish by either (a) combining his labor with natural resources (direct production) or (b) constructing a net and eventually combining his labor with this tool (a roundabout method of production). Let us assume that Crusoe could catch 2 fish per day by hand fishing, but could catch 3 fish per day if he constructed and used a net that would last for 330 days. Suppose it would take Crusoe 35 days to build the net. The opportunity cost of constructing the net would be 70 fish (2 per day for each of the 35 days Crusoe spent building the net). If Crusoe used the roundabout method of production, his output during the next year (including the 35 days required to build the net) would be 990 fish (3 per day for 330 days). Alternatively, hand fishing during the year would lead to an output of only 730 (2 fish per day for 365 days).

The capital-intensive, indirect method of production would be highly productive. Total output during the year would be expanded by 260 fish if the roundabout method of production were used. But the use of capital would also impose a current sacrifice. It will take time to build the net, and while Crusoe was constructing the net, his production of consumption goods (fish) would decline.

CONSUMPTION AND TIME PREFERENCE

Positive Rate of Time Preference: The desire of consumers for goods now rather than in the future.

Would you prefer to have a sporty new car now or next year? Or how about a very nice apartment—would you prefer to have it now or five years from now? If you are like most people, you have a preference for consumption goods sooner rather than later. On average, individuals possess a **positive rate of time preference.** By this we mean that people subjectively value goods obtained in the immediate or near future (including the present) more highly than goods obtained in the distant future.

There may be some exceptions. For example, a person with a large quantity of a perishable good, bananas, for example, might be willing to exchange 100 bananas now for fewer bananas in the future. In a modern economy, though, perishable goods can be exchanged for money, a nonperishable commodity.

There is nothing irrational or even shortsighted about a positive rate of time preference. Given the uncertainties of the world in which we live, it is perfectly reasonable to prefer the reality of current consumption to the uncertainty of some larger amount (in physical or monetary terms) of future consumption. As the saying goes, "A bird in the hand is worth two in the bush."

THE INTEREST RATE, CHOICES ACROSS TIME PERIODS, AND THE LOANABLE FUNDS MARKET

The decision of whether to use capital in production involves the comparison of a current cost (for example, the price of a machine) with future benefits (for example, a larger future output). Similarly, the decision as to whether to consume a good now or later involves the comparison of benefits and costs across time periods. When making decisions across time periods, the interest rate is of central importance because it links the future to the present. The interest rate allows individuals to place a current evaluation on future income and costs.

The interest rate is the price of earlier availability; it is the premium that must be paid if you want to acquire goods now rather than later. In a modern economy, people often borrow funds in order to finance current consumption and investment.

Because of this, the interest rate is often defined as the price of loanable funds. This definition is proper. But we should remember that it is the earlier availability of goods and services purchased, not the money itself, that is desired by the borrower.

THE DETERMINATION OF THE INTEREST RATE

The interest rate is determined by the demand and supply for loanable funds. Consumers demand loanable funds because they have a positive rate of time preference; they prefer earlier availability. Simultaneously, investors demand funds in order to finance capital assets that they believe will increase output and generate profit.

The demand of investors for loanable funds stems from the productivity of roundabout methods of production. People are willing to borrow in order to finance the use of capital in production because they expect that an expansion in future output will provide them with the resources to repay both the principal and interest on the loan. Our prior example of Robinson Crusoe illustrates this point. Remember, Crusoe could increase his output by 260 fish this year if he could take off 35 days to build a net. Crusoe's fish production, however, would decline (by 2 fish per day) while he was constructing the net. Crusoe might be on the verge of starvation. Suppose a fishing crew from a neighboring island visited Crusoe and offered to lend him 70 fish so that he could undertake the capital investment project (building the net). Crusoe would gain. If Crusoe could borrow the 70 fish (the principal) in exchange for, say 140 fish *a year later* (a 100 percent interest rate), the investment project would be highly profitable. Crusoe could repay the funds borrowed, plus the 100 percent interest rate, and still have 190 additional fish (the 260 additional fish caught minus the 70 fish paid in interest).

Crusoe's demand for loanable fish—and more generally, the demand of investors for loanable funds—stems directly from the productivity of the capital investment. Crusoe can gain by borrowing to finance the construction of a fishing net only because the net enables him to expand his total output during the year. Similarly, investors can gain by borrowing funds to undertake investment projects only when the capital assets purchased permit them to expand output (or reduce costs).

As Exhibit 1 illustrates, the interest rate brings the choices of consumers and investors wanting to borrow funds into harmony with the choices of lenders willing to supply funds. Higher interest rates make it more costly for consumers to buy now and for investors to undertake capital spending projects. Both consumers and investors will curtail their borrowing as the interest rate rises. Rather than pay the higher interest premium for earlier availability, some consumers will reduce their current consumption when the interest rate increases. Similarly, since some investment projects that would be profitable at a lower interest rate will be unprofitable at higher rates, investors will also borrow less as the interest rate increases. Therefore, the amount of funds demanded by borrowers is inversely related to the interest rate.

The interest rate also provides a reward to persons (lenders) willing to reduce their current consumption in order to provide loanable funds to others. If some individuals are going to borrow in order to undertake an investment project (or consume more than their current income), others must curtail their current consumption by an equal amount. In essence, the interest rate provides lenders with the incentive to reduce their current consumption so that borrowers can either invest or consume beyond their current income. Higher interest rates provide persons willing to save (willing to supply loanable funds) with *more future* goods in

EXHIBIT 1

The Determination of the Interest Rate

The demand for loanable funds stems from the consumer's desire for earlier availability and the productivity of capital. As the interest rate rises, current goods become more expensive in comparison with future goods. Therefore, borrowers will reduce the amount of loanable funds demanded. On the other hand, higher interest rates will stimulate lenders to supply additional funds to the market.

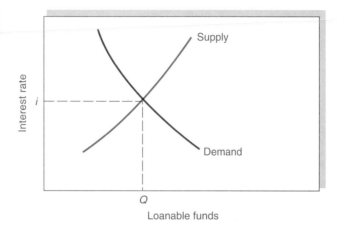

exchange for the sacrifice of current consumption. Even though people have a positive rate of time preference, they will give up current consumption to supply funds to the loanable funds market if the price is right—that is, if the interest rate is attractive enough. Therefore as the interest rate rises, the quantity of funds supplied to the loanable funds market expands.

As Exhibit 1 illustrates, the interest rate will bring the quantity of funds demanded into balance with the quantity supplied. At the equilibrium interest rate, the quantity of funds borrowers demand for investment and consumption now (rather than later) will just equal the quantity of funds lenders save.

MONEY RATE OF INTEREST AND REAL RATE OF INTEREST

Money Rate of Interest: The rate of interest in monetary terms that borrowers pay for borrowed funds. During periods when borrowers and lenders expect inflation, the money rate of interest exceeds the real rate of interest.

Real Rate of Interest: The money rate of interest minus the expected rate of inflation. The real rate of interest indicates the interest premium, in terms of real goods and services, that one must pay for earlier availability.

We have emphasized that the interest rate is a premium borrowers are willing to pay for earlier availability. During periods of inflation, the **money rate of interest,** determined by the forces of supply and demand in the loanable funds market, may be a misleading indicator of how much borrowers give up to obtain earlier availability. Suppose the money rate of interest is 10 percent at a time when prices are rising at an annual rate of 5 percent. A person borrowing $100 will have to pay back $110 one year later. During that year, however, the level of prices will have increased by 5 percent. The $110 paid to the lender one year later will not buy 10 percent more goods. Instead, it will buy only 5 percent more goods than the $100 provided to the borrower one year earlier. Therefore, when the rate of inflation is taken into account, the **real rate of interest** is only 5 percent.

Once decision-makers anticipate rising prices, the money rate of interest will include an inflationary premium compensating lenders for the expected decline in the purchasing power of their principal and interest over the duration of the loan. The real rate of interest is equal to the money rate of interest minus the premium for the expected rate of inflation.

Recognizing the decline in the purchasing power of the dollars with which they will be repaid, lenders will reduce the amount of money supplied to the loanable funds market unless they are compensated for the anticipated rate of inflation. Simultaneously, once borrowers become fully aware that they will be paying back their loans with dollars of less purchasing power, they will be willing to pay the inflationary premium as well as the real rate of interest. If borrowers and lenders fully anticipate a 5 percent rate of inflation, for example, they will be just as willing to agree on a 10 percent interest rate as they were to agree on a 5 percent interest rate when both anticipated stable prices. Under inflationary conditions, the money rate of interest will therefore incorporate an inflationary premium reflecting the expected future increase in prices. An increase in the expected rate of inflation in the future will cause money interest rates to rise. It should not be surprising, then, that higher money interest rates are often associated with high rates of inflation. The U.S. experience during the 1970s illustrates the point. Money interest rates soared to historical highs as double-digit inflation rates were observed during the period.

THE MULTIPLICITY OF INTEREST RATES

So far, we have proceeded as though there is a single interest rate. In the real world, of course, there are many interest rates. There is a mortgage rate, a prime interest rate (the rate charged to business firms with strong credit ratings), a consumer loan rate, and a credit card rate, to name only a few. These interest rates generally differ.

The interest rate on a given loan is influenced by (a) the cost of processing, (b) the risk associated with the borrower, and (c) the duration of the loan. The accounting costs associated with a loan of several hundred thousand dollars may actually be smaller than those for a consumer loan for a few hundred dollars, if, for example, the large loan is repaid in a lump sum at a designated time in the future and the small loan is repaid monthly. Since the bookkeeping costs per dollar loaned are generally higher for small loans, interest rates will be higher for such loans.

The interest rate on a loan is also influenced by the credit standing of the borrower and the risk associated with lending to that borrower. Banks are likely to charge an unemployed worker a higher interest rate than they charge General Motors. Since the probability of default is considerably greater for the unemployed worker than for General Motors, the former will have to pay a risk premium, which will be incorporated into the interest rate of the loan. Similarly, the interest rate on a "secured loan," such as a mortgage on a house, will be less than that on a unsecured loan, such as a credit card purchase.

The degree of risk involved in a loan also varies with the loan's duration. Lenders usually require higher interest rates for longer-term loans since they involve greater risk. The longer the time period, the more likely that the financial standing of the borrower will deteriorate substantially or that market conditions will change dramatically. Also, unless rates are believed to be unusually high, borrowers are willing to pay a premium to keep the funds for a longer period of time. Thus, long-term loans usually carry a premium that compensates for the additional uncertainties and additional benefits of the longer time period.

THE COMPONENTS OF AN INTEREST RATE—A SHORT SUMMARY

As Exhibit 2 illustrates, the money rate of interest on a loan has three components. The pure interest component is the market price one must pay for earlier availability. The inflationary premium component reflects the expectation that the loan will be repaid with dollars of less purchasing power as the result of inflation. The third component—the risk premium—reflects the risk imposed on the lender by the possibility that the borrower may be unable to repay the loan. The risk premium, therefore, is directly related to the probability of default by the borrower.

THE VALUE OF FUTURE INCOME

Suppose that one year from now someone will pay you $100. How much would that $100 be worth today? Clearly, it would be worth less than $100. If you deposited $100 today in a savings account earning 6 percent interest, you would have $106 one year from now.

EXHIBIT 2

Three Components of the Money Interest

The money interest rate reflects the following three components: (a) pure interest, (b) inflationary premium, and (c) risk premium. When decision-makers expect a high rate of inflation during the period in which the loan is outstanding, the inflationary premium will be substantial. Similarly, the risk premium will be large when probability of default by the borrower is substantial.

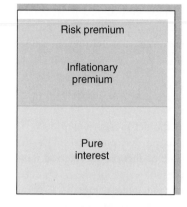

Net Present Value: The current worth of future income after it is discounted to reflect the fact that revenues in the future are valued less highly than revenues now.

The present value of $100 a year from now is equal to the amount that you would have to invest today in order to have $100 one year from now. The interest rate allows us to make this calculation. The interest rate connects the value of dollars (and capital assets) today with the value of dollars (and expected receipts) in the future. The interest rate is used to discount the value of a dollar in the future so that its present worth can be determined today.

The **net present value** (NPV) of a payment received one year from now can be expressed as follows:

$$NPV = \frac{\text{receipts one year from now}}{1 + \text{interest rate}}$$

If the interest rate is 6 percent, the current value of the $100 to be received one year from now is:

$$NPV = \frac{\$100}{1.06} = \$94.34$$

If you placed $94.34 in a savings account yielding 6 percent interest, during the year the account would earn $5.66 interest (6 percent of $94.34) and therefore grow to $100 one year from now. Thus, the present value of $100 a year from now is $94.34.

Discounting: The procedure used to calculate the present value of future income. The present value of future income is inversely related to both the interest rate and the amount of time that passes before the funds are received.

Economists use the term **discounting** to describe this procedure of reducing the value of a dollar to be received in the future to its present worth. Clearly, the value of a dollar in the future is inversely related to the interest rate. For example, if the interest rate were 10 percent, the net present value of $100 received one year from now would be only $90.91 (100 divided by 1.10).

The net present value of $100 received two years from now is:

$$NPV = \frac{\$100}{(1 + \text{interest rate})^2}$$

If the interest rate were 6 percent, $100 received two years from now would be equal to $89 today ($100 divided by 1.06^2). In other words, $89 invested today would yield $100 two years from now.

The net present value procedure can be used to determine the current value of any future income stream. If R represents receipts received at the end of the year and i represents the interest rate, the net present value of the future income stream[2] is:

$$\text{NPV} = \frac{R_1}{(1 + i)} + \frac{R_2}{(1 + i)^2} + \cdots + \frac{R_n}{(1 + i)^n}$$

Exhibit 3 shows the net present value of $100 received at various times in the future at several different discount rates. The chart clearly illustrates two points. First, the present value of income received at a date in the future declines with the interest rate. The present value of the $100 received one year from now, when discounted at a 4 percent interest rate, is $96.15, compared to $98.04 when a 2 percent discount rate is applied. Second, the present value of the $100 also declines as the date of its receipt is set farther into the future. If the applicable discount rate is 6 percent, the present value of $100 received one year from now is $94.34, compared to $89 if the $100 is received two years from now. If the $100 is received five years from now, its current worth is only $74.43. So, the present value of a future dollar payment is inversely related to both the interest rate and how far in the future the payment will be received.

---

[2]For a specific annual income stream in perpetuity, the net present value is equal simply to R/i, where R is the annual revenue stream and i the interest rate. For example, if the interest rate is 10 percent, the NPV of a $100 annual income stream in perpetuity is equal to $100/.10, or $1,000.

EXHIBIT 3 ■ The Net Present Value of $100 to be Received in the Future

The columns indicate the net present value of $100 to be received a designated number of years in the future for alternative interest rates. For example, at a discount rate of 2 percent, the net present value of $100 to be received five years from now is $90.57. Note that the net present value of the $100 declines as either the interest rate or the number of years in the future increases.

Years in the Future	Net Present Value of $100 to Be Received a Designated Number of Years in the Future for Alternative Interest Rates					
	2 Percent	4 Percent	6 Percent	8 Percent	12 Percent	20 Percent
1	98.04	96.15	94.34	92.59	89.29	83.33
2	96.12	92.46	89.00	85.73	79.72	69.44
3	94.23	88.90	83.96	79.38	71.18	57.87
4	92.39	85.48	79.21	73.50	63.55	48.23
5	90.57	82.19	74.73	68.06	56.74	40.19
6	88.80	79.03	70.50	63.02	50.66	33.49
7	87.06	75.99	66.51	58.35	45.23	27.08
8	85.35	73.07	62.74	54.03	40.39	23.26
9	83.68	70.26	59.19	50.02	36.06	19.38
10	82.03	67.56	55.84	46.32	32.20	16.15
15	74.30	55.53	41.73	31.52	18.27	6.49
20	67.30	45.64	31.18	21.45	10.37	2.61
30	55.21	30.83	17.41	9.94	3.34	0.42
50	37.15	14.07	5.43	2.13	0.35	0.01

MAKING INVESTMENT DECISIONS

Investment projects (roundabout methods of production) generally involve the purchase of long-lasting capital assets that are used to produce goods and services in the future. The additions to production and revenues derived from the employment of a capital asset are generally spread over several years. How can an investor compare the current asset cost with the future additions to revenue? The discounting procedure provides the answer. The discounting procedure allows an investor to determine the *present value* of the expected future net revenue generated by a capital asset and to compare this value to the cost of the asset. Thus, the procedure is particularly important to investors.

Profit-seeking investors will search for capital investments for which the present value of the revenues generated exceeds the cost of the project (or the capital asset). When the present value of the revenue derived from an investment exceeds the cost of the investment, the investor will earn economic profit. For profitable projects, the rate of return provided by the asset will exceed the market interest rate. On the other hand, if the cost of the project exceeds the discounted value of the future net receipts, losses will result. Losses indicate that the asset is earning less than the interest rate.

Let us consider an example. Suppose a truck rental firm is contemplating the purchase of a new $40,000 truck. Past experience indicates that after the operational and maintenance expenses have been covered, the firm can rent the truck for $12,000 per year (received at the end of each year) for the next four years, the expected life of the vehicle.[3] Since the firm can borrow and lend funds at an interest rate of 8 percent, we will discount the future expected income at an 8 percent rate. Exhibit 4 illustrates the calculation. Column 4 shows how much $12,000, available at year-end for each of the next four years, is worth today. In total, the net present value of the expected rental receipts is $39,744—less than the purchase price of the truck. Therefore, the project should not be undertaken.

The decision to accept or reject a prospective project is highly sensitive to the interest rate. If the interest rate in our example had been 6 percent, the net present value of the future rental income would have been $41,580.[4] Since it pays to purchase a capital good whenever the net present value of the income generated exceeds the purchase price of the capital good, the project would have been profitable at the lower interest rate.

---

[3]For the sake of simplicity, we assume that the truck has no scrap value at the end of four years.
[4]The derivation of this figure is shown in the following tabulation:

Year	Expected Future Income (dollars)	Discounted Value per Dollar (6% rate)	Present Value of Income (dollars)
1	12,000	0.943	11,316
2	12,000	0.890	10,680
3	12,000	0.840	10,080
4	12,000	0.792	9,504
			41,580

EXHIBIT 4 ■ **The Discounted Present Value of $12,000 of Truck Rental for Four Years (Interest Rate = 8 percent)**			
Year (1)	Expected Future Income (Received at Year-End) (2)	Discounted Value (8 Percent Rate) (3)	Present Value of Income (4)
1	$12,000	0.926	$11,112
2	12,000	0.857	10,284
3	12,000	0.794	9,528
4	12,000	0.735	8,820
			$39,744

EXPECTED FUTURE EARNINGS AND ASSET VALUES

The net present value of the expected revenue of an investment compared to the cost of the investment reveals whether a project should be undertaken. However, *once an investment project has been completed,* the present value of the expected future net earnings will determine the market value of the asset. If the present value of the expected net earnings rises (falls), so too, will the value of the asset.

How much would you be willing to pay for an asset that would provide you with $1,000 of income every year, indefinitely into the future? If the market interest rate were 10 percent, investors would be willing to pay $10,000 for the asset. When purchased at this price, the asset would provide an investor with the 10 percent market rate of return. Correspondingly, if an asset generates $2,500 of net earnings annually and the market interest rate were 10 percent, the asset would be worth $25,000. There is a direct relationship between the expected future earnings of an asset and the asset's market value.

This linkage between expected future earnings and the price of an asset provides a strong incentive for the owners of business assets to make sure that the assets are being used wisely. Some entrepreneurs are particularly good at (a) identifying a business that is poorly operated, (b) purchasing the business at a depressed price, (c) improving the operational efficiency of the firm, and (d) then reselling the business at a handsome profit. Suppose that a poorly run business currently has net earnings of $1 million per year. What is the market value of the business? If the firm is expected to continue earning $1 million per year, the market value of the firm would be $10 million if the interest rate is 10 percent. Suppose that an alert entrepreneur buys the business for $10 million, hires new management, and improves the operational efficiency of the firm. As the result of these changes, the annual net earnings of the firm increase to $2 million per year. Now how much is the firm worth? If the $2 million annual earnings are expected to continue into the future, the net present value of the firm would rise to $20 million. Thus, the entrepreneur who improved the performance of the firm would be able to sell the firm for a very substantial profit.

In a competitive environment, there is a strong incentive for business managers and asset owners to use the resources under their control efficiently. If they do not, the value of the assets will decline and the business will be vulnerable to a takeover by alert entrepreneurs capable of operating the firm more efficiently and using the assets more profitably.

INVESTORS AND CORPORATE INVESTMENTS

In modern market economies, investors typically are not entrepreneurs who personally decide which factories to expand, which machine tools to build, and which research investments to undertake. Instead, corporate officers under the scrutiny of corporate boards of directors, make the entrepreneurial capital investment choices. Nevertheless, individual investors (buyers and sellers of stock) influence that process through the stock market itself. Stock market investors who believe that a corporation is making sound investment decisions that are likely to yield future profits, will buy more of the corporation's stock, driving up its price. Similarly, stockholders who believe that the corporation's current investment decisions will not prove to be profitable, have an incentive to ''bail out'' by selling their stock holdings. Either way, the stock market price of a corporation's stock gives corporate officers very fast feedback on how market investors evaluate their investment decisions.

Since individual stockholders reap the benefit or pay the cost of their stock market decisions, each has a strong incentive to search for and invest in projects that will yield economic profit. Investment in profitable projects will increase the investor's wealth, while unprofitable investments will reduce it. The choices of investors reveal their evaluation of the investment projects undertaken by businesses. The choices of individual buyers (and nonbuyers) of the firm's product form the ultimate judgments on business performance. However, the choices of investors will provide early returns on the expected success of business ventures.

INVESTING IN HUMAN CAPITAL

In earlier chapters, we discussed the concept of human capital. A decision to invest in human capital—to continue in school, for example—involves all the ingredients of other investment decisions. Since the returns and some of the costs normally accrue in the future, the discounting procedure helps one to assess the present value of expected costs and revenues associated with a human capital investment.

Exhibit 5 illustrates the potential human capital decision confronting Susan, an 18-year-old high school graduate contemplating the pursuit of a bachelor's degree in business administration. Just as an investment in a truck would involve a cost in order to generate a future income, so too, does a degree in business administration. If Susan does not go to college, she will be able to begin work immediately at annual earnings of E_1. Alternatively, if she goes to college, she will incur direct costs (C_d) in the form of tuition, books, transportation, and related expenses. She will also bear the opportunity cost (C_o) of lower earnings while in college. However, the study of business will expand Susan's knowledge and skills, and thereby enable her to earn a higher future income (E_2 rather than E_1). Will the higher future income be worth the cost? To answer this question, Susan must discount each year's *additional* income stemming from completion of the business degree and compare that with the discounted value of the cost, including the opportunity cost of earnings lost during the period of study. If the discounted value of the additional future income exceeds the discounted value of the cost, acquiring the degree is a worthwhile human capital investment.

Of course, nonmonetary considerations may also be important, particularly for human capital investment decisions, since human capital is embodied in the

EXHIBIT 5

Investing in
Human Capital

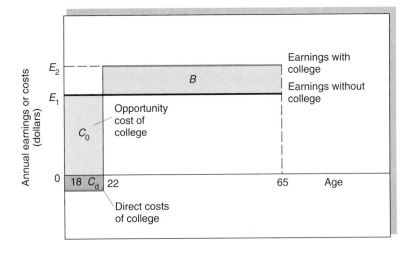

Here we illustrate the human capital investment decision confronting Susan, an 18-year-old
who just finished high school. If Susan goes to college and majors in business administration,
she will incur the direct cost (C_d) of the college education (tuition, books, transportation, and
so on) plus the opportunity cost (C_o) of earnings forgone while in college. However, with a
business degree, she can expect higher future earnings (B) during her career. If the
discounted present value of the additional future earnings exceeds the discounted value of
the direct and indirect cost of a college education, the business degree will be a profitable
investment for Susan.

individual. For example, Susan's preferences might be such that she would really
prefer working as a college graduate in the business world (rather than in the jobs
available to high school graduates) even if she did not make more money. Thus, the
nonpecuniary attractiveness of business may induce her to pursue the business
degree even if the monetary rate of return is low (or even negative).

Even though human capital investments can be analyzed in the same terms as
any other investment, the analysis is likely to be less precise, since it is difficult to
isolate the nonmonetary aspects of these decisions. However, the same methods—
the discounting procedures and the comparison of the present value of future
revenues (or benefits) with costs—can apply to both human and physical capital
investment decisions.

ECONOMIC PROFIT AND INVESTMENT

Why do individuals purchase long-lasting capital assets? Why do they invest in
education, training, and other forms of human capital? They do so because they
expect to profit—to do better than if they simply invested the funds at the market
rate of interest.

Economic Profit: A return to
investors that exceeds the
opportunity cost of financial
capital.

Economic profit is a return to investment in excess of the opportunity cost of
loanable funds. There are three basic sources of economic profit: (a) uncertainty, (b)
entrepreneurial alertness, and (c) monopoly.

PROFIT AND UNCERTAINTY

In a world of perfect knowledge and communication and no uncertainty, profits (and losses) would be completely absent. The real world, though, is one of change, disequilibrium markets, uncertainty, and imperfect knowledge. No one can predict the future with certainty. Unanticipated shifts in market prices or costs can cause the rate of return derived by investors to rise or fall. Investments (ownership of physical and human capital) expose one to additional uncertainty. In a sense, investing resembles a game of chance. Unanticipated changes, changes that no one could have foreseen, create winners and losers. If people did not care whether their income experienced substantial variability or not, the uncertainty accompanying investment projects would not affect the average rate of return. Most people, though, dislike uncertainty. They prefer the certain receipt of $1,000 to a 50-50 chance of receiving either nothing or $2,000. Therefore, people must be paid a premium if they are going to willingly accept the uncertainty that necessarily accompanies investments. This premium is a source of economic profit.

PROFIT AND ENTREPRENEURSHIP

While the world is characterized by uncertainty, some individuals are better than others at identifying potentially profitable opportunities. At any given time, there are virtually an infinite number of potential investment projects. Some will increase the value of resources and therefore lead to a handsome rate of return on capital. Others will reduce the value of resources, generating economic losses.

Alertness to potential opportunities to combine resources in a manner that increases their value is a source of economic profit. Economists refer to this source of profit as a return to entrepreneurship.

This component of profit reflects the ability of astute entrepreneurs to recognize and undertake economically beneficial projects that have gone unnoticed by others. Discovery of a lower-cost method of production, introduction of a new product highly valued relative to cost, development of an improved marketing technique, and the correct anticipation of a future market change provide examples of entrepreneurial behavior that markets reward with economic profit. Originality, quickness to act, and imagination are important aspects of entrepreneurship. Successful entrepreneurship involves leadership; most profits will be gone by the time the imitators arrive on the scene.

The great Harvard economist Joseph Schumpeter believed that entrepreneurship and innovative behavior were the moving forces behind capitalism. According to Schumpeter, this entrepreneurial discovery of new, improved ways of doing things led to a nation's continual improvement in its standard of living:

> The fundamental impulse that sets the capitalist engine in motion comes from the new consumer's goods, the new methods of production or transportation, and new markets, and the new forms of industrial organization that capitalist enterprise creates.[5]

Of course, entrepreneurial decision-making is always conducted in an atmosphere of uncertainty. It is important to be first and to be innovative, but it is also important to be correct. Frequently, the entrepreneur's vision turns out to have been a mirage. What appeared to be a profitable opportunity often turns out to have been an expensive illusion.

---

[5]Joseph A. Schumpeter, *Capitalism, Socialism, and Democracy* (New York: Harper Torchbooks, 1950), p. 83.

OUTSTANDING ECONOMIST

**Joseph Schumpeter
(1883–1950)**

Born in Austria, Schumpeter began his career practicing law, but soon turned to teaching economics. In 1932, he emigrated to the United States where he accepted a professorship at Harvard.

A former president of the American Economic Association (1949), Schumpeter is perhaps best known for his views on entrepreneurship and the future of capitalism. He believed that the progressive improvement in the economic well-being of the masses was the result of the creative and innovative behavior of business entrepreneurs. Entrepreneurs willing to risk their livelihood to pursue an innovative idea could be counted on to provide a steady stream of improved products at a reduced cost. These forces would generate widespread prosperity. As Schumpeter put it:

> Queen Elizabeth owned silk stockings. The capitalist achievement does not typically consist in providing more silk stockings for queens but in bringing them within the reach of factory girls in return for steadily decreasing amounts of effort.[6]

Despite his admiration for a dynamic capitalist system, Schumpeter thought that the system would generate the seeds of its own destruction. Unlike Marx, who argued that capitalism would break down under the weight of its own failures, Schumpeter thought that the success of capitalism would eventually "undermine the social institutions which protect it."[7] He believed that the growth of large, technologically efficient organizations would dampen innovative zeal. The daring entrepreneur would be replaced by the organization person, the committee, and the board of directors.

In addition, Schumpeter thought that the affluence produced by a capitalist system would breed a generation of flabby business leaders incapable of defending the system against its intellectual critics, who would turn the masses toward socialism. Is Schumpeter's indictment of capitalism correct? Only the future will tell.

[6]Schumpeter, *Capitalism, Socialism, and Democracy,* p. 67.
[7]Ibid., p. 61.

Entrepreneurship, like other resources, is scarce. Just as people differ with regard to other skills, so too, do they possess differing amounts of entrepreneurial ability. Potential entrepreneurs are confined to using their own wealth and that of co-venturers, in addition to whatever can be borrowed. Entrepreneurs with a past record of success will be able to attract funds more readily for investment projects. Therefore, in a market economy, previously successful entrepreneurs will exert a disproportionate influence over decisions as to which projects will be undertaken and which will not.

MONOPOLY PROFIT

As we discussed in previous chapters, profits may also originate from sole ownership of a key resource (as in the diamond industry), government regulation (as in the taxicab market of many cities), or a legally granted property right to a technical innovation (as for patented products). In such cases, the monopoly rights to the key resource, privileged license, or patent are worth the present value of the future return that is in excess of what could be earned in competitive markets. In contrast with the transitory profits earned in markets with low entry restraints,

"My ambition is to get so good at growing things, that the government will pay me not to."

Grin and Bear It by Fred Wagner © by and Permission of News America Syndicate.

monopoly profit may persist over a lengthy time period. What does economics say about monopoly profit? Two factors must be considered. First, as we pointed out previously, monopolists can gain from a "contrived" scarcity. They may choose to supply less of a product so that the price can be raised and profits increased. They may well forgo the production of units even though their marginal cost is less than the product price. If one considers only the static economic effects, allocative inefficiency will result.

Second, monopoly profit does not exist in a vacuum. In a dynamic economy, potential monopoly profit will induce competitors to follow pathways that lead to monopoly profit. If dynamic efficiency indicates that the investment resulting in monopoly profit is actually beneficial, this advantage must be weighed against the static allocative inefficiency. The protection of property rights to inventions, new products, and innovative production techniques falls in this category—economic activities of this variety, though they result in monopoly profits, can clearly lead to improvements in economic welfare. To encourage innovative activities, most countries have established a patent system, even though a temporary grant of monopoly power results.

Regardless of their source, the present value of future monopoly profits is incorporated into the value of the assets that provide the "monopoly rights." Licenses that protect their owners from competitors command high prices if they guarantee an above-market rate of return. Similarly, the market value of patent rights and specialized resources incorporates the present value of any future monopoly profits these assets might bestow on their owners. Once the monopoly profits are recognized by others, the market value of the monopoly-granting asset will rise until the monopoly profits have been eliminated.

INTEREST, PROFIT, AND RESOURCE ALLOCATION

Both interest and profit perform important allocation functions.[8] Interest induces people to forgo current consumption, a sacrifice that is a necessary ingredient for capital formation. Economic profit provides both human and physical capital decision-makers with the incentive to (a) undertake investments yielding an uncertain return and (b) discover and develop beneficial and productive investment opportunities.

---

[8]In addition to wages, interest, and profits, economists often discuss ''rent'' as a return to a factor of production. Economists define rent as a return to a factor the supply of which is perfectly inelastic. We have not included this discussion for two reasons. First, one can legitimately argue that the supply of all factors of production has some elasticity. After all, even the supply of usable land can be expanded through drainage, clearing, and conservation. Therefore, rent is always a matter of degree. Second, the term ''rent'' is used in a variety of ways, even by economists. The macroeconomic usage differs substantially from the usage in microeconomics. The term is sometime used to define the returns to a specialized resource, such as an actor's talent, even though training plays an integral part in the supply of the resource. Rent is also sometimes applied to a factor the supply of which is temporarily fixed, even though it can clearly be expanded in the future. Since the returns to capital can be adequately discussed without introducing rent, we concluded that the cost of the ambiguity of the term exceeded the benefits of an extended discussion.

APPLICATIONS IN ECONOMICS

Can Agricultural Price Supports Make Farming More Profitable?

Since the 1930s, the government has instituted various types of **price support programs** for agricultural products. Price supports are designed to increase the prices of crops such as wheat, cotton, tobacco, peanuts, rice, and feed grains and thereby increase farmers' incomes. However, there is good reason to question the programs' effectiveness.

Price Support Programs: Legislative action establishing a minimum price for an agricultural product. The government pledges to purchase any surplus of the product that cannot be sold to consumers at the support price.

Using wheat as an example, Exhibit 6 illustrates the nature of the early price support programs. These programs established a price floor (support) for wheat above the market equilibrium level and pledged that any wheat that could not be sold at the support price would be purchased by the government. Of course, the above-equilibrium price led to an excess supply of wheat. As Exhibit 6a illustrates, the excess supply was initially relatively small (A_1B_1), since both the demand for and the supply of wheat were highly inelastic in the short run. With the passage of time, however, both the demand and supply curves became more elastic. Given sufficient time to adjust, farmers both cultivated wheat land more intensively and

increased the amount of land allotted to wheat. Therefore, the excess supply the government had pledged to purchase continued to increase. (Compare the size of the excess supply of Exhibit 6b and 6a.)

The costs of storing the excess supply expanded rapidly. In fact, during the 1950s, these storage costs became a national scandal. The public outcry over the huge costs, economic waste, spoilage, and fraud eventually led to an alteration of the program.

In an effort to maintain a policy of support for farmers without creating surplus crops and the attendant problems, Congress adopted an **acreage restriction program** designed to reduce the output of agricultural products.

Although nonmonetary factors are more important in human capital decision-making, opportunity cost and the pursuit of profit guide human capital investors just as they guide physical capital investors. As with choosing to purchase a new machine, choosing a human capital investment project (obtaining a law degree, for example) involves cost, the possibility of profit, and uncertainty. In both instances, the expected return will influence the investor. Giving due consideration to nonmonetary factors, physical and human capital investors will both seek to undertake only those projects that they anticipate will yield benefits in excess of costs. To the extent they are correct, their actions will increase the value of resources—that is, they will create wealth.

LOOKING AHEAD

The agricultural price support program illustrates the importance of many of the concepts incorporated into this chapter. The competitive process and the normal rate of return, the relationship between the expected future income and the present value of an asset, and capitalization of the future value of monopoly profit—these concepts will help us understand the impact of agricultural price supports. For an analysis of this issue, see the accompanying Application in Economics box.

EXHIBIT 6

Impact of Agricultural Price Supports

When a price support program pushes the price of an agricultural product, such as wheat, above the market equilibrium, an excess supply of the product results. Initially, the excess supply may be small (A_1B_1 of frame a). However, as farmers adjust their planting and cultivation, the long-run supply of wheat becomes increasingly elastic, causing the excess supply to expand to (A_2B_2, frame b).

Acreage Restriction Program: A program designed to raise the price of an agricultural product by limiting the acreage planted with the product.

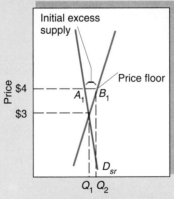

Bushels of wheat per year

(a)Impact in short run

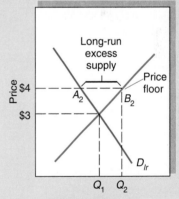

Bushels of wheat per year

(b)Impact in long run

Under this plan, price is still fixed above the market equilibrium, but the number of acres that farmers can plant is reduced to decrease supply and bring it into balance

with demand at the above-equilibrium support price. Each farm is granted an acreage allotment of wheat (and other *(Continued)* supported products), based on the acres planted during a base year. The allotments are attached to the farm. Owners of farms are prohibited from planting more than the specified number of acres for each product.

Exhibit 7 illustrates the economics of the acreage restriction program. By restricting the number of acres planted, the supply of the product is reduced until the price of the product rises to the support level. If the government has to purchase the product at the support price, it can reduce the acreage allotments of farmers during the next period. In contrast, if the market price rises above the support level, the government can relax the allotment a little during the next period. In this manner, the government is able to bring the amount demanded and amount supplied into balance at the supported price level (for

example, as Exhibit 7 illustrates, at the $4 price floor for wheat).

The acreage restrictions make it more costly to grow any given amount of a product. Normally, farmers would minimize their cost of growing more wheat (or any other product) by using a little more of each of the factors of production (land, labor, fertilizer, machinery, and so on). The acreage restriction program prohibits them from using more land. The support price provides farmers with an incentive to produce more wheat, for example, but they must do so by using factors of production other than land more intensively. Higher costs result, shifting the supply curve of Exhibit 7 to the left (to S_2). Supply curve S_1 is unattainable once the acreage restrictions are imposed, since it would require a larger amount of land than is permissible under the allotment program.

Is farming more profitable in the long run after the imposition of the acreage restrictions and price support programs? Surprisingly, the answer is no. To the extent that price supports make farming more profitable in the short run, the demand for land with acreage allotments increases (see Exhibit 8). Competition bids up the price of land with acreage allotments until the investors receive only the normal rate of return. Just as one cannot earn an abnormally high rate of return by purchasing stock ownership rights of a firm already earning monopoly profit, neither can a farmer earn an abnormally high rate of return by purchasing the ownership rights of farms with acreage allotments.

Suppose the price support program permitted wheat growers to earn an additional $100 each year from an acre of land planted in wheat. If that were true, the net

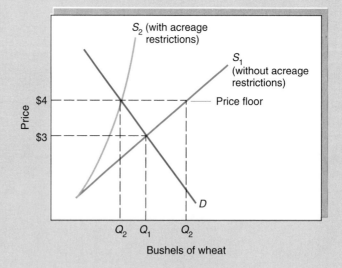

present value (NPV) of the land with a wheat allotment would rise by $100 divided by the interest rate. At a 10 percent rate of interest, the value of the additional $100 per year would equal $1,000 (NPV = R/i = $100/.10 = $1,000). The value of an acre of land with a wheat allotment would rise by $1,000. Essentially, the value of the monopoly-profit income stream derived from the price support program would be capitalized into the value of land with a wheat allotment.

The major beneficiaries of the price support/acreage restriction program have been the owners of land with an allotment at the time of the program's establishment. Competition for land with acreage allotments has driven the price of such land up until the rate of return on agricultural land with allotments is equal to the market rate of return. Thus, the profit rate of the current owners of the land is no higher than it would have been had Congress never adopted any kind of price support system in the first place.[9]

[9]For additional details on specific agricultural price support programs, see E. C. Pasour Jr., *Agriculture and the State: Bureaucracy and the Market Process* (San Francisco: The Independent Institute, 1989).

EXHIBIT 8

Rising Land Values and Capitalizing Profit

Since land with an acreage allotment permits one to plant wheat and sell it at the above-market-equilibrium price, the price support program makes such land more valuable. Competition drives the price of land *with an allotment* upward until the higher land values fully capture the larger profits resulting from the program. But once land values have risen, the farmer's rate of return on investment is no higher with the program than it was prior to the program's establishment. The major beneficiaries of price support programs have been those who owned land with acreage allotments *at the time the programs were established.*

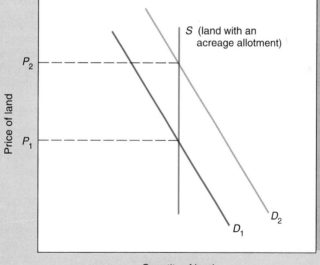

CHAPTER SUMMARY

1. We can often produce more consumption goods by first using our resources to produce physical and human capital resources and then by using the capital resources to produce the desired consumption goods. Resources used to produce capital goods will be unavailable for the direct production of consumption goods. Thus, when roundabout production methods are used, current consumption must be reduced.

2. People have a positive rate of time preference; they generally value present consumption more highly than future consumption.

3. Both consumers and investors contribute to the demand for loanable funds. The demand of consumers reflects their positive rate of time preference, while the demand of investors emanates from the productivity of roundabout production methods. Consumers are willing to pay a positive interest rate in order to achieve earlier availability and investors are willing to pay interest in order to finance projects expected to yield economic profit.

4. The interest rate is the price of earlier availability. Interest provides lenders with an incentive to curtail current consumption and to supply loanable funds to others. The market interest rate will bring the quantity of funds demanded by borrowers (to undertake current investments and to consume beyond their current income) into balance with the supply of funds provided by lenders willing to forgo current consumption in exchange for the interest premium.

5. During inflationary times, the money rate of interest incorporates an inflationary premium reflecting the expected future increase in the price level. Under these circumstances, the money rate of interest exceeds the real rate of interest.

6. The money rate of interest on a specific loan reflects three basic factors—the pure interest rate, an inflationary premium, and a risk premium that is directly related to the probability of default by the borrower.

7. Since a dollar in the future is valued less than a dollar today, the value of future receipts must be discounted to calculate their current worth. The discounting procedure can be used to calculate the net present value of an expected income stream from a potential investment project. A project should be undertaken only if the net present value of the expected income from the project exceeds its current cost (purchase price).

8. The expectation of economic profit influences investment decisions in both human and physical capital. Other things constant, the higher the expected profit, the more attractive the project to an investor.

9. The present value of expected future net earnings will determine the market value of *existing* assets. An increase (decline) in the expected future earnings derived from an asset will increase (reduce) the market value of the asset.

10. There are three basic sources of economic profit: (a) uncertainty, (b) entrepreneurial alertness, and (c) monopoly.

11. Since the future is uncertain, investors must expose themselves to uncertainty arising from unanticipated shifts in market demand and costs. Since most people dislike uncertainty, investors must be paid a premium (a return in excess of the interest rate) to induce them to accept the uncertainty that necessarily accompanies investment. This uncertainty premium is a source of economic profit.

12. Astute entrepreneurs are able to recognize and undertake economically beneficial investment opportunities that have gone unnoticed by others. Entrepreneurial alertness for potential opportunities to combine resources in a manner that increases their value is a source of economic profit.

13. Profits may also emanate from monopoly power—entry barriers that shield suppliers from competitive pressure. Sole ownership of a vital resource, legal restraint of entry, and patents can bestow monopoly rights on owners of assets. Monopoly profits encourage entrepreneurs to invest resources to acquire a monopoly privilege.

CRITICAL ANALYSIS QUESTIONS

1. Suppose U.S. investors are considering the construction of bicycle factories in two different countries, one in Europe and the other in Africa. Projected costs and revenues are at first identical, but the chance of guerilla warfare (and possible

destruction of the factory) is suddenly perceived in the African nation. In which country will the price of bicycles (and the current rate of return to bicycle factories) probably rise? Will the investors be better off in the country with the higher rate of return? Why or why not?

*2. How would the following changes influence the rate of interest in the United States?
   a. An increase in the positive time preference of lenders.
   b. An increase in the positive time preference of borrowers.
   c. An increase in domestic inflation.
   d. Increased uncertainty about a nuclear war.
   e. Improved investment opportunities in Europe.

3. Can you discover ways to make pure economic profits from an investment by reading about currently profitable investments in the *Wall Street Journal?* Why or why not?

4. "Any return to capital above the pure interest yield is unnecessary. The pure interest yield is sufficient to provide capitalists with the earnings necessary to replace their assets and to compensate for their sacrifice of current consumption. Any return above that is pure gravy; it is excess profit." Do you agree with this view? Why or why not?

5. How are human and physical capital investment decisions similar? How do they differ? What determines the profitability of a physical capital investment? Do human capital investors make profits? If so, what is the source of profit? Explain.

*6. Suppose you are contemplating the purchase of a minicomputer at a cost of $1,000. The expected lifetime of the asset is three years. You expect to lease the asset to a business for $400 annually (payable at the end of each year) for three years. If you can borrow (and lend) money at an interest rate of 8 percent, will the investment be a profitable undertaking? Is the project profitable at an interest rate of 12 percent? Provide calculations in support of your answer.

7. How do the accounting profits of corporations differ from economic profits? Do corporate profits incorporate an interest return? A risk return? A pure profit return? A monopoly profit return? As a percentage of corporate assets, how large do you think each of these returns is in most manufacturing industries? Explain.

*8. According to a news item, the owner of a lottery ticket paying $3 million over 20 years is offering to sell the ticket for $1.2 million cash *now.* "Who knows?" the ticket owner explained, "We might not even be here in 20 years, and I do not want to leave it to the dinosaurs."
   a. Assuming that the ticket pays $150,000 per year at the end of each year for the next 20 years, what is the present value of the ticket if the appropriate rate for discounting the future income is thought to be 10 percent?
   b. Assuming the discount rate is in the 10 percent range, is the offer price of $1.2 million reasonable?
   c. Can you think of any disadvantages of buying the lottery earnings rather than a bond?

*9. A lender made the following statement to a borrower, "You are borrowing $1,000, which is to be repaid in 12 monthly installments of $100 each. Your total interest charge is $200, which means your interest rate is 20 percent." Is the effective interest rate on the loan really 20 percent? Explain.

10. Which of the following options would you prefer: (a) your income during the next 12 months or (b) a 50-50 chance of either zero or twice your income during the next 12 months? Would you accept (b), if someone paid you a premium? If the premium were paid, would it be improper to call it "profit"?

11. Assuming that you can borrow and lend at a 12 percent rate of interest, which would you rather have: (a) $4 million paid in $200,000 end-of-the-year installments for each of the next 20 years, or (b) $1.5 million now? (You may ignore differences in tax treatment between the two alternatives.)

Asterisk denotes questions for which answers are given in Appendix C, Selected Answers.

*12. "Janet Jones is $20 million richer today. She just won the Florida lottery, which will pay her $1 million per year for each of the next 20 years." Evaluate. Is she really $20 million richer?

*13. A U.S. senator from a major agricultural state recently argued: "Subsidies are necessary to keep farmers in business. If all the farmers go out of business, we will starve to death."

    a. If all farm subsidies were abolished, would we have to worry about all (or even most) farmers going out of business? Why or why not?

    b. Should we subsidize automobile or shoe manufacturers for fear that, without subsidies, all producers in these industries will go out of business and leave us with neither automobiles nor shoes?

14. Suppose the current price support/acreage allotment program for wheat were abolished. What would be the impact on (a) the value of land with a wheat allotment, (b) the cost of producing wheat, (c) the amount of wheat exported, (d) the world price of wheat, and (e) the profitability of wheat farming?

*15. Farmers are often heard to complain that they are not helped by the price support/acreage allotment program, and yet they oppose its repeal. Explain why these seemingly contradictory views are not surprising.

*16. "Giant corporations today decide what will be available for consumers to buy. The investment decisions of a few corporate executives determine much of what our economic life will be like in the future. Ordinary citizens have no voice." Evaluate.

26

Labor Unions and Collective Bargaining

Analysts who have attributed national economic problems ranging from unemployment to wage inflation to low productivity to unions will have to find a new culprit to blame: unless there is a remarkable renaissance in unionism, critics won't have unions to kick around any more.[1]

Richard B. Freeman

CHAPTER FOCUS

■ How much of the U.S. work force is unionized?

■ How does the collective bargaining process work? How important is the "strike" in the bargaining process?

■ Can unions increase the wages of their members? What makes a union strong? What factors limit the power of a union?

■ Can unions increase the share of income going to labor?

■ Do unions cause inflation?

■ What impact have unions had on the legal structure of worker-management relations?

Labor Union: A collective organization of employees who bargain as a unit with employers.

*I*n an earlier chapter, we mentioned that labor unions may be able to establish institutional arrangements that will affect supply and demand, and therefore alter wage rates. We are now prepared to examine the labor market effects of unions. A **labor union** is an organization of employees, usually working either in the same occupation or industry, who have consented to joint bargaining with employers concerning wages, working conditions, grievance procedures, and other elements of employment. The primary objective of a labor union is to improve the welfare of its members.

Unions have historically been controversial. Some believe that labor unions are a necessary shield protecting workers from the beast of employer greed. Others charge that unions are monopolies seeking to provide their members with benefits at the expense of economic efficiency, consumers, and other workers. Still others argue that the economic influence of unions—both for good and for bad—is vastly overrated. This chapter will enhance our understanding of labor unions and the economic factors that influence their ability to achieve desired objectives.

UNION MEMBERSHIP AS A SHARE OF THE WORK FORCE

Historically, the proportion of the U.S. labor force belonging to a labor union has fluctuated substantially. In 1910, approximately 10 percent of the nonfarm employees belonged to a union. As Exhibit 1 shows, this figure rose to 18 percent in 1920. In the aftermath of the First World War, union membership declined, falling to 12 percent of the nonfarm work force by 1929. Favorable legislation adopted during the Depression of the 1930s encouraged unions and union membership as a share of the nonfarm labor force rose from 13.5 percent in 1935 to 30.4 percent in 1945. By 1954, one-third of the nonfarm work force in the United States was unionized.

Since the mid-1950s, however, union membership has waned. As Exhibit 1 illustrates, it declined slowly during 1955–1975, and then quite sharply since 1975. By 1990, union workers accounted for only 16.3 percent of nonfarm employment, down from 32 percent in 1954 (and 28 percent as recently as 1975).

Why have union members declined as a share of the U.S. work force in recent decades? Several factors have contributed to the decline. First, most of the recent growth in employment has been with relatively small firms (less than 100 employees) in service and high-tech industries. Small firms are costly to organize and unions have traditionally been weak in service and high-tech industries. Second, competition has eroded union strength in several important industries. Foreign producers have increased their market share in steel, mining, automobiles, and other heavy manufacturing industries. Employment has thus been shrinking in these areas of traditional union strength. Deregulation in transportation and communication industries has also reduced the effectiveness of unions. As these industries have become more competitive, unionized firms have faced increased competition from nonunion producers. Finally, even regional growth patterns have

[1]Richard B. Freeman, "Contraction and Expansion: The Divergence of Private Sector and Public Sector Unionism in the United States," *Journal of Economic Perspectives,* Vol. 2 (Spring, 1988), p. 86.

EXHIBIT 1

Changes in Union Membership as a Share of Nonagricultural Employment

Between 1910 and 1935, union membership generally ranged between 12 percent and 17 percent of nonagricultural employment. During the 1935–1945 period, union membership increased sharply to approximately one-third of the nonfarm work force. Since the mid-1950s, union membership has declined as a percent of nonfarm employment, and the decline has been particularly sharp since 1975.

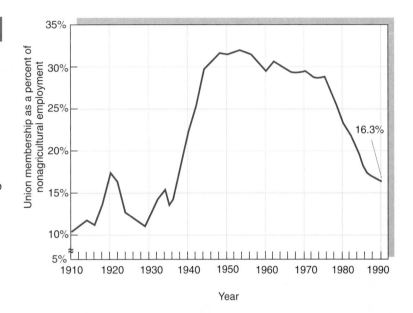

Source: Leo Troy and Neil Sheflin, *Union Source Book: Membership, Structure, Finance, Directory* (West Orange, NJ: Industrial Relations and Information Services, 1985) and *Employment and Earnings,* (various issues).

adversely affected union strength. During the 1960s and 1970s, population and employment grew rapidly in the sunbelt, while stagnating in the northeast and upper middle west. Since the former is an area of union weakness and the latter an area of strength, this pattern also retarded the growth of union membership.

All of these factors, of course, have to some extent been caused by union success in raising union wages. Wages that increase more than productivity act to retard the growth of employment in the geographic areas, the industries, and the classes of firms employing the high wage workers. In contrast, where wages are low relative to productivity, business investment and the growth of employment are encouraged.

As Exhibit 2 shows, there is substantial variation in the incidence of union membership across sex, race, and occupational groups. Men are more likely than women to belong to a union. In 1990, 19.3 percent of employed men were union members, while only 12.6 percent of women employees were unionized. Similarly, the incidence of unionization among blacks (21.1 percent) was a little higher than for whites (15.5 percent) and Hispanics (14.8 percent). There is substantial variation in unionization according to occupation. Only about 10 percent of the workers in technical, sales, clerical, and service occupations were unionized in 1990. In contrast, more than a quarter of the workers in craft, operative, and laborer occupations belonged to a union.

There is a major difference between the private and public sector in the degree of unionization. While only 12.1 percent of the private wage and salary workers are unionized, 36.5 percent of the government employees belong to a union. And while the share of the private work force belonging to a union has been shrinking, unionization has been increasing in the public sector. During the last three decades, the proportion of government employees belonging to a union has more than tripled, rising from 11 percent in 1960 to 36.5 percent in 1990.

EXHIBIT 2 ■ Differences in the Incidence of Union Membership According to Sex, Race, Occupation, and Sector, 1990.	
	Union Members as a percent of Group, 1990
By Sex	
Men	19.3
Women	12.6
By Race	
Whites	15.5
Blacks	21.1
Hispanics	14.8
By Occupation	
Technical, sales, and clerical	10.4
Service[a]	9.9
Precision production, craft, and repair	25.9
Operators, fabricators, and laborers	26.4
By Sector	
Private wage and salary	12.1
Government	36.5

[a]Excluding protective service workers.

Source: U.S. Department of Labor, *Employment and Earnings,* (January, 1990).

THE COLLECTIVE BARGAINING PROCESS

Collective Bargaining Contract: A detailed contract between (a) a group of employees (a labor union) and (b) an employer. It covers wage rates and conditions of employment.

Each year, **collective bargaining contracts** covering wages and working conditions for six to nine million workers are negotiated. A collective bargaining contract is a union-management agreement prescribing the conditions of employment. Union negotiators, acting as agents for a group of employees, bargain with management about the provisions of a labor contract. If the union representatives are able to obtain a contract they consider acceptable, they will typically submit it to a vote of the union members. If approved by the members, the contract establishes in detail wage rates, fringe benefits, and working conditions for a future time interval, usually the next two or three years. During that time interval, union and management alike must abide by the conditions of the contract. While the labor contract is between management and union, it also applies to the nonunion bargaining unit members who are employed by the firm or industry.

Union Shop: The requirement that all employees join the recognized union and pay dues to it within a specified length of time (usually 30 days) after their employment with the firm begins.

Some labor-management contracts contain a **union shop** provision. A union shop contract requires all workers to join the union after a specified length of employment, usually 30 days. Union proponents argue that since all workers in the bargaining unit enjoy the benefits of collective bargaining, all should be required to join and pay dues. In the absence of a union shop, individual workers might reap gains brought about by the union without incurring the costs.

Opponents of the union shop argue that all employees are not helped by a union. Some unions lack the necessary power to obtain wage increases. Some employees may feel that they would be better off if they could bargain for themselves. In addition, unions often engage in political activities, either directly or indirectly. These activities may run counter to the views of individual employees.

Right-to-Work Laws: Laws that prohibit the union shop— the requirement that employees must join a union (after 30 days) as a condition of employment. Each state has the option to adopt (or reject) right-to-work legislation.

Why should an employee be forced, as a condition of employment, to support activities he or she does not approve? In 1947, Congress passed the Taft-Hartley Act; Section 14-B allows states to enact **right-to-work laws** prohibiting union shop contracts. Thus, when a state has a right-to-work statute, a union-management contract cannot require a worker to join a union as a condition of employment. Currently, 21 states, most of them in the sunbelt, have adopted right-to-work legislation.

THE STRIKE AND COLLECTIVE BARGAINING

Typically, management and labor negotiators begin the bargaining process for a new labor contract several months, or even a year, before the termination of the current agreement. The new contract is usually approved before the old contract has terminated. However, at the termination of the old labor-management agreement, if the bargaining process has broken down and there is no agreement on a new contract, either side may use its economic power to try to bring the other to terms.

Employers can withhold employment from workers at the expiration of the old contract. However, since employers can unilaterally announce their terms for continued employment, they seldom discontinue operations.

Strike: An action of unionized employees in which they (a) discontinue working for the employer and (b) take steps to prevent other potential workers from offering their services to the employer.

The major source of work stoppage is the strike. A **strike** consists of two major actions by a union: (a) employees, particularly union employees, refuse to work, and (b) steps are taken to prevent other employees from working for the employer. Both conditions are essential to a strike. Without efforts to prevent other employees, often referred to as ''scabs'' or ''strike-breakers,'' from accepting jobs with the employer, a strike would merely be a mass resignation. A strike also involves picketing to restrict and discourage the hiring of other workers, actions to prevent free entry and exit from a plant, and perhaps even violence or the threat of violence against workers willing to cross the picket lines.

The purpose of a strike is to impose economic costs on an employer so that the terms proposed by the union will be accepted. When the strike can be used to disrupt the production process and interfere with the employer's ability to sell goods and services to customers, it is a very powerful weapon. Under such conditions, the employer may submit to the wage demands of the union, as a means of avoiding the costs of the strike.

Given the nature of the strike, it is not surprising that the ''right to strike'' has had an uneven history. At times, striking was prohibited because it was thought to interfere with the rights of nonunion workers. Before the passage of legislation in the early 1900s clearly establishing the right to strike, courts were sometimes willing to intervene and limit certain types of strikes. The role of law enforcement in strikes also has had a mixed history. In some areas, the police have given nonstrikers, who desire to continue working, protection to and from their jobs. In other cases, they have permitted pickets to block entry and have turned their backs on violence between strikers and nonstrikers. Even today, the protection a nonstriker can expect from the police varies from location to location.

The United States has established some limitations on the right to strike. The use of the strike by government employees—the single area of union growth—is substantially restricted. Most states limit the right of public employees to strike. Prohibitions against strikes by police and fire protection workers are particularly commonplace. Strikes by federal employees are also prohibited by law. When the air-traffic controllers' union called a strike during the summer of 1981, striking workers who refused to return to work were fired and eventually replaced. The Taft-Hartley Act allows the president to seek a court injunction prohibiting a private sector strike for 80 days when it is believed that the strike would create a "national emergency." During the 80-day period, work continues under the conditions of the old contract. If a settlement has not been reached during this "cooling-off" period, however, employees again have the option of using the strike as a weapon.

THE COST OF A STRIKE

A strike can be costly to both union and management. From the firm's viewpoint, a work stoppage may mean that it will be unable to meet the current demand for its product. It may lose customers, and they may be difficult to win back once they have turned to competitors during the strike. A strike will be more costly to the firm when (a) demand for its product is strong, (b) it is unable to stockpile its product, and (c) its fixed costs are high even during the strike. If the firm can stockpile its product in anticipation of a strike, a work stoppage may not have much impact on current sales. For example, automobile producers, particularly during slack times, often have an inventory of new cars that allows them to meet current demand during a 60- or even 90-day strike. In contrast, the shipping revenues of a trucking firm may be completely eliminated by a truckers' strike. The firm would be unable to deliver its service because of the strike, and potential customers would therefore turn to rail, air, postal, and other forms of shipping. The firm could suffer a permanent loss of sales.

Careful timing can also magnify the cost of a strike. Agricultural unions can threaten farmers with the loss of an entire year's income by striking at harvest time. Similarly, major league umpires can strengthen their position by striking at World Series time.

The nature of the product, the level of current demand, and the ability of the firm to continue to meet the requests of its customers during a strike all influence the effectiveness of the strike as a weapon. The more costly a work stoppage would be to a firm, the greater the pressure on it to yield to the demands of the union.

Strikes, particularly if they are long, are also quite costly to employees. Although a carnival attitude often prevails during the early days of a strike, a few weeks without paychecks impose an extreme hardship on most families. Strike funds are usually inadequate to deal with a prolonged strike. Some workers may be able to arrange for a temporary job to help pay the bills, but such employment will generally be much less attractive than their regular jobs. Therefore, as a strike continues, pressures build on the union to arrive at a settlement.

Strikes sometimes exert a substantial impact on secondary parties who are unable to influence union-management relations. For example, a prolonged strike in the steel industry might cause a loss of work time in automobile, construction, and other industries. A teachers' strike might force a working parent to quit his or her job to care for the children. A public transit strike in New York can paralyze Fun City. A coal miners' strike can leave Londoners without heat. Should third parties be protected when strikes involve the public interest? Many would answer this question in the affirmative. But, how can the public be protected without interfering with the bargaining process? These questions have not yet been fully answered.

KEEPING WORK STOPPAGES IN PERSPECTIVE

Since a strike is news, work stoppages receive considerable media exposure. Nevertheless, work stoppages due to strikes must be placed in proper perspective. The strike, or the threat of it, forces both management and labor to bargain seriously. Both have a strong incentive to settle without a work stoppage. This is

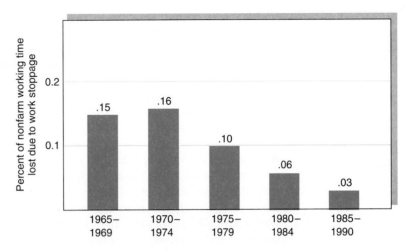

EXHIBIT 3

The Percentage of Work Time Lost Due to Strikes

Since 1965, only one-tenth of 1 percent of nonfarm working time has been lost due to labor disputes, and the figure has been declining.

Source: *Statistical Abstract of the United States* (annual) and *Monthly Labor Review* (various issues).

usually what happens. Each year an estimated 120,000 labor contracts are terminated. Thus, during the course of a year, 120,000 labor and management bargaining teams sit across the bargaining table from each other. They deal with the important issues of wages, fringe benefits, grievance procedures, and conditions of employment. More than 99 percent of the time, labor-management contracts are agreed to without the use of strikes. One seldom hears about these contracts because peaceful settlements are back-page news, at best. It is the strikes that rate the headlines.

As Exhibit 3 illustrates, very little potential work time is lost as the result of strikes. During the last 25 years, the number of worker-hours lost because of strikes was approximately one-tenth of 1 percent of the total working time—and the proportion has been falling. The amount of work time lost due to strikes is substantially less than the work time lost because of absenteeism.

HOW CAN UNIONS INFLUENCE WAGES?

The collective-bargaining process often gives one the impression that wages are established primarily by the talents of the union-management representatives who sit at the bargaining table. It might appear that market forces play a relatively minor role. However, as both union and management are well aware, market forces provide the setting in which the bargaining process is conducted. They often tip the balance of power one way or the other.

High wages increase the firm's costs. When union employers face stiff competition from nonunion producers or foreign competitors, they will be less able to pass along higher wage costs to their customers. Competition in the product market thus limits the bargaining power of a union. Changing market conditions also influence the balance of power between union and management. When the demand for a product is strong, the demand for labor will be high, and the firm will be much more willing to consent to a significant wage increase. When demand is weak, however, the product inventory level of the firm (or industry) is more likely to be high. The firm's current demand for labor will be weakened. It will be much less vulnerable to a union work stoppage. Under such conditions, wage increases will be much more difficult to obtain. (Note: When we speak of wage rates, we are referring to the total compensation package, including both fringe benefits and money wages.)

A union can use three basic strategies to increase the wages of its members: supply restrictions, bargaining power, and increase in demand. We will examine each of these in turn.

SUPPLY RESTRICTIONS

If a union can successfully reduce the supply of competitive labor, higher wage rates will automatically result. Licensing requirements, long apprenticeship programs, immigration barriers, high initiation fees, refusal to admit new members to the union, and prohibition of nonunion workers from holding jobs are all practices that unions have used to limit the supply of labor to various occupations and jobs. Craft unions, in particular, have often been able to obtain higher wages because of their successful effort to limit the entry of competitive labor. In the 1920s, unions successfully lobbied for legislation that reduced the torrent of worker-immigrants from abroad to a mere trickle. The tighter immigration laws considerably reduced the influx of new workers, reducing the growth of supply in U.S. labor markets and thus causing higher wages to prevail.

Exhibit 4a illustrates the impact of supply restrictions on wage rates. Successful exclusionary tactics will reduce supply, shifting the supply curve from S_0 to S_1. Facing the supply curve S_1, employers will consent to the wage rate W_1. Compared to a free-entry market equilibrium, the wage rate has increased from W_0 to W_1, but employment has declined from E_0 to E_1. At the higher wage rate, W_1, an excess supply of labor, *AB,* will result. The restrictive practices will prevent this excess supply from undercutting the above-equilibrium wage rate. Because of the exclusionary practices, the union will be able to obtain higher wages for E_1

EXHIBIT 4

Supply Restrictions, Bargaining Power, and Wage Rates

The impact of higher wages obtained by restricting supply is very similar to that obtained through bargaining power. As illustrated by frame a, when union policies reduce the supply of one type of labor, higher wages result. Similarly, when bargaining power is used in order to obtain higher wages (frame b), employment declines and an excess supply of labor results.

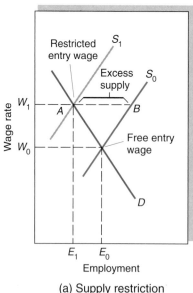

(a) Supply restriction

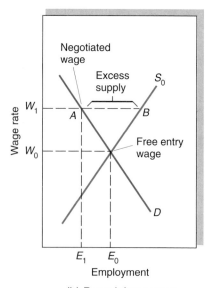

(b) Bargaining power

employees. Other employees who would be willing to accept work even at wage rate W_0 will now be forced into other areas of employment.

BARGAINING POWER

Must unions restrict entry? Why can they not simply use their bargaining power, enhanced by the strike threat, as a vehicle for raising wages? If they have enough economic power, this will be possible. A strike by even a small percentage of vital employees can sometimes halt the flow of production. For example, a work stoppage by airline mechanics can force major airlines to cancel their flights. Because the mechanics perform an essential function, an airline cannot operate without their services, even though they constitute only 10 percent of all airline employees.

If the union is able to obtain an above-free-entry wage rate, the impact on employment will be similar to a reduction in supply. As Exhibit 4b illustrates, employers will hire fewer workers at the higher wage rate obtained through bargaining power. Employment will decline below the free-entry level (from E_0 to E_1) as a result of the rise in wages. An excess supply of labor, AB, will exist, at least temporarily. More employees will seek the high-wage union jobs than employers will choose to hire. Nonwage methods of rationing jobs will become more important.

INCREASE IN DEMAND

Unions may attempt to increase the demand for union labor by appealing to consumers to buy only union-produced goods. Union-sponsored promotional campaigns instructing consumers to "look for the union label" or "buy American" are generally designed to increase the demand for union-made products.

Most people, however, are primarily interested in getting the most for their consumer dollar. Thus, the demand for union labor is usually determined primarily by factors outside of the union's direct control, such as the availability of substitute inputs and the demand for the product. Unions, though, can sometimes use their political power to increase the demand for their services. They may be able to induce legislators to pass laws requiring the employment of certain types or amounts of labor for a task (for example, unneeded firemen on trains, allegedly for safety reasons, or a certain number of stage engineers). Unions often seek import restrictions as a means of increasing the demand for domestic labor. For example, automobile workers generally support high tariffs and import quotas for foreign-made automobiles. Garment workers have used their political muscle to raise tariffs and reduce import quotas for clothing goods produced abroad. Such practices increase the demand for domestic automobiles and clothing, thereby increasing the demand for domestic auto and garment workers. It is not surprising that the management and union representatives of a specific industry often join hands in demanding government tariff protection from foreign competition. As Exhibit 5 illustrates, successful union actions to increase demand for the services of union members result in both higher wages and an expansion in employment, usually at the expense of consumers.

A union in a strong bargaining position may shift the firm off its demand curve. This can happen if the union offers an "all-or-none" settlement in which the union specifies both wage and the quantity of labor (or restrictive work rules). To get any labor at all in this case, the firm must hire more labor at the union wage than it wants. For example, the International Typographical Union has sometimes stipulated that advertisements printed from molded mats supplied by advertisers

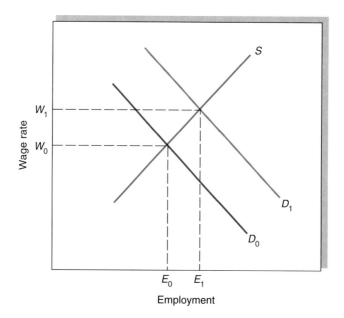

must be set, proofread, and corrected in the newspaper's composing room. This
"bogus type" was discarded. If the newspaper wanted any work—and no picket
lines—from typesetters, it had to either pay them to do "bogus" work or make
other bargaining concessions to induce the union to withdraw the rule. This type of
"make-work rule" is another way in which a union may be able to loosen the
connection between higher wages and lower levels of employment.

UNION POWER, EMPLOYMENT, AND MONOPSONY

Is unionization necessary to protect employees from the power of employers? When
there are a large number of employers in a market area, the interest of employees
will be protected by competition among employers. Under these circumstances,
each employer must pay the market wage to employees to keep them from shifting
to higher-paying alternative employers. In a modern society, labor is highly mobile.
Most employees work in a labor market in which there are many employers.
However, a few workers may confront a situation in which there is only a single
employer of labor, at least for the specific skill category of labor supplied by the
workers. For example, if a single large employer—perhaps a textile manufacturer
or lumber mill—dominates the labor market of a small town, local workers may
have few alternative employment opportunities.

Monopsony: A market in
which there is only one buyer.
The monopsonist confronts the
market supply curve for the
resource (or product) bought.

Analysis of resource markets under conditions of **monopsony** will help us
understand situations in which the market is dominated by a single employer or a
small number of employers. Monopsony refers to a market situation in which there
is a single buyer for a specific resource; for example, a specific skill category of
labor. As we previously discussed, when the seller has a monopoly, the seller can
profit by restricting output and charging a price above the marginal cost of

EXHIBIT 6

Labor Market Monopsony and Unionization

As frame a illustrates, the monopsonist's supply curve for labor will slope upward to the right. The marginal factor cost curve for labor will be steeper than the labor supply curve. The monopsonist will hire E_1 units of labor and pay a wage rate, W_1, along its labor supply curve. If a union establishes a wage floor, W_2 of frame b, for example, the monopsonist may hire additional workers (E_2 rather than E_1) at the higher wage rate.

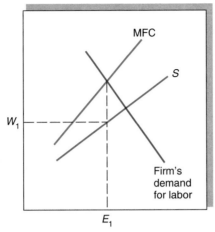

(a) Monopsony (without unionization)

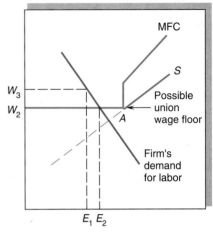

(b) Monopsony (with unionization)

Marginal Factor Cost: The cost of employing an additional unit of a resource. When the employer is small relative to the total market, the marginal factor cost is simply the price of the resource. In contrast, under monopsony, marginal factor cost will exceed the price of the resource, since the monopsonist faces an upward-sloping supply curve for the resource.

production. Under monopsony, the buyer has a monopoly. Since the alternatives available to sellers are limited, the monopsonist-buyer will be able to profit by restricting the purchase of the resource and paying a price (wage rate) that is less than the marginal revenue generated by the resource.

Exhibit 6 illustrates the impact of monopsony in the labor market. Since the monopsonist is the only employer (purchaser of labor), its supply curve for the resource in question will coincide with the market supply curve for that resource. The supply curve for the resource will slope upward to the right because higher wages are necessary to attract the additional workers desired. For now, we will assume that both the old and new employees will be paid the higher wage rates if employment is expanded. The **marginal factor cost** (MFC) curve indicates the marginal cost of labor to the monopsonist. The marginal factor cost of labor will exceed the wage rate because the higher wages necessary to attract each additional worker must be paid to all employees. As illustrated by Exhibit 6, this means that the monopsonist's marginal factor cost curve will be steeper than the labor supply curve.

How many workers should a profit-maximizing monopsony employ? The monopsonist's demand curve for labor indicates how much each additional worker adds to the firm's total revenue. The monopsonist will continue to expand employment as long as hiring additional workers adds more to total revenues than to total costs. This means that the monopsonist will choose employment level E_1, where the firm's demand curve, reflecting the marginal revenue product of labor, is just equal to the marginal factor cost of labor. A wage rate of W_1 will be sufficient to attract E_1 employees. For employment levels beyond E_1, it would cost the monopsonist more to hire an additional worker (MFC) than that worker would add to total revenue. As the result of this cost, the monopsonist firm will hire fewer employees than it would if it were not the only buyer in the labor market.

Exhibit 6b illustrates what would happen if a union established a wage floor—W_2, for example—for a monopsonist. The wage floor would prohibit the monopsonist from paying low wages even if employment dropped. The union would confront the employer with the supply curve W_2AS. In essence, the wage floor would become the firm's marginal factor cost curve until the wage floor intersected the labor supply curve at A. As long as the marginal factor cost of additional units of labor was less than the firm's demand curve, additional workers would continue to be employed. Thus, if a union imposed wage rate W_2, the monopsonist would expand employment to E_2. In this case unionization would result in both higher wages and an expansion in employment. If the union expanded the wage rate above W_3, employment would fall below E_1, the level employed by a nonunion monopsonist. But, for any wage floor less than W_3, the monopsonist would expand employment beyond E_1.

While this analysis is sound as far as it goes, there are three additional factors that should be considered.[2] First, a higher wage rate will obviously increase the firm's total costs of production. In the long run, when the firm sells its product in a competitive market, higher per unit costs will almost certainly force the firm to raise its price. A decline in the firm's market share and output is a likely result. As the firm's market share declines, employment of all factors of production, including labor, will fall.

Second, a monopsonist will often be able to confine the higher wage rates to new employees only. When this is the case, the marginal factor cost curve of the monopsonist will not differ from its labor supply curve. Rather than restricting employment to keep wages low, the firm may simply offer new employees (but not old ones) higher job classifications and more attractive employment conditions to obtain their services.

Third, given the speed of transportation, employers often draw workers from 30 to 50 miles away. In addition, many employees (particularly skilled workers, professionals, and managers) compete in a much broader labor market, a national labor market in some cases. Over a period of time, such workers will flow into and away from local labor markets. Given the mobility of labor, then, most employers will be small relative to their labor market, and their decisions to expand or contract their work force will not exert much impact on the market wage rate. Under these circumstances, marginal factor cost is nearly the same as the wage rate in the competitive market model. A rise in the wage rate will therefore almost certainly reduce employment.

The strength of these factors is enough to substantially reduce monopsony power. When economic researchers have compared the predictive power of the monopsony model with the competitive model, the latter has generally been shown to perform better. Empirical evidence thus indicates that unions normally operate in labor markets characterized by competition rather than monopsony.

WHAT GIVES A UNION STRENGTH?

Not all unions are able to raise the wages of their workers. What are the factors that make a union strong? Why are some unions able to maintain employee wages above free-entry level, while others have a negligible impact on wage rates?

Simply stated, if a union is to be strong, the demand for its labor must be inelastic. This will enable the union to obtain large wage increases while suffering

---

[2]See Armen Alchian and William Allen, *Exchange and Production: Competition, Coordination, and Control* (Belmont: Wadsworth, 1983), pp. 334–39, for additional theoretical analysis of monopsony.

only modest reductions in employment. In contrast, with an elastic demand for union labor, a substantial rise in wages will mean a large loss in jobs.

There are four major determinants of the demand elasticity for a factor of production: (a) the availability of substitutes, (b) the elasticity of product demand, (c) the share of the input as a proportion of total cost, and (d) the supply elasticity of substitute inputs.[3] We now turn to the importance of each of these conditions as a determinant of union strength.

THE AVAILABILITY OF GOOD SUBSTITUTE INPUTS

When it is difficult to substitute other inputs for unionized labor when producing a good, the union is strengthened. When this is the case, the demand for union labor will be more inelastic and reductions in employment will tend to be small if the union is able to use its bargaining power and the threat of a strike to push wages up. In contrast, when there are good substitutes for union labor, employers will turn to the substitutes and cut back on their use of union labor as it becomes more expensive. Under these circumstances, higher union wages will price the union workers out of the market and lead to a sharp reduction in their employment.

Some employers may be able to automate various production operations—in effect, substituting machines for union workers if their wages increase. When machines are a good substitute for union labor, the demand for union labor will be fairly elastic. An elastic demand for union labor will substantially reduce the ability of the union to gain above-market wages.

The best substitute for union labor is generally nonunion labor. The power of unions to gain more for their members will be directly related to their ability to protect themselves from competition with nonunion labor. When employers are in a position to substitute nonunion labor for unionized workers, it will be difficult for a union to push wages above the market level.

Within a given plant, a union will negotiate the wages and employment conditions for all workers, both union and nonunion. However, employers often will be able to *indirectly* substitute nonunion for union workers. For example, as union wages rise, it may be economical for unionized firms to contract with nonunion firms to handle specific operations or supply various components used in production. Thus, contracting out often permits employers to indirectly substitute nonunion for union labor. Many large firms in automobile, textile, and other manufacturing industries operate both union and nonunion plants. They may be able to substitute nonunion for union labor by shifting more and more of their production to their nonunion plants, including those located overseas or in right-to-work states where unions are generally weaker.

ELASTICITY OF DEMAND FOR THE PRODUCTS OF UNIONIZED FIRMS

Wages are a component of costs. An increase in the wages of union members will almost surely lead to higher prices for goods produced with union labor. Unless the demand for the good produced by union labor is inelastic, the output produced by unionized firms will decline if the union pushes up wages (and costs). If a union is going to have a significant impact on wages, its workers must produce a good for which the demand is inelastic.

Our analysis implies that a union will be unable to significantly increase wages above the free market rate when producing a good that competes with similar (or identical) goods produced by nonunion labor or foreign producers. The demand for

---

[3]Alfred Marshall, *Principles of Economics,* 8th ed. (New York: Macmillan, 1920).

the good produced by union labor will almost surely be highly elastic when the same product is available from nonunion and foreign producers. Thus, if the union pushes up wages and costs, the market share of unionized firms will shrink and the employment of union labor will fall substantially.

Both past history and recent events are consistent with this view. In the 1920s, the United Mine Workers obtained big wage gains in unionized coal fields. The union, however, was unable to halt the growth of nonunion mining, particularly in the strip mines of the West. The unionized mines soon lost the major share of their market to nonunionized fields, leading to a sharp reduction in the employment of unionized miners.

More recently, the strength of the Teamster's union was substantially eroded when deregulation subjected the unionized segment of the trucking industry to much more intense competition from nonunion firms in the early 1980s. With deregulation, nonunion firms with lower labor costs entered the industry. Given their labor-cost advantage, many of the new entrants cut prices to gain a larger share of the market. The market share of the unionized firms declined. More than 100,000 Teamsters lost their jobs. Given the sharp reduction in the employment of their members, the Teamsters eventually agreed to wage concessions and a reduction in their fringe-benefit package.[4]

Unions sometimes negotiate substantial wage increases, even though they may eventually result in significant reductions in employment. This appears to be the case in both the steel and automobile industries. The hourly earnings of production workers in these two industries rose sharply *compared with other workers in the private sector* during the 1970s. By 1982, the average hourly earnings of steel workers were 74 percent greater than for all private-sector workers, up from a 19 percent premium in 1969. The parallel wage premium in the automobile industry was 51 percent in 1982, up from 21 percent in 1969. These substantial wage increases during the 1970s pushed up the costs of American steel and automobile producers relative to their foreign competitors. Foreign producers were able to capture a larger share of the U.S. market and, as a result, the employment of unionized labor in both the steel and automobile industries declined sharply. Between 1978 and 1982, membership in the United Steel Workers Union fell by 45 percent. The United Automobile Workers (UAW) lost 142,000 members, approximately 16 percent of their total, in the late 1970s and early 1980s. The experience of workers in both the steel and automobile industries provides vivid evidence that higher wages at unionized firms will mean less employment when the unionized firms compete with nonunion and foreign competitors.

UNION LABOR AS A SHARE OF COST OF PRODUCTION

If the unionized labor input comprises only a small share of total production cost, demand for that labor will tend to be relatively inelastic. For example, since the wages of plumbers and pilots comprise only a small share of the total cost of production in the housing and air travel industries, respectively, a doubling or even tripling of the wages of plumbers or airline pilots would result in only a 1 or 2 percent increase in the cost of housing or air travel. A large increase in the price of such inputs would have little impact on product price, output, and employment.

---

[4]A recent study found that after the deregulation of the trucking industry, the wage premium of unionized truckers fell from 48 percent to 30 percent in the *regulated* sector of the industry. See Barry Hirsch, "Trucking Regulation, Unionization, and Labor Earnings," *The Journal of Human Resources,* Vol. 23 (Summer 1988), pp. 296–319.

This factor has sometimes been called ''the importance of being unimportant,'' because it is important to the strength of the union.

THE SUPPLY ELASTICITY OF SUBSTITUTE INPUTS

We have just explained that if wage rates in the unionized sector are pushed upward, firms will look for substitute inputs, and the demand for these substitutes will increase. If the supply of these substitutes (such as nonunion labor) is inelastic, however, their price will rise sharply in response to an increase in demand. The higher price will reduce the attractiveness of the substitutes. An inelastic supply of substitutes will thus strengthen the union by making the demand for union labor more inelastic.

WAGES OF UNION AND NONUNION EMPLOYEES

The precise impact of unions on the wages of their members is not easy to determine. In order to isolate the union effect, differences in other factors must be eliminated. Comparisons must be made between union and nonunion workers who have similar productivity (skills) and who are working on similar jobs.

Numerous studies have examined the effect of unions on wages. The pioneering work in this area was a 1963 study by H. Gregg Lewis of the University of Chicago.[5] Lewis estimated that, on average, union workers during the 1950s received wages between 10 and 15 percent higher than those of nonunion workers with similar productivity characteristics. The findings of other researchers using data from the 1950s and 1960s are generally consistent with the early work of Lewis.[6]

In a 1986 work, Lewis reviewed the evidence from nearly 200 studies on this topic and used more recent data to develop estimates of the union wage premium for the 1960s and 1970s.[7] Exhibit 7 summarizes the findings of Lewis's work and projects his estimates up to 1988–1990. Research in this area indicates that the union-nonunion wage differential widened during the 1970s.[8] Lewis estimates that union workers received an 18 percent premium compared with similar nonunion workers during the 1976–1979 period, up from a 12 percent premium during 1967–1970. During the early 1980s, the wages of union workers continued to grow more rapidly than their nonunion counterparts, leading to an estimated 20 percent differential for 1980–1982. Since 1983, however, the trend has reversed—the wages of nonunion workers have increased more rapidly than those of unionized workers. As of 1990, most researchers in this area estimate that the premium of

[5]H. Gregg Lewis, *Unionism and Relative Wages in the United States* (Chicago: University of Chicago Press, 1963).

[6]See Albert Rees, *The Economics of Trade Unions* (Chicago: University of Chicago Press, 1967) and Michael J. Boskin, ''Unions and Relative Wages,'' *American Economic Review,* Vol. LXII (June, 1972), pp. 466–72.

[7]H. Gregg Lewis, *Union Relative Wage Effects: A Survey* (Chicago: University of Chicago Press, 1986).

[8]See William J. Moore and John Raision, ''The Level and Growth of Union/Nonunion Relative Wage Effects, 1967–1977,'' *Journal of Labor Research,* Vol. 4 (Winter, 1983), pp. 65–79; Richard B. Freeman and James L. Medoff, *What Do Unions Do?* (New York: Basic Books, 1984); and Barry T. Hirsch and John T. Addison, *The Economic Analysis of Unions: New Approaches and Evidence* (Boston: Allen & Unwin, 1986) for evidence on this point.

EXHIBIT 7

The Wage Premium of Union Workers, 1950–1990

Most studies indicate that the wages of union workers have been between 10 percent and 20 percent higher than similar nonunion workers during the last several decades. The union-nonunion wage differential widened during the 1970s, but it has declined since 1982. On average, union workers earned between 12 percent and 16 percent more than similar nonunion workers in the late 1980s.

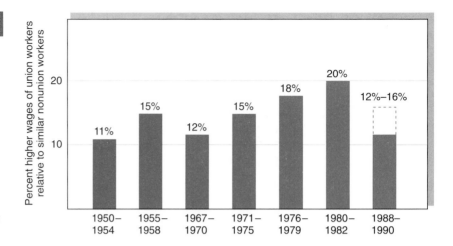

Source: H. Gregg Lewis, *Unionism and Relative Wages in the United States: An Empirical Inquiry* (Chicago: University of Chicago Press, 1963), p. 222; and H. Gregg Lewis, *Union Relative Wage Effects: A Survey* (Chicago: University of Chicago Press, 1986), p. 9. The 1980–1982 and 1988–1990 data are estimates by the authors based on the annual change in the Employment Cost Index of union and nonunion labor since 1979, as reported by the U.S. Department of Labor.

union members is in the 12 percent to 16 percent range, approximately the same as the estimated union-nonunion differential during the 1950–1975 period.[9]

Our theory indicates that some unions will be much stronger than others. Thus, there will be substantial variation in the ability of unions to achieve higher wages for their members. In some occupations, the size of the union-nonunion differential will be well above the average, while in other occupations, unions will exert little impact on wages.

Lewis estimated that strong unions, such as those of the electricians, plumbers, tool and die makers, metal craft workers, truckers (this was prior to the moves toward deregulation), and commercial airline pilots, were able to raise the wages of their members substantially more than the average for all unions. Other economists have also found substantial variation in the impact of unions on wages. In a study using 1973 data, Paul Ryscavage placed the union-nonunion wage differential at 29 percent for craft workers, 23 percent for operatives (machine operators), 44 percent for truck drivers (prior to deregulation) and 36 percent for laborers.[10]

Unionization appears to have had the least impact on the earnings of cotton textile, footwear, furniture, hosiery, clothing, and retail sales workers. In these areas, the power of the union has been substantially limited by the existence of a

---

[9]The studies referred to in the text compared the wages of similarly productive union and nonunion workers at a point in time. Another approach would be to compare the *change* in the wages of the same worker in cases where the worker moves from a union to a nonunion job and vice versa. Research using this approach has generally placed the union wage premium in the 10 percent range, somewhat smaller than the estimates derived from the cross-section studies. For evidence provided by studies using this methodology, see Wesley Mellow, "Unionism and Wages: A Longitudinal Analysis," *Review of Economics and Statistics,* Vol. 63 (February, 1981), pp. 43–52, and Richard B. Freeman, "Longitudinal Analysis and Trade Union Effects," *Journal of Labor Economics,* Vol. 2 (January, 1984), pp. 1–26.

[10]Paul M. Ryscavage, "Measuring Union-Nonunion Earnings Differences," *Monthly Labor Review,* Vol. 97 (December, 1974), pp. 3–9.

substantial number of nonunion plants in these industries. The demands of union workers in these industries are moderated by the fear of placing unionized employers at a competitive disadvantage in relation to the nonunion employers of the industry.

UNIONS, PROFITABILITY, AND EMPLOYMENT IN THE UNIONIZED SECTOR

If unions increase the wages of unionized firms above the competitive market level, the costs of those firms will rise unless (as seems unlikely) there is a corresponding increase in productivity. The higher costs will reduce the profitability of the unionized firm. Recent research indicates that this was true during the 1970s. Barry Hirsch of Florida State University found that as the union-nonunion wage premium increased during the 1970s, the profitability of unionized firms lagged behind the profitability of other firms.[11]

If unions are able to transfer profits from unionized firms to union workers, clearly this is a two-edged sword. In the long run, investment will move away from areas of low profitability. Like other mobile resources, capital may be exploited in the short run, but this will not be the case in the long run. Therefore, to the extent that the profits of unionized firms are lower, investment expenditures on fixed structures, research, and development will flow into the nonunion sector and away from unionized firms. As a result, the growth of both productivity and employment will tend to lag in the unionized sector. Investment, production, and employment will all shift away from unionized operations and toward nonunion firms.

The larger the wage premium of unionized firms, the greater the incentive to shift production toward nonunion operations. The recent findings of Linneman, Wachter, and Carter are highly supportive of this view.[12] They found that industries with the largest union wage premiums were precisely the industries with the largest declines in the employment of unionized workers. On the other hand, union employment tended to be either constant or increasing in those industries with only a small union wage premium. Viewed from this perspective, the sharp decline in union membership during recent years (see Exhibit 1) is at least partially the result of the union wage premium—and the increase in the size of that premium in important industries during the 1970s (see Exhibit 7).

IMPACT OF UNIONS ON THE WAGES OF ALL WORKERS

While unions have increased the average wages of their members, there is no reason to believe that they have increased the average overall compensation of workers—*both union and nonunion.* At first glance, this may seem paradoxical. However, the economic way of thinking enhances our understanding of this issue. As unions push wages up in the unionized sector, employers in this sector will hire fewer workers. Unable to find jobs in the high wage union sector, some employees will shift to the nonunion sector. This increase in labor supply will depress the wages of nonunion workers. Thus, higher wages for union members do not necessarily mean higher wages for *all* workers. (See accompanying Myths of Economics box for additional detail on this subject.)

With regard to the impact of unions on the overall level of wages, it is important to keep one other key point in mind. The general level of wages is dependent upon

---

[11]Barry Hirsch, *Labor Unions and the Economic Performance of Firms* (Kalamazoo, MI: Upjohn Institute for Employment Research, 1991). Also see Richard B. Freeman and James L. Medoff, *What Do Unions Do?* (New York: Basic Books, 1984), Chapter 12, for evidence that unions exert a negative impact on the profits of unionized firms.

[12]Peter D. Linneman, Michael L. Wachter, and William Carter, "Evaluating the Evidence on Union Employment and Wages," *Industrial and Labor Relations Review,* Vol. 44, (October, 1990).

MYTHS OF ECONOMICS

"Unions have increased the wages of workers and thereby expanded the share of income going to labor."

It is one thing for unions to increase the wages of *union members*. It is quite another for them to increase the wages of *all workers,* both nonunion and union. Neither economic theory nor empirical evidence indicates unions are able to increase the general level of wages. If unions were the primary source of high wages, the real wages of workers would be higher in highly unionized countries such as Australia, the United Kingdom, and most European countries than they are in the United States. But, this is not what we observe. For example, real wages are at least 40 percent lower in the United Kingdom than they are in the United States, even though half of the work force is unionized in the United Kingdom compared to less than 20 percent in the United States (see Exhibit 9).

The real source of high wages is high productivity, not labor unions. In turn, high productivity depends on abundant physical capital, the knowledge and skill of the work force, and institutional arrangements that encourage the creation of wealth.

To the extent unions increase the wages of union members, there is good reason to believe they do so primarily at the expense of nonunion workers. Higher union wages (and costs) will lead to a reduction in the output of products that intensively use union labor. This factor will cause employment in the unionized sectors to fall. What will happen to employees who are unable to find jobs in the unionized sector? They will compete for nonunion jobs, increasing supply and depressing nonunion wages. Labor economist Gregg Lewis has estimated that the real wages of nonunion workers, four-fifths of the labor force, are 3 to 4 percent lower than they would be in the absence of unionism.[13]

If labor unions increased the wages of all workers and therefore the share of income going to labor, we would expect labor's share of income to be directly related to union membership. Again, the evidence is inconsistent with this view. Exhibit 8 presents data on labor's share of income since 1930. Total employee compensation (including the social security contribution of the employer) has increased slightly since the Second World War. However, this is primarily a reflection of the decline in the number of self-employed persons in agriculture and the corresponding increase in the proportion of employed workers. Since the earnings of self-employed proprietors such as farmers, sales personnel, accountants, and small business operators emanate primarily from their labor services, a clearer picture of the labor-property owner components of income emerges when self-employment income is added to employee compensation. As Exhibit 8 shows, this measure of labor's share has been amazingly constant. Between 81 and 83 percent of national income in the United States has gone to labor

productivity—output of goods and services that people value. Income is simply the flip side of output. Increases in the general level of wages are dependent upon increases in productivity per hour. Of course, improvements in (a) technology, (b) the machines and tools available to workers (physical capital), (c) worker skills (human capital), and (d) the efficiency of economic organization provide the essential ingredients for higher levels of productivity. Higher real wages can be achieved only if the production of goods and services is expanded. Although unions can increase the wages of union workers, they cannot increase the wages of all workers unless their activities increase the total productivity of labor.

DO UNIONS CAUSE INFLATION?

Labor unions are often accused of pushing up wages and thereby triggering price increases that cause inflation. Inspection of this view, however, indicates that it

EXHIBIT 8

Labor's Share of National Income, 1930–1989

As a share of the nonfarm work force, union membership increased from less than 10 percent in the 1930s to nearly 35 percent in the mid-1950s. Since 1960, union membership has declined substantially as a proportion of the U.S. labor force (see Exhibit 1). Despite these fluctuations, the share of national income allocated to labor (employee compensation and self-employment income) has been virtually constant throughout the 1930–1989 period.

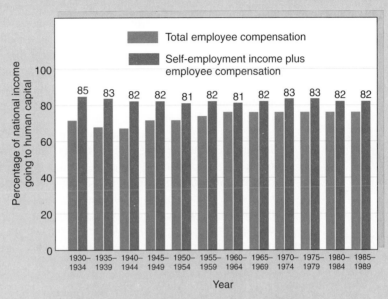

Source: Derived from the national estimates of the U.S. Department of Commerce published in *Survey of Current Business*.

during each five-year period since 1935. The share of national income going to labor did not rise as union membership grew as a proportion of the labor force during the 1935–1955 period. Neither has it fallen as union membership has declined since 1955.

In conclusion, while there is evidence that unions often increase the wages of their members, there is no evidence that they are able to increase the general level of real wages or the share of income earned by labor relative to physical capital.

[13]H. Gregg Lewis, *Unionism and Relative Wages in the United States* (Chicago: University of Chicago Press, 1963).

suffers from a major defect; it fails to incorporate the secondary effects of higher union wages. Let us consider this issue in more detail.

Suppose an economy were initially experiencing stable prices and the normal (natural) rate of unemployment. What would happen if a major union, that of the automobile workers, for example, used its economic power and the threat of a strike to obtain a very substantial increase in wages? The higher wages would trigger both direct and secondary effects. The increased labor costs would push up the prices of automobiles, trucks, and buses, particularly if imports could also be restrained. The direct effect of the higher automobile prices would be an increase in the consumer price index.

However, there would also be important secondary effects that are often overlooked. Confronting the higher automobile prices, consumers must either (a) purchase significantly fewer automobiles (quality-constant units) or (b) increase their expenditures on automobiles. To the extent that consumers purchased fewer (or less expensive) automobiles, the amount of labor services required by the automobile industry would decline. Automotive employment would fall (or at least expand by an abnormally small amount). Some workers who would have been able to find jobs in the automobile industry will now be forced into other lines of employment. The labor supply in these alternative employment areas would increase, placing *downward* pressure on wages and costs in these sectors.

On the other hand, if consumers increased their expenditures on automobiles, they would have less income to spend on other things. Consumers would be forced to cut back their spending in other areas. The demand for products, the consumption of which must now be forgone as a result of the increase in expenditures on automobiles, would decline. Market adjustments would place downward pressure on prices on these areas.

Clearly, neither of these secondary effects would trigger an inflationary spiral. In fact, quite the opposite is true. Both (a) and (b) would place downward pressure on costs and prices outside of the automobile industry, which would, at least partially, offset the impact of higher automobile prices on the general price level. Of course, relative prices would change. The prices of goods requiring the services of automobile workers would rise, but the prices (and costs) of other goods would decline (or rise less rapidly). Once we consider the secondary effects, there is no reason to expect that an increase in the wages of automobile or other unionized workers would trigger a sustained increase in the general price level.[14]

UNIONISM IN OTHER COUNTRIES

Exhibit 9 presents data on the level of unionism for several Western industrial economies. The data illustrates that union workers comprise a larger share of the labor force in other major industrial countries than they do in the United States. In 1986 and 1987, approximately half of the nonagricultural workers in both Australia and the United Kingdom were union members. The comparable figures in both Italy and Germany exceeded 40 percent. Correspondingly, unionization as a percent of the labor force in Canada and Japan was substantially greater than in the United States. Except for France, the degree of unionization in 1986–1987 in other major industrial countries was substantially greater than in the United States.

Not only is the rate of unionization higher in most other industrial countries, the gap has been widening. The share of the labor force that is unionized has been increasing or relatively constant in other large industrial countries (except for Japan), while the proportion has declined substantially in the United States.[15]

We must be cautious, however, in our interpretation of the international data on unionism. The role of unions varies substantially among countries. In Europe, unions are often more closely tied to a political party and are more heavily involved in political activities than unions in the United States. In contrast, unions are less

---

[14]For an in-depth analysis of the impact of unions on inflation, see Daniel J. Mitchell, *Unions, Wages, and Inflation* (Washington, D.C.: Brookings Institution, 1980).

[15]With regard to Canada, this statement should be qualified. Two-thirds of the public sector employees in Canada are unionized, compared to only 36.5 percent in the United States. Thus, much of the difference in unionization in Canada compared to the United States, is explained by the greater degree of public sector unionization in Canada. As in the United States, unionization in the *private sector* declined in Canada during the 1980s.

EXHIBIT 9 ■	Union Membership: An International Comparison	

	Union Membership as a Percent of Nonagricultural Employment	
Country	1970	1986–1987
Australia	52	56
United Kingdom	51	50
Italy	39	45
Germany	37	43
Canada	32	36
Japan	35	28
France	22	19
United States	31	17

Source: Richard B. Freeman, ''Contraction and Expansion: The Divergence of Private Sector and Public Sector Unionism in the United States,'' *Journal of Economic Perspectives* Vol. 2 (Spring, 1988), U.S. Department of Labor, Division of Foreign Labor Statistics, *Union Membership*, September 1988, and R. Bean (ed.), *International Labor Statistics: A Handbook, Guide, and Recent Trends* (London: Routledge, 1989).

political and more directly involved with the firm's personnel policies in Japan. Approximately 90 percent of the union members in Japan belong to an enterprise or ''company union,'' a type of organization that has been illegal in the United States since the passage of the Wagner Act in 1935. These variations in the role of unions contribute to the substantial differences in union membership among countries.

UNIONS AND THE NATURE OF THE WORKPLACE

If one talks to any worker long enough, and candidly enough, one discovers that his loyalty to the union is not simply economic. One may even be able to show him that, on a strictly cost-benefit analysis, measuring income lost from strikes and jobs lost as a result of contract terms, the cumulative economic benefits are delusions. It won't matter. In the end, he will tell you, the union is the only institution that ensures and protects his ''dignity'' as a worker.[16]

Irving Kristol

Economists generally focus on wages and employment when discussing the impact of unions. However, unions also exert important effects on the operation of the workplace and the *structure* of compensation. When evaluating the overall contribution and significance of unions, the following points should also be considered.

1. Unions Have Played a Central Role in the Development of Contractual or Formal Rules and Procedures that Govern Promotions, Raises, Layoffs, Terminations, and

---

[16]Irving Kristol, ''Understanding Trade Unionism,'' *Wall Street Journal* (October 23, 1978). Reprinted with permission of the *Wall Street Journal*.

Other Aspects of the Relationship Between Employers and Employees.   In essence, unions have established a system of "industrial jurisprudence" which protects workers against arbitrary actions by a supervisor or management representative. Labor contracts define a worker's rights and provide the worker with a series of industrial appeal courts. Specifically, a worker cannot be fired without good cause, which must be proved to the satisfaction of his or her union representative. Actions the worker considers arbitrary or unfair can be taken to a shop steward, appealed through labor-management channels, and eventually brought to an objective arbitrator. Production at multimillion-dollar plants has been brought to a halt because a single worker's rights, as specified by the collective bargaining agreement, were violated. In addition, these contractual procedures provide employers with a strong incentive to pay attention to the complaints of workers and to treat them with dignity.

The contribution of unions in this area may also enhance employer/employee relations in a nonunion setting. Many employers are anxious to avoid time-consuming procedures and inflexible rules that often accompany collective bargaining agreements. One of the best ways of doing that is to establish a positive work environment and open lines of communication with employees. Put another way, positive personnel relations deter union organizing. Thus, concern about possible unionization provides nonunion employers with a strong incentive to treat their employees right.

2.   Unions Tend to Elevate the Importance of Seniority.   In a union setting, employees with more seniority generally have more job security and protection than similar employees in a nonunion setting. Senior employees are also more likely to receive favorable treatment with regard to promotion. As a result of this emphasis on seniority, the managers of unionized firms generally have less opportunity for the subjective evaluation of employees than their nonunion counterparts. The greater weight given to seniority in the determination of wages in a union environment tends to reduce wage variation among workers. Thus, the *dispersion* of wages among workers in union plants is generally less than the *dispersion* in nonunion plants.

3.   In Unionized Firms, Fringe Benefits Usually Comprise a Larger Component of the Total Compensation Package than is True for Nonunion Firms.   Studies indicate that the fringe benefits of union employees, particularly deferred benefits for pensions and life, accident, and health insurance exceed the benefits of nonunion employees with similar pay rates. Senior union members are often more active and in positions of greater influence within the union than their younger counterparts. The higher pension and health benefits and greater protection against layoffs will also be particularly attractive to union members with substantial amounts of seniority.

4.   Unions Tend to Reduce the Turnover Rate of Employees.   Union employees are less likely to quit than their nonunion counterparts. This may partially reflect the union wage premium. But it may also reflect other factors. Freeman and Medoff argue that unions provide employees with a "collective voice" through which they can communicate their problems and grievances to management. This collective voice provides employees an alternative to quitting as a way for sending a message to management. The closer relationship between seniority and employee benefits (for example, pension benefits and job protection) in the unionized sector also reduces the incentive of employees to quit. These factors increase the work force stability of unionized firms relative to their nonunion counterpart. In turn, the greater stability reduces the firm's recruitment, hiring, and training costs. However, the more rigid system may also reduce the firm's ability to establish a close relationship between employee productivity and wage rates. Therefore, on balance, it is difficult to determine the impact of the unionized *wage structure* on the firm's costs.

Unions have played a central role in the shaping of the current work environment in both the union and nonunion sectors. Their role in the establishment of the governance system between employers and employees has been particularly important. In fact, many would argue that these nonwage effects of unions are even more important than their role in the determination of wage rates.

LOOKING AHEAD

The previous four chapters have analyzed markets for human and physical resources. Wages, prices, and employment levels in these markets determine our personal incomes. The next chapter will focus on the distribution of income among individuals.

CHAPTER SUMMARY

1. Union membership as a share of the nonagricultural labor force has fluctuated substantially during the last 80 years. During the 1910–1935 period, union workers generally comprised between 12 percent and 17 percent of the nonfarm labor force. Unionization increased rapidly during the 1935–1945 period, soaring to one-third of the nonfarm work force. Since the mid-1950s, union membership has waned. In 1990, only one in six nonfarm workers was a union member.

2. The strike is a major source of union power. A strike can cause the employer to lose sales while incurring continuing fixed cost. The threat of a strike, particularly when inventories are low, is an inducement for the employer to consent to the union's terms.

3. A strike is also costly to employees. Strike funds are usually inadequate to deal with a prolonged strike. The loss of just a few paychecks can impose extreme hardship on most families. The potential cost of a strike to both union and management provides each with an incentive to bargain seriously to avoid a work stoppage.

4. Agreement on most collective bargaining contracts is reached without a work stoppage. Since the Second World War, the number of work hours lost due to strikes is approximately one-tenth of one percent of the total work time—and the proportion of work time lost due to strikes has been declining.

5. There are three basic methods a union can use to increase the wages of its members: (a) restrict the supply of competitive inputs, including nonunion workers; (b) apply bargaining power enforced by a strike or threat of one; and (c) increase the demand for the labor service of union members.

6. When a large number of employers compete in the market for labor services, each employer will have to pay the market wage rate to keep employees from shifting to higher-wage alternatives. However, when monopsony is present, the single purchaser of labor may be able to profit by restricting employment and paying a wage rate that is less than the marginal revenue generated by the labor. Under these circumstances, a wage floor established by a union can result in both higher wages and increased employment.

7. If a union is going to increase the wages of its members without experiencing a significant reduction in employment, the demand for union labor must be inelastic. The strength of a union is enhanced if (a) there is an absence of good substitutes for this service, (b) the demand for the good it produces is highly inelastic, (c) the union labor input is a small share of the total cost of production, and/or (d) the supply of any available substitute is highly inelastic. An absence of these conditions weakens the power of the union.

8. Studies suggest that the wage premium of union members relative to similar nonunion workers increased during the 1970s, but declined during the 1980s. Most researchers placed the union-nonunion wage differential in the 12 percent to 16 percent range in 1990, down from approximately 20 percent in 1980.

9. Recent research indicates that the profitability of unionized firms is lower than the profitability of nonunion firms. Responding to the lower profitability rates, investment expenditures for fixed structures, research, and development have tended to flow into the nonunion sector and away from the unionized sector. As a result, employment in the unionized sector has declined, particularly in industries where the union wage premium is large.

10. Union workers are a substantially larger proportion of the work force in other industrial countries than they are in the United States. Since the role of unions varies among countries, this factor may contribute to the variation in the level of unionism among countries.

11. Even though unions have increased the average wage of their members, there is no indication that they have either increased the average wage of all workers or increased the share of national income going to labor (human capital rather than physical capital). Even though union membership rose sharply during the 1935–1955 period and declined sharply between 1975 and 1990, the share of national income going to labor (human capital) was virtually constant throughout the entire period. The real wages of workers are a reflection of their productivity rather than the share of the work force that is unionized. Thus, there is no relationship between the unionization of the labor force and real wages across countries.

12. An increase in the wages of union members will either reduce expenditures on goods produced by nonunion labor or increase the supply of nonunion labor. In either case, the secondary effects of higher union wages will tend to reduce prices in the nonunion sector. Thus, there is no reason to believe that unions cause sustained increases in the general price level (inflation).

13. Unions have played a central role in the development of the current system of industrial jurisprudence which governs the relationship between employers and employees. Many think that the positive role of unions in this area is as important, if not more important, than their role in the determination of wage rates.

CRITICAL ANALYSIS QUESTIONS

1. Assume that the primary objective of a union is to raise wages.
   a. Discuss the conditions that will help the union achieve this objective.
   b. Why might a union be unable to meet its goal?
*2. Suppose that Florida migrant farm workers are effectively unionized. What will be the impact of the unionization on (a) the price of Florida oranges, (b) the profits of Florida fruit growers in the short run and in the long run, (c) the mechanization of the fruit-picking industry, and (d) the employment of migrant farm workers?
*3. Unions in the North have been vigorously involved in efforts to organize lower-wage workers in the South. Union leaders often express their compassion for the low-money-wage southern workers. Can you think of a reason, other than

*Asterisk denotes questions for which answers are given in Appendix C, Selected Answers.

compassion, for northern union leaders' (and workers') interest in having the higher union scale extended to the South? Explain.

4. "Unions have brought a decent living to working men and women. Without unions, employers would still be paying workers a starvation wage." Analyze.

5. Evaluate the following statements.

   a. "An increase in the price of steel will be passed along to consumers in the form of higher prices for automobiles, homes, appliances, and other products made with steel." Do you agree or disagree?

   b. "An increase in the price of craft-union labor will be passed along to consumers in the form of higher prices of homes, repair and installation services, appliances, and other products that require craft-union labor." Do you agree or disagree?

   c. Are the interests of labor unions in conflict primarily with the interests of union employers? Explain.

6. "The purpose of unions is to push the wage rate above the competitive level. By their very nature, they are monopolists. Therefore, they will necessarily cause resources to be misallocated." Do you agree or disagree? Explain.

*7. "If a union is unable to organize all the major firms in an industry, it is unlikely to exert a major impact on the wages of union members." Indicate why you either agree or disagree.

8. The Retail Clerks Union has organized approximately one-third of the department stores in a large metropolitan area. Do you think the union will be able to significantly increase the wages of its members? Explain.

*9. "When an industry is highly unionized, higher labor costs will reduce industry profitability. Unions benefit workers at the expense of capitalists." True or false?

*10. "In the absence of unions, employers would be able to pay workers whatever they wanted." True or false?

11. Suppose that the United Automobile Workers (UAW) is able to substantially increase wages in the auto industry. What impact will the higher wages in the auto industry have on:

   a. the wages of nonunion workers outside of the automobile industry?

   b. the price of automobiles made by the UAW?

   c. the demand for foreign-produced automobiles?

   d. the profitability of U.S. automobile manufacturers?

*12. Even though the wage scale of union members is substantially greater than the minimum wage, unions have generally been at the forefront of those lobbying for higher minimum rates. Why do you think unions fight so hard for a higher minimum wage?

*13. Suppose that Congress were considering the following revenue measures: (a) a 10 cent per gallon increase in the gasoline tax or (b) an increase in the tariff (tax) on imported automobiles that would raise an equivalent amount of revenue. Which of the two options would the United Auto Workers be most likely to favor? Which would American automobile manufacturers be most likely to favor? Explain.

14. "Unions provide workers with protection against the greed of employers." Evaluate this statement. Be sure to consider the following questions:

   a. With whom do union workers compete?

   b. When union workers restrict entry into a market, who are they trying to keep out?

*15. A survey of firms in your local labor market reveals that the average hourly wage rate of unionized production workers is $1.50 higher than the average wage rate of nonunion production workers. Does this indicate that unionization increases the wage rates of workers in your area by $1.50? Why or why not?

27

Inequality, Income Mobility, and the Battle Against Poverty

All animals are equal, but some animals are more equal than others.[1]

George Orwell

CHAPTER FOCUS

- How much income inequality is there in the United States? What are the major factors that influence the distribution of income?

- Why has income inequality increased in recent years in the United States?

- How does the degree of income inequality in the United States compare with that of other countries?

- How much income mobility is there in the United States—do the rich remain rich while the poor remain poor?

- What are the characteristics of the poor? Have they changed in recent decades?

- How is the poverty rate derived? Have income transfers reduced the poverty rate?

*I*n a market economy, people have a strong incentive to produce goods and generate income. As we have explained, the personal income of market participants is determined by their productivity: those who use their human and physical resources to produce a lot of things that are highly valued by others will have very high incomes. The close link between personal prosperity and productivity provides market participants with a strong incentive to work, use their resources productively, and figure out better ways of doing things. Even Karl Marx acknowledged that market economies were enormously productive.

With markets, there is not a central distributing agency that carves up the economic pie and allocates slices to various individuals. Rather, the income of each individual is determined by what they receive from others in exchange for productive services or as a gift. But people differ with regard to their productive abilities, opportunities, preferences, and intestinal fortitude. Some will be able to hit a baseball, perform a rock concert, design a computer, or operate a restaurant so effectively that people will pay millions to consume their product. There will be others, however, with disabilities and few skills who may be unable to even support themselves. When markets are used to allocate resources, income inequality will result.

There is substantial income variation in all societies. Substituting politics and central planning for markets will not eliminate economic inequality. And, of course, differences in income provide individuals with productive incentives. Nonetheless, most of us are troubled by the extremes of inequality—extravagant luxury on the one hand and grinding poverty on the other. How much inequality is there in the United States? How do we measure poverty? How have income transfer programs influenced the distribution of income and the welfare of the poor? This chapter focuses on these questions and related issues.

INCOME INEQUALITY IN THE UNITED STATES

Money income is only one component of economic well-being. Such factors as leisure, noncash transfer benefits, the nonpecuniary advantages and disadvantages of a job, and the expected stability of future income are also determinants of economic welfare. Nevertheless, since money income represents command over market goods and services, it is highly significant. Moreover, it is readily observable. It is the most widely used measure of economic well-being and the degree of inequality.

Exhibit 1 indicates the share of *before-tax* annual money income received by quintile—that is, by each fifth of families ranked from the lowest to the highest. If there were total equality of annual income, each quintile (fifth) of the population would have received 20 percent of the aggregate income. Clearly that was not the case. In 1989, the bottom 20 percent of family income recipients received 4.6 percent of the total money income. At the other end of the spectrum, the 20 percent of families with the highest annual incomes received 44.6 percent of the total money income in 1989. The top quintile of income recipients thus received almost ten times as much money income as the bottom quintile of recipients.

---

[1]George Orwell, *Animal Farm* (New York: Harcourt Brace and Company, 1946), p. 112.

EXHIBIT 1 ■ Inequality in the Money Income of Families—Selected Years 1935–1989					
	Percentage of Before-Tax Aggregate Money Income Received by:				
	Lowest 20 Percent of Recipients	Second Quintile	Third Quintile	Fourth Quintile	Top 20 Percent of Recipients
1935–1936	4.1	9.2	14.1	20.9	51.7
1950	4.5	12.0	17.4	23.4	42.7
1960	4.8	12.2	17.8	24.0	41.3
1970	5.4	12.2	17.6	23.8	40.9
1980	5.2	11.5	17.5	24.3	41.5
1985	4.7	10.9	16.8	24.1	43.5
1989	4.6	10.6	16.5	23.7	44.6

Source: Bureau of the Census, *Current Population Reports*, Series P-60, No. 167 (Table 10) and No. 168 (Table 6).

As Exhibit 1 illustrates, there was a substantial reduction in income inequality between the mid-1930s and 1950. In 1950, the top five percent of recipients received 42.7 percent of the aggregate money income, down from 51.7 percent in the mid-1930s. Simultaneously, the income shares of the other quintile groupings increased during the 1935–1950 period. The trend toward less income inequality among families continued, albeit at a slower pace, during the 1950s and 1960s. By 1970, the income share earned by the bottom 20 percent of recipients had risen to 5.4 percent, up from 4.5 percent in 1950. Correspondingly, the income share of the top quintile declined from 42.7 percent in 1950 to 40.9 percent in 1970.

Since 1970, the trend toward less income inequality has reversed. The income share of the lowest quintile of income recipients fell to 4.6 percent in 1989, well below the 1970 figure. Simultaneously, the income share received by the top quintile of earners rose from 40.9 percent in 1970 to 44.6 percent in 1989. Because of the trend reversal during the 1970s and 1980s, the income shares received by each quintile grouping were approximately the same in 1989 as they were in 1950.

Two points emerge from Exhibit 1. First, there is a great deal of inequality in annual income in the United States. Second, after four decades of movement toward greater equality in family income, the trend has reversed. Inequality in income in the United States has increased since 1970.

A CLOSER LOOK AT THE FACTORS INFLUENCING THE INCOME DISTRIBUTION

How meaningful are the data of Exhibit 1? If all families were similar except in the amount of income received, the use of annual income data as an index of inequality would be far more defensible. However, this is not the case. The aggregate data lump together (a) small and large families, (b) prime-age earners and elderly retirees, (c) multi-earner families and families without any current earners, and (d) husband-wife families and single-parent families. Even if individual incomes over a lifetime were exactly equal, these factors would result in substantial inequality of annual income.

Consider just one factor, the impact of age, on the pattern of lifetime income. Typically, the annual income of young people is low, particularly if they are going to school or acquiring training. Many persons under 25 years of age studying to be lawyers, doctors, engineers, and economists will have a low annual income during this phase of their life. This does not mean they are poor, however, at least not in

EXHIBIT 2 ▫ The Differing Characteristics of High- and Low-Income Families, 1989		
	Bottom 20 Percent of Income Recipients, 1989	Top 20 Percent of Income Recipients, 1989
Mean years of schooling (household head)	10.3	14.7
Age of household head (percent distribution)		
Under 35	36	14
35–64	40	78
65 and over	24	8
Family status		
Married-couple family (percent of total)	52	94
Single-parent family (percent of total)	48	6
Persons per family	2.93	3.41
Earners per family	.82	2.31
Full-time earners per family	.37	1.84
Percent of married-couple families in which wife works	30	78
Percent of total weeks worked supplied by group	7	31

Source: U.S. Department of Commerce, *Money Income of Households, Families, and Persons in the United States: 1989,* Washington, D.C.: U.S. Government Printing Office, 1990.

the usual sense. After completing their formal education and acquiring work experience, individuals move into their prime working years. During this phase of life, annual income is generally quite high, particularly for families in which both husband and wife work. It is, however, also a time period when families are purchasing houses and providing for children. All things considered, annual income during the prime working years tends to overstate the economic well-being of most households. Finally, there is the retirement phase, characterized by less work, more leisure, and smaller family size. Even families who are quite well off tend to experience income well below the average for the entire population during the retirement phase.

Exhibit 2 highlights major differences between high- and low-income families that underlie the distributional data of Exhibit 1. The typical high-income family (top 20 percent) was headed by a well-educated person in the prime working-age phase of life whose income was supplemented with the earnings of other family members, particularly working wives. In contrast, persons with little education, nonworking retirees, younger workers (under age 35), and single-parent families are substantially overrepresented among low-income families (bottom 20 percent of income recipients). The mean number of years of schooling for the household heads of high-income families was 14.7 years, compared with only 10.3 years for heads of families with low annual incomes. Seventy-eight percent of the high-income families had household heads in the prime working age category (age 35 to 64), compared with only 40 percent of the low-income families. Only one parent was present in 48 percent of the low-income families, whereas 94 percent of the high-income group were husband-wife families. Contrary to the views of some, high-income families are larger than low-income families. In 1989, there were 3.41 persons per family in the top income quintile, compared to only 2.93 family members among the bottom quintile of income recipients.

There was a striking difference in the work time between low- and high-income families. No doubt, much of this difference reflected factors such as family size, age, working wives, and the incidence of husband-wife families. In high-income families, the average number of workers per family was 2.31, compared with .82 for low-income families. The difference was still greater for full-time workers. On average, there were 1.84 full-time workers per high-income family, compared with only .37 for low-income families. Thus, there were five times as many full-time workers per family among the high-income group as among the bottom quintile of income recipients. Seventy-eight percent of the high-income families were characterized by a working wife, compared with only 30 percent for low-income married families.

The top 20 percent of income recipients contributed 31 percent of the total number of weeks worked, while the low-income group contributed only 7 percent of the total work time. Thus, high-income families worked 4.4 times as many weeks as low-income families and earned almost 10 times as much income. This implies that the *earnings per week worked* of the top income recipients were only slightly greater than twice the *earnings per week worked* of the low-income recipients. Clearly, differences in the amount of time worked were a major factor contributing to the income inequality of Exhibit 1.

In summary, Exhibit 2 sheds substantial light on the distributional data of Exhibit 1. The high-income recipients were better educated, more likely to be in their prime working years, and they worked approximately 4.4 times as many weeks as low-income families in 1989. Given these factors, it is not surprising that the top 20 percent of recipients had substantially higher annual incomes than the bottom quintile.

The income data of Exhibit 1 represent income *before taxes*. Noncash income transfers are excluded. Families of varying size and at various stages of their lifetime earnings are lumped together. Suppose these factors were taken into account—that income comparisons were made *after taxes and noncash transfers* for families of the same size and age of household head. How much inequality would still be present?

A detailed study by Edgar Browning and William Johnson addresses this question. Browning and Johnson investigated the distribution of annual income after taxes and noncash transfers for three-person households headed by a 35- to 44-year-old.[2] With progressive taxation, taxes take a larger share of the income as income increases. Correspondingly, low-income households are the primary beneficiaries of noncash transfer programs which provide people with food (food stamps), health care, and housing. Before taxes, the top quintile of families in the study by Browning and Johnson received 41.0 percent of the aggregate income, compared with only 5.3 percent for the lowest one-fifth of income recipients. Thus, the degree of income inequality of the families in their study was similar to that of Exhibit 1. *After taxes and transfers,* the aggregate net income of the bottom quintile

[2]See Edgar K. Browning and William R. Johnson, *The Distribution of the Tax Burden* (Washington, D.C.: American Enterprise Institute, 1979).

rose to 9.2 percent, while the income share of the top quintile fell to 36.3 percent. Therefore, the top quintile received approximately 4 times the annual net income of the bottom 20 percent of recipients, compared with 8 times the amount of their income prior to taxes and transfers.

WHY HAS INCOME INEQUALITY INCREASED?

Exhibit 1 indicates that there has been an increase in income inequality in the United States during the last couple of decades. Why has the gap between the rich and the poor been growing? The answer to this question is a point of controversy among social scientists. No single factor can be isolated. Research in this area, however, indicates that at least three factors contributed substantially to the recent shift toward greater inequality.

1. The Increasing Proportion of Single Parent and Dual-Earner Families Has Contributed to the Increase in the Inequality of Family Income. The nature of the family and the allocation of work responsibilities within the family has changed dramatically in recent decades. In 1989, slightly more than one-fifth of all families were headed by a single parent, approximately double the figure of the mid-1960s. Simultaneously, the labor force participation rate of *married* women has approximately doubled during the last 25 years.

By way of comparison with the late 1960s and early 1970s, we now have both more single-parent families and more dual-earner families. Both of these changes tend to promote income inequality. Perhaps an example will illustrate why. Consider two hypothetical families, the Smiths and the Browns. In 1970, both were middle income families with two children and one market worker earning $30,000 (in 1990 dollars). Now consider their 1990 counterparts. The Smiths of 1990 are divorced and one of them, usually Mrs. Smith, is trying to work part-time and take care of the two children. The probability is very high that the single-parent Smith family of 1990 will be in the low, rather than middle, income category. They may well be in the bottom quintile of the income distribution. In contrast, the Browns of 1990 both work outside of the home and each earns $30,000 annually. Given their dual incomes, the Browns are now a high (rather than middle) income family. Along with many other dual-income families (see Exhibit 2), the Browns' 1990 family income will probably place them in the top quintile of income recipients.

Even if there were no changes in earnings between skilled and less-skilled workers, the recent changes within the family would enhance income inequality among families and households. More single-parent families like the Smiths increase the number of families with low incomes, while more dual-earner families like the Browns increase the number of high-income families. Both will promote income inequality.

2. Earnings Differentials between Skilled and Less-Skilled Workers Have Increased in Recent Years, Further Magnifying Income Inequality. In 1970, workers with little education who were willing to work hard, often in a hot and sweaty environment, were able to command high wages. This is less true today. Throughout the 1950s and 1960s, guidance counselors told high school students that a college education was essential for economic success. For a long time, it appeared that they were wrong. As Exhibit 3 shows, in 1974 the annual earnings of men who graduated from college were only 27 percent higher than the earnings of male high school graduates, hardly a huge payoff for the time and cost of a college degree. Since 1974, however, things have changed dramatically. By the late 1980s, the earnings

EXHIBIT 3 ■ The Increasing Earnings Differences According to Educational Attainment				
	Percent that Median Income of College Graduates Exceeds Median Income of High School Graduates		Percent that Median Income of High School Graduates Exceeds Median Income of Persons with 9 to 11 Years of Schooling	
Year	Males	Females	Males	Females
1974	27	54	27	34
1980	35	63	40	39
1984	49	74	50	41
1986	60	93	48	43
1988	53	89	51	55

Source: U.S. Commerce Department, Current Population Reports, Series P-60, No. 167, *Trends in Income, by Selected Characteristics: 1947 to 1988*, Table 50.

premium of college graduates relative to high school grads had risen to the 50 to 60 percent range, approximately twice the premium of 1974. Similarly, the earnings of women college graduates increased sharply relative to women with only a high school education during the 1974–1988 period.

Changes in the income of high school dropouts (persons with 9 to 11 years of schooling) relative to high school graduates provide further proof that income differences across skill categories have increased in recent years. While the earnings of high school graduates declined relative to college graduates in the late 1970s and early 1980s, they increased (for both men and women) relative to persons with only 9 to 11 years of schooling during the same time period (see Exhibit 3).

Why have the earnings of persons with more education (and skill) risen relative to those with less education (and skill)? Deregulation of the transport industry and the waning power of unions may have reduced the number of high-wage, blue-collar jobs available to workers with little education. No doubt, international competition has also played an important role here. Increasingly, American workers compete in a global economy. Recent innovations and cost reductions in both communications and transportation provide firms with greater flexibility with regard to location. Firms producing goods that require substantial amounts of low-skill labor are now better able to move to places such as Korea, Taiwan, and Mexico, where low-skill labor is cheaper. As firms using lots of low-skill labor move overseas, both the demand for and earnings of Americans with few skills and little education will decline. In an international setting, the U.S. will be far more attractive to firms requiring substantial amounts of high-skill, well-educated workers. Thus, the globalization of our economy tends to expand the earnings differences across skill categories in the United States.

3. As Marginal Tax Rates Were Reduced During the 1980s, the Observed Incomes of High-Income Americans Increased Sharply Because They Had More Incentive to Earn and Less Incentive to Engage in Tax Shelter Activities. Prior to 1981, high-income Americans confronted top marginal tax rates of up to 70 percent (50 percent on earnings). Such high marginal tax rates encouraged high-income earners to undertake investments and structure their business affairs in a manner that sheltered much of their income from the Internal Revenue Service. As we indicated in Chapter 5 (see pp. 117–20), the taxable incomes of the top 10 percent of earners expanded sharply when the top marginal tax rates were reduced to the 30 percent range during the 1980s. Some of this increase in income reflected greater work effort due to the increased incentive to earn. Much of it, however, merely reflected a reduction in tax shelter activities in response to the lower marginal tax rates. The flip side of the reduction in tax shelter activities accompanying the lower marginal tax rates of the 1980s was an increase in the *visible* income of the rich. In essence, after the rate cuts, the earnings of the rich were more readily observable. To the extent this factor contributed to the increase in the measured income of wealthy Americans, the increase in income inequality was more imaginary than real.

INCOME INEQUALITY IN OTHER COUNTRIES

How does income inequality in the United States compare with that in other nations? Exhibit 4 presents a summary of household income data compiled by the World

EXHIBIT 4 ■ Equality and Inequality Around the World			
	Percentage Share of Household Income Received by:		
Country (Year)	Bottom 20 Percent	Middle Three Quintiles	Top 20 Percent
Developing Nations			
India (1983)	8.1	50.5	41.4
Malaysia (1987)	4.6	44.2	51.2
Indonesia (1987)	8.8	49.9	41.3
Venezuela (1987)	4.7	44.7	50.6
Brazil (1983)	2.4	35.0	62.6
Colombia (1988)	4.0	43.0	53.0
Peru (1985)	4.4	43.7	51.9
South Korea (1981)	8.0	52.4	39.6
Mexico (1977)	2.9	39.4	57.7
Yugoslavia (1987)	6.1	51.1	42.8
Israel (1979–80)	6.0	54.1	39.9
Hong Kong (1980)	5.4	47.6	47.0
Developed Nations			
Sweden (1981)	7.4	50.9	41.7
United Kingdom (1982)	6.8	53.7	39.5
Japan (1979)	8.7	53.8	37.5
France (1979)	6.3	52.9	40.8
Germany (1984)	6.8	54.5	38.7
Canada (1987)	5.7	54.1	40.2
Switzerland (1982)	5.2	50.2	44.6
United States (1985)	4.7	53.4	41.9

Source: The World Bank, *World Development Report, 1990*, Table 30.

Bank. These data indicate that the degree of income inequality in the United States exceeds that of most other large industrial economies. Among the developed nations, income appears to be most equally distributed in Japan, Sweden, France, Germany (prior to unification) and the United Kingdom. In light of their relatively homogeneous populations—that is, uniformity with respect to race and ethnicity—and welfare state policies (except for Japan), the lesser degree of inequality in these countries is not surprising.[3]

The share of income going to the wealthy is usually greater in less developed countries. According to the World Bank study, the top 20 percent of income recipients received 62.6 percent of the aggregate income in Brazil, 57.7 percent in Mexico, 53 percent in Colombia, 51.9 percent in Peru, and 51.2 percent in Malaysia. Among the developing nations of Exhibit 4, India, Indonesia, South Korea, Yugoslavia, and Israel were marked by a degree of inequality similar to that of developed countries.

The data of Exhibit 4 are not adjusted for either differences across countries in size of households or the demographic composition of the population. In addition, procedures used to make the estimates and the reliability of the data vary across countries. Thus, these data should be interpreted with a degree of caution.

INCOME MOBILITY—DO THE POOR STAY POOR AND THE RICH STAY RICH?

Income Mobility: Movement of individuals and families either up or down income distribution rankings when comparisons are made at two different points in time. When substantial income mobility is present, one's current position will not be a very good indicator as to what one's position will be a few years in the future.

The distribution of annual income is like a snapshot. It presents a picture at a moment in time. However, since the picture does not reveal the degree of movement across income groupings, it may be misleading. Consider two countries with identical distributions of annual income.[4] In both cases, the annual income of the top quintile of income recipients is 8 times greater than the bottom quintile. Now, suppose that in the first country—we will refer to it as Static—the same people are at the top of the income distribution year after year. Similarly, the poor people of Static remain poor year after year. Static is characterized by an absence of **income mobility.** In contrast, earners in the second country, which we will call Dynamic, are constantly changing places. Indeed, every five years, each family spends one year in the upper-income quintile, one year in each of the three middle-income quintiles, and one year in the bottom-income quintile. In Dynamic, no one is rich for more than one year (out of each five) and no one is poor for more than a year. Obviously, the degree of economic inequality in Static and Dynamic is vastly different. You would not know it, though, by looking at their annual income distributions. In fact, the annual income distributions in the two countries are identical.

The contrast between Static and Dynamic indicates why it is important to consider income mobility when addressing the issue of economic inequality. Until

---

[3]See Gir S. Gupta and Ram D. Singh, ''Income Inequality Across Nations Over Time: How Much and Why,'' *Southern Economic Journal* 51 (July 1984), pp. 250–57 for an analysis of factors that influence income inequality among countries.

[4]The authors are indebted to Mark Lilla from whom this illustrative method was drawn. See Mark Lilla, ''Why the 'Income Distribution' Is So Misleading,'' *The Public Interest*, 77 (Fall 1984), pp. 63–76.

EXHIBIT 5 ■ Income Mobility—Family Income Ranking in 1984 Compared with Ranking in 1980						
Family Income Quintile, 1980	*Family Income Quintile, 1984*					
	Highest	Second	Third	Fourth	Lowest	Total
Highest	62.0	23.6	8.4	3.7	2.3	100%
Second	26.6	36.9	23.6	8.9	4.0	100%
Third	6.0	26.5	35.8	23.4	8.3	100%
Fourth	4.0	9.3	23.9	41.9	20.8	100%
Lowest	1.4	4.0	8.2	22.1	64.5	100%

Source: These data were supplied by the Institute for Social Research at the University of Michigan. An earlier version of this table was included in Greg J. Duncan et al., *Years of Poverty, Years of Plenty* (Ann Arbor: Institute of Social Research, 1984).

recently, detailed data on income mobility were sparse. Fortunately, this situation is changing, primarily as the result of a group of researchers at the University of Michigan's Survey Research Center. Under the direction of James Morgan and Greg Duncan, the Center collects detailed socioeconomic data on a representative sample of the U.S. population and tracks the same individuals and their families each year. With these data, it is now possible to see how income and other indicators of economic status change with time.

Since 1968, the University of Michigan has published panel income data that allow us to follow the income of families from year to year.[5] Exhibit 5 summarizes the major findings of the study with regard to income mobility. After grouping families by their income in 1980, the table then looks at the relative income position of the families four years later. For example, the first row indicates the relative income position in 1984 of families who were in the top quintile of income recipients in 1980. Surprisingly, only 62 percent of the Americans who were best off (the top quintile) in 1980 were able to retain the same position just four years later. Nearly 15 percent fell to the bottom three quintiles of the 1984 income distribution. The bottom row of Exhibit 5 tracks the experience of families in the lowest-income quintile in 1980. A little less than two-thirds (64.5 percent) of the families in the bottom-income quintile in 1980 remained there in 1984. On the other hand, 13.6 percent of the families at the bottom in 1980 were able to move into one of the top three income quintiles by 1984.

The diagonal (color) numbers of Exhibit 5 provide a measure of income mobility. If there were little or no income mobility within the American system, each diagonal number would be close to 100 percent. For the three middle-income quintiles, the diagonal numbers are approximately 40 percent, indicating that roughly two-fifths of the persons in each of these quintiles remained in the same quintile. Nearly three-fifths moved either up or down the income ladder between 1980 and 1984.

The data of Exhibit 5 focus on changes in the income of families. What can we say about income mobility across generations? If your parents are poor (or wealthy), does it mean you will be poor (or wealthy)? The Michigan panel data are just now

---

[5]Greg J. Duncan et al., *Years of Poverty, Years of Plenty: The Changing Fortunes of American Workers and Families* (Ann Arbor: Institute for Social Research, University of Michigan, 1984). Also see Bradley R. Schiller, "Relative Earnings Mobility in the United States," *American Economic Review*, vol. 67, no 5 (1977), pp. 926–39 for an earlier pioneer study of income mobility.

starting to yield information related to this issue. Nearly 1,500 young adults in the study have now left their parents and formed families of their own. Among those who came from families with incomes in the top quintile, 36 percent were able to attain this lofty ranking relative to the other newly formed families. In contrast, 41 percent of the offspring of families in the highest-income quintile fell to the bottom three income quintiles among the newly formed families. Among the offspring of poor families, less than half (44 percent) remained in the bottom quintile among the newly formed families. For middle-income families (the three middle quintiles), offspring were spread almost evenly among the five quintiles of the income distribution for newly formed families.

The data thus indicate that while high-income families are able to influence the economic status of their offspring, they are unable to pass along their lofty income position to most of their children. Similarly, the children of low-income families face disadvantages but they frequently achieve income levels well above those of their parents. For the three middle-income quintiles, parents fail to exert a systematic impact on the success or failure of their children. Thus, the *intergenerational* distribution of income approaches perfect mobility among the middle-income groupings.

The findings of the Michigan panel data are highly consistent with the findings of Christopher Jencks, based on a less detailed, but much earlier study by the Center for Educational Policy Research at Harvard. Writing in 1972, Jencks stated:

> Among men born into the most affluent fifth of the population . . . we estimate that less than half will be part of the same elite when they grow up. Of course, it is also true that very few will be in the bottom fifth. Rich parents can at least guarantee their children that much. Yet, if we follow families over several generations, even this will not hold true. Affluent families often have at least one relatively indigent grandparent in their background, and poor families, unless they are black or relatively recent immigrants, have often had at least one prosperous grandparent.[6]

Our analysis indicates that drawing conclusions from *annual* income data must be done with care. The annual data camouflage the fact that many high-income earners had much lower incomes just a few years before. Similarly, many with low current incomes have attained significantly higher incomes previously (and they can be expected to do so again in the future). Panel income data indicate that the inequalities observed at a point in time are substantially reduced over time as individuals and families exchange relative economic positions. This income mobility is particularly important across generations. The ability of American parents to pass along their economic status to their children is quite limited.

POVERTY IN THE UNITED STATES

In an affluent society such as the United States, income inequality and poverty are related issues. Poverty could be defined in strictly relative terms—the bottom one

---

[6]Excerpt from Christopher Jencks et al., *Inequality: Reassessment of the Effect of Family and Schooling in America,* (New York: Basic Books, Inc. 1972), p. 216.

MEASURES OF ECONOMIC ACTIVITY

Determining the Poverty Rate

Families and individuals are classified as poor or nonpoor based on the poverty threshold income level originally developed by the Social Security Administration (SSA) in 1964. Since consumption survey data indicated that low- and median-income families of three or more persons spent approximately one-third of their income on food, the SSA established the poverty threshold income level at three times the cost of an economical, nutritionally adequate, food plan. A slightly larger multiple was used for smaller families and individuals living alone. The poverty threshold income varies according to family size, because the food costs vary by family size and composition. The poverty threshold income level is adjusted annually to account for rising prices. The chart below illustrates how the poverty threshold for a family of four has increased as prices have risen:

Year	Poverty Threshold Income Level for a Family of Four
1959	$ 2,973
1970	3,968
1980	8,414
1990	13,360

Even though the poverty threshold income level is adjusted for prices, it is actually an *absolute* measure of economic status. As real income increases, the poverty threshold income will decline relative to the income of the general populace.

The official poverty rate is the *number of persons or families* living in households with a money income *below* the poverty income threshold *as a proportion of the total*. When determining a person's or family's income, the official poverty rate considers only money income. Income received in the form of *noncash* benefits such as food stamps, medical care, and housing subsidies, is completely ignored in the calculation of the official poverty rate.

Since noncash benefits targeted for low-income households have grown rapidly since the late 1960s, the failure of the official poverty rate to count this "income" reduces its accuracy as a measurement tool. To remedy this deficiency, Congress instructed the Bureau of Census to develop a poverty index that included noncash benefits as income. In addition to the official poverty rate, the Bureau now publishes annual

data for three "adjusted" poverty rates based on alternative methods of accounting for noncash benefits. Economists generally favor the use of the recipient value-adjusted poverty rate. This method values noncash benefits at the equivalent amount of cash income a recipient would be willing to exchange for the noncash benefits. It thus takes into account the possibility that recipients might rather have cash than the in-kind benefits.

When the value of noncash benefits is added to money income, the *adjusted* poverty rate for all age groups is reduced. For example, while the official poverty rate for families was 10.8 percent in 1989, the adjusted poverty rate based on the recipient value method of evaluating food, housing, and medical benefits was only 8.8 percent.

The poverty rate is calculated each year based on a current population survey of nearly 60,000 households designed to reflect the population of the United States. The most comprehensive source for detailed data on this topic is the Bureau of Census publication, "Money Income and Poverty Status in The United States" (annual).

Poverty Threshold Income Level: The level of money income below which a family is considered to be poor. It differs according to family characteristics (for example, number of family members) and is adjusted when consumer prices change.

fifth of all income recipients, for example. However, this definition would not be very helpful, since that would mean that poverty could never decline.

The official definition of poverty in the United States is based on the perceived minimum income necessary to provide food, clothing, shelter, and basic necessities economically for a family. This **poverty threshold income level** varies with family size and composition. The poverty threshold income is adjusted annually for changes in prices. For purposes of determining whether or not income is above the poverty threshold, the official poverty rate considers only money income. (See the Measures of Economic Activity box for additional details on how the poverty rate is measured.)

How many people are poor? According to the official definition of poverty, there were 31.5 million poor people and 6.8 million poor families in 1989. As Exhibit 6 indicates, 12.8 percent of the population and 10.3 percent of the families were officially classified as poor in 1989. During the 1950s and 1960s, the poverty rate declined substantially. By 1970, the official poverty rate for families had fallen to 10.1 percent, down from 18.1 percent in 1960 and 32.0 percent in 1947. During the 1970s, the overall poverty rate changed little. In fact, the official poverty rate was slightly higher in 1980 than it was in 1970. During the early 1980s, the poverty rate rose. Most commentators point to the stagnating economy during 1979–1982 and to cutbacks in transfer programs during the early years of the Reagan Administration as the source of the rising poverty rates in the 1980s. As we proceed, we will investigate the link between poverty and income transfers in more detail.

In recent years, the composition of the poverty population has changed substantially. As Exhibit 7 indicates, elderly persons and the working poor formed the core of the poverty population in 1959. Twenty-two percent of the poor families were headed by an elderly person in 1959. Most poor people (70 percent) worked at least some part of the year. By 1989, the picture had changed dramatically. In 1989, only 10 percent of the poor families were headed by an elderly person. In recent years, there has been a substantial growth in the proportion of female-headed families and an accompanying decline in the proportion of husband-wife families. Since the poverty rate of female-headed families is several times higher than the rate for husband-wife families (32.2 percent compared with 5.6 percent in 1989), an increase in family instability tends to push the poverty rate upward. In 1989, more than half (52 percent) of the poor families were headed by a female, compared with only 23 percent in 1959. Many of these women were not in the work force. As a result, only 49 percent of the heads of poor households worked at all during 1989, compared with 70 percent who worked in 1959.

The poverty rate of blacks in 1989 was 27.8 percent compared to 7.8 percent for whites. Nonetheless, 69 percent of the poor people in the United States were white. Perhaps the most tragic consequence of poverty is its impact on children. During the last two decades, the poverty rate among children has increased substantially. Nineteen percent of the children in the United States lived in poverty in 1989, up from 14.9 percent in 1976.

EXHIBIT 6 ■ The Poverty Rate of Persons and Families in the United States, 1947–1989		
	Poverty Rate (Percent)	
Year	Persons	Families
1947	n.a.	32.0
1960	22.2	18.1
1970	12.6	10.1
1980	13.0	10.3
1985	14.0	11.4
1987	13.4	10.7
1989	12.8	10.3

Source: Bureau of the Census, *Money Income and Poverty Status in the United States: 1989* (Tables 18 and 21), and *Economic Report of the President 1964* (Table 7).

TRANSFER PAYMENTS AND THE POVERTY RATE

In the mid-1960s, it was widely believed that an increase in income transfers directed toward the poor would substantially reduce, if not eliminate, the incidence of poverty. The *1964 Economic Report of the President* (p. 77) presented the dominant view. The report stated:

> Conquest of poverty is well within our power. About $11 billion [approximately $44 billion measured in 1990 dollars] a year would bring all poor families up to the $3,000 income level we have taken to be the minimum for a decent life. The majority of the nation could simply tax themselves enough to provide the necessary income supplements to their less fortunate citizens. The burden—one fifth of the annual defense budget, less than 2 percent of GNP—would certainly not be intolerable.

The 1965–1975 period was characterized by a rapid growth in income transfer programs. Overall transfers, including those directed toward the elderly, approximately doubled *as a proportion of personal income* between 1965 and 1975. As the War on Poverty programs of the Johnson administration were put in place, income transfers directed toward the poor also grew rapidly. Measured in 1987 dollars, **means-tested income transfers** tripled, expanding from $28 billion in 1965 to $79.6 billion in 1975 (Exhibit 8). As a proportion of personal income, means-tested transfers jumped from 1.5 percent in 1965 to 3.0 percent in 1975.

Means-Tested Income Transfers: Transfers that are limited to persons or families with an income below a certain cut-off point. Eligibility is thus dependent on low-income status.

Did the expansion in government income transfers reduce the poverty rate as the *1964 Economic Report of the President* anticipated? Exhibits 9 and 10 shed light on this question. Continuing the trend of the post-Second World War era, the official poverty rate fell throughout the 1960s. During the 1970s, however, the rate

EXHIBIT 7 ■ The Changing Composition of the Poor and the Poverty Rate of Selected Groups: 1959, 1976, and 1989			
	1959	1976	1989
Number of Poor Families (in millions)	8.3	5.3	6.8
Percent of Poor Families Headed by a:			
Female	23	48	52
Black	26	30	31
Elderly person (age 65 and over)	22	14	10
Prime working-age (25–64) person	57	72	77
Person who worked at least some during the year	70	55	49
Poverty Rate			
All families	18.5	10.1	10.3
Married-couple families	15.8	7.2	5.6
Female-headed families	42.6	32.5	32.2
Whites	16.5	8.1	7.8
Blacks	54.9	32.2	27.8
Children (under age 18)	26.9	14.9	19.0

Source: U.S. Department of Commerce, *Characteristics of the Population Below the Poverty Level: 1982* (Table 5), and *Money Income and Poverty Status in the United States: 1989* (Tables 21 and 23).

EXHIBIT 8 ■	The Path of Government Income Transfers, 1965–1987[a]		
		Means-Tested Transfer Payments	
Year	Total Transfer Payments as a Percent of Personal Income	Total (Billions of 1987 dollars)	As a Percent of Personal Income
1965	8.5	28.0	1.5
1975	17.4	79.6	3.0
1980	17.8	90.3	2.9
1987	19.4	102.0	2.7

[a]Includes noncash transfers such as food stamps, school lunch subsidies, public housing and other housing subsidies, Medicaid, and Medicare.

Source: *Economic Report of the President: 1991* (Table 25), and Department of Commerce, *Estimates of Poverty Including the Value of Noncash Benefits: 1987* (Table A), and *The Statistical Abstract of The United States: 1990* (Tables 576 and 580).

leveled off. By 1980, the official poverty rate was 10.3 percent, virtually unchanged from the 1968 rate.

After increasing during the sluggish economic conditions of the early 1980s, the official poverty rate for all families stood at 10.3 in 1989. Therefore, for nearly two decades, the poverty rate has stubbornly remained in the 10 to 11 percent range.

Aggregate poverty rate data as presented in Exhibit 9 conceal an important difference between the experience of the elderly and nonelderly that has largely gone unnoticed. Exhibit 10 highlights this point. The poverty rate for the elderly continued to decline throughout the 1970s. By 1989, the official poverty rate of the elderly had fallen to 6.6 percent, down from 17.0 percent in 1968 and 30.0 percent in 1959 (Exhibit 10a). The experience of working-age Americans, however, was vastly different. After falling for several decades, the official poverty rate of nonelderly families bottomed in 1968 and rose throughout the 1970s and early 1980s (Exhibit 10b). In 1989, the official poverty rate of nonelderly families was 11.0 percent, compared with 9.0 percent in 1968 (and 10.9 percent in 1965, just

EXHIBIT 9

The Poverty Rate, 1947–1989

The official poverty rate of families declined sharply during the 1950s and 1960s, changed little during the 1970s, and rose during the early 1980s. The shaded area of the bars indicates the additional reduction in the poverty rate when noncash benefits are counted as income. In 1989, the poverty rate adjusted for noncash benefits was 8.1 percent.

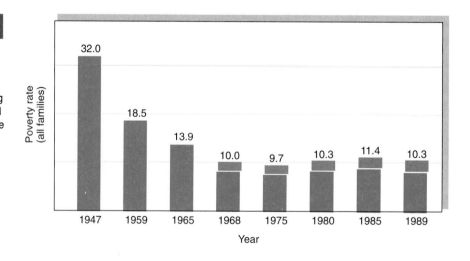

EXHIBIT 10

Changing Poverty Rates, the Differing Experience of the Elderly and Nonelderly, 1959–1989

Source: Derived from Department of Commerce, *Money Income and Poverty Status of Families and Persons in the United States: 1984* and *1989* and *Measuring the Effects of Benefits and Taxes on Income and Poverty, 1989.* See James Gwartney and Thomas S. McCaleb, ''Have Antipoverty Programs Increased Poverty?'' *The Cato Journal* (Spring/Summer, 1985).

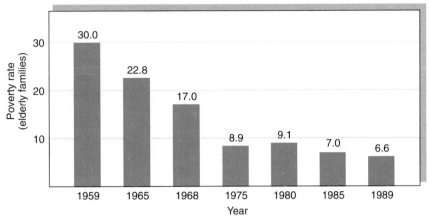

(a) The official poverty rate for elderly families has declined sharply since 1959.

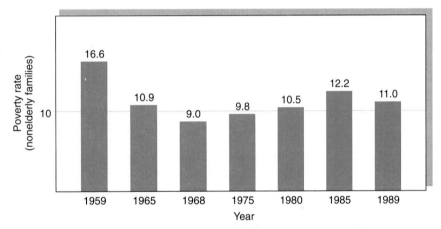

(b) In contrast, the official poverty rate for nonelderly families has been rising since the late 1960s.

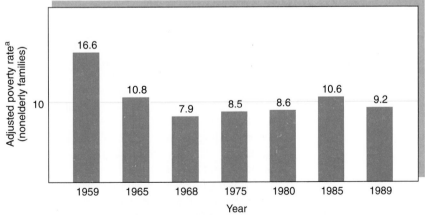

(c) Adjusting for noncash transfers reduces the poverty rate of the nonelderly but it does not alter the basic pattern.

[a]The recipient value method was used to adjust the poverty rate for noncash food, housing, and medical benefits. The 1989 figure is an estimate of the authors.

prior to the increase in expenditures on transfer programs accompanying the War on Poverty).

Why was so little progress made against poverty—particularly poverty among the nonelderly—during the War on Poverty era? For a time, it was widely believed that the stagnating poverty rate of the 1970s reflected the failure of the official data to count noncash benefits derived from programs such as Medicare, Medicaid, food stamps, public housing, and school lunches. Since in-kind transfers have grown rapidly since 1970, this is a potential source of bias. Addressing this issue, the Department of Commerce now publishes adjusted poverty rates that count the in-kind benefits. Given the size of noncash transfers, it is now possible to reconstruct adjusted poverty rate data for earlier time periods.[7]

As Exhibit 9 illustrates, once noncash benefits are counted, the poverty rate is reduced. Adjusting the poverty rate for the value of noncash benefits to recipients reduces the poverty rate of families to 8.1 percent in 1989, compared with the official rate of 10.8 percent. However, as Exhibit 10c illustrates, adjustment for noncash benefits does not significantly alter the picture for working-age Americans. Even after accounting for noncash benefits, the poverty rate of working-age families has been rising since 1968.

Economic and social changes have retarded progress against poverty. While the employment rate has increased during the last 15 years, real wage rates have stagnated. The real wages of workers with few skills and little education have actually declined in recent years. The failure of real wage increases during the 1970–1989 period to match their growth during the 1960s has contributed to the poverty of *working* Americans. In addition, increases in the divorce rate, births to unwed mothers, and the incidence of female-headed households have contributed to the problem. Nonetheless, the results achieved from expanded expenditures (compared with the mid-1960s) on transfer programs have been disappointing. Whether one looks at the official or adjusted poverty rates, the picture is the same. Except for the elderly, the steady progress of the 1950s and 1960s came to a halt during the 1970s and 1980s.

FACTORS LIMITING THE EFFECTIVENESS OF TRANSFER PROGRAMS

How can one explain the relative ineffectiveness, at least compared to what was expected, of income transfers as a weapon against poverty? Analysis of the impact of transfers on the incentive structure confronting the poor enhances our understanding of this issue. While government transfers improved the living standards of many poor people, the programs also severely penalized self-improvement efforts of low-income Americans.

It is important to recognize that the poor are not a monolithic group. In fact, the poor consist of at least two rather distinct groups. There is a hardcore group characterized by individuals who are generally victims of debilitating disease, or

---

[7]See James Gwartney and Thomas S. McCaleb, "Have Antipoverty Programs Increased Poverty?" *The Cato Journal* (Spring/Summer, 1985), for additional details on this topic.

physical, mental, or emotional disability. The hardcore poor remain poor during both the good times and the bad. There is also a second group, which might be called the marginal poor. The periods of poverty experienced by the marginal poor reflect factors such as loss of job, change in family status, premature termination of schooling (or training), or choice of a high-risk lifestyle. In contrast with the hardcore poor, the personal choices of the marginal poor exert an impact on the incidence and duration of their periods of poverty.

There are three major secondary effects that reduce the ability of transfer programs to uplift the living standards of the poor, particularly the marginally poor.

Marginal Tax Rate: The amount of one's additional (marginal) earnings that must be paid explicitly in taxes or implicitly in the form of a reduction in the level of one's income supplement. Since it establishes the fraction of an additional dollar earned that an individual is permitted to keep, it is an important determinant of the incentive to work.

1. High Implicit Marginal Tax Rates Reduce the Incentive of the Poor to Earn. The Net Increase in Income of the Poor is Thus Much Smaller Than the Transfer.   When the size of the transfer payments to the poor is linked to income, an increase in redistribution results in an increase in the implicit marginal tax rate of the poor. As the incomes of the poor rise, they qualify for fewer programs and the size of their transfer income is reduced. For the poor, higher earnings mean less transfer income. Under these circumstances, therefore, the link between additional earnings and additional net income is weakened for the income transfer recipient.

Transfer benefits derived from Aid for Families with Dependent Children (AFDC), food stamps, Medicaid, school lunch subsidies, rent supplements, and housing subsidies decline as income rises. The implicit marginal tax rate associated with individual programs appears to be quite reasonable. For example, food stamp benefits are reduced by $30 for each $100 of monthly earnings up to monthly earnings of $800 for a family of four. The implicit marginal tax rate for AFDC is higher, usually in the 50 percent range. The real problem arises, though, when the potential benefits from several programs are considered. Exhibit 11 illustrates this point for a mother with two children residing in Pennsylvania. If she earned no income, she would be eligible for annual cash and in-kind benefits of $7,568 from AFDC, food stamps, Medicaid, and the Earned Income Tax Credit. If the family's

EXHIBIT 11	■ The Effect of Transfer Benefits and Taxes on the Incentive of a Pennsylvania Mother with Two Children to Earn Income (September 1983)				
Annual Gross Wage	Transfer Benefits[a]	Income and Employment Taxes[b]	Spendable Income	Implicit Marginal Tax Rate
$0	$7,568	$ 0	$7,568	—
2,000	6,525	134	8,391	58.8
4,000	5,482	268	9,214	58.8
5,000	3,040	346	7,694	252.0
6,000	2,059	611	7,448	124.6
7,000	1,719	810	7,909	53.9
8,000	1,378	1,021	8,357	55.2
9,000	1,038	1,240	8,798	55.9
10,000	698	1,469	9,229	56.9

[a]The following benefits are included: AFDC, Earned Income Tax Credit, food stamps and Medicaid. The Medicaid benefits were valued at the 1978 national average adjusted for inflation between 1978 and 1982.

[b]Includes social security and federal and state income taxes.

Source: Data are derived from U.S. House of Representatives Committee on The Ways and Means, *Background Material on Poverty* (Washington, D.C.: Government Printing Office, 1983) Table 10, page 89.

earnings rose to $2,000, transfer benefits would be reduced and taxes increased, leaving the family with spendable income of $8,391. Additional earned income of $2,000 thus generates only $823 in additional spendable income, equivalent to a marginal tax rate of 58.8 percent. At higher levels of earned income, this implicit marginal tax rate is even greater. If earned income rose from $4,000 to $5,000, spendable income would *decrease* from $9,214 to $7,694, an implicit marginal tax rate of 252 percent. If income increased further to $6,000, the family would lose eligibility for AFDC, and its after-tax-and-transfer income would decrease again, this time by $246. In fact, a family earning $6,000 has less spendable income than a family with no earned income, and a family earning $10,000 each year (equivalent to a full-time year-round job paying $5 an hour) would have spendable income of $9,299, just $1,661 more than a family with no earned income at all. The loss in transfer benefits and the increased taxes when earnings rise from zero to $10,000 is equivalent to a tax rate of 83 percent on earned income.

Such extremely high marginal tax rates severely retard the incentive of persons with low income to earn. Many transfer recipients who would otherwise engage in market work decide to work fewer hours or not at all. (Note Exhibit 7 indicates that only 49 percent of the family heads of poor families worked at all during 1989 compared with 70 percent in 1959.) As a result, some portion of the transfer income is merely replacement income; it simply replaces income the recipient would have earned in the absence of the transfer. Thus, the net income of recipients increases by less than the amount of the transfer.

2. The Skills of the Poor Depreciate When They Opt Out of the Labor Force Due to the High Implicit Marginal Tax Rates. Declining Skills Further Limit Their Ability to Escape Poverty.   Individuals who do not use their skills for extended periods of time will find it difficult to compete with otherwise similar individuals with continuous labor force participation. The long-term consequences of an incentive structure that encourages nonwork is even more destructive than the short-term effects. As marginal poor people opt for nonwork, their work record deteriorates. With the passage of time, they become less and less able to support themselves. As the length of time out of the work force expands, marginally poor individuals move into the hardcore poor category.

3. Some Economists Believe that Transfer Programs May Encourage Individuals to Engage in Behavior that Can Lead to Poverty.   By insuring against adversity, these economists suggest, transfer programs reduce the opportunity costs of such activities as dropping out of school or drug and alcohol dependence. Furthermore, the detailed rules and guidelines intended to limit abuse of transfer programs tend to reduce the possibility of individually tailored solutions for recipients. Since the transfer programs provide potential recipients with a measure of protection against adversity arising from imprudent decisions, they tend to encourage choices that increase the likelihood of the adversity.

RECENT WELFARE REFORM

In an effort to minimize the perverse effects of welfare transfers, Congress passed the Family Support Act in 1988. This legislation provided for four major structural changes in transfer programs.

1. Child-Support Payments. The legislation requires states to establish a system of minimum child-support payments for absent parents that must be followed by judges (unless there is a written court finding explaining why the guidelines are inappropriate). All parents who are ordered to make child-support payments after January 1, 1994, will have the payments automatically deducted from their paychecks, just as payroll taxes are today. In the mid-1980s, only about half of the 4.4 million absent parents (mostly fathers) were making their court-mandated child-support payments. The new provision of the welfare reform legislation is designed to substantially increase that proportion, and thereby make absent parents more fully responsible for their children.

2. Extended Medicaid and Child-Care Benefits. Under the new legislation, welfare recipients who go to work will be eligible for continued Medicaid and day-care benefits for an additional 12 months. This provision is intended to reduce the work disincentive of income transfers.

3. Two-Parent Families Eligible For AFDC. The act requires all states to extend AFDC payments to two-parent families where the principal wage earner is unemployed. Twenty-three states had already adopted this provision prior to the 1988 legislation.

4. Work and Training Requirements. States must enact a program requiring able-bodied welfare recipients to engage in some form of work, training, or job preparation, unless the recipient takes care of a child under age 3 (or under age 6 if day care is unavailable). If the recipients are under age 16, a full-time student, or at least 3 months pregnant, they are exempted from this provision. States are also required to provide child care, if such care is necessary, for the recipient's participation in work or training programs.

Will the new legislation reduce the poverty rate? Economic analysis indicates that it will generate conflicting effects. Family dissolution is one of the major causes of poverty. Holding absent fathers responsible for the support of their children will enhance the welfare of single-parent families, while reducing the incentive of fathers to abandon their families in order to escape support responsibilities. Additionally, child-support payments do not deter the work incentive of mothers the way welfare transfers do. Thus, the combination of more reliable child-support payments from fathers and additional earnings of working mothers should push a number of families above the poverty line.

The impact of the other provisions is more ambiguous. While the 12-month extension of Medicaid and day-care benefits to welfare recipients who take a job increases the work incentive of current recipients, it also makes spells of welfare more attractive to families not currently on welfare. In 1980, there were more than one million single-parent families with incomes below or only slightly above the poverty rate who were not on welfare. Under the new legislation, the extended Medicaid and child-care benefits increase the incentive of these families to move, at least temporarily, onto the welfare rolls.

Additionally, there is little reason for optimism that the work/training requirements will be very effective. More than 90 percent of the current welfare recipients are exempt (primarily because of the presence of small children in the home) from the work-training provision. The results of past training programs designed to move chronic recipients from welfare to work have been disappointing. Finally, most families in poverty will continue to confront high marginal tax rates when the effects of multi-programs are considered. In some respects, the new legislation does constitute a break from the past approach. However, most of the perverse disincentive effects remain. Thus, there is good reason for skepticism that the new legislation will significantly reduce the incidence of poverty and dependency.

THE MECHANICS OF A SIMPLE NEGATIVE INCOME TAX

Negative Income Tax: A system of transferring income to the poor, whereby a minimum level of income would be guaranteed by the provision of income supplements. The supplement would be reduced by some fraction (less than 1) of the additional income earned by the family. An increase in earnings would always cause the disposable income available to the family to rise.

Break-Even Point: Under a negative income tax plan, the income level at which one neither pays taxes nor receives supplementary income transfers.

Would it be possible to devise an income transfer system that would avoid the disincentive effects associated with the current system? Some economists, most notably Milton Friedman, believe that the cost of redistribution would be substantially reduced if a simple **negative income tax** were substituted for the current jungle of complex and sometimes conflicting welfare programs.

How would the negative income tax work? To begin with, a base income level would be established. This guaranteed income level would reflect family size, with larger families receiving greater income supplements. As income was earned, the base income supplement would be reduced by a fraction of the family's outside income. This fraction would be the *marginal tax rate*. A family would always face a marginal tax rate of substantially less than 100 percent. (Most plans suggest a 33 or 50 percent rate.) Recipients would always get to keep a significant amount of any additional earnings.

Exhibit 12 illustrates the mechanics of a negative income tax. Under this plan, a family of four would be guaranteed an income of $4,000 and a marginal tax rate of 33 percent. As outside income rises, the family's disposable income increases by two-thirds of the amount earned. For example, initial earnings of $1,500 would increase the family's disposable income by $1,000, from $4,000 to $5,000. The family would receive more in supplementary income than it would pay in taxes until income reached $12,000, the **break-even point.** At the break-even point, the family's tax bill would equal the income supplement; beyond the break-even point, the family would face a positive tax bill.

Would a negative income tax help the poor without generating major counter-productive side effects? During the 1968–1982 period, the United States government funded a number of negative income tax experiments in New Jersey, rural Iowa, Gary (Indiana), Seattle, and Denver. The data generated by these experiments have been extensively analyzed by economists. The results indicate that even a negative income tax transfer program would result in a significant reduction in work effort by the poor. Philip Robins, of the University of Miami, summarizes the findings in the following manner:

> The labor supply responses from the four NIT [negative income tax] experiments are remarkably consistent. On average, husbands reduced labor supply by about the equivalent of two weeks of full-time employment. Wives and single female heads reduced labor supply by about the equivalent of three weeks of full-time employment. Youth reduced labor supply by about the equivalent of four weeks of full-time employment. Because women and youth work fewer hours per year than do husbands, their effects are correspondingly much larger in percentage terms. All of these responses may be viewed as those forthcoming from a fairly generous NIT program—one having a guarantee level equal to the poverty level and a tax rate equal to 50 percent.[8]

EXHIBIT 12

The Mechanics of the Negative Income Tax

The graph illustrates how a negative income tax with a 33 percent marginal tax rate and a minimum income of $4,000 for a family of four would work. If the family had zero earnings during the year, it would receive a $4,000 annual subsidy. As earnings rose, the family's after-tax income would increase by 67 cents (and the subsidy would decline by 33 cents) for every dollar of income earned, until the break-even income level of $12,000 was attained.

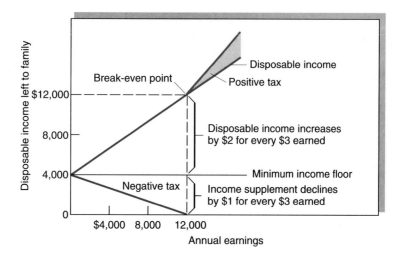

Once again, the NIT experiments indicate that in economics there are no solutions, only trade-offs.

ESTIMATING THE COSTS OF REDISTRIBUTION

Estimating the loss of output emanating from redistributive activities is a highly complex issue. Income transfers from the rich to the poor will increase the marginal tax rates (either explicit or implicit) of both. High marginal tax rates reduce the effectiveness of markets to allocate resources efficiently. They also tend to reduce labor supply. A recent study by Edgar Browning and William Johnson sought to measure the loss of output due to the reduction in the supply of labor associated with the rise in marginal tax rates accompanying income transfers.[9] Browning and Johnson estimated that it would cost $3.49 in terms of lost output to transfer an additional $1 from the top 60 percent to the bottom 40 percent of recipients under a negative income tax plan.

Transferring income from producers to nonproducers is an expensive undertaking. Perhaps a negative income tax might be able to reduce the loss of output compared to the current system. However, both the NIT experiments and the work of Browning and Johnson indicate that it is not a cure-all.

Are redistribution programs worth the cost? Economics cannot answer that question. It can only help identify and quantify the possibilities for redistributing income in relation to the total amount of income available to be distributed—the economic pie. Social security is the largest single income redistribution program. The accompanying Applications in Economics box focuses on this important income transfer program.

---

[8]Philip K. Robins, "A Comparison of the Labor Supply Findings from Four Negative Income Tax Experiments," *Journal of Human Resources* (Fall, 1985), p. 580.

[9]See Edgar K. Browning and William Johnson, "The Trade-off Between Equality and Efficiency," *Journal of Political Economy* (April, 1984).

APPLICATIONS IN ECONOMICS

Social Security and the Intergenerational Redistribution of Income

"Social security"—officially known as Old Age, Survivors, Disability and Health Insurance (OASDHI)—is by far, the largest income transfer program. It offers protection against the loss of income that usually accompanies old age or death or dismemberment of a breadwinner. Its Medicare provisions are designed to offset the heavier health care expenses often incurred by the elderly and the disabled. In 1989, more than $350 billion was paid out to 41 million recipients under the various provisions of OASDHI.

The Financing of Social Security

Private pension and insurance programs invest the current premiums of customers in stocks and bonds, which finance the development of real assets. In turn, the assets generate income, which increases the value of the pension funds and provides the resources with which the pension fund (or insurance company) fulfills the future obligations made to its customers. Social Security does not follow this saving and investment model. Most of the funds flowing into the system are paid out to current retirees and other beneficiaries of the program. In essence, the social security system is an intergenerational income transfer program. Taxes are collected from the present generation of workers and, for the most part, paid out to current beneficiaries.

The social security system is financed by a payroll tax of 7.65 percent levied on *both* the employee and the employer. Therefore, the total tax is equal to 15.3 percent of employee earnings. In 1991, the tax applied to all employee earnings up to $53,400. Thus, employees earning $53,400 or more paid $8,170 in social security taxes in 1991.

When the program was initiated in 1935, there were lots of workers and few eligible retirees. As recently as 1950, there were 16 taxpaying workers to finance the benefits of each social security recipient. As Exhibit 13 illustrates, by 1970 there were only 4 workers per social security recipient and the present ratio has fallen to 3. As the number of workers per social security recipient declined through the years, the taxes per worker increased sharply in order to maintain benefit levels. Measured in real dollars, the maximum social security tax in 1991 was more than six times the amount of 1960.

Winners and Losers Under Social Security

The primary beneficiaries of social security were persons close to retirement during periods when benefits were increased substantially. These workers paid lower tax rates (or higher rates for only brief periods of time). Yet, they received the higher benefits. Today's social security retirees are receiving real benefits of four or five times the amount they paid into the system. The return on the social security taxes they paid generally exceeds 25 percent, much better than they could have done had they invested the funds privately.

In contrast, studies indicate the workers paying for these large benefits will not do nearly as well. For example, those now at age 35 can expect to earn a real rate of return of only 2 or 3 percent on their social security tax dollars, less than what they could earn from personal investments. For two-earner couples just entering the labor force, the expected return from social security taxes is negative.

In summary, social security has been a good deal for current and past retirees. But, it is not a very good deal for younger workers. Workers now entering the labor force would probably be better off if they could invest their tax dollars elsewhere.

Fairness and Social Security

Fairness is not an economic concept. Nevertheless, economics does reveal information about benefits and costs that allow individuals to make more informed, subjective judgments. Three characteristics of the current social security system are important in this regard.

1. *The elderly are no longer the least well-off age group.* In the 1950s, the income status and poverty rate of the elderly indicated that they were significantly less well-off than the rest of the population. In the 1980s, this is not the case. Adjusted for family size, the income of the elderly is now higher than for any other age grouping. The wealth holdings (ownership of houses, stocks, bonds, and so on) of the elderly are much higher than for the rest of the population. The official poverty rate of the elderly in 1989 was 6.6 percent, compared to 11.0 percent for nonelderly families and an even 19 percent rate for children (Exhibits 7 and 10). In

EXHIBIT 13

The Declining Number of Workers per Social Security Recipient

In 1950, there were 16 workers for each social security beneficiary.

In 1970, there were 4 workers for each social security beneficiary.

In 1985, there were 3 workers for each social security beneficiary.

By 2025, there will be just 2 workers for each social security beneficiary.

Result: an increasing burden on each worker whose social security taxes support the program.

contrast with the situation two decades ago, the social security system today transfers income from persons who are, on average, less well-off (current workers) to people who are better off (current retirees).

2. *The social security retirement system transfers income from blacks to whites.* This is not the intent of the program. Nevertheless, it is a result. Since blacks generally begin working earlier and have a lower life expectancy, their tax payments relative to retirement benefits will be substantially greater than for whites. Consider the case of two 25-year-old men, one white and the other black. Given his life expectancy, the average 25-year-old black male who works and pays social security taxes can expect to receive only five months of retire-

ment benefits before his death. The white male of the same age can expect to draw benefits for 73 months, nearly 15 times longer than his black coworker. Similarly, a black female at age 25 can expect to draw social security retirements benefits for 8.3 years, compared to 13.0 years for her white counterpart.[10] Given the expected low or negative rate of return of youthful workers in general, the program clearly imposes a major net cost on blacks in general, and youthful workers in particular.

3. *The social security system taxes working wives while providing them little or no additional benefits.* The social security system was designed in the 1930s when few wives were in the labor force. Women are thus

permitted to draw benefits based on either the earnings of their husband or their personal earnings. Generally, the benefits based on the work history of the husband are greater. When this is the case, the working wife pays taxes into the system and receives no additional retirement benefits in return.

Planning for the Retirement of the Baby Boomers
During the 15 years following the Second World War, the birth rate in the United States was very high. (*Continued*)

---

[10]National Center for Policy Analysis, *Social Security and Race* (Dallas: National Center for Policy Analysis, 1987).

Demographers refer to this large group of people born during 1946–1960 as the "baby boom" generation. When these people retire between 2010 and 2025, they will place enormous strain on the social security system. The number of workers per beneficiary is expected to decline to only two by 2025 (see Exhibit 13). With so few workers per beneficiary, the social security system is projected to run a huge deficit during the 2025 to 2050 period.

Recognizing that the retirement of the baby boom generation will present a serious problem for the social security system, Congress increased social security taxes in 1983 and planned large surpluses for the system during the 1990–2010 period. In the mid-1990s, the system is expected to run $50 to $100 billion surpluses each year.

According to plan, the surpluses of the 1990–2010 period would then be used to help finance the deficit of the 2025–2050 period and cushion the tax burden during the latter period when there are so few workers per social security recipient. However, there is a major problem with this strategy: the surplus of the social security system is currently mixed with other government revenues and is being used to finance current government expenditures. There is no mechanism forcing politicians to keep their hands off of the social security surplus. Even with the social security surpluses, the federal government continues to run huge unified budget deficits. No funds are being set aside or invested to cover future benefit payments to social security recipients. Neither are the

surpluses being used to reduce government borrowing, lower interest rates, and thereby encourage private capital formation.

When the social security system reduces its holdings of government bonds during the system's deficit years (beginning in approximately 2015), other federal taxes will have to be raised (or additional funds borrowed) to finance the redemption of the bonds held by the social security trust fund. The current financing method will not reduce the overall tax burden required to finance the social security deficit during the 2020s and 2030s. It will merely *shift* some of that tax burden to income and other taxes which will have to be raised in order to finance the redemption of the government bonds held by the social security system.

CONCLUDING THOUGHTS

Throughout this chapter, we have presented descriptive data on income inequality and poverty. These data focus our attention on outcomes. When considering the significance of these data, two additional points should be kept in mind. First, positive economics does not indicate that one pattern of outcomes (distribution of income) is superior to another. Such a conclusion would involve interpersonal comparisons among individuals—the value judgment that some people (or groups) are more deserving than others. Modern economists are unwilling to make such comparisons.

Second, some would argue that the *pattern* of economic outcomes is not nearly so important as the *process* that generates the outcomes. According to this view, the fairness of the outcome should be judged by the fairness of the process, rather than the pattern of the income distribution. For example, suppose that an athlete, rock star, or business entrepreneur was able to provide a good or service that five million people per year were willing to pay a price large enough to generate the individual a net income of one dollar for each unit sold. As a result, this individual would have an annual income of $5 million, which would result in a substantial amount of income inequality. But the income inequality merely reflects voluntary exchanges between responsible individuals. What could be unfair about that? Those who stress

If the current real social security benefit levels are going to be maintained, staggering increases in taxes will be required. Fifty years from now, projections indicate that it will take 15 percent of national income just to finance this one program, up from 7 percent during the 1980s.

What might be done to reduce the burden accompanying the retirement of the baby boom generation? Several alternatives have been suggested. First, some advocate that the normal social security retirement eligibility age be raised with life expectancy. The retirement age is already scheduled to increase to age 67 after the turn of the century. Linking it to life expectancy would provide for additional increases in the eligibility age and thereby reduce the number of retirees per worker.

Second, Senator Patrick Moynihan of New York has introduced legislation that would reduce current social security taxes and eliminate the planned surpluses during the next 15 years. The proponents of this view believe that the lower taxes and the elimination of the social security surplus would leave people with more funds to plan for their own retirement and, once the cover of the social security surplus was removed, force Congress and the President to reduce the size of the current budget deficit.

Finally, some have suggested that individuals be allowed to substitute, at least partially, individual retirement accounts (IRAs) and/or the purchase of government bonds for social security taxes. Essentially, this plan would permit individuals to

use their social security tax dollars to acquire a property right to either a private investment fund or a government bond. Should the individual die prior to retirement, the property could be passed on to his or her heirs. As more people opt for this alternative plan over time, the provision of retirement benefits would shift away from social security and toward private investments and government bonds. This plan would also alleviate the adverse impact of the current system on blacks and working women. Interestingly, the United Kingdom has recently modified its social retirement system in this direction.

the importance of the process would generally conclude that since the process was fair, so too, was the outcome even though it resulted in substantial inequality. Thus, when evaluating the significance of income inequality, many social scientists believe that it is also important to consider the process underlying the economic outcomes.

CHAPTER SUMMARY

1. In the late 1980s, the annual income data before taxes and transfers indicate that the bottom 20 percent of families received slightly less than 5 percent of the aggregate income, while the top 20 percent received almost 45 percent of the total income.

2. During the 1940s, there was a substantial reduction in income inequality in the United States and the trend toward less inequality continued at a slower rate throughout the 1950s and 1960s. Since 1970, however, the earlier trend has reversed; there has been an increase in income inequality in the United States during the last two decades.

3. A substantial percentage of the inequality in the annual income distribution reflects differences in age, education, family status, number of earners in the family, and

time worked. Young, inexperienced workers, students, and retirees are overrepresented among those with low incomes. Persons in their prime working years are overrepresented among high-income recipients. Persons with high incomes have substantially more years of schooling. Married-couple families with multi-earners are overrepresented among the high-income recipients, while single-parent families with few earners make up a large share of the low-income recipients.

4. Differences in time worked contributed substantially to the inequality of annual income. While the income of families in the top earnings quintile were almost 10 times the income of families in the bottom quintile in 1989, the number of weeks worked by members of the top quintile of families was 4.4 times the weeks worked by families in the bottom quintile of income recipients. Thus, the before-tax income per week worked of the top earners was only about twice the income per week worked of the low-income families.

5. No single factor can explain the shift toward greater measured income inequality during the 1970s and 1980s in the United States. However, the following three factors contributed to this shift: (a) the increasing number of single-parent and dual-earner families, (b) an increase in earnings differentials between high and low skill (and education) groups, and (c) reduced tax shelter activities due to the sharp reduction in marginal tax rates during the 1980s.

6. Among the advanced industrial nations, there is less income inequality in Japan, Sweden, Germany, France, and the United Kingdom. Income inequality is greater in Canada, Switzerland, and the United States. In general, income is distributed more equally in the advanced industrial countries than in less developed nations.

7. In interpreting the significance of the annual income distribution, it is important to recognize that the annual data camouflage the movement of persons up and down the distribution over time. Many persons with middle and high current income had substantially lower incomes just a few years ago. Similarly, many low-income recipients have attained significantly higher incomes in the past (and many will do so again in the future).

8. There is substantial intergenerational income mobility in the United States. Of the children born to parents who are in the top 20 percent of all income recipients, studies indicate that only 36 percent are able to attain this high-income status themselves. Similarly, more than half of the children of families in the bottom quintile of the income distribution attain a higher relative position when they form their own families.

9. According to the official data, approximately 10 percent of the families in the United States were poor in 1989. Those living in poverty were generally younger, less educated, less likely to be working, and more likely to be living in families headed by a single parent than those who were not poor.

10. During the 1965–1975 period, transfer payments—including means-tested transfers—increased quite rapidly in both real dollars and as a share of personal income. As income transfers expanded, the poverty rate of the elderly continued to decline. However, beginning in the late 1960s, the poverty rate for working-age Americans began to rise. Even after adjustment for in-kind food, housing, and medical benefits, the poverty rate of working-age Americans has been rising gradually since the late 1960s.

11. When considering the impact of current income transfer programs on the poverty status of working-age persons, it is important to recognize the following points:

    a. When the transfer benefits of low-income families decline with income, the incentive of the poor to earn personal income is reduced. Thus, means-tested transfers tend to increase the *net* income of the poor by less than the amount of the transfer.

    b. When high marginal tax rates accompanying transfers induce the poor to opt out of the labor force, their skills depreciate, further limiting their ability to escape poverty.

c. The effectiveness of transfers may also be limited as the result of the tendency of programs designed to protect against adversity to encourage choices that actually increase the occurrence of the adversity.

12. Some economists believe that the cost of redistribution could be substantially lowered if the negative income tax were substituted for current social welfare programs. The major advantages of the negative income tax (relative to present programs) are (a) its simplicity and (b) its provision for the transfer of income to people because they are poor, rather than on the basis of other selective characteristics. However, the results of the negative income tax experiments indicate that it is no cure-all. Even transfers based on a negative income tax would reduce work effort and real output.

13. The social security program is primarily an intergenerational transfer program. At current levels of benefits and taxes, the program is expected to run a substantial surplus during the 1990–2015 period and a huge deficit during the 2025–2050 period, as individuals in the post-Second World War baby boom generation goes through their "prime working years" and then the "retirement phase" of their life cycle. Currently, the program surplus is being used to finance the budget deficit.

CRITICAL ANALYSIS QUESTIONS

1. Do you think the current distribution of income in the United States is too unequal? Why or why not? What criteria do you think should be used to judge the fairness of the distribution of income?

*2. Is annual money income a good measure of economic status? Is a family with a $50,000 annual income able to purchase twice the quantity of goods and services as a family with $25,000 of annual income? Is the standard of living of the $50,000 family twice as high as the $25,000 family? Discuss.

3. What is income mobility? If there is substantial income mobility in a society, how does this influence the importance of income distribution data?

*4. Consider a table such as Exhibit 5 in which the family income of parents is grouped by quintiles down the rows and the family income of their offspring is grouped by quintiles across the columns. If there were no intergenerational mobility in this country, what pattern of numbers would be present in the table? If the nation had attained complete equality of opportunity, what pattern of numbers would emerge? Explain.

5. Do individuals have a property right to income they acquire from market transactions? Is it a proper function of government to tax some people in order to provide benefits to others? Why or why not? Should there be any constitutional limitations on the use of the political process to take income from some in order to provide benefits to others? Discuss.

*6. Since income transfers to the poor typically increase the marginal tax rate confronted by the poor, does a $1,000 additional transfer payment necessarily cause the income of poor recipients to rise by $1,000? Why or why not?

*7. Sue is a single parent with two children considering a job at $800 per month ($5 per hour). She is currently drawing monthly cash benefits of $300, plus food stamp benefits of $100, and Medicaid benefits valued at $80. If she accepts the job, she will be liable for employment taxes of $56 per month and lose all transfer benefits. What is Sue's implicit marginal tax rate for this job?

8. Between 1965 and 1975, there was a substantial increase in transfer payments, both in real dollars and as a share of total income. What impact did the government's expanded tax-transfer role have on the distribution of income and the poverty rate? Discuss.

9. Some argue that taxes exert little effect on people's incentive to earn income. In considering this issue, suppose you were required to pay a tax rate of 50 percent on

---

*Asterisk denotes questions for which answers are given in Appendix C, Selected Answers.

all money income you earn while in school. Would this affect your employment? How might you minimize the personal effects of this tax?

*10. As Exhibit 8 indicates, transfer payments targeted to the poor make up only a small portion of the total government income transfers. Large income transfers are targeted toward the elderly, farmers, and the unemployed, regardless of their economic condition. Why do you think this is so? Does an expansion in the size of tax-transfer activities reduce income inequality?

11. "Welfare is a classic case of conflicting goals. Low welfare payments continue to leave people in poverty, but high welfare payments attract people to welfare roles, reduce work incentives, and cause higher rates of unemployment" (quoted from the *There Is No Free Lunch Newsletter*).
   a. Evaluate. (Hint: apply the opportunity cost concept.)
   b. Can you think of a plan to resolve the dilemma? Is the dilemma resolvable? Why or why not?

12. Suppose the government decides to increase taxes in order to provide a $2,000 per year real income supplement to persons age 65 year and over. Will the real income of the elderly be $2,000 greater in the future than it would have been in the absence of this program? Why or why not?

13. "Means-tested transfer payments reduce the current poverty rate. However, they also create an incentive structure that discourages self-provision and self-improvement. Thus, they tend to increase the future poverty rate. Welfare programs essentially purchase a lower poverty rate today in exchange for a higher poverty rate in the future." Evaluate.

*14. Under legislation passed in 1983, after-tax social security benefits are reduced as income increases for recipients with incomes above $25,000. Recently, some have advocated that social security benefits be completely eliminated for elderly persons with high incomes. Do you think this is a good idea? Why or why not? If social security benefits are reduced (and perhaps eliminated in some cases) as income increases, how will this influence the incentive of the elderly to save and provide income support for their own retirement? How will the number of low-income elderly be affected?

*15. From the viewpoint of the entire economy, can the benefits of a "pay-as-you-go" social security system be called wealth? Might future retirees treat the benefits as wealth? If so, what will happen to the rate of private saving relative to the saving rate if there were no social security program? (Assume that people consume a fixed fraction of their wealth each year.)

16. Why do you think the social security system is operated by the government? Could a private insurance company establish the same type of plan? Why or why not?

17. "The social security system ensures a minimum income for the elderly, but the system also transfers income from the young to the old, from blacks to whites, and from the relatively poor to the relatively well-to-do." Evaluate this statement.

28 Natural Resource and Environmental Economics

Barren timber for building is of great value in a populous and well-cultivated country, and the land which produces it affords a considerable rent. But in many parts of North America the landlord would be much obliged to any body who would carry away the greater part of his large trees.[1]

Adam Smith

CHAPTER FOCUS

■ Can people "create" natural resources? What role does human knowledge, ingenuity, effort, and culture play in determining our stock of energy and other natural resources?

■ How important are substitutes in the case of natural resources?

■ What are proved reserves, and how can they expand over time?

■ Why do we periodically see "doomsday" projections about natural resources? How accurate have they been?

■ Why are property rights important for natural resource management and for the preservation of environmental quality?

*T*he value of a resource depends very much on the situation in which it is found and on the people who have access to it. When Adam Smith wrote the sentences in the chapter-opening quote, and published them in 1776, large trees had great value in the British Isles, where the labor to use wood was cheap and trees were scarce. Large trees were often a nuisance in America, though, where labor was more scarce and trees were plentiful. It was costly even to remove the trees to make way for crops. In America today, workers armed with chain saws, lumber mills, and woodworking tools help make the big trees very valuable, and cleared farmland abounds. For these reasons, trees have increased in value over the years.

Natural resources, unlike manufactured items, are in one sense "gifts of nature." Crude oil, water, virgin forests, and native animal populations are examples of natural resources. They are not created by human hands. In most cases, though, their value (including even our esthetic appreciation of them) depends on human effort, technology, culture, and ingenuity. Wilderness, for example, was not appreciated by most people until recent decades. It was instead a problem to be overcome; now, wilderness is eagerly pursued by those in search of solitude and a pristine natural setting. Crude oil was simply bothersome—a sticky mess wherever it surfaced—until imagination and technology transformed it into "black gold."

When it comes to environmental resources, tastes and preferences matter as well as circumstances. Even today, only a few people appreciate the solitude and isolation of wilderness enough to spend extended periods of time without trails, cleared campsites, and the other amenities which by definition are missing in wilderness areas. Even the value of clean water and air depends both on circumstances and on the people who experience them. Hazy air is a larger problem when it obscures a magnificent vista than when no such view is available.

In this chapter we will examine the production and protection of natural resources and environmental quality. As we will see, the economic principles of earlier chapters are helpful in understanding people's choices and their decisions about natural resources. Economic principles apply here, just as they do in other decision-making situations.

The economic way of thinking can help us investigate and understand a great many issues and answer a great many questions. How responsive are mineral supplies and demands when mineral prices change? What is the role of technological change, and how important are property rights to the operation of these markets? As demands for water increase, will we have enough? What can we say about the long-run availability of minerals, which are in finite supply on Earth? What role do property rights play in the determination of environmental quality? How can environmental quality be improved? We will focus on these and related questions in this chapter.

IN NATURAL RESOURCE MARKETS, INCENTIVES MATTER

As in all markets, the quantity of a natural resource demanded will fall, and the quantity supplied will rise, when its price rises (other things constant). The higher price provides users with the incentive to conserve and to find substitutes for the

---

[1]Adam Smith, *Wealth of Nations*, Edwin Cannan, ed. (New York: The Modern Library, 1937), p. 163.

EXHIBIT 1 ■ How Water "Requirements" Can Vary

When the use of water is expensive, people find ways to use less of it. These numbers, all from actual industrial plants, demonstrate the wide variations possible, even within specific industrial use. How much water is needed to generate a unit of electricity? That depends very much on how costly water is, as the table shows. The "need" can vary from 1.32 gallons to 170 gallons. With time, technology can further expand this range of options.

Product or User and Unit	*Draft (in gallons)*		
	Maximum	Typical	Minimum
Steam-electric power (kw-h.)	170	80	1.32
Petroleum refining (gallon of crude oil)	44.5	18.3	1.73
Steel (finished ton)	65,000	40,000	1,400
Soaps, edible oils (pound)	7.5	—	1.57
Carbon black (pound)	14	4	0.25
Natural rubber (pound)	6	—	2.54
Butadiene (pound)	305	160	13
Glass containers (ton)	667	—	118
Automobiles (per car)	16,000	—	12,000
Trucks, buses (per unit)	20,000	—	15,000

Source: H. E. Hudson and Janet Abu-Lughod, "Water Requirements," *Water for Industry,* Jack B. Graham and Meredith F. Burrill, eds. Publication no. 45 (Washington, D.C.: American Association for the Advancement of Science, 1956), pp. 19–21.

resource that rose in price. The higher price also brings forth extra production, providing additional supplies. Lower prices have the opposite effect, reducing the quantity supplied of the resource, and increasing the quantity demanded.

The use of water by industry, as illustrated in Exhibit 1, provides a good example of the importance of substitution. When automakers, steel producers, or oil refineries need water for their production processes, the amount they use will depend on the price they must pay to get the water. Some processes use much more water than others, and where water costs are high, producers use processes requiring less water. The same is true for any other industry and any other resource. Consumers will respond in the same way, reinforcing the effect of price changes.

As in most markets, time is an important factor in determining the responsiveness of producers and users to a price change—the price elasticities of supply and demand. The longer a sharp rise or fall in price persists, the stronger the response to the change in price. Product innovation and technological change are among the factors that have greater impact over time. A consideration of energy markets will help us illustrate these points.

RESOURCE DEMAND IS FAR MORE ELASTIC IN THE LONG RUN THAN IN THE SHORT RUN

The *immediate* response of consumers to higher energy prices is likely to be relatively weak. In the short run, individuals will find it costly to reduce their

EXHIBIT 2

Supply and Demand in the Energy Market

As frame 2a illustrates, both the supply of and demand for energy products tend to be highly inelastic during the short run. However, as frame 2b shows, both will be considerably more elastic in the long run.

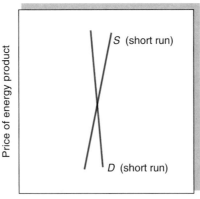

(a) Supply and demand in short run

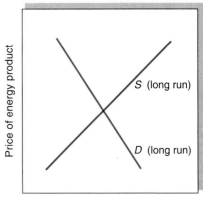

(b) Supply and demand in long run

consumption of electricity, fuel oil, and gasoline by a large amount, even if the prices of these energy products rise sharply. Of course, some energy-saving measures can be adopted immediately. More care can be taken to turn off the lights in unoccupied rooms. Warmer clothing can be substituted for heating oil in the winter, and fans can replace air conditioning in the summer. Nonessential driving can be curtailed. These adjustments, though, will be small *compared to the potential reduction over a longer period of time.*

Consumption adjustments that would be very costly in the short run become easier with time. Old and new houses will be better insulated. Higher gasoline prices will induce new car buyers to exchange some power and size for more fuel economy, and auto makers will design more fuel-efficient cars. Home appliances, farming, industrial processes, and vacation trips will become less energy intensive over time. Several years will pass, however, before old habits, old techniques, old buildings, and old machinery are completely replaced.

As Exhibit 2 illustrates, the demand for energy products can be highly inelastic in the short run. In the long run, though, energy-saving adjustments are more attractive. As our theory predicts, and as the boxed feature "Prices and Quantities: How Energy Buyers Respond" verifies, the demand for energy will be much more elastic in the long run than in the short run.

THE SHORT-RUN SUPPLY WILL BE INELASTIC DUE TO THE LENGTHY PRODUCTION CYCLE

New energy sources generally take years of development. Crude oil is a case in point. Oil companies will search more diligently for additional crude oil supplies when they believe the oil they find will be sold for a higher price. The search will take time, however. Promising areas must be tested, exploratory wells must be drilled, and production equipment must be put in place. These are time-consuming

APPLICATIONS IN ECONOMICS

Prices and Quantities: How Energy Buyers Respond

Economic theory tells us that the demand for a commodity depends on the price of the commodity, the income of buyers, and the price of both substitutes and complements. The theory is demonstrated clearly in energy markets.

Consumers determine how much electricity, gas, or other energy form is used. For example, in the case of electricity, they choose whether or not to use electric heat and how high to set the thermostat. But they also decide how much aluminum (made with large quantities of electricity) to buy and which producers (those using more electricity per ton of aluminum, or less per ton) to buy from. Higher electricity prices raise aluminum prices relative to the prices of substitute metals and increase costs more significantly for producers using more electricity per ton. Producers using techniques and equipment that conserve more fully on the use of materials that

are increasing in price will enjoy a competitive advantage. Thus, even with very little knowledge of how or why electricity prices are rising throughout the economy, consumers make choices that move sales away from the energy form rising fastest in cost, and toward conservation, other energy sources, and other means of satisfying their wants.

How much less will be consumed when the price of an energy form rises? Exhibit 3, summarizing the results of several statistical studies, provides some answers in the form of estimated price elasticities. For residential electricity, a 10 percent rise in price would lead to a 2 percent short-run reduction in quantity demanded. The short run here means one year. When buyers have up to 10 years to respond, the long-run elasticity indicates that the same 10 percent price rise would cause a 7 percent decline in

residential use of electricity, other factors held constant.

Price elasticities are useful in predicting fuel usage as fuel prices change. However, other factors, such as income and the price of substitutes, will also influence consumption. In addition, we cannot expect the same reaction to a price change from people in different situations. Once auto manufacturers have spent years in researching and developing techniques to save fuel, for example, even a return to the much lower gasoline prices of years past would not bring back the previous level of gas guzzling. Measured elasticities reflect history, but history can never be retraced exactly, even if the path of prices is somehow repeated. Estimated price elasticities are a rough but often useful guide to buyer behavior when prices of an important commodity such as energy change.

EXHIBIT 3 ■ **Price Responsiveness of Energy Forms: Estimated Price Elasticities**

	Estimated Elasticity[a]	
Fuel	Short Run	Long Run
Residential electricity	0.2	0.7
Residential natural gas	0.1	0.5
Gasoline	0.2	0.7

[a]When income and other factors such as other fuel prices are held constant, the elasticities indicate the ratio of percent change in quantity to the percent change in price causing the quantity change. Each elasticity is actually a negative number, since price and quantity demanded move in opposite directions.

Source: Douglas R. Bohi, *Analyzing Demand Behavior* (Baltimore: Johns Hopkins University Press, 1981), p. 159.

processes. It usually takes more than three years from the time the search begins until the refined product can be brought to market. Even though development and delivery can be somewhat accelerated (at a cost), higher product prices will have only a small effect on output in the short run.

As Exhibit 2b indicates, the supply response to an increase in price expands with time. Not only will more exploration and development of new wells occur, but additional extraction of oil from existing wells will be profitable at the higher price. On average, about two-thirds of a well's oil is left in an oil pool when the well is abandoned. Extracting the rest is too expensive. But, when oil prices rise, wells are not abandoned so quickly. The oil field can be flooded with water, or injected with steam or chemicals to increase total recovery. These measures take time and money, but higher production will result.

When high prices are expected to persist or to rise in the future, the incentive to innovate increases. Research and development activities will expand, and often lead to technological advances which lower the cost of finding, producing, and processing crude oil. When the reward for production is expected to be higher, added investments will speed the development of supply-enhancing technological changes.

INFORMATION IS COSTLY, AND THE FUTURE IS UNCERTAIN

What will be the long-run future availability of energy and other natural resources? Opinions differ, but no one really knows. Natural resources are different from manufactured goods, whose long-run availability depends mainly on the size of the work force and the factories we choose to build and maintain. In the short run, manufactured inventories determine what can be supplied. For a natural resource such as a mineral, long-run availability depends not only on "factories" (mining equipment and refining capacity) but also on the reserves of the raw material, such as ore, or crude oil in the ground.

Mineral reserves are frequently misunderstood by observers outside the industry. They often confuse total reserves that *can become* available with the reserves we know about now. Known reserves are naturally much smaller in quantity.

Why don't we know more about the quantity of reserves that might eventually be made available? To find oil or other mineral reserves not only takes time, it also requires the use of valuable equipment, skilled labor, and other factors of production. In other words, known, or "proved" reserves are expensive. **Proved reserves** are the discovered and verified quantity of resources that producers believe they can recover *at current prices and levels of technology*. To find and prove reserves too many years in advance would be wasteful, just as producing automobiles years before their use would be wasteful. Proved reserves, in fact, are similar to inventories in any other industry. To produce inventories too soon costs more than it is worth, and would reduce profits. Just as an auto dealer might hold a 2- to 3-month inventory of cars, oil and gas producers commonly hold a 10- to 15-year supply of oil and gas reserves. And, just as we do not worry about running

Proved Reserves: The verified quantity of a resource that can be recovered at current prices and levels of technology.

EXHIBIT 4	■ Proved Reserves: Inventories That Can Expand Even as They Are Used Up		
	Millions of Tons, Metal Content		
Mineral	Proved reserves 1950	Production 1950–80	Proved reserves 1980
Copper	100	156	494
Iron	19,000	11,040	93,466
Aluminum	1,400	1,346	5,200
Lead	40	85	127

Source: William Vogely, "Nonfuel Minerals and the World Economy," in Robert Repetto, ed., *The Global Possible,* (New Haven: Yale University Press, 1985), p. 458.

out of cars in 2 to 3 months, both logic and the available evidence indicate that we need not fear running out of oil in 10 to 15 years.

Using data for copper, iron, aluminum, and lead, Exhibit 4 illustrates that proved reserves are important only in the short run. Column 1 indicates the quantity of proved resources for each of these minerals in 1950. During the ensuing 30-year period, the production of each metal was greater than (or approximately equal to) the proved reserve level of 1950. Nonetheless, at the end of the 30-year period, the proved resources of each of the four metals had increased. In fact, the proved reserves of the metals in 1980 were several times greater than the level of 1950. New ore discoveries had been made, and new technologies had reduced the cost of finding and processing the minerals. These advances more than offset the production and use of the ore reserves known in 1950. As a result, the prices of these metals changed very little during the 30-year period.

RESOURCE DECISIONS ARE MADE AT THE MARGIN

In natural resource markets, as in all markets, decisions concern actions taken at the margin. In fact, two natural resources, diamonds and water, provide a classic way to explain the concept of marginal values. Writing before the discovery of the marginal principle, Adam Smith was puzzled by the fact that water, which is so valuable and necessary for life itself, is much cheaper than natural diamonds, which normally are "useless baubles." Modern economists know that price and market value are determined by the value of marginal units, rather than by the average value to buyers or sellers. Since the supply of water is very great compared to the supply of diamonds, the value of an *extra* unit of water is relatively small (at most times and in most places), even though the total value of the world's supply of water is far greater than the total value of its diamond supply.

Crude oil wells provide another example. As we said earlier, each well is abandoned when the marginal cost of pumping becomes greater than the value of the oil extracted. This typically occurs when only about one-third of the oil in the pool has been withdrawn. But, when the price of oil is high, additional expenses to extract more of the oil are justified.

Various uses of water provide yet another useful application of the marginal principle. The willingness of a farmer or a municipality to pay for water reflects the *marginal* value of the water in farming or in the city. In the water-short American West, the marginal values can be high, and the differences quite large. While demand for water by residential, commercial, and industrial users in cities is growing, roughly 90 percent of the water is still used by farmers. Urban water prices are often at least ten times as great as water prices for agriculture, so there are large potential gains from trade. Despite some legal obstacles, some of these trades are proceeding, moving water from agriculture to the higher-valued municipal and industrial uses.[2] Does this mean that industry and the cities are likely to draw all of the water out of agriculture? If you are tempted to answer "yes," remember that prices are determined at the margin. While nonagricultural users are willing to pay far more than the water is worth *at the margin* to farmers, each water trade reduces the value of additional water to the recipient, and increases the value of water to the seller. Suppose that cities and industries doubled their use of water, from 10 to 20 percent. Agriculture would still have about 80 percent of the total water in the West, and the marginal value of water to farmers would be higher, while the marginal value of water to others would be cut substantially by the doubling of their usage. Farmers will gain greatly from selling some of their water, but most of it will be retained. Trades tend to equalize the differing values of water at the margin, so agriculture is not likely to dry up and blow away.

In considering the problems and policy options for natural resources, it is essential to keep the marginal principle in mind. Prices and values are determined at the margin, and good decisions are made when the marginal effects of alternative choices are considered.

OPPORTUNITY COSTS ARE THE RELEVANT COSTS

Markets allocate scarce natural resources well because when a resource is more scarce, its price rises and users have an incentive to economize more intensively on its use. At the same time, producers have a stronger incentive to raise their output of the resource and its substitutes. As we have indicated earlier, especially in Chapter 4, property rights are crucial to the success of this market system of resource conservation and management. If government policy, for example, limits the ability of market participants to buy and sell a resource, then market trading may not establish the true opportunity cost as the resource price, and resource users will be reacting to something other than the opportunity cost in making decisions about using the resource.

Consider the case of federally owned hydropower—electricity generated by water falling through turbines in a dam built across a river. By law, such federally owned power must be sold "at cost," meaning the out-of-pocket costs of generating and delivering the electricity, not its opportunity cost. This electric power is usually generated at a cost far below the cost of power from other generating plants selling

---

[2]See Zach Willey and Tom Graff, "Federal Water Policy in the United States—An Agenda for Economic and Environmental Reform," *Columbia Journal of Environmental Law*, vol. 13, no. 2, 1988, for a description of these water markets.

electricity, including plants in the same delivery system. This low cost typically is lowered further by federal subsidies. The rights to purchase this power at the artificially low price are allocated politically to classes of users in the region. The rights (and thus the power) cannot be conserved and resold at a profit by those receiving the rights. For this reason, even when others would be willing to pay a price higher than its value to the current user, the other users cannot bid for it. The opportunity cost of the power is ignored.

Pacific Northwest electricity, generated mostly by dams on the Columbia River and sold by the federal Bonneville Power Administration (BPA), provides an example. It has been sold in recent years at prices far lower than other power in the region. Users pay only a fraction of the value of that power in other potential uses (a fraction of the opportunity cost). To see the inefficiency in the system, consider what would happen if users of electricity could sell their rights to the low-priced power. Suppose that each current user were given a certificate providing the right to continue purchasing power at the same price (adjusted periodically for utility cost increases, as before). But suppose also that the certificates could be sold, so that other electricity users, not now able to buy the cheap electricity, could buy the certificates from current users, thus obtaining the right to purchase the cheap power. If certificates were issued, and could be resold, some of the electric power would flow to users who valued it more highly than current users, who would find ways to conserve power and sell some of their certificates. With no increase at all in their power bills, users would notice the opportunity cost (offers made by others to get certificates) and have the appropriate incentive to conserve electricity. Both buyers and sellers would be better off, and the revenue to BPA would remain the same. Such efficient and mutually beneficial trades are not allowed, however. The profits to be made by the sale of certificates, allowing better use of electricity, are thought to be politically unacceptable, even though both buyers and sellers would gain. A side effect of the current policy is that with less conservation, growth in the region will require that additional nuclear or coal-fired power plants be built.

Water taken from the same river for irrigation provides another example. The federally financed Columbia River Project, designed to provide irrigation water for 1.1 million acres of farmland in the region, has been half completed. Completion of the remainder is proposed. The added construction would cost an estimated $5,000 per acre irrigated, in present value terms.[3] Of this, landowners receiving the water would pay an estimated $115 in present value. However, the water to be delivered would be drawn out of the river behind the Grand Coulee Dam, and thus would reduce the ability of that dam and the others below it on the Columbia to produce electric power. Additional coal or nuclear power plants would then be required to replace the power lost because of irrigation water withdrawals from the river, in addition to the electric power needed to pump the water up from the river's level to the farmland. The cost? Bonneville Power would have to charge its customers an estimated $110 million per year extra to pay the added power costs, which do not appear in the project's budget. That is an opportunity cost of about $4,050 per acre irrigated, in addition to the budgeted cost of delivering the proposed

---

[3]Data for this irrigation project are from a series of studies by Washington State University Professor of Agricultural Economics Norman K. Whittlesey and others. See Whittlesey, "Should We Finish the Columbia Basin Project?" a paper delivered to the Farm Forum in Spokane, Washington, in January 1984.

irrigation water. It would be spread over a great many power customers and taxpayers, few of whom are even aware of the proposed project.

Once again, project decision-makers and those lobbying for project completion would not face the full opportunity cost of their actions. If they could simply sell their rights to subsidized water to those who would gain from having the water left in the stream, they would do so, unless the benefits from the project truly exceeded its costs. The political process, however, may deliver quite different results because the property rights to the water (and the Treasury subsidies) are not clearly defined and tradeable. Under the current political rules, project decision-makers and those lobbying for project completion do not face the full opportunity cost of their actions.

National forests provide yet another example. What is the cost of managing a portion of a national forest for timber or for oil and gas production, rather than for wilderness? Environmentalists point out that when logging firms purchase the rights to cut timber on national forest lands, they frequently do not pay even the cost of preparing for the timber sale plus the cost of roads to serve the loggers, much less the cost of reduced wildlife habitat or the loss of roadless recreation. On the other hand, wilderness advocates (and users) generally pay nothing at all toward the cost of wilderness, even though official Wilderness designation precludes roads, logging, and, in effect, outlaws oil and gas extraction, which could be extremely valuable. Since the many would-be users do not pay the opportunity cost of what they get, agency decision-makers do not face the opportunity cost of the options they consider, and find it difficult even to estimate the size of those costs.

OPPORTUNITY COST AND BENEFIT-COST ANALYSIS

Benefit-Cost Analysis (B-C): A process used to determine the efficiency of a project by estimating each benefit and each cost. A project is said to be efficient if it generates more benefits than costs.

Economists often are asked to look at a government project and to determine whether it is an efficient use of resources. Such analysis involves the estimation of opportunity costs and benefits. **Benefit-cost analysis (B-C)** is a process to determine the efficiency of a project by examining every benefit and cost. It is intended to guide decision-makers who cannot observe market prices directly, and to help them achieve efficient outcomes without this market information. The project is said to be efficient if benefits exceed costs. The benefit-cost ratio is often calculated by simply dividing total benefits by total costs. An efficient project has a benefit-cost ratio greater than one.

The purpose of using B-C is to separate efficient projects from inefficient ones and to avoid the latter. Inefficient projects move resources from higher-valued uses to lower-valued ones. To do its job, B-C must correctly measure all of the benefits and all of the costs (present and future), implied by the choice being analyzed, and compare them properly. Then, the B-C must be used by decision-makers. There are thus three major reasons why even B-C may go astray:

1. Measurement Assigning a Dollar Amount to the Costs and Benefits Can Be Very Difficult. Goods and services involved in natural resource projects often are unpriced. They frequently involve publicly provided goods and services, which are not marketed. Because of this, it is difficult to determine their value and their opportunity cost. Costs and values are subjective, so when preferences are not revealed by offers to buy and to sell, objective estimates may be almost impossible. In recent years, some especially difficult issues have arisen regarding the preservation of natural areas. (See the Applications in Economics box, "Tough Issues in Natural Resource Preservation.") But, economists and other policy analysts work hard to approximate willingness-to-pay or opportunity costs, since

APPLICATIONS IN ECONOMICS

Tough Issues in Natural Resource Preservation

Some values claimed for natural resources are by their nature difficult to measure. An example of this is the **existence value** of a natural wonder, such as the Grand Canyon. Some people derive satisfaction just from knowing that the Grand Canyon exists in its unspoiled state. A few years ago, a dam for water storage and power generation to be built in the canyon was proposed. Some of the grandeur would be lost if the dam were built. The dam, like Hoover Dam farther west on the same river, would have a grandeur of its own, but it would certainly not be

Existence Value: The satisfaction people can derive simply from knowing that something—the Grand Canyon or Hoover Dam, for example—exists. It is extremely difficult to measure existence values.

Irreversibility: Once an action is taken, some physical effects may not be reversible—the prior physical conditions cannot be restored. Such a situation involves an irreversibility.

the same. Building the dam and harnessing the wild river would create existence value for some people and would destroy it for others. Since many of those who would appreciate the existence of either the unspoiled canyon or the dam would never visit the Grand Canyon, how can we take their evaluations into account? How can we estimate that component of the opportunity cost of building (or not building) the dam?

Voluntary organizations, such as those organized to preserve the Statue of Liberty or the Hawk Mountain Sanctuary, provide one way that existence values are expressed. People who never visit the sites contribute to their preservation. But, each of us who enjoys such value may choose to "free ride," leaving the cost of providing the existence value to others. In the end, existence values that individuals refuse to voluntarily support might have to be ignored. While existence values are everywhere, they are nearly impossible to estimate.

Another difficult issue in resource management is the problem of irreversible decisions. A dam built in the Grand Canyon

would have some permanent physical effects. **Irreversibility** means that once the action is taken, some physical effects could not be reversed. Once the dam is built, even removing it would not restore the original beauty of the Grand Canyon, because the water behind the dam would permanently change the appearance of its walls. Opponents of such a project argue that irreversibility puts the project in a special category, so that postponing the project to preserve the option for the future is an especially attractive option. Unfortunately, the situation is not so easy to analyze.

Suppose the project were actually beneficial, producing $1 million of net benefits in electricity and water storage services per year. To delay the project 5 years would mean giving up $5 million in benefits, and giving them up forever. At an interest rate of 10 percent, $5 million is equivalent to $500,000 per year forever. What permanent conservation (or other) goals could be purchased with that permanent stream of income? While a delay can preserve an option, the delay itself may have irreversible effects.

rational governmental decisions and policies may depend on the resulting estimates, even though they are imperfect.

2. An Inappropriate Rate of Interest May Be Used When Calculating the Benefits and Costs. The chapter on "Capital, Interest, and Profit," explained why comparing present and future dollar amounts requires the use of an interest rate and a discounting procedure. A dollar in benefits (or costs) today is worth more than a dollar next year. The choice of the appropriate interest rate can strongly influence estimated costs and benefits. That choice is not a simple one, however, and economists have long debated how the correct rate should be chosen. Governmental projects involving natural resources have often been the stage for those debates.

3. Policy-Makers May Fail to Use the B-C Analysis When Making Decisions on Resource Use.   Supporters of a project will usually lobby for it and opponents will lobby against it, regardless of the B-C results. Political considerations, rather than economics, may determine the outcome of the issue. Efficiency has no political constituency. Unlike private owners, whose wealth is dependent on efficient outcomes, the success of political decision-makers depends more on pleasing politically effective interest groups than on making efficient decisions.

THE FUTURE OF NATURAL RESOURCE MARKETS

Is the world running out of natural resources? (See the Myths of Economics box.) Can we forecast future supply and scarcity? What factors will determine the future of natural resource availability?

As we noted at the beginning of this chapter, the value of a resource depends on the knowledge and ingenuity possessed, and the circumstances faced by its potential users. In a very real sense, humankind creates resources, even though the physical resource is a gift of nature. The challenge, then, is to see that knowledge is created in a timely way, and ingeniously applied in a manner appropriate to the circumstances. Historically, the price system has provided information on approaching resource scarcity, and supplied inventors, innovators, and investors with the proper incentives to deal appropriately with the situation. For that to happen, however, prices must reflect the values and expectations of buyers and sellers, including speculators, on current and coming resource scarcities. Appropriate price signals, in turn, depend on the existence of well-defined, secure, and transferrable property rights.

PROPERTY RIGHTS BRING THE FUTURE INTO THE PRESENT

One benefit of private property rights is their ability to bring expected future effects of current decisions to bear now. Property rights provide long-term incentives for maximizing the value of a resource, even for owners whose personal outlook is short term. If land is used for the construction of a toxic waste dump, its future productivity may be reduced. If so, its value falls and the fall in the land's value reduces the owner's wealth. That happens because land's current worth reflects the value of its future services: the revenue from production or the services received directly from the land, minus the costs (including amounts that must be paid to anyone harmed by escaping wastes) required by the land's use.

Of course, the owner may seek to conceal the pollution in order to avoid the loss of wealth. But buyers have a strong incentive to investigate potential problems of this sort—indeed a much stronger incentive than does a bureaucrat who is charged with enforcing an anti-pollution law, but who has no direct financial exposure. Disclosure laws that govern real estate transactions, and the services of title insurance firms are meant to reduce problems of concealment.

An important feature of private ownership of a resource is that fewer services from the resource, or greater costs associated with it in the future, mean lower value (and less wealth for the owner) now. In fact, as soon as an appraiser or potential buyer can see future problems, the wealth of the owner declines by the amount of the reduction in potential buyers' willingness to pay for the resource. Not only does using land to store hazardous waste reduce future options for the land's productivity but the value also may be reduced by the risk of future lawsuits if the wastes leak and cause damage to other people or property. The key fact here is that any reduction in *future* services and *future* net value due to potential liability is visited on the owner now by its direct impact on the present capitalized value of the resource.

In effect, the value of the property right, which gives the resource owner the privilege as well as the responsibility of control, serves as a hostage to the owner's socially responsive stewardship of the resource. Any decision resulting in less value produced, either now or in the future, reduces the property's value now. The reverse also is true: Any new and better way employed to produce more value now or in the future is capitalized into the asset's present value. Even a short-sighted owner has the incentive to be alert to new possibilities and new dangers and to act as if he or she cares about the future usefulness of the land.

This is true even if the owner of the resource is a corporation, and the corporate officers, rather than the owner-stockholders, are in control. Corporate officers may be concerned mainly about the short term, not expecting to be present when future problems arise. However, property rights hold such decision-makers accountable. If current actions are known to cause future problems, or if current expenditures are seen to promise future benefits, those who buy and sell stock will push the stock price up or down accordingly, capturing the reduction or increase in future net benefits.

The average owner of stock is not a pollution expert, but can gain by reading the published reports of stock analysts who are tuned in to all phases of the industry they cover. Watchdog environmental groups also spread the word about suspected problems. It is in the stockholder's interest to keep an "ear to the ground" because correctly anticipating how the market will react can allow the discerning investor to buy before good news is fully captured in the stock price, or to sell before bad news is fully reflected in a falling stock price.

For better and for worse, even the rumor of future benefits or expenses can strongly influence today's stock price. It is not clear whether analysts, commentators, and interest groups publicizing future problems overreact or underreact to problems as they occur. But in either case, corporate decision-makers are immediately visited by stock market evaluations of their actions, even though the "bottom line" of the profit and loss statement may not reflect the results of bad decisions and good investments for a long time to come. Property rights, and market evaluations made by observers with their own wealth at stake and reflected in resource prices, bring expected future results to bear on current decision-makers today.

RESOURCE CONSERVATION IN MARKET AND SOCIALIST ECONOMIES

To see the importance of property rights and market pricing in resource conservation, consider resource use in developed market economies compared with those in developed socialist economies. In the latter, few resources are privately owned, and market prices have little influence in directing industrial production. Researcher Mikhail Bernstam, at Stanford University's Hoover Institution, recently compared the use of energy and steel in two groups of nations. The market economies included the United States, Japan, Canada, South Korea, and eight west European countries. The socialist group included the Soviet Union, North Korea,

MYTHS OF ECONOMICS

"We are running out of energy, minerals, timber and other nonrenewable natural resources. Doomsday is just around the corner."

The first recorded doomsday forecast, says J. Clayburn LaForce,[5] was the fifteenth-century prediction that England would run out of wood. "At the time, wood was the main source of fuel, and terrible consequences were expected. What happened? The price of that resource gradually rose as forests around urban centers receded. In response to higher prices, people gradually began to substitute coal for charcoal a wood derivative in both personal and commercial uses. England entered its greatest period of economic growth and that 'sceptered isle' still has forests."

Doomsday forecasts have been made ever since, often by very responsible people. In 1865, the noted economist William Jevons argued that the industrial growth of that century could not be maintained far into the future because the world was running out of coal, the primary energy resource at the time.[6]

Governments have made some of the worst forecasts. In 1905, Theodore Roosevelt predicted a timber famine if present rates of cutting continued. In 1914, the Bureau of Mines reported that the total U.S. supply of crude oil was approximately 6 million barrels. We now produce that much every 20 months.

A major energy crisis occurred in the United States in the early 1800s, when home lighting depended on lamps that burned whale oil, especially from the sperm whale. "As population rose," LaForce relates, "demand for this resource increased, and many predicted that soon there would be no more whales and that we would be faced with darkness during the winter nights."

The price of whale oil rose. Over some 30 to 40 years, the price of sperm whale oil rose from 43 cents per gallon to $2.55 a gallon, while the price of other whale oil rose from 23 cents to $1.42 a gallon. Higher prices motivated consumers and entrepreneurs to seek alternatives, Laforce explains, including distilled vegetable oils, lard oil, and coal gas. By the early 1850s, coal oil (kerosene) had won out. And very soon thereafter, a new substitute for whale oil appeared: petroleum replaced coal oil as the source of kerosene. A new industry was born.

As for whale oil, by 1896, its price had fallen to 40 cents per gallon, and even at that price few people used it. The whale oil crisis had passed.

"All this happened," says LaForce, "with no pretense of a national energy (or lighting) plan. There were no price controls.... Each change had been guided and coordinated by 'the invisible hand' of the market: the price mechanism."

Dire predictions about our natural resource future became a fad during the 1970s. The "year of exhaustion" of important natural resources, especially crude oil, was a popular news item. The arithmetic of the doomsday calculations was unassailable.

---

[5]Quoted from J. Clayburn LaForce, "The Energy Crisis: The Moral Equivalent of Bamboozle," International Institute for Economic Research, Original Paper 11 (Los Angeles, April 1978).
[6]In his book, *The Coal Question* (London: Macmillan, 1865), Jevons stated: "We cannot long maintain our present rate of increase of consumption; the cost of fuel must rise, perhaps within a lifetime, to a rate injurious of our commercial and manufacturing supremacy; and the conclusion is inevitable, that our present happy progressive condition is a thing of limited duration."

---

and six east European nations. He found that on average, energy use per $1,000 of national output was less than half as great in the market nations as in the socialist economies for 1980.[4] Energy efficiency was far greater where markets provided both signals and incentives for resource conservation. Energy is a key indicator of resource use because it comprises about half of all resource use in industrialized nations.

---

[4]Mikhail S. Bernstam, *The Wealth of Nations and the Environment,* (London: Institute of Economic Affairs, 1991), p. 24.

One simply found the current annual consumption rate (averaged over, say, the last two decades) and divided that number into the quantity of proved reserves of the resource. That provided the years of the resource remaining. Add that number to the current date, and we have the "year of exhaustion."

Why then have the years to exhaustion projections proved to be so wrong? There are two major reasons for their inaccuracy. First, "proved reserves" of a mineral resource are an inventory. *Proved reserves are costly to find and verify, so we do not want to bear the cost of "proving" a mineral deposit too many years in advance.* We want to produce inventories, including proved reserves, only a few weeks, months, or years ahead of the time we need them. The size of currently proved reserves says nothing at all about the sufficiency for the future of absolute reserves.

Second, doomsday predictions have generally failed to consider the role of price changes and technology. Both consumption rates and the expected recoverable supply are projected *assuming current technology and prices.* But when a resource becomes more scarce, its price rises. This provides additional incentive for

innovators, engineers, and inventors to alter technology in a manner that will (a) conserve on direct use of the resource, (b) provide substitutes for the resource, and (c) develop new methods of discovering and recovering larger quantities of the resource. In resource economics, it is critical to remember that we want the services gained by using the resource, not the resource itself. There are very few services that we could not find substitutes for, if we really needed to. For all these reasons, the cost of most natural resources has remained constant or fallen for decades, and in most cases, for centuries.

The classic study of Harold Barnett and Chandler Morse illustrates this point. Using data from 1870 to 1963, Barnett and Morse found that resource costs declined during that long period.[7] Far from suggesting that doomsday was around the corner, the facts of natural resource availability tell a much more optimistic story. Relative price data indicate that technology and the ever-increasing availability of substitutes have outrun our ability to use up scarce natural resources. When price changes are allowed to reflect changing scarcities, constructive human responses to specific

scarcities are an understandable and predictable occurrence. Just as they have been wrong in the past, future doomsday forecasts that fail to incorporate human response to relative price changes will prove to be wrong in the future.

[7]See Harold Barnett and Chandler Morse, *Scarcity and Growth: The Economics of Natural Resource Availability,* (Baltimore: The Johns Hopkins University Press for Resources for the Future, 1963). An update and extension of the data, reaching similar conclusions, is in Manuel H. Johnson, Fredrick W. Bell, and J. T. Bennett, "Natural Resource Scarcity: Empirical Evidence and Public Policy," *Journal of Environmental Economics and Management,* 7, (September 1980); pp. 258–69. Not all economists fully accept this view, however. See V. Kerry Smith, ed., *Scarcity and Growth Reconsidered* (Baltimore; The Johns Hopkins University Press for Resources for the Future, 1979).

In the socialist nations, energy efficiency fell as energy use per $1,000 of output rose by 8 percent from 1980 to 1986. By contrast, energy efficiency increased in the market nations. They used 9 percent *less* energy on average in 1986, per $1,000 of output, than they had in 1980.

In the use of steel, the results were similar. The market economies used less than half as much steel per unit of output in 1975, and that figure fell 24 percent by 1985. The socialist economies used more than twice as much steel per unit of output at the beginning of the same period, and the amount used rose by 12 percent, rather than falling, over the same 10-year period.

Without market prices to guide and provide incentives for resource conservation, socialist economies use resources far less efficiently than do market economies. Looking across many different resources, Bernstam concludes: ''First, resource use per unit of output is much higher in socialist than in market economies. . . . Second, inputs of basic resources declined in Western market economies during the last two decades of economic growth and technological progress. These inputs continually increased in socialist economies with or without economic growth.''[8]

The kind of conservation that leads to rising efficiency in market economies is shown in Exhibit 5. An important use of aluminum is for beverage cans. Competition among producers of steel and aluminum cans produced large reductions in the amount of aluminum needed per can. In turn, this saving meant a large reduction in the amount of electrical energy used to produce beverage cans.

Efficiency in resource use does more than increase the value of output per unit of resource input: Reducing waste means reducing pollution. The disposal of waste is the most common cause of environmental pollution. Smoke is unburned fuel, water pollution is unutilized mineral or chemical inputs, and much of the garbage in landfills is the unused portion of retail purchases. The inefficiency of the socialist economies is matched by the degree to which their air, water, and land are polluted by waste products.

Western observers were shocked at the levels of pollution found when the Berlin wall and the Iron Curtain fell, and the world was permitted to travel more freely in the socialist nations. Less efficient use of resources due to the absence of property rights and the resulting market prices, implies a larger pollution problem. We turn now to look at the importance of property rights, and the resulting market prices and incentives, for environmental quality.

PROPERTY RIGHTS AND ENVIRONMENTAL QUALITY

Environmental pollution generally is the disposal or leakage of potentially harmful waste products into air or water or onto the land of others. A pollutant becomes a problem when its concentration and its location cause harm.

Pollution is a property rights problem from two perspectives. First, if the resources going into the polluting waste product are owned and are valuable, then the owner has an incentive to conserve rather than waste them. The search for economical ways to conserve is part of the search to increase profits by reducing resource costs. Second, when property rights are established and enforceable, the owner of a harmed resource (human or otherwise) has an incentive to prevent the harm by enforcing the right to be free of harm caused by others. Thus a polluter is not only losing the resources going into the polluting waste stream, but is also liable for damages done to the resources of others.

---

[8]See Bernstam, cited above, p. 23.

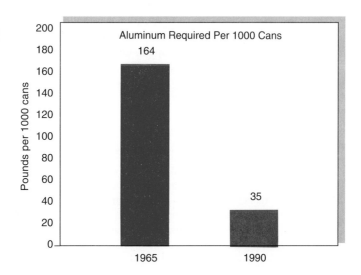

Source: Lynn Scarlett, "Make Your Environment Dirtier—Recycle," *Wall Street Journal*, Jan. 14, 1991.

Sometimes property rights can be enforced against polluters, even when the threatened water or the air is not privately owned. Consider the case of water pollution in England and Scotland. There, unlike the United States, sports and commercial fishing rights are privately owned and transferable even though the streams themselves are not. Owners of fishing rights can sue polluters of streams, and they can obtain damage awards and court injunctions to stop polluting activities. Such lawsuits occurred well before pollution control became part of the politically controlled public policy. Once established by precedent, such rights seldom need to be defended in court.[9]

Where property rights can be established and defended, owners have both the ability and the incentive to protect those rights, often more effectively through the courts than with extensive bureaucratic controls. Owners have good reason to do the job on a self-interested and cost-effective basis.

An important result of enforceable property rights is that both the owners of polluting resources and the owners of harmed resources have the authority and the incentive to reduce pollution and its damages. The polluter is held accountable for the results, partly by the cost of the polluting resource and partly by the liability for harm done to others and to the resources they own.

Unfortunately, property rights cannot always be used effectively to protect resources. If carbon dioxide and other gasses emitted by all animals, by rice crops, and even by volcanoes are found to cause a harmful level of global warming, as some scientists believe, then lawsuits against all these international sources are not a feasible answer to the problem. More direct governmental action may be required. Similarly, if the smog in the Los Angeles basin is found to cause serious harm, the

[9]See Jane S. Shaw and Richard L. Stroup, "Gone Fishin'," *Reason,* (August/September, 1988), pp. 34–37.

fact that it is caused by millions of automobiles and other such sources probably means that the right of individuals to be free from harm imposed by the pollution of others cannot be properly enforced simply by lawsuits. Governmental (political) action may be required.

LOOKING AHEAD

We have seen how market prices can provide both the signals and the incentives needed for resource conservation and pollution control when property rights are enforceable and tradable in markets and when their prices reflect opportunity costs. In the next two chapters we will use the economic way of thinking to analyze more fully the factors that may indicate the need for political (governmental) action and the problems that these actions themselves can bring.

CHAPTER SUMMARY

1. Natural resources are "gifts of nature," but their value depends on human effort, knowledge, culture, and ingenuity, and on the circumstances in which people have access to the resources.

2. As with other markets, incentives matter in resource markets. Both the quantity demanded of a resource and the quantity supplied depend on the resource price. Substitutes can be found everywhere. Both the demand and the supply curves will be more elastic when buyers and sellers have more time in which to respond to a price change.

3. Information about the future availability of a natural resource is costly, and proved reserves of a mineral resource are equivalent to an inventory. Discovering and verifying an oil field or a mineral deposit far in advance of when it will be used may be more costly than it is worth. Proved reserves of many minerals are growing, as prices and technologies change.

4. Resource values are determined at the margin, rather than by the average usefulness or average cost of the resource. When a resource is worth more at the margin in one use than in another, gains from trade are possible.

5. The opportunity cost of a resource is its relevant cost. Nonmarketed resources, and projects involving those resources, are difficult to evaluate. Benefit-cost analysis is a process to conduct project evaluation.

6. Neither economic analysis nor empirical evidence is supportive of the view that the world is about to run out of key natural resources. When private property rights are present, increased scarcity (relative to demand) of a natural resource will increase the price of the resource and thereby encourage conservation, the use of substitutes, and the development of new technologies capable of reducing our reliance on the resource. The fact that the real prices of most natural resources have declined during the last century is inconsistent with the doomsday view of resource scarcity.

7. In a market setting, the existence of secure, transferable property rights is a key to proper conservation and wise use of natural resources, as with all other goods and services. Comparisons of resource conservation between market and socialist economies confirm this point.

8. Environmental pollution can generally be viewed as a property rights problem. When people lack enforceable property rights to clean air and water, they may be harmed by the pollution of others. When rights can be enforced, as in the case of English fishing rights, pollution can be stopped by those harmed.

9. Enforceable property rights cannot always be put into place, so the preservation of environmental quality may require governmental intervention.

CRITICAL ANALYSIS QUESTIONS

*1. In what sense are crude oil and other natural resources "gifts of nature"? In what sense are they the result of human ingenuity?

2. Why is the price elasticity of demand for resources such as electricity and natural gas greater in the long run than the short run? What examples of responses to price changes can you think of that are more complete after one year than after one week?

*3. "Steel production typically requires 40,000 gallons of water per finished ton of steel. Steel is important to U.S. industry and our national defense. As water becomes more scarce in the nation, it is imperative that the required amounts of water be reserved for the steel industry." Evaluate.

4. "The federal government should do a complete survey of mineral availability in the nation. It is inexcusable that we do not know how much oil, for example, the country can ultimately produce." Evaluate.

*5. "If the federal government starts charging fees for outdoor recreation, only the rich will be able to participate. They will buy up all the opportunities, leaving none for the common citizen." Evaluate.

*6. Why will more oil *in total* be produced from an oil well, when the price of crude oil is higher?

*7. What is the difference between the total reserves of a mineral and its proved reserves? Why might both be important?

8. Will the world ever run out of any resource? Why are economists likely to answer in the negative? Does this imply that increasing resource scarcity will never be a problem?

*9. Does a resource that is not owned, and therefore is not priced, have a zero opportunity cost? Might it be treated as if it did? Explain.

10. Some of the oil now being produced in the world can be delivered to a Texas gulf-coast refinery for about $3 per barrel. Other oil now being produced costs more than $20 per barrel, delivered to the same refinery. What is the opportunity cost of selling the oil to the refinery, in each case?

*11. "Corporations should not be allowed to own forests. Corporate managers are just too short-sighted. Their philosophy is to make a profit now, regardless of the future consequences. For example, trees may be cut after growing 30 years to get revenue now, even though another 20 years' growth would yield a very high rate of return. The long-run health of our forests is too important to entrust them to this sort of management." Evaluate.

* 12. Suppose that you were the owner of some land scheduled to be irrigated by water from a heavily subsidized dam project being proposed in Congress. If the project is built, you would receive increased net farming revenues from your land. The project's costs would occur over the next 2 years, but the benefits would start later and continue for the next 50 years. Would you want the federal benefit-cost analysts, whose report will be available to Congress, to use a high or a low interest rate in their analysis? Why?

13. When farmers who receive water from federal irrigation projects repay project costs, they do so over a long period, often 50 years, with no payments due during the first 10 years. They pay no interest, but of course the federal government does pay interest on the funds borrowed to build the project. Suppose that the relevant interest

*Asterisk denotes questions for which answers are given in Appendix C, Selected Answers.

rate is 7 percent (a dollar doubles in value every 10 years at that rate), and the project built now costs $1 million. If the farmers simply give the federal government the full $1 million on a date 30 years after the project cost is paid, have they paid the full cost of the project? If not, how much is their subsidy?

14. "Since our National Forests are owned by all the people, their resources will be conserved for the benefit of all, rather than exploited in a shortsighted way, to produce benefits only for the owners." Evaluate.

PART FIVE

Public Choice

29 Problem Areas for the Market

The principal justification for public policy intervention lies in the frequent and numerous shortcomings of market outcomes.[1]

Charles Wolf

CHAPTER FOCUS

- Why do market decision-makers face inappropriate incentives when an externality is present?

- What role do imperfect information and imperfect property rights play in causing externalities?

- What can we learn from the theory of external effects about pollution problems and alternative solutions? Why are some solutions to pollution problems less effective than others?

- What is the "free rider" problem? What kinds of goods are likely to be susceptible to this problem?

- What can we say about buyers' and sellers' lack of knowledge in the market, and when is this problem likely to be most serious?

We have emphasized that a properly functioning market system uses prices to coordinate the decisions of buyers and sellers. Market prices give each decision-maker the information needed to make intelligent decisions, while weighing the relative desires of others. Equally important, prices provide the incentive to use that information. Even when they think only of themselves, decision-makers facing appropriate prices act as if they care about others. For example, to personally gain the largest return, resource owners have an incentive to move their resources to uses in which others value them most. Producers want to get the most highly valued production from the bundle of resources they use, and to minimize the cost (the value to others) of those resource inputs. Buyers have an incentive to economize on their consumption of each good and service in order to get as much satisfaction as possible from their limited budgets.

In short, the "invisible hand" of Adam Smith provides each decision-maker in the market economy with the information and incentive to act as if others matter. However, as we pointed out in Chapter 4, the invisible hand can slip. (At this point, the reader should review Chapter 4.) There are several potential causes of **market failure,** economic activity that results in allocative inefficiency relative to the hypothetical ideal of economists. The causes of market failure can be grouped into four general classes: (a) externalities, (b) public goods, (c) poorly informed buyers or sellers, and (d) monopoly.

In this chapter, we will delve more deeply into market failure and the possible responses to it, especially government responses. Since the impact of monopoly on the product and factor markets has already been investigated, this chapter will emphasize the other three categories of market failure.

Keep in mind that market failure is merely a failure to attain conditions of *ideal* efficiency. Alternative forms of economic organization will also have defects. Market failure creates an opportunity for government to improve the situation. In some circumstances, however, public-sector action will not be corrective. Sometimes there may even be good reason to expect it will be counterproductive. We will analyze market failure in this chapter and focus on the operation of the public sector in the next chapter.

Market Failure: The failure of the market system to attain hypothetically *ideal* allocative efficiency. This means that potential gain exists that has not been captured. However, the cost of establishing a mechanism that could *potentially* capture the gain may exceed the benefits. Therefore, it is not always possible to improve the situation.

EXTERNAL EFFECTS AND THE MARKET

The genius of a market exchange system lies in its ability to bring personal and social welfare into harmony. When two parties trade, and only they are affected, production and voluntary exchange also promote the *social* welfare. When externalities are present, though, production and exchange affect the welfare of nonconsenting secondary parties. The external effects may be either positive or negative.

If the welfare of nonconsenting secondary parties is adversely affected by actions not accounted for in market prices, the spillover effects are called **external costs.** A steel mill that belches smoke into the air imposes an external cost on surrounding residents who prefer clear air. A junkyard creates an eyesore, making an area less pleasant for passersby. Similarly, litterbugs, drunk drivers, muggers,

External Costs: Harmful effects of an individual's or a group's action on the welfare of nonconsenting secondary parties, not accounted for in market prices. Litterbugs, drunk drivers, and polluters, for example, create external costs.

---

[1]Charles Wolf, Jr. *Markets or Government,* (Cambridge: MIT Press, 1988), p. 17.

"In other words, what you'll have us believe, sir, is that all the fish in the river next to your plant suddenly died of old age."

Reproduced by Special Permission of Playboy Magazine © 1980 by Playboy.

External Benefits: Beneficial effects of group or individual action on the welfare of non-paying secondary parties.

and robbers impose unwanted costs on others. If the spillover effects enhance the welfare of secondary parties, they are called **external benefits.** A beautiful rose garden provides external benefits for the neighbors of the gardener. A golf course generally provides spillover benefits if others own the surrounding property.

When external costs and external benefits are present, market prices will not send the proper signals to producers and consumers. This situation results in market failure.

External Costs.

From the viewpoint of economic efficiency, an action should be undertaken only if it generates benefits in excess of its social costs. **Social costs** include (a) the private cost borne by the consenting parties and (b) any external cost imposed on nonconsenting secondary parties.

Social Costs: The sum of (a) the private costs that are incurred by a decision-maker and (b) any external cost of the action that are imposed on nonconsenting secondary parties. If there are no external costs, private and social costs will be equal.

When external costs are present, market prices understate the social cost generated by the use of resources or consumption of products. Decision-makers are not forced to fully bear the cost associated with their actions. Motivated by self-interest, they may undertake actions that generate a net loss to the community. The harm done to the secondary parties may exceed the net private gain. In such circumstances, private interest and economic efficiency are in conflict.

External Costs and Ideal Output.

Externalities may result from the actions of either consumers or producers. When the actions of a producer impose external costs on others, the costs of the firm, reflecting only private costs, are not an accurate indicator of the total social costs of production.

Exhibit 1 illustrates the impact of external costs on the socially desirable price and output. Suppose there are a large number of copper-producing firms. They are

EXHIBIT 1

Supply, Externalities, and Minimum-Cost Production of Copper

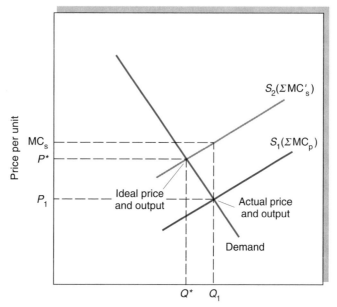

Supply curve S_2 reflects the social and private cost of producing copper. Supply curve S_1, however, reflects only the private costs paid by copper producers. The ideal output, considering both private and social cost, is Q^* and the optimal price (and producer cost) is P^*. But when producers are not forced to be responsible for social costs, we can expect a larger output Q_1 and a larger social marginal cost MC_s, even though buyers only pay P_1 for copper.

able to discharge their waste products (mainly sulfur dioxide) into the air without charge, even though the pollution damages people and property downwind from the discharge. These air pollution costs are external to the copper producers. If allowed to operate freely, the producers have little incentive to adopt either cleaner production techniques or control devices that would limit the costs inflicted on others. These alternatives would increase their private production cost without generating additional benefits (revenue) for the producer.

Since pollutants can be freely discharged into the atmosphere, each copper producer expands output as long as marginal private costs (MC_p) are less than price. This leads to market supply curve S_1, the horizontal summation of the *private* marginal cost curves of the copper producers. Given the demand, the equilibrium market price for copper is P_1. Producers supply Q_1 units of copper. At output level Q_1, however, the *social* marginal cost of copper is MC_s, an amount substantially in excess of both the private cost and the consumer's valuation (as indicated by the height of the demand curve at Q_1) of copper. As a result of the external costs, output is expanded beyond the ideal efficiency level. From the standpoint of efficiency, the market price, which fails to reflect the external cost, is too low. Additional units of copper are produced even though the value of the resources, as measured by the social marginal costs (and supply curve S_2) required to produce the units, exceeds the consumer's valuation of the units. A deterioration in air quality is a by-product.

When a producer's action imposes external costs on secondary parties, the producer's marginal costs will be understated. Therefore, the producer will produce more of a good and charge less for it (and probably use different techniques to produce it) as compared to outcomes consistent with ideal economic efficiency.

Private Property Rights: A set of usage and exchange rights held *exclusively* by the owner(s).

External Costs and Property Rights.   Clearly defined and enforced property rights are essential for the efficient operation of a market economy. The problems caused by externalities stem from a failure (or an inability) to clearly define and enforce property rights. Property rights help determine how resources will be used and who will be allowed to use them. **Private property rights** give owners the exclusive right to control and benefit from their resources as long as their actions do not harm others. It is important to recognize that private property rights do not include the right to use one's property in a manner that will injure others. For example, property rights do not grant the owners of rocks the right to throw them at automobiles.

Property rights also provide individuals with legal protection against the actions of parties who might damage, abuse, or steal their property. While property rights are often associated with selfishness on the part of owners, they could more properly be viewed as a means by which owners (including corporate owners) are protected against the selfishness of others. If adequately compensated, though, property owners often allow others to use their assets, even though the value of the assets will consequently fall. Rental car firms sell individuals the right to use their automobiles despite the reduction in the resale value of the car. Housing is often rented, even though normal use by the renter imposes a maintenance and upkeep cost on the homeowner. Since property rights are clearly defined and enforceable in these cases, the market exchange system induces people who use the property (including the owner, whose wealth is tied up in the value of the property) to fully consider the costs of their actions.

ENFORCEABLE PROPERTY RIGHTS AND INFORMATION

To legally enforce property rights, the owner must be able to show in court that those rights have in fact been violated. If John runs into Mary's car, the case is often fairly simple, and the parties may not even have to go to court. When John knows that Mary can prove him at fault and quantify the damages, he (or his insurance company) will simply compensate Mary for the damage done. (If John was insured, his rates will likely rise.) But, consider the case of Mr. Steel, the factory owner whose smoke fouls the air at Mary's home. Mary may have a right to clean air, which is violated by Mr. Steel's smoke. To receive compensation, however, she must be able to demonstrate in court: (a) the extent of the damage inflicted by the pollution, (b) that the pollutant in question actually caused the damage, and (c) that the pollutant came from Mr. Steel's plant. It is likely to be very costly, or even impossible, for her to do so. Her property rights, then, although defined, are probably not enforceable. They are useless, in effect, and external cost is the result.

The high cost (or the unavailability) of information can make property rights unenforceable, and bring about market failure. Unfortunately, the same lack of information may prevent governmental solutions from improving the situation. If we cannot estimate the consequences of certain actions, such as the emission of certain amounts of a pollutant at a specific time in a specific place, this lack of information will prevent any rational approach, private or public, to the problem.

COMMON PROPERTY RESOURCES AND EFFICIENCY

Property rights are sometimes held in common. A **common property resource** is one for which rights are held in common by a group of individuals, none of whom has a transferable ownership interest. Access to a common property resource may be unrestricted, as in the case of air, or may be controlled politically, as wildlife is controlled by state governments in the United States.

If access to the resource is unrestricted, it is an **open access resource.** When there is more of it than people wish to use, then the open access resource is not

Common Property Resource: A resource for which rights are held in common by a group of individuals, none of whom has a transferable ownership interest. Access to the resource may be open (unrestricted), or may be controlled politically.

Open Access Resource: A resource to which access is unrestricted. No one has the right to exclude others from using the resource. Overuse and abuse of such a resource is typical.

scarce and there is no problem. However, trouble arises when such a resource becomes scarce. (See the Applications in Economics box, ''The Importance of Common and Private Property Rights.'') Without some form of political control to replace the ownership functions of controlling access and of caring for or maintaining the resource, external costs are almost guaranteed. For example, when water users are harmed by pollution, but cannot sue for damages, then external costs due to pollution are likely to occur. The polluter (who does not own the water) has no incentive to curtail his activities that cause pollution. Streams, like other resources, are much more likely to be abused when they are treated as open access resources. We have established environmental control agencies in order to deal with the problems that arise when there is open access to a resource.

As we will see in more detail in the next chapter, political control of a common property resource, such as the air or a river, has its own problems. Typically, no one person or small, easily organized group has a large stake in seeing to it that decision-makers protect the resource and allocate its use efficiently. Would private ownership rights, then, be more efficient? Not necessarily. It is costly to establish and defend the property rights of certain resources.[2] Exclusive ownership can easily be defined and defended for such commodities as apples, cabbages, waterbeds, cars, and airline tickets, but how would one establish and defend property rights to salmon or whales, which travel thousands of miles each year? Similarly, who owns an oil pool that is located on the property of hundreds of different landowners? In the absence of clearly assigned property rights, spillover costs and overutilization are inevitable. Certain whales have been on the verge of extinction because no single individual (or small group) has an incentive to reduce its own current catch so that the future catch will be larger. Each tries to catch as many whales as possible now; someone else will catch those whales, the argument goes, if the first person (or group) does not. The same principle applies to oil-pool rights when many well owners can draw from the pool and no single owner can control the rate of withdrawal. In the absence of regulation, each oil-well operator has an incentive to draw the oil *from a common pool* as rapidly as possible. When all operators do so, though, the commonly owned oil is drawn out too rapidly and the total amount that can be withdrawn falls.

EXTERNAL BENEFITS AND MISSED OPPORTUNITIES

Spillover effects are not always harmful. Sometimes the actions of an individual (or firm) generate external benefits; gains that accrue to nonparticipating (and nonpaying) secondary parties. When external benefits are present, the personal gains of the consenting parties understate the total social gain, including that of secondary parties. Activities with greater social benefits than costs may not be undertaken because no single decision-maker will be able to fully capture all the gains. Considering only personal net gains, decision-makers will allow potential social gains to go unrealized.

As in the case of external costs, external benefits occur when property rights are undefined or unenforceable. Because of this, it is costly—or impossible—to

---

[2]The problems entailed in defining and enforcing private, transferable property rights are discussed in Terry L. Anderson and P. J. Hill, ''Privatizing the Commons: An Improvement?'' *Southern Economic Journal*, vol. 50., no. 2 (October 1983).

APPLICATIONS IN ECONOMICS

The Importance of Common and Private Property Rights

What is common to many is taken least care of, for all men have greater regard for what is their own than for what they possess in common with others.[3]

Aristotle

The point made by Aristotle more than 2,000 years ago is as true now as it was then. It is as important in primitive cultures as it is in developed ones. When resources are held in common and access is unrestricted, the resource typically is abused and endangered. In contrast, when the rights are held by an individual (or family), conservation and wise utilization generally result. The following examples from sixteenth-century England, nineteenth-century American Indian culture, present-day Africa, and ocean fisheries illustrate the point.

Cattle Grazing on the English Commons

Many English villages in the sixteenth century had commons, or commonly held pastures, which were available to any villagers who wanted to graze their animals. Since the benefits of grazing an additional animal accrued fully to the individual, whereas the cost of overgrazing was an external one, the pastures were grazed extensively. Since the pastures were communal property, there was little incentive for an *individual* to conserve grass in the present so that it would be more abundant in the future. When everyone used the pasture extensively, there was not enough grass at the end of the grazing season to provide a good base for next year's growth. What was

good for the individual was bad for the village as a whole. In order to preserve the grass, pastures were fenced in the enclosure movement. After the enclosure movement established private property rights, owners and managers saw to it that overgrazing no longer occurred.

The Property Rights of American Indians

Among American Indian tribes, common ownership of the hunting grounds was the general rule. Because the number of native Americans was small and their hunting technology was not highly developed, hunted animals seldom faced extinction. However, there were at least two exceptions.

One was the beaver hunted by the Montagnais Indians of the Labrador Peninsula. When the French fur traders came to the area in the early 1600s, the beaver increased in value and therefore became increasingly scarce. Recognizing the depletion of the beaver population and the animal's possible extinction, the Montagnais began to institute private property rights. Each beaver-trapping area on a stream was assigned to a family, and conservation practices were adopted. The last remaining pair of beavers was never trapped, since the taker would only be hurting his own family the following year. For a time, the supply of beavers was no longer in jeopardy. However, when a new wave of European trappers invaded the area, the native Americans, because they were unable to enforce their property rights, abandoned conservation to take the pelts while they could.[4] Individual

ownership was destroyed, and conservation disappeared with it.

Property Rights and African Elephants

The excessive exploitation of wildlife can be linked to an absence of property rights. Because herds of Great Plains buffalo were available for everyone to use, allowing individuals to kill animals without facing the costs of herd depletion, the buffalo suffered near-extinction during the nineteenth century.[5] Today, we see contrasting approaches to such a problem with the African elephant. In Kenya, elephants roam unowned on unfenced terrain. The Kenyan government tries to protect elephants from poachers seeking valuable ivory by banning all commercial use of the elephant except tourism. In the decade that this policy has been in effect, the Kenyan elephant population has fallen from 65,000 to 19,000. In other East and Central African countries that have followed the Kenyan approach, the collective elephant populations have dropped from 1,044,050 to 429,520 between 1979 and 1989.[6]

---

[3]Aristotle, as quoted by Will Durant in *The Life of Greece* (New York: Simon and Schuster, 1939), p. 536.
[4]For an economic analysis of the Montagnais management of the beaver, together with historical references, see Harold Demsetz, ''Toward a Theory of Property Rights,'' *American Economic Review* (May 1967), pp. 347–59.
[5]See Francis Haines, *The Buffalo* (New York: Crowell, 1970).
[6]Randy Simmons and Urs Kreuter, ''Herd Mentality: Banning Ivory Sales Is No Way to Save the Elephant,'' *Policy Review* (Fall 1989) pp. 46–49, provide the facts used in this section.

In Zimbabwe, by contrast, shops openly sell ivory and hides and legislation was passed giving the local people on whose land the elephant roam the right to hunt the elephants. This encourages them to preserve elephants and to permit controlled hunting by big-game hunters. Since assigning property rights in elephants, Zimbabwe has seen its elephant population grow from 30,000 to 43,000. Elephant populations in the countries adopting a similar approach—Botswana, South Africa, Malawi, and Namibia—are increasing at a rate of five percent a year.

Property Rights and Ocean Fisheries

Once, the waters off the northeastern United States teemed with Atlantic Cod, haddock, flounder, and pollock—fish that many people love to eat, and many fishermen love to catch. But fish populations have fallen sharply in recent years due to overfishing, a problem for wild fisheries all over the world.[7] Wild fisheries of the oceans are open access resources. The only way to claim ownership of fish is to catch them. In addition, there is no individual incentive to leave some fish for next year's catch; other fishermen will probably catch them. Without an authority, such as an owner, in place to control access, the fish population faces possible extinction.

When demand for the fish is high, and new fishermen enter so that overfishing occurs, fishermen suffer losses. As the population of fish falls, costs rise because the sparser population of fish requires a more intensive effort to find

them. The smaller catch may reduce supply enough to raise the price of fish, but entry will occur until there is no profit, and if the population is falling, profit is likely to turn negative. Yet, in the short run, fishermen will continue to fish so long as they can cover their variable costs, keep the fishing pressure intense, and further reduce the number of fish and the available breeding stock.

Compare this open access fishery with one where the fish population or its territory is owned by a person or group who can control the rate of take, practicing conservation to protect next year's profits, which, after all, belong to the owner. We would expect that more conservation would be practiced, and overfishing would not occur, so that the income of fishermen would be higher. Richard J. Agnello and Lawrence P. Donnelley found just such results when they compared open access and private property oyster beds.[8] Using data from Maryland, Virginia, Louisiana, and Mississippi, they found that from 1945 to 1970 the ratio of harvest in the earlier part of the season to the later part was 1.35 for open access oyster beds and 1.01 for the private-property oyster bed. In the open access fishery, each fisherman tried to catch as many fish as quickly as possible, just as our logic predicts. Too much fishing effort was expended all season, relative to the more efficient allocation of fishing effort under the private property regime. Fishermen in the private-property state of Louisiana earned $3,207, while their counterparts in the open access state of Mississippi earned

$807. Such a finding supports the expectation of higher incomes and larger harvests over the years, under the private property regime. These and other findings of the study indicate that property rights, by solving the open access problem, help conserve a fishery resource and manage it more efficiently.

Could property rights be established for fisheries on the high seas? Such a scheme is not costless, and both federal and state governments have held that private rights violate antitrust laws. Informal unions of fishermen have tried to limit entry, but they have had limited success. Any agreement is difficult to maintain without an authority to enforce it.[9]

Don Leal, Research Associate, Political Economy Research Center Bozeman, Montana

[7]See Jennifer A. Kingston, "Northeast Fishermen Catch Everything, and That's a Problem," *The New York Times,* November 13, 1988.
[8]Richard J. Agnello and Lawrence P. Donnelley, "Prices and Property Rights in the Fisheries," *Southern Economic Journal,* XLII (October 1979), pp. 253–62.
[9]Ronald N. Johnson and Gary D. Libecap, "Contracting Problems and Regulation: The Case of the Fishery," *American Economic Review,* (December 1982), pp. 1,005–1,022.

withhold these benefits from secondary parties and retain them for oneself at the same time. The producer of a motion picture has rights to the film and can collect a fee from anyone who sees or rents it. In contrast, a person who produces a beautifully landscaped lot that is visible from the street cannot collect a fee for the enjoyment that others derive from it. Some of the benefits of the landscaper's efforts accrue to secondary parties who probably will not help cover the cost.

Why should we be bothered if others benefit from our actions? Most of us are not, although it is quite possible, for example, that more people would better maintain their property if those who derived benefits from it helped pay for it. Generally, external benefits become important only when our inability to capture these potential gains forces us to *forgo* a socially beneficial activity. Exhibit 2 illustrates this point. Education adds to students' productivity, permitting them to attain higher future earnings. In addition, let us assume that those who receive at least a basic education may be better citizens, more competent voters, and may even commit fewer crimes. When some of the benefits of education accrue to the citizenry as a whole, not just to the students and their families, the private market demand curve understates the total social benefits of education. In the absence of government intervention, as shown in Exhibit 2, Q_1 units of education result from market forces. However, when external benefits MB are added to private benefits, the social gain from additional units of education exceeds the cost until output level Q_s is produced. The welfare of all in the community might thus be improved if output were expanded beyond Q_1 to Q_s, but since educational consumers cannot capture these external gains, they fail to purchase units beyond Q_1. The free market output is too small. A subsidy is required if the ideal output level Q_s is to be achieved.

When external benefits are present, the market demand curve understates the social gains of conducting the beneficial activity. Potential social gains go unrealized because no single decision-maker can fully appropriate or capture the gains; they are seen as "lost" when bestowed on nonpaying secondary parties. Decision-makers thus lack the incentive to carry an activity far enough to capture fully the potential social gains.

EXHIBIT 2

Adding External Benefits

The demand curve *D*, indicating only private benefits, understates the social benefits of education. At output Q_1, the social benefit of an additional unit of education exceeds the cost. Ideally, output should be expanded to Q_s, where the social benefit of the marginal unit of education would be just equal to its cost. A public subsidy of *AB,* per unit of education, would lead to this output level.

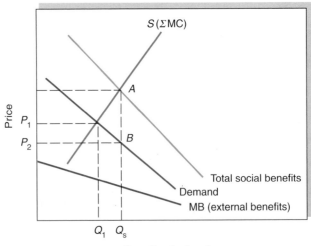

PUBLIC-SECTOR RESPONSES TO EXTERNALITIES

What can the government do to improve the efficiency of resource allocation when externalities are present? Sometimes private property rights can be more clearly defined and more strictly enforced. The granting of property rights to ranchers and homesteaders greatly improved the efficiency of land use in the Old West. More recently, the establishment of enforceable property rights to the oyster beds of the Chesapeake Bay improved the efficiency of oyster farming in the area. In many instances, however, it is difficult to delineate boundaries for a resource, determine who owns what portion, and enforce those rights. This is clearly the case with air and water rights. The clean-air rights of property owners often lack enforcement due to the high cost of information. In most states, water itself is not individually owned, although the right to use the water in certain ways may be privately held. Thus, the market process may fail to give good information and incentives to water users. External costs then result.

Why not simply prohibit activities that result in external cost? After all, why should we allow nonconsenting parties to be harmed? This approach has a certain appeal, but closer inspection indicates that it is often an unsatisfactory solution. Automobile exhaust imposes an external cost on bicyclists and, for that matter, on everyone who breathes. Dogs are notorious for using the neighbor's lawn for bone burying and relief purposes. Motorboats are noisy and frighten fish, much to the disgust of fishermen. Few people, though, would argue that we should do away with cars, dogs, and motorboats. From a social viewpoint, prohibition is often a less desirable alternative than tolerating the inconvenience of the external costs. The gains from the activity must be weighed against the costs imposed on those who are harmed, as well as against practical problems associated with controlling the activity.

When we cannot establish and enforce property rights, as in the case of our air resources, but we do not want simply to prohibit an activity, an alternative control strategy may be necessary. There are three general approaches that government might take. First, a government agency might act as a resource manager, charging the users of the resource a fee. Second, a regulatory agency might establish a maximum pollution emission standard and require that polluters attain at least that standard. Third, the agency might specify exactly what pollution control steps each polluter must take. We will consider each of these alternatives.

THE POLLUTION TAX APPROACH

Some economists favor a user's charge, which we will call a pollution tax. Exhibit 3 uses actual cost estimates from a copper smelter to illustrate the economics of this approach. The copper-producing firm has minimum costs of production when it spends nothing on pollution control. The marginal control cost curve reveals the cost savings (control costs avoided) that accrue to the firm when it pollutes. The marginal damage cost curve shows the cost ($32.50 per ton) imposed on parties downwind from the smelter. Without any tax or legal restraints, the smelter would emit 190,000 tons of sulfur dioxide into the air per year, causing $6.2 million in damage. A tax equal to the marginal damage cost of $32.50 per ton emitted would cause the firm to reduce its emissions to 17,100 tons per year and reduce pollution damage from $6.2 million to about $0.6 million per year. The control cost of reducing emissions to this level would be about $2.9 million per year. Total social

EXHIBIT 3

Taxing a Smelter's Emissions

The marginal control cost curve shows that the firm, if it pays no damage costs itself, will emit 190,000 tons per year while spending nothing on control costs. However, if taxed according to the marginal damages it imposes ($32.50 per ton), it will voluntarily cut back its emissions to 17,100 tons per year, which is the socially efficient level. Further control would cost more than its social benefit.

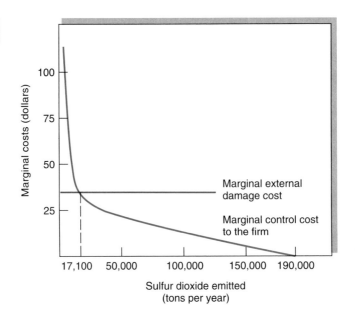

Source: Richard L. Stroup, "The Economics of Air Pollution Control" (Ph.D. diss., University of Washington, 1970).

costs each year would fall from $6.2 million (all borne by those suffering pollution damage) to $3.5 million (combined costs of pollution damage and control, paid entirely by the firm and its customers). The net social gain would be $2.7 million.

The tax approach would promote efficient resource allocation by altering several economic incentives in a highly desirable way. First, the pollution tax would increase the cost of producing pollution-intensive goods, causing the supply in these industries to decline. A properly set tax would approximate the ideal price and output conditions illustrated by Exhibit 1. The revenues generated by the tax could be used to compensate secondary parties harmed by the pollutants or to finance a wide range of projects, including applied research on alternative methods of improving air quality. Second, the pollution tax would give firms an economic incentive to use methods of production (and control technology) that would create less pollution. As long as it was cheaper for the firm to control harmful emissions than to pay the emission fee (tax), the firm would opt for control. Third, since firms would be able to lower their tax bills by controlling pollution, a market for innovative emission-control devices would exist. Entrepreneurs would be induced to develop low-cost control devices and market them to firms that would now have a strong incentive to reduce their levels of emissions.

The pollution tax is backed by some environmental advocacy groups, as well as many economists.[10] It has been criticized on several grounds by policy-makers, however. There are three common objections: first, to be efficient it must be based on damage costs of the emissions. It is difficult to estimate the size of these damages. Of course this same problem hinders any strategy which might be intended to be efficient. A second problem for the tax approach is that emissions would have to be monitored. Again, any efficient approach would require

[10]See for example Lester Brown, et al., eds. *State of the World, 1991,* (New York: W.W. Norton & Co., 1991), pp. 181–85.

knowledge of who is polluting, and how much. A third objection, which carries a lot of weight in the political arena, is that the tax approach would require payment from polluters who previously did not have to pay, so long as they met legal limits on how much of the pollutant they emitted. This would, in some cases, mean very large tax payments by polluters. Whole industries could be shaken up, and some firms put out of business. Lobbyists for polluters have successfully avoided such taxes up to this point.

Given the damage and control costs estimates of Exhibit 3, the pollution tax approach does not fully eliminate pollution emissions. Should it? Clearly, the answer is no. At pollution emission levels of less than 17,100 tons per year, the marginal costs of pollution control would exceed the marginal benefits of the control. In cases such as that illustrated by Exhibit 3, substantial improvement can be made at a modest cost. At some point, however, it will become extremely costly to make additional improvements.

The pollution tax approach recognizes that cleaning up the environment is like squeezing water from a wet towel. Initially, a great deal of water can be squeezed from the towel with very little effort, but it becomes increasingly difficult to squeeze out still more. So it is with the environment. At some point, the benefit of a cleaner environment simply becomes less than its cost. The optimal level of pollution is seldom zero.

People want clean air and water. However, since they want other things as well, those entrusted with the authority to control pollution should ask themselves two crucial questions: How many other goods and services are we willing to give up to fight each battle against pollution? And, how much would the public like us to spend, from its own pockets, to achieve additional freedom from pollution? Since we all want to obtain the maximum benefit from expenditures on pollution control, it is important that these questions be answered carefully, no matter which control strategy we adopt.

THE MAXIMUM EMISSION STANDARD APPROACH

Maximum Emission Standard: The maximum amount of pollution that a polluter is permitted to emit, established by the government or a regulatory authority. Fines are generally imposed on those who are unwilling or unable to comply.

Although economics suggests that the pollution tax approach would be much more efficient, a **maximum emission standard** is more often imposed. In this case, the regulatory agency forces all producers to reduce their emissions to a designated level. Producers who are unable to meet the standard are required to pay a fine or even to terminate production.

The problem with this approach is that the costs of eliminating pollution emissions generally vary widely among polluters. Some can control pollution much more cheaply than others, but the maximum emissions standard approach fails to use this fact to get more control per dollar of expenditure in control costs. It thus results in less pollution control per dollar than, for example, the pollution tax strategy.

Exhibit 4 illustrates why the standard emissions approach is an inefficient method of reducing the pollution level. Estimated minimum costs of added control by three particulate pollution emitters are listed. Suppose the regulatory agency wants to reduce the total particulate emissions from the three firms by three tons. The emission standards approach might accomplish this simply by requiring each firm to reduce its particulate emissions by one ton. The cost of these equal reductions will differ substantially among the firms; it will cost the electric utility $80, the steel plant $990, and the petroleum refiner $573. If this method is adopted, it will cost society $1,643 in control cost to meet the new maximum pollution standard, which is three tons below the previous level of emissions.

EXHIBIT 4

Controlling Pollution—
Cheaper for Some Than
for Others

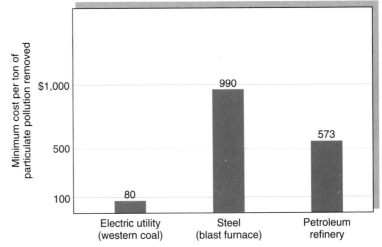

Source: EPA reports, summarized by Robert Crandall in *Controlling Industrial Pollution* (The Brookings Institution, Washington, D.C., 1983), page 36.

Some polluters face much higher control costs than others. If the authorities' control strategy does not properly take this into account, control may be needlessly expensive and opposition to control needlessly strong. If each polluter were required to reduce particulate pollution by one ton, total control costs for that change would be $80 + $990 + $573 = $1,643. But, if a pollution tax of $82.50 were levied, the steel and petroleum plants would pay it, while the electric utility would find it cheaper to control some of its particulate pollution, and a reduction of 3 tons of emissions would cost roughly $240 instead of more than $1,640.

Alternatively, the regulatory agency might levy a pollution tax and eliminate the same amount of pollution for much less. If we assume that a 3-ton reduction is small for each producer, so that each additional ton of pollution reduction raises control costs only by one dollar, then a tax of just $82.50 per ton would cause the electric utility to reduce particulate emissions by 3 tons, at a total cost of $243 ($80 + $81 + $82 = $243). That would allow the utility to escape 3 × $82.50 = $247.50 in added tax. The other polluters would not cut back emissions, but would choose to pay the tax, which is cheaper for them than the control costs. With the tax approach, which causes the cheapest control to take place, society buys the 3-ton reduction in pollution for $243, about one-seventh the cost incurred in the elimination of the same amount of pollution under the maximum emission control strategy.

TRANSFERABLE EMISSION RIGHTS

A much more efficient form of the maximum emission strategy is to require the same one-ton-per-firm reduction, but allow the remaining rights to pollute (their original pollution rate, minus one ton each) to be traded among the three. In this case, the electric utility would sell two tons of its rights-to-pollute, one to each of the other two firms. Why? It can profit by reducing its pollution by 3 tons for $243, then selling its "excess" pollution rights to the other two firms, saving the steel firm $990 and the refinery $573. The amount paid by the two firms to the utility for its service (added pollution control, beyond its own requirement) would be more than $80 per ton, but no higher than the $990 plus $573 saved by the other two. The net savings to society in getting the full 3-ton reduction in pollution is again the same as in the pollution tax case. The emission rights trading strategy also has an important political advantage: no large payments (or small ones either) have to be made by the firms to the tax collector.

Since each polluter has a different control cost schedule, either the pollution tax strategy or the emission rights trading strategy would result in the most pollution control per control dollar spent, and reach any desired pollution level at the lowest possible price. Some people object to the emissions trading strategy because pollution emitted at one location may cause more damage or less damage than the same pollution at another place. This is true, but any efficient strategy would have to make adjustments to recognize this fact. The emissions trading strategy might allow polluters in densely populated areas to exchange their pollution rights with polluters in a sparsely populated area with a bonus. Two tons of pollution rights in Manhattan might trade for three tons on a sparsely populated part of the coast, where the winds usually blow the particulates out to sea with much less damage.

The emissions trading strategy was incorporated, in a limited way, into the Clean Air Act Amendments of 1990. Beginning in 1995, power plants fueled by coal are required to scale back their emissions of sulfur dioxide by more than half from 1980 levels. Those who control more than required, however, will be able to sell their "allowances" (the amount they are allowed by the new law to emit) to other power plants. Other polluters are not affected, but if this project is judged to be a success, additional uses of this strategy can be expected.

THE SPECIFIC PRESCRIPTION APPROACH

We have shown how the emission standard approach (without emissions trading) is less efficient than the pollution tax. Even less efficient is the approach taken earlier by Congress requiring the EPA to implement the Clean Air Act of 1970, for coal-burning electric power plants. Rather than set emission standards, Congress ordered the EPA to require that new plants use specific kinds of pollution control apparatus—giant "scrubbers" to clean exhaust gases from new coal-burning electric power plants. Even though cheaper and more reliable means are frequently available to produce electricity with the same or less pollution, especially the use of clean coal, the far more expensive scrubbers were required. This favored certain regions of the country over others, and delayed the construction of newer, cleaner power plants, so that the air was dirtier than it would have been with the cheaper control methods. As ironic and as well known as this situation was,[11] more efficient approaches were not politically feasible until 1990, when the Clean Air Act Amendments began to focus on emission standards. For reasons that we will explore more fully in the next chapter, the government solution to market failure is often itself rather inefficient.

SHOULD THE GOVERNMENT ALWAYS TRY TO CONTROL EXTERNALITIES?

When an externality is present, ideal efficiency of resource allocation may not be attained. It does not follow, though, that the government can always improve the situation and bring the economy closer to its ideal allocation level. In evaluating the case for a public-sector response to externalities, one should keep in mind the following three points.

1. *Sometimes the Economic Inefficiency Resulting from Externalities Is Small. Therefore, Given the Cost of Public-Sector Action, Net Gain from Intervention Is Unlikely.* The behavior of individuals often influences the welfare of others. The

---

[11]See Robert Crandall, *Controlling Industrial Pollution: the Economics and Politics of Clean Air* (Washington: The Brookings Institution, 1983); and Bruce Yandle, *The Political Limits of Environmental Regulation: Tracking the Unicorn* (New York: Quorum Books, 1989), for fascinating accounts of the politics and economics of this situation. Eastern coal mine owners and the United Mine Workers Union joined forces with environmental interests in the West, who wanted less mining of the cleaner western coal. This coalition pushed through the requirement that costly scrubbers be used instead of allowing power plants to switch to cleaner western coal.

length of hair, choice of clothing, and personal hygiene of some individuals may affect the welfare of secondary parties. Should an agency in charge of personal appearance and hygiene be established to deal with externalities in these areas? Persons who value personal freedom would answer with a resounding no. From the standpoint of economic efficiency, their view is correct. The effects of externalities in these and similar areas are small. The costs of correcting externalities of this type would often be greater than the benefit.

Government intervention requires the use of scarce resources. Regulatory agencies must be established; suits and countersuits are typically filed. These actions require the use of scarce and costly legal resources. Most public-sector decision-makers lack the information necessary to determine which activities should be taxed and which should be subsidized. Administrative problems such as these greatly reduce the attractiveness of public-sector action. When the external effects are small, the cost of government intervention is likely to exceed the loss due to market inefficiency, *relative to the hypothetical ideal*. Under these circumstances, the best approach is usually to do nothing.

2. *The Market Often Finds Reasonably Efficient Means of Dealing with Externalities.* The existence of externalities implies the presence of *potential* gain. If the external effects are significant, market participants have an incentive to organize economic activity in a manner that will enable them to capture the potential gain. If the number of parties affected by the externality is small, they may be able to arrive at a multi-party bargain that will at least partially negate the inefficiency and loss resulting from the externality.

Some entrepreneurs have devised ingenious schemes to capture benefits that were previously external to private parties. Private developers of country clubs and golf courses can capture the benefits of these amenities by placing them on large tracts of land. The purchasers of lots and houses will benefit from trees, gardens, manicured lawns, and so on. If consumers are willing to pay for these amenities, as they often are, tract developers who provide such amenities will be able to benefit from their provision in the form of higher prices on the sale of surrounding lots.[12] The greater the potential gains, the greater the incentive to find answers to these kinds of problems. Thus, market participants will often devise efficient arrangements for dealing with external effects, when those effects become sufficiently large.

3. *Government Action May Also Impose an External Cost on Secondary Parties.* We have already mentioned that government intervention designed to correct the inefficiencies created by externalities is costly. Often, the costs of public-sector intervention exceed the benefits. Therefore, on efficiency grounds, intervention should be rejected. In addition, we should recognize that even democratic public-sector action results in the imposition of an externality—the

---

[12]The development of Walt Disney World in Florida is an interesting case in which entrepreneurial ingenuity made it possible to capture external benefits more fully. When Walt Disney developed Disneyland in California, the market value of the land in the immediate area soared as a result of the increase in demand for services (food, lodging, gasoline, and so on). Since the land in the area was owned by others, the developers of Disneyland were unable to capture these external benefits. However, when Walt Disney World was developed near Orlando, Florida, the owners purchased an enormous plot of land, far more than was needed for the amusement park. As was the case with Disneyland in California, the operation of Walt Disney World caused land values in the immediate area to rise sharply. However, since the developers of Walt Disney World initially purchased a large amount of land near the attraction, they were able to capture the external benefits by selling prime property to hotels, restaurants, and other businesses desiring a nearby location.

majority imposes an external cost on the minority, which is opposed to the action. Just as an individual may carry an activity too far when some of the costs are borne by others, a majority may also carry an action beyond the point of ideal efficiency. The gains that accrue to the majority may be less than the costs imposed on the minority. So, even though the government can potentially take corrective measures, counterproductive economic action by the democratic majority may result if the external costs imposed on the minority are not fully considered. (Limits to the effectiveness of government action will be discussed more fully in the next chapter.)

MARKET FAILURE: PUBLIC GOODS

Public goods comprise the extreme case of commodities, the consumption of which results in spillover benefits to secondary parties. In the original formulation by Paul Samuelson, there are two distinctive characteristics of public goods. First, the availability of a public good to one person makes it equally available to all others. Public goods must therefore be consumed jointly by all. Second, because of this joint consumption, it may be impossible to exclude nonpayers from the receipt of public goods. It is important to note that only goods with these two characteristics qualify as public goods in an economic sense. Goods provided in the public sector, ranging from medical services and education to trash collection, are *not* necessarily public goods. Examples of *pure* public goods are rare. National defense is one. The defense system that protects you provides similar protection to all other citizens. The quality of the atmosphere might also be classified as a public good.

THE FREE RIDER PROBLEM

Free Rider: One who receives the benefit of a good without contributing to its costs. Public goods and commodities that generate external benefits offer people the opportunity to become free riders.

Since nonpaying consumers cannot be excluded (at a reasonable cost), a sufficient amount of public goods may not be provided by the market mechanism. If public goods were provided through the market, each of us would have an incentive to become a **free rider,** one who receives the benefits of a good without paying toward its costs. Why contribute to the cost of supplying a public good? Your actions will have a negligible impact on the supply of clean air, pure water, national defense, and legal justice. The sensible path will lead you to do nothing. As long as you travel that path alone, you will ride along, free and easy. If everyone else joins you, however, the aggregate lack of action will lead to an insufficient quantity of public goods.

Suppose national defense were provided entirely through the market. Would you voluntarily help to pay for it? Your contribution would have a negligible impact on the total supply of defense available to each of us, even if you made a *large personal* contribution. Many citizens, even though they might value defense highly, would become free riders, and few funds would be available to finance the necessary supply. If the military-industrial complex were dependent on market forces, it would be small indeed!

The harmony between private and social interests tends to break down for public goods. The amount of a public good available to an individual (and others) will be virtually unaltered by whether or not the individual pays for it. Each individual thus has an incentive to become a free rider. When numerous individuals become free riders, however, less than the ideal amount of the public good is likely to be produced. (It should be noted that markets will sometimes supply public goods. See Applications in Economics box ''Private Provision of Public Goods.'')

APPLICATIONS IN ECONOMICS

Private Provision of Public Goods

An excellent example of a public good is the preservation of a locally or nationally significant form of wildlife. Hawks, sea lions, and wild geese belong to no one, but their survival keeps ecosystems in balance and intact. We all benefit when habitats are kept available to ensure that such species do not become extinct. Despite the fact that each of us can be a free rider if others make the effort and sacrifice needed to bring about such preservation, successful voluntary efforts in the private sector have done just that: thousands of organizations, each defying the free rider problem, have for many decades led the conservation movement, privately establishing successful conservation projects.

Some of these groups are very large. The Nature Conservancy owns and manages a national system of nearly 800 sanctuaries and has preserved some 2.4 million acres since 1951. The 1984 Annual Report of the President's Council of Environmental Quality reports that the National Audubon Society has a sanctuary system of over 63 units totalling over 250,000 acres. Others are small—a local garden club might own and manage two acres to preserve a particular wild flower.

Private groups have often been leaders in educating the public, and have been well ahead of government in providing their particular public good. Two examples involve hawks and sea lions.

Example 1:
The Hawk Mountain Sanctuary
In the 1930s, hawks were considered a nuisance or worse, since they killed certain other birds, including domestic chickens. There was often a bounty on them—the government would pay people who killed hawks. Conservationists, however, had begun to worry about the declining numbers of hawks, pointing out that among other things, hawks ate rodents, keeping down the grain losses experienced by farmers. The environmental movement was still very weak, however, and the slaughter of hawks continued.

In one area in particular, Hawk Mountain of eastern Pennsylvania, thousands of hawks were killed on certain days each year. So upset was Rosalie Edge, an early conservationist (and leading suffragist) that when reasoning with governmental authorities failed, she organized a small group of conservationists who simply bought Hawk Mountain for $3,500. They prevented further shooting from that critical spot and established a nonprofit educational and conservation group—the

NEAR PUBLIC GOODS

Few commodities are pure public goods, but a much larger set of goods are jointly consumed even though nonpaying customers can be excluded. For example, such goods as radio and television broadcasts, national parks, interstate highways, movies, and football games may be jointly consumed. Until congestion sets in, additional consumption of these "near public goods," *once they are produced,* is costless to society.

Should nonpaying customers be excluded when the marginal cost of providing the good to them is zero? Many economists argue that such near public goods as highways, national parks, and television programming should be provided free to consumers, at the expense of the taxpayers. Why exclude people from the consumption of these near public goods when their use of the goods does not add to the costs? The argument has a certain appeal.

We must be careful, however. Television programs, highways, parks, and other public goods are scarce. The consumption of other products must be sacrificed to produce such goods. If a zero price is charged, how does one determine whether or not consumers value additional units enough to cover their opportunity cost? How can an intensely concerned minority communicate its views as to the types of near

Hawk Mountain Sanctuary Association. Seven thousand members from all over the nation, in addition to admission fees paid by 50,000 visitors per year, support a visitor and education center at the mountain where previously the hawks were slaughtered by the thousands each year.

Example 2: Sea Lion Caves, Inc.
Like hawks, sea lions on the Oregon coast were formerly hunted, and bounties were paid to those who killed them. Sea lions feed on fish, and during the 1920s the state of Oregon paid $5 per sea lion killed. Several bounty hunters made their living in this fashion. The intent was to reduce sea lion consumption of coastal salmon. Earlier, commercial fishing interests hired professional hunters to exterminate the sea lion. However, one important area of the

sea lion's Oregon habitat was privately owned and used as a tourist attraction—Sea Lion Caves, where the animals could be viewed up close, in a natural setting. The owners of the caves had to spend a good deal of time driving off bounty hunters. By 1931, conservation legislation was passed to protect sea lions in most areas of the Oregon coast. Nevertheless, while the extermination pressure was on, the profit-seeking Sea Lion Cave operation played an important part in the survival of the sea-going mammals. The sea lions themselves are not owned, and their survival is largely a public good. But, private ownership of the habitat had concentrated enough of the benefits in the hands of a tourist-based business to help guarantee the survival of the endangered animals at a critical time.

* * *

Can private clubs and businesses eliminate the public goods problem? Not necessarily, since there is no guarantee that the optimal amount of public goods will be provided. The problem continues to exist and to be an important source of market failure. However, these private-sector philanthropic and entrepreneurial solutions to certain public goods problems do remind us that whenever the will exists to solve such problems, government action is not the only possible way. The same sort of informed and determined efforts needed to convince government to do the right thing can frequently find private solutions more quickly and cheaply.

public goods that should be produced? If some users become dissatisfied, will the government-funded producer have an incentive to consider change, as happens when users reduce their patronage of market establishments? Taxes will be necessary to cover the costs of making near public goods freely available. Will such taxes lead to inefficiency? These factors reduce the attractiveness of public-sector provision of jointly consumed commodities when exclusion of nonpaying consumers is possible.

MARKET FAILURE: POOR INFORMATION

In the real world, market choices, like other decisions, are made with incomplete information. Consumers do not have perfect knowledge about the quality of a product, the price of alternative products, or side effects that may result from a product. They may make incorrect decisions, decisions they will later regret, because they do not possess good information.

The reality of imperfect knowledge is not, of course, the fault of the market. In fact, the market provides consumers with a strong incentive to acquire information, and producers providing consumers with the best deal with an incentive to advertise that fact. Because consumers must bear the consequences of their mistakes, they certainly will seek to avoid the deliberate purchase of "lemon" products.

GETTING YOUR MONEY'S WORTH

Repeat-Purchase Item: An item purchased often by the same buyer.

The consumer's information problem is minimal if the item is purchased regularly. Consider the problem of purchasing a brand of soap. There is little cost associated with trying out brands. Since soap is a regularly purchased product, trial-and-error is an economical means of determining which brand is most suitable to one's needs. It is a **repeat-purchase item.** The consumer can use past experience to good advantage when buying repeat-purchase items such as soap, toothpaste, most food products, lawn service, and gasoline.

What incentive does the producer have to supply accurate information that will help the customer make a satisfying long-run choice? Is there a conflict between consumer and producer interests? The answers to these questions are critically affected by the seller's dependence on return customers.

If dissatisfaction on the part of *current* customers is expected to have a strong adverse effect on *future* sales, a business entrepreneur will attempt to provide accurate information to help customers make wise choices. The future success of business entrepreneurs who sell repeat-purchase products is highly dependent on the future purchases of currently satisfied customers. There is a harmony of interest because buyer and seller alike will be better off if the customer is satisfied with the product purchased.

LET THE BUYER BEWARE

Major problems of conflicting interests, inadequate information, and unhappy customers arise when goods either (a) are difficult to evaluate on inspection and are seldom repeatedly purchased from the same producer or (b) are potentially capable of serious and lasting harmful side effects that cannot be predicted by a layperson. Under these conditions, human nature being what it is, we would expect some unscrupulous producers to sell low-quality, defective, and even harmful goods.

When customers are unable to distinguish between high-quality and low-quality goods, their ability to police quality and price is weakened. When this is the case, business entrepreneurs have a strong incentive to cut costs by reducing quality. Consumers get less for their dollars. Since sellers are not dependent on repeat customers, they may survive and even prosper in the marketplace. The probability of customer dissatisfaction is thus increased because of inadequate information and poor quality. Accordingly, the case for an unhampered market mechanism is weakened.

Consider the consumer's information problem when an automobile is purchased. Are most consumers capable of properly evaluating the safety equipment? Except for a handful of experts, most people are not. Some consumers might individually seek expert advice. It may be more efficient, though, to prevent market failure by having the government regulate automobile safety and require certain safety equipment.

As another example of the problem of inadequate consumer information, consider the case of a drug manufacturer's exaggerated claims for a new product. Until consumers have had experience with the drug or have listened to others' experiences, they might make wasteful purchases. Government regulation might benefit consumers by forcing the manufacturer to modify its claims.

ENTREPRENEURS AND INFORMATION

Consumers have the incentive to seek good information, but that can be very expensive. Entrepreneurial sellers, when they are in fact providing good value, have an incentive to bridge the information gap, and to let consumers know it. How? Expert evaluations are one way that consumers can learn about the special characteristics built into complex products. For car buyers and computer buyers, for example, publishers market dozens of specialized magazines containing expert analyses and opinions from almost any point of view. Laboratory test results are provided by consumer organizations on a wide variety of goods available nationwide.

Franchises are another way that entrepreneurs have responded to the consumer need for more information, as we pointed out in Chapter 2. The tourist traveling through an area for the first time—and very possibly the last—may find that eating at a franchised food outlet and sleeping at a franchised motel is the cheapest way to avoid annoying and costly mistakes. The franchiser sets the standards for all firms in the chain and establishes procedures, including continuous inspection, designed to maintain the standards. Franchisers have a strong incentive to maintain their reputation for quality, because if it declines, their ability to sell new franchises is hurt. Even though the tourist may visit a particular establishment only once, the franchise turns that visit into a "repeat purchase," since the reputation of the entire national franchise operation is at stake.

Similarly, the advertising of a brand name nationally develops a reputation that is at stake when purchases are made. How much would the Coca Cola Company pay to avoid a dangerous bottle of Coke being sold? Surely, it would be a large sum. The company's reputation is a hostage to quality control. Advertising investments act as a signal that the firm is serious about its future business and has something important to lose if it cheats customers.

Johnson & Johnson's experience with Tylenol capsules is a concrete example of how far a company is willing to go to protect a brand name. In 1982, seven people died as a result of taking Tylenol capsules that had been laced with cyanide. Even though Johnson & Johnson, the producer of the capsules, was not at fault, the company spent at least $60 million to recall 31 million bottles of Tylenol, provide consumers and retailers with refunds, and introduce a new triple-sealed bottle of Tylenol. Although Tylenol's share of the market dropped to below 7 percent immediately following the tragedy, by 1984, its share was almost as high as the 35 percent it had before the deaths occurred, according to *Business Week* magazine.

In early 1986, though, Johnson & Johnson faced a replay of the situation when a woman died from taking cyanide-laced capsules. This time the company decided to stop making Tylenol capsules, because it was unable to ensure their safety. It recalled existing bottles of Tylenol capsules and offered to replace them with more tamper-resistant Tylenol "caplets." *The New York Times* estimated that this move to protect the reputation of Tylenol would cost Johnson & Johnson $100 million to $150 million.

As this example indicates, entrepreneurial measures such as assuring the quality of a franchiser or protecting a brand name can be both expensive and effective. They cannot, however, guarantee that customers will never be cheated or disappointed after a transaction. Despite the best efforts of entrepreneurs, the lack of consumer information will continue to assure that the market will remain imperfect relative to the economists' ideal, and that government will have a potential role to play in improving on the market's results.

ONE-SIDED INFORMATION

Asymmetric Information Problem: A problem arising when either buyers or sellers have important information about the product that is not possessed by the other side in potential transactions.

As useful and important as the published evaluations of experts, franchise operations, advertising and brand-name reputations are, they cannot solve a kind of information problem that has little to do with product design or manufacture. This is called the **asymmetric information problem,** and it can make markets themselves, for some products, difficult to operate effectively. The problem arises when either the potential buyer or potential seller has important information, but the other side does not have the same information.

Think for a moment about buyers trying to avoid "lemons" in the used car market. Sellers know which cars are above average quality and which are below average. Buyers on the other hand, cannot tell which is which simply by looking at and test-driving them. Thus buyers will be willing to pay no more than the average value of all cars they believe to be offered in the market. But if better-than-average cars cannot bring better-than-average prices, then fewer of them will be sold in the market, and if below-average cars bring average prices, then more of the below-average cars will be offered. Buyers understand this, so the average car they expect in such a market will be below the average of all existing cars of that age and type. Owners of better cars will be more reluctant to sell at the low market price. It will be hard to make a market for above-average quality cars, when buyers are not able to get good information about which cars are actually better.

Can anything be done to reduce this kind of asymmetric information problem? Even though the approaches listed above are aimed at large markets and have little value, we still can answer in the affirmative. Of course, sellers of the better used cars have an incentive to provide additional information in order to get a higher price for their superior goods. But how is this done? Who will believe their claims about their product being better? Car owners can support their claims in several ways. Some will keep their records of oil changes and lubrications, to show that these services, important to the long-run durability of a car, have actually been performed on schedule. Used car dealers whose mechanics inspect the cars before they are offered for sale, may offer money-back guarantees, or warranties that promise free repairs if needed within a specified time, on the most reliable cars they sell. The other cars they sell will be sold "as is" with no warranty. Sellers of products can even give price guarantees, as some stores do when they advertise that if the buyer finds a lower price for the same product within a specified period of time, the seller will refund the difference. By offering to bear such risks, sellers provide credibility to their claims about better products and prices. This gives information to buyers and provides some assurance they they will not later regard their purchase as a "lemon."

The problem of asymmetric information also arises when buyers know more than sellers. Consider the market for health insurance. If buyers know their own health problems better than insurance companies, then the one-price insurance offered will be most attractive to buyers with the greatest expected health problems. The buyers whose health history and life styles indicate greater potential health costs will pay the same, but later collect more from the insurance company. In contrast, the same insurance at the same price is less attractive to the healthiest people, and fewer of them will buy. When the company is unable to identify those with the greatest potential health costs and charge them more, it will have to charge their healthier customers a rate that exceeds their expected future insurance claims. But this would drive away even more of the healthier potential buyers, making the situation even worse. As in the case of used cars, asymmetric information reduces the effectiveness of the market. Just as the best used cars may be hard to sell, so, too, may the healthiest individuals be hard to insure when asymmetric information is present.

What can be done about asymmetric information when buyers have information, but sellers do not? Buyers, too, are willing to provide information to sellers, when it is to their advantage to do so. In the case of insurance buyers, those buyers with the best health record who are therefore least likely to have future insurance claims, can often get lower insurance rates by opening their private medical records to the insurance company. Sellers who otherwise have no right to see that information may find it gladly offered—at least by the healthiest buyers—when buyers with better records are offered lower insurance prices.

Another strategy sellers use to deal with the insurance problem, is to offer "bundle purchases." Knowing that some employees in any sizeable firm are likely to have good health, and some bad health, insurance companies find it economical to offer a "group rate" policy, covering all the employees of the firm. By screening out only the easily identified bad risks, so that it can save the cost of carefully screening every employee's medical history, it can offer moderate rates.

We have discussed many ways in which market participants can reduce the problem they face due to the scarcity and cost of information. These are not totally effective, however, and poor information remains a problem that keeps markets from reaching their hypothetical ideal.

LOOKING AHEAD

In this chapter, we focused on the failures of the market. In the next chapter, we will use economic analysis to come to a better understanding of the workings of the public sector. We will also discuss some of the expected shortcomings of public-sector action. Awareness of both the strengths and weaknesses of alternative forms of economic organization will help us to make more intelligent choices in this important area.

CHAPTER SUMMARY

1. The sources of market failure can be grouped into four major categories: (a) externalities, (b) public goods, (c) poor information, and (d) monopoly.

2. When externalities are present, the market may fail to confront decision-makers with the proper incentives. Since decision-makers are not forced to consider external cost, they may find it personally advantageous to undertake an economic activity even though it generates a net loss to the community. In contrast, when external benefits are present, decision-makers may fail to undertake economic action that would generate a net social gain.

3. When external costs originate from the activities of a business firm, the firm's costs will understate the social cost of producing the good. If production of the good generates external costs, the price of the product under competitive conditions will be too low and the output too large to meet the *ideal requirements* of economic efficiency.

4. External costs result from the failure or inability of a society to establish private property rights. Clearly established private property rights enable owners to prohibit others from using or abusing their property. In contrast, common property rights with open access normally result in overutilization, since most of the cost of overutilization (and misuse) is imposed on others.

5. When external benefits are present, the market demand curve will understate the social gains of conducting the activity. The consumption and production of goods that generate external benefits will tend to be lower than the socially ideal levels.

6. The efficient use of air and water resources is particularly troublesome for the market because it is often impossible to apportion these resources and determine ownership rights. A system of emission charges or of transferable emission rights can induce individuals to make wiser use of these resources. Either strategy will (a) increase the economic cost of producing pollution-intensive goods, (b) grant firms an incentive to use methods of production that create less pollution, and (c) provide producers with an incentive to adopt control devices when it is economical to do so.

7. When the marginal benefits (for example, cleaner air) derived from ending pollution are less than the social gains associated with a pollution-generating activity, prohibition of the activity that results in pollution (or other external cost) is not an ideal solution.

8. When the control costs of firms vary, the emission charge (pollution tax) approach will permit society to reduce pollution by a given amount at a lower cost than will the maximum emission standard methods, which is currently widely used. The marginal cost of attaining a cleaner environment will rise as the pollution level is reduced. At some point, the economic benefits of a still cleaner environment will be less than the costs.

9. In evaluating the case for government intervention in situations involving externalities, one must consider the following factors: (a) the magnitude of the external effects relative to the cost of government action; (b) the ability of the market to devise means of dealing with the problem without intervention; and (c) the possibility that the political majority may carry the government intervention too far if the external costs imposed on the minority are not fully considered.

10. When it is costly or impossible to withhold a public good from persons who do not or will not help pay for it, the market system breaks down because everyone has an incentive to become a free rider. When everyone attempts to ride for free, production of the public good will be lower than the socially ideal level.

11. The market provides an incentive for buyers and sellers to acquire information. When a business is dependent on repeat customers, it has a strong incentive to promote customer satisfaction. However, when goods are either (a) difficult to evaluate on inspection and seldom purchased repeatedly from the same producer or (b) have potentially serious and lasting harmful effects, consumer trial and error may be an unsatisfactory means of determining quality. Franchising and brand names often communicate reliable information on product quality to consumers and thereby reduce the likelihood that consumers will be cheated or misled, even in cases when the specific item is not purchased regularly. Asymmetric information provides an additional challenge to market participants.

CRITICAL ANALYSIS QUESTIONS

*1. When cattle grazed on the English commons—open access pastures—overgrazing took place. Eventually, many of the pastures became private property. What other option might have solved the open access problem?

2. Why might businesses operating currently, and causing pollution problems, prefer transferable emission rights to the pollution tax approach? When would they not have such a preference?

3. "Elementary education is obviously a public good. After all, it is provided by government." Evaluate.

*4. Why is it difficult to determine the proper output of a pure public good?

5. "Since free riders can enjoy public goods, there is no way that they will be provided privately." Evaluate.

*6. Are people more likely to take better care of an item they own jointly (communally) or one they own privately? Why? Does the presence of private property rights affect the behavior of persons in noncapitalist nations? Why or why not?

*Asterisk denotes questions for which answers are given in Appendix C, Selected Answers.

*7. **What's Wrong with This Way of Thinking?**
"Corporations are the major beneficiaries of our lax pollution control policy. Their costs are reduced because we permit them free use of valuable resources—clean water and air—in order to produce goods. These lower costs are simply added to the profits of the polluting firms."

8. **What's Wrong with This Way of Thinking?**
"Private property rights are a gamble. What if the owner doesn't take good care of what he owns? Communal property rights are better—there are more people to take care of what they own. Surely someone will exercise the needed care." (Hint: What was Aristotle's position on the issue?)

*9. Can you think of any public goods, or near public goods, that are supplied privately? Do such examples show that there is no such thing as a free rider problem?

*10. What factor limits the private supply of public goods?

*11. "Corporations in America are being persecuted unfairly by environmental legislation such as air pollution control laws. Corporate leadership is responsible and would work for cleaner air without all this legal hassle." Evaluate, using the economic way of thinking.

*12. In a small town located next to an interstate highway are two prospering family restaurants. Both are locally owned, but one is franchised, a part of a nationally advertised chain of such restaurants. The other does not advertise. Assuming that highway travelers and local residents have seen equal amounts of advertising from the chain, in which restaurant would you expect to find more highway travelers? Why?

13. Many consumers are willing to pay more for brand-name products (for example, Bayer aspirin or Minute Maid orange juice) than for generic versions of the same products. Is this irrational? Do consumers get anything for their additional expense? Explain.

14. It is reported that prior to the overthrow of the Bulgarian communist regime in 1989, industrial pollution damaged 70 percent of Bulgaria's farmland. If the farmland had been privately owned would you have expected the same damages to have occurred? Explain.

30 Public Choice: Understanding Government and Government Failure

It does not follow that whenever laissez faire falls short government interference is expedient; since the inevitable drawbacks of the latter may, in any particular case, be worse than the shortcomings of private enterprise.[1]

Harry Sidgwick 1887

CHAPTER FOCUS

- What are the major forces that determine outcomes under representative democracy?
- Can government action be mutually advantageous to all citizens? Does it sometimes reduce the economic welfare of citizens?
- Will government action sometimes be more efficient than market exchange? When is it likely to be less efficient?
- Why does representative democracy often tax some people in order to provide benefits to others? What types of income transfers are attractive to politicians?
- Can constitutional rules influence political outcomes? What types of constitutional rules and restraints make sense?

*A*bout two-fifths of U.S. national income is channeled through the various governmental departments and agencies. More than a third of the nation's land is owned by government, and the legal framework set by government establishes many of the "rules of the game" for the market sector. Government regulation of prices, of the use of land, water, and air, along with labor relations and business practices, exert a major impact on the operation of the economy. Given the size and influence of government, understanding how the political process works is a crucial issue.

During the last three decades, public choice economists have enhanced our knowledge of democratic politics. Public choice theory indicates that there are two general forces underlying political action: (a) the correction of market failure and (b) rent seeking—the pursuit of private gain at public expense. Citizens can reap gains from government action that reduces market inefficiency emanating from externalities, public goods, an absence of competition, and poor information. However, the political process is merely an alternative form of economic organization, not an automatic corrective device. It is not a pinch-hitter we can count on to supply a base hit whenever we fear the market might strike out.[1]

As with markets, there are categories of activity that economic theory indicates even democratic governments will do poorly. As we discussed briefly in Chapter 4, there is government failure, as well as market failure. **Government failure** is present when the political process leads to economic inefficiency and the waste of scarce resources.

Government Failure: Failure of government action to meet the criteria of ideal economic efficiency.

Public policy reflects the political decision-making rules and constitutional restraints of a society. Public choice theory enhances our knowledge of how alternative forms of political organization work and provides us with insight on how we might better design the rules of politics. As we proceed in this chapter, we will consider this issue. Most political decisions in Western countries are made legislatively. Therefore, we will focus our analysis on a democratic system of representative government. Let us see what the tools of economics reveal about the political process.

REPRESENTATIVE DEMOCRACY

In modern democratic countries, voters elect representatives to direct the actions of governments. In turn, the representatives establish agencies and hire bureaucrats to conduct the day-to-day government affairs. Voters, politicians, and bureaucrats are the major players in the democratic political process. Under representative democracy, government action is the result of a complex set of interrelationships among the members of these three groups. Like consumers in the market, voters use their electoral support, money, and other political resources to express their demand for legislation. Like business entrepreneurs, politicians are suppliers: they design and shape legislation. Finally, just as managers and employees are assigned the details of the production process in the market, bureaucrats perform this task in the public sector.[2]

---

[1]Quoted in Charles Wolf, Jr., *Markets or Government*, (Cambridge: MIT Press, 1988), p. 17.
[2]For a more comprehensive view of public choice theory and the operation of democratic governments, see James Gwartney and Richard Wagner (eds.), *Public Choice and Constitutional Economics* (Greenwich: JAI Press, 1988). Our analysis borrows from this work.

Economists use the self-interest postulate to enhance our understanding of consumer behavior, business decision-making, and resource supply decisions. Likewise, public choice economists apply the self-interest postulate to political decision-making. They assume that, just as people are motivated by personal wealth, power, and prestige in the market sector, so, too, will these factors influence them when they make decisions in the political arena.

Closely related to self-interest as a motivator for politicians and bureaucrats are the concepts of survival and expansion. In the private sector, even if there are some managers not primarily seeking profits, it will be the profit-making firms which are most likely to survive, expand, and be imitated. Similarly in the public sector, politicians and the bureaucrats they hire must often act in the narrow self-interest of their constituents (and thus in their own career self-interests) if they hope to survive. Those who cooperate most closely with powerful constituency groups will tend to survive, to obtain more political clout, and to lead larger government agencies.

THE VOTER-CONSUMER

How do voters decide whom to support? No doubt, many factors influence their decisions. Which candidate is the most persuasive, and which presents the best television image? Who appears to be honest, sincere, and effective? However, the self-interest postulate indicates that voters, like market consumers, will ask, "What can you do for me, and how much will it cost me?" The greater the voter's perceived net personal gain from a particular candidate's platform, the more likely it is that the voter will favor that candidate. In contrast, the greater the perceived net economic cost imposed on the voter by the positions of a candidate, the less inclined the voter will be to support the candidate. Other things equal, voters will tend to candidates whom they believe will provide them the most political goods, services, and transfer benefits, net of personal costs.

As we discussed in Chapter 4, when decisions are made collectively, the direct link between the individual voter's choice and the outcome of the issue is broken. The choice of a single voter is seldom decisive when the decision-making group is large. Recognizing that the outcome will not depend on one vote, the individual voter has little incentive to seek information (which is costly) on issues and candidates in order to cast a more informed vote. Economists refer to this phenomenon as the "rational ignorance effect" (see Chapter 4, pp. 94–96).[3]

The rational ignorance effect explains why few voters are able to accurately identify their congressional representatives, much less identify and understand their position on issues such as minimum wage legislation, tariffs, and agricultural price supports. The fact that voters acquire scanty information merely indicates that they are responding rationally to economic incentives.

It is interesting to compare the incentive of both consumers and voters to choose wisely. The consumer who makes a poor choice—for example by purchasing a product that does not work well—must bear the consequences. Thus, each consumer has a strong incentive to acquire information, choose wisely, and search for quality goods that are attractively priced. In contrast, there is little direct incentive for voters to be concerned about the quality of their choices of candidates. Even if informed about the candidates, individual voters will exert little impact on the outcome of congressional elections. Whether mistaken or not, there is only a

---

[3]The concept of rational ignorance among voters was initially developed by Anthony Downs. See Downs, *An Economic Theory of Democracy* (New York: Harper & Row, 1957).

minuscule chance that an individual voter's decision will decide the election. Therefore, it makes no sense for the voter to "waste" time and effort making a careful choice. Given this incentive structure, there is reason to believe that the choices of consumers will be better informed and more carefully made than those of voters.

To see in a more personal way why citizens are likely to make better informed decisions as consumers than as voters, imagine that you are planning to buy a car next week and also to vote for one of two Senate candidates. You have narrowed your car choice to either a Ford or a Honda. In the voting booth, you will choose between candidates Smith and Jones. Both the car purchase and the Senate vote involve complex tradeoffs for you. The two cars come with many options and you must choose among dozens of different combinations; the winning Senate candidate will represent you on hundreds of issues, although you are limited to voting for one of the two choices.

Which decision will command more of your scarce time for research and thinking about the best choice? Since your car choice is decisive, and you must pay for what you choose, an uninformed car purchase could be very costly for you. But if you mistakenly vote for the wrong candidate out of ignorance, it is very unlikely that your vote will decide the election. And if somehow your vote does swing the election, you will share the cost with all citizens with interests similar to yours. It would not be surprising, then, if you spent substantial time considering the car purchase and very little time becoming informed about either the candidates or the political issues at election time.

Car choices are not perfectly informed decisions, but the buyer is certain to benefit from giving careful consideration to the alternatives. As a result, car companies may well be guided by better-informed votes (dollar votes) than the United States Senate, even though Senate activities are far more important than cars to the voters as a group.

The fact that one's vote is unlikely to be decisive explains more than lack of information on the part of voters. It also helps to explain why many citizens fail to vote. Even when there is a presidential election, only about half of all voting-age Americans take the time to register and vote. Given the low probability that one's vote will be decisive, this low voter turnout should not be surprising. The rationality of voters is further indicated by the fact that when voters perceive that the election is close, voter turnout is larger.[4] A vote in a close election has a greater chance of actually making a difference.

THE POLITICIAN-SUPPLIER

Public choice theory postulates that pursuit of votes is the primary stimulus shaping the behavior of political suppliers. In varying degrees, such factors as pursuit of the public interest, compassion for the poor, and the achievement of fame, wealth, and power may influence the behavior of politicians. But regardless of ultimate motivation, the ability of politicians to achieve their objectives is sorely dependent upon their ability to get elected and reelected. Just as profits are the lifeblood of the market entrepreneur, votes are the lifeblood of the politician.

Rationally uninformed voters often must be convinced to "want" a candidate. Voter perceptions may be based on realities, but it is always perceptions, not the

---

[4]This and other results consistent with the rational actions of voters can be found in Yoram Barzel and Eugene Silberberg, "Is the Act of Voting Rational?" *Public Choice,* vol. XVI (Fall 1973), pp. 51–58.

realities themselves, that influence decisions. This is true regardless of whether the decisions are private or political. As a result, a candidate's positive attributes must be brought to the attention of the rationally ignorant voter, who may well be more interested in the local sports teams (which are probably more entertaining) than in seeking out detailed knowledge about the attributes of the various candidates. An expert staff, polls to ferret out which issues and which positions will be favored by voters, high quality advertising to present the candidate's image and favored positions, and other forms of political resources are of great value in politics. Thus, political campaigns are costly. Candidates campaigning for the 35 open Senate seats in 1990 spent $180 million. Senator Phil Gramm alone spent $12.5 million in his successful bid for re-election in Texas. Candidates for the House of Representatives that year spent $265 million.[5]

Are we implying that politicians are selfish, caring only for their pocketbooks and re-election chances? The answer is no. When people act in the political sphere, they may genuinely want to help their fellow citizens. Factors other than personal political gain, narrowly defined, influence the actions of many political suppliers. On certain issues, one may feel strongly that one's position is best for the nation, even though it may not be currently popular. The national interest as perceived by the political supplier may conflict with the position that would be most favorable to re-election prospects. Some politicians may opt for the national interest even when it means political defeat. None of this is inconsistent with an economic view of political choice.

However, the existence of political suicide does not change the fact that most politicians prefer political survival. There is a strong incentive for political suppliers to stake out positions that will increase their vote total in the next election. In fact, competition more or less forces politicians to make decisions in light of political considerations.

If a politician refuses to support policies that are vote-getters, perhaps because he or she thinks the policies are counterproductive or morally wrong, then he or she runs an increased risk of being replaced by a competitor who pays a closer attention to the acquisition of votes. Just as neglect of economic profit is the route to market oblivion, neglect of potential votes is the route to political oblivion.

CORRECTING MARKET FAILURE AND THE DEMAND FOR GOVERNMENT

People participate in market activity because it is productive. Production and exchange is a positive-sum activity: it is mutually beneficial. It allows individuals to achieve a higher level of wealth than would be possible in the absence of trade.

People also "demand" certain types of government action because they are productive. When market failure (externalities, public goods, monopoly, or poor information) is present, corrective action can increase the size of the economic pie, generating personal net benefits for individual voters. Each form of market failure discussed in the previous chapter provides a potential opportunity for productive government action, action that generates benefits in excess of costs.

---

[5]Data are from *Congressional Quarterly Weekly Report*, vol. 49, no. 8, p. 490.

The protective actions of the state—government actions that protect the lives and property of individuals against intruders—are highly productive because they reduce the incidence of activities that impose external costs on others. Violence, theft, and fraud impose external costs on nonconsenting parties. We all gain when each of us is free from serious worry that a criminal can threaten, injure, rob, or defraud us. Therefore, government prohibitions against such activities that generate large external costs are highly productive. When external costs are less severe (than those that endanger our lives and substantially affect our wealth), regulation or taxation can still reduce the negative side effects emanating from the failure of markets to hold private decision-makers fully accountable for their actions. When there are external benefits of activities insufficiently provided by private means, regulation and tax policy again can intervene. For example, sidewalks can be required in residential neighborhoods, and owners can be compelled to keep them snow-free, in order to provide external benefits to pedestrians. Similarly, tax breaks can be provided for nonprofit organizations that fight diseases, preserve natural areas, art, or architecture, or do other charitable works generating benefits for individuals who do not pay for them.

The theory of public goods explains why certain activities cannot easily be provided through markets. Since it is difficult, if not impossible, to restrict their consumption to those who pay for the service, markets tend to undersupply public goods. For example, it would be quite difficult, if not downright impossible, for someone who builds a dam to control flooding to withhold flood protection from those who do not pay. This being the case, market exchange often fails to provide a sufficient amount of flood control protection.

On a larger scale, national defense is a classic public good. Whoever protects the nation against foreign threats or invasion provides a service to all including those who would try to be free-riders and let others pay for defense. Markets will supply an insufficient amount of national defense due to the public-good nature of the service. In contrast, government can tax everyone and use the revenue to provide protection against foreign intruders. Clearly, such action is potentially productive.

Poorly informed consumers can also be helped by government action. Government certification or licensure of accountants, doctors, and lawyers can protect uninformed consumers from those who would practice without the training and experience necessary to perform effectively. Building codes can protect people against unsafe building practices, and so on. When the cost of uninformed choices is high, and the cost of consumer protection is low, appropriate government action can create net benefits for individuals at large.

When monopoly power causes output to be lower, and prices to be higher than they would be in competitive markets, several government policies can potentially help the consumer and the economy as a whole. Anti-trust activities, regulation of monopoly prices, and governmental provisions in place of market provision all have some potential for providing net gains to society.

The theory of market failure highlights the potential for productive governmental action—action that generates benefits in excess of costs. Will representative government lead to constructive action? When the cost of a government project is spread among voters in the same proportion as the benefits received, all voters will gain from productive projects and lose if counterproductive projects (measures for which benefits are insufficient to cover costs) are undertaken. Correspondingly, their representatives have an incentive to support productive measures and oppose wasteful ones. The larger the net gain from a project, the greater the incentive of a representative to support the proposal.

Perhaps surprising to some, when a government project is productive, there is the potential for unanimity (100 percent approval) among voters and their representatives. *When voters pay in proportion to benefits received,* all voters would gain if the government action were productive (and all would lose if it were counterproductive).[6] When voters pay in proportion to benefits received, there is a harmony between good politics and sound economics.

THE DISTRIBUTION OF BENEFITS AND COSTS

With public-sector action, the link between receipt of and payment for a good can be broken—the beneficiaries of a proposal may not bear its cost. Public choice theory indicates that the pattern of benefits and costs among voters will influence the workings of the political process. The benefits derived from a government action may be either widespread among the general populace or concentrated among a small subgroup (for example, farmers, students, or residents of northern Vermont). Similarly, the costs may be either widespread or highly concentrated among voters. As Exhibit 1 illustrates, there are four possible patterns of voter benefits and costs: (1) widespread benefits and widespread costs, (2) concentrated benefits and widespread costs, (3) concentrated benefits and concentrated costs, and (4) widespread benefits and concentrated costs.

When both the benefits and costs are widespread among voters (type 1), essentially everyone benefits and everyone pays. While the costs of type 1 measures may not be precisely proportional to benefits, there will be a rough relationship. When type 1 measures are productive, almost everyone gains, there will be little opposition, and political representatives have a strong incentive to support such proposals. In contrast, when type 1 proposals generate costs in excess of benefits, almost everyone loses and representatives will confront pressure to oppose such issues. Thus, for type 1 projects, the political process is consistent with economic efficiency.

Interestingly, the provision of traditional public goods—like provision of national defense, a legal system for the protection of persons and property and enforcement of contracts, and a monetary system to oil the wheels of exchange—best fits category 1. Nearly everyone pays and nearly everyone benefits from public-sector action of this type.

Similarly, there is reason to believe that the political process will work pretty well for type 3 measures—those for which both benefits and costs are concentrated on a small subgroup. In some cases, the concentrated beneficiaries may pay for the government to provide services. This would be the case when user charges finance public services (for example, air safety or garbage collection) benefitting subgroups

---

[6]The principle that productive projects generate the potential for political unanimity was initially articulated by Swedish economist Knut Wicksell in 1896. See Wicksell, ''A New Principle of Just Taxation,'' in James Gwartney and Richard Wagner (eds.), *Public Choice and Constitutional Economics* (Greenwich: JAI Press, Inc., 1988). Nobel laureate James Buchanan has stated that Wicksell's work provided him with the insights that led to his large role in the development of modern public choice theory.

EXHIBIT 1

The Distribution of
Benefits and Costs
Among Voters

Distribution of Benefits Among Voters

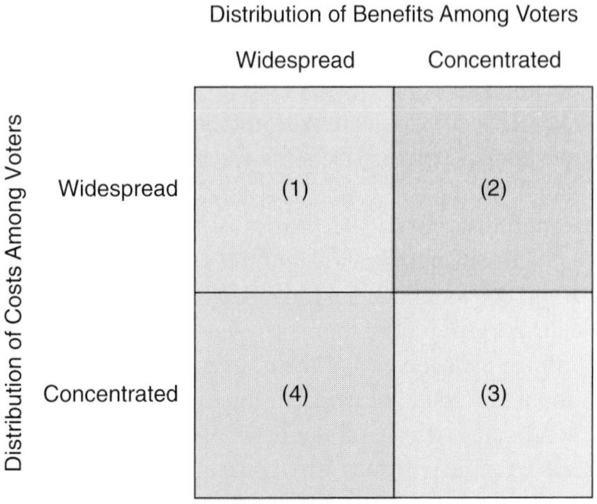

It is useful to visualize four possible combinations for the distribution of benefits and costs among voters and to consider how the alternative distributions affect the operation of representative government. When the distribution of benefits and costs are widespread among voters (1) or concentrated among voters (3), representative government will tend to undertake projects that are productive and reject those that are unproductive. In contrast, when the benefits are concentrated and the costs are widespread (2), representative government is biased toward adoption of counterproductive activity. Finally, when benefits are widespread but the costs concentrated (4), the political process may reject projects that are productive.

of the populace. Under these circumstances, voter support will provide politicians with an incentive to provide public services that generate value in excess of cost.

Of course, the subgroup of beneficiaries might differ from the subgroup footing the bill. But even in this case, if the benefits exceed the costs, the concentrated group of beneficiaries will have an incentive to expend more resources supportive of the measure than those harmed by it will expend opposing it. Thus, productive measures will tend to be adopted. Similarly, unproductive measures will tend to be rejected when both the benefits and costs are concentrated.

Problems are present, however, when the distribution of benefits differs substantially from the distribution of costs (categories 2 and 4 of Exhibit 1). In a democratic setting, representative government is biased toward adoption of type 2 proposals, even if they are counterproductive. Correspondingly, the democratic process may reject type 4 measures, even when they are productive. The following section will explain these biases and the accompanying economic problems.

RENT SEEKING, SPECIAL INTERESTS, AND GOVERNMENT FAILURE

Public-sector effects to alleviate problems arising from market failure explain a substantial amount of government activity. However, another substantial portion of public sector activity reflects neither gains from improved efficiency nor a preference for less economic inequality. Rather, it is reflective of rent-seeking behavior, the political actions of individuals and groups seeking personal advantage at the expense of others.[7]

Rent-seeking activities are most likely to be successful when an issue generates substantial personal benefits for a small number of constituents, while imposing a small individual cost on a large number of other voters (type 2 of Exhibit 1). Economists refer to measures of this type as special interest issues.

It is easy to see how politicians can improve their election prospects by catering to the views of special interests. Since their personal stake is large, members of the interest group (and lobbyists representing their interests) have a strong incentive to inform themselves and their allies and to let legislators know how strongly they feel about an issue of special importance. Many of them will vote for or against candidates strictly on the basis of whether they support their interests. In addition, such interest groups are generally an attractive source of campaign resources, including financial contributions. In contrast, most other voters will care little about a special interest issue. For the non-special interest voter, the time and energy necessary to examine the issue will generally exceed any possible personal gain from a preferred resolution. Thus, most non-special interest voters will simply ignore such issues.

If you were a vote-seeking politician what would you do? Clearly, little gain would be derived from supporting the interest of the largely uninformed and disinterested majority. Predictably, politicians will be led as if by an invisible hand to serve well-organized, concentrated interests. Support of such special interests will generate vocal supporters, campaign workers, and most importantly, campaign contributors. Corporations, unions, farm commodity groups, and other special interest organizations provide critical aid for increasingly costly political races. Media advertising is one of the critical (and expensive) elements of a modern political campaign. Television and radio advertising accounted for more than a third of the $180 million spent by candidates for the 35 Senate seats filled in the 1990 elections.[8] In the age of media politics, there is strong pressure for politicians to support special interests, tap them for campaign funds, and use the contributions to project a positive candidate image on television.[9]

The rational ignorance effect strengthens the power of special interests. Since the cost imposed on individual voters is small, and since the individual is unable to avoid the cost even by becoming informed, voters bearing the cost of special interest legislation tend to be uninformed. This will be particularly true if the complexity of the issue makes it difficult for voters to figure how an issue affects their personal welfare. Thus, politicians often make special interest legislation complex in order to hide the cost imposed on the typical voter.[10]

In addition, the interests of bureaucrats are often complementary with those of interest groups. The bureaucrats who staff an agency usually want to see their department's goals furthered, whether the goals are to protect more wilderness,

---

[7]For an excellent survey of the literature on rent seeking, see Robert D. Tollison, "Rent Seeking: A Survey," *Kyklos, 35* (March 1982), pp. 575–602.

[8]Data are from the *Congressional Quarterly Weekly Report*, vol. 49, no. 11 (Mar. 16, 1991), p. 647.

[9]For numerous examples of the link between special interest legislation and political contributions, see Brooks Jackson, *Honest Graft: Big Money and the American Political Process* (New York: Knopf, 1989).

[10]See Gordon Tullock, *Toward a Mathematics of Politics* (Ann Arbor: University of Michigan Press, 1966), pp. 103–106 for additional details on this topic.

build more roads, or provide additional subsidized irrigation projects. To accomplish these things requires larger budgets, which—not so incidently—are likely to provide the bureaucrats with expanded career opportunities while helping to satisfy their professional aspirations as well. Bureaus, therefore, are usually happy to work to expand their programs to deliver benefits to special interest groups, who, in turn, work with politicians to expand their bureau budgets and programs.

SPECIAL INTERESTS AND INEFFICIENT PUBLIC POLICY

The special interest bias of the political process helps to explain the presence of many programs that reduce the size of the economic pie. For example, consider the case of wool and mohair growers in the United States. During the Second World War, military planners found that U.S. wool producers could supply only half the wool wanted by the military. Partly for this reason, and partly to give added income to wool growers, the National Wool Act was passed in 1954. Mohair, produced by Angora goats, had no military use but was included as an offshoot of the wool industry. Wool was removed from the military's list of strategic materials in 1960, but the program survives and continues to grow.[11]

Under the Wool Act, growers are given subsidy checks to supplement what they receive in the market for their wool. In 1990, the wool subsidy rate was 127 percent. The farmer who got $1,000 for selling wool in the market, also got a $1,270 check from the government. Selling twice as much would have brought a check for $2,540 from the government. The subsidy rate for mohair was much larger, 387 percent. The subsidies are paid for by tariffs on imported wool. As a result, consumers pay more for imported wool, also driving up the market price they pay for domestic wool, which is a close substitute. The economy operates less efficiently, since less wool is imported even though the imported wool costs less. The subsidy program, together with the higher price caused by the wool tariff, means that domestic land, labor, and capital resources are withheld from more productive uses, and they are applied to the production of wool and mohair instead of to more highly valued goods.

Nevertheless, Congress continues to support the program. Thousands of very small checks are sent to small growers in every state. Almost half of the 1990 payments were less than $100. Many of those who receive the subsidies are willing to write letters and to vote for those who support the program. Nearly half of the money, though, goes to the one percent of the growers who are the largest producers. The largest checks—nearly 300 of them—averaged $98,000 and accounted for 27 percent of the program's 1990 cost. Recipients of these large checks can be counted on to contribute to organizing costs, and to give campaign donations to members of Congressional committees critical to the continuation of the subsidy program. By contrast, since American taxpayers pay only about $1 per family (1990 data), most are unaware of the program and of how their elected representatives voted on it. Even though their numbers are large and the total financial cost to them of the Wool Act is great, taxpayers individually lose so little that they do not become organized or knowledgeable on the topic. Thus the Wool Act, which harms the interests of the great majority of voters, has continued to survive.

This special interest effect also helps to explain the presence of tariffs and quotas on steel, automobiles, textiles, and several other products. Regulations

---

[11]The description and data on the Wool Act are from Jonathan Rauch, "The Golden Fleece," *National Journal*, vol. 23, no. 20 (May 18, 1991), pp. 1168–71.

mandating that Alaskan oil be transported by the high cost American maritime industry reflect the industry's political clout, not its economic efficiency. Federally funded irrigation projects, subsidized grazing rights, subsidized loans, subsidies to airports—the list goes on and on. Policy in each of these areas is rooted in the special interest effect and not in sound economic doctrine. While each such program individually imposes only a small drag on our economy, in the aggregate they drain our resources, and impair our standard of living.

LOGROLLING AND PORK BARREL LEGISLATION

Logrolling: The exchange between politicians of political support on one issue for political support on another issue.

Pork-Barrel Legislation: A package of spending projects benefiting local areas at federal expense. The projects typically have costs that exceed benefits, but each is intensely desired by the residents of the district getting the benefits without having to pay much of the costs.

Logrolling within a legislative assembly also strengthens the political clout of special interest groups. **Logrolling** is the practice of trading votes by a representative (and his or her constituents) in order to pass intensely desired legislation. Representative A promises to vote for measures favored by other representatives in exchange for their support of a measure that A strongly favors. With logrolling, legislative bodies often pass a bundle of proposals, each of which would be rejected if it were voted on separately.

Pork barrel legislation is a slight variant of logrolling. This type of legislation bundles together a set of projects to benefit regional interests (for example, water projects, dredging of harbors, or expenditures on military bases) at the expense of the general taxpayer. As in the case of logrolling, the bundle of pork barrel projects can often gain approval even if each is counterproductive and would individually be rejected by the legislative assembly.

Exhibit 2 provides a numeric illustration of the forces underlying logrolling and pork barrel legislation. Here we consider the operation of a five-member legislative assembly considering three projects: construction of a post office in district A, dredging of a harbor in B, and expenditures on a military base in C. In each case, the project is inefficient—the net cost of the project exceeds the net benefit (by a 12 to 10 ratio). If the projects were voted on separately, and the representatives reflected the views of their constituents, each project would lose by a 4 to 1 vote. However, when the projects are bundled together through either logrolling or pork-barrel legislation, representatives A, B, and C will vote yes. The legislative bundle will pass 3 to 2 even though it is counterproductive (on average, the projects, as a bundle, reduce the wealth of constituents by $6).[12]

Legislation providing subsidies to electricity consumers in California, Nevada, and Arizona illustrates the relevance of logrolling and pork-barrel legislation. Under legislation passed in 1937, electricity generated by Hoover Dam has been sold to residents in the three surrounding states at rates ranging between 10 percent and 25 percent of the market price. The law providing for the subsidized rates was scheduled to expire in 1987. However, before it did so, Congress extended the subsidies for another 30 years. The residents of many western states are the recipients of federally subsidized electricity. Every senator west of Missouri voted to continue the subsidized rates for electricity generated by Hoover Dam. In turn, they can expect senators and representatives from California, Arizona, and Nevada to support subsidized electricity rates in their states. In contrast, residents of other states will pay higher taxes so that many residents in western states can enjoy cheap electricity.

---

[12]Logrolling and pork barrel policies can lead to the adoption of productive measures. However, if a project is productive, there would always be a pattern of finance that would lead to its adoption even if logrolling were absent. Thus, the tendency for logrolling and pork barrel policies to result in the adoption of inefficient projects is the more significant point.

EXHIBIT 2 ■ Vote Trading and Passing Counterproductive Legislation				
	Net Benefits (+) or Costs (−) to Each Voter in District			
Voters of District[a]	Construction of Post Office in A	Dredging Harbor in B	Construction of Military Base in C	Total
A	+$10	−$ 3	−$ 3	+$4
B	−$ 3	+$10	−$ 3	+$4
C	−$ 3	−$ 3	+$10	+$4
D	−$ 3	−$ 3	−$ 3	−$9
E	−$ 3	−$ 3	−$ 3	−$9
Total	−$ 2	−$ 2	−$ 2	−$6

[a]We assume the districts are of equal size.

Why don't representatives oppose measures that force their constituents to pay for projects that benefit others? There is some incentive to do so, but the constituents of any one representative can capture only a small portion of the benefits of tax savings from improved efficiency, since they would be spread nationwide among all taxpayers. Just as we do not expect a corporation's president to devote the firm's resources to projects not primarily benefiting stockholders, we should not expect an elected representative to devote political resources to projects such as defeating pork-barrel programs, when the benefits of greater efficiency would not go primarily to that representative's constituents. Instead, each representative has a strong incentive to work for programs whose benefits are concentrated among his or her constituents—especially the organized interest groups who can help the representative be reelected. Heeding such incentives is a survival characteristic. It will enhance the politician's re-election prospects.

GOVERNMENT FAILURE: THE SHORT-SIGHTEDNESS EFFECT

How does the political process handle benefits and costs across time periods? What happens *prior* to the next election is of crucial importance to incumbent politicians. Since issues of public policy are usually complex, it is often difficult for voters to anticipate *future* benefits and costs accurately. Moreover, principles of rational ignorance suggest there is little payoff from doing so in any case. Instead, voters tend to rely on current conditions. To the voter, the best indicator of how well the incumbent has done may be the state of affairs close to election day.

Policies that look good around election day will thus enhance the image of incumbents, even if those policies are likely to have substantial negative side effects after the election. On the other hand, policies that generate pre-election costs in order to provide long-term gains that emerge only after the next election reduce the re-election prospects of incumbents. As a result, the political process is biased toward the adoption of shortsighted policies and against the selection of sound long-range policies, when they involve observable costs prior to the next election.

SHORT-TERM COSTS AND GOVERNMENT INACTION

It has been noted that public-sector action is "crisis-oriented." In recent years, we have experienced a welfare crisis, an inflation crisis, a poverty crisis, an energy crisis, and several environmental crises. One reason for this is that crises tend to loosen up budgetary purse strings; special interest groups, politicians, and agencies use a crisis to justify larger budget requests. Other crises, however, occur simply because important action was postponed. City governments, for example, often find it expedient to delay needed maintenance of roads, water systems, and sewers. Higher taxes would bring current political pain, but most of the benefit would lie in future decades. To postpone needed maintenance may be very costly, but most of the cost lies in the future. By the time the problem reaches crisis proportions, other politicians will be likely to have to deal with it. Rationally ignorant voters, after all, know more about the size of today's tax burden than about the problems that might result from delayed spending. Then, too, many of those affected in the future are not current voters.

How does this political tendency to put off needed expenditures compare with similar situations in the private sector? Wouldn't the owner of a hotel or a restaurant also be reluctant to bear the cost of shutting down the business temporarily and undertaking needed repairs? The owner also wants to avoid costs. But the distinction is that with private, transferable property rights, the value of the added future benefits is available immediately to the owner in the form of higher property values. The owner can immediately collect the *value* of the added future business revenue, either by borrowing against the increased value of the property, or simply by selling it. The salable property right makes the increased future benefits of investments available to the owner immediately. Of course the owner's wealth also falls immediately if the property deteriorates. Neither of these influences on the personal wealth of decision-makers is present in the public sector. In fact, one solution to the political problem of water supply, or public transportation investments, and so on, is to let private firms provide the capital facilities and supply the services.

Some cities take advantage of the private sector's willingness to invest by simply purchasing services or allowing customers to buy services, rather than by using government investments. For example, the subways in New York City were built by private companies, and the city took them over later only to keep subway fares well below costs—and still keep the wages of politically important subway workers high, at the expense of taxpayers. One result has been a deterioration of the subway system over time.

When competition among firms is too costly *within* the market, because one large firm can be more efficient than several small ones, then competition *for* the market is sometimes used to prevent problems of monopoly pricing.[13] Regulation is another alternative, but the shortsightedness effect indicates that political pressures to keep current prices down at the expense of future costs may be brought to bear on the regulators, just as they are brought to bear on politicians when government owns the facilities. Private solutions cannot always be found, but, unfortunately, economic theory suggests that pressures on democratic decision-makers, without transferable property rights, is often inconsistent with sensible long-range planning.

---

[13]See Steve H. Hanke (ed.), *Prospects for Privatization* (New York: Academy of Political Science, 1988) for a discussion of many such possibilities.

SHORT-TERM BENEFITS AND GOVERNMENT ACTION

While proposals with future benefits difficult to perceive are usually delayed, proposals with immediate benefits, at the expense of complex future costs—costs that will accrue after the next election—are very attractive to political entrepreneurs. Office-holders and candidates alike have a strong incentive to support such proposals and emphasize the immediate voter benefits.

Is there any evidence that the pursuit of short-term political gains has led to inappropriate public-sector action? Consider the issue of macroeconomic instability. In the 1960s and 1970s, inflationary expectations were relatively low, and slow to change. Expansionary monetary and fiscal policy could be used to "heat up" the economy and reduce the rate of unemployment in the short run. An overheated economy, though, leads to inflation. The shortsightedness effect predicts that the party in power would, in those circumstances, tend to follow an expansionary policy in the 12 to 24 months before an election, even if these policies would result in future inflation. The "stabilization" policies preceding the presidential elections of those two decades suggest the incumbent political suppliers made a substantial effort to give voters the impression that the economy was strong on election day. There is little doubt, however, that expansionary macropolicy overheated the economy in each case, causing the post-election increase in the rate of inflation. Once market participants began to recognize the inflationary effects of expansionary policy, the political profit from the policy fell. Expectations of inflation adjusted more quickly, and the expansionary portion of the cycle became more brief.

It is easy to think of other examples where positive short-term effects have increased the political attractiveness of policies that exert a long-term detrimental impact. Borrowing to finance short-term programs that benefit coveted voting blocks is attractive even though the long-term results will be higher real interest rates, less capital formation, and higher future taxes. Rent controls tend to reduce rental housing prices in the short term, even though housing shortages, black markets, and a deterioration in housing quality are the long-run result.

The shortsightedness effect can be a source of conflict between good politics and sound economics. Policies that are efficient from the standpoint of social benefits and costs are not necessarily the policies that will enhance a politician's election prospects. As a result, grossly inefficient projects may be undertaken and potentially beneficial projects may be ignored.

GOVERNMENT FAILURE: FEW INCENTIVES FOR INTERNAL EFFICIENCY

The day-to-day functions of government are performed by bureaus, which derive the major component of their revenues from the periodic appropriations of the legislature rather than from the direct sale of output to consumers. In effect, the legislative body supplies the bureau with a budget along with instructions for dealing with its assigned tasks. The function of the bureau is to transform the budget into public services.

What does economic analysis indicate about the cost-effectiveness of government-operated bureaus compared to private firms? In the private sector, there is a strong incentive to produce efficiently because lower costs will mean higher profits.

APPLICATION IN ECONOMICS

Can Educational Vouchers and Parental Choice Improve Our Schools?

There is widespread concern about the quality of education in the United States. The average achievement scores of current high school graduates are substantially lower than the scores of their parents 25 years ago. The math and science skills of American students rank near the bottom among industrial countries. In addition, the high school dropout rate is high. In the 1980s, approximately 30 percent of ninth graders dropped out of school prior to their graduation.

The declining level of performance does not reflect expenditures. *Measured in 1982 dollars*, expenditures per pupil on public elementary and secondary schools in the United States increased from $1,585 in 1967 to $3,575 in 1988, a real increase of 125 percent. During this same period, the SAT scores of high school seniors declined from 958 to 904. We are spending more, but the students are learning less.

Why are our schools failing? Many economists believe that part of the answer lies with the structure of the schooling system. In essence, public schools are government-operated firms with substantial monopoly power. They are protected from the competition of rivals because ''free'' education is only available to those who attend the local-district public school. If students (and their parents) choose a nonpublic school, they have to pay for their own education. In essence, they lose the government subsidy that would be theirs if they attended public schools. This makes it very costly to switch to rival suppliers. Thus, a public school has to be very bad before it loses many ''customers.''

Perhaps a thought experiment will help illuminate some of the problems with the current educational structure. Suppose that the restaurant industry in the United States were set up like our schools. A system of local ''restaurant districts'' would be established. Taxes would be levied to finance the cost of the government-operated restaurants in each district. Citizens would not be allowed to patronize public restaurants outside of their local district. If customers chose to patronize private restaurants, they would have to pay for the food *twice*—once as a taxpayer and again as a customer. Thus, if a private restaurant were to survive, it would have to figure out how to attract customers from the tax-financed public restaurants that are giving food away to district residents.

Clearly, there would be major problems with this organizational structure. Since the managers of the government-operated restaurants would derive their funds from the government, predictably they would spend more time satisfying those with political clout (including worker unions) and less time catering to the needs and preferences of customers. The incentive to keep costs low would be weak. After all, a lower quality of service would merely highlight the need for additional funding of the public-sector restaurants. Since consumers could not take their funding and go elsewhere, they would be in an extremely weak position to discipline the district restaurants that were not doing a good job. The outcome of this organizational structure is predictable. Compared to the current competitive system, restaurant food costs would rise and quality would deteriorate. We would get less for our food expenditure dollar.

What might be done to improve the current educational system? One idea that is currently being widely discussed is educational vouchers and market competition. Instead of providing aid directly to public schools, a voucher plan would provide parents with a

Even though the stockholders of a private firm can seldom identify good and bad individual decisions, they can easily observe a ''bottom line'' index of efficiency—the firm's rate of profit. Current profits, together with stockholder judgments about the firm's investment strategy, determine stock prices. In the private sector, a low stock price relative to the firm's assets is an invitation for a restructuring or a takeover in which management is ousted. Together with bankruptcy, these possibilities are deterrents to economic inefficiency.

In contrast, public sector bureaus confront an incentive structure that is less conducive to operating efficiency. Direct competition, in the form of other firms

certificate equal to the current educational expenditures per pupil. The parents could then use the voucher to finance their child's education at the public or private school that they think is best for their child.

In essence, a voucher plan would put competition to work to improve our schools. Since their revenues would be dependent upon their ability to attract students, schools would compete for students and parents would be free to choose among schools. The competition among schools would encourage innovative ideas and the discovery of more effective teaching techniques. It would also mean competition for first-rate educators. The demand for outstanding teachers would increase, which would increase salaries and help attract quality people to the teaching profession. Perhaps just as important, the demand for poor teachers would decline and many would shift to other careers.

A voucher system would also promote diversity and allow a larger number of Americans to choose and receive the type of schooling that they really want. Some parents would choose a highly structured school; others would prefer the open-school concept. Some would select a school that stresses religious values; others would opt for secularism in education. Some would choose a school with a traditional college prep program, while others would support schools that provide technical and vocational training. Under a system of parental choice, each of these diverse preferences could be satisfied.

Two major objections have been raised against a voucher system. First, some charge that the primary beneficiaries would be high-income Americans who already send their children to private schools. Second, others express a fear that a voucher plan would increase the racial imbalance among schools.

A modified voucher plan targeted toward low- and middle-income families would overcome both of these objections. For example, low-income families might be granted a voucher equal to the current full-cost per pupil of public spending on education, while the vouchers granted to middle-income families might be worth, say two-thirds of the public school cost, and the vouchers granted to high-income families worth even less. This type of voucher plan would enhance the educational opportunities available to the children of low- and middle-income families without providing a windfall gain to high-income families who send their children to private schools.

In addition, the modified voucher plan would actually promote racial and economic balance among schools. Since blacks and other minorities are overrepresented among the low-income families receiving the highest valued vouchers, those groups would also be overrepresented among families shifting to private schools (and high-quality public schools outside their district).

The experience of recent decades indicates that additional government spending is unlikely to improve our current educational system significantly. This should not be surprising to students of economics. There is little incentive for government firms operating in a protected market to provide high-quality service at a low cost. On the other hand, competition among rival suppliers works quite well in most markets. Many believe that it would also work well in education and help improve our schools.

trying to take an agency's customers, is rare in the public sector. And since there is no easily identified index of performance analogous to profit rates and stock prices, public-sector managers can often gloss over economic inefficiency. If a public-sector decision-maker spends money unwisely or uses resources primarily for personal benefit (such as excessive expenditures on plush offices or "business travel"), the burden of this inefficiency will fall on the taxpayer. The notorious and persistent cost overruns in the Pentagon are one example of the difficulty inherent in cost control without a profit motive and without vigorously competing firms. Public schools provide another example. (See the boxed feature, "Can Educational

Vouchers and Parental Choice Improve Our Schools?'' for a discussion of this problem. The public sector is also not subject to the test of bankruptcy, which tends to eliminate inefficient operations in the private sector. Political finesse is far more important to success in the public sector than operational efficiency. At election time, political candidates and parties must offer something more impressive than efficiency in government if they expect to win.

Taxpayers would be the major beneficiaries of reduced costs and an improvement in public-sector efficiency. A public-sector manager seldom reaps personal reward by saving the taxpayers money. In fact, if an agency fails to spend this year's allocation, its case for a larger budget next year is weakened. Agencies typically go on a spending spree at the end of a budget period if they discover that they have failed to spend all of this year's appropriation.

It is important to note that the argument of internal inefficiency is not based on the assumption that employees of a bureaucratic government are necessarily lazy or incapable. Rather, the emphasis is on the structure of information and incentives under which managers and other workers toil. No individual or relatively small group of individuals has much incentive to ensure efficiency. Their performances cannot readily be judged, and without private ownership their personal wealth would not be significantly increased or reduced by changes in the level of efficiency. Since public officials and bureau managers spend other people's money, they are likely to be less conscious of cost than they would be with their own resources. Attempts to control waste and abuse are made through rules that try to anticipate problems, rather than by an owner's drive toward profit and away from loss. Without a need to compare sales revenues to costs, there is no test by which to define economic inefficiency clearly or measure it accurately, much less eliminate it. The perverse incentive structure of a bureaucracy is bound to have an impact on its internal efficiency.

Research by economists over the last several years has tended to verify this line of reasoning. When private firms are compared to government agencies providing the same goods or services, the private firms generally have been shown to provide them more economically.[14]

THE PUBLIC SECTOR VERSUS THE MARKET: A SUMMARY

Throughout this text, we have argued that theory can explain why both market forces and public-sector action sometimes break down—that is, why they sometimes fail to meet the criteria for ideal efficiency. The deficiencies of one or the other sector will often be more or less decisive depending on the type of economic activity. Nobel laureate Paul Samuelson has stated, ''There are not rules concerning the proper role of government that can be established by *a priori* reasoning.''[15] This

---

[14]For a summary of many such studies, along with a detailed explanation of why these results are to be expected, see Louis De Alessi, ''The Economics of Property Rights: A Review of the Evidence,'' *Research in Law and Economics,* vol. 2 (Greenwich: JAI Press, Inc., 1980), pp. 1–47. Also see Anthony E. Boardman and Aidan R. Vining, ''Ownership and Performance in Competitive Environments: A Comparison of the Performance of Private, Mixed, and State-owned Enterprises'', *Journal of Law and Economics,* (April 1989), pp. 1–34.

[15]Paul A. Samuelson, ''The Economic Role of Private Activity,'' in *The Collected Scientific Papers of Paul A. Samuelson,* J. E. Stiglitz (ed.), vol. 2, (Cambridge: MIT Press, 1966), p. 1423.

does not mean, however, that economics has nothing to say about the *strength* of the case for either the market or the public sector in terms of specific classes of activities. Nor does it mean that social scientists have nothing to say about institutional arrangements for conducting economic activity. It merely indicates that each issue and type of activity must be considered individually.

The case for government intervention is obviously stronger for some activities than for others. For example, if an activity involves substantial external effects, market arrangements often result in economic inefficiency, and public-sector action may allow for greater efficiency. Similarly, when competitive pressures are weak and when there is reason to expect consumers to be poorly informed, market failure may result, and again government action may be called for. (See the Thumbnail Sketch for a summary of factors that influence the case for market or for public-sector action.)

THUMBNAIL SKETCH

These factors weaken the case for market-sector allocation:	These factors weaken the case for public-sector intervention:
1. External costs and benefits **2.** Public goods **3.** Monopoly **4.** Uninformed consumers	**1.** Voter ignorance, inability to recognize costs and benefits fully, and cost concealment **2.** The power of special interests **3.** The shortsightedness effect **4.** Little incentive for operational efficiency

---

The identical analysis holds for the public sector. When there is a good reason to believe that special interest influence will be strong, the case for government action to correct market failures is weakened. Similarly, the lack of a means of identifying and weeding out public-sector inefficiency weakens the case for government action. More often than not, the choice of proper institutions may be a choice among evils. For example, we might expect private-sector monopoly if an activity is left to the market and perverse regulation due to the special interest effect if we turn to the public sector. Understanding the shortcomings of both the market and the public sectors is important if we are to improve our current economic institutions.

ECONOMICS, POLITICS, AND THE TRANSFER SOCIETY

As Exhibit 3 illustrates, direct income transfers through the public sector have increased sharply during the last six decades. In 1929, income transfers accounted for only 1.8 percent of national income; by 1990, the figure had risen to 15.2 percent.

As in other areas, both the market failure and rent-seeking models of government underlie public-sector income transfers. As we discussed in Chapter 4,

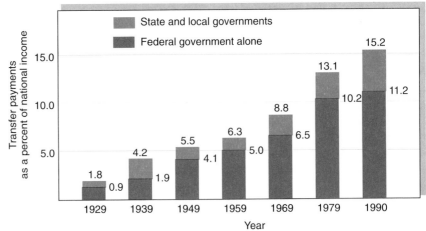

EXHIBIT 3

The Growth of Government Transfer Payments

The government now taxes approximately 15 percent of national income away from some people and transfers it to others. Means-tested income transfers—those directed toward the poor—account for only about one-sixth of the income transfers.

Source: *Economic Report of the President. 1991*, Tables B-24, B-80, B-81.

sometimes income transfers reflect the public good characteristics of antipoverty efforts. Since the number of poor people, like the strength of our national defense, is largely independent of one's personal contribution, individuals motivated by the desire to reduce poverty in general may simply become free-riders. When a large number of people become free-riders, though, less than the desired amount of antipoverty effort will be voluntarily supplied. If everyone is required to contribute through the tax system, then the free-rider problem can be overcome. Under these circumstances, transfers directed to the poor may be consistent with economic efficiency.

However, means-tested transfers, those directed toward the poor, constitute only about one-sixth of all income transfers. No income test is applied to the other five-sixths and they are generally directed toward groups that are either well organized or easily identifiable. The recipients of these transfers often have incomes well above the average. This suggests that the rent-seeking model of government also plays an important role in the allocation of income transfers.

Within the framework of public choice analysis, the relatively small portion of income transfers directed toward the poor is not surprising. There is little reason to believe that transfers to the poor will be particularly attractive to vote-seeking politicians. After all, in the United States, the poor are less likely to vote than middle and upper income recipients. They are less likely than others to be well-informed on political issues and candidates. They are not united. Neither are they a significant source of financial resources that exert a powerful influence on the political process.

Farm subsidies provide an excellent example of an income transfer program. The subsidies clearly reflect the rent-seeking model of government. In 1989 the federal government paid about $15 billion in direct crop subsidies to farmers. The subsidy programs distort resource use and generate market surpluses of agriculture products. As Exhibit 4 illustrates, the primary recipients of these income transfers are high income farmers. Only one-sixth of the farms in the United States had annual sales of $100,000 or more in 1989. Yet this small group of large farmers received more than two-thirds of the direct crop payments in 1989. More than six out of seven dollars of the transfer payments went to farmers with annual sales in

EXHIBIT 4 ■ Distribution of Government Income Transfers to Farmers by Farm Size, 1989			
		Direct Government Payments	
Farm Size (Annual Sales in Dollars)	Percent of Farms	Payments per Farm ($)	Percent of Payments Received
500,000 and over	2.0	48,400	13.0
250,000 to 500,000	3.9	28,100	19.6
100,000 to 250,000	11.1	16,100	34.4
40,000 to 100,000	13.7	8,900	19.3
10,000 to 40,000	22.7	4,500	11.0
10,000 or Less	46.6	1,700	2.7
All Farms	100.0	10,700	100.0

Source: Economic Research Services USDA (unpublished data).

excess of $40,000. The complex array of income transfers to farmers cost the average taxpayer-consumer about $100 per year, while generating an average gain in gross income of about $10,000 per participating farmer. The persistence of these programs indicates that the prospect of a $10,000 gain for a small subgroup is much more effective at generating political support than the prospect of a $100 savings is in generating political opposition. The result is highly consistent with the rent-seeking, special-interest view of how government programs are formulated.

Before leaving the topic of transfers, one final point should be stressed. Market adjustments and competition for the transfers will erode much of the long-run gain of the intended beneficiaries. This point follows from a standard proposition of economic theory: Competitors will be attracted to activities that yield abnormally high rates of return until the abnormally high profit is eroded. Application of this proposition to politics indicates that whenever the government establishes a criteria (as it must in a world of scarce resources) that must be met in order to qualify for transfers or other political favors, competition to meet the standard will erode the opportunity for profit. Unanticipated changes in public policy will impose temporary gains and losses on various groups. However, paradoxical as it may appear, it is extremely difficult to bestow favors upon a class of recipients in a manner that will *permanently* improve their well-being.

As people and markets adjust to the transfers, any abnormally high returns derived by recipients of government subsidies will dissipate. When one considers what one has to buy, or do, or be in order to qualify for transfers, it is clear that the net gain of the recipients is substantially less than the size of the transfers. In the case of the poor, high implicit marginal tax rates accompanying income-tested transfers severely retard the incentive of the poor to earn. Thus, the net increase in income of the poor is much less than the dollars transferred. To a large extent, the transfers merely replace income that would have been earned in their absence. The high implicit tax rates often induce the poor to drop out of the work force. When this happens the skills of the poor depreciate, further reducing their ability to support themselves and escape poverty. Government involvement in antipoverty transfers crowds out private charitable efforts by families, individuals, churches, and civic organizations. When taxes are levied to do more, predictably private individuals and groups will adjust and do less. When one considers these adjustments, it is not at all clear that the poor benefit from transfers, particularly in the long run.

If transfer programs fail to provide significant benefits to recipients beyond the windfall gains at the time the programs are instituted or unexpectedly expanded, what accounts for the continued political support for such programs? Gordon Tullock's work on the transitional gains trap provides the answer.[16] Elimination of the programs would be costly for recipients who have adjusted to or ''bought into'' the programs. Even though the programs do little to improve their welfare, the current beneficiaries would be harmed by the elimination or unexpected reduction in the programs. Thus, they form a vocal lobby supportive of the programs.

CONSTITUTIONAL ORGANIZATION AND GETTING MORE FROM GOVERNMENT

Public choice theory indicates that political action can, and often does, reduce economic inefficiency emanating from market failure. However, it also indicates that unconstrained democratic governments will often enact programs that waste resources and impair the general standard of living of citizens. How can we reap the benefits available from government while minimizing its unwanted, counterproductive activities?

An efficient political organization does not emerge naturally. It must be shaped by the legal environment. The ''founding fathers'' of the United States recognized this point. They sought to establish a constitutional order that would limit the misuse of the ordinary political process, while allowing government to undertake activities important to the welfare of citizens. With time, many of the safeguards embodied in the U.S. Constitution have either eroded or been modified. Nonetheless, the general idea was a sound one.

What would a constitutional structure consistent with economic efficiency look like? Interestingly, public choice analysis indicates that it would incorporate a number of the ideas emanating from the Philadelphia convention 200 years ago. First, it would seek to constrain rent-seeking activities—the use of the political process to take the rights and wealth from some in order to bestow them on others. The U.S. Constitution contains provisions designed to prevent such takings. The Fifth Amendment states, ''nor shall private property be taken for public use without just compensation.''[17] Article I, Section 10 mandates, ''No state shall . . . pass any . . . law impairing the obligations of contracts.'' These provisions might be strengthened and supplemented with prohibitions against the use of government to fix prices and to bar entry into the production of otherwise legal goods, both of which restrain trade and are indirect forms of taking property without compensation.

---

[16]Gordon Tullock, ''The Transitional Gains Trap,'' *Bell Journal of Economics,* 6 (Autumn 1975).

[17]For a detailed analysis of the importance of this clause from a law and economics viewpoint, see Richard A. Epstein, *Takings: Private Property and the Power of Eminent Domain* (Cambridge: Harvard University Press, 1985).

The federal government might also be barred from income transfer activities, other than those that are means-tested (directed toward the poor).

Second, the efficiency of the political process would be enhanced if the primary beneficiaries of government activities were required to foot the bill for their cost. Again, there is evidence that this is what the founding fathers had in mind. The U.S. Constitution, Article I, Section 8, states: "The Congress shall have power to lay and collect taxes, duties, imports and excises to . . . provide for the common defense and general welfare of the United States, but all duties, imports and excises shall be uniform throughout the United States." This constitutional provision indicates that it was the intent of the Founders that, at the federal level, uniformly levied taxes would be used only for the finance of expenditures yielding general benefits—the common defense and general welfare (type 1 issues of Exhibit 1). In order to assure stricter adherence to this substantive provision, tax and spending proposals at the federal level could be required to secure the approval of a supra-majority (for example, three-fourths) of the legislative members. Such a provision would reduce the power of interest groups and the viability of pork-barrel spending projects.

Finally, if we want efficiency in government, the constitutional structure should strengthen independent state and local governments. In *The Federalist Papers,* James Madison argues that competition among state and local governments will help check abusive and counterproductive government action.[18] Public choice analysis indicates that Madison's perception was correct. How might the constitutional order promote competition among governments? One way would be to require more inclusive majorities the higher the level of government. For example, local legislative bodies (city commissions, county commissions, regional authorities, and so on) might continue to act with the approval of only a simple majority, while a three-fifths majority might be required for legislative action at the state level, and a three-fourths majority at the federal level. The increasing majorities required for legislative action at higher levels of government would help remedy a deficiency of the current system—the tendency of federal and state governments to get involved with issues that are best dealt with at lower levels of governments. Decentralization in government would permit states and localities to adopt different governmental environments. Those that people like best—that supply public-sector goods that are highly valued relative to their tax cost—would grow and prosper relative to those people appreciate less. This structure would allow individuals and businesses to "vote with their feet," as well as with their ballots.

Of course, public choice theorists are continuing to investigate the operation of alternative forms of political organization. The challenge before us is to develop political institutions capable of bringing, to the fullest extent possible, the self-interest of politicians, bureaucrats, and voters into harmony with the general welfare of a society.

---

[18]See Charles Tiebout, "A Pure Theory of Local Expenditures," *Journal of Political Economy* (October 1956); Vincent Ostrom, *The Political Theory of a Compound Republic* (Fairfax: Center for Study of Public Choice, George Mason University, 1971); and Robert Bish, "Federalism: A Market-Economics Perspective" in James Gwartney and Richard Wagner (ed.), *Public Choice and Constitutional Economics* (Greenwich: JAI Press, 1988) for additional information on the importance of competition among governmental units.

LOOKING AHEAD

Democratic governments are a creation of the interactions of human beings. Public choice analysis helps us better understand these interactions and think more clearly about constitutional rules capable of improving the results achieved from government. As we consider trade among nations, how economies develop, and alternative forms of economic organization, public choice analysis will enhance our understanding of important issues in these areas.

CHAPTER SUMMARY

1. It is fruitful to analyze the public sector in the same way in which we analyze the private sector. The public sector is an alternative to the market—it provides an alternative means of organizing production and/or distributing output.

2. Voters cast ballots, make political contributions, lobby, and adopt other political strategies to demand public-sector action. Other things constant, voters have a strong incentive to support the candidate who offers them the greatest personal gain relative to personal costs. Obtaining information is costly. Since group decision-making breaks the link between the choice of the individual and the outcome of the issue, it is rational for voters to remain uninformed on many issues. Candidates are generally evaluated on the basis of a small subset of issues that are of the greatest personal importance to individual voters.

3. Under a democratic system, politicians have a strong incentive to follow a strategy that will enhance their chances of getting elected (and reelected). Political competition more or less forces politicians to focus on how their actions influence their support among voters.

4. Market failure presents government with an opportunity to undertake action that will result in additional benefits relative to costs. Other things constant, the greater the social loss resulting from the market failure, the stronger is the incentive for public-sector action. Ultimately, though, it is votes, not efficiency, which will determine political outcomes. The votes of citizens and their representatives will be influenced by the intensity as well as the direction of their preferences and interests. Logrolling and pork-barrel legislation are ways to make intensity more influential.

5. The distribution of the benefits and costs among voters influences how the political process works. When voters pay in proportion to the benefits they receive from a public-sector project, democratic decision-making works quite well. Productive projects tend to be approved and counterproductive ones rejected. However, problems arise when the pattern of benefits among voters differs from the pattern of costs.

6. There is a strong incentive for political entrepreneurs to support special interest issues and to make the issues difficult for the unorganized, largely uninformed majority to understand. Special interest groups supply both financial and direct elective support to the politician. Constitutional rules are one way to limit the power of special interests to use the political process to achieve their interests at the expense of the group as a whole.

7. In government, where decision-makers normally do not hold private property rights to the resources they control, the shortsightedness effect is another potential source of conflict between good politics and sound economics. Both voters and politicians tend to support projects that promise substantial current benefits at the expense of difficult-to-identify future costs. There is a bias against legislation that involves immediate and easily identifiable costs but complex future benefits.

8. The economic incentive for operational efficiency is small for public-sector action. No individual or relatively small group of individuals can capture the gains derived from improved operational efficiency. There is no force analogous to the threat of bankruptcy in the private sector that will bring inefficient behavior to a halt. Since public-sector resources, including tax funds, are communally owned, their users are less likely than private resource owners to be cost conscious.

9. A growing portion of public-sector activity involves income redistribution. Economic analysis indicates two potential sources of pressure for income redistribution: (a) the public-good nature of antipoverty efforts and (b) rent seeking. From the viewpoint of a vote-maximizing politician, there is incentive to support redistribution from unorganized to well-organized groups. Considerable income redistribution in the United States is of this type.

10. Keeping government from engaging in counterproductive activities, while encouraging it to undertake things that it does well, is difficult. Properly designed constitutional rules and restraints can help us achieve that objective.

CRITICAL ANALYSIS QUESTIONS

*1. "Voters should simply ignore political candidates who play ball with special interest groups, and vote instead for candidates who will represent all the people when they are elected. Government will work far better when this happens." Evaluate.

*2. "Government can afford to take a long view when it needs to, while a private firm has a short-term outlook. Corporate officers, for example, typically care about the next 3 to 6 months, not the next 50 to 100 years. Government, not private firms, should own things like forests, where centuries, rather than the next few months, are at stake." Evaluate.

3. Suppose that you are part of a group of nature enthusiasts, and have discovered a bog that the group would like to preserve, although the site might soon be transferred to another use. Your group has some cash and can spend it several ways: it could buy the land and lease it, obtaining the right to manage it as it wishes. Alternatively, it could lobby the local authorities to regulate the land's use, forcing the current owner not to change the bog's condition or use. Using economic thinking, what analysis of the options could you provide to the group? The group wants to get the most for its money in the long run, and prefers cooperation to conflict.

4. Do you think that advertising exerts more influence on the type of car chosen by a consumer than on the type of politician chosen by the same person? Explain your answer.

5. Do you think that the political process works to the advantage of the poor? Explain. Are the poor well organized? Do they make substantial campaign contributions to candidates? Are they likely to be well informed? Is it surprising that only about one-sixth of the approximately $700 billion of cash income transfer payments in the United States is directed toward the poor? Explain.

6. Which of the following public-sector actions are designed primarily to correct "market failure": (a) laws against fraud, (b) truth-in-lending legislation, (c) rate regulation in the telephone industry, (d) legislation setting emission control standards, (e) subsidization of pure research, and (f) operation of the Post Office? Explain your answer.

*7. "When an economic function is turned over to the government, social cooperation replaces personal self-interest." Is this statement true? Why or why not?

*8. The liquor industry contributes a large share of the political funds to political contests on the state level. Yet its contributions to candidates for national office are minimal. Why do you think this is true? (*Hint:* Who regulates the liquor industry?)

9. One explanation for the shortsightedness effect in the public sector is that future voters cannot vote now to represent their future interests. Are the interests of future generations represented in market decision? For example, if the price of chromium were expected to rise rapidly over the next 30 years due to increased scarcity, how could speculators grow rich while providing the next generation with more chromium at the expense of current consumers?

---

*Asterisk denotes questions for which answers are given in Appendix C, Selected Answers.

*10. **What's Wrong with This Way of Thinking?**
   "Public policy is necessary to protect the average citizen from the power of vested interest groups. In the absence of government intervention, regulated industries, such as airlines, railroads, and trucking, would charge excessive prices, products would be unsafe, and the rich would oppress the poor. Government curbs the power of special interest groups."

11. Are shoppers making decisions in the local supermarket likely to make better informed choices than voters making choices in political races? Why or why not?

12. Economics indicates that "principals" in both the private and public sector cannot be sure that their "agents" will act in their interests. Compare this principal-agent problem between a) stockholders and managers in the private sector and b) voters and politicians (and bureaucrats) in the public sector. Do you think inefficiencies arising from the principal-agent problem will be more or less severe in the public sector than in the private sector? Why?

13. Why might members of Congress who work for special interest and pork-barrel legislation under an unconstrained system of representative democracy nonetheless favor constitutional restraints limiting such spending?

14. Do you think a system of educational vouchers would improve the performance of schools in the United States? Why or why not? How do you think a voucher system would affect the educational opportunities of the following: (a) students in poor families? (b) students living in inner cities? (c) gifted students? What groups would you expect to oppose a voucher system? Why?

15. Many countries in Eastern Europe and the Soviet Union are moving toward democratic decision-making. Will democracy make these countries prosperous? Why or why not? Should these countries establish constitutional restraints limiting the economic role of government? If so, indicate what constitutional provisions you would recommend. Be specific.

PART SIX

International Economics and Comparative Systems

31 *Gaining from International Trade*

Free trade consists simply in letting people buy and sell as they want to buy and sell. It is protection [trade restrictions] that requires force, for it consists in preventing people from doing what they want to do. Protective tariffs are as much applications of force as are blockading squadrons, and their objective is the same—to prevent trade. The difference between the two is that blockading squadrons are a means whereby nations seek to prevent their enemies from trading; protective tariffs are a means whereby nations attempt to prevent their own people from trading.[1]

Henry George (1886)

CHAPTER FOCUS

■ How large is the international sector in the United States? What are the major import and export products of the United States? Which countries are the major trading partners of the United States?

■ Under what conditions can a nation gain from international trade?

■ How do trade restrictions affect the welfare of a nation?

■ Why do nations erect trade barriers? Are there valid economic arguments in support of trade restrictions?

■ Do trade restrictions create (or save) jobs?

■ Will free trade with low-wage countries cause wage rates in high-wage countries to decline?

e live in a shrinking world. Wheat raised on the flatlands of western Kansas may be processed into bread in a Russian factory. The breakfast of many Americans might include bananas from Honduras, coffee from Brazil, or hot chocolate made from Nigerian cocoa beans. The volume of international trade, enhanced by improved transportation and communications, has grown rapidly in recent years. Approximately 21 percent of the world's total output is now sold in a country other than that in which it was produced—double the figure of three decades ago.

Perhaps surprising to some, most international trade is not between the governments of the nations involved. Instead, international buying and selling of goods and services take place between individuals (or business firms) that happen to be located in different countries. International trade, like other voluntary exchange, results because both the buyer and the seller gain from it. If both parties did not expect to gain, there would be no trade.

THE COMPOSITION OF THE INTERNATIONAL SECTOR

Exhibit 1 illustrates the growth in the size of the trade sector during the 1965–1988 period. The proportion of total output exported to a purchaser in another country has grown in all major industrial countries. The size of the trade sector varies substantially among nations. International trade comprises more than one-half of the GNP of the Netherlands and more than one quarter of the GNP in Sweden, West Germany, and Canada. The relative size of the trade sector is smaller for Australia,

---

[1]Henry George, *Protection or Free Trade* (1886; reprinted edition, New York: Robert Schalkenbach Foundation, 1980), p. 47.

EXHIBIT 1 ■ The size of the Trade Sector for Selected Countries, 1965 and 1988		
	Exports as a Percentage of Total Output	
Country	1965	1988
Netherlands	43	55
Sweden	22	32
Germany	19	33
Canada	19	26
United Kingdom	18	23
France	13	22
Australia	15	17
Japan	11	13
United States	6	11
World (all countries)	12	21

Source: The World Bank, *World Development Report: 1990* (Table 9).

Japan, and the United States. The international trade sector accounts for approximately 11 percent of the GNP in the United States, up from 6 percent in 1965.

However, the size of the international sector relative to GNP understates the importance of trade. We are dependent on foreign producers for almost all of our coffee, bananas, bauxite, chromium, diamonds, tin, cobalt, nickel, manganese, and asbestos. The domestic price of these goods would rise dramatically if we could not import them. Because of comparative advantage, even items that are commonly produced in the United States would be more expensive without trade. Thus, the life-style of Americans (as well as of our trading partners) would change dramatically if international trade were halted or even substantially reduced.

Exhibit 2 summarizes the leading products that the U.S. imports and exports. The United States both imports and exports a substantial quantity of food and agricultural products. The major imported products, however, are generally quite different from primary products that are exported. Reflecting the temperate climate and fertile agricultural lands of the United States, wheat, corn, soybeans, and tobacco are the primary food and agricultural exports. In contrast, the primary imported products in this category are fish, fruits and nuts, coffee, and alcoholic beverages. The mineral and raw material products exported are also quite different from those that are imported. In this category, coal and plastics comprise the primary export goods, while petroleum (particularly crude oil) and diamonds are major imports. In the manufacturing area, automobiles and electronic equipment are

EXHIBIT 2 ■ The Major Import and Export Products of the United States by Categories

Exports	Value (in billions)	Percent of total exports	Imports	Value (in billions)	Percent of total imports
Food and Agriculture Products			*Food and Agriculture Products*		
Wheat	$ 5.1	1.7	Fish	$ 5.3	1.2
Corn	5.2	1.7	Fruits/Nuts	3.2	0.7
Soybeans	4.8	1.6	Coffee	2.0	0.5
Tobacco prod.	4.2	1.4	Alcoholic Bev.	3.4	0.8
Minerals and Raw Materials			*Minerals and Raw Materials*		
Coal	4.0	1.3	Petroleum	38.1	8.2
Plastics	7.3	2.4	Diamonds	4.3	1.0
Manufactured Goods			*Manufactured Goods*		
Automobiles	24.0	7.8	Automobiles	71.3	16.2
Computers	22.4	7.3	Office Mach.	22.6	5.1
Aircraft	20.0	6.5	Telecommunications equip.		
Power generating machinery	12.8	4.2	(incl. T.V. sets)	22.3	5.1
Scientific instruments	8.9	2.9	Clothing	21.5	4.9
Telecommunications Equip.			Paper	8.3	1.9
			Footwear (shoes)	8.0	1.8
(incl. T.V. sets)	6.5	2.1	Toys	6.5	1.5
Total	$308.4	—	Total	$441.3	—

Source: *Statistical Abstract of the United States, 1990*, pp.811–14.

major items among both imports and exports. The markets for automobiles, computer equipment, televisions, and stereos are world-wide markets. Therefore, in these markets U.S. producers sell substantial quantities abroad, while at the same time, many U.S. consumers purchase these goods from foreign manufacturers.

Clearly, international trade exerts a different impact on some industries than on others. In some industries, domestic producers find it very difficult to compete with their rivals abroad. For example, approximately 90 percent of the shoes purchased by Americans and nearly two-thirds of the radio and television sets, watches, and motorcycles are produced abroad. Imports also supply a high percentage of the clothing and textile products, paper, and toys consumed in the United States. On the other hand, a large proportion of the aircraft, power generating equipment, scientific instruments, construction equipment, and fertilizers produced in the United States is exported to purchasers abroad.

With which countries does the U.S. trade the most? As Exhibit 3 illustrates, Japan and Canada head the list. In 1989, more than one-third of U.S. exports were sold to purchasers in Canada and Japan. Almost 40 percent of U.S. imports were produced in those two countries. Mexico, and the nations of the European Economic Community (particularly West Germany, the United Kingdom, France,

EXHIBIT 3

The Leading Trading Partners of the United States, 1989

Canada, Japan, Mexico, and Western European countries are the leading trading partners of the United States. In recent years, South Korea, Hong Kong, and Brazil have also emerged as important trading partners of the United States.

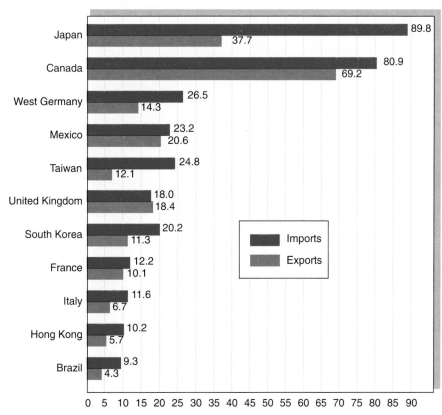

Value of U.S. exports and imports with selected countries, 1989
(billions of dollars)

Source: *Statistical Abstract of the United States: 1990,* (Table 1406).

and Italy) were also among the leading trading partners of the United States. During the 1970s, U.S. trade with petroleum-exporting countries such as Saudi Arabia and Venezuela grew rapidly. However, the volume of trade with these nations declined as the price of crude oil fell in the 1980s. Taiwan, South Korea, Hong Kong, and Brazil emerged as major trading partners of the United States during the 1980s.

GAINS FROM SPECIALIZATION AND TRADE

If a foreign country can supply us with a commodity cheaper than we ourselves can make it, [we had] better buy it of them with some part of our own industry, employed in a way in which we have some advantage.[2]

Adam Smith

Comparative Advantage:
The ability to produce a good at a lower opportunity cost than others can produce it. Relative costs determine comparative advantage. A nation will have a comparative advantage in the production of a good when its production costs for the good are low relative to its production costs for other goods.

The law of comparative advantage, which we discussed in Chapter 2, explains why mutual gains arise from specialization and exchange. According to the law of comparative advantage, trading partners are better off if they specialize in the production of goods for which they are a low opportunity cost producer and trade for those goods for which they are a high opportunity cost producer. Specialization in the area of one's **comparative advantage** minimizes the cost of production and leads to maximum joint output.

International trading partners can gain if they specialize in those things they do best. We know that different countries have drastically different resources. These differences in resource endowments influence costs and areas of specialization. For example, countries with warm, moist climates such as Brazil and Colombia find it advantageous to specialize in the production of coffee. Land is abundant in sparsely populated nations such as Canada and Australia. These nations tend to specialize in land-intensive products, such as wheat, feed grains, and beef. In contrast, land is scarce in Japan, a nation with a highly skilled labor force. The Japanese therefore specialize in manufacturing, using their comparative advantage to produce cameras, automobiles, and electronic products for export.

It is easy to see why trade and specialization expand joint output and lead to mutual gain when the resource bases of regions differ substantially. However, even when resource differences among nations are less dramatic, mutual gain is possible. Since failure to comprehend the principle of mutual gains from trade is often a source of "fuzzy thinking," we will take the time to illustrate the principle in detail.

Absolute Advantage:
A situation in which a nation, as the result of its previous experience and/or natural endowments, can produce more output (with the same resources) than another nation.

Suppose that the United States and Japan produce two products: food and clothing. Consider a case in which the output per worker of both food and clothing is higher for Japan than for the United States. Perhaps due to its previous experience or natural endowments, Japan has an **absolute advantage** in the production of both commodities. Using hypothetical data, Exhibit 4 illustrates this situation. Japanese workers can produce 3 units of food per day, compared with only 2 units per day for U.S. workers. Similarly, Japanese workers are able to produce 9 units of clothing per day, compared with only 1 unit of clothing per day for U.S. workers.

---

[2]Adam Smith, *An Inquiry into the Nature and Causes of the Wealth of Nations* (1776; Cannan's ed., Chicago: University of Chicago Press, 1976), pp. 478–79.

EXHIBIT 4 ■ The Relative Cost of Food and Clothing in the United States and Japan—Hypothetical Data

Gains from exchange depend on comparative advantage, not absolute advantage. Here we illustrate a case in which U.S. workers are able to produce 2 units of food per day, compared to 3 units per day for Japanese workers. Similarly, U.S. workers are able to produce only 1 unit of clothing per day, compared to 9 units per day for Japanese workers. However, even though it is at an absolute disadvantage in the production of both goods, the U.S. has a *comparative* advantage in the production of food. The opportunity cost of producing a unit of food in the U.S. is one-half unit of clothing, compared to an opportunity cost of food in Japan of 3 units of clothing. Thus, the U.S. is the low opportunity cost producer of food. On the other hand, in Japan production of a unit of clothing costs only one-third of a unit of food, compared with 2 units in the United States. Thus, Japan is the low opportunity cost producer of clothing.

Country	*Units of Output per Worker-Day*		*Opportunity Cost*	
	Food	Clothing	Food (in terms of clothing)	Clothing (in terms of food)
United States	2	1	½	2
Japan	3	9	3	⅓

Given that the Japanese workers are more efficient at producing *both* food and clothing than their American counterparts, are gains from trade possible? Perhaps surprising to some, the answer is yes. As long as *relative* production costs of the two goods differ between Japan and the United States, gains from trade are possible.

Suppose that the size of the labor force in the United States was 200 million worker-days while in Japan the labor force was 50 million worker-days. Given the productivity of workers in each country, Exhibit 5 illustrates the *pre-trade* production (and consumption) possibilities for both the United States and Japan. (For simplicity, we will assume that the relative cost of food and clothing in each country is independent of output. Relaxation of this assumption would not alter the basic analysis.) First, let us consider the pre-trade situation in the United States. If the United States used all of its 200 million worker-days in the food industry, it could produce 400 million units of food (2 units per worker-day) and zero units of clothing. Of course, the United States could produce clothing, but only if some of its workers were moved from food to clothing production. The opportunity cost of clothing in the U.S. is 2 units of food; the U.S. would have to sacrifice 2 units of food for each unit of clothing produced. Thus, if clothing output in the U.S. is expanded from zero to 50 million, in the absence of trade, U.S. food output will have to be cut back by 100 million units—from 400M to 300M. (M refers to millions of units). Given the productivity of its workers in both food and clothing, Exhibit 5a graphically illustrates the various combinations of food and clothing that could be produced with the 200 million worker-days available in the United States. If they were unable to engage in international trade, American consumers would choose to purchase 150 units of clothing and 100 units of food.

Exhibit 5b indicates the pre-trade production possibilities of Japan. If Japan uses all of its 50 million worker-days to produce clothing, 450 million units (9 per day times 50 million days) of clothing could be produced. It would thus be possible for Japan to produce the output combination of 450 million units of clothing and zero units of food. In the absence of trade, Japan must sacrifice 9 units of clothing for each 3 units of food it produces. A unit of food thus costs the Japanese 3 times

EXHIBIT 5

The Production Possibilities of the United States and Japan before Specialization and Trade

Here we illustrate the production possibilities of a U.S. labor force of 200 million worker-days and a Japanese labor force of 50 million worker-days, given the cost of producing food and clothing presented in Exhibit 4. The slope of the production possibilities constraint reflects the opportunity cost of food relative to clothing. Since Japan is the high opportunity cost producer of food, its production possibilities constraint is steeper than the constraint for the U.S. In the absence of trade, consumption in each country will be restricted by the country's production possibilities constraint. Prior to trade, the U.S. chooses combination P_4 (100M food, 150M clothing) and Japan chooses P_3 (75M food and 225M clothing). With trade however, *both* countries will be able to increase their consumption of *both* food and clothing. See Exhibit 6.

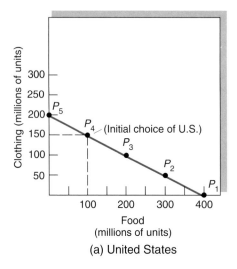

(a) United States

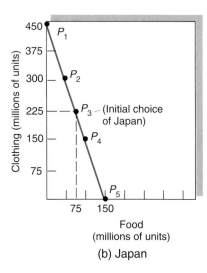

(b) Japan

as much as a unit of clothing. For example, if the Japanese want to produce 50 million units of food, they must be willing to sacrifice 150 million units of clothing, cutting clothing output from 450 million to 300 million. In the absence of trade, Exhibit 5b graphically illustrates the various combinations of food and clothing that the Japanese could produce with the employment of 50 million worker-days. In the absence of trade, the preferred bundle of Japanese consumers is 225 units of clothing and 75 units of food.

DIFFERENCES IN OPPORTUNITY COST— THE SOURCE OF GAINS FROM TRADE

As long as the opportunity cost of production of the two goods differs between Japan and the United States, potential gains from specialization and exchange are present. Consider the opportunity cost of food in each of the two countries. If Japanese workers produce 1 additional unit of food, they sacrifice the production of 3 units of clothing. In Japan, the opportunity cost of 1 unit of food is 3 units of clothing (see Exhibit 4). On the other hand, 1 unit of food can be produced in the U.S. at an opportunity cost of only ½ unit of clothing. *U.S. workers are therefore the low opportunity cost producers of food, even though they cannot produce as much food per day as the Japanese workers.* Both countries can gain if the U.S. trades food to Japan for clothing at a trading ratio greater than 1 food = ½ clothing (the U.S. opportunity cost of food) but less than 1 food = 3 clothing (the Japanese opportunity cost of food). Any intermediate trading ratio between these two extremes would permit the U.S. to acquire clothing cheaper than it can be produced in the U.S. and simultaneously permit Japan to acquire food at a lesser sacrifice than it can be produced in Japan.

EXHIBIT 6

The Effects of Trade on Production and the Consumption Possibilities of the United States and Japan

Prior to trade, the two countries produce and consume the combinations represented by US_1 (P_4 of Exhibit 5a) and J_1 (P_3 of Exhibit 5b). When trade takes place at an exchange ratio of one unit of food equals one unit of clothing, both countries gain by specializing in their area of comparative advantage. The U.S. specializes in the production of food, produces 400M units, and exports 200M units of food to Japan in exchange for 200M units of clothing. This permits the U.S. to consume the combination 200M food and 200M clothing (imported from Japan). Compared to the no-trade option chosen (150M clothing and 100M food), the U.S. is able to consume a larger quantity of both goods after trade.

Simultaneously, Japan can also increase its consumption of both goods. When Japan specializes in the production of clothing, it can produce 450M units, and export 200M units to the U.S. in exchange for 200M units of clothing. This permits Japan to consume 250M units of clothing and 200M units of food, compared to its initial preferred bundle of 225M clothing and 75M food. Specialization and trade thus expands the consumption possibilities of both countries.

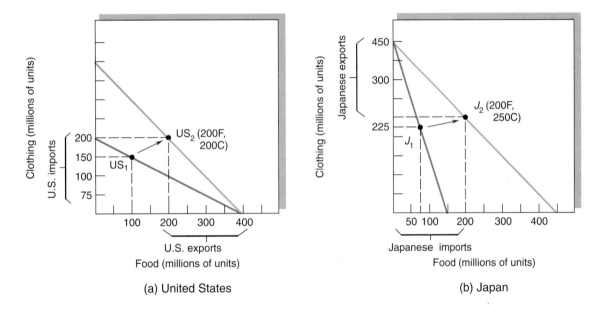

(a) United States

(b) Japan

Suppose the two countries agree to a trading ratio (an "intermediate price") in which 1 unit of food exchanges for 1 unit of clothing. This would allow each country to specialize in the area of its comparative advantage—food for the U.S. and clothing for the Japanese—while trading for the commodity for which it is a high opportunity cost producer. As Exhibit 6 shows, specialization and trade benefits both countries. Rather than producing and consuming its initially preferred combination of 150M clothing and 100M food, the U.S. could produce 400M food and import 200M clothing from Japan in exchange for 200M food. This would permit the U.S. to consume the combination 200M units of food and 200M units of clothing. Following trade, the U.S. is able to consume a larger quantity of both food and clothing than the preferred bundle in the absence of trade.

Similarly, the Japanese benefit from specialization and exchange. Prior to trade, the preferred bundle in Japan was 225M clothing and 75M food. With trade, the Japanese could specialize in the production of clothing. If the Japanese produce 450M units of clothing and export 200M to the U.S. in exchange for 200M units of food, they would be left with the combination 200M units of food (imported from the U.S.) and 250M units of clothing. As was the case for the U.S., the exchange permits the Japanese to consume a larger quantity of both commodities relative to their preferred pre-trade output combination.

Specialization and exchange leads to an expansion in the joint output of the two countries, and as a result, both countries can increase their consumption of both commodities. The chart below indicates the production and consumption combination for the two countries, *prior to trade*.

	Food	Clothing
U.S. Consumption	100	150
Japanese Consumption	75	225
Total	175	375

With specialization and trade, food production jumps to 400M units, an increase of 225M units over the pre-trade output level. Similarly, clothing production expands to 450M, an increase of 75M. Therefore, after specialization and exchange (at the price ratio where one unit of food exchanges for one unit of clothing), households in the two countries are now able to consume the following combination of food and clothing:

	Food	Clothing
U.S. Consumption	200	200
Japanese Consumption	200	250
Total	400	450

Comparisons of this chart with the above chart for the pre-trade consumption levels reveals that with trade, *both* countries are able to consume more of *both* commodities.

Mutual gains accrue to trading partners when each nation specializes in the production of those products for which it is a low opportunity cost producer and trades them for those goods for which it is a high opportunity cost producer. Such specialization and exchange will permit nations to maximize their joint output. A country can gain from trade even when it is at an absolute disadvantage in the production of all goods. Comparative advantage is the source of gains from trade, and a nation will always have a comparative advantage in the production of some goods as long as there is some variation in the relative opportunity cost of goods across countries.

Exhibits 4, 5, and 6 actually understate the potential of gains from trade across national boundaries. For simplicity, we assumed that each good was produced under conditions of constant cost. (This is why the production possibilities constraints of Exhibits 5 and 6 are straight lines.) Often, access to a larger market will lead to lower per unit costs, as the result of economies accompanying large scale production, marketing, and distribution. The aircraft industry illustrates this point. Approximately half of the jet planes of the major U.S. aircraft producers are sold abroad. Given the huge designing and tooling cost necessary for the production of a jumbo jet, the cost of airplanes to both domestic and foreign purchasers would be higher if it were not for international trade. Thus, economies accompanying an expansion in the size of the market will enlarge the gains from specialization and trade.

While our hypothetical example illustrates the case of complete specialization, a country need not specialize in the production of just a few products to realize gains from trade. The example of complete specialization was used for illustrative purposes only. Similarly, we ignored the potential importance of transportation costs. Of course, transportation costs reduce the potential gains from trade. Sometimes transportation costs, both real and artificially imposed, exceed the mutual gain. (See the Applications in Economics box, "Frédéric Bastiat on Obstacles to Gains from Trade.") When this is so, exchange does not occur. However, this does not negate the basic point: the potential realization of gains from specialization and exchange implied by the law of comparative advantage.

APPLICATIONS IN ECONOMICS

Frédéric Bastiat on Obstacles to Gains from Trade

Since voluntary exchange is a positive-sum economic activity, obstacles to mutually advantageous exchange are costly. As Frédéric Bastiat notes in the following essay,[3] tariffs limit the gains from voluntary exchange just as bad roads or high transportation costs do. Best known for his cutting satire, Bastiat chastises French legislators for spending tax funds to reduce the transport costs of goods and then turning around and erecting tariff barriers that, in effect, increase transportation costs. Even though it was written in 1845, the thrust of Bastiat's message remains valid today.

> The illusions of inventors are proverbial, but I am positively certain that I have discovered an infallible means of bringing products from every part of the world to France, and vice versa, at a considerable reduction in cost.

> It requires neither plans, estimates, preparatory study, engineers, mechanics, contractors, capital, shareholders, or government aid.

> Why does an article manufactured at Brussels, for example, cost dearer when it comes to Paris?

> Between Paris and Brussels *obstacles* of many kinds exist. First of all, there is distance, which entails loss of time, and we must either submit to this ourselves or pay another to submit to it. Then comes [sic] rivers, marshes, accidents, bad roads, which are so many difficulties to be surmounted. We succeed in building bridges, in forming roads, and making them smoother by pavement, iron rails, etc. But all this is costly, and the commodity must be made to bear the cost.

> Now, among these obstacles there is one which we have ourselves set up. . . . There are men who lie in ambush along the frontier, armed to the teeth, and whose business it is to throw difficulties into the way of transporting merchandise from the one country to another. They are called customs officials, and they act in precisely the same way as ruts and bad roads. . . .

> I often seriously ask myself how anything so whimsical could ever have entered into the human brain, as first of all to lay out many millions for the purpose of removing *natural obstacles* which lie between France and other countries, and then to lay out many more millions for the purpose of substituting *artificial obstacles*. . . so that the obstacle created and the obstacle removed neutralize each other.

> [The] problem is resolved in three words: Reduce your tariff. You will then have done what is equivalent to constructing the Northern Railway without cost. . . [emphasis in the original].

[3]Frédéric Bastiat, *Economic Sophisms*, trans. Patrick James Stirling (London: Unwin, 1909), pp. 68–70. Reprinted with permission of T. Fisher Unwin, Ltd./Ernest Benn, Ltd., London.

THE EXPORT-IMPORT LINK

Confusion about the merit of international trade often results because people do not consider all the consequences. Why are other nations willing to export their goods to the United States? So they can obtain dollars. Yes, but why do they want dollars? Would foreigners be willing to continue exporting oil, radios, watches, cameras, automobiles, and thousands of other valuable products to us in exchange for pieces of paper? If so, we could all be semiretired, spending only an occasional workday at the dollar printing press office! Of course, foreigners are not so naive. They trade goods for dollars so they can use the dollars to import goods and purchase ownership rights to U.S. assets.

Exports provide the buying power that makes it possible for a nation to import other goods. Nations export goods so that they will be able to import foreign products. If a nation does not import goods from foreigners, foreigners will not have the purchasing power to buy that nation's export products. Thus, the exports and imports of a nation are closely linked.

SUPPLY, DEMAND, AND INTERNATIONAL TRADE

How does international trade affect prices and output levels in domestic markets? Supply and demand analysis will help us answer this question. Given our modern transportation and communication networks, the market for many commodities is worldwide. When a product can be transported long distances at a low cost (relative to its value) the domestic price of the product is in effect determined by the forces of supply and demand in the worldwide market.

Using soybeans as an example, Exhibit 7 illustrates the relationship between the domestic and world markets for an internationally traded commodity. World-wide market conditions determine the price of soybeans. In an open economy, domestic producers are free to sell and domestic consumers are free to buy the product at the world market price (P_w). At the world market price, U.S. producers will supply Q_p, while U.S. consumers will purchase Q_c. Reflecting their comparative advantage, U.S. soybean producers will export $Q_p - Q_c$ units at the world market price.

Let us compare the open economy outcome with the situation in the absence of trade. If U.S. producers were not allowed to export soybeans, the domestic price would be determined by the domestic supply (S_d) and demand (D_d) only. A lower "no-trade" price (P_n) would emerge. Who are the winners and losers as the result of free trade in soybeans? Clearly, soybean producers gain. Free trade allows domestic producers to sell a larger quantity (Q_p rather than Q_n). As a result, the *net* revenues of soybean producers will rise by $P_w b c P_n$. On the other hand, domestic consumers of soybeans will have to pay a higher price under free trade. Consumers will lose both (a) because they have to pay P_w rather than P_n for the Q_c units they purchase, and (b) because they lose the consumer surplus on the $Q_n - Q_c$ units now purchased at the higher price. Thus, free trade imposes a net cost of $P_w a c P_n$ on consumers. As can be seen in Exhibit 7, however, the gains of producers outweigh the losses to consumers by the triangle *abc*. Free trade leads to a net welfare gain.

When one focuses only on an export product, it appears that free trade benefits producers relative to consumers. This is potentially quite misleading, however,

EXHIBIT 7

Producer Benefits from Exports

As frame b shows, the price of soybeans and other internationally traded commodities is determined by the forces of supply and demand in the world market. If U.S. soybean producers were prohibited from selling to foreigners, the domestic price would be P_n (frame a). Free trade permits the U.S. soybean producers to sell Q_p units at the higher world price (P_w). The quantity $Q_p - Q_c$ is exported abroad. Compared to the no-trade situation, the producers' gain from the higher price ($P_w bcP_n$) exceeds the cost imposed on domestic consumers ($P_w acP_n$) by the triangle *abc*.

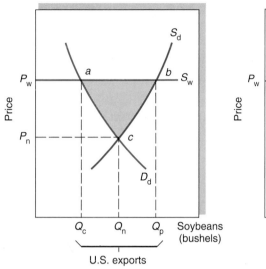

U.S. exports

(a) U.S. market for soybeans

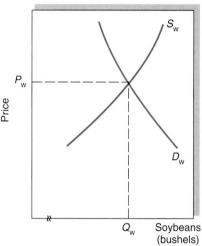

(b) World market for soybeans

because it ignores the secondary effects. How will foreigners generate the dollars they will need to purchase the export products of the United States? If foreigners do not sell goods to us, they will not have the purchasing power necessary to purchase goods from us. U.S. imports—that is, the purchase of goods from low-cost foreign producers—provide foreigners with the dollar purchasing power necessary to buy U.S. exports. In turn, the lower prices in the import-competitive markets will benefit the U.S. consumers who appeared at first glance to be harmed by the higher prices (compared to the no-trade situation) in export markets.

Exhibit 8 illustrates the impact of imports, using shoes as an example. In the absence of trade, the price of shoes in the domestic market would be P_n, the intersection of the domestic supply and demand curves. However, the world price of shoes is P_w. In an open economy, many U.S. consumers would take advantage of the low shoe prices available from foreign producers. At the lower world price, U.S. consumers would purchase Q_c units of shoes, importing $Q_c - Q_p$ from foreign producers.

Compared to the no-trade situation, free trade in shoes results in lower prices and an expansion in domestic consumption. The lower prices lead to a net consumer gain of $P_n abP_w$. Domestic producers lose $P_n acP_w$ in the form of lower sales prices and reductions in output. However, the net gain of consumers exceeds the net loss of producers by *abc*.

For an open economy, international competition directs the resources of a nation toward the areas of their comparative advantage. When domestic producers have a comparative advantage in the production of a good, they will be able to compete effectively in the world market and profit from the export of goods to foreigners. In turn, the exports will generate the purchasing power necessary to buy goods that foreigners can supply more economically than we can produce. Relative to the no-trade alternative, international trade and specialization result in lower prices (and higher consumption levels) for imported products and higher prices (and lower consumption levels) for exported products. More importantly, trade permits the producers of each nation to concentrate on the things they do best (produce at

Consumer Benefits from Imports

In the absence of trade, the domestic price of shoes would be P_n. Since many foreign producers have a comparative advantage in the production of shoes, international trade leads to lower prices. At the world price P_w, U.S. consumers will demand Q_c units, of which $Q_c - Q_p$ are imported. Compared to the no-trade situation, consumers gain $P_n abP_w$, while domestic producers lose $P_n acP_w$. A net gain of abc results.

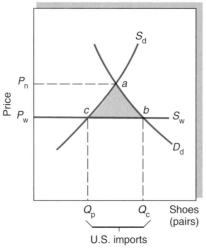

(a) U.S. market for shoes

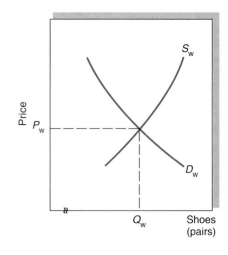

(b) World market for shoes

a low cost), while trading for those things which they do least well. The result is an expansion in both output and consumption compared to what could be achieved in the absence of trade.

The pattern of U.S. exports and imports is consistent with this view. The United States is a nation with a technically skilled labor force, fertile farm land, and substantial capital formation. Thus, we export computers, aircraft, power generating equipment, scientific instruments, and land-intensive agricultural products—items we are able to produce at a comparatively low cost. Simultaneously, we import substantial amounts of petroleum, textile (clothing) products, shoes, coffee, and diamonds—goods for which it is costly to produce additional units domestically. Clearly, trade permits us to specialize in those areas in which our comparative advantage is greatest and trade for those products we are least suited to produce.

THE ECONOMICS OF TRADE RESTRICTIONS

Tariff: A tax levied on goods imported into a country.

Despite the potential benefits from free trade, almost all nations have erected trade barriers. What kinds of barriers are erected? Tariffs and quotas are the two most commonly used trade-restricting devices. A **tariff** is nothing more than a tax on foreign imports. As Exhibit 9 shows, tariff barriers in the United States have fluctuated. Until the 1940s, tariffs of between 30 and 50 percent of product value were often levied. In recent years, the average tariff rate has been much lower. In 1988, the average tariff on imported goods was 4 percent.

Exhibit 10 illustrates the impact of a tariff on automobiles. In the absence of a tariff, the world market price of P_w would prevail in the domestic market. At that price, U.S. consumers purchase Q_1 units. Domestic producers supply Q_{d1}, while foreigners supply Q_1 minus Q_{d1} units to the U.S. market. When the United States levies a tariff t on automobiles, Americans can no longer buy cars at the world price.

EXHIBIT 9

How High Are U.S. Tariffs?

Tariff rates in the United States fell sharply during the period from 1930 to 1950. Subsequently, after rising slightly during the 1950s, they have trended downward since 1960. In 1988, the average tariff rate on duty-eligible imports was 4 percent.

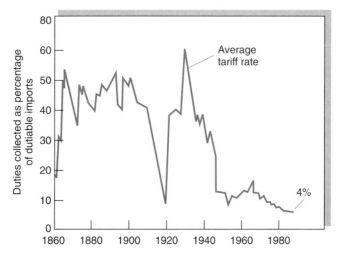

Source: U.S. Department of Commerce.

U.S. consumers have to pay $P_w + t$ to purchase an automobile from foreigners. The domestic market price thus rises to $P_w + t$. At that price, domestic consumers demand Q_2 units (Q_{d2} supplied by domestic producers and $Q_2 - Q_{d2}$ supplied by foreigners). The tariff results in a higher price and lower level of domestic consumption.

The tariff benefits domestic producers and the government at the expense of consumers. Since they do not pay the tariff, domestic producers will expand their output in response to the higher (protected) market price. In effect, the tariff acts as a subsidy to domestic producers. Domestic producers gain the area S (Exhibit 10) in the form of additional net revenues. The tariff raises revenues equal to the area T for the government. The areas U and V represent costs imposed on consumers that do not benefit either producers or the government. Simply put, U and V represent a deadweight loss (loss of efficiency) as the result of the tariff.

As the result of the tariff, resources that could have been used to produce goods that U.S. firms produce efficiently (compared to producers abroad) are diverted into the production of automobiles. Thus, we end up producing less in areas where we have a comparative advantage and more in areas where we are a high-cost producer. Potential gains from specialization and trade go unrealized.

Import Quota: A specific quantity (or value) of a good permitted to be imported into a country during a given year.

An **import quota,** like a tariff, is designed to restrict foreign goods and protect domestic industries. A quota places a ceiling on the amount of a product that can be imported during a given period (typically a year).

The United States imposes quotas on several products, including brooms, steel, shoes, textile products, sugar, dairy products, and peanuts. As in the case of tariffs, the primary purpose of quotas is to protect domestic industries from foreign competition.

Since 1953, the United States has imposed a quota, limiting the importation of peanuts to 1.7 million pounds per year, approximately two peanuts per American. Using peanuts as an example, Exhibit 11 illustrates the impact of a quota. If there were no trade restraints, the domestic price of peanuts would be equal to the world market price (P_w). Under those circumstances, Americans would purchase Q_1 units. At the price P_w, domestic producers would supply Q_{d1}, and the amount $Q_1 - Q_{d1}$ would be imported from foreign producers.

EXHIBIT 10

Impact of a Tariff

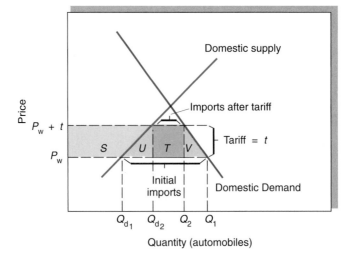

Here we illustrate the impact of a tariff on automobiles. In the absence of the tariff, the world price of automobiles is P_w: U.S. consumers purchase Q_1 units (Q_{d1} from domestic producers plus $Q_1 - Q_{d1}$ from foreign producers). The tariff makes it more costly for Americans to purchase automobiles from foreigners. Imports decline and the domestic price increases. Consumers lose the sum of the areas $S + U + T + V$ in the form of higher prices and a reduction in consumer surplus. Producers gain the area S and the tariff generates T tax revenues for the government. The areas U and V are deadweight losses due to a reduction in allocative efficiency.

Now consider what happens when a quota limits imports to $Q_2 - Q_{d2}$, a quantity well below the free trade level of imports. Since the quota reduces the foreign supply of peanuts to the domestic market, the price of the quota-protected product increases (to P_2). At the higher price, U.S. consumers will reduce their purchases to Q_2, and domestic producers will happily expand their production to Q_{d2}. With regard to the welfare of consumers, the impact of a quota is similar to that of a tariff. Consumers lose the area $S + U + T + V$ in the form of higher prices and the loss of consumer surplus. Similarly, domestic producers gain the area S, while the areas U and V represent deadweight losses from allocative inefficiency. However, there is a big difference between tariffs and quotas with regard to the area T. Under a tariff, the U.S. government would collect revenues equal to T, representing the tariff rate multiplied by the number of units imported. With a quota, however, these revenues will go to the foreign producers, who are granted import permits to sell in the U.S. market. Clearly, this right to sell at a premium price (since the domestic price exceeds the world market price) is extremely valuable. Thus, foreign producers will compete for the permits. They will hire lobbyists, make political contributions, and engage in other rent-seeking activities in an effort to secure the right to sell at a premium price in the U.S. market.

In many ways, quotas are more harmful than tariffs. With a quota, foreign producers are prohibited from selling additional units regardless of how much lower their costs are relative to domestic producers. In contrast with a tariff, a quota brings in no revenue for the government. While a tariff transfers revenue from U.S. consumers to the Treasury, quotas transfer these revenues to foreign producers. Obviously, this politically granted right creates a strong incentive for rent-seeking activities on the part of foreign producers. From the standpoint of economics, these

EXHIBIT 11

Impact of a Quota

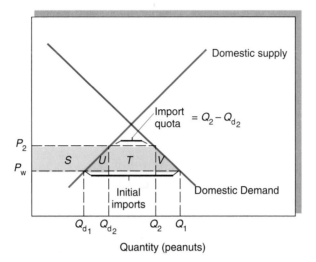

Here we illustrate the impact of a quota, such as the one the United States imposes on peanuts. The world market price of peanuts is P_w. If there were no trade restraints, the domestic price would also be P_w, and the domestic consumption would be Q_1. Domestic producers would supply Q_{d1} units, while $Q_1 - Q_{d1}$ would be imported. A quota limiting imports to $Q_2 - Q_{d2}$ would push up the domestic price to P_2. At the higher price, the amount supplied by domestic producers increases to Q_{d2}. Consumers lose the sum of the areas $S + U + T + V$, while domestic producers gain the area S. In contrast with tariffs, quotas generate no revenue for the government. The area T goes to foreign producers who are granted permission to sell in the U.S. market.

rent-seeking activities are a pure waste of resources. Nevertheless, many foreign producers will be helped by the quota. Thus, by rewarding both domestic producers with higher prices and foreign producers with valuable import permits, quotas generate two strong interest groups supportive of their continuation. As a result, removal of a quota is often even more difficult to achieve than a tariff reduction.

The United States generally perceives of itself as being a free trade country. As we have seen, this is not entirely true. The U.S. imposes tariffs and/or quotas on numerous goods. These trade barriers increase the prices that American consumers pay for products. Recent estimates indicate that each year trade barriers cost Americans between $500 and $750 per household, approximately 2 percent of our aggregate output.[4]

WHY DO NATIONS ADOPT TRADE RESTRICTIONS?

If trade restrictions promote inefficiency and reduce the potential gains from specialization and trade, why do nations adopt them? Three factors contribute to the existence of trade barriers: (a) partially valid arguments for the protection of specific

[4]See Murray Weidenbaum and Michael C. Munger, ''Protection at Any Price,'' *Regulation,* July/August 1983; Gary Clyde Hufbauer, Diane T. Berliner, and Kimberly Ann Elliot, *Trade Protection in the United States: 31 Case Studies* (Washington, D.C.: Institute for International Economics, 1986); and Michael C. Munger and Kathleen A. Rehbein, ''The High Cost of Protectionism'' *Europe,* May/June 1984.

industries under certain circumstances; (b) economic ignorance—a lack of knowledge as to who is helped and who is harmed by trade restrictions and which politicians support the costly restrictions; and (c) the special interest nature of trade restrictions. We now turn to a consideration of each of these factors.

PARTIALLY VALID ARGUMENTS FOR RESTRICTIONS

There are three major, at least partially valid, arguments for protecting certain domestic industries from foreign competitors.

1. National Defense Argument.   Certain industries—aircraft, petroleum, and weapons, for example—are vital to national defense. A nation might want to protect such industries from foreign competitors so that a domestic supply of these materials would be available in case of an international conflict. Would we want to be entirely dependent on Arabian or Russian petroleum? Would complete dependence on French aircraft be wise? Most Americans would answer no, even if trade restrictions were required to preserve these domestic industries.

The national defense argument is sound; however, it is often abused. Relatively few industries are truly vital to our national defense. In cases where a resource is important for national defense, often it would make more sense to stockpile the resource during peacetime, rather than follow protectionist policies to preserve a domestic industry. The U.S. strategic petroleum reserve incorporates elements of this strategy. Since the national defense argument is often used by special interests to justify protection for their industry, the merits of each specific case must be carefully evaluated.

2. The Infant-Industry Argument.   The advocates of this view hold that new domestic industries should be protected from older, established foreign competitors. As the new industry matures, it will be able to stand on its own feet and compete effectively with foreign producers.

The infant-industry argument has a long and somewhat notorious history. Alexander Hamilton used it to argue for the protection of early U.S. manufacturing. While it is an argument for only temporary protection, the protection, once granted, is often difficult to remove. Consumers often find that they pay higher prices now for little or no long-run benefits. For example, nearly a century ago, this argument was used to gain tariff protection for the young steel industry in the United States. Surely, today, steel is a very mature industry. Nevertheless, public policy has failed to remove the tariff.

Dumping: The sale of a good by a foreign supplier in another country at a price lower than the supplier sells it in its home market.

3. Anti-Dumping Argument.   **Dumping** is the sale of goods abroad at a price below their cost (and below their price in the domestic market of the exporting nation). In some cases, dumping merely reflects the exporter's desire to penetrate a foreign market. In other instances, dumping may emanate from export subsidies of foreign governments. At various times in the past, it has been alleged that Argentina has dumped textiles, Korea has dumped steel, and Canada has dumped radial tires into the U.S. market. Dumping is illegal. The Trade Agreements Act of 1979 provides for special anti-dumping duties (tariffs) when a good is sold in the United States at a price lower than that found in the domestic market of the exporting nation.

As in the case of imports, dumping generally benefits domestic consumers and imposes costs on domestic producers. The lower prices of the "dumped" goods permit consumers to obtain the goods more economically than they are available from domestic producers. Simultaneously, the lower prices make it more difficult for domestic producers to compete. Predictably, domestic producers (and their employees) are the major source of the charges that dumping is unfair.

Economists generally emphasize two points with regard to dumping. First, dumping can, in a few instances, be used as a weapon to gain monopoly power. For example, if the foreign firm temporarily cuts its price below cost, it might eliminate

MYTHS OF ECONOMICS

"Free trade with low-wage countries such as China and India would cause the wages of U.S. workers to fall."

Many Americans believe that trade restrictions are necessary to protect U.S. workers from imported goods produced by cheap foreign labor. How can U.S. labor compete with Indian and Chinese workers receiving $1 per hour? The fallacy of this argument stems from a misunderstanding of both the source of high wages and the law of comparative advantage.

High hourly wages do not necessarily mean high per unit labor cost. Labor productivity must also be considered. For example, suppose a U.S. steel worker receives an hourly wage rate of $20 and a steel worker in India receives only $2 per hour. Given the capital and production methods used in the two countries, however, the U.S. worker produces 20 times as many tons of steel per worker-hour as the Indian worker. Because of the higher productivity per worker-hour, labor cost *per unit of output* is actually lower in the United States than in India!

Labor in the United States possesses a high skill level and works with large amounts of capital equipment. These factors contribute to the high productivity and the high hourly wages of American workers. Similarly, low

productivity per worker-hour is the primary reason for low wages in such countries as India and China.

When analyzing the significance of wage and productivity differentials across countries, one must remember that gains from trade emanate from *comparative advantage,* not *absolute* advantage (see Exhibits 4, 5, and 6). The United States cannot produce everything cheaper than China or India merely because U.S. workers are more productive and work with more capital than workers in China and India. Neither can the Chinese and Indians produce everything cheaper merely because their wage rates are low compared to the U.S. When resources are directed by relative prices and the principle of comparative advantage, *both* high-wage and low-wage countries gain from the opportunity to specialize in those activities that, *relatively speaking,* they do best.

The comparative advantage of low-wage countries is likely to be in the production of labor-intensive goods such as wigs, rugs, toys, textiles, and assembled manufactured products. On the other hand, the comparative advantage of the United States, a country with a highly skilled labor force and an abundance of fertile farm land, lies in the production of high-technology manufacturing products (computers, aircraft, and scientific instruments, for example) and land-intensive agricultural

products (wheat, corn, and soybeans). The pattern of U.S. exports and imports confirms this point (see Exhibit 2).

Trade permits both high- and low-wage countries to reallocate their resources away from productive activities in which they are inefficient (relative to foreign producers) to activities in which they are highly efficient. The net result is an increase in output and consumption opportunities for both trading partners.

If foreigners, even low-wage foreigners, will sell us a product cheaper than we ourselves could produce it, we can gain by using our resources to produce other things. Perhaps an extreme example will illustrate the point. Suppose a foreign producer, perhaps a Santa Claus who pays workers little or nothing, were willing to supply us with free winter coats. Would it make sense to enact a tariff barrier to keep out the free coats? Of course not. Resources that were previously used to produce coats could now be freed to produce other goods. Output and the availability of goods would expand. The real wages of U.S. workers would rise. National defense aside, it makes no more sense to erect trade barriers to keep out cheap foreign goods than to keep out the free coats of a friendly, foreign Santa Claus.

domestic competition and later raise its price to a higher level after the domestic competitors have been driven from the market. However, this is usually not a feasible strategy. After all, domestic producers may re-enter the market if price is raised in the future. In addition, alternative foreign suppliers limit the monopoly power of a producer attempting this strategy.

Second, the law of comparative advantage indicates that a country (as a whole) can gain from the purchase of foreign-produced goods when they are cheaper than domestic goods. This is true regardless of whether the low price of foreign goods reflects comparative advantage, subsidies by foreign governments, or poor business practices. Unless the foreign supplier is likely to monopolize the domestic market, there is little reason to believe that dumping harms the economy receiving the goods.

TRADE BARRIERS AND JOBS

Part of the popularity of trade restrictions stems from their ability to protect easily identifiable jobs. Whenever foreign competitors begin to make inroads into markets that have traditionally been supplied by domestic producers, the outcry for ''protection to save jobs'' is sure to be raised. Many politicians will recognize the potential political gain from a protectionist policy and respond accordingly.

The recent history of the automobile industry in the United States illustrates this point. During the 1970s, imported automobiles gained a larger and larger share of the U.S. market. There were several reasons for these gains. High wages in the U.S. auto industry, improved efficiency of foreign producers, excessive government regulation of the domestic auto industry, and failure of U.S. producers to offer high performance small cars when gasoline prices soared during the 1970s were all contributing factors. The increased competition from imports encouraged both management and labor to seek trade restrictions.

The Reagan administration, firmly on record as favoring free trade, was reluctant to request either tariffs or quotas. Nevertheless, the administration bargained with the Japanese government, which eventually agreed to restrict ''voluntarily'' the number of Japanese automobiles sold in the U.S. market to 1.6 million. As is the case with quotas, voluntary restrictions push up prices in the domestic market. Robert Crandall of the Brookings Institution estimates that, in 1987, the restraints increased the price of Japanese automobiles sold in the United States by approximately $2,500 and the price of American models by around $750. When foreign producers limit their sales to the U.S. market, they can sell the restricted quantity at a higher *per unit* price. The voluntary restrictions of the Japanese illustrate this point. Prior to the restrictions, the price differential between a Toyota Corolla or a Nissan Sentra sold in Japan and the same automobiles sold in the U.S. was less than $500. After the restrictions, the Japanese-U.S. price differential for these automobiles jumped to approximately $3,000.[5] In large measure, Japanese producers were the primary beneficiaries of voluntary restrictions.

In the long run, trade restrictions such as quotas, tariffs, and allegedly voluntary limitations cannot protect jobs. Jobs protected by import restrictions will be offset by jobs destroyed in export industries. The choice is not whether automobiles (or some other product) will be produced in the United States or Japan. The real question is (a) whether our resources will be used to produce automobiles

---

[5] See Robert W. Crandall, ''Detroit Rode Quotas to Prosperity,'' *The Wall Street Journal,* January 29, 1986.

and other products for which we are a high opportunity cost producer or (b) whether the resources will be used for agriculture, high-technology manufactured goods, and other products for which we are a low cost producer.

What about industries that are long-time recipients of protection? Of course, sudden and complete removal of trade barriers would harm producers and workers. It would be costly to effect an immediate transfer of the protected resources to other areas and industries. Gradual removal of such barriers would minimize the cost of relocation and eliminate the shock effect. The government might also cushion the burden by subsidizing the retraining and relocation costs of displaced workers.

SPECIAL INTERESTS AND THE POLITICS OF TRADE RESTRICTIONS

Protectionism is a politician's delight because it delivers visible benefits to the protected parties while imposing the costs as a hidden tax on the public.

Murray L. Weidenbaum
(former Chairman of the President's Council of Economic Advisers)

Even when trade restrictions promote inefficiency and harm economic welfare, political entrepreneurs may be able to reap political gain from their enactment. Those harmed by a protectionist policy for industry X will individually bear a small and difficult-to-identify cost. Consumers who will pay higher prices for the products of a protected industry are an unorganized group. Most of them will not associate the higher product prices with the protectionist policy. Similarly, numerous export producers (and their employees) will individually be harmed only slightly. The rational ignorance effect implies that those harmed by trade restrictions are likely to be uninformed and unconcerned about our trade policy.

In contrast, special interest groups—specific industries, unions, and regions—will be very concerned with the protection of their industries. The benefits they derive will be quite visible. Thus, they will be ready to aid political entrepreneurs who support their views and penalize those who do not. Clearly, vote-seeking politicians will be sensitive to the special interest views.

Often, there will be a conflict between sound economics and good politics on trade restriction issues. Real-world public policy will, of course, reflect the politics of the situation.

EFFORTS TO LIMIT PROTECTIONISM

GATT AGREEMENTS

General Agreement on Tariffs and Trade (GATT): An organization composed of most non-Communist countries designed to set the rules for the conduct of international trade and reduce barriers to trade among nations.

After high tariffs restricted international trade during the early 1930s, Congress in 1934 adopted legislation authorizing the president to negotiate limited reductions in trade restrictions in exchange for similar concessions from our trading partners. Concern about the impact of trade restrictions on international economic health eventually led to the development of a multination organization called **General Agreement on Tariffs and Trade (GATT)** shortly after the Second World War. GATT has grown from 22 members to an international organization of 107 members representing nations that conduct approximately 85 percent of the world trade. GATT spells out the rules for international trade and oversees bargaining designed to reduce trade barriers among nations.

Modern U.S. trade policy conducted within the framework of GATT has substantially reduced tariffs. Under the Trade Expansion Act of 1962, Congress authorized the president to reduce tariffs by up to 50 percent and to completely eliminate duties of less than 5 percent. This led to the Kennedy Round of GATT negotiations that reduced tariffs on several industrial commodities. Legislation adopted in 1974 provided the president with similar authority and led to the Tokyo Round of tariff reductions which was completed in 1979. Authorizing the president to reduce tariffs within the framework of GATT without additional congressional action limits the ability of special interests to erect and maintain overt trade barriers. Thus, tariffs have declined substantially during the post-Second World War period (see Exhibit 9).

Paradoxically, while tariffs have been reduced, various nations have established quotas, price controls, and regulatory policies that also limit the freedom of international trade. Since 1986, the latest round of GATT negotiations (Uruguay Round) has targeted such thorny nontariff issues as quotas and agricultural subsidies. Currently, the talks are stalled over the agricultural subsidy issue. Several industrial countries impose tight import restrictions on agricultural products so they can fix the domestic prices of these products above the world market level. Without the restrictions, these price support/agricultural subsidy programs would collapse. The United States would like to see sharp reductions in these subsidy programs and the lifting of the trade restrictions that accompany them. Several European countries are unwilling to follow this course. In late 1990, the negotiations were broken off as the result of disagreements over the agriculture subsidy issue, but hopes were rekindled as the parties agreed to reconvene the negotiations during the spring of 1991.

THE CANADA-UNITED STATES FREE-TRADE AGREEMENT

As we previously discussed, Canada is the leading trading partner of the United States. Under an agreement ratified in 1988, Canada and the United States will (1) phase out all tariffs between the two countries during the next ten years, (2) reduce several nontariff trade barriers, (3) remove many of the restrictions on cross-border investment, and (4) create a U.S.-Canada Tribunal to settle trade disputes between the two countries. Approximately three-fourths of the trade between the two countries was tariff-free prior to the trade agreement. The pact phases out tariff barriers on seafood, forest products, textiles, petroleum products, and heavy equipment, either immediately or over time periods ranging from one to five years. The agreement is an important step toward the establishment of the world's largest (in terms of value of goods) free trade area.

Both Canada and the United States will reap substantial gains from the agreement. Domestic producers in both countries will now have free access to a larger market. Many products can be sold at a lower per-unit price if a larger volume of production can be planned and produced. When economies of scale are important, expansion in the size of the market generally leads to lower costs for producers and lower prices to consumers. Free access to the huge U.S. market will be particularly important to Canadian producers in markets where economies of scale are important. Elimination of trade barriers will also provide consumers with greater variety and an expanded choice among suppliers. Predictably, the domestic price of a product will fall when the nation's net imports of the good expand, and rise in response to the growth of net exports of the good. These price changes will direct resources into the areas where their comparative advantage is greatest. As a result, each country is able to specialize more fully in those products for which it is the low opportunity cost producer and to realize more fully the potential gains from economies of scale. The result will be a larger aggregate output and higher standard of living in both countries.

In the 1990s, free-trade agreements among countries are becoming more popular. In 1992, the countries of the European Economic Community are scheduled to abolish most of their internal trade barriers. Pacific Bloc nations are in the process of trying to create a multilateral free-trade agreement. There is also considerable discussion of lower trade barriers among the nations of South and Central America.

Most importantly to Americans, negotiations are well underway for the establishment of a free trade agreement between the United States and Mexico. Quite likely, an agreement gradually reducing trade barriers between the two countries during the 1990s will be approved in the near future.

Compared with the Canadian-American trade agreement, a free trade agreement with Mexico is much more controversial. As we have discussed, trade flows among nations are determined by comparative advantage, not relative wage rates. Nonetheless, many Americans still fear the competition from low-wage workers (see Myths of Economics box on free trade with low wage countries). As in the case of the U.S.-Canada agreement, economics indicates that a free trade agreement would help both the United States and Mexico. It would reduce the cost of labor-intensive goods to U.S. consumers while simultaneously increasing the availability of high-tech manufactured goods for Mexican consumers. As a result, both countries would be able to use more fully their resources in those areas where they have the greatest comparative advantage.

LOOKING AHEAD

There are many similarities between trade within national borders and trade across national boundaries. However, there is also a major difference. In addition to the exchange of goods for money, trade across national borders generally involves the exchange of national currencies. The next chapter deals with the financial arrangements under which international trade is conducted.

CHAPTER SUMMARY

1. The volume of international trade has grown rapidly in recent decades. In the late 1980s, approximately 21 percent of the world's output was sold in a different country than that in which it was produced.
2. The trade sector comprises approximately 11 percent of the U.S. GNP. More than half of all U.S. trade is with Canada, Japan, and the developed nations of Western Europe.
3. Comparative advantage rather than absolute advantage is the source of gains from trade. As long as the *relative* production costs of goods differ between nations, the nations will be able to gain from trade.
4. Mutual gains from trade accrue when each nation produces goods for which it is a low opportunity producer and trades for goods for which it is a high opportunity cost producer. This pattern of specialization and trade allows trading partners to maximize their joint output and expand their consumption possibilities.
5. Exports and imports are closely linked. The exports of a nation are the primary source of purchasing power used to import goods. When a nation restricts imports, it simultaneously limits the ability of foreigners to acquire the purchasing power necessary to buy the nation's exports.

6. International competition directs the resources of a nation toward their areas of comparative advantage. In an open economy, when domestic producers have a comparative advantage in the production of a good, they will be able to export their product and compete effectively in the world market. On the other hand, for commodities in which foreign producers have the comparative advantage, a nation could import the goods more economically (at a lower opportunity cost) than they can be produced domestically.

7. Relative to the no-trade alternative, international exchange and specialization result in lower prices for products that are imported and higher domestic prices for products that are exported. However, the net effect is an expansion in the aggregate output and consumption possibilities available to a nation.

8. The application of a tariff, quota, or other import restriction to a product reduces the amount of the product that foreigners supply to the domestic market. As a result of diminished supply, consumers face higher prices for the protected product.
Essentially, import restrictions are subsidies to producers (and workers) in protected industries at the expense of (a) consumers and (b) producers (and workers) in export industries. Restrictions reduce the ability of domestic producers to specialize in those areas for which their comparative advantage is greatest.

9. Both high-wage and low-wage countries gain from the opportunity to specialize in the production of goods that they produce at a low opportunity cost. If a low-wage country can supply a good to the United States cheaper than the U.S. can produce it, the U.S. can gain by purchasing the good from the low-wage country and using the scarce resources of the United States to produce other goods for which it has a comparative advantage.

10. National defense, infant-industry, and anti-dumping arguments can be used to justify trade restrictions for specific industries under certain conditions. It is clear, though, that the power of special interest groups and voter ignorance about the harmful effects of trade restrictions offer the major explanations for real-world protectionist public policy.

11. In the long run, trade restrictions do not create jobs. Jobs protected by import restrictions are offset by jobs destroyed in export industries. Since this result of restrictions often goes unnoticed, their political popularity is understandable. Nevertheless, trade restrictions are inefficient, since they lead to the loss of potential gains from specialization and exchange.

12. Even though trade restrictions promote economic inefficiency, they are often attractive to politicians because they generate visible benefits to special interests—particularly business and labor interests in protected industries—while imposing costs on consumers and taxpayers that are *individually* small and largely invisible.

CRITICAL ANALYSIS QUESTIONS

*1. "Trade restrictions limiting the sale of cheap foreign goods in the United States are necessary to protect the prosperity of Americans." Evaluate this statement made by an American politician.

2. Suppose at the time of the Civil War the United States had been divided into two countries and that through the years no trade existed between the two. How would the standard of living in the "divided" United States have been affected? Explain.

*3. Can both (a) and (b) be true? Explain.
   a. "Tariffs and import quotas promote economic inefficiency and reduce the real income of a nation. Economic analysis suggests that nations can gain by eliminating trade restrictions."
   b. "Economic analysis suggests that there is good reason to expect trade restrictions to exist in the real world."

*Asterisk denotes questions for which answers are given in Appendix C, Selected Answers.

4. "Tariffs and quotas are necessary to protect the high wages of the American worker." Do you agree or disagree? Why?

*5. "An increased scarcity of a product benefits producers and harms consumers. In effect, tariffs and other trade restrictions increase the domestic scarcity of products by reducing the supply from abroad. Such policies benefit domestic producers of the restricted product at the expense of domestic consumers." Evaluate this statement.

*6. The United States uses an import quota to maintain the domestic price of sugar well above the world price. Analyze the impact of the quota. Use supply and demand analysis to illustrate your answer. To whom do the gains and losses of this policy accrue? How does the quota affect the efficiency of resource allocation in the United States? Why do you think Congress is supportive of this policy?

7. Suppose that it costs American textile manufacturers $20 to produce a shirt, while foreign producers can supply the same shirt for $15. (a) Would a tariff of $6 per shirt help American manufacturers compete with foreigners? (b) Would a subsidy of $6 per shirt to domestic manufacturers help them compete? (c) Is there any difference between the tariff and a direct subsidy to the domestic manufacturers?

*8. "Getting more Americans to realize that it pays to make things in the United States is the heart of the competitiveness issue." (quote from an American business magazine)

   a. Would Americans be better off if more of them paid higher prices in order to "buy American" rather than purchase from foreigners? Would U.S. employment be higher? Explain.

   b. Would Californians be better off if they only bought goods produced in California? Would the employment in California be higher? Explain.

*9. It is often alleged that Japanese producers receive subsidies from their government that permit them to sell their products at a low price in the U.S. market. Do you think we should erect trade barriers to keep out cheap Japanese goods if the source of their low price is governmental subsidies? Why or why not?

10. How do tariffs and quotas differ? Can you think of any reason why foreign producers might prefer a quota rather than a tariff? Explain.

11. **What's Wrong with This Economic Experiment?**

   A researcher hypothesizes that higher tariffs on imported automobiles will cause total employment in the United States to increase. Automobile tariffs are raised and the following year employment in the U.S. auto industry increases by 50,000. The researcher concludes that the higher tariffs created 50,000 jobs.

*12. Does international trade cost American jobs? Does interstate trade cost your state jobs? What is the major effect of international and interstate trade?

13. "The United States is suffering from a huge excess of imports. Cheap foreign products are driving American firms out of business and leaving our economy in shambles." Evaluate this statement from an American politician.

14. Do you think the United States would benefit if all trade barriers with Mexico were eliminated? Would Mexico benefit? Would wages in the United States fall to the level of wages in Mexico? Why or why not?

*15. Tariffs not only reduce the volume of imports, they also reduce the volume of exports. (True or false? Explain.)

*16. Suppose that as the result of traveling abroad, you are permitted to bring a limited quantity of goods into the United States duty-free. Will the presence of a U.S. tariff on a good affect the likelihood that you will find a bargain on the good while abroad?

International Finance and the Foreign Exchange Market

There has been a remarkable increase in the degree of economic interdependence since World War II.[1]

Alan Deardorff and Robert Stern

CHAPTER FOCUS

■ What determines the exchange rate value of the dollar relative to other currencies?

■ What information is included in the balance of payments accounts of a nation? Why are these accounts important?

■ How do monetary and fiscal policy influence the exchange rate value of a nation's currency?

■ What is the significance of a current account deficit? Does a current account deficit indicate that a nation is in financial trouble?

■ What are the advantages and disadvantages of the current international monetary system?

Since the Second World War, the volume of international exchange has grown rapidly. As we discussed in the last chapter, voluntary exchange between persons of different nations is mutually advantageous to the trading partners. Since international trade fosters a more efficient use of resources, the world has benefited substantially from its growth.

International trade is complicated by the fact that it generally involves two different currencies. Farmers in the United States want dollars, not some foreign currency, when they sell their wheat. Therefore, foreign purchasers must exchange their currency for dollars before they buy U.S. wheat. Similarly, French wine makers want to be paid in francs, not dollars. Therefore, U.S. importers must exchange dollars for francs when they purchase French wines (or French exporters must obtain francs before they pay the winemakers).

Since 1971, most Western nations have permitted the value of their monetary unit relative to other currencies to be determined largely by market forces. In this chapter, we analyze how international currencies are linked and how the rates for their exchange are determined.

THE FOREIGN EXCHANGE MARKET

Foreign Exchange Market:
The market in which the currencies of different countries are bought and sold.

If you wanted to exchange dollars for a foreign currency, you would go to the foreign exchange market. The **foreign exchange market** is a widely dispersed, highly organized market in which the currencies of different countries are bought and sold. Commercial banks and currency brokers around the world are primary organizers of the market.

Let's assume you own a shoe store in the United States and are preparing to place an order for sandals from a manufacturer. You can purchase the sandals from a domestic manufacturer and pay for them with dollars. Alternately, you can buy them from a British manufacturer, in which case they must be paid for in pounds because the employees of the British manufacturer must be paid with pounds. If you buy from the British firm, either you will have to change dollars into pounds at a bank and send them to the British producer, or the British manufacturer will have to go to a bank and change your dollar check into pounds. In either case, purchasing the British sandals will involve an exchange of dollars for pounds.

Exchange Rate: The domestic price of one unit of foreign currency. For example, if it takes $1.50 to purchase one English pound, the dollar-pound exchange rate is 1.50.

If the British producer sells sandals for 10 pounds per pair, how can you determine whether the price is high or low? To compare the price of the sandals produced by the British firm with the price of domestically produced sandals, you must know the exchange rate between the dollar and the pound. The **exchange rate** is simply the price of one national currency (the pound, for example) in terms of another national currency (such as the U.S. dollar). Exchange rates enable consumers in one country to translate the prices of foreign goods into units of their own currency. For example, if it takes 1.50 dollars to obtain 1 pound, then the British sandals priced at 10 pounds would cost $15.00 (10 times the 1.50 dollar price of the pound).

---

[1]Alan V. Deardorff and Robert M. Stern, "Current Issues in Trade Policy" in Stern, (ed.), *U.S. Trade Policies in a Changing World Economy* (Cambridge: MIT Press, 1989), p. 17.

Suppose the dollar pound exchange rate is $1.50 = 1 pound and that you decide to buy 200 pairs of sandals from the British manufacturer at 10 pounds ($15) per pair. You will need 2,000 pounds in order to pay the British manufacturer. If you contact an American bank that handles exchange rate transactions and write the bank a check for $3,000 (the 1.50 exchange rate multiplied by 2,000), it will supply the 2,000 pounds. The bank will typically charge a small fee for handling the transaction.

Where does the American bank get the pounds? The bank obtains the pounds from British importers who want dollars to buy things from Americans. Note that the U.S. demand for foreign currencies (such as the pound) comes from the demand of Americans for things purchased from foreigners. On the other hand, the U.S. supply of foreign exchange comes from the demand of foreigners for things bought from Americans.

Exhibit 1 presents data on the exchange rate between the dollar and selected foreign currencies during the 1973–1991 period, as well as an index of the exchange rate value of the dollar against ten major currencies. Under the current flexible system, the exchange rate between currencies changes from day to day and even from hour to hour. Thus, the annual exchange rate data given in Exhibit 1 are really averages for each year.

Between 1980 and 1985, the exchange rate value of the dollar appreciated against the major foreign currencies. An **appreciation** in the value of a nation's

Appreciation: An increase in the value of a domestic currency relative to foreign currencies. An appreciation increases the purchasing power of the domestic currency over foreign goods.

EXHIBIT 1   ■   Foreign Exchange Rates, 1973–1991 (U.S. cents per unit of foreign currency)

Year	French Franc	German Mark	Japanese Yen	British Pound	Canadian Dollar	Index of Exchange Rate Value of the Dollar (Ten Currencies)[a]
1973	22.5	37.8	0.369	245.10	99.9	99.1
1975	23.4	40.7	0.337	222.16	98.3	98.5
1977	20.3	43.1	0.373	174.49	94.1	103.3
1979	23.5	54.6	0.458	212.24	85.3	88.1
1980	23.7	55.1	0.443	227.74	85.5	87.4
1981	18.4	44.4	0.45	202.43	83.4	102.9
1982	15.2	41.2	0.402	174.80	81.0	116.6
1983	13.1	39.2	0.421	151.59	81.1	125.3
1984	11.4	35.1	0.421	133.68	77.1	138.3
1985	11.1	34.0	0.419	129.74	73.2	143.2
1986	14.4	46.1	0.594	146.77	72.0	112.2
1987	16.6	55.6	0.691	163.98	75.4	96.9
1988	16.8	56.9	0.780	178.13	81.3	92.7
1989	15.7	53.2	0.724	163.82	84.4	98.6
1990	18.4	61.9	0.690	178.41	85.7	89.1
1991(May)	17.2	58.0	0.726	173.50	87.0	92.1

[a]March 1973 = 100. In addition to the five currencies listed above, the index includes the Belgian franc, Italian lira, Netherlands guilder, Swedish krona, and Swiss franc.

Source: Council of Economic Advisers, *Economic Report of the President* (Washington, D.C.: U.S. Government Printing Office, 1991) and *The Wall Street Journal*, May 24, 1991.

currency means that fewer units of the currency are now required to purchase one unit of a foreign currency. For example, in 1985 only 34 cents were required to purchase a German mark, down from 55 cents in 1980.[2] As the result of this appreciation in the value of the dollar relative to the mark, West German goods became less expensive to Americans. The direction of change in the prices that West Germans paid for American goods was just the opposite. An appreciation of the U.S. dollar in terms of the mark is the same thing as a depreciation in the mark relative to the dollar.

Depreciation: A reduction in the value of a domestic currency relative to foreign currencies. A depreciation reduces the purchasing power of the domestic currency over foreign goods.

A **depreciation** makes foreign goods more expensive, since it decreases the number of units of the foreign currency that can be purchased with a unit of domestic currency. As Exhibit 1 shows, the number of cents required to purchase a French franc, German mark, Japanese yen, or British pound rose substantially between 1985 and 1990. Thus, during this period the dollar depreciated against these currencies, increasing the price of goods purchased by Americans from producers in these countries.

The ten-currency index of the dollar's exchange rate value presented in Exhibit 1 provides evidence on what is happening to the dollar's general exchange rate value.[3] An increase in the index implies an appreciation in the dollar, while a decline is indicative of a depreciation in the dollar. During the 1970s, the ten-currency index changed by only small amounts from year to year. However, between 1980 and 1985, the index indicates that the exchange rate value of the dollar increased sharply each year. The dollar appreciated by more than 60 percent during the five-year period. In contrast, it depreciated by a similar amount during 1986–1990.

EXCHANGE RATES UNDER A FLEXIBLE EXCHANGE RATE SYSTEM

Flexible Exchange Rates: Exchange rates that are determined by the market forces of supply and demand. They are sometimes called "floating exchange rates."

What determines the exchange rate between two currencies? Under a system of **floating** or **flexible exchange rates,** the value of currencies in the exchange rate market is determined by market forces. Just as the forces of supply and demand determine other prices, so too, they determine the exchange rate value of currencies in the absence of government intervention.

To simplify our explanation of how the exchange rate market works, let us assume that the United States and Great Britain are the only two countries in the world. Under these circumstances, the supply and demand for pounds is the supply and demand for foreign exchange.

---

[2]Since an appreciation means a *lower* price of foreign currencies, some may think it looks like a depreciation. Just remember that a lower price of the foreign currency means that one's domestic currency will buy more units of the foreign currency and thus more goods and services from foreigners. For example, if the dollar price of the pound falls, this means that a dollar will buy more pounds and thus more goods and services from the British. Therefore, a lower dollar price of the pound means the dollar has appreciated relative to the pound.

[3]In the construction of this index, the exchange rate of each currency relative to the dollar is weighted according to the proportion of U.S. trade with the country. For example, the index weights the dollar-Japanese yen exchange rate more heavily than the dollar-Swiss franc exchange rate because the volume of U.S. trade with Japan exceeds the volume of trade with Switzerland.

In our two-country world, the demand for pounds in the exchange rate market originates from the demand of Americans for British goods, services, and assets (either real or financial). For example, when U.S. residents purchase men's suits from a British manufacturer, travel in the United Kingdom, or purchase the stocks, bonds, or physical assets of British business firms, they demand pounds from (and supply dollars to) the foreign exchange rate market to pay for these items. On the other hand, the supply of pounds (and demand for dollars) in the exchange rate market comes from the demand of the British for items supplied by Americans. When the British purchase goods, services, or assets from Americans, they supply pounds to (and demand dollars from) the foreign exchange market.

Exhibit 2 illustrates the demand and supply curves of Americans for foreign exchange; British pounds in our two-country case. The demand for pounds is downward sloping because a lower dollar price of the pound—this means a dollar will buy more pounds—makes British goods cheaper for American importers. The goods produced by one country are generally good substitutes for the goods of another country. This means that when foreign (British) goods become cheaper, Americans will increase their expenditures on imports (and therefore the quantity of pounds demanded will increase). Thus, Americans will increase their expenditures on the lower-priced (in dollars) British goods and therefore they will demand more pounds as the pound's dollar price declines.

Similarly, the supply curve for pounds is dependent on the purchases of American goods by the British. An increase in the dollar price of the pound means

---

EXHIBIT 2

Equilibrium in the Foreign Exchange Market

The dollar price of the pound is measured on the vertical axis. The horizontal axis indicates the flow of pounds to the foreign exchange market. The equilibrium exchange rate is $1.50 = 1 pound. At the equilibrium price, the quantity demanded of pounds just equals the quantity supplied. A higher price of pounds such as $1.80 = 1 pound would lead to an excess supply of pounds, causing the dollar price of the pound to fall. On the other hand, a lower price, for example $1.20 = 1 pound, would result in an excess demand for pounds, causing the pound to appreciate.

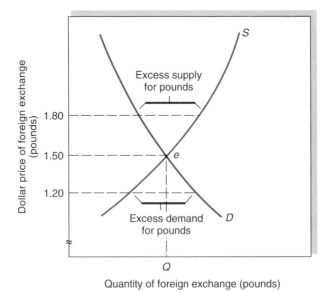

Quantity of foreign exchange (pounds)

that a pound will purchase more dollars and more goods priced in terms of dollars. The price (in terms of pounds) of American goods, services, and assets *to British consumers* declines as the dollar price of the pound increases. The British will purchase more from Americans and therefore supply more pounds to the exchange rate market as the dollar price of the pound rises. Because of this, the supply curve for pounds tends to slope upward to the right.

As Exhibit 2 shows, equilibrium is present at $1.50 = 1 pound—the dollar price of the pound that brings the quantity demanded and quantity supplied of pounds into balance. The market-clearing price of $1.50 per pound not only equates demand and supply in the foreign exchange market; it also equates (a) the value of U.S. purchases on items supplied by the British with (b) the value of items sold by U.S. residents to the British. Demand and supply in the currency market are merely the mirror images of (a) and (b).

What would happen if the price of the pound was above equilibrium—$1.80 = 1 pound, for example? At the higher dollar price of the pound, British goods would be more expensive for Americans. Americans would cut back on their purchases of English shoes, glassware, textile products, financial assets, and other items supplied by the British. Reflecting this reduction, the quantity of pounds demanded by Americans would decline. Simultaneously, the higher dollar price of the pound would make U.S. exports cheaper for the British. For example, an $18,000 American automobile would cost British consumers 12,000 pounds when one pound trades for $1.50, but it would cost only 10,000 pounds when one pound exchanges for $1.80. If the price of the pound were $1.80, the British would tend to supply more pounds to the exchange rate market to purchase the cheaper American goods. Thus, at the $1.80 = 1 pound price, the quantity of pounds demanded by Americans falls and the quantity supplied by the British increases. As can be seen in Exhibit 2, an excess supply of pounds results, causing the dollar price of the pound to decline until equilibrium is restored at the $1.50 = 1 pound price.

At a below-equilibrium price such as $1.20 = 1 pound, an opposite set of forces would be present. The lower dollar price of the pound would make English goods cheaper for Americans and American goods more expensive for the British. The quantity demanded of British goods and pounds by Americans would increase. Simultaneously, the quantity of American goods demanded and pounds supplied by the British would decline. An excess demand for pounds would result at the $1.20 = 1 pound price. The excess demand would tend to cause the dollar price of the pound to rise until equilibrium was restored at $1.50 = 1 pound.

CHANGING MARKET CONDITIONS AND EXCHANGE RATES

When exchange rates are free to fluctuate, the market value of a nation's currency will appreciate and depreciate in response to changing market conditions. Any change that alters the quantity of goods, services, or assets bought from foreigners relative to the quantity sold to foreigners will also alter the exchange rate. What types of change will alter the exchange rate value of a currency?

Changes in Income.   An increase in domestic income will encourage the nation's residents to spend a portion of their additional income on imports. When the income of a nation grows rapidly, the nation's imports tend to rise rapidly as well. As Exhibit 3 illustrates, an increase in imports also increases the demand for foreign exchange, the pound in our two-country case. As the demand for pounds increases, the dollar price of the pound rises (from $1.50 to $1.80). This depreciation of the

EXHIBIT 3

The Growth of Income and the Growth of Imports

Other things constant, if incomes grow in the United States, U.S. imports will grow. The increase in the imports will increase the demand for pounds, causing the dollar price of the pound to rise (from $1.50 to $1.80).

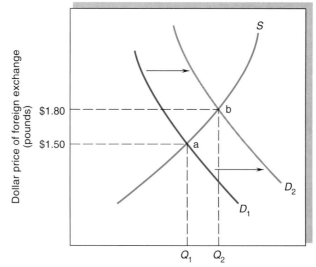

dollar reduces the incentive of Americans to import British goods and services, while increasing the incentive of the British to purchase U.S. exports. These two forces will restore equilibrium in the foreign exchange market at a new, higher dollar price of the pound.

Just the opposite takes place when the income of a trading partner (Great Britain in our example) increases. Rapid growth of income abroad will lead to an increase in U.S. exports, causing the demand for the dollar to rise. This will result in dollar appreciation—equilibrium at a new, lower dollar price of the pound.

What happens to the exchange rate if income increases in both countries? The key here is to identify the nation that is growing the fastest. For countries that are similar in size and propensity to import, the country that is growing the fastest will increase its demand for imports relatively more than will its trading partner, resulting in a decrease in the value of the more rapidly-growing nation's currency. Thus, as paradoxical as it may seem, sluggish growth of income relative to one's trading partners tends to cause the slow-growth nation's currency to appreciate, since the nation's imports decline relative to exports.

Differences in Rates of Inflation.   Other things constant, domestic inflation will cause a nation's currency to depreciate on the exchange market, whereas deflation will result in appreciation. Suppose prices in the United States rise by 50 percent, while our trading partners are experiencing stable prices. The domestic inflation will cause U.S. consumers to increase their demand for imported goods (and foreign currency). In turn, the inflated domestic prices will cause foreigners to reduce their purchases of U.S. goods, thereby reducing the supply of foreign currency to the exchange market. As Exhibit 4 illustrates, the exchange rate will adjust to this set of circumstances. The dollar will depreciate relative to the pound.

Exchange rate adjustments permit nations with even high rates of inflation to engage in trade with countries experiencing relatively stable prices. A depreciation in a nation's currency in the foreign exchange market compensates for the nation's

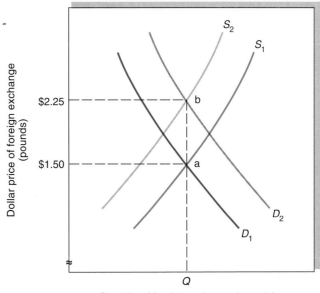

EXHIBIT 4

Inflation with Flexible Exchange Rates

If prices were stable in England while the price level increased 50 percent in the United States, the U.S. demand for British products (and pounds) would increase, whereas U.S. exports to Britain would decline, causing the supply of pounds to fall. These forces would cause the dollar to depreciate relative to the pound.

Quantity of foreign exchange (pounds)

inflation rate. For example, if inflation increases the price level in the United States by 50 percent and the value of the dollar in exchange for the pound depreciates 50 percent, then the prices of American goods measured in pounds are unchanged to British consumers. Thus, when the exchange rate value of the dollar changes from $1.50 = 1 pound to $2.25 = 1 pound, the depreciation in the dollar restores the original prices of U.S. goods to British consumers even though the price level in the U.S. has increased by 50 percent.

What if prices in both England and the United States are rising at the same annual rate, say 10 percent? The prices of imports (and exports) will remain unchanged relative to domestically produced goods. Equal rates of inflation in each of the countries will not cause the value of exports to change relative to imports. Identical rates of inflation will not disturb an equilibrium in the exchange market. Inflation contributes to the depreciation of a nation's currency only when a country's rate of inflation is more rapid than that of its trading partners.

Changes in Interest Rates.   Short-term financial investments will be quite sensitive to changes in real interest rates—that is, interest rates adjusted for the expected rate of inflation. International loanable funds will tend to move toward areas where the expected real rate of return (after compensation for differences in risk) is highest. If real interest rates increase in the United States relative to Western Europe, borrowers in Britain, France, and Germany will demand dollars (and supply their currencies) in the exchange rate market to purchase the high yield American assets. The increase in demand for the dollar and supply of European currencies will cause the dollar to appreciate relative to the British pound, French franc, and German mark.

In contrast, when real interest rates in other countries are high relative to the United States, short-term financial investors will move to take advantage of the improved earnings opportunities abroad. As investment funds move from the United

States to other countries, there will be an increase in the demand for foreign currencies and an increase in the supply of dollars in the foreign exchange market. A depreciation in the dollar relative to the currencies of countries experiencing the high real interest rates will be the result.

The accompanying Thumbnail Sketch summarizes the major forces that cause a nation's currency to appreciate or depreciate when exchange rates are determined by market forces.

THUMBNAIL SKETCH

Currency Appreciation and Depreciation with Freely Fluctuating Exchange Rates

These factors will cause a nation's currency to appreciate:

1. A slow rate of growth in income that causes imports to lag behind exports.
2. A rate of inflation that is lower than one's trading partners.
3. Domestic real interest rates that are greater than real interest rates abroad.

These factors will cause a nation's currency to depreciate:

1. A rapid rate of growth in income that stimulates imports relative to exports.
2. A rate of inflation that is higher than one's trading partners.
3. Domestic real interest rates that are lower than real interest rates abroad.

THE APPRECIATION AND DEPRECIATION OF THE DOLLAR, 1973–1991

During the late 1970s, the United States was in the midst of double-digit inflation. Compared to most of its major trading partners, the inflation rate was higher and real interest rates were lower in the United States. As our analysis indicates, a high inflation rate will discourage purchases by foreigners and a low real interest rate will lead to an outflow of capital. Both of these forces will cause a nation's currency to depreciate in the exchange rate market. This is precisely what happened, as the dollar fell to new lows against most major currencies during 1977–1979.

These forces reversed sharply during the early 1980s, as the U.S. shifted toward a more restrictive monetary policy and expansionary fiscal policy. Beginning in 1981, the more restrictive monetary policy retarded the inflation rate. The U.S. inflation rate plunged from the double-digit levels of 1979–1980 to 3.2 percent in 1983. Simultaneously, pushed along by both the restrictive monetary policy and huge budget deficits, real interest rates in the United States rose to historic highs. As Exhibit 5 illustrates, real interest rates in the United States were between 2 percent and 4 percent *higher than* real rates in Europe and Japan during 1981–1984. Attracted by the high real return, financial capital flowed into the United States. This combination of forces—a low inflation rate and capital inflow

(see Exhibit 5)

EXHIBIT 5

Real Interest Rates and the Exchange Rate Value of the Dollar, 1974–1991

Our model indicates that a reduction in real U.S. interest rates compared with the rates in other countries will, other things constant, cause the dollar to depreciate. As shown above, this is precisely what happened in the late 1970s, 1985–1987, and again in 1990. In contrast, when real interest rates are higher in the United States than in other countries, strong demand for dollars in order to make financial investments in the United States will cause the dollar to appreciate. The 1980–1984 period illustrates the potency of high real interest rates as a factor pushing the exchange rate value of the dollar upward.

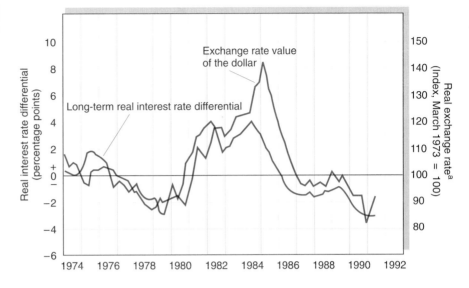

Source: Charles P. Thomas, "U.S. International Transactions in 1986," *Federal Reserve Bulletin* (May 1987); and Federal Reserve Bank of St. Louis, *International Economic Conditions* (monthly).
aWeighted average of the ten countries referred to in Exhibit 1.

Fixed Exchange Rate System: An international monetary system in which each country's currency is set at a fixed rate relative to all other currencies and governmental policies are used to maintain the fixed rate.

attracted by high real interest rates—sharply increased the demand for the dollar. The dollar appreciated by approximately 60 percent against an index of ten major currencies during 1980–1984.

However, beginning in early 1985, the situation again changed abruptly. As the low rate of inflation persisted, real interest rates declined in the United States. The inflow of foreign capital slowed. Simultaneously, the U.S. economy rebounded strongly from the 1982 recession. Responding to both the rapid economic growth and the strong dollar, U.S. imports surged relative to exports during 1983–1985. During 1985–1986, the low U.S. interest rates relative to other countries (see Exhibit 5), and fears arising from the large excess of imports compared to exports, resulted in a sharp decline in the exchange rate value of the dollar.

During the 1987–1990 period, real interest rates in the United States were lower than the real rates of our trading partners. Thus, the demand for dollars to undertake financial investments in the United States was weak and the exchange rate value of the dollar remained weak in the late 1980s.

THE OPERATION OF A FIXED EXCHANGE RATE SYSTEM

Between 1944 and 1971, most of the world operated under a system of fixed exchange rates. Under a **fixed exchange rate system,** each nation "pegs" the price of its currency to another currency, such as the dollar (or gold), for long periods of time. Governments intervene in the foreign exchange market or alter their economic policies in an effort to maintain the fixed value of their currency.

Fixing the price of a currency in the exchange market, like fixing other prices, results in surpluses and shortages. As market conditions change, the exchange rate that equates the quantity supplied of each currency with the quantity demanded of that currency also changes. What happens when the fixed rate differs from the equilibrium rate? Building on the analysis of Exhibit 2, suppose the equilibrium exchange rate was $1.50 = 1 pound. If the price of the pound is fixed at $1.80 = 1 pound, an excess supply of pounds will result. At the $1.80 = 1 pound rate, the pound is overvalued (and the dollar undervalued). At the $1.80 per pound exchange rate, the U.S. will persistently export more goods, services, and assets to the British than they will import from the British. The central bank in the United States will have to continually increase its holdings of pounds—that is, buy the excess supply of pounds, to maintain the above-equilibrium price of the pound. In essence, this situation leads to a surplus of exports over imports for the United States in its trade with England.

What would happen if the dollar price of the pound was set below equilibrium, such as $1.20 = 1 pound (Exhibit 2)? The below-equilibrium price of the pound would lead to an excess demand for pounds. Since the pound is undervalued (and the dollar overvalued) at the $1.20 per pound price, British imports are cheap to Americans (and U.S. exports expensive for the British). In its trade with the British, the U.S. would persistently buy (import) more than it sells (exports). To defend the $1.20 per pound fixed rate, the U.S. central bank would have to draw down its holdings of pounds, balances that were perhaps built up during periods when the dollar price of the pound was above equilibrium.

To make a fixed rate system work, each country must maintain a reserve balance of other currencies that will permit it to weather temporary periods of excess demand relative to supply. When the fixed rate system was put in place at the end of the Second World War, the **International Monetary Fund** (IMF) was established to perform this function. The IMF required each of its more than 100 member countries to deposit a specified amount of its currency into a reserve fund held by the IMF. Thus, it possessed substantial holdings of dollars, francs, pounds, marks, and other currencies of the participating nations. As the need arose, these reserves were loaned to nations experiencing difficulties with their balance of payments.

The premise of a fixed rate system is that a nation ordinarily pays for its imports with exports. Of course, countries may temporarily experience periods where imports exceed exports. During such periods, nations can draw down their reserve balance. However, chronic debtor nations—nations persistently importing more than they export—must take corrective action designed to bring exports and imports into balance. During the 1944–1971 period, the IMF provided discipline to the system by encouraging and in some cases requiring member nations as a condition for the receipt of loans, to adopt policies that would bring their exports and imports into balance.

What steps can a nation experiencing an excess of imports over exports take to remedy this situation under a fixed rate system? Basically, there are three alternatives.

1. A Nation Can Devalue Its Currency.   **Devaluation** is a one-step reduction in the value of a nation's currency under a fixed rate system. When a currency is

International Monetary Fund: An international banking organization, with more than 100 nation members, designed to oversee the operation of the international monetary system. Although it does not control the world supply of money, it does hold currency reserves for member nations and make currency loans to national central banks.

Devaluation: An official act that changes the level of the "fixed" exchange rate downward in terms of other currencies. In essence, it is a one-step depreciation of a currency under a fixed exchange rate system.

overvalued, a devaluation can restore equilibrium between the demand and supply of the currency in the exchange market. For example, if there is an excess supply of dollars (excess demand for pounds) in the exchange market when the fixed exchange rate is $1.20 = 1 pound, a devaluation of the dollar (perhaps to $1.50 = 1 pound) could restore balance. A devaluation makes imports more expensive to domestic consumers, while encouraging exports. It thus tends to correct an excess of imports relative to exports.

2. A Nation Can Heighten Trade Barriers, Adopting Tariffs and Quotas in an Effort to Reduce Imports and Bring the Value of Its Currency on the Foreign Exchange Market into Equilibrium. This strategy is in conflict with economic efficiency and the promotion of the free flow of trade between nations. Nevertheless, it was often adopted during the period from 1944 to 1971. Once a nation's exchange rate was established, it tended to become sacred. Politicians during that period, including many in the United States, frequently argued that even though they did not like to impose trade restrictions, the barriers were necessary to avoid devaluation. The balance of payments issue was an excellent excuse to promote trade restrictions—which were advocated by special interests—against low-cost foreign goods.

3. A Nation Can Follow Restrictive Macroeconomic Policy Designed to Promote Deflation (or at Least Retard Inflation) and High Interest Rates. Policy-makers might use restrictive monetary and fiscal policy to retard inflation and increase interest rates. A slower rate of inflation relative to one's trading partners would encourage exports and discourage imports. Higher domestic real interest rates would attract foreign investment and thereby increase the nation's supply of foreign exchange.

When a nation uses macroeconomic policy to restore balance in the exchange market, an important point emerges. This method of bringing about equilibrium in the exchange market attempts to manipulate the level of all other prices to maintain one price—the fixed exchange rate. In contrast, a flexible exchange rate system changes one price, the foreign exchange rate—to restore balance between what is bought from and what is sold to foreigners.

THE BALANCE OF PAYMENTS

Just as countries calculate their gross national product so that they have a general idea of their domestic level of production, most countries also calculate their balance of international payments in order to keep track of their transactions with other nations. The **balance of payments** account is a periodic report that summarizes the flow of economic transactions with foreigners. It provides information on the nation's exports, imports, earnings of domestic residents on assets located abroad, earnings on domestic assets owned by foreigners, international capital movements, and official transactions by central banks and governments.

Balance of payments accounts are kept according to the principles of basic bookkeeping. Any transaction that supplies the nation's domestic currency (or creates a demand for foreign currency) in the foreign exchange market is recorded as a debit, or minus, item. Imports are an example of a debit item. Transactions that create a demand for the nation's currency (or a supply of foreign currency) on the

Balance of Payments:

A summary of all economic transactions between a country and all other countries for a specific time period—usually a year. The balance of payments account reflects all payments and liabilities to foreigners (debits) and all payments and obligations (credits) received from foreigners.

foreign exchange market are recorded as a credit, or plus, item. Exports are an example of a credit item. Since the quantity demanded will equal the quantity supplied in the foreign exchange market, the total debits will equal the total credits.

The balance of payments transactions can be grouped into three basic categories: current account, capital amount, and official reserve account. Let us take a look at each of these.

CURRENT ACCOUNT TRANSACTIONS

Current Account: The record of all transactions with foreign nations that involve the exchange of merchandise goods and services or unilateral gifts.

All payments (and gifts) that are related to the purchase or sale of goods and services and income flows during the designated period are included in the **current account.** In general, there are four major types of current account transactions: the exchange of merchandise goods, the exchange of services, income from investments, and unilateral transfers.

Merchandise Trade Transactions.   The export and import of merchandise goods comprise by far the largest portion of a nation's balance of payments account. As Exhibit 6 shows, in 1989, the United States imported $490 billion of merchandise goods and exported only $369 billion. When Americans import goods from abroad, they also supply dollars to the foreign exchange market. Thus, imports are recorded as debits in the balance of payments accounts. In contrast, when U.S. producers export their products, foreigners demand dollars on the exchange market to pay for the U.S. exports. Exports are the credit item.

Balance of Merchandise Trade: The difference between the value of merchandise exports and the value of merchandise imports for a nation. The balance of merchandise trade is only one component of a nation's total balance of payments.

The difference between the value of a country's merchandise exports and the value of its merchandise imports is known as the **balance of merchandise trade.** If the value of a country's merchandise exports falls short of (exceeds) the value of its merchandise imports, it is said to have a balance of trade deficit (surplus). In 1989, the United States ran a balance of merchandise trade deficit of $121 billion.

Other things constant, a U.S. merchandise trade deficit implies that Americans are supplying more dollars to the exchange market in order to purchase foreign-made goods than foreigners are demanding for the purchase of American goods. If the merchandise trade deficit were the only factor influencing the value of the dollar on the exchange market, one could anticipate a decline in the foreign exchange value of the U.S. currency. However, several other factors also affect the supply of and demand for the dollar on the exchange market.

Service Exports and Imports.   The export and import of "invisible services," as they are sometimes called, also exert an important influence on the foreign exchange market. The export of insurance, transportation, and banking services generates a demand for dollars by foreigners just as the export of merchandise does. A French business that is insured with an American company will demand dollars with which to pay its premiums. When foreigners travel in the United States or transport cargo on American ships, they will demand dollars with which to pay for these services. These service exports are thus entered as credits on the current account.

On the other hand, the import of services from foreigners expands the supply of dollars to the exchange market. Therefore, service imports are entered on the balance of payments accounts as debit items. Travel abroad by U.S. citizens, the shipment of goods on foreign carriers, and the purchase of other services from foreigners are all debit items, since they supply dollars to the exchange market.

These service transactions are substantial. As Exhibit 6 illustrates, in 1989 the U.S. service exports were $107 billion, compared with service imports of $80 billion. Thus, the U.S. ran a $27 billion surplus on its service trade transactions.

EXHIBIT 6 ■ U.S. Balance of Payments, 1989

Item	Amount (billions of dollars)	Deficit(−) or Surplus (+) (billions of dollars)	Deficit (−) or Surplus (+) (billions of dollars)
Current Account			
1. Merchandise Trade		−121	
a. Merchandise Exports (including military sales)	+369		
b. Merchandise Imports (including military purchases)	−490		
2. Service Trade		+ 27	
a. Service exports	+107		
b. Service imports	− 80		
3. Income from investments		− 1	
a. Income from U.S. investments abroad	+128		
b. Income of foreigners from investments in U.S.	−129		
4. Net unilateral transfers abroad		− 15	
Current Account Balance			−110
Capital Account			
5. Outflow of U.S. capital		− 49	
a. U.S. direct investment abroad	− 27		
b. Loans to foreigners	− 22		
6. Inflow of foreign capital		+151	
a. Foreign direct investments in U.S.	+ 72		
b. Loans from foreigners	+ 79		
7. Statistical discrepancy		+ 23	
Capital Account Balance			+125
Official Reserve Account			
8. Increase (−) in U.S. official reserve assets		− 25	
9. Increase (+) in foreign official assets in U.S.		+ 10	
Official Reserve Balance			− 15
TOTAL		0.0	0.0

Source: *Federal Reserve Bulletin*, May 1991.

Balance of Trade: Exports of goods and services minus the imports of goods and services. It is often called net exports.

When we add the balance of service exports and imports to the balance of merchandise trade, we obtain "net exports," the overall **balance of trade,** including both merchandise and services. These net exports are a component of both GNP and aggregate demand. When net exports are positive, the foreign sector is adding stimulus to the aggregate demand for goods and services. On the other hand, when net exports are negative, the foreign sector exerts a drag on aggregate demand. In 1989, net exports were equal to minus $94 billion (the $121 billion merchandise trade deficit minus the $27 billion service trade surplus).

Income from Investments. In the past, Americans have made substantial investments in stocks, bonds, and real assets in other countries. As these investments abroad generate income, dollars will flow from foreigners to

Americans. Since the income of Americans from their investments abroad supplies foreign currency (and creates a demand for dollars) in the foreign exchange market, it enters as a credit item on the current account.

Correspondingly, foreigners hold substantial investments in the United States. As these investments earn dividends, interest, and rents, they earn income for foreigners. This income of foreigners leads to an outflow of dollars. As foreigners convert their dollar earnings to their domestic currency, the supply of dollars (and demand for foreign currency) increases on the foreign exchange market. Thus, the income of foreigners from their investments in the United States is a debit item in the balance of payments accounts.

As Exhibit 6 shows, in 1989 Americans earned $128 billion of income on their investments abroad, while foreigners earned $129 billion on their investments in the United States. Thus, the net flow of income from investments was minus $1 billion.

Unilateral Transfers.   Monetary gifts to foreigners, such as U.S. aid to a foreign government or private gifts from U.S. residents to their relatives abroad, supply dollars to the exchange market. These gifts are debit items in the balance of payments accounts. Monetary gifts to Americans from foreigners are credit items. Gifts in kind are more complex. When products are given to foreigners, goods flow abroad, but there is no offsetting influx of foreign currency—that is, a demand for dollars. Balance of payments accountants handle such transactions as though the United States had supplied the dollars with which to purchase the direct grants made to foreigners. So, these items are also entered as debits. Because the U.S. government (and private U.S. citizens) made larger grants to foreigners than we received, net unilateral transfers of $15 billion were entered as a debit item on the current accounts for 1989.

Balance on Current Account.   The difference between (a) the value of a country's current exports and earnings from investments abroad and (b) the value of its current imports and the earnings of foreigners on their domestic assets (plus net unilateral transfers to foreigners) is known as the **balance on current account.** Current account transactions involve only current exchanges of goods and services and current income flows (and gifts). They do not involve changes in the ownership of either real or financial assets. The current account balance provides a summary of all current account transactions. As with the balance of trade, when the value of the current account debit items (import-type transactions) exceeds the value of the credit items (export-type transactions), we say that the country is running a current account deficit. Alternatively, if the credit items are greater than the debit items, the country is running a current account surplus. In 1989, the United States ran a current account deficit of $110 billion.

Balance on Current Account: The import-export balance of goods and services plus net private and government transfers. If a nation's export of goods and services exceeds (is less than) the nation's import of goods and services plus net unilateral transfers to foreigners, a current account surplus (deficit) is present.

CAPITAL ACCOUNT TRANSACTIONS

In contrast with current account transactions, capital account transactions focus on changes in the ownership of real and financial assets. Capital account transactions are composed of (a) direct investments by Americans in real assets abroad (or by foreigners in the United States) and (b) loans to and from foreigners. If a U.S. investor purchases a shoe factory in Mexico, the Mexican seller will want to be paid in pesos. The U.S. investor will supply dollars (and demand pesos) on the foreign exchange market. U.S. investment abroad is thus entered on the balance of payments accounts as a debit item. On the other hand, foreign investment in the

United States creates a demand for dollars on the exchange market. Therefore, it is entered as a credit.

Investment abroad can be thought of as the import of an asset. Importing ownership of a financial (or real) asset from abroad has the same effect on the balance of payments as importing goods from abroad. Therefore, both are recorded as debits. Similarly, in a sense, we are exporting the ownership of capital when foreigners invest in the United States. These transactions enter as a credit.

As for domestic markets, many international transactions are conducted on credit. When a U.S. banker loans $100,000 to a foreign entrepreneur for the purchase of U.S. exports, the banker is in effect importing a foreign bond. Since the transaction causes an outflow of dollars, it is recorded as a debit. On the other hand, when Americans borrow from abroad, they are exporting bonds. Since this transaction creates an inflow of dollars (in order to supply the loanable funds), it is recorded as a credit in the U.S. balance of payments account.

In 1989, foreigners invested $72 billion in the United States and extended $79 billion in loans to Americans. In contrast, U.S. direct investment abroad was only $27 billion and Americans extended loans of $22 billion to foreigners. Since the inflow of capital was substantially greater than the outflow of capital, the United States ran a $125 billion capital account surplus in 1989.

THE OFFICIAL RESERVE ACCOUNT

Special Drawing Rights:
Supplementary reserves, in the form of accounting entries, established by the International Monetary Fund (also called ''paper gold''). Like gold and foreign currency reserves, they can be used to make payments on international accounts.

Governments maintain official reserve balances in the form of foreign currencies, gold, and **special drawing rights** (SDRs) with the International Monetary Fund, a type of international central bank. Countries running a deficit on their current and capital account balance can draw on their reserves. Similarly, countries running a surplus can build up their reserves of foreign currencies and reserve balances with the IMF. Under the fixed exchange system present during 1944–1971, these reserve transactions were highly significant. Countries experiencing balance of payments difficulties were forced to draw on their reserves to maintain their fixed exchange rate. Countries that were selling more to foreigners than foreigners were buying from them accumulated the currencies of other nations.

Under the current (primarily) flexible rate system, nations usually permit a rise or fall in the foreign exchange value of their currency to bring about equilibrium in the exchange rate market. Thus, changes in the official reserve account are generally quite small. However, sometimes nations have their central banks buy and sell currencies in an attempt to reduce sharp swings in the exchange rate. For example, the Reagan administration arranged for foreign governments to buy dollars in an effort to stem the sharp depreciation in the dollar during 1986–1987. In 1989, the net official reserve transactions were modest. The U.S. increased its holdings of foreign reserves by $25 billion, while foreign governments increased their holdings of dollars by $10 billion.

BALANCING THE ACCOUNTS

The aggregated balance of payments accounts must balance. The following balance of payments' identity must hold:

$$\text{current account balance} + \text{capital account balance} + \text{official reserve account balance} = 0$$

However, the specific components of the accounts need not balance. For example, the debit and credit items of the current account need not be equal. Specific components may run either a surplus or a deficit. Nevertheless, since the balance of payments as a whole must balance, a deficit in one area implies a surplus in another.

If a nation is experiencing a deficit on its current account balance, it must experience an offsetting surplus on the sum of its capital account and official reserve account balances. Under a pure flexible exchange system, official reserve transactions are zero. Therefore, under a flexible rate system, a current account deficit implies a capital account surplus. Similarly, under a flexible rate system, a current account surplus would imply a capital account deficit.

A current account deficit means that, in aggregate, the citizens of a nation are buying more goods and services from foreigners than they are selling to foreigners. Under a pure flexible rate system, this excess of expenditures relative to receipts is paid for by borrowing from and selling assets to foreigners.

The current system is a managed floating rate system because governments often engage in official reserve transactions. However, the volume of these transactions is usually small relative to the total. In 1989, the U.S. increased its net official reserve assets by $15 billion. The current account deficit was $110 billion, while the capital account surplus was $125 billion. Thus, the deficits and surpluses on current account, capital account, and net official reserve transactions summed to zero (see right column of Exhibit 6).

MACROECONOMIC POLICY IN AN OPEN ECONOMY

During the post-Second World War period, there has been a dramatic increase in international trade and in the flow of investment capital across national boundaries. This increasing mobility of both goods and capital influences the effects of macroeconomic policy, even in a country such as the United States with a relatively small trade sector. We now live in a global economy. No country can conduct its macroeconomic policy in isolation.

Throughout this text, we have focused on the impact of macroeconomic policy within the framework of an open economy. To date, however, we have paid little attention to the impact of macroeconomic policy on exchange rates and on the components of a nation's balance of payment accounts. We now turn to these issues.

MACROECONOMIC POLICY AND THE EXCHANGE RATE

Since monetary and fiscal policies exert an impact on income growth, inflation, and real interest rates, the policies will also influence exchange rates. Because these two major macropolicy tools differ with regard to their impact on the foreign exchange market, we will consider them separately.

Monetary Policy and the Exchange Rate.   Suppose the United States began to follow a more expansionary monetary policy. How would the more expansionary monetary policy influence the exchange rate market? When the effects are not fully anticipated, expansionary monetary policy will lead to more rapid economic growth, an acceleration in the inflation rate, and lower real interest rates.[4] As we previously discussed, each of these factors will increase the demand for foreign

---

[4]A complete analysis would show that neither growth nor the real interest rate will change if people fully anticipate the effects of the change in monetary policy on the price level. In this chapter, we assume for simplicity that the price level effects of monetary policy are unanticipated. This clearly is more relevant in the short run rather than in the long run.

exchange, causing the dollar to depreciate. The rapid growth of income will stimulate imports. Similarly, the acceleration in the U.S. inflation rate (relative to our trading partners) will make U.S. goods less competitive abroad, causing a decline in exports. Simultaneously, the lower real interest rate will encourage the flow of capital abroad. The expected short-run effect of an unanticipated shift to a more expansionary monetary policy is a depreciation in the exchange rate value of the dollar.

The expected outcome of an unanticipated switch to a more restrictive monetary policy will be just the opposite. The restrictive monetary policy will retard economic growth, decelerate the inflation rate, and push real interest rates upward. Exports will grow relative to imports. Investment funds from abroad will be drawn by the high real interest rates in the United States. Foreigners will demand more dollars with which to purchase goods, services, and real assets in the United States. The strong demand for the dollar will cause it to appreciate.

Fiscal Policy and the Exchange Rate. Fiscal policy tends to generate conflicting influences on the foreign exchange market. Suppose the United States unexpectedly shifts toward a more restrictive fiscal policy, planning a budget surplus or at least a smaller deficit. Just as with restrictive monetary policy, the restrictive fiscal policy will tend to cause a reduction in aggregate demand, an economic slowdown, and a decline in the rate of inflation. These factors will discourage imports and stimulate exports, placing upward pressure on the exchange rate value of the dollar. However, restrictive fiscal policy will also mean less government borrowing, which will reduce real interest rates in the United States. The lower real interest rates will cause financial capital to flow from the United States. This will increase the supply of dollars in the foreign exchange market, and thereby place downward pressure on the exchange rate value of the dollar.

Which of these two effects is likely to dominate? When answering this question, it is important to consider the mobility of capital relative to trade flows. Financial capital is highly mobile. Investors can and do quickly shift their funds from one country to another in response to changes in interest rates. In contrast, importers and exporters often enter into long-term contracts when buying and selling goods. Thus, they are likely to respond more slowly to changing market conditions. Therefore, to the extent that a more restrictive fiscal policy places downward pressure on interest rates, the outflow of capital is likely to dominate in the short run. At least a temporary depreciation in the nation's currency is the most likely outcome.

The analysis of expansionary fiscal policy is symmetrical. To the extent that larger budget deficits stimulate aggregate demand and domestic inflation, they will encourage imports, which will place downward pressure on the exchange rate value of a nation's currency. However, the increased borrowing to finance larger budget deficits will push real interest rates up and draw foreign investment to the United States, causing the dollar to appreciate. In the short run, the latter outcome is more likely.

MACROECONOMIC POLICY AND THE CURRENT ACCOUNT

How does macroeconomic policy affect a nation's balance on current account? When considering this question, it is important to remember that the current and capital account balances must sum to zero under a purely flexible rate system. Thus, any deficit on current (capital) account must be exactly offset by a capital (current) account surplus of equal size. Since unanticipated shifts in macroeconomic policy influence both the demand for imports and real interest rates, then, clearly, they will exert an impact on both current account and capital account balances.

Monetary Policy and the Current Account.
Suppose that the Federal Reserve suddenly increases the growth rate of the money supply. How will this shift to a more expansionary monetary policy influence the U.S. balance on current account? As we just indicated, the more rapid money growth will stimulate income, place upward pressure on the inflation rate, and reduce real interest rates. Think how this combination of factors will affect the current and capital accounts. The growth of income and higher domestic prices will stimulate imports, retard exports, and thus cause the current account to shift toward a larger deficit (or smaller surplus). At the same time, the lower domestic interest rates will encourage investors, both domestic and foreign, to shift funds from the United States to other countries where they can earn a higher rate of return. Predictably, this outflow of capital will cause a capital account deficit and depreciation in the exchange rate value of the dollar. In turn, the dollar depreciation will encourage exports, discourage imports, and act as a partial offset to the direct effects of the more rapid income growth. Since capital is far more mobile than goods in international markets, the outflow of capital effect will generally dominate in the short run. For a time, therefore, the shift to the expansionary monetary policy will tend to cause a capital account deficit (reflecting the outflow of capital) and a current account surplus.

Now consider the impact of an unanticipated shift to a more restrictive monetary policy on a nation's current account balance. The restrictive policy will tend to slow growth and inflation, which will reduce the demand for imports. However, it will also increase real interest rates, which will lead to an inflow of capital and appreciation in the nation's currency. In the short run, the inflow of capital will generally dominate. The expected result is a capital account surplus (reflecting the inflow of capital), currency appreciation, and at least a short-term current account deficit.

Fiscal Policy and Current Account.
What impact will large budget deficits have on a nation's current account? Expansionary fiscal policy will tend to stimulate aggregate demand and push domestic interest rates upward (the crowding-out effect). The increase in aggregate demand will encourage the purchase of imports, and thereby shift the current account toward a deficit (or smaller surplus). Simultaneously, the higher real interest rates will both attract foreign capital and help keep domestic capital at home. Predictably, there will be a net capital inflow, which will shift the capital account toward a surplus.

When fiscal policy is expansionary, both the increase in imports due to the demand stimulus and the increase in the net capital inflow as the result of the higher interest rates will shift the current account toward a deficit and the capital account toward a surplus. Thus, large budget deficits will also tend to result in large current account deficits.

Once again, the analysis is symmetrical. A shift to a more restrictive fiscal policy—for example, a reduction in the size of a budget deficit—will retard demand and reduce interest rates. As the result of the decline in aggregate demand, imports will tend to fall, shifting a nation's current account toward a surplus (or smaller deficit). Simultaneously, the low interest rates will lead to a net capital outflow, which will shift the capital account toward a deficit. Thus, restrictive fiscal policy will tend to cause a current account surplus and a capital account deficit.

The accompanying Thumbnail Sketch summarizes the expected impacts of unanticipated shifts in monetary and fiscal policy.

THUMBNAIL SKETCH

Macroeconomic Policy, Exchange Rates, and Balance of Payments

A. The impact of an unanticipated shift in monetary policy:

	Expansionary Monetary Policy	Restrictive Monetary Policy
Exchange Rate (value of currency)	depreciates	appreciates
Real Interest Rates	decline	increase
Flow of Capital	capital outflow	capital inflow
Current Account	shifts toward a surplus	shifts toward a deficit

B. The impact of an unanticipated shift in fiscal policy:

	Expansionary Fiscal Policy	Restrictive Fiscal Policy
Exchange Rate (value of currency)	uncertain, but the interest rate effect is likely to cause appreciation	uncertain, but the interest rate effect is likely to cause depreciation
Real Interest Rates	increase	decline
Flow of Capital	capital inflow	capital outflow
Current Account	shifts toward a deficit	shifts toward a surplus

---

MACROECONOMIC POLICY AND THE CURRENT ACCOUNT DEFICIT OF THE 1980s AND EARLY 1990s

We are now in a position to analyze the impact of recent macroeconomic policy on the foreign exchange value of the dollar and the current account of the United States. Responding to the double-digit inflation rates of 1979–1980, the Federal Reserve shifted toward a more restrictive monetary policy in the early 1980s. In addition, legislation passed in 1981 substantially reduced tax rates. Thus, in the early 1980s, monetary policy was more restrictive and fiscal policy was more expansionary. How will this macroeconomic policy combination affect exchange rates and a nation's current account? Look at the accompanying thumbnail sketch. Both a more restrictive monetary policy and a more expansionary fiscal policy will tend to cause currency appreciation, higher real interest rates, an inflow of capital, and a current account deficit.

This is precisely what occurred. As Exhibit 7a illustrates, the dollar appreciated sharply beginning in 1981 (see also Exhibit 1). Shortly thereafter, as Exhibit 7b shows, the current account began to shift dramatically toward a deficit position. The

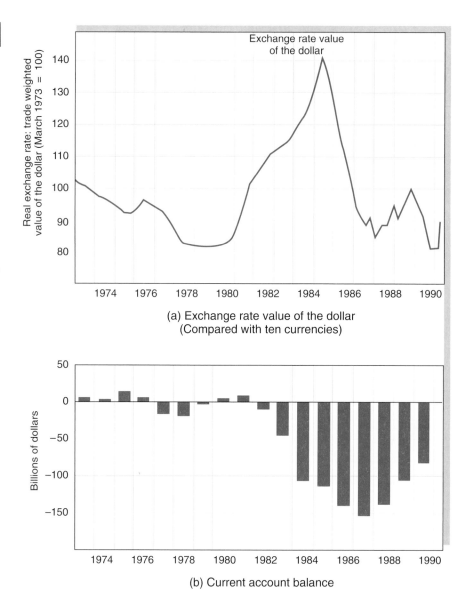

EXHIBIT 7

The Exchange Rate Value of the Dollar and the Current Account Deficit, 1973–1991

As the dollar appreciated during the early 1980s, the current account deficit of the United States soared. In early 1985, the dollar reversed course and began to depreciate. The current account deficit (frame b), however, continued to expand throughout 1986 and 1987. It was not until 1988, approximately three years after the dollar began to depreciate, that the current account deficit began to shrink. Just as the J-curve analysis indicates, there will be a substantial lag between a change in the exchange rate value of a currency and a change in a nation's current account balance.

(a) Exchange rate value of the dollar
(Compared with ten currencies)

(b) Current account balance

annual current account of the United States turned from a $6.9 billion surplus in 1981 to a $46 billion deficit in 1983 and continued upward, reaching a deficit of $154 billion in 1987. As the dollar appreciated throughout 1981–1985, capital continued to flow into the United States and the current account deficit continued to widen.

THE J-CURVE EFFECT

Beginning in 1985, the rise in the exchange rate value of the dollar reversed itself. The dollar depreciated sharply during 1986–1987. Why didn't the decline in the exchange rate value of the dollar reverse the current account deficit? It takes time for a depreciation in a nation's currency to turn around a current account deficit, and, initially, the depreciation generally enlarges rather than shrinks a trade deficit.

The impact of a currency depreciation on a current account deficit can be broken down into a "price effect" and a "quantity effect." A 10 percent depreciation in the dollar means that import prices increase by 10 percent in terms of dollars. Of course, this increase in the dollar price of imports will discourage purchases. However, the 10 percent depreciation also means that *for a given quantity sold,* foreigners will earn 10 percent more dollars. Therefore, unless Americans reduce the *quantity* of their imports by more than 10 percent, their *expenditures* on imports will *increase* in response to a depreciation in the dollar. Similarly, the depreciation will make U.S. exports 10 percent cheaper to foreigners. Unless foreigners increase their *quantity* purchased by more than 10 percent, their demand for dollars in the exchange market will *decrease* as the result of the depreciation.

Since American and foreign-produced goods are excellent substitutes for one another, there is good reason to expect that both the U.S. demand for imports and foreign demand for U.S. exports will be highly elastic in the long run. However, this may not be true in the short run. When the dollar depreciates, it will take time for American consumers to substitute away from the more expensive imports and for foreign consumers to adjust their consumption, purchasing more of the now cheaper American exports. The new suppliers (or new customers) must be contacted. New agreements must be completed. In some cases, these developments must await the expiration of prior contracts. Therefore, initially, the decrease in the *quantity* of exports may be less than the 10 percent reduction in price. If this is the case, for a time the depreciation will actually cause the current account deficit to worsen—the *dollar expenditures* on imports will rise while the *dollar sales* of exports will decline. Eventually, this situation will reverse. With the passage of time, the U.S. demand for imports and foreign demand for U.S. exports will become more elastic. The quantity effects will dominate and a depreciation will reduce the current account deficit.

J-Curve Effect: The tendency of a nation's current account deficit to widen initially before it shrinks in response to an exchange rate depreciation. This tendency results because the short-run demand for both imports and exports is often inelastic, even though the long-run demand is almost always elastic.

Economists refer to this time path of adjustment as the **J-curve effect.** According to this effect, a nation's current account deficit will initially widen (slide down the hook of the J) before it shrinks (moves up the stem of the J) as the result of a currency depreciation. This occurs because the *short-run* elasticity of domestic demand for imports and foreign demand for exports is inelastic. Thus, the depreciation initially increases import expenditures and export sales. However, in the long run, the demand for both imports and exports is elastic. Therefore, the depreciation of a nation's currency will eventually shrink the nation's current account deficit.[5]

Empirical studies are consistent with the J-curve analysis. There is often a lag of two or three years before a change in the exchange rate value of a nation's currency will exert a major impact on current account transactions. This lagged effect can be observed from the data of Exhibit 7. As Exhibit 7a illustrates, the exchange value of the dollar appreciated substantially (approximately 30 percent) during 1981 and 1982. Initially, however, there was little impact on current account transactions. The size of the current account deficit in 1981 and 1982 was not much different from the levels of 1979–1981. Beginning in 1983, two years after the dollar began to appreciate, the current account deficit began to widen considerably. Clearly, the appreciation in the dollar during 1981–1985 reduced the price of

[5]See Jeffery A. Rosensweig and Paul D. Koch, "The U.S. Dollar and the 'Delayed J-Curve,'" *Federal Reserve Bank of Atlanta, Economic Review,* (July/August 1988), pp. 2-15, for an interesting article on the J-curve effect as it applies to the trade imbalances of the United States during the 1980s.

imports (and increased the price of U.S. exports) and contributed to the sizable current account deficit during those years.

Beginning in mid-year 1985, the exchange rate value of the dollar took a sharp plunge. The purchasing power of the dollar in the foreign exchange market declined by 40 percent during 1986 and 1987. Nonetheless, the current account deficit continued to widen during 1986 and 1987. It was not until 1988, approximately two and a half years after the dollar began to depreciate, that the current account deficit began to shrink. Just as the J-curve analysis implies, there was a lengthy lag between the depreciation of the dollar and the reversal in the direction of the nation's current account deficit.

IS THE CURRENT ACCOUNT DEFICIT A PROBLEM?

Under a flexible exchange rate system, a current account deficit must be financed with a capital account surplus. A capital account surplus indicates that the net investment position of Americans is deteriorating relative to foreigners. Thus, the asset holdings of foreigners in the United States are rising relative to the asset holdings of Americans abroad. Is this bad? The answer to this question depends on why Americans are investing so little abroad and foreigners are investing so much in the United States. If it is because large budget deficits have induced Americans to consume beyond their means, and pushed up interest rates, then there is cause for concern. However, if this is the case, it is important to note that the problem is not the current account deficit, but rather large budget deficits which are encouraging current consumption and diverting the savings of Americans away from private capital formation. To the extent that Americans save and invest less as the result of budget deficits, the growth of their future income will be slower.

In recent years, some commentators have charged that current account deficits indicate that Americans are dangerously indebted to foreigners. This position is unduly alarmist. A nation's current account position is an aggregation of the voluntary choices of businesses and individuals. In contrast with the government's budget deficit, there is no legal entity that is responsible for the current account deficit. As Herbert Stein, a former Chairman of the President's Council of Economic Advisers, states:

> The fact is that a certain (unknown) number of Americans bought more abroad than they sold abroad and a certain other (unknown) number of Americans sold more than they bought abroad. The trade deficit is the excess of the net foreign purchases of the first group over the net foreign sales of the second group. The trade deficit does not belong to any individual or institution. It is a pure statistical aggregate, like the number of eggs laid in the U.S. or the number of bald-headed men living here.[6]

The U.S. deficit or surplus on current accounts depends not only upon the choices of Americans, but also upon those of foreigners. When Americans purchase goods, services, and assets abroad, foreigners acquire dollars. If foreigners spend these dollars only on current goods and services (U.S. exports), then the U.S. will tend to run a current account surplus. On the other hand, if foreigners find investment opportunities attractive in the United States, and therefore spend a large share of their acquired dollars on real and financial investments in the United States, then the U.S. will run a current account deficit (and a capital account surplus).

Whether a nation runs a current account deficit or surplus is dependent upon the investment opportunities in the country relative to the nation's saving rate. Under a

---

[6]Herbert Stein, "Leave the Trade Deficit Alone," *The Wall Street Journal,* March 11, 1987.

flexible exchange system, countries with more attractive investment opportunities and a lower saving rate than their trading partners will run current account deficits. Correspondingly, countries with less attractive investment opportunities and a higher saving rate will run a current account surplus.

How long can a nation continue to run a current account deficit? Perhaps surprising to some, the answer is a long time. A current account deficit is not like business losses or an excess of household spending relative to income—conditions that eventually force decision-makers to alter their ways. The United States ran a current (trade) account deficit almost every year from 1800–1875. On the other hand, the U.S. consistently ran current account surpluses during the 1946–1976 period. The trade accounts of other countries have followed similar lengthy periods of both deficits and surpluses.

Currently, the United States has a rapidly growing labor force (compared with Europe and Japan), a system of secure property rights, and political stability. This makes it an attractive country in which to invest. On the other hand, the saving rate of the United States, perhaps as the result of budget deficits, cultural factors, or less favorable tax treatment of saving, is low compared to our major trading partners. A continuation of this combination of factors—attractive investment opportunities and a low saving rate—will result in the long-term inflow of foreign capital and a corresponding current account deficit.

The forces underpinning the U.S. current account deficit may change in the near future. The growth rate of the U.S. labor force may slow, reducing the return on investment and the inflow of capital. Or a period of slow growth in the income of Americans may motivate them to save a larger proportion of their income. Correspondingly, as the income of foreigners increases, they may decide to consume more and save less. Perhaps the federal government will reduce the size of its deficit and thereby push U.S. interest rates lower. Changes of this type will close the current account deficit. But such changes need not take place. And if they do not, the current account deficit will continue, and there is little reason to believe that it is exerting a harmful impact on the U.S. economy.

THE CURRENT INTERNATIONAL MONETARY SYSTEM

The international monetary system in effect since 1973 might best be described as a managed flexible rate system. The system qualifies as a flexible rate system because all of the major industrial countries allow the exchange rate value of their currencies to float. Many small countries maintain fixed exchange rates against the dollar, the English pound, or some other major currency. Therefore, the exchange rate value of these currencies rises and falls with the major currency to which they are tied. The system is managed because the major industrial nations have from time to time altered their official reserve holdings in an effort to moderate major swings—say, swings of 20 percent or more within six months—in exchange rates.

Recent intervention has often involved coordinated efforts on the part of the major industrial nations. The macroeconomics policies and the purchases and sales of currency reserves of the Group of Seven (United States, Japan, France, United Kingdom, West Germany, Canada, Italy) have been conducted with an eye for exchange rate stability in recent years.

APPLICATIONS IN ECONOMICS

The Gold Standard International Monetary System

Throughout history, gold has played an important role in monetary matters. The gold standard is an international monetary system under which the value of each nation's currency (for example, the dollar, pound, or mark) is defined in terms of gold. The last time the world economy operated on a gold standard was during the period from the 1870s until the First World War.

When each currency is linked to gold, the precious metal in essence becomes a world currency. Suppose the U.S. pledged it would buy and sell gold from both domestic citizens and foreigners at a price of $\frac{1}{20}$ of an ounce = $1. Simultaneously, suppose other countries set the value of their currencies in terms of gold. Perhaps the English would set the value of a pound equal to $\frac{1}{10}$ of an ounce of gold and the French would set the value of the franc at $\frac{1}{40}$ of an ounce of gold. Under these circumstances, when each

country sets the value of its currency in terms of gold, the countries also establish a system of fixed exchange rates. For example, if a pound traded for twice as much gold ($\frac{1}{10}$ of an ounce rather than $\frac{1}{20}$ of an ounce) as the dollar, the fixed exchange rate value of the pound would be 1 pound = $2. No one would ever pay more for a pound than $2 because they could always buy $\frac{1}{10}$ of an ounce of gold for $2 and then use the gold to buy a pound. Similarly, the exchange rate between the French franc and the dollar would be $0.50 = 1 franc because the dollar exchanges for twice as much gold ($\frac{1}{20}$ versus $\frac{1}{40}$ of an ounce) as the franc. Since each currency is readily redeemable in gold, the currency of each nation is little more than a gold certificate under a gold standard system.

How did an economy adjust to the flow of international trade under a gold standard? Since domestic citizens could redeem

gold for money, an inflow of gold, in effect, increased the nation's money supply. Under a gold standard system, the flow of gold among countries tended to bring imports and exports of nations into balance. If a nation's imports exceed its exports, the differential was paid in gold. Thus, "trade-deficit" nations exported gold to "trade-surplus" nations. These gold transfers caused the money supply of trade-deficit nations to fall and the money supply of trade-surplus countries to rise. Prices soon reflected these changes in the supply of money. Prices declined in the trade-deficit nations as a result of the shrinking supply of money. The price reductions made the goods of the trade-deficit nations cheaper on international markets, stimulated exports, and thereby restored the balance of trade. Similarly, prices in the trade-surplus nations rose as these countries acquired gold and expanded their money supply. The

---

ADVANTAGES OF THE CURRENT SYSTEM

The proponents of the current system stress three major advantages of the structure. We will discuss each of these in turn.

1. The Current System Is Flexible Enough to Adjust to Major Shocks That Influence the Value of Currencies.   The system of floating exchange rates handled the inflation and soaring oil prices of the 1970s, the unanticipated plunge in oil prices in the 1980s, and the Gulf War of the 1990s with a minimum of difficulty. The volume of international trade continued to rise even during periods of instability.

2. The Current System Allows Countries to Pursue Independent Macroeconomic Policies.   When inflation rates and growth rates vary across nations, a change in only one price—the exchange rate—will bring the flow of international transactions into balance. In contrast, countries often had to follow macropolicy designed to deflate or inflate their economies in order to solve trade imbalances under a fixed rate system. Clearly, it is less painful to alter one price rather than the level of all prices.

3. The Current Structure Solves Trade Imbalances without Trade Restrictions.   Under the fixed rate system, nations often raised tariffs and imposed quotas in an

price inflation in the trade-surplus nations made their products less competitive. Exports declined, moving the trade balance of these countries toward equilibrium.

Despite the beauty of the system's simplicity, the gold standard had a number of drawbacks. First, real resources were tied up in the mining of gold so that it could be transferred between trading nations. Second, as the international sector grew in importance, the demand for exchange currency expanded. Since the supply of gold was virtually fixed, this expanding demand could not be satisfied without a decline in prices. Third, with gold-backed currency used for both domestic and foreign transactions, the system placed a stranglehold on monetary planners. While this might be considered an advantage during periods of inflation, dissatisfaction arose when a reduction in a nation's gold stock (as a result of a trade deficit) not

only placed downward pressure on prices but also caused a decline in employment and income. As the result of these disadvantages, the gold standard was abandoned in 1914.

While the gold standard is very much like a fixed exchange rate system, a fixed system can be maintained without linking currencies to gold. To make a fixed rate system work, countries must conduct their monetary policy *as if* they are on a gold standard. When a country runs a trade surplus, it should increase the growth rate of its money supply more rapidly. This will cause the domestic price level to rise, making its exports less competitive. Eventually, balance between what is sold to foreigners and what is bought from them will be restored. On the other hand, a country that is running a trade deficit should reduce its rate of monetary growth in order to reduce the domestic price level and make

its goods and services more competitive in the world market. The more restrictive monetary policy will eventually restore balance in the trade sector.

Despite the similarities, there is one crucial difference between a pure gold standard and a fixed rate system such as was present during the 1944–1971 period. The gold standard does not allow policy-makers a choice with regard to altering monetary policy. Under a pure gold standard, the money supply of nations experiencing a trade surplus increases automatically, while the money supply of trade deficit nations declines. The gold standard eliminates the discretion of the policy-makers. Proponents of the gold standard usually find this to be one of its most attractive features.

attempt to maintain the fixed exchange rate. Such policies retarded the potential gains from international exchange. With flexible exchange rates, minor changes in rates will generally handle small trade imbalances without generating much sentiment for protectionism. Wild currency value swings, however, may still generate pressures for protectionist policies.

DISADVANTAGES OF THE CURRENT SYSTEM

The current system is not without its critics. The critics of the system stress the following problems:

1. The Current System Leads to Volatile Exchange Rate Changes That Create Uncertainty.   During 1980–1985, the dollar appreciated by 50 percent or more against major currencies such as the French franc, German mark, and British pound. In contrast, the dollar depreciated by a similar amount against several leading currencies during 1986–1988 (see Exhibit 1). Critics of the current system argue that fluctuations of this type make it difficult for exporters and importers to plan for the future.

When evaluating the merit of this charge, one should keep in mind that futures markets allow buyers and sellers to hedge against currency fluctuations when they engage in long-term contracts in another currency. For example, an American business contracting to purchase Japanese houseware products to be delivered in six months can arrange now *at a designated current price* for the delivery of the yen needed to complete the transaction. Thus, if international traders want to avoid the uncertainty implied by potential fluctuations in the exchange rate, futures markets in currencies permit them to do so at a moderate cost. This helps to explain the fact that, even during periods of rapidly changing exchange rates, the volume of international trade has continued to grow.

2. Since the Current System Fails to Impose Macroeconomic Policy Discipline, We Can Expect More Inflation Than Under a Fixed Rate System.   Under a fixed rate system, inflationary policies lead to balance of payments deficits. Since policy-makers will not want to devalue the nation's currency, proponents of this view charge that fixed rates restrain policy-makers more than a flexible rate system. In essence, this view stresses the cost of providing macroeconomic policy-makers with greater independence—they are likely to abuse it.

3. Changes in Exchange Rates Alter Trade Balances Slowly, Only After the Passage of Time.   As we previously discussed, the demand for both imports and exports is often inelastic in the short run. When this is the case, a depreciation in a nation's currency will temporarily cause a current account deficit to increase. Thus, changes in exchange rates are a crude and uncertain instrument with which to deal with trade imbalances, according to this view.

CONCLUDING REMARKS

The current international monetary system is the product of an evolutionary process. Future changes are likely. However, a return to a system of fixed exchange rates such as existed for nearly three decades following the Second World War seems unlikely. Nations are simply unwilling to subject their monetary and fiscal policies to the constraints that a system of fixed rates would require. Currently, there is widespread recognition that the economic health of nations is influenced by the flow of international trade. Perhaps this recognition will lead to a greater coordination of monetary and fiscal policies among Western nations. Recent events at the annual economic summits of Western nations appear to point in this direction.

CHAPTER SUMMARY

1. The foreign exchange market is a highly organized market in which currencies of different countries are bought and sold. The exchange rate is the price of one national currency in terms of another. The exchange rate permits consumers in one country to translate the prices of foreign goods into units of their own currency.

2. When international trade takes place, it is usually necessary for one party to convert its currency to the currency of its trading partner. Imports of goods, services, and assets (both real and financial) by the United States generate a demand for foreign currency with which to pay for these items. On the other hand, exports of goods, services, and assets supply foreign currency to the exchange market because foreigners exchange their currency for the dollars needed to purchase the export items.

3. The value of a nation's currency on the exchange market is in equilibrium when the supply of the currency (generated by imports—the sale of goods, services, and assets to foreigners) is just equal to the demand for the currency (generated by exports—the purchasing of goods, services, and assets from foreigners).

4. Under a flexible rate system, if there is an excess supply of dollars (excess demand for foreign currencies) on the foreign exchange market, the value of the dollar will

depreciate relative to other currencies. A depreciation will make foreign goods and assets more expensive to U.S. buyers and U.S. goods and assets cheaper for foreign purchasers, reducing the value of our imports and increasing the value of our exports until equilibrium is restored. On the other hand, an excess demand for dollars (excess supply of foreign currencies) will cause the dollar to appreciate, stimulating imports and discouraging exports until equilibrium is restored.

5. With flexible exchange rates, a nation's currency tends to appreciate when (a) rapid economic growth *abroad* (and slow growth at home) stimulates exports relative to imports, (b) the rate of domestic inflation is below that of the nation's trading partners, and (c) domestic real interest rates increase relative to one's trading partners. The reverse of these conditions will cause a nation's currency to depreciate.

6. During the period from 1944 to 1971, most of the nations of the free world operated under a system of fixed exchange rates. Under this system, if the value of the goods, services, and capital assets exported to foreigners is less than the value of the items imported, there is an excess supply of the country's currency on the foreign exchange market. When this happens, the country must (a) devalue its currency, (b) take action to reduce imports (for example, heighten its trade barriers), or (c) pursue a restrictive macropolicy designed to increase interest rates and retard inflation. During the period when the fixed rates were in effect, corrective action taken to maintain the rates was often in conflict with free trade in international markets and the macropolicy objective of full employment.

7. The balance of payments accounts record the flow of payments between a country and other countries. Transactions (for example, imports) that supply a nation's currency to the foreign exchange market are recorded as debit items. Transactions (for example, exports) that generate a demand for the nation's currency on the foreign exchange market are recorded as credit items.

8. In aggregate, the balance of payment accounts must balance. Thus, (a) the current account balance plus (b) the capital account balance plus (c) the official reserve account balance must equal zero. However, the individual components of the accounts need not be in balance. A deficit in one area implies an offsetting surplus in other areas.

9. Under a pure flexible rate system, there will not be any official reserve account transactions. Under these circumstances, a current account deficit implies a capital account surplus (and vice versa).

10. An unanticipated shift to a more restrictive monetary policy will raise the real interest rate, reduce the rate of inflation, and, at least temporarily, reduce aggregate demand and the growth of income. These factors will in turn cause the nation's currency to appreciate on the foreign exchange market. In turn, the currency appreciation along with the inflow of capital will result in a current account deficit. In contrast, the effects of a more expansionary monetary policy will be just the opposite: lower interest rates, an outflow of capital, currency depreciation, and a shift toward a capital account surplus.

11. An unanticipated shift to a more expansionary fiscal policy will tend to increase real interest rates, lead to an inflow of capital, and cause the nation's current account to shift toward a deficit. The effects of a shift to a more restrictive fiscal policy will be just the opposite: lower interest rates, an outflow of capital, and movement toward a current account surplus.

12. Under a flexible exchange rate system, a nation's current account position is an aggregation of the voluntary choices of individuals and businesses. Some will have bought more abroad than they sold, while others will have sold more than they bought. The current account deficit simply indicates that the net foreign purchases (and unilateral gifts) of the first group exceed the net foreign sales of the latter group.

13. While flexible exchange rates bring the sum of the current and capital accounts into balance, they do not bring either component into balance. Thus, it is possible for a

country to experience a *long-term* current account deficit or surplus. Whether a country runs a current account deficit or surplus is dependent upon the attractiveness of domestic investment opportunities relative to the nation's saving rate. Countries with more attractive investment opportunities and a low saving rate will tend to run capital account surpluses and current account deficits. On the other hand, countries with less attractive investment opportunities and a high saving rate will tend to experience capital outflow and current account surpluses under a flexible rate system.

14. Since 1973, most countries have operated under a managed flexible rate system. It is a managed system because the major industrial nations have used their official reserve balances in an effort to moderate swings in exchange rates. Nevertheless, market forces now play the major role in the determination of exchange rates among the major industrial nations. Given the severe shocks that international markets have suffered since it was instituted in 1973, the current system appears to be working reasonably well.

15. Prior to the First World War, most countries set the value of their currency in terms of gold. When trade was conducted under the gold standard, the gold stock of a nation would fall if it imported more than it exported. The decline in the stock of gold would decrease the nation's money supply, causing prices to fall and making the nation's goods more competitive on the international market. In contrast, if a nation was a net exporter, its stock of gold would rise, causing inflation and making the nation's goods less competitive on the international market. However, alterations in the supply of gold often caused abrupt shifts in income and employment. The gold standard was abandoned in 1914.

CRITICAL ANALYSIS QUESTIONS

1. During the early 1980s, the United States shifted toward a more restrictive monetary policy that sharply decelerated the domestic inflation rate. Simultaneously, the federal government was running a large budget deficit. Explain how this policy mix influences the value of the dollar in the exchange rate market.

2. How do flexible exchange rates bring about balance in the exchange rate market? Do flexible exchange rates lead to a balance between merchandise exports and imports? Do you think the United States should continue to follow a policy of flexible exchange rates? Why or why not?

3. "If a current account deficit means that we are getting more items from abroad than we are sending to foreigners, why is it considered a bad thing?" Comment.

*4. Suppose the exchange rate between the United States and Mexico freely fluctuated in the open market. Indicate which of the following would cause the dollar to appreciate (or depreciate) relative to the peso.

   a. An increase in the quantity of drilling equipment purchased in the United States by Pemex, the Mexican oil company, as a result of a Mexican oil discovery.

   b. An increase in the U.S. purchase of crude oil from Mexico as a result of the development of Mexican oil fields.

   c. Higher real interest rates in Mexico, inducing U.S. citizens to move their financial investments from U.S. to Mexican banks.

   d. Lower real interest rates in the United States, inducing Mexican investors to borrow dollars and then exchange them for pesos.

   e. Inflation in the United States and stable prices in Mexico.

   f. Ten percent inflation in both the United States and Mexico.

   g. An economic boom in Mexico, inducing Mexicans to buy more U.S.-made automobiles, trucks, electric appliances, and television sets.

   h. Attractive investment opportunities, inducing U.S. investors to buy stock in Mexican firms.

*5. The chart below indicates the actual newspaper quotation of the exchange rate of various currencies:

*Asterisk denotes questions for which answers are given in Appendix C, Selected Answers.

	U.S. Dollar Equivalent	
	Feb. 1	Feb. 2
British pound	1.755	1.746
French franc	.1565	.1575

On Feb. 2, did the dollar appreciate or depreciate against the British pound? How did it fare against the French franc?

6. **What's Wrong with This Way of Thinking?**
"The government can change from fixed to flexible exchange rates, but we will continue to run a balance of payments deficit because foreign goods, produced with cheap labor, are simply cheaper than goods produced in the United States."

7. "A nation cannot continue to run a deficit on current account. A healthy growing economy will not persistently expand its indebtedness to foreigners. Eventually, the trade deficits will lead to national bankruptcy." Evaluate this view.

8. In recent years, a substantial share of the domestic capital formation in the United States has been financed by foreign investors. Is this inflow of capital from abroad indicative that the U.S. economy is in poor health? What does it indicate?

*9. Suppose that the United States were running a current account deficit. How would each of the following changes influence the size of the current account deficit?
   a. a recession in the United States?
   b. a decline in the attractiveness of investment opportunities in the United States?
   c. an improvement in investment opportunities abroad?

10. "Foreigners are flooding our markets with goods and using the proceeds to buy up America. Unless we do something to protect ourselves, the Japanese, Europeans, and Arabs are going to own America." Evaluate this recent statement of an American political figure.

*11. If foreigners have confidence in the U.S. economy and therefore move to expand their investments in the United States, how will the U.S. current account balance be affected? How will the exchange rate value of the dollar be affected?

12. Is a trade surplus indicative of a strong, healthy economy? Why or why not?

*13. If the dollar depreciates relative to the German mark, how will your ability to purchase the BMW you have longed for be affected? How will this change influence the quantity of BMWs purchased by Americans? How will it affect the dollar expenditures of Americans on BMWs?

14. What is the J-curve effect? According to the J-curve effect, how will a depreciation in a nation's currency affect its current account balance?

15. Explain why a current account balance and a capital account balance must sum to zero under a pure flexible exchange rate system.

*16. Changes in exchange rates will automatically direct a country to a current account balance under a flexible exchange rate system. True or false?

Economic Development and the Growth of Income

Certain fundamental principles—formulating sound monetary and fiscal policies, removing domestic price controls, opening the economy to international market forces, ensuring property rights and private property, creating competition, and reforming and limiting the role of government— are essential for a healthy market economy.

Economic Report of the President, 1991, p. 211.

CHAPTER FOCUS

■ How do economists differentiate between developed and less developed countries?

■ How wide is the economic gap between rich and poor nations?

■ Are economic growth and development the same thing?

■ What are the sources of economic growth?

■ Why do many nations remain poor, while other poor countries grow and become prosperous?

■ What can governments do to promote economic prosperity?

■ Is the economic gap between rich and poor nations narrowing or widening?

*T*hroughout history, economic growth and income levels substantially greater than those required for survival have been rare. In the battle with Nature for survival, human beings have usually had to struggle and toil merely to eke out a minimal living. The wheels of progress have moved forward slowly. Economic growth and the rising standard of living taken for granted by much of the Western world did not exist for extended periods of recorded history and still do not exist for many non-Western countries. For example, Phelps Brown showed that the real income of English building trade workers was virtually unchanged between 1215 and 1798, a period of nearly six centuries. The living conditions of peasants in such countries as India and Pakistan are not much different from those of their ancestors 1,000 years ago.

Against this background of poverty and stagnation, the economic record of the Western world during the last 250 years is astounding. In 1750, people all over the world struggled 50, 60, and 70 hours per week to obtain the basic necessities of life—food, clothing, and shelter. Manual labor was the major source of energy. Animals provided the means of transportation. Tools and machines were primitive by today's standards.

In the last two centuries, petroleum, electricity, and nuclear power have replaced human and animal power as the major sources of energy. Automobiles, airplanes, and trains are now the major means of transportation. Subsistence levels of food, shelter, and clothing are taken for granted, and the typical Western family worries instead about financing summer vacations, obtaining video cassette recorders, and providing for the children's college educations. For the first time in history, economic growth is such that subsistence-level living standards have been far surpassed in many parts of the world.

DEVELOPED AND LESS DEVELOPED COUNTRIES

Like the rich nations, the poor countries of the world differ from each other in many respects. Some have grown rapidly in recent years; others have continued to stagnate. War and political upheaval have contributed to the poverty of some; cultural and tribal stability dominate others. There is no sharp division between developed and **less developed countries.** If per capita income were used to distinguish between the two, there would be no significant difference between the income level of the wealthiest less developed country and that of the poorest developed nation. In many respects, the division between the developed and less developed countries is arbitrary. However, there is a set of characteristics generally shared by the less developed countries.

1. The Most Obvious Characteristic of Less Developed Nations Is Low Per Capita Income. Extreme poverty, hunger, and filth are a way of life throughout much of India, Pakistan, most of Asia, Africa, and much of Central and South America. Exhibits 1 and 2 present the harsh statistics. In 1988, per capita *annual* income was $120 in Ethiopia, $170 in Bangladesh, $330 in China, and $340 in India. Approximately 2.9 billion people—60.8 percent of the world's population—lived in the 42 poorest countries with a 1988 annual income per person of less than $500. Another 15.7 percent of the world's population lived in countries where the per

Less Developed Countries: Low income countries characterized by rapid population growth, an agriculture-household sector that dominates the economy, illiteracy, extreme poverty, and a high degree of income inequality.

EXHIBIT 1 ■ Annual Per Capita Output of Nations, 1988 (Derived by the Exchange Rate Conversion Method)							
Poorest Countries (Annual Output Less than $500)		Poor Countries (Annual Output $500 to $2,200)		Middle-Income Countries (Annual Output $2,200 to $6,000)		High-Income Countries (Annual Output Greater than $6,000)	
Selected Countries	Per Capita GNP,1988	Selected Countries	Per Capita GNP,1988	Selected Countries	Per Capita GNP,1988	Selected Countries	Per Capita GNP,1988
Ethiopia	$120	Bolivia	$ 570	South Africa	$2,290	Hong Kong	$ 9,220
Bangladesh	170	Philippines	630	Hungary	2,460	Australia	12,340
Zaire	170	Egypt	660	Uruguay	2,470	United Kingdom	12,810
Nigeria	290	Thailand	1000	Argentina	2,520	France	16,090
China	330	Turkey	1,280	Yugoslavia	2,520	Canada	16,960
India	340	Chile	1,510	Venezuela	3,250	Germany	18,480
Pakistan	350	Mexico	1,760	South Korea	3,600	United States	19,840
Haiti	380	Poland	1,860	Greece	4,800	Japan	21,020
Indonesia	440	Brazil	2,160	Libya	5,420	Switzerland	27,500

Source: The World Bank, *World Development Report, 1990* (Table 1).

capita GNP was between $500 and $2,200 in 1980. Even though these poor countries (the two poorest groups of Exhibits 1 and 2) contained three-fourths of the world's total population, they generated only 11.8 percent of the world's output. In contrast, 25 countries with a per capita GNP of $6,000 or more (the high-income countries) accounted for approximately one-sixth of the world's population in 1988, but they generated more than four-fifths of the world's output. The low-income status of the poor countries of Exhibits 1 and 2 reflects the absence of economic development. By the same token, the standard of living of the wealthy nations is the fruit of past economic development.

2. The Agriculture-Household Sector Dominates the Economy of Less Developed Nations.   Nearly two-thirds of the labor force of the low-income countries of Asia, Africa, and South America is employed in agriculture. In contrast, 2 percent of the U.S. labor force is employed in this sector. The size of the household (nonmarket) sector in less developed countries is generally far greater than in developed nations. Most households in less developed nations raise their own food, make much of their clothing, and construct the family shelter. The specialization and exchange that dominate developed economies are largely absent in less developed countries.

3. Rapid Population Growth Generally Characterizes Less Developed Nations.   The population of the poor countries of Asia, Africa, and South America has been expanding at an average annual rate of approximately 2.2 percent. The population of these nations doubles every 30 or 35 years. In contrast, the population growth of the developed nations of Europe and North America is generally less than 1 percent each year.

4. Income Is Usually More Unequally Distributed in Less Developed Countries.   Not only is the average income low in less developed countries, but most of the available income is allocated to the wealthy. The top 10 percent of all income recipients

EXHIBIT 2 ■ World Population and Output in 1988 by Income Level of Countries		

The 79 countries with per capita annual output of less than $2,200 accounted for 76.5 percent of the world's population but only 11.8 percent of the world GNP in 1988. In contrast, the 16.6 percent of the world's population living in countries with a per capita output of more than $6,000 produced 81.7 percent of the world GNP in 1988.

Category	Percent of World's Population	Percent of World GNP
42 Poorest Countries (Per capita output less than $500)	60.8	5.6
37 Poor Countries (Per capita output $500 to $2,200)	15.7	6.2
17 Middle-Income Countries (Per capita output $2,200 to $6,000)	6.9	6.5
25 High-Income Countries (Per capita output greater than $6,000)	16.6	81.7

Source: The World Bank, *World Development Report*, 1990 (Table 1). The GNP figures were converted to U.S. dollars using the exchange rate method. The data for the Soviet Union are not included in these figures.

usually receives a larger proportion of the aggregate income in less developed countries than in developed nations. Often, this reflects the existence of a two-sector economy—a trade and financial sector linked to the developed world and an agriculture-household sector bound by tradition. The incomes of persons employed in the trade and financial sectors may be comparable to those of individuals in developed nations, but most of the population belong to the dominant agriculture-household sector and languish in poverty.

5. Inadequate Health Care, Poor Educational Facilities, and Illiteracy Are Widespread in Less Developed Nations. While nearly all school-age children attend primary school in North America and the European nations, less than half do so in many less developed countries. One half or less of the adult population is literate in such countries as Bangladesh, Ethiopia, Pakistan, and India. Physicians and hospitals are unavailable in many parts of the less developed world. Most of the resources of these nations are allocated to the provision of basic necessities—food and shelter. Health care and education are luxuries most people cannot afford.

HOW WIDE IS THE ECONOMIC GAP BETWEEN THE DEVELOPED AND LESS DEVELOPED NATIONS?

Most countries of the continents of Asia, Africa, and South America possess the characteristics of less developed nations. Per capita income is low. The agriculture-household sector dominates the economy. Rapid population growth, economic inequality, and poverty abound. On the other hand, these indicators of underdevelopment are generally absent from North America, Europe, Oceania, and Japan. Although there are a few exceptions, these areas by and large comprise the developed nations of the world.

How wide is the economic gap between the developed and less developed world? This is a difficult question to answer. The gross national product per capita is a measure of the goods and services available to individuals, but how can we draw

Exchange Rate Conversion Method: Method that uses the foreign exchange rate value of a nation's currency to convert that nation's GNP to another monetary unit, such as the U.S. dollar.

meaningful comparisons when Mexico's GNP is measured in pesos, Brazil's GNP is measured in cruzeiros, France's GNP is measured in francs, and so on?

The simplest method used to deal with this problem is the **exchange rate conversion method.** This method uses the value of each nation's currency in the exchange rate market to convert the nation's GNP to a common currency, such as the U.S. dollar. For example, if the British pound is worth 1.5 times as much as the U.S. dollar *in the foreign exchange market,* then the GNP of the United Kingdom is converted to dollars by multiplying the British GNP *in pounds* by 1.5. Similarly, the exchange rate value of the currency of other nations is used to convert their GNP to dollars. Since the procedure is relatively simple, most international income comparisons are based on this technique.

Although the exchange rate conversion method is simple and straightforward, it may be a misleading indicator of differences in living standards among nations. The exchange rate of a currency reflects the relative purchasing power of the currency for goods traded in international markets. However, it may not be a reliable indicator of the relative purchasing power of the currency for goods and services not exchanged in international markets. For example, merely because a pound purchases 1.5 dollars in the foreign exchange market, it does not follow that it will purchase 1.5 times as much housing, education, recreation, child-care service and similar items in the United Kingdom as a dollar will purchase in the United States. Since many items are not traded in international markets, the *domestic* purchasing power of a currency may be either more or less than its purchasing power in the exchange market.

The quality of comparative international income data would be greatly improved if the conversion ratio between currencies were expressed in terms of the ability of the currencies to purchase a typical bundle of goods and services in the country of their origin. The United Nations International Comparison Project, an ongoing study conducted by the United Nations Statistical Office, the University of Pennsylvania, and the World Bank, has devised such a purchasing power index for several currencies. The **purchasing power parity method** compares the costs of purchasing a typical bundle of goods and services in the domestic markets for various nations. Each category in the bundle is weighted according to its contribution to GNP. The cost of purchasing the typical bundle in each nation is then compared to the dollar cost of purchasing the same bundle in the United States. Once the purchasing power of each nation's currency (in terms of the typical bundle) is determined, this information can be used to convert the GNP of each country to a common monetary unit (for example the U.S. dollar).

Purchasing Power Parity Method: Method for determining the relative purchasing power of different currencies by comparing the amount of each currency required to purchase a typical bundle of goods and services in domestic markets. This information is then used to convert the GNP of each nation to a common monetary unit.

Recently completed work by Robert Summers and Alan Heston of the University of Pennsylvania provides us with per capita output estimates for 130 countries derived by the purchasing power parity method.[1] Exhibit 3 presents these newly constructed estimates for several countries as well as the more widely cited per capita GNP estimates based on the exchange rate conversion method. Even though the purchasing power parity estimates of Exhibit 3 are for 1985, they are in 1980 dollars, since they are based on the typical bundle consumed in 1980.

---

[1]Robert Summers and Alan Heston, "A New Set of International Comparisons of Real Product and Price Levels—Estimates for 130 Countries, 1950–1985," *The Review of Income and Wealth,* 34 (March 1988), pp. 1–25. For additional detail on the construction of the purchasing power parity estimates, see I. B. Kravis, Alan Heston, and Robert Summers, *World Product and Income: International Comparisons of Real Gross Product* (Baltimore: Johns Hopkins Press, 1982).

EXHIBIT 3 ■	A Comparison of the Per Capita GNP of Selected Countries—the Exchange Rate Conversion Method Versus the Purchasing Power Parity Method	
Country	1988 Per Capita GNP in 1980 Dollars (Exchange Rate Conversion Method)	1985 Per Capita GNP in 1980 Dollars (Purchasing Power Parity Method)
China	$ 233	$ 2,444
India	240	750
Thailand	706	1,900
Brazil	1,526	3,282
Mexico	1,243	3,985
Argentina	1,780	3,486
Hong Kong	6,515	9,093
United Kingdom	9,050	8,665
France	11,370	9,918
Germany	13,056	10,708
United States	14,017	12,532
Japan	14,850	9,447
Switzerland	19,430	10,640

Source: The exchange rate conversion estimates are derived from the World Bank, *World Development Report, 1990* (Table 1). The purchasing power parity estimates are from Robert Summers and Alan Heston, ''A New Set of International Comparisons of Real Product and Price Levels—Estimates for 130 Countries, 1950–1985,'' *The Review of Income and Wealth,* 34 (March 1988).

In general, the income comparisons derived by the purchasing power parity method indicate that the exchange rate conversion method overstates the income of developed nations relative to less developed countries. For example, the per capita GNP estimate for India derived by the purchasing power parity method is approximately 3 times the exchange rate conversion estimate. For China, the per capita GNP figure derived by the purchasing power parity method is more than ten times ($2,444 compared to $233) the estimate based on exchange rate conversion! For most all less developed countries, including Thailand, Brazil, Mexico, and Argentina, the per capita GNP estimates based on the purchasing power parity method are substantially greater than the parallel estimates derived by exchange rate conversion. Just the opposite is the case for most developed countries. For the United Kingdom, France, Japan, United States, Switzerland, and several other industrial economies, the per capita GNP estimates based on the exchange rate conversion exceed the parallel estimates derived by the purchasing power parity method.

Exhibit 4 used both the exchange rate conversion and purchasing power parity methods to estimate the size of the gap between the industrial nations and less developed countries. According to the exchange rate conversion method, the per capita GNP of the market economies of North America, Europe, Oceania, and Japan was $17,080 in 1988, compared with only $750 for the less developed countries of the world. This exchange rate conversion income comparison suggests that the per capita GNP of developed nations was more than 22 times the comparable figure for less developed countries in 1988.

<table>
<tr><td colspan="3">EXHIBIT 4 ■ Measuring the Economic Gap Between
Developed and Less Developed Countries</td></tr>
</table>

If the per capita GNP of industrial, market-economy nations is estimated by the exchange rate conversion method, it is more than 22 times greater than that of less developed countries. However, if the more accurate purchasing power parity procedure is used, the gap narrows, indicating that the GNP per capita is approximately 6.5 times greater for industrial nations than for less developed countries.

	Per Capita GNP	
	Industrial Countries[a]	**Less Developed Countries**[b]
Exchange rate method		
1988 (in 1988 U.S. dollars)	$17,080	$750
1988 (industrial countries = 100)	100	4.4
Purchasing power parity method		
1985 (in 1980 U.S. dollars)	$9,660	$1,480
1985 (industrial countries = 100)	100	15.3

[a]North America, Europe, Japan, and Oceania. The Soviet Union and other centrally planned economies of Eastern Europe are not included in these data.

[b]Asia, Africa, South America, and Central America.

Source: The World Bank, *World Development Report, 1990* and Robert Summers and Alan Heston, "Improved International Comparisons of Real Product and its Composition: 1950–1985," *Review of Income and Wealth,* 34 (March 1988), pp. 1–25.

Using the purchasing power parity method, however, the estimated 1985 per capita GNP of industrial economies was $9,660, compared to $1,480 for the less developed nations (both figures are in 1980 dollars). This purchasing power parity comparison implies that in the mid-1980s the per capita GNP of the industrial economies was approximately 6.5 times the per capita GNP of less developed countries, a substantially smaller differential than the estimate based on exchange rate conversion.

Since they reflect the prices of a broader set of commodities rather than only items traded internationally, most economists believe that the purchasing power parity estimates are a more accurate indicator of international differences in per capita GNP than the more widely circulated estimates based on exchange rate conversions. Nevertheless, even the purchasing power parity method indicates the economic gap between developed and less developed countries is extremely large.

ARE GROWTH AND DEVELOPMENT THE SAME THING?

During the two decades following the Second World War, economists failed to draw a clear distinction between growth and development. Development was deemed present if a country was able to generate and sustain a significant rate of increase in GNP—for example, 3 percent or more. In recent years, it has become increasingly popular to define growth in strictly positive terms—the rate of change in GNP. Development is now widely perceived as a normative concept, encompassing not only growth but also distributional and structural changes that imply an improvement in the standard of living for most of the populace. Development requires not only growth in output per person but also an improvement in the availability of consumption goods for a wide spectrum of the populace, including those people in the bottom half of the income distribution.

Economic growth and development are closely related. Countries that grow rapidly generally experience economic development. There are exceptions, however. For example, during the 1965–1980 period, Brazil achieved substantial economic growth. The distribution of income in Brazil, however, was highly skewed. More than 60 percent of the aggregate income was allocated to the wealthiest 20 percent of the population. By way of comparison, the wealthiest one-fifth of the population earn between 40 and 45 percent of the aggregate income in the developed countries of Europe and North America. The economic growth of Brazil during the 1965–1980 period did little to alter the economic status of the overwhelming majority of its citizens. Thus, Brazil experienced growth, but was unable to achieve economic development.

Even though economic growth and development can be distinguished, it is obvious that growth is necessary for development. Without sustained economic growth, continuous improvement in the economic opportunities and status of a nation's populace, including those at the bottom of the economic spectrum, will be impossible.

Extensive Economic Growth: An expansion in the total output of goods and services, regardless of whether or not output per capita increases.

Intensive Economic Growth: An increase in output per person. When intensive economic growth is present, output is growing more rapidly than population.

It is important to understand the distinction between two types of growth—extensive and intensive growth. **Extensive economic growth** is present when the output of a nation, as measured by real GNP, for example, is expanding. A nation may experience extensive growth even though the output per person is stagnating. Since economists are interested primarily in the well-being of individuals, they generally focus on **intensive economic growth,** the expansion in the availability of goods and services per person. Per capita real output (or income) is a measure of intensive economic growth. If a society's production of goods and services is expanding more rapidly than is its population, per capita real income will rise. On average, the economic well-being of people will improve, reflecting the intensive economic growth. Conversely, if the population of the nation is expanding more rapidly than is production, per capita real income will decline. Economic regression, the opposite of intensive growth, will be the result.

SOURCES OF ECONOMIC GROWTH

Why do some countries grow rapidly while others stagnate? Lay persons often argue that natural resources are the key ingredient of economic growth. Of course, other things constant, countries with abundant natural resources do have an advantage. It is clear, though, that natural resources are neither a necessary nor sufficient condition for economic growth. Japan has few natural resources and imports almost all of its industrial energy supply. Similarly, Hong Kong has practically no raw materials, very little fertile soil, and no domestic sources of energy. Yet, the growth records of these two countries are envied throughout the world. In contrast, such resource-rich nations as Ghana, Kenya, and Bolivia are poor and experiencing only slow growth. Physical resources are not the key to economic progress.

If natural resources are not the key to growth, what is? Thus far, economists have been unable to construct a general theory of growth and development.

Therefore, we cannot fully determine the essential ingredients necessary for the transition from stagnation to economic progress and development. Economics is nevertheless capable of pinpointing certain important determinants. Three factors stand out. Clearly, (a) investment in physical and human capital, (b) technological advances, and (c) improvement in economic organization play important roles in the growth process.

INVESTMENT IN PHYSICAL AND HUMAN CAPITAL

Machines can have a substantial impact on a person's ability to produce. Even Robinson Crusoe on an uninhabited island can catch far more fish with a net than he can with his hands. Farmers working with modern tractors and plows can cultivate many more acres than their great-grandparents, who probably worked with hoes. Similarly, education and training that improve the knowledge and skills of workers can vastly improve their productivity. For example, a cabinet-maker, skilled by years of training and experience, can build cabinets far more rapidly and efficiently than can a lay person. Both physical capital (machines) and human capital (knowledge and skills) expand the productive capacity of a worker.

The acquisition of physical and human capital, though, involves an opportunity cost. When time and effort are expended on the production of machines or the development of skills, fewer resources are available for current production. There are no free lunches. The cost of additions to a nation's stock of physical and human capital is a reduction in current consumption, either domestically or abroad if the investment is financed by borrowing.

As we discussed in Chapter 2, *other things constant,* nations that invest more in human and physical capital tend to grow more rapidly. However, if investment is going to promote growth and development, it must be channeled into productive activities. Stated another way, the investment must be for goods and services that are valued more highly than the resources that were used in their production.

Some economists argue that less developed countries are trapped in their poverty because they cannot generate a sufficient amount of savings for the finance of capital formation. According to their view, less developed nations are caught in a **vicious circle of underdevelopment.**[2] Thus, the poverty of less developed nations becomes self-perpetuating: poor societies are unable to save and invest, and lacking capital formation, they are unable to escape their poverty.

This vicious circle of poverty theory has been severely criticized in recent years. The critics of the theory argue that the theory suffers from a major defect: the modern world is characterized by an international capital market. If investment in a poor country is productive, capital will be attracted from foreign investors. The critics of the vicious circle of underdevelopment argue that the problem is not an

Vicious Circle of Underdevelopment: A pattern of low income and low economic growth, which tends to perpetuate itself. Since the current consumption demands of poor nations are large in proportion to available income, the savings and investment rates of these nations are low. In turn, the low investment rate retards future growth, causing poor nations to remain poor.

---

[2]Ragnar Nurkse provides a clear statement of the vicious circle of underdevelopment:

In discussions of the problem of economic development, a phrase that crops up frequently is "the vicious circle of poverty."

A situation of this sort [the vicious circle of underdevelopment] relating to a country as a whole can be summed up in the trite proposition: "A country is poor because it is poor". . . . The supply of capital is governed by the ability and willingness to save; the demand for capital is governed by the incentives to invest.

On the supply side, there is the small capacity to save, resulting from the low level of real income. . . .

On the demand side, the inducement to invest may be low because of the small buying power of the people, which is due to their small real income, which again is due to low productivity.

See Ragnar Nurkse, *Problems of Capital Formation in Underdeveloped Countries* (New York: Oxford University Press, 1953), pp. 4–5.

absence of financing, but rather low rates of return often due to uncertainties emanating from insecure property rights and perverse government policies.[3]

TECHNOLOGICAL PROGRESS

Technological Advancement: The introduction of new techniques or methods of production that enable a greater output per unit of input.

Technological advancement—the adoption of new improved techniques or methods of production—enables workers to generate additional output with the same amount of resources. Such improvements reduce the cost of producing goods and services. Less human and physical capital per unit of output is required.

Technological advancement is brought about by capital formation and research investments. Modern technological breakthroughs are generally the result of systematic investments in research and development. Thus, advancements in science and technology, like other improvements requiring investment expenditures, necessitate the sacrifice of current consumption.

When analyzing the phenomenal growth of Western nations during the nineteenth century, economic historians often point to dramatic technological advancements as the major source of economic progress. This view certainly has some merit. From a technological viewpoint, a person living in 1750 would probably have felt more at home in the world at the time of Christ than in today's society. During the last 250 years, technology has radically altered our way of life. The substitution of power-driven machines for human labor, the development of new sources of energy (for example, the steam engine, the internal combustion engine, hydroelectric power, and nuclear power), and developments in transportation and communications are the foundation of modern society. Without them, the growth and development of the last 250 years would have been impossible.

Invention: The discovery of a new product or process, often facilitated by the knowledge of engineering and scientific relationships.

Obviously, technological progress encompasses **invention,** the discovery of new products or processes. But, it also includes **innovation,** the practical and effective adoption of new techniques. It is sometimes easy to overlook the significance of innovation, but it is crucial to economic development. Many innovators were not involved in the discovery of the products for which they are now famous. Henry Ford played a minor role in the discovery and development of the automobile. His contribution was an innovative one—the adoption of mass production techniques, which facilitated the low-cost production of reliable automobiles. Ray Kroc, the developer of the McDonalds fast food chain, did not invent anything. In fact, he was not even involved in the operation of the first McDonalds restaurant. But he recognized a good idea when he saw it. Kroc was an innovator. He franchised the business, trained operators of McDonalds, and in the process changed the eating habits of a nation. Inventions are important, but without innovators, inventions are merely ideas waiting to be exploited.

Innovation: The successful introduction and adoption of a new product or process; the economic application of inventions.

Although technological advancement has played an important role in the promotion of material progress, it is clearly not a sufficient condition for sustained economic growth. Modern technology is available to all, including the less developed nations. If technology were the only requirement for economic growth, the less developed nations would be growing rapidly.

Before modern technology can set growth in motion, the work force of a nation must be sufficiently knowledgeable to operate and maintain complex machines. Innovative entrepreneurs who are capable of adapting technology to the needs (and price structure) of a nation must be available and have access to resources.

---

[3]See Peter T. Bauer, *Equality, the Third World, and Economic Delusion* (Cambridge: Harvard University Press, 1981).

EFFICIENT ECONOMIC ORGANIZATION

Allocative Inefficiency: The use of an uneconomical combination of resources to produce goods and services, or the use of resources to produce goods that are not intensely desired relative to their opportunity cost.

Infrastructure: The provision of a legal, monetary, educational, transportation, and communication structure necessary for the efficient operation of an exchange economy.

The efficiency with which the economic activity of a country is organized will influence the country's output and growth rate. If the economic organization of a nation encourages waste and fails to reward the creation of wealth, economic growth will be stunted. Regardless of the form of economic organization present, certain basic conditions must be met if waste and inefficiency are to be avoided. The incentive structure must encourage production of the goods and services that are most desired by people (relative to their costs). **Allocative inefficiency** results when a nation's resources are used to produce the wrong products. For example, waste results when a nation whose people intensely desire more food and better housing, uses valuable resources to produce unwanted national monuments and luxurious vacations for political leaders. In the same way, waste results when a nation ill-equipped to manufacture steel and automobiles insists on using resources that could be productive in other areas (for example, agriculture) to produce these prestige goods.

Efficient economic organization must also encourage producers to choose low opportunity cost methods of production. Regardless of whether an economy is centrally planned or market directed, efficient production requires that the marginal productive contribution of each resource reflect its opportunity cost. Waste results when producers are discouraged from the adoption of the least-cost resource combination. For example, if unfavorable tax treatment or interest rate controls discourage the use of capital, economic waste and higher production costs will result.

The supply of public goods and goods that generate substantial external benefits is also an important ingredient of efficient economic organization. Broadly speaking, this issue relates to the provision of an economic infrastructure. **Infrastructure** is a term used by economists to describe the economy's legal, monetary, educational, transportation, and communication structure. The provision of an adequate infrastructure involves several things, including a legal system that clearly defines property rights and a monetary system that encourages the wise use of resources across time periods (that is, something approximating price stability). It also involves the provision of an educational system that encourages children of all social classes to develop their skills and abilities.

Finally, an efficient economy requires the development of highways, telephones, and power sources necessary for the realization of gains from specialization, division of labor, and mass production methods—the ''heart and soul'' of a modern exchange system. These networks often are provided by government, but each has also been provided privately since users can be made to pay for the benefits they receive through tolls and user charges. However they are provided, a sound infrastructure is an integral part of efficient economic organization.

WHY POOR NATIONS REMAIN POOR: SOURCES OF ECONOMIC STAGNATION

During the last 250 years, sustained growth has taken place throughout most of Europe, North America, and Oceania. More recently, living standards have improved substantially in Japan and several small countries in Asia. At the same time, poverty, subsistence-level living standards, and malnutrition have persisted throughout much of Asia, Africa, South America, and Central America. In these places, most people continue to live and die in a world of poverty, malnutrition, and disease, just as they have done for thousands of years.

Why have industrialization and economic growth bypassed these people? There is no single, comprehensive answer to this question. However, we can point to several factors that have retarded economic growth in less developed countries.

POLITICAL INSTABILITY DISCOURAGES INVESTMENT AND RETARDS GROWTH

As a rule of thumb, the more securely present and future property rights are defined, the more capital formation there will be. In contrast, insecurely defined property rights and a potentially volatile political climate will repel capital investment and retard economic growth.

Unfortunately, the political climate of many underdeveloped nations is highly unstable. Prejudice and injustice, a highly unequal distribution of wealth, and a history of political favoritism to a ruling class make political upheaval a distinct possibility. Wise investors, both domestic and foreign, avoid investment in real assets under these conditions. Those who do undertake business ventures find it advantageous to seek favors (and assurances) from the military and ruling classes. This may aggravate the situation in the long run. Unquestionably, several Latin American countries have suffered because of their political instability. Nationalization and the threat of expropriation have discouraged both domestic and foreign investment. Continued poverty and economic stagnation have been the results.

Political instability is a very difficult obstacle to overcome, even when countries adopt democratic political institutions. The level of poverty in many less developed countries is such that many are willing to support political revolution in the hope that it will better their lot. As the possibility of political upheaval increases, however, the investment necessary to improve the economic welfare of the citizenry comes to a standstill. In turn, the low rate of investment and accompanying economic stagnation make political revolution still more likely. Many underdeveloped nations will be unable to improve their economic conditions until they solve the problem of political instability.

PUBLIC POLICY OFTEN DISTORTS PRICES AND PROMOTES INEFFICIENCY

The economic policies of many less developed countries are often a major deterrent to economic prosperity. In a well-functioning economy, producers must be provided with an incentive to use resources wisely and to produce goods that consumers want. If they are not provided with these incentives, production costs will be high and resources will be wasted producing the wrong things.

Prices direct the choices of consumers, producers, and resource owners. If resources are going to be allocated efficiently, the relative prices of products and factors must reflect their relative scarcity and true value. Inappropriate pricing signals are a potential source of inefficiency for market and centrally planned economies alike—and for developed and less developed countries.

Unfortunately, public policy in less developed countries has often distorted pricing signals and directed resources away from areas of high productivity. For example, several less developed nations (particularly African countries) have adopted price controls on agricultural commodities that have depressed agricultural prices below world market levels, made farming unprofitable, and driven investment from agriculture. While the intent was to help urban consumers, the result was a decline in agricultural output and widespread food shortages.

In addition, the governments of many less developed countries, particularly those in Latin America and Africa, operate numerous business enterprises ranging from hotels to fertilizer plants. These state-owned enterprises are generally subsidized and protected from both foreign and domestic competition. They often pursue political objectives such as providing attractive jobs for political supporters and other favored groups. In essence, these state-owned enterprises combine the perverse incentive structure of government-operated firms with the protection from competition provided by the grant of monopoly power (or government subsidies). From the standpoint of economic efficiency, this is a disastrous combination. Since they are protected and subsidized, these state-owned enterprises are able to survive and even expand despite their notorious inefficiency. Scarce investment funds, including funds derived from foreign aid, are often squandered on these enterprises.

Less developed nations do not, of course, have a monopoly on foolish economic practices. Developed nations do silly things, too. However, the effects of policies that distort prices, impede business activity, and discourage production are more pronounced in the less developed world. In these cases, the results are sometimes catastrophic.

Since price distortions emanate from a variety of sources, it is not easy to quantify their effects. Economists are just beginning to undertake research in this area. Exhibit 5 summarizes the findings of a World Bank research project that analyzed the impact of price distortions on the growth rate of less developed countries.[4] The World Bank study focused on price distortions arising from foreign exchange controls, trade restrictions, wage, price, and interest rate controls, and inflation. A price distortion index for 31 less developed countries was derived. In turn, the price distortion index was related to economic growth. The study found that the nine "low-distortion" countries were able to achieve an average annual growth rate of 6.8 percent during the 1970s. In contrast, the average growth rate of the eleven "high-distortion," less developed countries was only 3.1 percent. In terms of *per capita* GNP, the growth rate of the low-distortion countries was 4.5 percent, compared with only 0.8 percent for the high-distortion countries. Thus, the per capita real growth of the low-distortion countries was more than five times the comparable rate for high-distortion countries.

A recent study by Gerald Scully of the University of Texas-Dallas also sheds light on the link between political interference with market exchange and economic growth. Scully's study covered 115 countries during the 1960–1980 period. Scully found that economies that relied more extensively on market prices, private property, and the rule of law grew between two and three times more rapidly than economies characterized by political controls and interference with market forces.[5]

MONETARY INSTABILITY AND CAPITAL MARKET RESTRICTIONS DISCOURAGE INVESTMENT AND GROWTH

Like political instability, monetary instability also discourages investment and other time-dimension exchanges (for example, the use of bonds, mortgages, and other forms of credit to finance the purchase of houses and other capital assets). When prices increase at 20, 50, or 100 percent per year, the uncertainty accompanying time-dimension contracts is enormous. When the purchasing power of the currency fluctuates wildly from year to year (and in extreme cases, month to month), it is virtually impossible to plan for the future in a sensible manner. Rather than dealing with the uncertainties that accompany double and triple-digit inflation rates, many

---

[4]The World Bank, *World Development Report: 1983*, Chapter 6.
[5]Gerald W. Scully, "The Institutional Framework and Economic Development," *Journal of Political Economy* 96 (June 1988), pp. 652–62.

EXHIBIT 5 ■ Price Distortions and Economic Growth— The Result of the World Bank Study		
	Annual Growth of Real GNP 1970–1979	
	Aggregate	**Per Capita**
Low-distortion countries[a]	6.8	4.5
Median-distortion countries[b]	5.7	2.9
High-distortion countries[c]	3.1	0.8

[a]The low-distortion countries were: Malawi, Thailand, Cameroon, South Korea, Malaysia, Philippines, Tunisia, Kenya, Yugoslavia, and Colombia.

[b]The median-distortion countries were: Ethiopia, Indonesia, India, Sri Lanka, Brazil, Mexico, Ivory Coast, Egypt, and Turkey.

[c]The high-distortion countries were: Senegal, Pakistan, Jamaica, Uruguay, Bolivia, Peru, Argentina, Chile, Tanzania, Bangladesh, Nigeria, and Ghana.

Source: The World Bank, *The World Development Report, 1983*, Table 6.1 and Table 19.

investors and business decision-makers will move their activities to countries with a more stable environment. Foreigners will invest elsewhere and citizens will often go to great lengths to get their savings (potential funds for investment) out of the country. As a result, potential gains from capital formation and business activities will be lost.

Of course, rapid growth in the money supply is the major cause of inflation. For decades, many less developed countries, particularly those in South America, have financed their government operations with printing-press money, rather than with taxes. Rapid inflation and the flight of capital from the country are the inevitable side effects of this policy.

Naturally, inflation leads to high interest rates once the rising prices are anticipated by borrowers and lenders. Many less developed countries have sought to suppress the high interest rates that inevitably accompany inflation. When they fix interest rates below the market level, however, domestic lenders invest their funds abroad. Similarly, potential foreign lenders are repelled from the market. In effect, monetary expansion, coupled with interest rate controls, destroys the private capital market.

The consequences of this policy are disastrous. The private capital market plays an important role in directing investment funds toward their highest valued uses. Investors who supply private capital to finance projects have a strong incentive to evaluate alternative projects carefully since their return is dependent upon the success of the venture. Private investors will tend to channel their funds into those projects that are most likely to succeed. In turn, successful (profitable) projects will increase the wealth of the nation. Without a private capital market, it is virtually impossible to attract funds and channel them into wealth-creating activities. Private capital formation is retarded, and public investment often results in the inefficient use of funds. With little productive capital formation, the income of many less developed countries continues to stagnate.

As Exhibit 6 illustrates, monetary expansion and interest rate controls have led to negative real interest rates in several less developed countries during the 1980s. Negative real interest rates, however, will result in capital flight. Investors channel

EXHIBIT 6 ■ Capital Markets, Real Interest Rates, and the Growth of Per Capita GNP in Developing Countries		
	Real Interest Rate 1987–1988[a]	Growth of Per Capita GNP, 1980–1988
Countries with Negative Real Interest Rates during the 1980s		
Mexico	−67	−1.7
Uganda	−65	−1.8
Zambia	−30	−2.0
Ghana	−21	−1.3
Ecuador	−19	−0.7
Venezuela	−18	−1.7
Nigeria	−15	−4.4
Countries with Positive Real Interest Rates during the 1980s		
Chile	+15	0.2
Cameroon	+13	2.2
Indonesia	+9	3.0
India	+9	3.0
Thailand	+9	4.1
Korea	+6	8.7
Hungary	+6	1.7
Singapore	+4	4.6
Malaysia	+3	2.0

[a]The real interest rate is equal to the average nominal lending interest rate in 1987–1988 minus the average inflation rate in 1987–1988

Source: World Bank, *World Development Report 1989 and 1990* and *World Tables: 1989–1990 Edition.*

their funds elsewhere. Lacking both financial capital and a mechanism to direct investment toward productive projects, productive investment in such countries comes to a standstill. Income stagnates and even regresses. The experience of Uganda, Mexico, Zambia, Ghana, Ecuador, Venezuela, and Nigeria illustrates this point. The real interest rate in each of these countries was negative during the 1980s. So, too, was their growth rate.

In contrast, the second set of less developed countries of Exhibit 6 followed more stable monetary policies and placed fewer restrictions on the loanable funds market. The real interest rate in these countries was positive. Thus, they were able to attract investment funds from both domestic and foreign investors. In turn, the capital formation contributed to the positive growth rate of their per capita GNP.

HIGH MARGINAL TAX RATES DISCOURAGE PRODUCTIVE ACTIVITY

When high marginal tax rates take a large share of the fruits generated by productive activities, the incentive of individuals to work and undertake business projects is reduced. High tax rates may also drive a nation's most productive citizens to other countries where taxes are lower. They also discourage foreigners from financing domestic investment projects. In short, economic theory indicates that high marginal tax rates will retard productive activity, capital formation, and economic growth.

The most detailed study of the impact of high marginal tax rates on the economic growth of less developed countries has been conducted by Alvin

Rabushka of Stanford University.[6] Rabushka undertook the tedious task of reconstructing the 1960–1982 tax structure for 54 less developed countries for which data could be obtained. He found that some countries levied very high marginal tax rates, which took effect only at very high income thresholds. Others levied high marginal rates on even modest levels of income. A few countries imposed only low or medium tax rates.

Rabushka found that countries which kept marginal tax rates low generally experienced more rapid economic growth. Summarizing the finding of his study, Rabushka concluded:

> Good economic policy, including tax policy, fosters economic growth and rising prosperity. In particular, low marginal income tax rates, or high thresholds for medium- and high-rate tax schedules, appear consistent with higher growth rates. The key in any system of direct taxation is to maintain low tax rates or high (income) thresholds.[7]

Exhibit 7 presents data similar to that used by Rabushka in his study. As Exhibit 7 shows, several less developed countries levy exceedingly high marginal tax rates and apply them at a very low income level. For example, in 1984 Peru taxed virtually all income at a marginal tax rate of 65 percent. Thus, people got to keep only about one-third of what they earned. Similarly, persons with equivalent incomes of less than $10,000 U.S. dollars confronted marginal tax rates of between 60 percent and 65 percent in India, Pakistan, Ghana, Kenya, and Zaire. Top marginal tax rates of 80 percent and 95 percent were levied in Zambia, and Tanzania. When people are not permitted to keep much of what they produce, they do not produce much. Unsurprisingly, the average growth of real per capita GNP for the high tax countries of Exhibit 7 was only 0.4 percent.

Exhibit 7 also presents parallel data for countries that levy lower marginal tax rates (or higher rates that apply only at a high income threshold). During the 1970s and early 1980s, Hong Kong, Paraguay, Indonesia, and Singapore levied the lowest marginal tax rates in the world. Interestingly, these less developed countries also enjoyed rapid economic growth. The average growth rate of real per capita GNP during the 1965–1984 period for the low-tax countries of Exhibit 7 was 3.4 percent, well above the rate for the high tax countries.

TRADE BARRIERS OFTEN PREVENT COUNTRIES FROM UTILIZING THEIR COMPARATIVE ADVANTAGE

In the absence of trade barriers, producers in various countries will be directed toward those areas where they have a comparative advantage. For example, a country such as Hong Kong with a skilled labor force will tend to focus on the manufacture and assembly of products. On the other hand, a country with an abundance of fertile land, Argentina for example, will tend to specialize in the production of grains and beef. Aggregate output is maximized and each trading partner gains when producers specialize in the areas in which they have a comparative advantage.

Unfortunately, countries often erect trade barriers which direct producers away from areas where they have a comparative advantage. Political leaders in less developed countries have often associated economic development with industrialization. Thinking it would promote development, many less developed countries

---

[6]See Alvin Rabushka, "Taxation, Economic Growth, and Liberty," *Cato Journal* (Spring/Summer, 1987), pp. 121–48.

[7]Alvin Rabushka, "Taxation and Liberty in the Third World," paper presented to a conference on Taxation and Liberty held in Santa Fe, New Mexico, September 26–27, 1985.

EXHIBIT 7 ■ Marginal Tax Rates and Economic Growth			
	Highest Marginal Tax Rate, 1984	Income at Which the Top Rate Takes Effect (in 1982 U.S. dollars)	Growth Rate of Per Capita GNP, 1965–1984
High Tax Countries			
Jamaica	58	$ 2,400	−0.4
Peru	65	40	−0.1
India	62	7,700	1.6
Pakistan	60	6,500	2.5
Philippines	60	24,350	2.6
Ghana	60	400	−1.9
Kenya	65	9,900	2.1
Zaire	60	1,350	−1.6
Zambia	80	10,700	−1.3
Tanzania	95	19,293	0.6
Average Growth Rate			**0.4**
Low Tax Rate Countries			
Hong Kong	25	$ 4,900	•6.2
Paraguay	30	8,200	4.4
Indonesia	35	44,750	4.9
Singapore	40	325,000	7.8
Guatemala	48	324,350	2.0
Honduras	46	476,400	0.5
Panama	56	192,500	2.6
Venezuela	45	1,110,000	0.9
Average Growth Rate			**3.4**

Source: The growth rate data are from the World Bank, *World Development Report: 1986*. The marginal tax rates and the income threshold at which they apply are from Price Waterhouse, *Individual Tax Rates, 1984*.

have tried to promote domestic manufacturing, even when the domestic producers were far less efficient than their foreign rivals. Since the domestic producers had higher costs, protectionist policies were required to insulate them from the competition of lower-cost foreign producers.

Seeking to promote industrialization, many less developed countries adopted high tariffs, quotas, and other international trade barriers. These trade barriers directed resources away from areas where domestic producers had a comparative advantage and into areas where domestic producers were relatively inefficient. Such policies wasted resources and reduced domestic incomes.

WHAT CAN GOVERNMENT DO TO PROMOTE PROSPERITY?

As we previously discussed, economists do not have a sure-fire recipe to promote growth and prosperity. However, both economic theory and historical experience do provide us with some knowledge of the conditions conducive to economic development. Foremost among these conditions are secure protection of private property, freedom of exchange, stable prices, and low marginal tax rates. As Adam Smith noted long ago, the wealth of nations is crucially dependent upon gains from (1) specialization and trade, (2) expansion in the size of the market, and (3) the discovery of better ways of doing things. Governments that respect property rights and freedom of exchange while following monetary (and fiscal) policies consistent with relatively stable prices establish the foundation for economic growth. All of the modern economic miracles from the recovery of West Germany and Japan following the Second World War to the more recent rapid growth of the "Asian tigers" (Hong Kong, South Korea, Indonesia, and Singapore) have been in countries which followed this strategy.

In contrast with this approach, governments around the world have often used price controls, regulations, and taxes to restrain both domestic and international trade. They have often followed monetary policies that resulted in double- and even triple-digit inflation rates, which erode the value of property and increase the risk of time-dimension exchange. Similarly, governments have often levied high marginal tax rates, which, in turn, discourage production and drive both capital and productive citizens elsewhere. To varying degrees, these types of policies plague almost all poor countries. This is a strategy that doesn't work. And countries that follow this course will continue to experience poverty and economic stagnation.

Perverse economic policies, including rapid monetary expansion, price (and interest rate) controls, high taxes, and trade restrictions have exerted a devastating impact in many less developed nations. In 1988, per capita income in Tanzania, Zaire, Zambia, Bolivia, and Jamaica was actually lower than it was in 1965. In Argentina and Peru, real income per capita was virtually unchanged during the 1965–1988 period. The per capita income of Mexico declined during the 1980s. See Applications in Economics box for evidence of differences in growth rates among less developed countries.

It is interesting to compare the economic policies of countries that have experienced substantial economic growth in recent decades with the policies followed by countries with stagnating economies. Exhibit 9 provides an overview of the policies followed by six high-growth countries during the 1980s compared with those of nine troubled economies. In general, the high growth countries followed far more restrictive monetary policies and, as a result, inflation was much less of a problem. Simultaneously, the high-growth countries shunned interest rate controls. Thus, the real interest rates in the high-growth countries were positive. In contrast, the stagnating economies generally imposed interest rate controls that resulted in negative real interest rates. In the area of tax policy, the high-growth countries tended to have lower marginal tax rates (or high rates that apply only at relatively high income levels) than the stagnating economies. Finally, the tariff rates of the high-growth economies were generally lower than the rates of the stagnating economies.

The winds of change are now beginning to blow; there is evidence of significant policy changes in several less developed countries. Among Latin American countries, Chile has already shifted substantially away from the policies of monetary expansion, price controls, and trade restrictions. The annual inflation rate in Chile during the 1980s was approximately 20 percent, down from 130 percent during the 1970s. Tariff rates were cut; the top marginal tax rate was reduced from 80 percent to 50 percent; and several state enterprises were privatized during the

APPLICATIONS IN ECONOMICS

Rich and Poor Nations—Are They Two Worlds Drifting Apart?

Since almost everyone was poor 250 years ago, people did not worry much about subsistence-level living standards and starvation in other countries. Of course, there were rich nations and poor nations, but the per capita income of the rich was seldom more than twice that of the poor.

During the eighteenth century, sustained economic growth took place throughout much of Europe and North America. By 1850, there was a virtual explosion of economic development, and it soon spread to Oceania and Japan. Not only did industrial nations grow rapidly during this period, but the fruits of growth were also widely dispersed. The living standards of the well-off and those not so well-off increased substantially. Today, even poor people in North America, Europe, Oceania, and Japan are far better off than most citizens of an underdeveloped nation, The present level of affluence in the developed nations is unprecedented.

Economic growth over the last century has created an enormous gulf between developed and less developed countries. The average income of people in developed nations today is more than six times the figure for less developed countries (see Exhibit 4). Some observers have argued that the world is comprised of growing industrial nations on the one hand and stagnating, less developed countries on the other. According to this view, the widening gap between rich and poor nations threatens to plunge the world into crisis. Evidence indicates this view is an oversimplification. The less developed countries are not a

monolithic block of humanity condemned forever to poverty and stagnation, but rather are nearly 100 nations with widely varying growth rates and records. Exhibit 8 highlights this diversity.

The less developed nations of the late-1980s can be broken down into several groups. (Even with this analysis, there will of course be some oversimplification.) First, there are nations that are losing the battle with economic growth. The per capita income of Ethiopia, Zaire, Uganda, Ghana, and Bolivia has actually declined since 1965. The twentieth century has passed by the people of these countries. Like their ancestors for centuries, these people spend their lives trying to eke out a bare subsistence living.

Fortunately, there is a second group of less developed countries that *has* achieved a very impressive growth record. As Exhibit 8 illustrates, the growth of per capita income in China, Indonesia, Egypt, Botswana, South Korea, Singapore, and Hong Kong has generally exceeded the growth rates of the wealthier developed countries. These countries are winning the race with scarcity.

The high-growth, less developed countries are a diverse group. Some are large; others are small. Some (China and Indonesia) are rich with minerals, but others (Hong Kong, Singapore, and Egypt) have few natural resources. But these high growth countries also have several things in common. First, they have an incentive structure that encourages farmers and business entrepreneurs to produce and earn income. Several of them (Hong Kong,

Indonesia, and Singapore) are characterized by low marginal tax rates. Even in China, recent reforms have increased the ability of agricultural workers to capture the benefits of increases in production. Second, during recent decades, property rights have been relatively secure in each of the less developed countries experiencing rapid growth, and as a result, each has attracted substantial foreign investment. Interestingly, with the possible exception of Egypt, aid from foreign governments has played little part in the rapid growth of these nations. Finally, these countries have done a reasonably good job of controlling inflation. They have not financed government operations with printing-press money. Thus, inflation in the high growth countries has generally been much less rampant than in other less developed countries.

Compared to industrial nations, the population growth of poor nations—both those achieving economic growth as well as those stagnating—has been quite rapid. While the population of the United States, Japan, and the developed nations of Europe has been expanding less than 1 percent annually, the population growth rate of the less developed countries has generally exceeded 2.5 percent annually. (See Exhibit 8, column 2.)

For less developed countries, the rapid population growth is both a problem and an opportunity. It is a problem because population expansion is clearly running a tight race with economic growth. However, it also presents an

EXHIBIT 8 ■ Wealth of Nations—Growth of Population and Income

Selected Countries	Per Capita GNP, 1988 (U.S. Dollars)[a] (1)	Average Annual Growth Rate		
		Population 1980–1988 (2)	Real Per Capita GNP	
			1965–1980 (3)	1980–1988 (4)
Poor country (slow growth in per capita income)				
Ethiopia	120	2.9	0.0	−1.5
Zaire	170	3.1	−1.4	−1.2
Tanzania	160	3.5	0.6	−1.5
Uganda	280	3.2	−2.1	−1.8
Ghana	400	3.4	−0.8	−1.3
Bolivia	570	2.7	2.0	−4.3
Peru	1,300	2.2	1.1	−1.1
Argentina	2,520	1.4	1.9	−1.6
Poor country (rapid growth in per capita income)				
China	330	1.3	4.2	9.0
Indonesia	440	2.1	5.6	3.0
Egypt	660	2.6	4.7	3.1
Thailand	1,000	1.9	4.3	4.1
Botswana	1,010	3.4	10.5	8.0
Malaysia	1,940	2.6	4.8	2.0
South Korea	3,600	1.2	7.6	8.7
Singapore	9,070	1.1	8.5	4.6
Hong Kong	9,220	1.5	6.6	5.8
Rich country				
Australia	12,340	1.4	2.2	1.9
United Kingdom	12,810	0.2	2.2	2.6
France	16,090	0.4	3.3	1.4
Canada	16,960	0.9	3.8	2.4
Germany	18,480	−0.1	3.0	1.9
Sweden	19,300	0.2	2.4	1.5
United States	19,840	1.0	1.7	2.3
Japan	21,020	0.6	5.3	3.3

[a]Derived by the exchange rate conversion method.

Source: The World Bank, *World Development Report, 1990.*

opportunity. If less developed countries can reduce their birth rates, the initial impact on their growth rates is likely to be quite positive. A reduction in a nation's birth rate will result in a smaller number of dependents per working-age adult, which would stimulate the growth in per capita income. Nations currently experiencing rapid growth in aggregate GNP can expect a period of very rapid growth in *per capita* income if they are able to reduce their birth rates. If this happens, less developed countries such as South Korea, Egypt, Thailand, Indonesia, and perhaps China may well follow in the footsteps of Japan and by the turn of the century begin to move rapidly up the ladder of economic development.

EXHIBIT 9 ■ A Comparison of the Monetary, Credit, Tax, and Trade Policies of High Growth and Stagnating Economies, 1980–1988					
	Growth Rate of the Money Supply 1980–1988[a]	Inflation Rate 1980–1988	Real Interest Rate, 1987–1988	Top Marginal Tax Rate, 1984 (percent)	Average Tariff Tax Rate on Imports, 1987	Growth of Per Capita GNP 1980–1988
High Growth Countries						
Hong Kong	7.7	6.7	+6	25[b]	0.8	8.8
Indonesia	18.7	8.5	+9	35	3.6	3.0
Korea	9.6	5.0	+6	65	8.8	8.7
Singapore	6.4	1.2	+4	40	0.5	4.6
Taiwan	14.8	8.8	+6	60	2.3	1.6
Malaysia	8.4	1.3	+3	45	4.9	2.0
Stagnating Countries						
Argentina	284.2	290.5	—	62	12.7	−1.6
Ecuador	29.8	31.2	−19	58	8.0	−0.7
Ghana	42.9	46.1	−21	60[b]	10.1	−1.3
Mexico	62.1	73.8	−67	55	2.2	−1.7
Peru	99.7	119.1	−36	65[b]	15.1	−1.1
Philippines	16.0	15.6	+ 5	60[b]	15.4	−2.4
Tanzania	19.5	25.7	− 5	95[b]	8.8	−1.5
Zambia	28.2	33.5	−33	80[b]	10.2	−2.8
Zaire	57.5	56.1	—	60[b]	10.4	−1.2

[a]The money supply data are for the actual growth rate of the money supply minus the growth rate of real GNP. Thus, the actual money supply data are adjusted to reflect the country's growth rate.

[b]Rate applies at an income threshold of less than $25,000.

Source: Derived from World Bank, *World Development Report, 1990* and *World Tables: 1989–1990;* International Monetary Fund, *Government Finance Statistics Yearbook, 1990;* and Price Waterhouse, *Individual Tax Rates, 1984.*

1980s. In recent years, Chile has become the growth economy of South America. During 1984–1989, the real GNP of the Chilean economy grew at a 6.3 percent annual rate.

Several other less developed countries in Latin America, Africa, and Asia now appear to be more receptive to sound economic policies than at any time in recent decades.[8] For example, Mexico has begun to move toward the liberalization of its economy. In the late 1980s, the Mexican government took some modest steps toward the decontrol of prices and privatization of state enterprises. The top marginal income tax rate was reduced to 35 percent in 1990, down from 60.5 percent in 1987. Approval of a US.–Mexico free trade agreement would be an additional major step toward liberalization. It will be exciting to monitor and analyze the results of these decontrol "experiments" during the 1990s.

---

[8]See the *Economic Report of the President, 1991* (Chapter 6) for additional details on recent changes in the economies of less developed countries.

LOOKING AHEAD

In the next chapter, we will use economic tools to analyze different economic systems. The economies of several Eastern European countries and even the Soviet Union are now in a period of transition. The following chapter will focus on the operation of centrally planned economies and the forces driving the current changes in Eastern Europe and the Soviet Union.

CHAPTER SUMMARY

1. For the first time in history, economic growth is such that per capita income far surpasses the subsistence level in most of Europe, North America, Oceania, and Japan. Living conditions have been transformed for the one-sixth of the world's population who reside in these regions.

2. The major characteristics of less developed countries are (a) low per capita income, (b) a large agriculture-household sector, (c) rapid population growth, (d) inequality of income distribution, and (e) widespread illiteracy coupled with poor educational and health facilities.

3. Although there is no sharp dividing line between developed and less developed countries, the nations of North America, Europe and Oceania, as well as Japan, can be classified as developed countries. In contrast, most of the countries of Asia, Africa, South America, and Latin America exhibit the characteristics of underdevelopment.

4. The exchange rate conversion method and the purchasing power parity method provide ways of comparing income among nations. Under the exchange rate conversion method, the exchange rate value of a nation's currency is used to convert the GNP of each nation into a common currency, usually the U.S. dollar. Alternatively, the purchasing power parity method uses data on the cost of purchasing a typical bundle of consumer goods and services to determine the relative purchasing power of each currency and to calculate the GNP of each nation in terms of a common currency. While the purchasing power parity method is likely to provide a more accurate measure of differences in living standards across countries, the data required to make the calculations are not readily available. As a result, most of the widely cited income comparisons are based on the exchange rate conversion method.

5. Income comparisons based on the exchange rate conversion method suggest that the per capita real GNP of industrial economies is more than 22 times the figure for less developed nations. However, recent comparisons based on the purchasing power parity method indicate that the exchange rate conversion method overstates the relative income of the industrial nations. When measured by the purchasing power parity method, the per capita GNP of industrial countries is estimated to be 6.5 times that of less developed countries.

6. Economic growth is a positive concept. Extensive growth is present when the real GNP of a nation expands. Intensive growth requires an increase in output per person. Economic development is a normative concept, encompassing distributional and structural factors as well as high per capita income. Economic development implies an advance in the standard of living for a broad cross-section of a nation's population, including those people in the bottom half of the income distribution.

7. The availability of domestic natural resources is not the major determinant of growth. Countries such as Japan and Hong Kong have impressive growth rates without such resources, while many resource-rich nations continue to stagnate.

8. While economists have been unable to develop a general theory of economic growth and development, several important determinants of economic progress have been pinpointed. The following factors have played an important role in the economic progress of developed nations: (a) investment in physical and human capital, (b) development and dissemination of technologically improved production methods and products, and (c) efficient economic organization.

9. Several factors have retarded economic growth in many less developed countries (LDCs) in recent years. Political instability in several LDCs has discouraged

investment. Price controls and protected (and subsidized) government enterprises have often resulted in the inefficient use of resources. Rapid monetary expansion has increased uncertainty and thereby discouraged both capital formation and business activity. In addition, several less developed countries have imposed high marginal tax rates and erected trade restrictions which have also retarded their growth.

10. As Adam Smith noted more than 200 years ago, the wealth of nations is dependent upon gains from (a) specialization and trade, (b) expansion in the size of the market, and (c) the discovery of better (more productive) ways of doing things. Governments that respect property rights, protect the freedom of exchange, and follow monetary and fiscal policies consistent with a stable price level help provide the framework for the creation of wealth.

11. The economic growth record of less developed countries is mixed. A large portion of the world's inhabitants live in countries characterized by both extreme poverty and per capita real income that is either stagnating or falling. The rates of population growth in these countries are among the highest in the world. Their economic prospects are bleak. In contrast, the recent economic growth record in other less developed countries, including Egypt, Hong Kong, Indonesia, Singapore, South Korea, Thailand, Brazil, Cameroon, and more recently China, has been highly impressive. These countries may well duplicate the post-Second World War "Japanese miracle" of economic development and join the developed world in the near future.

CRITICAL ANALYSIS QUESTIONS

1. Imagine you are an economic adviser to the president of Mexico. You have been asked to suggest policies to promote economic growth and a higher standard of living for the citizens of Mexico. Outline your suggestions and discuss why you believe they would be helpful.

*2. "Without aid from the industrial nations, poor countries are caught in the poverty trap. Because they are poor, they are unable to save and invest; and lacking investment, they remain poor," Evaluate this view.

*3. It is often argued that the rich nations are getting richer and the poor are getting poorer. Is this view correct? Is it an oversimplification? Explain.

*4. As the people of a nation become wealthier, do you think they will save a larger percentage of their income? Why or why not? As a nation becomes wealthier, do you think that length of the average workweek will decline? Why or why not? Does the experience of the United States support your answer? Explain.

5. The size of the population in some countries may partially reflect the desire of some people for additional security in the form of children to support them in their old age. Is this method of providing for one's retirement inferior to our system of compulsory social security? Why or why not?

6. Discuss the importance of the following as determinants of economic growth: (a) natural resources; (b) physical capital; (c) human capital; (d) technical knowledge; (e) attitudes of the work force; (f) size of the domestic market; and (g) economic policy.

7. What do the high growth countries among less developed nations have in common? How do they differ? What lessons of economic development can be drawn from the similarities and differences among these countries?

*8. Explain why the exchange rate conversion method may result in a misleading estimate for the per capita GNP of a country.

9. How do the exchange rate conversion and purchasing power parity methods differ as tools with which to compare relative incomes among countries? How do the estimated incomes of less developed countries compare with developed countries under the two methods?

*10. Do you think that the absence of international trade barriers will be more important for a small country like Costa Rica than for a larger country like Mexico? Explain.

*Asterisk denotes questions for which answers are given in Appendix C, Selected Answers.

Comparative Economic Systems

Less than 75 years after it officially began, the contest between capitalism and socialism is over: capitalism has won. The Soviet Union, China, and Eastern Europe have given us the clearest possible proof that capitalism organizes the material affairs of humankind more satisfactorily than socialism.[1]

Robert Heilbroner

CHAPTER FOCUS

■ Are there basic economic principles that apply to all economies?

■ What are the distinguishing characteristics of capitalism and socialism?

■ How is the Soviet economy organized? How does the economic record of the Soviet Union compare with market-directed economies?

■ How did the economic reforms of the late 1980s affect the Soviet economy?

■ What are the future prospects of the Soviet economy? What do the Soviets need to do to achieve economic success?

■ How has the economy of China changed in recent years? Have the changes affected economic performance?

■ How rapidly has the Japanese economy grown since 1950? How does the economic organization of Japan differ from that of other market economies?

*T*he institutions and organizations of an economy influence economic outcomes. In previous chapters, we have focused our analysis on the operation of mixed capitalistic economies such as those that exist in the United States, Canada, Australia, Japan, and throughout most of Western Europe. Market forces play an important role in the allocation of resources in these countries. Government action is also important. Private industries are often regulated by government. Government ownership and operation of utilities, transportation, communication, and educational facilities are not uncommon, even in Western countries. In addition, taxes and government subsidies are sometimes used to alter market outcomes. Throughout this book, we have used economic tools to help us understand the incentives and expected results of governmental policy that redirects market forces.

Today, nearly one-third of the world's population lives in the Soviet Union, Eastern Europe, and China. The economies of these countries are in the midst of enormous structural change. Until recently, these economies were characterized by central government planning and government ownership of productive assets. In this chapter, we will apply the tools of economics to the operation of centrally planned economies. Because of its size and importance, particular attention will be given to the organizational framework and recent economic developments in the Soviet Union. We will also take a closer look at distinctive characteristics and the economic performance of the Chinese and Japanese economies. The chapter concludes with a brief overview of the economic record of socialist and capitalist economies.

GENERAL APPLICATION OF BASIC ECONOMIC PRINCIPLES

All economic systems, despite their differences, face similar constraints. Scarcity of economic goods confronts individuals and nations alike with budgetary problems. No nation is able to produce as much as its citizenry would like to consume. Therefore, regardless of economic organization, choices must be made. The decision to satisfy one desire leaves many other desires unsatisfied. All economic systems are constrained by the bonds of scarcity.

Many of the economic concepts that have been discussed throughout this book apply to all economic systems. Let us reconsider and summarize four of these basic ideas.

1. Opportunity Cost.   An economy can be organized so that various goods can be provided without charge to the consumer, but economic organization cannot eliminate the opportunity costs associated with the provision of goods. The provision of additional medical services, even if distributed free, necessitates the use of resources that could have been used to produce other things. Similarly, if there is an expansion of the national defense sector, there must be a contraction of other sectors. Whenever productive resources have alternative uses, as they almost always do, the production of goods is costly, regardless of the form of economic organization.

[1]Robert Heilbroner "Reflections: The Triumph of Capitalism," *The New Yorker,* January 23, 1989, p. 98.

2. Diminishing Marginal Returns. According to the law of diminishing marginal returns, increased application of a variable resource to a fixed factor of production, such as land or natural resources, will expand output by a smaller and smaller amount. Other things being equal, a nation cannot continue to expand output proportionally by simply using more labor with the current stock of physical capital. Neither can proportional increases in agricultural output be achieved by using more and more fertilizer with the current stock of land. The law of diminishing returns limits the ability of both the Soviet Union and the United States to expand output from a given resource base. It is applicable to all economies. With the passage of time, of course, capital formation (an expansion in the resource base) and improved technology will permit us to loosen the bonds of scarcity. Without capital formation and improvements in technical knowledge, growth of output in capitalist and socialist countries alike will be severely retarded.

3. Comparative Advantage and Efficiency. Total production is greatest when each good is generated by the low opportunity cost producer. The assignment of the productive task to a high opportunity cost producer is inefficient (that is, output will be below its potential level), regardless of whether the activity takes place in a capitalist or a socialist economy. No matter what the type of economic organization, the goal of efficient production can best be attained by heeding the principle of comparative advantage.

4. The Law of Demand. Reflecting the law of diminishing marginal utility, the law of demand states that the quantity demanded of a good will be inversely related to its price. The law of demand is just as relevant in socialist countries as it is in capitalist countries. High prices will discourage consumption in both. For example, if socialist planners set the price of color television sets quite high, few will be purchased. On the other hand, if planners set zero or extremely low prices for medical services or basic housing, the quantity demanded will be large—often greater than the quantity supplied. Waiting lines and other forms of nonprice rationing will result.

INCENTIVES MATTER

Changes in the structure of incentives alter human behavior in both capitalist and socialist countries. For example, at one time in the Soviet Union, the managers of glass-producing firms were rewarded according to the tons of sheet glass produced. Not surprisingly, most plants produced sheet glass so thick that one could hardly see through it. The rules were changed so that the managers were rewarded according to the square meters of glass produced. The managers reacted in a predictable way. Under the new rules, Soviet firms produced very thin glass that broke easily. Incentives matter in the Soviet Union just as they do in the United States.

In our analysis of alternative economic systems, we will focus on how economic organization affects people's motivations. Marxists often have argued that communism would eventually alter basic human motivations. In their view, people would cease to respond in predictable, traditional ways to changes in personal costs and benefits. Perhaps this is so, but the experiences of the Soviet Union and other Communist countries have produced little evidence thus far to support this view. Therefore, until human nature does change radically, an analysis based on the postulate that incentives do affect human decisions is most relevant. This is not to say that only economic considerations matter. Religious, cultural, and political factors can and do influence economic behavior. The economic approach does not deny their importance.

CONTRASTING CAPITALISM AND SOCIALISM

Socialism: A system of economic organization in which (a) the ownership and control of the basic means of production rest with the state and (b) resource allocation is determined by centralized planning rather than by market forces.

Joseph Schumpeter, the renowned Harvard economist, defined **socialism** as:

> . . . an institutional pattern in which the control over means of production and over production itself is vested with a central authority—or, as we may say, in which, as a matter of principle, the economic affairs of society belong to the public and not the private sphere.[2]

As Schumpeter's definition implies, capitalist and socialist economic organizations differ in two important respects—ownership of physical capital and resource allocation.

OWNERSHIP OF PHYSICAL CAPITAL— PRIVATE OR GOVERNMENT

Every economic system has a legal framework within which the rights of resource owners are defined. Practically all economic systems guarantee the rights of individuals to sell their own human capital—their labor—to the highest bidder. Earnings are derived from the sale of labor services in capitalist and socialist societies alike. Under socialism, however, the rewards obtained from the use of physical capital (machines, buildings, and so on) in the production process accrue to the state. If the state actually owns the nonhuman productive resources, the earnings they generate go directly to the state. The state can also use taxation to gain at least partial control over earnings that would otherwise accrue to other owners of physical capital. In either case, under socialism, investment in physical capital reflects the views of those who control the state.

RESOURCE ALLOCATION—MARKETS OR CENTRAL PLANNING

Capitalism: An economic system based on private ownership of productive resources and allocation of goods according to the price signals provided by free markets.

Every economy must have a mechanism that coordinates the economic activity of microunits—business firms, individual resource owners, and consumers. The mechanism must solve such problems as the use of resources, the selective production of goods, and the distribution of income.

Under market-directed **capitalism,** economic activity is coordinated by contractual agreements between private parties who possess property rights to products and resources. There is no central planning mechanism. Market prices direct the actions of decentralized decision-makers. The forces of supply and demand push prices up or down in response to the decisions of individual buyers and sellers.

Under a socialist economic organization, resources are used and allocated in accordance with the centrally determined and administered scheme. Economic decisions, such as what and how much will be produced, what the relative proportions of investment and consumption will be, how resources will be used in production, and to whom the product will be distributed, are made by a central authority. The central plan may also include decisions on quantities of raw materials and inputs, techniques of production, prices, wages, locations of firms and industries, and the employment of labor. Socialist economic objectives generally reflect the preferences and value judgments of central planners. These objectives may or may not reflect the views of consumers.

---

[2]Joseph A. Schumpeter, *Capitalism, Socialism, and Democracy,* 3rd ed. (New York: Harper, 1950), p. 167.

EXHIBIT 1 ■ Contrasting Capitalism and Socialism		
	Capitalism	Socialism
Property rights	Nonhuman resources are owned by private parties (that is, individuals or corporations)	Nonhuman resources are owned by the government
Allocation of goods and resources	Determined by market forces	Determined by centralized planning
Employment	Workers are self-employed or employed by private firms	Workers are employed by the government or government-controlled cooperatives
Investment	Undertaken by private parties seeking profits and higher future incomes	Undertaken by the government in accordance with the objectives of the planners
Income distribution	Determined by market forces that reward productivity and ownership of economic resources	Determined by central planners who may seek to promote equality or some other pattern of income distribution

Exhibit 1 summarizes the distinctive characteristics of capitalist and socialist economic organization. Capitalist economies are characterized by private ownership of physical assets and the use of market forces to coordinate the actions of buyers and sellers and thereby determine the allocation of goods and resources. Markets also coordinate employment and investment decisions and determine the distribution of income under capitalism. In contrast, government ownership (or control) of physical assets and the allocation of resources by central planning are the distinctive characteristics of socialist economic organization. Under socialism, the central planners also determine the patterns of employment and investment as well as the distribution of income.

CLASSIFYING REAL-WORLD ECONOMIES

In reality, all modern economies use some combination of capitalist and socialist economic organization. Exhibit 2 classifies several economies according to their reliance on (a) private ownership or public ownership of assets and (b) market allocation compared to central planning. Economies characterized by both private ownership and market allocation best fit pure capitalism. Hong Kong, Japan, the United States, and Canada fall at the capitalism end of the spectrum (the southwest corner of Exhibit 2). On the other hand, economies characterized by government ownership of assets and central planning approximate pure socialism (the northeast corner of Exhibit 2). Even through the future structure of the economy is currently being reevaluated in both the Soviet Union and China, at present, these two economies fall at the socialist end of the spectrum.

Yugoslavia and Sweden are interesting exceptions to the pure capitalism or pure socialism classifications. In Yugoslavia, most of the means of production are owned by the government. Market prices, though, are widely used to allocate goods and resources. Thus, the Yugoslavian economy is something of a hybrid. In Sweden, most physical assets are owned by private individuals and corporations. Nevertheless, the government uses taxes, subsidies, and regulatory powers to shape the allocation of resources. Approximately three-fifths of the aggregate income of Sweden is channeled through government, a significantly larger proportion than for France, Germany, or the United Kingdom, for example. The Swedish economy, too, is something of a cross between capitalism and socialism.

EXHIBIT 2

The Classification of Economies

The Soviet Union and China most closely approximate pure socialism, while Hong Kong, and the United States come closest to pure capitalism. The Yugoslavian economy is characterized by government ownership coupled with substantial reliance on markets. Thus, it lies in the southeast corner of the diagram. On the other hand, Sweden has only modest government ownership, but government planning plays a major role in the allocation of resources. Therefore, it lies toward the northwest corner.

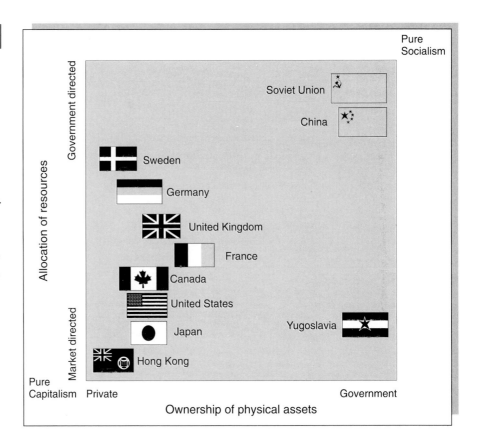

THE SOVIET ECONOMY

The Soviet Union is the largest socialist economy in the world. Except for a few small privately owned service businesses, the government owns and operates almost all of the business–industrial sector, including manufacturing firms, the wholesale and retail network, and the banking, finance, transportation, communications, and agricultural sectors. The government's central planning apparatus establishes production priorities and directs the activities of the government-owned enterprises.

Prodded along by poor economic performance, the socialist structure of the Soviet economy is currently under intense review. In some areas, modest reforms have already been instituted. Neither the current debate nor the prospects for successful reform can be understood without reference to the Soviet system of central planning. Thus, we will begin our analysis of the Soviet economy with a description of the structure of the economy as it existed for four decades following the Second World War.

THE STRUCTURE OF THE SOVIET ECONOMY

Organizationally, the state-operated Soviet economy is similar to a huge vertically and horizontally integrated corporation. Government central planners establish economic policy objectives; allocate resources to business firms (enterprises); and assign the firms directives which they are supposed to implement.

Command Economy:
An authoritarian socialist economy characterized by centralized planning and detailed directives to productive units. Individual enterprises have little discretionary decision-making power.

Gosplan: The central planning agency in the Soviet Union.

Material Balance Method:
A method of central planning employed in the Soviet Union whereby the planning agency keeps track of the physical units of resources and allocates them among state enterprises in a manner that will permit each enterprise to achieve its targeted output and thereby lead to the fulfillment of the economy's central plan.

Since the Soviet economy uses directives rather then prices to allocate resources, it is sometimes referred to as a command economy. A **command economy** is characterized by detailed directives—detailed instructions to productive agents concerning what they are to do and how they are to do it.

The **Gosplan,** the government's central planning agency, drafts the basic plan for the entire economy. This plan takes on the force of law when it is approved by the Soviet government. The central planning agency supplies each of the more than 200,000 Soviet enterprises with a thick document outlining their available resources and production targets. This planning document tells each enterprise what commodities are to be produced, the amounts of labor and raw materials it is allocated, new machinery that should be installed, the timing of available credit, and other operational details. The problem of the enterprise is to transform its allotted inputs into the target output. The operational targets of the annual plan are used as criteria in evaluating the performance of a firm at the end of the planning period and in rewarding it accordingly.

Under Soviet planning, commodities and raw materials are centrally rationed in physical terms. The central planners decide how much of each good will be produced and the quantity of resources, including intermediate goods, that will be used to produce the final output. How do Soviet planners accomplish this task? Essentially, they use the **material balance method** to reconcile the supply and demand for resources. Under this method, the central planning agency prepares a balance sheet of all available resource supplies and sources of resource demand. Beginning with the total supply of all productive resources—labor, raw materials, minerals, imports, and so on—the planning agency allocates these resources to individual enterprises in the quantities it believes will be necessary to produce the enterprise's targeted output. Simultaneously, the central planners assign each enterprise output targets that, when fulfilled, will produce the quantity of each good called for by the central plan. Of course, the Gosplan must ensure that the total quantity of each input allocated to the enterprises (the total demand for the input) balances with the total supply of the input.

Under the material balancing system, the output of one enterprise (steel, for example) is generally the input of another enterprise (a tractor-producing firm, for example). The failure of one firm to meet its production quota sets off a domino effect. Firms that are not supplied with adequate inputs fail to meet their production quotas unless they make adjustments.

The Soviet system of central planning poses an enormous coordination problem. Each enterprise must be supplied with just the right amount of labor and materials at just the right time in order to keep things moving smoothly. If one firm fails to meet its output quota, perhaps as the result of equipment failure or bad weather, other firms will lack the resources required for the achievement of their production targets. Thus, literally billions of output objectives must be both properly interfaced and achieved in a timely fashion. If they are not, the system tends to break down.

Consider the problem that arises if the target output for, say, trucks is increased by 20 percent. The planners must take additional steps to ensure that the truck-producing enterprises receive the right amount of labor, capital equipment, component parts manufactured by other enterprises, and raw materials such as steel, aluminum, glass, and copper. If other suppliers fail to meet their quotas to truck-manufacturing enterprises, the truck manufacturers will also fail to meet their quotas.

It is interesting to compare the response of a market system and a material balance planned system to an imbalance between supply and demand in the resource market. Under market allocation, if there is an excess supply of steel and excess demand for lumber, steel prices will fall and lumber prices will rise. These price changes will motivate literally millions of producers and users of steel and lumber to take the steps needed to restore balance between supply and demand in the two markets. Under material balance planning, an imbalance will trigger administrative action. In response to an excess demand for lumber, the planners could either increase their output target for enterprises producing lumber or reduce the allocation of lumber to enterprises using lumber. If the lumber output targets are increased, then inputs will have to be reallocated from other industries, such as steel, to lumber producers. On the other hand, if the allocation of lumber to users is reduced, planners will have to reduce the output targets of enterprises using lumber. In either case, the plans of numerous enterprises will have to be altered. Each revision will require administrative action at several different levels. Clearly, in a planned system the correction of even a simple supply and demand imbalance is a formidable task, one unlikely to be accomplished quickly.

MOTIVATING SOVIET MANAGERS

Although the central plan is prepared by the planners, it is the responsibility of the enterprise managers to carry out the plan. An incentive structure combining the "carrot" and the "stick" is used to motivate enterprise managers. Both pecuniary and nonpecuniary factors play a role. Managers who meet their production quotas are rewarded with bonuses and promotions. On the other hand, when the output of an enterprise falls short of its production quota, managers are often demoted.

How do the planning authorities know how much an enterprise is capable of producing? Just as a government bureau in the United States has an incentive to confront legislative authorities with the image of an over-worked agency squeezing the maximum output from an unrealistically small budget, so too, do Soviet enterprise managers have an incentive to project this image to the central planners. From the viewpoint of an enterprise manager, the ideal plan is one that provides a quantity of resources such that the firm's output target can be easily achieved. Managers thus have an incentive to provide the central planners with misleading and even false information with regard to the actual productive capability of the firm. Since high-level central planners have limited knowledge of the real output that an efficiently operated firm can achieve in its particular circumstances, they are in a weak position to control the actions of the enterprise managers.

Even if an enterprise manager is able to persuade the planners to provide sufficient resources for the easy achievement of the plan, they are unlikely to exceed the targeted output by much. After all, a large output relative to the target will reveal the true potential of the enterprise and lead to a substantially larger output target next year. Shrewd enterprise managers will prefer to stockpile resources or trade them to other enterprises for future favors, while exceeding this year's target by only a modest margin.

Of course, Soviet leaders are not unaware of these problems. Procedures designed to provide more accurate information and limit collusion have been established. The system, however, makes it difficult to detect misrepresentation and collusive behavior (the Russians call it "familyness") among enterprise managers and low-level planners.

THE GROSS OUTPUT SYSTEM

The Soviet planning system stresses "gross output" rather than value. The enterprises are rewarded on the basis of the weight, surface area, or number of units produced (relative to the target). Whether consumers actually value the output is of little importance to producers. Thus, the variety and quality of products is, at best, a secondary consideration. This focus on gross output leads to numerous anomalies and the wasteful use of resources. Consider the case of an enterprise that produces nails. When the central plan measures output in terms of *weight,* the enterprise will tend to produce mostly large nails. On the other hand, if output is measured in terms of *number* of nails, the enterprise will produce small nails (since they can be produced with a smaller quantity of inputs).

When output is measured in quantitative units rather than in value to users, it is extremely difficult to confront enterprises with a sensible incentive structure. Paul Craig Roberts and Karen LaFollette illustrate this point with regard to the Soviet petroleum industry:

> In the petroleum industry, geologists assigned to drill for oil are rewarded with premiums if they drill a specified number of meters per month. The geologists quite logically react by drilling only shallow holes, since the deeper they go, the slower the progress of the drilling. As a result, some geological expeditions in the Republic of Kazakhstan have not discovered a valuable deposit for many years, but they are considered successful because they have fulfilled their quota in terms of meters drilled. The geologists and ministers are paid handsomely for their efforts, everyone goes out and gets drunk, and no one cares that the whole exercise has been an extraordinary waste of time and money.[3]

Under the gross output planning system, the Soviet enterprise manager has little incentive to improve quality, to innovate, or to experiment with alternative production techniques. The potential gains associated with the discovery of better ways of doing things are small, while the risks are great if an innovative method proves to be a failure. In addition, resource combinations supplied by the central planning authority often limit the adoption of innovative production methods. As long as enterprise managers can get goods past the inspector, there is little incentive to worry about the quality, reliability, or durability of the product.[4]

PRIORITIES UNDER SOVIET PLANNING

With central planning, the allocation of resources is in accordance with the preferences of the planners. In the past, Soviet planners have consistently emphasized two priorities. First, heavy industries such as steel, mining, and

---

[3]Paul Craig Roberts and Karen LaFollette, *Meltdown: Inside the Soviet Economy,* (Washington, D.C.: Cato Institute, 1990), p. 10.

[4]Under the recent openness of the Gorbachev era, the problem of shoddy product quality has been well publicized. The Soviet magazine *Ogonek* reports that exploding TV sets caused 18,000 fires, 512 serious injuries, and 929 deaths between 1980 and 1986. The Soviet Union recently established independent quality inspector groups at 2,300 plants manufacturing consumer goods and machine tools. According to the Soviet press, up to 30 percent of the output in these plants was initially rejected. Seventy percent of the shoes at a factory in Volgograd were rejected and 40 percent of all products from plants in the Ukraine were rejected. As the result of the failure to meet the tighter quality control standards, many plant managers and workers lost bonuses. It remains to be seen whether the new firmness will exert any long-term impact on product quality. In addition to the problem of product quality, many household appliances, including automatic dishwashers and toasters, are simply unavailable in the Soviet Union. Hair dryers are allegedly produced, but no one knows where one could be bought. See Peter Galuszka and Bill Jovetski, "Reforming the Soviet Economy," *Business Week* (December 7, 1987) and Barry Newman, "Russians Want Stuff to Spend Money On," *The Wall Street Journal* (June 17, 1988).

EXHIBIT 3	■	The Functional Use of GNP in the United States and the Soviet Union

The Soviet economy, responding to the views of the planners, allocates a much larger share of GNP to investment and defense.

	Percent Share of Total GNP	
	United States	Soviet Union
Consumption	73	54–58
Defense	6	12–16
Investment	19	25–29
Government administration	3	3

Source: *Economic Report of the President: 1991;* Josef C. Brada and Ronald L. Graves, ''The Slowdown in Soviet Defense Expenditures,'' *Southern Economic Journal,* 54 (April 1988); and Svetozar Pejovich, *A Report Card on Socialism—Life in the Soviet Union* (Dallas: The Fisher Institute, 1979), pp. 65 and 98.

military hardware have been favored over light industries such as textiles and household goods. Second, investment goods have been emphasized relative to consumption goods. As Exhibit 3 shows, the Soviet Union allocates a much larger share of its GNP to investment and military defense and a much smaller share to consumption than does the United States. In fact, the investment rate of the Soviet Union is among the highest in the world. Centralized economic organization enables the planners to emphasize industrialization and capital accumulation, even though this may not reflect the views of the citizens. Current consumption, of course, is sacrificed as a result.

PRICES AND THE ALLOCATION OF SOVIET GOODS

The Soviet Union does use prices to ration goods among consumers. The prices, however, reflect the preferences of planners rather than market forces. Similarly, the supply of goods is determined by the objectives of planners, rather than prices relative to opportunity costs. When a good is in short supply, there is no assurance that more of it will be produced in the future. Neither does the accumulation of a good on the shelves of the state-operated stores necessarily mean that the production of the good will be curtailed.

Exhibit 4 illustrates the forces of supply and demand within the Soviet planning system. Like their counterparts in other countries, Soviet consumers will buy more at lower prices. Thus, the demand curve for goods is a downward sloping curve. The supply for each good, however, is determined by the priorities of the planners. Therefore, it is vertical at the quantity determined by resource scarcity and the decisions of the planners.

The central planners set the prices of more than 200,000 products and resources. Sometimes the planners attempt to set the price of a good at the level that will bring the quantity demanded into line with the available supply (for example, P_e of Exhibit 4). However, this is not always true. Prices of some goods are set at extremely low levels, presumably so that they will be affordable to all. When prices are set below the market clearing level, however, shortages develop and waiting lines form. The price of housing provides an example. Of course, almost all housing is owned by the state and is rented to households at very low prices. But the

EXHIBIT 4

Prices, Shortages, and Surpluses in the Soviet Union

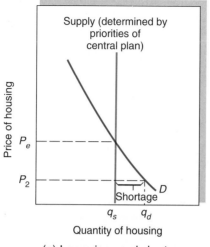

(a) Low prices and shortages

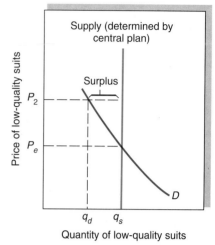

(b) High prices and surpluses

The supply of each good is determined in accordance with the priorities of the central plan. Thus, the supply curve is perfectly inelastic (vertical). However, the demand curve for goods such as housing and clothing will obey the law of demand. Soviet central planners also set the price of goods. Sometimes they will attempt to establish a price (such as P_e) that will equate amount demanded with the available supply. In other cases, the price of a good will be set either below or above equilibrium. When price is set below equilibrium, such as illustrated for the housing market (frame a), shortages and waiting lines will result. In contrast, when the price of a product, such as low-quality suits, is set above equilibrium (frame b), a surplus of unsold goods will develop.

availability of housing is substantially less than the quantity demanded. Thus, families wait for years before an apartment is available.[5] On the other hand, the price of some goods will exceed the equilibrium level. As Exhibit 4b illustrates, above equilibrium prices lead to surpluses (unsold goods). The presence of low-quality, poorly designed goods lingering on the shelves of Soviet stores indicates that the prices of these products exceed the market clearing level.

Until recently, the prices of products in the Soviet Union were seldom changed. Therefore, even if the price of a good approximated an equilibrium price when it was initially established, changing market conditions often resulted in either a shortage or a surplus as the price persisted year after year. Product prices in the Soviet Union do not reflect opportunity costs. In essence, the government supplies some goods at a substantial loss, while others are produced at a huge profit. Again, this incentive structure leads to waste and inefficiency. For example, when the government supplied bread at a price of approximately 3 cents (only a small fraction of its cost), farmers began feeding it to their chickens and hogs. When

---

[5]While the consumption of housing is highly subsidized, recent evidence indicates that the housing shortage in the Soviet Union is more severe than was previously thought. On average, Soviet families have 100 square feet of housing space *per person*. This implies that a typical family of four lives in a twenty foot by twenty foot apartment. In order to apply for a housing upgrade, a family's current per person housing space must be less than 36 square feet (for a family of four, this would imply a space approximately equal to an average-size American bedroom). Nonetheless, the Soviet press recently reported that nearly one-fifth of all Soviet families are wait-listed for a housing upgrade.

undergarments were provided at highly subsidized prices, many consumers bought them, ripped them up, and used the cloth to produce goods ranging from ski hats to bandages which were in short supply.

The results of Soviet price-setting policies are easily observable. Western tourists are nearly always struck by the simultaneous occurrence of (a) lengthy waiting lines, as consumers seek to purchase goods in short supply and (b) state-operated stores overflowing with unpurchased goods, particularly items that are less desired because of their poor quality relative to their price. This combination—shortages of some goods and unsold quantities of others—is precisely what one would expect given the Soviet system of price-fixing.

Hedrick Smith paints a vivid picture of the plight of the Soviet consumer:

> I had heard about consumer shortages before going to Moscow but at first it seemed to me that the stores were pretty well stocked. Only as we began to shop in earnest as a family did the Russian consumer's predicament really come through to me. First, we needed textbooks for our children (who went to Russian schools) and found that the sixth-grade textbooks had run out. A bit later, we tried to find ballet shoes for our 11-year-old daughter, Laurie, only to discover that in this land of ballerinas, ballet shoes size 8 were unavailable in Moscow. . . Goods are produced to fill the Plan, not to sell. Sometimes the anomalies are baffling. Leningrad can be overstocked with cross-country skis and yet go several months without soap for washing dishes. In the Armenian capital of Yenevan, I found an ample supply of accordians but local people complained they had gone weeks without ordinary kitchen spoons or tea samovars. In Rostov, on a sweltering mid-90s day in June, the ice cream stands were all closed by 2 p.m. and a tourist guide told me that it was because the whole area had run out of ice cream, a daily occurrence.[6]

These results are a natural outgrowth of a *centrally imposed* pricing structure.

THE AGRICULTURAL SECTOR IN THE SOVIET UNION

The agricultural sector in the Soviet Union comprises approximately one-fifth of the total economy. Nearly 98 percent of the land under cultivation in the Soviet Union is allocated to large state enterprises and collective farms. Like their counterparts in other areas, the managers and workers in the agricultural sector have little opportunity for independent decision-making. The central plan allocates them resources and assigns them a production quota. The job of the managers and workers is to transform the resources into the assigned output target.

The agricultural sector has consistently been a problem for the Soviet economy. It is easy to see why. Since the workers all receive virtually the same reward, they have little incentive to work intensely and productively. Neither the managers nor the collective farm workers own the farm equipment with which they work. Thus, their incentive to take good care of it and make sure that it is properly maintained is minimal. Since the farms are owned by the state, there is no small group of owners who can gain from lower costs, higher productivity, or a shift in production to a more highly valued product. Given the incentive structure of the collective farming system, the low productivity and perennial crop failures that have beset Soviet agriculture are not surprising.

In addition to regular work assignments, families living on collective farms are permitted to grow products on a small assigned plot—usually one acre in size.

---

[6]Hedrick Smith, *The Russians* (New York: Quadrangle/The New York Times Book Co., Inc., 1976), p. 60. Reprinted by permission of Times Books, a division of Quadrangle/The New York Times Book Co., Inc., New York.

EXHIBIT 5

Agriculture Production on Private Plots in the Soviet Union

Although the private agriculture plots constituted only 1.5 percent of the land under cultivation, output on these plots accounts for approximately 25 percent of the total value of agriculture production. Each year a large share of the aggregate output of several products is produced on these private plots.

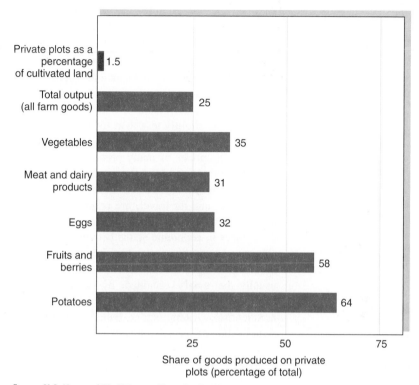

Source: *U.S. News and World Report,* November 9, 1981, p. 41. Also see A. Yemelyanov, ''The Agrarian Policy of the Party and Structural Advances in Agriculture,'' *Problems of Economics* (March 1975), pp. 22–34.

Products raised on the private plots may be consumed or sold in the market at prices determined by the fluctuations of supply and demand. In total, these private plots constitute slightly more than 1 percent of the total agricultural land under cultivation. Nevertheless, as Exhibit 5 illustrates, they account for approximately 25 percent of the total Soviet agricultural output. A major share of the total output of such products as eggs, potatoes, vegetables, fruits, meat, and dairy products is derived from these private plots.[7] Despite their less than optimal size, the private plots are an important source of agricultural production.

INCOME INEQUALITY IN THE SOVIET UNION

How does income inequality in the Soviet Union compare with that in Western nations? Comparable data are difficult to obtain. Exhibit 6 presents data on income shares of low- and high-income households for several countries. These data imply that the degree of income inequality in the Soviet Union is somewhat less than for the United States. After taxes, the bottom 20 percent of households received 8.7 percent of the aggregate personal income in the Soviet Union (1972–1974), compared to only 6.2 percent in the United States (1976). Correspondingly, the top

[7]The fact that more land-intensive agricultural products—grains and cotton, for example—are grown on the collective farms partially accounts for the fact that the productivity of these farms (measured in terms of value per acre) is lower than that of the private plots. However, the large disparity strongly suggests that incentives matter. Apparently, Soviet farmers cultivate the private plots, which generate personal gain, much more intensively than the collective farms, where most of the gains from efficiency accrue to others.

quintile of households received a smaller share of the aggregate income in the Soviet Union than in the United States. Similarly, there also appears to be somewhat less income inequality in the Soviet Union than in Canada.

On the other hand, the distribution of income in the Soviet Union is apparently not much different than in Japan and Sweden. In fact, the *before-tax* distribution of income in Japan is quite similar to the *after-tax* income distribution of the Soviet Union. Perhaps surprising to some, the degree of income inequality in Sweden appears to be slightly less than for the Soviet Union.

Income inequality data in the Soviet Union, though, should be interpreted with caution. The prices of many products purchased intensively by the poor (medical service, clothing, and food) are, relatively speaking, cheaper in the Soviet Union than they are in most Western economies. In contrast, most luxury goods, such as automobiles and air travel, are relatively more expensive in the Soviet Union. As the result of these structural factors, data on income inequality may overstate differences in economic status between the rich and the poor in the Soviet Union. Opposite biases, however, are also present. Soviet elites are often provided with special privileges that do not show up in the income statistics. Automobiles can usually be easily obtained by upper-level bureaucrats and, until recently, Communist party members. Soviet officials and members of favored groups, such as scientists, writers, actors, ballet stars, and economic managers, are granted the right to shop in special stores that offer goods at cut-rate prices and that stock many items unavailable to other citizens. Such products as choice meats, fine wines, fresh fruits and vegetables, French perfumes, Japanese electronic equipment, American cigarettes, and imported clothing are sold in these stores.[8] Since income data do not incorporate privileges of this types, they understate economic inequality in the Soviet Union.

---

[8]See Hedrick Smith, *The Russians*, pp. 26–30.

EXHIBIT 6 ■	The Distribution of Income Shares in the Soviet Union Compared to Selected Market Economies		
	Percentage of Aggregate Income Received		
Country and Year	**Bottom 20% of Households**	**Top 20% of Households**	**Top 10% of Households**
(After Taxes)			
Soviet Union, 1972–1974[a]	8.7	38.5	24.1
United States, 1976	6.2	42.0	—
Sweden, 1972	9.3	35.2	20.5
(Before Taxes)			
Canada, 1987	5.7	40.2	24.1
Japan, 1979	8.7	37.5	22.4

[a]For urban households only.

Source: The after-tax data for the Soviet Union (1972–1974) and Sweden (1972) are from Abram Bergson, "Income Inequality Under Soviet Socialism," *Journal of Economic Literature*, 22 (September 1984). The after-tax data for the United States (1976) are from Edgar K. Browning and Jacquelene M. Browning, *Public Finance and the Price System* (New York: MacMillan Publishing Co., 1983) (Table 8-7). The before-tax data are from *The World Development Report: 1990* (Table 30).

INCOME AND GROWTH IN THE SOVIET UNION

Since the Soviet Union does not use prices to allocate goods and resources, Soviet output cannot easily be compared with the output of market economies. Prior to the late 1980s, leading authorities in both the Soviet Union and the West estimated that the per capita GNP of the Soviet Union was approximately 50 percent of the parallel figure for the United States. Since the population of the Soviet Union is a little larger than the United States, in aggregate, the output of Soviet economy was thought to be between 55 and 60 percent as large as output in the United States.

Recent data accompanying the relaxation of political (and informational) controls in the Soviet Union indicate that these figures substantially over-estimated the size of the Soviet economy. A 1990 detailed study of the Soviet economy undertaken by four prestigious international organizations placed the 1989 per capita GNP of the Soviet Union at $1,780, compared to $20,900 for the United States.[9] Thus, according to this study Soviet output per capita was less than one-tenth of the comparable figure for the United States.

Exhibit 7 sheds light on the level of output and standard of living in the Soviet Union. Economic indicators such as percent of labor force in agriculture and life expectancy tend to reflect the income level of a country. In general, countries with higher income levels will have a smaller percent of their work force in agriculture, a longer life expectancy, and a lower infant mortality rate. Thus, these variables provide us with an indirect indicator of per capita GNP. As Exhibit 7 illustrates, all of the indirect indicators suggest that the per capita income of the Soviet Union is well below the figure for the United States, Western Europe (EEC), and Japan. In fact, the Soviet Union looks more like the World Bank's "upper-middle income countries," a group of countries with an average per capita GNP of $3,240. Data like that of Exhibit 7 have convinced most economists that the upper-bound estimate

[9]International Monetary Fund, The World Bank, Organization for Economic Co-operation and Development, and European Bank for Reconstruction and Development, *The Economy of the USSR* (Washington, D.C.: The World Bank, 1990).

EXHIBIT 7 ■ Economic Indicators: A Comparison of the Soviet Union, United States, European Economic Community (EEC), and Japan					
Economic Indicators	Soviet Union	Upper-Middle Income Countries[a]	United States	EEC[b]	Japan
Percent of labor force in agriculture	19	18	2	4	3
Life expectancy at birth	69	68	76	76	78
Infant mortality rate (per 1000 births)	25	42	10	9	5
Per capita GNP, 1988 (in U.S. dollars)	$1780 to $3500	$3240	$19,840	$11,075	$21,020
Aggregate GNP, 1988 (in trillions of U.S. dollars)	$0.5 to $1.0	—	$4.87	$3.59	$2.58

[a]The *World Development Report: 1990* included countries with a per capita GNP between $2,200 and $6,000 in this category. The following countries comprise the classification: South Africa, Algeria, Hungary, Uruguay, Argentina, Yugoslavia, Gabon, Venezuela, Trinidad and Tobago, South Korea, Portugal, Greece, Oman, Libya, Iran, Iraq, and Romania.

[b]The EEC countries are: Belgium, Denmark, France, Germany, Ireland, Italy, Greece, Netherlands, Portugal, Spain, and the United Kingdom.

Source: World Bank, *World Development Report: 1990* and International Monetary Fund, *The Economy of the USSR*.

of per capita GNP in the Soviet Union is approximately $3,500, less than one-fifth the comparable figure for the United States and Japan. Therefore, the per capita GNP figures imply that the aggregate GNP of the Soviet Union is between $500 billion and $1 trillion, much smaller than the size of the economies of the United States, Western Europe (EEC), and Japan.

Most Soviet watchers thought that the Soviet economy, spurred on by a high rate of capital formation, expanded at an annual rate of approximately 6 percent during the 1950s and 1960s. Given recent income estimates, it now appears that these growth rate estimates were too high. While the precise magnitude of Soviet growth during recent decades is still a topic for debate, a consensus view has emerged on one point: the Soviet growth rate has declined sharply in recent years. As Exhibit 8 illustrates, the average annual growth rate of the Soviet economy during the 1984–1990 period was 1.1 percent, down from 2.0 percent during 1976–1983 and 4.0 percent during 1966–1975. Since the mid-1970s, all of the major industrial market economies have out-performed the Soviet Union. During 1984–1990, the economies of Japan and the United States grew at annual rates of 4.8 percent and 3.4 percent respectively, three to four times the growth rate of the Soviet Union. The recent growth rate of the market economies of Western Europe has also exceeded that of the Soviet Union. Therefore, not only is the per capita income higher for the Western market economies, but the economic gap between these economies and the Soviet Union is widening.

EXHIBIT 8

The Average Annual Growth Rate of Gross National Product for the Major Economic Powers

The average annual growth rate of real GNP for the Soviet Union, United States, Japan, and the European Economic Community for selected periods during 1966–1990 are presented.

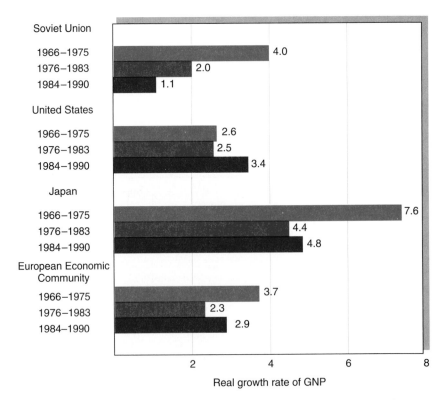

Source: *Economic Report of the President: 1991* (Table B–110).

Why did so many people over-estimate the size of the Soviet economy during the 1970s and 1980s? Three major factors contributed to this over-estimation. First, insufficient allowance was made for the poor product quality that is a predictable occurrence when enterprises are rewarded on the basis of the quantity (''gross output'') produced. Second, physical units of production were counted as output even though consumers would not buy them. Odd shoe sizes, outmoded foot-pedal sewing machines, and bulldozers that were too dangerous to operate and too costly to fix—the resource cost of producing these and numerous other items were added to GNP even though they were essentially worthless. Finally, since enterprises were rewarded on the basis of units produced, there was a strong incentive to pad the figures. Bureaucrats also looked good when the enterprises under their supervision met their quota. Thus, they had little incentive to control fraudulent reporting.

SOVIET ECONOMIC REFORMS DURING THE LATE 1980S

Prodded by slow economic growth, poor quality of goods, and continued shortages in many areas, Soviet leaders adopted several economic reforms during the late 1980s. The common thread running through most of the reforms was decentralization: less reliance on bureaucratic commands and greater freedom of action at the firm level. Let us consider a number of the more significant recent changes in the Soviet economy during this period.

1. An Expansion in the Freedom to Operate Small Private Businesses.   In 1987, the Soviet Union increased the number of categories where private individuals could legally offer their services to consumers. Self-employed individuals were legally allowed to operate taxicabs; tailor clothing; sand floors; and repair appliances, watches, and even automobiles. In all, 40 new categories of services were opened up to private enterprise. In order to operate legally in these areas, individuals needed only a license from the state. Family members were permitted to assist, but the business was not allowed to hire other workers. To a degree, this law merely recognized activities that were already quite widespread. According to recent estimates, several hundred thousand Soviet citizens were engaged in these private business activities by 1991.

2. An Expansion in Business Cooperatives.   Reforms during the late 1980s also permitted private cooperative businesses to operate restaurants, retail stores, small farms, and in some cases, small industrial firms; in essence, these cooperative businesses are joint ventures undertaken by up to 25 people. As of October 1990, there were approximately 250,000 cooperative enterprises employing about 5.2 million workers in the Soviet Union.

In the agricultural sector, the private cooperatives are called ''contract brigades.'' Under this arrangement, a small number of workers, often members of the same family, form a contract brigade which is assigned land by the collective farm. The ''brigade'' must also contract with the collective farm for both productive resources (machinery and fertilizer, for example) and the sale of its output. In turn, the members of the brigade are permitted to keep a share of the profits. To date, these private cooperatives have not caught on in the agricultural sector.[10] Most collective farm members are not anxious to make it easy for a subgroup to break away and enhance their income. This hostility substantially limits the attractiveness of private cooperatives since land, equipment, and other inputs must be obtained from the collective farm.

In recent years, cooperatives have also been operating in the industrial sector. In some cases, former managers of state-enterprises have formed cooperatives in order to lease and operate state-owned plants. However, the legality and future approval of these lease agreements is highly uncertain. Thus, the managers of the leased facilities have a strong incentive to maximize their short-term gain and little incentive to preserve the capital assets of the state.

3. Enterprises Were Given More Discretion in the Late 1980s.   The administration of President Gorbachev moved to expand the discretionary decision-making powers of plant managers and to relax the control of the central planners. Enterprises are now allowed to keep a portion of their net income, rather than return 100 percent of it to the government treasury. These funds may be used to either reward workers or expand productive capacity in ways other than those specified by the central plan. As the net income of enterprises provides a larger share of their investment funds, firms will be better able to produce goods that can be profitably sold, even if their production is not part of the central plan.

4. Price Reforms.   For years, the government has subsidized various goods and, in effect, taxed others at an exorbitant rate. Thus, there was little relationship between price and the production cost of goods in the Soviet Union. Recent price changes were supposed to bring the prices of goods more into line with their production costs. Under 1991 price reforms, the prices of some heavily subsidized staple products, such as bread and milk, did increase sharply. But this was not true for other heavily subsidized goods. In fact, total expenditures on price subsidies were projected to nearly double in 1991.

Under the reforms proposed by President Gorbachev and approved by the Supreme Soviet, eventually state enterprises are supposed to cover their costs, including their cost of capital. In turn, the enterprises would be permitted to charge prices that reflect their cost. To date, however, this has not happened. The state continues to fix the prices of both resources and the products available in the state-operated stores.

THE IMPACT OF THE REFORMS

Despite the reforms of the late 1980s, the Soviet economy continued to decline. The detailed system of central planning collapsed under the weight of both economic stagnation and the internal contradictions of policies. While some of the reforms

---

[10]As of July 1990 (three years after the private cooperatives were approved) there were only 30,000 private farms in the Soviet Union and more than four-fifths of these were in Georgia, Latvia, Lithuania, and Estonia. In contrast, there were fewer than 1,000 private farms in Russia and the Ukraine, even though more than two-thirds of the Soviet population lives in these two republics. Soviet history helps explain the lack of interest in the private agricultural cooperatives. During Lenin's New Economic Policy of the 1920s, the communist government established private property rights in the agriculture sector in order to encourage production. After many farmers expanded their output, both their produce and land were expropriated during the collectivization and Stalinist purges of the 1930s. Many were exiled to labor camps or executed during this era. Given knowledge of these events, the modest interest in private cooperative farms during the late 1980s is certainly understandable.

were positive steps, most reflected compromises with old-guard political leaders and top-level bureau administrators intent upon preserving their political power and that of the Communist Party. Thus, the late 1980s' reforms were half-way measures—a modest relaxation of control within the framework of a socialist, centrally planned economy. Enterprise managers were given more discretion, but the enterprises were not privatized. Central planners sought to bring the prices of goods more into line with their production costs, but prices were not decontrolled. Private farm cooperatives were permitted, but only within the framework of the collectivized agricultural system. Unfortunately, the incentive structure emanating from these half-way measures was often as bad or worse than that of detailed central planning.

Simultaneously, the government instituted other policies that undermined the reforms. During the late 1980s, a large portion of the government investment funds were financed with newly created money, rather than with taxes (or enterprise profits). This rapid expansion in the money supply increased the demand for goods. However, since most prices were fixed by the government, the higher level of demand merely resulted in shortages and longer waiting lines.

In 1991, the government ordered the withdrawal of all large-denomination bills (50- and 100-ruble notes) in circulation and gave people only three days to turn them in. No individual was allowed to exchange more than 1,000 rubles; many were unable to exchange their bills because of long waiting lines and banks that ran out of small-denomination bills. This policy was allegedly an attempt to punish black-marketers and fight inflation. However, its real effects were quite different. It undermined the confidence of people trying to operate businesses within the government's regulatory maze; it confiscated the savings of many Soviet citizens; and it reduced the money supply by approximately 25 percent. Within this environment, the worsening shortages and estimated 15 percent decline in Soviet output during 1990–1991 were understandable.

THE FUTURE OF THE SOVIET UNION

It was against this background that leading officials in the military, KGB, and Soviet central government attempted a coup during August of 1991. When the coup attempt failed, the Communist Party was publicly humiliated, and the democratic forces in the Soviet republics were greatly strengthened. Many old-line Communists, who had been able to weaken and block earlier reforms, were displaced. Many observers now believe that the door is open for real economic reform and the development of a market economy in the Soviet Union (or in several of the republics if the country fragments).

How can the Soviets transform their centrally directed socialist economy into a market economy? Four things are essential for this transition. First, they need to establish private property rights. A market economy cannot exist without private property. With regard to agricultural lands, houses, and small business, the Soviets should be able to move toward privatization quickly. For example, collective farm workers might be given five- or ten-acre plots (instead of the lease rights to a one-acre plot). Larger plots could be sold for a nominal price, auctioned to the highest bidder, or simply given to people willing to work the land for a specified number of years (as in the case of 19th-century homesteading in the United States). Similarly, government-owned housing might be given to people who have lived in the housing for the last five or ten years. Ownership rights to businesses might be given to workers or established through a lottery. The important factor is that private property rights are established. Precisely how they are established is of secondary importance. If assets end up in the hands of people who do not know how to use them wisely, there will be a tendency for resale to move the assets into the hands of better-qualified owners. In contrast with collective ownership, private owners will have a strong incentive to care for and develop property, expand output, strive for business efficiency, and improve the quality of products that they are producing.

Second, privatization and regulations must be supportive of competitive markets. As government-owned businesses are privatized, enterprises in the same industry need to be sold to different owners. Care should be taken to avoid the replacement of a government monopoly with a private monopoly. Restrictions limiting the ability of individuals to start businesses and hire workers need to be removed. Trade restrictions, taxes, and bureaucratic red tape must not limit foreign producers from entry into the Soviet market. Business competition is the life blood of a market economy.

Third, the Soviets must make the ruble fully convertible to hard currencies such as the dollar and the yen. In our modern world, if an economy is going to prosper and expand, it must attract products, investment, and business expertise from around the world. The Soviet economy will be unable to do so without a convertible currency. With free trade and a convertible currency, the relative prices of products traded in international markets will tend to reflect their opportunity cost. Producers will be directed into the production of those goods and services that are most highly valued relative to their costs. However, free trade and a convertible currency will require the Soviet government to abandon its control over prices, something that, as of late 1991, it was unwilling to do.

Finally, the Soviets must develop a capital market, a market capable of channelling savings into profitable investments. In order to do so, a stable currency must be established and strict limitations must be placed on the government's ability to create money. In order to give people confidence in the currency, the government may want to make it freely exchangeable into gold. Regulations limiting the use of stock ownership and bond financing must be removed. Under the socialist system, Soviet planners allocate funds for investment to enterprises. This system elevates the importance of political power, bureaucratic contacts, and out-right corruption. Unsurprisingly, it has not been able to direct funds toward wealth-creating business activities with any degree of consistency. As a result, a large portion of the Soviet investment funds in recent decades has been wasted on projects that transformed valuable resources into worthless (or less valuable) products.

The future of the Soviet economy is also complicated by an important political factor—disunity among the republics. More than 50 years ago, the Baltic states were annexed against their will as the result of an agreement between Stalin and Hitler. These three states (Estonia, Latvia, and Lithuania) declared their independence in 1991. Several other republics have also taken steps toward political independence. The huge Russian republic along with the Ukraine comprise a population of 200 million people, approximately 70 percent of the Soviet population. The future of the union will turn on the actions of these two republics.

Clearly, political controversies about who is in charge are likely to be an important source of economic uncertainty in the foreseeable future. Agreements about the ownership of resources and the legitimacy of rule-making authorities will have to be hammered out both (a) between independent republics and the Soviet Union and (b) among the republics that remain in the union. Will republics that break away be able to establish a sensible monetary policy? Will the central Soviet government be able to establish monetary arrangements that provide decision-makers with confidence? All of these factors are sources of economic uncertainty that, until they are successfully resolved, will impede the potential vitality of the Soviet economy.

Disunity among Soviet republics also raises the issue of trade restrictions. If the republics establish trade restraints that retard the flow of goods, this too will erode potential gains emanating from comparative advantage and the division of labor. From an economic standpoint, the best approach would be a loose federation where the functions of the central government would be limited to (a) the provision of national defense, (b) the establishment of a stable, convertible currency, and (c) the power to prohibit the republics from erecting internal trade barriers. Essentially, this is the model, which is implicit in the U.S. Constitution, that provided the foundation of the 19th-century prosperity of the 13 states and that comprised the original union of the United States. However, there is no assurance that anything approximating this model will evolve out of the current political upheaval in the Soviet Union.

THE CHINESE ECONOMY IN TRANSITION

Following the Second World War, China adopted a system of detailed central planning patterned after the Soviet Union. Prior to 1979, the Chinese economy encompassed the basic features of the Soviet model: state ownership, collectivization of agriculture, government-determined prices, and state directives to enterprises. Except for private agricultural plots, which comprised approximately 7 percent of the Chinese farm land, private enterprise was virtually exterminated from mainland China during the 1950–1978 period.

Following the death of Mao Zedong, the Chinese began to move away from detailed central planning in the late 1970s.[11] The initial reforms focused on agriculture, a sector of the economy that encompasses nearly three-fourths of the Chinese work force. Meeting in December 1978, the Third Plenum of the Eleventh Central Committee of the Communist Party stressed the importance of increasing the material rewards of farmers and expanding agricultural output. Shortly thereafter, reforms were adopted that led to the dismantling of the Chinese system of collective farms.

The Chinese established what they refer to as a "contract responsibility system" in agriculture. Under this system, individual families are permitted to lease land for up to 15 years in exchange for supplying the state with a fixed amount of production at a designated price (which is generally below the market price). Amounts produced over and above the required quota belong to the individual farmer. The output in excess of the production quota may either be consumed or sold at a free market price. In effect, this system of long-term land leases provides farmers with something akin to a private property right. Legal ownership remains with the state, but individual farmers are permitted to lease the land for long periods of time at a predetermined price. The farmer pays a 100 percent tax—the fixed amount of production owed the state for the land—on the first part of the produce,

[11]For additional detail on recent economic developments in China, see Dwight Heald Perkins, "Reforming China's Economic System," *Journal of Economic Literature,* 26 (June 1988), pp. 601–45; Luc DeWulf, "Economic Reform in China," *Finance and Development* (March 1985), pp. 8–11; and Alvin Rabushka, *The New China* (San Francisco: Pacific Institute for Public Policy, 1987).

but no tax at all on what is grown beyond the quota. Thus, the farmer's marginal tax rate is zero. Clearly, this system provides farmers with a strong incentive to produce.

Other reforms were adopted that enhanced the development of markets in agricultural products. Restrictions on individual stock breeding, household sideline occupations, transport of agricultural goods, and trade fairs (marketplaces) were removed. Farmers were permitted to own tractors and trucks, and even hire laborers to work in their "leased" fields. By the late 1980s, less than 15 percent of the grain (rice, wheat, and barley) produced in China was turned over to the state. The rest was marketed privately.

Production in agriculture expanded at an impressive rate as market forces replaced bureaucratic commands. Real output in agriculture expanded at an annual rate of 7 percent during 1980–1988, compared to 3 percent during 1965–1980.[12] Grain production increased by a third. The output of cash products, including cotton, sugar cane, fruits, and meats, increased even more rapidly—approximately doubling during the 1980–1988 period. Suddenly, China had evolved from an importer to an exporter of agricultural products.

The success in agriculture encouraged reforms in other sectors. Restrictions on the operation of small-scale service and retail businesses were relaxed. Private restaurants, stores, and repair shops sprang up and began to compete with state-operated enterprises. The share of total output produced by private enterprises rose from 19 percent in 1979 to 40 percent in 1987. By the mid-1980s, Chinese cities were teeming with side-walk vendors, restaurants, small retail businesses, and hundreds of thousands of individuals providing personal services. After losing their monopoly position, state enterprises began to stay open longer and pay more attention to serving their customers.[13]

Finally, China began to take steps toward greater reliance on markets in the production and distribution of industrial products. Measures incorporated into the Seventh Five-Year Plan (1986–1990) call for prices—whether state-controlled or not—that reflect production costs. The plan recognizes that this will mean increased prices for some commodities that are currently subsidized. In other cases, prices of commodities that are now taxed heavily will decline. Currently, China has a dual allocative system in the industrial sector. More than half of all industrial inputs and outputs continued to be produced and distributed at state administered prices. Many of these state enterprises continue to receive state subsidies and derive investment funds from the government budget (rather than internal financing). Often there is little relationship between the state-mandated prices and opportunity cost. As a result, some firms producing goods in short supply cannot expand because the sale price of their product is set below market equilibrium. Simultaneously, other firms do quite well turning out products with high state-mandated prices that go unsold in the state-operated stores. Moves that reform the industrial pricing system and rely more extensively on market forces have slowed in the industrial sector.

THE CHINESE ECONOMY: TODAY AND TOMORROW

Despite the continued problems with resource allocation in the industrial sector, the recent growth rate of China has been quite impressive. During 1980–1988, real GNP in China increased at an annual rate of 10 percent, compared with 4.5 percent

---

[12]The World Bank, *World Development Report, 1990* (Table 2).

[13]Dwight Heald Perkins, "Reforming China's Economic System," *Journal of Economic Literature* (June 1988), p. 619.

during the 1953–1980 period. The growth of output in the agricultural and service sectors—the two sectors that dominate the economy—was particularly striking. Nonetheless, China is still a very poor country by Western standards. In 1985, the per capita income of China was an estimated $2,444, compared with $12,532 for the United States.[14]

The Chinese economy is now going through a very sensitive period. After years of virtually stable prices (controlled by the state), consumer prices rose at an annual rate of 7.3 percent in 1987. A double-digit inflation rate occurred in 1988. Most economists, including those in China, attribute this inflation to a highly expansive monetary policy. Enterprises seeking funds to cover losses and undertake investments typically go to local banks for loans. An expansion in these loans leads to an increase in the money supply. According to International Monetary Fund data, the money supply in China increased at an annual rate of 26 percent during 1984–1988. Clearly, such rapid expansion in the money supply will generate inflationary pressures.

Even though the inflation emanates from monetary expansion, many people associate it with a general relaxation of government control over the economy. Thus, the inflation tends to weaken the political position of reformers favoring greater reliance on markets. There is already evidence for this. In 1988, the Communist Party Central Committee deferred for at least two years any further action toward the decontrol of prices and decreed that price decontrol would be carried out over a period of 20 years.

What does the future hold for the Chinese economy? Prior to the events of Tiananmen Square during June 1989, most observers believed that the Chinese economy would evolve toward greater reliance upon markets. Clearly, that process has now slowed. Viewing the events of Eastern Europe, powerful political leaders in China are now more fearful, and probably with good reason, that increased reliance upon markets will also mean the loss of political control. As a result, the trend toward markets in China has, at least for now, come to a standstill.

However, strong forces pushing China toward a market economy are still present. The recent failures of the hard-line communist forces in the Soviet Union will almost surely weaken their counterparts in China. China is surrounded by some of the most successful market economies in the world—including Japan, South Korea, Singapore, Taiwan, and Hong Kong. In 1997, the latter will become part of China. In contrast with the Soviet Union, many current-day Chinese have had prior experience with markets and private businesses. This enhances the likelihood of success where markets are adopted. The Chinese have been highly successful as entrepreneurs, developers, and traders throughout the world. In fact, they have succeeded economically just about everywhere *except* mainland China. In a world where the experience of other countries is increasingly visible, the success both of market economies and of people of Chinese descent in other areas strengthens the reform movement and reduces the likelihood that the evolutionary process toward a market economy will be permanently stifled.

---

[14]These figures are from Robert Summers and Alan Heston, "A New Set of International Comparisons of Real Product and Price Levels: Estimates for 130 Countries, 1950–1985," *The Review of Income and Wealth, 34* (March 1988). They were derived by the purchasing power parity method. Estimates derived by the exchange rate conversion method imply that the per capita income in China is substantially less than the above figures, but most economists believe that this method understates income in China. Other economists, however, suspect that output in the centrally planned sector of China is exaggerated, just as it was in the Soviet Union. Thus, the income estimates for China should be interpreted with caution.

EXHIBIT 9 ■ The Japanese "Miracle"			
	United States (1982 dollars)	Japan[a] (1982 dollars)	Japan as a Percentage of United States
Gross National Product (in billions)			
1950	1,204	82	6.8
1960	1,665	191	11.5
1970	2,416	529	21.9
1980	3,187	1,029	32.3
1988	4,017	2,125	52.9
Gross National Product per capita			
1950	7,905	1,004	12.7
1960	9,215	2,046	22.2
1970	11,782	5,007	42.5
1980	13,995	8,803	62.9
1988	16,365	17,336	106.0

[a]The Japanese data were converted to U.S. dollars by the exchange rate conversion method.
Source: U.S. Department of Commerce and *The World Development Report, 1990.*

THE JAPANESE "MIRACLE"

By American and European standards, the Japanese people in 1950 were poor and their methods of production primitive. Forty-two percent of the Japanese labor force was employed in agriculture, compared with 12 percent in the United States.[15] The per capita GNP of Japan was one-eighth that of the United States.

The transformation of the Japanese economy during the last three decades is the success story of the postwar era. Today, the Japanese economy is the third largest in the world, ranking behind only the U.S. and the integrated European economy. Adjusted for inflation, the GNP of Japan grew approximately 9.5 percent annually between 1950 and 1980. During that period, the income of the typical Japanese family, measured in dollars of constant purchasing power, doubled every eight years!

The data of Exhibit 9 illustrate the phenomenal economic growth of Japan. Measured in inflation-adjusted 1982 U.S. dollars, the Japanese per capita GNP in 1950 was $1,004, compared with $7,950 for the United States. During the 1950–1987 period, the real per capita GNP of Japan increased seventeenfold. By 1988, the World Bank data indicate that the *per capita* income of Japan exceeded that of the United States.

The land area of Japan is 10 percent smaller than that of California. Its population is approximately one-half as great as that of the United States. It lacks natural resources; almost all of Japan's petroleum is imported. On the surface, it

---

[15]By 1981, the percentage of the Japanese work force employed in agriculture had declined to 12 percent. Since labor productivity is generally higher in manufacturing than in agriculture, this shift from agriculture contributed to the rapid growth of Japan during 1950–1980.

would appear to be an overpopulated nation, lacking energy and natural resources. How can we explain the economic performance of Japan?

Several factors underlie the Japanese "miracle." Japan's economy is primarily a capitalist market economy. Nevertheless, it differs in several important respects from the market economies of Western Europe and North America. Let us consider some of the unique features of the Japanese economy.

THE JAPANESE LABOR MARKET

Lifetime Employment Commitment: An arrangement offered by most large firms in Japan whereby employees are guaranteed employment until the age 55 unless guilty of misconduct.

In contrast with laborers in most market economies, Japanese workers are intensely loyal to the firms in which they are employed. Two factors appear to explain this loyalty. First, the large Japanese firms make a **lifetime employment commitment** to their employees. After a probationary period, which is usually less than one year, employees acquire tenure. Henceforth, they cannot be discharged except for misconduct (for example, excessive absenteeism, commission of a crime, or fighting on the job). Since seniority largely determines the wage scales of blue- and white-collar workers, the lifetime employment commitment system provides workers with economic security. As long as the firm is able to meet its economic obligations, the employee need not worry about layoffs, unemployment, or loss of income. Of course, the employee may resign, but this is unusual. The tenure of the employee is maintained until he or she reaches the age of 55, when retirement is compulsory.

Second, employee unions in Japan are almost exclusively company unions, and they represent both white- and blue-collar workers rather than particular types of jobs, as in the United States. For this reason, national federations of unions in Japan have little to do with the establishment of compensation and working conditions; these matters are dealt with by labor and management at the company, rather than the industry, level. Approximately one-third of the Japanese labor force is unionized, compared to one-sixth in the United States. In contrast to U.S. labor-management relations, however, the union-management relationship in Japan is characterized by cooperation rather than conflict. Japanese unions often support wage reductions as a means of avoiding employment cutbacks during periods of weak demand for the product of their firm. Thus, unemployment in Japan is substantially lower than it is in the United States.[16] In contrast to the United States and Western European economies, the proportion of managers who are experienced union leaders is high in Japan. Consultation between management and employee representatives is an integral part of Japanese industrial relations. Each has certain areas of control: Unions play an important role in the establishment of wage differentials among jobs; management is given a great deal of flexibility in the assignment of employees, and the movement of employees among positions in the firm is seldom resisted by the union. Areas of joint labor-management consultation include future production plans, projected technological changes, and the transfer of personnel to new plants. Since the long-run economic prospects of employees, including provisions for retirement, are closely tied to the success of the firm, it is not unusual for management and the union to work out a temporary reduction in wages during an economic slowdown or in order to enable the firm to expand into a new market.

---

[16]For example, the Japanese unemployment rate in 1989 was 2.3 percent compared with 5.3 percent in the United States.

Ichiro Nakayama, a senior Japanese labor economist, summed up the labor-management relationship as follows:

> One of the facts that is frequently referred to as the most marked characteristic of labor-management relations in Japan is the relative absence of conflict between employer and worker in all phases of industrial relations. . . . This manifests in various features of the trade union organization known as the enterprise-wide union—for example, the lack of a strong feeling of confrontation at the collective bargaining table, the ambiguous distinction between union membership and employee's status . . . and the importance attached to the system of life-long employment. When compared with those in Western countries, labor-management relations in Japan are conspicuous, in the last analysis, by the common characteristic of a close human relationship between employers and employees.[17]

SAVINGS AND INVESTMENT

The savings and investment rates of Japan are much higher than those of other market economies. Urban workers in Japan save approximately 20 percent of their disposable income. Not surprisingly, the major share of corporate profits is rechanneled into investment. Since the Second World War, nearly one third of the GNP of Japan has been allocated to investment. No democratic market economy has ever chosen to allocate such a large share of its output to capital formation during peacetime.

The Japanese tax structure is at least partially responsible for these high rates of saving and investment. Capital gains derived from the sale of securities are not taxed in Japan. Businesses and land capital gains are taxed at much lower rates than they are in Western countries. Interest and dividends are taxed at a maximum rate of 25 percent, compared to marginal tax rates of 50 percent and more for income derived from interest and dividends in most Western nations. A system of tax credits encourages various forms of savings.

TAXES IN JAPAN

Although the Japanese tax structure is progressive, there are so many exemptions that high marginal rates can generally be avoided, particularly if one is willing to save. Until recent years, taxes were substantially lower in Japan than in the United States, Canada, and Western Europe. During the past decade, the size of the public sector has grown substantially in Japan. Thus, the "tax gap" between other industrial nations and Japan has narrowed. As Exhibit 10 illustrates, however, taxes still consume a smaller share of GNP in Japan than in any other market-directed economy except the United States. In 1988, tax revenues accounted for 29 percent of GNP in Japan, compared to approximately 40 percent in France, the United Kingdom, and West Germany and nearly 50 percent in Sweden. Many believe that low tax rates, particularly during the 1950–1976 period, have contributed to the impressive growth record of Japan.

THE ECONOMIC FUTURE OF JAPAN

In recent years, the phenomenal growth rate of Japan has slowed. The Japanese real GNP expanded at an annual rate of 4.6 percent during 1976–1990, compared with 7.6 percent during 1966–1975. Nevertheless, Japan is still growing more rapidly than any other major industrial nation (see Exhibit 8).

---

[17]As quoted in Hugh Patrick and Henry Rosovsky (eds.), *Asia's New Giant* (Washington, D.C.: Brookings Institution, 1976), p. 639.

EXHIBIT 10 ■ Taxes in Selected Western Countries, 1988	
Country	Tax Revenues as a Percentage of GNP, 1988
Sweden	49.3
France	41.5
West Germany	38.8
United Kingdom	37.1
Japan	29.2
United States	27.9

Source: International Monetary Fund, *Government Finance Statistics Yearbook 1990.*

The slowdown of the Japanese economy from the lofty growth records of 1950–1975 period was expected. During the 1950s and 1960s, Japan was able to profit by drawing on the technology and methods of production of more advanced countries.[18] Since Japanese manufacturing is now as modern as that of other industrial economies, this potential source of growth is no longer present. There is reason to question whether the Japanese growth rate will return to the levels of the 1960s. As real incomes of Japanese workers continue to expand, they are likely to opt for a shorter work week and longer vacations in the future. An increase in environmental pollution has accompanied Japan's rapid growth. The Japanese will probably allocate more resources to pollution control as their standard of living rises. These factors will most likely cause the growth rate of the Japanese GNP to fall well below the rate of the 1950–1975 period.

SOCIALISM AND CAPITALISM

Until recently, it was widely believed that centrally planned socialist economies were able to deliver the goods. Some economists even argued that it was only a matter of time before output in the Soviet Union would overtake the United States and Western Europe. The socialist model was thought to be particularly attractive for developing countries wanting to increase their standard of living rapidly. We are now in the midst of a widespread re-evaluation of these views.

Given differences in natural resources, cultural characteristics, and historical experiences among countries, it is not easy to isolate the importance of economic organization. However, there are a few cases where *similar people* have opted for alternative forms of economic organization in recent decades. For example, the resource endowments and cultural characteristics of the population are similar between North Korea and South Korea, China, and Hong Kong (and Taiwan), and what was, prior 1990, East Germany and West Germany. Though similar in many other respects, these countries have had different forms of economic organization

[18]A study by the Brookings Institution found that the major determinants of the growth rate differential between Japan and other major market economies were (a) rapid capital formation, (b) advances in knowledge and technology, and (c) economies of scale. See Edward F. Denison and William K. Chung, ''Economic Growth and Its Source,'' in Patrick and Rosovsky, *Asia's New Giant.*

during the last four decades. Did these differences in economic organization affect economic conditions?

Economic indicators suggest that they did. Recent data indicates that, prior to their unification, the per capita GNP of West Germany was approximately twice the comparable figure for East Germany. Similarly, in 1988 the per capita income levels for the predominantly market economies of South Korea, Hong Kong, and Taiwan were two or three times the parallel figures for North Korea and China. Comparison of data on life expectancy, infant mortality rates, and the share of the labor force in agriculture also indicates that the market economies of West Germany, South Korea, Hong Kong, and Taiwan delivered a higher standard of living during the post-Second World War period than their socialist counterparts in East Germany, North Korea, and China.

Income comparisons like these, along with recent information indicating that living standards in the Soviet Union are much lower than was previously thought, have caused many to question whether detailed central planning can deliver rapid economic growth, quality products, and sustained prosperity. (See Chapter opening quotation of Robert Heilbroner, one of the leading defenders of socialism during the 1970s and most of the 1980s.) No socialist country has been able to provide the abundance and diversity of goods and services available to consumers in the high-tech industrial market economies of North America, Western Europe, and Japan. Neither has any less-developed socialist economy been able to match the impressive growth rates of the market-directed economies of Hong Kong, Singapore, South Korea, Taiwan, and Indonesia during the 1975–1990 period, to say nothing of the post-1950 record of Japan.

The economic performance of socialism should not come as a surprise to those who believe that incentives exert a powerful influence on human behavior. If we are going to make the most of our resources, goods must be produced efficiently (at a low cost); resources must be used to produce things that people value; and investments must be channeled into activities that are wealth-creating (that increase the value of resources). These laws of economics apply to all economies — capitalist and socialist alike.

From the standpoint of economic efficiency, the problem with socialism is the structure of incentives. Compared with their market counterparts, the managers of government-operated firms have less incentive to keep production costs down and respond to the preferences of consumers. Neither do they have much incentive to innovate — to figure out better ways of doing things. While a centrally planned economy can channel resources disproportionally into investment, there is no assurance that the funds will be invested wisely. Socialist economies do not have a mechanism like the capital market that is capable of assuring that investments will be directed toward wealth-creating projects. When politics replaces profit in the allocation of investment funds, projects that reduce (rather than enhance) the value of resources are far more likely to occur and persist into the future. Finally, when property rights are clearly defined, there are good reasons to believe that market prices will more closely reflect the marginal opportunity cost of goods than prices set by government planners. Thus, resources are more likely to be directed toward projects that are highly valued relative to their cost under markets than under central planning. Compared to socialism, markets provide a stronger incentive for (1) firms to produce efficiently, (2) investment funds to be allocated productively, and (3) enterprises to produce things that consumers value highly (relative to their costs).

Given this incentive structure, it would be surprising if the economic performance of market economies were not superior to that of socialist economies.

Of course, a comparison of economic systems involves more than material goods and economic data. One's view of human nature, personal freedom, and equality are also important considerations. However, recent events in socialist countries highlight the importance of economic performance. Clearly, disappointment in the economic record of socialism has been a driving force for economic change in China, Eastern Europe, and the Soviet Union. It is not obvious where these changes will lead. But one thing is certain: analysis of these changes will be an integral and exciting part of economics in the 1990s.

CHAPTER SUMMARY

1. Basic economic concepts, such as opportunity cost, diminishing marginal returns, comparative advantage, and the law of demand apply to socialist and capitalist economies alike. Different forms of economic organization can change the incentives faced by decision-makers (for example, managers and workers), but basic economic principles do not differ from one type of economy to another.

2. Capitalist economies are characterized by private ownership of productive assets and the use of markets to allocate goods and resources. The distinguishing characteristics of socialist economies are government ownership of physical capital and resource allocation by central planning.

3. The Soviet Union is the largest socialist economy in the world. Except for a few small, privately owned service businesses, the government owns and operates almost all business enterprises. The Gosplan, a central planning agency, presents state enterprises with an allocation of inputs and target levels for output. Key commodities and raw materials are centrally rationed in physical terms. The rewards of managers and workers are affected by their success at meeting the targets of the central planning authority.

4. The Soviet planning system stresses "gross output," rather than value. Since Soviet enterprises are rewarded on the basis of their output relative to their production target, they have little incentive to improve quality, to innovate, or to discover superior production procedures.

5. The supply of goods in the Soviet Union is determined by the priorities of the central plan. While prices are used to ration goods among consumers, the prices reflect the preference of planners rather than market forces. Planners do not necessarily expand the production of goods in short supply. Neither do they necessarily curtail production when inventories accumulate in state stores. Sometimes the planners will attempt to set the price of a good at a level that will bring the quantity demanded into balance with the available supply. However, this is not always the case. Shortages and surpluses occur when the planners set the prices of various goods either below or above the market-clearing price.

6. Approximately 98 percent of the land under cultivation in the Soviet Union is allocated to state enterprises and collective farms. This system of collectivization in agriculture does not provide much incentive for workers to produce, conserve resources, or take good care of the equipment with which they work. Therefore, the productivity on the collective farms is low. Even though small, private plots constitute slightly more than 1 percent of the land under cultivation in the Soviet Union, they have accounted for approximately one fourth of the total value of Soviet agricultural production in recent years.

7. The distribution of income in the Soviet Union is probably less unequal than for the United States. The distribution of income shares in Japan and Sweden, however, appears to be quite similar to that of the Soviet Union.

8. The per capita GNP of the Soviet Union is substantially lower than was thought during the 1970s and 1980s. Recent estimates indicate that the per capita GNP of the Soviet Union is approximately one-fifth that of the United States and Japan, and one-third that of the European Economic Community. The growth rate of the Soviet economy has fallen sharply in recent years, plunging to only about 1 percent during 1984–1990.

9. Slow economic growth, poor quality of goods, and shortages of many products provided the foundation for economic reforms in the Soviet Union in the late 1980s. These reforms expanded the number of categories where small-scale private businesses were permitted, encouraged the development of private cooperative businesses, and expanded the discretionary decision-making powers of plant managers.

10. The reforms of the late 1980s were half-way measures that failed to correct the basic problems of the Soviet planning system. In the aftermath of the failed coup attempt of August 1991, more meaningful reforms may now be possible. However, political disunity and uncertainty about the future direction of economic policy cloud the future of the Soviet economy.

11. For three decades following the Second World War, the Chinese economy was characterized by Soviet-style detailed central planning. Beginning in the late 1970s, China began to move away from collectivism and toward market allocation. A system of long-term land leases to family farmers replaced collectivization in agriculture. Restrictions limiting the operation of small-scale service and retail businesses were relaxed. Some industrial prices were deregulated. Rapid growth of GNP, particularly in the agricultural and service sectors, accompanied the recent reforms of the Chinese economy. However, the political unrest of the late 1980s has, for now, brought the movement toward a market economy in China to a halt.

12. The growth record of Japan has been the most impressive of the major industrial nations during the postwar period. The following factors have contributed to this rapid growth:

    a. institutional arrangements that have encouraged harmonious labor-management relations,

    b. very high rates of saving and capital formation, and

    c. low tax rates.

CRITICAL ANALYSIS QUESTIONS

1. Compare and contrast the role of business managers of firms in the United States and the Soviet Union. In which country would managers have the greatest incentive to operate the firm efficiently?

2. What do you think are the major advantages of a centrally planned economy? What are the major disadvantages? Do you believe that market allocation is superior or inferior to centralized planning? Explain your answer.

3. Under the Soviet planning system, the managers of state enterprises are told what resources to use, what price to charge, and how many units to produce. Why aren't instructions of this type given to owners and managers of firms in a market setting? Who controls the actions of firms in a market economy?

4. "Socialism means production for use, not for profit. Workers contribute according to their qualifications, and they are rewarded according to egalitarian principles. Socialism takes power from the business elite and grants it to the workers, who, after all, produce the goods." Analyze this point of view.

*5. What major factors have contributed to the rapid economic growth of Japan? Do you think the Japanese economy will grow as rapidly in the future as it has in the past? Why or why not?

6. Do you think the United States should encourage firms to adopt the lifetime employment commitment offered by the major firms in Japan? Why or why not? What are the advantages and disadvantages of this system?

*7. **What's Wrong with This Way of Thinking?**
"Central planning makes it possible for an economy to invest more and to expand at a more rapid rate. Consumer incomes, stimulated by the high rates of capital formation, also increase rapidly. Thus, the consumer is the major beneficiary of central planning, which stresses a rapid rate of capital formation."

*8. "Capitalism is better at producing wealth; socialism is better at distributing it fairly." Evaluate.

9. What major economic reforms have recently taken place in China? What have been the effects of these reforms?

*10. Socialists often claim that under capitalism resources are wasted producing luxury goods for the rich. Evaluate the charge.

11. If the investment funds of a country are going to promote prosperity, they must be directed toward the production of goods that are valued more highly than the resources used in their production. Why is this important? Will additional investment always increase the wealth of a nation? Explain.

12. Suppose you were hired as a consultant to develop a comprehensive economic reform plan that would improve the standard of living in the Soviet Union. What *specific* reforms would you suggest? Indicate why you think they would be effective.

---

*Asterisk denotes questions for which answers are given in Appendix C, Selected Answers.

APPENDIX A

Production Theory and Isoquant Analysis

When analyzing production theory and input utilization, economists often rely on isoquant analysis. Since the technique is widely used at the intermediate level, some instructors explain the concept in their introductory course.

WHAT ARE ISOQUANTS?

Generally, several alternative input combinations can be used to produce a good. For example, 100 bushels of wheat might be produced with 2 acres of land, 5 bushels of seed, and 100 pounds of fertilizer. Alternatively, the wheat could be produced with more land and less fertilizer, or more seed and less land, or more fertilizer and less seed. Many input combinations could be used to produce 100 bushels of wheat.

Isoquant: A curve representing the technically efficient combinations of two inputs that can be used to produce a given level of output.

The word "isoquant" means "equal quantity." An **isoquant** is a curve that indicates the various combinations of two inputs that could be used to produce an equal quantity of output. Exhibit 1 provides an illustration. The isoquant labeled "100 units of cloth" shows the various combinations of capital and labor that a technically efficient producer could use to produce 100 units of cloth. Every point on an isoquant is technically efficient. By that we mean that it would not be possible, given the current level of technology, to produce a larger output with the input combination. If a producer wanted to produce a larger output, 140 units of cloth, for example, it would be necessary to use more of at least one of the resources. Since larger output levels require additional resources, isoquants representing larger levels of output always lie to the northeast of an isoquant diagram.

CHARACTERISTICS OF ISOQUANTS

Isoquant analysis must be consistent with the laws of production. What do the laws of production imply about the characteristics of isoquants?

1. *Isoquants Slope Downward to the Right.* Within the relevant range of utilization, an increase in the usage level of an input makes it possible to expand output. If, for example, the use of the labor input is expanded, it is possible to produce the same output level (stay on the same isoquant) with a smaller quantity of capital. Since both labor and capital can be used to increase production, they can be substituted for each other. Constant output can be maintained either by (a) using more labor and less capital or (b) by using more capital and less labor. Thus, every isoquant runs from the northwest to the southeast, as illustrated by Exhibit 1.

2. *Isoquants Are Convex When Viewed from the Origin.* The convexity of isoquants stems from the fact that as one continues to substitute labor for capital, larger and larger amounts of labor are required to maintain output at a constant level. As labor is used more intensively, it becomes increasingly difficult to substitute labor for each additional unit of capital. Since larger and larger amounts of labor are required to compensate for the loss of each additional unit of capital (and thus maintain the constant level of output), the isoquant becomes flatter as labor is used more intensively (see Exhibit 2, point B).

On the other hand, when capital is used more and more intensively, larger and larger amounts of capital are required to compensate for the loss of a unit of labor. Thus, an isoquant becomes steeper as capital (the *y* factor) is used more intensively (see Exhibit 2, point *A*). It is convex when viewed from the origin.

EXHIBIT 1

The Isoquant

An isoquant represents all input combinations that, if used efficiently, will generate a specific level of output. As illustrated here, 100 units of cloth could be produced with the input combinations L_1K_1 or L_2K_2 or any other combination of labor and capital that lies on the isoquant representing 100 units of cloth.

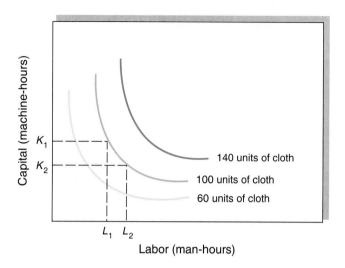

3. *The Slope of the Isoquant Is the Marginal Product of Labor Divided by the Marginal Product of Capital.* The slope of the isoquant is determined by the amount of labor that must be added to maintain a constant level of output when one less unit of capital is used. This slope is dependent on the marginal productivity of labor relative to capital. When labor is used intensively relative to capital, its marginal product is low, relative to capital. Under these circumstances, as Exhibit 2 (point B) illustrates, the slope of the isoquant is small (the isoquant is relatively flat). In contrast, when capital is used intensively (Exhibit 2, point A), the marginal product of labor is high, relative to capital. The steepness of the isoquant reflects this fact. At any point on the isoquant, the slope of the isoquant is equal to MP_L/MP_K.

EXHIBIT 2

Convexity and the Slope of the Isoquant

When labor is used intensively relative to capital (point B), the slope of the isoquant is much flatter than it is when capital is used more intensively (point A). The slope of an isoquant is the ratio of the marginal products of the two factors (MP_L divided by MP_K). When labor is used more intensively relative to capital, its marginal product falls (and that of capital increases). Since the marginal product of labor is low (and the marginal product of capital is high) when labor is used intensively (as at point B), the isoquant is relatively flat.

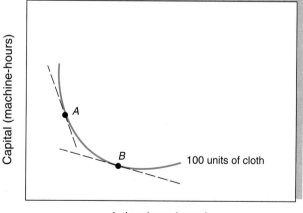

THE ISOCOST LINE

Isocost Line: A line representing the various combinations of two factors that can be purchased with a given money budget (cost).

A set of isoquants outlines the technically efficient input combinations that could be used to produce alternative levels of output. Before we can determine the economically efficient input combination for producing a level of output, we must also incorporate information about cost and resource prices.

Firms generally can purchase inputs at a fixed price per unit. The **isocost line** shows the alternative combinations of inputs that can be purchased with a given outlay of funds. As the term implies, the cost of purchasing an input combination on the isocost line is equal to the cost of purchasing any other input combination on the same line. To construct an isocost line, two pieces of information are required: (a) the prices of the resources and (b) the specific outlay of funds. Exhibit 3 illustrates the construction of three different isocost lines, assuming that the price of labor is $5 per unit and that the price of capital is $10 per unit. Consider the $500 isocost line. If all funds were spent on labor, 100 units of labor could be purchased. Alternatively, if the entire $500 were expended on capital, 50 units of capital could be purchased. It would be possible to purchase any input combination between these two extremes—for example, 80 units of labor and 10 units of capital—with the $500. The input combinations are represented by a line connecting the two extreme points, 100 units of labor on the *x*-axis and 50 units of capital on the *y*-axis. Note that the slope of the isocost line is merely the price of labor divided by the price of capital (P_L/P_K).

If the outlay of funds were to increase, it would be possible to purchase more of both labor and capital. Thus, as Exhibit 3 illustrates, the isocost lines move in a northeast direction as the size of the outlay of funds increases.

MINIMIZING THE COST OF PRODUCTION

A profit-seeking firm will want to choose the minimum-cost method of production. We can combine isoquant analysis and the isocost line to derive the minimum-cost input combination for producing a given output level. As Exhibit 4 illustrates, the

EXHIBIT 3

The Isocost Line

The isocost line indicates the alternative combinations of the resources that can be purchased with a given outlay of funds. When the price of a unit of labor is $5 and that of a unit of capital is $10, the three isocost lines shown here represent the alternative combinations of labor and capital that could be purchased at costs of $500, $1000 and $1500. The slope of the isocost line is equal to P_L/P_k ($5/$10 = ½ in this case).

EXHIBIT 4

The Cost-Minimization Resource Combination

When the cost of producing an output level (for example, 100 units of cloth) is minimized, the isoquant is tangent to the isocost line. At that point (A), $MP_L/MP_K = P_L/P_K$.

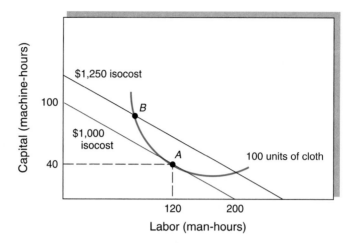

minimum-cost input combination for producing 100 units of cloth is represented by the point at which the lowest isocost line just touches (is tangent to) the isoquant for 100 units of cloth. At that point (*A* of Exhibit 4), the producer will be able to combine 120 units of labor purchased at a cost of $600 ($5 per unit) with 40 units of capital purchased at a cost of $400 ($10 per unit) to produce 100 units of cloth. The total cost of the 100 units is $1,000 ($10 per unit).

Of course, other input combinations could be used to produce the 100 units of cloth. However, they would be more costly, given the current prices of labor and capital. For example, if the input combination *B* were used to produce the 100 units, the total cost would be $1,250 ($12.50 per unit).

When costs are at a minimum, the isoquant is tangent to the isocost line. The slopes of the two are equal at that point. In other words, when the cost of producing a specific output is at a minimum, the MP_L/MP_K (the slope of the isoquant) will be equal to P_L/P_K (the slope of the isocost line). Since:

$$\frac{MP_L}{MP_K} = \frac{P_L}{P_K}$$

then:

$$\frac{MP_L}{P_L} = \frac{MP_K}{P_K}$$

The latter equation represents precisely the condition that our earlier analysis, in the chapter devoted to supply of and demand for productive resources, indicated would be present if the cost of production were at a minimum.

The isoquant analysis indicates that when a firm chooses the minimum-cost method of production, the ratio of the price of labor to the price of capital will equal the ratio of the marginal productivities of the factors. This makes good economic sense. It implies, for example, that if capital is twice as expensive per unit as labor, the firm will want to substitute the cheaper labor for capital until the marginal product of capital is twice that of labor.

COST MINIMIZATION AND CHANGES IN RESOURCE PRICES

The minimum-cost input combination is dependent on both (a) the technical relationship between the productive inputs and output, as illustrated by the isoquant, and (b) the price of the factors, represented by the isocost line. If the ratio of the price of labor to the price of capital changes, the minimum-cost input combination will be altered.

Exhibit 5 illustrates this point. Exhibit 4 shows that if the price of labor were $5 and the price of capital were $10, the minimum-cost input combination to produce 100 units of cloth would be 120 units of labor and 40 units of capital. The total cost of the 100 units would be $1,000. Exhibit 5 indicates what would happen if the price of labor increased from $5 to $10. At the higher price of labor, a $1,000 outlay of funds would now purchase only 100 units of labor, (rather than 200). As a result of the increase in the price of labor, the isocost line would become steeper, as indicated by the change in isocost lines from *MN* to *OP*. The lowest isocost line that is tangent to the isoquant for 100 units would now be *OP*. The new minimum-cost input combination would be 90 units of labor and 60 units of capital. Cost-minimizing producers would substitute capital for labor. The cost of producing the 100 units would rise (from $1,000 to $1,500).

THE SIGNIFICANCE OF ISOQUANT-ISOCOST ANALYSIS

Isoquant-isocost analysis is most applicable in the long run, when all factors are variable and the possibilities for substitution are greatest. It is a conceptual tool, more suitable for illustrating principles than for solving management problems. Few firms would try to design their production activities by drawing isoquants, although some managers might make mental use of the model to design numerical techniques for minimizing costs. In any case, firms that do maximize profits behave as though they were using the analysis.

Isoquant-isocost analysis helps clarify the production conditions that must be met if a firm is to minimize its production cost and get the largest possible output from a specific outlay of funds.

EXHIBIT 5

The Impact of an Increase in the Price of a Resource

The slope of the isocost line increases as the price of a unit of labor rises from $5 to $10. As a result of the increase in the price of labor, (a) cost-minimizing producers substitute capital for the more expensive labor, and (b) the minimum cost of producing 100 units of cloth rises.

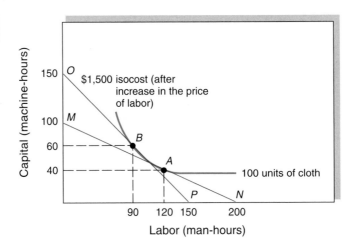

APPENDIX B

General Business and Economic Indicators

| SECTION 1   ■   National Income and Product Accounts* | | | | | | | | |

	The Sum of These Expenditures				EQUALS	LESS	EQUALS	LESS	EQUALS
	Personal Consumption Expenditure	Gross Private Domestic Investment	Government Purchases of Goods and Services	Net Export of Goods and Services	Gross National Product (GNP)	Capital Consumption Allowances	Net National Product (NNP)	Indirect Business Taxes	National Income
Year				*Billions of Dollars*					
1929	77.3	16.7	8.9	1.1	103.9	9.9	94.0	7.1	84.7
1930	69.9	10.3	9.2	1.0	90.4	8.0	82.4	7.2	75.4
1932	48.6	1.0	8.1	0.4	58.0	7.4	50.7	6.8	42.8
1933	45.8	1.6	8.3	0.4	56.0	7.6	48.4	7.1	39.4
1934	51.3	3.3	9.8	0.6	65.1	6.8	58.2	7.8	49.5
1936	61.9	8.5	12.0	0.1	82.5	7.0	75.4	8.7	65.0
1938	63.9	6.5	13.0	1.3	84.7	7.3	77.4	9.2	67.4
1939	67.0	9.5	13.6	1.2	91.3	9.0	82.3	9.4	71.2
1940	71.0	13.4	14.2	1.8	100.4	9.4	91.1	10.1	79.6
1941	80.8	18.3	25.0	1.5	125.5	10.3	115.3	11.3	102.8
1942	88.6	10.3	59.9	0.2	159.0	11.3	147.7	11.8	136.2
1943	99.5	6.2	88.9	−1.9	192.7	11.6	181.1	12.8	169.7
1944	108.2	7.7	97.1	−1.7	211.4	12.0	199.4	14.2	182.6
1945	119.6	11.3	83.0	−0.5	213.4	12.4	201.0	15.5	181.6
1946	143.9	31.5	29.1	7.8	212.4	14.2	198.2	17.1	180.7
1947	161.9	35.0	26.4	11.9	235.2	17.6	217.6	18.4	196.6
1948	174.9	47.1	32.6	7.0	261.6	20.4	241.2	20.1	221.5
1949	178.3	36.5	39.0	6.5	260.4	22.0	238.4	21.3	215.2
1950	192.1	55.1	38.8	2.2	288.3	23.6	264.4	23.4	239.8
1951	208.1	60.5	60.4	4.5	333.4	27.2	306.2	25.3	277.3
1952	219.1	53.5	75.8	3.2	351.6	29.2	322.5	27.7	291.6
1953	232.6	54.9	82.8	1.3	371.6	30.9	340.7	29.7	306.6
1954	239.8	54.1	76.0	2.6	372.5	32.5	340.0	29.6	306.3
1955	257.9	69.7	75.3	3.0	405.9	34.4	371.5	32.2	336.3
1956	270.6	72.7	79.7	5.3	428.2	38.1	390.1	35.0	356.3
1957	285.3	71.1	87.3	7.3	451.0	41.1	409.9	37.4	372.8
1958	294.6	63.6	95.4	3.3	456.8	42.8	414.0	38.6	375.0
1959	316.3	80.2	97.9	1.5	495.8	44.6	451.2	41.7	409.2
1960	330.7	78.2	100.6	5.9	515.3	46.4	468.9	45.3	424.9

	The Sum of These Expenditures				EQUALS	LESS	EQUALS	LESS	EQUALS
	Personal Consumption Expenditure	Gross Private Domestic Investment	Government Purchases of Goods and Services	Net Export of Goods and Services	Gross National Product (GNP)	Capital Consumption Allowances	Net National Product (NNP)	Indirect Business Taxes	National Income
Year				*Billions of Dollars*					
1961	341.1	77.1	108.4	7.2	533.8	47.8	486.1	48.0	439.0
1962	361.9	87.6	118.2	6.9	574.6	49.4	525.2	51.5	473.0
1963	381.7	93.1	123.8	8.2	606.9	51.4	555.5	54.6	500.3
1964	409.3	99.6	130.0	10.9	649.8	53.9	595.9	58.7	537.6
1965	440.7	116.2	138.6	9.7	705.1	57.4	647.7	62.5	585.2
1966	477.3	128.6	158.6	7.5	772.0	62.1	709.9	65.2	642.0
1967	503.6	125.7	179.7	7.4	816.4	67.4	749.0	70.1	677.7
1968	552.5	137.0	197.7	5.5	892.7	73.9	818.7	78.7	739.1
1969	597.9	153.2	207.3	5.6	963.9	81.4	882.5	86.3	798.1
1970	640.0	148.8	218.2	8.5	1,015.5	88.8	926.6	94.0	832.6
1971	691.6	172.5	232.4	6.3	1,102.7	97.5	1,005.1	103.4	898.1
1972	757.6	202.0	250.0	3.2	1,212.8	107.9	1,104.8	111.1	994.1
1973	837.2	238.8	266.5	16.8	1,359.3	118.1	1,241.2	120.8	1,122.7
1974	916.5	240.8	299.1	16.3	1,472.8	137.5	1,335.4	129.0	1,203.5
1975	1,012.8	219.6	335.0	31.1	1,598.4	161.8	1,436.6	140.0	1,289.1
1976	1,129.3	277.7	356.9	18.8	1,782.8	179.2	1,603.6	151.7	1,441.4
1977	1,257.2	344.1	387.3	1.9	1,990.5	201.5	1,789.0	165.7	1,617.8
1978	1,403.5	416.8	425.2	4.1	2,249.7	229.9	2,019.8	178.1	1,838.2
1979	1,566.8	454.8	467.8	18.8	2,508.2	265.8	2,242.4	189.4	2,047.3
1980	1,732.6	437.0	530.3	32.1	2,732.0	303.8	2,428.1	213.3	2,203.5
1981	1,915.1	515.5	588.1	33.9	3,052.6	347.8	2,704.8	251.5	2,443.5
1982	2,050.7	447.3	641.7	26.3	3,166.0	383.2	2,782.8	258.8	2,518.4
1983	2,234.5	502.3	675.0	−6.1	3,405.7	396.6	3,009.1	282.6	2,719.5
1984	2,430.5	664.8	735.9	−58.9	3,772.2	415.5	3,356.8	331.9	3,028.6
1985	2,629.0	643.1	820.8	−78.0	4,014.9	437.2	3,577.6	333.6	3,234.0
1986	2,797.4	659.4	872.2	−97.4	4,231.6	460.1	3,771.5	348.9	3,412.6
1987	3,009.4	699.5	921.4	−114.7	4,515.6	487.0	4,028.6	367.8	3,660.3
1988	3,238.4	747.1	962.5	−74.1	4,873.7	514.3	4,359.4	388.7	3,984.9
1989	3,450.1	771.2	1,025.6	−46.1	5,200.8	554.4	4,646.4	414.0	4,223.3
1990	3,657.3	741.0	1,098.1	−31.2	5,465.1	575.6	4,889.5	469.4	4,420.1

*Details may not add to totals due to rounding and to minor statistical discrepancies.
Source: *Economic Report of the President, 1991* and *Economic Report of the President, 1970*.

SECTION 2   ■   Real Output and Prices

	GROSS NATIONAL PRODUCT, 1929–1990			PRICE INDEXES: 1929–1990			
				GNP Deflator		Consumer Price Index	
Year	1982 Prices (billions of dollars)	Annual Real Rate of Growth	Real GNP Per Capita (1982 dollars)	Index (1982 = 100)	Annual Percentage Change	Index (1982–84 = 100)	Annual Percentage Change (Dec. to Dec)
1929	709.6	-	5,828	14.6	-	17.1	0.0
1930	640.0	−9.8	5,243	14.2	−3.2	16.7	−2.5
1931	587.2	−8.2	4,735	12.9	−9.2	15.2	−8.8
1932	503.3	−14.3	4,111	11.5	−11.0	13.6	−10.3
1933	496.4	−1.0	3,952	11.2	−2.3	12.9	−5.1
1934	538.8	8.5	4,276	12.2	8.6	13.4	3.4
1935	589.4	9.4	4,632	12.4	1.9	13.7	2.5
1936	673.9	14.3	5,216	12.5	0.4	13.8	1.0
1937	706.0	4.8	5,481	13.1	4.8	14.3	3.4
1938	673.9	−4.5	5,164	12.8	−2.4	14.1	−1.9
1939	726.4	7.8	5,554	12.7	−0.7	13.9	1.4
1940	772.9	6.4	5,850	13.0	2.0	14.0	1.0
1941	909.4	17.7	6,817	13.8	6.2	14.7	5.0
1942	1,080.3	18.8	8,011	14.7	6.6	16.3	10.7
1943	1,276.2	18.1	9,333	15.1	2.6	17.3	6.1
1944	1,380.6	8.2	9,976	15.3	1.4	17.6	1.7
1945	1,354.8	−1.9	9,682	15.7	2.9	18.0	2.3
1946	1,096.9	−19.0	7,758	19.4	22.9	19.5	8.7
1947	1,066.7	−2.8	7,401	22.1	13.9	22.3	14.4
1948	1,108.7	3.9	7,561	23.4	7.0	24.1	2.7
1949	1,109.0	0.0	7,434	23.5	−0.5	23.8	−1.8
1950	1,203.7	8.5	7,905	23.9	2.0	24.1	5.8
1951	1,328.2	10.3	8,576	24.9	4.8	26.0	5.9
1952	1,380.0	3.9	8,759	25.4	1.5	26.5	0.9
1953	1,435.3	4.0	8,960	25.9	1.6	26.7	0.6
1954	1,416.2	−1.3	8,687	26.3	1.6	26.9	−0.5
1955	1,494.9	5.6	9,009	27.2	3.2	26.8	0.4
1956	1,525.6	2.1	9,032	28.1	3.4	27.2	2.9
1957	1,551.1	1.7	9,019	29.1	3.6	28.1	3.0
1958	1,539.2	−0.8	8,801	29.7	2.1	28.9	1.8

	GROSS NATIONAL PRODUCT, 1929–1990			PRICE INDEXES: 1929–1990			
				GNP Deflator		Consumer Price Index	
Year	1982 Prices (billions of dollars)	Annual Real Rate of Growth	Real GNP Per Capita (1982 dollars)	Index (1982 = 100)	Annual Percentage Change	Index (1982–84 = 100)	Annual Percentage Change (Dec. to Dec)
1959	1,629.1	5.8	9,161	30.4	2.4	29.1	1.7
1960	1,665.3	2.2	9,217	30.9	1.6	29.6	1.4
1961	1,708.7	2.6	9,302	31.2	1.0	29.9	0.7
1962	1,799.4	5.3	9,646	31.9	2.2	30.2	1.3
1963	1,873.3	4.1	9,899	32.4	1.6	30.6	1.6
1964	1,973.3	5.3	10,284	32.9	1.5	31.0	1.0
1965	2,087.6	5.8	10,744	33.7	2.7	31.5	1.9
1966	2,208.3	5.8	11,235	34.9	3.6	32.4	3.5
1967	2,271.4	2.9	11,431	35.9	2.6	33.4	3.0
1968	2,365.6	4.1	11,786	37.7	5.0	34.8	4.7
1969	2,423.3	2.4	11,956	39.8	5.6	36.7	6.2
1970	2,416.2	−0.3	11,783	42.0	5.5	38.8	5.6
1971	2,484.8	2.8	11,966	44.4	5.7	40.5	3.3
1972	2,608.5	5.0	12,428	46.5	4.7	41.8	3.4
1973	2,744.1	5.2	12,949	49.5	6.5	44.4	8.7
1974	2,729.3	−0.5	12,762	54.1	9.1	49.3	12.3
1975	2,695.0	−1.3	12,478	59.3	9.8	53.8	6.9
1976	2,826.7	4.9	12,961	63.1	6.4	56.9	4.9
1977	2,958.6	4.7	13,431	67.3	6.7	60.6	6.7
1978	3,115.2	5.3	13,993	72.2	7.3	65.2	9.0
1979	3,192.4	2.5	14,182	78.6	8.9	72.6	13.3
1980	3,187.1	−0.2	13,994	85.7	9.0	82.4	12.5
1981	3,248.8	1.9	14,114	94.0	9.7	90.9	8.9
1982	3,166.0	−2.5	13,614	100.0	6.4	96.5	3.8
1983	3,279.1	3.6	13,964	103.9	3.9	99.6	3.8
1984	3,501.4	6.8	14,771	107.7	3.7	103.9	3.9
1985	3,618.7	3.4	14,981	110.9	3.0	107.6	3.8
1986	3,717.9	2.7	15,385	113.8	2.6	109.6	1.1
1987	3,845.3	3.4	15,761	117.4	3.2	113.6	4.4
1988	4,016.9	4.5	16,305	121.3	3.3	118.3	4.4
1989	4,117.7	2.5	16,550	126.3	4.1	124.0	4.6
1990	4,157.3	1.0	16,530	131.5	4.1	130.7	6.1

Source: *Economic Report of the President (various years)* and *The Statistical History of the United States.*

SECTION 3 ■ Population and Employment

	Population and Labor Force				Unemployment Rates			
Year	Civilian Noninstitutional Population Age 16 and over[a] (Millions)	Civilian Labor Force (Millions)	Civilian Labor Force Participation Rate	Employment Population Ratio (Including Armed Forces)	All Workers	Both Sexes, Age 16–19 Years	Men Age 20+	Women Age 20+
1929	85.6	49.2	57.5	55.9	3.2	—	—	—
1930	87.1	49.8	57.2	52.5	8.7	—	—	—
1931	88.2	50.4	57.1	48.4	15.9	—	—	—
1932	89.3	51.0	57.1	43.8	23.6	—	—	—
1933	90.5	51.6	57.0	43.1	24.9	—	—	—
1934	91.7	52.2	56.9	44.9	21.7	—	—	—
1935	92.9	52.9	56.9	45.8	20.1	—	—	—
1936	94.1	53.4	56.7	47.5	16.9	—	—	—
1937	95.2	54.0	56.7	49.0	14.3	—	—	—
1938	96.5	54.6	56.6	46.2	19.0	—	—	—
1939	97.8	55.2	56.4	47.2	17.2	—	—	—
1940	100.4	55.6	55.4	47.8	14.6	—	—	—
1941	101.5	55.9	55.0	51.2	9.9	—	—	—
1942	102.6	56.4	55.0	56.3	4.7	—	—	—
1943	103.7	55.5	53.5	61.2	1.9	—	—	—
1944	104.6	54.6	52.2	62.5	1.2	—	—	—
1945	105.6	53.9	51.0	60.9	1.9	—	—	—
1946	106.5	57.5	54.0	55.1	3.8	—	—	—
1947	101.8	59.4	58.3	58.3	3.9	—	—	—
1948	103.1	60.6	58.8	58.4	3.8	9.2	3.2	3.6
1949	104.0	61.3	58.9	57.7	5.9	13.4	5.4	5.3
1950	105.0	62.2	59.2	56.6	5.2	12.2	4.7	5.1
1951	104.6	62.0	59.3	58.2	3.2	8.2	2.5	4.0
1952	105.2	62.1	59.0	58.2	2.9	8.5	2.4	3.2
1953	107.1	63.0	58.8	58.0	2.8	7.6	2.5	2.9
1954	108.3	63.6	58.7	56.4	5.4	12.6	4.9	5.5
1955	109.7	65.0	59.3	57.5	4.3	11.0	3.8	4.4
1956	111.0	66.6	60.0	58.2	4.0	11.1	3.4	4.2
1957	112.3	66.9	59.6	57.8	4.2	11.6	3.6	4.1
1958	113.7	67.6	59.5	56.1	6.6	15.9	6.2	6.1
1959	115.3	68.4	59.3	56.7	5.3	14.6	4.7	5.2

	Population and Labor Force				Unemployment Rates			
Year	Civilian Noninstitutional Population Age 16 and over[a] (Millions)	Civilian Labor Force (Millions)	Civilian Labor Force Participation Rate	Employment Population Ratio (Including Armed Forces)	All Workers	Both Sexes, Age 16–19 Years	Men Age 20+	Women Age 20+
1960	117.2	69.6	59.4	56.8	5.4	14.7	4.7	5.1
1961	118.8	70.5	59.3	56.1	6.5	16.8	5.7	6.3
1962	120.1	70.6	58.8	56.3	5.4	14.7	4.6	5.4
1963	122.4	71.8	58.7	56.1	5.5	17.2	4.5	5.4
1964	124.5	73.0	58.6	56.4	5.0	16.2	3.9	5.2
1965	126.5	74.5	58.9	56.9	4.4	14.8	3.2	4.5
1966	128.1	75.8	59.2	57.6	3.7	12.8	2.5	3.8
1967	130.0	77.3	59.5	58.0	3.7	12.9	2.3	4.2
1968	132.0	78.7	59.6	58.2	3.5	12.7	2.2	3.8
1969	134.3	80.7	60.1	58.7	3.4	12.2	2.1	3.7
1970	137.1	82.8	60.4	58.0	4.8	15.3	3.5	4.8
1971	140.2	84.4	60.2	57.2	5.8	16.9	4.4	5.7
1972	144.1	87.0	60.4	57.5	5.5	16.2	4.0	5.4
1973	147.1	89.4	60.8	58.3	4.8	14.5	3.3	4.9
1974	150.1	91.9	61.2	58.3	5.5	16.0	3.8	5.5
1975	153.2	93.8	61.2	56.5	8.3	19.9	6.8	8.0
1976	156.2	96.2	61.6	57.3	7.6	19.0	5.9	7.4
1977	159.0	99.0	62.3	58.3	6.9	17.8	5.2	7.0
1978	161.9	102.3	63.2	59.7	6.0	16.4	4.3	6.0
1979	164.9	105.0	63.7	60.3	5.8	16.1	4.2	5.7
1980	167.7	106.9	63.8	59.6	7.0	17.8	5.9	6.4
1981	170.1	108.7	63.9	59.4	7.5	19.6	6.3	6.8
1982	172.3	110.2	64.0	58.2	9.5	23.2	8.8	8.3
1983	174.2	111.6	64.0	58.3	9.5	22.4	8.9	8.1
1984	176.4	113.5	64.4	59.9	7.4	18.9	6.6	6.8
1985	178.2	115.5	64.8	60.5	7.1	18.6	6.2	6.6
1986	180.6	117.8	65.3	61.1	6.9	18.3	6.1	6.2
1987	182.8	120.0	65.6	61.9	6.1	16.9	5.4	5.4
1988	184.6	121.7	65.9	62.6	5.4	15.3	4.8	4.9
1989	186.4	123.9	66.5	63.3	5.2	15.0	4.5	4.7
1990	188.0	124.8	66.4	63.0	5.4	15.5	4.9	4.8

[a]Prior to 1947 the data are for persons age 14 and over

Source: *Economic Report of the President, 1991* and *1967,* and *The Statistical History of the United States.*

SECTION 4 ■ Money Supply, Interest Rates, and Federal Finances

Year	Money Supply M1 (billions of dollars)	Annual Change In M1	Interest Rate of Corporate Bonds (Moody, Aaa Percent)	Federal Budget Totals (billions of dollars)			National Debt	
				Fiscal Year Outlays	Fiscal Year Receipts	Surplus or Deficit (−)	Billion of Dollars	As a Percent of GNP
1929	26.5	—	4.73	3.1	3.9	0.7	16.9	16.3
1930	25.4	− 4.2	4.56	3.3	4.1	0.8	16.1	17.8
1931	23.6	− 7.1	4.58	3.6	3.1	− 0.5	16.8	22.2
1932	20.7	− 12.3	5.01	4.7	1.9	− 2.7	19.5	33.6
1933	19.5	− 5.8	4.49	4.6	2.0	− 2.6	22.5	40.5
1934	21.5	0.3	4.60	6.6	3.0	− 3.6	27.7	42.5
1935	25.6	19.1	3.60	6.5	3.7	− 2.8	28.7	39.8
1936	29.1	13.7	3.24	8.4	4.0	− 4.4	38.5	46.7
1937	30.3	4.1	3.26	7.7	5.0	− 2.8	41.3	45.7
1938	30.1	− 0.7	3.19	6.8	5.6	− 1.2	42.0	50.0
1939	33.6	11.6	3.01	9.1	6.3	− 3.9	45.0	49.7
1940	39.0	16.1	2.84	9.5	6.5	− 2.9	48.5	48.3
1941	45.4	16.4	2.77	13.7	8.7	− 4.9	55.3	44.1
1942	55.2	21.6	2.83	35.1	14.6	− 20.5	77.0	48.4
1943	72.3	31.0	2.73	78.6	24.0	− 54.6	140.8	73.1
1944	86.0	18.9	2.72	91.3	43.7	− 47.6	202.6	95.8
1945	99.2	15.3	2.62	92.7	45.2	− 47.6	259.1	121.4
1946	106.0	6.9	2.53	55.2	39.3	− 15.9	269.9	127.1
1947	113.1	6.7	2.61	34.5	38.5	4.0	258.4	109.0
1948	111.5	− 1.4	2.82	29.8	41.6	11.8	252.4	96.5
1949	111.2	− 0.3	2.66	38.8	39.4	0.6	252.8	97.1
1950	116.2	4.5	2.62	42.6	39.4	− 3.1	257.4	89.3
1951	122.7	5.6	2.86	45.5	51.6	6.1	255.3	76.6
1952	127.4	3.8	2.96	67.7	66.2	− 1.5	259.2	73.7
1953	128.8	1.1	3.20	76.1	69.6	− 6.5	266.1	71.6
1954	132.3	2.7	2.90	70.9	69.7	− 1.2	271.3	72.8
1955	135.2	2.2	3.06	68.4	65.5	− 3.0	274.4	67.6
1956	136.9	1.3	3.36	70.6	74.6	3.9	272.8	63.7
1957	135.9	−0.7	3.89	76.6	80.0	3.4	270.6	60.0
1958	141.1	3.8	3.79	82.4	79.6	− 2.8	276.4	60.5
1959	140.0	0.1	4.38	92.1	79.2	− 12.8	284.8	57.4

Year	Money Supply M1 (billions of dollars)	Annual Change In M1	Interest Rate of Corporate Bonds (Moody, Aaa Percent)	Federal Budget Totals (billions of dollars)			National Debt	
				Fiscal Year Outlays	Fiscal Year Receipts	Surplus or Deficit (−)	Billions of Dollars	As a Percent of GNP
1960	140.7	0.5	4.41	92.2	92.5	0.3	286.5	55.6
1961	145.2	3.2	4.35	97.7	94.4	− 3.3	289.2	54.2
1962	147.9	1.9	4.33	106.8	99.7	− 7.1	298.6	52.0
1963	153.4	3.7	4.26	111.3	106.6	− 4.8	306.5	50.5
1964	160.4	4.6	4.40	118.5	112.6	− 5.9	312.5	48.1
1965	167.9	4.7	4.49	118.2	116.87	− 1.4	317.9	45.1
1966	172.1	2.5	5.13	134.5	130.8	− 3.7	320.0	41.5
1967	183.3	6.5	5.51	157.5	148.8	− 8.6	322.3	39.5
1968	197.5	7.7	6.18	178.1	153.0	− 25.2	344.4	38.6
1969	204.0	3.3	7.03	183.6	186.9	3.2	351.7	36.5
1970	214.5	5.1	8.04	195.6	192.8	− 2.8	369.0	36.3
1971	228.4	6.5	7.39	210.2	187.1	− 23.0	396.3	35.9
1972	249.3	9.2	7.21	230.7	207.3	− 23.4	425.4	35.1
1973	262.9	5.5	7.44	245.7	230.8	− 14.9	456.4	33.6
1974	274.4	4.4	8.57	269.4	263.2	− 6.1	473.2	32.1
1975	287.6	4.8	8.83	332.3	279.1	− 53.2	532.1	33.3
1976	306.4	6.5	8.43	371.8	298.1	− 73.7	619.2	34.7
1977	331.3	8.1	8.02	409.2	355.6	− 53.6	697.6	35.0
1978	358.5	8.2	8.73	458.7	399.7	− 59.0	767.0	34.1
1979	382.9	6.8	9.63	503.5	463.3	− 40.2	819.0	32.7
1980	408.9	6.8	11.94	590.9	517.1	− 73.8	906.4	33.2
1981	436.5	6.7	14.17	678.2	599.3	− 78.9	996.5	32.6
1982	474.5	8.7	13.79	745.7	617.8	−127.9	1,140.9	36.0
1983	521.2	9.8	12.04	808.3	600.6	−207.8	1,375.8	40.4
1984	552.1	5.9	12.71	851.8	666.5	−185.3	1,559.6	41.3
1985	620.1	12.3	11.37	946.3	734.1	−212.3	1,821.0	45.6
1986	724.7	16.9	9.02	990.3	769.1	−221.2	2,122.7	50.0
1987	750.4	3.5	9.38	1,003.8	854.1	−149.7	2,347.8	52.0
1988	787.5	4.9	9.71	1,064.1	909.0	−155.1	2,599.9	53.3
1989	794.8	0.9	9.26	1,144.1	990.7	−153.4	2,836.3	54.5
1990	825.5	3.9	9.32	1,251.7	1,031.3	−220.4	3,210.9	58.8

Source: *Economic Report of the President* (various years).

SECTION 5 ■ Size of Government as a Share of GNP, 1929–1990				
Federal, State, and Local Government				
Year	Expenditures (Percent of GNP)	Revenues (Percent of GNP)	Purchase of Goods and Services (Percent of GNP)	Non-Defense Purchases of Goods and Services (Percent of GNP)	Transfer Payments to Persons (Percent of GNP)
---	---	---	---	---	---
1929	10.0	11.9	8.2	—	0.9
1933	19.2	16.7	14.4	—	3.8
1937	16.6	17.0	13.2	—	2.7
1939	19.3	16.9	14.9	13.3	2.8
1940	18.4	17.7	14.1	11.8	2.7
1941	22.9	19.9	19.9	8.8	2.1
1942	40.3	20.6	37.6	6.5	1.7
1943	48.4	25.5	46.1	4.6	1.2
1944	48.8	24.2	45.9	4.3	1.4
1945	43.5	25.0	38.9	4.2	2.8
1946	22.2	24.8	13.7	5.9	6.2
1947	18.5	24.6	11.2	7.0	5.6
1948	19.5	22.8	12.5	8.1	5.5
1949	23.0	21.7	15.0	9.6	6.5
1950	21.3	24.1	13.5	8.4	6.2
1951	23.8	25.7	18.1	7.8	4.4
1952	26.8	25.7	21.6	8.3	4.1
1953	27.4	25.6	22.3	9.1	4.1
1954	26.2	24.3	20.4	9.2	4.6
1955	26.5	25.0	18.6	8.9	4.6
1956	24.5	25.7	18.6	9.1	4.3
1957	25.7	25.9	19.4	9.5	4.9
1958	28.1	25.3	20.9	10.8	5.8
1959	26.6	26.3	19.7	10.5	5.6
1960	26.6	27.2	19.5	10.9	5.7
1961	28.1	27.3	20.3	9.7	6.3
1962	28.1	27.5	20.6	11.7	6.1

	Federal, State, and Local Government				
Year	Expenditures (Percent of GNP)	Revenues (Percent of GNP)	Purchase of Goods and Services (Percent of GNP)	Non-Defense Purchases of Goods and Services (Percent of GNP)	Transfer Payments to Persons (Percent of GNP)
1963	27.9	28.0	20.4	12.1	6.1
1964	27.4	27.0	20.0	12.2	5.9
1965	26.9	27.0	19.7	12.4	5.9
1966	27.9	27.8	20.5	12.5	6.0
1967	30.0	28.3	22.0	13.0	6.7
1968	30.5	29.8	22.1	13.3	7.0
1969	30.1	31.1	21.5	13.3	7.2
1970	31.3	30.2	21.5	13.9	8.3
1971	31.5	29.7	21.1	14.4	9.1
1972	31.1	30.8	20.6	14.2	9.2
1973	30.3	30.9	19.6	13.9	9.3
1974	31.7	31.4	20.3	14.7	10.2
1975	34.1	30.0	21.0	15.4	11.9
1976	34.0	30.8	20.0	14.8	11.6
1977	31.9	31.0	19.5	14.4	11.1
1978	30.9	30.9	18.9	14.1	10.6
1979	30.6	31.1	18.7	13.8	10.7
1980	32.6	31.3	19.4	14.2	11.7
1981	33.0	32.0	19.3	13.8	11.9
1982	35.1	31.6	20.3	14.1	12.8
1983	35.0	31.2	19.9	13.5	12.8
1984	33.9	31.0	19.5	13.2	11.9
1985	35.1	31.6	20.4	13.8	12.0
1986	35.1	31.7	20.6	14.1	12.0
1987	34.8	32.5	20.4	14.0	11.8
1988	33.9	32.0	19.7	13.8	12.0
1989	34.1	32.4	19.7	13.9	11.9
1990	34.9	32.6	20.1	14.4	12.3

Source: *Economic Report of the President* (various years)

Country (ranked according to GNP per capita)	Population (millions) 1988	GNP per Capita		Average Annual Growth Rate (Percent) 1980–88	Adjusted Average Annual Growth Rate of the Money Supply 1980–1988[a]	Average Annual Inflation Rate 1980–1988
		Dollars 1988				
Switzerland	6.6	27,500		1.6	6.1	3.8
Japan	122.6	21,020		3.3	5.9	1.3
Norway	4.2	19,990		3.5	8.3	5.6
United States	246.3	19,840		2.3	6.0	4.0
Sweden	8.4	19,300		1.5	9.0	7.5
Germany	61.3	18,480		1.9	3.9	2.8
Denmark	5.1	18,450		2.2	13.4	6.3
Canada	26.0	16,960		2.4	4.5	4.6
France	55.9	16,090		1.4	8.1	7.1
Netherlands	14.8	14,520		1.1	4.2	2.0
Belgium	9.9	14,490		1.4	5.4	4.8
Italy	57.4	13,330		2.0	10.0	11.0
United Kingdom	57.1	12,810		2.6	10.4	5.7
Australia	16.5	12,340		2.9	9.4	7.8
New Zealand	3.3	10,000		1.4	14.6	11.4
Hong Kong	5.7	9,220		5.8	—	6.7
Singapore	2.6	9,070		4.6	6.4	1.2
Spain	39.0	7,740		2.0	7.2	10.1
Greece	10.0	4,800		0.9	23.7	18.9
Korea, Rep. of	42.0	3,600		8.7	9.6	5.0
USSR	288.0	1,780–3,500		2.0	7.1	—
Yugoslavia	23.6	2,520		0.7	65.7	66.9
Argentina	31.5	2,520		−1.6	284.2	290.5
Uruguay	3.1	2,470		−1.0	57.5	57.0
Brazil	144.4	2,120		0.7	—	188.7
Mexico	83.7	1,760		−1.7	63.1	73.8
Syria	11.6	1,680		−3.1	19.3	12.9
Chile	12.8	1,510		0.2	—	20.8
Peru	20.7	1,300		−1.1	99.7	119.1
Turkey	53.8	1,280		3.0	45.0	39.3
Paraguay	4.0	1,180		−1.5	18.3	22.1
Colombia	31.7	1,180		1.3	25.3	24.1
Thailand	54.5	1,000		4.1	12.0	3.1
Guatemala	8.7	900		−3.1	14.9	13.3
Honduras	4.8	860		−1.9	10.0	4.7
Egypt	50.2	660		3.1	16.5	10.6
Bolivia	6.9	570		−4.3	590.8	462.8
Indonesia	174.8	440		3.0	18.7	8.5
India	815.6	340		3.0	11.8	7.4
China	1,088.4	330		9.0	15.6	4.9
Nigeria	110.1	290		−4.4	13.0	11.6

[a]The money supply data are for the actual money supply divided by real GNP. Thus, it is the actual supply of money adjusted to reflect the country's growth rate. The money supply data are for a broad measure similar to M2 in the United States.

Source: The World Bank, *World Development Report 1990* and *The World Bank Atlas: 1990*.

APPENDIX C

Answers to Selected Questions

CHAPTER 1

2. Production of scarce goods always involves a cost; there are no free lunches. When the government provides goods without charge to consumers, other citizens (taxpayers) will bear the cost of their provision. Thus, provision by the government affects *how* the costs will be covered, not whether they are incurred.

4. The legislation would increase the cost of traveling by air with a small child. Given the higher cost, some parents may choose to drive rather than fly. Since auto travel is more dangerous than air travel, then an increase in injuries and fatalities due to the additional automobile travel — a secondary effect — must also be considered.

6. For most taxpayers, the change will reduce the *after-tax* cost of raising children. Other things constant, one would predict an increase in the birth rate.

7. False. The key to sound policy is not the intentions of the advocate, but rather the ability of the policy to bring individual self-interest and the general welfare into harmony. People are not like pieces on a chess board. They have self will and personal interests. As Adam Smith pointed out in the *The Theory of Moral Sentiments* (1759), ''In the great chess board of human society, every single piece [individual] has a principle of motion of its own, altogether different from that which the legislature might choose to impress on it. If the two coincide [the self-interest of individuals and the objectives of a policy], the game of human society will go on easily and harmoniously, and is very likely to be happy and successful. If they are opposite or different, the game will go on miserably, and the society must be at all times in the highest degree of disorder.''

9. Raising the price of new cars by requiring safety devices, which customers would not have purchased if given the choice, slows the rate of sales for new cars. Thus the older, less safe cars are driven longer, partially offsetting the safety advantage provided by the newer, safer cars. Also, drivers act a bit differently when they are told that the new cars have the safety devices. They count on them for help in the event of an unexpected accident. In fact, economist Gordon Tullock says that the greatest safety device of all might be a dagger built into the center of the steering wheel, pointed directly at the driver's chest!

10. Money has nothing to do with whether an individual is economizing. Any time a person chooses, in an attempt to achieve a goal, he or she is economizing.

CHAPTER 2

2. Even though the productivity of painters has changed only slightly, rising productivity in *other areas* has led to higher wages in *other occupations,* thereby increasing the opportunity cost of being a house painter. Since people would not supply house painting services unless they were able to meet their opportunity costs, higher wages are necessary to attract house painters from competitive (alternative) lines of work.

6. The statement reflects the ''exchange is a zero sum game'' view. The view is false. No private business can force customers to buy. Neither can a customer force a business to sell. Unless both buyer and seller believe the exchange is in their interest, they will not enter into the exchange. Mutual gain provides the foundation for voluntary exchange.

9. Yes. The market value of the land will increase in anticipation of the future harvest, as the trees grow and the expected day of harvest moves closer. Thus, with transferable private property, the tree farmer will be able to capture the value added by his planting and holding the trees for a few years even if the actual harvest does not take place until well after his death.

10. In general, it sanctions all forms of competition except for the use of violence (or the threat of violence), theft, or fraud.

12. When used to generate *personal* services for the owner, *private property rights* permit owners to satisfy their own preferences while ignoring the wishes of others, if they so choose. However, when property is used for investment purposes or put up for sale, owners must cater to the preferences of others, if they want to maximize the return on sale value of the property. Finally, private property rights do provide legal protection against selfish persons who would use violence or theft to take the property of another.

14. If the food from land, now and in the future, is worth more than the housing services from the same land, then developers will not be able to bid the land away from farmers. However, since it is comparative advantage that determines the efficient use of a resource, even the best farm land, if situated in the right location, may be far more valuable for buildings. Other, poorer land can always be made more productive by the use of different (and more costly) farming techniques, irrigation, fertilizer, and so on. Physical characteristics alone do not determine the value or the most valuable use of a resource.

16. A large number of people feel that safety is priceless — that no price is too high to pay for something that saves lives. However, there is a problem with this view: It ignores opportunity costs. If we want more safety we will have to give up other things. Sometimes the opportunity cost of the additional safety will exceed its value. Consider travel safety. We could save lives if we cut our current speed limits in half, doubled the width of every road, and allowed only tank-like automobiles on the roads. But we would have to give up other things — things that are valued more highly than the lives saved — if we did. You could reduce your likelihood of accidental death by refusing to travel by automobile, train, or airplane. However, most people do not choose to do this,

because they value the travel more than the additional safety. Remember, economics is about trade-offs, not absolutes.

CHAPTER 3

1. a. and b. would increase the demand for beef; c. and d. would affect primarily the supply of beef, rather than the demand; e. leads to a change in quantity demanded, not a change in demand.

4. a. Reductions in the supply of feed gains and hay led to sharply higher prices. b. The higher feed grain and hay prices increased the cost of *maintaining* a cattle herd and thereby caused many producers to sell (an increase in *current* supply), depressing cattle prices in 1988. c. The reduction in the size of cattle herds led to a smaller future supply and higher cattle prices in 1989.

6. Agreement of both buyer and seller is required for an exchange. Price ceilings push prices below equilibrium and thereby reduce the quantity sellers are willing to offer. Price floors push prices above equilibrium and thereby reduce the quantity consumers wish to buy. Both decrease the actual quantity traded in the market.

8. True, "somebody" must decide who will be the business winners and losers. Neither markets nor the political process leave the determination of winners and losers to chance. Under market organization, business winners and losers are determined by the decentralized choices of millions of consumers who use their dollar votes to reward firms that provide preferred goods at a low cost and penalize others who fail to do so. Under political decision-making, the winners and losers are determined by political figures and planning boards who use taxes, subsidies, regulations, and mandates to favor some businesses and penalize others.

10. a. Profitable production increases the value of resources owned by people and leads to mutual gain to resource suppliers, consumers, and entrepreneurs. b. Losses reduce the value of resources which reduces the well-being of at least some people. c. No.

12. In the absence of trade restrictions, modest price increases in France will attract wheat from other regions, minimizing the effects in the drought region and resulting in slightly higher prices worldwide.

14. Rationing by price encourages future output; waiting in a line does not. Like a higher price, a longer wait in line rations the *current* supply by increasing the consumer's opportunity cost. However, the consumer's cost of waiting in line is wasted. It generates nothing for suppliers. In contrast, while a higher price also increases the consumer's opportunity cost, this cost transfers resources to suppliers, increases their returns, and thereby encourages them to expand the future availability of the good.

16. a. Demand would increase, rising vertically by $3 per meal—the added per-meal cost previously paid separately. b. Both price and quantity will rise in response to the rise in demand.

CHAPTER 4

2. When payment is not demanded for services, potential customers have a strong incentive to attempt a "free ride." However, when the number of nonpaying customers becomes such that the sales revenues of sellers are diminished (and in some cases eliminated), the sellers' incentive to supply the good is thereby reduced (or eliminated).

5. Disagree. As long as changes in personal costs and benefits influence choices predictably, theories for both market and public-sector action can be developed and tested against real-world events. Theory building and testing are the essential ingredients of a positive science.

6. The antimissile system is a public good for the residents of Washington, D.C. Strictly speaking, none of the other items are public goods since each could be provided to some consumers (paying customers, for example) without being provided to others.

9. In both markets and government, mutual consent is the only conclusive test of whether an action is productive. If all parties affected by an activity agree to it, then it is productive. Projects favored by a majority are not necessarily productive because the cost imposed on the nonconsenting minority may exceed the net gain to the majority.

11. The invisible hand principle is present only when the self-interest of individuals is consistent with the general welfare. Both the special interest effect and the shortsightedness effect indicate that this will not always be the case, even when political choices are made democratically.

12. True. Since individual computer customers both decide the issue (what computer, if any, will be purchased) and bear the consequences of a mistaken choice, they have a strong incentive to acquire information that will help them make a wise choice. In contrast, voters recognize that their choice, even if mistaken, will not decide the congressional election. Thus, they have little incentive to search for information that will help them make a better choice.

14. When Jack sells his stock, its price will reflect the value of future profits from the investment being undertaken now in lieu of dividends paid. The GM investment reduces Jack's income now, but increases the value of his stock by enough to make up for the loss. But there is no way for him to recapture the value of the tax payments without continuing to live in Los Angeles. (But if he owned a home, the sale price of the home would reflect the value of better city services, such as better streets serving his neighborhood.)

CHAPTER 5

2. Local and state governments operate in a more competitive setting than does the federal government. The competition reduces their ability to exploit taxpayers. Taxpayers who feel they are paying high taxes and getting little in return can vote with their feet; they can move to another local (or state) governmental unit that offers them more value for their tax dollars.

3. User charges differ from general taxation in that they impose the cost of a government activity on users in proportion to their consumption of the good. If you do not use the good, you do not have to pay for it. Taxes earmarked to finance specific activities may approximate user charges, but general taxation does not. The use of general taxes to finance a government activity breaks the link between consumption and payment and thereby forces nonusers to pay for things enjoyed by others. Like market prices, user charges provide valuable information about value relative to cost. If the revenue from a user charge is sufficient to cover opportunity cost, this is strong evidence that consumers value the good more than the alternatives forgone. Conversely, if user charges are insufficient to cover cost, this is evidence that consumers place a higher value on other things that might be produced.

6. True. In addition to the outlay cost of the project, the collection cost of the taxes and the deadweight losses emanating from the taxes implied by the project must also be covered if the project is going to enhance economic welfare.

7. High marginal tax rates make tax-deductible expenditures (for example, business entertainment, elegant office, or luxury automobile for business use) cheap *to the purchaser* (but not to society). A reduction in marginal tax rates will increase the purchaser's cost of deductible expenditures, since the lower rates reduce the tax savings accompanying deductible expenditures. Thus, lower marginal rates will tend to reduce expenditures on deductible items and other forms of tax avoidance.

10. False. Just as businesses do not pay taxes, neither do inanimate objects such as trucks. Only people pay taxes. In this case, the increased costs accompanying the tax translates into higher freight rates. These costs will be paid by consumers of the products transported (in the form of higher prices), by truck owners (in the form of lower profits), and by trucking employees (in the form of lower earnings).

CHAPTER 6

1. a., c., f., and g. will exert no impact on GNP; b. and d. will increase GNP by the amount of the expenditure; and

e. will increase GNP by $250 (the commission on the transaction).

3. Since the furniture was produced last year, the sale does not affect GNP this year. It reduces inventory investment by $100,000 and increases consumption by $100,000, leaving GNP unchanged.

5. The reliability of GNP comparisons over long periods of time is reduced because the leisure and human costs may change substantially between the two years, and because the types of goods available for consumption during the two years may be vastly different. Likewise, GNP may not be a good index of output differences between countries (for example, the United States and Mexico) for the same reasons. In addition, there may be substantial differences between countries in the production of (1) economic "bads," (b) goods in the household sector, and (c) the size of the underground economy.

7. $269.55

9. a. $1,000 b. $600 c. $200 d. 0 e. $10,000

11. a. False. Inventory investment indicates whether the holdings of unsold goods are *rising* or *falling*. A negative inventory investment (economists refer to this as disinvestment) means that inventories were drawn down during the period. b. False. If gross investment is less than the depreciation of capital goods during the period, net investment would be negative. Net investment in the United States was negative for several years during the Great Depression of the 1930s. c. Not necessarily. Rather, it may be the result of an increase in prices, population, or hours worked.

12. Neither the receipts nor the expenditures on payouts would count toward GNP since they are merely transfers—they do not involve production. However, expenditures on operations, administration, and government-provided goods and services from lottery proceeds would add to GNP.

14. a. 0 b. 0 c. $500 d. $300 e. $300 f. 0 g. 0

17. Consideration of this question illustrates some of the problems accompanying income comparisons across widely separated time periods when the bundle of goods available differs substantially. Of course, the price level has risen approximately sevenfold since 1929, so that $40,000 of income in 1929 would be comparable to $280,000 in 1989. However, even with $280,000 of income in 1929, you could not have purchased a C.D. player, color television, personal computer or an airplane ticket for New York to Los Angeles. Neither could you have purchased an automobile that would deliver the service and dependability of even today's economy model. The number of people you could have contacted via telephone would have been limited. Modern household appliances that most people take for granted would have been unavailable. Of course, you could have purchased a lot of other goods, including clothing, land, and wood for heating. Even so, we suspect that many would prefer the choices available today at a lower level of real income.

CHAPTER 7

1. Job seekers do not know which employers will offer them the more attractive jobs. They find out by searching. Job search is "profitable" and consistent with economic efficiency as long as the marginal gain from search exceeds the marginal cost of searching.

4. The wages people earn are also prices (prices for labor services) and like other prices they usually rise as the general level of prices increases. The statement ignores this factor. It implicitly assumes that money wages are unaffected by inflation; that they would have increased by the same amount (6 percent) even if prices would have been stable. Generally, this will not be the case.

6. One of the most harmful side effects of inflation is the uncertainty it creates with regard to time dimension contracts. As the statement indicates, it tends to undermine the ability of markets to allocate goods and resources to those who value them the most. In effect, it encourages speculation rather than production. The "well known" economist who made the statement referred to in the question was John Maynard Keynes. See *The Economic Consequences of Peace* (New York: Harcourt Brace, 1920, pages 235–36).

7. When the *actual* unemployment rate is equal to the *natural* rate of unemployment, cyclical unemployment is absent and potential GNP is at its sustainable rate. When *actual* unemployment rate is greater (less) than the *natural* rate of unemployment, cyclical unemployment is positive (negative) and potential GNP is less (greater) than its sustainable rate.

8. a. 60 percent **b.** 8.3 percent **c.** 55 percent

9. No. No. It means that there were no jobs available at wage rates acceptable to the potential workers who were unemployed. Thus, they continued to search for more attractive opportunities.

11. The inflation will tend to increase the wealth of **a.** and **e.** because it will increase the nominal value of their assets and reduce their real liabilities. It will hurt **b.**, **c.**, and **f.** because their income will rise less rapidly than prices. With regard to **d.**, it depends on whether his indebtedness is at a fixed or variable interest rate. If it is fixed, the inflation will reduce his real indebtedness, but if it is variable (tied to an interest rate than can be expected to increase with the inflation rate), his interest cost will rise with inflation.

13. Since most of the government's indebtedness is at a fixed interest rate, the unanticipated jump in the inflation rate transfers wealth away from the bondholders to the government. However, if the inflation continues and is eventually anticipated, higher nominal interest rates will result.

15. Each will encourage additional search.

CHAPTER 8

4. If the inflation rate unexpectedly falls from 3 percent to zero, the real wages of union members will rise. If other unions have similar contracts, the unemployment rate will increase because employment costs have risen relative to product prices. Profit margins will be cut and producers will respond by reducing output and laying off workers. In contrast, if the inflation rate rises to 8 percent, profit margins will improve, producers will expand their output, and the unemployment rate will decline.

7. The key things held constant when constructing the demand and supply schedules for a specific good are: demand (consumer income, prices of related goods, consumer preferences, expected future price of the good, and number of consumers) and supply (resource prices, technology, and expected future price of the good). Changes in these factors shift the relevant schedule.

The key things held constant when constructing the *aggregate* schedules are: *AD* (money supply, the government's tax and spending policies, real wealth, real income of one's trading partners, consumer preferences, and the expected future price level); *LRAS* (size of resource base, technology, and institutional structure of the economy); and *SRAS* (factors held constant in the *LR* plus resource prices and the expected price level). Again, change in these factors will shift the schedules indicated.

10. They are all equal.

11. Negative real interest rates are realized when the money interest rate is less than the inflation rate. This generally occurs when decision-makers (particularly lenders) underestimate the future rate of inflation and therefore agree to an inflationary premium that proves to be insufficient to compensate for the effects of inflation. This was the case for many loans in the United States during the sharp acceleration in inflation in the mid-1970s. Negative real interest rates are unlikely to persist because lenders losing real purchasing will alter their expectations of the inflation rate upward and therefore demand a larger inflationary premium.

12. $10,000; $20,000

14. Inversely; an increase in interest rates is the same thing as a reduction in bond prices.

CHAPTER 9

1. a. would decrease *AD;* **b.**, **c.**, and **d.** would increase it; and **e.** would leave it unchanged. For the "why" part of the question, see the section "Shifts in Aggregate Demand," pp. 205–208.

2. a., b., c., and d. will reduce *SRAS;* e. will increase it.

4. When an economy is operating at less than full employment, weak demand in resource markets will tend to reduce (a) the real rate of interest and (b) resource prices *relative to product prices* and thereby restore normal profit and the incentive of firms to produce the long-run potential output level. If resource prices and the real interest rate were inflexible downward, the self-correcting mechanism would not work.

6. At the lower than expected inflation rate, real wages (and costs) will increase *relative* to product prices. This will squeeze profit margins and lead to reductions in output and employment, causing the unemployment rate to rise.

8. Tightness in resource markets will result in rising resource prices *relative to product prices,* causing the SRAS to shift to the left. Profit margins will decline, output rate will fall, and long-run equilibrium will be restored at a higher price level. The above normal output cannot be maintained because it reflects input prices that people would not have agreed to and output decisions they would not have chosen if they had anticipated the current price level (and rate of inflation). Once they have a chance to correct these mistakes, they do so; and output returns to the economy's long-run potential.

9. Real wages will tend to increase more rapidly when the unemployment rate is low because a tight labor market (strong demand) will place upward pressure on wages.

12. In the short run, the unanticipated expansion in demand will tend to increase output and employment, while exerting modest upward pressure on the price level. In the long run, the primary impact will be a higher price level, with no change in output and employment.

CHAPTER 10

2. a. Increase current consumption, as the expectation of rising future prices will induce consumers to buy now. b. Decrease current consumption, as people will attempt to save more for hard times. c. Increase current consumption, as the result of an expansion in disposable income. d. May have little effect. However, the tendency will be toward a reduction in consumption, since households have an incentive to save more at the higher interest rate. e. Decrease consumption, as falling stock prices will reduce the wealth of consumers. f. and g. Increase consumption, as the young and the poor typically have a higher marginal propensity to consume than the elderly and wealthy.

4. It is the concept that a change in one of the components of aggregate demand, investment, for example, will lead to a far greater change in the equilibrium level of

income. Since the multiplier equals 1/1 − MPC), its size is determined by the marginal propensity to consume. The multiplier makes stabilizing the economy more difficult, since relatively small changes in aggregate demand have a much greater impact on equilibrium income.

7. The funds for the additional spending must come from either a decline in saving or an increase in borrowing. The model implicitly assumes one of the following: either (a) the changes in saving and borrowing exert no impact on the real interest rate or (b) the level of current investment, consumption, and government expenditure is insensitive to changes in the real rate of interest. In essence, the model ignores the interrelation between the goods and services market and the loanable funds markets.

9. The statement fails to recognize that association does not imply a direction of causation. The investment demand conditions differ during the periods of boom and recession. During an expansionary boom, investment demand is strong. In turn, the strong investment demand pushes interest rates up, not vice versa. Similarly, during a recession, weak investment demand leads to lower interest rates. Thus, it is the fluctuations in investment demand (shifts of the schedule) that explain the pattern of interest rates over the business cycle.

11. When the change is unanticipated and when it is expected to persist for a substantial period of time. In contrast, changes in expenditures that are anticipated and expected to be temporary will exert little impact on the rate of production. For example, even though expenditures on goods such as lawn mowers, swim suits, toys, and skiing equipment are much higher at certain times of the year, the production and employment of firms producing these goods is relatively stable since the changes in expenditures are both anticipated and expected to be temporary.

13. None. The Keynesian model assumes that wages and prices are inflexible downward. It will take an increase in aggregate expenditures to restore full employment.

15. Recession is an expected impact. The Keynesian model suggests that a stock market crash will tend to adversely affect business and consumer optimism, resulting in a reduction in planned aggregate demand, which in turn is magnified by the multiplier.

In the AD/AS model, the impact of the decline in business and consumer optimism is less predictable. If businesses and consumers become more pessimistic and therefore reduce their spending, a reduction in business borrowing and an increase in household saving is implied. These forces will place downward pressure on the real interest rate, which will stimulate demand and thereby help cushion any reduction in AD emanating from the increased pessimism. Thus, the AD/AS model indicates that the stability characteristics of a market economy are not nearly so fragile as the Keynesian model implies.

CHAPTER 11

2. The crowding-out effect is the theory that budget deficits will lead to higher real interest rates, which retard private spending. The crowding-out effect indicates that fiscal policy would not be nearly so potent as the simple Keynesian model implies. The new classical theory indicates that anticipation of higher future taxes (rather than higher interest rates) will crowd out private spending when government expenditures are financed by debt.

4. Automatic stabilizers are built-in features (unemployment compensation, corporate profit tax, progressive income tax) that tend automatically to promote a budget deficit during a recession and a budget surplus (or smaller deficit) during an inflationary boom. Automatic stabilizers have the major advantage of providing needed restraint, or stimuli, without congressional approval which, in turn, minimizes the problem of proper timing.

8. This statement depicts the views of many economists two decades ago. Today, most economists recognize that it is naive. Given our limited ability to accurately forecast future economic conditions, timing of fiscal policy is more difficult than it was previously thought. Political considerations— remember, the government is merely an alternative form of social organization, not a corrective device—reduce the likelihood that fiscal policy will be used as a stabilization tool. Changes in interest rates and private spending may offset fiscal actions and thereby reduce the potency of fiscal policy. All factors considered, it is clear that the use of fiscal policy to stabilize the economy is both difficult and complex.

10. There is a major defect in this view. If the budget deficits stimulated demand and thereby output and employment, we would have expected the inflation rate to accelerate. This was not the case; in fact, the inflation rate declined. The failure of the inflation rate to accelerate during the expansion of the 1980s strongly suggests that factors other than demand stimulus were at work.

13. This is an accurate statement of what economists refer to as the balanced budget multiplier. It is correct under very restrictive assumptions. However, it ignores the secondary effects in the loanable funds market. If the taxes of consumers rise by $10 billion and consumers reduce their spending by only $7.5 billion, then a $2.5 billion reduction in the supply of loanable funds is implied. This will place upward pressure on the real interest rate, which under normal circumstances will crowd out $2.5 billion dollars of private spending. Thus, when the secondary effects are considered, the validity of the statement is highly questionable.

14. Yes. Only the lower rates would increase the incentive to earn marginal income and thereby stimulate aggregate supply.

CHAPTER 12

1. A liquid asset is one that can easily and quickly be transformed into money without experiencing a loss of its market value. Assets such as high-grade bonds and stocks are highly liquid. Assets such as real estate, a family-owned business, business equipment, and artistic works are generally illiquid.

3. Money is valuable because of its scarcity relative to the availability of goods and services. The use of money facilitates (reduces the cost of) exchange transactions. Money also serves as store of value and a unit of account. Doubling the supply of money, holding output constant, would simply cause its purchasing power to fall without enhancing the services that it performs. In fact, *fluctuations* in the money supply would create uncertainty as to its future value and reduce the ability of money to serve as a store of value, accurate unit of account, and medium of exchange for time-dimension contracting.

6. a. No change; currency held by the public increases, but checking deposits decrease by an equal amount. b. Bank reserves decrease by $100. c. Excess reserves decrease by $100 minus the required reserve ratio multiplied by $100.

8. Answers b., e., and f. will reduce the money supply; a. and c. will increase it; if the Treasury's deposits (or the deposits of persons who receive portions of the Treasury's spending) are considered part of the money supply, then d. will leave the money supply unchanged.

10. While the transformation of deposits into currency does not *directly* affect the money supply, it does reduce the excess reserves of banks. The reduction in excess reserves will cause banks to reduce their outstanding loans and thereby shrink the money supply. Therefore, an increase in the holding of currency relative to deposits will tend to reduce the supply of money.

12. There are two major reasons. First, the money supply can be altered quietly via open market operations, while a reserve requirement change focuses attention on Fed policy. Second, open market operations are a fine tuning method, while a reserve requirement change is a blunt instrument. Generally, the Fed prefers quiet, marginal changes to headline-grabbing, blunt changes which are more likely to disrupt markets.

13. a. False; statements of this type often use money when they are really speaking about wealth (or income). b. False; the checking deposit also counts as money. In addition, the deposit increases the reserves of the receiving bank, and thereby places it in a position to extend additional loans which would increase the money supply. c. False; only an increase in the availability of goods and services valued by people will improve our standard of living. Without an additional supply of goods and services, more money will simply lead to a higher price level.

CHAPTER 13

1. **a.** and **c.** would increase your incentive to hold money deposits; **b.** and **d.** would reduce your incentive to hold money.

2. **a.** The cost of *obtaining* the house is $100,000, but the cost of *holding* it is the interest forgone on the $100,000 sales value of the house. **b.** The cost of *obtaining* a dollar is the amount of goods one must give up in order to acquire a dollar. For example, if a pound of sugar sells for 50 cents, the cost of obtaining a dollar in terms of sugar is two pounds. As in the case of the house, the cost of *holding* a dollar is the interest forgone.

8. If the time lag is long and variable (rather than short and highly predictable), it is less likely that policy-makers will be able to time monetary policy so that it will exert a countercyclical impact on the economy. They will be more likely to make mistakes and thereby exert a destabilizing influence. Such destabilizing effects would be reduced if the policy-makers followed the monetary rule of expanding the money supply at a constant rate. Thus, if the effectiveness lag is long and variable, the case for discretionary monetary policy is weakened and the case for a monetary rule is strengthened.

9. It strengthens the case for discretion and weakens the case for a rule. Discretionary changes in monetary policy could be used to offset fluctuations in the velocity of money. For example, if velocity fell, the money supply could be expanded more rapidly in order to prevent a reduction in aggregate demand and income. Correspondingly, if velocity fluctuates, it means that steady growth in the money supply would fail to stabilize the growth of demand, output, and employment.

11. Association does not reveal causation. Decision-makers—including borrowers and lenders—will eventually anticipate a high rate of inflation and adjust their choices accordingly. As the expected rate of inflation increases, the demand for loanable funds will increase and the supply will decrease. This will lead to higher nominal interest rates. Thus, economic theory indicates that the causation tends to run the opposite direction from that indicated by the statement.

12. Aggregate demand will decline as individuals and businesses reduce spending in an effort to build up their money balances.

14. The change in the money supply (M) plus the change in velocity (V) must equal the change in real output (Y) plus the change in the price level. Historically, the growth rate of real output (Y) in the United States has averaged approximately 3 percent. During the 1990s, if real output and velocity both grow at a 3 percent annual rate, then the money supply will have to remain constant (zero growth rate) for price stability to be achieved.

CHAPTER 14

4. Traditional monetary and fiscal policy are designed to maintain a high level of aggregate demand to combat the unemployment problem in the short run. The microapproach, on the other hand, is not such a quick-fix strategy. It emphasizes the relative price effects, the microstructure of the economy, and long-run policy prescriptions. If monetary and fiscal policy cannot permanently reduce the long-run natural rate of unemployment, then the microapproach is a viable substitute for traditional macropolicies.

6. Economists in the mid-1970s thought inflation would reduce unemployment; they failed to recognize that decision-makers would eventually come to anticipate the inflation. The modern view of the Phillips curve incorporates expectations into the analysis.

9. Compared to the early views of the Phillips curve, modern theory indicates that inflationary policies will be less attractive. Acceptance of the modern view by policy-makers will reduce the likelihood of inflationary policies.

12. A recent National Bureau of Economic Research study by Bruce Meyer (see footnote 11) found that the chances of an unemployed person getting a job quadrupled between the sixth week before the end of benefits and one week before the benefits expire. Meyer estimates that a ten percent increase in the share of after-tax earnings replaced by unemployment benefits lengthens the average unemployment spell by one and one-half weeks. Lowering the benefits after a couple of months of job searching reduces both the employment disincentive effects of the benefits and the natural rate of unemployment.

14. With unanticipated inflation, real wages fall because many workers, who did not anticipate the inflation, accepted explicit and implicit contracts at wage rates they would have found unacceptable had they correctly anticipated the magnitude of the price increase. Job search time will decline because many workers will accept jobs at money wage rates they would have rejected if they had been fully aware of how much inflation had increased money wages. Both of these factors will temporarily reduce the unemployment rate. When the inflation is anticipated, it will be fully reflected in long-term wage agreements. Thus, the inflation will fail to reduce real wage rates. Similarly, job search time will be normal because workers will recognize how much inflation has increased the money wages of potential jobs. Thus, anticipated inflation fails to reduce the unemployment rate.

16. **a.** A change in the expected rate of inflation; **b.** changes in factors that influence the natural rate of unemployment.

17. A major problem is that of differentiating between unemployed workers and workers out of the labor force. The payments provide persons out of or marginally attached to the

labor force with an incentive to indicate that they are available for work in order to receive the benefits. This would increase *measured* unemployment.

CHAPTER 15

4. Compared with earlier periods, the United States has experienced less economic instability during the last four decades. There is reason to believe that a more stable monetary policy has contributed to the increase in stability. See text Exhibits 1 and 3.

5. Nonactivists think that a monetary rule would result in less instability from monetary sources. The changing nature of money may reduce the stabilizing effects of a monetary rule.

9. Activists argue that it has been during only the last four decades that policy-makers have attempted to adjust macroeconomic policy in light of economic conditions. According to the activist view, the improved stability reflects the use of discretionary policy. Nonactivists point out that fluctuations in policy, particularly monetary policy (see Exhibit 3), have declined in recent years, and that the increased economic stability merely reflects the more stable policies. According to nonactivists, this linkage indicates that still more stable policies, such as would result from a monetary rule, would lead to a still more stable economy.

11. An unexpected shift to more expansionary monetary policy might temporarily reduce real interest rates. However, persistent use of expansionary policy in an attempt to push real interest rates below market levels will result in inflation (and high nominal interest rates). Once decision-makers anticipate an inflation rate, even high rates of inflation will fail to reduce real interest rates.

14. It implies that Americans tend to vote their pocketbooks, and as a result, the latter set of factors are much less important than is generally believed.

CHAPTER 16

1. No. Both private corporations and governments can, and often do, have continual debt outstanding. Borrowers can continue to finance and refinance debt as long as lenders have confidence in their ability to pay. This will generally be the case as long as the interest liability is small relative to income (or the potential tax base).

4. No. Remember, trade is a positive-sum game. Bonds are sold to foreigners because they are offering a better deal (acceptance of a lower interest rate) than is available elsewhere. Prohibiting the sale of bonds to foreigners would result in higher real interest rates and less investment, both of which would adversely affect Americans.

5. A failure to anticipate fully the future taxes accompanying debt implies an underestimation of the true cost of government. Since politicians will want to exaggerate the benefits and conceal the cost of their actions, the ability of debt to hide the true cost of government increases its attractiveness with vote-seeking politicians.

6. Rather than defaulting, the federal government could, as a last resort, meet its debt obligations by borrowing from the Fed. In essence, this means the government is paying its debts with printing-press money. It would lead to inflation.

8. It increases. Yes, if inflation reduced the real outstanding national debt by a larger amount than the budget deficit. See the next question for an illustration of this point.

9. **a.** $100 billion **b.** $2,625 billion **c.** $2,500 billion. Real indebtedness declined.

10. No. Yes.

14. In responding to this question, reflect on the following: Will Congressional representatives, subject to political pressures, be more or less likely to adopt an antiinflationary policy than relatively anonymous central banking policy-makers (for example, the Board of Governors of the Fed)? The empirical evidence indicates that the politicians will be more likely to adopt inflation-generating policies. The central banks of many countries, particularly those in South America, are under the direct control of the political authorities. The inflation rates in these countries are generally quite high.

15. Lower; voters do not enjoy paying taxes and therefore, voter dissatisfaction places a restraint on higher taxes, which would also restrain expenditures if the budget had to be balanced. More efficient; the restraint of tax increases would tighten the budget constraint and make the reality of opportunity cost more visible to both voters and politicians.

CHAPTER 17

1. **a.** increase demand; **b.** decrease demand; **c.** decrease incentive to develop nongasoline powered car; **d.** leave *demand* unchanged, *quantity demanded* declined; **e.** increase demand.

3. **a.** 0.21; 1.2. **b.** substitutes; higher fuel oil prices lead to an increase in demand (and consumption) for insulation.

8. Water is usually cheaper than oil because its *marginal utility* at current consumption levels is less than that of oil. Since water is so abundant relative to oil, the benefit derived from an *additional* quart of water is less than the benefit from an *additional* quart of oil, even though the *total utility* from all units of water is far greater than the *total utility* from all units of oil. However, the price of a product will reflect marginal utility, not total utility.

9. Both income and time constrain our ability to consume. Since, in a wealthier society, time becomes more binding and income less binding, time-saving actions will be more common in a wealthier society. As we engage in time-saving actions (fast food, automatic appliances, air travel, and so on) in order to shift the time restraint outward, our lives become more hectic.

12. All three statements are true.

13. a. No; even for things we like, we will experience diminishing returns. Eventually, the cost of additional units of pizza will exceed their benefits. b. Perfection in any activity is generally not worth the cost. For example, reading every page of this text 3, 4, or 5 times may improve your grade, but it may not be worth it. One function of a text is to structure the material (highlighted points, layout of graphs, and so on) so that the reader will be able to learn quickly (at a lower cost).

14. Carole.

15. False. Since the demand for agricultural products is generally inelastic, farm incomes may well increase. But the total utility of farm output reflects not only the sales revenues but also the consumer surplus. *For the units produced,* the utility is unchanged as the loss of consumer surplus by consumers is exactly offset by higher payments to farmers. However, both the payments to farmers and consumer surplus are lost *for those units not produced.* Therefore, the decline in production will reduce the total utility of farm output and the nation will be worse off as a result

18. Deceit and dishonesty will be encouraged by methods of organization that increase the returns to such behavior. The returns to deceitful and dishonest claims will be inversely related to the ease with which they can be countered by rivals. Other things constant, the presence of rivals will tend to reduce deceitful behavior. Is a politician more or less likely to tell the truth when he or she regularly confronts rivals? Is the news media more or less likely to be balanced and trustworthy when it faces rivals in the news business? Is a court witness more or less likely to tell the truth when there are other witnesses and cross-examination can be expected? Is a firm selling automobiles, cough drops, or hamburgers more or less likely to be honest when it faces competitors? Answers to such question are obvious.

19. The deadweight loss is the loss of the potential gains of buyers and sellers emanating from trades that are squeezed out by the tax. It is an excess burden because even though the exchanges that are squeezed out by the tax impose a cost on buyers and sellers, they do not generate tax revenue (since the trades do not take place).

production process. Accounting profit often excludes the opportunity cost of certain resources—particularly the equity capital of the firm and any labor services provided by an owner-manager. Zero economic profit means that the resources owned by the firm are earning their opportunity cost—that is, the rate of return is as high as the highest valued alternative forgone. Thus, the firm would not gain by pursuing other lines of business.

2. a. sunk costs are irrelevant; b. there is an opportunity cost of one's house; c. sunk costs should not affect one's current decision; d. there is an opportunity cost of public education even if it is provided free to the consumer.

9. Since owners receive profits, clearly profit maximization is in their interest. Managers, if they are not owners, have no property right to profit and therefore no *direct* interest in profit maximization. Since a solid record of profitability tends to increase the market value (salary) of corporate managers, they do have an indirect incentive to pursue profits. However, corporate managers may also be interested in power, nice offices, hiring friends, expansion of sales and other activities, which may conflict with profitability. Thus, the potential for conflict between the interests of owners and managers is present.

10. a. The interest payments b. the interest income forgone. The tax structure encourages debt rather than equity financing since the firm's tax liability is *inversely* related to its debt/equity ratio.

11. True. If it could produce the output at a lower cost, its profit would be greater.

13. Did your marginal cost curve cross the ATC and AVC curves at their low points? Does the vertical distance between the ATC and AVC curves get smaller and smaller as output increases? If not, redraw the three curves correctly. See Exhibit 6b.

17. $2,500; the $2,000 decline in market value during the year plus $500 of potential interest on funds that could be obtained if the machine were sold new. Costs associated with the decline in the value of the machine last year are sunk costs.

18. Because they believe they will be able to restructure the firm and provide better management so that the firm will have positive net earnings in the future. If the firm is purchased at a low enough price, this will allow the new owners to cover the opportunity cost of their investment and still earn an economic profit. Alternatively, they may expect to sell off the firm's assets, receiving more net revenue than the cost of purchasing the firm.

CHAPTER 18

1. The economic profit of a firm is its total revenues minus the opportunity cost of all resources used in the

CHAPTER 19

1. In a highly competitive industry such as agriculture, lower resources prices might improve the rate of profit in the

short run, but in the long run, competition will drive prices down until economic profit is eliminated. Thus, lower resource prices will do little to improve the long-run profitability in such industries.

2. New firms will enter the industry and the existing firms will expand output; market supply will expand, causing the market price to fall until economic profit is eliminated.

6. The statement is nonsense. If a reduction in demand leads to losses and exits from the industry, this reduction in supply will lead to a higher price and the restoration of normal returns.

8. a. increase **b.** increase **c.** increase, firms will earn economic profit **d.** rise (compared with its initial level) for an increasing cost industry, but return to initial price for a constant cost industry **e.** increase even more than it did in the short run. **f.** economic profit will return to zero.

9. a. decline **b.** increase **c.** decline **d.** decline.

11. The firms are unable to earn long-term economic profit because the barriers to entry into a competitive industry are low. Thus, profit attracts rival firms who ''spoil the market.'' Even though competitive firms earn only normal returns in the long run, profits and losses direct entrepreneurs into the production of those goods that are in short supply *relative to their cost* in the short run. This is a vitally important function.

14. a. room prices (including the tax) will increase **b.** decline in the short run. In the long run, supply will fall and profit will return to normal **c.** increase when the demand for rooms in the city is inelastic, but decline when demand is elastic.

16. True. Sellers undercut other sellers in order to gain business. Buyers outbid other buyers in order to obtain a good.

17. b. Six or seven tons; $250 profit. **c.** seven or eight tons; $600 profit **d.** five or six tons; $50 loss; Since the firm can cover its variable cost, it should stay in business if it believes that the low ($450) price is temporary.

CHAPTER 20

1. Profits cannot exist in the long run without barriers to entry because without them new entrants seeking the profits would increase supply, drive down price, and eliminate the profits. But as the chapter shows, barriers to entry are no guarantee of profits. Sufficient demand is also a necessary condition.

3. No; no; no

7. With a single tuition for all, it can nevertheless price-discriminate by giving financial aid to effectively lower the cost for students from lower-income families. These students presumably are more sensitive to higher tuition, so that their elasticity of demand for the university's services is greater.

9. Once an item has been invented and patented, short-run efficiency is indeed reduced by the monopoly given by the patent. The market will probably be under-stocked, with a price set higher than marginal cost. Patents are inefficient in this sense. Over time, however, consumers benefit by the efforts of innovators and the investors who support them. These efforts would be smaller if there were no patents to provide some monopoly power to successful innovators.

12. No. The firm's new profit-maximizing output rate will be 10 percent larger, but the profit-maximizing price will be unchanged. Construct a graph that illustrates this point.

13. Yes; **b.** implies that in the observed price range, the demand for petroleum products was inelastic. But a monopolist would never set price in this range—the inelastic portion of the demand curve—because a higher price would both increase revenues and reduce cost (since fewer units are produced and sold).

15. Reductions in the cost of transportation generally increase competition because they force firms to compete with distant rivals and permit consumers to choose among a wider range of suppliers. As a result, the U.S. economy today is generally more competitive, in the rivalry sense, than it was 100 years ago.

18. The Sonics do have a monopoly on NBA basketball in Seattle. But there are many other college and high school teams, and there are other professional sports to watch in Seattle, such as football. In addition there are numerous other forms of entertainment available in Seattle. All of these options (and more) compete for the entertainment dollars of fans.

CHAPTER 21

2. Building the new resort is more risky (and less attractive) because if the market analysis is incorrect, and demand is insufficient, it probably will be difficult to find other uses for the newly built resort. If the airline proves unprofitable, however, the capital (airplanes) should be extremely mobile. However, the resort would have one offsetting advantage: If demand were stronger than expected, and profits larger, it would take competitors longer to enter the market (build a new resort), and they would be more reluctant to make the more permanent investment.

5. The stock price, when the uncle bought the stock, no doubt reflected the well-known profits of Mammoth. The previous owners of the stock surely would not have sold it at a low price that failed to reflect the future dividends. In the language of the text, the uncle was not an ''early bird.'' It is unlikely that he will profit, in the economic sense, from the purchase.

6. Product variation provides each firm in the oligopoly a chance to "cheat" by raising the quality of its product in order to entice customers from rivals. This raises cost and helps to defeat the purpose, for the oligopolistic group, of controlling price. But if collusion has raised price much above marginal cost, there will be a powerful incentive for each firm to compete in a hidden way to get more customers.

9. The concentration ratio of an industry depends very much on how the industry is defined by the analyst calculating the ratio. It can overstate or understate the market power of the firms in question. Even potential entrants may influence price decisions by market producers. But sellers in local markets may have much more market power than the concentration ratio indicates. And finally, even a monopoly does not guarantee the ability to cover costs, much less a large profit. The firm's costs, as compared to willingness of consumers to pay, and number of such consumers, also must be considered.

12. The amount of variety is determined by the willingness of consumers to pay for variety relative to the cost of providing it. If consumers value variety highly and the added costs of producing different styles, designs, and sizes is low, there will be a lot of variety. Alternatively, if consumers desire similar products or if variation can be produced only at a high cost, little variety will be present. Apparently, consumers place a substantial value (relative to cost) on variety in napkins, but not in toothpicks.

13. The tax would increase the price of lower quality (and lower priced) automobiles by a larger percentage than higher quality automobiles. Consumers would substitute away from the lower quality autos since their relative price has increased. This substitution would increase the average quality of automobiles sold. Since the funds from the tax are rebated back to citizens through the lottery, one would expect this substitution effect to dominate any possible income effect.

CHAPTER 22

1. Employment in manufacturing is declining, but output is not. Manufacturing productivity is rising, and the sector is holding its own as a share of the economy. The trend for more than a century (see Exhibits 1 and 2), has been away from blue-collar occupations and toward information-related service occupations, including managers, professional and technical workers, and sales personnel. Noninformation service jobs have risen only a little. Incomes per worker have been rising—not an indication of a second-rate economy.

4. Reduced competition is a potential danger for consumers. But if a merger makes a firm more efficient and better able to undercut the prices of other competitors, it may in effect increase the degree of competition, even as the firm increases its share of the market.

6. Making cars more safe is good, but if the cost has previously kept consumers from demanding the safety measures, it is possible that they are not worth the cost to many consumers. Some very expensive cars, such as Mercedes-Benz, had air bags when there was no requirement, but Volkswagen did not. Should only the more costly cars be sold? If so, then some people, probably the less affluent, will drive older, even less safe cars. This is not a clearcut issue.

8. Profitability may be adversely affected in the short run, but in the long run prices will rise enough for the firms to cover their opportunity cost of production. Consumers bear the cost of such legislation and get the association benefits, large or small.

9. Since this would increase competition from foreign sources, the effect should be to reduce the fears of market power being held by domestic firms. The need for antitrust action should decline.

12. Existing airlines could be expected to define "necessary" in such a way that no new service would be allowed. Service by existing firms would always, in their view, be sufficient. Customers would be expected to favor (and thus define as necessary) any new service that would reduce prices and/or increase service with a sufficiently small price increase. Since the airlines are far fewer in number and better organized politically than customers, we would expect the airline view of "necessary" to prevail, as it did until the regulatory system grew so that it stifled competition, and prices became so demonstrably high that deregulation occurred and the CAB was abolished.

15. The statement is essentially true. In the short run, capital may be invested in an industry such that it cannot easily be moved elsewhere. If customer demand is elastic, the industry may bear a large part of the cost burden in the short run. In the long run, however, capital is mobile. Factories don't have to be replaced, for example. If costs in the industry are high, relative to the revenues, then capital will migrate over time to other industries, and supply in the regulated industry will fall until the price buyers will pay is again high enough to provide the market rate of return to capital.

17. Experts often do know far more about the technical options than do consumers, although consumers can and do read the advice of experts. Suppliers of safer products also make it a point to advertise data and expert opinion indicating their products are indeed safer. Nevertheless, experts usually do understand the technologies better. On the other hand, experts cannot know about how products will be used. A consumer may prefer to pay for a high degree of safety for the family car, which will carry the whole family at high speeds over long distances, while preferring a much cheaper, less reliable car for running errands near home. Such choices are

hard to allow if all vehicles are strictly regulated for safety. Decision-maker knowledge (and incentives) is, in some cases, better with consumer choice than with thorough and strict regulation.

CHAPTER 23

3. a. five **b.** $350 **c.** four The firm will operate in the short run but it will go out business in the long run unless the market prices rises.

4. Yes. General increases in the productivity of the labor force will cause a general increase in wages. The higher general wage rates will increase the opportunity cost of barbering and cause the supply of barbers to decline. The reduction in the supply of barbers will place upward pressure on the wages of barbers, even if technological change and worker productivity have changed little in barbering.

8. No. The dressmaker needs to employ more capital and less labor because the marginal dollar expenditures on the former are currently increasing output by a larger amount than the latter.

10. Other things constant, a lengthy training requirement to perform in an occupation reduces supply and places upward pressure on the earnings level. However, resource prices, including those for labor services, are determined by *both* demand and supply. When demand is weak, earnings will be low even though a considerable amount of education may be necessary to perform in the occupation. For example, the earnings of people with degrees in English literature and world history are generally low, even though most people in these fields have a great deal of education.

12.b. 4 **c.** Employment would decline to 3.

CHAPTER 24

2. U.S. workers are more productive. By investing in human capital, the laborers are somewhat responsible, but the superior tools and physical capital that are available to U.S. workers also contribute to their higher wages.

6. While this statement often made by politicians sounds true, in fact, it is false. Output of goods and services valued by consumers, not jobs, is the key to economic progress and a high standard of living. Real income cannot be high unless real output is high. If job creation was the key to economic progress it would be easy to create millions of jobs. For example, we could prohibit the use of farm machinery. Such a prohibition would create millions of jobs in agriculture. However, it would also reduce output and our standard of living.

8. The opportunity cost of leisure (nonwork) for higher wage workers is greater than for lower wage workers.

9. a. decreases **b.** increases **c.** decreases **d.** increases.

10. False. Several additional factors including differences in preferences (which would influence time worked, the trade-off between money wage and working conditions, and evaluation of alternative jobs), differences in jobs, and imperfect labor mobility would result in variations in earnings.

12. a., b., e., and **f.** will generally increase hourly earnings; **c.** and **d.** will generally reduce hourly earnings.

13. a. The increase the cost of employment. Yes. **b.** Sure, if the higher wages are sufficient to compensate for the absence of the fringe benefits. **c.** No. Employees pay for them in the form of lower money wages than could be earned on comparable jobs that do not provide the fringe benefits.

15. a. The cost of employing part-time workers would rise and their employment level would fall. **b.** The *money* wages of part-time workers would fall; the higher fringe benefits would increase the supply of workers willing to work at a given *money* wage, and thereby reduce the wage.

16. Hourly wages will be highest in B because the higher wages will be necessary to compensate workers in B for the uncertainty and loss of income during layoffs. Annual earnings will be higher in A in order to compensate workers in A for the additional hours they will work during the year.

17. The employment level of low-skill workers with large families would decline. Some would attempt to conceal the presence of their large family in order to get a job.

19. Not necessarily. Compared with married men, single men tend to be younger, have fewer dependents, are more likely to drop out of the labor force, and less likely to receive earnings-enhancing assistance from another person. All of these factors will reduce their earnings relative to married men.

CHAPTER 25

2. All of the changes would increase interest rates in the United States.

6. The project is profitable at 8 percent but not at 12 percent. Use Exhibit 3 to calculate the present value of $400 received at the end of each of the next three years at the two interest rates.

8. a. approximately $1.277 million **b.** yes. **c.** The lottery earnings are less liquid. Since there is not a well-organized market transforming lottery earnings into present income, the transaction costs of finding a "buyer" (at a price equal to the present value of the earnings) for the lottery earnings "rights" may be higher than for the bond, if one wants to sell in the future.

9. No. The *average* outstanding balance during the year is only about half of $1,000. Therefore, the $200 interest charge translates to almost a 40 percent annual rate of interest.

12. No. At an 8 percent discount rate, the present value of her earnings is equal to approximately $10.6 million (assuming the first $200,000 is paid now). At a 12 percent discount rate, the present value of the earnings is approximately $8.366 million. In addition, she will confront a tax liability on the earnings.

13. a. and b. The ''we will all starve'' argument is irrelevant and illustrates a lack of understanding about how markets work. If a decline in agriculture output accompanied the abolition of farm subsidies (a highly questionable assumption), agricultural prices would rise, providing farmers with additional incentive to produce a larger output. The same process also applies to automobiles, shoes, and other goods.

15. To the extent that the price supports increase farm revenues, the larger income stream drives up the price of land with allotments. Therefore, at the higher level of land prices, farming is no more profitable with the supports than it would be in their absence. Thus, today's farmers are not helped by the program. However, since repeal would reduce the current value of their land, the reluctance of farmers to support the repeal of the programs is understandable.

16. The investment choices of ordinary citizens exert an impact on the stock prices of corporations. If investors believe that consumers will value the product offered more than what it costs to produce it, the price of the corporation's stock will rise. If investors do not think consumers will like the product, the price of the corporation's stock will fall. Thus, ordinary citizens as investors provide almost instant feedback to corporate decision-makers and the behavior of investors limits the ability of corporate executives to raise funds to finance projects that investors believe are in conflict with the preferences of consumers.

CHAPTER 26

2. If the union is able to raise the wages of the farm workers: (1) The cost of Florida oranges will rise, causing supply to decline and their price to rise in the long run; (b) profits of the Florida orange growers will decline in the short run, but in the long run they will return to the normal rate; (c) mechanization will be encouraged; and (d) the employment of fruit pickers will decline—particularly in the long run.

3. The higher wages in the South would increase the costs of the southern firms and thereby make them less competitive with their northern rivals.

7. If only part of an industry is unionized, the costs of nonunion firms in the industry will be lower than the costs of unionized firms, if the unionized firms have higher wage rates. If the union wages are much higher than nonunion wages, then the unionized firms will be unable to compete successfully.

9. False. Investors do not have to supply capital to an industry. If the expected profit rate of a highly unionized industry is low, then investment funds will flow elsewhere. An *unanticipated* increase in union wages might reduce profitability in the short run, but it will not be able to do so in the long run. The primary effects of the higher wages will be higher prices. Consumers, rather than investors, will bear the primary cost of high union wages.

10. False. Competition constrains both employers and employees. Employers must compete with *other employers* for labor services. In order to gain the labor services of an employee, an employer must offer a compensation package superior to what the employee can get elsewhere. If the employer does not offer a superior package, the the employee will work for a rival employer or choose self-employment.

Similarly, employees must compete with *other employees*. Therefore, their ability to demand whatever wage they would like is also restrained. Thus, competition prevents both the payment of low (below market) wages by employers and the imposition of high (above market) wages by employees.

12. Remember, union members compete with *other workers,* including less skilled workers. An increase in the minimum wage makes unskilled, low-wage workers more expensive. A higher minimum wage increases the demand for high-skill employers who are good substitutes for the low-skill workers. Union members are over-represented among the high-skill group helped by an increase in the minimum wage. Therefore, while union leaders will generally pitch their support for a higher minimum wage in terms of a desire that all workers be paid a ''decent wage,'' the impact of the legislation on union members suggests that self-interest rather than altruism underlies their support for the legislation.

13. The union and the manufacturer would be most likely to favor the tariff because it would make foreign-produced automobiles more expensive and thereby increase the demand for American-made automobiles and the labor with which they are made. In contrast, the higher gasoline tax makes driving more expensive. In response, the demand for higher-gasoline-consumption automobiles will fall, which will adversely affect both American automobile manufacturers and workers.

15. Not necessarily. Adjustment must be made for differences in (a) the productivity characteristics of the union and nonunion workers and (b) the types of jobs they occupy (for example, work environment, job security, likelihood of

layoff, and so on). Adjustment for these factors may either increase or reduce the $1.50 differential.

CHAPTER 27

2. Differences in family size, age of potential workers, nonmoney "income," taxes, and cost-of-living among areas reduce the effectiveness of annual money income as a measure of economic status. In general, high-income families are larger, more likely to be headed by a prime-age worker, have less nonmoney income (including leisure), pay more taxes, and reside in higher cost-of-living areas (particularly large cities). Thus, money income comparison between high- and low-income groups often overstates the economic status of the former relative to the latter.

4. If there were no intergenerational mobility, the diagonal numbers would all be 100 percent. If there were complete equality of opportunity and outcomes, the numbers in each column and row would be 20 percent.

6. No. The increase in marginal tax rates will reduce the incentive of the poor to *earn* income. Therefore, their income will rise by $1,000 minus the reduction in their personal earnings due to the disincentive effects of the higher marginal tax rates.

7. 67 percent.

10. Here, as in other areas, it is important to remember that government is merely an alternative form of social organization, rather than a corrective device. The structure of income transfers reflects political clout. The elderly, farmers, and business and labor interests are easily identifiable, politically potent interest groups. In contrast, the poor have a low voter participation rate and offer little in the way of financial support to politicians. Given these factors, it is not surprising that most income transfers go to the nonpoor.

14. Adjustment of individuals to redistributive programs often leads to unintended side effects. If a higher income from private saving means a lower level of social security benefits, people will save less for retirement. Other things constant, the number of low-income (and therefore high-benefit) elderly will grow. Stated another way, programs that subsidize low-income status (and penalize high-income status) during retirement will expand the number of people in the former category and reduce the number in the latter category with the passage of time.

15. Under a pay-as-you-go system, social security benefits do not constitute societal wealth because the benefits imply a liability of equal size. However, *individuals* may treat the expected future benefits as wealth and reduce their saving accordingly. If they do, a society with a pay-as-you-go social security system will have a lower rate of saving and capital formation than a society without such a program.

CHAPTER 28

1. Crude oil, for example, is a gift of nature in the sense that it was put in place without the help of human beings. But as a resource, it is not simply a gift of nature, because human ingenuity and effort are required to make the naturally occurring substance valuable.

3. The "requirement" of water for the steel industry depends on the value placed on water, as well as on the value placed on steel. The same amount of steel can be produced with vastly differing amounts of water, as illustrated in Exhibit 1 of this chapter. Also, steel itself is not indispensable in all its uses, including national defense uses. There are many substitutes, not only for water in the making of steel, but also for steel in the making of tanks, and for tanks in providing national defense. So a given amount of water for steel is not really a requirement.

5. Remember, the marginal principle. There are a limited number of rich people, and they have a limited amount of time to spend on recreation. It is unlikely that the rich will be willing or able to "buy up all the recreation opportunities." Remember also that if the price of the best fly fishing access, for example, rises because rich people like it, then more such areas will be provided by profit-seeking entrepreneurs who can improve existing streams and create additional habitat, when it is profitable to do so.

6. Wells are abandoned by producers when the cost of extracting and delivering additional oil exceeds its value. When the value of crude oil rises, additional oil can be produced since water flooding, steam and chemical measures—all of which are costly—can be paid for by the higher prices gained from the extra oil.

7. Total reserves of a mineral include all the resources that are in place, and which might become available in the future, given sufficiently high prices or technological advances. Proved reserves are the resources which producers believe they can produce with current technology, at today's prices. Proved reserves are what count in the short term, but if we are concerned with the long-run prospect of much greater scarcity, with higher prices and incentives for technological advances in mineral exploration and production, then total reserves might also become important.

9. The use of an unowned, unpriced resource might have a high opportunity cost. Yet if there is no owner to protect it, or to allocate it to its highest-valued use, then it might indeed be treated as if it had no opportunity cost. If it is valuable, however, then it might pay an entrepreneur to find a way to establish ownership. That, in fact, is the history of many natural resources in the United States. Ownership of land, for example, was often not established until it became economically attractive enough to reward the initial claimants who established ownership.

11. If an investment, such as leaving the trees to grow

another 20 years, yields a higher return than other investments, then the stock price will fall if the trees are cut too soon, or will go higher if a new, more profitable investment path (leaving the trees to grow) is announced. Either way, the stock price immediately rewards good long-term decisions and penalizes bad ones.

12. A lower interest rate would increase the present value of benefits, which occur farther in the future, relative to a high interest rate. (See our earlier chapter on Capital, Interest, and Profit, if this is confusing to you.) Since the project's costs occur sooner, the interest rate chosen has less impact on the present value of costs than on the present value of benefits. As a result, a lower interest rate would make this project look more attractive. A person trying to get the project approved by Congress would want a low interest rate used in the benefit-cost analysis.

CHAPTER 29

1. The commons could have been managed politically, without any private ownership. The open access problem is the absence of *both* private property and of political control of access to the resource.

4. By definition, a public good cannot be marketed, because free riders (nonpayers) can consume it. There is little incentive for the consumer to state his or her true preference, even if asked. So a producer, including government, has a difficult time knowing how much an extra unit of the public good is worth.

6. We expect that private ownership, which concentrates both the costs and the benefits of stewardship on the owner(s), will result in better care than will joint ownership, at least if the joint owners are many. In the latter case, the benefits are spread among the joint owners, while the costs of care fall on the person doing the care—unless, of course, the group arranges to assign and enforce duties, or to jointly pay for care.

7. Permitting all firms to use air and water resources for "free garbage disposal" services would reduce the producer's costs of supplying pollution-intensive goods. However, as long as free entry is present, the lower cost would lead to lower prices not higher profits. Except for unanticipated changes in pollution control policy, competition will drive the profit rate of all firms, including those in industries that pollute, toward the normal rate of return.

9. Many goods with public-good aspects are provided privately. Free museum admission, free concerts, wildlife preservation, and so on defy the free-rider problem But the public good problem is still with us, and we cannot know whether the right amounts are produced when goods have public goods aspects.

10. An inability to exclude nonpaying consumers. Since consumers cannot be prevented (at least not at a low cost) from consuming a public good if they fail to pay, each has an incentive to "free ride," which undermines the private supplier's ability to cover the cost of production.

11. Economics doesn't say what is fair, but corporations—like all firms—want to minimize their costs in order to maximize profits. If they can reduce costs by emitting more pollution into the air and by avoiding costly abatement measures, then they are likely to do so. And those who do will gain a competitive advantage over those who do not, so long as the legal system does not hold polluters responsible for downwind damages. Without effective court procedures or bureaucratic action on behalf of those harmed by the pollution it would be folly to expect even public-spirited corporate executives to sacrifice profits to gain a public good—air quality, if their competitors were allowed to pollute.

12. Knowing that the firm's national reputation is at stake at every franchise, travelers would probably find the nationally advertised restaurant more appealing. Also, if they had seen the advertising, they would have a better idea of what sort of food is available. Their relative lack of knowledge about the unadvertised place probably deters their using it. In contrast, the local people would know more than the travelers about the local restaurant, as the result of personal experience or by talking with friends who had tried it.

CHAPTER 30

1. It is difficult for the voter to know what a candidate will do once elected, and the rationally ignorant voter is usually not willing to spend the time and effort required to understand issues, since his or he vote will not be the decisive one anyway. Special interest voters, on the other hand, will know which candidate has promised them the most on their issue. Also, the candidate who is both competent and prepared to ignore special interests will have a hard time getting these facts to voters without financial support from special interest groups. Each voter has an incentive to be a "free rider" on the "good government" issue. Controlling government on behalf of society as a whole is a public good, requiring much private activity. Like other public goods, it tends to be underproduced.

2. Corporate officers, while they surely care about the next few months and the profits during that time, care also

about the value of the firm and its stock price. If the stock price rises sufficiently in the next few months—as it will if investors believe that current investments in future-oriented projects (planting new trees, for example) are sound—then the officers will find their jobs secure even if current profits do not look good. Rights to the profits from those (future) trees are saleable now in the form of the corporation's stock. There is no such mechanism to make the distant fruits of today's investments available to the political entrepreneurs who might otherwise fight for the future-oriented project. Only if the project appeals to today's voters, and they are willing to pay today for tomorrow's benefits, will the program be a political success. In any case, the wealth of the political entrepreneur is not directly enhanced by his or her successful fight for the project.

7. No. The government is merely an alternative form of organization. Government organization does not permit us to escape either scarcity or competition. It merely affects the nature of the competition. Political competition (voting, lobbying, political contributions, taxes, and politically determined budgets) replaces market competition. Neither is there any reason to believe that government organization modifies the importance of personal self-interest.

8. The regulatory and taxation policy toward the liquor industry is usually conducted at the state, rather than at the federal level. Thus, liquor industry interests will be more likely to use lobbying and campaign contributions to influence the action of state-level politicians.

10. When the welfare of a special interest group conflicts with that of a widely dispersed, unorganized majority, the legislative political process can reasonably be expected to work to the benefit of the special interest.

CHAPTER 31

1. Availability of goods and services, not jobs, is the source of economic prosperity. When a good can be purchased cheaper abroad than it can be produced at home, a nation can expand the quantity of goods and services available for consumption by specializing in the production of those goods for which it is a low-cost producer and trading them for the cheap (relative to domestic costs) foreign goods. Trade restrictions limiting the ability of Americans to purchase low-cost goods from foreigners stifles this process and thereby *reduce* the living standard of Americans.

3. Answers a. and b. are not in conflict. Since trade restrictions are typically a special interest issue, political entrepreneurs can often gain by supporting them even when they promote economic inefficiency.

5. True. The primary effect of trade restrictions is an increase in domestic scarcity. This has distributional consequences, but it is clear that as a whole, a nation will be harmed by the increased domestic scarcity accompanying the trade restraints.

6. The quota reduces the supply of sugar to the domestic market and drives up the domestic price of sugar. Domestic producers benefit from the higher prices at the expense of domestic consumers (See Exhibit 11). Studies indicate that the quota expanded the gross income of the 11,000 domestic sugar farmers by approximately $130,000 per farm in the mid-1980s, at the expense (in the form of higher prices of sugar and sugar products) of approximately $6 per year to the average domestic consumer. Since the program channels resources away from products for which the U.S. has a comparative advantage, it reduces the productive capacity of the United States. Both the special interest nature of the issue and rent-seeking theory explain the political attractiveness of the program.

8. a. No. Americans would be poorer if we used more of our resources to produce things for which we are a high opportunity-cost producer and less of our resources to produce things for which we are low opportunity-cost producer. Employment might either increase or decrease, but the key point is that it is the value of goods produced, not employment, which generates income and provides for the wealth of a nation. The answer to b. is the same as a.

9. In thinking about this issue, consider the following points. Suppose the Japanese were willing to give products such as automobiles, electronic goods, and clothing to us free of charge. Would we be worse off if we accepted the gifts? Should we try to keep the free goods out? What is the source of real income—jobs or goods and services? If the gifts make use better off, doesn't it follow that partial gifts would also make us better off?

12. While trade reduces employment in import-competing industries, it expands employment in export industries. On balance, there is no reason to believe that trade either promotes or destroys jobs. The major effect of trade is to permit individuals, states, regions, and nations to generate a larger output by specializing in the things they do well and trading for those things that they would produce only at a high cost. A higher real income is the result.

15. True. If country A imposes a tariff, other countries will sell less to A and therefore acquire less purchasing power in terms of A's currency. Thus, they will have to reduce their purchases of A's export goods.

16. Yes. The price equalization theorem indicates that goods will tend to sell for similar prices in all markets except for differences due to taxes and transport costs. Therefore, except in cases where there is a high tariff (or some other U.S. tax) on a good, it is unlikely that the good will be much cheaper abroad than it is in the United States.

CHAPTER 32

4. Answers **a.** and **g.** would cause the dollar to appreciate; **b., c., d., e.,** and **h.** would cause the dollar to depreciate,   would leave the exchange rate unchanged.

5. On February 2, the dollar appreciated against the pound and depreciated against the franc.

9. Each of the changes would reduce the size of the current account deficit.

11. The current account balance will move toward a larger deficit (or smaller surplus) and the dollar will appreciate.

13. The depreciation will make the dollar price of BMWs more expensive which will reduce the *quantity purchased* by Americans. If the American demand for BMWs is inelastic (elastic), then the dollar expenditures on BMWs will rise (fall).

16. False. Flexible exchange rates bring the *sum* of the current and capital accounts into balance, but they do not necessarily lead to balance for either component.

CHAPTER 33

2. Many economists believe that this view is essentially true. However, there are reasons for doubt. Foreign aid has not played a significant role in the progress of most of the high growth, less developed countries. Often, financial aid disrupts markets and retards the incentive of producers in less developed countries. Finally, attractive investment alternatives will draw investment from abroad even if domestic saving is inadequate. Thus, the efficacy of aid as a tool to promote economic growth is highly questionable.

3. There is considerable diversity among the poor nations. The real GNP of several poor countries has declined during the last two decades (see Exhibit 8). Others have stagnated or experienced only slow growth. Still others have experienced rapid growth. On the encouraging side, the average growth rates of per capita GNP in China and India (the two most populous less developed countries) were 5.7 percent and 1.8 percent during the 1965–1988 period. These rates—particularly the rate for China—compare quite favorably with the growth rates of industrial developed economies. If these two giants are able to follow the path of Japan, and more recently Hong Kong, South Korea, Singapore, and Indonesia, perhaps two-thirds of the world's population will have incomes well above subsistence levels early in the next century.

4. The evidence indicates that as nations become wealthier their saving rate increases only slightly, if at all, while the length of the work week declines. The U.S. experience is consistent with this general pattern. The length of the average work week in the United States has steadily declined for at least 100 years, while the saving/GNP rate has changed little.

8. In order to make comparisons among countries, we must estimate the purchasing power of each nation's currency in terms of a common currency (such as the U.S. dollar). The exchange rate value of a nation's currency may be a misleading indicator of its domestic purchasing power over a broad range of goods typically purchased by households. Only a small portion of the typical bundle of goods consumed by households is traded in international markets. In addition, exchange rates are influenced by factors such as interest rate differentials and capital movements among countries. Thus, the relative exchange rate value of a nation's currency may fail to accurately reflect the currency's purchasing power over a broad bundle of consumer goods. When this is the case, the exchange rate conversion method will yield a misleading estimate of the nation's income in terms of the common currency.

10. Yes. Trade barriers limit the ability of both businesses and consumers to benefit from economies associated with an expansion in the size of the market. This limitation will be more restrictive for small countries than for large countries because the latter will often have sizable domestic markets.

CHAPTER 34

5. The taxes on productive effort in Japan are low compared with taxes in the United States and other Western nations. Similarly, the rates of saving and investment are high in Japan compared with those of other countries. Think about how these factors affect the rate of growth in Japan. The importation of advanced technology from other countries also contributed to the rapid Japanese growth rate during the 1950–1975 period. Since Japanese technology generally lagged behind other industrial nations during the 1950s and 1960s, they were able to copy innovative technologies developed elsewhere. Since the application of technology to production is now up-to-date in Japan, they can no longer borrow previously developed technologies from more advanced economies. This restraint is likely to slow the growth rate of Japan compared with the growth rate achieved during the 1950–1975 period.

7. This view ignores the fact that additional current investment necessitates a reduction in current consumption. Thus, while *future* consumers may gain from a high level of capital formation, *current* consumers clearly must sacrifice consumption, when a large share of resources is allocated to investment.

8. Points to consider in your answer: What kinds of wealth do the two systems produce? Is there more personal security under socialism? If wealth is acquired from production and exchange that does not involve the use of theft, violence, or fraud, is it fair for the wealth to be taken and given to someone else?

10. Under capitalism, mass production and market penetration lead to wealth. But you cannot have large scale production without pricing the product so that it will be affordable to the mass consumer market. Thus, a market system rewards producers who figure out how to make products affordable to lots of consumers rather than just the rich. The careers of Henry Ford and Sir Henry Royce illustrate this point. Ford became a multimillionaire by bringing a low-cost automobile within the budget of mass consumers. In contrast, Royce died a man of modest wealth. He engineered the Rolls Royce, a car far superior to the Ford, but he designed it for the rich. The market rewarded him accordingly.

GLOSSARY

A

Ability-to-Pay Principle: The equity concept that people with larger incomes (or more consumption or more wealth) should be taxed at a higher rate because their ability to pay is presumably greater. The concept is subjective and fails to reveal how much higher the rate of taxation should be as income increases.

Absolute Advantage: A situation in which a nation, as the result of its previous experience and/or natural endowments, can produce a product with fewer resources than another nation.

Accounting Profits: The sales revenues minus the expenses of a firm over a designated time period, usually one year. Accounting profits typically make allowances for changes in the firm's inventories and depreciation of its assets. No allowance is made, however, for the opportunity cost of the equity capital of the firm's owners, or other implicit costs.

Acreage Restriction Program: A program designed to raise the price of an agricultural product by limiting the acreage planted with the product.

Active Budget Deficits: Deficits that reflect planned increases in government spending or reductions in taxes designed to generate a budget deficit.

Activist Strategy: The view that deliberate changes in monetary and fiscal policy can be used to inject demand stimulus during a recession and apply restraint during an inflationary boom and thereby minimize economic instability.

Adaptive Expectations Hypothesis: The hypothesis that economic decision-makers base their future expectations on actual outcomes observed during recent periods. For example, according to this view, the rate of inflation actually experienced during the last two or three years would be the major determinant of the expected rate of inflation for next year.

Administrative Lag: The time period between when the need for a policy change is recognized and when the policy is actually administered.

Aggregate Demand Curve: A downward sloping curve indicating an inverse relationship between the price level and the quantity of goods and services that households, business firms, governments and foreigners (net exports) are willing to purchase during a period.

Aggregate Supply Curve: A curve indicating the relationship between the price level and quantity of goods supplied by producers. In the short run, it is probably an upward sloping curve, but in the long run most economists believe the aggregate supply curve is vertical (or nearly so).

Allocative Efficiency: The allocation of resources to the production of goods and services most desired by consumers. The allocation is "balanced" in such a way that reallocation of resources could not benefit anyone without hurting someone else.

Allocative Inefficiency: The use of an uneconomical combination of resources to produce goods and services that are not intensely desired relative to their opportunity cost.

Anticipated Change: A change that is foreseen by decision-makers, in time for them to adjust.

Anticipated Inflation: An increase in the general level of prices that is expected by economic decision-makers. Past experience and current conditions are the major determinants of an individual's expectations with regard to future price changes.

Appreciation: An increase in the value of a domestic currency relative to foreign currencies. An appreciation increases the purchasing power of the domestic currency over foreign goods.

Asymmetric Information Problem: A problem arising when either buyers or sellers have important information about the product that is not possessed by the other side in potential transactions.

Automatic Stabilizers: Built-in features that tend automatically to promote a budget deficit during a recession and a budget surplus during an inflationary boom, even without a change in policy.

Automation: A production technique that reduces the amount of labor required to produce a good or service. It is beneficial to adopt the new labor-saving technology only if it reduces the cost of production.

Autonomous Expenditures: Expenditures that do not vary with the level of income. They are determined by factors (such as business expectations and economic policy) that are outside the basic income-expenditure model.

Average Fixed Costs: Fixed cost divided by the number of units produced. It always declines as output increases.

Average Product: The total product (output) divided by the number of units of the variable input required to produce that output level.

Average Tax Rate: One's tax liability divided by one's taxable income.

Average Total Cost: Total cost divided by the number of units produced. It is sometimes called per unit cost.

Average Variable Cost: The total variable cost divided by the number of units produced.

B

Balance of Merchandise Trade: The difference between the value of merchandise exports and the value of merchandise imports for a nation. The balance of trade is only one component of a nation's total balance of payments.

Balance of Payments: A summary of all economic transactions between a country and all other countries for a specific time period—usually a year. The balance of payments account reflects all payments and liabilities to foreigners (debits) and all payment and obligations (credits) received from foreigners.

Balance on Current Account: The import-export balance of goods and services plus net private and government transfers. If a nation's export of goods and services exceeds (is less than) the nation's import of goods and services plus net unilateral transfers to foreigners, a current account surplus (deficit) is present.

Balanced Budget: A situation in which current government revenue from taxes, fees, and other sources is just equal to current expenditures.

Barriers to Entry: Obstacles that limit the freedom of potential rivals to enter an industry.

Benefit-cost Analysis (B-C): A process used to determine the efficiency of a project by estimating each benefit and each cost. A project is said to be efficient if it generates more benefits than costs.

Break-Even Point: Under a negative income tax plan, the income level at which one neither pays taxes nor receives supplementary income transfers.

Budget Constraint: The constraint that separates the bundles of goods that the consumer can purchase from those that cannot be purchased, given a limited income and the prices of products.

Budget Deficit: A situation in which total government spending exceeds total government revenue during a specific time period, usually one year.

Budget Surplus: A situation in which total government spending is less than total government revenue during a time period, usually a year.

Business Cycle: Fluctuations in the general level of economic activity as measured by such variables as the rate of unemployment and changes in real GNP.

C

Capital Formation: The production of buildings, machinery, tools, and other equipment that will enhance the ability of future economic participants to produce. The term can also be applied to efforts to upgrade the knowledge and skill of workers and thereby increase their ability to produce in the future.

Capitalism: An economic system based on private ownership of productive resources and allocation of goods according to the signals provided by free markets.

Cartel: An organization of sellers designed to coordinate supply decisions so that the joint profits of the members will be maximized. A cartel will seek to create a monopoly in the market.

Choice: The act of selecting among alternatives.

Classical Economists: Economists from Adam Smith to the time of Keynes who focused their analyses on economic efficiency and production. With regard to business instability, they thought market prices would adjust quickly in a manner that would guide an economy out of a recession back to full employment.

Collective Bargaining Contract: A detailed contract between (a) a group of employees (a labor union) and (b) an employer. It covers wage rates and conditions of employment.

Collective Decision-making: The method of organization that relies on public-sector decision-making (voting, political bargaining, lobbying, and so on). It can be used to resolve the basic economic problems of an economy.

Collusion: Agreement among firms to avoid various competitive practices, particularly price reductions. It may involve either formal agreements or merely tacit recognition that competitive practices will be self-defeating in the long run. Tacit collusion is difficult to detect. The Sherman Act prohibits collusion and conspiracies to restrain interstate trade.

Command Economy: An authoritarian socialist economy characterized by centralized planning and detailed directives to productive units. Individual enterprises have little discretionary decision-making power.

Commercial Banks: Financial institutions that offer a wide range of services (for example, checking accounts, savings accounts, and extension of loans) to their customers. Commercial banks are owned by stockholders and seek to operate at a profit.

Common Property Resource: A resource for which rights are held in common by a group of individuals, none of whom has a transferable ownership interest. Access to the resource may be open (unrestricted), or may be controlled politically.

Competition as a Dynamic Process: A term that denotes rivalry or competitiveness between or among parties (for example, producers or input suppliers), each of which seeks to deliver a better deal to buyers when quality, price, and product information are all considered. Competing implies a lack of collision among sellers.

Complements: Products that are usually consumed jointly (for example, lamps and light bulbs). An increase in the price of one will cause the demand for the other to fall.

Concentration Ratio: The total sales of the four (or sometimes eight) largest firms in an industry as a percentage of the total sales of the industry. The higher the ratio, the greater is the market dominance of a small number of firms. The ratio can be seen as a measure of oligopolistic power.

Conglomerate Merger: The combining under one ownership of two or more firms that produce *unrelated products*.

Constant Cost Industry: An industry for which factor prices and costs of production remain constant as market output is expanded. Thus, the long-run market supply curve is horizontal.

Constant Returns to Scale: Unit costs are constant as the scale of the firm is altered. Neither economies nor diseconomies of scale are present.

Consumer Price Index: An indicator of the general level of prices. It attempts to compare the cost of purchasing the market basket bought by a typical consumer during a specific period with the cost of purchasing the same market basket during an earlier period.

Consumer Surplus: The difference between the maximum amount a consumer would be willing to pay for a unit of a good and the payment that is actually made.

Consumption: Household spending on consumer goods and services during the current period. Consumption is a flow concept.

Consumption Function: A fundamental relationship between disposable income and consumption. As disposable income increases, current consumption expenditures will rise, but by a smaller amount than the increase in income.

Consumption Opportunity Constraint: The constraint that separates the consumption bundles that are attainable from those that are unattainable. In a money income economy, it is usually called a budget constraint.

Countercyclical Policy: A policy that tends to move the economy in an opposite direction from the forces of the business cycle. Such a policy would stimulate demand during the contraction phase of the business cycle and restrain demand during the expansionary phase.

Credit Unions: Financial cooperative organizations of individuals with a common affiliation (such as an employer or labor union). They accept deposits, including checkable deposits, pay interest (or dividends) on them out of earnings, and channel funds primarily into loans to members.

Crowding-Out Effects: A reduction in private spending as a result of high interest rates generated by budget deficits that are financed by borrowing in the private loanable funds market.

Current Account: The record of all transactions with foreign nations that involve the exchange of merchandise goods and services or unilateral gifts.

Cyclical Unemployment: Unemployment due to recessionary business conditions and inadequate aggregate demand for labor.

D

Dead-End Jobs: Jobs that offer the employee little opportunity for advancement or on-the-job training.

Deadweight Loss: A net loss associated with the forgoing of an economic action. The loss does not lead to an offsetting gain for other participants. It thus reflects economic inefficiency.

Decreasing Cost Industries: Industries for which costs of production decline as the industry expands. The market supply is therefore inversely related to price. Such industries are atypical.

Deflationary Gap: The situation present when the short-run equilibrium output is less than full employment potential. Weak demand conditions place downward pressure on prices.

Demand Deposits: Noninterest-earning deposits in a bank that either can be withdrawn or made payable on demand to a third party via check. In essence, they are "checkbook money" because they permit transactions to be paid for by check rather than by currency.

Demand for Money: At any given interest rate, the amount of wealth that people desire to hold in the form of money balances; that is, cash and checking account deposits. The quantity demanded is inversely related to the interest rate.

Dependency Ratio: The number of children (under a specific age—14, for example) and the number of the elderly (age 65 and over) living in a country, divided by the total population. An increasing ratio indicates that a larger burden is being placed on the productive-age work force.

Deposit Expansion Multiplier: The multiple by which an increase (decrease) in reserves will increase (decrease) the money supply. It is inversely related to the required reserve ratio.

Depreciation: A reduction in the value of a domestic currency relative to foreign currencies. A depreciation reduces the purchasing power of the domestic currency over foreign goods.

Depression: A prolonged and very severe recession.

Derived Demand: Demand for an item based on the demand for products the item helps to produce. The demand for resources is a derived demand.

Devaluation: An official act that changes the level of the "fixed" exchange rate in a downward direction. In essence, it is a one-step depreciation of a currency under a fixed exchange rate system.

Differentiated Products: Products distinguished from similar products by such characteristics as quality, design, location, and method of promotion.

Discount Rate: The interest rate the Federal Reserve charges banking institutions for borrowing funds.

Discounting: The procedure used to calculate the present value of future income. The present value of future income is inversely related to both the interest rate and the amount of time that passes before the funds are received.

Discouraged Workers: Persons who have given up searching for employment because they believe additional job search would be fruitless. Since they are not currently searching for work, they are not counted among the unemployed.

Discretionary Fiscal Policy: A change in laws or appropriation levels that alters government revenues and/or expenditures.

Discretionary Monetary Policy: Changes in monetary policy instituted at the discretion of policy-makers. The policy is not predetermined by rules or formulas.

Disposable Income: The income available to individuals after personal taxes. It can either be spent on consumption or saved.

Division of Labor: A method that breaks down the production of a commodity into a series of specific tasks, each performed by a different worker.

Dumping: The sale of a good by a foreign supplier in another country at a price lower than the supplier sells it in its home market.

E

Economic Efficiency: Economizing behavior. When applied to a community, it implies that (a) an activity should be undertaken if the sum of the benefits to the individuals exceeds the sum of their costs and (b) no activity should be undertaken if the costs borne by the individuals exceed the benefits.

Economic Good: A good that is scarce. The desire for economic goods exceeds the amount that is freely available from Nature.

Economic Profit: A return to investors that exceeds the opportunity cost of financial capital.

Economic Regulation: Regulation of product price or industrial structure, usually imposed on a specific industry. By and large, the production processes used by the regulated firms are unaffected by this type of regulation.

Economic Theory: A set of definitions, postulates, and principles assembled in a manner that makes clear the "cause-and-effect" relationships of economic data.

Economies of Scale: Reductions in the firm's per unit costs that are associated with the use of large plants to produce a large volume of output.

Economizing Behavior: Choosing the objective of gaining a specific benefit at the least possible cost. A corollary of economizing behavior implies that when choosing among items of equal cost, individuals will choose the option that yields the greatest benefit.

Elasticity of Supply: The percentage change in quantity supplied, divided by the percentage change in the price that causes that change in quantity supplied.

Employment Discrimination: Unequal treatment of persons on the basis of their race, sex, or religion, which restricts their employment and earnings opportunities compared with others of similar productivity. Employment discrimination may stem from the prejudices of employers, consumers and/or fellow employees.

Entrepreneur: A profit-seeking decision-maker who decides which projects to undertake and how they should be undertaken. A successful entrepreneur's actions will increase the value of resources.

Equation of Exchange: $MV = PQ$, where M is the money supply, V is the velocity of money, P is the price level, and Q is the quantity of goods and services produced.

Equilibrium: A balance of forces permitting the simultaneous fulfillment of plans for buyers and sellers.

Escalator Clause: A contractual agreement that periodically and automatically adjusts the wage rates of a collective-bargaining agreement upward by an amount determined by the rate of inflation.

Eurodollar Deposits: Deposits denominated in U.S. dollars at banks and other financial institutions outside the United States. Although this name originated because of the large amounts of such deposits held at banks in Western Europe, similar deposits in other parts of the world are also called Eurodollars.

Excess Burden of Taxation: A burden of taxation over and above the burden associated with the transfer of revenues to the government. An excess burden usually reflects losses that occur when beneficial activities are forgone because they are taxed.

Excess Reserves: Actual reserves that exceed the legal requirement.

Excess Supply of Money: Situation in which the actual money balances of individuals and business firms are in excess of their desired level. Thus, decision-makers will increase their spending on other assets and goods until they reduce their actual balances to the desired level.

Exchange Rate: The domestic piece of one unit of foreign currency. For example, if it takes $1.50 to purchase one English pound, the dollar-pound exchange rate is 1.50.

Exchange Rate Conversion Method: Method that uses the foreign exchange rate value of a nation's currency to convert that nation's GNP to another monetary unit, such as the U.S. dollar.

Exclusive Contract: An agreement between manufacturer and retailer that prohibits the retailer from carrying the product lines of firms that are rivals of the manufacturer. Such contracts are illegal under the Clayton Act when they "lessen competition."

Existence Value: The satisfaction people can derive simply from knowing that something—the Grand Canyon or Hoover Dam, for example—exists. It is extremely difficult to measure existence values.

Expansionary Fiscal Policy: An increase in government expenditures and/or a reduction in tax rates such that the expected size of the budget deficit expands.

Expansionary Monetary Policy: An acceleration in the growth rate of the money supply.

Explicit Costs: Money paid by a firm to purchase the services of productive resources.

Exports: Goods and services produced domestically but sold to foreigners.

Extensive Economic Growth: An expansion in the total output of goods and services, regardless of whether or not output per capita increases.

External Benefits: Beneficial effects of group or individual action on the welfare of nonpaying secondary parties.

External Costs: Harmful effects of an individual's or a group's action on the welfare of nonconsenting secondary parties, not accounted for in market prices. Litterbugs, drunk drivers, and polluters, for example, create external costs.

External Debt: That portion of the national debt owed to foreign investors.

Externalities: The side effects of an action that influence the well-being of nonconsenting parties. The nonconsenting parties may be either helped (by external benefits) or harmed (by external costs).

F

Fallacy of Composition: Erroneous view that what is true for the individual (or the part) will also be true for the group (or the whole).

Federal Funds Market: A loanable funds market in which banks seeking additional reserves borrow short-term (generally for seven days or less) funds from banks with excess reserves. The interest rate in this market is called the federal funds rate.

Federal Reserve System: The central bank of the United States; it carries out banking regulatory policies and is responsible for the conduct of monetary policy.

Fiat Money: Money that has little intrinsic value; it is neither backed by nor convertible to a commodity of value.

Final Goods and Services: Goods and services purchased by their ultimate users.

Fiscal Policy: The use of government taxation and expenditure policies for the purpose of achieving macroeconomic goals.

Fixed Costs: Cost that does not vary with output. However, fixed cost will be incurred as long as a firm continues in business and the assets have alternative uses.

Fixed Exchange Rate System: An international monetary system in which each country's currency is set at a fixed rate relative to all other currencies and governmental policies are used to maintain the fixed rate.

Flexible Exchange Rates: Exchange rates that are determined by the market forces of supply and demand. They are sometimes called "floating exchange rates."

Foreign Exchange Market: The market in which the currencies of different countries are bought and sold.

Fractional Reserve Banking: A system that enables banks to keep less than 100 percent reserves against their deposits. Required reserves are a fraction of deposits.

Free Rider: One who receives the benefit of a good without contributing to its costs. Public goods and commodities that generate external benefits offer people the opportunity to become free riders.

Frictional Unemployment: Unemployment due to constant changes in the economy that prevent *qualified* unemployed workers from being immediately matched up with existing job openings. It results from lack of complete information on the part of both job seekers and employers and from the amount of unemployed time spent by job seekers in job searches (pursuit of costly information).

Fringe Benefits: Benefits other than normal money wages that are supplied to employees in exchange for their labor services.

Full Employment: The level of employment that results from the efficient use of the civilian labor force after allowance is made for the normal (natural) rate of unemployment due to dynamic changes and the structural conditions of the economy. For the United States, full employment is thought to exist when between 94 and 95 percent of the labor force is employed.

G

General Agreement on Tariffs and Trade (GATT): An organization composed of most non-Communist countries designed to set the rules for the conduct of international trade and reduce barriers to trade among nations.

GNP Deflator: A price index that reveals the cost of purchasing the items included in GNP during the period relative to the cost of purchasing these same items during a base year (currently, 1982). Since the base year is assigned a value of 100, as the GNP deflator takes on values greater than 100, it indicates that prices have risen.

Going Out of Business: The sale of a firm's assets, and its permanent exit from the market. By going out of business, a firm is able to avoid fixed cost, which would continue during a shutdown.

Goods and Services Market: A highly aggregate market encompassing all final user goods and services during a period. The market counts all items that enter into GNP. Thus, real output in this market is equal to real GNP.

Gosplan: The central planning agency in the Soviet Union.

Government Failure: Failure of government action to meet the criteria of ideal economic efficiency.

Government Purchases: Current expenditures on goods and services provided by federal, state, and local government; They exclude transfer payments.

Gross National Product: The total market value of all ''final product'' goods and services produced during a specific period, usually a year.

H

Head Tax: A lump-sum tax levied on all individuals, regardless of their income, consumption, wealth, or other indicators of economic well-being.

Herfindahl Index: A measure of industry concentration, calculated by squaring the percentage share of each firm in the industry, then summing the squares. The index can range from zero to 10,000. It is a more sophisticated measure of concentration than the traditional concentration ratio, and is used by the Justice Department in antitrust policy.

Homogeneous Product: A product of one firm that is identical to the product of every other firm in the industry. Consumers see no difference in units of the product offered by alternative sellers.

Horizontal Merger: The combining of the assets of two or more firms engaged in the production of *similar products into a single firm.*

Human Resources: The abilities, skills, and health of human beings that can contribute to the production of both current and future output. Investment in training and education can increase the supply of human resources.

I

Impact Lag: The time period between when a policy change is implemented and when the change begins to exert its primary effects.

Implicit Costs: The opportunity costs associated with a firm's use of resources that it owns. These costs do *not* involve a direct money payment. Examples include wage income and interest forgone by the owner of a firm who also provides labor services and equity capital to the firm.

Import Quota: A specific quantity (or value) of a good permitted to be imported into a country during a given year.

Imports: Goods and services produced by foreigners but purchased by domestic consumers, investors, and governments.

Income Effect: That part of an increase (decrease) in amount consumed that is the result of the consumer's real income (the consumption possibilities available to the consumer) being expanded (contracted) by a reduction (increase) in the price of a good.

Income Elasticity: The percent change in the quantity of a product demanded divided by the percent change in consumer income. It measures the responsiveness of the demand for a good to a change in income.

Income Mobility: Movement of individuals and families either up or down income distribution rankings when comparisons are made at two different points in time. When substantial income mobility is present, one's current position will not be a very good indicator as to what one's position will be a few years in the future.

Increasing Cost Industries: Industries for which costs of production rise as the industry output is expanded. Thus, the long-run market supply is directly related to price.

Index of Leading Indicators: An index of economic variables that historically has tended to turn down prior to the beginning of a recession and turn up prior to the beginning of a business expansion.

Indexing: The automatic increasing of money values as the general level of prices increases. Economic variables that are often indexed include wage rates and tax brackets.

Indifference Curve: A curve, convex from below, that separates the consumption bundles that are more preferred by an individual from those that are less preferred. The points *on* the curve represent combinations of goods that are equally preferred by the individual.

Industrial Capacity Utilization Rate: An index designed to measure the extent to which the economy's existing plant and equipment capacity is being used.

Inferior Goods: Goods for which the income elasticity is negative. Thus, an increase in consumer income causes the demand for such a good to decline.

Inflation: A continuing rise in the general level of prices of goods and services. The purchasing power of the monetary unit, such as the dollar, declines when inflation is present.

Inflationary Gap: The situation present when the short-run equilibrium output exceeds full employment potential GNP. The strong demand places upward pressure on prices.

Inflationary Premium: A component of the money interest rate that reflects compensation to the lender for the expected decrease, due to inflation, in the purchasing power of the principal and interest during the course of the loan. It is equal to the expected rate of future inflation.

Infrastructure: The provision of a legal, monetary, educational, transportation, and communication structure necessary for the efficient operation of an exchange economy.

Innovation: The successful introduction and adoption of a new product or process; the economic application of inventions.

Intensive Economic Growth: An increase in output per person. When intensive economic growth is present, output is growing more rapidly than population.

Intermediate Goods: Goods purchased for resale or for use in producing another good or service.

International Monetary Fund: An international banking organization, with more than 100 nation members, designed to oversee the operation of the international monetary system. Although it does not control the world supply of money, it does hold currency reserves for member nations and make currency loans to national central banks.

Invention: The discovery of a new product or process, often facilitated by the knowledge of engineering and scientific relationships.

Inventory Investment: Changes in the stock of unsold goods and raw materials held during a period.

Investment: The flow of expenditures on durable assets (fixed investment) plus the addition to inventories (inventory investment) during a period. These expenditures enhance our ability to provide consumer benefits in the future.

Investment in Human Capital: Expenditures on training, education, and skill development designed to increase the productivity of an individual.

Invisible Hand Principle: The tendency of market prices to direct individuals pursuing their own interests into productive activities that also promote the economic well being of the society.

Irreversibility: Once an action is taken, some physical effects may not be reversible—the prior physical conditions cannot be restored. Such a situation involves an irreversibility.

J

J-Curve Effect: The tendency of a nation's current account deficit to widen initially before it shrinks in response to an exchange rate depreciation. This tendency results because the short-run demand for both imports and exports is often inelastic, even though the long-run demand is almost always elastic.

K

Kinked Demand Curve: A demand curve that is highly elastic for a price *increase* but inelastic for a price *reduction*. These differing elasticities are based on the assumption that rival firms will match a price reduction but not a price increase.

L

Labor Force: The portion of the population 16 years of age and over who are either employed or unemployed.

Labor Union: A collective organization of employees who bargain as a unit with employers.

Laffer Curve: A curve illustrating the relationship between tax rates and tax revenues. The curve reflects the fact that tax revenues are low for both very high and very low tax rates.

Law of Comparative Advantage: A principle that states that individuals, firms, regions, or nations can gain by specializing in the production of goods that they produce cheaply (that is, at a low opportunity cost) and exchanging those goods for other desired goods for which they are high opportunity cost producers.

Law of Demand: A principle that states that there is an inverse relationship between the price of a good and the amount of it buyers are willing to purchase.

Law of Diminishing Marginal Utility: A basic economic principle that states that as the consumption of a commodity increases, the marginal utility derived from consuming more of the commodity (per unit of time) will eventually decline. Marginal utility may decline even though total utility continues to increase, albeit at a reduced rate.

Law of Diminishing Returns: The postulate that as more and more units of a variable resource are combined with a fixed amount of other resources, employment of *additional* units of the variable resource will eventually increase output only at a decreasing rate. Once diminishing returns are reached, it will take successively larger amounts of the variable factor to expand output by one unit.

Law of Supply: A principle that states that there will be a direct relationship between the price of a good and the amount of it offered for sale.

Less Developed Countries: Low income countries characterized by rapid population growth, an agriculture-household sector that dominates the economy, illiteracy, extreme poverty, and a high degree of inequality.

Lifetime Employment Commitment: An arrangement offered by most large firms in Japan whereby employees are guaranteed employment until age 55 unless guilty of misconduct.

Liquid Asset: An asset that can be easily and quickly converted to purchasing power without loss of value.

Loanable Funds Market: A general term used to describe the market arrangements that coordinate the borrowing and lending decisions of business firms and households. Commercial banks, savings and loan associations, the stock and bond markets, and insurance companies are important financial institutions in this market.

Logrolling: The exchange between politicians of political support on one issue for political support on another issue.

Long Run: A time period of sufficient length to enable decision-makers to adjust fully to a market change. For example, in the long-run, producers will have time to alter their utilization of all productive factors, including the heavy equipment and physical structure of their plants.

Long Run (in Production): A time period long enough to allow the firm to vary all factors of production.

Loss: Deficit of sales revenue relative to the cost of production, once all the resources used have received their opportunity cost. Losses are a penalty imposed on those who use resources in lower rather than higher valued uses, as judged by buyers in the market.

M

Macroeconomics: The branch of economics that focuses on how human behavior affects outcomes in highly aggregated markets, such as the markets for labor or consumer products.

Mandated Benefits: Government mandated fringe benefits that must be included in the total compensation package of employees.

Marginal: Term used to describe the effects of a change, given the current situation. For example, the marginal cost is the cost of producing an additional unit of a product, given the producer's current facility and production rate.

Marginal Cost: The change in total cost required to produce an additional unit of output.

Marginal Factor Cost: The cost of employing an additional unit of a resource. When the employer is small relative to the total market, the marginal factor cost is simply the price of the resource. In contrast, under monopsony, marginal factor cost will exceed the price of the resource, since the monopsonist faces an upward-sloping supply curve for the resource.

Marginal Product: The increase in the total product resulting from a unit increase in the employment of a variable input. Mathematically, it is the ratio of (a) change in total product to the (b) change in the quantity of the variable input.

Marginal Propensity to Consume: Additional current consumption divided by additional current disposable income.

Marginal Rate of Substitution: The change in the consumption level of one good that is just sufficient to offset a unit change in the consumption of another good without causing a shift to another indifference curve. At any point on an indifference curve, it will be equal to the slope of the curve at that point.

Marginal Revenue: The incremental change in total revenue derived from the sale of one additional unit of a product.

Marginal Revenue Product: The change in the total revenue of a firm that results from the employment of one additional unit of a factor of production. The marginal revenue product of an input is equal to its marginal product multiplied by the marginal revenue (price) of the good or service produced.

Marginal Tax Rate: Additional tax liability divided by additional income. Thus, if $100 of additional earnings increases one's tax liability by $30, the marginal tax rate would be 30 percent.

Marginal Utility: The additional utility received by a person from the consumption of an additional unit of a good within a given time period.

Market: An abstract concept that encompasses the trading arrangements of buyers and sellers that underlie the forces of supply and demand.

Market Failure: The failure of the market system to attain hypothetically *ideal* allocative efficiency. This means that potential gain exists that has not been captured. However, the cost of establishing a mechanism that could *potentially* capture the gain may exceed the benefits. Therefore, it is not always possible to improve the situation.

Market Mechanism: A method of organization that allows unregulated prices and the decentralized decisions of private property owners to resolve the basic economic problems of consumption, production, and distribution.

Market Power: The ability of a firm that is not a pure monopolist to earn unusually large profits, indicating that it has some monopoly power. Because the firm has a few (or weak) competitors, it has a degree of freedom from the discipline of vigorous competition.

Material Balance Method: A method of central planning employed in the Soviet Union and other Eastern European countries whereby the planning agency keeps track of the physical units of resources and allocates them among state enterprises in a manner that will permit each enterprise to achieve its targeted output and thereby lead to the fulfillment of the economy's central plan.

Maximum Emission Standard: The maximum amount of pollution that a polluter is permitted to emit, established by the government or a regulatory authority. Fines are generally imposed on those who are unwilling or unable to comply.

Means-tested Income Transfers: Transfers that are limited to persons or families with an income below a certain cut-off point. Eligibility is thus dependent on low-income status.

Measure of Economic Welfare: A new measure of economic well-being that focuses on the consumption of goods and services during a period. It differs from GNP in that (a) the estimated cost of various economic "bads" are deducted, (b) expenditures on "regrettable necessities" are excluded, and (c) the estimated benefits of leisure and various nonmarket productive activities are included.

Microeconomics: The branch of economics that focuses on how human behavior affects the conduct of affairs within narrowly defined units, such as individual households or business firms.

Middleman: A person who buys and sells, or who arranges trades. A middleman reduces transaction costs, usually for a fee or a markup in price.

Minimum Wage Legislation: Legislation requiring that all workers in specified industries be paid at least the stated minimum hourly rate of pay.

Monetarists: A group of economists who believe that (a) monetary instability is the major cause of fluctuations in real GNP and (b) rapid growth of the money supply is the major cause of inflation.

Monetary Base: The sum of currency in circulation plus bank reserves (vault cash and reserves with the Fed). It reflects the stock of U.S. securities held by the Fed.

Monetary Policy: The deliberate control of the money supply and, in some cases, credit conditions for the purpose of achieving macroeconomic goals.

Money Interest Rate: The interest rate measured in dollars. It overstates the real cost of borrowing during an inflationary period. When inflation is anticipated, an inflationary premium will be incorporated into the nominal value of this rate.

Money Rate of Interest: The rate of interest in monetary terms that borrowers pay for borrowed funds. During periods when borrowers and lenders expect inflation, the money rate of interest exceeds the real rate of interest.

Money Supply: The supply of currency, checking account funds, and traveler's checks. These items are counted as money since they are used as the means of payment for purchases.

Money Supply (M1): The sum of (a) currency in circulation (including coins), (b) demand deposits, (c) other checkable deposits of depository institutions, and (d) traveler's checks.

Money Supply (M2): Equal to M1, plus (a) savings and time deposits (accounts of less than $100,000) of all depository institutions, (b) money market mutual fund shares, (c) money market deposit accounts, (d) overnight loans from customers to commercial banks, and (e) overnight Eurodollar deposits held by U.S. residents.

Money Supply (M3): Equal to M2, plus (a) time deposits

(accounts of more than $100,000) at all depository institutions and (b) longer-term (more than overnight) loans of customers to commercial banks and savings and loan associations.

Monopolistic Competition: A situation in which there are a large number of independent sellers, each producing a differentiated product in a market with low barriers to entry. Construction, retail sales, and service stations are good examples of monopolistically competitive industries.

Monopoly: A market structure characterized by a single seller of a well-defined product for which there are no good substitutes and by high barriers to the entry of any other firms into the market for that product.

Monopsony: A market in which there is only one buyer. The monopsonist confronts the market supply curve for the resource (or product) bought.

Multiplier: The ratio of the change in equilibrium output to the independent change in investment, consumption, or government spending that brings about that change. Numerically, the multiplier is equal to $1/(1-MPC)$ when the price level is constant.

Multiplier Principle: The concept that an induced increase in consumption, investment, or government expenditures leads to additional income and consumption spending by secondary parties and therefore expands total spending by a larger amount than the initial increase in expenditures.

Mutual Savings Banks: Financial institutions that accept deposits in exchange for interest payments. Historically, home mortgages have constituted their primary interest-earning assets. Under recent banking legislation, these banks, too, are authorized to offer interest-bearing checkable accounts.

N

National Debt: The sum of the indebtedness of the federal government in the form of outstanding interest-earning bonds. It reflects the cumulative impact of budget deficits and surpluses.

National Income: The total income payments to owners of human (labor) and physical capital during a period. It is also equal to NNP minus indirect businesses taxes.

Natural Monopoly: A market situation in which the average costs of production continually decline with increased output. Therefore, average costs of production will be lowest when a single large firm produces the entire output demanded.

Natural Rate of Unemployment: The long-run average of unemployment due to frictional and structural conditions of labor markets. This rate is affected both by dynamic change and by public policy. It is sustainable in the future.

Negative Income Tax: A system of transferring income to the poor, whereby a minimum level of income would be guaranteed by the provision of income supplements. The supplement would be reduced by some fraction (less than 1) of the additional income earned by the family. An increase in earnings would always cause the disposable income available to the family to rise.

Net Federal Debt: The portion of the national debt owed to domestic and foreign investors. It does *not* include bonds held by agencies of the federal government or the Federal Reserve.

Net National Product: Gross national product minus a depreciation allowance for the wearing out of machines and buildings during the period.

Net Present Value: The current worth of future income after it is discounted to reflect the fact that revenues in the future are valued less highly than revenues now.

Neutral Tax: A tax that does not (a) distort consumer buying patterns or producer production methods or (b) induce individuals to engage in tax avoidance activities. There will be no excess burden if a tax is neutral.

New Classical Economists: Modern economists who believe there are strong forces pushing a market economy toward full employment equilibrium and that macroeconomic policy is an ineffective tool with which to reduce economic instability.

Nominal GNP: GNP expressed at current prices. It is often called money GNP.

Nominal Values: The value of economic variables such as GNP and personal consumption expressed in current prices. A general increase in prices will cause nominal values to rise even when there is no real change in the variable (quantity produced or consumed).

Nonactivist Strategy: The maintenance of the same monetary and fiscal policy—that is, no change in money growth, tax rates, or expenditures—during all phases of the business cycle.

Nonhuman Resources: The durable, nonhuman inputs that can be used to produce both

current and future output.
Machines, buildings, land, and
raw materials are examples.
Investment can increase the
supply of nonhuman resources.
Economists often use the term
"physical capital" when
referring to nonhuman
resources.

**Nonpecuniary Job
Characteristics:** Working
conditions, prestige, variety,
location, employee freedom and
responsibilities, and other
nonwage characteristics of a job
that influence how employees
evaluate the job.

Nonpersonal Time Deposits:
Time deposits owned by
businesses or corporations.

Normative Economics:
Judgments about "what ought
to be" in economic matters.
Normative economic views
cannot be proved false, because
they are based on value
judgments.

O

Oligopoly: A market situation in
which a small number of sellers
comprise the entire industry. It
is competition among the few.

Open Access Resource: A
resource to which access is
unrestricted. No one has the
right to exclude others from
using the resource. Overuse and
abuse of such a resource is
typical.

Open Market Operations: The
buying and selling of U.S.
government securities (national
debt) by the Federal Reserve.

Opportunity Cost: The highest
valued benefit that must be
sacrificed (forgone) as the result
of choosing an alternative.

Opportunity Cost of Capital:
The implicit rate of return that
must be paid to investors to
induce them to continuously

supply the funds necessary to
maintain a firm's capital assets.

P

Passive Budget Deficits: Deficits
that merely reflect the decline in
economic activity during a
recession.

Patent: The grant of an exclusive
right to use a specific process or
produce a specific product for a
period of time (17 years in the
United States).

Permanent Income Hypothesis:
The hypothesis that
consumption depends on some
measure of long-run expected
(permanent) income rather than
on current income.

Personal Income: The total
income received by individuals
that is available for
consumption, saving, and
payment of personal taxes.

Phillips Curve: A curve that
illustrates the relationship
between the rate of change in
prices (or money wages) and
the rate of unemployment.

Policy Ineffectiveness Theorem:
The proposition that any
systematic policy will be
rendered ineffective once
decision-makers figure out the
policy pattern and adjust their
decision-making in light of its
expected effects. The theorem is
a corollary of the theory of
rational expectations.

Political Good: Any good (or
policy) supplied by the political
process.

Pork-Barrel Legislation: A
package of spending projects
benefiting local areas at federal
expense. The projects typically
have costs that exceed benefits,
but each is intensely desired by
the residents of the district
getting the benefits without
having to pay much of the
costs.

Positive Economics: The

scientific study of "what is"
among economic relationships.

**Positive Rate of Time
Preference:** The desire of
consumers for goods now rather
than in the future.

Potential Output: The level of
output that can be achieved and
sustained into the future, given
the size of the labor force,
expected productivity of labor,
and natural rate of
unemployment consistent with
the efficient operation of the
labor market. For periods of
time, the actual output may
differ from the economy's
potential.

**Poverty Threshold Income
Level:** The level of money
income below which a family is
considered to be poor. It differs
according to family
characteristics (for example,
number of family members) and
is adjusted when consumer
prices change.

Predatory Pricing: The practice
by which a dominant firm in an
industry temporarily reduces
price to damage or eliminate
weaker rivals, so that prices can
be raised above the level of
costs at a later time.

Price Ceiling: A legally
established maximum price that
sellers may charge.

Price Discrimination: A practice
whereby a seller charges
different consumers different
prices for the same product or
service.

Price Elasticity of Demand: The
percent change in the quantity
of a product demanded divided
by the percent change in the
price causing the change in
quantity. Price elasticity of
demand indicates the degree of
consumer response to variation
in price.

Price Equalization Principle:
The tendency for markets, when

trade restrictions are absent, to establish a uniform price for each good throughout the world (except for price differences due to transport costs and differential tax treatment of the good).

Price Floor: A legally established minimum price that buyers must pay for a good or resource.

Price Searcher: A seller with imperfect information, facing a downward sloping demand curve, who tries to find the price that maximizes profit.

Price Support Programs: Legislative action establishing a minimum price for an agricultural product. The government pledges to purchase any surplus of the product that cannot be sold to consumers at the support price.

Price Takers: Sellers who must take the market price in order to sell their product. Because each price taker's output is small relative to the total market, price takers can sell all of their output at the market price, but are unable to sell any of their output at a price higher than the market price. Thus, they face a horizontal demand curve.

Principal-Agent Problem: The incentive problem arising when the purchaser of services (the principal) lacks full information about the circumstances faced by the seller (the agent) and thus cannot know how well the agent performs the assigned activity. The agent may to some extent work toward objectives other than those sought by the principal paying for the service.

Private Property Rights: Property rights that are held exclusively by an owner, and that can be transferred to others at the owner's discretion.

Production Possibilities Curve: A curve that outlines all possible combinations of total output that could be produced, assuming (a) the utilization of a fixed amount of productive resources, (b) full and efficient use of those resources, and (c) a specific state of technical knowledge. The slope of the curve indicates the rate at which one product can be traded off to produce more of the other.

Productivity: The average output produced per worker during a specific time period. It is usually measured in terms of output per hour worked.

Profit: An excess of sales revenue relative to the cost of production. The cost component includes the opportunity cost of all resources, including those owned by the firm. Therefore, profit accrues only when the value of the good produced is greater than the sum of the values of the individual resources utilized.

Progressive Tax: A tax that requires those with higher taxable incomes to pay a larger percentage of their incomes to the government than those with lower taxable incomes.

Property Rights: The right to use, control, and obtain the benefits from a good or service.

Proportional Tax: A tax for which individuals pay the same percentage of their income (or other tax base) in taxes, regardless of income level.

Proved Reserves: The verified quantity of a resource that can be recovered at current prices and levels of technology.

Public Choice Analysis: The study of decision-making as it affects the formation and operation of collective organizations, such as governments. The discipline bridges the gap between economics and political science.

In general, the principles and methodology of economics are applied to political science topics.

Pure Competition: A model of industrial structure characterized by a large number of small firms producing a homogeneous product in an industry (market area) that permits complete freedom of entry and exit.

Public Goods: Jointly consumed goods. When consumed by one person, they are also made available to others. National defense, poetry, and scientific theories are all public goods.

Purchasing Power Parity Method: Method for determining the relative purchasing power of different currencies by comparing the amount of each currency required to purchase a typical bundle of goods and services in domestic markets. This information is then used to convert the GNP of each nation to a common monetary unit.

Q

Quantity Theory of Money: A theory that hypothesizes that a change in the money supply will cause a proportional change in the price level because velocity and real output are unaffected by the quantity of money.

R

Rate of Employment: The number of persons 16 years of age and over who are employed as a percentage of the total noninstitutional population 16 years of age and over. One can calculate either (a) a civilian rate of employment, in which only civilian employees are included in the numerator, or

(b) a total rate of employment, in which both civilian and military employees are included in the numerator.

Rate of Labor Force Participation: The number of persons 16 years of age or over who are either employed or actively seeking employment as a percentage of the total noninstitutional population 16 years of age and over.

Rate-of-Return Equalization Principle: The tendency for capital investment in each market to move toward a uniform or normal rate of return. An abnormally high return in a market will attract additional investment which will drive returns down. Conversely, an abnormally low return will result in investment flight from the market which will eventually lead to the restoration of normal returns.

Rate of Unemployment: The percent of persons in the civilian labor force who are not employed. Mathematically, it is equal to:

$$\frac{\text{Number of persons unemployed}}{\text{Number in civilian labor force}} \times 100$$

Rational Expectations Hypothesis: This viewpoint expects individuals to weigh all available evidence, including information concerning the probable effects of current and future economic policy, when they formulate their expectations about future economic events (such as the probable future inflation rate).

Rational Ignorance Effect: Voter ignorance that is present because people perceive their individual votes as unlikely to be decisive. Voters rationally have little incentive to inform themselves so as to cast an informed vote.

Rationing: An allocation of a limited supply of a good or resource to users who would like to have more of it. Various criteria, including charging a price, can be utilized to allocate the limited supply. When price performs the rationing function, the good or resource is allocated to those willing to give up the most ''other things'' in order to obtain ownership rights.

Real Balance Effect: The increase in wealth emanating from an increase in the purchasing power of a constant money supply as the price level declines. This wealth effect leads to a negative relationship between price (level) and quantity demanded in the goods and services market.

Real GNP: GNP in current dollars deflated for changes in the prices of the items included in GNP. Mathematically, real GNP_2 is equal to nominal GNP_2 multiplied by (GNP $Deflator_1$/ GNP $Deflator_2$). Thus, if prices have risen between periods 1 and 2, the ratio of the GNP deflator in period 1 to the deflator in period 2 will be less than 1. This ratio will therefore deflate the nominal GNP for the rising prices.

Real Interest Rate: The interest rate adjusted for expected inflation; it indicates the real cost to the borrower (and yield to the lender) in terms of goods and services.

Real Price: The cost of an item, corrected for inflation. For example, if the price of oil doubles while the prices of all other goods also double, the real price of oil is unchanged. Decisions are generally based on real prices, rather than the money (nomimal) prices.

Real Rate of Interest: The money rate of interest minus the expected rate of inflation. The real rate of interest indicates the interest premium, in terms of real goods and services, that one must pay for earlier availability.

Real Values: The measurement of a variable after it has been adjusted for changes in the general level of prices.

Recession: A downturn in economic activity characterized by declining real GNP and rising unemployment. In an effort to be more precise, many economists define a recession as two consecutive quarters in which there is a decline in real GNP.

Reciprocal Agreement: An agreement between firms whereby the buyer of a product requires the seller to purchase another product as a condition of sale. The practice is illegal under the Clayton Act when it substantially reduces competition.

Recognition Lag: The time period between when a policy change is needed from a stabilization standpoint and when the need is recognized by policy-makers.

Regressive Tax: A tax that takes a smaller percentage of one's income as one's income level increases. Thus, the proportion of income allocated to the tax would be greater for the poor than for the rich.

Rent Seeking: Actions by individuals and interest groups designed to restructure public policy in a manner that will either directly or indirectly redistribute more income to themselves.

Repeat-Purchase Item: An item purchased often by the same buyer.

Required Reserve Ratio: A percentage of a specified liability category (for example, transaction accounts) that banking institutions are required to hold as reserves against that type of liability.

Required Reserves: The minimum amount of reserves that a bank is required by law to keep on hand to back up its deposits. Thus, if reserve requirements were 15 percent, banks would be required to keep $150,000 in reserves against each $1 million of deposits.

Reserves: Vault cash plus deposits of the bank with Federal Reserve Banks.

Residual Claimant: Individual in a firm who receives the excess of revenues over costs. A residual claimant gains if the firm's costs are reduced and if revenues are increased.

Resource: An input used to produce economic goods. Land, labor, skills, natural resources, and capital are examples.

Resource Market: A highly aggregate market encompassing all resources (labor, physical capital, land, and entrepreneurship) that contribute to the production of current output. The labor market forms the largest component of this market.

Resource Markets: Markets in which business firms demand factors of production (for example, labor, capital, and natural resources) from household suppliers. The resources are then used to produce goods and services. These markets are sometimes called factor markets.

Resource Mobility: A term that refers to the ease with which factors of production are able to move among alternative uses. Resources that can easily be transferred to a different use or location are said to be highly mobile. In contrast, when a resource has few alternative uses, it is immobile. For

example, the skills of a trained rodeo rider would be highly immobile, since they cannot be easily transferred to other lines of work.

Restrictive Fiscal Policy: A reduction in government expenditures and/or an increase in tax rates such that the expected size of the budget deficit declines (or the budget surplus increases).

Restrictive Monetary Policy: A deceleration in the growth rate of the money supply.

Right-to-Work Laws: Laws that prohibit the union shop—the requirement that employees must join a union (after 30 days) as a condition of employment. Each state has the option to adopt (or reject) right-to-work legislation.

Roundabout Method of Production: The use of productive effort to make tools and other capital assets, which are then used to produce the desired consumer good.

S

Saving: Disposable income that is not spent on consumption. Saving is a ''flow'' concept. Thus, it is generally measured in terms of an annual rate.

Savings and Loan Associations: Financial institutions that accept deposits in exchange for shares that pay dividends. Historically, these funds have been channeled into residential mortgage loans. Under recent banking legislation, S & Ls are now permitted to offer checkable deposits (NOW accounts) and extend a broad range of services similar to those of commercial banks.

Say's Law: The view that production creates its own demand. Thus, there cannot be a general over-supply because

the total value of goods and services produced (income) will always to available for purchasing them.

Scarcity: Fundamental concept of economics which indicates that less of a good is freely available than consumers would like.

Scientific Thinking: Development of theory from basic postulates and the testing of the implications of that theory as to their consistency with events in the real world. Good theories are consistent with and help explain real-world events. Theories that are inconsistent with the real world are invalid and must be rejected.

Secondary Effects: Economic consequences of an initial economic change, even though they are not immediately identifiable. Secondary effects will be felt only with the passage of time.

Shirking: Working at less than a normal rate of productivity, thus reducing output. Shirking is more likely when workers are not monitored, so that the cost of lower output falls on others.

Shortage: A condition in which the amount of a good offered by sellers is less than the amount demanded by buyers at the existing price. An increase in price would eliminate the shortage.

Short Run: A time period of insufficient length to permit decision-makers to adjust fully to a change in market conditions. For example, in the short run, producers will have time to increase output by using more labor and raw materials, but they will not have time to expand the size of their plants or to install additional heavy equipment.

Short Run (in Production): A time period so short that a firm is unable to vary some of its factors of production. The firm's plant size typically cannot be altered in the short run.

Shortsightedness Effect: Misallocation of resources that results because public-sector action is biased (a) in favor of proposals yielding clearly defined current benefits in exchange for difficult-to-identify future costs and (b) against proposals with clearly identifiable current costs yielding less concrete and less obvious future benefits.

Shutdown: A temporary halt in the operation of a business. The firm does *not* sell its assets. Its variable cost will be eliminated, but the firm's fixed costs will continue. The shut-down firm anticipates a return to operation in the future.

Social Costs: The sum of (a) the private costs that are incurred by a decision-maker and (b) any external cost of the action that are imposed on nonconsenting secondary parties. If there are no external costs, private and social costs will be equal.

Socialism: A system of economic organization in which (a) the ownership and control of the basic means of production rest with the state and (b) resource allocation is determined by centralized planning rather than by market forces.

Special Drawing Rights: Supplementary reserves, in the form of accounting entries, established by the International Monetary Fund (also called "paper gold"). Like gold and foreign currency reserves, they can be used to make payments on international accounts.

Special Interest Issue: An issue that generates substantial individual benefits to a small minority while imposing a small individual cost on many other voters. In total, the net cost to the majority might either exceed or fall short of the net benefits to the special interest group.

Stagflation: A period during which an economy is experiencing both substantial inflation and a slow growth in output.

Strike: An action of unionized employees in which they (a) discontinue working for the employer and (b) take steps to prevent other potential workers from offering their services to the employer.

Structural Unemployment: Unemployment due to structural changes in the economy that eliminate some jobs while generating job openings for which the unemployed workers are *not* well qualified.

Substitutes: Products that are related such that an increase in the price of one will cause an increase in demand for the other (for example, butter and margarine, Chevrolets and Fords).

Substitution Effect: That part of an increase (decrease) in amount consumed that is the result of a good being cheaper (more costly) in relation to other goods because of a reduction (increase) in price.

Sunk Costs: Costs that have already been incurred as a result of past decisions. They are sometimes referred to as historical costs.

Supply Shock: An unexpected event that temporarily either increases or decreases aggregate supply.

Supply-Side Economists: Modern economists who believe that changes in marginal tax rates exert important effects on aggregate supply.

Surplus: A condition in which the amount of a good that sellers are willing to offer is greater than the amount that buyers will purchase at the existing price. A decline in price could eliminate the surplus.

T

Tariff: A tax levied on goods imported into a country.

Tax Base: The level of the activity that is taxed. For example, if an excise tax is levied on each gallon of gasoline, the tax base is the number of gallons of gasoline sold. Since higher tax rates generally make the taxed activity less attractive, the size of the tax base is inversely related to the rate at which the activity is taxed.

Tax Incidence: The manner in which the burden of the tax is distributed among economic units (consumers, employees, employers, and so on). The tax burden does not always fall on those who pay the tax.

Tax Rate: The per-unit or percentage rate at which an economic activity is taxed.

Tax Shelter Industry: Business enterprises that specialize in offering investment opportunities designed to create a short-term accounting or "paper" loss, which can then be deducted from one's taxable income; at the same time, future "capital gain" income is generated, which is sometimes taxable at a lower rate.

Technological Advancement: The introduction of new techniques or methods of production that enable a greater output per unit of input.

Technology: The body of skills and technological knowledge available at any given time. The level of technology establishes the relationship between inputs and the maximum output they can generate.

Thrift Institutions: Traditional savings institutions, such as savings and loan associations, mutual savings banks, and credit unions.

Total Cost: The costs, both explicit and implicit, of all the resources used by the firm. Total cost includes an imputed normal rate of return for the firm's equity capital.

Total Product: The total output of a good that is associated with alternative utilization rates of a variable input.

Transaction Accounts: Accounts including demand deposits, NOW accounts, and other checkable deposits against which the account holder is permitted to transfer funds for the purpose of making payment to a third party.

Transaction Costs: The time, effort, and other resources needed to search out, negotiate, and consummate an exchange.

Transfer Payments: Payments to individuals or institutions that are not linked to the current supply of a good or service by the recipient.

Trickle-Down Theory: The theory that intensive economic growth will eventually lead to an improvement in the standard of living of the entire society, even for persons at the bottom of the economic spectrum.

U

Unanticipated Change: A change that decision-makers could not reasonably foresee. Thus, choices made prior to the event did not take the event into account.

Unanticipated Inflation: An increase in the general level of prices that was not expected by

most decision-makers. Thus, it catches them by surprise.

Underground Economy: Unreported barter and cash transactions that take place outside recorded market channels. Some are otherwise legal activities undertaken to evade taxes. Others involve illegal activities such as trafficking in drugs, prostitution, extortion, and similar crimes.

Unemployed: The term used to describe a person, not currently employed, who is either (a) actively seeking employment or (b) waiting to begin or return to a job.

Union Shop: The requirement that all employees join the recognized union and pay dues to it within a specified length of time (usually 30 days) after their employment with the firm begins.

Utility: The benefit or satisfaction expected from a choice or course of action.

V

Value Marginal Product: The marginal product of a resource multiplied by the selling price of the product it helps to produce. Under perfect competition, a firm's marginal revenue product will be equal to the value marginal product.

Variable Costs: Costs that vary with the rate of output. Examples include wages paid to workers and payments for raw materials.

Velocity of Money: The average number of times a dollar is used to purchase final goods and services during a year. It is equal to GNP divided by the stock of money.

Vertical Merger: The creation of a single firm from two firms,

one of which was a supplier or customer of the other—for example, a merger of a lumber company with a furniture manufacturer.

Vicious Circle of Underdevelopment: A pattern of low income and low economic growth that tends to perpetuate itself. Since the current consumption demands of poor nations are large in proportion to available income, the savings and investment rates of these nations are low. In turn, the low investment rate retards future growth, causing poor nations to remain poor.

W

Work-Leisure Substitution Effect: The substitution of leisure time for work time when higher tax rates reduce after-tax personal earnings. In effect, the reduction in the take-home (after-tax) portion of earnings reduces the opportunity cost of leisure, and thereby induces individuals to work less (and less intensively). Of course, lower tax rates would exert the opposite effect.

Y

Youth Work Scholarship: A proposed scholarship providing subsidies to younger workers who maintain jobs. Some scholarships would limit the subsidies to employment that offered on-the-job training.

INDEX

D
E
F
G
H
I
J
3
4
5
6
7
8
9
0
1

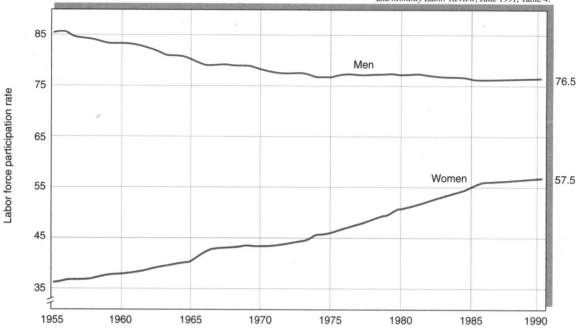

Source: *Economic Report of the President, 1989,* Table B-36 and *Monthly Labor Review,* June 1991, Table 4.

EXHIBIT E The Labor Force Participation Rate of Men and Women, 1955–1990 During the last several decades, the labor force participation of women has steadily increased while the rate for men has fallen.

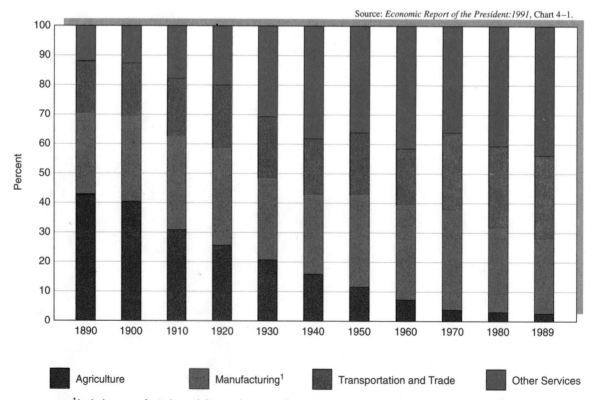

Source: *Economic Report of the President: 1991,* Chart 4–1.

■ Agriculture   ■ Manufacturing[1]   ■ Transportation and Trade   ■ Other Services

[1] Includes manufacturing, mining, and construction.

EXHIBIT F Labor Force Transition, 1890–1989 During the last 100 years, the U.S. labor force has moved out of agriculture and first into manufacturing and later into service industries.